THE NEW AMERICAN ROGET'S COLLEGE THESAURUS IN DICTIONARY FORM

Revised Edition Prepared by

Philip D. Morehead

A MERIDIAN BOOK

MERIDIAN
Published by the Penguin Group
Penguin Books USA Inc., 375 Hudson Street, New York, New York 10014, U.S.A.
Penguin Books Ltd, 27 Wrights Lane, London W8 5TZ, England
Penguin Books Australia Ltd, Ringwood, Victoria, Australia
Penguin Books Canada Ltd, 10 Alcorn Avenue, Toronto, Ontario, Canada M4V 3B2
Penguin Books (N.Z.) Ltd, 182–190 Wairau Road, Auckland 10, New Zealand

Penguin Books Ltd, Registered Offices: Harmondsworth, Middlesex, England

Published by Meridian, an imprint of Dutton Signet, a division of Penguin Books USA Inc.

First Meridian Printing, July, 1985
25 24 23 22 21 20 19

Library of Congress Catalog Card Number: 84-61835

Prepared and edited by
The National Lexicographic Board

ALBERT H. MOREHEAD, *Chairman and General Editor*
WALDEMAR VON ZEDTWITZ, *President*
LOY C. MOREHEAD, *Vice President & Secretary;* LOYD F. GEHRES, SALVATORE RAMONDINO, *Vice Presidents;* DONALD D. WOLF, WILLIAM C. CAMPBELL, GEORGE H. COPELAND, JACK LUZZATTO.

Staff for
The New American Roget's College Thesaurus
JACK LUZZATTO *and* LOY MOREHEAD, *Editors*
WILLIAM C. CAMPBELL, WILLIAM T. ATWOOD, BETTY BRINKERHOFF, ELIZABETH MACLEAN, *Associate Editors.*

PRINTED IN THE UNITED STATES OF AMERICA

HOW TO USE THIS THESAURUS

PETER MARK ROGET was an English Physician who was born in 1779 and died in 1869. As a hobby he liked to make lists of words and group them together when they were related to one another. Some were related because they were synonyms, such as *illegal* and *unlawful*; some because they were antonyms, such as *peaceful* and *warlike*; some because they were reminders of one another, such as *father* and *mother*. Altogether Mr. Roget made a thousand different groups, or *categories*, of related words. Every word he knew or could find in the dictionaries that he had was classified in one or more of these categories.

In 1852 Mr. Roget's list of words was published. He called the book a thesaurus, or treasury, of words. There were not many words in the first ROGET'S THESAURUS, compared to the number in a volume like this, but his book was the first collection of synonyms, antonyms, and other related words. Not only writers, but many others found it invaluable. Dozens of editors, beginning with Mr. Roget's son, have revised the original Thesaurus, added to it, and brought it up to date (for many of the words in the original Roget list are now obsolete and many common words of today were unknown in his time); but virtually every edition is still called ROGET'S THESAURUS in honor of the man who first had the idea.

This edition of ROGET'S THESAURUS is both a dictionary of synonyms and a thesaurus or "treasury" of related words. It combines, in one easy-to-use alphabetical list, *categories* (very much like those in Roget's original thesaurus) and a list of words with their close synonyms. For clarity, each category is printed the full width of the page and set off in a box, while the synonym listings are printed half-page width.

To find *synonyms* for a word, first look up the word in the alphabetical list. In most cases, you will find what you are looking for immediately under that word. Reference to more synonyms is indicated by words printed in SMALL CAPITALS. If you look up the word or words referred to, you will find additional synonyms and other words related to the word you were looking up. Most references are to categories, where you will also find words of related meaning but different parts of speech.

To find *antonyms* for a word, look up the word in the alphabetical listing and refer to the appropriate category (as indicated by SMALL CAPITALS); references for where to look for antonyms will be found at the end of the category.

Suppose you were looking for synonyms and antonyms for *proximity*. In the alphabetical word list under *proximity* you will find the synonyms NEARNESS, *vicinity, propinquity, neighborhood*. NEARNESS is in small capitals. When you refer to it, you will find many more words related to *proximity*, not only nouns, but also verbs, adjectives, and adverbs. By further reference to the words in small capitals in the category NEARNESS—or by looking up in the alphabetical word list some of the other synonyms given for *proximity* (such as *vicinity*)—you can explore in even greater depth the various aspects of the idea with which you began. At the end of the category NEARNESS, you are referred for antonyms to the category DISTANCE, where you find *distance, remoteness, farness*, and many other words of different parts of speech expressing the opposite of *proximity*.

Frequently only one form of a word is entered in the alphabetical word list. You will find synonyms for the other forms by referring to the entries printed in SMALL CAPITALS under the listed word. For example, to find synonyms for *proximate*, look under *proximity* in the alphabetical word list and refer to the category NEARNESS, where you find *adjacent, adjoining* and other related adjectives.

A word or phrase in parentheses—()—is explanatory or shows how the preceding word is to be used in a sentence. Brackets—[]—indicate that the bracketed letters, word, or phrase may or may not be used with the adjoining word, depending on the preference of the writer.

In the listings, synonyms for different senses of the listed word are separated by semicolons (;). Colloquial and slang *senses* of the entry word are labeled *colloq*. or *slang* at the beginning of each sense; colloquial and slang *synonyms* for all senses of the entry word are listed separately, headed respectively by *Colloq*. or *Slang*. Moreover, entry words or individual synonyms may be labeled to indicate special or substandard usage. The most commonly used labels—in addition to *colloq*. and *slang*—are *dial*. (dialectal), *Brit*. (British), *poetic*, and *archaic*.

Familiar dictionary abbreviations are used for parts of speech: *n*., noun; *v*., verb; *v.i.*, intransitive verb; *v.t.*, transitive verb; *adj*., adjective; *adv*., adverb; *pron*., pronoun; *prep*., preposition; *conj*., conjunction; *interj*., interjection.

This is not a dictionary. It does not define words, except to the extent that they are defined in their synonyms. A word that has no natural synonyms is not entered merely to define it. Moreover, alternate spellings for a word are generally not given. The publishers of this Thesaurus also publish a companion volume, THE NEW AMERICAN WEBSTER HANDY COLLEGE DICTIONARY, which was the authority for the preferred spellings used herein and in which may be found definitions of the words in this book.

Antonyms formed by simply adding *un-*, *in-*, *dis-*, etc., are not given, nor are words listed when they are simple negatives of other words. For example, such a word as *unloved* is not entered, since one may merely look up the positive term, but *unbearable* is entered because the positive term has various dissimilar meanings.

FOREIGN PHRASES. This Thesaurus includes foreign words and phrases related to English words and phrases; but foreign words and phrases that are not wholly anglicized are not listed in regular alphabetical order. They are collected on the final pages of this book, with definitions and with reference to the entries or categories in which their synonyms and related English phrases may be found.

—Philip D. Morehead

A

aback, *adv.* rearwards, behind. See REAR, DIFFICULTY.

abaft, *adv.* aft, astern, behind. See REAR.

abandon, *v.t.* relinquish, resign, give up, forgo, surrender, discontinue, waive, abdicate; leave, quit, evacuate, withdraw (from); desert, forsake, maroon, discard, drop; let go, throw up, pull out of, have done with, turn one's back on, wash one's hands of; pull out on. See RELINQUISHMENT, RESIGNATION, DISUSE. —*n.* RASHNESS, recklessness, impetuosity, impulsiveness, audacity.

abandoned, *adj.* dissipated, immoral, reprobate, dissolute, depraved; lost; unbridled. See IMPURITY, RASHNESS.

abase, *v.t.* humble (see ABASH); demean, degrade; dishonor; cast down. See HUMILITY, SERVILITY.

abash, *v.t.* humiliate, humble, shame; embarrass, disconcert; mortify, crush, take down a peg. See HUMILITY.

abate, *v.* DECREASE, lessen, moderate, diminish, subside; allay, slake, slacken, subdue; curtail, remit; let down (on), take off the edge (of).

abattoir, *n.* slaughterhouse (see KILLING).

abbé, *n.* See CLERGY.

abbey, *n.* See TEMPLE.

abbreviate, *v.* abridge, condense, contract, shorten, curtail, digest, truncate, prune. See SHORTNESS, DEDUCTION.

abdicate, *v.* relinquish, resign, renounce, abandon, quit, surrender. See RELINQUISHMENT, RESIGNATION.

abdomen, *n.* belly, paunch, epigastrium, venter; midriff. *Colloq.*, corporation, solar plexus, guts. See INTERIOR.

abduct, *v.t.* kidnap, carry off, steal, spirit away, shanghai, snatch. See STEALING.

abeam, *adv.* sideways (see SIDE).

aberration, *n.* DEVIATION, variation, distortion, disorientation; aberrance, INSANITY; ERROR.

abet, *v.t.* AID, assist, support; encourage.

abeyance, *n.* suspension. See END, LATENCY.

abhor, *v.t.* HATE.

abide, *v.* dwell, reside, live, stay; tolerate, endure, submit (to); remain, stay. See ABODE, DURABILITY, FEELING.

ability, *n.* POWER, SKILL, competency, capacity, capability, aptitude, faculty, talent. *Colloq.*, know-how. *Slang,* what it takes.

abject, *adj.* servile, contemptible; miserable, wretched, hangdog; base. See SERVILITY, IMPROBITY, CONTEMPT.

abjure, *v.* forswear, renounce, repudiate. See NEGATION, NULLIFICATION.

ablaze, *adj.* afire, burning; aglow. See HEAT, LIGHT, RESENTMENT.

able, *adj.* capable, competent, skillful, talented. See POWER, SKILL.

able-bodied, *adj.* fit, robust. See STRENGTH, HEALTH.

ablution, *n.* cleansing, washing. See CLEANNESS.

abnegate, *v.* See NEGATION.

abnormal, *adj.* unusual, aberrant, eccentric, irregular, anomalous; insane; monstrous. See UNCONFORMITY, INSANITY.

aboard, *adv. & prep.* on, on board. *Colloq.*, astride. See PRESENCE, SHIP.

ABODE

Nouns—1, abode, dwelling, residence, domicile, address, habitation, berth, seat, lodging[s], lodging place, quarters, headquarters, base, depot, housing, place; habitat. *Colloq.*, place to hang one's hat. *Slang,* dump, joint. See LOCATION.

2, home, homeplace, homestead, hearth, hearthstone, fireside, inglenook, ingleside, household, ménage, roof; ancestral hall[s], fatherland, native land *or* soil, country. *Colloq.*, roost.

3, retreat, asylum, cloister, hermitage, hideaway, hiding-place, sanctuary, arbor, *sanctum sanctorum,* cave, nest, den, cell, dugout, hive, hole, lair, haunt. *Slang,* hangout, hideout, stamping ground *or* place. See SECLUSION.

4, camp, barrack[s], bivouac, encampment, casemate; stopover; tourist camp, trailer camp. *Slang,* [hobo] jungle.

5, house, dwelling[-place], building; hall; *casa,* mansion, palace, villa, dacha, lodge, castle (see DEFENSE), chalet, bungalow, manor-house; brownstone [house], flat, apartment [house], two-(*etc.*)family house, farmhouse, ranch house, split-level, town house, condominium, cooperative, penthouse, tenement, loft; ark; temple; rectory; [residential] hotel; skyscraper; [housing] development, [building] project; trailer. *Colloq.*, diggings, digs; condo, co-op. *Slang,* pad, cheesebox.

6, hut, adobe, bunkhouse, hogan, cabin, cottage, hovel, igloo, tupek, lean-to, log cabin, Quonset hut, rancho, shack, shanty, tent, tepee, wickiup, wigwam, kiosk.

7, inn, caravansary, club, hospice, hostel, hostelry, hotel, motel, motor hotel, motor court, rooming house, bread and breakfast, dormitory; harem; resort, spa.

8, barn, cowshed, doghouse, kennel, pound, henhouse, hutch, warren, pen, [pig]sty, apiary, shed, stable, stall, booth, coop, dovecote, aviary, birdcage, birdhouse, roost.

9, estate, hacienda, ranch, plantation, farm, domain.

10, village, hamlet, town, pueblo; municipality, metropolis, city, suburb (see REGION); inner city, ghetto, slum, quarter; colony; commune, kolkhoz.

11, sanatorium, sanitarium, asylum, [health] resort, [convalescent, nursing, *or* rest] home. *Colloq.*, old folks' home. See REMEDY.

12, see INHABITANT.

Verbs—**1,** inhabit, domesticate, colonize, naturalize; take root, sit down, settle [down], take up one's abode, establish oneself, squat, perch, pitch one's tent, put up at, keep *or* set up house; bivouac, stop over, encamp, rough it.

2, abide, occupy, people, dwell, reside, stay, sojourn, live, put up, tenant, lodge, nestle, board, live in, camp out. *Colloq.*, roost. See INHABITANT.

3, accommodate, lodge, put up, board.

Adjectives—**1,** dwelling, residing, in residence, at home.

2, urban, suburban, provincial; metropolitan, cosmopolitan; domestic, foreign.

---

abolish, *v.t.* annul, cancel, abrogate; exterminate, wipe out. See NULLIFICATION, DESTRUCTION.

abominable, *adj.* detestable. See HATE, UNCLEANNESS.

aboriginal, *adj.* primitive, primeval; indigenous. See OLDNESS, INHABITANT.

abortion, *n.* miscarriage; premature delivery *or* birth; FAILURE, fiasco; monstrosity, freak. See END.

abound, *v.i.* teem, swarm, be plentiful. See SUFFICIENCY.

about, *adv.* around, round, on all sides; approximately; nearly, almost. See RELATION, NEARNESS. —*prep.* concerning, regarding, anent, respecting.

about-face, *n.* turnabout, reversal, volte-face. See INVERSION.

above, *adv.* aloft, overhead, up; earlier, before. See HEIGHT. —*prep.* over, beyond; surpassing; more than, exceeding.

aboveboard, *adj.* candid (see PROBITY).

abracadabra, *n.* mumbo-jumbo (see SORCERY).

abrade, *v.t.* wear (away), grind. See FRICTION.

abreast, *adv.* side-by-side; to the same degree. See SIDE, EQUALITY.

abridge, *v.* CONDENSE, shorten, compress, contract. See SHORTNESS.

abroad, *adv.* overseas, away, outside; roaming, wandering, at large. See TRAVEL, ABSENCE, DISTANCE.

abrogate, *v.t.* repeal, annul, retract. See REJECTION, NULLIFICATION.

abrupt, *adj.* sudden, precipitate, short, curt; steep, precipitous, sheer; sudden *or* sharp (turn, *etc.*); jerky. See INSTANTANEITY.

abscess, *n.* ulcer, boil. See DISEASE.

abscond, *v.i.* decamp, bolt, run away, flee, fly, take off. See AVOIDANCE.

ABSENCE

Nouns—**1,** absence, nonresidence, noninhabitance, nonpresence, nonattendance, absenteeism, truancy, hooky, French leave; NONEXISTENCE.

2, emptiness, void, vacuum, vacuity, vacancy; blank, clean slate. See SPACE, INSUBSTANTIALITY.

3, absentee, truant; missing person, M.I.A.; absentee landlord. *Colloq.,* no-show.

4, nobody present, not a soul, nary a soul, nobody under the sun, nary a one, no one, no man, never a one.

Verbs—be absent, absent oneself, stay *or* keep away, keep out of the way, play truant, play hooky, take French leave, go A.W.O.L., absent oneself without [official] leave; slip away (see ESCAPE); keep *or* hold aloof; withdraw, vacate (see DEPARTURE). *Colloq.,* not show up, make oneself scarce. *Slang,* cut [out].

Adjectives—**1,** absent, nonattendant, not present, away, nonresident, missing, missing in action, lost, wanting, omitted, nowhere to be found, out of sight, gone, lacking, away from home, truant, absent without [official] leave, A.W.O.L.; abroad, oversea[s], on vacation. *Colloq.,* minus.

2, empty, vacant, void, vacuous, untenanted, unoccupied, uninhabited, tenantless; devoid, bare, hollow, blank.

Adverbs—nowhere; elsewhere; neither here nor there; somewhere else, not here. *Dial.,* nowheres.

Prepositions—*in absentia,* without, less, minus, *sans;* wanting (see INSUFFICIENCY).

Antonyms, see PRESENCE.

---

absent-minded, *adj.* See INATTENTION.

absolute, *adj.* complete, perfect, thorough; sheer; fixed, positive; unrestricted, unbounded, full, plenary; despotic, autocratic, supreme. See COMPLETION, GREATNESS, CERTAINTY.

absolution, *n.* cleansing, FORGIVENESS, shrift, dispensation; discharge. See ACQUITTAL, EXEMPTION.

absolutism, *n.* despotism, autocracy; dogmatism. See AUTHORITY, CERTAINTY.

absolve, *v.t.* forgive, cleanse, shrive, pardon, discharge. See FORGIVENESS.

absorb, *v.* assimilate, take in, suck up; incorporate, integrate; engross, preoccupy, obsess. See THOUGHT, RECEIVING, ATTENTION, USE, COMBINATION, LEARNING.

abstain, *v.i.* forbear, refrain. See AVOIDANCE, MODERATION, ASCETICISM, DISUSE.

abstemious, *adj.* abstaining, abstinent; temperate, sober. See MODERATION, ASCETICISM.

abstract, *adj.* theoretical, metaphysical; abstruse, recondite. See SUPPOSITION. —*v*. excerpt (from); remove. See STEALING. —*n*. compendium, summary, epitome, précis, abridgment. See SHORTNESS.

abstruse, *adj*. profound, recondite, esoteric, subtle, deep; obscure, enigmatical. See UNINTELLIGIBILITY, OBSCURITY.

ABSURDITY

Nouns—**1,** absurdity, absurdness, nonsense; paradox, inconsistency; inanity (see FOLLY); ludicrousness, ridiculousness, comicality.

2, muddle, [Irish] bull; bathos; song and dance; travesty (see RIDICULE).

3, jargon, doubletalk, twaddle, gibberish, fustian, empty talk, galimatias. *Colloq*., poppycock, stuff and nonsense. *Slang,* hot air. See UNMEANINGNESS.

4, theater of the absurd; dada[ism].

Verbs—**1,** play the fool, talk nonsense, talk through one's hat, go from the sublime to the ridiculous.

2, make a fool of, make absurd, burlesque (see RIDICULE).

Adjectives—absurd, nonsensical, preposterous, senseless, inconsistent, illogical, paradoxical, ridiculous, extravagant, fantastic, silly, funny, comic[al], unmeaning, without rhyme or reason, fatuous, ludicrous, laughable. *Slang,* screwy, cockamamie, cock-and-bull.

Antonyms, see MEANING.

---

abundance, *n*. plenty, SUFFICIENCY, profusion, luxuriance, fullness; affluence, opulence, wealth.

abuse, *v.t.* misuse, misapply; mistreat, injure, damage; malign, scold, berate, vilify, curse; flay. —*n*. injury, desecration; insult. See DISAPPROBATION, BADNESS, DECEPTION, IMPURITY, WRONG.

abut, *v*. touch, border (on). See CONTACT.

abysmal, *adj*. abyssal; deficient, below par, miserable. See DEPTH, INFERIORITY.

abyss, *n*. abysm, deep, DEPTH[s], gulf, chasm, [bottomless] pit, chaos, HELL. See INTERVAL.

academic, *adj*. scholastic, collegiate; educational; scholarly, erudite; theoretical. See TEACHING, LEARNING.

academy, *n*. SCHOOL, college, preparatory *or* finishing school; [learned] society.

accede, *v.i*. agree, ASSENT, CONSENT, acquiesce, yield, comply; attain (see ARRIVAL). See SUBMISSION.

accelerate, *v*. hasten, expedite, anticipate, speed (up), quicken. See EARLINESS, HASTE.

accelerator, *n*. gas pedal, throttle. See INSTRUMENTALITY, VELOCITY.

accent, *v*. accentuate, emphasize, stress. —*n*. emphasis, stress, tone, dialect, pronunciation. See SPEECH, SOUND.

accept, *v*. ASSENT; take; adopt, believe; honor, admit. See RECEIVING, CONSENT, INCLUSION.

acceptation, *n*. sense, MEANING.

access, *n*. APPROACH, avenue, way; admittance, entrée. *Colloq*., (an) in; a line (to). See PASSAGE, INGRESS, POSSIBILITY.

accession, *n*. acceding, ASSENT; increase, ADDITION, ACQUISITION; attainment. See TRANSFER.

accessory, *adj*. contributory; helping; AUXILIARY, incident (to). —*n*. accomplice, assistant, confederate. See AID, ACCOMPANIMENT.

accident, *n*. mishap, injury, casualty; CHANCE, fortuity. See ADVERSITY, OCCURRENCE.

acclaim, *v.t*. applaud; praise, hail, salute. —*n*. praise. See APPROBATION.

acclamation, *n*. acclaim, applause; unanimity. See APPROBATION.

acclimate, acclimatize, *v.t.* accustom, inure, habituate. See HABIT.
acclivity, *n.* ASCENT, rise, incline, pitch, slope, grade.
accolade, *n.* honors, laurels, tribute, reward; decoration, embrace, kiss. See APPROBATION.
accommodate, *v.* adapt, adjust, conform, fit, suit; oblige, help out; lend money (to); put up; lend (to). See AID, AGREEMENT, DEBT, PACIFICATION, ABODE.

ACCOMPANIMENT

Nouns—**1,** accompaniment, concomitance, company, association, companionship, [co]partnership, fellowship, coefficiency. See SYNCHRONISM, SEQUENCE.
2, concomitant, accessory, adjunct, corollary, coefficient; companion, attendant, fellow, associate, consort, spouse, colleague, comrade; accompanist; [co]partner, satellite, hanger-on, shadow; convoy, cortege, escort, bodyguard, chaperon (see SAFETY); retainer[s], following (see SERVANT); cavalier, squire; camp follower. *Slang,* pard. See FRIEND, MARRIAGE.
Verbs—accompany. attend, hang on, wait on, go along with, go hand in hand with, keep company, row in the same boat, associate *or* consort with, take up with, hang around; string along; escort, chaperon, convoy, squire, see out.
Adjectives—accompanying, attendant, concomitant, fellow, associated, coupled, accessory.
Adverbs—hand-in-hand, arm-in-arm, side-by-side, cheek-to-cheek, hand-in-glove, together, at one's side; in tow; on one's coattails. *Colloq.,* cheek-by-jowl.
Prepositions—with, together with, along with, in company with.
Conjunctions—and, both, also.
Antonyms, see DISJUNCTION.

---

accomplice, *n.* accessory, abettor, confederate, crony; partner, colleague. *Colloq.,* sidekick. See AUXILIARY.
accomplish, *v.t.* do, complete, fulfill, perform, effect, execute, achieve, consummate. See COMPLETION.
accomplished, *adj.* proficient, versed; talented. See SKILL.
accord, *v.i.* harmonize, conform, agree. See AGREEMENT, ASSENT. —*v.t.* grant, bestow; concede. See GIVING. —*n.* AGREEMENT.
accordingly, *adv.* hence, so, therefore, thus. See CIRCUMSTANCE.
according to, *adv.* consistent with, in keeping with; based on. See CONFORMITY, EVIDENCE.
accordion, *n.* concertina. See MUSIC.
accost, *v.t.* greet, hail, address. See COURTESY.
account, *v.i.* report, relate, narrate. See DESCRIPTION. —*v.t.* attribute. See CAUSE. —*n.* report, recital, narrative, DESCRIPTION, story, tale, history, chronicle, statement; ACCOUNTING.

ACCOUNTING

Nouns—**1,** accounting, accountance, bookkeeping, audit, calculation (see NUMERATION), commercial *or* business arithmetic.
2, accountant, bookkeeper, actuary, Certified Public Accountant, C.P.A., chartered accountant (*Brit.*); auditor, bank examiner; clerk. See INQUIRY.
3, accounts, books, finances, budget, money matters, figures.
4, ledger, journal, day book, cash book, petty-cash book, bank book, pass book, balance sheet, profit-and-loss statement, accounts-payable *or* -receivable ledger, sales ledger.

5, asset, liability; expenditure (see PAYMENT); bill, invoice, statement [of account]; balance, account, A/C; CREDIT, debit (see DEBT); net worth.

Verbs—**1,** keep accounts, keep the books, enter, post, book, CREDIT, debit, carry over, balance [accounts *or* the books]; bill, invoice, dun, settle accounts; take stock, take inventory; audit, examine the books; open *or* close the books.

2, falsify *or* doctor accounts; embezzle (see STEALING). *Slang,* cook the books.

---

accouter, *v.t.* outfit, attire. See CLOTHING.

accredit, *v.* authorize, license, certify; believe; attribute. See BELIEF, COMMISSION, ATTRIBUTION.

accretion, *n.* See INCREASE.

accrue, *v.* accumulate, grow. See INCREASE, RECEIVING, DEBT.

accumulate, *v.* amass, gather; aggregate, collect, hoard, bank; pile up. See ACQUISITION, ASSEMBLAGE, STORE.

accurate, *adj.* correct, exact; precise, truthful. *Colloq.,* on the button *or* nose, to the penny. See TRUTH, RIGHTNESS.

ACCUSATION

Nouns—**1,** accusation, charge, incrimination, inculpation; CONDEMNATION, denunciation, invective, implication, imputation, blame, reproach, recrimination. See DISAPPROBATION.

2, LAWSUIT, plaint, complaint, citation, allegation; indictment, arraignment, impeachment, true bill; libel, slander (see DETRACTION).

3, accuser, plaintiff, complainant; prosecutor, district attorney, attorney general. *Colloq.,* D.A.

4, accused, defendant, respondent, co-respondent, libelee.

Verbs—**1,** accuse, charge, tax (with), incriminate; allege, impute; inculpate, blame, complain against *or* of, reproach, indict, arraign, impeach, implicate, cite; have something on. *Colloq.,* throw the book at.

2, denounce, inform (against), take to task, call to account, lay at one's door, give the lie (to); trump up a charge; tell on, tattle (on); cast the first stone. *Slang,* put the finger on, point the finger (at), rat (on); frame.

Adjectives—accusing, accusatory; incriminatory, recriminatory, reproachful; imputative.

Antonyms, see APPROBATION, VINDICATION.

---

accustom, *v.* habituate, familiarize, inure. See HABIT.

ace, *n.* expert, adept; particle, iota. See SKILL, LITTLENESS. —*adj.* excellent, first-rate. See SUPERIORITY.

ache, *n.* PAIN. —*v.i.* hurt, smart, throb, PAIN; yearn (see DESIRE).

achieve, *v.t.* accomplish, attain, reach. See COMPLETION.

acid, *adj.* sour, bitter, tart, vinegary; acrimonious, cutting, caustic. See SOURNESS, DISCOURTESY.

acknowledge, *v.* admit, confess, own; ANSWER, receipt. See DISCLOSURE, EVIDENCE, GRATITUDE.

acme, *n.* summit, pinnacle (see HEIGHT).

acolyte, *n.* altar boy; attendant, assistant; novice. See RELIGION, AUXILIARY, BEGINNING.

acoustic, *n.* See SOUND.

acquaint, *v.t.* inform, notify, tell; familiarize, teach. See INFORMATION, FRIEND, LEARNING.

acquaintance, *n.* familiarity, experience, KNOWLEDGE, ken; FRIEND.

acquiesce, *v.t.* agree, accede, ASSENT, concur, CONSENT. See OBEDIENCE, SUBMISSION.

ACQUISITION

Nouns—**1,** acquisition, acquirement, accession, obtainment, procurement; collection, accumulation, amassing, gathering, reaping, gleaning, picking (up). See RECEIVING, POSSESSION, ASSEMBLAGE, STORE.

2, seizure, confiscation, commandeering, attachment, appropriation, apprehension, expropriation, dispossession; abduction, kidnaping; annexation; STEALING, theft.

3, haul, catch; windfall; spoils, plunder, loot, booty, payoff, split. *Colloq.*, pickings. *Slang,* the take, gravy, velvet.

4, acquirer, obtainer, *etc.;* buyer, purchaser, vendee; inheritor, legatee; good bargainer *or* trader; winner, captor, thief. *Colloq.,* horsetrader.

5, acquisitiveness, ambition, hunger; covetousness, avarice; greed, voracity. See DESIRE.

6, claw, talon, pincer, tongs, pliers.

Verbs—**1,** acquire, get, find, gain, obtain, come by, dig up *or* out; secure, win, earn, pull down, realize, receive, take; collect, amass, reap, crop, gather, glean, scare *or* scrape up, scrape together; inherit, come in for, come by honestly; PURCHASE. *Colloq.,* step into; get hold of, pick up, rake in. *Slang,* clean up, help oneself (to), line one's pockets *or* purse.

2, appropriate, take over, assume, take possession of, commandeer, confiscate, expropriate, arrogate; annex, attach; preempt, usurp; catch, nab, bag, pocket; capture, seize; take away; grasp, clinch, clutch, grip, grab, snatch, seize, cop, snap up, lay hold of, lay one's hands on. *Slang,* latch on to, hook, snag.

Adjectives—acquisitive, avaricious, greedy, grasping, covetous. *Slang,* on the make.

Antonyms, see GIVING, RELINQUISHMENT, LOSS, POSSESSION.

---

acquit oneself, *v.* behave; conduct; comport, *or* bear oneself; pay off, settle, square. See CONDUCT, PAYMENT.

ACQUITTAL

Nouns—acquittal, quittance, exoneration, VINDICATION; discharge, release, reprieve, absolution. See FORGIVENESS, LIBERATION.

Verbs—acquit, exculpate, exonerate, clear, absolve; pardon, grant amnesty to, reprieve, discharge, release. *Colloq.,* whitewash; let off.

Adjectives—acquitted, vindicated, *etc.;* quit, free, clear; in the clear.

Antonyms, see CONDEMNATION.

---

acrid, *adj.* pungent, biting, acid; corrosive, caustic. See SOURNESS, PUNGENCY.

acrimony, *n.* bitterness, rancor, acerbity, asperity, RESENTMENT, DISCOURTESY, PUNGENCY.

acrobat, *n.* gymnast, tumbler, contortionist. See DRAMA, EXERTION, ELASTICITY.

across, *adv.* crosswise, athwart. —*prep.* on, over, athwart. See CROSSING.

act, *n.* & *v.* See ACTION, DRAMA, CONDUCT, AFFECTATION, REPRESENTATION, RULE.

acting, *adj.* substitute, representative, DEPUTY. See SUBSTITUTION.

ACTION

Nouns—**1,** action, performance, operation, execution, PRODUCTION; process, procedure, proceeding, transaction; CONDUCT; EXERTION.
2, affair, effort, job, deed, business, work; stunt; LAWSUIT; battle (see WARFARE, CONTENTION).
3, doer (see AGENT).
Verbs—act, do, execute, perform, function; operate, work, practice, exercise, commit, perpetrate; raise *or* lift a finger *or* a hand; militate; take care of; take effect; progress (see PROGRESSION); labor, toil, drudge, ply.
Adjectives—acting, active, operative, in operation, in action, at work, on duty; functional, effective, efficient. *Colloq.,* in harness.
Adverbs—in the act, conspicuously, flagrantly, *in flagrante delicto,* red-handed.
Antonyms, see INACTIVITY, NEGLECT, REPOSE.

ACTIVITY

Nouns—**1,** activity, activeness, business, ENERGY, liveliness, animation; briskness, quickness, alertness; wakefulness, vigil; alacrity, zeal, dash, fervor, eagerness, vivacity, VIGOR, spirit; activism. See ACTION.
2, movement, fuss, ado, bustle (see AGITATION); three-ring circus; high gear; industry, diligence, assiduity, assiduousness; activities, comings and goings, goings-on.
3, activist, new broom; fan, devotee, addict. *Colloq.,* hustler, go-getter, ball of fire. *Slang,* live wire; freak.
Verbs—**1,** be active, busy, *etc.,* have one's hands full, have other fish to fry; bestir oneself, come to life, come alive, get up, go about *or* at, look alive, bustle, fuss; feel one's oats. *Slang,* get on the stick. See HASTE.
2, activate, animate; awaken, [a]rouse, build a fire under.
Adjectives—**1,** active, busy, astir, at it, in the swim; brisk, alert, spry, smart, quick, spanking; energetic, lively, alive, vivacious, keen, eager; frisky, feisty, forward, spirited; up and doing, quick on the trigger, on the jump, on the go, on the job, on one's toes, in high gear, in full swing, on the fly *or* the job. *Colloq.,* snappy, psyched up.
2, working, on duty, at work; in commission, in circulation; in effect, in force; industrious, diligent, assiduous. *Colloq.,* in harness.
Adverbs—actively, *etc.* See HASTE.
Antonyms, see INACTIVITY, REPOSE.

actor, actress, *n.* performer, player; tragedian, comedian, Thespian; play-actor; doer, worker. See AGENT, DRAMA.

actual, *adj.* real, veritable, true, genuine; concrete, factual. See EXISTENCE, PRESENT, TRUTH.

actuate, *v.* move, induce, compel, persuade; start, get under way. See CAUSE, BEGINNING.

acumen, *n.* discernment, shrewdness, penetration; INTELLIGENCE.

acute, *adj.* shrewd, discerning, astute; sharp, poignant, keen, pointed, severe. See INTELLIGENCE, CUNNING, SHARPNESS.

ad, *n.* See ADVERTISEMENT.

adage, *n.* proverb, saw, saying, aphorism, motto, MAXIM.

adamant, *adj.* adamantine, hard; inflexible, immovable, firm. See HARDNESS, OBSTINACY.

adapt, *v.* suit, conform, regulate, fit; adjust, convert, reconcile. See AGREEMENT.

add, *v.* See ADDITION, NUMERATION.
addendum, *n.* ADDITION; appendix.
adder, *n.* puff adder, VIPER.
addict, *n.* devotee, fan, enthusiast; user, slave (to). *Slang,* head, junkie, freak, mainliner. See HABIT, ACTIVITY.

ADDITION

Nouns—**1,** addition, INCREASE, EXPANSION, annexation, accession; corollary, concomitant (see ACCOMPANIMENT). See SEQUENCE.
2, adjunct; affix, prefix, suffix; appendix, INSERTION, postscript, epilogue, addendum, supplement, attachment, appendage; extension, annex, wing; rider, codicil; flap, tab, tag; bonus; grace period.
Verbs—add, affix, annex, superimpose, append, subjoin, figure in; tack on to. *Colloq.,* hitch on.
Adjectives—added, *etc.;* additive, supplementary, additional, another, further, extra.
Adverbs—in addition, again, more, plus, extra, besides, also, too, at that, and then some, to boot, as well, into the bargain, for good measure, over and above, and so forth, and so on; by the way, by the bye, on the side, in passing.
Prepositions—apart from, aside from; together with, let alone, not to mention, much less, not to speak of, to say nothing of, as well as.
Conjunctions—and, in addition to being.
Antonyms, see DEDUCTION.

address, *v.t.* direct; court, woo; accost, greet, approach, speak to. —*n.* street and number; residence, home; SPEECH, discourse, oration; cleverness, dexterity. See DIRECTION, INDICATION, ABODE, COURTESY, SKILL.
adduce, *v.t.* present, bring forward, cite, mention. See EVIDENCE.
adept, *adj.* skillful, dexterous, apt; practiced, expert, proficient. —*n.* expert, master. See SKILL.
adequate, *adj.* enough, sufficient; serviceable; satisfactory, ample. See SUFFICIENCY, UTILITY.
adhere, *v.i.* cling (to), stick; hold closely to. See COHERENCE, DUTY.
adherent, *n.* follower, believer; partisan, disciple. See LEARNING, AUXILIARY.
adhesive, *adj.* sticky, gluey, tenacious. See COHERENCE.
adieu, *n.* farewell (see DEPARTURE).
adjacent, *adj.* near, close by, next to; touching, bordering, contiguous, neighboring. See CONTACT.
adjoin, *v.* touch, abut, border, meet, neighbor. See CONTACT.
adjourn, *v.* defer, postpone; discontinue; END. See LATENESS.
adjudicate, *v.* judge (see JUDGMENT).
adjunct, *n.* ADDITION, appendix, appendage, annex; accessory, extension, postscript; complement, INSERTION; ACCOMPANIMENT.
adjure, *v.t.* charge, bind, command. See REQUEST.
adjust, *v.t.* fix, adapt, true, regulate, straighten; settle, compensate; equalize, rate. See AGREEMENT, EQUALITY.
adjutant, *n.* assistant (see AUXILIARY).
ad-lib, *v., colloq.,* extemporize, improvise. See UNPREPAREDNESS.
administer, *v.t.* govern, rule, manage, control; give, dose, dispense. See AUTHORITY, GIVING, APPORTIONMENT, CONDUCT.
admire, *v.t.* esteem, idolize, venerate, RESPECT; regard; WONDER, marvel.
admission, *n.* confession, DISCLOSURE; entry, admittance, INGRESS; cover [charge], charge, minimum; CONSENT. See INCLUSION.
admit, *v.t.* let in; induct, matriculate; concede, acknowledge; receive, allow. *Colloq.,* fess *or* own up. See DISCLOSURE, RECEIVING, PERMISSION.

admonition, *n.* reproof (see DISAPPROBATION); caution, WARNING.
ado, *n.* bustle, ACTIVITY; fuss, commotion, DISORDER.
adolescence, *n.* YOUTH, minority, juvenility; teens, teen-age, nonage; puberty.
adopt, *v.t.* embrace, take to oneself, assume; foster, give a home to, provide a home for, accept as one's own. See CHOICE.
adore, *v.t.* LOVE, WORSHIP, idolize.
adorn, *v.t.* ORNAMENT, embellish, deck, garnish, beautify.
adrift, *adj.* afloat; drifting, loose. See DISJUNCTION, DISPERSION, CHANGEABLENESS.
adroit, *adj.* dexterous, deft, skillful. See SKILL.
adulate, *v.* flatter (see FLATTERY).
adult, *adj.* grown[-up], full-grown, mature, ripe. —*n.* grown-up, big person; major, senior. See AGE, MALE, FEMALE.
adulterate, *v.t.* mix, water down, weaken, dilute; debase, corrupt. See DETERIORATION, MIXTURE, WEAKNESS.
adultery, *n.* infidelity, fornication, licentiousness. See IMPURITY.
advance, *v.* progress, go forward, proceed; further, second, AID. —*n.* progress, rise; success, gain; prepayment. See PROGRESSION, DEBT, OFFER.
advantage, *n.* SUPERIORITY, upper hand, leverage, the better (of); gain, profit, benefit, odds, favor. *Colloq.*, ace in the hole. See CHANCE, SUCCESS.
advent, *n.* See APPROACH.
adventitious, *adj.* foreign, EXTRINSIC.
adventure, *n.* enterprise, UNDERTAKING; happening, event; risk, hazard, venture. See CHANCE. —*v.* embark upon; dare. See DANGER.
adventurer, *n.* voyager, traveler, wanderer, roamer; gambler, fortune hunter, free lance, soldier of fortune; adventuress (*derog.*). See TRAVEL, CHANCE.
adversary, *n.* opponent (see OPPOSITION).

ADVERSITY

Nouns—**1,** adversity, affliction; bad, ill, adverse, *or* hard luck *or* fortune; evil lot; frowns of fortune; evil star *or* genius; ups and downs of life; hard case *or* lines; peck of troubles, hell upon earth; slough of despond. See EVIL, FAILURE, PAIN, DIFFICULTY.
2, trouble, hardship, bother, curse, POVERTY, tough sledding; hot seat.
3, evil day; time out of joint; hard times, a dog's life; rainy day; gathering clouds, ill wind; visitation, infliction, distress; bitter pill; trial, ordeal.
4, mishap, mischance, misadventure, misfortune; disaster, calamity, fatality, catastrophe; accident, casualty, cross, reverse, check, *contretemps,* rub; losing game.
Verbs—go hard *or* ill with, weigh on; fall on evil days; go downhill; go to rack and ruin; go to the dogs, touch *or* hit bottom; fall from high estate; be badly off, have seen better days, have two strikes against one; come to grief. *Slang,* draw a blank; lose one's shirt.
Adjectives—**1,** unfortunate, unblest, ill-fated, unhappy, unlucky; in adverse circumstances, unprosperous, luckless, hapless, out of luck, down on one's luck; in trouble, in a bad way, in an evil plight, in Dutch; under a cloud; bleak, clouded; ill *or* badly off; poor, down in the world, down at heel, hard put [to it], down and out, undone; underprivileged; born under an evil star. *Slang,* on the ropes, in a jam, out on a limb.
2, adverse, untoward; disastrous, calamitous, ruinous, dire.
Adverbs—if the worst comes to the worst; from bad to worse; out of the frying pan into the fire.

Antonyms, see PROSPERITY.

---

advertisement, *n.* announcement, [public] notice; commercial, [want, classified, personal, *etc.*] ad; publicity. *Colloq.*, plug, blurb. See PUBLICATION.

ADVICE

Nouns—**1,** advice, counsel, suggestion, recommendation; exhortation, expostulation; admonition (see WARNING); guidance, instruction; charge.
2, adviser, prompter, counselor; mentor (see TEACHING).
3, guide; consultation, conference; INFORMATION, NEWS.

Verbs—**1,** advise, counsel, suggest, recommend, prescribe, exhort; kibitz; instruct; expostulate, dissuade; warn (see WARNING).
2, advise with; consult together; compare notes; hold a council, deliberate, be closeted with, confer, consult.

Adjectives—**1,** advisory, consultative, consultant; recommendatory, hortative, persuasive, dissuasive, admonitory, WARNING.
2, advisable, desirable, commendable.

Antonyms, see DISSUASION.

advocate, *v.* favor, plead; recommend, suggest; support. —*n.* patron, supporter; lawyer. See FRIEND, AUXILIARY, LAWSUIT.

aerate, *v.t.* AIR; carbonate.

aerial, *adj.* airy, atmospheric; lofty, soaring; graceful, ethereal; visionary. See AIR, HEIGHT, INSUBSTANTIALITY, IMAGINATION. —*n.* rabbit ears (see COMMUNICATION).

aeronautics, *n.* See AVIATION.

aesthetic, *adj.* See ESTHETIC.

afar, *adv.* at a DISTANCE.

affable, *adj.* friendly, sociable, gracious; approachable. See COURTESY.

affair, *n.* occasion, event, happening, OCCURRENCE; BUSINESS; party (see SOCIALITY); amour, love affair, liaison (see LOVE).

affect, *v.t.* INFLUENCE, touch; concern, relate to; move, stir. See RELATION, DISEASE, FEELING.

AFFECTATION

Nouns—**1,** affectation, affectedness, artificiality, insincerity, histrionics, OSTENTATION; charlatanism, quackery (see DECEPTION); pretense, gloss, veneer, façade; pose, pretension, airs; pedantry, euphuism; preciosity, preciousness; mannerism, conceit, foppery, dandyism, coxcombry. *Slang,* side. See FALSEHOOD.
2, stiffness, formality; prudery, coquetry; crocodile tears.
3, fop, coxcomb, dandy, blade, sport, dude; attitudinarian; poser, poseur, pretender, hypocrite; faker, sham, pedant, bluestocking, prude, prig; charlatan, deceiver. *Colloq.*, nice Nelly.

Verbs—affect, act, put on *or* give oneself airs, feign, sham; simper, mince; attitudinize, pose, assume *or* strike an attitude.

Adjectives—affected, pretentious, artificial, insincere, pedantic, stilted, stagy, theatrical, sham, histrionic; unnatural, self-conscious, stiff, starchy, formal, prim, smug, prudish, priggish, foppish, dandified; precious, mannered, mincing, namby-pamby; glib, butter wouldn't melt in one's mouth. *Colloq.*, art[s]y.

Antonyms, see SIMPLENESS, MODESTY, PROBITY.

affection, *n.* LOVE, regard, esteem, liking. See FEELING, ENDEARMENT.

affidavit, *n.* deposition, attestation. See EVIDENCE.

affiliate, *v.i.* join, unite. —*n.* associate; branch, subsidiary. See COOPERATION, COMBINATION.

affinity, *n.* liking, ATTRACTION; RELATION, SIMILARITY.

AFFIRMATION

Nouns—**1,** affirmation, statement, allegation, assertion, predication, declaration, averment. See INFORMATION.

2, asseveration, swearing, oath, deposition (see EVIDENCE); avouchment, avowal; protestation, profession; ASSENT.

3, observation, expression; saying, dictum. See CERTAINTY.

4, PROMISE, pledge, vow.

Verbs—**1,** affirm, assert, say, predicate, declare, state; emphasize, protest, profess; have one's say, declare oneself, nail one's colors to the mast, speak up, give voice *or* utterance (to); stand up and be counted.

2, put forth, put forward, express; allege, set forth, hold out, maintain, contend, pronounce. *Colloq.,* claim.

3, depose, depone, aver, avow, avouch, asseverate, swear; take one's oath; make an affidavit; kiss the book, vow, swear till one is black *or* blue in the face, stand by; cross one's heart [and hope to die]; be sworn, call Heaven to witness; vouch, warrant, certify; swear by bell, book, and candle; hammer [away] at.

4, PROMISE, warrant.

Adjectives—declaratory, predicatory, pronunciative, affirmative; positive, certain; express, emphatic; unretracted; predicable.

Adverbs—affirmatively, in the affirmative, *etc.;* with emphasis, *ex cathedra,* without fear of contradiction; on one's honor.

Antonyms, see NEGATION, NULLIFICATION.

---

affix, *v.t.* fasten, attach; append. See ADDITION, CONNECTION.

afflict, *v.t.* beset, trouble; burden (with). See PAIN, ADVERSITY.

affluent, *adj.* flowing; abundant, plentiful; rich, wealthy. See MONEY, PROSPERITY, FLUIDITY.

afford, *v.t.* manage, bear; supply, yield, produce; make available, furnish. See GIVING, PROVISION.

affront, *v. & n.* insult, slight, snub. See DISRESPECT.

afire, aflame, *adj.* See HEAT.

afloat, *adj.* floating; in circulation. See PUBLICATION, LEVITY.

aforesaid, *adj.* former, aforementioned. See PRECEDENCE.

afoul, *adv.* entangled (see DIFFICULTY).

afraid, *adj.* See FEAR.

aft, *adv.* abaft, astern, rearward. See REAR.

after, *prep.* past, beyond, behind. —*adj.* later, subsequent, following. —*adv.* afterward, subsequently, not now, later. See SEQUENCE, PURSUIT.

aftermath, *n.* results, consequence[s]. See EFFECT.

afternoon, *n. post meridiem,* p.m.; twilight hour. See CHRONOMETRY.

afterthought, *n.* reflection; hindsight. See LATENESS.

again, *adv.* once more, afresh, anew, repeatedly, twice; encore; in ADDITION. See REPETITION.

against, *prep.* in OPPOSITION to, counter *or* contrary to; dead against, at cross purposes; in exchange for. See CONTACT, SUBSTITUTION, PREPARATION.

agape, *adj.* See OPENING, WONDER.

AGE

Nouns—**1,** age, OLDNESS; old *or* advanced age, senility; senescence; years, anility, gray hairs, climacteric, menopause; declining years, decrepitude (see DETERIORATION), superannuation; second childhood, dotage; vale of years, decline of life, three-score years and ten; ripe [old] age; longevity; gerontology, geriatrics. See TIME.

2, adulthood, manhood, maturity; legal *or* lawful age; prime of life; years of discretion, majority; seniority, eldership; primogeniture.

3, elder, doyen, father, matron; senior citizen, old-timer, graybeard; veteran; firstling. *Slang,* fossil.

Verbs—**1,** grow old, age, decline, senesce; be aged.

2, come of age, mature, ripen, mellow; come to man's estate, attain majority, have cut one's eyeteeth, have sown one's wild oats.

Adjectives—**1,** aged, old, elder[ly], senior, senile; aging, graying, senescent; matronly, anile; [along *or* on] in years; ripe, mellow, run to seed, declining, past one's prime; grayheaded, hoary, venerable, gray, timeworn; antiquated (see OLDNESS); decrepit, superannuated; advanced in life *or* years; stricken in years; wrinkled; having one foot in the grave.

2, of [full] age, out of one's teens, grown up, mature, full grown, over age; in one's prime, middle-aged, adult; womanly, matronly; marriageable (see MARRIAGE); of a certain age, no [spring] chicken, over the hill, old as Methuselah; patriarchal, ancient.

Antonyms, see YOUTH.

---

ageless, *adj.* perpetual, young at heart. See PERPETUITY.

agelong, *adj.* lengthy, protracted. See DURABILITY.

AGENCY

Nouns—**1,** agency, operation; working, POWER, function; office, exercise, play, work; interworking, interaction; causality, causation (see CAUSE); INSTRUMENTALITY, action, MEANS; mediation, medium; METHOD, *modus operandi.*

2, AGENT, doer, performer, perpetrator, operator; executor, executrix, administrator, administratrix; practitioner, worker, stager.

3, actor, actress; workman, operative, artisan; craftsman, mechanic; working *or* laboring man *or* woman; hewer of wood and drawer of water, laborer, navvy; handyman, journeyman, hack; tool, beast of burden, drudge; maker, artificer, ARTIST, wright, manufacturer, architect, builder, mason, smith, mechanic, engineer.

Verbs—**1,** operate, execute, work; act upon; perform, play, support, sustain, maintain; take effect, quicken, strike.

2, come *or* bring into operation *or* play, activate; have free play *or* rein; bring to bear upon.

Adjectives—operative, efficient, efficacious, practical, effectual; at work, on foot; acting, doing; in operation, in force, in action, in play; acted upon.

---

agenda, *n.* things to be done, order of the day, schedule, calendar, docket, program, PLAN. See BUSINESS.

AGENT

Nouns—**1,** agent, representative, delegate, emissary, envoy, deputy, proxy, broker, factor, attorney; commissary, commissioner; trustee, nominee; salesman, saleswoman (see SALE); middleman, go-between; spokesperson, spokesman, spokeswoman; commission agent, auctioneer, one's man of business, [personal] secretary; ambassador, diplomat, legate, minister, apostle, messenger; advertising, book, press, publicity, *or* theatrical agent.
2, lieutenant, henchman; legman; vicar; assistant, right-hand man; man *or* girl Friday; handmaiden, SERVANT, slave; midwife, *accoucheur,* obstetrician; robot, cat's paw. *Colloq.,* stooge. See INSTRUMENTALITY.
3, representation, SUBSTITUTION.
Verbs—represent (see SUBSTITUTION); appoint (see COMMISSION).

---

aggrandize, *v.t.* enlarge, extend (see EXPANSION); exaggerate (see EXAGGERATION).
aggravate, *v.* worsen, intensify, INCREASE; *colloq.,* irritate, annoy, exacerbate (see RESENTMENT).
aggregate, *n.* total, sum, WHOLE; combination. See QUANTITY.
aggression, *n.* offense, ATTACK, war, invasion; belligerence.
aghast, *adj.* awestruck, agape. See FEAR, WONDER.
agile, *adj.* nimble, active, spry; quick, acrobatic, athletic. See ACTIVITY.

AGITATION

Nouns—**1,** agitation, stir, tremor, shake, ripple; trepidation, quiver, quaver, dance; flutter. *Colloq.,* sweat.
2, perturbation, commotion, disquiet, tumult, dither, bustle, fuss, EXCITEMENT, flurry; ebullience; turmoil, hurly-burly, turbulence (see VIOLENCE); demonstration (see REVOLUTION).
3, spasm, throe, fit, throb[bing], crick, stitch, twinge, palpitation, convulsion, paroxysm; disturbance, DISORDER; restlessness, CHANGEABLENESS; fever, frenzy; ferment, froth, foam, surf, fermentation; ebullition, effervescence. *Slang,* heebie-jeebies. See EXCITABILITY.
4, bundle of nerves, fussbudget; agitator.
Verbs—**1,** agitate, shake, tremble, quiver, quaver, quake, shiver, twitch, vellicate, twitter, toss, stagger, bob, reel, sway; wag, wiggle, waggle; wriggle [like an eel]; dance, stumble; throb, pulsate, beat, palpitate, go pit-a-pat; be nervous, flutter, flitter, bustle, fidget, have ants in one's pants.
2, ferment, effervesce, fizzle, foam; seethe, boil (over), bubble (up); toss about; shake like an aspen leaf; shake to its foundations.
3, convulse, toss, tumble; flap, brandish, flourish; jiggle, joggle, ruffle, flurry, disturb, fan, stir; whip *or* shake up, churn; jounce, bounce.
4, perturb, ruffle, fluster, disturb, startle, shock, give one a turn; pique, infuriate, madden, make one's blood boil, lash into a fury, get on one's nerves, give one fits, give one a hard time, give one gray hair, tie in knots, shake up, throw for a loss.
Adjectives—shaking, agitated, tremulous; giddy; convulsive, unquiet, restless, at loose ends, restive, all atwitter, nervous, jittery, jumpy; choppy; ebullient. *Slang,* strung out, all shook up, in a lather, up-tight.

Antonyms, see REPOSE.

agnostic, *n.* skeptic, doubter (see DOUBT).

ago, *adv.* since, over, PAST.

agony, *n.* PAIN, torture; anxiety, anguish; throes of DEATH.

agree, *v.* yield, CONSENT; coincide, harmonize; conform (see AGREEMENT).

agreeable, *adj.* pleasant, congenial, compatible, harmonious; compliant (see CONSENT). See AGREEMENT, SOCIALITY, PLEASURE.

AGREEMENT

Nouns—**1,** agreement, accord, accordance; unison, harmony, concord, concordance, coincidence, concert; affinity; CONFORMITY, conformance; consonance, consistency, congruity, keeping; congeniality; CORRESPONDENCE, apposition, union. See RIGHTNESS, UNITY.

2, unanimity, common consent, acclamation, chorus; *vox populi,* public opinion; the silent majority; concurrence, COOPERATION, consensus.

3, fitness, aptness, aptitude, appropriateness; coaptation, propriety, compatibility; cognation (see RELATION); right person, woman, *or* man in the right place; very thing; decorum, just the thing.

4, adaptation, adjustment, accommodation, reconciliation; CONSENT, ASSENT, concurrence. See PREPARATION.

5, compact, contract, pact, bargain, meeting of minds, covenant.

Verbs—**1,** agree, accord, concur, harmonize, get along, get on; CONSENT, ASSENT; correspond, tally, go with, go together; meet, befit; fall in with, chime in with, fit [right] in, square with, comport with; dovetail, fit like a glove, lend itself to; get together, match, become one; close ranks; see eye to eye. *Colloq.,* jibe; fill the bill. See SIMILARITY.

2, fit, suit, adapt, tailor, accommodate, adjust; harmonize, reconcile; dovetail, square.

3, contract, covenant; engage (see PROMISE); stipulate; make *or* come to terms, settle, strike a bargain, come to an understanding.

Adjectives—**1,** agreeing, suiting, in accord, accordant, concordant, consonant, congruous, congruent, correspondent, congenial; harmonious, reconcilable, conformable; in accordance, harmony, *or* keeping with; at one with, of one mind, of one piece; consistent, compatible, proportionate; in phase.

2, unanimous, agreed on all hands, carried [by acclamation].

3, apt, apposite, pat; to the point *or* purpose; happy, felicitous; adapted, apropos, cut out for, in line with, in place, in tune, made-to-order, in character, appropriate, decorous, seasonable, suitable, meet.

Adverbs—unanimously, with one voice, with one accord, by common consent, in chorus, to a man, without a dissentient voice; as one man, one and all, on all hands.

Antonyms, see DISAGREEMENT, DISCORD.

AGRICULTURE

Nouns—**1,** agriculture, cultivation, husbandry, farming, tillage, culture, agronomy, gardening; horticulture, arboriculture, floriculture, forestry, vintage; landscape gardening; georgics, geoponics; green thumb.

2, husbandman, horticulturist, gardener, florist; agriculturist; gentleman farmer, country squire; yeoman, farmer, granger, cultivator, tiller of the soil; sharecropper; plowman, reaper, sower; rustic; woodsman. *Colloq.,* hayseed, hick, rube, peasant, [country] bumpkin, clod[hopper]. See POPULACE.

3, farm, grange; field, lawn, garden; nursery, greenhouse, hothouse, conservatory; bed, border, seed plot, parterre; plantation, ranch, homestead (see ABODE); arboretum, orchard, vineyard, vinery.

4, crop, yield, harvest, product; cash crop; truck (see VEGETABLE); wheat, alfalfa, corn, soybean, *etc.*

5, veterinarian (see DOMESTICATION); school of agriculture. *Colloq.*, horse doctor. *Slang,* cow college.

Verbs—cultivate, till the soil, farm, garden; sow, plant, set out, put in; reap, harvest; mow, dress the ground; dibble, hoe, plow, harrow, rake, weed; take root, grow.

Adjectives—agricultural; arable; praedial, rural, rustic, country, georgic; horticultural.

---

aground, *adj.* stranded, grounded. See DIFFICULTY.

ague, *n.* chill. See DISEASE.

ahead, *adv.* before, in advance (of); leading, winning. See PRIORITY, SUPERIORITY, FRONT.

AID

Nouns—**1,** aid, assistance, help, succor, RELIEF; support, advance, furtherance, promotion; patronage, auspices, favor, INFLUENCE; ministration, subministration; accommodation. See BENEVOLENCE, INSTRUMENTALITY, UTILITY.

2, helper, assistant, aid, aide; accessory, partisan, supporter, confederate; AGENT; ally, co-worker; supplies, reinforcements, backup; crutch; patron, fairy godmother. *Colloq.*, angel. See AUXILIARY.

Verbs—**1,** aid, assist, help [out], be of service, succor, come to the aid of, get behind; lend one's aid, lend oneself to, contribute, subsidize, subscribe to, advocate; reinforce; give *or* lend a hand, give one a lift, take in tow; oblige, accommodate, encourage.

2, relieve, rescue, set on one's legs, pull *or* see through; give new life to, be the making of; push forward, give a lift to, give a leg up; promote, further, forward, advance; speed, expedite (see HASTE); support, sustain, uphold.

3, nourish, nurture, foster, cherish; feed *or* fan the flames; serve; do service to, administer to.

4, second, stand by, stick by, stand *or* stick up for; back [up], abet, take up the cudgels for; espouse [the cause of], advocate, give moral support to, keep in countenance, patronize; smile upon, favor, side with, take the part of, play the game of, go to bat for; be of use to, benefit.

5, turn to, fall back on.

Adjectives—aiding, auxiliary, adjuvant, helpful, coadjuvant; ministrant, ancillary, accessory, subsidiary; favorable; obliging.

Adverbs—with *or* by the aid of; on *or* in behalf of, in back of; on account of; for the sake of; on the part of.

Antonyms, see HINDRANCE.

---

aide, *n.* assistant; aide-de-camp. See AID, AUXILIARY.

ail, *v.i.* be ill, suffer, fail (in health). See DISEASE, PAIN.

aim, *n.* purpose, INTENTION, goal, end. —*v.* point, direct; aspire to, try for. See DIRECTION.

aimless, *adj.* random, undirected, CHANCE; driftless, idle; wanton. See DISORDER.

AIR

Nouns—**1,** air, atmosphere, ether, ozone; ventilation, fresh *or* open air; sky, welkin, blue sky; oxygen, nitrogen, hydrogen, *etc.* See VAPOR.
2, troposphere, tropopause, layer, ozone layer, stratosphere, thermosphere, [Kennelly-]Heaviside layer, ionosphere, exosphere.
3, weather, climate, rise and fall of the barometer, isobar, weather map; aerology, meteorology, climatology; aneroid barometer, baroscope.
4, airpipe, air shaft, airway; funnel, vent, tube, flue, chimney, ventilator; nostril, nozzle, blowhole; windpipe, spiracle, larynx, throat; pipe. See PASSAGE.

Verbs—air, ventilate, fan; aerate. See WIND, REFRESHMENT.

Adjectives—**1,** windy (see WIND).
2, atmospheric, airy, aerial, aeriform; meteorological.

Adverbs—outdoors, *al fresco.*

Antonyms, see LAND, WATER.

---

airline, *n.* [air] carrier, airways; air shuttle. See AVIATION.

airplane, airship, *n.* See AVIATION.

airport, *n.* airfield, landing strip, airstrip. See AVIATION.

airs, *n. pl.* pretension[s], façade. See AFFECTATION, VANITY.

airtight, *adj.* hermetic; flawless. See CLOSURE, STRENGTH.

aisle, *n.* passageway, path, corridor. See OPENING.

ajar, *adj.* open, agape; discordant. See OPENING, DISCORD.

akin, *adj.* related, kindred, like. See RELATION, SIMILARITY.

alacrity, *n.* promptness, speed; zeal, eagerness. See ACTIVITY, EARLINESS, DESIRE.

alarm, *n.* alarum, WARNING; tocsin; S.O.S., siren, danger signal, red light *or* flag; condition red; FEAR, unease. —*v.* frighten, panic, scare; shock, horrify; make uneasy; sound the alarm, bell, *or* tocsin; alert, warn; cry wolf. See FEAR.

alarmist, *adj. & n.* terrorist, panic- *or* scaremonger. See FEAR.

alas, *interj.* alack! woe is me! (see LAMENTATION).

album, *n.* scrapbook, RECORD; looseleaf book; ASSEMBLAGE.

alchemy, *n.* See SORCERY.

alcoholic, *adj.* beery, winy; spirituous. See DRINKING.

alcove, *n.* recess, niche. See RECEPTACLE, CONCAVITY.

ale, *n.* porter, stout. See DRINKING.

alert, *adj.* watchful, on guard, wary; quick, ready. See CARE, ACTIVITY. —*v.* See WARNING.

alias, *n.* assumed name, pseudonym, *nom de plume* or *de guerre;* nickname. —*adv.* also known as, a.k.a. See NOMENCLATURE.

alibi, *n., colloq.,* excuse (see VINDICATION).

alien, *adj.* foreign, strange. —*n.* foreigner, stranger, immigrant. See UNCONFORMITY, EXTERIOR.

alienate, *v.t.* estrange, make hostile. *Colloq.,* turn off. See DISCORD.

alienist, *n.* psychiatrist. See INTELLECT.

alight, *v.i.* descend, get off, land; dismount; arrive, disembark. See ARRIVAL, DESCENT. —*adj.* glowing, lighted; on fire, burning. See LIGHT, HEAT.

align, *v.* line up, true, range, straighten; regulate; array, take sides. See ARRANGEMENT, STRAIGHTNESS, DIRECTION.

alike, *adj.* analogous, resembling, like; akin. See SIMILARITY.

aliment, *n.* FOOD, sustenance.

alimony, *n.* maintenance; child support. See PAYMENT, RECEIVING.

alive, *adj.* living (see LIFE); quick-witted, alert, brisk, spry; susceptible.

See INTELLIGENCE, ACTIVITY, SENSIBILITY.

all, *n.* See WHOLE, GENERALITY.

allay, *v.t.* lessen; soothe, mitigate, ease; calm. See MODERATION, RELIEF.

allege, *v.* state, assert, affirm; imply; accuse. See ACCUSATION, AFFIRMATION.

allegiance, *n.* loyalty, devotion; DUTY. See OBEDIENCE.

allegory, *n.* parable, fable. See FIGURATIVE.

allergy, *n.* sensitivity, reaction. See SENSIBILITY, DISEASE.

alleviate, *v.* lessen, mitigate; relieve. See MODERATION, RELIEF.

alley, *n.* PASSAGE, lane, walk. See OPENING.

alliance, *n.* association, federation, league; COMBINATION; treaty, accord; marriage; connection. See COOPERATION, RELATION.

allocate, *v.t.* allot, assign. See APPORTIONMENT.

allot, *v.* appoint, assign; distribute, parcel out. See APPORTIONMENT.

allow, *v.* grant, permit; concede; tolerate, suffer, let. See DISCLOSURE, CONSENT, PERMISSION.

allowance, *n.* stipend; DISCOUNT, concession; admission, sanction, PERMISSION. See GIVING, QUALIFICATION.

alloy, *n.* compound, MIXTURE; admixture. See COMPOSITION. —*v.* mix, combine; adulterate. See COMBINATION.

allude, *v.* refer (see INFORMATION).

allure, *n.* ATTRACTION, charm. —*v.* tempt, attract, charm, entice. See DESIRE.

allusion, *n.* reference, suggestion, hint, mention. See INFORMATION, FIGURATIVE.

ally, *n.* FRIEND, confederate, supporter. See AID, AUXILIARY.

almanac, *n.* calendar, ephemeris. See CHRONOMETRY, PUBLICATION.

almighty, *adj.* all-powerful, omnipotent. See DEITY, POWER.

almost, *adv.* nearly, not quite, all but, approximately. See NEARNESS.

alms, *n.* charity, dole. See GIVING.

aloft, *adv.* on high, overhead, above, up; in the air; in the rigging. See HEIGHT.

alone, *adj.* apart, solitary, single. —*adv.* individually, solely, singly. See UNITY, SECLUSION.

along, *adv.* lengthwise; onward; together (with). See LENGTH, PROGRESSION, ACCOMPANIMENT.

alongside, *adv.* beside, neck-and-neck, abreast, side-by-side. See SIDE.

aloof, *adj.* distant, unneighborly, reserved, remote; indifferent. See SECLUSION, INDIFFERENCE.

aloud, *adv.* audibly; vociferously, loudly, with full voice. See LOUDNESS, HEARING.

alphabet, *n.* letters; ABC's, crisscross row. See WRITING, BEGINNING.

already, *adv.* by now, previously. See PRESENT, PART, PRIORITY.

also, *adv.* too, further[more], besides, likewise. See ADDITION, ACCOMPANIMENT.

also-ran, *n.* runner-up, second best. See INFERIORITY.

altar, *n.* communion *or* Lord's table; shrine. See TEMPLE.

alter, *v.* modify, CHANGE.

altercation, *n.* See DISCORD.

alternate, *n.* substitute, stand-in, proxy. —*v.* take turns, change, vacillate. See OSCILLATION, INTERCHANGE, DISCONTINUANCE.

alternative, *n.* CHOICE, option; PLAN.

although, *conj.* notwithstanding, albeit, though. See COMPENSATION.

altitude, *n.* HEIGHT, elevation.

altogether, *adv.* entirely, all, collectively, totally. See WHOLE.

altruism, *n.* BENEVOLENCE; selflessness; generosity, LIBERALITY, philanthropy, UNSELFISHNESS.

alumna, alumnus, *n.* graduate, fellow. See SCHOOL.

always, *adv.* at all times, invariably, continually, ever. See GENERALITY, DURABILITY, PERPETUITY.

amalgamation, *n.* MIXTURE, blend, COMBINATION; unification, merger, federation, UNITY.

amass, *v.t.* collect, accumulate; pile

or heap up, STORE. See ASSEMBLAGE, ACQUISITION.

amateur, *n.* nonprofessional, beginner; dilettante; volunteer. See BEGINNING, TASTE.

amative, amatory, *adj.* loving, affectionate; amorous, ardent; erotic. See LOVE.

amaze, *v.t.* astonish, astound, SURPRISE.

ambassador, *n.* envoy, emissary; consul; deputy. See SUBSTITUTION.

ambient, *adj.* surrounding, neighboring. See ENVIRONMENT.

ambiguous, *adj.* vague, undecided, uncertain; obscure, undefined. See DOUBT, LATENCY, OBSCURITY, UNINTELLIGIBILITY.

ambition, *n.* purpose, wish, hope, desire, INTENTION; aspiration, goal, end; resolve; zeal. See DESIRE.

ambush, *n.* ambuscade; hiding-place, cover, camouflage; pitfall, trap; bushwhacking. —*v.t.* lie in wait for; bushwhack. See CONCEALMENT, ATTACK.

ameliorate, *v.* get better (see IMPROVEMENT).

amenable, *adj.* agreeable; pliant, yielding, submissive; liable. See DUTY, CONSENT.

amend, *v.* change; correct, rectify; improve; (*pl.*) recompense (see ATONEMENT). See IMPROVEMENT.

amenities, *n. pl.* See COURTESY.

amiable, *adj.* friendly, agreeable, kindly, pleasant; likable. See COURTESY, BENEVOLENCE, FRIEND.

amicable, *adj.* friendly (see FRIEND).

amid, amidst, *prep.* among, midst, mid. See MIXTURE.

amiss, *adv.* WRONG, ill; badly, improperly. See EVIL.

ammunition, *n.* ammo, bullets, *etc.* See ARMS.

amnesia, *n.* loss of memory (see OBLIVION).

amnesty, *n.* pardon, remission, moratorium. See FORGIVENESS.

among, *prep.* in the middle (of), midst, included in, with. See MIXTURE.

amorous, *adj.* loving, passionate, amative. See LOVE.

amorphous, *adj.* shapeless, formless; heterogenous, vague. See FORMLESSNESS.

amount, *n.* QUANTITY, sum, total, aggregate; DEGREE; PRICE.

amphitheater, *n.* gallery, ARENA. See DRAMA.

ample, *adj.* sufficient, copious, plenty; large, expansive, spacious. See GREATNESS, SPACE, SUFFICIENCY.

amplify, *v.t.* enlarge, swell, magnify. See EXPANSION.

amputate, *v.* sever, cut off. See DISJUNCTION, DEDUCTION.

amulet, *n.* charm, token, talisman, good-luck piece. See CHANCE, SORCERY.

AMUSEMENT

Nouns—**1,** amusement, entertainment; diversion, *divertissement,* distraction; recreation, hobby, avocation, relaxation, pastime, sport; labor of love, PLEASURE; night life; time of one's life.

2, fun, frolic; laughter (see REJOICING), drollery, tomfoolery, mummery; pleasantry (see WIT). See CHEERFULNESS.

3, play, game, gambol, romp, prank, antic, lark, escapade, spree, skylarking; monkeyshine, monkey trick, practical joke.

4, dance, ball, masquerade; reel, rigadoon, saraband, hornpipe, bolero, fandango, cancan, minuet, waltz, polka, galop, jig, fling, *allemande,* gavotte, mazurka, kozotzky, morisco, morris dance, quadrille, country dance, cotillion, *cotillon;* one-step, two-step, fox trot, turkey trot, Charleston, jitterbugging, bunnyhop, black bottom, cakewalk; bossa nova, tango, cha-cha, mambo, samba; soft shoe. *Colloq.,* drag, hop, prom.

5, festivity, merrymaking (see SOCIALITY); fete, festival, gala, revel, revelry, carnival, Mardi Gras, brawl, saturnalia, high jinks; banquet, wassail, carouse, carousal; picnic, field day; jubilee (see CELEBRATION). *Slang,* jamboree.

6, theater, ballroom, music hall, honky-tonk, discotheque; circus, big top; park, arbor, bowling green *or* alley, rink, casino, fun fair, amusement park, theme park, resort, watering place; midway, boardwalk. See ARENA.

7, game[s]; billiards, bowls; cards, chess, checkers, draughts, backgammon, dominoes, solitaire; gambling (see CHANCE); fishing, hunting; aquatics, swimming; sports (see CONTENTION).

8, toy, plaything, bauble; doll, puppet, teetotum, knickknack.

Verbs—**1,** amuse, entertain, divert, distract, recreate.

2, amuse oneself; play (games, pranks, tricks, *etc.*); sport, disport, toy, revel, drown care; make merry, drive dull care away; frolic, gambol, frisk, romp, caper; sow one's wild oats, have one's fling, live it up, cut up; fool, mess, play, *or* monkey around; take one's pleasure; make holiday, go a-Maying, while away the time, kill time, dally; step out, have fun, have a ball *or* a time, cut a caper, horse around, paint the town [red], carry on, cut loose, whoop it up, make a night of it, go to town, let one's hair down, blow *or* let off steam, roister.

Adjectives—**1,** amusing, entertaining, diverting, recreative; festive; roguish, rompish, frisky, playful [as a kitten], sportive.

2, amused, entertained, diverted, *etc.*

Adverbs—on the town; for fun, for the devil of it.

Antonyms, see WEARINESS, PAIN.

---

anachronism, *n.* misdate, prolepsis, anticipation; metachronism, parachronism, prochronism. See TIME, ERROR.

analogous, *adj.* like, parallel; related; corresponding, similar. See SIMILARITY, IDENTITY.

analysis, *n.* breakdown, separation, disintegration; investigation, study; abstract, summary. See INQUIRY, DECOMPOSITION.

anarchy, *n.* lawlessness, terrorism, DISORDER, disorganization; nihilism.

anathema, *n.* curse, execration, IMPRECATION. See DETRACTION.

anatomy, *n.* structure, framework; zootomy; analysis. See FORM, INQUIRY.

ANCESTRY

Nouns—**1,** ancestry, paternity, maternity, origins, background, parentage, breeding; house, stem, trunk, branch, tree, stock, stirps, pedigree, lineage, blood, kin, line, family, tribe, sept, race, clan; family tree, genealogy, descent, extraction, birth; forefathers, patriarchs. See PRECEDENCE, PRIORITY.

2, ancestor, predecessor, forebears; grandsire, grandfather; grandmother, granddam.

3, parent; father, sire, dad, papa, paterfamilias, genitor, progenitor, procreator; motherhood, maternity; mother, dam, ma, mama, materfamilias.

4, genealogist, archivist.

Adjectives—parental, paternal, maternal, fatherly, motherly; family, ancestral, linear, patriarchal; direct, lineal, collateral.

Antonyms, see POSTERITY.

---

anchor, *n.* grapnel, kedge; mainstay, safeguard. —*v.* fasten, attach, fix; hold fast. See STABILITY, CONNECTION.

anchorage, *n.* mooring, road[stead], harbor. See SAFETY, LOCATION.

ancient, *adj.* aged, venerable; antique, antiquated; archaic, hoary. See AGE, OLDNESS.

and, *conj.* moreover, also, in addition; plus, to boot, besides. See ADDITION, ACCOMPANIMENT.

anecdote, *n.* sketch, story, tale, narrative; joke. See DESCRIPTION.

anemia, *n.* bloodlessness. See WEAKNESS.

anesthesia, *n.* See INSENSIBILITY.

anew, *adv.* again (see REPETITION).

ANGEL

Nouns—**1,** angel, archangel; celestial being, invisible choir, heavenly host; seraph, cherub; ministering spirit, guardian angel. See HEAVEN, GOODNESS.
2, angelology; seraphim, cherubim, thrones, dominations *or* dominions, virtues, powers, principalities, archangels, angels.

Adjectives—angelic, seraphic, cherubic, celestial.

Antonyms, see DEMON.

---

anger, *n. & v.* See RESENTMENT.

angle, *n.* corner (see ANGULARITY); aspect, guise, point of view; approach. See APPEARANCE. —*v.i.* fish. See PURSUIT.

anguish, *n.* agony, anxiety, PAIN.

ANGULARITY

Nouns—**1,** angularity, OBLIQUITY; angle, notch, fork, bifurcation; elbow, knee, knuckle, ankle, shoulder, groin, crotch, crutch, crane, fluke; zigzag; corner, coign, quoin, dovetail, nook, recess, niche, oriel, peak; salient, projection. See SHARPNESS, CURVATURE.
2, angulation; right, acute, obtuse, *or* oblique angle; angular measurement, elevation, distance, velocity; trigonometry, trig; goniometry; altimeter, clinometer, graphometer, goniometer; theodolite; sextant, quadrant.
3, triangle, trigon, wedge; rectangle, square, lozenge, diamond; rhomb, rhombus; quadrangle, quadrilateral; parallelogram; quadrature; polygon, pentagon, hexagon, heptagon, octagon, decagon; cube, rhomboid; tetrahedron, octahedron, dodecahedron, icosahedron; prism, pyramid, block, brick; parallelepiped.
4, lankiness, boniness, ungainliness (see NARROWNESS).

Verbs—angle, fork, bifurcate.

Adjectives—angular, crooked; deltoid, triangular, rectangular, square, *etc.;* aquiline, sharp; jagged, serrated; falciform, furcated, forked, bifurcate; zigzag; knockkneed, akimbo, geniculated; oblique (see OBLIQUITY).

Antonyms, see CURVATURE, STRAIGHTNESS.

---

anile, *adj.* childish, foolish, simple; senile. See AGE.

animadversion, *n.* criticism, reflection. See DISAPPROBATION.

ANIMAL

Nouns—**1,** animal, beast, brute, creature, living thing, creeping thing, dumb animal; domestic animal; wild animal, game; flesh, flesh and blood; corporeality, carnality; animation, animality. See DOMESTICATION.

2, natural science, zoology, biology, mammalogy, ornithology, herpetology, ichthyology, entomology; animal kingdom, animal life, animalia, fauna; animal morphology, anatomy, zootomy, histology, cytology, embryology, paleontology; zoo-, bio-(*etc.*)physics, chemistry, *etc.;* ENVIRONMENT, balance of nature, ecology, bionomics, ethology, teleology, zoography, zoogeography, *etc.*

3, zoologist, zoographist, naturalist; biologist, bionomist, *etc.;* bird watcher, nature lover.

4, vertebrate, invertebrate; quadruped, biped; mammal, marsupial, cetacean; bird, fowl; reptile, snake, amphibian; fish, crustacean, shellfish, mollusk, worm; insect, arachnid; zoophyte; protozoan, animalcule.

5, livestock; cattle, kine, bird, poultry, fowl, swine; beasts of the field.

6, yearling, youngling, colt, filly, whelp, cub (see YOUTH).

7, zoological garden, zoo, [wild] animal farm, menagerie, *Tiergarten* (see ABODE).

Adjectives—**1,** animal, bestial, carnal, corporal, corporeal, physical, fleshly; sensual; human.

2, mammalian, cetaceous, avian, reptilian, vermicular, piscatory; piscine, molluscous; aquatic, terrestrial; domestic, wild; carnivorous, herbivorous, insectivorous, omnivorous; equine, bovine, canine, feline, *etc.*

3, zoological, morphological, anthropological, *etc.*

---

animate, *v.* liven, impel; cheer, enliven, enspirit, encourage, inspire. —*adj.* lively; living. See CHEERFULNESS, EXCITEMENT, ACTIVITY, CAUSE, LIFE.

animosity, *n.* antipathy, ill will, enmity. See RESENTMENT, DISLIKE.

annals, *n.pl.* chronicle, archive[s], RECORD.

annex, *v.* add, attach, affix. See ADDITION, JUNCTION, ACQUISITION.

annihilate, *v.* demolish, destroy; eliminate, exterminate. See DESTRUCTION, NONEXISTENCE.

anniversary, *n.* jubilee (see REGULARITY).

annotate, *v.* comment on, gloss, explain. See INTERPRETATION.

announce, *v.* tell, proclaim, publish, make known; broadcast, report. See INFORMATION, PREDICTION, PUBLICATION.

annoy, *v.* vex, tease, harass, disturb, molest, trouble, bother, irritate, PAIN. *Colloq.,* peeve. See MALEVOLENCE.

annual, *adj.* yearly, seasonal, anniversary. See REGULARITY. —*n.* yearbook, [annual] report. See RECORD.

annul, *v.t.* cancel, abolish, repeal, rescind, retract, revoke, nullify, quash; dissolve (a marriage); set aside, invalidate. See NULLIFICATION, DIVORCE.

anoint, *v.* oil, salve. See RITE.

anonymous, *adj.* unnamed, nameless, incognito. See NOMENCLATURE.

another, *adj.* different; one more. See DIFFERENCE, ADDITION.

ANSWER

Nouns—**1,** answer, response, reply, rescript; acknowledgment; rebuttal, riposte, rejoinder, return, retort; repartee; antiphon; password (see INDICATION); echo, feedback; answering machine *or* service. *Colloq.,* comeback.

2, discovery, DISCLOSURE, solution, explanation; clue (see INDICATION). See INTERPRETATION.

Verbs—**1,** answer, respond, reply; rebut, retort, rejoin; give answer; acknowledge, echo; confute (see CONFUTATION); answer *or* talk back (see INSOLENCE).

2, satisfy, resolve, set at rest; find out, determine, solve, explain; figure *or* dope out, work out.

Adjectives—answering, responsive, conclusive.

Antonyms, see INQUIRY.

---

answerable, *adj.* accountable, liable. See LIABILITY.

antagonism, *n.* animosity, antipathy, enmity; hostility, OPPOSITION.

antecede, *v.t.* go before, precede. See PRIORITY.

antechamber, anteroom, *n.* waiting room, INGRESS; lobby, vestibule, foyer. See RECEPTACLE.

antenna, *n.* aerial, rabbit ears, mast, tower. See COMMUNICATION.

anthem, *n.* song, hymn, chorale; national anthem. See MUSIC, WORSHIP.

anthology, *n.* collection, miscellany, garland. See ASSEMBLAGE.

antic, *n.* caper, escapade, prank, gambol. See AMUSEMENT.

anticipate, *v.* await, expect; precede; forestall; foresee. See PREPARATION, PRIORITY, FUTURITY, EARLINESS.

antidote, *n.* antitoxin, REMEDY.

antipathy, *n.* DISLIKE; repugnance, aversion. See OPPOSITION.

antiquary, *n.* archaeologist, historian, student of the PAST.

antiquated, *adj.* antique; outdated, behind the times, outmoded; obsolete. See OLDNESS, AGE.

antique, *n.* relic. See OLDNESS.

antiquity, *n.* old[en] times; the PAST, ancient history; OLDNESS.

antisocial, *adj.* cynical, misanthropic. See MALEVOLENCE.

antithesis, *n.* contrast, opposition. See DIFFERENCE.

anxiety, *n.* concern, CARE; FEAR, mental anguish, PAIN. See EXPECTATION, DOUBT, JEALOUSY.

anyhow, *adv.* anyway; at any rate; nevertheless. See COMPENSATION.

apart, *adv.* separately, alone, independently; away; in pieces. See DISTANCE, DISJUNCTION.

apartment, *n.* flat, suite, rooms, maisonette, tenement, walk-up; condominium, co-op. See ABODE, RECEPTACLE.

apathy, *n.* coldness, INDIFFERENCE, unconcern.

ape, *n.* gorilla, anthropoid, simian; imitator, mimic. —*v.* imitate, copy, mimic. See IMITATION.

apex, *n.* peak, climax. See HEIGHT.

aphorism, *n.* MAXIM, adage, proverb.

apiece, *adv.* for each, for one, respectively, individually. See SPECIALITY.

aplomb, *n.* poise, [self-]assurance. See INEXCITABILITY.

apology, *n.* excuse, justification, VINDICATION; regret, amends. See ATONEMENT, PENITENCE.

apostate, *n.* backslider, renegade, turncoat, deserter, traitor, recreant; double dealer, opportunist. See CHANGEABLENESS, IMPIETY, HETERODOXY, EVILDOER, DISSENT.

apostle, *n.* disciple; evangelist. See LEARNING, RELIGION.

appall, *v.t.* horrify, shock; disgust, revolt. See FEAR, PAIN.

apparatus, *n.* machine, machinery; equipment, instruments. See INSTRUMENTALITY, PROVISION.

apparel, *n.* See CLOTHING.

apparent, *adj.* plain, obvious, visible; EVIDENT, manifest, perceptible. See APPEARANCE, VISIBILITY.

apparition, *n.* phantom, ghost, specter; dream. See DEMON, IMAGINATION.

appeal, *n.* entreaty, plea, begging, petition; resort; attractiveness, ATTRACTION. See REQUEST, LAWSUIT.

APPEARANCE

Nouns—**1,** appearance, sight, show, scene, view; outlook, prospect, vista, angle, perspective, bird's-eye view; scenery, landscape, picture, tableau; display, setting, *mise en scène*. See VISIBILITY.

2, peep show, magic lantern, phantasmagoria, panorama, diorama; spectacle, pageantry (see OSTENTATION).

3, aspect, phase, seeming, semblance; shape (see FORM); guise, façade, look, complexion, color, image, mien, air, cast, carriage, port, demeanor; presence, expression, first blush; point of view, light. See FASHION.

4, lineament, feature; contour, face, countenance, physiognomy, visage, cast of countenance, figure, profile, cut of one's jib. *Slang,* phiz.

Verbs—appear, become visible, materialize; put in *or* make an appearance, darken one's door, show up, turn out, crop *or* turn up; seem, look, show; have, take on, *or* assume the appearance *or* semblance of; look like; cut a figure, figure; present to the view. See ARRIVAL.

Adjectives—apparent, seeming, ostensible; on view; evident, manifest.

Adverbs—apparently, ostensibly, seemingly, as it seems, on the face of it, *prima facie;* at first blush *or* sight; in the eyes of; to the eye.

Antonyms, see ABSENCE, DISAPPEARANCE, INVISIBILITY.

---

appease, *v.t.* mollify, pacify, soothe, placate; satisfy, slake. See PACIFICATION, MODERATION, SUFFICIENCY.

append, *v.t.* add, attach (to), affix. See ADDITION.

appendix, *n.* supplement (see ADDITION).

appetite, *n.* hunger, DESIRE, craving.

appetizer, *n.* relish; hors d'oeuvre, antipasto; dainty. See FOOD, TASTE, PRECEDENCE.

applause, *n.* clapping; praise. See APPROBATION.

appliance, *n.* device, machine, implement; attachment, accessory. See INSTRUMENTALITY, REMEDY.

applicable, *adj.* fitting, suitable, appropriate, relevant, pertinent. See UTILITY, AGREEMENT.

application, *n.* diligence, assiduity; suitability, relevancy; form, blank. See REQUEST, RELATION, ATTENTION, USE.

apply, *v.* put *or* lay on, USE; ask, REQUEST; work, persevere (see RESOLUTION).

appoint, *v.* prescribe, assign, ordain; place, designate, nominate; equip, rig. See COMMISSION, COMMAND.

appointment, *n.* meeting, interview, engagement; office; rendezvous, tryst. *Colloq.,* date. See BUSINESS, SOCIALITY, COMMISSION.

APPORTIONMENT

Nouns—**1,** apportionment, allotment, consignment, allocation, assignment; appropriation; dispensation, distribution, division, partition, deal. See DISPERSION, PART.

2, dividend, portion, contingent, share, lot, measure, dose; dole, meed, pittance; quantum, ration; ratio, proportion, quota, modicum, allowance.

Verbs—apportion, admeasure, divide, budget; distribute, consign, dispense; billet, allot, detail, cast, share, mete; choose up sides; portion, allocate, disburse, ration; dish, hand, give, parcel, *or* dole out, farm out; deal, carve, administer; partition, assign, appropriate, appoint. *Colloq.,* go halves. *Slang,* divvy (up). See COOPERATION.

Adjectives—apportioning; respective; proportional, proportionate, commensurate; divisible.

Adverbs—respectively, *pro rata,* each to each, severally, individually; *per stirpes, per capita. Slang,* per.

Antonyms, see ACQUISITION.

---

appraise, *v.* evaluate, assess, PRICE. See MEASUREMENT.
appreciable, *adj.* tangible; measurable. See SUBSTANCE.
appreciate, *v.* prize, esteem, value; INCREASE [in value]; comprehend, understand; realize worth. See APPROBATION, KNOWLEDGE, MEASUREMENT, GRATITUDE.
apprehend, *v.* seize, arrest; grasp, see, understand, perceive. See RESTRAINT, KNOWLEDGE.
apprehension, *n.* FEAR, anxiety; arrest, seizure; understanding. See KNOWLEDGE, RESTRAINT, EXPECTATION.
apprenticeship, *n.* training, probation. See LEARNING.

APPROACH

Nouns—**1,** approach, nearing, approximation; imminence; CONVERGENCE.
2, access, entrance, advent; PASSAGE, INGRESS. See NEARNESS.
Verbs—approach, approximate; near, lower, draw near, come *or* step up; come to close quarters; move toward, come at; drift; make up to; gain upon, pursue, tread on the heels of; hug the shore; loom ahead, impend, stare one in the face (see DESTINY).
Adjectives—approaching, near[ing], approximate; impending, brewing, preparing, forthcoming, oncoming, imminent, destined; on the horizon, on the brink *or* verge of, in the wind; approachable, accessible, *etc.*
Antonyms, see REGRESSION, DISTANCE, AVOIDANCE, RECESSION.

APPROBATION

Nouns—**1,** approbation, approval, sanction; esteem, good opinion, favor, countenance; admiration (see RESPECT); appreciation, popularity, kudos, credit.
2, commendation, praise, laudation; good word; meed, tribute, encomium; eulogy, panegyric; benediction, blessing, benison.
3, applause, plaudit, ovation, clapping [of hands]; acclaim, acclamation, cheer; paean, hosanna; thumbs up; claque. See CONGRATULATION.
4, award, trophy, medal, prize, cup, loving cup, statuette; palm, laurel, garland of bays; crown, wreath, feather in one's cap, honor, decoration; Oscar, Emmy, Edgar, Obie, Tony, Grammy.
Verbs—**1,** approve, O.K.; think good, much, well, *or* highly of; esteem; value, prize; set great store by; do justice to, appreciate; like, favor, take kindly to. *Colloq.,* hand it to.
2, stand *or* stick up for; clap *or* pat on the back; endorse, give credit, recommend; commend, praise, laud, compliment, pay a tribute, applaud, cheer, encore; congratulate (see CONGRATULATION); panegyrize, eulogize, cry up, puff, extol, magnify, glorify, exalt, make much of; bless, give a blessing to; have *or* say a good word for; speak well *or* highly of; sing, sound, *or* resound the praises of. *Slang,* give a big hand, root for.
3, be praised; receive honorable mention; be in [high] favor with; ring with the praises of, gain credit, stand well in the opinion of; pass muster; bring down the house, stop the show; be popular, catch on.
Adjectives—**1,** approving, commendatory, complimentary, benedictory, laudatory, panegyrical, eulogistic, lavish of praise; in favor of.
2, approved, praised, popular; in good odor; exemplary; in high esteem, respected, riding high, in one's good graces *or* books; in [good] with.
3, deserving, worthy, praiseworthy, commendable, meritorious, estimable,

creditable, unimpeachable; beyond all praise. *Colloq.*, in one's good books.
Adverbs—with credit, well; on approval.
Interjections—hear, hear! bravo! bravissimo! olé! nice going! so far so good! viva! encore!

Antonyms, see DISAPPROBATION.

---

appropriate, *adj.* proper, fit, timely, suitable. See AGREEMENT. —*v.t.* take, seize, confiscate; allot, assign. See STEALING, ACQUISITION, APPORTIONMENT.

approve, *v.t.* accept, like, support, recognize, ratify, endorse. *Colloq.*, O.K. See APPROBATION.

approximate, *adj.* near, close, rough. See NEARNESS, SIMILARITY, RELATION.

apron, *n.* bib, smock; flap, strip. See CLOTHING, AVIATION.

apt, *adj.* suitable, appropriate, fitting; quick, clever; likely. See AGREEMENT, SKILL, TENDENCY.

aquatic, *adj.* watery; oceanic, marine, fresh- *or* salt-water. See WATER.

aquiline, *adj.* beaked, curved, hooked, Roman. See ANGULARITY.

arable, *adj.* tillable, farmable; fertile. See AGRICULTURE.

arbitrary, *adj.* despotic, dictatorial; capricious; unreasonable; discretionary, willful. See ILLEGALITY, AUTHORITY, WILL.

arbitration, *n.* intervention, mediation, settlement (of dispute). See JUDGMENT, COMPROMISE.

arbitrator, *n.* judge, referee, umpire, mediator. See JUDGMENT, COMPROMISE.

arbor, *n.* bower, pergola; shaft. See ABODE, ROTATION.

arcade, *n.* corridor (see PASSAGE); penny arcade (see AMUSEMENT).

arcane, *adj.* SECRET.

arch, *n.* curve, arc, vault. See CONVEXITY, CONCAVITY, CURVATURE. —*adj.* CUNNING, roguish; preeminent, chief. See SUPERIORITY.

archaeology, *n.* See PAST.

archaic, *adj.* old, ancient; antiquated, obsolete, outdated; historic. See PAST, OLDNESS.

archer, *n.* bowman. See COMBATANT.

archetype, *n.* model, prototype. See PREPARATION.

architect, *n.* planner, designer, creator. See AGENCY, ARTIST.

architecture, *n.* design, FORM.

archive, *n.* chronicle, annal, RECORD.

arctic, *adj.* boreal. See COLD.

ardent, *adj.* warm, passionate, zealous, fervent; glowing, fiery; eager. See FEELING, HEAT, ACTIVITY.

ardor, *n.* fervor, passion, enthusiasm, élan, zeal; HEAT. See FEELING, VIGOR.

arduous, *adj.* onerous, wearisome. See DIFFICULTY, WEARINESS.

area, *n.* tract, territory; SPACE; expanse; scope. See REGION.

ARENA

Nouns—**1,** arena, field, theater; amphitheater, coliseum, Colosseum, stadium, bowl; hippodrome, circus, race course *or* track, turf, cockpit; playground, gymnasium, ring, rink, lists, tilting ground; stage. See AMUSEMENT, CONTENTION. **2,** theater [of war]; battlefield, battleground, front, field of combat. See WARFARE.

---

argument, *n.* debate, dispute; EVIDENCE, case. See REASONING, DISCORD, THOUGHT.

aria, *n.* song, air (see MUSIC).

arid, *adj.* dry, parched; jejune, barren; uninteresting. See DRYNESS, WEARINESS, USELESSNESS.

arise, *v.i.* get up, awake; originate, begin. See BEGINNING, ASCENT, EFFECT.

aristocracy, *n.* NOBILITY. See AUTHORITY.

arithmetic, *n.* mathematics, computation (see NUMERATION).

arm, *n.* limb, member; branch, wing; weapon, strength. See ARMS, POWER, PART. —*v.* See PROVISION.

armistice, *n.* truce, respite, lull, peace. See PACIFICATION.

armor, *n.* steel plate, mail, shielding. See DEFENSE.

armory, *n.* arsenal. See STORE.

ARMS

Nouns—**1,** arms, weapon[s], weaponry, firearms, armament, engine of war, materiel; panoply, stand of arms, military establishment; armory, arsenal (see STORE); armor (see DEFENSE). See WARFARE, PROVISION.

2, ammunition, munitions, explosive; ball, bolt, shot, grape [shot], chain shot, pellet, bullet, dumdum bullet, cartridge, shell, fragmentation shell, shrapnel; missile, projectile, grenade, bomb, depth charge, ashcan, atomic bomb, A-bomb, fission bomb, hydrogen bomb, H-bomb, thermonuclear bomb, blockbuster; torpedo, guided missile, Nike, I.C.B.M. (intercontinental ballistic missile), rocket, V1, V2; [thermo]nuclear warhead, neutron bomb. *Colloq.,* Molotov cocktail. *Slang,* hardware.

3, artillery, gun[s], gunnery, cannon, battery, ordnance, ballistics; piece, fieldpiece, howitzer, mortar; siege, coast, *or* field artillery; Big Bertha, French 75, two-pounder, ten-pounder, 8-inch, 16-inch, *etc.;* carronade, culverin, basilisk, falconet, jingle, swivel, petard; antiaircraft, A.A., ackack. See PROPULSION.

4, machine gun, submachine gun, pompom, Gatling gun, Maxim gun, Bren gun, Thompson *or* Tommy gun. *Slang,* chopper.

5, small arms; musket[ry], carbine, rifle, shotgun, fowling piece, breechloader, muzzle-loader, chassepot, blunderbuss, harquebus, arquebus, matchlock, flintlock, flint-and-steel; .22, .25, .32., .38, .44, .45, .30-30, .30-06, *etc.;* 8-, 12-, 16-gauge, *etc.;* Kentucky long rifle, Springfield, Enfield, Winchester, Lee-Enfield, Garand, *etc.;* pistol, automatic, semiautomatic, derringer, repeater, revolver, hammerless [revolver], six-shooter, six-gun; Colt, Smith and Wesson, Luger, Beretta, *etc. Slang,* gat, rod, heater, zip gun.

6, armored vehicle, tank.

7, sword, saber, broadsword, cutlass, falchion, scimitar, bilbo, rapier, skean, claymore, creese, kris; dagger, dirk, hanger, poniard, stiletto, stylet, dudgeon, bayonet; foil, épée, blade, steel; ax, poleax, battleax, halberd, tomahawk; bowie knife, bolo, kukri, pigsticker, switchblade knife, yataghan; cold steel. See SHARPNESS.

8, pike, lance, spear, spontoon, javelin, dart, djerrid, arrow, reed, shaft, bolt, boomerang, harpoon, gaff; fishing spear.

9, club, mace, truncheon, staff, bludgeon, cudgel, life-preserver, shillelagh; quarterstaff; battering ram (see IMPULSE); bat, knuckle-duster, brass knuckles *or* knucks; blackjack, sap, billy, nightstick.

10, bow, crossbow, arbalest; catapult, sling; bola.

11, warship (see SHIP).

12, [poison *or* nerve] gas, chemical agent; [nuclear] fallout.

13, armsmaker, fletcher.

Verbs—arm, equip, PROVISION.

Adjectives—armed, equipped, *etc.;* armed [to the teeth], in arms.

---

army, *n.* troops, soldiers, [military] force; host, crowd, throng. See COMBATANT, MULTITUDE.

aroma, *n.* fragrance, smell; quality, characteristic (see SPECIALITY). See ODOR.

around, *adv. & prep.* surrounding, about; near, neighboring. See NEARNESS, ENVIRONMENT.

arouse, *v.* rouse, awaken; stir, excite, stimulate, whet. See EXCITEMENT, ACTIVITY.

arraign, *v.t.* indict, charge, accuse. See ACCUSATION, LAWSUIT.

ARRANGEMENT

Nouns—arrangement, plan, PREPARATION, disposition, distribution, sorting; configuration, FORM, format, grouping, assortment, triage; METHOD; allotment (see APPORTIONMENT); taxonomy, organization, classification (see CLASS); register, file (see LIST); echelon; ORDER, array, system. See SYMMETRY.

Verbs—**1,** arrange, dispose, line up, place, form; put, set, *or* place in order; set out, collate, pack, marshal, range, size, rank, group; dispose of, compartmentalize, pigeonhole, assign places to; assort, sort; put *or* set to rights, align, line up, put in shape *or* in array, reduce to order, put up; stack.
2, classify, alphabetize, file; string together, register (see LIST); graduate (see DEGREE); regulate, systematize, coordinate, organize, straighten up.

Adjectives—arranged, methodical, orderly, tidy, neat, regular, systematic.

Adverbs—methodically, systematically, like clockwork, in apple-pie order.

Antonyms, see DISORDER.

arrant, *adj.* thorough, outright. See COMPLETION, DISREPUTE.

array, *n.* CLOTHING, apparel; host, MULTITUDE; ARRANGEMENT. See ASSEMBLAGE, OSTENTATION, CONTINUITY, ORDER.

arrears, *n.pl.* See DEBT.

arrest, *v.* seize, apprehend, capture; stop, halt; retard, suspend. *Colloq.,* nab. *Slang,* pinch, bust. See END, RESTRAINT.

ARRIVAL

Nouns—**1,** arrival, advent, landing; debarkation, disembarkation; homecoming, return, rencounter.
2, home, goal, landing-place, destination (see END); harbor, haven, port, port of call; terminus; attainment (see COMPLETION).
3, newcomer, visitor; Johnny-come-lately; *colloq.,* newborn child.

Verbs—**1,** arrive, get to, come to, reach, attain; come up with *or* to; catch up (to); overtake.
2, light, alight, dismount; land, go ashore, debark, disembark; detrain, deplane; put in[to], visit, cast anchor, pitch one's tent; sign *or* check in, get to one's journey's end, end up; come *or* get back, come home, return; appear, put in an appearance, come in, drop in, darken one's door. *Slang,* blow in, hit town; make the scene.

Antonyms, see DEPARTURE.

arrogance, *n.* haughtiness, self-importance; INSOLENCE, presumptuousness. See SEVERITY, VANITY.

arrogate, *v.* usurp, claim, seize; assume, appropriate, take. See ACQUISITION.

arrow, *n.* shaft, bolt; pointer. See ARMS, DIRECTION.

arsenal, *n.* armory, storehouse, supply; resources. See STORE.

art, *n.* craft, SKILL; CUNNING; science,

technics; fine arts (see REPRESENTATION). See BUSINESS.

artery, *n.* vessel, vein, channel. See PASSAGE.

artful, *adj.* See CUNNING, SKILL.

article, *n.* item; object, thing; story, piece, essay, report. See SUBSTANCE, INFORMATION, BELIEF, PART, UNITY.

articulate, *adj.* jointed, segmented (see JUNCTION); distinct, intelligible; literate, lucid. —*v.* pronounce, enunciate, utter, put in words, verbalize; unite, join. See SPEECH, MEANING.

artifice, *n.* trick, stratagem, ruse; device; CUNNING. See DECEPTION.

artificial, *adj.* handmade, handcrafted, synthetic; false, sham, fake, deceptive; affected, unnatural. See AFFECTATION, DECEPTION, PRODUCTION, INELEGANCE.

artillery, *n.* cannon, ordnance. See ARMS.

artisan, *n.* mechanic, craftsman, workman. See AGENCY, SKILL, ARTIST.

ARTIST

Nouns—**1,** artist, virtuoso, master, maestro, academician; craftsman, artisan; old master. See AGENCY, SKILL.

2, a. painter, limner, drawer, sketcher; illustrator, portraitist, watercolorist, miniaturist, pointillist, surrealist, genre painter, landscapist, landscape artist, seascapist; engraver, designer, etcher; reetcher, retoucher; cartoonist, caricaturist; copyist, draftsman; commercial artist, advertising artist, layout man. See PAINTING. **b.** sculptor, sculptress, carver, chaser, modelist, chiseler (see SCULPTURE). **c.** author, writer, novelist (see WRITING); poet (see POETRY). **d.** dramatist, actor, actress, Thespian, performer (see DRAMA); dancer, ballerina; musician, composer, arranger, orchestrator, soloist, pianist, *etc.* (see MUSIC). **e.** architect, builder; landscape architect *or* gardener. **f.** photographer, cameraman, cinematographer. **g.** decorator; interior decorator; window dresser.

Antonyms, see UNSKILLFULNESS.

artistic, *adj.* talented, accomplished; cultural; beautiful, esthetic; skillful, masterly. See BEAUTY, TASTE, ELEGANCE.

artless, *adj.* simple; ingenuous, unsophisticated, naïve; guileless, innocent. See INNOCENCE.

ASCENT

Nouns—**1,** ascent, ascension, mounting, rising, rise, leap; upswing, upsurge; acclivity, hill; flight of steps *or* stairs, stairway, staircase; ladder, accommodation ladder, fire escape; incline, ramp, gangway; elevator, lift, escalator (see ELEVATION). See OBLIQUITY.

2, mountaineer, mountain climber.

Verbs—ascend, rise, mount, arise, uprise; ride *or* crawl up; spring *or* shoot up; step up; climb, clamber, surmount, scale the heights; tower, soar; LEAP.

Adjectives—rising, scandent, buoyant; in the ascendant.

Adverbs—up, uphill; upstairs, abovestairs.

Antonyms, see DESCENT.

ascertain, *v.t.* find, discover, learn; determine, establish, fix; certify, ensure, settle, clinch. See CERTAINTY, DISCLOSURE, LEARNING.

ASCETICISM

Nouns—**1,** asceticism, puritanism, austerity; abstinence, abstemiousness; [self-] mortification, [self-]denial, maceration, sackcloth and ashes, hair shirt, flagellation; penance, fasting. See ATONEMENT.

2, ascetic, anchoret, anchorite, hermit, recluse; fakir; puritan, sabbatarian.

Verbs—fast, do penance; abstain, eat like a bird; mortify the flesh, flagellate; eat worms.

Adjectives—ascetic, austere, puritanical, anchorite; abstinent, abstemious.

Antonyms, see PLEASURE, GLUTTONY.

---

ascribe, *v.t* impute, accredit, attribute (see ATTRIBUTION).

ashamed, *adj*. abashed, embarrassed, mortified. See REGRET, HUMILITY.

ashen, *adj*. ashy, pale, bloodless, wan, gray. See COLORLESSNESS.

ashore, *adj*. on land *or* shore. See LAND.

aside, *adv*. apart, aloof, away. See DISTANCE, SIDE. —*n*. parenthesis; [stage] whisper. See SPEECH.

asinine, *adj*. mulish, donkeyish; silly. See FOLLY, ABSURDITY.

ask, *v*. interrogate, question; inquire; invite; REQUEST, demand. See INQUIRY, BARTER.

askance, *adv*. sideways; distrustfully. See SIDE, DOUBT.

askew, *adj*. crooked, awry, lopsided, oblique. See DISTORTION.

asleep, *adj*. sleeping; dozing, napping; quiescent, dormant; numb; dead (see DEATH). See INACTIVITY, INATTENTION.

aspect, *n*. look, APPEARANCE, side, view; expression, mien; phase, stage. See LOCATION.

aspire, *v.i*. DESIRE, strive (for).

ass, *n*. donkey, jackass, burro; fool, simpleton. See TRANSPORTATION, FOLLY.

assail, *v.t*. ATTACK, set upon, assault; criticize.

assassin, *n*. killer, slayer, murderer, thug. See KILLING.

assault, *v*. & *n*. See ATTACK.

ASSEMBLAGE

Nouns—**1,** assemblage, assembly, gathering, meeting, forgathering, convocation, congregation, council, caucus, conclave, congress, diet, convention; symposium, panel; concourse, conflux; muster, levy, posse, *posse comitatus*, roundup; caravan, convoy. See SOCIALITY, PRESENCE.

2, compilation, collection, anthology, album, compendium; miscellany (see MIXTURE); library, treasury, museum, menagerie (see STORE).

3, crowd, throng, rabble, mob, press, crush, horde, body, tribe (see POPULACE); audience (see HEARING); crew, gang, knot, squad, band, PARTY; swarm, shoal, school, covey, flock, flight, herd, drove; array, bevy, galaxy, constellation; clique, coterie, set; fleet; corps, company, troop; host (see MULTITUDE).

4, shower, group, cluster, clump, set, batch, lot, pack; battery; bunch, bundle, fascine, bale; wisp, shock, rick, fardel, stack, sheaf, haycock.

5, accumulation, congeries, heap, pile, drift, aggregate, agglomeration, conglomeration, aggregation, concentration, QUANTITY. See ACQUISITION.

Verbs—**1,** assemble, be *or* come together, collect, muster; meet, unite, rejoin; cluster, flock, swarm, surge, stream, herd, crowd, throng, associate; congregate, conglomerate, concentrate; rendezvous, resort; come, flock, *or* get together; forgather, huddle.

2, get *or* bring together, assemble, muster, collect, collocate, call up, gather, convene, convoke, convocate; rake up, dredge; heap, mass; agglomerate, aggregate; sheaf, collate, compile, take up; group, concentrate, amass, accumulate; scare up, round up.

Adjectives—assembled, closely packed, massed, serried, crowded, teeming, swarming, populous; cumulative.

Adverbs—en masse, in force, in a crowd.

Antonyms, see DISPERSION.

ASSENT

Nouns—**1,** assent, acquiescence; nod, accord, accordance; concord (see AGREEMENT); recognition, concurrence.

2, ratification, confirmation, corroboration; approval, acceptance (see APPROBATION); CONSENT, willingness. See PERMISSION.

3, yes-man, company man; rubber stamp; signator[y], signer.

Verbs—**1,** assent, nod, acquiesce, agree; accept, accede, accord, concur; lend oneself to, CONSENT; go with, go along (with), chime in, jump at, recognize; subscribe (to), say yes; say the word, ditto, amen, *or* aye (to), O.K.; ratify, validate, approve (see APPROBATION); countersign; corroborate; let ride.

2, come to an understanding, come to terms, see eye to eye; swim with the stream; be in the fashion, join in the chorus.

3, be ratified, carry, pass, go through.

Adjectives—**1,** assenting, of one accord *or* mind, of the same mind, at one with; agreed, acquiescent, willing.

2, uncontradicted, unchallenged, unquestioned, uncontroverted; carried, agreed.

Adverbs—**1,** yes, yea, aye; true, good, well, very well, well and good; granted; even so, just so, to be sure; truly, exactly, precisely, that's just it, indeed, certainly, of course, indubitably, unquestionably, surely, sure, assuredly, by all [manner of] means, no doubt, doubtless, and no mistake; be it so, so be it, amen; willingly; to a man.

2, affirmatively, in the affirmative.

3, willingly, fain, freely; heart and soul; with pleasure, nothing loath, graciously, without reluctance, of one's own accord.

Interjections—yes sirree! yes sirree Bob! you said a mouthful! you said it! and how! right on!

Antonyms, see DISSENT.

---

assert, *v.t.* avow, declare, say, claim, affirm, state. See AFFIRMATION.

assertive, *adj.* positive, dogmatic. See CERTAINTY, INSOLENCE.

assess, *v.t.* value, appraise, price, estimate; charge, tax. See JUDGMENT, MEASUREMENT, PAYMENT.

assets, *n.pl.* possessions, PROPERTY; capital; resources. See ACCOUNTING.

assiduous, *adj.* diligent, attentive. See ACTIVITY.

assign, *v.* hand over; allot, distribute; delegate, COMMISSION; appoint, designate; ascribe (see ATTRIBUTION). See APPORTIONMENT, GIVING, TRANSFER, BUSINESS.

assimilate, *v.t.* digest, absorb; incorporate, merge (with). See SIMILARITY, IMITATION, LEARNING.

assist, *v.t.* AID, help, second, support; attend (see PRESENCE).

assistant, *n.* See AUXILIARY.

associate, *v.* join, fraternize, ally, combine (with); unite, connect, relate, link. See CONNECTION, RELATION. —*n.* FRIEND, comrade; colleague, co-worker, partner. See ACCOMPANIMENT, AUXILIARY, COMBINATION.

association, *n.* club, organization (see PARTY); fraternity; partnership, COMBINATION, league; analogy (see RELATION). See ACCOMPANIMENT, COOPERATION.

assort, *v.t.* arrange, classify; mix. See ARRANGEMENT, MIXTURE.

assuage, *v.t.* lessen (see RELIEF).

assume, *v.t.* suppose, take for granted; put on, affect; appropriate. See SUPPOSITION, AFFECTATION, ACQUISITION.

assurance, *n.* confidence, CERTAINTY, BELIEF; INSOLENCE, boldness; pledge, guarantee, PROMISE.

astern, *adv.* aft, to the rear, abaft, See REAR.

astir, *adv.* afoot; moving; up and about. See ACTIVITY.

astonish, *v.t.* SURPRISE, amaze, astound.

astray, *adv.* lost, wandering; in ERROR. See DEVIATION.

astringent, *adj.* binding, styptic; severe (see SEVERITY). See CONTRACTION, PUNGENCY.

astrology, *n.* horoscopy, stargazing. See PREDICTION.

ASTRONAUTICS

Nouns—**1,** astronautics, space travel *or* flight; space *or* celestial navigation, astrogation, astronavigation; outer- *or* interplanetary space; aerospace.

2, rocket, space ship *or* shuttle, spacecraft, lunar module, L.E.M., space probe; space station; [communications, weather, observation, *etc.*] satellite; probe; [ascent *or* descent] stage, drop-off, capsule; free fall, weightlessness; docking; injection *or* insertion [into orbit]; launch site, Cape Kennedy, Cape Canaveral, cosmodrome; escape velocity, launch window, reentry corridor; countdown, [number for] go; launch; payload.

3, astronaut, cosmonaut, spaceman *or* -woman.

Verbs—launch, blast off; dock; touch down; inject *or* insert into orbit.

---

astronomy, *n.* cosmology, cosmogony. See UNIVERSE.

astute, *adj.* clever, shrewd, CUNNING. See INTELLIGENCE.

asunder, *adv.* apart (see DISJUNCTION, DISTANCE).

asylum, *n.* retreat, refuge, sanctuary, shelter; home, orphanage, sanitarium, sanatorium; mental hospital, psychopathic ward. See SAFETY, INSANITY, ABODE.

asymmetric, asymmetrical, *adj.* uneven, irregular. See DISTORTION, IRREGULARITY.

atheist, *n.* heretic, unbeliever. See IRRELIGION, HETERODOXY.

athletic, *adj.* sporting, gymnastic, acrobatic; agile, strong. See STRENGTH, AMUSEMENT, EXERTION.

atlas, *n.* See PLAN.

atmosphere, *n.* AIR, sky, ether, ozone; exosphere; mood, aura, ambience, ENVIRONMENT.

atom, *n.* particle, iota, speck. See LITTLENESS, POWER.

atomize, *v.t.* vaporize; pulverize. See VAPOR, POWDERINESS.

ATONEMENT

Nouns—**1,** atonement, reparation; COMPENSATION, quittance, quits; expiation, redemption, reclamation, propitiation. See PENITENCE, ASCETICISM.

2, amends, apology, *amende honorable,* satisfaction, RESTORATION; peace offering, burnt offering; sacrifice, sacrificial lamb.

3, penance, fasting, maceration, sackcloth and ashes, white sheet, shrift, flagellation, lustration; purgation, purgatory.

Verbs—**1,** atone (for); expiate; propitiate; make amends, pay for, make good; reclaim, redeem, redress, repair; ransom, purge, shrive; do penance, repent [in sackcloth and ashes] (see PENITENCE); set one's house in order; wipe off old scores; make matters up; pay the penalty; take back, eat one's words, eat humble pie, eat crow; live down.
2, apologize, beg pardon, ask forgiveness, give satisfaction; fall on one's knees.
Adjectives—propitiatory, conciliatory, expiatory; sacrificial, piacular; apologetic.
Antonyms, see IMPENITENCE, IMPIETY.

---

atrocity, *n.* enormity; outrage. See MALEVOLENCE, BADNESS.

atrophy, *n.* degeneration, DETERIORATION.

attachment, *n.* ADDITION, adjunct, appendage; legal seizure (see ACQUISITION); affection, LOVE, loyalty, devotion. See JUNCTION.

ATTACK

Nouns—**1,** attack; assault, assault and battery; onset, onslaught, charge; aggression, offense; incursion, inroad, invasion; counterattack; irruption, outbreak; sally, sortie, raid, foray; boarding, *escalade;* siege, investment, besiegement, beleaguerment; storm[ing], bombing, air attack, air raid, blitz[krieg], bombardment, barrage, cannonade. See WARFARE, COMBATANT.
2, volley, fusillade, broadside; salvo; raking, crossfire; cut, thrust, lunge, pass; kick, punch. See IMPULSE.
3, assailant, aggressor, offender, invader; pusher, go-getter.
Verbs—**1,** attack, assault, charge, assail; set *or* fall upon; raid; ambush; make *or* go to war (on *or* against), break a lance with, enter the lists, aggress; assume *or* take the offensive, strike the first blow, throw the first stone; lift a hand *or* draw the sword (against), take up the cudgels; march against *or* upon, invade; take by storm, blitz; harry, show fight.
2, strike (at), thrust at, hit, kick, slap, cut, pelt; take a punch, poke, *or* sock at; deal a blow (at), tee off at, lash out, fetch one a blow, fling oneself at *or* upon, lunge at, pounce upon; lace, lay, rip, light, sail, plow, tear, *or* pitch into, launch out against, go at *or* for; bait, slap on the face; make a pass at; bear down upon, close with, come to grips with, come to close quarters, bring to bay; rush, run, fly, *or* have at, ride full tilt against, let fly at, turn on; attack tooth and nail; press hard; run down, strike at the root of; lay about one, run amuck; gang up on *or* against. *Colloq.,* whale away. See IMPULSE.
3, fire at, shoot at, open up on; pepper, bombard, shell, pour a broadside into; open fire, fire a volley; beset, besiege, beleaguer; lay siege to, invest; sap, mine; storm, board, scale the walls; cut and thrust, bayonet, butt, batter; bomb, strafe, dive-bomb, blitz.
4, draw fire, be a sitting duck.
Adjectives—**1,** attacking, aggressive, offensive, pushy; up in arms, on the warpath; forceful, belligerent, combative, warlike.
2, under attack *or* fire, under siege.
Adverbs—on the offensive.
Antonyms, see DEFENSE.

---

attain, *v.t.* achieve, accomplish; reach. See ARRIVAL, SUCCESS.

attempt, *n. & v.* try, endeavor, essay; ATTACK. See UNDERTAKING.

attend, *v.* accompany, escort; be present; heed, listen; minister to, serve. See ACCOMPANIMENT, ATTENTION, PRESENCE, REMEDY.

ATTENTION

Nouns—**1,** attention, mindfulness, intentness, attentiveness, THOUGHT, thoughtfulness, advertence, CARE; observance, observation, consideration, heed, notice, look, note, regard; vigil; circumspection, study, scrutiny, inspection (see INQUIRY); fixation. See RESPECT, INFORMATION.

2, diligence, application, attention to detail, absorption (of mind), preoccupation (with).

3, calling *or* drawing attention to (see INDICATION).

Verbs—**1,** attend (to), observe, look, watch, notice, regard, take notice, mark; give *or* pay [close] attention, have an ear to the ground, prick up the ears, keep the eyes open *or* peeled; be all ears, hang on one's words, harken, heed, be attentive, listen, lend *or* give an ear to; hang on the words *or* lips of; trouble one's head about, give a thought to, occupy oneself with; contemplate; look [in]to, see to; turn the mind to, apply oneself to, buckle *or* knuckle down, have an eye to; bear in mind, take into account *or* consideration; keep in sight *or* view, keep one's eye on the ball; have a regard to; take cognizance of, entertain; make *or* take note *or* notice of, note, see about. *Colloq.*, get with it.

2, examine closely *or* intently, consider; inspect, review, take stock of; fix, rivet, *or* devote the mind *or* thoughts on *or* to, zero in on; lose oneself, have eyes only for; go over with a fine-tooth comb.

3, catch *or* strike the eye; attract attention *or* notice, cut a swath, awaken *or* invite interest; hold the stage, be arresting *or* absorbing; engage, intrigue; be uppermost in one's mind; monopolize, engross, tie up.

4, indicate, bring to one's notice, point out, lay the finger on; bring, direct, call, *or* draw attention to; show.

Adjectives—**1,** attentive, mindful, observant, regardful, assiduous; alive *or* awake to; observing, occupied with, engrossed, thoughtful, wrapped up in, absorbed, rapt, all ears *or* eyes; intent (on), open-eyed, on the watch *or* ball, alert, [broad *or* wide] awake, vigilant; watchful, wakeful, Argus-eyed, expectant.

2, absorbing, engrossing, eye-catching, catchy.

Adverb—in mind.

Interjections—see! look! mark! lo! behold! hark! mind! observe! lo and behold! attention!; *nota bene, N.B.;* this is to give notice.

Antonyms, see INATTENTION.

---

attenuate, *v.* weaken; thin out, rarefy. See DECREASE, NARROWNESS, WEAKNESS.

attest, *v.* testify, bear witness, depose, certify, swear, vouch. See EVIDENCE.

attic, *n.* loft, garret. See RECEPTACLE.

attire, *n.* dress, CLOTHING, garb.

attitude, *n.* stand, pose, posture, position. See LOCATION, FORM, CIRCUMSTANCE.

attorney, *n.* lawyer, AGENT. See LAWSUIT.

ATTRACTION

Nouns—**1,** attraction, attractiveness; drawing to, pulling towards, adduction, magnetism, gravity, gravitation; affinity. See TRACTION.

2, allurement, seduction, fascination, appeal, enticement, temptation (see DESIRE); lodestone, lodestar, polestar; magnet, electromagnet, siderite, alnico; lure, glamour, charm; decoy, bait.

Verbs—**1,** attract; draw *or* pull towards; adduce.

2, allure, seduce, interest, charm, captivate, fascinate, tempt, entice, lure, lead on; rope in; make one's mouth water.

Adjectives—**1,** attracting, attrahent, attractive, adducent, adductive; magnetic.

2, attractive, charming, alluring, engaging, interesting, winning, prepossessing, captivating, bewitching, fascinating, seductive; mouth-watering. See BEAUTY.

Antonyms, see REPULSION.

ATTRIBUTION

Nouns—**1,** attribution, ascription, assignment, reference to; accounting for; imputation, derivation from, credit; explanation, reason, motive (see CAUSE); etiology; INTERPRETATION. See EFFECT.

2, attribute, trait, characteristic, quality, property. See INDICATION, SPECIALITY.

Verbs—attribute, ascribe, assign, impute, accredit; refer, lay, point, *or* trace to; set *or* put down to; credit with *or* to; ground on; lay at the door of; put words in one's mouth; charge *or* chalk up to; account for, derive from, read into; blame on *or* to, charge with *or* to, fix responsibility *or* blame (see ACCUSATION).

Adjectives—attributed, attributable, referable, assignable, ascribably; due to, derivable from, owing to.

Adverbs—**1,** hence, thence, therefore, since, on account of, because, owing *or* due to; on that account; thanks to, forasmuch as; whence, *propter hoc*; duly.

2, why? wherefore? whence? *Colloq.,* how come?

---

attrition, *n.* abrasion (see DETERIORATION, FRICTION).

auction, *n.* bidding, vendue, SALE; offering.

audacity, *n.* boldness, COURAGE; impudence; RASHNESS, INSOLENCE.

audible, *adj.* See HEARING.

audience, *n.* HEARING, interview; onlookers, hearers; assembly. See DRAMA, CONVERSATION.

auditorium, *n.* hall, meeting place; theater. See DRAMA, AMUSEMENT.

augment, *v.* See INCREASE.

augur, *v.* foretell, prophesy; signify, presage. See PREDICTION.

august, *adj.* noble, exalted, imposing; eminent. See REPUTE.

aura, *n.* atmosphere, air; emanation. See WIND, ENVIRONMENT.

auspice, *n.* omen, token; (*pl.*) patronage, protection, protectorship. See PREDICTION, AID.

auspicious, *adj.* favorable, promising, propitious; fortunate. See HOPE, PREDICTION, OCCASION.

austere, *adj.* harsh, stern, severe, rigorous; ascetic, simple. See SEVERITY, ASCETICISM.

authentic, *adj.* genuine, real, authoritative, trustworthy. See TRUTH, AUTHORITY.

authenticate, *v.t.* verify, confirm. See EVIDENCE, DEMONSTRATION.

author, *n.* creator, originator; writer, inventor. See PRODUCTION, WRITING, ARTIST, CAUSE.

authoritative, *adj.* official, decisive; imperative, peremptory; truthful, reliable; scholarly. See AUTHORITY, CERTAINTY.

AUTHORITY

Nouns—**1,** authority, POWER, right, jurisdiction, title, prerogative; INFLUENCE, patronage; prestige (see REPUTE); command, control, rule, sway; dominion, domination, predominance, sovereignty, empire, supremacy; lordship, suzerainty, seigniory; the crown, the sovereign; the state, commonwealth, realm, body politic, polity; divine right, dynasticism, dynasty, regime.

2, mastery, hold, grasp, grip; octopus, fangs, clutches, talons; rod of empire, scepter, throne. See SUPERIORITY.

3, administration, governance, ministration; direction, management, government, conduct, legislation, regulation, guidance; reins [of government]; supervision, superintendence, surveillance, oversight; control, charge; capital, seat [of government]. See LEGALITY.

4, government, administration, headquarters; autocracy, autarchy, aristocracy, oligarchy, hierarchy, theocracy, patriarchy, plutocracy, democracy; monarchy, absolute monarchy, kingdom, chiefdom; caliphate, pashalik; proconsulship, consulship; prefecture, magistracy; directory, triumvirate, *etc.;* absolutism, despotism, tyranny, imperialism, czarism, dictatorship, authoritarianism, fascism, nazism, monolithic government, *Führer Prinzip,* boss rule; communism, Marxism, socialism, syndicalism, collectivism, People's Republic; anarchism, nihilism (see ILLEGALITY); bureaucracy, red tape, officialdom; feudalism, feudality; gynarchy, gynocracy, matriarchy, petticoat government; autonomy, home rule, representative government, republic, free enterprise (see FREEDOM); constitutional government, constitutional *or* limited monarchy. *Colloq.,* brass, the man, big brother.

5, directorship, presidency, premiership, senatorship; chair, portfolio; stewardship, proctorship, jurisdiction.

6, sovereign, ruler, emperor, empress, crowned head, king, queen, prince, princess (see NOBILITY); potentate, liege, suzerain, monarch; czar, tsar, kaiser; boss, dictator, Duce, Führer, despot, tyrant, pharaoh; judge, autocrat; president, chairperson, the chair, premier, prime *or* first minister; potentate, patriarch, chief, chieftain, sachem, ataman, hetman, caliph, sultan, pasha, emir, sheik; master.

7, accession, succession, installation, coronation, crowning.

8, master, lord, *padrone;* employer; superior, DIRECTOR; mayor, majordomo, prefect, regent, chancellor, provost, magistrate, *alcalde,* burgomaster, seneschal, warden; commandant, commander, captain, skipper, commanding officer; governor, leader, higher-up. *Colloq.,* Simon Legree. *Slang,* top banana, top dog, [head] honcho, whole cheese *or* show, the man.

9, usurpation, assumption, *or* arrogation of authority (see ILLEGALITY).

Verbs—**1,** have *or* wield authority; head, lead, command; dominate, control, boss; dictate, dispose, rule, govern, administer; preside; wear the crown, ascend the throne; have the upper *or* whip hand, wear the pants *or* trousers; rule the roost, throw one's weight around, ride roughshod over; lord it over, bend to one's will, give the law to, lay down the law; have under one's thumb, hold in the hollow *or* palm of one's hand.

2, direct, manage, govern, conduct; order, prescribe, cut out work for; head, lead, boss; superintend, supervise, overlook, keep in order, look after, see to, legislate for; administer, ministrate; have care *or* charge of, have *or* take the direction, take over, take charge, pull the strings *or* wires, call the shots *or* the tune; hold office, preside; take, occupy, *or* be in the chair, take over; pull the stroke oar; carry the ball.

3, be under, subject to, *or* in the power of (see SUBJECTION).

4, authorize, empower, put in authority (see PERMISSION).

Adjectives—**1,** ruling, regnant, at the head, in command, dominant, predominant, preponderant, in the ascendant, influential; paramount, supreme (see SUPERIORITY); imperious; authoritative, executive, administrative, clothed with authority, official, *ex officio, ex cathedra;* imperative, peremptory, overruling, absolute; arbitrary; dictatorial, tyrannical, bossy; regal, sovereign, royal, monarchical, kingly, imperial, princely; presidential, gubernatorial, mayoral, *etc.;* directing, managing, governing, *etc.;* hegemonic.

2, at one's command; in one's power; under one's control.

3, governmental, civic.

Adverbs—**1,** in authority, in charge, at the helm *or* head of, on the throne, in the hand of, in the saddle, on top, in the driver's seat, behind the wheel.

2, at one's pleasure; by a stroke of the pen; *ex cathedra;* with a high hand.

Antonyms, see SUBJECTION, OBEDIENCE, DISORDER, SERVANT.

---

authorization, *n.* PERMISSION.

autocrat, n. dictator, czar, despot, monarch. See AUTHORITY.

autograph, *n.* signature; manuscript, holograph. See WRITING.

automatic, *adj.* mechanical; self-operating; instinctive, reflex. See NECESSITY, INTUITION.

automobile, *adj.* self-propelled. See PROPULSION. —*n.* auto, car. See VEHICLE.

autonomy, *n.* self-government; independence. See FREEDOM, AUTHORITY.

autopsy, *n.* post-mortem, examination. See INQUIRY.

autumn, *n.* fall, harvest TIME.

AUXILIARY

Nouns—auxiliary, assistant, adjuvant, adjutant, adjunct, help, helper, helpmate, helpmeet, helping hand; colleague, partner, mate, confrère; cooperator, coadjutor, collaborator; ally, confederate, accomplice, accessory, *particeps criminis;* AID, aide, aide-de-camp; secretary, amanuensis, clerk, associate, right hand [man], man *or* girl Friday; handmaid, SERVANT; satellite, adherent; disciple, devotee, votary; acolyte; seconder, backer, upholder, abettor, advocate, partisan, champion, exponent, friend at court; friend in need, guardian angel. See ACCOMPANIMENT.

Verbs—help, AID, assist, second.

Adjectives—auxiliary, helping, helpful, accessory; subsidiary, subservient; supplementary, reserve, extra.

Antonyms, see HINDRANCE, OPPOSITION.

---

avail, *v.* serve, do, suffice; help, benefit. See SUCCESS, UTILITY.

available, *adj.* handy, ready, convenient; obtainable; usable. See UTILITY.

avalanche, *n.* snowslide; landslide. See DESCENT, SUCCESS.

avant-garde, *n.* See PRECEDENCE.

avarice, *n.* greed. See DESIRE.

avenge, *v.t.* See RETALIATION.

avenue, *n.* thoroughfare, boulevard, artery; MEANS, access. See PASSAGE.

aver, *v.t.* See AFFIRMATION.

average, *n.* normal, norm, MEAN, standard. —*adj.* MEAN, normal, ordinary. See UNIMPORTANCE, MEDIOCRITY, GENERALITY.

averse, *adj.* loath, reluctant; unwilling, opposed. See OPPOSITION, HATE, UNWILLINGNESS, DISLIKE.

avert, *v.t.* keep off, turn aside, ward off; turn away; prevent. See HINDRANCE, DEVIATION.

AVIATION

Nouns—**1,** aviation, flight, flying; navigation, aerial navigation; aeronautics, aerodynamics, aerostatics, avionics; air power, air transportation; ballooning, balloonery; skydiving, soaring, [hang] gliding; gliding.

2, [scheduled *or* nonscheduled] airline, air coach; airways; airport, airfield, airdrome, flying field; landing field, landing strip, runway; control tower, windsock.

3, air warfare; air force, RAF, Luftwaffe; formation flying, echelon; bombing, dive-bombing, pursuit, dogfight; group, wing, flight, squadron.

4, aircraft: **a.** lighter-than-air, aerostat; [captive, observation, *or* barrage] balloon; airship, dirigible, Zeppelin, blimp, kite, box kite; glider, crate, box, ship, jenny; parachute. **b.** heavier-than-air, airplane, aeroplane, plane, monoplane, biplane, wedgewing, seaplane, amphibian, hydroplane, flying boat; airliner, transport; pursuit plane, interceptor, fighter, flying fortress, bomber; jet plane, turbojet, propjet, J.A.T.O. (jet-assisted take-off), S.T.O.L. (short take-off and landing), V.T.O.L. (vertical take-off and landing); Caravelle, Concorde, airbus, *etc.;* autogiro, helicopter, whirlybird, Sikorsky.

5, fuselage, tail, rudder, fin, stabilizer; cockpit, gondola, nacelle; propeller, prop; reciprocating, radial, *or* jet engine, rocket; airfoil, wing, aileron, elevator; stick, Joyce *or* joy stick; landing gear, pontoon; altimeter, artificial horizon, artificial pilot, tachometer, airspeed indicator, rate-of-climb indicator, turn-and-bank indicator, inclinometer; bomb bay, inflatable slide, safety *or* emergency doors.

6, takeoff, landing, three-point landing, pancake; zoom, loop, loop the loop, soar, climb, glide; Immelmann turn, barrel roll; dive, nosedive, spiral, spin, tailspin; buzz, hedgehopping; thrust, lift, drag; airstream, slipstream, backwash, sideslip, drift; flying circus, barnstorming, stunt flying; skywriting; point of no return; visibility, ceiling, ceiling zero; air pocket, headwind, tailwind; airsickness.

7, flier, aviator, aeronaut, airman, balloonist, pilot, co-pilot, navigator, bombardier; Daedalus, Icarus, Darius Green, Amelia Earhart, Eddie Rickenbacker; air marshal, flying officer; airborne troops, paratroops; passenger (see TRAVEL). *Colloq.,* no-show.

8, space travel (see ASTRONAUTICS).

Verbs—aviate, fly, pilot, go by air; zoom, climb, stall, yaw, pitch, roll, bank, dive, cruise, soar, glide, taxi, take off, land; stunt, buzz, hedgehop; peel off; nose down, over, *or* up; strafe, divebomb; crash, crack up, prang, conk out, bail out. *Slang,* skyjack.

Adjectives—aeronautic; airworthy; airsick; airborne, aloft, on the wing.

---

avidity, *n.* eagerness, longing, DESIRE; keenness, alarity; avarice, greed, voracity.

avocation, *n.* hobby, sideline. See AMUSEMENT, BUSINESS.

AVOIDANCE

Nouns—**1,** avoidance, evasion, default, circumvention, elusion, dodge, sidestep; abstinence, forbearance, refraining (see ASCETICISM); DEPARTURE; ESCAPE, flight; truancy, hooky, French leave (see ABSENCE); subterfuge, quibble, equivocation; CIRCUITY; brush-off. *Colloq.,* the slip, the go-by, the runaround; tax shelter. *Slang,* cop-out. See NEGLECT, UNWILLINGNESS.

2, shirker, slacker, quitter, malingerer, deserter, dodger, truant, fugitive, runaway, absconder, refugee; welsher; abstainer, teetotaler; nonparticipant. *Colloq.,* goldbrick.

Verbs—**1,** avoid, shun, sidestep, shirk, circumvent, eschew, refrain (from), not do, let alone, steer clear of, give a wide berth to, fight shy of; pass the buck; abstain, keep aloof, keep one's distance; evade, elude, dodge, lead a merry chase, get around, get by, give the runaround; put off, defer (see LATENESS); set one's face against; shy away from; make way for, give place to; take no part in, have no hand in; hem and haw, fudge, waffle. *Colloq.*, take the fifth. *Slang,* lay off.

2, malinger, shirk, slack off; beg off. *Slang,* cop out, fob off.

3, flee, desert, take French leave, abscond; show *or* take to one's heels, beat a retreat, turn tail, run for it, cut and run, steal away, make off, slip off, take off; walk out on, go back on; skip *or* jump bail. *Colloq.*, shake off. *Slang,* take it on the lam.

Antonyms, see PURSUIT.

---

avow, *v.* declare, confess; assert. See AFFIRMATION, DISCLOSURE.

await, *v.* expect, wait for, anticipate, look forward to; impend, lie in store (see DESTINY). See EXPECTATION, LATENESS.

awake, *adj.* alert, heedful, observant, attentive; keen, knowing; informed, astute, watchful, on guard, unsleeping, vigilant. See CARE, KNOWLEDGE, ATTENTION. —*v.* awaken. *Slang,* knock up. See ACTIVITY, EXCITEMENT.

award, *n.* prize, medal; COMPENSATION; decision, adjudication. See GIVING, JUDGMENT, APPROBATION.

aware, *adj.* cognizant, informed; alert (to). See KNOWLEDGE.

away, *adv.* absent, elsewhere, far-off, gone. See DISTANCE, ABSENCE.

awe, *n.* FEAR, dread; WONDER.

awful, *adj.* horrible, dreadful; tremendous. See FEAR, WONDER.

awkward, *adj.* clumsy, ungraceful, ungainly; gauche; embarrassing. See UNSKILLFULNESS, DIFFICULTY.

awry, *adj.* askance, crooked, askew; out of order; mistaken, amiss, WRONG. *Slang,* cockeyed, screwy. See OBLIQUITY, DISORDER.

ax, axe, *n.* chopper, hatchet; instrument (see MUSIC). See ARMS, SHARPNESS. — *v., slang,* dismiss (see EJECTION).

axiom, *n.* law, proposition; aphorism, MAXIM.

axis, *n.* shaft, pivot. See ROTATION, MIDDLE.

axle, *n.* shaft, pin. See ROTATION.

azure, *adj.* blue, sky-blue, cerulean. See COLOR.

B

babble, *v.i.* chatter, prattle, gossip; rave, gibber; gurgle. See LOQUACITY, UNMEANINGNESS.

baby, *n.* infant, babe, child, tot; nursling, suckling; offspring. *Colloq.*, kid. See YOUTH.—*v.t.* pamper. See LENIENCY.

bachelor, *n.* celibate, Coelebs; widower, divorcé; licentiate, [post-] graduate. See CELIBACY, SCHOOL.

back, *n.* See REAR. —*v.t.* support; AID; promote, fund, finance (see MEANS); stand behind, encourage. —*v.i.* move backward, reverse. See REGRESSION.

backbite, *v.* attack, revile. See DETRACTION.

backbone, *n.* spine, spinal column; COURAGE, RESOLUTION. See SUPPORT.

backfire, *v.i.* boomerang, go awry. See FAILURE, VIOLENCE, RECOIL.

background, *n.* setting, ENVIRONMENT; experience, training; family (see ANCESTRY). See KNOWLEDGE, DISTANCE, REAR.

backlash, *n.* reaction; RECOIL.

backsliding, *n.* recidivism, REGRESSION, lapse; apostasy (see IMPIETY); relapse.

backup, *n.* substitute, alternate. See SUBSTITUTION, AID.

backward, *adj.* retarded, slow, underdeveloped; third-world; delayed, tardy; unwilling, loath, shy. See REAR, UNWILLINGNESS, LATENESS.

backwoods, *adj.* rustic; primitive, uncouth. See VULGARITY.

badge, *n.* emblem, sign. See INDICATION.

badger, *v.t.* nag, pester, tease. See DISCONTENT.

BADNESS

Nouns—**1,** badness, hurtfulness, virulence, perniciousness, malignancy, malignity; insalubrity; ill *or* bad turn, evil star, ill wind; bane, pest, plague-spot, scourge; pestilence (see DISEASE); skeleton in the closet, thorn in the side *or* in the flesh. *Slang,* bummer. See EVIL.

2, ill-treatment, molestation, abuse, oppression, persecution, outrage; atrocity, torture. See MALEVOLENCE.

3, misbehavior, mischief; depravity, vice (see IMPURITY); GUILT; IMPROBITY, knavery.

4, bad influence, bad *or* evil genius. *Colloq.,* hoodoo, jinx; rotten egg. *Slang,* Jonah.

5, IMPERFECTION, defectiveness, poor quality, MEDIOCRITY, INFERIORITY.

Verbs—**1,** WRONG, aggrieve, oppress, persecute; trample, tread, *or* put upon, overburden, weigh down, victimize.

2, be vicious; sin, fall, err, transgress, go astray, forget oneself; misdo, misbehave; trespass, deviate, sow one's wild oats, act up, carry on; horse, fool, monkey, play, *or* mess around. *Colloq.,* cut up, hack off *or* around.

Adjectives—**1,** bad, ill, untoward, as bad as can be, dreadful; horrid, horrible; rank, rotten [at *or* to the core], decayed, decomposed, putrid, tainted. *Slang,* cheesy, punk, lousy.

2, hurtful, harmful, baneful, baleful; detrimental, pernicious; mischievous, full of mischief, mischief-making, full of the Old Nick *or* the devil; malefic, malignant, noxious, nocuous, noisome; unlucky, sinister; obnoxious; inauspicious; oppressive, burdensome, onerous; malign, malevolent; virulent, venomous, envenomed, corrosive; poisonous, toxic.

3, mean, paltry; injured, deteriorated, unsatisfactory, exceptionable, indifferent; below par, inferior, imperfect; ill-contrived, ill-conditioned; wretched, abysmal, pitiful, pathetic, sad, grievous, deplorable, lamentable; pitiable; unfortunate (see ADVERSITY).

4, EVIL, WRONG; depraved, vile, base; flagrant, nefarious; reprehensible, heinous, hateful (see DISAPPROBATION); wicked, sinful. *Colloq.,* beastly, ungodly.

Adverbs—badly, amiss, awry, WRONG, ill; to one's cost; where the shoe pinches.

Antonyms, see GOODNESS, CONDUCT.

---

baffle, *v.* foil, frustrate, balk, block; puzzle, nonplus; muffle. See HINDRANCE, DOUBT, SILENCE.

bag, *n.* RECEPTACLE, case, container, pouch, sack. —*v.* trap, capture, take, catch; sag, droop, hang; bulge, protrude, swell. See ACQUISITION, PENDENCY, CONVEXITY.

baggage, *n.* luggage, impedimenta; trunks, suitcases, valises. See POSSESSION, TRANSPORTATION.

bagpipe, *n.* musette, doodlesack, union pipes; chanter. See MUSIC.

bail, *n.* SECURITY, bond, pledge; guarantee, surety.

bailiff, *n.* constable, beagle, bailie;

sheriff, marshal, officer. See SAFETY, AGENT.

bailiwick, *n.* district, REGION; area of concern, BUSINESS.

bait, *n.* lure, temptation. —*v.t.* decoy, lure, tempt; tease, torment, badger. See ATTRACTION, MALEVOLENCE, DISCONTENT.

bake, *v.* roast, cook; harden, dry; fire. See HARDNESS, HEAT, FOOD.

balance, *n.* equilibrium, steadiness, stability; surplus, excess, rest, REMAINDER; scales. —*v.* offset, even, square; equalize, level, adjust; equal, match. See EQUALITY, COMPENSATION, SYMMETRY, MEAN, GRAVITY, ACCOUNTING.

balcony, *n.* gallery, loggia, porch, portico; tier, loge, mezzanine, dress circle. *Slang,* peanut gallery, paradise. See DRAMA, RECEPTACLE.

bald, *adj.* hairless; treeless; bare, unadorned; undisguised. See DIVESTMENT, SIMPLENESS.

bale, *n.* bundle (see ASSEMBLAGE); sorrow, woe, DEJECTION.

baleful, *adj.* hostile; malignant; hurtful, injurious. See BADNESS.

balk, *v.* rebel; stop, shy; hinder, thwart, foil, frustrate. See HINDRANCE, REFUSAL, DISAPPOINTMENT.

ball, *n.* dance, cotillion; shot, projectile; sphere, globe. See AMUSEMENT, ARMS, ROTUNDITY.

ballad, *n.* song, chantey, spiritual; calypso. See MUSIC, POETRY.

ballast, *n.* counterbalance (see COMPENSATION, GRAVITY).

ballet, *n.* concert *or* classical dance, choreography; corps de ballet. See DRAMA.

balloon, *n.* aerostat, blimp; free, sounding, kite, pilot, *or* dirigible balloon; fire balloon, montgolfier. See AVIATION. —*v.i.* swell. See CONVEXITY.

ballot, *n.* vote, CHOICE, poll; franchise, voice.

ballroom, *n.* dance hall. See AMUSEMENT.

balm, *n.* balsam, salve; analgesic, sedative, anodyne. See MODERATION, REMEDY, COMPENSATION, FRAGRANCE.

ban, *n.* PROHIBITION, restriction, proscription, interdict.

banal, *adj.* common[place], trite. See HABIT.

band, *n.* strip, stripe, FILAMENT; brassard; belt, strap; group, crowd; orchestra, brass *or* military band. See ASSEMBLAGE, MUSIC.

bandage, *n.* tourniquet, dressing; Band-Aid. See REMEDY.

bandit, *n.* highwayman, brigand, outlaw. See STEALING.

bane, *n.* poison, venom; curse, mischief; thorn in the side; bale, scourge, nuisance, pest; harm, injury, DESTRUCTION; trouble. See EVIL, BADNESS.

bang, *n.* clap, crash (see LOUDNESS). —*v.* slam, pound, batter; smash, damage. See IMPULSE, DESTRUCTION. —*adv.* See INSTANTANEITY.

bangle, *n.* bracelet, anklet. See ORNAMENT.

banish, *v.t.* exile, dismiss, expel. See EJECTION, PUNISHMENT, EXCLUSION.

bank, *n.* slope, hillside; mound, heap, ridge; tier; beach, shore, shoal; depository, vault. See OBLIQUITY, LAND, STORE. —*v.* tilt, angle, slope; deposit. See EDGE, AVIATION.

banknote, *n.* paper *or* folding MONEY; bill.

bankrupt, *adj.* insolvent, ruined; bereft, indigent, penniless, destitute. *Slang,* broke. —*v.* impoverish; pauperize. See DEBT, POVERTY, FAILURE.

banner, *n.* flag, pennant; symbol, badge; headline. See INDICATION.

banquet, *n.* feast, regale. *Colloq.,* big feed. *Slang,* shindig. See FOOD, AMUSEMENT.

banter, *n.* jest, chaff, badinage. See WIT, RIDICULE.

baptize, *v.* sprinkle, immerse, dip; name, christen; cleanse. *Colloq.,* dunk. See NOMENCLATURE, RITE.

bar, *n.* barrier, obstacle; barroom (see DRINKING); hurdle; legal profession, court, bench; rod, bolt, rail; measure; stripe. See LAWSUIT, LENGTH. —*v.* forbid; exclude, restrict, reject; lock, bolt, fasten. See EXCLUSION, CLOSURE, PROHIBITION.

barb, *n.* spike, arrowhead. See SHARPNESS.

barbarian, *n.* foreigner, outsider, alien, savage; ruffian (see EVILDOER). See UNCONFORMITY.

barbarism, n. solecism; barbarity, savagery, brutality, inhumanity, VIOLENCE; ignorance, rudeness, VULGARITY. See DISCOURTESY, MALEVOLENCE, INELEGANCE.

barbecue, *n.* cookout; rotisserie, spit. See FOOD.

barber, *n.* hair stylist, coiffeur, coiffeuse. See BEAUTY.

bare, *adj.* unclothed, naked, nude; uncovered; empty, unfurnished; mere, simple. See DIVESTMENT, SIMPLENESS, ABSENCE.

barefaced, *adj.* brazen, shameless, impudent. See INSOLENCE.

barely, *adv.* only, just. See NARROWNESS.

bargain, *n.* deal, AGREEMENT, transaction; good buy (see CHEAPNESS). —*v.* negotiate, haggle, BARTER.

barge, *n.* scow (see SHIP).

barge in, *v.i., colloq.,* crash, bust, *or* burst in. See INGRESS.

bark, *n.* COVERING, rind, skin, shell; yelp, yap, bay (see CRY); barque, brig (see SHIP).

barn, *n.* stable, mews. See ABODE.

barracks, *n.pl.* caserne, bivouac. See ABODE.

barrage, *n.* ATTACK, bombardment.

barrel, *n.* keg, tun, cask, vat; cylinder, tube. See RECEPTACLE, ROTUNDITY.

barren, *adj.* infertile, unprofitable, unproductive; sterile; stark, bare. See USELESSNESS.

barricade, *n.* blockade, stockade; fence, barrier. See DEFENSE, ENCLOSURE, CLOSURE.

barrier, *n.* obstacle, impediment, HINDRANCE. See ENCLOSURE, DEFENSE.

BARTER

Nouns—**1,** barter, exchange, truck, INTERCHANGE; marketing, trade, commerce, buying and selling, traffic, BUSINESS, custom, shopping; commercial enterprise, speculation, [stock-]jobbing, brokerage, stockbroking, agiotage; reciprocation; trading, dealing, transaction, negotiation; free trade, open market; black market. See SALE.

2, trading stamps; trade-in; horse trade. See TRANSFER.

3, dealer, trader, merchant, businessman, AGENT. *Slang,* wheeler-dealer.

Verbs—**1,** barter, exchange, truck, INTERCHANGE; trade, traffic, buy and sell, give and take; carry on, ply, *or* drive a trade; be in business, be in the city; keep a shop; deal in, employ one's capital in. *Slang,* wheel and deal.

2, speculate, give a sprat to catch a herring, buy in the cheapest and sell in the dearest market; rig the market.

3, trade (in), deal *or* have dealings with, transact *or* do business with, open *or* keep an account with, patronize; drive *or* make a bargain, negotiate, bargain, bid for, haggle, palter, dicker; cheapen, beat down; outbid, underbid; ask, charge; strike a bargain, contract, *or* compact. See AGREEMENT.

Adjectives—commercial, mercantile, trading; interchangeable, marketable, staple, for sale; wholesale, retail.

Adverbs—across the counter; in *or* on the market.

---

base, *n.* basis, foundation, groundwork, SUPPORT; basement, substructure; headquarters, depot; root; footing, floor; pavement; bottom;

bedrock. —*v*. found, establish; predicate; ground, rest, *or* build upon. See CAUSE, ABODE. —*adj*. debased, impure; counterfeit, spurious; low, vile. See DISREPUTE, IMPURITY, BADNESS, SERVILITY, COWARDICE, IMPROBITY.

basement, *n*. cellar, vault (see LOWNESS).

bashful, *adj*. shy, diffident, timid. See MODESTY.

basic, *adj*. fundamental, essential; alkaline. See INTRINSIC.

basin, *n*. bowl, vessel, sink; hollow, valley. See CONCAVITY, RECEPTACLE.

basis, *n*. See BASE.

bask, *v.i*. luxuriate, revel, [take] delight *or* PLEASURE in; prosper, flourish; sunbathe, sun. See PROSPERITY, HEAT.

basket, *n*. hamper, pannier; hoop. See RECEPTACLE.

bass, *adj*. low, deep[-toned]; bass, [bass-]baritone. —*n*. basso [profundo]. See LOWNESS, MUSIC.

bastard, *n*. illegitimate [child], love child; sham, counterfeit, fraud. —*adj*. illegitimate, natural, misgotten; false, spurious; mongrel, hybrid. See IMPURITY, DECEPTION, POSTERITY.

bastion, *n*. fort; rampart, fortification. See DEFENSE.

bat, *n*. cudgel, club, stick, nightstick; brickbat. See ARMS.

batch, *n*. baking; set, series, run, lot, QUANTITY. See ASSEMBLAGE.

bath, *n*. wash(ing); dip, plunge; whirlpool, Jacuzzi; Turkish *or* Swedish bath. See CLEANNESS, WATER.

bathhouse, *n*. cabaña, bathing hut. See RECEPTACLE, CLEANNESS.

bathroom, *n*. toilet, facilities, head, water closet, W.C. See CLEANNESS.

batter, *v*. smash, beat, pound. See DESTRUCTION, IMPULSE.

battery, *n*. assault, ATTACK; guns, artillery; array, ASSEMBLAGE; Leyden jar, voltaic cell, accumulator, [wet *or* dry] cell, solar *or* storage battery. See ARMS, STORE, POWER, COMBATANT.

battle, *n*. fight, engagement, combat; contest. See CONTENTION, ACTION, ATTACK.

battlefield, *n*. battleground. See WARFARE.

battleship, *n*. man-of-war, SHIP of the line, dreadnaught; battle wagon.

bawdy, *adj*. coarse, ribald, gross, lewd. See IMPURITY.

bawl, *v*. yell, bellow; CRY, sob.

bawl out, *v.t*. reprimand, reprove. See DISAPPROBATION.

bay, *n*. estuary, bayou, fiord, sound; alcove, niche; inlet; laurel. See WATER, RECEPTACLE, CONCAVITY.

bazaar, *n*. market [place], fair; street fair. See BUSINESS.

be, *v*. exist, breathe; occur, take place. See EXISTENCE.

beach, *n*. shore, coast[line]; strand, sands, shingle. —*v*. ground, run aground *or* ashore, strand. *Colloq*., hit the beach. See NAVIGATION, LAND.

beacon, *n*. lighthouse, buoy, lightship; beam; signal fire; signal, guide. See INDICATION, LIGHT, WARNING.

bead, *n*. drop; pellet, ball. See ROTUNDITY.

beak, *n*. nose, bill, nib. *Slang*, magistrate. See CONVEXITY, FRONT.

beam, *v*. shine, glow; smile. —*n*. ray, gleam; joist, timber. See LIGHT, SUPPORT.

bear, *v*. endure, tolerate; suffer; render, yield; hold, sustain; carry, transport, convey. See FEELING, PRODUCTION, SUPPORT, TRANSPORTATION.

beard, *n*. whiskers; goatee, vandyke; stubble. See ROUGHNESS.

bearded, *adj*. hairy, whiskered, awned, hirsute. See ROUGHNESS.

beardless, *adj*. [clean-]shaven, smooth-faced; hairless; youthful. See YOUTH, DIVESTMENT.

bearing, *n*. course, trend; carriage, manner, CONDUCT; MEANING, significance; RELATION. See DIRECTION.

beast, *n*. brute, quadruped; blackguard (see DISCOURTESY). See ANIMAL, TRANSPORTATION.

beat, *n*. throb, stroke, accent, rhythm;

pulse; route. See BUSINESS, REGION. —*v*. throb, pulsate; strike, batter; conquer, defeat. See REGULARITY, IMPULSE, SUPERIORITY, AGITATION.

beatify, *v*. sanctify, hallow, consecrate, bless. See PIETY.

beatnik, *n*. beat, hipster, Bohemian. See UNCONFORMITY.

beat-up, *adj*., *slang*, dilapidated, broken-down. See DETERIORATION.

BEAUTY

Nouns—**1,** beauty, the beautiful; form, ELEGANCE, grace, charm, beauty unadorned; SYMMETRY; loveliness, attractiveness, comeliness, fairness, pulchritude, good looks, body beautiful; style, polish, gloss (see SMOOTHNESS); bloom, brilliancy, radiance, splendor, gorgeousness, magnificence, glory; delicacy, refinement.

2, a. Venus, Hebe, the Graces, peri, houri, goddess; witch, enchantress; reigning beauty, beauty queen, Miss America, Miss U.S.A., Miss Universe, *etc.;* charmer, belle [of the ball]; poster girl, pin-up [girl]. *Colloq.*, eyeful, picture, dream, stunner, [Georgia] peach, doll, knockout, raving beauty, good-looker, cover girl. **b.** Mr. America, Adonis, Narcissus. *Colloq.*, ladykiller, ladies' man.

3, a. beautifying; make-up, cosmetics, vanishing cream, *etc.*, vanity case; decoration, adornment, embellishment, ornamentation (see ORNAMENT); manicure, pedicure; beautician, make-up artist; hairdresser, coiffeur, coiffeuse; manicurist, pedicurist; beauty salon *or* parlor. **b.** barber, hair stylist; haircut; barber shop.

Verbs—beautify; make up, do, paint; adorn, embellish (see ORNAMENT); prettify; style.

Adjectives—**1,** beautiful, beauteous, handsome, prepossessing; pretty, lovely, graceful, elegant; delicate, dainty, refined; fair, personable, comely, seemly, bonny, good-looking, eye-filling, cute; photogenic, telegenic; well-favored, well-made, well-formed, well-proportioned, curvaceous; proper, shapely; symmetrical, regular, harmonious, sightly. *Colloq.*, easy on the eyes, sight for sore eyes, cutesy, nifty, stunning, devastating, long on looks, [well-]built.

2, brilliant, shining, radiant; splendid, resplendent, dazzling, glowing; glossy, sleek; rich, gorgeous, superb, magnificent, grand, fine, sublime.

3, artistic, esthetic; picturesque, well-composed, well-grouped; enchanting, attractive, becoming, ornamental; undeformed, undefaced, unspotted; spotless, immaculate; perfect, flawless (see PERFECTION).

Antonyms, see UGLINESS.

---

because, *adv*. by reason of, owing to, on account of. —*conj*. since, for, for the reason that, as. See CAUSE, REASONING.

beckon, *v*. signal, summon; lure, entice. See INDICATION, ATTRACTION.

become, *v.t*. befit, accord with, behoove; turn into, CHANGE [in]to. See DUTY, AGREEMENT.

becoming, *adj*. fit, proper, seemly; attractive, ornamental. See BEAUTY, RIGHTNESS, EXPEDIENCE.

bed, *n*. couch, cot, resting place; base, foundation; garden. See SUPPORT, AGRICULTURE, LAYER.

bedlam, *n*. asylum, madhouse; confusion, uproar, turmoil. See INSANITY, DISORDER.

beer, *n*. bock, dark, *or* light beer, lager [beer], two-percent beer, hops, malt; ginger beer. See DRINKING.

befit, *v.t*. suit, harmonize with, fit; become, behoove. See AGREEMENT, DUTY.

before, *adv*. foremost, ahead; forward; beforehand, sooner, previously, heretofore. See PRIORITY, PRECEDENCE.

beg, *v.* implore, beseech; ask alms. See POVERTY, REQUEST.

beget, *v.t.* engender, procreate, generate. See REPRODUCTION.

beggar, *n.* suppliant; pauper, mendicant. See POVERTY, REQUEST, POPULACE.

BEGINNING

Nouns—**1,** beginning, commencement, opening, outset, incipience, inception; alpha, initial; installation, inauguration, debut; foundation, reaction, initiation; embarkation, rising of the curtain, kickoff, take-off; outbreak, onset; initiative, first move, foot in the door, running start, foothold; thin end of the wedge; fresh start, new departure. *Colloq.,* coming out. See OLDNESS.

2, origin, CAUSE; source, rise; bud, seed, germ, egg, embryo, nucleus; root, radix, radical, etymon; stem, stock, stirps, trunk, taproot; genesis, birth, nativity; nest, cradle, infancy, womb, nidus, birthplace, hotbed; start, starting point; dawn, morning. See PRIORITY.

3, title page; head, heading, introduction, prelude (see PRECEDENCE); FRONT, forefront, van, vanguard; curtain raiser, appetizer, *etc.*

4, entrance (see INGRESS); outskirts.

5, rudiments, basics; primer, alphabet, ABC's, first principles. See PREPARATION.

6, beginner, tyro, novice, neophyte, acolyte, freshman, rookie, recruit, cub, learner, amateur, first-time Charlie, low man on the totem pole (see INFERIORITY).

7, founder, initiator, creator; aborigine, native.

Verbs—**1,** begin, commence, rise, arise, originate, see the light of day, open its doors, initiate, introduce, inaugurate, set up; install; open, dawn, set in, enter upon; set out, depart, embark on; make one's debut, take up; set about, start out *or* in, get off *or* away, get under way, go ahead, get down to, get going, get to, turn on, start up, kick off, strike up, set to work, fall to, dig in, make a beginning *or* start; take the first step, get one's feet wet, break ground, break the ice, break cover, cross the Rubicon, open fire; undertake; come on *or* up. *Colloq.,* get going, pitch in; get the show on the road *or* off the ground; get to first base; get off on the wrong foot.

2, usher in, preface; lead off, lead the way, take the lead, start from scratch, take the initiative; inaugurate, swear in; call to order, head, lay the foundations, prepare, break in, found, CAUSE, set up, set on foot, start the ball rolling, launch, broach; open the door to.

Adjectives—initial, initiatory, initiative; primary, pristine, maiden; inceptive, introductory, incipient; inaugural; embryonic, rudimentary; primeval, primordial, primitive, aboriginal, natal.

Adverbs—at first blush, glance, *or* sight, at *or* in the beginning, [at] first, in the first place, *imprimis,* first and foremost; in the bud, in its infancy; from the beginning, from [its] birth, from scratch, from the ground up, *ab initio*. *Colloq.,* from the word go, at the drop of a hat.

Antonyms, see END.

beguile, *v.t.* delude, deceive; amuse, divert. See DECEPTION, PLEASURE.

behalf, *n.* interest, benefit, advantage. See UTILITY.

behave, *v.i.* bear, CONDUCT, *or* comport oneself, act.

behead, *v.t.* decapitate, decollate. See KILLING, PUNISHMENT.

behind, *adv.* rearward, aft, backward; after, subsequently; slow. *—prep.* in back of, following. See REAR, LATENESS, REGRESSION, SEQUENCE.

behold, *v.* see, espy; look at, watch, observe. *—interj.* lo [and behold]! *ecce!* look! *voilà!* See VISION, ATTENTION.

being, *n.* LIFE, EXISTENCE; person, creature. See SUBSTANCE, HUMANITY.

belch, *v.* eructate; gush, issue. See EJECTION.

BELIEF

Nouns—**1,** belief, credence, credit, assurance, [good] faith, trust, troth, confidence, presumption; dependence on, reliance on. *Colloq.,* store. *Slang,* stock. See SUPPOSITION, PIETY.

2, persuasion, conviction, CERTAINTY; [matter of] opinion, mind, view, viewpoint, outlook; impression, notion, idea; surmise, conclusion (see JUDGMENT).

3, tenet, dogma, principle, article of faith; school, doctrine, articles, canon[s]; declaration *or* profession of faith, constitution, manifesto, creed, tenets, orthodoxy; cult, ism. See RELIGION, HETERODOXY.

4, credibility, believability, plausibility, probability.

5, [true] believer; devotee, zealot, disciple; fanatic.

Verbs—**1,** believe, credit, accredit, give credence to, give the benefit of the doubt, take at face value; take for; consider, esteem (see SUPPOSITION); count, rely, figure, *or* depend on, pin one's faith on, swear by; take on trust *or* credit; take for granted *or* gospel. *Colloq.,* set store by, bet on, bank on, bet one's bottom dollar on, have the courage of one's convictions; buy, swallow [whole] (see CREDULITY); take stock in.

2, confide in, believe in, put one's trust in; take one's word for, take at one's word; pin one's hopes on (see HOPE).

3, think, hold, opine, be of the opinion, conceive, fancy, apprehend; have, hold, entertain, hazard, *or* cherish a belief *or* an opinion.

4, satisfy, persuade, assure, convince, convert, bring round, indoctrinate, teach, bring home to; be convincing, carry conviction.

Adjectives—satisfied, confident, unhesitating, convinced, unsuspecting, secure; indubitable, undeniable, indisputable, incontrovertible; credible, trustworthy, to be depended on; satisfactory; probable, odds-on; persuasive, impressive, convincing.

Adverbs—no doubt, on faith, on the strength of.

Antonyms, see DOUBT, CERTAINTY.

---

belittle, *v.t.* run down, disparage, deprecate. See DETRACTION.

bell, *n.* chime, ring; flare. See INDICATION, EXPANSION.

belligerent, *adj.* bellicose, warlike, pugnacious, quarrelsome. See CONTENTION, ATTACK. *—n.* COMBATANT.

bellow, *v.i.* roar, shout, bawl. See CRY.

belly, *n.* stomach, tummy; abdomen; paunch, potbelly; underside. *Colloq.,* breadbasket; pod, bay window, beer belly, pot, gut, swagbelly. *Slang,* corporation. *—v.* bulge, swell, billow. See CONVEXITY, RECEPTACLE, INTERIOR.

belong, *v.i.* form part of; be someone's; relate to. See POSSESSION, RELATION.

beloved, *adj.* See LOVE.

below, *adv.* subordinate, lower, underneath. *—prep.* under, beneath. See INFERIORITY, LOWNESS.

belt, *n.* girdle, band; stripe; zone; circuit. *—v.t.* bind, encircle; gird; whip. See CIRCULARITY, CIRCUMSCRIPTION, IMPULSE.

bench, *n.* seat, settee; court, bar, the judiciary; board. See SUPPORT, LAWSUIT, COUNCIL.

bend, *n.* curve, turn. —*v.i.* give, yield; curve. —*v.t.* control; shape. See SOFTNESS, AUTHORITY, CURVATURE, OBLIQUITY.

beneath, *adv.* underneath, under, below. —*prep.* under; unworthy of. See LOWNESS, INFERIORITY.

benediction, *n.* See BLESSING.

benefactor, *n.* See BENEVOLENCE.

beneficial, *adj.* useful, helpful, salutary, advantageous. See GOODNESS, UTILITY.

beneficiary, *n.* legatee, donee. See RECEIVING.

benefit, *n.* profit, advantage, gain, good, avail; fund-raiser. —*v.* help, serve, assist; improve. See BENEVOLENCE, UTILITY, AID, REQUEST, GOODNESS, MEANS.

BENEVOLENCE

Nouns—**1,** benevolence, Christian charity, good will; God's grace; altruism, philanthropy, unselfishness; good nature, kindness, kindliness, loving-kindness, benignity, brotherly love, charity, humanity, fellow-feeling, sympathy, goodness of heart, heart of gold, open heart, *bonhomie,* kindheartedness; amiability, milk of human kindness, tenderness, LOVE, friendship; consideration, mercy (see PITY).

2, generosity, LIBERALITY, bounty, almsgiving; good works, beneficence, act of kindness, good turn; good offices, labor of love; public service, social science, sociology.

3, philanthropist, benefactor, good Samaritan; good citizen; sympathizer, altruist, humanitarian. See GIVING, GOODNESS.

Verbs—bear good will, mean well by, wish well, take an interest in, sympathize with, feel for; have one's heart in the right place; do as you would be done by; meet halfway; treat well, give comfort, do a good turn, benefit, render a service, open one's heart, be of use; give of oneself; AID, philanthropize; heap coals of fire on a person's head.

Adjectives—**1,** benevolent, benign, kindly, well-meaning; amiable, good-natured, cordial, obliging, courteous (see COURTESY); gracious, unselfish, magnanimous; considerate, sympathetic, tender, warmhearted, kindhearted; charitable, liberal, generous, beneficent, altruistic, humane, bounteous, bountiful; public-spirited; well-intentioned, well-meant.

2, fatherly, motherly, brotherly, sisterly; paternal, maternal, fraternal.

Adverbs—benevolently, charitably, with good *or* the best intentions; with all one's heart; liberally, generously.

Antonyms, see MALEVOLENCE.

---

benign, *adj.* gracious; favorable. See HEALTH, BENEVOLENCE.

bent, *n.* TENDENCY, inclination, nature, propensity. See DESIRE.

bequest, *n.* legacy. See GIVING, RECEIVING, TRANSFER.

bereft, *adj.* bereaved, deprived of. See LOSS.

berth, *n.* bunk, compartment; couchette; dock, slip; position, office; lodging. See BUSINESS, SUPPORT, ABODE.

beseech, *v.t.* beg, implore. See REQUEST.

beset, *v.t.* besiege, ATTACK, invest; stud (see ORNAMENT).

beside, *prep.* by, near, alongside, abreast. See NEARNESS, SIDE.

besides, *adv.* also, further, moreover. See ADDITION.

besiege, *v.t.* beset, surround, beleaguer, invest; plague, pester. See ATTACK.

best, *adj.* choice, unequalled, unparalleled. See GOODNESS, PERFECTION. —*v.t.* defeat, surpass. See SUPERIORITY.

bestial, *adj.* beastlike, brutal, brutish, ANIMAL. See VIOLENCE.

bestow, *v.t.* donate, present, confer, bequeath. See GIVING.

bet, *v.* wager, stake, gamble, play, lay odds. See CHANCE, IMPROBITY.

betray, *v.* play false; divulge, reveal. See INFORMATION, IMPROBITY, DISCLOSURE.

betrothal, *n.* engagement. See MARRIAGE, PROMISE.

better, *v.t.* mend, correct, relieve. See IMPROVEMENT, SUPERIORITY.

BETWEEN

Nouns—**1,** interjacence, intervenience, interlocation, interpenetration; interjection, interpolation, interlineation, interspersion, intercalation; interlocution, intervention, interference, interposition, intrusion, obtrusion, insinuation, INSERTION.

2, parenthesis, episode; flyleaf; embolism; partition, septum, diaphragm, midriff; party-wall; panel, halfway house; interim. See MIDDLE, TIME.

3, intermediary, go-between, middleman, medium (see AGENT); intruder, interloper, trespasser, meddler; kibitzer. *Slang,* buttinsky, chiseler, gate-crasher.

Verbs—**1,** intervene, come between, step in, slide in, interpenetrate; interfere, put an oar in, thrust one's nose in, cut in; intrude, obtrude; have a finger in the pie. *Slang,* butt in, horn in, barge in, muscle in; tamper with. See HINDRANCE.

2, put between, introduce, insinuate, import; interpose, interject, intercalate, interpolate, interline, interleave, intersperse, interweave, interlard, insert, sandwich; throw, let, wedge, edge, drag, worm, run, *or* work in; dovetail, splice, mortise (see JUNCTION).

Adjectives—interjacent, intervenient, intervening, intermediate, intermediary, intercalary, interstitial; embolismal; parenthetical, episodic; mediterranean; intrusive, interfering, meddlesome, officious, obtrusive.

Adverbs—between, betwixt; among[st], amid[st], in the thick (of), in the middle; betwixt and between; parenthetically, *obiter dictum.*

Antonyms, see EXTERIOR, END, SIDE.

---

bevel, *v.* slant, slope. See OBLIQUITY.

beverage, *n.* liquor, drink, potable. See DRINKING.

bevy, *n.* flock (see ASSEMBLAGE).

beware, *v.* take care, be on guard; avoid, shun. See WARNING.

bewilder, *v.t.* puzzle, confuse, perplex; daze. See DOUBT, WONDER.

bewitch, *v.t.* fascinate, charm; enchant. See SORCERY, PLEASURE.

beyond, *adv.* farther, yonder. —*prep.* over; past. See DISTANCE, SUPERIORITY.

bias, *n.* prejudice, partiality; bent, inclination; slope, diagonal. —*v.t.* INFLUENCE, sway, prejudice. See OBLIQUITY, TENDENCY, INJUSTICE.

Bible, *n.* See SACRED WRITINGS.

bicker, *v.i.* quarrel, wrangle, dispute; flicker, flutter; gurgle, ripple. See DISCORD, AGITATION.

bicycle, *n.* tandem, two-wheeler. *Colloq.,* bike. See VEHICLE.

bid, *n.* OFFER; effort, try (see UNDERTAKING); invitation. —*v.* COMMAND, enjoin; invite, REQUEST.

bier, *n.* litter, catafalque. See INTERMENT.

big, *adj.* large, bulky, huge; mountainous, enormous; massive, impressive; important, weighty. See GREATNESS, SIZE.

bigot, *n.* dogmatist, zealot; racist. See CERTAINTY, HETERODOXY, INJUSTICE.

bilateral, *adj.* two-sided, symmetrical. See SIDE, SYMMETRY.

bill, *n.* score, reckoning; invoice, statement, dun; account, charges; [bank]note, greenback; beak. See ACCOUNTING, MONEY, PRICE, LEGALITY, CONVEXITY.

billboard, *n.* bulletin *or* message board. See PUBLICATION.

billfold, *n.* wallet. See STORE.

billow, *v.i.* surge, swell. —*n.* undulation, wave. See WATER, CONVEXITY.

bin, *n.* compartment, crib, bunker. See RECEPTACLE.

bind, *v.t.* restrain, secure, fasten; obligate. See RESTRAINT, DUTY, COMPULSION, JUNCTION.

binge, *n., slang,* see DRINKING.

bingo, *n.* lotto, beano. See AMUSEMENT.

biography, *n.* life story, history, memoirs. See DESCRIPTION.

bird, *n.* fowl; songbird, warbler; cock, hen; nestling, fledgling. See ANIMAL.

birth, *n.* origin, creation; genesis, inception; childbirth, parturition. See REPRODUCTION.

biscuit, *n.* cracker, hardtack, cookie; bun, cake. See FOOD.

bisect, *v.* bifurcate, halve. See DISJUNCTION, NUMERATION.

bishop, *n.* prelate, lawn sleeves; overseer; episcopacy. See CLERGY.

bit, *n.* scrap, mite; slice, piece; tool, drill; curb; *colloq.,* routine. See PART, LITTLENESS, SPECIALITY.

bite, *n.* morsel, scrap; nip. —*v.* cut; snap, snip; corrode; sting. See FOOD, LITTLENESS, PUNGENCY.

biting, *adj.* sharp, piercing, keen; pungent, acrid; forceful, telling. See VIGOR, PUNGENCY, COLD.

bitter, *adj.* stinging, cutting; spiteful; rigorous; acrid, unpalatable. See MALEVOLENCE, RESENTMENT, PUNGENCY, COLD.

bivouac, *n.* barracks (see ABODE).

bizarre, *adj.* grotesque, odd. See UNCONFORMITY.

blab, blabber, *v.i.* babble, chatter; tattle, gossip. See LOQUACITY, DISCLOSURE.

black, *n.* darkness, midnight, Stygian hue; Negro. —*v.t.* shine, polish (shoes). See COLOR, DARKNESS.

blackball, *v.* exclude, ostracize, reject, boycott. See EXCLUSION.

blacken, *v.t.* besmirch; smudge; malign, slander. See COLOR, DETRACTION.

blackguard, *n.* rascal, villain; scoundrel. See EVILDOER.

blacklist, *v.* ostracize, exclude (see EXCLUSION).

blackmail, *n.* extortion, hush money, protection. *Slang,* shakedown. See STEALING, PAYMENT, THREAT.

bladder, *n.* sac, vesicle, blister. See RECEPTACLE.

blade, *n.* cutter, edge; sword; knife; leaf (of grass); dandy, sport. See SHARPNESS, IMPURITY, AFFECTATION.

blame, *n.* criticism, censure; culpability, GUILT. —*v.t.* charge, reproach, condemn. See ACCUSATION, DISAPPROBATION, WRONG.

blanch, *v.* whiten; scald. See COLORLESSNESS, FOOD.

bland, *adj.* suave; affable, gracious; mild, unflavored. See COURTESY, INSIPIDITY.

blandish, *v.t.* coax, cajole. See FLATTERY.

blank, *adj.* empty, unfilled; vacant, vacuous, expressionless; unloaded. See NONEXISTENCE, INSUBSTANTIALITY, ABSENCE, FORMLESSNESS.

blanket, *n.* See COVERING. —*adj.* widespread, comprehensive. See GENERALITY.

blare, *n.* blast, fanfare. See LOUDNESS.

blasé, *adj.* bored (see WEARINESS).

blasphemy, *n.* irreverence, profanity; heresy. See IMPIETY.

blast, *n.* explosion; discharge; gust; harangue (see SPEECH). —*v.t.* destroy, shatter, ruin; explode. See VIOLENCE, DESTRUCTION.

blatant, *adj.* noisy, obtrusive. See LOUDNESS, OSTENTATION.

blaze, *n.* fire, flame; mark, spot. See HEAT, INDICATION.

blazon, *v.* proclaim, advertise; embellish, decorate. See PUBLICATION, ORNAMENT.

bleach, *v.t.* whiten, blanch, lighten. See COLORLESSNESS.

bleak, *adj.* raw, desolate, unsheltered; COLD; discouraging, inauspicious. See ADVERSITY.

blear, *adj.* blurred; bloodshot. See VISION, DIMNESS.

bleed, *v.* flow, hemorrhage; let blood; overcharge, fleece; suffer. *Slang,* soak, skin. See PAIN, STEALING, FLUIDITY.

blemish, *n.* flaw, defect, IMPERFECTION; spot, taint, mark; smear, smudge. —*v.* disfigure, mar; bruise, rot; stain, spot; injure, hurt; sully, disgrace, tarnish. See UNCLEANNESS, UGLINESS, DETERIORATION, DISREPUTE.

blend, *n.* COMBINATION, MIXTURE; crossbreed. —*v.* merge, amalgamate.

bless, *v.t.* hallow, consecrate; praise; thank. See DEITY, PIETY, APPROBATION.

blessing, *n.* benediction, commendation; godsend, boon. See APPROBATION, GOODNESS, PROSPERITY.

blight, *n.* decay, rot; rust, smut. —*v.t.* stunt, rot, impair, corrupt; thwart, foil. See DETERIORATION, HINDRANCE, DESTRUCTION.

blimp, *n.* dirigible (see AVIATION).

blind, *n.* ambush, screen; shade, shutter; DECEPTION, ruse, subterfuge. —*adj.* See BLINDNESS, INATTENTION, CONCEALMENT.

blindfold, *n.* blinders. See DIMNESS, DECEPTION.

BLINDNESS

Nouns—**1,** blindness, sightlessness, anopsia; blind spot; amaurosis; cataract; dimsightedness, benightedness; night blindness, snow blindness, *etc.;* darkness.
2, Braille, Moon's type, New York point, American Braille; seeing-eye dog, white cane, talking book.

Verbs—**1,** be blind, not see; lose sight; grope in the dark, feel one's way.
2, blind, darken, benight, put one's eyes out, gouge; blindfold, hoodwink, throw dust into one's eyes, dazzle; screen, hide (see CONCEALMENT).

Adjectives—blind, eyeless, sightless, unseeing; dark, stone-blind; undiscerning, unperceiving; blind as a bat, a mole, *or* an owl, dimsighted.

Adverbs—blindly, sightlessly, gropingly; blindfold; darkly.

Antonyms, see VISION.

blink, *v.* wink; flash, twinkle; glimmer; disregard, ignore. See VISION, NEGLECT.

bliss, *n.* happiness, ecstasy, rapture, PLEASURE.

blister, *n.* vesicle; bubble, sac. See RECEPTACLE.

blithe, *adj.* gay, lighthearted, merry. See CHEERFULNESS.

blitz, blitzkrieg, *n.* See ATTACK.

blizzard, *n.* snowstorm, whiteout. See WIND, COLD.

bloat, *v.* distend, swell, puff up. See CONVEXITY.

blob, *n.* drop, bubble, lump. See ROTUNDITY.

bloc, *n.* PARTY, faction, ring; union, alliance, coalition. See COOPERATION.

block, *n.* HINDRANCE, blockage, obstruction; row, street, square (see ABODE); mass, lump, cube (see DENSITY). —*v.t.* impede, check, stop, bar; thwart, foil. See CLOSURE, IDENTITY.

blockade, *n.* barrier, stoppage; embargo, siege. —*v.t.* obstruct, bar, barricade. See CLOSURE, HINDRANCE.

blond, *adj.* light-colored, fair-skinned; light-haired, yellow, flaxen, platinum. See COLORLESSNESS, COLOR.

blood, *n.* serum, essence; sap; gore; kindred; lineage, heritage. See RELATION, FLUIDITY, ANCESTRY, CLASS.

bloodless, *adj.* anemic; pale; unfeeling, cold; peaceful; cowardly. See COLORLESSNESS, COWARDICE, INSENSIBILITY.

bloodletting, *n.* phlebotomy, venesection; bloodshed. See REMEDY, KILLING.

bloodshed, *n.* killing, slaughter.

bloodthirsty, *adj.* murderous, sanguinary. See KILLING, MALEVOLENCE.

bloody, *adj.* gory, sanguinary, bleeding; red. See KILLING.

bloom, *n.* blossom, flower; glow; flowering. —*v.i.* blossom; mature; glow, flourish, thrive. See HEALTH, PROSPERITY, VEGETABLE.

blossom, *v.* flower, bloom; develop, flourish. See VEGETABLE, PROSPERITY.

blot, *v.* stain, blemish, spot; sully. —*n.* spot, smear, blemish. See DISREPUTE, UNCLEANNESS, GUILT.

blow, *n.* knock, stroke, hit; DISAPPOINTMENT; blast, WIND, breeze, gale. See IMPULSE, SURPRISE. —*v.* brag; gasp, pant, puff; SOUND; storm, breeze, whiff, waft; *slang,* miss; *slang,* squander. See FAILURE, WASTE.

blowup, *n.* explosion; outburst; enlargement. See EXPANSION, VIOLENCE.

blue, *adj.* azure, indigo, sapphire (see COLOR); delft; severe, puritanical; sad, dejected, depressed, dispirited, downhearted; risqué, profane. See IMPURITY, DEJECTION.

bluejeans, *n.* jeans, dungarees. See CLOTHING.

blues, *n.* melancholy, despondency. See DEJECTION.

bluff, *n.* cliff, bank, headland; hoax. —*v.* mislead; brag; intimidate. See BOASTING, DECEPTION, VERTICAL. —*adj.* frank, abrupt. See DISCOURTESY.

blunder, *n.* slip, botch, mess; solecism. —*v.i.* botch, fail, err; bungle, flounder. See ERROR, UNSKILLFULNESS.

blunt, *v.t.* dull, deaden, numb; moderate. —*adj.* dull; direct; brusque; undiplomatic, forthright. See DISCOURTESY, DULLNESS, INSENSIBILITY, MODERATION.

BLUNTNESS

Nouns—bluntness, dullness; obtundity; obtuseness.
Verbs—blunt, full, take off the edge *or* point of, obtund.
Adjectives—blunt, dull, edgeless, obtundent, unpointed, unsharpened; obtuse.
Antonyms, see SHARPNESS.

---

blur, *v.* blot, smear; obscure, dim; swim, be indistinct. See DIMNESS, OBSCURITY, UNCLEANNESS.

blurt, *v.t.* blab (see DISCLOSURE).

blush, *v.i.* COLOR, flush, glow; redden (see MODESTY). See FEELING.

bluster, *n.* bravado; braggadocio, BOASTING; bullying, hectoring; front. —*v.i.* swagger; play the bully, hector, vapor; roar (see LOUDNESS). See INSOLENCE, THREAT.

board, *n.* COUNCIL, cabinet, panel, committee, directorate; plank; cardboard; provisions, fare. —*v.* lodge, feed; embark (see DEPARTURE). See FOOD, ATTACK, LAYER.

BOASTING

Nouns—**1,** boasting, boast, vaunt[ing], puff, *fanfaronnade,* bluster, gasconade, braggadocio, bravado, swagger, exultation; buncombe (see ABSURDITY); bounce (*Brit.*); rodomontade, bombast, bluff, tall talk, magniloquence, grandiloquence, heroics, chauvinism; EXAGGERATION, much cry and little wool. *Slang,* dog, side, bunk, hot air, front. See VANITY, REJOICING, OSTENTATION.

2, boaster, braggart, Gascon, pretender, *soi-disant,* blusterer. *Slang,* blowhard, windbag, loudmouth. See EVIDENCE, INSOLENCE.

Verbs—boast, make a boast of, brag, vaunt, puff, swagger, roister; preen *or* plume oneself; bluster, bluff; exult, gloat, crow over, neigh, throw up one's cap. *Colloq.*, talk big, show off, blow *or* toot one's own horn. *Slang,* give oneself airs, put on the side *or* dog, put up a big front.
Adjectives—boastful, magniloquent, *soi-disant;* vainglorious, bombastic, pompous, chauvinist, extravagant, high-flown, ostentatious, heroic, grandiose; exultant; in high feather, flushed with victory, cock-a-hoop, on stilts.
Adverbs—boastfully, bombastically, *etc.*

Antonyms, see MODESTY.

---

boat, *n.* See SHIP.
bob, *v.t.* dock, cut, curtail. —*v.i.* jerk, LEAP, float; nod, bow, curtsy. —*n.* weight, float; bobsled; shilling. See AGITATION, OSCILLATION, SHORTNESS.
bodily, *adj.* corporeal, physical, material. —*adv.* wholly, entire. See WHOLE, SUBSTANCE.
body, *n.* anatomy, torso; SUBSTANCE; ASSEMBLAGE, aggregate; solid; person, thing, figure; WHOLE. See PARTY.
bodyguard, *n.* [armed] escort, retinue. See DEFENSE, ACCOMPANIMENT.
bog, *n.* swamp, morass, quagmire, marsh, fen. See WATER.
boggle, *v.t.* amaze, astound. See SURPRISE.
bogus, *adj.* fake, counterfeit, spurious. See DECEPTION.
bogy, bogie, *n.* hobgoblin, gremlin. See DEMON.
boil, *n.* sore, suppuration. See CONVEXITY. —*v.* bubble, seethe; scald; cook; fume, rage. See DISEASE, HEAT, VIOLENCE, AGITATION, EXCITABILITY, FOOD.
boisterous, *adj.* noisy, clamorous, vociferous; unrestrained, rambunctious, riotous, stormy, uproarious. See EXCITEMENT, VIOLENCE, LOUDNESS.
bold, *adj.* daring, audacious, forward; intrepid, brave; impudent. See COURAGE, INSOLENCE, DEFIANCE, VIGOR.
bolt, *n.* lock, latch, bar; thunderbolt, stroke, flash. See CLOSURE, LIGHT. —*v.* dash, run [away]; winnow, sift; gobble, gulp. See ESCAPE, GLUTTONY, VELOCITY, FOOD.
bomb, *n.* [bomb]shell; *slang,* flop (see FAILURE). See ARMS.
bombast, *n.* BOASTING, braggadocio, grandiloquence, EXAGGERATION.
bonanza, *n.* [gold] mine, mother lode (see MONEY, STORE).
bond, *n.* union, CONNECTION, tie; accord, sympathy; guaranty, pledge; shackle. See RELATION, SECURITY, CONNECTION, RESTRAINT.
bondage, *n.* slavery, serfdom, SUBJECTION; helotry, peonage.
bone, *n.* whalebone, ivory, *etc.* See DENSITY.
bonus, *n.* premium, extra, dividend. See GIVING, ADDITION, PAYMENT.
bony, *adj.* skeletal, stiff; osseous; lank, lean. See HARDNESS, NARROWNESS.
booby, *n.* dunce, boob (see FOLLY).
book, *n.* novel, opus; volume, folio; handbook, textbook, *etc.* See PUBLICATION, WRITING.
bookkeeping, *n.* See ACCOUNTING.
bookmaker, *n.* gambler. *Slang,* bookie. See CHANCE.
bookworm, *n.* scholar, pedant; bibliophile. *Colloq.*, grind. See KNOWLEDGE.
boom, *v.* push, boost, plug; flourish; thunder, drum, rumble (see LOUDNESS). —*n.* beam, spar, jib; PROSPERITY. See PUBLICATION, SHIP.
boon, *n.* benefit; favor. See ACQUISITION, REQUEST.
boondocks, *n., slang,* wilderness. See REGION.
boorish, *adj.* ill-mannered, vulgar, rude; rustic, clownish. See VULGARITY, DISCOURTESY.
boost, *n.* AID, help, endorsement; lift, hoist. —*v.i.* assist, promote, recommend; lift, hoist. See APPROBATION, ELEVATION.

boot, *n.* footwear, shoe; Hessian boot; blucher, hip *or* jack boot; seven-league boot; brogan, buskin, chukka. See CLOTHING. —*v.t., slang,* kick out, dismiss, give the boot. See EJECTION.

booth, *n.* hut; compartment, stall. See RECEPTACLE, ABODE.

booty, *n.* spoil, plunder, prize, loot; graft, swag, boodle; pork barrel, pickings; pillage, blackmail; prey. See ACQUISITION.

border, *n.* EDGE, LIMIT, margin, rim; frontier, boundary; trim (see ORNAMENT). See NEARNESS, CONTACT, AGRICULTURE.

bore, *n.* diameter, caliber; nuisance. —*v.* drill, pierce; tire, weary, annoy. See BREADTH, WEARINESS, OPENING.

borough, *n.* See REGION.

borrow, *v.* take, receive (as a loan); appropriate, adopt, imitate, make use of; plagiarize, copy. See DEBT, STEALING.

bosh, *n.* nothing; nonsense, bunk. See ABSURDITY.

bosom, *n.* breast, bust; heart (see FEELING). See CONVEXITY. —*adj.* intimate, close, confidential. See FRIEND.

boss, *n.* knob, stud; manager, supervisor. See CONVEXITY, AUTHORITY, —*v.* oversee, direct; bully, domineer. See AUTHORITY, FEAR.

botany, *n.* See VEGETABLE.

botch, *v.* bungle, blunder, butcher; mar, spoil; mismanage. See UNSKILLFULNESS.

both, *pron.* the two, twain, pair. —*adj.* dually, equally, as well as, together. See EQUALITY, ACCOMPANIMENT.

bother, *n.* nuisance, annoyance; trouble; perplexity, worry. —*v.t.* irritate, pester, worry. See PAIN, ADVERSITY, DISCONTENT.

bottle, *n.* carafe, decanter; carboy; flacon, phial; canteen. See RECEPTACLE.

bottleneck, *n.* obstruction (see CLOSURE).

bottom, *n.* base, foot, sole; foundation; buttocks. See SUPPORT, LOWNESS, REAR. —*v.* fathom; run aground. See DEPTH.

bottomless, *adj.* unfathomable. See DEPTH, INFINITY.

boudoir, *n.* bedroom, sitting room. See RECEPTACLE.

bough, *n.* limb, branch. See PART.

boulder, *n.* See LAND.

boulevard, *n.* avenue, promenade. See PASSAGE.

bounce, *v.* rebound, RECOIL; LEAP; *slang,* eject (see EJECTION).

bound, *v.* LIMIT, confine, delimit, demarcate; LEAP, spring, vault. See CERTAINTY, DUTY.

boundary, *n.* LIMIT, border, confines. See EDGE.

boundless, *adj.* infinite, endless, limitless, illimitable. See INFINITY, SPACE.

bounty, *n.* grant, subsidy; premium; generosity, munificence. See REWARD, LIBERALITY.

bouquet, *n.* FRAGRANCE, perfume, aroma; corsage, boutonnière, nosegay, garland. See ORNAMENT.

bourgeois, *adj.* middle-class; conservative. See MEDIOCRITY.

bout, *n.* contest, match; turn, round; prizefight. See CONTENTION, REGULARITY.

boutique, *n.* specialty store, shop[pe]. See BUSINESS.

bow, *n.* obeisance, curtsy, kowtow, salaam; FRONT, prow. —*v.i.* nod, incline, bend; yield, concede; [make one's] debut. See COURTESY, RESPECT, SUBMISSION, BEGINNING.

bow, *n.* curve, arc, crescent; bowknot; crossbow. See CURVATURE, ARMS.

bowels, *n.pl.* intestines, guts, viscera, innards; depths, recesses. See INTERIOR, DEPTH.

bower, *n.* arbor, grotto. See RECEPTACLE.

bowl, *n.* basin, vessel, dish; cup, breaker; ARENA. See RECEPTACLE, CONCAVITY.

bowling, *n.* tenpins, duckpins, candlepins; ninepines, skittles; lawn bowling, bowls. See AMUSEMENT.

box, *n.* chest, case, carton, container; coffin. See RECEPTACLE. —*v.* fight, spar, come to blows. See CONTENTION.

boy, *n.* lad, YOUTH.

boycott, *v.t.* shun; blackball. See RESISTANCE.

brace, *v.t.* invigorate, stimulate; SUPPORT, prop, strengthen. See REFRESHMENT. —*n.* bracket, stay, girder; bit, stock; pair. See STRENGTH, NUMERATION, POWER.

bracelet, *n.* armlet, wristlet, bangle; handcuffs, manacles. See ORNAMENT, RESTRAINT, CIRCULARITY.

brag, *v.i.* See BOASTING.

braid, *n.* trim, ribbon. —*v.t.* intertwine, interweave, plait. See CROSSING, ORNAMENT, TEXTURE.

brain, *n.* cerebrum, cerebellum; mentality, INTELLECT, intelligence, mind; gray matter. —*v.t.* See KILLING.

brainchild, *n.* creation (see IMAGINATION).

brainstorm, *n.* inspiration (see IMAGINATION).

brainwash, *v.t.* [counter]indoctrinate, misinform. See DECEPTION, FALSEHOOD.

brake, *v.* retard, check, curb; slow down, stop. See SLOWNESS, RESTRAINT.

branch, *n.* member, arm, bough, limb, ramification; shoot, offshoot; PART. See ANCESTRY. —*v.i.* fork, divide, bifurcate; radiate, diverge. See DISJUNCTION.

brand, *n.* kind, sort, stamp; stigma, stain; mark, identification, trademark; ember; branding iron; torch. See DISREPUTE, HEAT, INDICATION, FUEL.

brandish, *v.t.* flourish, wave, make a show of, flaunt, display. See AGITATION, OSTENTATION.

brat, *n.* pest, *enfant terrible,* monster. See DISOBEDIENCE, YOUTH.

bravado, *n.* See BOASTING, INSOLENCE.

brave, *adj.* courageous, valiant. —*v.t.* face, defy. See COURAGE, DEFIANCE. —*n.* buck, redskin (*derog.*).

bravura, *n.* daring, COURAGE.

brawl, *n.* fight, free-for-all; revel. See CONTENTION, AMUSEMENT.

brawn, *n.* STRENGTH, muscle.

breach, *n.* split, rift, schism; dissension, DISCORD; hole, chasm, OPENING; violation, infringement. See ILLEGALITY, INTERVAL.

bread, *n.* staff of life; white, rye, pumpernickel, sourdough, whole wheat, *etc.* bread; *slang,* MONEY.

BREADTH

Nouns—breadth, width, broadness, scope, extent, latitude, amplitude, spaciousness, expanse; diameter, bore, caliber, radius; thickness, bulk, corpulence (see SIZE). See EXPANSION, SPACE, GENERALITY, LIBERALITY.

Verbs—broaden, widen, amplify, extend, enlarge, expand; thicken.

Adjectives—broad, wide, ample, extended; thick; outspread, outstretched; vast, spacious, comprehensive, extensive.

Antonyms, see NARROWNESS.

---

break, *n.* interruption, disconnection; breach, fracture, fissure, crack; pause; boon, advantage. —*v.* crack, fracture, shatter; tame, subdue; CHANGE; train; surpass; violate, infringe. See BRITTLENESS, DOMESTICATION, DISCONTINUANCE, DESTRUCTION.

breakdown, *n.* collapse, FAILURE; [nervous] prostration, crack-up. See INSANITY.

breakneck, *adj.* hazardous (see RASHNESS).

breakthrough, *n.* discovery, development; penetration. See DISCLOSURE, ATTACK.

break-up, *n.* ruin, disintegration. See DECOMPOSITION, DESTRUCTION.

breakwater, *n.* mole, sea wall, jetty. See HINDRANCE.

breast, *n.* bosom, bust, mamma; spirit. See CONVEXITY, FEELING. —*v.* face, brave. See OPPOSITION.

breath, *n.* respiration, inhalation, exhalation; breeze. See LIFE, WIND.

breathless, *adj.* puffing, panting, short-winded, out of breath *or* wind; excited, overcome. See WONDER, WEARINESS, FEELING.

breathtaking, *adj.* See SURPRISE.

breeches, *n.pl.* knickers, knickerbockers; trousers, pantaloons. See CLOTHING.

breed, *v.* create, multiply; generate, produce. —*n.* strain, race, stock. See RELATION, CLASS, REPRODUCTION.

breeding, *n.* background; culture, gentility, lineage. See COURTESY, ANCESTRY, FASHION.

breeze, *n.* zephyr, breath [of air]. See WIND.

brevity, *n.* concision, briefness, SHORTNESS, TRANSIENTNESS.

brew, *v.* stew, cook, steep, simmer; ferment, distill; scheme, foment, PLAN. —*n.* beer, ale; soup, stew; MIXTURE. See FOOD.

bribe, *n.* graft, bait, grease, payola. *Slang,* fix, hush money. —*v.t.* overtip; suborn, tempt, corrupt, grease [the palm]. See OFFER, PURCHASE.

bric-a-brac, *n.* knickknacks, curios. See ORNAMENT.

brick, *n.* block; adobe, clay; loaf, lump, bar, briquet[te]. See MATERIALS, DENSITY.

bridal, *adj.* nuptial, connubial. See MARRIAGE.

bridge, *n.* span, trestle, viaduct, causeway. —*v.t.* connect, span, link, cross. See CONNECTION, CROSSING.

bridle, *v.* curb, check; harness; bristle. See RESTRAINT, RESENTMENT.

brief, *adj.* short, succinct, terse; quick, fleeting. —*n.* summary, argument. —*v.t.* instruct. See INFORMATION, LAWSUIT, SHORTNESS.

briefcase, *n.* valise, portfolio. See RECEPTACLE.

brigand, *n.* bandit, thug, highwayman, robber, pirate. See STEALING.

bright, *adj.* brilliant, shining, glistening; luminous; clever, intelligent; gay, flashing, sparkling. See COLOR, INTELLIGENCE, LIGHT.

brilliant, *adj.* resplendent, radiant; luminous, sparkling, bright; intelligent, clever, quick-witted. See BEAUTY, INTELLIGENCE, LIGHT.

brim, *n.* EDGE, rim, brink.

brindled, *adj.* particolored, banded, tabby. See VARIEGATION.

bring, *v.t.* fetch, carry, convey, conduct; command (a price); CAUSE, occasion. See TRANSPORTATION.

brink, *n.* EDGE, brim, rim, bluff; verge, turning point.

brisk, *adj.* alert, quick, lively, animated, sprightly; cool, sharp. See ACTIVITY, COLD, REFRESHMENT.

bristle, *n.* hair, stubble. —*v.i.* stand, stick up; stiffen. See SHARPNESS, RESENTMENT, ROUGHNESS.

BRITTLENESS

Nouns—**1,** brittleness, fragility, friability, frangibility, frailty; crispness, delicacy, crumbliness. See POWDERINESS.

2, glass, porcelain, *etc.;* shortbread.

Verbs—break, crack, snap, split, shiver, splinter, shatter, fracture; bust, fall to pieces, break up, disintegrate, fragment; crisp.

Adjectives—brittle, frangible, friable, fragile, breakable, frail, gimcrack, shivery, splintery; splitting; eggshell, delicate; crisp, crumbly, short, brittle as glass, glassy, vitreous.

Antonyms, see COHERENCE.

---

broach, *v.t.* launch, introduce; tap, open. See BEGINNING, OPENING.

broad, *adj.* wide; widespread, extensive; marked (as an accent); sweeping, comprehensive; liberal, tolerant. See BREADTH, LIBERALITY, GENERALITY, IMPURITY.

broadcast, *v.* scatter, distribute, disseminate; spread, transmit, publish. —*n.* program, show, telecast. See DISPERSION, COMMUNICATION, PUBLICATION, DISCLOSURE.

broadminded, *adj.* liberal, unbiased. See LIBERALITY.

brochure, *n.* pamphlet, booklet, leaflet; tract, treatise; literature. See PUBLICATION.

broil, *v.* cook, grill, charbroil; fret, stew. See HEAT, RESENTMENT. —*n.* brawl, riot. See CONTENTION.

broke, *adj.* penniless, flat broke. See DEBT, POVERTY.

broker, *n.* AGENT, jobber, middleman, factor; pawnbroker, stockbroker.

brood, *n.* hatch, progeny. See POSTERITY. —*v.i.* ponder, mope, meditate, ruminate; sit (on eggs). See THOUGHT.

brook, *n.* stream, creek, rivulet, run. See WATER.

broom, *n.* brush, besom, whisk. See CLEANNESS.

broth, *n.* stock, bouillon, consommé; decoction, potion, elixir. See FOOD, REMEDY.

brothel, *n.* bawdy house, house of ill repute. See IMPURITY.

brother, *n.* friar, *frère, Frater;* cadet; kinsman, sibling; fellow, colleague, associate; soul brother. See CLERGY, FRIEND.

brotherhood, *n.* kinship, family; association, fraternity, fellowship. See PARTY, FRIEND, SOCIALITY.

brow, *n.* forehead; summit, crest. See FRONT, HEIGHT, EDGE.

browbeat, *v.t.* bully (see FEAR).

brown, *v.t.* toast, braise, singe; sunburn, tan, bronze. See COLOR, HEAT.

browse, *v.* graze, feed, nibble, pasture. See FOOD, INQUIRY.

bruise, *n.* contusion, black-and-blue spot; mouse, black eye, shiner. —*v.t.* batter, contuse; crush. See IMPULSE.

brunet, brunette, *adj.* dark, dark-haired, dark-complexioned; brown, swarthy. See DARKNESS.

brush, *n.* thicket, scrub, shrubbery; broom. —*v.* sweep; graze. See CLEANNESS, ROUGHNESS, TOUCH, PAINTING, CONTENTION.

brusque, *adj.* gruff, curt, abrupt. See DISCOURTESY.

brutal, *adj.* cruel, inhuman; crude, coarse. See MALEVOLENCE, DISCOURTESY.

brutalize, *v.t.* See DETERIORATION.

brute, *n.* beast, ANIMAL; ruffian, scoundrel, bull. See EVILDOER.

bubble, *n.* globule, blob. See ROTUNDITY, DECEPTION. —*v.i.* effervesce, boil, gurgle. See AGITATION, TRANSIENTNESS, WATER.

bucket, *n.* pail, tub; scoop. See RECEPTACLE.

buckle, *n.* clasp, fastening. —*v.* bend, twist, crumple; collapse. See CONNECTION, CONVOLUTION, FAILURE.

bucolic, *adj.* rustic, rural; pastoral. See REGION, POETRY.

bud, *v.i.* sprout, shoot; germinate; burgeon; mature. See BEGINNING, EXPANSION.

buddy, *n., colloq.,* comrade, pal, chum, FRIEND.

budge, *v.* move, stir, shift; alter, change, INFLUENCE. See MOTION.

budget, *n.* APPORTIONMENT, allowance; [estimate of] expenses. See ACCOUNTING, PLAN.

buff, *v.* polish (see SMOOTHNESS, FRICTION). —*n.* See COLOR.

buffer, *n.* fender, bumper; polisher. See SAFETY, HINDRANCE, SMOOTHNESS.

buffet, *v.t.* beat, slap; pelt. —*n.* slap, stroke, blow. See IMPULSE.

buffet, *n.* sideboard, cupboard, cabinet; refreshments, smorgasbord; counter. See RECEPTACLE, FOOD.

buffoon, *n.* fool, clown, jester; comedian, mountebank. See DRAMA, WIT.

bug, *n.* insect, arthropod, mite, nit, bedbug; vermin; *slang,* [wire]tap; *slang,* flaw, defect, fault, IMPERFECTION; *slang,* enthusiast (see ACTIVITY). See ANIMAL, LITTLENESS. —*v., slang,* [wire] tap; pester, annoy, bother. See DISCONTENT, INQUIRY.

bugbear, *n.* bogy, bugaboo. See FEAR.

build, *v.t.* construct, make, fashion; erect; found. See FORM, PRODUCTION. —*n.* physique, body.

building, *n.* edifice, structure; house, ABODE; skyscraper, high- *or* low-rise, *etc.* See FORM.

bulb, *n.* knob, globe; tuber, corm; lamp. See CONVEXITY, VEGETABLE, LIGHT, ROTUNDITY.

bulge, *v.* swell, protrude, bag. See CONVEXITY.

bulk, *n.* SIZE, QUANTITY, measure, amount, volume; mass, expanse; body; generality, majority.

bullet, *n.* missile, shot, ball, lead, slug; buckshot, B.B. shot. See ARMS.

bulletin, *n.* report, statement, INFORMATION. *Colloq.,* flash. See COMMUNICATION, NEWS.

bullfighter, *n.* matador; picador, banderillo; toreador. See AMUSEMENT.

bull's-eye, *n.* target, black. See MIDDLE.

bully, *n.* hector, brawler; plug-ugly; tyrant. —*v.t.* intimidate, browbeat, hector, bulldoze. See EVILDOER, INSOLENCE, THREAT.

bulwark, *n.* fortification, rampart; safeguard; barrier, parapet. See DEFENSE.

bum, *n., slang,* beggar, loafer. See INACTIVITY.

bump, *v.* collide, knock, strike, hit. See IMPULSE.

bun, *n.* roll, sweet roll, Danish [pastry], hot-cross bun; knot, chignon. See FOOD, ROUGHNESS.

bunch, *n.* crowd, group; cluster, bundle. See CONVEXITY, ASSEMBLAGE.

bundle, *n.* package, parcel, packet; bunch, bale; *colloq.,* riches, wealth. See ASSEMBLAGE, MONEY.

bung, *n.* stopper, cork, plug. See CLOSURE.

bungle, *v.* spoil; botch; blunder, goof. See UNSKILLFULNESS.

bunk, *n.* bed, berth, cot; *colloq.,* applesauce, nonsense, buncombe, claptrap, humbug, bosh. See SUPPORT, ABSURDITY.

buoy, *n.* float; marker; bellbuoy, lifebuoy. See NAVIGATION, INDICATION.

buoyant, *adj.* light, floating; resilient, springy; confident, sanguine. See ASCENT, HOPE, CHEERFULNESS, ELASTICITY.

burden, *n.* HINDRANCE; load, weight, encumbrance; charge; refrain. See GRAVITY, REPETITION.

bureau, *n.* department, office; chest, dresser; secretary, desk; division, branch, section, AGENCY. See RECEPTACLE.

bureaucracy, *n.* officialism; officiousness; red tape. See AUTHORITY.

burgeon, *n.* bud, sprout. See VEGETABLE, EXPANSION.

burglar, *n.* housebreaker, second-story man. See STEALING.

burlesque, *n.* farce, parody; comedy, buffoonery. —*v.t.* satirize, parody, mimic, caricature. See IMITATION, RIDICULE, DRAMA.

burn, *v.* oxidize, consume; blaze, flame; fire; sear, char, scorch; destroy. See HEAT, DESIRE, EXCITABILITY.

burrow, *n.* hole, tunnel, excavation, foxhole. —*v.* dig, mine. See CONCAVITY.

bursary, *n.* treasury; scholarship. See STORE, MEANS.

burst, *v.* rupture, break, rend; explode, shatter. *Slang,* bust. See VIOLENCE, DISJUNCTION.

bury, *v.t.* inter, inhume, immure; cover, sink. See INTERMENT, DEPTH, CONCEALMENT.

bus, *n.* omnibus, motorbus, coach, jitney, trolley [bus]. See VEHICLE.

bush, *n.* shrub, clump, thicket, hedge; scrub; wilderness. See VEGETABLE, USELESSNESS.

bushy, *adj.* hairy, shaggy, dense, bushlike. See ROUGHNESS.

BUSINESS

Nouns—**1,** business, occupation, employment, pursuit; venture (see UNDERTAKING); task, work, job, chore, errand, commission, charge, care, assignment; busy work; racket. *Slang,* bag.

2, province, function, bailiwick, lookout, department, station, capacity, sphere, orb, field, line, DUTY; affair, concern, matter, case; walk [of life]; beat, round, range, routine; career, vocation, calling, profession; art, craft, handicraft; trade, commerce, industry.

3, place, post, position, incumbency, living; situation, berth, employ; service; appointment, engagement; avocation (see AMUSEMENT). See ACTIVITY.

4, market, market place, mart, agora, fair, bazaar; industrial park; store, shop, stall, booth, workshop; office, bureau; [stock] exchange, curb, bourse, rialto, pit, Wall Street, the street; bank; firm, concern, establishment, house, company, limited company, conglomerate, corporation, [co-]partnership; concession; facility.

5, businessman, merchant, banker, broker, buyer, seller; bear, bull; financier, speculator; man in the gray flannel suit; white-collar worker. See SALE, PURCHASE.

Verbs—**1,** busy *or* occupy oneself with; undertake, attempt, turn one's hand to; do business, keep a shop, ply one's trade; talk shop *or* turkey; play the market. See ACTIVITY.

2, serve *or* act as, do duty as, discharge the duties of, hold office, fill *or* hold [down] a situation; be engaged in, have in hand; have on one's hands, bear the burden, have one's hands full. *Colloq.,* hold down a job, be into (something).

Adjectives—businesslike, orderly, thorough, methodical, efficient, systematic, workaday; professional, vocational; official, functional; authoritative; busy, in hand, afoot; on foot, on the fire; going on, acting.

Antonyms, see INACTIVITY, REPOSE.

---

bust, *n.* bosom, breast; statuette; *colloq.,* FAILURE; *colloq.,* spree, fling. See CONVEXITY, REPRESENTATION, AMUSEMENT. —*v.i., colloq.,* burst (see BRITTLENESS). —*v.t., slang,* arrest (see RESTRAINT).

bustle, *n.* stir, rustle, fluster, flurry, ado. See ACTIVITY, AGITATION, HASTE.

busy, *adj.* occupied, engaged, engrossed; employed; meddlesome. See ACTIVITY, BUSINESS.

busybody, *n.* meddler, snooper, gossip, talebearer, kibitzer. See CURIOSITY.

but, *conj.* still, yet, however.—*prep.* except, save, saving, excepting. See COMPENSATION, UNCONFORMITY.

butcher, *v.t.* slaughter, kill; bungle, spoil. See KILLING, UNSKILLFULNESS, FOOD.

butt, *n.* target, goat, laughingstock; handle. See RIDICULE, END. —*v.* abut; collide, strike. See IMPULSE, CONTACT.

butte, *n.* hill (see HEIGHT).

buttocks, *n.* rump, seat, hindquarters, breech. See REAR.

button, *n.* fastener; disk, boss; badge, emblem; pushbutton. —*v.* fasten, loop, close. See CLOSURE, JUNCTION, CONNECTION, INDICATION, INSTRUMENTALITY.

buttress, *n.* flying buttress; SUPPORT; prop, brace. See DEFENSE.

buy, *v.* See PURCHASE.

buzz, *v.* drone, hum, whirr; whisper, gossip; *colloq.,* bustle, fuss, hurry; *colloq.,* telephone, ring up. —*n.* hum, whirr, *etc.; colloq.,* [telephone] call, ring. See SOUND, EXCITEMENT.

by, *adv. & prep.* beside, alongside; past, beyond; no later than; through. See INSTRUMENTALITY, CAUSE, SIDE.

bygone, *adj.* former, PAST; antiquated, obsolete. See OBLIVION.

by-pass, *n.* detour, roundabout. See CIRCUITY, DEVIATION.

bystander, *n.* spectator, onlooker. See PRESENCE.

byway, *n.* lane, byroad. See PASSAGE.

byword, *n.* proverb; motto, slogan; shibboleth, password. See MAXIM, INDICATION, NOMENCLATURE.

C

cab, *n.* taxi[cab], hack[ney], hansom; cockpit. See VEHICLE, RECEPTACLE.

cabal, *n.* junto, conspiracy; plot. See PLAN, CONCEALMENT.

cabaret, *n.* nightclub, bistro, night spot. See FOOD, DRINKING.

cabin, *n.* shack, shed, shanty, lodge, hut, cottage; stateroom, cockpit. See RECEPTACLE, ABODE.

cabinet, *n.* room, boudoir, chamber, closet; *étagère,* case; repository; ministry, board, COUNCIL. See RECEPTACLE.

cable, *n.* rope, line, cord; cablegram. See FILAMENT, COMMUNICATION.

cache, *n.* hiding place, stash. See CONCEALMENT.

cad, *n.* scoundrel, bounder, churl. See EVILDOER, DISCOURTESY.

cadaver, *n.* body (see DEATH).

cadet, *n.* recruit (see COMBATANT).

café, *n.* coffeehouse; saloon, bar; cabaret, bistro. See FOOD.

cafeteria, *n.* restaurant, Automat. See FOOD.

cage, *n.* ENCLOSURE, bars; aviary, pen. —*v.t.* restrain, imprison, incarcerate, pen. See RESTRAINT.

cajole, *v.* flatter, wheedle, inveigle; beguile, blandish; coax. See FLATTERY, DECEPTION.

cake, *v.i.* harden; consolidate, cohere; thicken, congeal, condense. See COHERENCE. —*n.* mass, brick, block, floe; torte. See DENSITY, FOOD.

calamity, *n.* catastrophe, disaster. See ADVERSITY, EVIL.

calculate, *v.* compute, reckon; count, appraise; estimate; *colloq.,* consider, deem, figure. See NUMERATION, EXPECTATION, PLAN.

calculating, *adj.* scheming, crafty, designing, CUNNING. See PLAN.

calendar, *n.* almanac; diary, journal, log; register, schedule; docket. See CHRONOMETRY.

calf, *n.* dogie, weaner. See YOUTH.

caliber, *n.* gauge, bore; quality; ability, capability. See SIZE, BREADTH, INTELLIGENCE, DEGREE.

calibrate, *v.t.* graduate; rectify. See MEASUREMENT.

calisthenics, *n.* gymnastics, workout. See EXERTION.

call, *v.* CRY, shout, yell; summon, bid; convoke, muster; choose, appoint, elect; name, designate; visit, interview. —*n.* summons, demand; shout, yell; signal; impulse, urge; visit. See CHOICE, ASSEMBLAGE, COMMAND, NOMENCLATURE, SOCIALITY.

calling, *n.* vocation, profession; occupation, trade, BUSINESS; DUTY.

callous, *adj.* horny, tough; unfeeling, insensitive, hardened. See HARDNESS, INSENSIBILITY.

callow, *adj.* featherless, unfledged; immature, inexperienced. See YOUTH.

calm, *adj.* placid, serene, unruffled, cool, composed, undisturbed; phlegmatic, sedate; tranquil, still, motionless, halcyon; peaceful, pacific. —*v.t.* still, pacify. See REPOSE, PACIFICATION, DISSUASION, INEXCITABILITY.

calumny, *n.* slander (see DETRACTION).

camera, *n.* See OPTICAL INSTRUMENTS.

camouflage, *v.t.* disguise, conceal. —*n.* disguise, mask; pretense. See CONCEALMENT.

camp, *n.* encampment, bivouac, cantonment; group, clique. See ABODE, PARTY.

campaign, *n.* operations; PLAN. —*v.i.* canvass, electioneer; fight, war. See WARFARE, CONDUCT.

campus, *n.* grounds, quadrangle, quad. See SCHOOL.

can, *n.* tin, container; *slang,* jail; *slang,* toilet. See RECEPTACLE, PRISON, CLEANNESS.

canal, *n.* channel, waterway; ditch, culvert, conduit. See PASSAGE.

cancel, *v.t.* delete; offset, neutralize; void, annul; postmark. See NULLIFICATION, COMPENSATION, INDICATION, NONPAYMENT.

cancer, *n.* carcinoma, sarcoma, malignancy. See DISEASE.

candid, *adj.* frank, straightforward; outspoken, blunt. See TRUTH.

candidate, *n.* nominee, office-seeker; applicant, aspirant; probationer. See DESIRE, CHOICE.

candle, *n.* taper, wax, cierge. See LIGHT.

candor, *n.* honesty, sincerity, frankness; simplicity, naïveté, INNOCENCE. See TRUTH.

candy, *n.* confection, sweet, bonbon, kiss. See SWEETNESS.

cane, *n.* switch, stick, rod, birch; walking *or* swagger stick; canebrake. —*v.* thrash, flog, switch, beat. See PUNISHMENT, SUPPORT.

canister, *n.* caddy, container. See RECEPTACLE.

cannibal, *n.* man-eater, savage, anthropophagus. See EVILDOER.

cannon, *n.* gun, field gun *or* piece; artillery, ordnance, battery. See ARMS.

canny, *adj.* wary, sagacious. See CUNNING.

canoe, *n.* dugout, kayak, bungo, pirogue. See SHIP.

canon, *n.* decree, code, law; principle; criterion; round, catch. See CLERGY, MUSIC, RELIGION, RULE, BELIEF, RITE.

canopy, *n.* awning, tester; vault, sky; pavilion, cope; howdah. See COVERING.

cant, *n.* pretense, hypocrisy, insincerity; tilt, OBLIQUITY; argot, lingo, jargon. See IMPIETY, FALSEHOOD, CONCEALMENT, SPEECH.

cantankerous, *adj.* cross, ill-natured. See IRASCIBILITY.

canteen, *n.* flask, waterbag; commissary. See RECEPTACLE, STORE, FOOD.

canvas, *n.* sail, tarpaulin, tent; circus; PAINTING. See COVERING, SHIP.

canvass, *v.t.* examine, sift, discuss; solicit, campaign, poll, survey. See INQUIRY, REQUEST.

canyon, *n.* ravine, defile, gorge, gulch, chasm. See INTERVAL.

cap, *n.* skullcap, tam-o'-shanter, beret, beanie, kepi, glengarry; acme, top; climax; bottlecap. —*v.* cover; outdo, excel; complete, climax. See COVERING, CLOTHING, SUPERIORITY, SPACE, COMPLETION.

capable, *adj.* able, competent, proficient; susceptible. See SKILL, POWER.

capacity, *n.* content, volume; aptitude, faculty, ability. See SIZE, INTELLIGENCE, POWER, BUSINESS.

cape, *n.* mantle, cloak, tippet, fichu, pelerine, bertha; shawl; headland, promontory, point, tongue, peninsula. See CLOTHING, CONVEXITY.

caper, *v.i.* LEAP; cavort, gambol, frisk, frolic, prance, skip. —*n.* LEAP, capriole; prank, antic, trick. See AMUSEMENT.

capital, *adj.* excellent, paramount, first-rate, first-class, unequaled; important, primary, principal; metropolitan; upper-case. See GOODNESS, HEIGHT, PUNISHMENT. —*n.* metropolis, seat; funds, assets, resources. See MONEY, IMPORTANCE, MEANS.

capitol, *n.* statehouse. See COUNCIL.

capitulate, *v.i.* surrender. See SUBMISSION.

caprice, *n.* fancy, humor (see CHANGEABLENESS).

capsize, *v.* overturn, upset, turn turtle, turn *or* tip over. See INVERSION.

capsule, *n.* pill (see REMEDY).

captain, *n.* commander, skipper; leader; chief, headman. See AUTHORITY.

caption, *n.* title, subtitle, headline, heading, subhead, legend. See INDICATION.

captious, *adj.* caviling, carping, hairsplitting, faultfinding, hypercritical. See DISAPPROBATION.

captivate, *v.t.* charm, fascinate, enchant, enamor; enthrall; bewitch. See PLEASURE, ATTRACTION.

captive, *n.* prisoner (see PRISON, RESTRAINT).

capture, *v.t.* seize, apprehend, arrest; grab; bag, snare, trap. *Colloq.*, nab. *Slang*, collar. See RESTRAINT.

car, *n.* See VEHICLE.

caravan, *n.* procession, motorcade; van. See TRAVEL, VEHICLE.

carcass, *n.* corpse, remains, shell, hull. See REMAINDER, DEATH.

card, *n.* tarot, playing card; visiting *or* calling card; *colloq.*, character, oddball. See INDICATION, UNCONFORMITY.

CARE

Nouns—**1,** care, concern, consideration, solicitude, anxiety, heed, heedfulness; conscientiousness, watchfulness, vigilance, surveillance, eyes of Argus; watch, vigil, lookout, weather eye, watch and ward. See SAFETY.

2, alertness, ATTENTION, charge; precaution, prudence, circumspection, CAUTION.

3, tidiness, orderliness, cleanliness, accuracy, exactness, minuteness, attention to detail, meticulousness, *etc.*

Verbs—**1,** be careful, take care, have a care, deliberate, take pains, be cautious, take precautions; pay attention to, take care of, look *or* see to, look *or* see after, keep an eye on; double check; keep in sight *or* view, mind; mind one's business; keep tabs on.

2, have all one's wits about one; watch for, expect (see EXPECTATION); mind one's P's and Q's, weigh one's words, put one's best foot forward, speak by the card, pick one's steps.

3, observe, heed; do one's duty; make good, keep one's word *or* promise.

4, stop, look, and listen (see CAUTION).

Adjectives—**1,** careful, regardful, heedful; particular, painstaking, prudent, cautious, discreet; considerate, thoughtful, solicitous; deliberative, provident, prepared.

2, accurate, exact, deliberate, studied; fastidious, dainty, meticulous, conscientious.

Adverbs—carefully, *etc.;* with care, gingerly.

Antonyms, see NEGLECT.

---

careen, *v.* sway, lean; career, speed. See OBLIQUITY, VELOCITY.

career, *n.* profession, calling, lifework; history. See BUSINESS. —*v.* race, dash. See VELOCITY.

careless, *adj.* carefree, nonchalant; casual, offhand; negligent, slack, slovenly; reckless, rash, indiscreet. See INDIFFERENCE, NEGLECT, INATTENTION, RASHNESS.

caress, *v.t.* fondle, pet, stroke. See ENDEARMENT.

careworn, *adj.* worried, anxious. See FEAR.

cargo, *n.* freight, lading, shipment, load. See TRANSPORTATION.

caricature, *n.* burlesque, travesty; sketch. —*v.t.* satirize, take off, distort. See RIDICULE, IMITATION, EXAGGERATION.

carnage, *n.* massacre, slaughter; shambles, butchery. See KILLING.

carnal, *adj.* bodily, fleshly; worldly, sensual. See ANIMAL, IRRELIGION, INTEMPERANCE.

carnival, *n.* festival, fête, gala; masquerade, bacchanal; revelry. *Slang,* jamboree. See AMUSEMENT.

carnivorous, *adj.* flesh-eating; predatory, predaceous. See FOOD.

carol, *n.* noël. See MUSIC.

carom, *n.* cannon; rebound. See RECOIL.

carouse, *v.i.* feast, revel; debauch, drink. See DRINKING.

carpenter, *n.* cabinetmaker, woodworker, joiner. See PRODUCTION.

carpet, *n.* rug, drugget; wall-to-wall, broadloom, oriental, *etc.* See COVERING.

carriage, *n.* bearing, mien, behavior, CONDUCT, front; wagon, cart, stage-[coach], coach, equipage. See APPEARANCE, VEHICLE, TRANSPORTATION.

carrion, *n.* flesh, carcass, remains. See DECOMPOSITION.

carrousel, *n.* merry-go-round, whirligig (see ROTATION).

carry, *v.t.* uphold, SUPPORT; transport, convey, bear; adopt; [have *or* keep in] stock. See TRANSPORTATION, STORE, ASSENT.

cart, *n.* tumbrel, tumbril; pushcart, dogcart; gocart. See TRANSPORTATION, VEHICLE.

cartel, *n.* syndicate (see PARTY).

carton, *n.* box (see RECEPTACLE).

cartoon, *n.* sketch, drawing; caricature; comic strip, comics, funnies, funny papers. See PAINTING, RIDICULE.

cartridge, *n.* shell; case, cassette. See ARMS, ENCLOSURE.

carve, *v.i.* cut, slice; shape, fashion; chisel, engrave, SCULPTURE. See DISJUNCTION, FORM, ENGRAVING.

cascade, *n.* waterfall (see WATER).

case, *n.* instance, situation, plight; sheath, scabbard, holster; portfolio; suit, action, litigation; argument, proposition; box, container, carton, casket, cabinet; bag, suitcase, handbag, grip, valise. See BUSINESS, COVERING, LAWSUIT, RECEPTACLE, CIRCUMSTANCE.

cash, *n.* MONEY, specie, ready money, hard cash, currency. *Slang,* brass, dust.

cashier, *n.* teller, clerk. See SALE. —*v.t.* fire, dismiss. See EJECTION.

casing, *n.* shell (see COVERING).

cask, *n.* barrel, hogshead, keg, butt. See RECEPTACLE.

casket, *n.* coffin; reliquary, chest, box. See RECEPTACLE.

cast, *v.t.* throw, toss, heave, hurl, sling, fling; shed; mold; plan, compute. See EJECTION, FORM, PROPULSION. —*n.* APPEARANCE, aspect, air; company, actors, *dramatis personae;* casting, COPY, mold, sculpture. See DRAMA, COLOR.

caste, *n.* CLASS, rank.

castigate, *v.t.* criticize; correct, punish. See DISAPPROBATION, PUNISHMENT.

castle, *n.* fort[ress], stronghold; donjon, keep; rook. See DEFENSE, ABODE.

castrate, *v.t.* emasculate, unman; geld. See IMPOTENCE.

casual, *adj.* accidental, CHANCE; careless, cursory; irregular, occasional; informal; happy-go-lucky. See NEGLECT, IRREGULARITY.

casualty, *n.* accident; disaster, calamity. See ADVERSITY, EVIL, OCCURRENCE.

cat, *n.* feline, puss[y], tomcat, tabby, grimalkin, alley cat, mouser, kitten; lion, tiger, leopard, cougar, catamount, lynx, cheetah, liger, *etc.* See ANIMAL.

cataclysm, *n.* upheaval, disaster. See VIOLENCE, DESTRUCTION.

catacombs, *n.* charnel house; vaults, tombs. See INTERMENT.

catalog, *n.* LIST, index, register.

catastrophe, *n.* calamity, disaster, upheaval, cataclysm, paroxysm. See ADVERSITY, DESTRUCTION, EVIL.

catcall, *n.* boo, hiss. See DISAPPROBATION.

catch, *v.t.* take, seize; overtake; land, net, hook; surprise, detect; snare, trap; capture, arrest, apprehend; snatch. *Colloq.,* nab. See RESTRAINT, DECEPTION, DIFFICULTY, HINDRANCE.

catching, *adj.* infectious (see TRANSFER).

catchy, *adj.* tricky, deceptive; attractive. See DECEPTION, ATTENTION.

category, *n.* CLASS; status, place; pigeonhole.
cater, *v.i.* purvey (see PROVISION); indulge, humor. See PLEASURE.
cathartic, *adj.* laxative, physic, purgative, aperient, purifying. See REMEDY, CLEANNESS.
cathedral, *n.* cathedral church, *duomo*. See TEMPLE.
catholic, *adj.* tolerant, liberal; universal, general. See GENERALITY, LIBERALITY.
cattle, *n.* livestock; kine, cows, bulls, steers. See ANIMAL.
caucus, *n.* meeting, smoky *or* smoke-filled room. See ASSEMBLAGE.

CAUSE

Nouns—**1,** cause, origin, source, wellspring, principle, element; leaven; groundwork, base, basis, foundation (see BEGINNING); pivot, hinge, key; straw that breaks the camel's back.
2, causality, causation, origination; ground[s], reason [why]; motive, ax to grind; why and wherefore, rationale, occasion, derivation, root; etiology. See ATTRIBUTION.
3, weight, sway, leverage (see INFLUENCE); motive, impetus, impulse, consideration, motivation; temptation, enticement (see ATTRACTION); inspiration, exhortation, persuasion; goad, spur.
4, occasioner, prime mover, author, creator, producer, progenitor; mainspring, agent (see AGENCY); rabblerouser.

Verbs—**1,** cause, be the cause of, originate, give rise to, occasion, bring, sow the seeds of, engender, [en]kindle; bring to pass, effectuate, bring about; produce, create, give birth to, generate; set up, set afloat, set on foot, found, broach, carry through, bring on, institute, lay the foundation of (see BEGINNING); lie at the root of.
2, procure, induce; draw down, open the door to, let; evoke, entail, elicit, provoke; conduce to, contribute; have a hand in, have a finger in the pie; determine, decide, turn *or* tip the scale *or* balance.
3, have a common origin, derive from (see EFFECT).
4, move, prompt, motivate, put up to; sway, persuade, talk into, bear upon, prevail upon, twist one's arm; inspire, inspirit, stimulate, rouse, animate, incite, stir *or* whip up; set *or* touch off, precipitate, instigate (see ACTIVITY); urge, exhort, spur, goad, egg on.

Adjectives—causal, causative, efficient, original; primary, primitive, primordial; aboriginal; radical; seminal, germinal; at the bottom of, [in] back of.

Adverbs—because, by reason of, on account of, due to; since, for as much as, inasmuch as, what with, in consideration of, in view of, in [the] light of, therefore; by, per, in *or* by virtue of; now that.

Antonyms, see EFFECT.

causeway, *n.* highway (see PASSAGE).
caustic, *adj.* corrosive, burning; mordant, sarcastic, satirical, biting, acrimonious; severe. See DISCOURTESY, RESENTMENT, DETRACTION, FEELING.

CAUTION

Nouns—**1,** caution, cautiousness, discretion, prudence, heed, circumspection, calculation; deliberation, forethought, foresight; vigilance, CARE; WARNING.
2, coolness, self-possession, presence of mind, *sang-froid;* worldly wisdom, Fabian policy.

Verbs—**1,** be cautious, take care, take heed, have a care, watch it, look sharp, watch *or* look out, keep an eye out; mind, be on one's guard, keep watch, keep one's eyes open *or* peeled, sleep with one eye open, be on one's toes; watch one's step, make assurance doubly sure, think twice, look before one leaps, count the cost, look to the main chance, feel one's way, see how the land lies, wait to see how the cat jumps; bridle one's tongue; let well enough alone, keep out of harm's way; keep at a respectful distance; be on the safe side, play it safe.

2, *timeo Danaos, festina lente; cave canem; caveat emptor;* stop, look, and listen.

Adjectives—cautious, prudent, wary; alert, guarded, on one's guard, on the *qui vive,* on the alert, on watch, on the lookout; awake, broad awake, vigilant; watchful, wakeful, Argus-eyed, wide-awake, expectant; noncommittal; gingerly.

Antonyms, see RASHNESS.

---

cavalcade, *n.* procession, caravan. See CONTINUITY, TRAVEL.

cavalier, *n.* horseman, knight; escort. See ACCOMPANIMENT, TRAVEL.—*adj.* haughty, disdainful. See CONTEMPT, DISCOURTESY.

cavalry, *n.* horse soldiers, horsemen, dragoons, hussars; armored *or* mechanized cavalry. See COMBATANT.

cave, cavern, *n.* recess, grotto; lair, burrow, den. See CONCAVITY, ABODE.

cavernous, *adj.* hollow, gaping. See CONCAVITY.

cavil, *v.i.* carp, find fault, take exception; be captious, quibble. See DISAPPROBATION, DISSENT.

cavity, *n.* hole, excavation, hollow, pit; OPENING, depression, pocket, dent. See CONCAVITY.

cavort, *v.i.* See CAPER.

cease, *v.* stop, desist, discontinue, END. See DISCONTINUANCE.

cease-fire, *n.* truce (see PACIFICATION).

ceaseless, *adj.* continual, incessant (see CONTINUITY).

cede, *v.t.* yield, relinquish; grant, assign, TRANSFER; surrender, hand over. See RELINQUISH, SUBMISSION.

ceiling, *n.* roof, cupola, vault, canopy; maximum, LIMIT. See COVERING.

CELEBRATION

Nouns—**1,** celebration, solemnization, jubilee, commemoration; ovation, paean (see APPROBATION); triumph, jubilation; RITE. See REJOICING, OSTENTATION.

2, bonfire, salute, salvo; flourish [of trumpets], fanfare, colors flying, illuminations, fireworks; trophy, triumphal arch.

3, fete, festival, festivity, gala, gala occasion, holiday (see REGULARITY); love-in; harvest home; red-letter day; thanksgiving; inauguration, coronation, *etc.* (see REPUTE). *Slang,* jamboree.

Verbs—**1,** celebrate, keep, signalize, do honor to, commemorate, solemnize, hallow.

2, pledge, drink to, toast; rejoice, make merry, kill the fatted calf, hold jubilee, jubilate, kick up one's heels. See REJOICING.

Adjectives—celebrated, famous (see REPUTE); festive, gala.

Antonyms, see INDIFFERENCE, LAMENTATION.

---

celebrity, *n.* star, notable, lion, [big] name; eminence, fame, renown. See REPUTE.

celestial, *adj.* heavenly, divine, holy; unearthly, supernal; empyreal. See DEITY, HEAVEN, UNIVERSE, ANGEL.

CELIBACY

Nouns—**1,** celibacy, singleness, single blessedness; bachelorhood, bachelorship, spinsterhood; misogamy, misogyny; virginity, *pucelage,* maidenhood; chastity.
2, bachelor, Coelebs, agamist, misogamist, misogynist, monk, priest, lone wolf; spinster; maid, maiden, virgin, *femme sole,* old maid.

Verbs—take the vow, save oneself.

Adjectives—celibate, unmarried, unwed[ded], wifeless, spouseless; single, lone; maiden, virgin, chaste.

Antonyms, see MARRIAGE.

---

cell, *n.* protoplasm; cage, jail; compartment, room, vault; dry *or* wet cell, battery. See ORGANIC MATTER, PRISON, ABODE.

cellar, *n.* basement, subcellar; vault, shelter; wine, cyclone, *etc.* cellar. See RECEPTACLE, LOWNESS.

cement, *n.* mortar, concrete, grout, Portland cement; adhesive, glue, mucilage, paste. See CONNECTION, COHERENCE, UNITY.

cemetery, *n.* graveyard, necropolis, burial ground *or* mound. See INTERMENT.

censor, *n.* reviewer, critic; faultfinder; watchdog. —*v.t.* expurgate, delete; cut, edit; suppress, muzzle, silence. See DEDUCTION, SECRET.

censorious, *adj.* critical, faultfinding, condemnatory. See DISAPPROBATION.

censure, *v.t.* upbraid, chide, reprove; criticize, blame. *Slang,* hit, knock, pan. —*n.* reproof, blame, criticism, disapproval. See DISAPPROBATION, CONDEMNATION.

census, *n.* enumeration, count. See NUMERATION.

center, *n.* See MIDDLE.

ceramics, *n.pl.* pottery, clay-working; SCULPTURE; crockery, earthenware, china, porcelain, ironstone, faience, stoneware; enamel, cloisonné; brick, terra cotta, adobe, glass. See MATERIALS.

cereal, *n.* grain, seed, corn; porridge, gruel, pabulum. See FOOD.

ceremony, *n.* ritual, formality, punctilio, protocol; form, observance, RITE, sacrament, function. See OSTENTATION.

certain, *adj.* some; specified. See QUANTITY, SPECIALITY, CERTAINTY.

CERTAINTY

Nouns—**1,** certainty, certitude, confidence, sureness, conviction, surety, assurance; dead *or* moral certainty; positiveness, assuredness; dogmatism, absolutism; infallibility, reliability; NECESSITY.
2, dogmatist, doctrinaire, bigot, opinionist, Sir Oracle.
3, fact, matter of fact; AFFIRMATION; *fait accompli,* sure thing, shoo-in; *ipse dixit;* guarantee.

Verbs—**1,** be certain, stand to reason, admit of no doubt, go without saying; render certain, ensure, insure, assure, clinch, make sure; determine, ascertain, decide, settle; fix, button, *or* nail down; set at rest, make assurance doubly sure; convince, persuade.
2, dogmatize, lay down the law, make no bones about; bet one's bottom dollar, one's life, *or* one's boots; know like a book *or* like the back of one's hand; know [for certain].

Adjectives—**1,** certain, sure, assured; solid, well-founded; unqualified, absolute, positive, determinate, definite, clear, unequivocal, categorical, unmistakable, cut-and-dried, black-and-white, decisive, decided, on ice, sewed up, ascertained, known, proven.

2, inevitable, unavoidable; sure as fate, sure as death and taxes; unerring, infallible; utter; unchangeable; to be depended on, trustworthy, reliable; bound.

3, unimpeachable, undeniable, unquestionable, indisputable, incontestable, incontrovertible, indubitable; irrefutable, conclusive, without power of appeal; beyond a doubt, without question, beyond a shadow of a doubt; past dispute, beyond [all] question; undoubted, doubtless; clear as day, crystal-clear, evident.

4, assertive, dogmatic; doctrinaire; authoritative, authentic, official, magisterial, *ex cathedra* (see AUTHORITY); straight from the horse's mouth.

Adverbs—certainly, for certain, for sure, certes, sure, no doubt, doubtless, by all odds; and no mistake, sure enough, to be sure, of course, as a matter of course; at any rate, at all events; without fail, come what may *or* will, sink or swim, rain or shine; sight unseen; truly (see TRUTH), no question.

Antonyms, see DOUBT, QUALIFICATION.

---

certificate, *n.* certification, warrant, diploma; testimonial; policy, debenture, stock. See EVIDENCE, SECURITY, RECORD.

certify, *v.* attest (see AFFIRMATION, EVIDENCE).

cessation, *n.* See END.

chafe, *v.t.* abrade, wear, rub; vex, anger, annoy, eat. See FRICTION, RESENTMENT, PAIN, DISCONTENT.

chaff, *n.* husks; banter, jesting, raillery. See REMAINDER, RIDICULE.

chagrin, *n.* mortification, vexation. See DEJECTION, DISAPPOINTMENT.

chain, *n.* series, progression, course, row, string; bond, fetter. See CONTINUITY, CONNECTION, RESTRAINT.

chair, *n.* chairperson, -man, *or* -woman, convenor, coordinator, moderator, speaker, master of ceremonies, M.C., emcee, toastmaster; seat (see SUPPORT); professorship, judgeship, fellowship. *Slang,* roastmaster. See DIRECTOR.

challenge, *v.* query, question; controvert, dispute; dare, defy, stump. —*n.* exception; invitation, dare. See DEFIANCE, DOUBT.

chamber, *n.* room, bedroom; cavity, cell; hall; legislature, assembly. See RECEPTACLE, CONCAVITY, COUNCIL.

chameleon, *n.* turncoat, renegade, Proteus. See ANIMAL, CHANGEABLENESS, VARIEGATION.

champion, *n.* defender, protector, squire, knight; backer, supporter; conqueror, victor, winner, champ. — *v.t.* defend, protect; support. See DEFENSE, SUCCESS, AUXILIARY, SUPERIORITY.

CHANCE

Nouns—**1,** chance, accident, lot; fate, kismet, karma (see DESTINY); luck, fortune, hap, hazard; contingency, adventure, fortuity; indetermination.

2, speculation, venture, gamble, random shot, guessing game, blind bargain, shot *or* leap in the dark, pig in a poke; calculated risk; long shot, dark horse; fluke; potluck. See DANGER, RASHNESS.

3, a. gambling, risk, gaming, betting, dicing, bookmaking; bet, stake, wager. **b.** casino, gambling *or* gaming house, gambling hell, gaming table[s], roulette wheel, craps table, slot machine, one-armed bandit, *etc.;* race track, the turf, the horses, the dogs, parimutuel window[s], racing forms, tout sheets; bucket shop, off-track betting, O.T.B.; wheel of fortune, tossup, toss of the dice, Russian roulette, heads or tails, turn of the card[s] *or* wheel; lottery, raffle, sweepstakes, numbers game. **c.** gambler, gamester, dicer, horseplayer, better, crapshooter, pokerface, *etc.;* adventurer, speculator, entrepreneur; bookmaker. *Slang,* bookie.

4, probability, POSSIBILITY, expectancy (see EXPECTATION); odds, odds-on, edge, advantage; theory of probabilities, theory of games, law of averages.

5, good-luck piece, talisman, four-leaf clover, rabbit's foot; lucky number.

6, see OCCASION, OPPORTUNITY.

Verbs—**1,** chance, befall, hap, turn up; fall to one's lot, be one's fate; happen, hit *or* light upon, run into *or* across, stumble on.

2, chance [it], gamble, risk, venture, speculate; try one's luck, tempt fortune, take a chance, trust to chance; draw lots, toss a coin; shoot the works, go for broke; game, [set at] hazard, stake, bet, wager, play (for); go out on a limb, lay on the line.

3, be possible *or* probable; have *or* stand a chance; bid fair, seem likely; expect, think likely, dare say, flatter oneself.

Adjectives—**1,** chance, random, accidental, adventitious, casual, fortuitous, contingent, eventual, causeless, indeterminate, uncontrollable; indiscriminate; hit-or-miss, catch-as-catch-can; aleatory, aleatoric; lucky.

2, unintentional, undirected, aimless, purposeless, undirected, haphazard, unpremeditated, unwitting, inadvertent.

3, probable, possible, likely, in the cards.

4, at stake *or* risk, on the line; out on a limb.

Adverbs—**1,** by chance, casually, at random, haphazard; incidentally, *en passant,* by the way; as luck would have it.

2, possibly, probably, likely; perhaps, perchance, peradventure; maybe, mayhap, haply (see DOUBT); God willing, *Deo volente, D.V.,* wind and weather permitting. *Colloq.,* like as not, dollars to doughnuts, on the off chance.

Antonyms, see NECESSITY, IMPROBABILITY, CERTAINTY.

---

chancellor, *n.* minister; judge. See AUTHORITY, LAWSUIT.

chandelier, *n.* candelabra, electrolier, luster. See PENDENCY.

CHANGE

Nouns—**1,** change, alteration, mutation, permutation, variation, modification, modulation, innovation, metastasis; transition; menopause; deviation, flux, turn; shift; diversion, break; reform, revision, REVOLUTION; radicalism, revisionism; New Deal, New Frontier, *etc.;* vicissitude.

2, transformation, transfiguration; evolution, metamorphosis; transmutation; transubstantiation; metagenesis, transanimation, transmigration, metempsychosis; alternative.

3, conversion; alchemy; REVOLUTION, reversal; transposition; sex change; transference, TRANSFER; CHANGEABLENESS, tergiversation. See DIFFERENCE, INTERCHANGE.

4, progressive, reformer, revisionist, socialist, communist, revolutionary, radical; convert.

Verbs—**1,** change, alter, vary, wax and wane; temper, modulate, tamper with; turn, shift, veer, tack, swerve; change one's tune, whistle *or* sing a different tune, dance to another tune, reconsider, work a change, modify.

2, transform, translate, transfigure, transmute, transume, make over; metamorphose, ring the changes; convert, innovate, introduce new blood, shuffle the cards; influence, turn the scale *or* the tide; shift the scene, turn over a new leaf; recast, remodel, revamp; reverse, overturn, upset; transpose; reform, reorganize; come round; take a turn for the better *or* worse.

3, be converted (into), turn into, become, evolve, come to; grow, mature, mellow, ripen; resolve into; inflect; assume the form, *etc.* of.

Adjectives—**1,** changed, altered; new-fangled, novel (see NEWNESS); changeable, variable; transitional; modifiable.

2, progressive, reform, revisionary, radical, unconservative, leftish, communist[ic], socialist[ic], pink[ish], red. *Slang,* commie, pinko.

Antonyms, see STABILITY, PERMANENCE, REVERSION.

CHANGEABLENESS

Nouns—**1,** changeableness, alterability; mutability; inconstancy, fickleness; inconsistency; versatility; instability, vacillation, irresolution; fluctuation, fluidity, alternation (see OSCILLATION); restlessness, unrest; AGITATION; iridescence. See IRREGULARITY, DOUBT.

2, moon, Proteus, Cheshire cat, chameleon, quicksilver, mercury, shifting sands, weathervane, kaleidoscope, harlequin, Cynthia of the minute, April showers; wheel of fortune; flibbertigibbet; double-dealer, tergiversator; fair-weather friend. See TRANSIENTNESS.

3, caprice, whimsy, vagary, notion, coquetry, fad; capriciousness.

Verbs—fluctuate, flitter, shuffle, vacillate, turn and turn about, ring the changes; sway *or* shift to and fro; change one's mind, play fast and loose, play the field; change horses in midstream; blow hot and cold, oscillate; have as many phases as the moon. See CHANGE.

Adjectives—changeable, changeful; changing; alterable, mutable, movable, variable; kaleidoscopic, ever-changing, protean; versatile; inconstant, unsteady, unstable, unfixed, unsettled, adrift; fluctuating, restless, agitated; erratic, fickle; irresolute, capricious, whimsical; volatile, mercurial; touch-and-go; fitful, roving, wayward; alternating; transient; iridescent, chatoyant; convertible, modifiable.

Adverbs—seesaw; off and on; off again, on again.

Antonyms, see STABILITY.

---

changeless, *adj.* unchanging. See STABILITY.

changeling, *n.* See SUBSTITUTION.

channel, *n.* duct, conduit, PASSAGE; wavelength, band; artery, vein, blood vessel. —*v.* FURROW, groove.

chant, *n.* Gregorian, Roman, *or* Anglican chant; plainsong *or* -chant; intonation, incantation; psalm, canticle, requiem. See MUSIC, RITE.

chaos, *n.* DISORDER, confusion, jumble, disorganization; abyss, void. See FORMLESSNESS.

chapel, *n.* oratory (see TEMPLE).

chaperon, *n.* attendant, escort; matron, monitor. See SAFETY, ACCOMPANIMENT.

chaplain, *n.* padre. *Slang,* sky pilot. See CLERGY.

chapter, *n.* division, section, PART, verse, canto; branch, lodge, post, corps. See COUNCIL.

char, *v.t.* burn, singe, scorch, sear, carbonize. See HEAT.

character, *n.* kind, CLASS; nature, disposition, temperament, personality; part, rôle; sign, brand, stamp; figure, letter, hieroglyphic, ideograph, pictograph; *colloq.,* personage, eccentric, crank, original. See WRITING, SPECIALITY, INTRINSIC, IDENTITY, DRAMA.

characteristic, *adj.* distinctive, typical, peculiar. —*n.* quality, trait, mark, lineament, feature, peculiarity, attribute, distinction. See INDICATION, SPECIALITY, ATTRIBUTION, INTRINSIC.

charade, *n.* pantomime (see DRAMA).

charge, *v.* COMMAND, exhort, instruct; assess, tax; set a price; burden; debit; strike, ATTACK; fill, load, prepare; accuse, blame. —*n.* ACCUSATION, allegation, impeachment, indictment; COMMAND, order, mandate, requirement; onset, onslaught, ATTACK; PRICE, expense, tax, burden, LIABILITY, encumbrance, assessment, rate, debit; supervision, custody, ward, trust, CARE; load, blast. See ADVICE, DEBT, PAYMENT, COMMISSION.

chariot, *n.* carriage, phaeton (see VEHICLE).

charisma, *n.* See SPECIALITY.

charitable, *adj.* generous, liberal, kindly, Christian, forgiving; altruistic, eleemosynary. See BENEVOLENCE, LIBERALITY, PITY.

charlatan, *n.* quack, pretender, fraud, mountebank. See DECEPTION, FALSEHOOD.

charm, *v.t.* fascinate, hypnotize, enamor, bewitch, enchant, disarm, captivate, attract; soothe, calm, allay. —*n.* attractiveness, personality, captivation, fascination; amulet, talisman, good-luck piece; incantation, spell, magic. See LOVE, PLEASURE, SORCERY, ATTRACTION, BEAUTY.

chart, *n. & v.* map, PLAN; graph. See INFORMATION, RECORD.

charter, *n.* grant, sanction, license, franchise; constitution. —*v.* establish, license, empower; rent, lease, hire, let, book. See PERMISSION, COMMISSION, LEGALITY, SECURITY.

chase, *v.t.* pursue, follow, hunt; dispel, put to flight, rout, repel; tool, engrave. See PURSUIT, ORNAMENTATION.

chasm, *n.* canyon, crevasse, rift, fissure, cleft; abyss. See INTERVAL.

chaste, *adj.* virtuous, pure, undefiled, clean, innocent; simple, classic, severe. See INNOCENCE, SIMPLENESS, ELEGANCE, CELIBACY, CLEANNESS.

chastise, *v.t.* chasten, castigate, discipline. See PUNISHMENT.

chat, *n. & v.* See CONVERSATION.

chatter, *n.* prattle, talk, gabble, gibberish, patter, gossip. See LOQUACITY, SPEECH.

chauffeur, *n.* driver. See TRANSPORTATION.

chauvinist, *n.* nationalist, patriot; jingo, warmonger; macho. *Slang,* [male] chauvinist pig. See WARFARE, BOASTING.

CHEAPNESS

Nouns—**1,** cheapness, inexpensiveness, cut rates, low price; good buy, loss leader, markdown, bargain, pig in a poke; SALE, discount, depreciation, price war; drug on the market; loss leader; irregulars, seconds; bargain basement, dime store, five-and-dime, five-and-ten; cutthroat competition. *Colloq.,* steal.

2, triviality, paltriness, insignificance; trashiness, worthlessness. *Slang,* chicken feed. See UNIMPORTANCE.

3, gratuity (see NONPAYMENT).

4, see PARSIMONY.

Verbs—be cheap, cost little; come down in price, be marked down; get *or* buy for a song; buy at a bargain, buy dirt cheap; get one's money's worth; depreciate, undervalue, discount; cut (competitor's) throat. *Colloq.,* beat down. See ECONOMY.

Adjectives—**1,** cheap, underpriced, low-priced; moderate, reasonable, inexpensive; worth the money, economical, cheap at the price, dirt-cheap; reduced, cut-rate, half-price, marked down; depreciated, unsalable.

2, gratuitous, gratis, free, for nothing, without charge, untaxed, scot-free, free of cost, complimentary; honorary. *Colloq.*, on the house, dime a dozen; five-and-ten.

3, trivial, paltry, insignificant; trashy, worthless.

Adverbs—cheaply, inexpensively; for a song, at cost [price], at a reduction, at wholesale; below cost.

Antonyms, see DEARNESS.

---

cheat, *v.* deceive, defraud (see DECEPTION).

check, *v.t.* control, test, verify, tally, count; restrain, repress, halt, stop, arrest, impede, interrupt, curb; stunt. —*n.* draft, money order; interruption, rebuff; setback, reverse, stop, RESTRAINT; supervision, control, tab; check-up; drag, block, brake; plaid, tartan, checkerboard; ticket, token, bill, stub; counter, chip. See ADVERSITY, HINDRANCE, MONEY, VARIEGATION, EXPERIMENT.

checkered, *adj.* varied, irregular; colorful; checked, plaid. See VARIEGATION, IRREGULARITY.

cheek, *n.* jowl; INSOLENCE, impertinence, sauce, impudence, effrontery, face. *Colloq.*, brass. *Slang*, nerve, gall, sass. See SIDE.

CHEERFULNESS

Nouns—**1,** cheerfulness, geniality, gaiety, sunniness, good nature; cheer, good humor, spirits, high spirits, animal spirits; glee, high glee, light heart; optimism (see HOPE). See PLEASURE.

2, liveliness, vivacity, animation. See ACTIVITY.

3, mirth, merriment, hilarity, exhilaration; joviality, jollity, levity; jocularity (see WIT); playfulness, laughter, merrymaking, fun, AMUSEMENT. See REJOICING.

4, contentment, contentedness; happiness, peace of mind (see CONTENT).

Verbs—**1,** be cheerful, have the mind at ease, put a good face upon, keep up one's spirits; see the bright side; cheer up, brighten up, light up, bear up; take heart, cast away care, drive dull care away, perk up, snap out of it; rejoice, carol, chirrup, chirp; frisk, lilt. *Slang,* feel one's oats, kick up one's heels.

2, cheer [up], enliven, elate, exhilarate, gladden, hearten, inspirit, animate, raise the spirits, buck up, inspire; encourage, refresh. *Slang,* jazz up, give a shot in the arm.

Adjectives—**1,** cheerful, genial, happy, glad, cheery, of good cheer, good-natured, smiling, sunny, blithe; in good spirits, high-spirited, happy as the day is long, gay [as a lark]; light, lightsome, lighthearted; buoyant, free and easy, airy, jaunty.

2, lively, sprightly, spirited, animated, vivacious; sparkling, full of play, full of spirit, all alive.

3, merry as a cricket *or* grig, joyous, joyful, jocund, jovial, jolly, blithesome, gleeful, hilarious; playful [as a kitten], tricksy; mirthloving, laughter-loving, mirthful, rollicking; elated, jubilant, REJOICING; cock-a-hoop; cheering, inspiriting, exhilarating; pleasing.

Adverbs—cheerfully, cheerily, with relish, with zest; in fine fettle, in high spirits *or* feather; [sitting] on top of the world, flying *or* riding high.

Antonyms, see DEJECTION.

cheerless, *adj.* See DEJECTION.
cheesy, *adj., colloq.,* shoddy, second-rate. See INFERIORITY.
chef, *n.* [head] cook (see FOOD).
chemical, *n.* See INORGANIC MATTER.
cherish, *v.t.* nurture, nourish, foster, protect, nurse; entertain, harbor, cling to; prize, treasure, hold dear, revere. See LOVE, AID, ENDEARMENT.
cherub, *n.* cupid, amor; child, moppet, urchin; infant. See ANGEL, YOUTH.
chest, *n.* case, box, casket; coffer; cabinet, commode, locker, bureau; thorax, breast. See RECEPTACLE, CONVEXITY.
chew, *v.* masticate, gnaw, grind, champ. See FOOD.
chic, *n. & adj.* See FASHION.
chicanery, *n.* trickery (see DECEPTION, CUNNING).
chicken, *n.* fowl, cock, hen, pullet; fryer, broiler, capon; *slang,* coward (see COWARDICE). See ANIMAL, FOOD.
chide, *v.* scold, lecture, reprove. See DISAPPROBATION.
chief, *n.* chieftain, leader, president; captain, commander, general; superior, foreman, overseer; elder. See AUTHORITY. —*adj.* principal, foremost, leading, supreme. See IMPORTANCE.
child, *n.* See YOUTH.
childbirth, *n.* delivery, parturition, labor pains; natural childbirth, Lamaze, *etc.* method. See REPRODUCTION.
childhood, *n.* infancy, YOUTH.
childish, *adj.* infantile, puerile, juvenile, youthful, babyish; brattish; senile, simpleminded, weak, silly; credulous, naïve, trustful. See CREDULITY, YOUTH.
chill, *n.* shivering, shakes, ague; chilliness; frost. See COLD. —*v.* ice, frost; discourage, dispirit. See DISSUASION.
chime, *n.* [tubular] bell; doorbell. See MUSIC.
chime in, *v.i.* See ASSENT.
chimera, *n.* fancy, fantasy; monster; vain HOPE. See IMAGINATION, MYTHICAL DEITIES, NONEXISTENCE.
chimney, *n.* smokestack, spout, flue; vent. See OPENING.
china, *n.* chinaware, dishes, crockery; stoneware. See RECEPTACLE.
chip, *n.* piece, splinter, fragment, flake; counter, check. See PART, MONEY. —*v.t.* break, split. See DISJUNCTION.
chisel, *v.* trim, pare, sculpt, carve; *slang,* swindle, cheat. See DECEPTION, SCULPTURE, FORM.
chivalrous, *adj.* knightly, gallant, noble, courteous, brave. See COURTESY, COURAGE, UNSELFISHNESS.

CHOICE

Nouns—**1,** choice, option, selection, determination, pick, preference; volition, DESIRE; adoption, JUDGMENT; triage; alternative. See EXCLUSION, FREEDOM.
2, election, poll, ballot, vote, straw vote; voice, suffrage; plebiscite, referendum; *vox populi;* electioneering; voting; [split *or* straight] ticket; franchise.
3, voter, balloter, elector; suffragist; electorate, constituency.
4, elect, chosen one, pick of the crop, favorite, favorite son; lame duck.

Verbs—**1,** choose, elect, opt, fix upon; determine, make up one's mind (see RESOLUTION); exercise one's option, do as one pleases; adopt, take up, embrace, espouse; take sides.
2, vote, poll, ballot; hold up one's hand; thumbs up *or* down.
3, select, pick, designate, call, pick and choose, hand-pick; nominate, put up; pick over; pick *or* single out, cull, glean, winnow, sift; pick up, pitch upon; pick one's way; indulge one's fancy; set apart, mark out for; prefer, have rather, have as lief; DESIRE; take a decisive step, commit oneself to a

course, throw one's hat in the ring, stand for; cross the Rubicon; cast in one's lot with (see COOPERATION); take for better or for worse.

Adjectives—optional, elective; discretionary, voluntary, selective, preferential; either; eclectic; chosen; choice (see GOOD); on approval; on the bandwagon; choosy.

Adverbs—optionally, at pleasure, at will, at one's discretion; at the option of; whether or not; if anything; once and for all; for one's money; by choice, by preference; rather, before, sooner.

Antonyms, see NECESSITY, REJECTION, WILL.

---

choke, *v.* strangle, suffocate, garrote; stifle, obstruct, clog, jam, plug. See CLOSURE, KILLING.

choose, *v.* See CHOICE.

choosy, *adj., colloq.,* fussy, finicky. See TASTE.

chop, *v.* cut, mince; cleave, lop, hack, hew; strike. See DISJUNCTION.

choppy, *adj.* rough, jerky. See AGITATION.

chord, *n.* cord; harmony; triad, arpeggio. See MUSIC, FILAMENT.

chore, *n.* job, task, assignment; (*pl.*) housework, rounds. See BUSINESS, WEARINESS.

chorus, *n.* choir, singers, choristers; chorus line, dancers; refrain, burden. See MUSIC, CRY.

christen, *v.t.* baptize, sponsor, name; initiate. See NOMENCLATURE, RITE.

Christian, *n.* believer, gentile, churchman. See RELIGION, PIETY.

Christmas, *n.* yule, *Noël.* See TIME.

chronic, *adj.* continuing, persistent, constant; inveterate, rooted. See CONTINUITY, HABIT.

chronicle, *n.* history, annals, RECORD. See CHRONOMETRY, DESCRIPTION.

chronological, *adj.* dated, sequential, in SEQUENCE. See CHRONOMETRY.

CHRONOMETRY

Nouns—**1,** chronometry, horometry, chronology, horology; date, epoch; era, times.

2, calendar, date; millennium, century, decade, year, month (January, February, *etc.*), week, fortnight; day (Sunday, Monday, *etc.*); second, minute, hour; sunrise, morning, evening, noon, midday, afternoon, twilight, sunset, night, midnight; season, spring, summer, fall, autumn, winter; term, semester, trimester, quarter; turn of the century.

3, clock, watch, digital *or* analog watch, Big Ben; self-winding, quartz, *or* electric clock; chronometer, chronoscope, stopwatch, chronograph; [taxi]meter; repeater; clock-radio; timekeeper, timepiece; dial, sundial, gnomon, pendulum, hourglass, water glass, clepsydra; time signal. See TIME.

Verbs—fix *or* mark the time; date, register, chronicle; keep, measure, beat, *or* mark time; bear date; time.

Adjectives—**1,** chronometrical, chronological, chronoscopic, chronographical.

2, hourly, diurnal, daily, weekly, fortnightly, monthly, menstrual, yearly, annual, biennial, centennial; morning, matutinal, antemeridian; evening, vesper, crepuscular; nocturnal, nightly; vernal, estival, autumnal, wintry, brumal.

Adverbs—on the hour, minute, *etc.*

---

chubby, *adj.* plump, stout, obese; overweight. See SIZE.

chuckle, *v. & n.* chortle, cluck, snicker, cackle. See REJOICING.

chum, *n.* pal, buddy (see FRIEND).

chunk, *n.* lump, hunk. See PART.

church, *n.* WORSHIP, service; ministry; denomination; Christendom, Holy Church; chapel, cathedral, synagogue, TEMPLE. See RELIGION.
churl, *n.* villein, ceorl; peasant, rustic, yokel; boor, varlet, knave. See DISCOURTESY, POPULACE.
churn, *v.* agitate, whip; seethe, boil. See AGITATION.
chute, *n.* fall, DESCENT; rapids; white water; shoot, slide, trough, hopper. See WATER, PASSAGE.
cigar, *n.* cheroot, stogie; panatela, perfecto, corona, belvedere; cigarillo; Havana. See PUNGENCY.
cigarette, *n.* smoke; regular, king-size, long[-size], plain, oval, cork-tip, filter tip, 100's; butt. *Slang,* coffin nail, cig, fag, gasper, tube, weed, reefer. See PUNGENCY.
cinch, *n.* girth; *colloq.,* certitude, sure thing. See FACILITY, CIRCULARITY.
cinder, *n.* slag, ash[es]; brand, ember, coal; lava. See REMAINDER, HEAT, FUEL.
cinema, *n.* See DRAMA.
cipher, *n.* naught, zero; nonentity; cryptogram, codes, cryptology; monogram, device. See CONCEALMENT, INSUBSTANTIALITY, NUMBER.
circa, *prep.* about (see NEARNESS).
circle, *v.* encircle, ring, girdle; circumnavigate; circumscribe, compass. —*n.* circumference; CIRCUIT; ring, circlet; disk; set, clique. See PARTY, CIRCULARITY, CIRCUMSCRIPTION.

CIRCUIT

Nouns—circuit, circumference, circle, compass; itinerary, excursion; cycle; perimeter, round, contour, outline; turn, curvet; circumnavigation, circumambulation; route, orbit; period, *etc.;* circulation, CIRCULARITY. See TRAVEL.
Verbs—circuit, circle, round; circumnavigate, circumambulate, make the tour of, go the round, make the rounds of; put a girdle around the earth, orbit; go round the horn.
Adjectives—circumnavigatory, circumambulatory; excursionary.
Antonyms, see STRAIGHTNESS, DIRECTION.

CIRCUITY

Nouns—circuity, circuition, circumvention, circumlocution, indirectness; bypass, roundabout way, ambages, detour, loop, winding, zigzag, DEVIATION. See AVOIDANCE, CONVOLUTION.
Verbs—bypass, circumvent; go roundabout, go out of one's way; detour, meander; beat around *or* about the bush; veer, tack, twist.
Adjectives—circuitous, indirect, roundabout; zigzag, deviating, wandering, circumlocutory; devious.
Antonyms, see DIRECTION.

CIRCULARITY

Nouns—**1,** circularity, roundness; sphericity, ROTUNDITY.
2, circle, circlet, circumference, ring, areola, hoop, annulus, annulet, bracelet, armlet, ringlet; eye, grommet, loop; wheel, round, rundle, trolley; orb, ball, sphere, globe (see ROTUNDITY); orbit (see CIRCUIT); zone, belt, cordon, band (see CIRCUMSCRIPTION); wreath, garland; crown, corona, halo; coronet, diadem; chaplet, snood, necklace, collar, noose, lasso; napkin ring; meridian, equator, parallel, tropic.

3, ellipse, oval, ovoid, ellipsoid, spheroid, cycloid; epicycloid, epicycle; hemisphere, semicircle; quadrant, sextant, sector, segment.
Verbs—circle, surround; enclose, encompass; rotate, revolve (see ROTATION).
Adjectives—circular, round, rounded, annular, coronary; oval, ovate; elliptical, egg-shaped; rotund, spherical (see ROTUNDITY).

Antonyms, see ANGULARITY.

---

circulate, *v.* pass, go about, change hands, mix, move; spread, publish, diffuse, disseminate, propagate. See MONEY, PUBLICATION, ROTATION.

circumference, *n.* perimeter, boundary, compass. See CIRCUIT, ENVIRONMENT.

circumlocution, *n.* paraphrase, periphrasis, indirection. See AVOIDANCE, DIFFUSENESS.

CIRCUMSCRIPTION

Nouns—**1,** circumscription, circumjacence; limitation, ENCLOSURE; confinement, RESTRAINT; bound, LIMIT, boundary. See CIRCUIT.
2, zone, belt, cordon, band; sash, girdle, cestus, cincture, baldric, fillet.
Verbs—circumscribe, LIMIT, bound, confine, enclose; [en]circle, girth, gird, surround, compass about, close in, immure; imprison, restrict, restrain; wall in, fence in, hem in, hedge round; picket, pen, corral, enkraal; enclose, embrace, wrap *or* tie up; besiege (see ATTACK).
Adjectives—circumscribed, begirt, lapped, buried *or* immersed in; hemmed in, pent in *or* up, mewed up; immured, imprisoned; landlocked, seagirt.
Adverbs—out of bounds.

Antonyms, see FREEDOM, SPACE.

---

circumspect, *adj.* careful, discreet. See CARE.

CIRCUMSTANCE

Nouns—**1,** circumstance, situation, condition, case, phase, position, posture, attitude, place, ENVIRONMENT; footing, standing, status, state; OCCASION, eventuality, juncture, conjuncture; contingency, event; quandary, dilemma, predicament (see DIFFICULTY); emergency; exigency, crisis, pinch, pass, push; turning point; bearings, lay of the land, how the land lies.
2, OCCURRENCE, incident, fact, happening, phenomenon.
Verbs—occur; undergo, fall to the lot of, be one's lot; find oneself; shape up.
Adjectives—circumstantial, given, conditional, provisional (see QUALIFICATION); contingent, incidental; adventitious, EXTRINSIC; occasional.
Adverbs—**1,** in *or* under the circumstances, thus, in such wise, accordingly; therefore, consequently, that *or* such being the case, that being so, since, seeing that, so, then; conditionally, provided, if, in case; if so, in the event of; so *or* as long as; in such a contingency *or* case; occasionally; provisionally, unless, except, without (see QUALIFICATION); according to the circumstances, according as, as the case may be, as the wind blows. *Colloq.,* thusly.
2, eventually, in the [natural] course [of things]; as things go.

Antonyms, see NONEXISTENCE.

---

circumvent, *v.t.* evade; outwit. See DECEPTION, AVOIDANCE.

circus, *n.* ring, ARENA; carnival, menagerie; sideshow, midway, the big top, greatest show on earth; travesty. See AMUSEMENT, DRAMA.

cistern, *n.* tank, reservoir; rain barrel. See STORE, RECEPTACLE.

citadel, *n.* fortress. See DEFENSE.

cite, *v.t.* mention, bring forward, quote; arraign, summon; commend. See EVIDENCE, DEMONSTRATION, REPUTE.

citizen, *n.* resident, INHABITANT; civilian, native.

city, *n.* town, municipality; capital, metropolis, megalopolis, cosmopolis; city-state. *Colloq.*, burg, big town. See ABODE.

civil, *adj.* courteous, mannerly, polite; civic, secular, lay. See COURTESY, AUTHORITY.

civilize, *v.t.* educate, cultivate, refine; reclaim, enlighten. See IMPROVEMENT, COURTESY, FASHION.

claim, *v.t.* ask, demand, requisition, require; lay claim to; *colloq.*, contend, allege, assert. —*n.* demand, requisition, requirement, prerogative; lien, hold; plea, counterclaim; title. See AFFIRMATION, COMMAND, LAWSUIT, POSSESSION, RIGHTNESS, JUSTICE.

claimant, *n.* pretender, pleader, claimer, heir. See REQUEST.

clairvoyance, *n.* second sight, foreknowledge; fortune-telling, divination; insight. See INTUITION, PREDICTION.

clamber, *v.i.* scramble, crawl, shin up. See ASCENT.

clammy, *adj.* moist, damp, sweaty. See MOISTURE.

clamor, *n.* outcry, hallubaloo, uproar, racket, tumult, din. See CRY, LOUDNESS, DISAPPROBATION.

clamp, *n.* grip, vise; fastener, clasp. See RETENTION.

clan, *n.* family, tribe, sept; brotherhood, association; breed, caste; clique. See ANCESTRY, PARTY, CLASS.

clandestine, *adj.* SECRET, furtive, sly, undercover; veiled; illicit, fraudulent. See CONCEALMENT.

clang, *v.i.* peal, toll, ring. See LOUDNESS.

clap, *v.* applaud, acclaim; strike, slap, bang, slam; impose, put. See APPROBATION, IMPULSE.

clarify, *v.t.* filter, refine, purify; render; explain, elucidate, throw light on, clear up. See PURITY, INTERPRETATION.

clarity, *n.* clearness, TRANSPARENCY. See MEANING.

clash, *v.* collide, conflict; disagree, dispute, differ, contend. —*n.* collision, impact, concussion, conflict, DISAGREEMENT. See IMPULSE, CONTENTION, DISCORD.

clasp, *v.t.* hug, embrace, enfold; fasten, hook, buckle; clutch, hold. See COHERENCE, ENDEARMENT, CONNECTION.

CLASS

Nouns—**1,** class, division, category, head, section; department, province, domain (see PART); order, family, genus, species, variety; race, tribe, sept, clan; breed; type, sect, set, genre; coterie, clique (see PARTY); estate; assortment; feather, stripe, blood, ilk, kidney, the likes of; suit; gender, sex, kin; kind, sort, manner, description, denomination, designation (see NOMENCLATURE); character, stamp.

2, classification, organization, ARRANGEMENT, ORDER.

3, rank, standing, status, station, condition, [social] level, caste; rating, quality; class warfare *or* struggle. See DEGREE.

Verbs—class, classify, sort, screen; rank, rate, organize, arrange, catalog[ue], categorize; characterize, type, put *or* set down.

Adjectives—classified, specified; systematic, ordered, organized.

Antonyms, see WHOLE.

---

classic, *adj.* standard; chaste, simple. See SIMPLENESS, ELEGANCE.

classification, *n.* grouping, category, allocation; ARRANGEMENT, systematization, taxonomy, ORDER. See CLASS, SECRET.

classy, *adj., slang,* modish, chic. See FASHION.

clatter, *n.* rattle, racket, din. See LOUDNESS.

clause, *n.* article, paragraph, section; proviso, condition, stipulation. See QUALIFICATION, PART.

claw, *n.* talon, nail, hook; pincer, nipper. See ACQUISITION.

clay, *n.* earth, potter's clay, kaolin; mud, loam; flesh. See LAND, SUBSTANCE.

CLEANNESS

Nouns—**1,** cleanness, cleanliness, PURITY, spotlessness; purification, circumcision; purgation, lustration, ablution; cleansing, wash[ing], lavation; dry-cleaning; sanitation, disinfection; fumigation; irrigation, lavage; drainage, sewerage, plumbing.

2, bath, shower [bath], sponge bath; lavatory, lavabo, bathhouse, public bath, swimming pool, Turkish *or* steam bath, Swedish *or* Finnish bath, sauna, Jacuzzi; laundry, washhouse; washroom, washstand, toilet, bathroom.

3, brush, broom, besom; mop, hose, sponge, swab; carpet sweeper, dustpan, dust mop, vacuum, cleaner; washing machine; duster; washcloth, washrag; towel, napkin; soap, detergent, scouring powder, cleanser, disinfectant; purgative, cathartic; filter.

4, washerwoman, laundress; charwoman, maid, day-worker; houseman; janitor, cleaning man *or* woman, street-sweeper *or* -cleaner. *Colloq.,* whitewing.

5, see SIMPLENESS, IMPROVEMENT.

Verbs—**1,** clean [up], cleanse, do up; keep house; rinse, flush, irrigate; dry-clean; wipe, mop, sponge, scour, rub, swab, scrub; dust, brush up; vacuum; sandblast; wash, lave, launder; purify, expurgate, lustrate, clarify, refine; filter, filtrate; drain, strain, percolate, lixiviate, leach; elutriate.

2, disinfect, freshen, purge, sterilize, fumigate, deodorize.

3, sift, winnow, weed; groom, comb, rake, brush, sweep, card; sieve.

Adjectives—**1,** clean, cleanly, sanitary; pure, chaste, immaculate; spotless, stainless; without a stain, unstained, unspotted, unsoiled, unsullied, untainted, unadulterated, uninfected, sterile; sweet; neat, spruce, tidy, trim; bright as a new penny; snowy, snow-white, white; spic and span, clean as a whistle.

2, [hand *or* machine] washable, cleanable, wash and wear, drip-dry, permanent press.

Antonyms, see UNCLEANNESS.

---

clear, *adj.* clear-cut, plain, sharp, understandable; fair, unclouded, cloudless, fine; open, evident; lucid, pellucid, transparent, limpid; liquid, pure, silvery; innocent. See CERTAINTY, TRANSPARENCY, ACQUITTAL, VISION, PAYMENT.

cleave, *v.* stick, hold fast, adhere, cling; sever, shear, split, rive, rend, divide. See COHERENCE, DISJUNCTION.

cleft, *n.* split, rift, fissure, crack, crevice. See INTERVAL.

clemency, *n.* mildness, mercy, LENIENCY.

CLERGY

Nouns—**1,** clergy, ministry, priesthood, rabbinate, abbacy, ulema, imamate; the cloth, Roman collar. See RELIGION, WORSHIP.

2, clergyman, cleric, divine, ecclesiastic, churchman, priest, minister, preacher, dominie, pastor, leader of the flock, shepherd; father, father in Christ; padre, abbé, curé; patriarch; reverend; confessor.

3, Pope, pontiff, cardinal, eminence, reverence, primate, metropolitan, archbishop, bishop, prelate, diocesan, suffragan; rabbi, caliph, imam, muezzin; dean, subdean, archdeacon, prebendary, canon, rector, parson, vicar, chaplain, curate; deacon, preacher, reader, lecturer; missionary, propagandist, Salvationist, revivalist, gospel singer *or* preacher, evangelist; almoner, verger, beadle, sexton, sacristan; druid.

4, a. cenobite, conventual, abbot, prior, monk, friar, brother; lay brother, pilgrim. **b.** abbess, prioress, canoness; mother superior, nun, sister, novice, postulant. **c.** Jesuits, Franciscans, Gray Friars, Friars minor, Minorites; Capuchins, Dominicans, Black Friars; Carmelites, White Friars; Augustinians, Austin Friars; Carthusians, Benedictines, Cistercians, Trappists, Cluniacs, Maturines; Templars, Hospitallers.

5, holy orders, ordination, consecration, induction; clericalism, theocracy, hierarchy, ecclesiology; monasticism, monkhood, ASCETICISM, cloistered life; papacy, pontificate; prelacy.

6, vestments, canonicals; cloth; habit; robe, gown, frock, surplice, cassock, scapular[y], cope, scarf, amice, chasuble, alb, stole; fanon; tonsure, cowl, coif, hood; calotte; bands; pontificals, pall; miter, tiara, triple crown; cardinal's *or* red hat, biretta; crozier, pastoral staff; thurible.

7, consistory, synod, council, Sanhedrin.

Verbs—call, ordain, consecrate, induct; take orders *or* vows, take the veil.

Adjectives—ordained, in holy orders, called to the ministry; clerical, priestly, ecclesiastical, pastoral, ministerial; episcopal, hierarchical; pontifical, papal.

Antonyms, see LAITY.

---

clerk, *n.* salesperson, -man, *or* -woman; registrar, scribe, secretary; copyist, writer. See WRITING, ACCOUNTING, AUXILIARY.

clever, *adj.* adroit, skillful; talented, adept, gifted; smart, cute. See SKILL, CUNNING.

cliché, *n.* stereotype, plate, cut (see PRINTING); truism, commonplace, platitude; banality, triviality. *Colloq.*, bromide. See MAXIM.

click, *v., colloq.*, fall into place, jibe; go over, succeed, make the grade. See SUCCESS.

client, *n.* customer, buyer, patron. See PURCHASE.

cliff, *n.* precipice, palisade, crag, bluff, steep. See HEIGHT, VERTICAL.

climate, *n.* weather; temperature, rainfall, precipitation, *etc.;* REGION. See AIR.

climax, *n.* acme, zenith, summit, pinnacle; turning point, culmination; orgasm. See HEIGHT.

climb, *v.* mount, scale, ascend, rise, go up; succeed; clamber, scramble, shin[ny]. See ASCENT, DESCENT.

clinch, *v.t.* confirm; fasten, secure, rivet, clamp; clench, grapple; seize, grasp. —*v.i., colloq.*, embrace. See COMPLETION, JUNCTION, CERTAINTY, ACQUISITION, RETENTION.

cling, *v.i.* stick, hold, cleave, adhere; grasp, hold on to, hug. See COHERENCE, LOVE.

clinic, *n.* dispensary, hospital, polyclinic, ward; workshop, seminar. See REMEDY, SCHOOL

clip, *v.t.* cut, snip, scissor, trim, shorten; prune, mow; dock; *slang,* gyp, fleece. See SHORTNESS, DECEPTION.

clique, *n.* set, circle, group, coterie. See PARTY, ASSEMBLAGE, EXCLUSION.

cloak, *n.* cape, wrap, mantle, robe, burnoose, domino; shield, disguise. See CLOTHING, CONCEALMENT.

clobber, *v.t., slang,* pummel, punish; defeat. See IMPULSE, SUCCESS.

clock, *n.* timepiece, chronometer (see CHRONOMETRY).

clog, *v.t.* obstruct, block, congest, choke; hamper, encumber, jam, impede, restrain. See HINDRANCE, CLOSURE.

cloister, *n.* abbey, priory, convent, hermitage, monastery; retreat, sanctuary; arcade, colonnade. See SECLUSION, ABODE, TEMPLE.

clone, *n. & v.* COPY.

close, *adj.* compact, dense, firm; stifling, oppressive, muggy, stale, stuffy; stingy, tight-fisted, niggardly; taut; confining, constrictive; near, intimate; secretive, reticent, reserved; approximate. See DENSITY, HEAT, JUNCTION, NEARNESS, PARSIMONY, NARROWNESS, TACITURNITY. —*v. & n.* See CLOSURE, END, CONTENTION.

closet, *n.* cupboard, locker, wardrobe, clothespress. See RECEPTACLE, STORE.

close-up, *n.* See NEARNESS.

CLOSURE

Nouns—**1,** closure, occlusion; blockade, obstruction; shutting up; constipation, bottleneck; embolism; blind alley, dead end, stone wall, *cul de sac;* imperforation, imperviousness, impermeability. See HINDRANCE, RESTRAINT.
2, stopper, plug, seal[er] valve, cork, bung, stopcock, stopple, tamp, spike, ramrod, wad[ding], stuffing, pad[ding]; barrier, tourniquet; latch, bolt, lock.

Verbs—close, occlude, plug, choke up; lid, cork; button [up]; stop, shut, *or* dam up, fill in; block, blockade, clog, obstruct, congest; hinder; fasten, bar, bolt, barricade, latch, lock, stop, seal, plumb; fence in (see ENCLOSURE); choke, strangle, throttle; shut the door (on); confine, restrain (see RESTRAINT).

Adjectives—closed, shut, unopened, hermetic; unpierced, imporous, imperforate, impervious, impermeable; impenetrable, impassable; untrodden; unventilated; airtight, watertight, waterproof; vacuum-packed, hermetically sealed; tight, snug.

Antonyms, see OPENING.

clot, *n.* lump, clump, blob, dollop. —*v.* coagulate, thicken; clabber, curdle. See DENSITY.

cloth, *n.* material, stuff, fabric, textile; fiber, synthetic; [dry, bolt, *or* piece] goods, remnant; napkin, dust cloth, *etc.* See MATERIALS.

CLOTHING

Nouns—**1,** clothing, clothes, apparel, wear, dress, attire, array, raiment, garments, garb, costume, outfit; trousseau; millinery, hosiery, headwear, footwear, underwear, outerwear; equipment, accouterments, trappings, gear; uniform, dress uniform, fatigues, mufti; civilian clothes; vestments (see CLERGY). *Colloq.,* get-up, civvies, togs, duds, threads.
2, a. suit, dress *or* leisure suit; evening clothes, formal wear *or* attire, tails, tuxedo; coat, dinner coat *or* jacket, jacket, blazer; caftan; cutaway, frock coat, Prince Albert; overcoat, Mackinaw, mackintosh, lumberjacket, raincoat, slicker, Inverness, ulster, pea-jacket; cape, cloak. *Colloq.,* tux, best bib and

tucker, Sunday best. *Slang*, glad rags, soup and fish. **b.** shirt, sportshirt; sweater, cardigan, pullover, vest, blouse, tunic, waistcoat. **c.** trousers, pants, breeches, slacks, Levis, overalls, dungarees, jeans; shorts, Bermuda shorts, cut-offs. **d.** underwear, linen, undershirt, underpants, [under]shorts, loincloth, drawers, union suit, B.V.D.'s; supporter, jockstrap, codpiece. **e.** dressing gown, smoking jacket; nightclothes, pajamas, P.J.'s, nightshirt. **f.** shoe, boot, riding boot, Oxford, brogan, loafer, sneakers, moccasin; overshoes, galoshes, rubbers; gaiter, spats, garters, chaps, leggings, puttees. **g.** hat, headgear, tophat, silk hat, opera hat, topper, gibus, derby, Homburg, fedora, porkpie, felt hat; straw, panama, *or* beaver hat, cap, nightcap, sailor, beret, beanie, skullcap, sombrero, shako, helmet, busby, kepi, overseas cap. *Colloq.*, stovepipe. **h.** collar; scarf, muffler; sash; tie, necktie, cravat, Ascot, bow tie, four-in-hand. **i.** sock, hose.

3, a. dress, gown, frock, housedress; suit, tailormade; jumpsuit, pant suit pant dress, body suit *or* stocking. **b.** blouse, bodice, middy blouse, sweater, shirtwaist, tunic; shawl, stole, mantle. **c.** skirt, jumper, hoopskirt, crinoline. **d.** housecoat, smock, apron, negligee, robe, tea gown, kimono, sari; coat, jacket, shortie. **e.** foundation garment, underwear, undies, woolies, panties, lingerie, slip, half-slip, petticoat, camisole, chemise, shift; corset, girdle, foundation, garter belt, stepins, brassiere, bra, bandeau. **f.** nightgown, pajamas. **g.** shoe, pump, Oxford, wedgie, casuals, sandal, slipper, mules, walking shoe. **h.** hat, bonnet, cloche, chapeau, hood, veil, cowl, snood; hose, hosiery, stockings, nylons.

4, tailor, clothier, dressmaker, couturière.

Verbs—clothe, dress, attire, garb, costume, gown, do up; dress up; wrap *or* bundle up; invest; don, put on, wear, have on; accouter, equip, rig out, fit out; drape; tailor.

Adjectives—clothed, costumed, attired, dressed, clad.

Antonyms, see DIVESTMENT.

---

cloud, *n.* haze (see CLOUDINESS); flight (see ASSEMBLAGE).

cloudburst, *n.* downpour, deluge, spate, thundershower. See WATER.

CLOUDINESS

Nouns—cloudiness, cloud cover, overcast; cloud cumulus, altocumulus, cirrus, cirro-cumulus, stratus, cirro-stratus, nimbus; scud, raincloud, thunderhead; fog, mist, VAPOR, haze, haziness, veil; murk, murkiness; shade. *Colloq.*, [pea] soup, smog. See DARKNESS, DIMNESS, OBSCURITY.

Verbs—cloud, cloud over, shadow, obscure, overcast, shade.

Adjectives—cloudy, clouded, overcast, murky, misty, foggy, hazy, dirty, turbid, muggy; threatening, lowering; shady, gray; umbrageous; obfuscated; opaque.

Antonyms, see LIGHT.

---

clout, *n.* belt, swat, whack; *slang*, INFLUENCE, pull, impact. See IMPULSE.

clown, *n.* buffoon, comic, comedian, jester; boor, rustic (see POPULACE). See DRAMA, WIT.

cloy, *v.* glut, satiate, surfeit, sate; pall, bore. See SUFFICIENCY, WEARINESS.

club, *n.* cudgel, stick, bat, bludgeon; society, fraternity, sorority, association; nightclub; trefoil. See ARMS, ASSEMBLAGE, ABODE, SOCIALITY, PARTY.

clubfoot, *n.* splayfoot, Dutch-foot, taliped, talipes. See DISTORTION.

clue, *n.* suggestion, intimation, hint, key, guide. See ANSWER, INDICATION, DISCLOSURE.

clump, *n.* cluster, bunch, patch, thicket, grove; lump. See ASSEMBLAGE, DENSITY.

clumsy, *adj.* awkward, lumbering; bungling, bumbling, left-handed; cumbersome, unwieldy. See UNSKILLFULNESS, GRAVITY, UGLINESS.

cluster, *n.* bunch, clump, group. See ASSEMBLAGE.

clutch, *v.t.* hold fast, grip, cling to, clench; snatch, seize, grasp, grab, collar; clasp, squeeze, embrace. See ACQUISITION, RETENTION.

clutter, *n.* DISORDER, mess, jumble; litter, debris.

coach, *v.t.* teach, help, tutor, train. —*n.* trainer, director, teacher; stage-[coach], bus, omnibus, car, carriage, Pullman. See TEACHING, VEHICLE.

coagulate, *v.* clot, clabber, thicken, curdle; set, congeal. See DENSITY, COHERENCE.

coal, *n.* ember, cinder; charcoal, briquette (see FUEL). See HEAT.

coalesce, *v.* unite, consolidate. See COMBINATION.

coalition, *n.* union, alliance, league, axis; merger, bloc. See PARTY, COMBINATION.

coarse, *adj.* rough, harsh-textured, coarse-grained; uncouth, rude, crude, crass, vulgar, gross, unrefined; broad, bawdy, ribald. See ROUGHNESS, DISCOURTESY, IMPURITY, TEXTURE.

coast, *n.* shore, tideland, shoreline, waterfront, seacoast, beach. See LAND.

coat, *v.t.* cover, crust; plaster, paint, varnish, glaze; plate; protect. —*n.* jacket, overcoat, ulster, sack, cutaway, tunic; coating; tegument, shell, envelope, skin, peel, rind, surface, cover. See CLOTHING, COVERING, LAYER.

coax, *v.* cajole, inveigle, wheedle, persuade. See FLATTERY.

cockeyed, *adj.* cross-eyed, strabismic; *slang,* drunk (see DRINKING); *slang,* twisted. See VISION, DISTORTION.

cocktail, *n.* mixed drink; martini, old-fashioned, daiquiri, *etc.*; salad, appetizer. See FOOD, DRINKING.

cocky, *adj.* conceited (see VANITY).

coddle, *v.t.* humor, pamper. See LENIENCY.

code, *n.* cipher, secret writing, cryptogram; law, canon, principle, codex, constitution, system, standard, RULE. See CONCEALMENT, LEGALITY, INTERPRETATION.

coerce, *v.t.* compel, force, make. See COMPULSION.

coexist, *v.i.* coincide, live and let live, tolerate. See SYNCHRONISM, COOPERATION.

coffee, *n.* mocha, espresso, cappuccino; Sanka; percolated, drip, instant, freeze-dried, *etc.* coffee. *Slang,* java, mud. See DRINKING.

coffer, *n.* chest, strong box, vault; (*pl.*) treasury. See RECEPTACLE.

coffin, *n.* casket, pine box, sarcophagus. See INTERMENT.

cogent, *adj.* potent, forceful, convincing, persuasive, weighty, compelling. See POWER, VIGOR.

cogitate, *v.* reflect, think, muse, ponder, mull, consider, meditate; PLAN, think up. See THOUGHT.

cognizant, *adj.* sensible, aware, conscious. See KNOWLEDGE.

cohabit, *v.i.* live *or* sleep together; live in sin. *Slang,* shack up. See ACCOMPANIMENT.

COHERENCE

Nouns—**1,** coherence, adherence, adhesion, cohesion, adhesiveness; concretion, accretion; conglutination, coagulation, agglutination; set, gel, jell, jelly, cementation; sticking, soldering; TENACITY, stickiness, viscosity; inseparability; conglomerate, concrete. See DENSITY, UNITY, JUNCTION.

2, paste, gum, glue, lute, mucilage, size; jelly, gelatin, starch, gluten, albumen; mire, mud, slush, ooze; syrup, molasses.

Verbs—**1,** cohere, adhere, stick, cling, cleave; hold, take hold of, hold fast, close with, clasp; grow together, hang together; twine around; stick like a leech; stick close; cling like ivy, cling like a burr.

2, glue; agglutinate, conglutinate; cement, lute, paste, gum; solder, weld; cake, solidify, gel, jell, jelly, set.

Adjectives—**1,** cohesive, adhesive, adhering, tenacious, sticky; united, unseparated, sessile, inseparable, indivisible, inextricable, unbreakable, shatterproof, infrangible; compact, dense, solid, thick.

2, mucilaginous, gelatinous, glutinous, gluey; viscid, viscous, semiliquid; mucid, mucous, tacky; deliquescent, emulsive.

Antonyms, see DISJUNCTION.

---

cohort, *n.* band, company. See ASSEMBLAGE.

coiffure, *n.* hairdo, headdress. See BEAUTY.

coil, *n.* spiral, curl, roll, winding, circle, CONVOLUTION.

coin, *v.t.* mint, strike, stamp; invent, originate. See IMAGINATION, FORM. —*n.* MONEY, specie, currency, change, piece; gold, silver, copper, nickel, dime, cent, *etc. Colloq.,* tin, brass.

coincidence, *n.* concurrence, conjunction, concomitance, correspondence, AGREEMENT. See IDENTITY, SYNCHRONISM.

colander, *n.* strainer, sieve, sifter, riddle. See OPENING.

COLD

Nouns—**1,** cold, coldness, frigidity, severity, iciness, winter, cold wave *or* snap; Siberia, Arctic, Antarctic, polar regions.

2, ice, snow, snowflake, snow flurry, snowfall, snowstorm, blizzard; snowdrift; sleet, freezing rain; hail, hailstone, rime, frost, hoarfrost; icicle, iceberg, ice floe, ice field, glacier.

3, chilliness, chill, coolness; shivering, goose flesh, rigor, horripilation, chattering of teeth; frostbite, chilblains.

4, refrigeration; refrigerator, icebox, cooler, ice tray; ice cube *or* block, dry ice; refrigerant, ammonia, freon; freezer, deepfreeze, storage, locker.

Verbs—be cold, shiver, quake, shake, tremble, shudder, quiver (see AGITATION); perish with cold; cool, chill, ice, freeze, congeal, quickfreeze, freeze-dry, refrigerate; freeze over, snow under (see COVERING).

Adjectives—cold, cool; chill[y]; gelid, frigid, frozen, algid; brisk, crisp, fresh, keen, bleak, raw, bitter, biting, cutting, nipping, piercing, pinching; icy, glacial, frosty, freezing, wintry, boreal, arctic, Siberian, polar; icebound, snowbound; shivering, frostbitten, frost-nipped; stone cold, cold as marble *or* charity; blue with cold; quickfrozen, freeze-dried.

Adverbs—under refrigeration, on ice.

Antonyms, see HEAT.

---

cold-blooded, *adj.* merciless, unfeeling, cruel, ruthless, heartless. See MALEVOLENCE.

colic, *n.* indigestion; bellyache, stomachache; gripe. See DISEASE, PAIN.

coliseum, *n.* See ARENA.

collaborate, *v.i.* cooperate, pull together, pitch in; fraternize. See COOPERATION, IMPROBITY.

collage, *n.* montage. See REPRESENTATION.

collapse, *v.i.* break down, fail; cave

or fall in. —*n*. prostration, dejection, breakdown, exhaustion; downfall, ruin; cave-in. See FAILURE, IMPOTENCE, CONTRACTION, DETERIORATION, INSANITY.

collar, *n*. neckband, neckwear; necklace; gorget, bertha, dicky; harness. See CLOTHING, CIRCULARITY. —*v.t.*, *slang*, nab, arrest, catch. See RESTRAINT.

collate, *v.t.* assemble, gather, compile. See ASSEMBLAGE, ARRANGEMENT.

colleague, *n*. associate, partner; coworker, confrère. See FRIEND, ACCOMPANIMENT, AUXILIARY.

collect, *v*. gather, collate, assemble, amass, compile; throng, congregate, flock; scrape *or* round up, garner, accumulate, save. See ASSEMBLAGE, ACQUISITION.

collective, *adj*. combined, aggregate; general. See GENERALITY.

college, *n*. SCHOOL, academy, university, seminary, institute; junior college; finishing *or* preparatory school; association, guild. See PARTY.

collide, *v.i.* bump, crash, clash, conflict; interfere, impinge. See IMPULSE.

collision, *n*. impact, concussion; smashup, crash; clash, opposition, interference; conflict, engagement. *Colloq.*, fender-bender. See CONTENTION, IMPULSE.

colloquial, *adj*. idiomatic, informal, conversational, vernacular; chatty. See CONVERSATION, FIGURATIVE.

collusion, *n*. conspiracy, scheme, intrigue, cabal; conniving, DECEPTION; logrolling, pricefixing. *Colloq.*, hookup, cahoots. See PLAN, COOPERATION.

cologne, *n*. toilet, bay, *or* lavender water, eau de Cologne. See ODOR.

colonize, *v.t.* settle, establish, found, populate. See LOCATION, ABODE.

colony, *n*. settlement, community; territory; swarm, hive. See ASSEMBLAGE, INHABITANT.

COLOR

Nouns—**1,** color, hue, tint, tinge, shade, dye, complexion, tincture, cast, coloration, glow, flush; tone, key; color organ.

2, pure, primary, positive, *or* complementary color; three primaries; spectrum, chromatic dispersion; secondary color, tertiary color; coloring, pigmentation, perspective, value; brilliance, saturation; light, dark, medium; chromatics; spectrum analysis, prism, spectroscope, VIBGYOR (the spectrum: violet, indigo, blue, green, yellow, orange, red); rainbow, kaleidoscope. See VARIEGATION.

3, pigment (see PAINTING).

4, a. black, jet, ink, ebony, coal, pitch, soot, crow, lampblack, blueblack, India ink, sable, sloe-black, charcoal. **b.** blue, ultramarine, cobalt, Prussian blue, indigo, lapis lazuli, sapphire, turquoise, delft, azure, sky blue, sea blue, royal blue, copen. **c.** brown, ocher, umber, sienna, sepia, bay, tan, sorrel, auburn, chestnut, bronze, copper, rust, cinnamon, russet, chocolate, walnut, mahogany, khaki, cocoa, coffee, drab. **d.** gray, neutral, silver, dun, slate. **e.** green, Paris green, emerald green, vert, celadon, verdancy, olive. **f.** orange, ocher, cadmium, apricot, tangerine. **g.** purple, amethyst, lilac, heliotrope, violet, plum, magenta, puce. **h.** red, scarlet, cinnabar, lake, cochineal, vermilion, red lead, madder, rouge, crimson, pink, carmine, cardinal, cerise, maroon, carnation, ruby, blood, beet, brick, Chinese red. **i.** white, milkiness, snow, ivory, oyster. See COLORLESSNESS. **j.** yellow, gold, gamboge, yellow ocher, chrome yellow, banana, lemon, chartreuse, gold, saffron, cream, amber, ecru, buff, beige.

5, VARIEGATION, iridescence, play of colors; chameleon.

Verbs—color, dye, tinge, stain, tint, shade, paint, wash; illuminate, emblazon; bedizen, imbue; suffuse; blush, change color. See PAINTING.

Adjectives—**1,** colored, colorific, chromatic, prismatic; full-colored, high-colored; double-dyed; polychromatic; bright, brilliant, vivid, intense, deep; fresh, unfaded; rich, gorgeous, gay; gaudy, florid, garish, showy, flaunting, flamboyant, flashy; raw, crude; glaring, flaring; discordant, harsh, clashing, inharmonious; mellow, harmonious, pearly, sweet, delicate, tender, refined; off-color.

2, (*See also Nouns, 4*) **a.** inky, coal-black, jet-black, pitchy, sooty. **b.** cerulean. **c.** coppery. **d.** steel-gray, French-gray, ashen, silvery, dove-gray, slaty, drab, mousy. **e.** pea-green, sea-green, bottle-green. **f.** flame-colored. **g.** plum-colored. **h.** ruby-red, blood-red, beet-red, brick-red, rosy, roseate. **i.** snowy, milky, chalky, creamy, pearly, off-white, oyster-white. **j.** golden, sallow, cream-colored, xanthic, xanthous.

3, variegated (see VARIEGATION).

Antonyms, see COLORLESSNESS.

---

colored, *adj.* Negro, black; biased, deceptive. See DECEPTION.

colorful, *adj.* picturesque, vivid; dramatic. See COLOR, VARIEGATION, DRAMA.

COLORLESSNESS

Nouns—colorlessness, achromatism; decoloration, discoloration; pallor, pallidity; paleness, etiolation; neutral tint, monochrome, black-and-white. See WEAKNESS.

Verbs—lose color, fade, turn pale, pale, change color; decolorize, discolor, bleach, achromatize, blanch, etiolate, wash *or* tone down.

Adjectives—colorless, uncolored, achromatic, aplanatic, hueless, pale, pallid; pale-faced; faint, dull, muddy, leaden, gray, dun, wan, sallow, dead, dingy, ashy, ashen, pasty, lurid, ghastly, bloodless, deathly, ghostly, cadaverous, glassy, lackluster; blond, ash-blond, platinum-blond, fair; white; pale as death, pale as a ghost; white as a sheet; bleached.

Antonyms, see COLOR, VARIEGATION.

---

colossus, *n.* giant, titan, monster, prodigy. See SIZE.

colt, *n.* foal. See YOUTH, ANIMAL.

column, *n.* pillar, shaft; formation (of troops, figures, *etc.*); article, byline. See CONTINUITY, ROTUNDITY, SUPPORT, COMBATANT, NEWS, HEIGHT.

coma, *n.* unconsciousness; stupor, torpor. See INSENSIBILITY, INACTIVITY.

comb, *v.t.* scrape; card; dress, tease, back-comb; search. See CLEANNESS, INQUIRY.

combat, *n.* conflict, WARFARE; battle, close combat—*v.t.* fight, oppose. See CONTENTION.

COMBATANT

Nouns—**1,** combatant, disputant, litigant, belligerent; fighter, assailant; swashbuckler, fire-eater, duel[l]ist, bully; fighting-man, prizefighter, pugilist, boxer, bruiser, gladiator, wrestler; swordsman.

2, levy, draft; conscript, recruit, cadet, draftee, selectee, enlistee.

3, warrior, soldier, man-at-arms; campaigner, veteran; military man, G.I., doughboy, Tommy Atkins, *poilu;* armed force, troops, soldiery, forces, the army, standing army, regulars, militia, volunteers, auxiliaries, reserves, national guard, beefeater; guards, guardsman.

4, janizary, myrmidon, spahi, Cossack; irregular, mercenary; guerrilla, partisan; commando.

5, private, rank and file, trooper, legionnaire, legionary, cannon fodder; officer, commander, subaltern, ensign, standard bearer; archer, [long]bowman; spearman, pikeman; halberdier, lancer; musketeer, rifleman, sharpshooter, sniper, skirmisher; grenadier, fusileer.

6, horse, *or* foot-soldier; infantry[man], artillery[man], cavalry[man], horse; tanks, panzer, armor (see ARMS); paratrooper, paramarine; Uhlan, dragoon, hussar; cuirassier; gunner, cannoneer, bombardier; sapper, miner, engineer; light infantry, rifles, *chasseur,* zouave, camel corps, cameleers.

7, army, host; division, column, wind, detachment, garrison, brigade, regiment, corps, battalion, squadron, company, platoon, battery, squad; guard, legion, phalanx, cohort; troops.

8, marine, navy, naval forces; fleet, flotilla, armada, squadron; man-of-war (see SHIP); sailor, seaman (see NAVIGATION). *Slang,* leatherneck.

9, air force, air arm, Luftwaffe, R.A.F. (see AVIATION).

Antonyms, see PACIFICATION.

---

combative, *adj.* pugnacious, aggressive. See ATTACK.

combat fatigue, *n.* shell shock, war neurosis, trauma. See DISEASE.

COMBINATION

Nouns—**1,** combination, composite, synthesis, MIXTURE; JUNCTION, union, unification; incorporation, merger, amalgamation, embodiment, coalescence, crasis, fusion, blending, absorption, centralization; compound, amalgam, composition, alloy; resultant; impregnation. *Slang,* combo. See UNITY.

2, coalition, alliance, syndicate, consortium, federation, affiliation, association. See COOPERATION, PARTY.

Verbs—combine, unite, incorporate, amalgamate, affiliate, compound, embody, absorb, reembody, blend, merge, fuse, melt into one, consolidate, coalesce, centralize; put *or* lump together; cement a union, marry; federate, associate, syndicate, fraternize; gang up, throw *or* go in with, join up with.

Adjectives—combined, affiliated, allied, united; impregnated with, ingrained. *Colloq.,* in cahoots.

Antonyms, see DECOMPOSITION, DISJUNCTION.

---

combustible, *adj.* inflammable, burnable, flammable. See FUEL.

come, *v.i.* arrive, reach; APPROACH, move toward, near; befall, happen, occur. See ARRIVAL, OCCURRENCE.

comeback, *n., colloq.,* recovery, revival, RESTORATION, return; retort, rejoinder. See ANSWER.

comedian, *n.* See WIT.

comedown, *n.* DESCENT, decline; setback, reverse; DISAPPOINTMENT, letdown. See HUMILITY.

comedy, *n.* satire, parody, burlesque, travesty; comedy of errors; tragicomedy; humor, WIT, AMUSEMENT. See DRAMA.

comely, *adj.* attractive, good-looking, handsome, fair, pleasing. See BEAUTY.

come-on, *n., slang,* lure, gimmick. See DECEPTION.

comeuppance, *n., slang,* reward, [just] deserts. See RETALIATION.

comfort, *n.* luxury; ease, coziness; enjoyment, satisfaction; solace, consolation; cheer, air. See PLEASURE, RELIEF, CONTENT.

comforter, *n.* quilt, bedspread. See COVERING.

comic, *adj.* comical, funny, hilarious, laughable, sidesplitting, clownish, ludicrous, droll, slapstick, farcical. —*n.* comedian, stand-up comic. See ABSURDITY, WIT.

COMMAND

Nouns—**1,** command, commandment, order, ordinance, fiat, bidding, dictum, behest, call, beck, nod; direction, injunction, charge; instructions. *Colloq.,* say-so. See AUTHORITY, RULE.

2, demand, exaction, imposition, requisition, claim, ultimatum, terms, requirement, directive.

3, dictation, dictate, mandate; caveat, decree, rescript, precept; bull, edict, prescription, brevet, ukase, *mittimus, mandamus,* summons, subpoena, *nisi prius,* citation; word of command; bugle *or* trumpet call, beat of drum, tattoo; order of the day.

Verbs—command, order, decree, ordain, dictate, direct, give orders; prescribe, set, appoint, mark out; set *or* impose a task; set to work; bid, enjoin, charge, call upon, instruct; require, exact, impose, tax, task; demand, insist on, compel (see COMPULSION); claim, lay claim to, reclaim; cite, summon; call *or* send for, subpoena, beckon; make a requisition, decree, *or* order, issue a command; give the word *or* signal; call to order; lay down the law; assume command (see AUTHORITY); remand.

Adjectives—in command (see AUTHORITY); demanding, exacting, insistent.

Adverbs—in demand, at *or* on sight, on call, to order.

Antonyms, see OBEDIENCE.

commandeer, *v.t.* confiscate, usurp, appropriate, seize. See ACQUISITION.

commander, *n.* captain, commanding officer, skipper, commodore; chief, headman, chieftain, leader. See DIRECTOR, COMBATANT.

commando, *n.* ranger, raider, guerrilla, saboteur. See COMBATANT.

commemorate, *v.t.* celebrate, solemnize, observe, keep, memorialize. See RECORD, CELEBRATION, MEMORY.

commence, *v.* See BEGINNING.

commend, *v.t.* praise, applaud, cite, acclaim, approve, compliment; recommend; entrust. See APPROBATION, COMMISSION.

comment, *n.* observation, remark, note, reflection, criticism, annotation; aside, opinion; talk, gossip. See INTERPRETATION, CONVERSATION.

commentator, *n.* reviewer, critic, editor, news analyst, newscaster. See INTERPRETATION, INFORMATION.

commerce, *n.* BUSINESS, trade, BARTER; CONVERSATION.

commercial, *adj.* mercantile, trade; salable. See BARTER, SALE. —*n.* advertisement, spot [announcement]. See PUBLICATION.

commiserate, *v.t.* PITY, condole.

commissary, *n.* commissar; store, canteen, Post Exchange, P.X. See PROVISION, SALE.

COMMISSION

Nouns—**1,** commission, delegation; consignment, assignment; deputation, legation, mission, embassy; committee (see COUNCIL); agency, power of attorney; task, errand, charge, mandate; diploma; permit (see PERMISSION).

2, appointment, nomination, charter; ordination, installation, induction, investiture, coronation, enthronement.

3, deputy, proxy, AGENT; commissionaire, errand-boy; diplomate.
4, commissioner, commissar; minister, mayor, warden, councilor.

Verbs—commission, delegate, depute; consign, assign; charge, entrust, commit, commend; authorize, empower, permit; put in commission, accredit; engage, hire, employ; appoint, name, nominate; ordain, install, induct, invest, crown; sign up, take on; rent, hire out; lease; demise.

Adjectives—commissioned, delegated, assigned, *etc.;* sent to committee.

Adverbs—for, instead of, in place of, in lieu of, as proxy for.

Antonyms, see NULLIFICATION.

---

commit, *v.t.* perpetrate, perform, do; refer, consign, entrust; confide, commend; take in custody, confine. See ACTION, COMMISSION, LAWSUIT, PROMISE.

commitment, *n.* commission; committal, PROMISE, pledge; involvement.

committee, *n.* See COUNCIL, COMMISSION.

commodious, *adj.* spacious, capacious, ample, roomy. See SPACE.

commodity, *n.* article, product; goods, wares. See SALE.

common, *adj.* ordinary, standard, usual, conventional; joint, shared; prevalent, general, universal, popular, customary, vulgar, illbred, plebeian, coarse. See CONFORMITY, HABIT, GENERALITY, POPULACE.

commoner, *n.* gentleman, freeman, yeoman, tradesman, bourgeois; plebeian; citizen, subject. See POPULACE.

commonplace, *adj.* ordinary, usual, everyday; prosy, monotonous, stale, tedious, hackneyed, threadbare, trite, banal. See HABIT.

commonwealth, *n.* state, community, body politic, government. See AUTHORITY.

commotion, *n.* stir, fuss, ferment, hurlyburly, ado; turmoil, AGITATION, tumult, DISORDER, disturbance, unrest, EXCITEMENT, turbulence.

communal, *adj.* public, common. See HUMANITY.

commune, *v.i.* communicate, converse. See CONVERSATION. —*n.* community; collective, mir, kolkhoz, kibbutz. See ABODE.

COMMUNICATION

Nouns—**1,** communication; message, tidings, NEWS (see INFORMATION).
2, communicator, messenger, nuncio; herald, crier, trumpeter, bellman, courier, runner; postman, letter carrier; Mercury, Iris, Ariel; operator (radio, telephone, switchboard, *etc.*). See TRANSPORTATION.
3, the media, radio, television, cable, wireless, telephone, radiotelephony, telegraphy, *etc.;* broadcast, cablecast, simulcast; newspapers, press, fourth estate; magazines, reviews, journals; public-address system; switchboard; press box. *Slang,* idiot box. See PUBLICATION.
4, bulletins; wire *or* press service, syndicate; telegram, cable, wire, night *or* day letter; carrier pigeon; heliograph, wigwag, semaphore, signal; news flash, press release.
5, correspondence, letter, epistle, note, billet, billet doux, love letter; [picture] postcard; poison-pen letter; missive, favor; dispatch, these presents; rescript (see ANSWER); form letter, circular; round robin, chain letter; first-, second-(*etc.*)class mail; express mail, post, mail, air mail, special delivery *or* handling, priority mail, *etc*.
6, [mental] telepathy, thought transference, telekinesis, extrasensory perception, E.S.P.; spiritualism, spirit-rapping.

7. aerial, antenna; dipole, parabolic, *etc.* antenna; community antenna, C.A.T.V.; rabbit ears.

8, intercourse, CONVERSATION, exchange of talk *or* ideas. See SPEECH.

9, newsman (see NEWS); publisher; correspondent, pen pal; medium, spiritualist; messenger (see AGENT).

Verbs—**1,** communicate, send messages, broadcast, publish, write, preach, disseminate news *or* information; radio, telegraph, wire, cable; call [up], ring up, phone, give a ring *or* buzz, telephone; signal; sign on *or* off.

2, correspond (with), write to, send *or* post a letter to, keep up a correspondence (with); write back, acknowledge, ANSWER, reply; intercommunicate; keep track (of), keep in touch.

Adjectives—communicative, talkative; outgoing, extrovert; correspondent, corresponding, epistolary, postal; multimedia; on the air.

Antonyms, see CONCEALMENT, SILENCE.

---

communion, *n.* talk, CONVERSATION, intercourse, communication; concord, unity; sympathy; mass, Lord's Supper, Sacrament, Eucharist. See RITE, SOCIALITY, PARTY.

communiqué, *n.* bulletin (see NEWS).

communist, *n.* communalist, leftist, Red, fellow traveler, [parlor] pink. See CHANGE.

community, *n.* neighborhood, district, commonwealth; body, group; partnership, society. See PARTY, SOCIALITY, REGION.

commute, *v.* See INTERCHANGE, TRAVEL.

compact, *n.* contract, covenant; subcompact, mini; make-up *or* vanity case. See AGREEMENT, VEHICLE, BEAUTY.

companion, *n.* associate, colleague; pal, chum, comrade; shadow; escort; accomplice. See ACCOMPANIMENT, FRIEND.

company, *n.* companionship, fellowship; association, corporation, partnership, firm; cast, troupe; group, assembly; troop, platoon, squad; society; gang. *Colloq.,* crowd, party. See ACCOMPANIMENT, ASSEMBLAGE, DRAMA, COMBATANT, BUSINESS, SOCIALITY.

compare, *v.* contrast; place side by side; collate, confront, parallel, relate, test. See RELATION, SIMILARITY, DEGREE.

compartment, *n.* section, chamber, bin, cell. See RECEPTACLE.

compass, *v.* encompass, bound, surround, define, encircle; beset, besiege; reach, accomplish, effect. —*n.* bounds, extent, scope, area, circumference, range; gamut; needle (*naut.*). See DIRECTION, LIMIT, CIRCUIT, ENVIRONMENT, SPACE, CIRCUMSCRIPTION.

compassion, *n.* sympathy, tenderness, kindness, mercy, condolence; PITY, ruth, commiseration, heart.

compatible, *adj.* harmonious, well-matched, suitable, congruous; consistent; congenial. See AGREEMENT.

compatriot, *n.* countryman; *colloq.,* colleague. See FRIEND, INHABITANT.

compel, *v.t.* See COMPULSION.

compendium, *n.* abstract, précis, epitome, summary, digest, synopsis; compilation, anthology. See ASSEMBLAGE, SHORTNESS.

COMPENSATION

Nouns—**1,** compensation, satisfaction, indemnification, indemnity; COMPROMISE; counteraction, [equal and opposite] reaction; measure for measure; RETALIATION, backlash; equalization (see EQUALITY); robbing Peter to pay Paul, an eye for an eye [and a tooth for a tooth]; offset, counterpoise, counterbalance, ballast, equipoise.

2, equivalent, *quid pro quo,* consideration; fee, recompense (see PAYMENT); reward, award; due; amends, ATONEMENT; reparation, requital, redress, damages, balm.

Verbs—make compensation, compensate, indemnify; counteract, countervail, counterpoise, balance, counterbalance, set off, offset, cancel [out]; outbalance, overbalance; hedge, make up for, cover, fill up, make good; recoup, square oneself, redeem, atone. *Colloq.,* lean over backwards.

Adjectives—compensating, compensatory; counteracting, countervailing, *etc.;* equivalent, equal.

Adverbs—in return, in consideration; but, however, yet, still, notwithstanding, despite, in spite of, in the face of, in any case *or* event; nevertheless, anyhow; although, though; albeit; at all events, at any rate; be that as it may, just *or* all the same, for all that, even so, on the other hand, at the same time, at least, at [the] most; at that, however, that may be; after all, after all is said and done; duly; taking one thing with another; come hell or high water, come what may.

Antonyms, see LOSS.

---

compete, *v.i.* vie, contend, rival. See CONTENTION.

competence, *n.* capability, capacity, ability, efficiency, proficiency; MEANS, resources, income, SUFFICIENCY. See SKILL.

competition, *n.* See CONTENTION.

compile, *v.t.* collect, arrange; edit, write, make. See ASSEMBLAGE.

complacent, *adj.* CONTENT, pleased; self-satisfied, smug; apathetic, blasé, indifferent. See INDIFFERENCE, VANITY.

complaint, *n.* ACCUSATION, charge; DISEASE, ailment, sickness, indisposition, disorder; lament, grievance (see LAMENTATION).

complement, *n.* rest, extra, counterpart, opposite; personnel, staff. —*v.t.* complete, realize, fulfill, fill *or* round out; balance, offset, neutralize. See COMPLETION, PART.

COMPLETION

Nouns—**1,** completion; accomplishment, achievement, fulfillment, realization, fruition; execution, performance; dispatch; consummation, culmination; finish, close, END; terminus (see ARRIVAL); issue, outcome (see EFFECT); final, crowning, *or* finishing touch, epilogue, *coup de grâce; fait accompli;* feat; missing link, makeweight; PERFECTION; elaboration; exhaustion. See PRODUCTION, SUCCESS.

2, completeness, totality (see WHOLE).

3, fullness, impletion, repletion, saturation, high water; fill, load, bumper, brimmer; bellyful. *Colloq.,* full house, the works, the business. See SUFFICIENCY.

Verbs—**1,** complete, effect; accomplish, achieve, compass, consummate, go through with; bring to maturity; bring to perfection, perfect, elaborate.

2, do, execute, make, follow out; go *or* get through, knock *or* pull off; bring about *or* off, bring to pass, dispatch, polish off, make short work of, dispose of, mop up, set at rest; perform, discharge, fulfill, realize; put through, put in practice, carry out, make good, be as good as one's word; drive home, do thoroughly, not do by halves, go the whole hog, shoot the works, do up brown, do to a turn, go all out, go to any length; see out *or* through; round out, complement; be in at the death, carry through, play out, exhaust; do the job, fill the bill, turn the trick; deliver.

3, conclude, finish, close, END, wrap up; clinch, seal, set the seal on, put the seal to; cross the wire; give the final touch to, put the last hand to; crown (see SUPERIORITY).

4, ripen, mature, culminate; run its course, run one's race, reach the goal, arrive; get in the harvest.

5, fill, charge, load; fill *or* piece out, replenish, eke out; fill up, saturate. See SUFFICIENCY.

Adjectives—**1,** complete, perfect, consummate, full-fledged; diametric[al]; entire, WHOLE; thorough, plenary; solid, undivided, with all its parts; exhaustive, sweeping, encyclopedic, thoroughgoing, out-and-out, utter, arrant, radical; crowning, final; abundant, sufficient.

2, completing, supplemental, supplementary, complementary.

3, ripe, mature.

Adverbs—completely, altogether, outright, downright, wholly, soundly, totally, *in toto,* quite, from soup to nuts; hook, line, and sinker; thoroughly, conclusively, finally; effectually, for good and all, nicely, fully, all of, in all respects, in every respect; through and through, out and out, leaving no stone unturned, all told, to all intents and purposes; utterly, to the utmost, all out, all hollow, stark; heart and soul, root and branch, down to the ground; head over heels; lock, stock, and barrel; inside out; bag and baggage; to the top of one's bent, to the limit, as far as possible; throughout, from first to last, from beginning to end, from hell to breakfast, from end to end, from one end to the other, from head to foot, *cap-a-pie,* from top to toe, from top to bottom, from the ground up, backward and forward, fore and aft, every whit, every inch, to the nines; up to the brim, up to the ears; with a vengeance, to a fare-thee-well, for fair, but good, all the way, down the line, to the full, to the hilt; to the bone; to the bitter end.

Antonyms, see INCOMPLETENESS.

---

complex, *adj.* intricate, manifold, complicated, involved, knotty.—*n.* tangle, knot, maze; *colloq.,* obsession, fixation; inferiority, persecution, Oedipus, *etc.* complex. See DISORDER, INSANITY, INTELLECT.

complexion, *n.* hue, COLOR, tinge, tint; skin texture; aspect, APPEARANCE.

complicate, *v.t.* involve, embarrass, confuse; perplex; aggravate, compound. See DISORDER, DIFFICULTY.

complicity, *n.* guilt by association; collusion, participation, connivance, conspiracy. See COOPERATION.

compliment, *v.t.* praise, flatter, commend, congratulate. See APPROBATION, CONGRATULATION, COURTESY.

complimentary, *adj.* commendatory; courteous, polite; [con]gratulatory, laudatory, favorable; free, gratis, on the house. See APPROBATION, CHEAPNESS, CONGRATULATION.

comply, *v.t.* CONSENT, conform, yield, submit, obey. See OBEDIENCE, CONFORMITY, SUBMISSION.

component, *n.* PART, element, factor, constituent, ingredient; makings, fixings; link, feature, member.

comport, *v.* behave *or* CONDUCT oneself; suit, fit (see AGREEMENT).

composed, *adj.* cool, unruffled, collected, self-possessed; calm, tranquil. See INEXCITABILITY.

composer, *n.* See ARTIST.

COMPOSITION

Nouns—**1,** composition, constitution, construction, formation; COMBINATION, setup; INCLUSION.

2, contents, make-up, constituent parts, makings, fixings; capacity, volume;

cargo, freight, load[ing]; cupful, basketful, bottleful, *etc.;* stuffing, packing, filling, wadding. See PART.

Verbs—**1,** be composed of, be made of, be formed of; consist of, be resolved into; include, hold (see INCLUSION).

2, compose, compound, constitute, form, make, put together, make up; enter into the composition of, be a component, figure in, have a part in.

Adjectives—composite; composing, containing, constituting, *etc.*

Antonyms, see DECOMPOSITION, INSUBSTANTIALITY.

---

composure, *n.* placidity, serenity, self-possession, calmness. See REPOSE, INEXCITABILITY.

compound, *v.t.* combine, compose, concoct, amalgamate, mix; join, unite. See MIXTURE, JUNCTION, COMBINATION, COMPOSITION.

comprehend, *v.t.* comprise, embrace, include; grasp, apprehend, conceive, understand, see, know. See KNOWLEDGE, INCLUSION, INTELLIGENCE.

comprehensive, *adj.* full, inclusive, all-embracing. See GENERALITY, BREADTH, INCLUSION.

compress, *v.t.* reduce, digest, abridge, consolidate, condense; crowd, squeeze, contract. See DENSITY, CONTRACTION.

comprise, *v.t.* consist of, involve, embrace, cover, embody; include, comprehend, contain. See INCLUSION.

COMPROMISE

Nouns—**1,** compromise; mediation, arbitration, negotiation; settlement, concession, appeasement, COMPENSATION; terms; middle ground, mid-course. See PACIFICATION.

2, arbitrator, mediator, middleman, negotiator.

Verbs—**1,** compromise, take the mean, split the difference, strike a balance *or* a happy medium; meet one *or* go halfway, go fifty-fifty, give and take; come to terms, settle out of court; submit to arbitration; patch up, bridge over, arrange; adjust differences; agree; make the best of, make a virtue of necessity; take the will for the deed.

2, mediate, arbitrate, intercede; negotiate, bargain; reconcile, iron out; plea bargain.

Adjectives—conciliatory, diplomatic, give-and-take; mediatory, mediating, intermediary, intercessory.

Antonyms, see OBSTINACY, RESOLUTION.

COMPULSION

Nouns—compulsion, coercion, coaction, constraint, duress, obligation; enforcement, pressure; [physical, brute, *or* main] force; the sword, martial law, strong arm [of the law]; draft, conscription; RESTRAINT; requirement, NECESSITY, *force majeure;* Hobson's choice. See SEVERITY.

Verbs—compel, force, make, drive, coerce, constrain, enforce, necessitate, oblige; force one's hand, impose on, twist one's arm; force upon, press; cram, ram, thrust, *or* force down the throat; make a point of, insist upon, take no denial; put down; require, exact, tax, put in force, put teeth in; restrain, hold down; draft, conscript, impress, shanghai.

Adjectives—compulsory, compelling; coercive, coactive; obligatory, stringent, peremptory; forcible, not to be trifled with; irresistible; compulsive.

Adverbs—compulsorily, by force, by force of arms; on *or* under compulsion, perforce; at sword's point, forcibly; under protest, in spite of; against one's will; under press of; *de rigueur,* willy-nilly.

Antonyms, see FREEDOM.

---

compunction, *n.* See PENITENCE.

compute, *v.* figure, calculate, reckon. See NUMERATION.

computer, *n.* calculator (see NUMERATION).

comrade, *n.* FRIEND, companion, mate, fellow, associate; communist. See ACCOMPANIMENT.

con, *v.t.* steer, pilot (see DIRECTION); *slang,* swindle (see DECEPTION).

concatenate, *v.t.* link (see CONTINUITY, CONNECTION).

CONCAVITY

Nouns—**1,** concavity, depression, dip, hollow, indentation, cavity, hole, dent, dint, dimple, follicle, pit, *sinus alveolus;* excavation, crater, pocket; trough, FURROW, burrow; cup, basin, bowl (see RECEPTACLE); intaglio (see SCULPTURE); coil; socket. See DEPTH, INTERIOR.

2, valley, vale, dale, dell, dingle, bottom, blade, gully, cave, cavern, cove; grotto, grot; alcove; *cul-de-sac;* arch, bay, *etc.*

3, excavator, sapper, miner, digger, [steam] shovel, spade, *etc.* (see RECEPTACLE).

Verbs—cave in, depress, hollow, scoop [out], gouge, indent, dent, dint; excavate, mine, sap, undermine, burrow, tunnel; stave in.

Adjectives—concave, depressed, hollow, pitted, stove in; retiring; retreating, cavernous; cellular, porous; spongy, honeycombed, alveolar; infundibular, funnel-shaped, cupular; bell-shaped, campaniform; capsular, vaulted, arched.

Antonyms, see CONVEXITY.

CONCEALMENT

Nouns—**1,** concealment; hiding[-place]; curtain, screen, blind; smoke screen, ambush, camouflage; hideaway; trench, foxhole, *etc.;* disguise, costume, mask, domino, masquerade, shroud, curtain, cloak, veil; invisible ink; incognito, pseudonym; cryptography, steganography, cipher, code. See INVISIBILITY.

2, stealth, stealthiness; slyness, CUNNING; privacy, SECLUSION; secrecy, secretness (see SECRET).

3, reticence, silence, TACITURNITY; *arrière pensée,* suppression, circumlocution (see AVOIDANCE); evasion, equivocation, white lie, misprision (see DECEPTION); cover-up; underhand dealing; closeness, secretiveness, mystery; LATENCY; stowaway; jargon, cant, officialese, shop talk, gobbledygook, double-talk. *Colloq.,* poker face.

4, operative, sleuth, private investigator, undercover agent, secret agent, spy, plainclothesman.

Verbs—**1,** conceal, hide, secrete, put out of sight, stow; launder; lock up, bottle up; cover, screen, cloak, veil, shroud; draw the veil *or* curtain, curtain, shade, eclipse, becloud, mask, camouflage, disguise; dissemble (see DECEPTION); ensconce, muffle. *Slang,* stash, plant. See COVERING.

2, keep from, keep to oneself, keep dark, bury, sink, suppress, keep out of sight, keep in the background; stifle, hush up, gloss over, black out, cover up, smother, withhold, reserve; keep a secret, keep one's own counsel, hold one's tongue; not let the right hand know what the left is doing; hide one's light under a bushel.

3, be concealed *or* hidden; hide oneself, cover one's tracks, lie in ambush, lie in wait, lie low, lurk, sneak, skulk, slink, prowl; lay for; bury one's head in the sand; play hide and seek; take to the woods; hide in holes and corners.

Adjectives—**1,** concealed, hidden; behind the scenes; up one's sleeve; SECRET, recondite, arcane, Masonic, mystic; cabalistic, cryptic; privy, clandestine.

2, undercover, in ambush, in hiding, in disguise; in the dark; clouded, invisible; buried, underground, *perdu;* secluded (see SECLUSION); undisclosed, untold; cloak-and-dagger; covert, mysterious, unintelligible (see UNINTELLIGIBILITY); confidential, classified, top *or* most secret; latent.

3, furtive, stealthy; skulking, surreptitious, underhand, hole and corner; sly, CUNNING; secretive, evasive; reserved, reticent, uncommunicative, buttoned up, taciturn.

Adverbs—secretly, in secret, privately, in private; in the dark; behind closed doors, in closed session, hugger-mugger; under the rose, the counter, *or* the table; *sub rosa,* in the background, aside, on the sly, with bated breath, *sotto voce,* in a whisper; under cover *or* wraps; in [strict] confidence; confidentially, off the record, between ourselves, between you and me, *entre nous, in camera;* underhand, by stealth, like a thief in the night, stealthily; behind the scenes, behind one's back; incognito.

Antonyms, see DISCLOSURE.

---

concede, *v.t.* CONSENT, yield, give in, allow; accede; grant, admit, acknowledge, confess; RELINQUISH, cede, give up, surrender. See DISCLOSURE, GIVING, PERMISSION, COMPROMISE.

conceit, *n.* VANITY, PRIDE, egotism, self-esteem; epigram, *bon mot,* quip; whim, fantasy, fancy, caprice, notion, quirk. See WIT, IMAGINATION, FIGURATIVE.

conceive, *v.* devise, frame, imagine, visualize, fancy; grasp, realize, take in, understand; become pregnant. *Colloq.,* get in a family way. See IMAGINATION, KNOWLEDGE, REPRODUCTION.

concentrate, *v.* distill, condense, consolidate; intensify, fix, aim, focus; converge, center, localize; collect, assemble, gather. See ASSEMBLAGE, CONVERGENCE.

concentration camp, *n.* See PRISON.

concentric, *adj.* See MIDDLE.

concept, *n.* conception, conceit, THOUGHT; INTERPRETATION.

conception, *n.* idea, notion; pregnancy, fertilization; BEGINNING. See IMAGINATION, REPRODUCTION.

concern, *v.t.* regard, affect, relate, refer to, pertain to, have to do with, bear upon, belong to, treat of; interest; disturb, trouble. —*n.* matter, affair; CARE, anxiety, worry, solicitude, regard; significance, import, interest; firm, BUSINESS. See RELATION, IMPORTANCE, DOUBT.

concert, *n.* recital, program, serenade, musicale; COOPERATION, AGREEMENT, harmony, accord; conspiracy. See MUSIC, UNITY.

concession, *n.* COMPROMISE; grant, franchise (see BUSINESS).

conciliate, *v.t.* reconcile; pacify, appease, placate, mollify, propitiate; win, curry favor. See CONTENT, FORGIVENESS, PACIFICATION.

concise, *adj.* succinct, short, brief, terse, laconic, epigrammatic, summary, compact. See SHORTNESS.

conclave, *n.* assembly (see ASSEMBLAGE).

conclude, *v.* END, close, finish, wind up, terminate; infer, deduce; arrange, settle; resolve, judge, determine. See RESOLUTION, JUDGMENT.

conclusive, *adj.* decisive. See CERTAINTY, DEMONSTRATION.

concoct, *v.t.* prepare, invent, devise, contrive; brew; mix, cook; PLAN, make up, hatch. See PREPARATION, FALSEHOOD.

concord, *n.* accord, harmony, AGREEMENT, ASSENT; sympathy, rapport, congruousness, congruence; concurrence; union, UNITY; peace; alliance, league, compact; treaty, entente, understanding.

concourse, *n.* throng, crowd; arcade, square. See ASSEMBLAGE, PASSAGE.

concrete, *adj.* actual, real, tangible, solid; specific, definite, exact, particular. See SUBSTANCE, HARDNESS, COHERENCE, SPECIALITY. —*n.* See CEMENT.

concubine, *n.* hetaera; mistress, paramour, kept woman; wench, harem girl, odalisque; demimondaine, courtesan, prostitute. See IMPURITY.

concur, *v.i.* agree, ASSENT, harmonize; coincide; see eye to eye (with), pull together, parallel; acquiesce. *Colloq.*, jibe. See AGREEMENT, SYNCHRONISM, COOPERATION, UNITY.

concussion, *n.* shock, blow, impact. See IMPULSE, PAIN.

CONDEMNATION

Nouns—condemnation, conviction, proscription, damnation, doom; death warrant; attainder, attainture, attaintment; denunciation, commination; DISAPPROBATION, disapproval, censure. See ACCUSATION, JUDGMENT, IMPRECATION.

Verbs—condemn, convict, find guilty, damn, doom, sign the death warrant, sentence, pass sentence on, send up; attaint, proscribe, sequestrate; disapprove, censure, denounce, blame.

Adjectives—condemnatory, damnatory; denunciatory; condemned, damned, convicted; self-convicted.

Antonyms, see ACQUITTAL.

---

condense, *v.* abridge, digest, abbreviate, shorten, cut, epitomize; compress, compact, thicken, concentrate, distill. See DENSITY, SHORTNESS, CONTRACTION, LIQUEFACTION.

condescend, *v.i.* stoop, deign, descend, vouchsafe. See HUMILITY, PRIDE.

condiment, *n.* seasoning, sauce, spice, relish, chutney; herb, caraway; salt, pepper, cayenne, mustard, curry, onion, garlic, pickle, catsup, vinegar, mayonnaise, olive oil, salad dressing. See TASTE, FOOD, PUNGENCY.

condition, *n.* fitness; state, birth, rank, place, estate, station, CLASS; demand, QUALIFICATION, proviso; plight, situation, status, position, pass, case, circumstances. See REPUTE, CIRCUMSTANCE.

condolence, *n.* LAMENTATION, sympathy, PITY, consolation, commiseration.

condominium, *n.* co-operative [apartment house], co-op. See ABODE.

condone, *v.t.* See FORGIVENESS.

conduce, *v.i.* lead, tend, contribute. See TENDENCY, CAUSE, UTILITY.

CONDUCT

Nouns—**1,** conduct, dealing, transaction, ACTION, business; tactics, game plan, policy; generalship, statesmanship, seamanship; strategy, strategics; PLAN, program, execution, manipulation, treatment, campaign; husbandry, housekeeping, stewardship; *ménage,* regime; management, government, direction (see AUTHORITY).

2, behavior, deportment, comportment; carriage, demeanor, mien, bearing, manner; line of conduct, course of action; rôle, process, ways, practice, procedure, *modus operandi,* METHOD. *Colloq.,* goings-on.

3, see DIRECTOR.

Verbs—**1,** conduct, transact, execute, administer, deal with, have to do with; treat, handle, manipulate; play someone for; take steps, take measures; dispatch; proceed with, discharge; carry on *or* through, put into practice; direct, officiate.

2, conduct, behave, comport, deport, demean, carry *or* acquit oneself; do by; act one's age, give a good account of oneself, mind one's P's and Q's; run a race, lead a life, play a game; take *or* adopt a course; steer *or* shape one's course, play one's part *or* cards; shift for oneself, paddle one's own canoe.

Adjectives—strategical, tactical, businesslike, practical, executive.

Adverbs—on one's good *or* best behavior.

Antonyms, see BADNESS, NEGLECT.

---

conductor, *n.* guide, escort, DIRECTOR; manager, operator, supervisor; guard; drum major, leader, maestro, choirmaster; transmitter, conveyor. *Colloq.,* time beater. See TRANSPORTATION, MUSIC.

cone-shaped, *adj.* conic[al], conoid[al]; coniferous, pyramidal. See SHARPNESS, ROTUNDITY.

confederacy, *n.* confederation, league, federation, union, alliance; compact, combine. See PARTY.

confederate, *n.* aide, ally; accomplice; companion, associate. See AID, AUXILIARY, COOPERATION.

confer, *v.* converse, discuss, consult, debate, deliberate, talk, parley, palaver; give, grant, bestow. See ADVICE, CONVERSATION, GIVING.

confess, *v.* acknowledge, avow, own, admit; disclose, tell, reveal, unbosom, unburden, divulge. See DISCLOSURE, PENITENCE, RITE.

confidant, confidante, *n.* FRIEND, intimate.

confide, *v.* trust, believe in, rely on; entrust, commit; tell, divulge, unbosom, unburden. See BELIEF, DISCLOSURE.

confidence, *n.* assurance, CERTAINTY, positiveness; spirit, boldness, self-reliance; communication; privacy, SECRET; faith, trust. See BELIEF, COURAGE, HOPE.

confidential, *adj.* SECRET, private; intimate. See CONCEALMENT.

configuration, *n.* FORM, shape, figure, contour; grouping, ARRANGEMENT.

confine, *v.t.* imprison, incarcerate, immure, jail, detain; cage, pen; restrict, bound, LIMIT. See CIRCUMSCRIPTION, ENCLOSURE, RESTRAINT.

confinement, *n.* childbirth, childbed; imprisonment, incarceration, captivity, custody, detention; CIRCUMSCRIPTION, limitation, restriction. See RESTRAINT, REPRODUCTION.

confirm, *v.t.* establish, strengthen; ratify, validate, approve, endorse; verify, substantiate, prove, corroborate. See ASSENT, STRENGTH, EVIDENCE, DEMONSTRATION.

confiscate, *v.t.* take, seize, commandeer, appropriate. See ACQUISITION, CONDEMNATION.

conflict, *n.* battle, combat, strife, fight, encounter, clash, collision, struggle; discord, antagonism, dissension, hostility. See CONTENTION, DISAGREEMENT.

CONFORMITY

Nouns—**1,** conformity, conformance; conventionality, HABIT, custom, formality; AGREEMENT, compliance; uniformity, orthodoxy.

2, object lesson, example, instance, specimen, sample, swatch; run of the mill *or* mine, RULE, exemplification, case in point; pattern, prototype; master, master copy. See FASHION.

3, conformist, conventionalist, formalist; stickler, bookman.

Verbs—**1,** conform, follow suit, be regular, run true to form; follow, go by, *or* observe the rules, go by the book; comply with, chime in with, fall in with; be guided by; follow the fashion *or* crowd, lend oneself to; assimilate, pass muster, come up to scratch, shape up; toe the mark, walk the chalk, play the game, do as others do, in Rome do as the Romans do; go *or* swim with the stream *or* current, keep in step.

2, exemplify, be a model for, set the pace *or* fashion; stand on ceremony.

Adjectives—conformable; conforming, regular (see REGULARITY); well-regulated, orderly; conventional, customary, ordinary, common, habitual, usual; typical, normal, formal, par for the course, all in a day's work; exemplary; canonical, orthodox, uniform (see RULE).

Adverbs—conformably, by rule; agreeably to; in conformity with, in accordance with, in keeping with, in step; according to, consistent with, as usual; of course, as a matter of course; *pro forma,* for form's sake, by the book, according to rule, according to Hoyle; to scale; for example, for instance, for one [thing].

Antonyms, see UNCONFORMITY.

---

confound, *v.t.* confuse, bewilder, perplex, nonplus, dumfound, dismay, mix up, puzzle; rout, overcome, overthrow. See SURPRISE, SUCCESS.

confrere, *n.* colleague, associate, FRIEND. See AUXILIARY.

confront, *v.t.* face, oppose; resist, brave. See OPPOSITION, COURAGE.

confuse, *v.t.* perplex, confound, disconcert; embroil, muddle; abash, embarrass. See DISORDER, HUMILITY, UNINTELLIGIBILITY.

CONFUTATION

Nouns—confutation, refutation, disproof, rebuttal; *reductio ad absurdum;* knockdown argument, clincher. *Colloq.,* squelcher, crusher. See NULLIFICATION, NEGATION.

Verbs—confute, refute, disprove, show up, show the fallacy of, rebut, defeat; demolish, destroy, tear down, blow sky high; overwhelm, overthrow, overturn, squash, squelch; scatter to the winds, explode; put *or* reduce to silence, shut up; clinch an argument; not leave a leg to stand on, cut the ground from under one's feet.

Adjectives—confuting, confuted, confutative, negative (see NEGATION); refuted, refutable; condemned on one's own showing, condemned out of one's own mouth.

Antonyms, see DEMONSTRATION, EVIDENCE.

---

congeal, *v.* solidify, harden, fix, gel, jell, set, coagulate, stiffen, thicken; freeze; condense. See DENSITY, HARDNESS.

congenial, *adj.* compatible, agreeable, pleasing, sympathetic, kindred, harmonious. See AGREEMENT.

congest, *v.t.* overfill, clog, block; plug, stop, *or* stuff up; [over]crowd, jam, choke, cram; constipate. See CLOSURE.

conglomerate, *adj.* gathered, assembled. See ASSEMBLAGE. —*n.* concrete (see COHERENCE); diversified company (see BUSINESS).

CONGRATULATION

Nouns—congratulation, gratulation, felicitation; salute; compliments, compliments of the season, *etc;* pat on the back. See APPROBATION.

Verbs—congratulate, gratulate, felicitate, wish one joy; compliment, tender *or* offer one's congratulations, wish many happy returns of the day; pat on the back, shake one's hand; take a bow. See REJOICING.

Adjectives—congratulatory, complimentary.

Antonyms, see REGRET, DISAPPROBATION.

---

congregation, *n.* ASSEMBLAGE, assembly, gathering, collection, meeting, aggregation; church, parish, flock, fold, brethren. See RELIGION.

congress, *n.* assembly, legislature, parliament; meeting, convention; intercourse. See ASSEMBLAGE, COUNCIL, CONVERSATION.

conjecture, *n.* SUPPOSITION, hypothesis, extrapolation, speculation, guess; inference, surmise.

conjugal, *adj.* connubial (see MARRIAGE).

conjugate, *adj.* yoked, united, mated; related, paronymous, coderived. See JUNCTION.

conjure, *v.* cast spells, enchant; invoke, summon up; beseech, implore, beg. See SORCERY, REQUEST.

CONNECTION

Nouns—**1,** connection, bond, tie, link, concatenation; connective, interconnection; nexus, neck, isthmus; nape; bridge, tunnel, causeway, viaduct, *etc.* See CONTACT.

2, ligature, ligament; chain, sinew, tendon, umbilical cord; strap; fastening, clasp, buckle, button, snap, hook [and eye], zipper, Velcro fastener; lacing, latch, anchor, moorings, guy rope, hawser, grappling iron, painter; leash; knot, slipknot, running knot, bowknot, surgeon's knot, square knot, granny knot, *etc.;* bracket, brace, clevis.

3, nail, brad, finishing nail, spike, screw, toggle bolt, staple, tack, thumbtack, rivet (see JUNCTION).

4, cement, glue, paste, mucilage, gum; mortar, stucco, putty, lime, plaster, solder (see COHERENCE.)

Verbs—**1,** connect, link, join; tie in, plug in, hook up; associate, relate. See JUNCTION, RELATION.

2, attach, affix, fasten, bind, secure; blend, merge, fuse; tie, sew, stitch, tack, knit, button, hitch, knot, lash, truss, bandage, braid, splice, gird, tether, moor, picket, harness, chain; fetter, lock, latch, leash, couple, link, yoke, bracket, span, marry, wed.

3, pin, nail, bolt, clasp, clamp, clinch, screw, rivet, solder, weld, mortise, miter, dovetail, graft, entwine; interlace, entangle, intertwine.

Adjectives—firm, fast, tight, taut, secure, set, inseparable, indissoluble; mixed up.

Antonyms, see DISJUNCTION.

---

connivance, *n.* COOPERATION, collusion, complicity; PERMISSION, sufferance.

connoisseur, *n.* critic, gourmet, epicure, adept. See TASTE.

connotation, *n.* implication, suggestion, association, MEANING.

conquer, *v.t.* overcome, overthrow,

vanquish, subdue, subjugate. See SUCCESS.

conquest, *n.* victory (see SUCCESS).

consanguinity, *n.* See RELATION.

conscience, *n.* See PROBITY.

conscientious, *adj.* faithful, honorable, upright, trusty, scrupulous, meticulous; religious; thorough, particular, careful, painstaking. See PROBITY, CARE, DUTY.

conscious, *adj.* sensible, cognizant, percipient, understanding; awake, aware, sentient. See INTELLECT, KNOWLEDGE, SENSIBILITY.

conscription, *n.* enlistment, draft, impressment. See COMPULSION, WARFARE.

consecrate, *v.t.* bless, sanctify, hallow; seal, dedicate, devote. See PIETY, REPUTE, CLERGY.

consecutive, *adj.* See CONTINUITY, SEQUENCE.

consensus, *n.* concord, ASSENT, AGREEMENT; general *or* popular opinion, common belief; poll[ing], sampling; silent majority.

CONSENT

Nouns—consent, ASSENT, acquiescence; approval, APPROBATION; compliance, AGREEMENT, concession; yielding, accession, allowance, acceptance; ratification, confirmation; permit, PERMISSION, PROMISE.

Verbs—consent, ASSENT, yield, allow, concede, grant, deign; come over, come [a]round; give in, give consent, comply with, acquiesce, agree to, fall in with, accede, accept, embrace an offer, close with, take at one's word, have no objection; satisfy, meet one's wishes, come to terms; turn a willing ear (see WILLINGNESS); jump at; deign, vouchsafe.

Adjectives—consenting, acquiescent, compliant, willing, easy, docile, amenable, agreeable; permissible; agreed; unconditional.

Adverbs—yes, by all means, willingly, if you please, as you please; be it so, amen, so be it, well and good, of course.

Antonyms, see REFUSAL.

---

consequence, *n.* EFFECT, end, result, sequel, outcome, product, fruit; import, account, concern, interest, significance, matter, moment; notability, esteem, greatness, value, prominence; self-importance, arrogance, pomposity. See IMPORTANCE.

consequential, *adj.* consequent, sequential; inferable, deducible; indirect, resultant, resulting; important, of consequence. See EFFECT, IMPORTANCE, CIRCUMSTANCE.

conservation, *n.* maintenance, protection, keeping, PRESERVATION. See STORE.

conservative, *adj.* unprogressive; moderate; protective; unchanging, stable; reactionary, mossback, diehard, Tory. See PERMANENCE.

conservatory, *n.* greenhouse, nursery; SCHOOL, academy. See AGRICULTURE.

conserve, *v.t.* See STORE, PRESERVATION.

consider, *v.* deliberate, ponder, brood, contemplate, meditate, ruminate, reflect; speculate, turn, revolve, weigh, muse; believe, judge, deem; regard, take into account, heed, mark, notice, mind; entertain; esteem. See ATTENTION, THOUGHT, RESPECT, JUDGMENT, BELIEF.

considerable, *adj.* large, sizable, substantial, important, big; tolerable, fair, respectable; material, noteworthy, weighty. See GREATNESS, SIZE.

considerate, *adj.* thoughtful, kind, humane, sympathetic. See CARE, BENEVOLENCE.

consideration, *n.* THOUGHT, deliberation, contemplation, reflection, rumination; CARE, regard; esteem, deference; ATTENTION, notice; IM-

PORTANCE, consequence; motive, reason, ground, basis; gratuity, fee, COMPENSATION. See BENEVOLENCE, RESPECT, CAUSE, QUALIFICATION.

consign, *v.t.* deliver, commit, assign, delegate; remit, remand; send, dispatch, ship, condemn. See TRANSFER, COMMISSION, APPORTIONMENT.

consignee, *n.* committee; functionary, curator, treasurer; AGENT, factor, bailiff, clerk, proctor, underwriter, factotum, DIRECTOR; negotiator, go-between; middleman; employee; SERVANT, caretaker.

consignment, *n.* goods, shipment; delivery, consignation, commitment; allotment, assignment. See APPORTIONMENT, COMMISSION, TRANSFER.

consist, *v.i.* lie, reside, inhere; include, comprise. See EXISTENCE, COMPOSITION.

consistency, *n.* solidity, DENSITY; harmony, correspondence. See AGREEMENT, REGULARITY.

consistent, *adj.* accordant, coherent, uniform, congruous, compatible, consonant, harmonious; reconcilable; homogeneous, regular. See AGREEMENT, UNITY, REGULARITY.

consolation, *n.* condolence, solace, sympathy; assuagement, sop; encouragement. See RELIEF.

console, *v.t.* See RELIEF. —*n.* SUPPORT, bracket; cabinet, floor model. See RECEPTACLE.

consolidate, *v.t.* unite, join, combine, federate, syndicate, merge, pool, fuse, incorporate; compress, solidify, strengthen. See COMBINATION, DENSITY, UNITY.

consonance, *n.* AGREEMENT, harmony; UNITY, accordance, concord.

consort, *n.* spouse, husband, wife. See ACCOMPANIMENT. —*v.* associate, fraternize. See SOCIALITY.

consortium, *n.* cartel, syndicate; meeting, colloquium. See COMBINATION, CONVERSATION.

conspicuous, *adj.* prominent, notable, eminent, outstanding; signal, striking, salient, noticeable, obvious, marked; glaring, obtrusive, notorious, flagrant. See REPUTE, VISIBILITY.

conspire, *v.i.* plot, intrigue, collude, scheme; concur, combine. See PLAN, COOPERATION.

constant, *adj.* stanch, steadfast, loyal; fast, firm, unwavering, unchanging, unswerving, unflagging; permanent, abiding, enduring; steady, stable; regular, even; continual, incessant. See PROBITY, STABILITY, FREQUENCY, PERPETUITY, TENACITY, PERMANENCE, CONTINUITY, REGULARITY.

constellation, *n.* cluster, asterism; sign of the zodiac; ASSEMBLAGE, confluence, gathering. See UNIVERSE.

consternation, *n.* dismay, FEAR.

constipate, *v.t.* clog, stop up (see CLOSURE, DENSITY).

constituency, *n.* constituents, following; clientele; electorate, voters; district, ward. See CHOICE.

constituent, *adj.* integral, formative; elective, appointive, electoral. —*n.* component, PART; voter, supporter, elector (see CHOICE).

constitute, *v.t.* form, be, make, frame, compose; total; set up, establish, found; appoint. See COMPOSITION, PRODUCTION.

constitution, *n.* nature, make-up, temperament, physique, disposition; structure, construction; state, condition; bylaws, code, charter; designation, settlement; creation, foundation. See COMPOSITION, LEGALITY, INTRINSIC.

constraint, *n.* pressure, force, stress; RESTRAINT, confinement, repression; reserve, embarrassment, stiffness; COMPULSION, coercion, NECESSITY, duress. See MODESTY.

constrict, *v.t.* hamper, limit, contract, bind, cramp, squeeze, compress; choke, strangle, strangulate. See CONTRACTION.

construction, *n.* building, fabrication, COMPOSITION; formation, structure, erection; conformation; creation; explanation, INTERPRETATION. See FORM, PRODUCTION.

consul, *n.* emissary, resident. See AGENT.

consult, *v.* confer, refer (to). See ADVICE, CONVERSATION.

consume, *v.t.* destroy, demolish, annihilate; burn, decompose, corrode; devour, swallow, eat, drink; exhaust, drain, use up, expend. See DESTRUCTION, USE, WASTE.

consumer, *n.* customer, purchaser, user. See PURCHASE, USE.

consummate, *adj.* complete, perfect, finished, absolute. —*v.t.* complete, achieve, accomplish; perfect. See COMPLETION, PERFECTION.

consumption, *n.* DESTRUCTION, USE, burning; tuberculosis. See DISEASE, WASTE.

CONTACT

Nouns—contact, contiguity, abutment, TOUCH, CONNECTION; osculation; meeting, encounter, border[land], frontier, tangent. See NEARNESS.

Verbs—be in contact, be contiguous, join, adjoin, abut; butt; TOUCH, meet, encounter, run *or* bump into, meet up with, come *or* chance upon, happen on, run *or* come across, fall on; osculate, come in contact, march with, rub elbows *or* shoulders, keep in touch, hobnob. See JUNCTION.

Adjectives—in contact, contiguous, adjacent, touching; bordering, neighboring; conterminous, end to end, osculatory; tangent, tangential; hand to hand; close to, in touch with, shoulder to shoulder, cheek by jowl.

Prepositions—against, upon.

Antonyms, see INTERVAL, DISTANCE.

contagion, *n.* infection; epidemic, pestilence, virus; TRANSFER, transmission. See DISEASE.

contagious, *adj.* catching, infectious, epidemic, communicable, transmittable, pestilential, noxious, contaminative. See TRANSFER, DISEASE.

contain, *v.t.* include, comprise, incorporate, embrace, embody, comprehend, hold; restrain, check. See INCLUSION, RESTRAINT.

container, *n.* See RECEPTACLE.

contaminate, *v.t.* corrupt, infect, taint, pollute, soil; defile, sully, befoul, stain, dirty; debauch, deprave, degrade. See DETERIORATION, UNCLEANNESS.

contemplate, *v.* consider, meditate, ponder, muse, reflect; view, behold; propose, purpose, PLAN, mean, aim, intend, design. See THOUGHT, VISION, EXPECTATION, INTENTION, LEARNING.

contemporary, *adj.* simultaneous; coexistent, contemporaneous, coeval, synchronous, coincident, concomitant. See TIME, SYNCHRONISM.

CONTEMPT

Nouns—contempt, contemptuousness, disdain, scorn, despisal, contumely; slight, cold shoulder; sneer; DETRACTION, DISAPPROBATION; derision, DISRESPECT; DEFIANCE; arrogance (see INSOLENCE); RIDICULE, mockery; hoot, catcall. *Colloq.*, dig, cut. *Slang,* slam.

Verbs—**1,** be contemptuous of, despise, contemn, scorn, disdain, feel contempt for; disregard, slight; not mind, pass by, look down upon; hold cheap, hold in contempt, think nothing of, think small beer of; underestimate; take no account of, care nothing for, set no store by, not care a straw, set at naught.

2, laugh up one's sleeve, snap one's fingers at, shrug one's shoulders; snub, turn up one's nose at, pooh-pooh, damn with faint praise; sneeze at, sneer at; curl one's lip, toss one's head, look down one's nose at; draw oneself up; laugh at *or* off, brush off; be disrespectful, point the finger of scorn, hold up to scorn, laugh to scorn; scout, hoot, flout, hiss, scoff at, jeer, revile, taunt (see RIDICULE); turn one's back, turn a cold shoulder, leave in the lurch *or* out in the cold; trample upon *or* underfoot, spurn, kick, fling to the winds. *Colloq.*, cut. See AVOIDANCE.

Adjectives—**1,** contemptuous, disdainful, scornful; withering, contumelious, supercilious, cynical, haughty, cavalier; derisive.

2, contemptible, despicable; pitiable, pitiful; unimportant, despised, downtrodden; unenvied.

Adverbs—contemptuously, arrogantly, insolently, *etc.*

Interjections—bah! pooh! pshaw! tut! fiddle-de-dee!; away with! *Slang,* in your hat! come off it!

Antonyms, see APPROBATION, RESPECT.

---

contend, *v.i.* struggle (see CONTENTION); dispute, debate (see DISCORD); maintain, assert, argue, hold, allege. See AFFIRMATION.

CONTENT

Nouns—content, contentment, contentedness; complacency, satisfaction, ease, peace of mind; serenity, euphoria; CHEERFULNESS; gratification; comfort, well-being, life of Riley, bed of roses. See PLEASURE, RELIEF.

Verbs—**1,** rest satisfied, let well enough alone, feel *or* make oneself at home, hug oneself, take in good part; take heart, take comfort, breathe easily *or* freely; rest on one's laurels.

2, tranquilize, set at rest *or* ease, comfort, set one's heart *or* mind at ease *or* rest; speak peace; content, satisfy, gratify, please, soothe, assuage, mollify. See PACIFICATION.

Adjectives—**1,** content[ed], satisfied, at [one's] ease, at rest, serene, at home, in clover, on cloud nine; with the mind at ease, *sans souci,* easygoing, not particular; complacent, imperturbable; unrepining; resigned, patient, cheerful; unafflicted, unvexed, unmolested, unplagued; snug, comfortable [as an old shoe], in one's element.

2, satisfactory, tolerable, adequate, bearable, acceptable, desirable.

Adverbs—contentedly, to one's heart's content; all for the best.

Interjections—very well! so much the better! well and good!; that will do!

Antonyms, see DISCONTENT, PENITENCE.

CONTENTION

Nouns—**1,** contention, strife, contest, contestation, altercation; struggle; belligerency, pugnacity, combativeness (see IRASCIBILITY); competition, rivalry; litigation (see LAWSUIT); OPPOSITION.

2, controversy, polemics (see DISCORD, REASONING).

3, battle, conflict, skirmish, dogfight, row, mixup; encounter, *rencontre,* rencounter; collision, affair, brush, fight; battle royal, pitched battle, *casus belli,* WARFARE; combat, action, engagement, joust, tournament; tilt[ing], tourney, list; death struggle, Armageddon; fracas, clash of arms; tussle, scuffle, brawl, fray; melée, scrimmage, bush-fighting; naval engagement, sea fight. *Colloq.*, set-to, free-for-all. *Slang,* shindy, scrap, run-in, hassle. See OPPOSITION.

4, duel, single combat, monomachy; feud, vendetta; satisfaction, passage of arms, affair of honor.

5, sports, games of skill, gymkhana, round robin, tug-of-war; athletics; gymnastics; wrestling; pugilism, boxing, fisticuffs, prize-fighting, spar, mill, round, bout, game, event; martial arts, jujitsu, judo, kung fu, karate, aikido, *etc*.

6, match, race, relay race; foot race, dash, hurdles; automobile race, Indianapolis 500, drag race; bicycle race, tour; boat race, regatta, America's cup; horse-racing, sport of kings, turf, heat, steeplechase, handicap, claiming race, stake race, sweepstakes, trot, pace, Derby; bullfight, cockfight, *etc*.

7, contender, contestant, competitor, competer, entry; soldier (see COMBATANT).

Verbs—**1,** contend, contest, oppose, strive, struggle, fight, combat, battle, engage, skirmish; make something of; contend, grapple, *or* close with; try conclusions with, have a brush with, join issue, start something, come to blows, fall to, be at loggerheads, set to, come to scratch, meet hand to hand.

2, wrangle, scramble, wrestle, spar, exchange blows *or* fisticuffs, square off, pitch into, tussle, scuffle, tilt, box, stave, fence, encounter, take on, lay *or* light into, fall foul of, cross *or* measure swords; take up cudgels, the glove, *or* the gauntlet, enter the lists, couch one's lance; shoot it out; give satisfaction; lay about one, break the peace, lift one's hand against. *Colloq.*, pitch into. *Slang,* [put up a] scrap.

3, compete, cope, vie, *or* race with; contend for, run a race. *Slang,* drag.

Adjectives—contending, at loggerheads, at war, at swords' points, at issue; competitive, rival, cutthroat; belligerent; contentious, combative, bellicose, unpeaceful; warlike (see WARFARE); quarrelsome, pugnacious; pugilistic, fistic.

Antonyms, see PACIFICATION.

---

contents, *n.* See COMPOSITION.

contest, *v.t.* See CONTENTION.

contestant, *n.* contender, competitor, competer, *etc*. (see CONTENTION).

context, *n.* setting, background, position, situation. See ENVIRONMENT.

contiguity, *n.* juxtaposition, abutment, union, meeting. See CONTACT.

continence, *n.* self-restraint (see MODERATION).

continental, *adj.* mainland (see LAND); cosmopolitan, sophisticated, worldly, urbane; charming. See FASHION, COURTESY.

contingency, *n.* CHANCE, POSSIBILITY, likelihood, accident, casualty, prospect; situation, predicament, case. See CIRCUMSTANCE, LIABILITY, EXPECTATION.

contingent, *adj.* possible; provisional, conditional, provisory, dependent; incidental, accidental, casual. See CHANCE, LIABILITY, CIRCUMSTANCE, QUALIFICATION.

continual, *adj.* constant; repeated, frequent. See FREQUENCY, CONTINUITY.

continuance, *n.* CONTINUITY; persistence, perseverance, endurance; postponement, extension, prolongation. See LATENESS.

continue, *v.* persist; keep, go, carry, run, *or* hold on; maintain, keep up, sustain, uphold; prolong, remain, last, endure, withstand; protract, persevere, be permanent, stay, stick, abide; resume. See DURABILITY, CONTINUITY.

CONTINUITY

Nouns—continuity, continuum, SEQUENCE; round, suite, progression, series, train, chain; continuance, continuation, PERPETUITY; concatenation, scale; course; procession, column; retinue, caravan, cortege, cavalcade, rank and file, line of battle, array; running fire; pedigree, genealogy (see ANCESTRY, POSTERITY); rank, file, line, row, range, string, thread, suit; colonnade. See FREQUENCY, INFINITY, DURABILITY.

Verbs—**1,** continue, follow in a series, form a series; fall in; arrange in a series, string together, thread, graduate; tabulate, list, file.

2, keep at, on, *or* up, carry on *or* over, keep the ball rolling, stick with, go on.

Adjectives—continuous, continued; consecutive, progressive, serial, unbroken, linear; in a line, row, *or* column; uninterrupted, unintermitting, unremitting, endless, incessant, unceasing, ceaseless; perennial, evergreen; constant, chronic, continual, repeated, persistent, repeating, persisting; year-round.

Adverbs—continuously, *etc.; seriatim;* running, step by step, at a stretch; all along, all the time *or* while, around the clock, at every turn, day and night.

Antonyms, see DISCONTINUANCE.

---

contortion, *n.* DISTORTION, twist, dislocation, deformity; grimace. See CONVOLUTION.

contour, *n.* outline, profile, shape, FORM, conformation, figure. See APPEARANCE, CIRCUIT.

contraband, *adj.* forbidden, banned, prohibited; smuggled. See PROHIBITION, ILLEGALITY.

contraception, *n.* birth control, planned parenthood; rhythm method, condom, intrauterine device, I.U.D., diaphragm, the pill; zero population growth. See HINDRANCE.

contraceptive, *adj.* See HINDRANCE.

contract, *n.* compact, AGREEMENT, PROMISE, bargain, covenant, stipulation, convention.

CONTRACTION

Nouns—**1,** contraction, reduction, diminution; DECREASE; shrinking, astringency; emaciation, attenuation, consumption, tabescence; abbreviation. See LITTLENESS, NARROWNESS.

2, condensation, compression, compactness; squeezing, strangulation (see CLOSURE); cramp, seizure, contractility, compressibility. See DENSITY.

Verbs—**1,** contract, become small[er]; DECREASE, shrink, narrow, shrivel, collapse, lose flesh, reduce, deflate; decay, deteriorate (see DETERIORATION).

2, diminish, draw in, narrow; constrict, constringe, astringe; condense, compress, squeeze, cramp, crimp, crush, crumple up, purse up; wind up, tighten, pinch, strangle; stunt, dwarf; empty; waste away; pare, attenuate, shorten (see SHORTNESS).

Adjectives—contracting, contractive, contractile; tabescent; styptic, astringent; shrunk, strangulated, wizened, stunted; compact.

Antonyms, see EXPANSION.

---

contractor, *n.* builder, architect, *padrone;* entrepreneur. See PRODUCTION, UNDERTAKING.

contradict, *v.t.* gainsay, deny, belie, controvert, refute, disprove, overthrow; dispute, DISSENT. See NEGATION.

contraption, *n., colloq.,* gadget, contrivance (see INSTRUMENTALITY).

contrariety, *n* OPPOSITION, OBSTINACY; antagonism, DISAGREEMENT, DISOBEDIENCE.

contrary, *adj.* opposed, opposite, counter, conflicting, contradictory; unfavorable, adverse; captious, willful, perverse; hostile, antagonistic. See OPPOSITION, NEGATION, OBSTINACY.

contrast, *n.* DIFFERENCE, opposition, foil, dissimilarity, unlikeness, disparity.

contravene, *v.t.* violate, infringe upon; oppose, contradict, conflict with, defy. See OPPOSITION, NEGATION, ILLEGALITY.

contretemps, *n.* embarrassment; mischance, mishap. See DIFFICULTY.

contribute, *v.* give, subscribe, donate; help, AID, assist; conduce, advance, tend, serve, redound, go. See GIVING, CAUSE.

contributor, *n.* giver, subscriber, donor; author, correspondent, editor, columnist, reviewer, stringer; helper. See PUBLICATION, GIVING.

contrite, *adj.* penitent, sorry (see PENITENCE).

contrivance, *n.* device, invention, construction, machine, apparatus; PLAN, scheme, trick, stratagem. *Colloq.,* contraption. See INSTRUMENTALITY, CUNNING.

control, *v.t.* command, dominate, govern, rule, regulate, direct, master; restrain, subdue, modify, check; test, verify. —*n.* COMMAND, mastery, domination, sway, upper hand, POWER, regimentation, government, direction, management, dominion; RESTRAINT, ceiling, regulation. See AUTHORITY, EVIDENCE.

controversy, *n.* contention, dispute, argument, DISCORD, discussion, debate, quarrel, wrangle, altercation.

controvert, *v.t.* deny, contradict, contravene, traverse (*legal*), impugn, refute, confute, oppose, argue against, dispute, counter, debate. See NEGATION.

contumacy, *n.* rebelliousness, DISOBEDIENCE.

contumely, *n.* insult, abuse. See CONTEMPT, DISAPPROBATION, DISRESPECT.

contusion, *n.* bruise, black-and-blue [mark]. See DISEASE.

conundrum, *n.* riddle, enigma, puzzle. See SECRET.

convalesce, *v.i.* recover, recuperate, rally, revive, improve. See HEALTH, RESTORATION.

convene, *v.* assemble, gather, collect, congregate, meet, convoke. See ASSEMBLAGE.

convenience, *n.* accessibility, handiness, availability, suitability; advantage, accommodation, comfort, opportunity, ease. See UTILITY, EXPEDIENCE.

convent, *n.* cloister, nunnery. See TEMPLE.

convention, *n.* assembly, gathering, congregation, congress, meeting, caucus, COUNCIL; convocation; RULE, custom, usage, formality, practice; propriety, conventionality. See FASHION, ASSEMBLAGE, CONFORMITY.

conventional, *adj.* customary, accepted, orthodox, approved, habitual, usual; formal. See CONFORMITY, HABIT.

CONVERGENCE

Nouns—convergence, confluence, conflux, concourse; centralization, concentration, corradiation; appulse, meeting; focus, focal point, asymptote. See APPROACH, ASSEMBLAGE, NEARNESS.

Verbs—converge, come together, unite; meet, close with, close in upon; centralize, center round, center in; enter in; pour in; concentrate, bring into focus; home in (on); crowd, press.

Adjectives—convergent, confluent, concurrent; centripetal; asymptotic.

Antonyms, see DEVIATION.

---

conversant, *adj.* acquainted, [well-] informed; skilled, versed, practiced, proficient. See KNOWLEDGE, SKILL.

CONVERSATION

Nouns—**1,** conversation, interlocution, intercourse; collocution, colloquy, converse, discussion, talkfest; confabulation; talk, discourse; oral communication, communion, commerce; dialogue, duologue. *Colloq.,* confab. *Slang,* bull session.

2, chat, chit-chat, *causerie;* small talk, table talk, idle talk; comment, gossip (see INFORMATION); tittle-tattle, prattle (see LOQUACITY); *on dit;* talk of the town.

3, conference, consortium, parley, palaver, consultation; interview, audience, press conference, audition, *pourparler, tête-à-tête; conversazione;* congress, COUNCIL; debate, logomachy, war of words. *Colloq.,* powwow, huddle.

4, interlocutor, conversationalist, colloquist, dialogist, talker, spokesman, interpreter; Paul Pry; chatterer (see LOQUACITY).

Verbs—**1,** converse, talk together, discuss; confabulate; hold a conversation, carry on *or* engage in a conversation, make conversation; put in a word; shine in conversation; bandy words, parley, palaver, chat, gossip; fence *or* spar with; compare notes. *Colloq.,* go into a huddle, rap. *Slang,* chat, chew the fat *or* the rag; shoot, fan, *or* bat the breeze. See SOCIALITY.

2, discourse, confer, consult, advise, confer, *or* commune with; hold converse, hold a conference; interview; talk it over, hash out, go into; be closeted with, talk in private.

Adjectives—conversing, talking; interlocutory; conversational, conversationable, discursive, chatty, sociable; colloquial.

---

converse, *adj.* transposed, reversed, turned about; reciprocal; other, opposite, contrary. See OPPOSITION. —*n.* reverse, contrary, opposite; counterpart, reciprocal; vice versa. —*v.* See CONVERSATION.

conversion, *n.* reduction, CHANGE; retooling, changeover, adaptation; transmogrification; alchemy; RESOLUTION, assimilation; reformation; sex change.

convert, *v.t.* CHANGE, make over; retool, adapt; reorganize, remodel, regenerate; reduce, transmute, transform, transmogrify, render; exchange. —*n.* neophyte, disciple; renegade, apostate; transsexual.

CONVEXITY

Nouns—**1,** convexity, prominence, projection, swell[ing], bulge, protuberance, protrusion, growth, lump; stud. See ROTUNDITY.

2, excrescence, tumescence, outgrowth, tumor, tubercle, tuberosity; hump, hunch, bunch; tooth, knob, elbow; bulb, node, nodule; tongue; pimple, wen, weal, postule, sarcoma, carbuncle, corn, wart, furuncle, polyp, fungus, blister, boil (see DISEASE); papilla; breast, bosom, nipple, teat, mammilla; nose, proboscis, beak, snout; belly; withers, humpback; shoulder, lip. *Colloq.,* pot. *Slang,* corporation.

3, hill, HEIGHT, cape, promontory, headland; peninsula, neck, isthmus, point of land; reef; mole, jetty, ledge, spur.

4, cupola, dome, vault, arch, extrados, balcony, eaves; pilaster; boss; relief, bas-relief, cameo.

Verbs—project, bulge, protrude, pout, bunch; billow; jut, stand, stick, *or* poke out; start up, shoot up *or* out; arch, vault; swell, bag, bloat, intumesce, hang over, bend over; beetle; raise, emboss, chase.

Adjectives—convex, prominent, protuberant; projecting; bossed; nodular, bunchy; clavate; mammiform, papulous; hemispheric, bulbous; bowed, parched; bold; bellied; tuberous, tuberculous; humpbacked, gibbous; tumid, tumorous; cornute, odontoid; lentiform, lenticular; salient, in relief, raised, repoussé; bloated.

Antonyms, see CONCAVITY.

---

convey, *v.t.* bear, carry, transport; transmit, impart, communicate; TRANSFER, grant, cede, will. See INFORMATION, TRANSPORTATION.

conveyance, *n.* VEHICLE; TRANSFER, assignment, sale, legacy, disposal; transmission, communication. See INFORMATION.

convict, *v.t.* condemn, find guilty, doom. See CONDEMNATION, JUDGMENT. —*n.* criminal, felon, jailbird, prisoner, captive. See PRISON.

conviction, *n.* BELIEF, persuasion, faith, opinion, view; CONDEMNATION, sentence, penalty.

convince, *v.t.* persuade, satisfy. See BELIEF.

conviviality, *n.* SOCIALITY, sociability, festivity, gaiety, joviality.

convoke, *v.t.* convene, assemble, summon, call, collect, gather. See ASSEMBLAGE.

CONVOLUTION

Nouns—**1,** convolution, winding; involution, circumvolution; wave, undulation, tortuosity, anfractuosity; intricacy; sinuosity, sinuation; meandering, circuit; twist, twirl, windings and turnings; ambages; torsion; reticulation (see CROSSING). *Colloq.,* body English. See CIRCUITY, ROTATION.

2, coil, roll, curl, curlicue, buckle, spiral, helix, corkscrew, worm, volute, tendril; skein; scallop, escalop; serpent, eel; maze, labyrinth.

Verbs—convolve, be convoluted, wind, twine, turn and twist, twirl; wave, undulate, meander; entwine, twist, coil, roll; wrinkle, curl [up], crisp, friz[z], frizzle; crimp, scallop; wring, intort, contort.

Adjectives—convoluted; winding, twisting, tortile, tortuous; wavy; undulatory; circling, snaky, snakelike, serpentine; anguilliform, vermiform, vermicular; mazy, sinuous, involute, flexuous, sigmoidal; spiral, coiled, helical, turbinated; involved, intricate, complicated, perplexed (see DISORDER); labyrinthine.

Adverbs—convolutely, in and out, round and round.

Antonyms, see DIRECTION.

---

convoy, *v.t.* accompany, escort, conduct; guard, support. See ACCOMPANIMENT. —*n.* escort, [body]guard, safe-conduct; caravan. See ACCOMPANIMENT, ASSEMBLAGE, SAFETY.

convulse, *v.t.* agitate, shake, disturb, trouble, excite, stir; rend, wring, hurt. See AGITATION, PAIN, REVOLUTION, VIOLENCE.

cook, *v.t.* prepare, concoct, fix, make; roast, broil, boil, fry, *etc.; colloq.,* doctor; *slang,* ruin, spoil. See FOOD, HEAT, DETERIORATION, FALSEHOOD.

cookery, *n.* cooking, cuisine; culinary art. See PREPARATION.

cookie, *n.* wafer, biscuit; shortbread, sugar cookie, gingersnap, *etc.* See FOOD.

cool, *v.* chill, refrigerate, ice, freeze, harden; calm, allay. See DISSUASION, REFRESHMENT. —*adj.* COLD, chilly, frigid; inexcitable, self-controlled, calm, deliberate, composed; indifferent, unemotional, self-possessed; easygoing, placid; unfriendly, distant, lukewarm. See COLD, MODERATION, INEXCITABILITY, MALEVOLENCE.

COOPERATION

Nouns—**1,** cooperation, coadjuvancy, coadjutancy; coagency, coefficiency, concert, concurrence, participation, collaboration, coexistence; COMBINATION, collusion, complicity, conspiracy, connivance.
2, association, alliance, colleagueship, [co]partnership; confederation, affiliation, coalition, bloc, fusion (see COMBINATION); cooperative, co-op, commune; logrolling, give-and-take; common ground, unanimity (see ASSENT); esprit de corps, party *or* team spirit; clanship, partisanship. See PARTY, AGREEMENT.

Verbs—**1,** cooperate, coexist; concur; conspire, collaborate, collude, connive, concert, lay heads together, get together; confederate, affiliate, be in league with; unite one's efforts; keep, pull, club, hang, hold, league, *or* band together; be banded together, stand shoulder to shoulder, be in the same boat, act in concert, put their heads together, pool resources, line up, gang up, join forces, understand one another, get along, hunt in couples; split the difference (see COMPROMISE). *Colloq.*, play ball.
2, side with, go *or* play along with, sign up, go hand in hand with, join hands with, make common cause with, chime in, pitch in, unite *or* join with, mix oneself up with, pull one's weight, hold up one's end, take part in, cast in one's lot with, enter into partnership with, throw in with, line up with; go around with, hang *or* stick together; play politics. *Slang*, play footsie with.
3, be a party to, be in on, lend oneself to, participate, have *or* keep a hand in, have a finger in the pie, take part in, chip in; second, AID.

Adjectives—cooperating, in cooperation *or* league; coadjuvant, coadjutant; cooperative, coefficient; participatory, partaking; favorable to; unopposed. *Colloq.*, in cahoots with.

Adverbs—cooperatively; as one man, together, unanimously, shoulder to shoulder, side by side, hand in hand, hand in glove, in common, share and share alike, *pro rata*.

Antonyms, see OPPOSITION.

---

coordinate, *v.t.* equalize, adapt, harmonize, synchronize, adjust; organize. See ARRANGEMENT.

cop, *v.* seize, grap, take; steal, filch, pilfer; win, capture. See ACQUISITION, STEALING. —*n.*, *slang*, policeman (see SAFETY).

cope, *v.i.* contend, strive, deal with; face; manage, handle. See CONTENTION.

copious, *adj.* abundant, plentiful, ample, overflowing; wordy, profuse, diffuse, prolix. See SUFFICIENCY.

copulate, *v.i.* unite, join, couple; mate; have coitus *or* sex; cohabit, breed, fornicate, make love, live together, have relations. See MARRIAGE, JUNCTION.

COPY

Nouns—**1,** copy, facsimile, counterpart, effigy, form, semblance, cast[ing], ecotype, fake; IMITATION; model, study, portrait (see REPRESENTATION); tracing; duplicate; photocopy, instant copy, ditto; transcript[ion]; reflex, reflection, mirror; replica, clone; shadow, echo; chip off the old block; reprint, reproduction, second edition; REPETITION, apograph, fair copy. *Slang*, dupe, spit and image, dead ringer. See PRINTING, WRITING, IDENTITY, SIMILARITY.
2, parody, caricature (see RIDICULE); paraphrase; counterfeit (see DECEPTION).
3, copyist, transcriber; scribe, plagiarist; ape, parrot (see IMITATION).

Verbs—copy, duplicate, imitate, reproduce, trace, transcribe; photocopy;

plagiarize, crib; parody, mimic, forge, counterfeit; echo; reprint; clone. *Colloq.*, fake.

Adjectives—faithful; lifelike, similar (see SIMILARITY).

Antonyms, see IDENTITY, DIFFERENCE.

---

coquette, *n.* flirt. See ENDEARMENT.

cord, *n.* string, rope, band, bond, twine; tendon; cable. See FILAMENT, CONNECTION.

cordial, *adj.* sincere, heartfelt; hearty, genial, friendly, amicable, kindly. See COURTESY, FEELING. —*n.* liqueur (see DRINKING).

core, *n.* center, interim, heart, nucleus, kernel, pith; nut, nub, SUBSTANCE, gist. See MIDDLE, IMPORTANCE, INTRINSIC.

cork, *n.* stopper, plug, bung; float, bob. —*v.t.* stop, plug, bung, seal. See CLOSURE, MATERIALS.

corkscrew, *n.* bottle opener (see OPENING). —*adj.* twisted, tortuous. See CONVOLUTION.

corner, *n.* angle; nook, niche; control, monopoly; predicament; tight spot. See ANGULARITY, POSSESSION, DIFFICULTY.

cornucopia, *n.* horn of plenty *or* of Amalthea. See SUFFICIENCY.

corny, *adj., slang,* sentimental, mushy, sticky; old-fashioned, stale, musty, banal, sticky. See SENSIBILITY.

corollary, *n.* adjunct, offshoot. See JUDGMENT, ACCOMPANIMENT.

coronary, *adj.* coronal, crownlike, ringlike, round, circular. See CIRCULARITY. —*n.* [coronary] thrombosis, heart attack, apoplexy, paralysis, stroke. See DISEASE.

coronation, *n.* crowning, investment. See COMMISSION.

corporation, *n.* association, syndicate, company, society, partnership, merger, trust. See PARTY, BUSINESS.

corps, *n.* body, company, outfit, branch, service. See ASSEMBLAGE, COMBATANT.

corpse, *n.* cadaver (see DEATH).

corpulence, *n.* fatness, fleshiness, obesity, plumpness, portliness, bulk. See SIZE, ROTUNDITY.

corral, *n.* pen, yard. See ENCLOSURE.

correct, *v.t.* improve, rectify, [set] right, remedy, repair, amend, reform, better; edit, mark; reprove, punish, chastise, discipline; counteract, neutralize. See IMPROVEMENT, PUNISHMENT. —*adj.* right, regular, true, strict, accurate, exact, precise, perfect; proper, *comme il faut*. *Slang,* right on. See RIGHTNESS, ELEGANCE.

correlation, *n.* correlativity; reciprocation, reciprocity; mutuality; interrelation, correspondence; analogy, likeness. See RELATION.

corridor, *n.* hall, hallway, gallery, arcade, PASSAGE; skyway, airway, route.

corrigible, *adj.* amendable, rectifiable; amenable, tractable, docile. See IMPROVEMENT.

corroborate, *v.t.* confirm (see EVIDENCE, ASSENT, DEMONSTRATION).

corrode, *v.* consume, gnaw, rust, decay, wear; eat, etch. See DETERIORATION.

corrugate, *v.t.* FURROW, wrinkle, groove. See ROUGHNESS.

corrupt, *v.t.* demoralize, vitiate, deprave, defile, degrade, debase, debauch; bribe, pervert; contaminate, spoil, taint. —*adj.* wicked, demoralized, immoral, impure, dissolute, depraved, profligate, base; vicious; rotten, infected, tainted, spoiled. See IMPROBITY, UNCLEANNESS, EVIL, DECOMPOSITION, DETERIORATION, WRONG.

corsage, *n.* bouquet, boutonnière. See ORNAMENT.

cortege, *n.* procession; retinue. See CONTINUITY, ACCOMPANIMENT.

cosmetic, *adj.* beautifying, adorning, decorative. —*n.* preparation, makeup. *Slang,* war paint, face, mask. See BEAUTY.

cosmic, *adj.* universal, galactic, heavenly; vast, grandiose; harmonious, orderly. See UNIVERSE, ORDER.

cosmopolitan, *adj.* sophisticated, urbane, polished; informed, tolerant. See KNOWLEDGE, COURTESY, ABODE.

cost, *n.* PRICE, charge, expense; expenditure, outlay, disbursement, PAYMENT.

costly, *adj.* expensive, high-priced, dear, precious, valuable; extravagant; gorgeous, sumptuous. See DEARNESS.

costume, *n.* CLOTHING; fancy dress, uniform; outfit, rig. See CONCEALMENT.

cot, *n.* bed, pallet, couch. See SUPPORT.

coterie, *n.* set, clique. See PARTY.

cotillion, *n.* german; ball, square dance. See AMUSEMENT.

cottage, *n.* bungalow (see ABODE).

couch, *n.* bed, cot, pallet; lounge, divan, settee, convertible, davenport, chaise longue. See SUPPORT, LAYER, HORIZONTAL.

cough, *n.* hack, racking cough. See DISEASE.

COUNCIL

Nouns—**1,** council, committee, subcommittee, panel, advisory council, brain trust, comitia, chamber, board, bench, directory, chapter, syndicate, junta; cabinet, privy council; senate, upper house, house of representatives, lower house; parliament, chamber of deputies, legislature, congress, diet, divan; county council, city council; court, forum, tribunal, court of appeal[s]; consistory; diocesan, plenary, *or* ecumenical council; vestry.

2, convention, assembly (see ASSEMBLAGE).

3, statesman, senator, congressman, representative, member of parliament, M.P., councilor, councilman, assemblyman, legislator; majority leader, minority whip *or* leader; conventioneer; jurist, judge, justice.

Verbs—sit, assemble; sit on; deliberate, debate; serve, attend, hold court.

Adjectives—consultative, consultatory, consultory; bicameral, unicameral.

Adverbs—in council, committee, session, executive session, conference, *etc.*

---

counsel, *v.t.* & *n.* See ADVICE.

count, *v.* enumerate, tell, score, figure, account; matter, reckon; deem, consider, estimate. See JUDGMENT, NUMERATION, NUMBER.

countenance, *n.* face, features, visage, physiognomy; expression, complexion, aspect; approval, sanction, acceptance, favor, patronage. *Slang,* mug. See APPEARANCE, APPROBATION, FRONT.

counter, *adj.* opposing, opposite, contrary, counterclockwise, cross, against. See OPPOSITION.

counteract, *v.t.* check, thwart, nullify, negate, frustrate; counterbalance, offset; contervail, neutralize, render harmless. See OPPOSITION, COMPENSATION.

counterattack, *n.* reprisal, RETALIATION.

counterfeit, *adj.* false, sham, fake, forged, bogus, bastard, spurious. *Colloq.,* phony. —*n.* forgery, fake, slug, sham, brummagem, dummy, pretense. *Colloq.,* phony. See DECEPTION, IMITATION, COPY.

countermand, *v.t.* revoke, overrule. See NULLIFICATION.

counterpane, *n.* bedspread, coverlet. See COVERING.

counterpart, *n.* COPY, duplicate, double, facsimile, replica; likeness, image, similitude, match, parallel, twin, mate; complement. See SIMILARITY.

counterpoise, *n.* balance, equilibrium, equipoise; counterweight. See COMPENSATION.

countersign, *n.* password, shibboleth, watchword. See INDICATION.

countless, *adj.* innumerable, infinite, numberless, uncountable, incalculable, illimitable. See MULTITUDE, INFINITY.

country, *n.* land, REGION, tract, district, territory; countryside, plain, fields; state, people, fatherland, home, nation; power. *Colloq.*, the sticks.

countryman, *n.* national, citizen, compatriot; rustic, farmer. *Colloq.*, hayseed. *Slang,* rube, hick. See FRIEND, POPULACE.

coup, *n.* stroke, master stroke. See IMPULSE, SKILL, CUNNING.

couple, *v.t.* join, tie, link; yoke, unite, pair; marry. See JUNCTION, MARRIAGE.

coupon, *n.* certificate, ticket, slip; premium *or* trading stamp. See INDICATION, RECORD.

COURAGE

Nouns—**1,** courage, bravery, valor; boldness, strength; daring, gallantry, heroism, intrepidity; DEFIANCE, audacity; RASHNESS, brinkmanship; confidence, self-reliance; chivalry, prowess, derring-do; RESOLUTION.

2, manliness, manhood; nerve, pluck, backbone, grit, mettle, game; heart, heart of grace; hardihood, fortitude; heart of oak. *Colloq.*, spunk, sand, what it takes; shot in the arm. *Slang,* guts, crust, moxie.

3, exploit, feat, enterprise, [heroic] deed *or* act; bold stroke.

4, man *or* woman of courage *or* mettle; hero[ine], demigod[dess]; lion, tiger, panther, bulldog; fire-eater.

Verbs—**1,** be courageous, dare, venture, make bold, brave, beard, defy, face up to, face, meet, stand up to; put a bold face upon, show fight, brave it out; go through fire and water, run the gantlet; bell the cat, take the bull by the horns, beard the lion in his den.

2, take muster; summon up, screw up, *or* pluck up courage; get up the nerve, nerve oneself, take heart, keep one's chin up, keep a stiff upper lip; hold up one's head, screw one's courage to the sticking place, whistle in the dark; come up to scratch, stand to one's guns, stand against; bear up (against). *Slang,* stand the gaff.

3, give *or* inspire courage, hearten, reassure, encourage, nerve, put upon one's mettle, rally, raise a rallying cry; make a man of. See CHEERFULNESS.

Adjectives—**1,** courageous, brave; valiant, valorous; gallant, intrepid; mettlesome, plucky, gritty, bold as brass; manly, manful; resolute; stout, hardy, stouthearted; iron-hearted, lion-hearted; enterprising, adventurous, venturous, venturesome; dashing, chivalrous; soldierly, warlike, heroic; strong-minded, hardy, doughty; firm, determined, dogged, indomitable, persevering. *Slang,* gutsy.

2, bold, bold-spirited, daring, audacious, game; fearless, dauntless, undaunted, unappalled, undismayed, unawed, unabashed, unalarmed, unflinching, unshrinking, unblenching, unapprehensive; confident, self-reliant; bold as a lion, cool as a cucumber.

Antonyms, see COWARDICE, MODESTY, FEAR.

courier, *n.* messenger, runner. See COMMUNICATION.

court, *v.t.* solicit, invite; curry favor, cultivate, cajole, praise; woo, sue, make love to. *Colloq.,* spark. —*n.* ENCLOSURE, [court]yard, quadrangle, patio; tribunal, bench, bar, jurisdiction, session; courtship, addresses, attention; palace, hall; retinue, following, train. See ENDEARMENT, ENCLOSURE, FASHION, FLATTERY, LAWSUIT, SERVANT, ABODE, COUNCIL, JUDGMENT.

courtesan, *n.* harlot, prostitute. See IMPURITY.

COURTESY

Nouns—**1,** courtesy, courteousness; RESPECT; good manners, behavior, *or* breeding; manners, politeness, urbanity, comity, gentility, breeding, cultivation, polish, grace, civility, culture, civilization, social graces; tact, diplomacy; amenity, suavity; good *or* easy temper, good humor, amiability, gentleness, soft tongue; HUMILITY. affability, gallantry, chivalry, bushido. See SOCIALITY.

2, compliment; fair, soft, *or* sweet words, honeyed phrases; salutation, reception, presentation, introduction, mark of recognition, nod, recognition; welcome, respects, devoir, welcome mat; valediction, farewell, goodbye; regards, remembrances; kind regards *or* remembrances.

3, obeisance, reverence, bow, curtsy, salaam; kneeling, genuflection (see WORSHIP); salute, hand-shake, grip of the hand, embrace, hug, squeeze; accolade. *Colloq.,* high sign, glad hand.

Verbs—**1,** be courteous, show courtesy, keep a civil tongue in one's head; receive, do the honors, usher, greet, hail, bid welcome, accost, welcome [with open arms]; shake hands; hold out, press, *or* squeeze the hand; bid Godspeed, see off; speed the parting guest. *Colloq.,* have one's latch string out.

2, embrace, kiss hands, kiss on the cheek; drink to, pledge, hob and nob; move to, nod to; smile upon; touch *or* take off the hat, doff the cap, uncover, cap; present arms, salute; make way for, bow, make one's bow; curtsy, bob [a curtsy], kneel, bend the knee, prostrate oneself.

3, visit, wait upon, present oneself, pay one's respects, pay a visit (see SOCIALITY); pass the time of day; dance attendance on (see SERVILITY); pay attentions to, do homage to (see RESPECT).

4, mind one's P's and Q's, behave oneself, be all things to all men, conciliate, speak one fair, take in good part; look as if butter would not melt in one's mouth; mend one's manners.

5, polish, cultivate, civilize, humanize.

Adjectives—courteous, polite, civil, mannerly, urbane, continental, cosmopolitan; well-behaved, well-mannered, wellbred, well brought up, gentlemanly, courtly, gallant, chivalrous; good-mannered, polished, civilized, cultivated, refined (see TASTE); fine-spoken, fair-spoken, soft-spoken; honey-mouthed *or* -tongued; mealy-mouthed; obliging, conciliatory, on one's good behavior, ingratiating, winning; genteel; gentle, mild; good-humored, cordial, gracious, affable, amiable, familiar, suave; neighborly.

Adverbs—courteously; with a good grace, with open *or* outstretched arms.

Antonyms, see DISCOURTESY.

---

courtier, *n.* flatterer, sycophant. See FLATTERY, SERVILITY.

courtly, *adj.* elegant, refined. See ELEGANCE, COURTESY.

courtship, *n.* flirtation, wooing. See ENDEARMENT.

courtyard, *n.* court, square (see ENCLOSURE).

cove, *n.* inlet, bay, lagoon; nook. See CONCAVITY, WATER.

covenant, *v.* contract, agree, undertake, stipulate, engage, bargain, PROMISE. —*n.* AGREEMENT, contract, bargain, pact, PROMISE, SECURITY.

COVERING

Nouns—**1,** covering, cover; superposition, superimposition.

2, ceiling, canopy, awning, tent, pavilion, marquee; umbrella, parasol, sunshade; veil, shade, visor; hood, dome (see CONVEXITY); shelter, shield, DEFENSE; CLOTHING. See CONCEALMENT.

3, coverlet, counterpane, sheet, quilt, blanket, bedclothes, bedding; rug, carpet, linoleum; tapestry, drugget; tarpaulin, canvas; housing.

4, peel, crust, bark, rind, cortex, husk, shell, nutshell, coat, jacket; capsule, house; scab; sheath, sheathing, sleeve; pod; casing, case; wrapper, wrapping; envelope, vesicle.

5, overlay, film; veneer, facing; pavement; scale, LAYER; coating, paint (see PAINTING); masking tape; varnish; incrustation, ground; whitewash, plaster, stucco, compo; siding; lining; cerement.

6, integument; skin, pellicle, fleece, feathers, fell, fur, hide; pelt, peltry; cuticle; epidermis.

Verbs—cover, mask; superpose, superimpose; overlay, overspread; drape; wrap, encase, do up; face, case, veneer, pave, paper; tip, cap; coat, paint, varnish, incrust, stucco, dab, plaster, tar; wash; besmear, smear; bedaub, daub; anoint, do over; veil; glaze, gild, plate, japan, lacquer, enamel, whitewash; overlie, overarch, overlap, overhang; conceal; insulate.

Adjectives—**1,** covering; cutaneous, dermal, epidermal, cortical, cuticular, tegumentary, skinlike, skinny, scaly, squamous.

2, covered, imbricated, armor-plated, ironclad; under cover (see CONCEALMENT).

Antonyms, see DIVESTMENT.

---

covert, *adj.* SECRET, hidden, sheltered. See CONCEALMENT.

coverup, *n.* whitewash (see CONCEALMENT).

covet, *v.t.* DESIRE, long for, crave, want, envy. See JEALOUSY.

covey, *n.* flock, brood, bevy. See ASSEMBLAGE.

cow, *n.* bovine, calf, heifer; (*pl.*) kine, cattle. See ANIMAL. —*v.t.* intimidate, frighten. See FEAR.

COWARDICE

Nouns—**1,** cowardice, cowardliness, pusillanimity, poltroonery, baseness; dastardness, dastardy; abject fear, funk; Dutch courage; FEAR, white feather, faint heart, cold feet. See WEAKNESS.

2, coward, poltroon, dastard, sneak, craven, recreant, scaredy- *or* fraidy-cat; milksop, whiteliver, mama's boy, sissy, rabbit; runagate, runaway. *Slang,* chicken[-liver].

Verbs—be cowardly, be a coward; cower, skulk, sneak; quail, flinch, shy, fight shy, slink, turn tail; run away (see AVOIDANCE); show the white feather, have cold feet; be psyched out. *Slang,* chicken out.

Adjectives—coward[ly], fearful, shy; poor-spirited, spiritless, soft, effeminate; weak-minded; weak-, faint-, chicken-, lily-, *or* pigeon-hearted, lily- *or* white-livered; pusillanimous, spineless, bloodless; unable to say "Boo" to a goose, afraid of one's shadow; dastard[ly]; base, craven, sneaking, recreant; unwarlike, unsoldierlike, unmanned, unmanly; frightened, afraid (see FEAR). *Colloq.,* yellow[-bellied]. *Slang,* chicken[-livered].

Antonyms, see COURAGE.

---

cowboy, *n.* cowherd, cowman, cowgirl, cowpoke; cattleman *or* -woman, cowpuncher, cowhand, buckaroo; wrangler, broncobuster; trail boss, top hand; vaquero, gaucho, ranchero. *Slang,* pard[ner]. See DOMESTICATION.

cower, *v.i.* cringe, shrink, crouch, quail; fawn, grovel. See COWARDICE, SERVILITY, FEAR, RECOIL.

co-worker, *n.* associate, confrere, colleague. See AGENT.

coy, *adj.* bashful, reserved; chary; shrinking, shy, demure, retiring; coquettish. See MODESTY.

cozy, *adj.* snug, comfortable, homey, *gemütlich;* warm, plush. See PLEASURE, SOCIALITY.

crabbed, *adj.* crabby, ill-tempered, irascible, surly, growly, cross, peevish; cramped, illegible, squeezed. See IRASCIBILITY, UNINTELLIGIBILITY.

crack, *v.t.* pop, rend, explode, bang; crackle; break, split, burst, cleave, fracture, crush; *colloq.,* fail, bust, break down. —*n.* snap, break, fracture; crevice, crackle, craze, chink, flaw, cleft, rift, rent, fissure; slit, rut, groove, seam; pop, crash, clap; *slang,* attempt, try; *slang,* gibe (see WIT). See INTERVAL, DISJUNCTION, LOUDNESS, BRITTLENESS, FURROW, UNDERTAKING. —*adj., colloq.,* expert (see SKILL).

crackpot, *n., slang,* eccentric, screwball. See UNCONFORMITY.

cradle, *n.* crib; origin[s], infancy. See BEGINNING, SUPPORT.

craft, *n.* SKILL, expertise; art, handicraft; trade; vessel, SHIP, boat; CUNNING, artfulness, deceit, trickery. See BUSINESS.

craftsman, *n.* artisan. See ARTIST, AGENCY.

crafty, *adj.* guileful, CUNNING.

crag, *n.* rock, boulder. See LAND.

cram, *v.* crowd, stuff, press, force, jam, pack, choke; satiate, surfeit, gormandize, gorge, guzzle; study, burn the midnight oil. See CLOSURE, GLUTTONY, LEARNING.

cramp, *v.t.* restrict, hamper, handicap; compress, confine; fasten; cripple, paralyze, incapacitate. —*n.* seizure, spasm. *Colloq.,* charley horse. See HINDRANCE, IMPOTENCE, PAIN, CONTRACTION.

crane, *n.* heron; derrick. See ELEVATION, ANGULARITY. —*v.* stretch, rubberneck. See VISION.

crank, *n.* handle, winder, key; quirk; eccentric, oddball, fanatic. *Colloq.,* grouch, crab. *Slang,* crackpot, screwball, nut. —*v.* crank up, start; wind, turn, twist. See UNCONFORMITY, ROTATION, ELEVATION.

cranky, *adj.* irritable (see IRASCIBILITY).

crash, *n.* collision, shock, smash, shattering; FAILURE, collapse, downfall; burst, blast. See DESTRUCTION, IMPULSE, LOUDNESS.

crass, *adj.* coarse, crude, gross, unrefined, raw; obtuse, dense, stupid. See VULGARITY, IGNORANCE.

crate, *v.* pack, box, encase. —*n.* box, shipping case. See RECEPTACLE.

crater, *n.* volcano; hole, OPENING, depression, pit, mouth. See CONCAVITY.

crave, *v.t.* DESIRE, long *or* yearn for; ask, beg, seek, solicit, supplicate, beseech, pray, petition; need, require. See NECESSITY, REQUEST.

craven, *adj. & n.* See COWARDICE.

craving, *n.* DESIRE.

crawl, *v.i.* creep, lag, drag; cringe, fawn, cower, grovel. See SERVILITY, SLOWNESS, LOWNESS.

crayon, *n.* grease *or* wax pencil, pastel, chalk. See PAINTING.

craze, *v.t.* derange, unbalance, madden, unsettle. See INSANITY. —*n.* fad, rage. See FASHION.

crazy, *adj.* insane (see INSANITY).

creak, *v.i.* squeak, stridulate. See LOUDNESS.

cream, *n. crème,* top milk, rich milk; best, flower, pick, elite; gist, kernel; paste, lotion. See GOODNESS, FLUIDITY, IMPORTANCE.

crease, *n.* FOLD, pleat; bend; mark, wrinkle, FURROW; scrape, wound, cut. —*v.* mark, FOLD, pleat, FURROW, wrinkle, wound.

create, *v.t.* CAUSE, make, form, bring into being, EFFECT, fashion, originate, occasion; produce, procreate, propagate, breed; devise, design, conceive, invent, construct; bring to pass; imagine, visualize, envisage. See PRODUCTION, IMAGINATION.

creator, *n.* God, Supreme Being;

author, maker, fashioner, originator, producer, inventor, designer. See CAUSE, PRODUCTION, DEITY.

creature, *n.* ANIMAL, beast; creation, being, thing; human being, individual, mortal; SERVANT, instrument, slave, tool, dependent; critter (*dial.*). See SUBSTANCE.

credence, *n.* BELIEF.

credentials, *n.pl.* papers, documents, dossier; voucher, pass, passport, license; diploma, *etc.* See INDICATION.

credible, *adj.* believable (see BELIEF).

CREDIT

Nouns—**1,** credit, trust, score, tally, account, tab; loan (see DEBT); letter of credit, draft, paper credit, floating capital; charge account; credit *or* debit card. *Colloq.,* tick. See ACCOUNTING.

2, creditor, lender, lessor, mortgagee.

Verbs—credit, charge; keep an account with, run up an account with; entrust, accredit; place to one's credit *or* account; give *or* take credit. *Slang,* fly a kite.

Adjectives—crediting, credited; accredited.

Adverbs—on credit, to the account *or* credit of, on deposit; on account; on time. *Colloq.,* on tick. *Slang,* on the cuff.

Antonyms, see DEBT.

creditable, *adj.* praiseworthy, honorable. See VIRTUE, RESPECT.

credo, *n.* creed, credenda. See BELIEF.

CREDULITY

Nouns—**1,** credulity, credulousness, gullibility; self-delusion, self-deception; superstition; one's blind side; blind faith. See BELIEF.

2, dupe, gull, April fool. *Colloq.,* sucker.

Verbs—**1,** be credulous, swallow [whole], gulp down, eat *or* lap up, swallow hook, line and sinker, fall for; take on trust *or* faith, take for granted, take for gospel; run away with a notion *or* idea, jump *or* rush to a conclusion; take the shadow for the substance; catch at straws; bite, take the bait; knock on wood.

2, impose upon, dupe, gull, delude, deceive (see DECEPTION).

Adjectives—credulous, gullible; easily deceived, unsuspecting, simple, green, soft, childish, silly, stupid; overcredulous, overconfident; superstitious.

Antonyms, see INCREDULITY.

creed, *n.* credo, BELIEF, tenet, doctrine, persuasion, dogma, faith; sect, denomination. See RELIGION.

creek, *n.* stream, brook. See WATER.

creep, *v.i.* crawl, worm, grovel. See SLOWNESS.

cremation, *n.* burning, incineration, suttee. See HEAT, INTERMENT.

crescent, *adj.* crescent-shaped, lunate, moon-shaped, luniform. See CURVATURE.

crest, *n.* crown, tuft, topknot, comb, plume; summit, peak, ridge, tip, HEIGHT, top; seal, device; culmination, climax. See PERFECTION.

crestfallen, *adj.* abashed, dejected. See DEJECTION.

crevice, *n.* cleft, split, fissure, break, breach, opening, DISJUNCTION, hole, slit, chink; nook, cranny, space, INTERVAL, cavity; crevasse.

crew, *n.* force, gang, band, set, squad; ASSEMBLAGE, company; sailors. See INHABITANT, PARTY.

crib, *n.* manger, trough, box, stall, bin; cot, bed, cradle; translation, key; *colloq.,* pony, trot. See RECEPTACLE, SUPPORT, STEALING.

crime, *n.* offense, WRONG; misdemeanor, felony, outrage; transgression, sin, evil, wrongdoing; ILLEGALITY, lawbreaking.

criminal, *n.* offender, malefactor, felon, sinner, culprit, convict. See ILLEGALITY, EVILDOER.

crimp, *v.t.* wave, curl, crinkle, wrinkle, ripple; gather, bunch, pinch, tighten, FOLD, pleat, plait. —*n.* curl; notch. See CONVOLUTION, FURROW.

cringe, *v.i.* cower, stoop, flinch, wince, crouch, shrink; fawn, truckle, crawl, grovel; sneak. See RECOIL, FEAR, SERVILITY.

crinkle, *v.* wrinkle, roughen, crease, crumple, rumple, ripple, FOLD, crimp, corrugate. —*n.* wrinkle, crease. See FURROW.

cripple, *v.t.* disable, incapacitate, unfit; lame, paralyze, maim; hurt, enfeeble, cramp. See IMPOTENCE, HINDRANCE, WEAKNESS.

crisis, *n.* turning point, juncture; exigency, emergency, extremity, pinch, trial, crux, crunch, climax. See CIRCUMSTANCE, DIFFICULTY, OCCASION.

crisp, *adj.* brittle, curly, blunt, friable; short, crunchy, crumbly; pithy, terse; COLD, stiff; firm, fresh; bracing. See BRITTLENESS, NEWNESS, SHORTNESS.

crisscross, *adj. & n.* See CROSSING.

criterion, *n.* standard, model, rule, test, measure, norm, touchstone. See MEASUREMENT.

critic, *n.* judge, connoisseur, expert, reviewer, commentator; censor, censurer. See DETRACTION, TASTE.

critical, *adj.* exacting, captious, censorious, faultfinding, disparaging; judicious, accurate, analytical; decisive; urgent, crucial; dangerous, risky. See DISAPPROBATION, IMPORTANCE, DETRACTION.

criticize, *v.t.* judge, censure, excoriate, blame, reprove, flay; examine, dissect, analyze, review; nitpick. *Slang,* roast, pan; badmouth. See DISAPPROBATION, DETRACTION, JUDGMENT.

critique, *n.* review, criticism. See JUDGMENT.

crockery, *n.* pottery, earthenware, ceramics. See MATERIALS.

crone, *n.* hag, witch. See AGE.

crony, *n.* chum, pal, FRIEND.

crook, *n.* bend, curve, hook; thief, robber. See CURVATURE, ILLEGALITY, STEALING.

crooked, *adj.* bent, curved, angular, sinuous, winding, askew, zigzag, twisted, warped; false, dishonest, fraudulent, deceptive, sneaking; oblique, aslant, distorted, awry. See IMPROBITY, DISTORTION.

croon, *v.* sing, serenade. See MUSIC.

crop, *n.* craw, gorge; whip; harvest, yield, fruit, product. See EFFECT, PUNISHMENT, AGRICULTURE.

cross, *n.* rood, crucifix; crosspiece, cross mark, X, ex; gibbet; burden, trial, trouble, ADVERSITY, affliction; hybrid, MIXTURE, crossbreed; halfcaste, halfbreed; (*cap.*) Christianity, the Church, Gospel. —*v.* crossbreed, cross-pollinate, mix; traverse, go across, ford; mark out, cancel, strike out; pass over, lie across *or* athwart; bar, line, crosshatch; circumvent, thwart, frustrate, foil, oppose, hinder, obstruct. See CROSSING, NULLIFICATION, OPPOSITION, TRAVEL. —*adj.* opposite, converse; peevish (see IRASCIBILITY).

cross-examine, *v.t.* See INQUIRY.

CROSSING

Nouns—**1,** crossing, intersection, crossroad[s], grade crossing; underpass, bridge, tunnel. See JUNCTION, CONNECTION.

2, crisscross; textile, fabric; decussation, transversion; intertexture, reticulation, network, net, plexus, web, mesh, twill, tissue, lace; warp, woof; wicker; mat[ting]; plait, trellis, wattle, lattice, grate, grating, grill[e], grid[iron], tracery, fretwork, reticle (see ORNAMENT); cross, braid, cat's cradle, knot; entanglement (see DISORDER). See CONVOLUTION, OBLIQUITY, TEXTURE.

Verbs—cross, go over, intersect, crisscross, interlace, intertwine, intertwist, interweave, interlink; decussate; twine, entwine, weave, inweave, reticulate, twist, wreathe; mat, plait, braid, twill; tangle, entangle, ravel; net, knot; raddle (*dial.*).

Adjectives—crossing, crossed, crisscross, antiparallel; matted, transverse; cross[-shaped], cruciate, cruciform, crucial, decussate; retiform, reticular, reticulate[d]; areolar, cancellated, grated, barred, streaked; textile.

Adverbs—across, athwart, transversely; crosswise, obliquely, sidewise.

Antonyms, see SIMILARITY.

---

crotch, *n.* fork, divergence, branch, corner; groin, inguinal region, inguen; genitals, genitalia. See ANGULARITY.

crouch, *v.i.* bend, squat, stoop; cower, cringe. See DEPRESSION, SERVILITY, FEAR.

crow, *v.* caw; brag, boast, gloat. See BOASTING, CRY. —*n.* raven, blackbird.

crowd, *n.* gathering, concourse, horde, press, mass, gang, mob, MULTITUDE; host, herd, swarm, rout, crush, throng; *colloq.*, set, coterie, clique; POPULACE, rabble, *hoi polloi.* See ASSEMBLAGE.

crown, *v.t.* coronate, wreathe, enthrone, adorn, invest, install; top, cap, head, crest; complete, perfect, round out, finish. See COMPLETION, IMPULSE, HEIGHT. —*n.* chaplet, circlet, diadem, coronet, aureole; laurel, wreath, garland, reward, prize; pate, crest, top. See CIRCULARITY, APPROBATION.

crucial, *adj.* decisive, determining, final; urgent, critical, supreme; trying, severe; cruciform. See IMPORTANCE, CROSSING.

crucifix, *n.* cross (see CROSSING).

crucify, *v.t.* See KILLING.

crude, *adj.* rough, raw, unfinished, imperfect, plain, unwrought, unrefined, incomplete; unprepared, sketchy; coarse, crass, rude, tasteless, gross, immature, vulgar, uncouth. See INELEGANCE, IMPERFECTION, UNPREPAREDNESS, VULGARITY.

cruel, *adj.* coldblooded, harsh, pitiless. See MALEVOLENCE, SEVERITY.

cruise, *n.* voyage, journey, *etc.;* sail; ride, flight. —*v.i.* voyage, sail, yacht, steam; soar, coast; wander, rove, roam, meander, range, hunt. See TRAVEL, NAVIGATION, AVIATION.

crumb, *n.* bit, fragment, scrap, mite, morsel, jot, ort; leaving, leftover. See PART, LITTLENESS, REMAINDER, POWDERINESS.

crumble, *v.i.* disintegrate, break up, fall to pieces; decay, degenerate. See DESTRUCTION, DETERIORATION, POWDERINESS, WEAKNESS.

crumple, *v.t.* rumple, wrinkle; *colloq.*, collapse. See FOLD, CONTRACTION, DESTRUCTION.

crunch, *v.* chew, crush, grind. See FOOD, POWDERINESS.

crusade, *n.* Holy War, jihad; campaign, cause, drive. See WARFARE.

crush, *v.t.* press, mash, squash, squeeze, bruise; overcome, conquer, vanquish, subdue, quell, overwhelm, suppress, blot out; shame, disconcert. See CONTRACTION, DESTRUCTION, POWDERINESS, HUMILITY. —*n.* press, pressure; crowd; *slang,* infatuation. *Slang,* thing. See ASSEMBLAGE, LOVE.

crust, *n.* cake, coating, rind, shell, hull, incrustation; *slang,* nerve (see COURAGE). See COVERING.

crutch, *n.* staff, walking stick; SUPPORT; crotch (see ANGULARITY).

crux, *n.* gist, key; crisis. See IMPORTANCE, DIFFICULTY.

CRY

Nouns—**1,** cry, shout, call (see *Verbs*); vociferation, exclamation, outcry, hullaballoo, chorus, clamor, hue and cry; Bronx cheer; plaint (see LAMENTATION); stentor (see LOUDNESS); bark, ululation. See SPEECH, SOUND.
2, crier, street vendor, hawker (see SALE), barker, herald.

Verbs—cry, roar, shout, bawl, bellow, halloo, halloa, whoop, yell, howl, give a cry, scream, screech, shriek, squeak, squeal, squall; whine, pule; pipe; call, caw, bark, bray, mew, mewl, ululate; weep (see LAMENTATION); cheer, hoot, shrill; snore, snort; vociferate, ejaculate; cry, call, *or* sing out, raise *or* lift up the voice, exclaim; strain the throat, voice *or* lungs, rend the air, thunder, shout at the top of one's voice *or* lungs.

Adjectives—crying, clamant, clamorous; vociferous; stentorian (see LOUDNESS).

Antonyms, see SILENCE.

---

crypt, *n.* vault, tomb. See INTERMENT, TEMPLE

cryptic, *adj.* hidden, SECRET, occult. See CONCEALMENT.

cryptograph, *n.* cipher, cryptogram, code. See CONCEALMENT.

crystal, *adj.* lucid, pellucid, crystalline, clear. See TRANSPARENCY.

cub, *n.* offspring, whelp, youngster, pup[py]; novice. See ANIMAL, YOUTH, BEGINNING.

cubbyhole, *n.* cubby, nook, compartment. See RECEPTACLE.

cube, *n.* solid, square, die; hexahedron. See ANGULARITY, NUMERATION. —*v.i.* dice, chop. See DISJUNCTION.

cuddle, *v.* snuggle, nestle, curl up, huddle; clasp, fondle. See ENDEARMENT.

cudgel, *n.* club, bludgeon, staff, shillelagh, stick. See ARMS.

cue, *n.* hint, clue, intimation; catchword, signal, password; cuestick. See INDICATION, INFORMATION, MEMORY.

cuisine, *n.* kitchen; cookery. See FOOD.

cull, *v.t.* select (see CHOICE).

culminate, *v.* crown; come to a head; conclude, finish. See COMPLETION, HEIGHT.

culpable, *adj.* guilty (see GUILT).

culprit, *n.* offender, malefactor, wrongdoer, EVILDOER. See GUILT.

cult, *n.* cultus, sect, RELIGION, denomination; WORSHIP, devotion; school [of thought], BELIEF; mystique, fad, craze, vogue.

cultivate, *v.t.* farm, till, work, grow, develop; civilize, refine; pursue, court; foster, advance, cherish. See AGRICULTURE, IMPROVEMENT.

cultivation, *n.* farming, tillage, husbandry, AGRICULTURE; elevation, civilization, refinement, breeding; learning, education; pursuit. See IMPROVEMENT, COURTESY.

culture, *n.* cultivation, tillage; development, education, learning; enlightenment; refinement, breeding, polish; civilization. See AGRICULTURE, COURTESY, IMPROVEMENT, KNOWLEDGE.

culvert, *n.* conduit, drain. See PASSAGE.

cumbersome, *adj.* cumbrous, unwieldy, clumsy, burdensome, ponderous, oppressive. See HINDRANCE.

CUNNING

Nouns—**1,** cunning, craft, craftiness; gumption; slyness; subtlety, finesse, maneuvering. See SKILL, INTELLIGENCE.
2, chicane, chicanery, knavery, guile. See DECEPTION, IMPROBITY.
3, art, artifice; device, machination; diplomacy, Machiavellianism; plot,

PLAN, maneuver, coup, stratagem, contrivance, feint, gambit, dodge, artful dodge, wile, trick; trickery, DECEPTION; ruse, side-blow, shift, go by, subterfuge; *tour de force,* tricks of the trade.

4, schemer, intriguer, strategist; diplomat, politician; Machiavelli; sly boots, knave, fox, Renard. *Colloq.,* slicker, grafter, Philadelphia lawyer.

Verbs—be cunning, contrive, machinate, PLAN, live by one's wits; chicane (see DECEPTION); play both ends against the middle; maneuver, scheme, finagle, play a deep game, play tricks (with); be too much for, get the better of.

Adjectives—cunning, crafty, clever, calculating, artful; skillful (see SKILL); subtle, feline, vulpine; roguish; cunning as a fox, cunning as the serpent; deep[-laid]; arch, designing, scheming, contriving; strategic, diplomatic, politic, Machiavellian, artificial, tricky, shifty, wily, sly (see DECEPTION); shrewd, acute; sharp [as a needle]; canny, astute, knowing, up to snuff, too clever by half.

Adverbs—cunningly, slyly, on the sly.

Antonyms, see UNSKILLFULNESS.

---

cup, *n.* mug, tankard, chalice, goblet; [Holy] Grail; excavation, hollow, crater. See RECEPTACLE, CONCAVITY, APPROBATION.

cupboard, *n.* closet, storeroom; buffet, locker, press; pantry. See RECEPTACLE.

cupola, *n.* vault, dome. See CONVEXITY.

curate, *n.* See CLERGY.

curator, *n.* librarian; custodian, overseer, guardian. See SAFETY, DIRECTOR.

curb, *v.t.* restrain, subdue, control, check, repress; guide, manage; slacken, retard. —*n.* RESTRAINT, check, control; curb market; curbstone. See HINDRANCE.

curdle, *v.* clabber; curd, clot, thicken, coagulate, congeal, lump; separate; spoil, turn, sour. See DENSITY, DETERIORATION, SOURNESS.

cure, *v.t.* heal, restore, relieve; preserve, dry, smoke, tan, pickle. See REMEDY, PRESERVATION.

curfew, *n.* bedtime, vespers; siren, tocsin, whistle. See INDICATION.

curio, *n.* bric-a-brac, knickknack, objet d'art, ORNAMENT, whatnot, antique, gewgaw, gimcrack.

CURIOSITY

Nouns—**1,** curiosity, curiousness; interest, thirst for knowledge; inquiring mind; inquisitiveness; meddling, nosiness; sightseeing; voyeurism. See INFORMATION.

2, sightseer; questioner (see INQUIRY); gossip, busybody, quidnunc; peeping Tom, voyeur, Paul Pry; eavesdropper. *Colloq.,* snooper, nosy Parker. *Slang,* rubberneck.

Verbs—be curious, take an interest in; stare, prick up the ears; sightsee, see sights; pry, peep, eavesdrop; gossip; meddle. *Colloq.,* snoop. *Slang,* rubberneck, dish the dirt.

Adjectives—curious, inquisitiveness, burning with curiosity, overcurious, curious as a cat; inquiring (see INQUIRY); prying, nosy, meddlesome; inquisitorial.

Antonyms, see INDIFFERENCE.

---

curl, *v.* roll, wave, ripple, spiral, twist, coil. See CONVOLUTION, CURVATURE.

curlicue, *n.* curl, twist. See CONVOLUTION.

currency, *n.* MONEY, coin, specie;

publicity, circulation; topicality, timeliness. See PUBLICATION, NEWNESS.

current, *adj.* common, prevalent, PRESENT, in vogue, prevailing; accepted, abroad, rife; existing, circulating, rumored. See PUBLICATION, GENERALITY, NEWS. —*n.* stream, flow; movement, tendency; draft. See WIND, WATER, DIRECTION, COURSE.

curse, *v.* execrate, damn, swear, denounce; blaspheme. —*n.* malediction, IMPRECATION, execration, anathema; bane, plague. See EVIL, ADVERSITY.

cursory, *adj.* hasty, superficial. See HASTE.

curt, *adj.* short, concise, brief, succinct; snappish, tart, rude, brusque, bluff, blunt, abrupt. See SHORTNESS, DISCOURTESY.

curtail, *v.t.* shorten, clip, cut, abbreviate; abate, diminish, reduce, lessen, abridge; deprive. See SHORTNESS, DECREASE, DISCONTINUANCE.

curtain, *n.* screen, veil, valance, drapery, portiere, hanging, blind, shade. See CONCEALMENT.

curtsy, *n.* bow, reverence. See COURTESY.

curvaceous, *adj., colloq.,* buxom, voluptuous. See BEAUTY.

CURVATURE

Nouns—**1,** curvature, curving, curvity, curvation; incurvity, incurvation; flexure, crook, hook, bend[ing]; deflection, inflection; arcuation, devexity, turn; recurvity, recurvation; ROTUNDITY; curl[ing], sinuosity (see CONVOLUTION). See CIRCULARITY, CONVEXITY, CONCAVITY, FOLD.

2, curve, arc, arch, vault, bow, crescent, half moon, horseshoe, crane-neck, parabola, hyperbola; caternary, festoon; conchoid, cardioid, caustic; tracery (see ORNAMENT).

Verbs—**1,** be curved, sweep, swag, sag; turn, incurve.

2, curve, bend, incurve, incurvate, double up; deflect, inflect; crook; turn, round, arch, arcuate, arch over, bow, curl, recurve.

Adjectives—curved, curviform, curvilineal, curvilinear; recurved, recurvate; bowed, vaulted, hooked; falciform, falcated; semicircular, crescentic; liniform, lunilar; semilunar; conchoidal; cordiform, cordated; heart-, bell-, pear-, *or* fig-shaped; cardioid; hook-shaped, crescent[-shaped]; kidney-shaped, reniform; lens-shaped, lentiform, lenticular; arcuate[d]; bowlegged (see DISTORTION).

Antonyms, see STRAIGHTNESS, ANGULARITY.

---

cushion, *n.* pillow, bolster; ottoman. hassock; fender, bumper, *etc.;* buffer. —*v.t.* pad, soften, ease, absorb; protect, buffer, come between; soften the blow, let down easy. See SUPPORT, SOFTNESS, RELIEF.

custody, *n.* care, [safe]keeping, charge, protection; imprisonment, bondage. See SAFETY, RESTRAINT, RETENTION.

custom, *n.* practice, use, usage, wont, FASHION, precedent, RULE; HABIT, *mores,* convention; patronage, support, trade; (*pl.*) [import] duties. See CONFORMITY, PRICE, REGULARITY, PLAN.

customer, *n.* buyer (see PURCHASE).

cut, *v.t.* incise, carve, dissect, slice, shave, trim, shape; separate, divide, split, sever; abridge, shorten, diminish, reduce, curtail; hurt, sting, wound, snub, ignore; reap, gather. See DISJUNCTION, SHORTNESS, WEAKNESS, NEGLECT, DISCOURTESY, PAIN. —*n.* style, manner; woodcut (see ENGRAVING). See FORM.

cutback, *n.* reduction; retrenchment. See DECREASE, ECONOMY.

cute, *adj.* attractive, pretty; coy. *Colloq.,* cutesy. See BEAUTY.

cut-rate, *adj.* cheap, reduced. See CHEAPNESS.

cutthroat, *n.* murderer, thug. See KILLING. —*adj.* relentless. See SEVERITY, CONTENTION.

cutting, *adj.* sharp, incisive, keen-edged; biting, stinging, acrimonious, sarcastic, caustic, tart; bitter, raw, nippy. See DISAPPROBATION, SHARPNESS, COLD, RIDICULE.

cycle, *n.* period, age, epoch; circle, round; bicycle, velocipede, tricycle; motorcycle. See REGULARITY, CIRCUIT, VEHICLE.

cyclone, *n.* tornado, twister, gale, hurricane; vortex. See VIOLENCE.

cylinder, *n.* barrel, tube, roller, *etc.* See ROTUNDITY.

cynic, *n.* misanthrope, pessimist; philosopher. See THOUGHT, MALEVOLENCE.

cynical, *adj.* misanthropic, sneering, satirical, pessimistic, distrustful, sarcastic, cutting, disdainful, contemptuous, censorious; surly, snarling, captious. See CONTEMPT, DISAPPROBATION, MALEVOLENCE.

czar, *n.* tsar, emperor, caesar, kaiser, king, Czar of all the Russias; despot. See AUTHORITY.

D

dab, *n.* spot, pinch, bit. See LITTLENESS. —*v.* pat, tap. See IMPULSE.

dabble, *v.* splash, spatter; patter, trifle, fritter away. See WATER, INACTIVITY.

daffy, *adj., colloq.,* daft, crazy, silly. See FOLLY, INSANITY.

dagger, *n.* dirk, stiletto, poniard, knife, bodkin. See ARMS.

daily, *adj.* everyday, diurnal, quotidian; once a day. See FREQUENCY, REGULARITY.

dainty, *adj.* delicate, exquisite; fastidious, neat; delicious. See BEAUTY, TASTE, CARE, FOOD.

dais, *n.* platform, stage. See SUPPORT.

dally, *v.i.* delay, prolong, idle; trifle, flirt, philander. See AMUSEMENT, LATENESS.

dam, *n.* dike, seawall, levee, breakwater, embankment, floodgate. —*v.t.* embank, sandbag; clog, plug, stop up, jam. See ENCLOSURE, HINDRANCE, CLOSURE.

damage, *v.t.* harm, injure, mar, impair. —*n.* DETERIORATION, harm, injury; (*pl.*), amends, recompense (see COMPENSATION). See WEAKNESS, WRONG.

damn, *v.t.* See CONDEMNATION, DISAPPROBATION, IMPRECATION.

damp, *adj.* dank, humid, moist. —*v.t.* dampen, dispirit, deaden; smother, muffle, subdue; wet, moisten. See SILENCE, MODERATION, DEJECTION, DISSUASION, MOISTURE.

dance, *n.* ball; hop, prom. —*v.i.* glide, jug, flutter. *Colloq.,* trip the light fantastic. See AGITATION, AMUSEMENT, LEAP, OSCILLATION.

dandy, *n.* beau, coxcomb, dude, fop, macaroni. See AFFECTION. —*adj.* fine, excellent. See GOODNESS.

DANGER

Nouns—**1,** danger, peril, jeopardy, risk, hazard, THREAT, adventure, insecurity, precariousness, slipperiness; Russian roulette (see CHANCE).

2, exposure, vulnerability; vulnerable point, Achilles' heel, glass jaw.

3, forlorn hope, dangerous course, leap in the dark (see RASHNESS), road to ruin; hairbreadth escape; cause for alarm, breakers ahead, storm brewing, gathering clouds; apprehension (see WARNING).

4, pitfall; trap, snare; whirlpool, maelstrom, ambush, *etc.;* clay pigeon.

Verbs—**1,** be in danger; be exposed to danger, run into *or* encounter danger; run a risk, lay oneself open to (see LIABILITY); lean on a broken reed, feel the ground sliding *or* slipping from under one; have to run for it; have the odds against one; sit, sleep, *or* stand on a volcano, hang by a thread, totter [on the brink], sit on a barrel of gunpowder, sit on a powderkeg, sit on dynamite, live in a glass house.

2, endanger; bring, place, *or* put in danger, expose to danger, imperil, jeopardize, compromise, throw to the wolves.
3, adventure, play with fire, tempt fate, take a chance, take one's life in one's hands, skate on thin ice, risk one's neck; run the gantlet, go through the mill, go through hell and high water; dare (see COURAGE); engage in a forlorn hope, sail too near the wind (see RASHNESS). See CHANCE, DEFIANCE.
4, be dangerous, bear watching.

Adjectives—**1,** dangerous, hazardous, perilous, parlous, fateful; at stake, in question; precarious, ticklish, slippery, fraught with danger; built on sand, hanging *or* trembling in the balance, touch and go; threatening (see WARNING); explosive. *Slang,* hairy.
2, in danger, endangered, unsafe, unprotected, insecure; defenseless, unshielded, vulnerable, pregnable, exposed, open (to); at bay, on the rocks; hanging by a thread, between life and death, between Scylla and Charybdis, between two fires, between the Devil and the deep blue sea; on the edge, in deep [water], out on a limb, on the brink *or* verge of a precipice, in the lion's den, on slippery ground, on thin ice, under fire, not out of the woods; with one's back to the wall, on the spot; unprepared, off one's guard; helpless, in a bad way, in the last extremity.

Antonyms, see SAFETY.

---

dangle, *v.i.* hang, suspend; swing. See PENDENCY.

dank, *adj.* humid, moist. See MOISTURE.

dapper, *adj.* neat, trim; diminutive. See FASHION, LITTLENESS.

dare, *v.t.* face, defy, challenge, brave; venture upon *or* into. See DEFIANCE, COURAGE, RASHNESS.

daredevil, *adj.* rash, reckless. See RASHNESS.

DARKNESS

Nouns—**1,** darkness, dark; blackness, OBSCURITY, gloom, murk; dusk (see DIMNESS); CLOUDINESS; shade, shadow, umbra, penumbra; skiagraphy; shading.
2, Cimmerian darkness, Stygian darkness, night, midnight, dead of night, witching hour, dark of the moon.
3, obscuration, adumbration, obfuscation; extinction, extinguishment, [total *or* partial] eclipse; blackout, dimout; darkroom, camera obscura.

Verbs—darken, bedarken, obscure, shade; black out; dim; overcast, overshadow (see CLOUDINESS); eclipse; obfuscate, adumbrate, cast into the shade *or* shadow; cast, throw, *or* spread a shadow; put, blow, *or* snuff out, extinguish, douse; turn out *or* off.

Adjectives—dark, darksome, darkling, darkened; obscure, tenebrous, somber, pitch dark, pitchy, Cimmerian, Stygian; black (see COLOR); sunless, moonless, lightless; dusky; unilluminated; nocturnal; lurid, gloomy, murky, shady, umbrageous; dark as pitch *or* as a pit.

Adverbs—darkly, in the dark, in the shade.

Antonyms, see LIGHT.

---

darling, *n.* sweetheart, dearest, dear one, angel, treasure; hero, pet, idol, fair-haired boy. —*adj.* beloved, favorite; charming, winsome, adorable, cute. See ENDEARMENT.

dart, *v.* hurl, cast, throw; spring, rush; dartle. —*n.* spear, javelin, arrow; dash; seam. See ARMS, VELOCITY, HASTE, PROPULSION.

dash, *v.* shatter, smash; frustrate,

dishearten; hurl, cast; dart. See DESTRUCTION, DEJECTION, HASTE, PROPULSION. —*n.* élan, spirit; spurt, *soupçon,* trace. See ACTIVITY, VELOCITY, LITTLENESS, ENERGY, OSTENTATION.

dashing, *adj.* high-spirited, gay; showy, stylish. See FASHION.

data, *n.pl.* facts, EVIDENCE, INFORMATION.

date, *n.* day, TIME, moment; age, era, epoch; *colloq.,* rendezvous, tryst; *colloq.* escort, suitor, steady, blind date. —*v.* place [in time], begin, start; outmode, age; *colloq.,* court, escort, take out, show the town *or* a good time, go [out] with, go steady. See SOCIALITY, CHRONOMETRY, OLDNESS.

daub, *v.* smear, spread. See COVERING.

daunt, *v.t.* intimidate, cow, dismay, discourage. See FEAR, DEJECTION.

dawdle, *v.i.* idle, loiter, loaf, waste *or* kill time. *Colloq.,* goldbrick. *Slang,* goofoff. See INACTIVITY, SLOWNESS.

dawn, *n.* BEGINNING, origin, inception. See DIMNESS.

day, *n.* daytime, LIGHT; dawn, daybreak; around the clock; era, period. See TIME.

daybreak *n.* dawn, sunrise. See EARLINESS.

daydream, *n.* reverie, castle in the air, fancy. See HOPE, IMAGINATION, INATTENTION.

daze, *v.t.* confuse, dazzle, bewilder, awe; stun, shock, stupefy. See SURPRISE, INSENSIBILITY.

dazzle, *v.t.* blind; impress, overpower; dumfound, bewilder. See RESPECT, SURPRISE, VISION.

dead, *adj.* deceased, perished, defunct; lifeless, inanimate; obsolete, extinct. See DEATH, NONEXISTENCE, INSENSIBILITY.

deadbeat, *n., slang,* sponger. See DEBT, NONPAYMENT.

deaden, *v.t.* benumb; muffle; damp. See INSENSIBILITY, IMPOTENCE, SILENCE.

deadline, *n.* time LIMIT.

deadlock, *n.* impasse, bottleneck, stalemate; standoff, tie, draw, even match; hung jury. See EQUALITY, DIFFICULTY.

deadly, *adj.* lethal, fatal; malignant; *colloq.,* dull. See KILLING, DISEASE, WEARINESS.

deadpan, *adj., slang,* expressionless. See UNMEANINGNESS.

DEAFNESS

Nouns—**1,** deafness, hardness of hearing, surdity; deafmutism.
2, lip-reading, deaf-and-dumb alphabet, dactylology, manual alphabet, hand signals, signing; closed *or* open captions.
3, deafmute, lip reader, deaf-and-dumb person.
4, see INATTENTION.

Verbs—**1,** be deaf, have no ear; shut *or* close one's ears, turn a deaf ear to.
2, deafen, stun, split the ears.

Adjectives—**1,** deaf, earless, surd; hard *or* dull of hearing, unhearing; deafmute, deaf and dumb; stone-deaf, deafened, deaf as a post; tone deaf.
2, inattentive, oblivious of (see INATTENTION).

Antonyms, see HEARING.

---

deal, *v.t.* apportion, allocate, allot, distribute; BARTER; inflict; give, bestow, dole. See APPORTIONMENT, GIVING.

dear, *adj.* expensive (see DEARNESS); precious, beloved, cherished, darling. —*n.* darling, beloved, love, dearie, honey, sweetheart. See LOVE, ENDEARMENT.

DEARNESS

Nouns—dearness, costliness, high *or* famine price, pretty penny; overcharge; extravagance, exorbitance; heavy pull upon the purse, an arm and a leg; inflation (see INCREASE). *Slang,* highway robbery.

Verbs—be dear, cost much, cost a pretty penny; rise in price, look up; overcharge, jack up [the price]; soak, bleed [white], fleece, extort (see STEALING); pay too much; pay through the nose, pay dear.

Adjectives—dear, high, high priced; of great price, expensive, costly, precious, dear bought; unreasonable, excessive, extravagant, exorbitant, extortionate; at a premium, not to be had for love or money, beyond *or* above price; priceless, of priceless value, invaluable; worth its weight in gold, more precious than rubies, more precious than life itself. *Colloq.,* pricy.

Adverbs—dear, dearly; at great cost.

Antonyms, see CHEAPNESS.

DEATH

Nouns—**1,** death, expiration, decease, demise, the grave; END, cessation; loss, extinction, *or* ebb of life; dissolution, departure, passing on *or* away; release, [eternal] rest, quietus, fall; loss, bereavement.

2, death warrant, death watch, death rattle, deathbed; stroke, agonies, *or* shades of death; valley of the shadow of death, jaws *or* hand of death; last breath, last gasp, last agonies; dying day *or* breath; swan song; *rigor mortis;* Stygian shore. *Slang,* curtains, last roundup.

3, Death, King of terrors, King of Death; Grim Reaper, angel of death, Azrael; mortality, doom.

4, natural, sudden, *or* violent death, untimely end, drowning, watery grave; suffocation, asphyxia; DISEASE, fatality; death blow; euthanasia; suicide (see KILLING).

5, necrology, bills of mortality; obituary, obit; death song (see LAMENTATION).

6, corpse, body, cadaver, carcass; [mortal] remains; [dry] bones, skeleton, relics; dust, ashes, earth, clay; mummy, fossil, carrion, food for worms *or* fishes; tenement of clay, this mortal coil; the deceased, the decedent, the departed; zombie; shade, ghost. *Slang,* stiff.

Verbs—**1,** die [off], expire, perish, go; drown, smother; suffocate; meet one's death *or* end; pass away, be taken, yield *or* resign one's breath, resign one's being *or* life, end one's days *or* life, breathe one's last, cease to live *or* breathe, depart this life; be no more; lose, lay down, relinquish, *or* surrender one's life; sink into the grave, close one's eyes, fall dead, drop [down] dead, succumb; break one's neck, give up *or* yield the ghost; die in harness; walk the plank; die with one's boots on *or* in one's boots; die a violent death. *Colloq.,* bite the dust, cash in [one's chips]. *Slang,* kick off, kick the bucket, check out, croak, pop off, take a ride, sign off, turn up one's toes.

2, put to death (see KILLING); pay the debt to nature, shuffle off this mortal coil, take one's last sleep, go the way of all flesh; come, turn, *or* return to dust, cross the Styx, go to one's long account *or* one's last home, go west, go to Davy Jones' locker, cross the bar; receive one's death warrant, make one's will, die a natural death, go out like a candle; come to an untimely end; catch one's death.

Adjectives—**1,** dead, lifeless; deceased, demised, departed, defunct; late, gone, no more; asleep; exanimate, inanimate; out of the world, taken off, released, departed this life, dead and gone, launched into eternity, gathered to one's fathers, numbered with the dead; stillborn, extinct. *Colloq.*, dead as a doornail, stone dead, stiff.

2, fatal, deadly (see KILLING).

3, dying, moribund, *in extremis,* in the jaws of death; mortally ill *or* wounded; going [off], on one's deathbead; at the point of death, at death's door, at the last gasp, done for, on one's last legs, on the spot; with one foot in the grave, as good as dead, done for.

Antonyms, see LIFE.

---

deathless, *adj.* immortal, lasting. See PERPETUITY.

debacle, *n.* FAILURE; stampede, panic. See REVOLUTION, DESTRUCTION.

debar, *v.t.* exclude, shut out. See EXCLUSION, PROHIBITION.

debasement, *n.* abasement, debauchery, corruption, degradation, DISREPUTE; adulteration, impairment, impurity. See WEAKNESS, DETERIORATION.

debate, *n.* argument, dispute, controversy; forum, panel discussion; war of words. —*v.* argue, discuss, dispute; bandy words, take sides, lock horns, contend; reflect, consider. See CONVERSATION, REASONING.

debauch, *v.* corrupt, ruin. See IMPURITY.

debilitate, *v.t.* See WEAKNESS.

debit, *n.* & *v.* See DEBT.

debonair, *adj.* courteous; gay, affable. See CHEERFULNESS.

debris, *n.* rubbish, rubble, detritus, wreckage, ruins, trash. See REMAINDER, PART.

DEBT

Nouns—**1,** debt, indebtedness, obligation, LIABILITY, debit, score; charge, charge account; arrears, deferred payment, deficit, default; insolvency, nonpayment, bankruptcy, bad debt; interest, usury; floating debt *or* capital. See ACCOUNTING, INSUFFICIENCY, FAILURE, POVERTY, NONPAYMENT.

2, debtor, debitor; mortgagor; defaulter; borrower. *Slang,* deadbeat.

3, lending, loan, advance, accommodation; encumbrance; financing, mortgage; borrowing, raising money, pledging, hypothecation, pawning.

4, lender, banker, mortgagee, pawnbroker, pawnshop.

Verbs—**1,** be in debt, owe; incur *or* contract a debt; run up a bill *or* a score, run up an account; borrow; run *or* get into debt; accrue debts; outrun the constable; answer for, go bail for, bail out. *Colloq.,* run a tab, go on tick. *Slang,* touch, go broke.

2, lend, advance, finance, accommodate (with), loan, encumber; mortgage, hypothecate, pledge, pawn, borrow from Peter to pay Paul. *Colloq.,* hock.

3, repudiate, stop payment, dishonor; charge *or* write off. See NONPAYMENT.

Adjectives—**1,** indebted, liable, chargeable, answerable for, in debt, in embarrassed circumstances, in difficulties, encumbered, involved, plunged *or* deep in debt, short, up against it, in the red, in the hole, fast tied up; bankrupt, insolvent; minus, out of pocket. *Colloq.,* in hock. *Slang,* broke, on the cuff.

2, unpaid; unrequited, unrewarded; owing, due, past due, in arrears, outstanding; delinquent.

Antonyms, see PAYMENT, CREDIT.

debut, *n*. See BEGINNING.

decadent, *adj*. ruined, fallen; depraved, debauched, dissolute; sentimental, nostalgic; blasé, cynical. See DETERIORATION, IMPURITY.

decapitate, *v.t*. behead, chop off one's head. See KILLING.

decay, *n*. DECOMPOSITION, DETERIORATION, disintegration, dilapidation, putrefaction, rot, caries. —*v.i*. rot, putrefy, mortify; disintegrate. See OLDNESS, UNCLEANNESS.

decease, *n*. & *v*. See DEATH.

deceive, *v*., **deceit,** *n*. See DECEPTION.

decent, *adj*. decorous, chaste, pure in heart; acceptable, reasonable, tolerable; virtuous, modest, respectable. See PROBITY, REPUTE, MODESTY.

DECEPTION

Nouns—**1,** deception, deceptiveness; falseness, FALSEHOOD, untruth; imposition, imposture, misinformation; fraud, fraudulence, deceit, deceitfulness, speciousness, guile, bluff; bad *or* rubber check, bad paper; knavery (see CUNNING). See ERROR.

2, delusion, illusion, gullery; juggling, jugglery; sleight of hand, legerdemain, prestidigitation, magic (see SORCERY); trickery, chicanery; cozenage, circumvention, collusion; treachery (see IMPROBITY); practical joke, trick, hoax, cheat, blind, feint, plant; bubble (see IMAGINATION); fetch, catch, juggle, reach, hocus, hokey-pokey, fake, hanky-panky, blarney; weasel words; thimble-rig, card-sharping, artful dodge, swindle, racket, shell game; stratagem, artifice. *Slang,* sell, spoof, con game, gyp, scam, sting.

3, snare, trap, springe, gin, decoy, come-on; bait, decoy duck, baited trap (see ATTRACTION); mousetrap, beartrap, steel trap, mantrap; cobweb, net, toils; trapdoor, sliding panel, false bottom; spring-net, spring-gun, masked battery; booby trap. *Slang,* clip joint.

4, mockery, IMITATION, counterfeit, sham, make-believe, forgery, fraud, fake, lie; hollow mockery; whited sepulcher; tinsel, paste, false *or* counterfeit jewelry, glass; man of straw; ormolu; jerrybuilding; mirage; German silver; Britannia metal. *Colloq.,* phony. *Slang,* gold brick.

5, deceiver, trickster, sharper, swindler, liar, snake [in the grass]; humbug, charlatan, quack, mountebank, fast talker; impostor, fraud, fake[r], sham, hoax[er], cheat; pretender, Judas; wolf in sheep's clothing, cheat; magician, conjuror; dodger, swindler, *etc*. *Slang,* con man, fourflusher, ringer. See STEALING.

6, dupe, gull, victim. *Colloq.,* sucker. *Slang,* pigeon. See CREDULITY.

Verbs—**1,** deceive, take in; defraud, cheat, jockey, cozen, fleece, nab, play one false, do in, bilk, bite, pluck, swindle, hustle, victimize, gull, hoax, dupe, take, rope in; stuff the ballot box; abuse, mystify, blind one's eyes; kid; blindfold, hoodwink, take for a ride; throw dust into the eyes; impose, practice, play, put, palm, *or* foist upon; snatch a verdict; palm off; circumvent, overreach, outreach, outwit, outmaneuver, finagle, get around, cross up; steal a march upon, give the go-by, leave in the lurch. *Colloq.,* gouge, slip one over on, diddle. *Slang,* clip, give the runaround, chisel, con.

2, set *or* lay a trap, lay a snare for; bait the hook, spread the toils, decoy, lure, beguile, delude, inveigle, suck in; hook, trick, entrap, ensnare, throw a curve, trip up; nick, springe; catch in a trap; hocus, practice on one's credulity, fool, befool, pull the wool over one's eyes, pull one's leg; humbug, bamboozle, flimflam, bilk, put one *or* something over (on); stuff up, sell; play a trick upon; play a practical joke upon; send on a fool's errand, make a game of, make a fool of, make an April fool of, make an ass of; come over, dissemble, lie (see FALSEHOOD); misinform, brainwash, mislead (see ERROR); throw off the scent; betray. *Slang,* fourflush.

3, load the dice, stack the cards *or* deck; live by one's wits, play at hide and seek; obtain money under false pretenses (see STEALING); conjure, juggle, practice chicanery; pass, palm, foist, *or* fob off.

Adjectives—**1,** deceived, caught; hoist with one's own petard.

2, deceiving, guileful, CUNNING, deceptive, deceitful, devious, delusive, delusory, colored; illusive, illusory; elusive, insidious; untrue (see FALSEHOOD); mock, sham, make-believe, counterfeit, pseudo, spurious, so-called, pretended, feigned, trumped up, bogus, fraudulent, tricky, factitious, artificial, bastard, fake; surreptitious, underhand[ed], illegitimate, contraband, adulterated, sophisticated; unsound, rotten at the core; disguised, meretricious; tinsel, pinchbeck; catchpenny; brummagem; simulated, plated. *Colloq.,* doctored, phony.

Adverbs—deceptively, *etc.;* under false colors, under cover of; behind one's back, cunningly; slyly; on the sly.

Antonyms, see PROBITY, TRUTH.

---

decide, *v.* determine, elect, choose, settle, fix; make up one's mind; arbitrate. See RESOLUTION, CHOICE, CERTAINTY, CAUSE.

decimate, *v.* destroy, wipe out. See KILLING, DESTRUCTION.

decipher, *v.t.* make out, decode; translate, interpret. See INTERPRETATION.

decision, *n.* firmness, RESOLUTION; JUDGMENT, determination; verdict, finding. See LAWSUIT.

decisive, *adj.* final, conclusive, resolute. See RESOLUTION, CERTAINTY.

deck, *n.* floor, platform, flooring; quarterdeck, forecastle, fo'c'sle; after, boat, flight, *etc.* deck; pack [of cards]. —*v.t.* deck out, bedeck, ORNAMENT, array, adorn, decorate; *slang,* knock down (see IMPULSE). See COVERING, SHIP.

declaim, *v.i.* recite, harangue, rant. See SPEECH.

declaration, *n.* AFFIRMATION, proclamation, statement, assertion, avowal. See SPEECH, EVIDENCE.

decline, *n.* droop, slant, slope; decadence, wasting, aging, DETERIORATION. —*v.* worsen, slump; refuse, turn down (an offer). See OLDNESS, AGE, REFUSAL, DESCENT, WEAKNESS, RECESSION.

DECOMPOSITION

Nouns—decomposition, disintegration, decay, corruption (see UNCLEANNESS); analysis, dissection, resolution, dissolution, break-up; DISPERSION; DISJUNCTION.

Verbs—decompose, decompound, disintegrate; corrupt; analyze, dissolve; resolve, separate into its elements; catalyze, electrolyze; dissect, break up *or* down; disperse; unravel, unroll; crumble into dust.

Adjectives—decomposed, corrupt, decayed; analytical.

Antonyms, see COMPOSITION.

---

decor, *n.* decoration. See ORNAMENT.

decoration, *n.* ORNAMENT, garnishment, trimming; trophy, ribbon, *etc.* (see APPROBATION).

decorum, *n.* decency; protocol. See AGREEMENT, FASHION.

decoy, *v.t.* entice, lure, entrap. See ATTRACTION, DECEPTION.

DECREASE

Nouns—**1,** decrease, diminution; lessening, subtraction (see DEDUCTION); reduction, abatement; shrinking, CONTRACTION, extenuation; cut back, discount. See SHORTNESS.

2, subsidence, wane, ebb, decline; let up; decrement, reflux, depreciation; DETERIORATION; mitigation (see MODERATION).

Verbs—**1,** decrease, diminish, lessen, shrink; drop, fall, *or* tail off; fall away, wane, ebb; descend, subside, let up; melt, die, *or* fade away; retire into the shade, fall to a low ebb, die down; run low, out, dry, *or* short, wear away; dwindle, slacken, peter out.

2, abate, bate; discount, depreciate, lower; attenuate, extenuate, mitigate, moderate; cut to the bone; cut back, down, *or* into; curtail, reduce; step, turn, *or* scale down, take in; demote, downgrade.

Adjectives—unincreased, decreased, decreasing, short, diminishing, waning, wasting away, wearing out, reduced, lessening, ebbing, dwindling, petering out, fading, disappearing, vanishing, falling off; dwarfish.

Adverbs—on the wane, on the decrease, smaller and smaller, less and less.

Antonyms, see INCREASE.

---

decree, *n.* COMMAND, edict, ordinance, law, fiat; JUDGMENT. See LEGALITY.

decrepit, *adj.* delapidated, broken-down; shaky; doddering, senile. *Colloq.*, on one's last legs, ready for the scrap heap. See DETERIORATION, DISEASE, WEAKNESS.

decry, *v.* blame, censure. See DISAPPROBATION.

dedicate, *v.t.* devote, consecrate; inscribe. See USE, REPUTE.

deduce, *v.* infer, conclude, derive; reason, reckon, assume, opine, think, believe. See REASONING.

DEDUCTION

Nouns—**1,** deduction, removal, excision; subtraction, subtrahend, minuend; minus, minus sign; abstraction, abbreviation, curtailment (see SHORTNESS); reduction (see DECREASE); retrenchment; amputation, truncation.

2, decrement, discount, rebate.

3, censorship, expurgation, bowdlerization; castration, circumcision; excision, deletion, editing; editor, censor.

Verbs—**1,** deduct, subduct, subtract, take away; remove, excise, cut out, rub off, wipe out, rule out; abstract, abbreviate, curtail; reduce; retrench; amputate, dock, truncate; deduce, discount; abate, rebate, write off; pare, shave, prune.

2, censor, expurgate, bowdlerize, cut, edit; castrate, circumcise; excise, delete, edit; abridge (see SHORTNESS).

Adjectives—deducted, deductive, deducible, subtractive; sawed off.

Prepositions—minus, diminished by, less; without, except, barring, excluding.

Antonyms, see ADDITION.

---

deed, *n.* act, ACTION, feat, achievement, exploit; conveyance, TRANSFER. See COURAGE, RECORD.

deem, *v.* consider, judge, regard; assess. *Colloq.,* calculate, reckon. See JUDGMENT.

deep, *adj. & n.* See DEPTH, CUNNING.

deface, *v.t.* mar, disfigure, mutilate, blemish; maim, mangle, scar. See DETERIORATION, FORMLESSNESS.

defame, *v.t.* traduce, vilify, revile, calumniate, asperse, abuse, malign, slander. See DISREPUTE, DETRACTION.

default, *n.* omission, breach, NEGLECT; NONPAYMENT, delinquency, arrears; AVOIDANCE, nonappearance. See DEBT. —*v.* back out, NEGLECT, disregard; not pay; absent oneself, be missing. *Colloq.*, renege, welsh.

defeat, *v.t.* thwart, frustrate, foil, outwit; rout, conquer, overcome, beat, vanquish, subdue. *Colloq.*, lick. —*n.* frustration, setback, loss, rout, vanquishment. See FAILURE, SUCCESS, CONFUTATION.

defect, *n.* blemish, fault, flaw, IMPERFECTION; deficiency, lack, INCOMPLETENESS. —*v.i.* desert, flee, abandon. See RELINQUISHMENT, ESCAPE.

defendant, *n.* accused, suspect, [co]-respondent. See LAWSUIT, ACCUSATION.

DEFENSE

Nouns—**1,** defense, protection, guard, ward; shielding, PRESERVATION, guardianship; self-defense, self-preservation; resistance; safeguard (see SAFETY).

2, shelter, fortification; bulwark; foss[e], moat, entrenchment; foxhole; dike, parapet, embankment, mound, mole, bank; earthwork; fieldwork; fence, wall, dead wall; paling, sunk fence, haha, palisade (see ENCLOSURE), barrier, barricade; portcullis, *chevaux de frise,* abatis; battlement, rampart, scarp; glacis, casemate, buttress, abutment; breastwork, curtain, bastion, redan, ravelin; redoubt; lines, loophole, machicolation; barrage balloon, radar screen, D.E.W. (*D*istant *E*arly *W*arning) line.

3, hold, stronghold, fastness; sanctuary, refuge (see SAFETY); keep, dungeon, fortress, citadel, castle; tower, tower of strength; fort, blockhouse; air-raid shelter.

4, armor, shield, buckler, aegis, breastplate, cuirass, habergeon, mail, coat of mail, hauberk, lorication, helmet, steel helmet, siege cap, casque, cask, shako, bearskin; weapon (see ARMS).

5, defender, protector, guardian, guard, bodyguard, champion, knight [errant]; garrison, patrol, watch, national guard (see COMBATANT); sentinel, sentry, lookout; keeper, watchman; watchdog. See SAFETY.

Verbs—defend, go to bat for, stick up for, take up the cudgels for; forfend, fend off; shield, screen, fence round (see CIRCUMSCRIPTION); entrench, dig in; guard (see SAFETY); guard against; take care of, bear harmless; keep, ward, stave, fight, *or* beat off, parry; put to flight; hold *or* keep at bay, keep at arm's length; stand *or* set on the defensive; man the barricades, hold the fort; show fight; maintain *or* stand one's ground; stand by, hold a brief for; hold one's own; bear the brunt; fall back upon, hold. *Slang,* stonewall.

Adjectives—defending, defensive; protective, preservative; fortified, armored, armed, armed at all points, armed to the teeth; embattled; panoplied, ironplated, ironclad; loopholed, castellated, machiocolated, casemated; defended, invulnerable, impervious, proof (against).

Adverbs—defensively; on the defense *or* defensive; in defense; at bay.

Antonyms, see ATTACK.

---

defenseless, *adj.* helpless, exposed, unprotected, open, bare, vulnerable. See WEAKNESS, DANGER.

defer, *v.* delay, suspend, postpone, stay, procrastinate; submit, yield, give in, abide by, RESPECT. See LATENESS, SUBMISSION.

DEFIANCE

Nouns—defiance, dare, challenge, THREAT; provocation; warcry, warwhoop; rebellion (see DISOBEDIENCE); INSOLENCE; contempt; daring. See RASHNESS, OPPOSITION.

Verbs—defy, dare, double-dare, beard, brave (see COURAGE); bid defiance to, set at naught, set at defiance, provoke; hurl defiance at; face down, fly in the face of, brazen it out; dance the war dance; snap one's fingers at, bite the thumb, thumb one's nose at, laugh to scorn; disobey; show fight, show one's teeth, show a bold front, call a bluff; look big, stand akimbo; double *or* shake the fist, threaten (see THREAT); throw in the teeth; throw down the gauntlet, gage, *or* glove; challenge, call out; toss one's hat in the ring.

Adjectives—defiant; defying, daring; with arms akimbo; insolent, contemptuous, bold, rebellious.

Adverbs—defiantly, in defiance, in the teeth of; under one's very nose.

Antonyms, see OBEDIENCE, FEAR.

---

deficient, *adj.* lacking, wanting, inadequate, insufficient, imperfect, incomplete. See INFERIORITY, IMPERFECTION, INSUFFICIENCY.

deficit, *n.* shortfall (see DEBT).

defile, *v.t.* dirty, [be]foul, tarnish, blacken; corrupt, debauch, contaminate; dishonor, debase, sully, drag in the dust, give a bad name. See UNCLEANNESS, IMPURITY, DISREPUTE. —*n.* ravine, gorge, passage. See INTERVAL.

define, *v.t.* explain, interpret; prescribe; describe, circumscribe, LIMIT, demarcate. See INTERPRETATION.

definite, *adj.* exact, explicit, plain, limited, precise, unequivocal. See SPECIALITY, LIMIT, CERTAINTY, TRUTH.

definitive, *adj.* conclusive, fixed, final. See CERTAINTY, END.

deflate, *v.t.* exhaust, empty; reduce, humble, lower. See HUMILITY, CONTRACTION.

deflect, *v.* bend, curve, twist; deviate, avert, swing, sidetrack. See DEVIATION, CURVATURE.

deflower, *v.t.* ravish, despoil. See IMPURITY.

deformity, *n.* malformation, disfigurement, DISTORTION, UGLINESS, IMPERFECTION, FORMLESSNESS.

defraud, *v.t.* swindle, cheat, dupe, fleece. See STEALING, DECEPTION.

defray, *v.* reimburse (see PAYMENT).

defy, *v.t.* See DEFIANCE.

degeneracy, *n.* DETERIORATION, demoralization; viciousness, depravity, turpitude, vice.

degrade, *v.* humiliate, shame, debase, demean; degenerate. See DETERIORATION, DISREPUTE.

DEGREE

Nouns—degree, grade, extent, measure, amount, ratio, standard, height, pitch; reach, amplitude, range, scope, caliber; gradation, graduation, shade; echelon; station, estate, status, rank, hole, notch; standing (see CLASS); rate; point, mark (see INDICATION); intensity; proportion. See MEASUREMENT, QUANTITY.

Verbs—compare; rank, SIZE, graduate, grade.

Adjectives—comparative, relative; gradual, shading off.

Adverbs—by degrees, gradually, step by step, bit by bit, little by little, inch by inch, drop by drop; by inches, by slow degrees; in some degree, in some measure; so *or* as far as; to some extent, to a degree, rather; in the least, at all. *Colloq.*, kind of, sort of.

dehydrate, *v.* dry [out], dessicate, evaporate. See DRYNESS, PRESERVATION.

deign, *v.* condescend, lower oneself, stoop; vouchsafe, CONSENT. See HUMILITY.

DEITY

Nouns—**1,** Deity, Divinity; Godhead, Godship; Omnipotence, Providence.
2, God, Lord; Jehovah, Yahweh, Jah, JHVH, Tetragrammaton; Supreme Being, First Cause; Author *or* Creator of all things; the Infinite, the Eternal; the All-powerful, -wise, -merciful, *or* -holy.
3, (attributes:) infinite power, omnipotence; infinite wisdom, omniscience; goodness, justice, truth, mercy; omnipresence; unity, immutability, holiness, glory, majesty, sovereignty, infinity, eternity.
4, The Trinity, Holy Trinity, *or* Trinity in Unity: **a.** God the Father, Maker, Creator, *or* Preserver; creation, preservation, divine government; theocracy, thearchy; Providence, ways *or* dispensation of Providence. **b.** God the Son, Jesus, Christ, the Messiah, Anointed, Saviour, Redeemer; the Son of God, Man, *or* David; the Lamb of God, the Word [Incarnate]; Emmanuel, Immanuel; the King of Kings and King of Glory, Prince of Peace, Good Shepherd, Light of the World, the Incarnation; salvation, redemption, atonement, propitiation, mediation, intercession, judgment. **c.** God the Holy Ghost, the Holy Spirit, Paraclete; inspiration, unction, regeneration, sanctification, consolation. **d.** special providence, *Deus ex machina;* avatar.
5, Allah; God of Abraham, *etc.;* Lord of Hosts, the Lord God.
6, joss. See MYTHICAL DEITIES.

Verbs—**1,** create, uphold, preserve, govern, atone, redeem, save, propitiate, predestinate, elect, call, ordain, bless, justify, sanctify, glorify.
2, deify (see IDOLATRY, REPUTE).

Adjectives—almighty, holy, hallowed, sacred, divine, heavenly, celestial, sacrosanct, superhuman, supernatural; omnipotent, omnipresent, omniscient; ghostly, spiritual, hyperphysical, unearthly; theistic, theocratic; anointed.

Adverbs—divinely, by divine right; with the help of God.

Antonyms, see MANKIND, DEMON.

DEJECTION

Nouns—**1,** dejection, dejectedness, depression; lowness *or* depression of spirits; weight *or* damp on the spirits; low, bad, drooping, *or* depressed spirits; sinking heart, heaviness of heart; heaviness, gloom; weariness, disgust of life; homesickness; melancholy, sadness, melancholia, doldrums, vapors, megrims, spleen, *mal de siècle;* blue Monday; horrors, hypochondria, pessimism; despondency, dismay, slough of despond; disconsolation, DISCONTENT; hope deferred, blank despondency. See DISAPPOINTMENT, PAIN.
2, grief, chagrin, sorrow, heartache, heavy heart, prostration, blues, dumps; broken heart; despair; gravity, solemnity; straight, long, *or* grave face; death's-head at the feast. *Colloq.,* blue devils.
3, hypochondriac, pessimist; mope, killjoy. *Slang,* sourpuss, wet blanket, crepe hanger. See HOPELESSNESS.

Verbs—**1,** be dejected, grieve, mourn, lament (see LAMENTATION); take on, give way, lose heart, despond, languish, flag, droop, sink, lower, look downcast, frown, pout, hang down the head, pull *or* make a long face, laugh on the wrong side of the mouth, grin a ghastly smile, look blue; lay *or* take to heart; mope, brood (over), fret, sulk, pine, repine, despair, dismay.

2, deject, depress, discourage, dishearten, demoralize, daunt, dispirit, damp[en], dash, cast *or* knock down; unman, prostrate, break one's heart, cast a gloom *or* shade on, sadden; damp, dash, *or* wither one's hopes; weigh *or* lie heavy on the mind; prey on the mind; depress the spirits.

Adjectives—**1,** dejected, cheerless, joyless, spiritless; uncheerful, unlively, unhappy, sad, triste, gray, melancholy; oppressed with *or* a prey to melancholy; downcast, downhearted; down in the mouth, down on one's luck; heavy, heavyheart; [down] in the dumps, in the sulks, in the doldrums; in bad humor, sullen, mumpish, dumpish; mopish, moping, moody, blue, glum, sulky, discontented, out of sorts, out of humor, out of spirits; ill at ease, low-spirited, in low spirits; weary, discouraged, disheartened; despondent, chapfallen, crestfallen.

2, sad, pensive, tristful, doleful, woebegone, tearful, lachrymose, in tears, melancholic, hypochondriacal, bilious, jaundiced, atrabilious, saturnine, splenetic; lackadaisical; grave, sober [as a judge], solemn, grim, grim-faced, grim-visaged, rueful, long-faced.

3, disconsolate, inconsolable, forlorn, comfortless, desolate; sick at heart, soul-sick, heart-sick, in despair, lost; overcome, broken down, borne *or* bowed down; heart-stricken, cut up, dashed, sunk; unnerved, unmanned; downfallen, downtrodden; heartbroken, brokenhearted; careworn.

Adverbs—dejectedly, with a long face, with tears in one's eyes; sadly, *etc*.

Antonyms, see CHEERFULNESS.

---

delay, *v.* put off, retard, defer, postpone; linger, dally, loiter, procrastinate. —*n.* postponement, stay; procrastination. See LATENESS, SLOWNESS, HINDRANCE, DURABILITY.

delectable, *adj.* delightful, delicious, exquisite. See PLEASURE.

delegate, *n.* deputy, envoy, emissary, AGENT. —*v.t.* COMMISSION, entrust, depute, empower. See SUBSTITUTION.

delete, *v.t.* erase, cancel, expunge, take out, cross out, excise, dele. See NULLIFICATION, DEDUCTION.

deleterious, *adj.* injurious. See WRONG, INEXPEDIENCE.

deliberate, *adj.* intentional, studied; cool, careful, thoughtful, unhurried, See CARE, SLOWNESS. —*v.i.* ponder, consider, think, weigh. See THOUGHT, ADVICE, CAUTION, PLAN.

delicacy, *n.* sensitiveness, tact, nicety; frailty, daintiness, exactness; tidbit, dainty; discrimination, TASTE, fastidiousness. See BEAUTY, FOOD, SKILL, PLEASURE, BRITTLENESS.

delicious, *adj.* delectable, delightful, luscious, toothsome, palatable, savory. See TASTE.

delight, *n.* joy, rapture. —*v.* please, thrill. See PLEASURE.

delightful, *adj.* pleasing, enjoyable, charming, attractive, alluring. See PLEASURE, BEAUTY.

delineate, *v.t.* sketch, draw, limn, portray, outline, depict, describe. See PLAN, REPRESENTATION.

delinquent, *adj.* neglectful, negligent, defaulting, undutiful; culpable. —*n.* defaulter; transgressor, troublemaker, lawbreaker; juvenile delinquent, J.D. See DEBT, EVILDOER, GUILT, ILLEGALITY, NEGLECT.

delirious, *adj.* mad, raving, wandering, unbalanced, frenzied. See INSANITY, FEELING.

deliver, *v.* discharge, give forth, emit, deal; [set] free, liberate, release, emancipate; save, rescue, redeem; convey, carry to; rid; grant, cede, surrender; pronounce, speak, utter; give birth (to), produce; *colloq.*, make good. *Slang*, deliver the goods. See GIVING, SPEECH, LIBERATION, TRANSPORTATION, RELIEF.

delivery, *n.* surrender; conveyance; childbirth, parturition; rescue, ESCAPE, salvation, redemption (see

LIBERATION); address (see SPEECH).

delude, *v.t.* See DECEPTION.

deluge, *n.* flood, inundation; downpour, spate; plethora. See SUFFICIENCY, WATER.

delusion, *n.* DECEPTION; illusion, fantasy, misconception, hallucination. See ERROR.

de luxe, *adj.* elegant, sumptuous, luxurious. See OSTENTATION.

delve, *v.i.* research, dig. See INQUIRY.

demand, *v.t.* require, charge; levy, exact, order, call for, claim, requisition. See COMMAND, NECESSITY. —*n.* requirement, requisition; ultimatum; market; COMMAND. See PRICE, JUSTICE.

demanding, *adj.* arduous, difficult; insistent, exacting. See DIFFICULTY, COMMAND.

demarcation, *n.* boundary (see LIMIT).

demean, *v.t.* debase, lower. See HUMILITY.

demeanor, *n.* behavior, bearing. See CONDUCT, APPEARANCE.

demented, *adj.* deranged, crazed. See INSANITY.

demerit, *n.* black mark, minus, fault; defect, failing. See ERROR, DISAPPROBATION.

demobilize, *v.* discharge, muster out, send home; disarm, demilitarize; disband, scatter. See LIBERATION, DISJUNCTION.

democratic, *adj.* unsnobbish; popular. See AUTHORITY.

demolish, *v.t.* raze, level, ruin, wreck, destroy, wipe out. See DESTRUCTION, CONFUTATION.

DEMON

Nouns—**1,** demon, demonry, demonology; evil genius, fiend, familiar, devil; bad spirit, unclean spirit; cacodemon, incubus, succubus; Frankenstein's monster; Ahriman; fury, harpy. See MYTHICAL DEITIES, FEAR, IDOLATRY.

2, the Devil, Lucifer, Mephistopheles, Belial; Beelzebub, Asmodeus, Apollyon; the tempter, EVIL, the evil one, the evil spirit, the Prince of Darkness, the cloven hoof; Pluto, god of the underworld; the foul fiend, the archfiend; the Devil incarnate; the serpent, 666 (*Rev. or Apoc.* 13:18). *Slang,* the deuce, the dickens, old Nick, old Scratch, old Harry.

3, vampire, ghoul; ogre, ogress; gnome, affreet, genie, imp, kobold, fairy, brownie, pixy, elf, gremlin, dwarf, urchin, Puck, leprechaun, troll, sprite, bad fairy, nix, will-o'-the-wisp, poltergeist.

4, ghost, specter, apparition, spirit, shade, shadow, vision, hobgoblin; bugaboo, bogy; zombi; wraith, spook, banshee; evil eye. See HELL.

5, mermaid, merman, merfolk; siren; satyr, faun; changeling, elf-child.

Verbs—possess, obsess, bewitch.

Adjectives—demonic, demoniacal; supernatural, weird, uncanny, unearthly, spectral; ghostly, ghostlike; elfin, elflike; fiendish, fiendlike; impish, haunted; satanic, Mephistophelian; diabolic[al], devilish; infernal, hellish, hell-born, Plutonic.

Antonyms, see ANGEL.

DEMONSTRATION

Nouns—demonstration, substantiation, proof, probation, verification, authentication; confirmation, corroboration, EVIDENCE; conclusiveness; test (see EXPERIMENT); argument (see REASONING). See DEMONSTRATION.

Verbs—**1,** demonstrate, prove, confirm, substantiate, uphold, corroborate, establish; make good, show, bring home; evince, verify; settle the question;

make out, make out a case; go to show *or* prove; prove one's point, have the best of the argument.

2, follow, stand to reason; hold good, hold water (See TRUTH).

Adjectives—**1,** demonstrating, demonstrative, probative, unanswerable, convincing, conclusive; apodictic, irresistible, irrefutable, irrefragable; categorical, decisive, crucial; demonstrated, proven; unanswered, unrefuted; evident.

2, demonstrable, deducible, consequential, inferential, following, valid.

Adverbs—of course, in consequence, consequently, as a matter of course, *quod erat demonstrandum,* Q.E.D.

Antonyms, see CONFUTATION.

---

demoralize, *v.t.* disconcert, dishearten; disorganize, confuse; corrupt, deprave. See IMPOTENCE, DEJECTION, IMPROBITY.

demote, *v.t.* downgrade, reduce, degrade. *Slang,* bust. See PUNISHMENT, DECREASE.

demur, *v.i.* take exception, hesitate, object, scruple. —*n.* objection; irresolution, delay. See DOUBT, DISSENT, UNWILLINGNESS.

demure, *adj.* sedate, staid; modest, diffident, prim, coy. See INEXCITABILITY, MODESTY.

den, *n.* lair, cavern; sanctum, study; dive, haunt, hangout. See ABODE, RECEPTACLE, PRISON.

denial, *n.* NEGATION, repudiation, REFUSAL, contradiction; abnegation, temperance; disown, renounce. See ASCETICISM.

denigrate, *v.t.* blacken, defame. See DETRACTION.

denizen, *n.* dweller, INHABITANT.

denomination, *n.* NOMENCLATURE, name, title; CLASS, SCHOOL, PARTY, kind, sect, persuasion. See HETERODOXY.

denote, *v.t.* designate, signify, indicate, express, mean, specify. See EVIDENCE, MEANING, INDICATION.

denouement, *n.* resolution, solution, END, outcome, EFFECT. See DISCLOSURE.

denounce, *v.t.* stigmatize, condemn, decry, censure; arraign, charge, accuse; curse, rail at. See ACCUSATION, CONDEMNATION.

DENSITY

Nouns—**1,** density, denseness, solidity, solidness; impenetrability, impermeability; incompressibility; imporosity; cohesion (see COHERENCE); constipation; consistency, spissitude; specific gravity.

2, condensation, solidification, consolidation, concretion, coagulation, petrifaction; crystallization, precipitation; thickening, indissolubility, infrangibility. See HARDNESS.

3, solid, mass, block, knot, lump; concrete, conglomerate; precipitate; cake, brick, clot, stone, curd; gob, clump; bone, gristle, cartilege.

Verbs—solidify, concrete, set, take a set, consolidate, congeal, coagulate; curd, curdle; fix, clot, cake, precipitate, deposit; cohere, crystallize; petrify, harden; condense, thicken, inspissate; compress, constipate; compact, jell, jellify.

Adjectives—dense, solid, solidified, coherent, cohesive (see COHERENCE); compact, close, serried, firm, thickset; massive, lumpish; impenetrable, impermeable, imporous; incompressible; constipated; concrete, knotted, knotty; crystalline; thick, stuffy; undissolved, unmelted, unliquefied, unthawed; indivisible, indissolvable, indissoluble, infusible.

Antonyms, see RARITY, VAPOR.

dent, *n.* indentation, depression, hollow, dimple. —*v.t.* indent, buckle, mar. See CONCAVITY.

denunciation, *n.* ACCUSATION; DISAPPROBATION, censure, CONDEMNATION, arraignment; malediction, IMPRECATION, diatribe, anathema; THREAT.

deny, *v.t.* contradict, negate; refuse, withhold; DOUBT. reject; oppose, protest; renounce, doom. See NEGATION. REFUSAL. REJECTION.

deodorant, *n.* antiperspirant, [air] freshener; cream, spray, *or* roll-on deodorant. See ODOR.

department, *n.* PART, section, division; service, agency, bureau; sphere, domain, jurisdiction, BUSINESS, concern; REGION.

DEPARTURE

Nouns—**1,** departure, leaving, parting, decampment; DISAPPEARANCE; retreat, embarkation; outset, start; removal, exit, EGRESS. exodus, hejira, evacuation; flight (see ESCAPE); RECESSION.

2, leave-taking, valediction, adieu, farewell, goodbye, word of parting, send-off; stirrup-cup, gold watch, *etc.*

3, starting point, gate, *or* post; jumping-off point, point *or* place of departure *or* embarkation; port of embarkation.

Verbs—**1,** depart; go [away]; take one's departure, set out, set off, march off, put off, start off, be off, move off, get off, pack off, go off, take oneself off; start, issue, march out, debouch; go forth, sally [forth], set forth *or* forward; break camp, pull up stakes; be gone, shake the dust off one's feet. *Slang,* toddle *or* mosey along.

2, leave, quit, vacate, evacuate, abandon (see RELINQUISHMENT), go off the stage, make one's exit; retire, retreat, withdraw, remove, check *or* sign out; go one's way, go along, head out, go from home; show *or* take to one's heels, beat a retreat, make oneself scarce, run for it, cut and run, steal away, slip *or* take off; take flight, take wing; spring, fly, flit, wing one's way, fly away, embark; go on board, go aboard; set sail, put to sea, go to sea, sail, push off; take ship, get under way, weigh anchor, strike tents, decamp, clear out, bow out; take leave, excuse oneself; see off, say *or* bid goodbye, disappear, take French leave; elope, bolt, abscond, run away, make off, shove off, vamoose; avoid (see AVOIDANCE); light *or* skip out. *Slang,* skedaddle, skiddoo, head for the hills, take it on the lam, beat it, blow, lam, go fly a kite, hit the road, strike out.

Adjectives—departing, leaving; valedictory; outward bound; outgoing, retiring.

Adverbs—whence, hence, thence; with a foot in the stirrup; on the wing, on the move.

Interjections—farewell! adieu! goodbye! byebye! till we meet again! God be with you! Godspeed! fare you well!; *adieu! adios! au revoir! arrivederci! ciao! auf Wiedersehen! aloha! ave! shalom! sayonara! pax vobiscum!;* see you [later]! so long! cheerio! have a nice day!

Antonyms, see ARRIVAL.

---

depend, *v.i.* rely, trust; dangle, hang; be contingent, rest. See BELIEF. PENDENCY. EFFECT. SUBJECTION.

dependency, *n.* dependence, reliance; appurtenance; territory, colony. See BELIEF. POSSESSION.

depict, *v.t.* delineate, picture, limn, portray. See REPRESENTATION.

deplete, *v.* exhaust (see INSUFFICIENCY).

deplorable, *adj.* lamentable, sad, regrettable, disastrous. See BADNESS. PAIN. REGRET.

deploy, *v.* send, spread, *or* fan out; distribute, locate. See EXPANSION.

deport, *v.t.* conduct (oneself), behave; expel, send away, banish, exile, expatriate. See EJECTION, TRANSFER, CONDUCT.

depose, *v.* swear, affirm, testify; dethrone, uncrown, unseat, oust, disbar. See NULLIFICATION, EVIDENCE.

deposit, *n.* precipitate, sediment, dregs, lees; vein; pledge, PAYMENT, SECURITY. See REMAINDER.

deposition, *n.* affidavit, testimony, AFFIRMATION; dethronement, deposal. See EVIDENCE, NULLIFICATION.

depository, *n.* storehouse, warehouse, depot, vault, bank, treasury. See STORE.

depot, *n.* warehouse, depository; station. See STORE, LOCATION.

depravity, *n.* degeneracy, corruption, turpitude, degradation, perversion. See BADNESS, DETERIORATION, IMPURITY.

deprecate, *v.t.* protest, regret, disfavor, disapprove; expostulate, inveigh, *or* remonstrate (against). See DISAPPROBATION, DISSUASION.

depreciate, *v.* disparage, derogate, discredit, belittle; cheapen, slump, fall. *Colloq.*, run down. *Slang,* knock. See DETRACTION, CHEAPNESS, DECREASE.

DEPRESSION

Noun—**1,** depression, lowering; dip (see CONCAVITY); abasement, debasement; reduction.

2, overthrow, overset, overturn; upset; prostration, subversion, precipitation; bow; curtsy; genuflection, kowtow, obeisance. See RESPECT.

Verbs—**1,** depress, lower; let *or* take down, take down a peg; cast; let drop *or* fall; sink, debase, bring low, abase, reduce, pitch, precipitate; dent (see CONCAVITY).

2, overthrow, overturn, overset; upset, subvert, prostrate, level, fell; cast, take, throw, fling, dash, pull, cut, *or* knock down, lay out; raze [to the ground]; trample in the dust; pull about one's ears.

3, sit [down]; couch, crouch, squat, stoop, bend, bow; courtesy, curtsey; bob, duck, dip, kneel; bend, bow the head, bend the knee; slouch; bow down; cower.

Adjectives—depressed; at a low ebb; prostrate, overthrown; downcast.

Antonyms, see ELEVATION.

---

deprive, *v.t.* dispossess, divest, denude, bereave, strip; despoil, usurp; take [away] from; withhold. See LOSS, STEALING, INSUFFICIENCY.

DEPTH

Nouns—depth; deepness, profundity; depression, CONCAVITY, shaft, well; bowels of the earth, bottomless pit; HELL; abyss, chasm (see INTERVAL); deep sea, deeps, depths, ocean bottom, Davy Jones' locker; soundings; submersion; draft; plummet, plumbline, sound, probe, sounding rod *or* line; lead. See LOWNESS.

Verbs—deepen; submerge, bury, sink, plunge; sound, have the lead, take soundings, plumb; dig, excavate.

Adjectives—deep, deep-seated, profound; sunk, buried; submerged, subaqueous, submarine, subterranean, underground; bottomless, soundless, fathomless; unfathomed, unfathomable; abysmal; abyssal; deep as a well, yawning; knee-deep, ankle-deep, *etc.*

Adverbs—beyond one's depth, out of one's depth; over head and ears.

Antonyms, see SHALLOWNESS, HEIGHT.

---

deputy, *n.* AGENT, representative, delegate; substitute, proxy; envoy; factor; deputy sheriff. See SUBSTITUTION, COMMISSION.

derangement, *n.* craziness (see INSANITY); disturbance, upset, imbalance; confusion, turmoil, DISORDER; disconcertment, discomfiture, discomposure. See DISEASE.

derelict, *n.* wreck, hull; outcast; slacker, drifter, beachcomber, castaway. —*adj.* castaway, wrecked, stranded, abandoned, deserted, forsaken; delinquent, negligent, neglectful, remiss. See NEGLECT, RELINQUISHMENT.

derisive, *adj.* derisory, mocking, sarcastic, contemptuous, supercilious, disdainful. See RIDICULE, DISRESPECT, CONTEMPT, DETRACTION.

derive, *v.* get, obtain; deduce, originate, arise; infer. See RECEIVING, CAUSE, REASONING, ATTRIBUTION, EXTRACTION.

derogatory, *adj.* depreciative, disparaging, defamatory, humiliating. See DISREPUTE, DETRACTION.

derrick, *n.* crane; [oil] rig. See ELEVATION, HEIGHT.

descant, *n.* variation; counterpoint. See MUSIC. —*v.i.* discourse, comment. See DIFFUSENESS.

descendant, *n.* See POSTERITY.

DESCENT

Nouns—**1,** descent, descension (*rare*), declension, declination, inclination, fall; falling, drop, subsidence, lapse; comedown, downfall, tumble, slip, cropper, stumble, nosedive, crash dive; declivity, incline, dip, hill (see OBLIQUITY); avalanche, debacle, landslip, landslide, chute. *Colloq.,* spill.

2, speleology; speleologist.

Verbs—**1,** descend; go, drop, *or* come down, fall, dive, gravitate, drop, slip, slide, settle, subside, lapse, decline, set, sink, plummet.

2, dismount, climb down, alight, light, get off *or* down; swoop, fall prostrate, precipitate oneself, come a cropper; let fall; tumble, stumble, flop, topple, take a spill *or* header; topple *or* tumble down *or* over, plump down.

Adjectives—descending, descendent; decurrent, decursive; deciduous; nodding to its fall.

Adverbs—down, downhill, downward, downstream, downstairs.

Antonyms, see ASCENT, LEAP.

DESCRIPTION

Nouns—**1,** description, account, exposé (see DISCLOSURE); specification, particulars; summary (see SHORTNESS); guidebook (see INFORMATION); delineation, REPRESENTATION, sketch, portrait; minute, detailed, circumstantial, *or* graphic account; narration, recital, rehearsal, relation, recitation. See LIST, NEWS.

2, history; biography, autobiography; necrology, obituary; narrative, memoir; annals, chronicle, legend, story, tale, yarn, anecdote, historiette; personal narrative, journal, life, adventures, fortunes, experiences, confessions; work of fiction, novel, novelette, novella, romance, love story; detective story, thriller; fairy tale, nursery tale; fable, parable, apologue. *Slang,* whodunit.

3, narrator, relator, historian, recorder, biographer, fabulist, novelist; raconteur, anecdotist, story-teller. See WRITING.

Verbs—describe, narrate, relate, recite, recount; set forth, draw a picture, limn, picture; portray, represent, characterize, particularize; sum up, run over, recapitulate, rehearse, fight one's battles over again; unfold, tell, give *or* render an account of, write up, [make a] report, draw up a statement; enter into details *or* particulars, specify.

Adjectives—descriptive, graphic, narrative, well-drawn; historical, epic, suggestive, traditional; fabulous, legendary; picaresque, anecdotal, expository, storied; biographical, autobiographical; fictional, fictitious.

Antonyms, see DISTORTION.

---

desecrate, *v.t.* profane. See DISRESPECT.

desert, *n.* waste, wilderness, solitude. See USELESSNESS, SECLUSION.

desert, *v.* leave, forsake, abandon; secede, run away; leave in the lurch, be faithless. *Slang,* ditch. See AVOIDANCE, RELINQUISHMENT. —*n.* reward, due, merit. See JUSTICE.

deserve, *v.t.* merit, be worthy of, be entitled to. See JUSTICE.

design, *n.* PLAN, INTENTION, scheme, project; REPRESENTATION, drawing, diagram, pattern; decoration; purpose, METHOD. —*v.t.* PLAN, intend; draw, sketch. See PAINTING.

designate, *v.t.* name, specify, indicate, point out; appoint. See NOMENCLATURE, CHOICE, INDICATION.

designing, *adj.* artful, CUNNING.

DESIRE

Nouns—**1,** desire, wish, fancy, fantasy; want, need (see NECESSITY).

2, mind, inclination, devices, animus, partiality, penchant, predilection; weakness, proclivity (see TENDENCY); WILLINGNESS; liking, LOVE, fondness, relish; CHOICE. *Colloq.,* yen. See INTENTION.

3, longing, hankering, avidity, longing *or* wistful eye; solicitude, yearning, coveting, envy; aspiration, [vaulting] ambition; alacrity, eagerness, impatience, overanxiety; HOPE.

4, [sharp] appetite, keenness, hunger, torment of Tantalus, ravenousness, voracity, GLUTTONY; thirst, thirstiness; itch[ing]. *Colloq.,* sweet tooth.

5, avarice, greed[iness], itching palm, covetousness, acquisitiveness, grasping, craving, rapacity, passion, rage, furor, mania, dipsomania, kleptomania; prurience, cacoëthes, cupidity, lust, concupiscence.

6, desirer, lover (see LOVE), votary, devotee, fiend, aspirant, social climber, solicitant, candidate. *Colloq.,* fan.

7, desideratum, want, requirement; consummation devoutly to be wished; height of one's ambition, whim[sy].

Verbs—**1,** desire, wish (for); be desirous, have a longing; HOPE; care for, like, list (*archaic*), take to, take kindly to, cling to, take a fancy to, fancy; prefer, choose (see CHOICE); have an eye *or* mind to; have a fancy for, set one's eyes upon; take into one's head, have at heart, be bent upon; set one's cap for, set one's sights, have one's eye on, set one's heart *or* mind upon, covet, envy, want, miss, need, feel the want of, feel like; would fain have *or* do; would be glad of.

2, be hungry, have a good appetite; hunger, thirst, crave, lust, itch, *or* hanker after, make a play for; die for; burn to, have one's fingers itch to; desiderate; sigh, cry, gasp, pine, pant, languish, yearn, *or* long for; be on thorns for hope for; aspire after; champ at the bit; catch at, grasp at, jump at; fish for, whistle for.

3, cause, create, excite, *or* provoke desire, whet the appetite; appetize, titillate, take one's fancy, tempt; hold out temptation, tantalize, make one's mouth water.

Adjectives—**1,** desirous, desiring, inclined, fain, wishful, optative.

2, craving, hungry, sharp-set, peckish, ravening, with an empty stomach, pinched with hunger, famished; hungry as a hunter, horse, *or* churchmouse; thirsty, athirst, parched with thirst, dry; greedy [as a hog], piggish; overeager; voracious, omnivorous, ravenous, open-mouthed, covetous, avaricious, rapacious, grasping, extortionate, exacting, sordid, insatiable, insatiate; unquenchable, quenchless; unsatisfied, unsated, unslaked.

3, eager, avid, keen; burning, fervent, impatient; set, bent, *or* intent on, mad after, rabid, dying for, bad off for, devoured by desire; aspiring, ambitious, vaulting, sky-aspiring. *Slang,* horny, hard up.

4, desirable; desired, sought after, in demand; pleasing (see PLEASURE); appetizing, tantalizing.

Adverbs—desirously, wistfully, fain, would that, if only; solicitously, yearningly, fondly, ambitiously, *etc.;* with bells on.

Antonyms, see HATE, SUFFICIENCY, INDIFFERENCE

---

desist, *v.i.* stop, cease, abstain, quit, forbear. See END, DISCONTINUANCE.

desk, *n. escritoire,* secretary, lectern, counter; bureau. See RECEPTACLE.

desolate, *adj.* bleak, barren, inhospitable, unpeopled; lonely, abandoned, forlorn; comfortless, miserable. See ABSENCE, SECLUSION, DEJECTION. —*v.t.* waste, depopulate, devastate. See DESTRUCTION.

despair, *n.* HOPELESSNESS, sadness, DEJECTION, despondency, discouragement.

despatch, *n.* See DISPATCH.

desperado, *n.* bravo, outlaw, cutthroat, ruffian, thug. See RASHNESS, EVILDOER.

desperate, *adj.* hopeless, incurable; reckless, rash, foolhardy; furious, heroic. See RASHNESS, HOPELESSNESS.

despicable, *adj.* detestable, hateful, contemptible. See HATE, CONTEMPT.

despise, *v.t.* scorn, disdain, hold in CONTEMPT, HATE.

despite, *prep.* in spite of, regardless of, notwithstanding; contrary to [expectations], in the teeth *or* face of. See OPPOSITION, COMPENSATION.

despoil, *v.t.* pillage, plunder. See STEALING.

despondent, *adj.* downcast, melancholy, depressed, dejected, disconsolate, wretched; discouraged, dispirited, prostrate. *Colloq.,* down in the mouth. See DEJECTION, HOPELESSNESS.

despotism, *n.* dictatorship, autocracy, tyranny, oppression. See SEVERITY, AUTHORITY, ILLEGALITY.

dessert, *n.* sweet, savory, confection, treat, trifle. See SWEETNESS, FOOD.

destination, *n.* goal, terminus, port; DESTINY, END, objective. See INTENTION.

DESTINY

Nouns—**1,** destiny, future state, next world, world to come (see FUTURITY).

2, fate, kismet, God's will, act of God, the will of God *or* Allah; Karma; doom, determinism, fatalism, predestination, predetermination, NECESSITY, inevitability; luck, star, lot, fortune, destination; a cross to bear, a row to hoe; wheel of fortune, spin *or* turn of the wheel, fall of the dice *or* cards; the Fates; the mills of the gods; hour of destiny.

Verbs—**1,** impend, hang *or* lie over, loom, approach, stare one in the face.

2, ordain, foreordain, preordain; predestine, doom, have *or* lie in store.

Adjectives—destined, impending, fated, about to be *or* happen, coming, in store, to come, instant, at hand, near; near *or* close at hand; overhanging, hanging over one's hand, imminent, fateful; in the wind, in the cards, in the offing, in reserve; in prospect, expected (see EXPECTATION), looming in the distance *or* future *or* on the horizon; inevitable.

Adverbs—**1,** in time, in the long run; all in good time; eventually, whatever may happen, as chance *or* luck would have it.

2, fatally, fatalistically, imminently, *etc.;* in the hands of fate, in the lap of the gods, in God's hands; out of luck, in luck; by chance.

Antonyms, see CHANCE, CHOICE, WILL.

---

destitute, *adj.* wanting, lacking; stripped, bereft, penniless, poverty-stricken. *Slang,* down-and-out. See INSUFFICIENCY, POVERTY.

DESTRUCTION

Nouns—**1,** destruction, waste, dissolution, break[ing] up; disruption; consumption; disorganization. See LOSS.

2, fall, downfall, ruin, perdition, crash, smash, havoc, debacle, breakup; desolation, bouleversement, wreck, shipwreck, catastrophe, cataclysm; extinction, annihilation; destruction of life (see KILLING); obliteration; knockdown blow; [crack of] doom.

3, destroying, demolition, demolishment; overthrow, subversion, REVOLUTION, sabotage; vandalism; abolition; NULLIFICATION; sacrifice, ravage, devastation, incendiarism, extirpation, extermination, eradication; mayhem; road to ruin; dilapidation (see DETERIORATION).

4, destroyer, exterminator; nihilist; bane, blight, moth, locust; executioner.

Verbs—**1,** destroy, do *or* make away with, exterminate, kill off; nullify, annul (see NULLIFICATION); obliterate, eradicate, stamp *or* wipe out; sacrifice, demolish, dismantle (see USEFULNESS); tear up *or* down; overturn, overthrow, overwhelm; disrupt, upset, subvert, put an end to, seal the doom of; break up, cut up; break, cut, pull, mow, *or* beat down; cut short, take off, blot out; dispel, consume, burn out *or* up; disorganize, play *or* raise havoc with. *Slang,* total.

2, be destroyed, perish, fall [to the ground]; tumble, topple (see DESCENT); go *or* fall to pieces, break up, crack up, crumble to dust; go to smash, pot, *or* wreck, go to the dogs, go to the wall, go to wrack and ruin; go by the board, go all to smash; be all up *or* over with; cook one's goose; totter to its fall; [self-]destruct.

3, smash, dash, quell, squash, squelch, crumple up, shatter, shiver (see BRITTLENESS); tear, cut, crush, pull, *or* pick to pieces; nip [in the bud]; ruin; strike out; throw *or* knock down, lay low; fell, sink, swamp, scuttle, wreck, shipwreck, engulf, submerge; lay in ashes *or* ruins; sweep away, eradicate, erase, expunge; raze, level. *Slang*, trash.

4, deal destruction, lay waste, ravage; gut; swallow up, devour, desolate, devastate, sap, mine, blast, bang up; sabotage; extinguish, quench; annihilate; snuff, put, *or* stamp out; trample under foot; make short work of, make a clean sweep of, make mincemeat of; cut up root and branch; fling *or* scatter to the winds, throw overboard; strike at the root of, sap the foundations of, spring a mine, blow up.

Adjectives—**1,** destroyed; disrupted; perishing, trembling; nodding *or* tottering to its fall; in course of destruction; done for; extinct. *Colloq.*, kaput.

2, destructive, subversive, ruinous, incendiary, deletory; destroying, suicidal; deadly (see KILLING).

Antonyms, see PRODUCTION.

---

desultory, *adj.* aimless, fitful, rambling, unmethodical, erratic. See DISORDER, IRREGULARITY, DEVIATION, DIFFUSENESS, DISCONTINUANCE.

detach, *v.t.* separate, disconnect, remove, unfix, unfasten. See DISJUNCTION.

detached, *adj.* separate, independent; aloof, preoccupied. See DISJUNCTION, INATTENTION.

detachment, *n.* separation, isolation, DISJUNCTION; preoccupation, aloofness, abstraction; PART; detail. See INATTENTION, COMBATANT.

detail, *n.* PART, unit, item; particular, trifle; detachment. —*v.t.* particularize, itemize, enumerate; appoint, assign. See SPECIALITY, APPORTIONMENT, ORNAMENT, UNITY, UNIMPORTANCE.

detain, *v.t.* delay, check, hold back; hold in custody; keep, retain. See HINDRANCE, RESTRAINT.

detect, *v.t.* discover, find out, perceive, espy, ferret out. See LEARNING, KNOWLEDGE, DISCLOSURE.

detective, *n.* investigator, agent; policeman, plainclothesman, operative, shadow, undercover man; house detective, floorwalker; private investigator, private eye; Sherlock Holmes. *Colloq.*, sleuth[hound]. *Slang,* gumshoe, shamus, house dick, Fed. See INQUIRY.

detent, *n.* catch, pawl. See HINDRANCE.

détente, *n.* truce, relaxation (of international relations). See PACIFICATION.

deter, *v.t.* restrain, hinder, discourage, give pause. See HINDRANCE, FEAR.

detergent, *adj.* detersive, clean[s]ing, washing; solvent, saponaceous. —*n.* clean[s]er, soap, wetting agent, solvent. See CLEANNESS.

DETERIORATION

Nouns—**1,** deterioration, debasement; wane, ebb (see DECREASE); decline, declension; relapse, backsliding (see REGRESSION); RECESSION.

2, degeneracy, degeneration, degenerateness, degradation; depravation; depravity, perversion, retrogression; decadence. See UNCLEANNESS, OLDNESS.

3, impairment, injury, damage, detriment; vitiation; discoloration, oxidation; disrepair; debasement; poisoning, pollution, contamination, corruption; adulteration, alloy. See WEAKNESS.

4, decay, DECOMPOSITION, dilapidation, decrepitude, ravages of time, wear and tear; corrosion, erosion; moldiness, rottenness; moth and rust, dry rot, mildew, blight; atrophy, attrition, DESTRUCTION. See POWDERINESS.

Verbs—**1,** deteriorate, degenerate; have seen better days, fall off; wane, ebb (see DECREASE); retrograde (see REGRESSION); decline, go down, sink, go downhill, go from bad to worse, go into a tailspin *or* nosedive, take a turn for the worse, go down in the world, go to the dogs, go to wrack and ruin; jump out of the frying pan into the fire; go *or* run to seed, run down, lapse, be the worse for; break down; spring a leak, crack; shrivel (see CONTRACTION); fade, wilt, go off, wither, molder, rot, decay, go bad; lose ground; cave in; rust, crumble, collapse, go to pieces, totter [to its fall]; perish (see DEATH). *Colloq.,* go to pot.

2, weaken (see IMPOTENCE); taint, infect, contaminate, poison, envenom, canker, corrupt, pollute, vitiate, debase, denaturalize; debauch, defile (see IMPURITY); play havoc with; deprave, degrade; pervert, prostitute, discolor, alloy, adulterate, tamper with, gum up; do a job on; fester; curdle; blight, corrode, erode; wear away *or* out, fray; eat [away *or* out], gnaw [at the root of]; sap, mine, undermine, sap the foundations of, destroy (see DESTRUCTION).

3, injure, impair, damage, harm, hurt, scathe, spoil, mar, dilapidate; mangle, mutilate, disfigure, blemish, deface. *Colloq.,* cook.

Adjectives—**1,** deteriorated, altered [for the worse]; injured, sprung; withering, spoiling, on the wane, on the decline; degenerate, effete; depraved; worse, the worse for; in disrepair; out of order, kilter, commission, *or* whack, out of repair *or* tune, ramshackle, on the blink; adulterated, base; imperfect (see IMPERFECTION); the worse for wear; battered, weathered, weatherbeaten; stale; dilapidated, ragged, frayed, faded, wilted, shabby, threadbare; seedy, grungy, run-down; worn [to a thread *or* to a shadow], worn to rags; reduced to a skeleton; at a low ebb, in a bad way, on one's last legs, down on one's luck; undermined; deteriorative, ruinous, deleterious (see BADNESS). *Colloq.,* tacky.

2, decayed, motheaten, wormeaten; mildewed, rusty, moldy, spotted, timeworn, moss-grown; discolored; wasted, crumbling, moldering, rotten, cankered, blighted, tainted; decadent, decrepit; broken down; done for, done up; worn out, used up.

Adverbs—for the worse, out of the frying pan into the fire; if worst comes to worst.

Antonyms, see IMPROVEMENT.

---

determinate, *adj.* fixed, definite. See CERTAINTY.

determination, *n.* RESOLUTION, WILL, firmness; JUDGMENT; MEASUREMENT.

determine, *v.t.* decide, resolve; END, settle, ANSWER; delimit, define, bound; find out, ascertain; specify, restrict, differentiate. See RESOLUTION, LEARNING, CERTAINTY, CHOICE.

deterrent, *adj.* preventive, retardative, prohibitive, defensive. —*n.* preventative, RESTRAINT; obstacle, HINDRANCE, stumbling block. See DISSUASION.

detest, *v.t.* HATE, abhor, despise, abominate.

dethrone, *v.t.* depose; oust. See NULLIFICATION.

detonate, *v.* set, touch, *or* let off; discharge, explode, blow up, shoot [off], fire; go off. See LOUDNESS, VIOLENCE.

detonator, *n.* [fuse] cap, squib, powder, primer. See VIOLENCE.

detour, *n.* DEVIATION, digression, excursion; byway, bypass.

DETRACTION

Nouns—**1,** detraction, derogation, disparagement, dispraise, depreciation, disvaluation, vilification, obloquy, scurrility, scandal, defamation, aspersion, traducement, slander, calumny, evil-speaking, backbiting, vituperation; underestimation; libel; lampoon, derision (see RIDICULE); criticism, invective. *Colloq.,* bringdown, headhunting. See DISAPPROBATION, DISRESPECT, IMPRECATION.

2, detractor, derogator, *etc.* (see *Verbs*); cynic, critic; hatchetman; muckraker, mudslinger.

Verbs—detract, derogate, decry, depreciate, discount, disparage, denigrate; underestimate, belittle, cut down to size, put in one's place, minimize, run down, cry down, sneer at (see CONTEMPT); deride, RIDICULE; criticize, pull *or* pick to pieces, pick apart, pick holes in, asperse, cast aspersions, blow upon, bespatter, blacken, run *or* tear down, take down a peg; vilify, revile, give a dog a bad name, sell short, malign, backbite, libel, lampoon; vituperate, traduce, slander, defame, calumniate, bear false witness against; stab in the back; speak ill of, call names, anathematize, dip the pen in gall, view in a bad light. *Slang,* badmouth.

Adjectives—detracting, detractory, derogatory, defamatory, disparaging, libelous; caustic, critical, scurrilous; abusive; slanderous, calumnious, calumniatory, sarcastic, satirical, cynical.

Antonyms, see APPROBATION, EXAGGERATION, FLATTERY.

---

detriment, *n.* harm, injury, DETERIORATION; LOSS, liability; discredit, prejudice, disgrace; obstacle, impediment. See DISREPUTE, BADNESS.

devaluate, devalue, *v.* See CHEAPNESS.

devastate, *v.t.* [lay] waste, ravage, desolate, pillage; ruin, raze, destroy, demolish; disappoint, crush. See DESTRUCTION, DISAPPOINTMENT.

develop, *v.* evolve, unfold, mature, grow; bring about, cultivate, produce, amplify; elaborate, train, improve. See INCREASE, TEACHING, IMPROVEMENT, EXPANSION.

development, *n.* outgrowth, consequence; growth, EXPANSION; CHANGE, evolution; [building] project, housing development. See INCREASE, EFFECT, IMPROVEMENT, ABODE.

DEVIATION

Nouns—deviation; swerving, warp, refraction; deflection, declination; diversion, divergence, digression, excursion, departure from, aberration; zigzag; siding; detour, bypass, byroad, circuit; wandering; sidling, knight's move. See CIRCUITY, AVOIDANCE, OBLIQUITY, IRREGULARITY.

Verbs—**1,** deviate, alter one's course, turn off; depart from, turn, bend, curve (see CURVATURE); swerve, heel, bear off, deflect, head off, divert [from its course], distract; put on a new scent, shift, shunt, draw aside, warp.

2, stray, straggle; sidle, diverge, part, separate; jump the track; digress, divagate, wander, wind, twist, meander, roam, zigzag, veer, tack; come round; turn aside, avert, turn a corner, turn away from; wheel, steer clear of; ramble, rove, drift; go astray, go adrift; yaw, dodge, step aside; ease off, make way for, shy; fly off at a tangent; glance off; wheel *or* face about; turn to the right about; go out of one's way, lose one's way *or* bearings.

Adjectives—deviating, deviative, aberrant, errant, roundabout; excursive, discursive; devious, desultory, rambling; stray, erratic, undirected, divergent, radial, forked, centrifugal; circuitous, indirect, zigzag; crablike; off center; off one's beat, off the beaten track.

Adverbs—astray from, round about, wide of the mark; to the right about, all manner of ways; circuitously; obliquely, sidling.

Antonyms, see DIRECTION, CONVERGENCE.

---

device, *n.* scheme, trick, stratagem, ruse, expedient; badge, emblem, motto; mechanism, contrivance, instrument, invention, gadget; (*pl.*) inclination, pleasure. See INSTRUMENTALITY, PLAN, DESIRE, CUNNING.

devil, *n.* DEMON; wretch, unfortunate (see EVILDOER). —*v.t., colloq.,* bother, torment. See DISCONTENT.

devious, *adj.* See DEVIATION, CIRCUITY, DECEPTION.

devise, *v.t.* bequeath, will; produce, invent, fashion, concoct. See GIVING, IMAGINATION, PLAN, TRANSFER.

devoid, *adj.* lacking, without, destitute, empty. See ABSENCE, INSUFFICIENCY.

devote, *v.t.* give to, employ at; destine,

dedicate, consecrate. See UNDERTAKING, ATTENTION, USE, RESOLUTION, WORSHIP.

devotee, *n.* enthusiast, zealot, fanatic, votary, follower, disciple. *Colloq.*, fan, addict. See DESIRE, PIETY, AUXILIARY.

devotion, *n.* dedication; PIETY, godliness; affection, LOVE; (*pl.*) prayers, WORSHIP.

devour, *v.t.* eat, wolf [down]; consume, destroy. See FOOD, GLUTTONY, DESTRUCTION, USE.

devout, *adj.* pious, reverent, religious, godly, worshiping, fervent, sincere. See PIETY, FEELING.

dew, *n.* dewdrops, night damp. See MOISTURE.

dexterous, *adj.* skillful (see SKILL, FACILITY).

diabolic, *adj.* devilish, demoniac, wicked, impious, malevolent. See DEMON, BADNESS, MALEVOLENCE.

diadem, *n.* crown, tiara. See CIRCULARITY, ORNAMENT.

diagnosis, *n.* diagnostics; analysis, examination, explanation; symptomatology, semiology; conclusion, finding. See INTERPRETATION, IDENTITY.

diagonal, *adj.* aslant, oblique; catty-corner; inclined; tilted, pitched. See OBLIQUITY.

diagram, *n.* PLAN, sketch, chart, blueprint, map. —*v.t.* draw, outline, layout. See FORM.

dial, *n.* face, indicator, gauge; disk. See INDICATION, COMMUNICATION, MEASUREMENT.

dialect, *n.* language, tongue; vernacular, idiom, argot, patois, jargon, cant. See SPEECH.

dialogue, *n.* CONVERSATION; part, speeches, lines, script. See DRAMA.

diameter, *n.* BREADTH, thickness, width, caliber, bore. See LENGTH.

diametrical, *adj.* absolute, complete. See COMPLETION.

diamond, *n.* gem[stone], jewel, sparkler; engagement ring; parallelogram, lozenge, rhomb[oid], rhombus; check. *Slang,* ice. See ORNAMENT, ANGULARITY, GOOD.

diaper, *n.* breech cloth, napkin. See CLOTHING.

diaphragm, *n.* midriff; pessary. See BETWEEN.

diarrhea, *n.* dysentery, Montezuma's revenge. *Slang,* trots, runs. See DISEASE, EXCRETION.

diary, *n.* journal, log, chronicle; memoirs. See WRITING, RECORD.

diatribe, *n.* denunciation (see DISAPPROBATION).

dice, *n.pl. Slang,* cubes, ivories; cheaters, doctors. —*v.t.* cube, cut up. See DISJUNCTION.

dicker, *v.i.* bargain, negotiate, haggle; trade, BARTER.

dictate, *v.t.* enjoin, COMMAND; draw up, say for transcription; domineer, browbeat. See INSOLENCE.

dictatorial, *adj.* dogmatic, opinionated, despotic, arbitrary. See SEVERITY, INSOLENCE, AUTHORITY.

diction, *n.* expression; enunciation. See SPEECH.

dictionary, *n.* wordbook, lexicon, vocabulary. See PUBLICATION.

dictum (*pl.* **dicta**) *n.* saying, MAXIM; decision, judgment; pronouncement. See AFFIRMATION.

die, *v.i.* perish (see DEATH). —*n.* mold, matrix, punch, thread-cutter, prototype, perforator; cube, *etc.* See FORM, ENGRAVING.

diehard, *adj.* stubborn, obstinate; inflexible, dogmatic. —*n.* reactionary, conservative; fanatic, bigot. See PERMANENCE, STABILITY, OBSTINACY.

diet, *n.* parliament, congress; food, aliment, edibles, intake, victuals; regimen. *Slang,* grub, chow. See FOOD, REMEDY, ASSEMBLAGE, COUNCIL.

DIFFERENCE

Nouns—difference, differentness, unlikeness, variance, variation, variety;

diversity, dissimilarity, multiformity; divergence, dissimilitude; odds, incompatibility (see DISAGREEMENT); uniqueness, novelty (see UNCONFORMITY); DEVIATION; disparity, INEQUALITY, distinction, contradistinction; nice, fine, delicate, *or* subtle distinction; generation gap; incongruence, shade of difference, nuance; discordance, discrimination; antithesis, contrast; moods and tenses; different thing, far cry, horse of a different *or* another color, different story, something else again; this, that, and the other; no such thing; grab bag. See CHANGE.

Verbs—be different, differ, vary, mismatch, contrast, compare; diverge, deviate, branch out, disagree with; ring the changes; differentiate, draw a line, tell apart; specialize (see SPECIALITY); diversify; vary, CHANGE; discriminate, distinguish, set off, separate the men from the boys.

Adjectives—differing, different, distinct, diverse, disparate, heterogeneous, eclectic, all manner of; distinguishable, varied, modified; diversified, various, divers, all manner of; variform; daedal; incongruous, incompatible; distinctive, characteristic; discriminative; other, another, not the same; unequal, unmatched; widely apart, dissimilar, poles apart.

Adverbs—differently; otherwise, else; alongside of; on the one *or* other side.

Antonyms, see IDENTITY, SIMILARITY.

---

differentiate, *v.t.* isolate, particularize, set off *or* apart; discriminate, distinguish, alter, CHANGE. See DIFFERENCE, SPECIALTY.

DIFFICULTY

Nouns—**1,** difficulty, hardness, impracticability, hard work, uphill work, hurdle; hard task, Herculean task, large order, hard row to hoe; task of Sisyphus, Sisyphean labor; tough job; hard way.

2, dilemma, horns of a dilemma, predicament; embarrassment, contretemps; perplexity, entanglement; growing pains; awkwardness, Gordian knot, maze; coil (see CONVOLUTION); nice *or* delicate point; vexed question, poser, enigma, puzzle, riddle, paradox, knotty point, snag; hard nut to crack; bone to pick. See INQUIRY, SECRET.

3, quandary, strait, pinch, [pretty] pass, plight, critical situation, crisis; trial, rub, crux, emergency, exigency; quagmire, hot water, hornet's nest; sea of troubles, deep water; pretty kettle of fish, fat is in the fire, the devil to pay, can of worms, where the shoe pinches; imbroglio, mess, impasse, deadlock; scrape, *cul de sac,* hitch, catch; stumbling block, HINDRANCE. *Colloq.,* pickle, stew, fix, hole. *Slang,* jam. See ADVERSITY.

Verbs—**1,** be difficult, go against the grain, try one's patience, put one out; put to one's wits' end; go hard with, be on one's back; try one; pose, perplex, distress, bother, take aback, nonplus, bring to a deadlock; be impossible.

2, meet with difficulties, labor under difficulties *or* a disadvantage; be in difficulty, run afoul of; fish in troubled waters, buffet the waves, swim against the stream *or* tide; have much ado with, have a hard time of it, eke out; bear the brunt, carry *or* bear one's cross; grope in the dark, lose one's way; be in a corner.

3, get into difficulties, get into a scrape, burn one's fingers, take it on the chin; stir up a hornet's nest, bring a hornet's nest about one's ears, put one's foot in it; ask for *or* borrow trouble; flounder, boggle, struggle; not know which way to turn (see DOUBT); stick at, stick in the mud, stick fast; come to a standstill. *Slang,* get all balled up.

4, encumber, embarrass, ravel, entangle, complicate, involve; put a spoke in the wheel, hinder (see HINDRANCE); play the devil *or* hob with; stump; tree.

Adjectives—**1,** difficult, not easy, hard, tough, troublesome, toilsome, irksome; laborious (see EXERTION); onerous, arduous, demanding, Herculean, formidable; sooner *or* more easily said than done; difficult *or* hard to deal with; ill-conditioned.

2, awkward, unmanageable; intractable, stubborn, obstinate (see OBSTINACY); knotted, knotty; pathless, trackless, labyrinthine, convoluted (see CONVOLUTION); intricate, complicated, tangled, afoul; impracticable, desperate, hopeless (see HOPELESSNESS); embarrassing, perplexing, uncertain (see DOUBT); at the end of one's rope *or* tether, at one's wits' end, at a standstill; at sea, nonplused; stranded, aground, stuck fast; up a tree, out on a limb, at bay, driven into a corner, driven from pillar to post, driven to extremity, driven to the wall, on the ropes *or* rocks; in a bind, hole, box, *or* spot, up against it; out of one's depth, in deep, thrown out. *Slang,* behind the eight ball, in the soup, up the creek [without a paddle].

Adverbs—with difficulty, with much ado; hardly, uphill; against the stream *or* grain; coming and going; in the teeth of, in a pinch; at long odds.

Antonyms, see FACILITY.

DIFFUSENESS

Nouns—**1,** diffuseness, expatiation, enlargement, expansion, development, dilation, dilating; verbosity, LOQUACITY; peroration, REPETITION; pleonasm, exuberance, redundance, thrice-told tale; prolixity, circumlocution; penny-a-lining; richness.

2, see DISPERSION.

Verbs—be diffuse, be loquacious, run on, descant, expatiate, enlarge, dilate, expand; harp upon, repeat, iterate, dwell upon, insist upon; digress, divagate, maunder, ramble, beat about the bush, perorate, enlarge *or* expand [up]on, verbalize.

Adjectives—diffuse, profuse, wordy, verbose; copious, exuberant, pleonastic, longwinded, desultory, long-drawn-out, spun out, protracted; prolix; maundering, digressive, discursive, rambling, episodic; circumlocutory, periphrastic, roundabout; flatulent, frothy.

Adverbs—diffusely, redundantly, *etc.,* at large, *in extenso.*

Antonyms, see TACITURNITY.

---

dig, *v.* shovel, spade, excavate, grub, delve; labor, speed; unearth; *slang,* enjoy (see PLEASURE). See CONCAVITY, EXERTION.

digest, *v.t.* transform; absorb, assimilate; ruminate, ponder, weigh; shorten, abridge, condense. See THOUGHT, SHORTNESS, FOOD. —*n.* list, catalog; abstract, condensation, compendium. See WRITING.

digit, *n.* member, finger, toe; dewclaw; figure, numeral, cipher, NUMBER.

dignitary, *n.* official, officer. See IMPORTANCE.

dignity, *n.* REPUTE; nobility, eminence; PRIDE, stateliness, decorum; greatness, station, honor.

digress, *v.i.* diverge, ramble, deviate, wander. See DEVIATION.

LOQUACITY, DIFFUSENESS.

dike, *n.* embankment, levee; ditch. See ENCLOSURE, DEFENSE.

dilapidated, *adj.* decayed, disintegrating, crumbling, tumbledown, ramshackle. See DETERIORATION.

dilate, *v.* expatiate, descant; stretch, distend, enlarge. See INCREASE, EXPANSION, DIFFUSENESS.

dilatory, *adj.* delaying, procrastinating. See LATENESS.

dilemma, *n.* predicament, perplexity, quandary. See DOUBT, DIFFICULTY.

dilettante, *n.* amateur, enthusiast; dabbler, poetaster; lightweight, poseur, pretender, faker. See TASTE, IGNORANCE.

diligence, *n.* application, industry, assiduity, ACTIVITY; stagecoach (see VEHICLE). See ATTENTION.

diluted, *adj.* thin, weak, watery. See WATER, WEAKNESS.

dimension, *n.* amplitude, area, extent, measurement, SIZE, LENGTH.

diminish, *v.* lessen, reduce, shrink, abridge; wane, dwindle, peter out, DECREASE. See LITTLENESS, CONTRACTION.

diminutive, *adj.* small, little, tiny, wee. See LITTLENESS.

DIMNESS

Nouns—dimness, OBSCURITY, shadow, shade; DARKNESS, opacity; partial darkness, partial shadow, partial eclipse; CLOUDINESS; dusk, gloaming, twilight, evening, shades of evening; moonlight, moonbeam, moonshine, starlight, candlelight, firelight; paleness, half-light, faintness, nebulosity, glimmer[ing], aurora, daybreak, dawn. See COLORLESSNESS, INVISIBILITY.

Verbs—be *or* grow dim; flicker, twinkle, glimmer (see LIGHT); loom; fade, pale; dim, bedim, obscure, blur, cloud, mist; fog, befog; shadow, overshadow.

Adjectives—dim, dull, lackluster, dingy, darkish, dark; obscure, indistinct, faint, shadowed; cloudy, misty, blear, opaque; nebulous, nebular; looming; pale, colorless.

Antonyms, see LIGHT.

---

dimple, *n.* hollow, dent. See CONCAVITY.

dimsighted, *adj.* nearsighted (see VISION).

dimwit, *n., slang,* dunce (see IGNORANCE).

din, *n.* noise, clamor (see LOUDNESS); DISCORD, cacophony.

diner, *n.* dining car, luncheonette, lunchroom. *Colloq.,* eatery. See FOOD.

dingy, *adj.* discolored, grimy, dirty, tarnished. See DIMNESS, COLORLESSNESS, UNCLEANNESS.

dinner, *n.* supper, buffet, T.V. dinner; banquet. See FOOD.

diocese, *n.* district, REGION.

dip, *n.* plunge, dive; declivity, slope; hollow, depression; swim. —*v.t.* immerse, plunge; scoop; sink. See OBLIQUITY, WATER, CONCAVITY.

diploma, *n.* certification, COMMISSION, franchise; degree. *Colloq.,* sheepskin. See EVIDENCE.

diplomacy, *n.* statesmanship, statecraft, negotiation; shuttle diplomacy; finesse, tact, *savoir-faire;* SKILL, CUNNING, shrewdness, strategy. See COURTESY.

diplomat, *n.* envoy, ambassador; statesman; foreign-service officer. See CUNNING, COMPROMISE, AGENT.

dipper, *n,* scoop, ladle. See RECEPTACLE.

dire, *adj.* appalling, calamitous, fateful, dreadful, ominous; deplorable. See FEAR, ADVERSITY.

direct, *v.t.* guide, lead; regulate, govern, CONDUCT, head, manage, supervise, boss, rule; aim, point; order, COMMAND, prescribe, bid, instruct, teach, coach, prompt; show *or* lead the way; address. See AUTHORITY. —*adj.* straight, undeviating (see DIRECTION); blunt (see DISCOURTESY).

DIRECTION

Nouns—**1,** direction, bearing, course, set, drift, tenor, orientation, TENDENCY; incidence; tack, aim, line of fire; collimation. See STRAIGHTNESS.

2, point of the compass, cardinal points: north; east, orient, sunrise; south; west, occident, sunset; rhumb, azimuth, line of collimation; arrow.

3, line, path, course, road, range, quarter, line of march; alignment. See MOTION, TRAVEL.

4, helm, rudder, joystick; needle, compass; guiding star, loadstar, lodestar, polestar, North Star, Polaris; cynosure.

5, director, guide, cicerone, pilot, helmsman, steersman; driver, Jehu, charioteer.

Verbs—**1,** direct, tend, incline; take aim, point toward, face, aim at, draw a bead on, zero in on, level at, set one's sights on; go toward, set out for, head for, make [a beeline] for, steer toward; keep *or* hold a course; be bound for, bend one's steps toward; direct, steer, bend, *or* shape one's course; go straight [to the point].

2, ascertain one's direction, orient, get one's bearings, see which way the wind blows; box the compass; follow one's nose.

3, lead *or* show the way, take the lead, lead on; guide, steer, pilot; take the helm; take, hold, have, *or* handle the reins.

Adjectives—**1,** direct, straight, undeviating, unswerving, straightforward; directed *or* pointing toward, bound for.

2, northern, boreal; southern, austral; eastern, oriental; western, occidental.

3, directional; north-, south-, east-, *or* westbound.

Adverbs—directly, directionally, straight, northward, northerly, *etc.;* hither, thither, whither; straight as an arrow, as the crow flies, pointblank, head-on, in a line with; full tilt at; before the wind, windward, leeward; in all directions, hither and thither, here and there, everywhere, far and near; in all manner of ways, every which way.

Prepositions—through, via, by [the] way of; toward.

Antonyms, see DEVIATION.

---

directive, *n.* instruction. See COMMAND.

directly, *adv.* straightway, immediately, instantly, promptly; bluntly, flatly, unequivocally; expressly; straight. See INSTANTANEITY, DIRECTION.

DIRECTOR

Nouns—**1,** director, manager, governor, rector, comptroller, controller; superintendent, supervisor; executive director; overseer, foreman, overlooker; inspector, visitor, ranger, surveyor, aedile, moderator, monitor, taskmaster; employer; master, leader, ringleader, demagogue, conductor, precentor, bellwether, agitator, boss. *Colloq.,* straw boss.

2, head, president; chairman, -woman, *or* -person, speaker, chair; captain, superior; mayor; vice president, prime minister, premier, officer, functionary, minister, official, bureaucrat; officeholder; statesman, strategist, legislator, lawgiver, politician; Minos, Draco; arbiter, judge (see JUDGMENT); board, COUNCIL; secretary of state.

3, vicar, deputy, steward, factor; AGENT, bailiff, middleman; factotum, majordomo, seneschal, housekeeper; shepherd; croupier; proctor, procurator.

---

directory, *n.* index, guide; COUNCIL. See DIRECTION.

dirge, *n.* requiem, threnody, funeral hymn, elegy. See LAMENTATION.

dirigible, *n.* airship, blimp. See AVIATION.

dirt, *n.* earth, soil; dust, mud, *etc.;* gossip. See LAND, UNCLEANNESS, INFORMATION.

dirty, *adj.* unclean, filthy, soiled, foul; murky, miry, stormy; vile, sordid, mean; pornographic; dishonest. See UNCLEANNESS, DIMNESS, IMPURITY, CLOUDINESS.

disable, *v.t.* incapacitate, cripple, damage, unfit, maim. See IMPOTENCE.

disadvantage, *n.* drawback, check, HINDRANCE. See EVIL.

DISAGREEMENT

Nouns—**1,** disagreement, DISCORD, discordance; dissonance, dissidence, discrepancy; UNCONFORMITY, incongruity, incongruence; discongruity, misalliance; jarring; DISSENT, dissension, conflict; OPPOSITION; disunity.

2, mismatch, misjoining, disproportion, disproportionateness, variance, divergence; repugnance. See DIFFERENCE.

3, unfitness, inaptitude, impropriety; inapplicability; inconsistency, irrelevancy, irrelation; fish out of water.

Verbs—disagree; clash, jar, contend (see CONTENTION); diverge; come amiss; not concern, mismatch.

Adjectives—**1,** disagreeing, discordant, discrepant, incongruous; repugnant, incompatible, irreconcilable, inconsistent with; unconformable; disproportionate, unharmonious, unconsonant; divergent.

2, inapt, unapt, inappropriate, improper; impertinent; unsuited, unsuitable; inapplicable, beside the point *or* question, neither here nor there; unfit[ting], unbefitting, unbecoming; ill-timed, unseasonable, *mal à propos*, inadmissible; inapposite, irrelevant; uncongenial; ill-assorted, mismatched, misjoined, misplaced; unaccommodating; irreducible, uncommensurable; out of character, keeping, proportion, line, joint, tune, place, *or* season; out of its element; at odds *or* variance with, out of whack.

Adverbs—in disagreement; discordantly.

Antonyms, see AGREEMENT, RELATION.

DISAPPEARANCE

Nouns—disappearance, evanescence; eclipse (see CONCEALMENT); occultation; exit, DEPARTURE; vanishing point; dissolving views. See INSUBSTANTIALITY, NONEXISTENCE.

Verbs—disappear, vanish, dissolve, evanesce, fade, melt away, pass, go; be gone; leave no trace, evaporate; undergo an eclipse; retire from sight; lose sight of; depart (see DEPARTURE); dry up, go up in smoke, fade into thin air, dissolve, melt away, go down the drain, pass *or* go by the board; make away with.

Adjectives—disappearing, vanishing, evanescent; missing, lost; lost to sight *or* view; gone [with the wind].

Antonyms, see APPEARANCE.

DISAPPOINTMENT

Nouns—disappointment, sad *or* bitter disappointment, chagrin, frustration, letdown, comedown; blighted hope, balk, blow, bitter pill, cold comfort; slip 'twixt cup and lip, trick of fortune, false *or* vain expectation, forlorn hope; MISJUDGMENT, miscalculation; mirage, fool's paradise; disillusion[ment]. *Colloq.*, body blow. See FAILURE, DISCONTENT, REGRET, HOPELESSNESS.

Verbs—**1,** be disappointed, not realize one's hopes, have one's heart sink; look blue; find to one's cost; laugh on the wrong side of one's mouth.

2, balk, jilt, bilk; play one false, play one a trick; dash the cup from the lips, cut the ground from under; disillusion, devastate, let down; dissatisfy (see DISCONTENT).

Adjectives—disappointed, disconcerted; out of one's reckoning; crushed, dashed, *etc.*; disappointing.

Adverbs—disappointingly, not up to par.

Antonyms, see EXPECTATION, SUCCESS.

DISAPPROBATION

Nouns—**1,** disapprobation, disapproval; DISLIKE.

2, discommendation, demerit; blame, DETRACTION, CONDEMNATION.

3, animadversion, reflection, stricture, objection, exception, criticism; hypercriticism, picking; sardonic grin *or* laugh; left-handed compliment; sneer, derision (see CONTEMPT); taunt, DISRESPECT. *Slang,* knock, slam.

4, cavil, carping, censure, censoriousness; reprehension, remonstrance, expostulation, reproof, reprobation, reproach; chiding, upbraiding, rebuke, reprimand, castigation, lecture, scolding, trimming, dressing down (see *Verbs, 3*), rating, what-for, calling down; setdown, rap on the knuckles; frown, scowl, black look, evil eye; tirade, tongue-lashing, blowup. *Colloq.*, talking-to.

5, abuse, vituperation, objurgation, contumely; hard, bitter, *or* cutting words, dirty look; clamor, outcry, hue and cry; hiss[ing], catcall.

Verbs—**1,** disapprove; DISLIKE; object to, take exception to; be scandalized at, think ill of, take a dim view of, view with disfavor *or* with jaundiced eyes.

2, frown upon, scowl, look grave, knot one's brows, shake one's head, shrug one's shoulders; turn up one's nose (see CONTEMPT); look askance, make a wry face at; set one's face against.

3, discommend, speak ill of, not speak well of, denounce, damn, condemn; blame, lay blame upon, censure, reproach, pass censure on, reprobate, impugn; remonstrate, expostulate, recriminate, call to account; reprehend, chide, take to task, reprove, lecture, read the riot act, tell a thing or two, give a piece of one's mind; call on the carpet, chew out, get after, get on one's case, pick on, bring to book, rebuke, bawl out, reprimand, chastise, castigate, lash, rap one's knuckles, trounce, jump all over, come down hard on, trim, tongue-lash, flay, call *or* dress down, tell off, rip into, haul *or* rake over the coals, rap, give what-for, pin one's ears back; sail, tear, lay, *or* light into. *Colloq.*, lace into, skin alive. *Slang,* knock, roast, jaw.

4, exprobate, look daggers, vituperate, sound off, dish it out; abuse, scold, rate, objurgate, upbraid, rail (at), bark at; rave, fulminate, exclaim, protest, inveigh, declaim, cry out, *or* raise one's voice against; decry, run down; clamor, hiss, hoot, mob; draw up *or* sign a round robin; animadvert upon, reflect upon; cast reflection *or* a slur upon, damn with faint praise.

5, find fault with, criticize, give a hard time, jump down one's throat, cut up; be on one's back, pick on, draw a bead on; pull *or* pick to pieces; take exception; cavil, carp at; be censorious, pick holes, make a fuss about, kick against. See DETRACTION, CONTEMPT, DISRESPECT.

6, incur disapprobation, incur blame, scandalize, shock, revolt; get a bad name, forfeit one's good name, get the eye, be on one's bad side; be under a cloud (see DISREPUTE); bring a hornet's nest about one's ears; be in one's bad books; take blame, stand corrected; catch it *or* get it in the neck; have to answer for.

Adjectives—**1,** disapprobatory, disapproving, scandalized; disparaging, condemnatory, damnatory, denunciatory, reproachful, abusive, objurgatory, clamorous, vituperative; defamatory (see DETRACTION); satirical, sardonic, cynical; censorious, critical, faultfinding, captious, carping, hypercritical, catty; sparing *or* grudging of praise.

2, disapproved, in bad odor, unapproved, in one's bad graces, unblest, in bad; at a discount, exploded; weighed in the balance and found wanting; blameworthy, reprehensible, to blame, worthy of blame; answerable, uncommendable, objectionable, exceptionable, not to be thought of, beyond the pale; bad, vicious (see IMPROBITY). *Slang,* in the doghouse.

Adverbs—with a wry face; reproachfully, *etc.*

Interjections—thumbs down! it won't do [at all]! it will never do!; God forbid! Heaven forbid!; away with!; shame! for shame!

Antonyms, see APPROBATION.

---

disarm, *v.* demilitarize (see PACIFICATION); pull one's teeth; pacify, appease, charm. See IMPOTENCE, LOVE.

disarray, *n.* confusion, DISORDER.

disaster, *n.* calamity, cataclysm, misfortune, catastrophe, tragedy. See ADVERSITY, EVIL.

disband, *v.* break up, dismiss, dissolve. See DISJUNCTION, DISPERSION.

disbelief, *n.,* **disbelieve,** *v.t.* See DOUBT, IRRELIGION.

disburse, *v.t.* pay out, spend, expend, lay out; allot, apportion. See PAYMENT, APPORTIONMENT.

discard, *v.t.* cast off, reject, abandon, repudiate, throw aside. See NULLIFICATION, EJECTION, DISUSE, RELINQUISHMENT.

discern, *v.t.* espy; discover, perceive, distinguish, detect, discriminate. See VISION, VISIBILITY, INTELLIGENCE, DIFFERENCE.

discharge, *v.t.* dismiss, deselect, retire; expel, emit; shoot, fire; perform, do; settle, pay; unload; free, acquit. See LIBERATION, CONDUCT, PAYMENT, ACQUITTAL, COMPLETION, EJECTION, EXCRETION, EXEMPTION.

disciple, *n.* follower, devotee, adherent, pupil. See LEARNING, AUXILIARY.

discipline, *n.* training, regimen, drill, practice; OBEDIENCE, RESTRAINT, control, repression; PUNISHMENT, correction; course of study. See TEACHING, BUSINESS, ORDER.

disclaim, *v.t.* disavow, deny, repudiate; disown, renounce. See NULLIFICATION, NEGATION.

DISCLOSURE

Nouns—**1,** disclosure, divulgence, unveiling, revealing, revealment, revelation; exposition, exposure, expose; whole truth; telling (see INFORMATION); acknowledgment, admission, concession; exposé; avowal; confession, shrift; denouement, manifestation, PUBLICATION; clue, hint, intimation. See VISIBILITY, PENITENCE, TRUTH.

2, discovery, detection, ascertainment, find[ing], unearthing; ANSWER; first sight *or* glimpse; disinterment, exhumation.

Verbs—**1,** disclose, uncover, discover, detect, find, unmask, expose; lift *or* raise the veil *or* curtain; reveal, unveil, unfold, unseal, break the seal; lay open *or* bare, show up, bring to light, let into the secret; tell, inform (see INFORMATION); breathe, utter, blab, divulge, give away, let out, let fall, let drop, let slip, come out with, let the cat out of the bag, blow the lid off; betray; air *or* wash one's dirty linen in public; bruit abroad, broadcast; tell tales [out of school]; come out with, give vent *or* utterance to, blurt out, spill the beans, open the lips, vent; hint, intimate, whisper about; speak out, make manifest *or* public; exhume, disinter. *Slang,* peach, squeal, fink; spill the beans, give the show away.

2, acknowledge, allow, concede, admit, own [up], let on, confess, speak up *or* out, avow, shoot off one's mouth; turn inside out, make a clean breast, declare oneself, give oneself away, open up, show one's hand *or* cards, let it all hang out, unburden oneself *or* one's mind, open *or* lay bare one's mind, unbosom oneself, confide (in), let one's hair down, show one's [true] colors; get off one's chest; say *or* speak the truth; turn King's, Queen's, *or* state's evidence. *Colloq.,* come clean, sing. *Slang,* spill one's guts.

3, be disclosed, transpire, come to light, come out [in the wash]; come in sight (see APPEARANCE); become known, escape the lips; come *or* leak out, crop up; show its face *or* colors; break through the clouds, flash on the mind.

4, discover, spot; solve, unravel, smell *or* nose out, see through. *Slang,* dope out. See LEARNING, INQUIRY.

Adjectives—disclosed, expository, revelatory, *etc.*

Antonyms, see CONCEALMENT.

---

discolor, *v,* stain; fade. See DETERIORATION, COLORLESSNESS.

discomfort, *n.* uneasiness, distress, annoyance, embarrassment; PAIN, soreness.

disconcert, *v.t.* upset, discompose, embarrass; perplex, confuse; frustrate, thwart. See HINDRANCE, PAIN, DISCONTENT.

disconnect, *v.t.* detach, unplug. See DISJUNCTION.

disconsolate, *adj.* inconsolable, comfortless, hopeless; melancholy, forlorn, sad. See DEJECTION.

DISCONTENT

Nouns—**1,** discontent, discontentment, displeasure; dissatisfaction, RESENTMENT; inquietude, vexation, soreness, heartburning (see DEJECTION); querulousness (see LAMENTATION); dissidence, DISSENT; hypercriticism. *Colloq.,* gripe. *Slang,* the blahs.

2, malcontent, grumbler, growler, croaker, fussbudget. *Colloq.,* grouch, griper, crab. *Slang,* grouser.

3, thorn in the flesh *or* in one's side (see DISAPPOINTMENT).

Verbs—**1,** be discontented *or* dissatisfied; quarrel with one's bread and butter; repine, REGRET; take on, take to heart; shrug the shoulders, make a wry face, pull a long face, knot one's brows, look blue *or* black, look blank, look glum; cut off one's nose to spite one's face; take in bad part, take ill; fret, chafe, grumble, croak; lament (see LAMENTATION). *Colloq.,* gripe. *Slang,* grouse.

2, cause discontent, displease, dissatisfy, not sit right with; be a pain in the neck, vex, disappoint, chagrin, distress, exercise, afflict, annoy, ail, bother, badger, pester, lacerate, besiege, disconcert, harass, molest, nettle, heckle, persecute, get under one's skin, stick in one's craw *or* crop, put one's nose out of joint, rub the wrong way, jangle. *Colloq.,* bug, put off, devil.

Adjectives—**1,** discontented, dissatisfied, ill at ease, unsatisfied, ungratified;

dissident, dissenting, malcontent (see DISSENT); exigent, exacting, hypercritical; repining, regretful; down in the mouth, morose, dejected (see DEJECTION); in high dudgeon, in the dumps, in bad humor, glum, sulky, sullen, querulous; sour[ed], out of humor *or* temper, grumpy. *Colloq.*, sore, grouchy.

2, disappointing, unsatisfactory; pesky, annoying; ungrateful.

Antonyms, see CHEERFULNESS, PLEASURE, CONTENT.

DISCONTINUANCE

Nouns—discontinuance, discontinuity; disruption; DISJUNCTION, disconnection, interruption, letup, break, gap, INTERVAL, *caesura;* broken thread; intermission, half-time. See DISUSE, IRREGULARITY, RELINQUISHMENT.

Verbs—be discontinuous, alternate, intermit; discontinue, call off, pause, disrupt, interrupt, break into, hang up, cut short, break off, lay off; stop, cease, desist, give over, knock off, call it a day *or* quits, grind to a halt; draw *or* pull up, intervene, break in upon; interpose (see BETWEEN); break the thread; drop out; disconnect, disjoin, dislocate; cut, shut, *or* turn off, curtail, close *or* shut down, shut up shop, suspend, have done with, quit, throw in the sponge, give up the argument (see RESIGNATION). See END.

Adjectives—discontinuous, discrete, unsuccessive, broken, interrupted, disconnected, unconnected; parenthetical, episodic, fitful, irregular (see IRREGULARITY); spasmodic, desultory, intermitting, intermittent; alternate, recurrent, periodic; few and far between; abrupt.

Adverbs—discontinuously, sporadically, at intervals; by snatches, by fits and starts, fitfully; so much for.

Antonyms, see CONTINUITY.

DISCORD

Nouns—**1,** discord, discordance, disaccord, dissidence, DISAGREEMENT, dissonance; friction, incompatibility; variance, DIFFERENCE, dissension, DISSENT; misunderstanding, cross purposes, odds; division, rupture, disrupture, DISORDER, house divided against itself; breach.

2, quarrel, falling-out, dispute, debate, argument, discussion, controversy, squabble, tiff, altercation, hassle, [high] words, wrangling, bicker, flap, spat, jangle, cross questions and crooked answers, war of words; polemics (see REASONING).

3, strife, WARFARE, open rupture, declaration of war; jar[ring], clash, imbroglio, crossfire, *etc.* (see CONTENTION.)

4, subject of dispute, ground of quarrel, battleground, disputed point; bone of contention, bone *or* crow to pick; apple of discord, *casus belli*; question at issue, vexed question. *Colloq.,* hot potato. See INQUIRY.

5, dissonance, cacophony, caterwauling; harshness, stridency, din; babel.

Verbs—**1,** be discordant, disagree; clash, jar; misunderstand, differ, DISSENT; have a bone to pick with.

2, fall out, quarrel, dispute, litigate, squabble, wrangle, bicker, have words (with), have it out, set to, fall foul of; break, part company (with); declare war; try conclusions, join an issue, pick a quarrel, sow dissension; embroil, widen the breach; set at odds, pit against.

Adjectives—**1,** discordant; disagreeing, out of tune, ajar, on bad terms; dissenting, unreconciled, unpacified; quarrelsome, unpacific; controversial, polemic, disputatious, factious; litigious, litigant; pettifogging; at odds, at

loggerheads, at variance, at issue, at cross purposes, at sixes and sevens, up in arms, in hot water, embroiled; torn, disunited, divisive, disruptive.
2, discordant, dissonant, out of tune, off-key; tuneless, unmusical, unmelodious, unharmonious, harsh, cacophonous.

Antonyms, see AGREEMENT.

---

discotheque, *n.* disco, nightclub. See AMUSEMENT.

discount, *v.t.* rebate, allow, reduce; deduct, lessen, diminish; mark down, lower (the price); disregard, ignore; belittle. —*n.* allowance, qualification; markdown, rebate, refund, deduction; percentage. See DECREASE, CHEAPNESS, DETRACTION, DEDUCTION, SALE.

discountenance, *v.t.* disconcert, abash; disapprove of. See HINDRANCE, DISAPPROBATION.

discourage, *v.t.* depress, dishearten, dismay; dissuade, deter. See DEJECTION, DISSUASION, FEAR.

discourse, *v.i.* converse, talk, discuss; declaim, hold forth, dissertate. See CONVERSATION, SPEECH.

DISCOURTESY

Nouns—**1,** discourtesy, discourteousness; ill-breeding; rudeness, ill *or* bad manners. *Slang,* boardinghouse reach.
2, uncourteousness, inurbanity; illiberality, incivility, DISRESPECT; offense, insult, INSOLENCE, impudence; barbarism, barbarity, brutality, misbehavior, blackguardism, conduct unbecoming (a gentleman, lady, *etc.*), VULGARITY; churlishness, sullenness, IRASCIBILITY; tartness, acrimony, acerbity.
3, scowl, black look, frown; short answer, rebuff, slap in the face, cold shoulder; hard words, contumely; unparliamentary language *or* behavior.
4, bear, brute, boor, churl, cad, heel, blackguard, saucebox, beast; frump; bull in a china shop; cold fish. *Colloq.*, crosspatch.

Verbs—**1,** be discourteous, be rude; speak out of turn; insult, cut, treat with discourtesy; take a name in vain; make bold *or* free with, take a liberty; stare out of countenance; ogle, point at, put to the blush; turn one's back upon, turn on one's heel, give the cold shoulder, cold-shoulder; keep at a distance *or* at arm's length; look coldly upon; show the door to, give the brush-off, brush off; answer back, send away with a flea in the ear, add insult to injury; lose one's temper; sulk, frown, scowl, glower, pout; snap, snarl, growl.
2, wear out one's welcome, get the brush-off.

Adjectives—**1,** discourteous, uncourteous; uncourtly; ill-bred, ill-mannered, disrespectful, ill-behaved, unmannerly, impolite; unpolished, uncivilized, ungentlemanly; unladylike; blackguard; vulgar, indecorous; foul-mouthed, abusive, uncivil, ungracious, unceremonious, cool; pert, forward, direct, obtrusive, impudent, rude, coarse, curt, saucy; precocious. *Slang,* fresh, sassy, high-hat.
2, repulsive, unaccommodating, unneighborly, ungentle, ungainly; rough, bluff, blunt, gruff, churlish, nasty, boorish, bearish; brutal, brusque, snarling, harsh, cavalier, tart, crabbed, sharp, short, trenchant, sarcastic, biting, caustic, virulent, bitter, acrimonious, venomous, contumelious; distasteful; perverse; dour, sullen, peevish, irascible.

Adverbs—with a bad grace.

Antonyms, see COURTESY.

discover, *v.t.* uncover, reveal, disclose, manifest; find, espy, descry; detect, unearth; realize. See DISCLOSURE, VISION, KNOWLEDGE, LEARNING.

discovery, *n.* revelation, DISCLOSURE; detection, first sight *or* glimpse; unearthing; find[ing]; invention, innovation. See NEWNESS, ANSWER.

discredit, *v.t.* disparage, stigmatize, shame; doubt, disbelieve, impeach. See DISREPUTE, DOUBT.

discreditable, *adj.* blameworthy, disreputable, reprehensible. See IMPROBITY.

discreet, *adj.* prudent, judicious, careful, tactful, cautious. See CAUTION, CARE.

discrepancy, *n.* inconsistency, DISAGREEMENT.

discrete, *adj.* separate, distinct; discontinuous. See DISJUNCTION, DISCONTINUANCE.

discretion, *n.* JUDGMENT; tact, finesse, TASTE. See CAUTION, WILL.

discrimination, *n.* differentiation, DIFFERENCE, distinction; TASTE, JUDGMENT, insight, critical perception, discernment; bias, prejudice, EXCLUSION. See ELEGANCE, INTELLIGENCE.

discursive, *adj.* wandering, rambling, desultory, digressive. See DEVIATION.

discuss, *v.t.* talk over, debate, canvass, argue; analyze, explain. See REASONING, CONVERSATION.

disdain, *n.* scorn, CONTEMPT; arrogance, hauteur. See INATTENTION, INDIFFERENCE.

DISEASE

Nouns—**1,** disease, illness, sickness, ailment, ailing; morbidity, infirmity, ailment, indisposition; complaint, disorder, malady; distemper; breakdown, debility (see INSANITY); visitation, attack, seizure, stroke, fit, cramp, convulsion; allergy, allergic reaction; decay (see DETERIORATION); motion sickness; jet lag.

2, delicacy, loss of health, invalidism, cachexia, atrophy, marasmus; indigestion, dyspepsia, infantile paralysis, poliomyelitis, muscular dystrophy; paresis; [nervous, heat, *etc.*] prostration; fever, malaria, typhoid, typhus, scarlet fever; tuberculosis, [galloping] consumption, T.B.; nausea; coronary; cough; combat fatigue; malnutrition; infection, plague; rabies, colic; shock; rheumatism; seasickness; dysentery; scurvy; sunstroke.

3, sore, ulcer, abscess, boil, growth; tumor; bruise, contusion; pimple, swelling, carbuncle, rot, canker, cancer, carcinoma, caries, mortification, corruption, gangrene, brown *or* black lung, leprosy, eruption, rash, breaking out, inflammation.

4, invalid, patient, case; cripple, leper, consumptive, paralytic, *etc.*

5, pathology, etiology, therapeutics, diagnosis.

6, insalubrity, insalubriousness, unhealthiness; taint, pollution, infection, contagion, septicity, toxicity, epidemic, endemic; plague, pestilence, virus, pox.

Verbs—**1,** be ill, ail, run a temperature; suffer, labor under, be affected *or* afflicted with; complain of; droop, flag, languish, halt; sicken, peak, pine; keep [to] one's bed; feign sickness, malinger; catch, pick up, *or* come down with (a disease), fall *or* take sick *or* ill, catch one's death of.

2, disease, sicken, derange, attack; lay up; fester; infest.

Adjectives—**1,** diseased, ailing, ill (of), taken ill, seized with; indisposed, unwell, sick, squeamish, queasy, poorly, seedy, under the weather; laid up, confined, bedridden, invalided, in the hospital, on the sick list, in sick bay (*naut.*); out of health *or* sorts; valetudinary. *Colloq.,* off one's feed, green around the gills.

2, unsound, unhealthy; sickly, infirm, drooping, flagging, lame, palsied, paralytic, dyspeptic, weak (see IMPOTENCE); crippled, halt, halting; decrepit; decayed, deteriorated; incurable, in declining health; in a bad way, in danger, prostrate; moribund (see DEATH).
3, insalubrious, unhealthful, morbid, gangrenous, tainted, vitiated, contaminated, poisoned, poisonous, venomous; noxious, toxic, septic, virulent; harmful, unsanitary; contagious (see TRANSFER).
Antonyms, see HEALTH.

---

disembark, *v.i.* land; deplane, detrain, *etc.* See ARRIVAL.
disenchant, *v.* See DISILLUSION.
disengage, *v.t.* cut loose, [set] free, release. See LIBERATION, DISJUNCTION.
disentangle, *n.* extricate, [set] free; untangle, unsnarl; organize; comb, card. See DISJUNCTION, LIBERATION, FREEDOM.
disfavor, *n.* displeasure, disesteem. See DISRESPECT.
disfigure, *v.t.* deface, mar, mutilate, blemish. See DETERIORATION, DISTORTION, FORMLESSNESS, UGLINESS.
disgorge, *v.t.* vomit (see EJECTION).
disgrace, *v.t.* degrade, abase, dishonor, humiliate; shame, discredit. See DISREPUTE, HUMILITY.
disgruntled, *adj.* cross (see IRASCIBILITY).
disguise, *n.* camouflage, make-up, dissimulation, CONCEALMENT, mask.
disgust, *v.t.* nauseate, sicken, revolt, repel, offend. —*n.* aversion, nausea, loathing, abhorrence. See PAIN, DISLIKE.
dish, *n.* plate, saucer, *etc.;* serving; recipe; (*pl.*) tableware. See RECEPTACLE, FOOD.
dishearten, *v.t.* discourage, dispirit. See DEJECTION.
dishevel, *v.t.* muss, tousle. See DISORDER.
dishonest, *adj.* false, untrustworthy, deceitful, cheating, fraudulent, crooked. See FALSEHOOD, IMPROBITY.
dishonor, *n.* treachery, infamy, perfidy; infidelity, adultery; disgrace. —*v.t.* disgrace, shame; default (on) (see NONPAYMENT). See DISRESPECT, DISREPUTE, IMPROBITY, WRONG.
disillusion, *n.* disillusionment, disenchantment, revelation; DISAPPOINTMENT, cynicism. —*v.t.* disenchant, disabuse, remove the scales from one's eyes, enlighten; disappoint, puncture one's balloon, pour cold water on, deflate, bring down to earth. *Colloq.,* debunk. See DISCLOSURE.
disincline, *v.t.* dissuade, indispose, discourage. See DISLIKE, DISSUASION.
disinfect, *v.t.* sterilize, sanitize, purify, fumigate. See CLEANNESS.
disinherit, *v.t.* disown, cut off, deprive. See NULLIFICATION.
disintegrate, *v.* break up, separate, decompose; decay, crumble, dissolve, fall apart. See DISJUNCTION, DECOMPOSITION.
disinter, *v.t.* dig up, unearth. See INTERMENT, DISCLOSURE.

DISJUNCTION

Nouns—**1,** disjunction, disconnection, disunity, disunion, disassociation, disengagement; isolation, separateness, DISPERSION.
2, separation, parting, detachment, segregation; DIVORCE; *caesura,* division, schism, subdivision, break, fracture, rupture; dismemberment, disintegration; dislocation, luxation (see DISPLACEMENT); severance, disseverance; scission, rescission, abscission; section, resection, cleavage; dissection; DECOMPOSITION.
3, discontinuity, interruption (see DISCONTINUANCE).
4, fissure, rent, crevice, gash (see INTERVAL).

Verbs—**1,** be disjoined, come off, fall off, fall to pieces; peel off; get loose; branch [off], bisect, fork.

2, disjoin, disconnect, disengage, disunite, dissociate, DIVORCE, PART, detach, separate, cut loose *or* off, filter out, break off, segregate; set *or* keep apart; isolate; estrange, cut adrift, cast off *or* loose; loose[n], unloose, undo, unbind, unchain, untangle, disentangle; set free, demobilize, liberate (see LIBERATION).

3, sunder, divide, subdivide, sever, dissever, cut, saw, chop, cube, dice, mince, cleave, rive, rend, split, splinter, chip, crack, snap, break, tear, rip, burst; rend asunder, wrench, rupture, shatter, shiver; hack, hew, slash; amputate. *Colloq.*, smash to smithereens.

4, cut up, carve, gash, dissect, anatomize; cut, take, pull, *or* pick to pieces; disintegrate, dismember, disbranch, disband, disperse, displace, dislocate, disjoint, luxate; take *or* tear down; break up; apportion (see APPORTIONMENT).

Adjectives—disjoined, discontinuous, multipartite, inarticulate, disjunctive; isolated, separate, disparate, discrete, apart, asunder, far between, loose, free; detached, unattached, unannexed, unassociated, distinct; adrift, straggling, unconnected; scissile, divisible; several.

Adverbs—disjunctively, separately; one by one, severally, apart; adrift, asunder, in twain; in the abstract, abstractedly.

Antonyms, see JUNCTION, COHERENCE.

---

disk, *n.* plate, record, discus; face; floppy *or* fixed disk; wafer; wheel. See CIRCULARITY, FRONT, LAYER. —*v.* plow, harrow. See AGRICULTURE, PREPARATION.

DISLIKE

Nouns—**1,** dislike, distaste, disinclination; reluctance; backwardness (see UNWILLINGNESS); repugnance, disgust, nausea, loathing; antipathy, aversion, enmity, HATE, animosity; phobia (see FEAR).

2, *persona non grata*; unpopularity, lack of favor.

Verbs—**1,** dislike, mislike; mind, object to (see DISAPPROBATION); not care for; have, conceive, entertain, *or* take a dislike to; have no taste for, have no use for, have no stomach for; shun, avoid (see AVOIDANCE); shudder at, turn up the nose at, look askance at; abhor, HATE.

2, cause *or* excite dislike; disincline, repel, sicken; make sick; turn one's stomach, nauseate, disgust, go against the grain; stick in the throat; make one's blood run cold; pall. *Slang,* turn off.

Adjectives—**1,** disliking, averse, loath; shy of, sick of, disinclined.

2, disliked, uncared for, unpopular, out of favor; repulsive, repugnant, repellent; abhorrent, insufferable, fulsome, nauseous, sickening, disgusting, disagreeable.

Antonyms, see APPROBATION, LOVE.

---

dislocate, *v.t.* displace, disarrange; disjoin, disarticulate. See DISJUNCTION, DISCONTINUANCE.

dislodge, *v.t.* displace, topple; expel, evict, drive out. See EJECTION, DISPLACEMENT.

disloyal, *adj.* unfaithful, false; untrue, inconstant. See IMPROBITY.

dismal, *adj.* cheerless, depressing, gloomy; doleful, somber, funereal. See DEJECTION.

dismantle, *v.t.* take apart; raze,

demolish; disrobe, undress. See DIVESTMENT, USELESSNESS, DISUSE.

dismay, *n.* consternation, terror; discouragement. —*v.t.* appall; discourage. See FEAR, DEJECTION.

dismember, *v.t.* disjoint, disarticulate, dissect, tear limb from limb, cut to pieces. See DISJUNCTION.

dismiss, *v.t.* send away; discharge, liberate, disband; cancel (*law*). See NULLIFICATION, EJECTION, LIBERATION.

dismount, *v.t.* take apart, dismantle. See DISJUNCTION. —*v.i.* get off, climb down. See ARRIVAL, DESCENT.

DISOBEDIENCE

Nouns—**1,** disobedience, insubordination, contumacy; infraction, infringement; naughtiness; violation, noncompliance; recusancy; nonobservance.

2, revolt, rebellion, outbreak; rising, uprising (see REVOLUTION); insurrection; civil disobedience, nonviolence, sit-down strike, sit-in; [wildcat] strike, RESISTANCE; DEFIANCE; mutiny, mutinousness, mutineering; sedition, lese majesty. *Colloq.,* walkout. See ILLEGALITY.

3, insurgent, mutineer, rebel, revolter, rioter, seceder, runagate, brat, brawler.

Verbs—disobey, violate, infringe; defy; riot, run riot, run amuck, fly in the face of; take the law into one's own hands; kick over the traces; strike, resist (see OPPOSITION); revolt, secede; mutiny, rebel; turn restive, champ at the bit, strain at the leash. *Colloq.,* walk out.

Adjectives—disobedient, uncomplying, uncompliant, unsubmissive, naughty, unruly, restive, ungovernable, insubordinate, refractory, contumacious, recalcitrant; resisting (see OPPOSITION); lawless, mutinous, seditious, insurgent, riotous, rebellious, defiant.

Antonyms, see OBEDIENCE.

DISORDER

Nouns—**1,** disorder, derangement; irregularity; misrule, anarchy, anarchism; untidiness, disunion; disquiet, DISCORD; confusion, confusedness; disarray, jumble, huddle, litter, mess, mishmash, muddle (see MIXTURE); disorganization, dishevelment; laxity; imbroglio, chaos, havoc, ado, clutter, muss, medley, commotion. See VIOLENCE, FORMLESSNESS.

2, complexity, complexness, complication, implication; intricacy, intrication; perplexity; network (see CROSSING), maze, labyrinth; wilderness, jungle, involution, entanglement; coil, CONVOLUTION, tangled skein, [Gordian] knot, wheels within wheels. See UNINTELLIGIBILITY.

3, turmoil, ferment, AGITATION, row, disturbance, tumult, uproar, riot, pandemonium, bedlam, scramble, fracas, embroilment, melee, rough and tumble; whirlwind; Babel, Saturnalia, Donnybrook Fair; confusion twice confounded.

Verbs—**1,** be disorderly; kick up a fuss *or* a row *or* dust, raise the roof, raise Cain *or* the devil.

2, throw into disorder *or* confusion, put out of order, derange, ravel, ruffle, rumple, mess, mix up, muss, dishevel; complicate, [en]tangle; disorganize, disorder, disrupt; rock the boat, upset the apple cart. *Slang,* foul up.

3, perplex, confound, distract, disconcert, flurry, addle, fluster, bewilder; mix, embroil, muddle, disarrange, misplace.

Adjectives—**1,** disorderly, orderless, out of order, out of place, irregular, desultory; unmethodical, unsymmetric, unsystematic; untidy, slovenly, mussy, messy, sloppy; dislocated; promiscuous, indiscriminate; chaotic; anarchical, unarranged, disarranged, confused, deranged, mixed-up, topsy-turvy, helter-skelter, harum-scarum; aimless, shapeless; awry, haywire, disjointed, out of order, out of joint; all over the place, rough and tumble. *Colloq.*, out of kilter *or* whack. *Slang,* balled *or* fouled up.

2, complex, confused, intricate, complicated, perplexed, involved, labyrinthine, entangled, knotted, tangled, inextricable; tumultuous, riotous.

Adverbs—irregularly, by fits and starts; pell-mell, in a ferment, at sixes and sevens, at cross purposes; upside down, higgledy-piggledy, harum-scarum, willy-nilly, any *or* every which way.

Antonyms, see ORDER, SIMPLENESS, ARRANGEMENT.

---

disorganize, *v.t.* upset, disrupt, DISORDER, derange. See DESTRUCTION.

disown, *v.t.* disinherit; disclaim, repudiate, deny, disavow. See NEGATION, NULLIFICATION.

disparage, *v.t.* depreciate, discredit, belittle, decry, run down; asperse, traduce. See DETRACTION, DISAPPROBATION, DISRESPECT.

dispatch, *v.t.* send; expedite; kill; accomplish. —*n.* message, telegram; promptness, expedition, HASTE, speed; consummation, KILLING. See COMPLETION, NEWS, CONDUCT, EARLINESS.

dispel, *v.t.* scatter, dissipate, disperse, dissolve. See DESTRUCTION, DISPERSION.

dispense, *v.t.* distribute, apportion; administer; excuse, exempt. See GIVING, APPORTIONMENT, EXEMPTION.

DISPERSION

Nouns—dispersion, diffuseness; DISJUNCTION, scattering, dissemination, diffusion, dissipation, distribution, APPORTIONMENT, spread, disbanding, DECOMPOSITION. See WASTE.

Verbs—disperse, scatter, stud, sow, distribute, broadcast, disseminate, diffuse, shed, spread, overspread; dispel, disband, apportion; blow off, let out, dispel, cast forth, strew, sprinkle; intersperse; cast adrift, scatter to the winds, dissipate; spread like wildfire.

Adjectives—dispersed, diffuse, disseminated, broadcast, widespread; epidemic (see GENERALITY); adrift, stray; streaming; dispersive, distributive.

Adverbs—here and there; all over, everywhere, to the four corners *or* winds.

Antonyms, see ASSEMBLAGE.

---

dispirit, *v.t.* discourage, dishearten. See DEJECTION.

DISPLACEMENT

Nouns—**1,** displacement, misplacement, dislocation (see DISJUNCTION); transposition; EJECTION, dislodgment, exile; removal (see TRANSPORTATION); fish out of water; dispossession, disestablishment; migration.

2, displaced person, D.P.; expatriate, refugee, evacuee; Ishmael, outcast; exile, émigré, emigrant. See EXCLUSION.

Verbs—displace, dislocate, displant, dislodge, disestablish; dispossess; exile, seclude, transpose; set aside, move, remove; take away *or* off; unload, empty (see EJECTION); TRANSFER, cart off *or* away; dispel; disarrange, DISORDER; vacate, depart (see DEPARTURE).

Adjectives—displaced, misplaced, dislocated, unplaced, unhoused, unharbored, unestablished, unsettled; dispossessed, homeless; out of place; out of its element.

Antonyms, see LOCATION.

---

display, *n.* show, exhibition; pomp, OSTENTATION. —*v.t.* show, manifest, exhibit, disclose; flaunt, show off. See EVIDENCE, APPEARANCE.

displease, *v.* offend, vex, annoy, irritate, disturb. See PAIN, DISCONTENT, RESENTMENT.

dispose, *v.t.* arrange; regulate, adjust; incline. See AUTHORITY, ARRANGEMENT, TENDENCY.

disposed, *adj.* tending, inclined, prone, bent (upon), fain. See WILL.

disposition, *n.* ARRANGEMENT, classification, disposal, distribution, state; temperament, temper, nature, spirit; inclination, TENDENCY, propensity. See SALE.

dispossess, *v.t.* evict, dislodge; confiscate, usurp. See DISPLACEMENT, ACQUISITION.

disprove, *v.t.* refute, confute, explode, defeat. See NEGATION, CONFUTATION.

dispute, *v.* contradict, controvert, DOUBT, contest, question; argue, debate, quarrel, bicker, wrangle. —*n.* disputation, debate, argument, disagreement. See DISCORD, NEGATION, REASONING.

disqualify, *v.t.* disable, unfit, incapacitate, disfranchise. See IMPOTENCE.

disquiet, *n.* disquietude, AGITATION, uneasiness, anxiety, unrest; commotion. See DISORDER, FEAR, EXCITABILITY.

disregard, *v.t.* ignore, NEGLECT, overlook; disobey, defy; underestimate. See DISRESPECT, CONTEMPT.

disrepair, *n.* impairment, dilapidation. See DETERIORATION.

DISREPUTE

Nouns—**1,** disrepute, disreputableness, discredit, ill repute, bad name, bad odor, ill favor; DISAPPROBATION; ingloriousness, derogation, debasement; degradation, obloquy, ignominy; dishonor, disgrace, DISRESPECT; detriment, shame, humiliation; notoriety, scandal, baseness, vileness, infamy, opprobrium. See HUMILITY.

2, tarnish, taint, defilement, stigma, stain, blemish, blot, spot, brand, reproach, imputation, slur; badge of infamy, blot on one's escutcheon; bend *or* bar sinister. Slang, black eye.

Verbs—**1,** be in disrepute, be discredited, incur disgrace, lose face, fall from grace, have a bad name, have one's name be mud; disgrace oneself, soil *or* dirty one's hands, stoop, foul one's own nest, look foolish, cut a sorry figure, slink away; draw fire. *Slang,* be in the doghouse.

2, shame, disgrace, put to shame, dishonor, defame, reflect dishonor upon; be a reproach to, derogate from; stigmatize, blemish, tarnish, stain, blot, sully, taint; discredit, degrade, debase, defile; impute shame to, brand, post, vilify, defame, slur, give a bad name; not be caught dead.

Adjectives—**1,** disreputable, shameful, disgraceful, discreditable, despicable, heinous, questionable; unbecoming, unworthy; derogatory, degrading, humiliating, ignoble, *infra dignitatem*, undecorous; scandalous, infamous, too bad, deplorable, unmentionable; arrant, shocking, outrageous, notorious; ignominious, scrubby, dirty, abject, vile, beggarly, pitiful, low, mean, knavish, shabby, base, dishonorable (see IMPROBITY).

2, in disrepute, at a discount, under a cloud, out of favor, down in the world, down at heel; stigmatized, discredited, disgraced; inglorious, nameless, unhonored, unglorified.

Antonyms, see REPUTE.

DISRESPECT

Nouns—**1,** disrespect, disesteem, disregard, disestimation, disfavor, DISREPUTE, disparagement (see DISAPPROBATION); DETRACTION; irreverence; slight, superciliousness, CONTEMPT; contumely, affront, dishonor, insult, snub, indignity, outrage, DISCOURTESY; practical joking, left-handed compliment, scurrility, scoffing, derision; mockery, RIDICULE, sarcasm.

2, hiss, hoot, gibe, flout, jeer, slap in the face. *Slang,* razzberry.

Verbs—**1,** hold in disrespect, despise; disregard, slight, trifle with, set at naught, pass by, push aside, turn one's back upon, laugh up one's sleeve; spurn, scorn.

2, be disrespectful, be discourteous, treat with disrespect, set down, dishonor, desecrate; insult, affront, outrage; speak slightingly of; disparage; call names, drag through the mud, point at, indulge in personalities, bite the thumb; burn *or* hang in effigy.

3, deride, scoff, sneer, RIDICULE, gibe, mock, jeer (see CONTEMPT); make game of, make a fool of, play a practical joke, lead one a dance; scout, hiss, hoot, mob. *Colloq.,* razz. *Slang,* give the razz[berry].

Adjectives—disrespectful, irreverent, disparaging; insulting, supercilious; rude, derisive, sarcastic; scurrilous, contumelious; unrespected, unenvied, unsaluted, unregarded, disregarded.

Antonyms, see RESPECT.

---

disrobe, *v.* undress (see DIVESTMENT).

disrupt, *v.* disorganize, disturb, upset; turn inside out *or* upside down; mess up, play havoc with; separate. See DESTRUCTION, DISCONTINUANCE, DISORDER.

dissatisfy, *v.t.* DISCONTENT, displease, disappoint; vex, annoy, anger.

dissect, *v.t.* cut up, anatomize; examine, analyze. See DISJUNCTION, INQUIRY, DECOMPOSITION.

dissemble, *v.* pretend, feign, dissimulate; camouflage, conceal. See CONCEALMENT, FALSEHOOD.

disseminate, *v.* distribute (see DISPERSION).

DISSENT

Nouns—**1,** dissent, dissension, dissidence, DISCORD, discordance, DISAGREEMENT, nonagreement; difference *or* diversity of opinion; UNCONFORMITY; protestantism, recusancy, schism; secession (see RELINQUISHMENT); apostasy; caviling, protest, hue and cry, objection, demur, exception; contradiction (see NEGATION). See HETERODOXY.

2, dissentient, dissenter; recusant, schismatic, nonconformist; protestant, sectarian.

Verbs—dissent, demur; call in question, differ, beg to differ, disagree, contradict (see NEGATION); say no, refuse assent, refuse to admit; cavil, object, quibble, split hairs, protest, raise one's voice against, take issue; repudiate; shake the head, shrug the shoulders; secede (see RELINQUISHMENT). *Slang,* kick.

Adjectives—dissenting, dissident, dissentient; negative (see NEGATION), unconsenting, noncontent; protestant, recusant; unconvinced, unconverted; sectarian, denominational, schismatic; unavowed, unacknowledged; out of the question; discontented (see DISCONTENT); unwilling.
Adverbs—dissentingly, at variance, at issue with; under protest.
Interjections—God forbid! not for the world! by no means! not on your life! no sir[r]ee! not by a long shot!; pardon me!

Antonyms, see ASSENT.

---

dissertation, *n.* lecture, sermon, tract; discussion, disquisition; treatise, discourse; exposition, study, critique (see INTERPRETATION). See REASONING, PUBLICATION.
disservice, *n.* disfavor, wrong, INJUSTICE. See EVIL.
dissidence, *n.* DISAGREEMENT, DISSENT, DISCORD, DISCONTENT.
dissimilarity, *n.* See DIFFERENCE.
dissimulate, *v.* disguise, feign; dissemble. See FALSEHOOD.
dissipate, *v.t.* scatter, dispel, diffuse; WASTE, squander. See USE, DISPERSION, IMPURITY.
dissipated, *adj.* dissolute, profligate, debauched, licentious; dispersed (see DISPERSION). See INTEMPERANCE, IMPURITY.
dissolute, *adj.* vicious, dissipated. See INTEMPERANCE, IMPURITY.
dissolve, *v.* liquefy, break up, end; melt, vanish, evaporate, fade, disintegrate. See DECOMPOSITION, DISAPPEARANCE.
dissonance, *n.* DISCORD, cacophony, inharmoniousness; DISAGREEMENT, dissension.

DISSUASION

Nouns—dissuasion, determent, deterrent, dehortation, expostulation, remonstrance, admonition, WARNING; deprecation; discouragement, damper, cold water, wet blanket; RESTRAINT, curb; ADVICE.
Verbs—dissuade, dehort, cry out against, remonstrate, expostulate, warn; advise; disincline, indispose, discourage, talk out of, deter; hold *or* keep back, restrain; repel, turn aside; wean from; act as a drag, hinder; throw cold water on, quench, damp, cool, chill, calm; deprecate.
Adjectives—dissuading, dissuasive; dehortatory, expostulatory; monitory.

Antonyms, see INFLUENCE, CAUSE.

DISTANCE

Nouns—**1,** distance, remoteness, farness; offing, background; perspective, parallax; reach, span, stride; MEASUREMENT. See LENGTH, BREADTH.
2, outpost, outskirt; horizon; aphelion; foreign parts, *ultima Thule, ne plus ultra,* antipodes, interstellar space; long haul *or* pull; long range, giant's stride.
Verbs—be distant; extend, reach, spread, *or* stretch to; range; remain at a distance, stand off; keep *or* stand away, keep off, stand aloof, sit back, steer *or* stand clear of. See DISCOURTESY.
Adjectives—distant, remote; telescopic; far off, faraway; wide of; stretching to; yon[der]; ulterior, transmarine, overseas, transpontine, transatlantic, transpacific, transalpine; tramontane, ultramontane, ultramundane; hyperborean, antipodean; inaccessible, out of the way, unapproachable; unapproached, incontiguous. *Colloq.*, God-forsaken, to hell and gone, back of beyond.
Adverbs—far off, far away, afar, off, away, a long way off; wide *or* clear of;

out-of-the-way, far-out, out of reach; abroad, overseas, yonder, farther, further, beyond; far and wide, over the hills and far away; from pole to pole, to the ends of the earth, all over, out of this world; aside, out of hearing; nobody knows where; wide of the mark, a far cry from, not nearly, [wide] apart, [wide] asunder; at arm's length.

Phrase—a miss is as good as a mile.

Antonyms, see NEARNESS.

---

distaste, *n.* aversion, DISLIKE.

distasteful, *adj.* unpalatable, unappetizing, unattractive, unpleasant, uninviting, disagreeable, offensive. See SOURNESS, DISCOURTESY.

distend, *v.* stretch, expand, dilate, inflate, swell. See EXPANSION.

distill, *v.* extract, express, concentrate; drip, trickle, evaporate; purify. See PURITY, EXTRACTION, VAPOR.

distinct, *adj.* separate, unattached, discrete; definite, different, explicit; sharp, unmistakable, clear, well-defined. See DISJUNCTION, DIFFERENCE, VISIBILITY.

distinction, *n.* DIFFERENCE, separateness, variation; discrimination; dignity, refinement, elegance; eminence, importance, REPUTE. See TASTE, FASHION, SPECIALITY.

distinctive, *adj.* distinguishing, characteristic. See SPECIALITY, DIFFERENCE.

distinguish, *v.t.* differentiate, characterize; separate, discriminate; discern, pick out; honor. See DIFFERENCE, TASTE, VISION.

distinguished, *adj.* notable, renowned, celebrated, eminent. See REPUTE.

DISTORTION

Nouns—**1,** distortion, contortion; twist, torque, torsion; crookedness, OBLIQUITY; grimace; deformity, deformation, malformation, monstrosity, UGLINESS; asymmetry, anamorphosis; mutilation, disfigurement; talipes, clubfoot.

2, contortionist; freak [of nature], monster, monstrosity; elephant man.

3, perversion, misinterpretation, misconstruction; misrepresentation, FALSEHOOD, EXAGGERATION.

Verbs—**1,** distort, contort, twist, warp, wrest, writhe, deform, misshape, mutilate, disfigure; make a face.

2, pervert, misinterpret, misconstrue; misquote, twist, garble.

Adjectives—distorted, contorted, out of shape, irregular, unsymmetrical, awry, wry, askew, crooked, cockeyed; asymmetrical; not true, not straight; on one side, one-sided, deformed, misshapen, misproportioned, ill-proportioned, ill-made; monstrous, grotesque, gnarled, hump- *or* hunchbacked; bandy-[legged], bowlegged; knockkneed; taliped, splay-footed, clubfooted; round-shouldered; snub-nosed; stumpy, gaunt, thin, *etc.;* bloated.

Adverbs—distortedly, crookedly, *etc.*

Antonyms, see SYMMETRY, INTERPRETATION, REPRESENTATION.

---

distract, *v.t.* divert, turn aside; confuse, bewilder; derange, madden; entertain, amuse. See DEVIATION, AMUSEMENT, INSANITY.

distracted, *adj.* agitated, frenzied, frantic; distraught, bewildered. See EXCITEMENT, INSANITY, INATTENTION.

distress, *n.* discomfort, PAIN; trouble, affliction, trial, privation, harassment, grief, anxiety; calamity, ADVERSITY. See POVERTY, DIFFICULTY.

distribute, *v.t.* allot, parcel, apportion; disperse, scatter; divide, classify. See APPORTIONMENT, ARRANGEMENT, DISPERSION.

district, *n.* REGION, province, ward, quarter, section, tract, bailiwick.

distrust, *n.* DOUBT, suspicion, disbelief. —*v.t.* suspect, disbelieve, mistrust, FEAR. See JEALOUSY.

disturb, *v.t.* worry, agitate, disquiet, trouble; disarrange, confuse; interrupt, unsettle. See AGITATION, DISORDER.

disturbance, *n.* confusion, tumult, riot, DISORDER; commotion, AGITATION, perturbation.

disturbed, *adj.* unbalanced, touched. See INSANITY.

DISUSE

Nouns—**1,** disuse, forbearance, abstinence; obsoleteness, obsolescence; RELINQUISHMENT; cessation, DISCONTINUANCE. See REJECTION.

2, desuetude, disusage, want of habit *or* practice, unaccustomedness, newness to; nonprevalence.

Verbs—**1,** disuse, not use; do without, dispense with, let alone, not touch, forbear, abstain, spare, waive, neglect; keep back, reserve.

2, lay up *or* by, lay on the shelf, shelve; set, put, *or* lay aside; obsolesce, supersede (see SUBSTITUTION); taper off.

3, discard, abandon, throw aside *or* away, toss *or* throw out, relinquish; make away with, cast overboard, cast to the winds, jettison; dismantle, *etc.*

4, be unaccustomed to, break *or* wean oneself of a habit.

Adjectives—**1,** disused, not used, unemployed, unapplied, undisposed of, unspent, unexercised, untouched, untrodden, unessayed, ungathered, unculled; uncalled for, not required; run down, obsolete, obsolescent.

2, unused, unseasoned; new, green; unhackneyed. See OLDNESS.

Antonyms, see HABIT, USE.

---

ditch, *n.* channel, trench, gully, canal, moat, watercourse. See FURROW. —*v.t., slang,* cast off. See RELINQUISHMENT.

dither, *n.* fluster, commotion, twitter, flurry, confusion. See AGITATION, EXCITEMENT.

ditto, *adv.* as before, again, likewise; in the same way. See COPY.

ditty, *n.* song (see MUSIC).

diva, *n.* prima donna (see MUSIC).

divagate, *v.i.* stray, digress. See DEVIATION, DIFFUSENESS.

divan, *n.* sofa, couch; COUNCIL. See SUPPORT.

dive, *n.* plunge, dip, swoop; nose dive, power dive. *Slang,* honkytonk. See DESCENT, DRINKING.

diverge, *v.i.* separate, branch off, fork; sunder; divaricate, deviate; differ, vary, disagree; veer, swerve; detach; go off at a tangent; radiate. See DIFFERENCE, DEVIATION, DISAGREEMENT.

divergence, *n.* DIFFERENCE; DEVIATION; dispersion; fork[ing], branching off; ramification, variation; DISAGREEMENT; divergency.

diverse, *adj.* unlike, varied. See DIFFERENCE.

diversify, *v.* vary; variegate. See DIFFERENCE, VARIEGATION.

diversion, *n.* AMUSEMENT, entertainment, divertisement, pastime, recreation, sport; variation, change, DEVIATION. See REFRESHMENT.

diversity, *n.* DIFFERENCE, dissimilarity, variation, variety. See VARIEGATION.

divert, *v.t.* amuse, beguile, entertain; distract, turn aside. See AMUSEMENT, DEVIATION.

DIVESTMENT

Nouns—**1,** divestment, divestiture; taking off, undressing; [de]nudation;

decortication, depilation, excoriation, desquamation; molting, ecdysis; exfoliation.

2, nudity, bareness, undress, dishabille, the buff, the raw; calvities, baldness. *Colloq.*, the altogether. *Slang,* cheesecake.

Verbs—**1,** divest; uncover, denude, bare; strip, undress, disrobe, uncoif; dismantle; get, put, *or* take off; doff, cast, *or* slough off, shed; take off one's hands.

2, peel, pare, shell, decorticate, excoriate, skin, scale; scalp, shave, shear; flay; expose, lay open; exfoliate, molt; cast the skin.

Adjectives—divested, denuded, bare, naked, shorn, nude, in a state of nature, in one's birthday suit, with nothing on, stark naked, in the buff, [in the] raw; undressed, undraped, exposed, in dishabille; threadbare, out at elbows, ragged; bald[-headed], balding, bald as an egg; bare as the back of one's hand; barefoot; leafless, napless, hairless, beardless, clean-shaven. *Colloq.*, in the altogether.

Antonyms, see CLOTHING, COVERING.

---

divide, *v.* separate; partition, allot, assign; split [up], part; distribute, share. See APPORTIONMENT, DISJUNCTION.

dividend, *n.* share, part, portion; interest, bonus, plum. See APPORTIONMENT, PAYMENT.

divination, *n.* PREDICTION, prophecy, augury, guess; SORCERY.

divine, *adj.* godlike, superhuman; celestial, heavenly; holy, spiritual; religious. See DEITY, RELIGION, GOODNESS.

division, *n.* severance, separation, disunion, DISCORD, DISJUNCTION, schism; APPORTIONMENT, partitionment; PART, section; unit, group. See CLASS, COMBATANT.

DIVORCE

Nouns—**1,** divorce, divorcement, separation, annulment, parting of the ways, break-up, split-up. See DISJUNCTION.

2, divorce[e], grass widow[er].

Verbs—divorce, get a divorce *or* an annulment; separate, break up, split [up]. *Colloq.*, go to Reno, call it quits, get unhitched, cut loose.

Adjectives—divorced, separated, split. *Colloq.*, unhitched, in circulation.

Antonyms, see MARRIAGE.

---

divulge, *v.t.* disclose, reveal, let slip, tell. See DISCLOSURE.

dizzy, *adj.* giddy, lightheaded; *slang,* silly, mixed-up, flighty. See INSANITY.

do, *v.t.* perform, achieve, contrive, manage; solve, finish, work out; serve, render; *colloq.*, swindle, defraud. See ACTION, COMPLETION, PRODUCTION.

docile, *adj.* gentle, tractable, teachable, submissive. See CONSENT, SUBMISSION.

dock, *n.* dockage, mooring; berth, wharf, pier, slip, quay; anchorage, marina, boat *or* ship's basin; drydock, jetty; harbor, haven, prisoner's dock, witness stand. See ABODE. —*v.* cut, trim, curtail, reduce, deduct; fine, penalize. See SHORTNESS, PUNISHMENT, DEDUCTION.

docket, *n.* calendar, agenda, register; label. See RECORD, INDICATION.

doctor, *n.* physician, surgeon; learned man, sage. See REMEDY.

doctrinaire, *adj.* theoretical; dogmatic. See CERTAINTY.

doctrine, *n.* creed, theory, dogma,

tenet, principle. See BELIEF.

document, *n.* instrument, writing, RECORD, EVIDENCE.

dodder, *v.i.* tremble, totter, shake. See WEAKNESS.

dodge, *v.* elude, evade, escape, avoid, duck. See DEVIATION, AVOIDANCE, CUNNING.

doer, *n.* See AGENT.

doff, *v.t.* take off (see DIVESTMENT).

dog, *n.* canine, cur, whelp; pup[py], tyke, bitch, slut. *Colloq.,* doggy. *Slang,* pooch, mutt. See ANIMAL.

dogged, *adj.* obstinate, persistent. See OBSTINACY.

dogma, *n.* doctrine, tenet, precept. See BELIEF.

dogmatic, *adj.* dictatorial, imperious, arrogant, peremptory, positive, opinionated. See CERTAINTY, MISJUDGMENT, SEVERITY, RELIGION.

doldrums, *n.pl.* lull, calm; depression, despondency, DEJECTION; blues, dumps.

dole, *n.* alms, pittance. *Slang,* handout. See INSUFFICIENCY, GIVING.

doleful, *adj.* sorrowful, sad. See DEJECTION.

doll, *n.* dolly; kewpie doll, Barbie [doll]; puppet, Muppet, marionette, figurine; voodoo; *slang,* babe, baby[doll], sweetheart. See AMUSEMENT, BEAUTY.

dollar, *n.* single, one. *Slang,* buck, bean, iron man, simoleon, cartwheel. See MONEY.

dolorous, *adj.* mournful (see DEJECTION).

dolphin, *n.* porpoise, sea hog *or* pig, cetacean. See ANIMAL.

dolt, *n.* dunce (see IGNORANCE).

domain, *n.* realm, dominion, territory; REGION, land, sphere [of action]; estate (see ABODE).

dome, *n.* vault, cupola. See COVERING, CONVEXITY.

domestic, *adj.* household, homely; family, home; internal; native, home-grown, home-bred; tame. See SECLUSION, DOMESTICATION, INHABITANT.

DOMESTICATION

Nouns—**1,** domestication, taming; animal husbandry; cattle raising, dairy farming, ranching, stock breeding, horse training; veterinarianism, veterinary medicine. See ANIMAL.

2, menagerie, zoo, aquarium; stable, barn (see ABODE); corral, ranch; fishpond, hatchery.

3, husbandman, breeder, keeper, dairy farmer, rancher; groom, stableman; cowboy, cowgirl, cowherd, herder, cowman, cowpoke, cattleman, cowpuncher, cowhand, buckaroo; wrangler, trail boss, top hand; vaquero, gaucho, ranchero, broncobuster; shepherd, sheepherder, herdsman; swineherd; apiarist, beekeeper; handler, trainer. *Slang,* pard[ner].

4, veterinary, veterinarian, vet, horse doctor.

Verbs—domesticate, tame, breed, rear, train, break, ride herd, feed, water, milk, shear, rub down; round up, corral, housebreak.

Adjectives—domesticated, domestic, tame, gentle, broken; housebroken, trained.

Antonyms, see VIOLENCE.

---

domicile, *n.* See ABODE.

dominate, *v.t.* govern, control; domineer, overbear, tyrannize; predominate, stand out. See AUTHORITY, SUPREMACY.

domineer, *v.i.* tyrannize, overbear, bully. See INSOLENCE, SEVERITY.

dominion, *n.* power, AUTHORITY; domain, state, territory. See REGION, POSSESSION.

domino, *n.* bone; cloak, half-mask. See CONCEALMENT.

don, *v.t.* assume, put on. See CLOTHING.

donation, *n.* contribution, gift, present, benefaction, grant. See GIVING, LIBERALITY.

donkey, *n.* ass, jackass, burro; blockhead, fool. See ANIMAL, FOLLY.

do-nothing, *n.* fence-sitter, [time-] waster, drone, idler. See INACTION.

doodle, *n., slang,* scribble, sketch. See PAINTING.

doom, *n.* DESTINY, lot, fate, fortune; JUDGMENT, damnation, CONDEMNATION; DESTRUCTION, DEATH. See NECESSITY.

door, *n.* doorway, gate, portal, entrance, exit; barrier; inlet, outlet, path. See OPENING, INGRESS, EGRESS.

doorkeeper, *n.* doorman, porter, gatekeeper, *concierge,* sentry. See SAFETY.

dope, *n.* hint, INFORMATION; *colloq.,* drug, stimulant; *slang,* dunce. See REMEDY, IGNORANCE.

dormant, *adj.* torpid; quiescent. See LATENCY, INACTIVITY.

dormitory, *n.* quarters, hostel, bunks. *Colloq.,* dorm. See ABODE.

dose, *n.* dosage, measure, portion; mouthful, *etc.* See REMEDY, APPORTIONMENT, PART.

dossier, *n.* file, folder, papers, documents, RECORD.

dot, *n.* spot, speck, point; jot, whit, iota; dowry. See LITTLENESS, POSSESSION.

dotage, *n.* senility, feebleness; fondness. See AGE, ENDEARMENT.

dote, *v.i.* like, be fond of; worship, adore, be infatuated (with). See LOVE.

double, *adj.* twofold, duplicate, duplex, dual. —*v.t.* duplicate, increase, twofold; FOLD. —*n.* duplication; twin, counterpart; understudy, stand-in. See COPY, SIMILARITY, SUBSTITUTION.

double-cross, *slang, v.t.* betray. —*n.* betrayal. See IMPROBITY.

double-dealing, *adj. & n.* See FALSEHOOD.

double-talk, *n.* gibberish, jargon, nonsense, cant. See ABSURDITY.

DOUBT

Nouns—**1,** doubt, dubiousness, dubiety; unbelief, skepticism, pyrrhonism, disbelief; agnosticism, IRRELIGION; incredulity, discredit; credibility gap. See IMPROBABILITY, DEJECTION.

2, JEALOUSY, suspicion, distrust, anxiety, concern.

3, uncertainty, uncertainness, incertitude; hesitation, hesitancy, suspense; perplexity, irresolution, indecision; demur, scruple, qualm, misgiving; dilemma, quandary; bewilderment, vacillation, CHANGEABLENESS; vagueness, OBSCURITY; riskiness, precariousness, insecurity. *Colloq.,* dark horse, cliffhanger.

4, doubter, unbeliever, skeptic, pyrrhonist, agnostic, doubting Thomas, man from Missouri.

Verbs—**1,** doubt, be doubtful, disbelieve, discredit; misbelieve; refuse to admit *or* believe, doubt the truth of, be skeptical, not believe one's ears *or* eyes, distrust, mistrust, suspect, have doubts, harbor suspicions, have one's doubts, have cold feet; take with a grain of salt; be from Missouri.

2, demur, stick at, pause, hesitate, think twice, falter, scruple. *Slang,* smell a rat.

3, cast doubt upon, raise a question, give pause, bring *or* call in question; question, challenge, dispute, deny, cause *or* raise a doubt *or* suspicion; leave hanging [in the air].

4, be unbelievable, fill with doubt, startle, stagger; shake *or* stagger one's faith *or* belief.

5, be uncertain, wonder whether, waver, hover, see-saw, teeter, hem and haw, sit on the fence; not know which way to turn *or* jump; hang by a thread *or* a hair, hang in the balance.

6, confuse, bewilder, baffle, stump.

Adjectives—**1,** doubting, unbelieving, incredulous, skeptical; uncertain, irresolute; distrustful, suspicious, *or* shy of; heretical, faithless; dubious, scrupulous. **2,** doubtful, disputable, debatable, controversial, questionable, moot, problematical, suspect, under a cloud, unsettled, undecided, in midair, up in the air; open to suspicion *or* doubt; far-fetched; staggering, fabulous, hard to believe, unbelievable, incredible, not to be believed, inconceivable, fishy; ambiguous; fallible; undemonstrable; controvertible.

Adverbs—with a grain of salt, with reservations, maybe; betwixt and between.

Phrases—tell it to the Marines!

Antonyms, see BELIEF, CERTAINTY, RESOLUTION.

---

doubtless, *adv.* unquestionably (see CERTAINTY).

doughnut, *n.* cruller, *beignet,* friedcake. *Slang,* dunker, tire. See FOOD.

doughty, *adj.* redoubtable, fearless, strong, brave, bold, gallant, daring, spunky. See COURAGE.

dour, *adj.* sour, sullen; harsh, hard. See SEVERITY, DISCOURTESY.

douse, *v.* soak, drench, souse; put out, extinguish. See WATER, DARKNESS.

dowager, *n.* widow; matron, *grande dame,* beldam. *Slang,* battle-ax. See FEMALE.

dowdy, *adj.* frumpy, frowsy, down-at-heels; inelegant, old-fashioned. See INELEGANCE, VULGARITY.

dower, *n.* See DOWRY.

down, *adv.* downward; under, beneath, below. See LOWNESS, DESCENT.

down-and-out, *adj.* needy, destitute, poor, on the skids. See POVERTY.

downcast, *adj.* downhearted, dejected, modest, bashful. See HUMILITY, DEJECTION.

downfall, *n.* drop, comedown, disgrace, demotion; overthrow, defeat; collapse, crash. See DESCENT, FAILURE, DESTRUCTION.

downgrade, *v.t.* demote (see DECREASE). —*n.* See OBLIQUITY.

downhearted, *adj.* dejected, discouraged, downcast, sad. See DEJECTION.

downpour, *n.* cloudburst, deluge. See WATER.

downright, *adv.* plainly, bluntly; extremely; thoroughly, completely. —*adj.* unqualified, frank, absolute; direct, plain, blunt; complete, utter, absolute. See COMPLETION.

downtrodden, *adj.* oppressed, subjugated; in the dust *or* mire, treated like dirt; underprivileged. See SUBJECTION.

downward, *adj. & adv.* See DESCENT.

downy, *adj.* fluffy, feathery, fleecy, flocculent, soft. See SOFTNESS.

dowry, *n.* dower, dot; inheritance. See POSSESSION.

doze, *n. & v.i.* snooze, nap, drowse. See REPOSE.

drab, *adj.* grayish, brownish, dun; monotonous, dull, humdrum, uninteresting. See WEARINESS, COLOR.

draft, *n.* sketch, outline; breeze, air current, WIND; drink, dram; conscription, levy; load, pull, displacement; check, bill of exchange, demand note. See DRINKING, MONEY, CREDIT, DEPTH. —*v.t.* outline; draw, sketch, formulate; conscript, enlist, impress. See COMPULSION, PLAN, TRACTION, WRITING.

draftee, *n.* recruit, inductee, conscript. *Slang,* rookie. See COMBATANT.

draftsman, *n.* delineator; ARTIST, drafter.

drag, *v.* draw, pull, tow, tug, haul; protract, draw out; lag, dawdle, inch along; *slang,* race. See SLOWNESS, TRACTION, LATENESS.

drain, *v.* draw off, empty, exhaust, leak, drip, dry up. —*n.* outlet, spout, sewer, ditch, gutter. See WATER, USE, DRYNESS, EGRESS, WASTE, CLEANNESS.

dram, *n.* draft, drink. See DRINKING.

DRAMA

Nouns—**1,** drama; the drama, the stage, the theater, legitimate theater, street theater; show business, theatricals, theatrics; theater of the absurd, the mind, cruelty, involvement, protest, *etc.*; dramaturgy, stagecraft, histrionics, sock and buskin; Muse of Tragedy, Melpomene; Muse of Comedy, Thalia; Thespis; puppetry, Punch and Judy. *Slang,* legit.

2, play, drama, stage play, piece, vehicle, tragedy, comedy, tragicomedy; opera, operetta, musical comedy, review, road show, vaudeville, variety, burlesque, farce, divertissement, skit, playlet, extravaganza, harlequinade, pantomime, *opéra bouffe*, ballet, spectacle, masque, melodrama; monologue, duologue, dialogue; trilogy, tetralogy, *etc.;* charade; mystery, morality, *or* miracle play; puppet show; audition (see EXPERIMENT); libretto.

3, act, scene, tableau; introduction, prologue, curtain raiser; turn, number; entr'acte, intermission, intermezzo, interlude, half-time; epilogue, afterpiece; curtain; curtain call, encore.

4, performance, REPRESENTATION, *mise en scène,* stagery, stagecraft; acting, impersonation; stage business, slapstick, buffoonery; showmanship; part, rôle, character, cast, *dramatis personae*, road company; repertory, repertoire; summer theater, amateur theatricals, [summer] stock. *Colloq.,* gag. *Slang,* ham acting.

5, motion *or* moving picture, film, cinema, talking picture, silver screen; photoplay, screenplay. *Colloq.,* movie [show], talkie. *Slang,* flickers.

6, a. theater, house; legitimate theater, playhouse, opera house, music hall, movie theater, off- *or* off-off-Broadway theater; amphitheater, circus, hippodrome; puppet *or* marionette theater. See ARENA. **b.** auditorium, front of the house, stalls, boxes, orchestra, balcony, loges, gallery, peanut gallery; greenroom. **c.** stage, proscenium; the scene, the boards; trap; wings, flies; float, light, spotlight, footlight; orchestra pit, dressing room, quick-change room; scenery, flat, drop, screen, side-scene; transformation scene, curtain. **d.** make-up, greasepaint; theatrical costume; properties, props.

7, a. actor, player, stage player, performer, trouper, vaudevillian, Thespian; showman; star, hero, headliner, matinee idol; protagonist, leading man *or* woman; comedian, tragedian, villain, heavy; ingenue, soubrette; foil, straight man; pantomimist, mummer, masker, clown, harlequin, buffo, buffoon, farceur, Pantaloon, Columbine; Punch, Punchinello; tumbler, juggler, acrobat; contortionist. *Colloq.,* stooge. *Slang,* ham [actor]. **b.** supporting cast, super[numerary], extra spear carrier, bit player. **c.** librettist, scenario-writer, dramatic author; playwriter, playwright; dramatist. **d.** [stage] director; producer, impresario; prompter; stage manager; set, costume, *etc.* designer; stagehand. *Slang,* grip, gaffer. **e.** audience, public, theatergoer, spectator.

Verbs—act, play, perform; mount, put on the stage; impersonate (see REPRESENTATION); mimic, IMITATE, enact; play *or* act [out] a part; rehearse; tread the boards; hold the stage; blow *or* fluff one's lines; star, figure in; overact, upstage, steal the show; adapt for the stage, dramatize. *Slang,* ham [it up], mug, chew the scenery.

Adjectives—dramatic, theatrical, scenic, histrionic, comic, tragic, farcical, tragicomic, melodramatic, colorful, operatic; first- *or* second-run; stagy.

Adverbs—on the stage *or* boards; before the footlights.

drape, *n.* drapery, curtain, tapestry; hang, fall, look. —*v.t.* hang (curtains, *etc.*); shape, cut; dress, clothe, caparison; swathe, shroud, veil. See PENDENCY, CLOTHING.

drastic, *adj.* radical, extreme, stringent, severe; rash, impulsive. See SEVERITY.

draw, *v.t.* haul, drag, pull, tub, extract; attract, allure; depict, sketch; draft; win, receive; displace; inhale; elicit, get; disembowel, eviscerate. See ATTRACTION, PAINTING, TRACTION. —*n.* tie. See EQUALITY.

drawback, *n.* HINDRANCE, handicap, clog, encumbrance, restraint; objection, disadvantage. See EVIL.

drawing, *n.* picture, sketch, plan; delineation. See PAINTING.

dread, *v.t. & n.* See FEAR.

dreadful, *adj.* fearful, dire, frightful, shocking, horrible; awful, bad. See FEAR, BADNESS.

dream, *n,* vision, reverie, fantasy, fancy; daydream, chimera, nightmare; delusion, hallucination. See IMAGINATION, INSUBSTANTIALITY.

dreary, *adj.* drear, cheerless, gloomy, somber; depressing, lonely, wearisome, tedious. See DEJECTION, WEARINESS.

dregs, *n.* residue, sediment, silt, lees, grounds, heeltaps; scum, riffraff, off-scourings. See REMAINDER, POPULACE, UNCLEANNESS.

drench, *v.t.* douse, souse, soak, wet, saturate. See WATER, MOISTURE.

dress, *v.* clothe, attire, array; scold, reprove, berate, whip; adorn, garnish, decorate; align, equalize; prepare, bandage. See CLOTHING, DISAPPROBATION, ORNAMENT, REMEDY. —*n.* CLOTHING, costume, vesture, garb, raiment, apparel, habit; frock, gown.

dresser, *n.* bureau, chest [of drawers], vanity [table], dressing table. See RECEPTACLE.

dressing, *n.* decoration, ORNAMENT; sauce, seasoning, condiment; stuffing; garnish; bandage, application. See FOOD, REMEDY.

dressmaker, *n.* seamstress; stylist, fashion designer, *modiste, couturier, couturière*. See CLOTHING.

dressy, *adj.* stylish, fashionable, smart, chic; formal, fancy, showy. See OSTENTATION, FASHION.

dribble, *v.* slaver, drivel; trickle. See EGRESS, EXCRETION.

drift, *n.* pile, heap, deposit; movement, DEVIATION; TENDENCY, MEANING. See ASSEMBLAGE, MOTION, DIRECTION. —*v.i.* proceed aimlessly; pile up.

drill, *v.* pierce, bore; train, exercise, practice; quiz. See OPENING, TEACHING, EXERTION, REPETITION.

DRINKING

Nouns—**1,** drinking, imbibing, potation, libation.

2, a. drink, beverage, draft, impotation, liquor, nectar, broth, soup; potion. **b.** hard liquor, alcoholic drink, spirits, the bottle, little brown jug; home brew; brandy, cognac, applejack, hard cider; beer, ale; gin, rum, whiskey, cocktail, mixed drink, nightcap, pick-me-up; liqueur, cordial; the grape, [white, red, *or* rosé] wine, malmsey, retsina, champagne; grog, toddy, flip, punch, negus, cup, wassail. *Colloq.,* moonshine, hair of the dog [that bit one], booze. *Slang,* hooch, sauce. **c.** nonalcoholic beverage, soft drink' cola; coffee, chocolate, cocoa, tea. **d.** dram, draft, draught, nip, sip, sup, gulp, pull, swill. *Colloq.,* swig.

3, drunkenness, intoxication; INTEMPERANCE; inebriety, inebriation; ebriety, ebriosity; insobriety; wine bibbing; bacchanals, bacchanalia, libations; alcoholism, dipsomania, oenomania; delirium tremens, D.T.'s. *Colloq.,* bust, hangover. *Slang,* binge, tear, bat, toot, jag, bender, pink elephants; the morning after.

4, drunkard, drunk; alcoholic, dipsomaniac, sot, toper, tippler, bibber, wine bibber, guzzler; hard drinker; soaker, sponge, tosspot; thirsty soul, reveler, carouser; Bacchanal, Bacchanalian, Bacchante, devotee of Bacchus. *Colloq.*, boozer, barfly. *Slang,* souse, wino, lush, tank, rumhound, dipso, rummy.
5, tavern, inn; public house, pub (both *Brit.*); barroom, taproom, rathskeller, bar [and grill], alehouse, saloon, [cocktail] lounge; bistro, cabaret; bartender. *Slang,* gin mill.

Verbs—**1,** drink, imbibe, quaff, sip, lap; take a drop, tipple, guzzle, squizzle, soak, sot, carouse, tope, swill; take to drink; drink up, drink hard, drink like a fish; drain the cup, take a hair of the dog [that bit one]; wet one's whistle, crack a bottle, pass the bottle; toss off; wash down. *Colloq.*, booze, swig.
2, be *or* get drunk; fall off the wagon; see double. *Slang,* feel no pain; liquor up, lush, get high, hit the bottle *or* the sauce, go on a toot, paint the town red, hang one on, have an edge on, have a jag on, pass out [cold].
3, make drunk, intoxicate, inebriate, [be]fuddle, besot, go to one's head. *Slang,* plaster, pollute.

Adjectives—**1,** on the rocks, straight up, neat; potable, bibulous.
2, drunk, tipsy, intoxicated, inebrious, inebriate[d], in one's cups, in a state of intoxication, cut, fresh, merry, elevated, flush[ed], flustered, disguised, topheavy, overcome, maudlin, crapulous, dead *or* roaring drunk, drunk as a lord *or* an owl. *Colloq.,* boozy, mellow, high [as a kite]. *Slang,* off the wagon; boiled, soused, shellacked, fried, polluted, tanked, cockeyed, squiffed, stinko, tight, three sheets to the wind, out cold, stiff, blotto, feeling no pain, out of it.
3, intoxicating, heady.

Antonyms, see MODERATION.

---

drip, *v.i.* drop, dribble, trickle; leak, percolate. See WATER.

drive, *v.t.* propel, impel; urge forward, pursue; steer, control; conduct, carry out; ram, hammer, thrust; urge, force, compel, coerce. See COMPULSION, TRAVEL, PROPULSION, ENERGY, HASTE.

drivel, *n.* drool, slaver, slobber; nonsense, babble. —*v.i.* drool, slobber, babble, talk nonsense, dote. See ABSURDITY, LOQUACITY, UNMEANINGNESS, EXCRETION.

driver, *n.* chauffeur, teamster, wagoner, cabman, hack, cabby. See VEHICLE, TRANSPORTATION.

drizzle, *n. & v.* sprinkle, mist, rain, spray. See WATER.

droll, *adj.* comical, amusing. See AMUSEMENT.

drone, *n.* monotone, hum, buzz. See REPETITION.

drool, *v.i.* drivel, slaver. See EXCRETION.

droop, *v.* bend, loll, slouch, sag; sink, languish, decline, waste; wilt. See DEJECTION, DISEASE, WEAKNESS, PENDENCY.

drop, *v.* let fall; give up, abandon; fall, plunge; faint, collapse; cease, terminate, END; drip; dismiss, let go. See DESCENT, RELINQUISHMENT, IMPOTENCE. —*n.* globule, bead; minim; bit, mite; DESCENT. See LITTLENESS, PENDENCY, ROTUNDITY, WATER, WEAKNESS.

dross, *n.* refuse; slag; waste. See USELESSNESS, REMAINDER.

drought, *n.* aridity, DRYNESS, thirst; lack, scarcity. See INSUFFICIENCY.

drown, *v.* suffocate; submerge, inundate; muffle, overpower, go down for the third time. See WATER, KILLING, SILENCE, DEATH, LOUDNESS, FAILURE.

drowsy, *adj.* sleepy, somnolent; lazy, languid. See WEARINESS.

drudge, *v.i.* toil, slave, grub, plod, hack, grind, plug. See EXERTION.

drug, *n.* medicine, physic, elixir,

preparation, prescription, REMEDY; narcotic, dope; white elephant, a drug on the market. —*v*. narcotize, dope; medicate, dose; knock out, put to sleep. See INSENSIBILITY, SUFFICIENCY.

druggist, *n*. apothecary, pharmacist, chemist. See REMEDY.

DRYNESS

Nouns—**1,** dryness, aridity, aridness; desiccation, dehydration, anhydration; thirst; drainage; curing, mummification, freeze-drying (see PRESERVATION); evaporation.

2, drought; ebb tide, low water.

Verbs—dry (up), soak (up), sponge, swab, wipe; evaporate, desiccate; drain, parch, sear, scorch, wither; smoke, dehydrate.

Adjectives—**1,** dry, anhydrous, dehydrated, arid; dried, undamped; juiceless, sapless; sere, sear; thirsty, husky; rainless, without rain; *sec, brut*, fine; dry as a bone, a stick, a mummy, *or* a biscuit, bone-dry, dry-as-dust; waterproof, watertight; desertlike, unirrigated, waterless, parched.

2, drying, [de]siccative, dehydrating.

Antonyms, see MOISTURE.

dual, *adj*. duplex, twofold, double, duplicate, twin, binary. See NUMERATION.

dub, *v.t.* name, call, invest. See NOMENCLATURE.

dubious, *adj*. doubtful, uncertain; questionable, unreliable. See DOUBT.

duck, *v*. drake; nod, bob; dodge, avoid, elude; dip, immerse, plunge. See AVOIDANCE, WATER.

duct, *n*. channel, canal, tube, pipe, flue. See PASSAGE.

ductile, *adj*. tractile, malleable; yielding, pliant; compliant, docile, obedient. See SOFTNESS, OBEDIENCE, ELASTICITY.

dud, *n*. FAILURE; (*pl.*) *colloq*., CLOTHING.

due, *adj*. owed, owing, payable, outstanding, unpaid; rightful, proper, fit, appropriate, apropos; lawful, licit. See JUSTICE, RIGHTNESS, EXPEDIENCE, DEBT, DUTY, EFFECT. —*n*. reward, deserts. See COMPENSATION, JUSTICE, ATTRIBUTION.

duel, *n*. single combat, contest, competition, rivalry; affair of honor. See CONTENTION.

dues, *n.pl*. assessment, fee; deserts. See PAYMENT, PRICE.

dull, *adj*. unsharp, blunt; deadened, numb; stupid; tedious, uninteresting, boring; spiritless, vapid, vacuous; dead, lifeless; sluggish, listless, lethargic; lackluster, dim, cloudy, obscure, stale, jaded. —*v.t.* blunt. See SLOWNESS, BLUNTNESS, DIMNESS, WEARINESS, COLORLESSNESS.

duly, *adv*. properly; punctually. See ATTRIBUTION, EARLINESS.

dumbness, *n*. aphonia, muteness, aphony, mutism; deaf-mutism, voicelessness; SILENCE, TACITURNITY, inarticulateness; *colloq*., stupidity (see IGNORANCE).

dumfound, *v.t.* confound, flabbergast, disconcert; astonish. See SURPRISE.

dummy, *n*. [deaf-]mute; puppet, manikin, proxy, agent, stand-in. *Colloq*., stooge. See REPRESENTATION, SUBSTITUTION, SILENCE.

dump, *v*. drop, let fall; discharge, unload; abandon, jettison, scrap, junk, discard; flood the market. *Slang*, ditch. See REJECTION. —*n*. trashheap, junkpile, midden; STORE, depot, depository; den. *Slang*, dive, joint, greasy spoon, flophouse, flea trap. See ABODE, UNCLEANNESS.

dun, *v.t.* bill, press for payment. See ACCOUNTING.

dunce, *n*. dullard, moron, fool, dunderhead, simpleton, simple Simon, nitwit; dolt, oaf, clod. *Slang,* bonehead, meathead, boob, dope. See IGNORANCE, FOLLY.

dungarees, *n.pl.* jeans, overalls, Levis, chinos. See CLOTHING.

dungeon, *n.* pit, cell; jail, donjon, PRISON; black hole of Calcutta. See DEFENSE, LOWNESS.

dunk, *v.t.* dip (see WATER).

dupe, *n.* gull, victim, cully, cat's-paw; fool; puppet, tool; butt, laughingstock, April fool. *Colloq.,* sucker, chump. *Slang,* easy mark, soft touch, pushover, pigeon. —*v.t.* cheat, defraud, swindle; hoodwink, deceive, delude. See CREDULITY, DECEPTION.

duplicate, *n.* facsimile, duplication, double, reproduction, replica, COPY, reduplication; iteration, REPETITION; renewal; counterpart; gemination, twin. —*adj.* double[d], bifold, biform, bilateral, two-fold, two-sided, duplex; double-faced; twin, ingeminate; second. —*v.* [re]double, reduplicate, geminate, COPY, repeat.

duplicity, *n.* double dealing, two-facedness, treachery, deceitfulness, fraud, guile, hypocrisy. See FALSEHOOD, IMPROBITY.

DURABILITY

Nouns—**1,** durability, durableness, lastingness, CONTINUITY, standing; STABILITY, survival, longevity, AGE; distance, protraction, *or* prolongation (of time). See RESISTANCE.

2, diuturnity; age, century, eternity, aeon, years on end; lifetime; PERPETUITY, PERMANENCE. *Colloq.,* long haul, blue moon, month of Sundays. *Slang,* dog's *or* coon's age.

Verbs—**1,** endure, last, stand [up], remain, abide, bear up, hold good, hold on, linger, continue; wear well; tarry, drag on, hold, protract, prolong; tide over; drag, spin, eke, *or* draw out; temporize, gain *or* make time, talk against time; outlast, outlive, survive; land on one's feet, keep body and soul together; sit through; last *or* live out, live to fight again; live on borrowed time; take it.

2, perpetuate, immortalize, maintain (see PERPETUITY).

Adjectives—durable, lasting, hardy, heavy-duty; of long duration *or* standing, chronic, long-standing; intransient, intransitive; intransmutable, lifelong, livelong; everlasting, immortal; longeval, long-lived; diuturnal, evergreen, perennial; never-ending, unremitting; perpetual, interminable, eternal; unfailing; lingering, protracted, prolonged, spun-out, long-pending, long-winded; slow.

Adverbs—**1,** durably, long; for a long time, for an age, for ages, for ever so long, from way back; for many a long day; long ago; all day long, all year round, the live-long day, as the day is long; morning, noon, and night; day in and day out; hour after hour, day after day; for good, permanently.

2, always, ever, evermore, forever, for keeps, for good, till Hell freezes over, till the cows come home; for aye, world without end, perpetually.

Antonyms, see TRANSIENTNESS.

---

duration, *n.* term, TIME, period; continuance, persistence. See PERMANENCE.

duress, *n.* coercion; RESTRAINT, imprisonment. See COMPULSION.

during, *prep.* pending, through, in the time of, until. See TIME.

dusk, *n.* twilight, gloaming; semi-darkness, gloom, half-light, shadow; swarthiness. See DIMNESS, DARKNESS.

dust, *n.* powder; earth, soil; dirt, lint, ash, soot, flue. See POWDERINESS, UNCLEANNESS.

DUTY

Nouns—**1,** duty, moral obligation, accountability, LIABILITY, onus, responsibility; bounden duty; call of duty; allegiance, fealty, tie; engagement, PROMISE; part, function, calling, BUSINESS.
2, morality, morals, ethics; Ten Commandments; conscientiousness, conscience, inward monitor, still small voice; sense of duty, VIRTUE.
3, propriety, fitness, the [proper] thing (see AGREEMENT).
4, observance, fulfillment, discharge, acquittal, performance (see COMPLETION).

Verbs—**1,** be the duty of, be incumbent on, be responsible, behoove, become, befit, beseem; belong to, pertain to; fall to one's lot; devolve on, lie upon, lie on one's head, lie at one's door, rest with, rest on the shoulders of.
2, take upon oneself, PROMISE, be bound to, be sponsor for; incur a responsibility; be *or* stand under obligation; have to answer for, be answerable for, owe it to oneself.
3, impose a duty, enjoin, require, exact (see COMPULSION); pass the buck, let George do it.
4, enter upon, perform, observe, fulfill, discharge, satisfy, *or* acquit oneself of a duty *or* an obligation; adhere to; act one's part, redeem one's pledge, do justice to, be at one's post; do one's duty; be on good behavior, mind one's P's and Q's.

Adjectives—**1,** obligatory, binding, imperative, behooving, incumbent on; obligated, under obligation; obliged, bound, *or* tied by; saddled with; due to, beholden to, bound to, indebted to, duty bound, tied down; compromised; amenable, liable, accountable, responsible, answerable; right, meet, due; moral, ethical, casuistical, conscientious.
2, dutiful, duteous, loyal, diligent, obedient, submissive. See OBEDIENCE.

Adverbs—dutifully, in duty bound, on one's own responsibility, at one's own risk; in the line of duty.

Antonyms, see NEGLECT.

---

dwarf, *n.* midget, pygmy, Lilliputian, runt, shrimp. See LITTLENESS, DEMON. —*v.* stunt; tower over. See SHORTNESS, CONTRACTION, INFERIORITY.

dwell, *v.i.* live, reside, abide; *slang,* harp, iterate. *Slang,* hang out. See PRESENCE, REPETITION, ABODE, INHABITANT.

dwelling, *n.* See ABODE.

dwindle, *v.i.* diminish, shrink, lessen, run low, waste away. See DECREASE.

dye, *v.t. & n.* COLOR, tint, stain.

dynamic, *adj.* forceful, vigorous, potent, impelling; propulsive. See POWER, IMPULSE.

dysentery, *n.* flux; diarrhea; cramps. *Slang,* the grips, trots, *or* runs. See DISEASE, EXCRETION.

E

each, *adv.* apiece, severally, seriatim, respectively. See SPECIALITY. —*adj.* every. See GENERALITY.

eager, *adj.* desirous, keen, fervent, fervid, hot-headed, earnest, intent; zealous, ardent, agog; avid, anxious, athirst. See ACTIVITY, DESIRE, EXPECTATION, FEELING, HASTE.

eagle, *n.* bald, sea, *or* golden eagle, erne, ringtail, eaglet, harpy. See ANIMAL.

ear, *n.* head, spike; auricle, concha; handle, knob; heed, observance. See ATTENTION, HEARING.

earful, *n., colloq.,* harangue, tirade; gossip, tip; a piece of one's mind, bawling out. *Slang,* the lowdown, info. See NEWS, SPEECH, INFORMATION.

EARLINESS

Nouns—**1,** earliness, punctuality, promptitude, alacrity, dispatch, expedition, readiness (see PREPARATION); HASTE. See UNPREPAREDNESS.
2, prematurity, precocity, precipitation, anticipation; a stitch in time. See PREDICTION, PRIORITY, OCCASION.

Verbs—**1,** be early, be beforehand, jump the gun, take time by the forelock, anticipate, forestall; have the start; steal a march upon, get *or* have the jump on, steal one's thunder *or* the spotlight, take the words out of one's mouth; take advantage of; gain time, preempt, bespeak.
2, see INSTANTANEITY.

Adjectives—**1,** early, timely, punctual, forward; prompt, instant, ready.
2, premature, precipitate, precocious; prevenient, anticipatory, ahead of time; forward, advanced; imminent.

Adverbs—**1,** early, soon, anon, betimes, duly, ere *or* before long, punctually, promptly, on time *or* schedule, on the dot, to the minute, in due course *or* season, in [good] time *or* season, in due time, time enough, bright and early.
2, beforehand, prematurely, precipitately, hastily, too soon, before its time; in anticipation; unexpectedly.
3, briefly, shortly, presently, at the first opportunity, by and by, in a while, directly.

Antonyms, see LATENESS.

---

earmark, *n.* & *v.t.* See INDICATION.

earn, *v.t.* work for, gain, win; deserve, merit, rate; make a living, be gainfully employed. See ACQUISITION, JUSTICE.

earnest, *adj.* intent, intense, serious, grave, solemn, sober, weighty, purposeful, determined; sincere; IMPORTANT; diligent; eager, impassioned, animated, cordial, zealous, fervent, ardent. See FEELING, IMPORTANCE, RESOLUTION.

earnings, *n.pl.* pay, PAYMENT.

earsplitting, *adj.* See LOUDNESS.

earth, *n.* planet, globe, world; ground, LAND, dirt, soil, mold. See UNIVERSE.

earthbound, *adj.* mundane, temporal. See LIMIT, POSSIBILITY.

earthenware, *n.* crockery, china, pottery, ceramics, stoneware. See MATERIALS.

earthling, *n.* earthdweller, mortal, terrestrian; flesh and blood. See HUMANITY.

earthly, *adj.* terrestrial; material, worldly, sensual, temporal, mundane, secular; *colloq.,* possible, conceivable. See IRRELIGION, LAND, POSSIBILITY.

earthquake, *n.* tremor, seism, quake, shock. See VIOLENCE.

earthshaking, *adj., colloq.* See LOUDNESS, IMPORTANCE.

earthwork, *n.* rampart (see DEFENSE).

earthy, *adj.* earthly; popular, vulgar, crude, unrefined; elemental, simple, primitive, down-to-earth; robust, vigorous, Rabelaisian; lewd, racy, bawdy. *Slang,* gutsy. See SIMPLENESS, IMPURITY, POPULACE.

ease, *n.* comfort, luxury; rest, repose; CONTENT, enjoyment, complacency; RELIEF; leisure, convenience; FACILITY, readiness, expertness; unconstraint, naturalness. See PLEASURE, ELEGANCE.

easel, *n.* tripod. See SUPPORT.

eastern, *adj.* east, oriental. See DIRECTION.

easy, *adj.* comfortable, restful, indolent, unconcerned, untroubled; free, unembarrassed, careless, smooth, unconstrained, natural, graceful; effortless (see FACILITY); mild, gentle, indulgent; tractable, compliant; light, unexacting. See ELEGANCE, MODERATION, CONSENT, CONTENT.

easygoing, *adj.* happy-go-lucky, cheerful; unconcerned, untroubled, careless; effortless, facile; tractable, compliant. See CONTENT, LENIENCY.

eat, *v.* consume, devour, eat up, feed, fare; erode, corrode, wear, rust. See FOOD, DETERIORATION.

eavesdrop, *v.i.* listen in, spy, snoop, overhear; bug, tap. See HEARING, CURIOSITY.

ebb, *v.i.* recede, fall back, outflow, withdraw; decline; waste, decay. See DECREASE, REGRESSION, WASTE.

ebullient, *adj.* excited; boiling. See EXCITEMENT, AGITATION.

eccentric, *adj.* elliptic[al], parabolic, hyperbolic; irregular, deviating; peculiar, queer, odd, strange, bizarre, singular; erratic, cranky, abnormal. See IRREGULARITY, FOLLY, INSANITY, UNCONFORMITY, ROTUNDITY.

ecclesiastical, *adj.* churchly, sacerdotal, priestly, clerical. See CLERGY.

echelon, *n.* See DEGREE, ARRANGEMENT.

echo, *v.* reverberate, resound, reply, ring; repeat, reproduce. See IMITATION, RECOIL, ANSWER, COPY. —*n.* reverberation, REPETITION, response, repercussion.

eclectic, *adj.* selective. See CHOICE, DIFFERENCE.

eclipse, *v.t.* obscure, darken, cloud, hide, conceal; outshine, surpass, overshadow. See DARKNESS, REPUTE, CONCEALMENT.

ecology, *n.* conservation; ecosystem; autecology, *etc.* See ENVIRONMENT.

ECONOMY

Nouns—**1,** economy, thriftiness, frugality, thrift, care, husbandry, housekeeping, ménage, good housewifery, good management *or* administration, retrenchment, cutback. See ORDER, PRESERVATION.

2, savings, reserves; savings account, Christmas Club; PARSIMONY, cheeseparing, stinginess, scrimping. See CHEAPNESS.

Verbs—economize, save, scrimp; retrench, tighten one's belt; cut corners, skimp, make [both] ends meet, meet one's expenses, pay one's way; husband, save money, lay by *or* away, put by, lay aside, store up; hoard, accumulate, amass, salt away; provide for a rainy day; feather one's nest.

Adjectives—economical, frugal, careful, thrifty, saving, chary, sparing, parsimonious, stingy, scrimping.

Adverbs—sparingly, frugally, thriftily, economically, carefully, parsimoniously.

Antonyms, see WASTE.

ecstasy, *n.* rapture, joy, transport, bliss, exaltation; gladness, intoxication, enthusiasm; trance, frenzy, inspiration. See PLEASURE, FEELING, IMAGINATION.

ecumenical, *adj.* See GENERALITY.

eddy, *n.* countercurrent, vortex, whirlpool. See WATER, ROTATION.

EDGE

Nouns—**1,** edge, verge, brink, brow, brim, curb, margin, LIMIT, boundary, border, skirt, rim, flange, SIDE; mouth, jaws, lip; frame, fringe, flounce, frill, trim[ming], edging, skirting, hem, welt, furbelow, valance, salvage.

2, threshold, entrance, gate[way], coast, bank, shore; quay.

Verbs—edge, verge, border, bound, skirt, rim, fringe; sidle *or* inch along.

Adjectives—border, bordering, rimming, fringing, marginal, skirting; labial, labiated, marginated.

Adverbs—edgewise, edgeways, sidewise, sideways, edge on.

Antonyms, see INTERIOR, MIDDLE.

---

edgy, *adj.* irritable, nervous. See IRASCIBILITY, EXCITABILITY.

edible, *adj.* See FOOD.

edict, *n.* decree, bull, law, fiat, proclamation. See COMMAND.

edification, *n.* instruction, enlightenment, education. See TEACHING.

edifice, *n.* building, structure; palace, church. See PRODUCTION.

edit, *v.t.* redact, revise, arrange, digest, correct, prepare; select, adapt, compose, compile; issue, publish. See IMPROVEMENT, PUBLICATION.

edition, *n.* redaction; issue, impression, printing. See PUBLICATION.

editorialize, *v.* expatiate, expound, spout; use the editorial "we." *Slang,* sound off, put in one's two cents. See JUDGMENT, TEACHING.

educate, *v.t.* teach, train, instruct, enlighten, edify, school; develop, cultivate; discipline, form. See TEACHING.

educated, *adj.* lettered, literate. See KNOWLEDGE.

educe, *v.t.* draw forth, bring out, develop, elicit; deduce, infer, evoke. See EXTRACTION.

eerie, *adj.* weird, uncanny. See FEAR.

efface, *v.t.* obliterate, erase, expunge, excise, delete, dele, strike, cancel, wipe out, blot. See NULLIFICATION.

EFFECT

Nouns—**1,** effect, consequence, result, upshot, issue, outcome, denouement; outgrowth, development, aftermath, aftereffect, fallout; OCCURRENCE; corollary. *Slang,* payoff. See SEQUENCE.

2, product, output, work, handiwork, performance; creature, creation; offspring, offshoot, fruit, first fruits, crop, harvest; effectiveness.

Verbs—**1,** effect, CAUSE, create, effectuate, produce, bring about, give rise to.

2, be the effect of; be due *or* owing to; originate in *or* from; rise, ensue, arise, spring, proceed, emanate, come, grow, issue, *or* result from; come out of, follow, come to; cut both *or* two ways, pan out, fare; hinge on.

Adjectives—**1,** owing to, resulting from, due to, attributable to, caused by, dependent upon, derived *or* evolved from; derivative, hereditary.

2, consequent, resultant, contingent, eventual, consequential.

Adverbs—of course, it follows that, so that, in effect, therefore, hence, naturally, consequently, as a consequence, in consequence, in the wake of, through, necessarily, eventually.

Antonyms, see CAUSE.

---

effective, *adj.* efficacious, effectual, productive, adequate, telling, potent, active, operative, dynamic; successful; causative; efficient, capable. See POWER, UTILITY, AGENCY, SUCCESS, VIGOR.

effeminate, *adj.* womanish, unmanly. See WEAKNESS, FEMALE.

effervesce, *v.i.* bubble, hiss, ferment, foam, fizz. See AGITATION.

effete, *adj.* exhausted, spent, depleted; barren, sterile, fruitless; weak, corrupt, decadent. See DETERIORATION, USELESSNESS.

efficient, *n.* effective, effectual, efficacious, operative; skillful, capable, productive, competent; causative. See POWER, SKILL, AGENCY, CAUSE, UTILITY.

effigy, *n.* dummy, icon, caricature; COPY, counterpart, replica, simulacrum; substitute; Guy Fawkes. See REPRESENTATION.

effort, *n.* EXERTION, endeavor; strain, stress, attempt; achievement. *Colloq.,* push. See ACTION.

effortless, *adj.* easy, facile; natural, simple. See FACILITY.

effrontery, *n.* shamelessness, brazenness, INSOLENCE, audacity.

egg, *n.* egg cell, ovum, embryo; oval. See BEGINNING, REPRODUCTION, ROTUNDITY. —*v.* incite, goad. See CAUSE.

egg-shaped, *adj.* oviform, oval, ovate, ovoid, elliptical. See ROTUNDITY.

ego, *n.* self, personality, I. See INSUBSTANTIALITY, IDENTITY.

egoism, *n.* individualism, SELFISHNESS, self-seeking, conceit. See VANITY.

egotism, *n.* VANITY, self-exaltation, [self-]conceit. See SELFISHNESS.

EGRESS

Nouns—**1,** egress, exit, issue, emergence, eruption, emanation, exudation, leakage, oozing, gush, outpouring, effluence, effusion, drain, drainage, outflow; discharge (see EXCRETION).

2, export, expatriation, emigration, exodus, DEPARTURE; emigrant, migrant, colonist.

3, outlet, vent, spout, tab, sluice, floodgate; exit, way out, mouth, OPENING.

Verbs—**1,** emerge, emanate, issue, pass off; exit, exeunt, depart, ESCAPE; emigrate.

2, leak, run out, percolate, exude, strain, drain, ooze, filter, filtrate, dribble, gush, spout, flow, well out, pour, trickle; effuse, debouch, come forth, break *or* burst out, fall out, let out.

Adjectives—emergent, emerging, outgoing, emanative, effluent, eruptive, leaky; migrant.

Adverbs—out of, from, away.

Antonyms, see INGRESS.

---

either, *adj.* See CHOICE.

ejaculate, *v.t.* eject, discharge, spew *or* shoot out; exclaim, blurt out. See PROPULSION, CRY.

EJECTION

Nouns—**1,** ejection, emission, effusion, rejection, expulsion, eviction, extrusion, discharge, EXCRETION; evacuation, vomiting, eructation. See PROPULSION.

2, deportation, banishment, exile, excommunication, relegation, extradition, dislodgment, DISPLACEMENT; dismissal, ouster; riddance. *Slang,* the gate, the sack, the ax, the air, the bum's rush. See EXCLUSION, RELINQUISHMENT.

Verbs—**1,** give vent to, let out *or* off, send out, shed, void, eliminate, evacuate, emit, vomit, spew, eruct; extrude, effuse, spend; squirt, spurt, spill; throw up *or* heave; spit up.

2, eject, reject, expel, discard; cast out, throw *or* push out, off, away, *or* aside; shovel *or* sweep out; dispose of, get out of one's hair; brush off, cast adrift, turn *or* bundle out; unburden; throw overboard; get rid of, shake off; send packing, turn out, pack off, dismiss, dump; bow out, show the door to; boycott; discharge, cashier, read out of, send flying, kick upstairs. *Slang,* give the gate, the sack, *or* the bum's rush to, give *or* get the air; bounce.

3, evict, oust, dislodge, relegate, deport, banish, exile, extradite; kick *or* boot out; excommunicate; run out; clear off *or* out, clean out, make a clean sweep of, purge; displace; give one one's walking papers; smoke out.

4, be dismissed. *Slang,* get the ax, the sack, the bounce, the gate, *or* the hook.

5, unpack, unlade, unload, unship.

Adjectives—emitting, emissive, ejective, expulsive, eliminative.

Interjections—begone! get you gone! get away! go away! off with you! go about your business! be off! avaunt! *Slang*, take off! get lost! beat it! scram! drop dead!

Antonyms, see RECEIVING.

---

eke out, *v.t.* manage, just *or* barely make, squeeze out. See DIFFICULTY, PROVISION.

elaborate, *v.* work out, develop, devise, perfect, embellish, refine. See COMPLETION, VARIEGATION.—*adj.* labored, studied, complicated, detailed, painstaking, finished, perfected; intricate, involved. See DISORDER.

elapse, *v.i.* slip away, pass, expire, intervene, glide by. See TIME, COURSE.

ELASTICITY

Nouns—**1,** elasticity, springiness, spring, resilience, buoyancy, extensibility, ductility, stretch, rebound, adaptability. See VIGOR, EXPANSION.

2, rubber, India rubber, caoutchouc, whalebone, elastomer, baleen, gum elastic.

3, gymnast, contortionist.

Verbs—be elastic, spring back, rebound, stretch, expand.

Adjectives—elastic, tensile, springy, resilient, buoyant, extensible, ductile, stretchable, adaptable.

Antonyms, see INELASTICITY.

---

elate, *v.t.* excite, enliven, exhilarate, exalt, animate, lift up, flush, elevate; please, gratify, gladden, delight. See CHEERFULNESS, EXCITEMENT.

elbow, *n.* bend, angle, dogleg. See ANGULARITY, CONVEXITY. —*v.* jab, poke; push, prod, shove; jostle, make one's way through. See IMPULSE.

elder, *adj.* older, earlier, superior, senior; elderly. —*n.* ancestor, senior. See AGE, OLDNESS.

elect, *v.t.* choose, select, decide on, fix upon; call, ordain. See CHOICE.

electric, *adj.* voltaic, magnetic, galvanic; thrilling, exciting, stimulating. See FEELING, POWER.

electrify, *v.t.* galvanize, magnetize, charge; excite, thrill, stimulate, animate; stun, bewilder, startle. See POWER, WONDER, EXCITEMENT.

electrode, *n.* terminal; anode, cathode; conductor. See POWER.

ELEGANCE

Nouns—**1,** elegance, refinement, ease, grace, gracefulness, polish, finish, good TASTE, harmonious simplicity, rhythm, harmony, symmetry. See BEAUTY.

2, [good] style, euphony, classicism, purism; purist, classicist, stylist.

Verbs—show elegance *or* refinement; discriminate; round a period.

Adjectives—**1,** elegant, polished, classic[al], courtly, correct, artistic, chaste, pure, appropriate, refined, graceful, felicitous, in good taste, harmonious; genteel.

2, easy, fluent, flowing, mellifluous, balanced, euphonious; neatly put, well expressed.

Antonyms, see VULGARITY, INELEGANCE.

elegy, *n.* dirge, lament, requiem, threnody. See LAMENTATION, POETRY.

element, *n.* component, PART, substance, constituent, ingredient; factor, principle, rudiment, fundamental. See CAUSE, COMPOSITION.

elementary, *adj.* rudimentary, incipient, primary, fundamental, basic; introductory; simple, uncompounded. See INTRINSIC, SIMPLENESS.

elephantine, *adj.* huge, mammoth. See SIZE.

ELEVATION

Nouns—**1,** elevation; raising, lifting, erection; uplift. See ANGULARITY, VERTICAL.

2, prominence, eminence; HEIGHT, hill, mount, mountain.

3, lever, crank, block and tackle, crane, derrick, windlass, capstan, winch, crowbar, jimmy, pulley, jack, dredge, elevator, lift, dumbwaiter, hoist, escalator, moving stairway.

Verbs—elevate, heighten, raise, lift, erect, jack up, set up, stick up, heave, buoy, weigh, pick up; take up, fish up; cast up; dredge; hold up (see SUPPORT).

Adjectives—**1,** elevated, raised, lifted up; on a pedestal; aweigh; erect, VERTICAL.

2, eminent, prominent.

Antonyms, see DEPRESSION.

---

elevator, *n.* lift; granary, silo. See ELEVATION, STORE.

elf, *n.* sprite, fairy, imp, puck, pixy; gnome, goblin. See MYTHICAL DEITIES, DEMON.

elicit, *v.t.* draw forth, extract, evoke, educe, extort. See EXTRACTION, CAUSE.

elide, *v.t.* omit, suppress. See NEGLECT.

eligible, *adj.* qualified, fitted, suitable, desirable. See EXPEDIENCE.

eliminate, *v.t.* expel, excrete, secrete; remove, get rid of, exclude, set aside, drop, cast out, eradicate; omit, ignore, leave out, NEGLECT, pass over; suppress, extract. See EXTRACTION, EJECTION, EXCLUSION.

elite, *adj.* select, choice, prime. —*n.* [the] elect, choice, cream, flower; chosen people; inner circle, aristocracy, *beau* or *haut monde*; the four hundred; cream of the crop, *crème de la crème*. See SUPERIORITY, GOODNESS.

elixir, *n.* potion, essence, quintessence; philosophers' stone. See REMEDY.

elliptical, *adj.* oval, egg-shaped; condensed, cut, lacunal. See ROTUNDITY, SHORTNESS.

elongate, *v.* lengthen, extend, string out. See LENGTH.

elope, *v.t.* run away, decamp, abscond. See MARRIAGE, ESCAPE.

eloquence, *n.* oratory, rhetoric, power; fluency, persuasiveness, volubility. See LOQUACITY, SPEECH.

elsewhere, *adv.* somewhere else. See ABSENCE.

elucidate, *v.t.* clarify, illuminate, illustrate; explain, interpret. See INTERPRETATION.

elude, *v.t.* ESCAPE, evade, avoid; dodge, foil, baffle. See AVOIDANCE.

elusive, *adj.* elusory, evasive, slippery, shifty, tricky, baffling; deceptive, illusory, intangible, fugitive. See TRANSIENTNESS, DECEPTION.

emaciated, *adj.* starveling, thin, haggard, wasted, gaunt, drawn, scrawny. *Colloq.,* skin and bones. See NARROWNESS.

emanate, *v.* effuse, exhale, radiate; flow, proceed, issue, come, spring, arise. See EGRESS, EFFECT, FRAGRANCE.

emancipate, *v.t.* liberate, free, release, deliver, manumit, set free, enfranchise. See LIBERATION.

emasculate, *v.t.* unman, castrate, geld, alter, effeminize; devitalize, debilitate; dispirit, demoralize. See WEAKNESS, IMPOTENCE.

embalm, *v.t.* preserve, mummify. See INTERMENT, PRESERVATION.

embankment, *n.* dike, mole, bulwark, bank, wall, levee; barrier, rampart. See DEFENSE, ENCLOSURE.

embargo, *n.* restriction, RESTRAINT, HINDRANCE, PROHIBITION.

embark, *v.t.* ship, board, set sail; sail; begin, engage. See DEPARTURE, UNDERTAKING, BEGINNING.

embarrass, *v.t.* discomfort, demoralize, disconcert, discomfit, nonplus, bother, abash, encumber, trouble, hamper, complicate, perplex. See DIFFICULTY, HINDRANCE, DISCONTENT.

embassy, *n.* mission, ministry, legation, consulate. See COMMISSION.

embattled, *adj.* armed, arrayed; fortified. See DEFENSE.

embellish, *v.t.* ORNAMENT; embroider (see EXAGGERATION).

ember, *n.* coal, brand (see FUEL).

embezzle, *v.* steal, misappropriate, misapply, peculate, defalcate. See STEALING.

embitter, *v.t.* sour, envenom, poison, anger, irritate. See RESENTMENT.

emblem, *n.* symbol, token, sign; flag, badge, *etc.* See INDICATION.

embody, *v.t.* incorporate, join, unite, organize, impersonate, personify, incarnate; comprise, contain, include; express. See REPRESENTATION, COMBINATION, SUBSTANCE, WHOLE.

emboss, *v.* knob, stud, engrave, chase. See CONVEXITY, ORNAMENT.

embrace, *v.t.* clasp, clutch, hold, fold, hug; include, comprehend, take in, comprise, involve, embody; encircle, enclose, surround; receive, welcome; take up, adopt, espouse. See CHOICE, INCLUSION, ENVIRONMENT, ENDEARMENT, CIRCUMSCRIPTION.

embroidery, *n.* needlework, crewelwork, gros *or* petit point. See ORNAMENT, EXAGGERATION.

embroil, *v.t.* complicate, throw into DISORDER.

embryo, *n.* fetus, egg, germ, bud; incipience, conception. See BEGINNING.

emerge, *v.i.* issue, appear; arise, come forth. See EGRESS.

emergency, *n.* juncture, crisis; exigency, NECESSITY, pinch, extremity. See CIRCUMSTANCE, DIFFICULTY.

emigrant, *n.* See EGRESS.

emigration, *n.* migration, departure, exodus. See EGRESS.

eminence, *n.* height, altitude, ELEVATION; distinction, rank, REPUTE, importance; hill, HEIGHT. See CLERGY.

emissary, *n.* messenger, AGENT.

emit, *v.t.* discharge, emanate, radiate, breathe, exhale, send forth, throw off, issue; deliver, voice, utter. See EJECTION, SPEECH.

emollient, *n.* ointment, balm. See REMEDY, SOFTNESS.

emotion, *n.* FEELING, sentiment, passion, SENSIBILITY, sensation.

empathy, *n.* understanding, comprehension. See PITY, FRIEND.

emperor, *n.* Caesar, kaiser, tsar; empress. See AUTHORITY, NOBILITY.

emphasize, *v.t.* accentuate, stress, mark, underline, underscore. See AFFIRMATION, IMPORTANCE.

empire, *n.* realm, domain, imperium; sovereignty, sway. See AUTHORITY, REGION.

empirical, *adj.* experiential, perceptual, practical, firsthand; commonsense, pragmatic; by trial and error, by feel. See EXPERIMENT.

employ, *v.t.* USE, occupy; hire, engage. See COMPARISON, BUSINESS.

employee, *n.* SERVANT, helper, [hired] hand; clerk, assistant.

employer, *n.* user, consumer; boss, *padrone*. See USE, DIRECTOR.

emporium, *n.* See SALE.

empower, *v.t.* enable, endow, invest; authorize, license, COMMISSION. See PERMISSION, POWER.

empress, *n.* czarina, queen, [maha]rani, begum; consort. See AUTHORITY.

empty, *v.* void, deplete, exhaust, evacuate, drain, deflate, discharge, unload. See CONTRACTION, EJECTION. —*adj.* hollow, vacant, depleted, untenanted, devoid; hungry; vain, substantial, useless, foolish, trivial, unfeeling, fruitless, inane. See ABSENCE, USELESSNESS, WASTE.

empyrean, *adj.* heavenly, empyreal, celestial, sublime; fiery. See UNIVERSE.

emulate, *v.t.* rival, vie, compete, strive, contend. See OPPOSITION, REPUTE, IMITATION.

enable, *v.t.* empower, invest, endow; authorize. See POWER.

enact, *v.t.* decree, make, pass, order, ordain; play, execute, perform, do. See DRAMA, COMMAND.

enamor, *v.t.* charm, captivate. See LOVE.

enchant, *v.t.* bewitch, conjure; captivate, please, charm, delight, fascinate. See PLEASURE, SORCERY.

encircle, *v.t.* environ, surround, embrace, encompass, enclose; span, ring, loop, girdle. See ENVIRONMENT, CIRCUMSCRIPTION.

ENCLOSURE

Nouns—**1,** enclosure, envelope, case, cartridge, RECEPTACLE, wrapper, COVERING, girdle. See REGION.

2, pen, fold; enclave; sheepfold, paddock, pound, coop, sty, pigsty, stall, kennel, corral, net, kraal, compound; courtyard; patio, yard, *etc.*

3, wall; hedge, fence, pale, paling, balustrade, rail[ing], dike, ditch, fosse, moat, levee, embankment; dam. See DEFENSE.

4, barrier, barricade, parapet, rampart, stockade; jail (see PRISON).

Verbs—enclose, confine, surround, circumscribe, envelop, hedge about *or* in, pen in, hem in, impen, impound, close in, dam up. See CIRCUMSCRIPTION.

Antonyms, see EXTERIOR, SPACE.

encompass, *v.t.* surround, encircle; contain. See INCLUSION, ENVIRONMENT.

encounter, *v.t.* meet, come across; engage, struggle, contend. —*n.* meeting, interview; collision, combat, battle, skirmish, brush, engagement. See CONTENTION, IMPULSE, OPPOSITION, OCCURRENCE, CONTACT.

encourage, *v.t.* animate, strengthen, hearten, fortify, inspirit, cheer, inspire, reassure, rally, comfort; abet, embolden, incite, urge, instigate; help, foster, promote, advance, advocate. See HOPE, CHEERFULNESS, AID.

encroach, *v.i.* advance, infringe, usurp, invade, trespass, intrude, overstep, violate; make inroads. See ILLEGALITY, OVERRUNNING.

encumber, *v.t.* burden, hamper, load, clog, oppress; obstruct, hinder, impede, embarrass, retard, check, handicap. See HINDRANCE, DIFFICULTY, DEBT.

encyclopedic, *adj.* extensive, exhaustive, comprehensive. See INCLUSION, COMPLETION, GENERALITY.

END

Nouns—**1,** end[ing], close, termination, conclusion, wind-up, finis, finish, finale, period, terminus, stopping [point]; halt, cessation, desistance, cloture, abortion, curtailment, stop[page], expiration, halt. See DISCONTINUANCE.

2, extreme, extremity; acme, peak (see HEIGHT); tip, nib, point; tail [end], fag *or* tag end, bitter end; peroration. *Colloq.,* shank. See LIMIT.

3, consummation, COMPLETION, denouement, finish, doomsday, crack of doom, Day of Judgment, final curtain, last stages, last word, expiration, DEATH, end of all things, quietus, finality. *Slang,* payoff, curtains.

4, finishing stroke, death blow, knockout. K.O., *coup de grâce;* last straw; straw that breaks the camel's back.

5, goal, destination, object, purpose (see INTENTION).

Verbs—**1,** end, close, finish, terminate, conclude, be all over, expire, die (see DEATH); come to a close, run its course, run out, pass away, be through, end up; have done, leave off. *Colloq.,* wind up, the jig *or* game is up.

2, bring to an end, put an end to, make an end of, lay to rest; determine; complete; stop, turn, *or* cut off; close *or* shut the door, shut up shop, ring down the curtain; call a halt, blow the whistle on, rain out; flag down; stop cold *or* dead, stop in one's tracks; put out, extinguish.

3, cease, halt, arrest, desist, expire, lapse, stop; sign off; curtail, choke off, cut short (see SHORTNESS); abort, drop. *Slang,* cut out.

Adjectives—**1,** ending, final, terminal, definitive, crowning, completing, last [but not least], ultimate, extreme, conclusive, last-ditch.

2, end, at an end, settled, decided, over, played out.

Adverbs—finally, definitely, conclusively; at the last, when the chips are down; in time; once and for all, to the bitter end; all over but the shouting; that is that.

Antonyms, see BEGINNING.

---

endanger, *v.t.* imperil. See DANGER.

ENDEARMENT

Nouns—**1,** endearment, caress; fondling, billing and cooing, dalliance, embrace, kiss, buss, smack, osculation. See FLATTERY, FEELING.

2, courtship, affections, wooing, suit, addresses, *amour,* lovemaking, petting; flirting, flirtation, gallantry; coquetry. *Colloq.,* spooning. *Slang,* necking, smooching. See LOVE.

3, lover's knot, love token, love letter; *billet-doux,* valentine.

4, engagement, betrothal, MARRIAGE; honeymoon.

5, flirt, coquette, *femme fatale;* philanderer, lover, Don Juan, Casanova; paramour. *Colloq.,* loverboy. *Slang,* vamp, gold digger; wolf, sheik.

6, dear, darling, sweetheart, precious, love, honey, honeybunch, pet, *etc.*

Verbs—**1,** caress, fondle, pet; cosset, coddle, make much of; cherish, foster; clasp, hug, cuddle, nuzzle, snuggle, fall all over, enfold, fold in one's arms, nestle; embrace, kiss, buss, smack.

2, make love, bill and coo, pet; toy, dally, flirt, coquet, philander; court, woo, pay addresses; set one's cap for, be sweet on; ogle, cast sheep's eyes on, make eyes at; pop the question. *Colloq.,* pitch woo, spark, spoon, make time. *Slang,* smooch, neck, make out, play footsie; make a pass at, make a play for.

3, fall in love with; propose, pop the question; plight one's troth.

Adjectives—**1,** endearing, winsome, lovable, kissable, affectionate, caressing.

2, lovesick, lovelorn. *Colloq.,* spoony.

Antonyms, see DETRACTION, HATE.

---

endeavor, *v.i.* try, attempt, seek, struggle, strive, essay, labor, aim, offer. —*n.* trial, try, attempt, effort, struggle, EXERTION, offer. See INTENTION, UNDERTAKING.

endless, *adj.* incessant, uninterrupted,

unceasing, continuous, perpetual; never-ending, unending, everlasting, continual, undying, eternal; boundless, indefinite, illimitable, unlimited, immeasurable. See CONTINUITY, PERPETUITY, INFINITY.

endorse, *v.t.* approve, support, second; recommend; subscribe (to); sign. See APPROBATION.

endow, *v.t.* dower, settle upon, bequeath, bestow, enrich, endue; furnish, invest, clothe. See GIVING.

endowment, *n.* property, fund, foundation; gift, bestowal, dower, dowry; POWER; ability, faculty, aptitude, capacity, talent, bent. See GIVING, SKILL, POSSESSION.

endue, *v.t.* endow, clothe, furnish. See POWER.

endure, *v.* continue, remain, wear, last; abide, bear, suffer, bear up, sustain, undergo; tolerate, put up with, stand, brook, permit. See RESISTANCE, FEELING, DURABILITY, EXISTENCE.

enemy, *n.* foe, opponent (see OPPOSITION).

ENERGY

Nouns—**1,** energy, POWER, STRENGTH; VIGOR, vim, punch; intensity, go, dash, drive, high pressure; RESOLUTION; EXERTION, excitation. *Colloq.,* ginger. *Slang,* pep, moxie, socko, zip, vinegar.

2, ACTIVITY; effervescence, fermentation (see AGITATION); radioactivity, kinetic *or* dynamic energy, driving force; erg, dyne.

3, dynamo, generator; motor, engine; FUEL, electricity, atomic power, *or* energy; stimulant.

4, life of the party. *Slang,* live wire, human dynamo, go-getter, hustler.

Verbs—energize, stimulate, intensify. *Slang,* pep up, give a shot in the arm.

Adjectives—energetic, active, intense; keen, vivid, incisive, trenchant, brisk, rousing, electrifying. *Slang,* full of steam, raring to go.

Adverbs—energetically, strongly, with might and main, in earnest. *Colloq.,* like mad, hammer and tongs.

Antonyms, see WEAKNESS.

---

enervate, *v.t.* weaken, devitalize, unnerve, paralyze, soften, emasculate, unman, debilitate, enfeeble, effeminate. See IMPOTENCE, WEAKNESS.

enfold, *v.t.* envelop, enclose, encompass; embrace. See ENDEARMENT, CIRCUMSCRIPTION.

enforce, *v.t.* compel, force, oblige; urge, lash, goad; strengthen; execute, sanction, put in force. See COMPULSION, CAUSE.

enfranchise, *v.t.* liberate, set free, release; naturalize; empower, license, qualify. See PERMISSION, LIBERATION.

engage, *v.t.* bind, obligate, pledge, PROMISE; betroth; hire, enlist, employ, book, retain; reserve, secure; occupy, interest, engross, attract, entangle, involve, interlock; set about, take up; fight, contend. See COMMISSION, UNDERTAKING, ATTENTION, CONTENTION.

engagement, *n.* betrothal, obligation, PROMISE, agreement, pledge; appointment, interview; occupation, employment; battle, action, skirmish, brush, encounter. See DUTY, BUSINESS, CONTENTION, SOCIALITY, MARRIAGE.

engender, *v.t.* CAUSE; beget, procreate. See REPRODUCTION.

engine, *n.* motor, machine; device; engine of war. See ARMS, INSTRUMENTALITY, POWER.

ENGRAVING

Nouns—**1,** engraving; line, mezzotint, *or* stipple engraving; drypoint, etching, copperplate; steel *or* wood engraving; xylography, chalcography, glyptography, cerography, lithography, photolithography, glyphography; gravure, photogravure, rotogravure; photoengraving.
2, impression, print, plate, etching, lithotint, cut, linoleum cut, wood cut, xylograph; mezzotint, aquatint. See PRINTING.
3, graver, burin, etching-point, style; plate, stone, woodblock, negative, die, punch, stamp.
Verbs—engrave, grave, stipple, etch, bute, lithograph.
Adjectives—sculptured, engraved, graven; carved, carven, chiseled.

---

engross, *v.t.* monopolize, control; absorb; occupy, engage; copy, write, transcribe. See ATTENTION, THOUGHT, WRITING.

engulf, *v.t.* swamp, flood, immerse, engorge, swallow up; encircle, envelop, encompass. See DESTRUCTION, WATER.

enhance, *v.t.* intensify; exaggerate; advance, augment, INCREASE, elevate. See EXAGGERATION, IMPROVEMENT.

enigma, *n.* riddle, mystery, puzzle, conundrum, SECRET. See DIFFICULTY, UNINTELLIGIBILITY.

enjoin, *v.t.* COMMAND, bid, direct, order, instruct, charge; counsel, admonish; prohibit, forbid, restrain; exact, require. See ADVICE, DUTY, PROHIBITION.

enjoy, *v.t.* like, relish, love, gloat over, delight in; experience; hold, possess. See PLEASURE, POSSESSION.

enkindle, *v.t.* See EXCITEMENT, HEAT, CAUSE.

enlarge, *v.t.* increase, extend, widen, broaden; aggrandize, amplify, magnify, augment, expand, elaborate, expatiate; dilate, distend, swell. See INCREASE, GREATNESS, DIFFUSENESS, BREADTH.

enlighten, *v.t.* brighten, illuminate; educate, civilize, instruct, inform, teach, edify. See LIGHT, TEACHING, INFORMATION.

enlist, *v.* volunteer, sign up, enroll, recruit, draft, muster, press [into service], impress. See WARFARE, COMPULSION.

enliven, *v.t.* animate, exhilarate, inspirit, quicken, fire, brighten, stimulate, rouse, invigorate; cheer, elate, encourage. See CHEERFULNESS, EXCITEMENT.

enmity, *n.* hostility, unfriendliness, antagonism, OPPOSITION, HATE, ill-will; grudge, rancor, anger, spite, animus, animosity, DISLIKE, antipathy; feud, vendetta.

ennoble, *v.t.* dignify, exalt, raise, elevate, glorify, uplift. See REPUTE.

enormity, *n.* wickedness, atrociousness; atrocity, outrage; immensity, enormousness, GREATNESS. See GUILT.

enormous, *adj.* monstrous, atrocious, excessive; large, titanic, tremendous, huge, immense, colossal, gigantic, vast, prodigious, stupendous. See SIZE, BADNESS.

enough, *adj.* adequate, sufficient, satisfactory, equal; ample, abundant, plenteous. See SUFFICIENCY.

enrage, *v.t.* anger, exasperate, provoke, incense, irritate; madden, flame, infuriate. See RESENTMENT.

enrapture, *v.t.* transport, enravish, entrance, enchant; please, delight, charm, captivate, bewitch. See PLEASURE.

enrich, *v.t.* endow, aggrandize, make wealthy; embellish, ORNAMENT, adorn, beautify; fertilize; cultivate, develop. See IMPROVEMENT, MONEY.

enroll, *v.* LIST, RECORD, enter, register; enlist, serve.

en route, *adv.* on *or* along the way; in

transit, on the road. See TRAVEL.

ensemble, *n.* See WHOLE.

enshrine, *v.t.* consecrate, hallow; cherish; commemorate. See MEMORY, WORSHIP, PIETY.

ensign, *n.* flag; badge, emblem, insignia; standard-bearer. See INDICATION, COMBATANT.

enslave, *v.t.* subjugate, enthrall, suppress, dominate, hold dominion over; oppress, tyrannize; addict. See SUBJECTION, HABIT.

ensnare, *v.t.* [en]trap, catch, net, bag; entangle, ensnarl, entoil (*archaic*); bait, decoy; seduce, entice. See DECEPTION.

ensue, *v.* follow, succeed, supervene, happen, result; pursue, seek after. See EFFECT, SEQUENCE.

ensure, *v.t.* secure, guarantee; protect. See SECURITY, SAFETY, CERTAINTY.

entail, *v.t.* involve, imply, call for, require; CAUSE. See NECESSITY.

entangle, *v.t.* tangle, ravel, mesh, entrap, mat, ensnare, inveigle, twist, snarl; perplex, involve, embroil, embarrass. See DIFFICULTY, DISORDER.

enter, *v.* penetrate, pierce; go *or* come in; insert; trespass, invade, board; begin, start, take up; LIST, RECORD, inscribe, enroll, register, file; join. See COMPOSITION, INGRESS, ACCOUNTING.

enterprise, *n.* project, scheme, venture, UNDERTAKING; business; energy. *Colloq.,* push, go-ahead. See COURAGE.

enterprising, *adj.* energetic, venturesome, adventurous; eager, ambitious. *Colloq.,* pushing. See COURAGE.

entertain, *v.* receive, welcome; amuse, divert, regale; harbor, shelter, cherish; maintain, keep up; consider, dwell upon, heed. See ATTENTION, THOUGHT, AMUSEMENT.

enthrall, *v.t.* enslave, subjugate; captivate, fascinate, charm. See PLEASURE, SUBJECTION.

enthusiasm, *n.* ecstasy, frenzy, fanaticism; fire, spirit, force; ardor, zeal, fervor, vehemence, eagerness; optimism, assurance. See FEELING, HOPE, EXCITABILITY, VIGOR.

entice, *v.* [al]lure, tempt, attract; induce, coax, cajole, woo; bewitch, enchant, seduce; deceive, hoodwink. See ATTRACTION, PLEASURE.

entire, *adj.* complete, absolute, unqualified; total, gross, all; WHOLE, intact, undiminished, unimpaired, perfect, unbroken; undivided, unalloyed.

entitle, *v.t.* qualify, fit, capacitate, authorize; name, call, designate, dub, style. See NOMENCLATURE, JUSTICE, PERMISSION.

entity, *n.* thing, being; whole, UNITY; abstraction, EXISTENCE. See SUBSTANCE.

entourage, *n.* retinue, train. See ASSEMBLAGE, SERVANT.

entr'acte, *n.* interval. See DRAMA.

entrails, *n.* viscera, intestines, bowels; insides, guts. See INTERIOR.

entrance, *n.* entry, INGRESS, entree, incoming, ingoing; debut, induction; admission, access, admittance, APPROACH; aperture, door, lobby, gate, portal, way, OPENING; BEGINNING, start, commencement, introduction; invasion, penetration. See EDGE. —*v.t.* enrapture, delight; spellbind. See PLEASURE, SORCERY.

entrap, *v.t.* See ENSNARE.

entreat, *v.t.* REQUEST, beg, crave, pray, beseech, implore, supplicate, plead.

entrepreneur, *n.* producer, angel, impresario; investor. See CHANCE, UNDERTAKING, DRAMA.

entrust, *v.t.* COMMISSION, charge, delegate; confide, trust, consign, commit; charge; show faith *or* reliance in.

entry, *n.* ENTRANCE, memorandum, RECORD, posting, listing; entrant, contestant, contender, competitor. See CONTENTION.

entwine, *v.* twine, interlace, twist, wreathe, weave. See CROSSING.

enumerate, *v.t.* count, tell off, number; name over, mention, recount, rehearse, recapitulate, detail, specify. See NUMERATION.

enunciate, *v.* announce, state, proclaim, declare; pronounce, articulate. See AFFIRMATION, SPEECH.

envelop, *v.t.* cover, wrap, enshroud, enfold, surround, enclose, hide. See CIRCUMSCRIPTION, COVERING.

envelope, *n.* COVERING, wrapper, casing, capsule; film, skin, integument, shell, sheath; receptacle. See ENCLOSURE.

ENVIRONMENT

Nouns—environment, encompassment, circumjacence, circumference; atmosphere, ambience, aura, medium, surroundings (see CIRCUMSTANCE); environs, outposts, outskirts, suburbs, purlieus, precincts, neighborhood, vicinity, background, setting, habitat, *milieu*, stamping ground; ecology, ecosystem. *Colloq.*, neck of the woods; context. *Slang*, hangout. See NEARNESS, CIRCUMSCRIPTION.

Verbs—lie around *or* about, environ, surround, compass, encompass, enclose, encircle, embrace.

Adjectives—circumjacent, circumambient, ambient, surrounding, encompassing, enclosing, suburban, neighboring, vicinal.

Adverbs—around, about; on every side, on all sides, all around, round about.

Antonyms, see DISTANCE.

envoy, *n.* diplomat, AGENT; messenger (see COMMUNICATION); postscript (see ADDITION).

envy, *n.* enviousness, JEALOUSY; covetousness, cupidity, spite; ill-will, malice; greenness. —*v.* begrudge; DESIRE, crave, covet, hanker, turn green.

eon, *n.* age, [long] TIME, epoch. *Colloq.*, dog's *or* coon's age.

ephemeral, *adj.* short-lived, fugitive, transient, transitory, fleeting, evanescent, momentary. See TRANSIENTNESS.

epic, *adj.* heroic, majestic, elevated, noble; Homeric, Virgilian; larger than life, on a grand scale. See GREATNESS. —*n.* saga, edda; epos, tale; rhapsody, eulogy. See POETRY, WRITING.

epicure, *n.* epicurean, *bon vivant, gourmet*. See TASTE, PLEASURE, GLUTTONY.

epidemic, *n.* DISEASE, pestilence, plague, contamination. —*adj.* pestilential, infectious, contagious; raging, rife, pandemic, ubiquitous. See GENERALITY.

epigram, *n.* aphorism, bon mot, saying, MAXIM. See WIT.

epilogue, *n.* afterword, postscript, postlude; summation; valedictory, last word. See ADDITION, COMPLETION, DRAMA.

episode, *n.* digression, excursus; OCCURRENCE, incident, happening, action. See BETWEEN.

epistle, *n.* letter, COMMUNICATION, missive.

epitaph, *n.* inscription, *hic jacet, requiescat in pace,* R.I.P. See INTERMENT.

epithet, *n.* byname (see NOMENCLATURE).

epitome, *n.* compendium, abridgment, abstract, synopsis, summary, brief. See SHORTNESS.

epoch, *n.* date; period, era, age. See TIME, CHRONOMETRY.

EQUALITY

Nouns—**1,** equality, parity, coextension; symmetry, balance, evenness, level, equivalence; balance of power, standoff; equipoise, equilibrium; par, quits;

IDENTITY, SIMILARITY; equalization, equation, coordination, adjustment. See SYMMETRY, INDIFFERENCE.

2, tie, draw, dead heat, standoff, even match, photo finish; equalizer.

3, match, peer, compeer, equal, mate, fellow, brother, equivalent, parallel; tit for tat; a Roland for an Oliver, an eye for an eye.

Verbs—**1,** equal, match, keep pace *or* up with, come up to, be on a level *or* par with, balance, measure up to, be equal to, having nothing on (someone), hold a candle *or* stick to.

2, make equal, equalize, level, balance, equate, trim, adjust, poise, fit, strike a balance, equilibrate, restore equilibrium, readjust; handicap; share and share alike; break even.

Adjectives—**1,** equal, even, level, coequal, symmetrical, coordinate; on a par with, abreast, coextensive; up to the mark.

2, equivalent, tantamount; homologous, synonymous, analogous, similar, as broad as it is long, much the same, the same; equalized, drawn, neck-and-neck; half-and-half. *Colloq.,* quits; fifty-fifty.

Adverbs—equally, both, to the same degree; to all intents and purposes, nip and tuck, abreast; on even footing, with the best; up to par, scratch, *or* snuff; from scratch.

Antonyms, see INEQUALITY.

---

equanimity, *n.* evenness, composure, repose, poise; calmness, serenity, tranquility, self-possession, self-control, INEXCITABILITY.

equestrian, *adj.* equine. See ANIMAL. —*n.* horseman *or* -woman, rider. See TRAVEL.

equilibrium, *n.* balance, equipoise, STABILITY; moderation, neutrality; EQUALITY, parity, symmetry; composure, self-possession, [self-]restraint. See INEXCITABILITY.

equip, *v.t.* furnish, outfit, rig [out], provide; accouter, appoint, dress, accommodate, array, attire; arm, gird. See CLOTHING, PREPARATION, PROVISION.

equipage, *n.* carriage; outfit, equipment. See VEHICLE, PROVISION.

equipment, *n.* furnishings, gear, harness, supplies, apparatus, accouterment, appointment, outfit, apparel. See CLOTHING, INSTRUMENTALITY, PROVISION.

equipoise, *n.* equilibrium; counterbalance. See EQUALITY.

equitable, *adj.* fair, just, ethical, honest; unbiased, dispassionate, even-handed, fair-and-square; deserved, merited, condign, due. *Colloq.,* on the up-and-up. See JUSTICE.

equivalent, *adj.* equal, tantamount, synonymous; analogous, correspondent, interchangeable; convertible, reciprocal. —*n.* equal; worth; analogue. See COMPENSATION, SUBSTITUTION, EQUALITY, INTERPRETATION.

equivocation, *n.* equivocalness; quibble, quibbling; evasion, shiftiness; ambiguity, double meaning, *double-entendre;* prevarication, white lie; half-truth, sophistry, casuistry; dodge, subterfuge, smoke screen, red herring. See CONCEALMENT, FALSEHOOD, AVOIDANCE.

era, *n.* See TIME, CHRONOMETRY.

eradicate, *v.t.* abolish; blot out, erase, extirpate, exterminate, weed out, eliminate, uproot. See DESTRUCTION, EXTRACTION.

erase, *v.t.* efface, rub out, expunge, cancel, obliterate, blot out. See NULLIFICATION, DESTRUCTION, EXTRACTION.

erect, *v.t.* raise, exalt; rear; build, construct; establish, set up, institute; create. See ELEVATION, PRODUCTION. —*adj.* upright, straight, VERTICAL, perpendicular; uplifted.

erosion, *n.* eating *or* wearing away, disintegration. See DETERIORATION, FRICTION.

erotic, *adj*. sexual, sensual; carnal, lascivious; obscene, pornographic; hot, spicy. *Slang,* sexy, raunchy, X-rated. See IMPURITY, LOVE.

err, *v.t.* mistake, misjudge; nod, slip, go astray, trip, blunder; sin, transgress; fall, wander, stray. See ERROR, BADNESS, IMPROBITY.

errand, *n*. BUSINESS, COMMISSION, mission, charge, task, message; trip.

errant, *adj*. wandering, roving; deviating. See DEVIATION.

erratic, *adj*. abnormal, eccentric, odd, capricious, queer, peculiar; wandering, off course; uncertain, changeable. See CHANGEABLENESS, IRREGULARITY, DEVIATION.

ERROR

Nouns—**1,** error, fallacy; falsity (see FALSEHOOD), untruth; misconception, misapprehension, misunderstanding; inexactness, inaccuracy; anachronism; misconstruction, misinterpretation, miscomputation, MISJUDGMENT, misstatement; aberration. See HETERODOXY, WRONG, NEGLECT, UNSKILLFULNESS.
2, mistake, miss, fault, blunder; oversight; misprint, erratum; slip, flaw, trip, stumble; slip of the tongue, *lapsus linguae,* slip of the pen, lapse; solecism; typographical *or* clerical error; malapropism, blooper; bull, break; demerit. *Colloq.,* boner, howler, typo.
3, delusion, illusion, false impression, self-deception; heresy; hallucination, optical illusion (see DECEPTION).

Verbs—**1,** mislead, misguide, lead astray, lead into error, beguile, misinform, delude, give a false impression, misstate.
2, err, be in error, be mistaken, goof; mistake, receive a false impression, be in the wrong, stray, not have a leg to stand on; take for; blunder, put one's foot in one's mouth; misapprehend, misconceive, misinterpret, misunderstand, miscalculate, misjudge; be at cross purposes, slip up, slip a cog *or* gear. *Colloq.,* bark up the wrong tree.
3, trip, stumble, lose oneself, go astray.

Adjectives—**1,** erroneous, untrue, fallacious; apocryphal, ungrounded; groundless, unsubstantial; heretical, unsound, illogical; unauthenticated; exploded, refuted.
2, inexact, inaccurate, incorrect, ungrammatical, faulty. See WRONG.
3, illusive, illusory, delusive; spurious.
4, in error, mistaken, aberrant, wide of the mark, out of line, astray, faulty, at fault, on a false scent, at cross purposes. *Slang,* all wet, off base.

Adverbs—by error, by mistake.

Antonyms, see TRUTH, GRAMMAR.

---

erudite, *adj*. learned, literate, wise; authoritative. See LEARNING, KNOWLEDGE.

eruption, *n*. efflorescence, rash; outbreak, commotion; discharge, expulsion. See DISEASE, EGRESS, VIOLENCE.

escalate, *v*. intensify, worsen (see INCREASE).

escalator, *n*. moving staircase. See ELEVATION.

escapade, *n*. jaunt, adventure, prank; frolic, caper, spree. See AMUSEMENT.

ESCAPE

Nouns—**1,** escape, elopement, flight; evasion (see AVOIDANCE); retreat; narrow escape *or* squeak, hairbreadth escape; deliverance, LIBERATION; jailbreak, freedom. *Colloq.,* close call *or* shave. *Slang,* getaway, lam. See RECESSION, DEPARTURE.

2, outlet, loophole (see EGRESS); puncture, aperture; safety-valve, fire escape, ladder, parachute; refuge, sanctuary, asylum, See SAFETY.
3, refugee, fugitive, escapee, runaway, runagate, deserter.
4, escapism, withdrawal, fantasy, flight. See INSANITY.
Verbs—escape, get off, get well out of, save one's bacon, weather the storm; bolt, elope, abscond, defect; evade (see AVOIDANCE); show *or* take to one's heels, beat a retreat, flee, bail out, make oneself scarce, run away *or* off, [make a] run for it, cut and run, steal away, slip off, take off, vamoose; elude, make off, give one the slip, slip through the fingers, dig [oneself] out; wriggle out of; break out *or* loose, make a getaway; get away with, get off easy; find a loophole; drop, draw, fade, *or* fall back, back out. *Colloq.*, skip out; get away with murder. *Slang,* skedaddle, skiddoo, take a powder, fly the coop, take it on the lam, lam out.
Adjectives—escaping, escaped, fled, free, scotfree, at large, well out of.
Adverbs—on the run. *Slang,* on the lam, over the hill.

Antonyms, see RESTRAINT.

---

escarpment, *n.* cliff (see HEIGHT).
escort, *v.t.* accompany, conduct, convoy, guard, walk, attend, usher. —*n.* attendant, companion, conductor, convoy, bodyguard. See SAFETY, ACCOMPANIMENT.
esoteric, *adj.* select, mysterious. See SECRET.
espionage, *n.* intelligence, reconnaissance, investigation; counterespionage, counterintelligence; cloak-and-dagger *or* undercover work. See INQUIRY.
esplanade, *n.* promenade, boardwalk, quadrangle, mall. See PASSAGE, HORIZONTAL.
essence, *n.* being, SUBSTANCE, element, entity, reality, nature, life; extract, distillation; perfume; principle, inwardness; sense, gist, core, kernel, pith, quintessence, heart, purport. See EXTRACTION, ODOR, IMPORTANCE, INTRINSIC.
essential, *adj.* substantial, material, constitutional, fundamental, elementary, absolute; necessary, needful, requisite, cardinal, indispensable, vital; inherent, INTRINSIC, basic. See NECESSITY, PART, IMPORTANCE.
establish, *v.t.* confirm, fix, settle, secure, set, stabilize; sustain, install, root, ensconce; appoint, enact, ordain; found, institute, constitute, create, organize, build, set up; verify, prove, substantiate; determine, decide. See EVIDENCE, PRODUCTION, STABILITY, DEMONSTRATION, LOCATION.
estate, *n.* state, status, rank, condition, station, DEGREE; property, fortune, possessions, effects, interest, land, holdings; ABODE. See POSSESSION, CLASS.
esteem, *n.* RESPECT, regard, favor, admiration, estimation, honor; reverence, worship. See APPROBATION.
esthetic, *adj.* artistic, tasteful, beautiful. See BEAUTY, SENSIBILITY.
estimable, *adj.* meritorious, worthy. See APPROBATION.
estimate, *v.t.* consider, gauge, judge; value, appraise, evaluate, rate, assess, measure; compute, reckon, calculate. —*n.* JUDGMENT, opinion, appraisal, report, criticism; calculation.
estrange, *v.t.* alienate, separate, withdraw; fall out, be unfriendly; disunite, part, wean; transfer. See DISJUNCTION.
estuary, *n.* arm, inlet, firth, fjord; mouth, delta. See OPENING.
etch, *v.* engrave, incise, scratch, carve, corrode. See ENGRAVING.
eternal, *adj.* perpetual, endless, everlasting, continual, ceaseless; timeless, infinite, unending; incessant, constant; immortal, imperishable, deathless. See DURABILITY, PERMANENCE, PERPETUITY.

ethereal, *adj.* airy, delicate, light, tenuous, fragile, fairy; heavenly, celestial, empyreal. See INSUBSTANTIALITY, HEAVEN.

ethics, *n.* morals, morality, rules of conduct. See DUTY, VIRTUE.

etiquette, *n.* manners, decorum, custom, formality, good form. See FASHION.

Eucharist, *n.* Communion, Mass, viaticum, sacrament. See RITE.

eulogize, *v.t.* praise, compliment, celebrate, glorify, laud, panegyrize, extol. See APPROBATION.

euphoria, *n.* elation, high spirits, PLEASURE, well-being; the pink of condition. *Slang,* high. See CONTENT.

euthanasia, *n.* mercy-killing (see DEATH, KILLING).

evacuate, *v.t.* empty, clear; eject, expel, purge; discharge, excrete, defecate, void, emit; leave, quit, vacate. See DEPARTURE, EJECTION, EXCRETION.

evade, *v.t.* avoid, elude; dodge, shun; baffle, foil, parry; ESCAPE, slip away; ignore, violate, NEGLECT; equivocate. See AVOIDANCE.

evaluate, *v.t.* value, appraise, estimate, assess, PRICE. See MEASUREMENT.

evanesce, *v.i.* disappear, fade away. See DISAPPEARANCE.

evangelical, *adj.* proselytizing, apostolic, missionary. See RELIGION, SACRED WRITINGS.

evaporate, *v.* emanate, pass off, escape; vaporize, distill; condense, solidify, dehydrate, desiccate; vanish, disappear. See DRYNESS, INSUBSTANTIALITY, VAPOR, TRANSIENTNESS.

evasion, *n.* elusion, AVOIDANCE, ESCAPE; equivocation; trick, subterfuge. See NONPAYMENT.

even, *adj.* level, equal, smooth, flat, flush, uniform, regular, unvaried, parallel; equable, even-tempered, unruffled, placid; equitable, fair, impartial, just; straightforward, plain, direct; abreast, alongside; true, plumb, straight. See HORIZONTAL, EQUALITY, STRAIGHTNESS, SMOOTHNESS.

evening, *n.* dusk, nightfall, eventide, close of day; gloaming, twilight; sundown, sunset; curfew; eve, even (*poetic*); decline, old age, sunset years. See DIMNESS, TIME, AGE.

event, *n.* OCCASION, OCCURRENCE, happening; affair, episode, incident; gala affair *or* occasion, holiday; experience; circumstance, issue, outcome, result.

eventful, *adj.* bustling; momentous. See OCCURRENCE, IMPORTANCE.

eventual, *adj.* final, ultimate, coming; contingent. See FUTURITY, CHANCE, EFFECT.

ever, *adv.* always, at all times, eternally, perpetually, incessantly, continually, constantly, forever; once, at any time; in any case, at all. See DURABILITY, PERPETUITY.

everlasting, *adj.* unending, never-ending, without end; ageless, sempiternal; constant, ceaseless, wearisome, perpetual, continual, incessant. See PERPETUITY, DURABILITY.

every, *adj.* each, all; complete, entire. See GENERALITY.

everyday, *adj.* habitual, usual, routine, workaday. See HABIT, MEDIOCRITY.

everyone, *n.* everybody, *tout le monde*. See GENERALITY.

everywhere, *adv.* wherever; all over, far and wide. See SPACE.

evict, *v.t.* eject, oust, remove, expel, put out, dispossess. See EJECTION.

EVIDENCE

Nouns—**1,** evidence, facts, premises, data, grounds, DEMONSTRATION, confirmation, corroboration, support, ratification, authentication, acknowledgment, proof; state's, king's, queen's, oral, documentary, hearsay, external, extrinsic, internal, intrinsic, circumstantial, *ex parte,* presumptive, collateral, *or* constructive evidence; control. See LAWSUIT, TRUTH.

2, testimony, attestation, declaration, deposition, AFFIRMATION; examination; exhibit.

3, citation, reference, authority, warrant, credential, testimonial; diploma, voucher, affidavit, certificate, INDICATION; RECORD, document; signature, seal, identification. See PROMISE.

4, witness, indicator, eyewitness, deponent, sponsor, [innocent] bystander, testifier, attestor, onlooker.

Verbs—**1,** evidence, evince, manifest, display, exhibit, show; betoken, tell of, indicate, denote, imply, argue, bespeak; have *or* carry weight, tell, speak volumes, speak for itself; hold up.

2, rest *or* depend upon; bear witness, give evidence, testify, depose, witness, vouch for; sign, seal, set one's hand and seal, certify, attest, acknowledge. *Colloq.,* make out.

3, confirm, ratify, corroborate, support, bear out, uphold, warrant, establish, authenticate, prove, substantiate, verify, validate, demonstrate, lend *or* give color to. *Colloq.,* see the color of one's money.

4, adduce, attest, cite, quote, refer, bring into court; produce witnesses; collect evidence, examine, make out a case; have *or* get the goods on one.

Adjectives—evidential, documentary; indicative, indicatory, deducible; grounded on, founded on, based on, corroborative, confirmatory; supportive, authentic, conclusive; circumstantial, by inference, according to, *a fortiori*.

Antonyms, see NEGATION, CONFUTATION.

---

evident, *adj*. apparent, plain, obvious, distinct; broad, unmistakable, palpable, patent, open, manifest, clear; downright, overt, indubitable. See APPEARANCE, CERTAINTY, DEMONSTRATION, VISIBILITY.

EVIL

Nouns—**1,** evil, ill, harm, hurt; mischief, nuisance; disadvantage, drawback; disaster, casualty, mishap, misfortune, calamity, catastrophe, tragedy, ADVERSITY; abomination, peccancy; bane, curse, scourge, Jonah. *Colloq.,* jinx. *Slang,* bad news.

2, BADNESS, wickedness, sin, vice, iniquity, IMPIETY, immorality, corruption. See MALEVOLENCE.

3, outrage, WRONG, injury, foul play; bad *or* ill turn; disservice, spoliation, grievance, crying evil.

4, see EVILDOER.

Verbs—harm, hurt, injure, wrong, outrage, dishonor, victimize.

Adjectives—**1,** evil, bad, ill, sinful, peccant, wicked, wrong, vicious, immoral, corrupt; unrighteous.

2, harmful, hurtful, noisome, injurious; malevolent; prejudicial, disastrous.

Adverbs—badly, amiss, wrong, ill, to one's cost.

Antonyms, see GOODNESS.

EVILDOER

Nouns—**1,** evildoer; sinner, transgressor, profligate, libertine; oppressor, despot, tyrant (see AUTHORITY); incendiary, anarchist, destroyer, vandal, iconoclast, terrorist; arsonist. *Colloq.,* firebug.

2, savage, brute, ruffian, barbarian, caitiff, desperado; bully, rough, hooligan, hoodlum, gangster, tough, plug-ugly, hellion, gorilla; fraud, swindler, confidence man, thief (see STEALING); murderer, gunman, killer (see KILLING); villain, miscreant, rascal, knave, cad, scalawag, rogue, badman, scapegrace, rowdy, scamp, apache; pimp, procurer, whoremaster, white slaver; criminal, felon, convict (see PRISON); delinquent, troublemaker; forger; black sheep, blackguard, prodigal son, fallen angel, ne'er-do-well. *Slang,* hood, mobster.
3, hag, beldam[e], Jezebel, jade, nag, shrew, fishwife; murderess; ogress, harpy, Fury, maenad; adulteress, paramour, mistress; prostitute, whore (see IMPURITY); dragon, harridan, vixen, virago; witch, siren, Circe, Delilah, Medusa, Gorgon; enchantress, sorceress.
4, monster, fiend, DEMON, devil, devil incarnate, fiend in human shape; Frankenstein's monster; cannibal, bloodsucker, vampire, ghoul, vulture, ogre.
5, culprit, offender, malefactor; recidivist; traitor, betrayer, Judas [Iscariot], Benedict Arnold, Quisling; conspirator, snake in the grass; turncoat, renegade, apostate; informer. *Slang,* rat, squealer, bad *or* rotten egg, bad actor. See IMPROBITY.

Antonyms, see GOODNESS, BENEVOLENCE.

---

evince, *v.t.* exhibit, display, show, manifest, evidence, demonstrate, disclose, indicate, prove. See DEMONSTRATION.

eviscerate, *v.t.* disembowel. See EXTRACTION, WEAKNESS.

evoke, *v.t.* draw forth, summon, invoke; envision, imagine; suggest, bring to mind; produce, CAUSE. See EXCITEMENT.

evolution, *n.* evolvement, unfolding, growth, expansion, development, elaboration; Darwinism, natural selection; mutation. See CHANGE, IMPROVEMENT.

exacerbate, *v.* aggravate, intensify, worsen; enrage, embitter, irritate, vex. See INCREASE, RESENTMENT.

exact, *v.t.* require, claim, demand; extort, take, wring, wrest, force, impose. See COMMAND, COMPULSION.—*adj.* strict, rigorous; accurate, precise, delicate, nice, fine, correct, literal, verbatim; faithful, lifelike, close; definite, absolute, direct. See RIGHTNESS, SIMILARITY, TRUTH.

EXAGGERATION

Nouns—exaggeration, magnification, overstatement, hyperbole, stretch, strain, [high *or* false] coloring, caricature, extravagance; Baron Munchausen; fringe, embroidery, traveler's tale, yarn, tall story *or* tale, overestimation, tempest in a teapot; much ado about nothing; puffery, BOASTING, rant; figure of speech, stretch of the imagination; flight of fancy. See DISTORTION, FIGURATIVE.

Verbs—exaggerate, magnify, pile up, amplify, build up, expand, overestimate, hyperbolize; gild *or* paint the lily; overstate, overdraw, overpraise, overshoot the mark, strain, stretch, strain *or* stretch a point, spin a long yarn, make a mountain out of a molehill; draw the longbow, run riot, glorify, heighten, overcolor, embellish, enhance, embroider, misrepresent, puff, boast; bite off more than one can chew. *Colloq.,* carry on, put on, lay it on [thick].

Adjectives—exaggerated, overwrought; bombastic, florid, flowery, magniloquent, high-flown, hyperbolical, fabulous, extravagant, preposterous; egregious, outré; high-flying, tall, steep.

Antonyms, see TRUTH, MODESTY, DETRACTION.

exalt, *v.t.* elevate, raise, lift up, dignify, honor; praise, glorify, magnify, extol, aggrandize, elate, uplift; intensify, heighten. See APPROBATION, REPUTE, INCREASE.

examination, *n.* test; midterm, final; physical [examination]. *Colloq.*, exam. See INQUIRY.

examine, *v.t.* investigate, inspect, survey, prove, canvass, search; scrutinize, peruse, dissect, scan; test, interrogate, try, question; audit, review. See ATTENTION, INQUIRY, EVIDENCE.

example, *n.* sample, specimen, piece; instance, case, illustration; pattern, type, standard, copy, model, idea; precedent; warning; problem, exercise. See CONFORMITY, IMITATION.

exasperate, *v.t.* anger, enrage, infuriate; irritate, vex, nettle, provoke, roil, peeve, annoy. See RESENTMENT.

excavation, *n.* cavity, hole, pit, mine, shaft, quarry, opening. See CONCAVITY.

exceed, *v.t.* transcend, surpass, excel, outdo, outstrip, beat; overstep, pass, overdo, go beyond. See SUPERIORITY.

exceedingly, *adv.* extremely. See SUPERIORITY.

excel, *v.* exceed, surpass, eclipse, outdo, outstrip. See UNCONFORMITY, VIRTUE, GOODNESS.

except, *prep.* unless, saving, save, but, excepting, barring. See UNCONFORMITY, CIRCUMSTANCE, DEDUCTION.

exception, *n.* EXCLUSION, omission, rejection, reservation, limitation; objection, cavil, complaint; irregularity. See DISAPPROBATION, UNCONFORMITY, DISSENT, EXEMPTION, QUALIFICATION.

exceptionable, *adj.* objectionable. See DISAPPROBATION.

exceptional, *adj.* abnormal; unusual, uncommon, extraordinary, rare; special, superior. See UNCONFORMITY, SPECIALITY.

excerpt, *n.* extract, quote, citation, selection; sentence, verse, section, passage. See PART.

excess, *n.* immoderation, INTEMPERANCE, dissipation, indulgence; superabundance, superfluity, extravagance, exorbitance; redundance, REMAINDER. See SUFFICIENCY.

excessive, *adj.* immoderate, inordinate, extravagant, exorbitant, unreasonable, outrageous; superfluous, extreme. See DEARNESS.

exchange, *n.* reciprocity, substitution; trade, BARTER, commerce; conversion, INTERCHANGE; market. See BUSINESS, TRANSFER.

EXCITABILITY

Nouns—**1,** excitability, impetuosity, impatience, intolerance; irritability (see IRASCIBILITY); disquiet[ude], AGITATION, jitters. See SENSIBILITY, FEELING.

2, VIOLENCE, fierceness, rage, mania, madness (see INSANITY), frenzy, hysterics, fanaticism.

3, hothead, madcap; nervous Nellie, nervous wreck, bundle of nerves.

Verbs—**1,** be excitable *or* impatient, champ at the bit, be in a stew, fidget, toss, jump, twitch, jerk, jitter; choke up.

2, lose one's temper, burst out; fly off [at a tangent]; explode, flare up, burn; boil [over], foam, fume, seethe, rage, rave, rant, have a fit, run wild, go mad; go into hysterics; run riot, run amuck, go off half-cocked; climb the wall, go off the deep end, go overboard. *Slang*, get one's goat; fly off the handle, flip one's lid, blow one's top; push the panic button, have kittens.

Adjectives—**1,** excitable, seething, hot, boiling, burning; impatient, intolerant; feverish, frenzied, febrile, hysterical, unstrung; highstrung, mettlesome, jumpy, nervous, jittery, edgy, on edge, on pins and needles; skittish; mercurial (see CHANGEABLENESS); impulsive, impetuous, tempestuous, passionate, uncontrolled, ungovernable, irrepressible, madcap. *Colloq.*, flappable. *Slang,* uptight.

2, violent, wild, fierce, fiery, hot-headed, irritable, irascible; demonstrative, boisterous, enthusiastic, impassioned, fanatical, rabid.

Antonyms, see INEXCITABILITY.

EXCITEMENT

Nouns—**1,** excitement, excitation; stimulation, piquancy, provocation; animation, AGITATION, perturbation; intoxication, high pressure; passion, thrill, flame. See VIOLENCE.

2, commotion, to-do, buzz, dither, fluster, bustle, hurly-burly, hullabaloo, pandemonium, furor[e], upheaval.

3, EXCITABILITY, turbulence; exuberance, effervescence, ebullition.

Verbs—**1,** excite, move; strike, interest, animate, enliven, inspire, impassion, stir *or* warm the blood; awaken, evoke, provoke; raise, arouse, stir; fire, get going, [en]kindle, set on fire, inflame, fan the flames, heat, warm, foment, raise to fever heat. *Slang,* rev up, jazz up.

2, stimulate, inspirit, stir up, elate, work up, sharpen, spice, whet, incite, give a fillip, put on one's mettle; stir *or* play on the feelings; touch a chord, go to one's heart, touch to the quick.

3, intoxicate, electrify, turn one's head, carry *or* sweep off one's feet, carry away, warm the blood.

4, be excited, flare up, catch fire; work oneself up, lose one's grip; seethe, boil, simmer, foam, fume, rage, rave (see EXCITABILITY).

Adjectives—**1,** excited; worked, keyed, *or* wrought up, on the *qui vive,* in a quiver, in a fever, in hysterics; black in the face, overwrought; hit, flushed, feverish; all atwitter; flaming, boiling [over], ebullient, seething, foaming [at the mouth], fuming, raging; wild, frantic, mad, hectic, distracted, beside oneself, out of one's mind *or* wits, ready to burst, stung to the quick. *Colloq.,* hot and bothered, gung ho. *Slang,* switched on.

2, exciting, warm, glowing, fervid, swelling, heart-stirring, thrilling; striking; soul-stirring, spine-tingling, agonizing, sensational, hysterical; overpowering, overwhelming, piquant, spicy, heady, provocative, tantalizing. *Colloq.*, mind-blowing.

Adverbs—excitedly, excitingly, in a dither, all agog; with bated breath.

Antonyms, see INDIFFERENCE, INEXCITABILITY.

---

exclaim, *v.* cry out, shout, ejaculate, clamor, vociferate; exclaim *or* inveigh against, denounce, condemn. See CRY, SPEECH, DISAPPROBATION.

EXCLUSION

Nouns—**1,** exclusion, omission, exception, REJECTION, relegation; preclusion, elimination, DISPLACEMENT; separation, discrimination, segregation, quarantine, isolation, ostracism; PROHIBITION; exile, banishment, EJECTION.

2, clan, clique (see PARTY); silent treatment, blacklist.

Verbs—exclude, [de]bar; prohibit, preclude; freeze out, edge out; leave out, rule *or* count out, reject, blackball; lay, put, *or* set aside; relegate, pass over, omit, eliminate, weed out, throw over, throw overboard; strike out; separate, segregate, isolate, insulate, ostracize, weed out; displace; blacklist, keep *or* shut out, except; exile, banish, eject. See DEDUCTION.

Adjectives—exclusive, cliquish, clannish; closed; sole, unique; one and only, barring all others; exclusory, prohibitive; select, restrictive; excluded, left out, isolated, solitary, banished, inadmissible, unacceptable.

Prepositions—exclusive of, outside of, barring, except; with the exception of; save.

Antonyms, see INCLUSION.

---

excommunicate, *v.t.* expel, curse, unchurch. See EJECTION.

excrement, *n.* See EXCRETION.

excrescence, *n.* outgrowth, protuberance, appendage. See CONVEXITY.

EXCRETION

Nouns—**1,** excretion, discharge, exhalation, exudation, extrusion, secretion, effusion, egestion, extravasation, evacuation, dejection, defecation, EJECTION.
2, perspiration, sweat, saliva, rheum, sputum, spittle, spit, salivation, catarrh, diarrhea, *ejecta, dejecta, excreta,* urine, offal, feces, excrement; hemorrhage, bleeding, flux.

Verbs—excrete, eject, discharge, emit, evacuate, defecate; exhale; secrete, exude, perspire, sweat; extrude, effuse, extravasate; cast off; salivate, dribble, slaver.

Adjectives—excretive, excretory, ejective, eliminative; fecal, urinary; sweaty.

Antonyms, see RECEIVING.

---

excruciating, *adj.* torturing, painful, agonizing, racking, acute. See PAIN.

excursion, *n.* expedition, trip, sally, tour, outing, JOURNEY, jaunt; digression, DEVIATION.

excuse, *v.t.* pardon, remit, overlook, condone, forgive, extenuate, justify; exonerate, absolve, acquit, exempt, free, apologize. See VINDICATION, EXEMPTION, FORGIVENESS.

execrable, *adj.* abominable, bad, detestable; poor, inferior, wretched. See BADNESS.

execute, *v.t.* perform, do, accomplish, make, administer, enforce, effect; finish, complete, fulfill; kill, put to death, behead, lynch, hang, gas, electrocute; enact; seal, sign. See COMPLETION, PUNISHMENT, ACTION, AGENCY, CONDUCT.

executive, *n.* DIRECTOR, manager, official, administrator. *Slang,* brass.

exemplary, *adj.* commendable; model; typical, illustrative. See APPROBATION, CONFORMITY.

exemplify, *v.t.* typify; illustrate, explain, quote. See CONFORMITY.

EXEMPTION

Nouns—exemption, FREEDOM, immunity, impunity, privilege, liberty, release, excuse, dispensation, exception, absolution, discharge; [bill, act, covenant, *or* deed of] indemnity. See PERMISSION, UNCONFORMITY.

Verbs—exempt, release, discharge, liberate, free, set at liberty; indemnify; let off, pass over, spare, excuse, dispense with, give dispensation; stretch a point.

Adjectives—**1,** exempt, free, at liberty, scot-free, released, unbound, unencumbered, unaccountable, not answerable, immune, privileged, excusable, off the hook.
2, not having, devoid of, destitute of, without, unpossessed of, unblest with, exempt from, off one's hands; tax-free, untaxed, untaxable, tax-exempt.

Antonyms, see LIABILITY, DUTY.

exercise, *n.* drill (see EXERTION); (*pl.*) ceremonies (see RITE). —*v.* perform, USE; train, drill; disturb (see DISCONTENT).

EXERTION

Nouns—**1,** exertion, ENERGY, effort, strain, tug, pull, stretch, struggle, trouble, pains, endeavor, ACTION.

2, gymnastics, exercise, workout, athletics, calisthenics, acrobatics; training, sport, play, drill, daily dozen, warm-up, sitting-up exercises; ado.

3, labor, work, toil, task, travail, manual labor, sweat of one's brow, elbow grease, wear and tear, toil and trouble, yeoman work, uphill work, drudgery, slavery, heavy duty, run for one's money.

4, laborer, worker, toiler, drudge, slave; workhorse, packhorse, galley slave, Trojan; roustabout, odd-job man. *Slang,* workaholic.

Verbs—**1,** exert oneself, put one's back to it, go to *or* take the trouble, set *or* put one's hand to, roll up one's sleeves, strive, strain, pull, tug, ply, struggle, try; lay, fall, *or* turn to; fall over oneself, fall over backwards, sink one's teeth into, go out of one's way, knock oneself out.

2, labor, work, toil, moil, sweat, plug, plod, drudge, slave; buckle down, dig in, bear down, wade into, come to grips; put one's shoulder to the wheel, lay, sail, *or* pitch into; work like a horse; burn the candle at both ends; work one's fingers to the bone, keep one's nose to the grindstone, persevere, take pains, do one's best, bend over backwards, strain every nerve, spare no pains, move heaven and earth, burn oneself out; work off; hammer out (see PRODUCTION). *Slang,* sweat blood, go to town, blow one's brains out, break one's neck, burn the midnight oil.

3, exercise, work out, warm up, train, drill.

Adjectives—laboring; laborious; strained, toilsome, troublesome, wearisome, uphill, Herculean; hardworking, painstaking, strenuous, energetic; workaday.

Adverbs—laboriously, lustily; with might and main, with all one's might, tooth and nail, hammer and tongs, heart and soul; by the sweat of one's brow; energetically. *Colloq.,* like mad.

Antonyms, see REPOSE.

---

exhale, *v.t.* breathe, expel, emanate, emit, expire, transpire, respire, blow. See EXCRETION, WIND, ODOR.

exhaust, *v.t.* drain, empty, let out, deflate; weaken, deplete, overtire, prostrate, fag, fatigue; spend, consume, USE, expend; develop, finish, end. See COMPLETION, WEARINESS.

exhibit, *v.* show, present, display, produce, demonstrate, stage, expose, evince; reveal; flaunt. See EVIDENCE, OSTENTATION.

exhilarate, *v.t.* elate, exalt, inspirit; enliven, animate, cheer, make merry, invigorate, gladden. See CHEERFULNESS.

exhort, *v.* incite, urge, prompt, admonish. *Colloq.,* egg on. See ADVICE, WARNING, CAUSE.

exhume, *v.t.* dig up, disinter, excavate; discover, locate; call up, recall. See MEMORY, DISCLOSURE, PAST.

exigency, *n.* demand, need, NECESSITY, distress, DIFFICULTY, extremity, urgency, pressure, pinch, crisis, emergency, juncture. See CIRCUMSTANCE.

exile, *v.i.* expel, remove, banish, expatriate. See DISPLACEMENT, EJECTION, EXCLUSION, SECLUSION.

EXISTENCE

Nouns—**1,** existence, LIFE, being, entity, *ens, esse,* subsistence, PRESENCE. **2,** reality, actuality; positiveness, fact, matter of fact, stubborn fact, not a dream, no joke, sober reality, actual existence. *Colloq.,* what's what.

Verbs—exist, be; have being, subsist, live, breathe; stand, obtain, be the case; consist in, lie in, have place, prevail, endure, find oneself; vegetate, come alive *or* to life; come *or* bring into existence (see OCCURRENCE).

Adjectives—**1,** existing, existent, extant; in existence, current, prevalent. **2,** real, actual, positive, absolute, authentic, true; big *or* large as life, big as life and twice as natural; in person, in the flesh; matter-of-fact; substantial, substantive, enduring, well-founded.

Adverbs—actually, really, truly, positively, in fact, in point of fact, for that matter, in reality, indeed, *de facto, ipso facto;* as far as that goes *or* is concerned.

Antonyms, see NONEXISTENCE.

---

exit, *n.* DEPARTURE, withdrawal. See EGRESS.

exodus, *n.* DEPARTURE, flight, migration, EGRESS, issue.

exonerate, *v.t.* exculpate, free, clear, absolve, acquit. See VINDICATION, ACQUITTAL.

exorbitant, *adj.* excessive, immoderate, inordinate, unreasonable; extravagant, expensive, dear. See DEARNESS.

exorcise, *v.t.* expel, drive *or* cast out; adjure, conjure. See SORCERY.

exotic, *adj.* foreign, alien; strange, outlandish, *outré,* bizarre, rare; vivid, colorful, extravagant. See UNCONFORMITY.

expanse, *n.* stretch, spread, reach, extent, BREADTH. See SPACE.

EXPANSION

Nouns—expansion, INCREASE, enlargement, extension, augmentation, amplification, dilation, aggrandizement, spread, growth, development, turgescence, turgidness, turgidity; obesity, dropsy, tumefaction, tumescence, flare, swell[ing], tumor, tumidity; diastole, distension; puffiness, inflation; overgrowth, hypertrophy; blow-up. See ADDITION, ELASTICITY, SPACE.

Verbs—**1,** expand, widen, enlarge, extend, grow, augment, INCREASE, swell, mushroom, fill out; dilate; deploy; stretch, spread, flare, bell; spring up, bud, burgeon, sprout, put forth, open, burst forth, gain flesh, flesh out *or* up; draw out; outgrow, overrun, be larger than.
2, aggrandize, distend, develop, amplify, blow up, widen, inflate, stuff, pad, cram, exaggerate; fatten.

Adjectives—expanded, larger, swollen, expansive, widespread, overgrown, exaggerated, bloated, fat, turgid, tumid, hypertrophied, pot-bellied; obese, puffy, distended, bulbous, full-blown, full-grown, big.

Antonyms, see CONTRACTION.

---

expatiate, *v.i.* enlarge, descant, dilate, expand; rant. See DIFFUSENESS.

expatriate, *n.* exile, displaced person; exurbanite. See DISPLACEMENT, EGRESS.

EXPECTATION

Nouns—**1,** expectation, expectancy, anticipation, reckoning, calculation, foresight,

PREDICTION, imminence, contingency; contemplation, lookout, prospect, outlook, perspective, horizon. See DESTINY, INTUITION, FUTURITY.

2, suspense, waiting, anxiety, presentiment, apprehension; HOPE, BELIEF, faith.

Verbs—expect, look for, look out for, look forward to; hope for, anticipate, figure *or* plan on, take in stride; have in prospect, keep in view, wait *or* watch for, keep a sharp lookout for, await; bide one's time, hold one's breath, hang on; foresee, prepare for, predict, second-guess, count upon, believe in, think likely, bargain for *or* in; push *or* press one's luck.

Adjectives—**1,** expectant, expecting; open-mouthed, agape, all agog, on tenterhooks; ready, curious, eager, anxious, apprehensive.

2, expected, foreseen, in prospect, prospective, in view, impending, imminent. *Colloq.*, on deck, in the cards.

Adverbs—expectantly, on the watch, with bated breath, with ears pricked up, on edge.

Interjections—no wonder! of course! small wonder!

Antonyms, see DOUBT, UNPREPAREDNESS, SURPRISE, WONDER.

EXPEDIENCE

Nouns—expedience, expediency, desirableness, desirability, advisability, eligibility, seemliness, fitness, UTILITY, propriety, opportunism, opportunity, convenience, timeliness, suitability. See POSSIBILITY.

Verbs—be expedient *or* suitable, suit *or* befit the occasion, strike the right note.

Adjectives—expedient, acceptable, convenient, worthwhile, meet, fitting, fit, due, proper, eligible, seemly, becoming, opportune, in season, suitable, timely, well-timed, auspicious, right, seasonable.

Adverbs—expediently, conveniently; in the right place, at the right moment.

Antonyms, see INEXPEDIENCE.

---

expedition, *n.* HASTE, dispatch, promptness, speed, alacrity; journey, quest, tour, trip, jaunt, excursion; crusade, campaign. See EARLINESS, WARFARE, TRAVEL.

expel, *v.t.* eject, extrude, excrete, discharge, dispel, eliminate; exclude, remove, evict, dislodge, dispossess, oust; excommunicate; banish, exile, deport, expatriate. See EJECTION.

expend, *v.t.* spend, lay out, pay [out], disburse; USE, consume; exhaust; give; WASTE, use up. See PAYMENT.

expenditure, *n.* expense[s], outlay, spending, PAYMENT, cost[s]; disbursement, outgo, overhead; PURCHASE[s]; PRICE. See ACCOUNTING.

expensive, *adj.* costly, dear, high, exorbitant. See DEARNESS.

experience, *v.t.* have, know, see, meet, encounter; undergo, suffer, brave, sustain; enjoy, realize, apprehend, understand. See FEELING, KNOWLEDGE, OCCURRENCE.

EXPERIMENT

Nouns—**1,** experiment, experimentation, essay, attempt; venture, adventure, speculation; trial, probation, proof (see DEMONSTRATION); test, check, tryout, assay, ordeal; empiricism, rule of thumb, trial and error; criterion, golden rule. *Colloq.*, go, whack. *Slang,* shot, crack.

2, feeler; trial balloon, test flight, scout, straw in the wind, speculation, random shot, leap *or* shot in the dark; road test; tryout, screen test, audition.

Verbs—**1,** experiment, essay, try, endeavor, strive, attempt; venture, adventure, speculate, take a chance, tempt fortune, try one's luck *or* hand, have a go at, shoot at, make a go of it, give it a whirl; put on trial, put to the test *or* proof, try *or* check out, cross-check, shake down, put through one's paces, try on; test, practice upon; try one's strength, test one's wings.

2, grope, feel *or* grope one's way; throw out a feeler, send up a trial balloon, see how the land lies, see how the wind blows, feel the pulse, beat the bushes, try one's fortune; explore, inquire. *Colloq.,* see how the ball bounces; fiddle, monkey, mess, play, *or* fool around.

Adjectives—experimental, probative, probationary, tentative, empirical, on probation, on trial.

Adverbs—experimentally, tentatively, on trial, by rule of thumb.

---

expert, *n. & adj.* See SKILL.

expertise, *n.* SKILL, skillfulness, KNOWLEDGE, LEARNING, facility, proficiency, mastery; professionalism, *savoir-faire. Colloq.,* know-how. See PERFECTION.

expiate, *v.t.* atone for (see ATONEMENT).

expire, *v.* exhale, breathe out, emit; die, perish; END, cease, terminate, stop. See DEATH, WIND.

explain, *v.t.* expound, solve, elucidate, resolve, fathom, account for; demonstrate, construe, interpret, define, describe, develop, detail, criticize, comment. See ANSWER, ATTRIBUTION, INTERPRETATION.

expletive, *n.* oath, IMPRECATION.

explicit, *adj.* express, written, plain, positive, clear, unambiguous, open, definite; unreserved, outspoken. See INFORMATION, MEANING.

explode, *v.* destroy; burst, detonate, fire, discharge; reject; refute, discredit, expose, disprove. See CONFUTATION, VIOLENCE, EXCITABILITY.

exploit, *v.t.* utilize, profit by, milk, work; abuse, misapply. See USE. —*n.* deed, act, feat, achievement. See COURAGE.

explore, *v.t.* seek, search, fathom, prospect, penetrate, range, examine, investigate, inquire into. See INQUIRY.

explosive, *adj.* See VIOLENCE, DANGER. —*n.* dynamite, T.N.T., nitroglycerin. See VIOLENCE, ARMS.

exponent, *n.* expounder, representative; backer, defender; power, superscript. See TEACHING, AUXILIARY.

export, *n.* commodity, exportation. See EGRESS, SALE.

expose, *v.t.* disclose, reveal, divulge, unearth, unmask, denude, bare, uncover; exhibit, display; offer, submit; subject to, risk, weather, lay open, endanger, imperil; turn out, cast out, abandon; denounce, brand. See DANGER, DISAPPROBATION, DISCLOSURE, DIVESTMENT, VISIBILITY. —*n.* exposure, unmasking.

exposition, *n.* explanation, exegesis, elucidation, commentary; show, exhibition, fair; statement, discourse; exposure, abandonment. See DISCLOSURE, INTERPRETATION, REASONING, BUSINESS.

expostulate, *v.i.* remonstrate, reason; object, protest, rebuke. See ADVICE, DISAPPROBATION, DISSUASION.

expound, *v.t.* state, express, set forth; explain, interpret, elucidate. See TEACHING, SPEECH, INTERPRETATION.

express, *v.t.* squeeze, press out, exude; represent, symbolize, show, reveal, denote, signify, delineate, depict; state, tell, frame, enunciate, expound, couch, utter, voice, communicate, speak; ship. See MEANING, SPEECH, TRANSPORTATION, HASTE, INFORMATION, EXTRACTION. —*adj.* manifest, explicit, precise; special. See SPECIALITY.

expression, *n.* REPRESENTATION, symbolization, INDICATION; statement, utterance, wording, communication; modulation, shading, interpretation; idiom, phrase, term; aspect, look, pose; token; saying. See AFFIRMATION, APPEARANCE, MEANING, SPEECH, NOMENCLATURE.

expropriate, *v.t.* dispossess (see ACQUISITION).

expulsion, *n.* EJECTION, eviction, ousting, dislodgement, dismissal; banishment, exile, deportation, expatriation, ostracism; EXCRETION, discharge.

expunge, *v.t.* erase; efface. See DEDUCTION, DESTRUCTION.

expurgate, *v.t.* bowdlerize; purge, purify, cleanse; emasculate, castrate. See PURITY.

exquisite, *adj.* accurate, exact, fastidious, appreciative, discriminating; accomplished, perfected; intense, keen, sharp; choice, selected, refined, rare; excellent, delicate, beautiful, matchless, dainty, charming, delightful. See FEELING, SUPERIORITY.

extant, *adj.* surviving, existent. See EXISTENCE.

extemporaneous, *adj.* unpremeditated, spontaneous, extempore, improvised, impromptu, offhand, unprepared. See IMPULSE, UNPREPAREDNESS.

extemporize, *v.* improvise. *Colloq.*, fake, wing it. See UNPREPAREDNESS, INTUITION.

extend, *v.* continue, lengthen, elongate, widen, enlarge, stretch, draw out, prolong, protract, expand, spread, broaden; increase; hold out, proffer, OFFER, impart, bestow. See INCREASE, LENGTH.

extension, *n.* widening, enlargement, stretching, EXPANSION, amplification, distension, ADDITION, continuance, continuation, lengthening, protraction, prolongation, protrusion, projection, ramification; comprehension; expanse, sweep, stretch. See INCREASE, SPACE, LENGTH.

extensive, *adj.* broad, comprehensive. See BREADTH, GENERALITY, SPACE.

extent, *n.* LIMIT, measure, range; span, longitude, LENGTH, BREADTH; compass, proportions, SIZE.

extenuate, *v.t.* excuse, forgive, pardon, mitigate, palliate; attenuate; diminish, weaken. See VINDICATION, WEAKNESS, DECREASE.

EXTERIOR

Nouns—**1,** exterior, exteriority, outwardness, externality, extraneousness.
2, outside, surface, finish, superficies; skin (see COVERING), superstratum, facet, SIDE.

Verbs—be exterior, be outside; lie around, surround (see CIRCUMSCRIPTION).

Adjectives—exterior, external, outer, outmost, outside, outermost, outward, outdoor, round about, outside of, surface, superficial, skin-deep, EXTRINSIC.

Adverbs—externally, outwardly, out, without, outward[s]; out-of-doors, in the open air, *al fresco*.

Antonyms, see INTERIOR.

---

exterminate, *v.t.* abolish, destroy, annihilate; extirpate, eradicate, root out. See DESTRUCTION.

external, *adj.* EXTERIOR; foreign; perceptible, visible, physical; extraneous, superficial. See VISIBILITY, UNCONFORMITY.

extinct, *adj.* extinguished, quenched; exterminated, nonexistent, obsolete; died out, gone. See OLDNESS, PAST, NONEXISTENCE, DEATH, DESTRUCTION.

extinguish, *v.t.* destroy, annihilate, eradicate, suppress, end; quench, choke, put *or* blow out, douse, snuff; smother, suffocate; quell, subdue. See DARKNESS, DESTRUCTION.

extol, *v.t.* praise, applaud, commend,

glorify, celebrate, exalt. See APPROBATION.

extort, *v.t.* elicit, extract, draw, exact; wring, wrench, force; squeeze. See STEALING, COMPULSION, EXTRACTION, THREAT.

extra, *adj.* additional, AUXILIARY, accessory, spare, supplementary, redundant. See ADDITIONAL.

EXTRACTION

Nouns—**1,** extraction, removal; elimination, extrication, eradication, evulsion; expression, squeezing; extirpation, suction.

2, evolution (see ANCESTRY).

3, extractor, corkscrew, forceps, pliers, wrench; pump, pulmotor, vacuum cleaner.

4, extract, essence, juice, *etc.*

Verbs—**1,** extract; draw, pull, tear, *or* pluck out; wring from, extricate, wrench, extort; root, dig, *or* rout out, weed out; grub up, rake out, uproot, pull up; eviscerate; extirpate, eradicate, eliminate, remove; express, squeeze out; distill; pump, milk; soak [up].

2, educe, elicit, evolve, extract, derive, bring forth *or* out.

Antonyms, see INSERTION.

extradite, *v.t.* deliver, deport, expel; turn *or* hand over. See EJECTION, TRANSFER.

extraneous, *adj.* foreign, alien; ulterior, exterior, external, outlandish; excluded, inadmissible, exceptional. See EXTRINSIC.

extraordinary, *adj.* unusual, singular, uncommon, remarkable, phenomenal, abnormal; eminent, rare, notable. See GREATNESS, UNCONFORMITY, SPECIALITY.

extravagant, *adj.* profuse, prodigal, lavish, excessive, extreme; wasteful, profligate, rampant, wild; bombastic, fantastic; high, exorbitant, unreasonable; unreal, flighty, visionary, absurd, fanciful, grotesque. See IMAGINATION, ABSURDITY, DEARNESS, FOLLY, BOASTING, EXAGGERATION, WASTE.

extreme, *adj.* remote, utmost, farthest, last, final, ultra, radical, drastic; excessive, inordinate, deep, intense, desperate, outrageous, immoderate, greatest. See END, GREATNESS.

extremist, *n.* radical. See CHANGE.

extremity, *n.* utmost, LIMIT, EDGE, boundary, tip; limb (of the body); destitution, need, distress. See END, POVERTY.

extricate, *v.t.* free, disentangle, loose, liberate, disengage. See LIBERATION, EXTRACTION.

EXTRINSIC

Nouns—**1,** extrinsicality, outwardness, extraneousness, foreignness, objectivity. See EXTERIOR, AUXILIARY, CIRCUMSTANCE.

2, accessory, appendage, extra, appurtenance, supplement, adjunct; accident; contingency, incidental.

Verbs—be extrinsic, lie outside *or* beyond.

Adjectives—**1,** extrinsical, external, outward, objective, circumstantial, contingent, foreign, impersonal.

2, unessential, nonessential, extraneous, accessory, adventitious, extra, AUXILIARY, incidental, fortuitous, casual.

Antonyms, see INTRINSIC.

exuberance, *n.* zest, enthusiasm, VIGOR, ebullience, energy, EXCITEMENT, high spirits, abundance, bounty, effusion. See FEELING, DIFFUSENESS.

exude, *v.* emit, discharge, ooze, leak, trickle, drain. See EGRESS, EXCRETION.

exult, *v.i.* rejoice, vaunt, jubilate, gloat, crow, triumph, glory. See BOASTING, REJOICING.

eye, *v.t.* watch, ogle, stare, view, observe, scrutinize, inspect. See VISION. —*n.* orb, visual organ; optic; eyesight, perception; VISION; opinion, view; hook, loop, OPENING. See CIRCULARITY.

eyesight, *n.* See VISION.

eyesore, *n.* offense, blemish. See UGLINESS.

eyewitness, *n.* bystander, witness. See PRESENCE, EVIDENCE.

F

fable, *n.* parable, allegory, moral tale; apologue; myth, legend, fiction. See DESCRIPTION, FALSEHOOD, FIGURATIVE.

fabric, *n.* cloth, textile, material, tissue; structure, framework. See PRODUCTION, MATERIALS, CROSSING, TEXTURE.

fabricate, *v.t.* build, construct, manufacture; invent, make up, trump up, concoct. See PRODUCTION, IMAGINATION, FALSEHOOD.

fabulous, *adj.* legendary, mythical; incredible, stupendous, prodigious. See DESCRIPTION, EXAGGERATION, DOUBT, NONEXISTENCE.

façade, *n.* FRONT; APPEARANCE, aspect, style; pretense, false front, mask, persona; stimulation, AFFECTATION. See SHALLOWNESS, FALSEHOOD.

face, *n.* facing; countenance, visage, physiognomy, lineaments, features; FRONT, façade, facet, obverse; van, first line; prestige, reputation; effrontery, INSOLENCE. *Slang,* mug, map, puss, phiz. See APPEARANCE, REPUTE. —*v.* encounter, confront; veneer, plate, sheathe; look out on. See OPPOSITION, COVERING, DIRECTION.

facet, *n.* face, surface, plane, bezel, culet; aspect, phase. See EXTERIOR.

facetious, *adj.* whimsical, joking, tongue-in-cheek; ironic[al], sarcastic, satirical, derisive. See WIT, RIDICULE.

FACILITY

Nouns—**1,** facility, ease; easiness; capability, feasibility, practicability; dexterity, SKILL; plain *or* smooth sailing, smooth water, fair wind, clear coast *or* stage; line *or* path of least resistance; sinecure, child's play; full *or* free play (see FREEDOM). *Colloq.,* [lead-pipe] cinch, breeze, bed of roses. *Slang,* snap, picnic, duck soup, fun and games; gravy train, pushover.

2, manageability, submissiveness (see *Adjectives,* 2).

3, see BUSINESS, UNCLEANNESS.

Verbs—**1,** be easy, be feasible; go *or* run smoothly; have full *or* free play (see FREEDOM); work well; flow *or* swim with the stream, drift *or* go with the tide; see one's way; have it all one's own way, have the game in one's own hands; walk over the course; win in a walk, win hands down; take in one's stride; make light *or* nothing of; be at home in.

2, facilitate, smooth, ease, lighten [the labor]; popularize; free, clear; disencumber, disembarrass, disentangle, disengage; disobstruct, unclog, extricate, unravel; leave the matter open; give the reins to; make way for, open the door to; prepare the ground *or* way, smooth *or* clear the ground; leave a loophole; spoonfeed. *Colloq.,* grease the ways *or* wheels.

Adjectives—**1,** facile, simple, easy, effortless; feasible, practicable; easily managed *or* accomplished, nothing to it, easy as falling off a log, like water off a duck's back, like taking candy from a baby, easy as pie, hands-down; within reach, accessible, easy of access, open to. *Colloq.*, gut, painless. *Slang*, no sweat.

2, manageable, wieldy, tractable, submissive, yielding, ductile; pliant, soft; glib; unburdened, disburdened, disencumbered, unembarrassed, unloaded, unobstructed, in the clear, untrammeled, unrestrained, free; at ease, dexterous, light; at home, in one's element.

Adverbs—facilely, easily; readily, handily, smoothly, swimmingly, on easy terms, without a hitch; single-handed; without striking a blow.

Antonyms, see DIFFICULTY.

---

facsimile, *n.* duplicate, reproduction, replica. See IDENTITY.

fact, *n.* reality, actuality, CERTAINTY; OCCURRENCE, phenomenon. See EXISTENCE, TRUTH, EVIDENCE.

faction, *n.* clique, cabal, splinter party; sect, denomination; DISCORD, dissidence, dissension. See PARTY, HETERODOXY.

factor, *n.* component, element, PART, constituent, condition; AGENT.

factory, *n.* manufactory, mill, shop, works, facilities, workshop. See PRODUCTION.

faculty, *n.* ability, aptitude, POWER, talent, knack; professorate, [teaching] staff. See SKILL, SCHOOL, INTELLECT.

fad, *n.* craze, rage, vogue; fancy, hobby. See CHANGEABLENESS, FASHION.

fade, *v.* pale, dim, bleach, whiten; vanish, disappear; languish, wither, shrivel. See DIMNESS, COLORLESSNESS, NONEXISTENCE, DETERIORATION, DISAPPEARANCE, WEAKNESS, TRANSIENTNESS, OBLIVION.

failing, *n.* fault, frailty, shortcoming; foible. See GUILT, IMPERFECTION.

FAILURE

Nouns—**1,** failure, unsuccessfulness, nonsuccess, nonfulfillment; dead failure, abortion, miscarriage, malfunction, outage; labor in vain; no go; inefficacy; vain *or* abortive attempt, slip 'twixt cup and lip. See INSUFFICIENCY, NEGLECT.

2, mistake (see ERROR); mess, fiasco, breakdown, collapse, fall, crash, downfall, ruin, perdition, grief; bankruptcy; wild-goose chase; losing game. *Colloq.*, has-been. *Slang*, flop, turkey, bomb, washout.

3, rebuff, defeat, rout, debacle, beating, drubbing; checkmate, stalemate. *Colloq.*, death knell.

4, also-ran, flash in the pan; underdog; house of cards, dud; bankrupt. *Colloq.*, bust, lemon. *Slang*, flop, goner.

Verbs—**1,** fail, be unsuccessful, not succeed; labor *or* toil in vain; lose one's labor; bring to naught, make nothing of; roll the stone of Sisyphus; do by halves; lose ground (see REGRESSION); fall short of. *Colloq.*, peter out. *Slang*, flop, not get to first base.

2, miss, miss one's aim, miss the boat *or* bus, miss the mark, miss by a mile; make a slip, blunder (see ERROR); make a mess of; miscarry, misfire, hang fire, backfire, abort; go up like a rocket and come down like a stick; reckon without one's host, back the wrong horse. *Colloq.*, blow.

3, limp, hobble; fall, lose one's balance; overreach oneself; flounder, falter; stick in the mud, run aground; tilt at windmills; come up against a stone wall; burn one's fingers; break one's back; break down, sink, go under, drown, founder, have the ground cut from under one; get into trouble, get into a mess *or* scrape; come to grief (see ADVERSITY); go to the wall, go under, go to the dogs, go to pot.

4, bite the dust, be defeated, take it on the chin, meet one's Waterloo, have the worst of it, lose the day; come off second best, bring up the rear, lose, lose out; succumb, buckle, drop *or* fall by the wayside; not have a leg to stand on. *Colloq.,* flunk [out]; have two strikes against one. *Slang,* fall down on, lay an egg, fold up.

5, come to nothing *or* naught, end in smoke; go bankrupt, close its doors, come a cropper, fizzle [out], die *or* wither on the vine; fall through, fall flat; give out, give way, fall down on the job; slip through one's fingers; hang fire; collapse; topple down; go to wrack and ruin; go amiss, go hard with; go wrong, go on a wrong tack, take a wrong turn; sow the wind and reap the whirlwind; jump out of the frying pan into the fire. *Slang,* fold up; the jig is up.

6, cause to fail, fix one's wagon, dash one's hopes.

Adjectives—**1,** failing, unsuccessful; abortive, stillborn; fruitless; bootless; ineffectual, ineffective, inefficacious; inefficient; impotent (see IMPOTENCE); lame, hobbling; insufficient (see INSUFFICIENCY); unavailing, useless (see USELESSNESS).

2, aground, grounded, swamped, stranded, cast away, wrecked, foundered, capsized, shipwrecked; foiled, defeated, vanquished, conquered; struck, borne, *or* broken down; downtrodden, overborne, overwhelmed; all up with; lost, undone, ruined, broken, bankrupt (see DEBT); done up, done for, dead beat, knocked on the head; thrown off one's balance; unhorsed; in a sorry plight; hard hit; left in the lurch; stultified, befooled, hoist by one's own petard; victimized, sacrificed; wide of the mark (see ERROR); thrown away (see WASTE); unattained; uncompleted. *Colloq.,* whipped, licked, kaput, out of the running. *Slang,* washed out; dished.

Adverbs—unsuccessfully; to little or no purpose, in vain, to no avail; about *or* on one's head; about *or* around one's ears.

Antonyms, see SUCCESS.

---

faint, *v.i.* swoon; lose heart *or* courage; fail, fade, weaken. *Colloq.,* pass out. —*adj.* pale, indistinct; feeble, weak. See WEAKNESS, COLORLESSNESS, IMPOTENCE, SILENCE, DIMNESS.

fainthearted, *adj.* See COWARDICE.

fair, *adj.* beautiful, handsome, good-looking, pretty, comely; blonde, light; unsullied, unblemished; pleasant, fine; impartial, equitable, unbiased, just; moderate, passable; clear, sunny, cloudless. See BEAUTY, COLORLESSNESS, JUSTICE, PROSPERITY. —*n.* sale, bazaar. See BUSINESS.

fairy, *n.* fay, sprite, pixy, elf, brownie, gnome, leprechaun. See MYTHICAL BEINGS, DEMON.

faith, *n.* trust, reliance, confidence, EXPECTATION; BELIEF, creed; loyalty; RELIGION.

faithful, *adj.* loyal, devoted; conscientious, trustworthy; exact, lifelike. See PROBITY, OBEDIENCE, PIETY.

faithless, *adj.* unfaithful, disloyal, untrue, inconstant, treacherous. See IMPROBITY, DOUBT.

fake, *n.* counterfeit, imposture, make-believe; impostor. See DECEPTION, FALSEHOOD. —*v., colloq.,* pretend, feign; IMITATE; improvise. *Colloq.,* wing it. See UNPREPAREDNESS.

fakir, *n.* ascetic, dervish; yogi[n]. See ASCETICISM.

fall, *v.i.* plunge, drop, sink, tumble, topple; perish; be deposed, come to grief; happen, occur, take place; sin, misbehave, lapse. —*n.* slope, declivity; downfall, defeat, comedown; drop, slump; plunge, tumble, header; autumn. See DESCENT, DE-

STRUCTION, DETERIORATION, OBLIQUITY, BADNESS, FAILURE, DEATH.

fallacy, *n.* ERROR, flaw, misconception; false meaning.

fallible, *adj.* unreliable, untrustworthy. See DOUBT.

fallout, *n.* radioactive dust, contamination; aftereffect, EFFECT.

fallow, *adj.* uncultivated, untilled, unsown. See NEGLECT, UNPREPAREDNESS.

FALSEHOOD

Nouns—**1,** falsehood, falseness; falsity, falsification; DECEPTION, untruth; lying, misrepresentation; mendacity, perjury, forgery, invention, fabrication.
2, perversion *or* suppression of truth, fiction, romance; perversion, DISTORTION, false coloring; EXAGGERATION, prevarication, equivocation, mystification (see CONCEALMENT); simulation, IMITATION, dissimulation, dissembling; whitewash; sham, make-believe, pretense, pretending, malingering. *Colloq.,* play-acting, bunk.
3, lip service; hollowness; duplicity, double-dealing, insincerity, hypocrisy, façade, cant, humbug; pharisaism; Machiavellianism; crocodile tears, mealy-mouthedness, quackery; charlatanism, charlatanry; cajolery, FLATTERY; Judas kiss; perfidy, bad faith, unfairness (see IMPROBITY); misstatement (see ERROR). *Colloq.,* front. *Slang,* fourflushing.
4, lie, half-truth, white lie, fable, pious fraud, song and dance; irony.
5, liar, fibber, prevaricator, falsifier, perjurer; charlatan; Ananias, Baron Munchhausen. *Slang,* baby kisser.

Verbs—**1,** be false, speak falsely, tell a lie, lie, fib; lie like a trooper, forswear, perjure oneself, bear false witness; belie, falsify, pervert, distort, misquote; put a false construction upon, misinterpret; misinform, mislead; prevaricate, equivocate, quibble; fence, mince the truth, beat about the bush, blow hot and cold, play fast and loose; garble, gloss over, disguise, color, varnish, dress up, embroider; pad the bill; exaggerate. *Slang,* throw the bull; cook.
2, invent, fabricate; trump up, get up; forge, hatch, concoct; romance, imagine (see IMAGINATION); cry "wolf!"; dissemble, dissimulate, palter; feign, assume, put on, pretend, make believe (see AFFECTATION); play false, play a double game; pull out of a hat; act *or* play a part; affect, simulate; palm off, pass off for; counterfeit, sham, make a show of, malinger; cant, fob off, put on, play the hypocrite, sail under false colors, deceive (see DECEPTION); go through the motions. *Colloq.,* let on, play-act, play possum, put on a front. *Slang,* fourflush.

Adjectives—false, deceitful, mendacious, unveracious, fraudulent, dishonest, make-believe, faithless, truthless, trothless; unfair, uncandid, evasive; uningenuous, disingenuous; hollow, insincere, forsworn; canting; hypocritical, pharisaical; Machiavellian, two-faced, double-dealing; Janus-faced; smooth-faced, -spoken, *or* -tongued, tongue-in-cheek; mealy-mouthed; affected; collusive, collusory, perfidious (see IMPROBITY); spurious, deceptive (see DECEPTION); untrue, falsified; ungrounded, unfounded.

Adverbs—falsely; slyly, crookedly, *etc.*

Antonyms, see TRUTH, REASONING.

falter, *v.i.* hesitate, waver, hang back, vacillate; shuffle, stumble, totter; stammer. See DOUBT, SLOWNESS, STAMMERING, FAILURE, HOPELESSNESS.

fame, *n.* REPUTE, renown, prestige, celebrity; honor, distinction, glory, eminence; notoriety. See NEWS.

familiar spirit, *n.* See MYTHICAL DEITIES, DEMON.

familiarity, *n.* intimacy, acquaintance, fellowship; KNOWLEDGE; informality, forwardness, impudence. See FRIEND, SOCIALITY, INSOLENCE.

familiarize, *v.t.* acquaint; accustom. See INFORMATION, HABIT.

family, *n.* household; forefathers, children, descendants, lineage, family tree; clan, tribe, kindred; group, association, classification, CLASS. See ANCESTRY.

famish, *v.* starve, die of hunger, be hungry; pinch, exhaust. See PARSIMONY.

famous, *adj.* noted, famed, renowned, celebrated, well-known. See REPUTE.

fan, *n.* fanner, blower, winnower, flabellum, ventilator; wind; *colloq.,* devotee, follower, enthusiast, supporter. *Slang,* rooter, addict, groupie. See ACTIVITY. *—v.t.* blow, winnow, cool, refresh, ventilate, stir up; *slang,* strike out. See AIR, WIND, AGITATION, REFRESHMENT.

fanatic, *n.* zealot, enthusiast, dogmatist. See EXCITABILITY, FEELING, HETERODOXY, INSANITY.

fanciful, *adj.* whimsical, capricious, fantastic, quaint, bizarre; quixotic, imaginary. See UNCONFORMITY, IMAGINATION.

fancy, *n.* IMAGINATION; idea, caprice, whim; preference, DESIRE; reverie, daydream. *—v.t.* imagine; believe, suppose, assume; like, DESIRE, take to. See BELIEF, SUPPOSITION. *—adj.* ornate, showy; superior, extravagant. See ORNAMENT, OSTENTATION.

fancy-free, *adj.* carefree, unattached. See FREEDOM.

fanfare, *n.* flourish, tantara; CELEBRATION, OSTENTATION.

fang, *n.* tooth, eyetooth, tusk. See SHARPNESS.

fantastic, *adj.* bizarre, grotesque; imaginative, fanciful; extravagant, irrational, absurd. See IMAGINATION, ABSURDITY.

far, *adv.* remotely, distantly, widely, afar. *—adj.* far off, remote, distant. See DISTANCE.

farce, *n.* buffoonery, burlesque, travesty; mockery, fiasco. See WIT, DRAMA.

fare, *v.i.* get on, make out, get along; prosper, thrive; eat, dine, regale oneself. *—n.* passage, carfare, token; luck, outcome; FOOD, diet, table, board, provisions. See TRAVEL, PRICE, EFFECT.

farewell, *interj.* See DEPARTURE.

farfetched, *adj.* forced, strained. See IMPROBABILITY.

farm, *n.* ranch, rancho, plantation, farmstead, grange. See ABODE. *—v.* cultivate, till. See AGRICULTURE.

farsighted, *adj.* hypermetropic, eagle-eyed; foresighted, longheaded, prudent, provident. See PREDICTION, VISION.

farther, *adj.* more distant, further, additional. *—adv.* beyond. See DISTANCE.

fascination, *n.* charm, attraction, allurement, captivation; bewilderment; enchantment, spell; obsession. See PLEASURE, WONDER.

fascism, *n.* totalitarianism, authoritarianism; dictatorship; reactionism, nationalism; national socialism, red fascism, falangism, nazism; neofascism. See AUTHORITY.

FASHION

Nouns—**1,** fashion, style, [*bon*] *ton,* society; good society, polite society; drawing room, civilized life, civilization; town; *haut* or *beau monde,* high life, court; world; *haute couture,* high fashion *or* style; fashionable world; Vanity Fair; show, OSTENTATION.

2, manners, breeding, politeness (see COURTESY); air, demeanor, APPEARANCE; *savoir faire;* gentlemanliness, gentility, suavity; decorum, propriety,

convention, conventionality, punctilio; form, formality; etiquette, social usage, custom, HABIT; mode, vogue, go, rage, furor, fad, chic, TASTE, distinction; dress (see CLOTHING). *Slang,* the last word, *le dernier cri.*
3, man *or* woman of fashion, man *or* woman of the world; height of fashion; leader of fashion, socialite; arbiter; upper ten thousand (see NOBILITY); elite. *Colloq.,* upper crust, the four hundred; jet set, café society.

Verbs—be fashionable, be the rage; follow the fashion, conform to the fashion, get on the bandwagon, go with the stream (see CONFORMITY); keep up appearances, behave oneself (see CONDUCT); set the style *or* fashion; bring into style *or* fashion, come in. *Colloq.,* be in the swim.

Adjectives—fashionable, in fashion, modish, chic, dressy, formal, stylish, sharp [as a tack]; recherché; newfangled, *à la mode, comme il faut*; presentable; conventional, customary, genteel, continental; well-bred, well-mannered, well-behaved, well-spoken; gentlemanly, ladylike; civil, polite, courteous (see COURTESY); polished, refined, thoroughbred, courtly; *distingué; dégagé,* suave, jaunty, switched-on; dashing, fast. *Colloq.,* in, natty, snappy.

Antonyms, see VULGARITY, UNCONFORMITY.

---

fast, *v.i.* starve, diet, abstain. See ASCETICISM. *—adj.* swift, speedy, fleet, quick, rapid; secure, firm, permanent, steadfast, profound; wild, rakish, dissipated. See VELOCITY, JUNCTION, IMPURITY, TENACITY, FASHION.

fasten, *v.t.* secure, make fast, attach, fix, bind, lock up. See JUNCTION, CLOSURE, RESTRAINT.

fastening, *n.* fastener, lock, catch, clasp, latch, hook, CONNECTION; button, zipper, hook [and eye], buckle; nail, tack, staple, screw, bolt, rivet, peg; thread; glue, cement.

fastidious, *adj.* finicky, [over]nice, fussy, crotchety. See TASTE.

fasting, *n.* fast, starvation, hunger, famishment; hunger strike. See ASCETICISM, ATONEMENT.

fat, *adj.* plump, stout, corpulent, obese, portly, chubby; fertile, profitable, fruitful, rich; greasy, unctuous. See SIZE, ROTUNDITY, SMOOTHNESS, PRODUCTION.

fatal, *adj.* deadly, lethal, mortal; fateful, critical. See KILLING, DEATH, IMPORTANCE.

fatalism, *n.* determinism, predestination; submission, apathy, nonresistance; passivity, stoicism. See DESTINY.

fatality, *n.* mortality, deadliness; casualty, accident, DEATH. See ADVERSITY, NECESSITY.

fate, *n.* DESTINY, lot, fortune, doom, predestination, CHANCE. See NECESSITY.

father, *n.* sire, forefather; founder, patriarch; priest, pastor; the Father, God. See ANCESTRY, CLERGY, DEITY.

fatherland, *n.* homeland, native country, home. See ABODE.

fathom, *v.t.* measure, take a sounding; plunge, reach the bottom of; investigate, probe, study, delve into. See MEASUREMENT, INQUIRY.

fathomless, *adj.* bottomless, abyssal; cryptic, mystifying, insoluble, puzzling, enigmatic. See DEPTH, UNINTELLIGIBILITY.

fatigue, *v.* weary, tire, exhaust; jade, fag; bore, irk, wear; weaken, debilitate, overstrain, overtax, overwork. *—n.* tiredness, WEARINESS, exhaustion, lassitude, feebleness; exertion, strain; faintness, labor, work, toil, drudgery; ennui, boredom; (*pl.*) work clothes (see CLOTHING).

fatten, *v.* feed, flesh out; enrich, INCREASE. See EXPANSION, FOOD, PROSPERITY.

fatuous, *adj.* vain, foolish, inept; inane, silly. *Slang,* dumb, sappy. See FOLLY, ABSURDITY.

faucet, *n.* tap, spigot, cock, spout,

valve; spile, bung. See CLOSURE, OPENING.

fault, *n.* failing, shortcoming, peccadillo; flaw, blemish, defect, IMPERFECTION; ERROR, slip, inadvertency; sin, [venial] sin, [minor] vice. See GUILT, FAILURE.

faultfinding, *adj.* captious, carping, caviling, critical, censorious. See DISAPPROBATION.

faultless, *adj.* flawless, perfect, correct, impeccable; irreproachable, *sans peur et sans reproche*. See PERFECTION, INNOCENCE, PURITY.

faulty, *adj.* defective; erroneous, wrong. See IMPERFECTION, ERROR.

favor, *n.* good will, esteem, APPROBATION, approval; partiality, bias, favoritism; patronage, backing; concession, dispensation; kindness, service, good turn; token, badge. See AID, PERMISSION, GIVING, LENIENCY.

favorable, *adj.* auspicious, propitious, advantageous, opportune, commendatory, well-inclined; affirmative. See OCCASION, AID.

favorite, *n.* darling, pet; idol, hero, jewel; apple of one's eye; CHOICE, preference; spoiled child *or* darling. *Colloq.*, teacher's pet, fair- *or* white-haired boy. —*adj.* dearest; beloved, preferred, CHOICE. See LOVE.

fawn, *v.i.* cringe, grovel, toady, truckle, cower, ingratiate, curry favor. See SERVILITY, FLATTERY.

fay, *adj.* elfin, impish, pixie, fey; coy, arch; *slang,* effeminate. See MYTHICAL BEINGS, FEMALE.

faze, *v.t., colloq.*, deter, daunt, ruffle; disconcert, bother, rattle, hold back, interfere with. See HINDRANCE.

FEAR

Nouns—**1,** fear, fearfulness, phobia; timidity, timorousness, diffidence; solicitude, anxiety, worry, CARE, apprehension; apprehensiveness, misgiving, mistrust, DOUBT, suspicion, qualm; hesitation, irresolution; fright, alarm, dread, horror, awe, terror, dismay, consternation, panic, scare, stampede.

2, nervousness, restlessness, inquietude, disquietude; flutter, trepidation, fear and trembling, buck fever, jitters, creeps, shivers; goose flesh, bumps, *or* pimples; butterflies [in the stomach]; perturbation, tremor, quivering, shaking, trembling, palpitation, cold sweat; abject fear (see COWARDICE); hangup. *Colloq.*, funk. *Slang,* heebie-jeebies.

3, intimidation, terrorism, reign of terror, THREAT, menace.

4, bugbear, bugaboo; scarecrow; hobgoblin, DEMON; nightmare, Gorgon, ogre; *bête noire;* alarmist.

Verbs—**1,** fear, stand in awe of, be afraid, have qualms, be apprehensive, distrust, DOUBT; hesitate; funk, cower, crouch; skulk (see COWARDICE); take fright, take alarm, panic, stampede.

2, start, wince, flinch, cringe, shy, shrink; fly, flee (see AVOIDANCE); tremble, shake, jump out of one's skin; shiver [in one's boots *or* shoes]; shudder, flutter; tremble like a leaf *or* an aspen leaf, quake, quaver, quail; grow *or* turn pale; blench, stand aghast, throw up one's hands in horror. *Slang,* sweat blood.

3, inspire *or* excite fear *or* awe; raise apprehensions; alarm, startle, scare, cry "wolf!", disquiet, dismay; fright[en]; affright, terrify; scare *or* frighten out of one's wits, scare the daylights out of; awe, strike terror (into), appall, unman, petrify, horrify; make one's flesh creep, make one's hair stand on end, curl one's hair; make one's blood run cold, turn to ice, *or* freeze, make one's teeth chatter; take away one's breath, make one's heart stand still; make one tremble; haunt; prey *or* weigh on the mind.

4, put in fear, terrorize, intimidate, cow, daunt, take aback, overawe, deter, discourage; browbeat, bully, boss; threaten (see WARNING), menace.

Adjectives—**1,** fearing, frightened, in fear, in a fright, afraid, scared, fearful, timid, timorous, cowardly (see COWARDICE); nervous, diffident, faint-hearted, tremulous, shaky, panicky, afraid of one's shadow, mousy, apprehensive, irresolute; restless, fidgety, on pins and needles; having one's heart in one's mouth *or* boots; paranoid; careworn, anxious.

2, aghast; alarmed; awestricken, horror-, terror-, *or* panic-stricken; frightened to death, white as a sheet; pale as death, ashes, *or* a ghost; breathless, in hysterics. *Colloq.,* yellow. *Slang,* chicken.

3, inspiring fear, fearsome, alarming; formidable, redoubtable; forbidding, dreadful, fell; dire, direful; shocking, terrible, terrifying, terrific, spine-chilling, alarmist; tremendous; horrid, horrible, horrific; ghastly; awful, awe-inspiring, eerie.

Adverbs—in fear, for fear, for dear life, fearfully, with fear and trembling, with the tail between the legs.

Antonyms, see HOPE, COURAGE.

---

fearless, *adj.* courageous, dauntless, daring, valorous, valiant, intrepid, unafraid. See COURAGE.

feasible, *adj.* practicable, possible, workable; suitable. See POSSIBILITY, FACILITY.

feast, *n.* banquet, spread, repast; holiday, holy day, festival. See FOOD, RITE, SUFFICIENCY, GLUTTONY, PLEASURE.

feat, *n.* deed, gest, accomplishment, exploit; stunt. See COURAGE, COMPLETION.

feather, *n.* plume, plumage, down, aigrette; kind, sort, variety. See COVERING, DIFFERENCE, CLASS, ROUGHNESS.

feature, *n.* lineament, aspect; trait, peculiarity, property, characteristic; presentation, film, story. See FORM, INDICATION, IMPORTANCE, FRONT, SPECIALITY, APPEARANCE, PART.

fecund, *adj.* fertile, prolific, inventive, creative. See IMAGINATION, PRODUCTION.

federation, *n.* league, union, [con]-federacy, association, alliance. See COOPERATION, PARTY, COMBINATION.

fee, *n.* PAYMENT, pay; COMPENSATION, emolument; assessment, dues, tax; gratuity, tip.

feeble, *adj.* See WEAKNESS.

feed, *v.* eat, dine, consume, devour; graze; nourish, nurture, bait; supply, provide, furnish; satisfy, gratify. See FOOD, SUFFICIENCY, FUEL.

feedback, *n.* response, ANSWER.

feeler, *n.* antenna, tentacle, palp[us], vibrissa, whisker; test, probe, trial balloon. See TOUCH, INQUIRY.

FEELING

Nouns—**1,** feeling, sensation, sentience, emotion, SENSIBILITY, sensitivity; endurance, tolerance, sufferance, experience, response; PITY, pathos, sympathy, LOVE, vibrations; impression, inspiration, affection, tenderness; warmth, glow, unction, gusto, vehemence; fervor, fervency, fire; heart, breast; heartiness, cordiality; earnestness, eagerness; ardor, élan, zeal, passion, enthusiasm, verve, furor, fanaticism; EXCITEMENT; EXCITABILITY, ecstasy; PLEASURE. *Colloq.,* vibes.

2, blush, suffusion, flush; tingling, thrill; turn, shock (see SURPRISE); AGITATION, quiver, throb[bing]; heartstrings, heartthrob; lump in the throat; sob story.

3, TOUCH, tangibility, contact, manipulation; TASTE.

Verbs—**1,** feel, receive an impression; be impressed with; entertain, harbor, *or* cherish feeling; respond; catch fire, catch infection; enter the spirit of.
2, bear, suffer, support, sustain, endure, abide, experience, TASTE, prove; labor *or* smart under; bear the brunt of.
3, swell, glow, warm, flush, blush, change color, mantle; turn color, turn pale, turn black in the face; tingle, thrill, heave, pant, throb, palpitate, go pit-a-pat, tremble, quiver, flutter, twitter; wear one's heart on one's sleeve, take to heart; shake, be agitated, be excited, look blue, look black; wince, draw a deep breath. *Colloq.,* blow off steam. See AGITATION.
4, TOUCH, handle, finger, paw, fumble, grope.
Adjectives—**1,** feeling, sentient, sensuous; sensorial, sensory; emotive, emotional; tactile, tactual, tangible, palpable.
2, warm, quick, lively, smart, strong, sharp, acute, cutting, piercing, incisive; keen, exquisite, intense, razor-sharp; trenchant, pungent, racy, piquant, poignant, caustic.
3, impressive, deep, profound, indelible; pervading, penetrating, absorbing; deep-felt, heartfelt; swelling, soul-stirring, electric, thrilling, rapturous, ecstatic.
4, earnest, wistful, eager, breathless; fervent, fervid; gushing, passionate, warmhearted, hearty, cordial, sincere, devout, zealous, enthusiastic, flowing, ardent, burning, consumed with, red-hot, fiery, flaming; seething, boiling; rabid, raving, feverish, delirious, fanatical, hysterical; impetuous, excitable. *Colloq.,* gung-ho.
5, impressed by, moved by, touched, affected, seized by, imbued with; devoured by; wrought up, excited, struck all of a heap; misty- *or* dewy-eyed; rapt, in a quiver, enraptured.
Adverbs—feelingly, with feeling, heart and soul, with all one's heart, from the bottom of one's heart, at heart, *con amore, con brio,* heartily, devoutly, head over heels.

Antonyms, see INSENSIBILITY.

---

feign, *v.t.* simulate, pretend, counterfeit, sham. See FALSEHOOD, AFFECTATION.

feint, *n.* diversion, trick; pretense, artifice, evasion; sleight-of-hand, legerdemain; bobbing and weaving; red herring. See CUNNING, DECEPTION.

feisty, *adj.* quarrelsome; frisky. See IRASCIBILITY, ACTIVITY.

felicitate, *v.t.* See CONGRATULATION.

felicitous, *adj.* happy, well-chosen, pertinent, apt, pat, neat. See AGREEMENT, ELEGANCE, SUCCESS.

feline, *adj.* catlike, cattish, *etc.;* stealthy, CUNNING; catty.

fell, *v.t.* bring, cut, *or* chop down, drop. See DISJUNCTION. —*adj.* ruthless, terrible. See FEAR.

fellow, *n.* comrade, associate, colleague; compeer, mate, equal; scholar; *colloq.,* person, man, boy, chap, guy. See MANKIND, FRIEND, EQUALITY, ACCOMPANIMENT, MALE.

fellowship, *n.* companionship, camaraderie, comradeship; neighborliness, amity; sodality, sorority, fraternity; scholarship, bursary. See SOCIALITY, FRIEND, PARTY, COOPERATION, PAYMENT, ACCOMPANIMENT.

felon, *n.* criminal (see EVILDOER).

felony, *n.* crime. See ILLEGALITY.

FEMALE

Nouns—**1,** female, womankind, womanhood, femininity, muliebrity; fair sex, weaker sex; feminist, suffragist (see CHOICE). *Slang,* femme; [beach] bunny;

frail, dame, skirt, broad, sister, tomato (*all offensive*). See HUMANITY, POPULACE.

2, madam, madame, mistress, Mrs., Ms., lady, donna, belle, matron, dowager, goody, gammer; matriarch; crone (see EVILDOER); good woman, goodwife; squaw; wife (see MARRIAGE); matronhood; miss, mademoiselle; girl, lass (see YOUTH).

3, hen, bitch, sow, doe, roe, mare, she-goat, nanny-goat, ewe, cow, lioness, tigress, vixen, *etc.*

Adjectives—female, feminine; womanly, ladylike, matronly, maidenly; womanish, effeminate, unmanly; maternal.

Antonyms, see MALE.

---

feminist, *n.* suffragist, suffragette. See FEMALE.

fence, *n.* barrier, barricade, wall, stockade, paling, hedge, railing. —*v.i.* enclose; fight, thrust and parry; parry, evade. See DEFENSE, ENCLOSURE, CONTENTION.

fend, *v.* defend, protect, take care of; ward, hold, *or* stave off; avert; shift [for oneself], be on one's own. See DEFENSE, REPULSION.

fender, *n.* fire screen; bumper. See HEAT, SAFETY.

ferment, *n.* yeast, leaven; uproar, turmoil, AGITATION, DISORDER. See SOURNESS. —*v.i.* effervesce, work, raise; seethe, arouse.

ferocity, *adj.* fierceness, savagery, brutality, cruelty. See MALEVOLENCE, VIOLENCE.

ferret out, *v.t.* spy, fish, search, *or* hunt out. See INQUIRY.

ferry, *n.* ferryboat, scow, lighter, barge, raft, launch, tender; shuttle, air lift, airdrop. —*v.* convey, transport, shuttle. See TRANSPORTATION.

fertile, *adj.* prolific, productive, fruitful, rich; creative, inventive. See PRODUCTION, IMAGINATION.

fertilization, *n.* impregnation, procreation, pollination; enrichment. See PRODUCTION.

fertilizer, *n.* manure, compost, guano. See AGRICULTURE.

fervent, *adj.* earnest, fervid, ardent, eager; vehement, impassioned, intense; hot, glowing. See DESIRE, FEELING, HEAT.

fervor, *n.* intenseness, enthusiasm, ardor, passion, zeal. See ACTIVITY, FEELING, HEAT.

fester, *n.* suppurate, ulcerate, rankle; infect. See DISEASE, DETERIORATION.

festivity, *n.* merrymaking, REJOICING; gaiety, jollity; (*pl.*) festival. See AMUSEMENT, CELEBRATION.

fetch, *v.t.* retrieve, bring, carry; heave, deal, yield; sell *or* go for. See TRANSPORTATION, PRICE.

fetid, *adj.* stinking, malodorous, foul, smelly, noisome. See MALODOROUSNESS.

fetish, *n.* charm, amulet, totem, talisman; obsession, mania. See IDOLATRY.

fetter, *v.t.* shackle, manacle, handcuff, [en]chain, put in irons; tie up, tie hand and foot, hobble, hogtie, strap down; check, restrain. See RESTRAINT.

fetus, *n.* embryo. See BEGINNING.

feud, *n.* CONTENTION, quarrel, strife, conflict; rancor, grudge, rivalry, revenge, vendetta. —*v.i.* quarrel, struggle. See RETALIATION.

feudalism, *n.* vassalage, serfdom. See AUTHORITY, SUBJECTION.

fever, *n.* pyrexia; frenzy, delirium. See DISEASE, AGITATION, HEAT.

feverish, *adj.* febrile, hectic, hot; restless, agitated. See HEAT, EXCITEMENT, EXCITABILITY.

few, *adj.* not many, little; scant[y], meager, scarce, rare; infrequent; several, two or three, hardly any. See RARITY.

fiancé(e), *n.* affianced, betrothed, engaged, *or* pledged [one]; husband- *or* bride-elect. *Colloq.*, intended. See PROMISE.

fiasco, *n.* FAILURE, miscarriage, slip, misfire; botch, mess.

fiat, *n.* decree, COMMAND, edict, mandate; sanction, PERMISSION.

fib, *n.* white lie. See FALSEHOOD.

fiber, *n.* FILAMENT, thread, strand; shred; TEXTURE, structure.

fickle, *adj.* capricious, unstable, inconstant. See CHANGEABLENESS.

fiction, *n.* fabrication, FALSEHOOD; romance, myth, hypothesis. See DESCRIPTION.

fictitious, *adj.* imaginary, fictional, fictive; feigned, false. See IMAGINATION, DECEPTION.

fiddle, *n.* violin (see MUSIC). *—v.i.* trifle. See UNIMPORTANCE.

fidelity, *n.* faithfulness, reliability, loyalty; exactness, accuracy. See TRUTH, PROBITY.

fidget, *v.i.* toss, squirm, twitch, twiddle. See AGITATION, EXCITABILITY.

field, *n.* clearing, grassland; expanse, range, plot; playground, links, court, airport, aerodrome, ARENA; scope, sphere, realm; battlefield, WARFARE. See REGION, BUSINESS, AGRICULTURE, SPACE.

fiend, *n.* DEMON, imp; *colloq.*, addict, buff, fan, fanatic, enthusiast, nut. See DESIRE, FEELING, EVILDOER, ACTIVITY.

fierce, *adj.* ferocious, truculent; tigerish, savage; intense, violent; aggressive, bellicose; vehement. See VIOLENCE, EXCITABILITY.

fiery, *adj.* impetuous, passionate, hot-tempered, fervid; irritable; blazing, glowing; inflamed. See HEAT, EXCITEMENT, IRASCIBILITY, EXCITABILITY.

fiesta, *n.* CELEBRATION, holiday, fête, festival.

fight, *n.* battle, affray, brawl, quarrel; contest, struggle; pugnacity. *Slang,* scrap. See CONTENTION, IRASCIBILITY, RESOLUTION.

fighter, *n.* COMBATANT; boxer, prize fighter, pugilist, bruiser. *Slang,* pug.

figment, *n.* invention, fantasy, chimera, pipe dream. See IMAGINATION.

FIGURATIVE

Nouns—figurativeness, figure of speech; metaphor; way of speaking, colloquialism; phrase; figure, trope, metonymy, enallage, catachresis, synecdoche, autonomasia; symbolism; irony; image, imagery; metalepsis, type, anagoge, simile, personification, allegory, apologue, parable, fable; hendiadys; litotes; allusion, adumbration; hyperbole, EXAGGERATION.

Verbs—speak figuratively, employ figures of speech, metaphor, *etc.;* verbalize; personify, allegorize, symbolize, adumbrate; apply, allude to.

Adjectives—figurative, metaphorical, catachrestic, typical, parabolic, symbolic, allegorical, allusive, anagogical; ironical; colloquial.

Adverbs—figuratively, metaphorically; so to speak, so to say, in a sense, as it were; in a manner of speaking.

Antonyms, see MEANING.

---

figure, *n.* FORM, shape, configuration, outline; body; REPRESENTATION, image, effigy; APPEARANCE; pattern, diagram; figure of speech (see FIGURATIVE); emblem, symbol, NUMBER, digit; figurehead; cast, bust, statue. *—v.* ORNAMENT, decorate; symbolize, represent, signify, delineate, embody; imagine, conceive, picture; draw, outline; compute, calculate, do sums; appear, perform, act; cut a figure, matter, stand out. See IMAGINATION, NUMERATION, ACTION.

FILAMENT

Nouns—**1,** filament, line; fiber, fibril; funicle, vein, hair, capillament, capillary, cilium, tendril, gossamer; hairline.

2, string, chord, thread, cotton, sewing silk, twine, twist; whipcord, tape, ribbon, strap, strand, cord, rope, lariat, yarn, hemp, oakum, jute.

3, strip, shred, list, band, fillet, ribbon; lath, splinter, shiver, shaving; cable, wire.

Verbs—roll, spin, shred.

Adjectives—filamentous, filaceous, filar, filiform; fibrous, fibrilous; threadlike, wiry, stringy, ropy; capillary, capilliform; funicular, wire-drawn; anguilliform; flagelliform; hairy, ciliate.

---

file, *n.* ARRANGEMENT, classification; LIST, dossier, record, catalogue, inventory; folder; row, column; rasp. —*v.t.* classify, arrange, STORE; catalogue, record; submit, deliver; rasp. See CONTINUITY, FRICTION.

filial, *adj.* dutiful; sonlike, daughterly. See POSTERITY.

filigree, *n.* ornamentation, tracery, scrollwork, arabesque. See ORNAMENT.

fill, *v.t.* complete, load, pervade, permeate; plug, cork; occupy, serve well, satisfy; carry out. See LAYER, SUFFICIENCY, PRESENCE, CLOSURE, BUSINESS.

film, *n.* coating, membrane, haze, blur, scum; movie (see DRAMA). See COVERING, NARROWNESS.

filter, *v.* filtrate, strain, sieve; percolate, pass through; purify, refine, leach. See CLEANNESS, EGRESS. —*n.* strainer, sifter, sieve, screen, percolator; cheesecloth; optical *or* audio filter. See OPENING, DISJUNCTION.

filth, *n.* dirt, ordure; obscenity. See UNCLEANNESS, IMPURITY.

fin, *n.* flipper, process, lobe, pinna; propellor, rudder; lug, ear, blade. See NAVIGATION, PART.

finagle, *v.* wangle; maneuver. See CUNNING, DECEPTION.

final, *adj.* last, ultimate; decisive. See END, JUDGMENT.

finance, *v.t.* capitalize, back, fund, subsidize; put up money for; underwrite, guarantee. See DEBT, PAYMENT. —*n.* high finance, banking; budget, purse, treasury. See MONEY, ACCOUNTING, MEANS.

find, *v.t.* discover, detect, espy; get, obtain; learn, ascertain, perceive; provide; decide, declare. See ACQUISITION, DISCLOSURE, JUDGMENT.

finding, *n.* find, discovery, ACQUISITION, windfall; JUDGMENT, verdict. See DISCLOSURE.

fine, *n.* penalty, forfeit, amercement. —*v.t.* amerce, mulct, penalize. See PUNISHMENT. —*adj.* pure, superior, admirable, excellent; small, tiny, slender, flimsy, delicate; worthy, estimable; skilled, accomplished; refined, polished; subtle, nice, keen, sharp; fair, pleasant. See PURITY, BEAUTY, LITTLENESS, NARROWNESS, RARITY.

finery, *n.* frippery, frills, tinsel. See ORNAMENT.

finesse, *n.* craft, CUNNING; SKILL.

finger, *n.* digit; pointer, trigger finger, pinky. See TOUCH. —*v.t.* TOUCH, feel, toy with; *slang,* tell on (see INFORMATION).

finish, *v.t.* END, terminate, complete, conclude; USE up, polish off. —*n.* COMPLETION, conclusion; poise, polish; surface, patina. See ELEGANCE, EXTERIOR, TEXTURE.

finite, *adj.* limited (see LIMIT).

fire, *n.* flame, blaze, conflagration, holocaust; enthusiasm, verve. —*v.t.* kindle, ignite; shoot, detonate; inspire, arouse; dismiss, discharge. See HEAT, PROPULSION, EXCITEMENT, FUEL, VIGOR.

fireman, *n.* firefighter; stoker. See INCOMBUSTIBILITY, TRAVEL.

fireplace, *n.* hearth, ingle[nook], chimney. See HEAT.

fireproof, *adj.* See INCOMBUSTIBILITY.

firewood, *n.* faggots, logs, kindling. See FUEL.

fireworks, *n.pl.* pyrotechnics; firecrackers, sparklers, Roman candles, rockets, *etc.* See HEAT.

firm, *adj.* immovable, secure; unalterable, steadfast; solid, hard; steady, vigorous; unalterable, resolute, determined. See STABILITY, PROBITY, DENSITY, RESOLUTION. —*n.* partnership, company, house. See BUSINESS, PARTY.

firmament, *n.* sky, vault of HEAVEN; welkin, empyrean; starry cope. See UNIVERSE.

first, *adj.* earliest, original, prime; leading, chief, fundamental. —*adv.* firstly, originally, at first; before, ahead; sooner, rather. See BEGINNING, PRIORITY, PRECEDENCE.

first-class, first-rate, *adj.* choice, excellent, four-star, top-drawer, A-one, first-water; best, outstanding, palmary; de luxe, swanky, luxurious. *Slang,* ritzy. See SUPERIORITY.

fish, *v.* angle; pull out, dredge; solicit; search. See PURSUIT, DESIRE. —*n.* sport *or* game fish; shellfish; Pisces. See ANIMAL.

fisher, *n.* fisherman *or* -woman, angler, piscator; whaler, clam digger, *etc.* See PURSUIT.

fission, *n.* cleavage, scission, DISJUNCTION; nuclear fission, splitting the atom, atom-smashing.

fissure, *n.* cleft, chink, opening, crack, rift, breach. See INTERVAL.

fit, *n.* caprice, whim, fancy, notion; paroxysm, convulsion, seizure, outburst. See AGITATION. —*v.* equip, furnish, outfit; grace, beautify; accommodate; clothe; suit, meet, conform; adapt. See AGREEMENT, EQUALITY, PREPARATION, CLOTHING. —*adj.* appropriate, suitable, fitting, proper; expedient, advantageous; vigorous, well, sound. See AGREEMENT, HEALTH, VIOLENCE, EXPEDIENCE, DISEASE.

fitful, *adj.* intermittent. See DISCONTINUANCE.

fix, *v.t.* stabilize, establish; repair, adjust, mend; settle, decide; place; fasten; prepare; *slang,* bribe; *colloq.,* spay, castrate. See STABILITY, RESTORATION, JUNCTION, CERTAINTY, LOCATION, DENSITY.—*n., colloq.* predicament (see DIFFICULTY).

fixation, *n.* focus, ATTENTION; *idée fixe,* obsession, compulsion, mania. *Colloq.,* bee in one's bonnet. *Slang,* hangup. See INSANITY.

fixture, *n.* attachment, fitting, appendage. See PERMANENCE.

fizzle, *v.i.* fizz, effervesce, bubble, ferment, foam; sizzle, hiss; *colloq.,* collapse, disintegrate, fade *or* die out, fail, flop, conk out. See FAILURE, AGITATION.

flabby, *adj.* limp, soft, flaccid; feeble. See SOFTNESS, WEAKNESS.

flaccid, *adj.* flabby, soft. See SOFTNESS.

flag, *n.* banner, pennant, ensign, standard; iris; flagstone. See INDICATION. —*v.i.* droop, pine, languish. See INACTIVITY, DEJECTION, DISEASE.

flagon, *n.* flask, bottle, carafe, mug. See RECEPTACLE.

flagrant, *adj.* glaring, notorious, outrageous, shocking. See BADNESS.

flair, *n.* judgment, discernment, TASTE; talent, gift, bent, TENDENCY, SKILL; verve, style, bravura, flourish.

flake, *n.* fleck, floccule, scale, chip, shaving; snowflake. See LAYER, COLD.

flamboyant, *adj.* extravagant, showy, ostentatious; pompous, strutting, highflown, grandiloquent. *Colloq.,* splendiferous. See OSTENTATION.

flame, *n.* blaze, fire; EXCITEMENT, passion, zeal; *slang,* sweetheart. See HEAT, LOVE.

flange, *n.* rim, collar, EDGE.

flank, *n.* SIDE, wing (of an army). —*v.t.* skirt, circle around.

flap, *n.* tab, fly, lap, tag; FOLD; argument, controversy. See DISCORD, ADDITION. —*v.* swing, sway, flop, beat, wave. See AGITATION.

flare, *v.* blaze [up], burst into flame; shine, glow; spread out, swell, splay. —*n.* torch, flambeau, signal [light]; curvature, swelling; outburst. See LIGHT, EXPANSION.

flash, *v.i.* flare, blaze; burst, streak; gleam, scintillate; retort. See LIGHT.

flashy, *adj.* gaudy, showy, garish. See ORNAMENT.
flask, *n.* bottle, vial, flacon, ampoule. See RECEPTACLE.
flat, *adj.* level, smooth, plane; even, flush; positive, exact; dull, stale, INSIPID; *slang,* penniless. See HORIZONTAL; CERTAINTY, POVERTY. —*n.* plain, shoal; apartment (see ABODE).

FLATTERY

Nouns—**1,** flattery, adulation, blandishment, cajolery; fawning, wheedling, coquetry, sycophancy, flunkeyism, SERVILITY, toadying, incense, honeyed words, flummery, blarney; lip service, unctuousness. *Colloq.,* soft soap, sweet talk. *Slang,* snow job, banana oil. See FALSEHOOD.
2, flatterer, adulator; eulogist; toady, flunky, sycophant, courtier; puffer, touter, *claquer;* parasite, hanger-on (see SERVILITY); coquette.
Verbs—flatter, adulate, praise to the skies, puff; wheedle, cajole, coax; fawn (upon); blandish, humor, soothe, pet; overpraise, turn one's head; pay court to, court, curry favor with; overestimate, exaggerate (see EXAGGERATION). *Colloq.,* soft soap, butter up, lick one's boots, lay it on thick, pull one's leg, string along. *Slang,* snow, grease.
Adjectives—flattering, adulatory; mealy- *or* honey-mouthed, honeyed, buttery, fawning, smooth, smooth-tongued; soapy, oily, unctuous, specious; fine-spoken, sycophantic, fulsome, courtly.
Adverbs—flatteringly, fulsomely, fawningly, *etc.*
Antonyms, see DETRACTION.

---

flatulence, *n.* windiness, belching, eructation, gassiness; conceit, pompousness. See OSTENTATION, VAPOR.
flaunt, *v.* parade, display; brandish. See OSTENTATION.
flavor, *n.* TASTE, seasoning, savor.
flavorless, *adj.* tasteless, flat, insipid. See INSIPIDITY.
flaw, *n.* IMPERFECTION, defect, fault, mar, crack; ERROR, mistake, gust, squall, flurry. See WIND, INTERVAL.
flawless, *adj.* See PERFECTION.
flay, *v.t.* skin, peel; criticize. See DIVESTMENT, DISAPPROBATION.
fleck, *n.* speck, speckle, flyspeck, spot. See LITTLENESS.
flee, *v.i.* run away, fly, abscond. See AVOIDANCE, ESCAPE.
fleece, *v.t.* swindle, despoil, rob, strip. See STEALING, DECEPTION. —*n.* coat (see COVERING).
fleet, *n.* navy; flotilla, squadron, argosy, armada. See SHIP, COMBATANT, ASSEMBLAGE. —*adj.* swift, speedy, nimble; transient, brief. See VELOCITY, TRANSIENTNESS.
flesh, *n.* animal tissue, meat, pulp; HUMANITY, materiality, carnality; blood relative. See FOOD, IMPURITY.
flexible, *adj.* pliant, limber, lithe, supple; adaptable. See SOFTNESS, ELASTICITY.
flicker, *v.i.* waver, flutter, quiver, blink. See IRREGULARITY, LIGHT.
flier, *n.* aviator, aeronaut, airman, astronaut, pilot, co-pilot; leaflet, handbill, circular. *Slang,* birdman, flyboy. See AVIATION, PUBLICATION.
flight, *n.* decampment, hegira, ESCAPE, elopement; course, onrush; covey, flock, shower, volley; wing, squadron. See AVOIDANCE, MOTION, ASSEMBLAGE, AVIATION, VELOCITY.
flighty, *adj.* lightheaded; scatterbrained, capricious, frivolous. See INATTENTION, INSANITY.
flimsy, *adj.* sleazy, gossamer, fragile; tenuous, unsubstantial; feeble, weak. See WEAKNESS.
flinch, *v.i.* wince, shrink, RECOIL. See COWARDICE, FEAR.
fling, *v.t.* throw, cast, hurl, sling. See PROPULSION.
flippant, *adj.* pert, impertinent;

thoughtless, frivolous. *Colloq.*, flip. See INSOLENCE.

flirt, *n.* coquette, philanderer. *Slang,* vamp. —*v.i.* coquet, philander, dally. See ENDEARMENT. —*v.t.* jerk, fling, throw, toss. See PROPULSION.

flit, *v.i.* fly, dart, take wing. See DEPARTURE, MOTION, TRAVEL, TRANSIENTNESS.

float, *v.* glide, drift, be wafted, hover, soar, be buoyed up. —*n.* ferry, SHIP, raft; launch. See ASCENT.

flock, *n.* drove, herd; covey, flight, bevy; congregation. See MULTITUDE, RELIGION.

flog, *v.t.* thrash (see PUNISHMENT).

flood, *n.* deluge, inundation, torrent, freshet, cloudburst, spate; superabundance. See SUFFICIENCY, WATER, ASSEMBLAGE.

floodgate, *n.* dam, spillway, weir, lock; sluice[-gate], conduit; flume, penstock; control, inhibition. See HINDRANCE, EGRESS.

floor, *n.* flooring, deck, pavement, terrazzo; story, level; rostrum. See COVERING, HORIZONTAL, LAYER.

flop, *v.i.* fall, drop, thud, plump down; loll, idle; flutter, flap; *slang.*, fail; *slang,* sleep, bed down. *Colloq.*, bust. *Slang,* lay an egg. See DESCENT, FAILURE, REPOSE. —*n., slang,* FAILURE. *Slang,* bust, turkey.

florid, *adj.* ruddy, flushed; showy, rococo, flowery. See COLOR, OSTENTATION.

flounder, *v.i.* wallow, welter, struggle, stagger, fumble, grope. See FAILURE, UNSKILLFULNESS.

flourish, *v.t.* wave, wield, flaunt, brandish. See AGITATION. —*v.i.* grow, prosper, thrive. See PROSPERITY. —*n.* fanfare; ORNAMENT. See MUSIC, OSTENTATION.

flout, *v.* mock, scoff (at). See CONTEMPT, DISRESPECT.

flow, *v.i.* run, glide, trickle, stream, sweep along; circulate; issue. See MOTION, WATER, FLUIDITY.

flower, *n.* bloom, blossom, posy; elite, elect, best, pick; ORNAMENT. See VEGETABLE, GOODNESS.

flowery, *adj.* florid, high-flown, flamboyant; blossomy. See ORNAMENT, OSTENTATION.

flowing, *adj.* running, gliding; fluent, graceful, smooth; loose, billowy. See WATER, ELEGANCE.

fluctuate, *v.i.* alternate, wave, vacillate, vary, shift. See CHANGEABLENESS, OSCILLATION.

fluent, *adj.* flowing, graceful, voluble. See ELEGANCE, LOQUACITY.

fluffy, *adj.* downy, flocculent, cottony. See SOFTNESS.

fluid, *n.* See FLUIDITY.

FLUIDITY

Nouns—**1,** fluidity, liquidity, serosity, liquidness; fluid, liquid, liquor; lymph, juice, sap, serum, plasma, blood, ichor; solubility, solubleness, LIQUEFACTION; fluidics, hydrostatics, hydrodynamics; stream (see WATER). See MOTION.

2, fluid, liquid, juice, sap, lymph, plasma, blood, ichor; gas, VAPOR; solution, decoction, brew (see DRINKING).

3, see CHANGEABLENESS.

Verbs—be fluid, flow, bleed; liquefy (see LIQUEFACTION).

Adjectives—fluid, liquid, serous, juicy, watery (see WATER); succulent, sappy; affluent, fluent, flowing; liquefied, uncongealed, soluble (see LIQUEFACTION).

Antonyms, see DENSITY.

flunky, *n.* lackey; toady. See SERVANT, FLATTERY.

flurry, *n.* squall, gust, scud, blast; hubbub, ferment. See WIND, ACTIVITY. —*v.t.* ruffle, excite, fluster. See AGITATION.

flush, *v.* blush, redden; elate, thrill; rinse; start, rouse. See HORIZONTAL. —*n.* blush, redness, glow, elation, thrill; gush, rush. See

HEAT, FEELING, COLOR, CLEANNESS.

fluster, *v.t.* confuse; excite. See EXCITEMENT, INATTENTION.

flute, *n.* groove, FURROW, channel; pipe, piccolo, fife. See MUSIC.

flutter, *v.* flicker, tremble, flap, shake, whip, wave; bustle, fidget, twitter, quiver; agitate, ruffle; hover. See AGITATION, OSCILLATION, FEAR.

flux, *n.* flow, current, course; MOTION, CHANGE, transition; continuum; solvent; EXCRETION.

fly, *v.* soar, wing, aviate; float, wave; speed, bolt, dart; flee, decamp, disperse, scatter. See AVIATION, VELOCITY, ESCAPE.

foam, *n.* froth, suds, lather, spume. —*v.i.* froth, spume. See AGITATION, EXCITABILITY.

focus, *n.* point; focal *or* central point; concentration, CONVERGENCE; center, hub, core, heart, nucleus; sharpness. —*v.* concentrate, converge; centralize, contract; rally, gather, meet. See MIDDLE, VISION.

foe, *n.* enemy, adversary, antagonist, opponent. See OPPOSITION.

fog, *n.* mist, smog, vapor, haze, cloud; uncertainty, OBSCURITY. See CLOUDINESS, MOISTURE.

fogy, *n.* See PERMANENCE.

foible, *n.* whimsy, WEAKNESS.

foil, *v.t.* frustrate, battle, balk, circumvent. See HINDRANCE. —*n.* contrast, setoff; leaf, sheet (of metal); sword, épée. See OPPOSITION, LAYER, ARMS.

foist, *v.t.* palm off (see DECEPTION).

FOLD

Nouns—**1,** fold, crease, bend, lapping, plait; wrinkle, corrugation; flap, lapel, turnover, dogear; ply (see LAYER); tuck, gather, pleat, ruffle, flounce; crow's-feet. See FURROW.

2, see RELIGION, ASSEMBLAGE.

Verbs—fold, double (over), crease, crimp, bend; pucker, knit, corrugate, wrinkle, FURROW; tuck, gather, pleat; double back; turn over, dogear; crumple, rumple, crinkle; friz[zle], crisp.

Adjectives—folded, creased, *etc.*

Antonyms, see SMOOTHNESS, HORIZONTAL.

---

folder, *n.* booklet; cover, portfolio, loose-leaf [folder]. See WRITING, RECEPTACLE.

foliage, *n.* leafage, verdure. See VEGETABLE.

folk, *n.* people, commonalty, race; kin. See HUMANITY, POPULACE.

folklore, *n.* mythology, legends, old wives' tales. See KNOWLEDGE, MYTHICAL DEITIES.

follow, *v.* go *or* come after; succeed; tread on the heels of; come *or* be next; pursue (see PURSUIT); attend, associate with, go with, accompany; adhere to, support; obey, heed; understand; copy, imitate, emulate, practice; ensue, result, be the outcome of. See SEQUENCE, IMITATION, EFFECT, ACCOMPANIMENT, REAR.

following, *n.* followers, adherents; attendance, train, retinue. See ACCOMPANIMENT.

FOLLY

Nouns—**1,** folly, silliness, foolishness, inanity, idiocy; frivolity, ineptitude; giddiness; INATTENTION; irrationality, eccentricity (see INSANITY); extravagance, nonsense, ABSURDITY; RASHNESS. See SHALLOWNESS.

2, fool, dunce, idiot, tomfool, wiseacre, simpleton, imbecile, donkey, ass, goose, ninny, nincompoop, dolt, numskull, bonehead, boob[y]; trifler, babbler; oaf, lout, loon, ass, dullard, dunderhead, blockhead, loggerhead;

halfwit, nitwit, lackwit; harebrain; clod, clodhopper. *Colloq.*, chump, loony, chucklehead, fathead. *Slang,* jerk, sap, duffer, dumbbell, square, rube, dimwit, goof, dumb bunny.

3, antic (see AMUSEMENT).

4, innocent, milksop, sop (see CREDULITY); dotard, driveler; old fogy, old woman; crone, grandmother.

5, greenhorn, dupe, ignoramus (see IGNORANCE); lubber, bungler, blunderer; madman (see INSANITY).

6, jester (see WIT).

Verbs—**1,** be a fool, fool, drivel, have rocks in one's head; play the fool, talk nonsense, take leave of one's senses. *Slang,* horse around.

2, make a fool *or* monkey of (see RIDICULE).

Adjectives—**1,** foolish, silly, senseless, inane, irrational, giddy, fatuous, nonsensical, inept.

2, unwise, injudicious, imprudent, unreasonable, without reason, ridiculous, silly, stupid, asinine, ill-advised, ill-judged, extravagant, idle, useless (see USELESSNESS); inexpedient, frivolous, trivial (see UNIMPORTANCE).

Antonyms, see KNOWLEDGE, REASONING.

---

foment, *v.t.* stir up, incite. See EXCITEMENT.

fond, *adj.* affectionate, tender; foolish, doting. See LOVE.

fondle, *v.t.* pet, caress, cosset. *Slang,* feel up. See ENDEARMENT.

font, *n.* fount[ain], spring, source, basin, baptistery, reservoir; type, case, face. See RECEPTACLE, PRINTING.

FOOD

Nouns—**1,** food, aliment, nourishment, nutriment; aliment[ation], sustenance, nurture, subsistence, provender, fodder, PROVISION, ration, keep, commons, board; fare, cheer; diet, regimen; bread, staff of life; forage, pasture, pasturage; comestibles, eatables, victuals, edibles; groceries; meat, viands; fast food, convenience food; delicacy, dainty; fleshpots; festive board; ambrosia; good cheer; hearty meal; soul food. *Slang,* grub, chow; junk food.

2, meal, repast, feed, spread; mess; dish, plate, course; REFRESHMENT; refection, collation, picnic; feast, banquet (see AMUSEMENT); breakfast; *déjeuner,* lunch, luncheon; dinner, supper, snack, dessert; potluck [supper], wiener roast, barbecue, fish fry; buffet, smorgasbord; *table d'hôte*; table, cuisine, bill of fare, menu; chow line. *Colloq.*, brunch; square meal.

3, pancake, cereal; appetizer, antipasto; meat, joint, roast, sausage, hamburger, frankfurter, fish-and-chips; *pièce de résistance, entrée, hors d'oeuvre;* hash, stew, ragout, fricassee; vegetable, cabbage, *etc.*; pottage, potage, gruel, porridge, broth, soup, consommé, purée; salad; pie, pasty, *vol-au-vent;* pudding, omelet; bread, biscuit, bun, roll; pastry, cookie, pie, cake, tarte; dessert, sweets (see SWEETNESS); condiment, jam, dressing, sauce. *Slang,* slop.

4, drink (see DRINKING).

5, eating, ingestion, mastication, manducation, rumination; GLUTTONY; mouth, jaws, mandible, chops; carousal (see AMUSEMENT); digestion, chyle.

6, restaurant, steak house, diner, eatery, café, eating house, roadhouse, cafeteria, automat, canteen; dining room, refectory, mess hall. *Colloq.*, greasy spoon, hash house.

7, chef, cook, short order chef *or* cook; salad chef, pastry chef, *etc.*

8, eater, brown-bagger; gourmet, gourmand (see GLUTTONY).

Verbs—**1,** eat, feed, fare, devour, swallow, take; gobble, gulp, bolt, snap; fall to; dispatch, partake of, eat up; take, get, wolf, *or* gulp down; lay *or* tuck in; lick, pick (at), peck, eat like a bird (see ASCETICISM); gormandize (see GLUTTONY); bite, champ, munch, crunch, chew, masticate, nibble, gnaw; live, feed, batten, *or* fatten on, feast upon; browse, graze, crop; regale, carouse; eat heartily, do justice to; banquet; break bread, break one's fast; breakfast, lunch, dine, take tea, sup; eat out; ration (see APPORTIONMENT). *Colloq.*, put away. *Interjections*—come and get it!; soup's on!

2, nourish, nurture; digest; stick to one's ribs.

3, cook, grill, fry, brown, bake, broil, boil, parboil, toast, roast, charbroil, steam, scald, simmer; warm up, reheat; smoke.

Adjectives—eatable, edible, esculent, comestible, alimentary; cereal; dietetic; fast-food; culinary; nutritive, nutritious; succulent; omnivorous, carnivorous, herbivorous, graminivorous; macrobiotic, organic.

Adverbs—at table.

---

fool, *n.* See FOLLY. —*v.* dupe, mislead; idle away; tamper. See DECEPTION, CHANGE, INACTIVITY.

foolhardy, *adj.* daring, brash, reckless, venturesome. See RASHNESS.

foolish, *adj.* See FOLLY.

foolproof, *adj.* safe, fail-safe. See STRENGTH.

foot, *n.* base, bottom, footing; hoof, paw; foot soldiers, infantry. See SUPPORT, COMBATANT.

foothold, *n.* [toe]hold, footing, grip, SUPPORT; BEGINNING, start, access, opportunity, first rung on the ladder.

footing, *n.* foothold; basis, base, foundation, status, rank. See SUPPORT.

footstool, *n.* ottoman, hassock. See SUPPORT.

fop, *n.* dandy, dude, swell, buck, [gay] blade, coxcomb, macaroni, exquisite, Beau Brummel, Dapper Dan. *Slang,* clotheshorse. See AFFECTATION, OSTENTATION.

forage, *n.* fodder, feed, FOOD; pasturage, herbage. —*v.* pasture, graze, feed; hunt, search, beat the bushes; raid, maraud, pillage, plunder, loot, ravage, scrounge around. See STEALING, INQUIRY, PROVISION.

foray, *n.* & *v.i.* raid, ATTACK; pillage (see STEALING).

forbearance, *n.* [self-]restraint; patience, long-suffering; temperance, clemency, LENIENCY; mercy, pardon. See AVOIDANCE, DISUSE, RESIGNATION.

forbid, *v.t.* prohibit, inhibit, interdict, ban, taboo. See PROHIBITION.

forbidding, *adj.* prohibitive; repellent, fearsome (see FEAR); unpleasant, abhorrent; stern, menacing; unfriendly, distant; disagreeable. See UGLINESS, HINDRANCE, SEVERITY, PROHIBITION.

force, *n.* COMPULSION, coercion; STRENGTH, brawn, POWER, might; MEANING, import, effect; troops, soldiery, army (see COMBATANT). See VIGOR.

ford, *n.* wading place; shoal. —*v.* wade, cross. See PASSAGE, SHALLOWNESS.

fore, *adj.* foremost; former, prior, previous. See FRONT.

forebear, *n.* See ANCESTRY.

foreboding, *n.* portent; presentiment, premonition, apprehension. See PREDICTION, WARNING, THREAT.

forecast, *v.t.* predict, divine, prognosticate; foretell, presage, portend. See PREDICTION, PLAN.

forefathers, *n.pl.* ancestors, forebears, progenitors. See ANCESTRY.

foregoing, *adj.* preceding, previous, aforesaid. See PRIORITY.

foregone, *adj.* PAST, previous.

foreground, *n.* proscenium, FRONT.

forehead, *n.* brow, sinciput; head, temples. See FRONT.

foreign, *adj.* alien, strange, exotic; extraneous, unrelated. See EXTRINSIC, ABODE.

foreman, forewoman, *n.* supervisor, superintendent, overseer. *Colloq.*, straw boss. See DIRECTOR.

foremost, *adj.* leading, first, precedent; chief, best, principal. See BEGINNING, PRIORITY, FRONT, SUPERIORITY.

forensic, *adj.* legal, juridical; controversial. See LEGALITY, REASONING.

forerunner, *n.* precursor, predecessor; harbinger; herald, announcer; Elijah, John the Baptist, *etc.;* leader, vanguard, scout, picket. See PRIORITY, PREDICTION.

foreshadow, *v.t.* prefigure, foretoken (see PREDICTION).

foresight, *n.* forethought, PREPARATION; foreknowledge, prescience; clairvoyance, prevision. See PREDICTION, CAUTION, EXPECTATION.

forest, *n.* wood[s], tall timber, timberland, woodland; grove, coppice, copse, thicket. See VEGETABLE.

forestall, *v.t.* thwart, prevent. See HINDRANCE, EARLINESS.

forestry, *n.* woodcraft, silviculture; dendrology, forestage; conservation; [re]forestation. See AGRICULTURE.

foretell, *v.t.* presage, portend; forecast, prognosticate, predict. See PREDICTION.

forethought, *n.* prudence, providence; premeditation, anticipation. See PREPARATION, CAUTION.

foretoken, *n.* omen. —*v.t.* foreshadow. See PREDICTION.

forever, *adv.* always, ever, eternally; incessantly, unceasingly. See DURABILITY, PERPETUITY.

foreword, *n.* preface, prologue, introduction, *avant-propos,* preamble; [address] to the reader. See PRECEDENCE.

forfeit, *n.* penalty, fine; deposit. See LOSS, PUNISHMENT.

forge, *v.t.* make, fabricate; invent, counterfeit; hammer. See PRODUCTION, FALSEHOOD, COPY.

forgery, *n.* IMITATION, counterfeit. *Slang,* kited, rubber, bum, *or* phony check. See FALSEHOOD, DECEPTION.

forget, *v.t.* disregard, overlook, dismiss, omit. See NEGLECT, OBLIVION, FORGIVENESS.

FORGIVENESS

Nouns—forgiveness, pardon, condonation, grace, remission, absolution, amnesty, oblivion; indulgence; reprieve; excuse, exoneration, exculpation (see ACQUITTAL); conciliation, reconciliation; placability (see PACIFICATION). See OBLIVION.

Verbs—**1,** forgive, pardon, condone, think no more of, let bygones be bygones, shake hands, forget an injury, forgive and forget, live and let live; excuse, pass over, overlook; wink at (see NEGLECT); bear with; allow for, make allowances for; let one down easily, not be too hard upon, bury the hatchet; write off; let off, remit, absolve, give absolution, reprieve; acquit (see ACQUITTAL).

2, beg, ask, *or* implore pardon, excuse oneself; conciliate, propitiate, placate; make one's peace with, make up a quarrel (see PACIFICATION).

Adjectives—forgiving, placable, conciliatory, indulgent; forgiven, unresented, unavenged, unrevenged.

Antonyms, see RETALIATION.

---

forgo, *v.t.* relinquish, abandon; deny oneself, give up, do without, pass up. See RELINQUISHMENT.

fork, *v.i.* bifurcate, diverge, separate, branch off. See DISJUNCTION, ANGULARITY.

forlorn, *adj.* abandoned, deserted, forsaken; hopeless, wretched, miserable. See RELINQUISHMENT, HOPELESSNESS, DEJECTION.

FORM

Nouns—**1,** form, formation, forming, figure, shape; make[-up], conformation, configuration; make, frame[work], construction, cut, set, build, trim, cut of one's jib; stamp, type, cast, mold; organization, ARRANGEMENT, disposition, stratification; fashion; contour, outline, silhouette; lines, features, lineaments; skeleton, broad outline; architecture, structure; sculpture. See SYMMETRY, ORDER.

2, feature, lineament, anatomy, profile; turn; phase, aspect, APPEARANCE; posture, attitude, pose.

3, morphology, histology, structural botany; isomorphism.

Verbs—form, shape, figure, fashion, carve, cut, chisel, hew, cast; rough-hew, rough-cast; sketch, silhouette, delineate; block out, hammer out; trim; lick *or* put into shape; model, knead, work up into, set, mold, SCULPTURE; tailor; cast, stamp; build, construct.

Adjectives—formed, formative; plastic, fictile; isomorphous.

Antonyms, see FORMLESSNESS.

formal, *adj.* structural; external, superficial, outward; stylized, conventional, ceremonial, ritual[istic], conventional, traditional; solemn, dignified; stuffy, strict, prim; correct, proper. See CONFORMITY, FASHION, AFFECTATION. —*n.* evening dress; black tie, white tie [and tails]. See CLOTHING.

formality, *n.* formalness (see FORMAL); punctilio, convention, etiquette; due course, process, *or* form, red tape; mere formality, lip service. See CONFORMITY, AFFECTATION, FASHION.

format, *n.* form, ARRANGEMENT, PLAN, make-up, layout, design; style.

former, *adj.* erstwhile, whilom, sometime, quondam; foregoing, preceding. See PAST, PRIORITY.

formidable, *adj.* appalling, tremendous; arduous, Herculean. See FEAR, DIFFICULTY.

FORMLESSNESS

Nouns—formlessness, shapelessness, amorphism, informity; deformity, disfigurement, defacement, derangement, mutilation; DISORDER, chaos, DISTORTION.

Verbs—deface, disfigure, deform, mutilate, truncate, misshape; derange, DISORDER, distort.

Adjectives—formless, shapeless, amorphous; unformed, unhewn, uncut, unfashioned, unshapen; rough, rude, rugged, barbarous, chaotic; blank, vague, nebulous, half-baked; misshapen, disordered, distorted.

Antonyms, see FORM.

formula, *n.* RULE; expression, equation; recipe. See MAXIM.

formulate, *v.t.* frame, devise, concoct, formularize. See METHOD, PLAN.

forsake, *v.t.* desert, abandon; renounce, quit, forswear. See RELINQUISHMENT.

forswear, *v.* deny, abjure; commit perjury. See NEGATION, FALSEHOOD.

fort, *n.* fortress, stronghold, fortification. See DEFENSE.

forth, *adv.* forward, onward; out (of), from; away (from). See PROGRESSION.

forthcoming, *adj.* imminent; available. See APPROACH, PREPARATION.

forthright, *adj.* downright, straightforward, frank, candid, outspoken; unequivocal, explicit, honest. *Colloq.,* straight from the shoulder. See PROBITY.

fortify, *v.t.* strengthen, buttress, barricade; uphold, sustain. See POWER, DEFENSE, STRENGTH.

fortitude, *n.* COURAGE, patience, endurance. See INEXCITABILITY.

fortuitous, *adj.* casual, CHANCE.

fortunate, *adj.* lucky, blest, to be congratulated; auspicious, propitious, opportune. *Colloq.,* born under a lucky star *or* with a silver spoon in one's mouth. See PROSPERITY, SUCCESS, OCCASION.

fortune, *n.* fate, lot, DESTINY; CHANCE, luck; wealth, possessions, property; MONEY.

fortuneteller, *n.* clairvoyant, crystal-gazer, astrologer, numerologist, phrenologist, palmist, palm-reader. See PREDICTION.

forum, *n.* market place, agora; court, tribunal, COUNCIL; colloquium, symposium, panel, town meeting. See CONVERSATION.

forward, *adj.* FRONT, anterior, foremost; precocious; ready, eager, prompt; enterprising, aggressive; intrusive, officious; pert, saucy, flip; future, coming. —*v.t.* impel, dispatch, deliver, further, advance, encourage. See AID, TRANSPORTATION, PROGRESSION.

fossil, *n.* relic, petrification; fogy. See OLDNESS, AGE.

foster, *v.t.* nourish, nurture, cherish; encourage, support. See AID, ENDEARMENT.

foul, *adj.* dirty, soiled, disgusting; stormy, unpleasant; obscene, indecent; clogged, choked, entangled; unfair, underhand. See UNCLEANNESS, IMPURITY, IMPROBITY.

found, *v.t.* establish, institute, originate; cast. See BEGINNING, FORM.

foundation, *n.* base; basis; endowment; institution. See SUPPORT, PARTY, CAUSE, PREPARATION.

founder, *n.* producer, establisher, originator. See BEGINNING. —*v.i.* sink, be swamped; go lame. See NAVIGATION, FAILURE.

foundling, *n.* waif, orphan, bastard. See YOUTH, RELINQUISHMENT.

foundry, *n.* works, iron- *or* steelworks, smelter; smithy. See PRODUCTION.

fountain, *n.* spring, jet, spray; fount, source. See CAUSE, WATER.

fowl, *n.* bird; hen, stewing chicken. See ANIMAL, FOOD.

fox, *n.* reynard, slyboots. See ANIMAL, CUNNING.

foxhole, *n.* pit, trench. See DEFENSE.

foxy, *adj.* clever, sly, CUNNING.

foyer, *n.* lobby, vestibule, anteroom, entry, entrance hall. See RECEPTACLE, INGRESS.

fracas, *n.* uproar, disturbance. See DISORDER, LOUDNESS.

fraction, *n.* PART; half, quarter, eighth, *etc.;* portion, piece, bit; scrap, fragment.

fracture, *n.* break, split, crack, cleft. See DISJUNCTION, BRITTLENESS.

fragile, *adj.* delicate, frail, breakable; tenuous, gossamer. See BRITTLENESS, WEAKNESS.

fragment, *n.* bit, PART, scrap.

frail, *adj.* fragile, brittle, delicate; weak, infirm, weak-willed. See BRITTLENESS, WEAKNESS.

frame, *v.t.* construct, fashion, fabricate; devise, compose, formulate; enclose; *slang,* incriminate, trump up. See PRODUCTION, ACCUSATION, PLAN. —*n.* framework, skeleton; EDGE, boundary, confines; temper, state, humor; FORM; shape; plot, conspiracy. See SUPPORT, WILL.

franchise, *n.* privilege, right, prerogative. See FREEDOM, CHOICE.

frank, *adj.* ingenuous, candid, straightforward, forthright, sincere, open. See TRUTH.

frankfurter, *n.* frankfurt, sausage, wiener. *Colloq.,* frank. *Slang,* wienie, hot dog, red-hot. See FOOD.

frantic, *adj.* distraught, frenzied, wild. See INSANITY, EXCITEMENT.

fraternity, *n.* brotherhood, fellowship, secret society, club. See PARTY, SOCIALITY.

fraternize, *v.i.* associate, band together; consort *or* mingle with; collaborate. See SOCIALITY, COMBINATION, IMPROBITY.

fraud, *n.* DECEPTION, swindle; imposture, artifice; confidence man; impostor, humbug. *Colloq.*, bunco. See EVILDOER, STEALING.

fraught, *adj.* filled with, loaded, laden, beset. See COMPLETION.

fray, *n.* fracas, fight, battle, skirmish; brawl, melee, free-for-all. See CONTENTION. —*v.* ravel, rub, wear. See FRICTION, DETERIORATION.

frazzle, *v.t., colloq.*, fray, abrade, wear out; vex, exasperate, get on one's nerves. See RESENTMENT, WEARINESS.

freak, *n.* abnormality, fluke, monstrosity; caprice, sport, whim. See UNCONFORMITY, CHANGEABLENESS.

FREEDOM

Nouns—**1,** freedom, liberty, independence; license, PERMISSION; FACILITY; immunity, EXEMPTION; release, parole, probation, discharge.

2, scope, range, latitude, play; free hand *or* rein; free *or* full play, full scope; [full] swing, elbow room, margin, rope, wide berth.

3, franchise; emancipation (see LIBERATION); enfranchisement; autonomy, self-government, self-determination; liberalism, free trade; nonintervention, noninterference, Monroe Doctrine; free speech, freedom of speech *or* of the press.

4, freeman, freedman.

5, free land, freehold; allodium; mortmain.

Verbs—**1,** be free, have scope, have the run of, have one's own way, have a will of one's own, have one's fling; do what one likes, wishes, pleases, *or* chooses, see one's way clear; go at large, feel at home; fend for oneself; paddle one's own canoe; stand on one's rights; be one's own man; shift for oneself, stand on one's own [two] feet, hoe one's own row; take a liberty; make free with, make oneself at home; take leave, take French leave.

2, set free, liberate, release, let go; parole; permit (see PERMISSION); allow *or* give scope to, open the door; give [free] rein; give a horse his head; make free of; give the freedom of; give the franchise; enfranchise; *laisser faire*; live and let live; leave to oneself, leave alone, let alone. *Colloq.*, give one leeway, give one enough rope.

3, unfetter, untie, loose, unchain, unshackle, unbind; disengage, disentangle, clear, extricate, unloose.

Adjectives—**1,** free, free as air; independent, at large, loose, scot-free; left alone, left to oneself, on the loose; free and easy; at one's ease; *dégagé*, quite at home; wanton, rampant, irrepressible, unvanquished; freed, liberated, rid of, hands-off; freeborn; out from under; autonomous, freehold, allodial, on one's own [account *or* hook], under one's own steam; in the clear (see ACQUITTAL).

2, in full swing, uncaught, unconstrained, unbuttoned, unconfined, unrestrained, unchecked, unprevented, unhindered, unobstructed, unbound, uncontrolled, untrammeled, unsubject, ungoverned, unenslaved, unenthralled, unchained, unshackled, unfettered, unreined, unbridled, uncurbed, unmuzzled; catch as catch can, freewheeling, fancy-free, carefree; out of control; unrestricted, unlimited, unconditional; absolute; discretionary, optional (see CHOICE); exempt; unforced, uncompelled; unbiased, spontaneous.

Adverbs—*ad libitum,* at will, freely, *etc.*

Antonyms, see SUBJECTION, RESTRAINT.

---

free-for-all, *n., colloq.,* fight, melee, brawl, fracas; knock-down-drag-out [affair]. See CONTENTION.

free-loader, *n., slang,* parasite, sponge. See SERVILITY.

freethinker, *n.* skeptic, agnostic, doubter; iconoclast. See IRRELIGION.

freeway, *n.* highway, parkway, boulevard, expressway. See PASSAGE.

freewheeling, *adj., colloq.,* nonchalant, carefree. See FREEDOM.

freeze, *v.* congeal, turn to ice, make ice; harden; die; immobilize; chill, ice, frost, refrigerate; kill; fix, stabilize. See COLD, DEATH, PERMANENCE.

freight, *n.* cargo, load, shipment; burden. See TRANSPORTATION, GRAVITY.

freighter, *n.* cargo ship, lighter, trader, [tramp] steamer, transport, tanker. See SHIP.

frenetic, *adj.* frantic, frenzied, hectic, distraught, jittery. See EXCITABILITY, VIOLENCE.

frenzy, *n.* fury, AGITATION; EXCITEMENT, enthusiasm; delirium, furor. See VIOLENCE, INSANITY, EXCITABILITY.

FREQUENCY

Nouns—frequency, oftenness; REPETITION, recurrence, persistence; perseverance; prevalence; continuance.

Verbs—do frequently; do nothing but, keep on, continue (see CONTINUITY); persist; recur; repeat, hammer [away] at (see REPETITION).

Adjectives—frequent, many times, not rare, incessant, continual, constant; everyday, repeated (see REPETITION); habitual (see HABIT).

Adverbs—often, oft, ofttimes, oftentimes, frequently, every time one turns around; repeatedly (see REPETITION); not unfrequently; in rapid succession; many a time, daily, hourly, every day; perpetually, continually, constantly, incessantly, without ceasing, at all times, night and day, day after day; morning, noon and night; ever and anon; most often; commonly, habitually (see HABIT); sometimes, occasionally, between times, at times, [every] now and then, [every] once in a while, [every] now and again, from time to time, often enough, again and again, every so often; more often than not, in general. *Colloq.,* a lot.

Antonyms, see RARITY.

---

fresh, *adj.* novel, recent; new, unfaded, unjaded, unhackneyed, unused; healthy, vigorous; rested, unfatigued; unsalted; cool, refreshing, brisk, keen; inexperienced; *slang,* insolent. See NEWNESS, COLD, HEALTH, REFRESHMENT, INSOLENCE.

freshen, *v.t.* refresh, revive, brace up; renovate, spruce up; ventilate, air out, cool off; deodorize, sweeten. See RESTORATION, CLEANNESS, REFRESHMENT.

freshman, *n.* plebe, underclassman; novice, greenhorn, tenderfoot. *Colloq.,* frosh. See BEGINNING, SCHOOL.

fret, *v.* agitate, irritate, vex; worry, chafe, rub, fume, complain. See DISCONTENT, PAIN, RESENTMENT, DEJECTION.

friar, *n.* monk, brother; fra. See CLERGY.

FRICTION

Nouns—friction, attrition, rubbing; frication, confrication, abrasion, sanding, sandpapering, erosion, limation, rub; massage. See TRACTION, RESISTANCE.
Verbs—rub, scratch, abrade, file, rasp, scrape, scrabble, grate, scrub, fray, chafe, scuff, graze, curry, buff, scour, polish, rub up; work in; rub down, wear away *or* out; sandpaper, grind (see POWDERINESS); massage, knead.
Adjectives—frictional, abrasive, attritive.

Antonyms, see SMOOTHNESS.

FRIEND

Nouns—**1,** friend, acquaintance, neighbor, well-wisher; alter ego; bosom *or* fast friend, gentleman *or* lady friend; partner; *fidus Achates; persona grata;* associate, compeer, comrade, mate, companion, confrère, colleague, compatriot, brother, intimate, confidant[e], hail-fellow; countryman. See ACCOMPANIMENT.

2, patron, Maecenas; tutelary saint, guardian angel, good genius, advocate, partisan, sympathizer; ally; friend-in-need; associate. See BENEVOLENCE.

3, crony, chum, playfellow, playmate; schoolfellow, schoolmate; shopmate, shipmate, messmate, roommate; fellow, boon companion; regular guy *or* fellow. *Colloq.,* sidekick. *Slang,* pal.

4, Pylades and Orestes, Castor and Pollux, Nisus and Euryalus, Damon and Pythias, David and Jonathan, Three Musketeers.

5, friendship, friendliness, amity, brotherhood; harmony, concord, peace; cordiality, fraternization; fellowship, familiarity, intimacy, comradeship, common touch. See SOCIALITY, BENEVOLENCE.

Verbs—make friends with, receive with open arms; fraternize (see SOCIALITY), get along with; chase *or* run after; befriend, take up with, warm up to. *Colloq.,* hit it off, take to, stand in with. *Slang,* cozy up, shine up to.
Adjectives—friendly, amicable, cordial; hospitable, neighborly, brotherly, sisterly; hearty, bosom, warmhearted, familiar; on good terms, friends with, in with, on one's good side.

Antonyms, see OPPOSITION.

fright, *n.* dread, terror, panic, alarm, consternation. See FEAR.

frightful, *adj.* horrible, shocking; *colloq.,* unpleasant, disagreeable. See FEAR, UGLINESS.

frigid, *adj.* COLD, icy, freezing; passionless, cold-blooded, formal. See INSENSIBILITY.

frill, *n.* trimming, decoration, ORNAMENT; ruffle, flounce, furbelow; extra. *Colloq.,* icing [on the cake]. See EDGE.

fringe, *n.* EDGE, border, outskirts; edging; perimeter.

frisk, *v.t.* caper, cavort, frolic; cut up, carry on; *slang,* search, shakedown, fan. *Slang,* horse around. See AMUSEMENT, INQUIRY.

frisky, *adj.* playful, pert, peppy. *Colloq.,* full of beans. See AMUSEMENT, ACTIVITY.

fritter, *v.t.* squander, WASTE, dissipate.

frivolity, *n.* levity, flightiness, giddiness, FOLLY. See UNIMPORTANCE.

frock, *n.* gown, dress; smock. See CLOTHING.

frolic, *v.i.* play, gambol, caper, romp, disport. See AMUSEMENT.

from, *prep.* away, out of. See EGRESS.

FRONT

Nouns—**1,** front, forefront, fore, forepart; foreground; face, disk, frontage, façade, proscenium, frontispiece; obverse; BEGINNING. See PRECEDENCE.
2, front rank, front lines; flagship; van, vanguard; advanced guard; outpost. See PRIORITY.
3, face, brow, forehead, visage, physiognomy, countenance, features; rostrum; beak; bow, stem, prow, jib. *Slang,* mug, puss, kisser.
Verbs—be *or* stand in front, head [up]; front, face, confront, look in the eye *or* face, defy (see DEFIANCE); bend forward; come to the front *or* the fore.
Adjectives—front, fore, frontal, forward.
Adverbs—frontward, in front, to the fore; before, in the van, ahead, right ahead; foremost, headmost; in the foreground, in the lee; in one's face, before one's face *or* eyes, dead ahead; face-to-face, vis-à-vis.

Antonyms, see REAR.

---

frontier, *n.* borderland, outskirts; wilderness. See LIMIT, CONTACT.

frost, *n.* rime, hoarfrost, cranreuch; icing, coldness, COLD.

froth, *n.* foam, suds, lather, spume; head, cream, collar; scum; levity, triviality, frivolity. —*v.i.* foam, spume, effervesce, ferment, bubble, fizz. See AGITATION, UNIMPORTANCE.

frown, *v.i.* scowl, lower, glower; look askance. —*n.* scowl. See IRASCIBILITY, DISAPPROBATION, DEJECTION.

frowsy, *adj.* unkempt, slovenly, frumpy. See UNCLEANNESS, VULGARITY.

frozen, *adj.* glacial, gelid; frostbitten, COLD; motionless, paralyzed, petrified; coldhearted, frigid, insensitive. See INSENSIBILITY.

frugal, *adj.* prudent, saving, provident, thrifty; sparing, stinting. See ECONOMY.

fruit, *n.* product, yield, harvest; offspring, result, consequence, outgrowth. See PRODUCTION, EFFECT.

fruitful, *adj.* productive, fertile; prolific; profitable. See PRODUCTION, PROSPERITY.

fruition, *n.* realization, attainment. See COMPLETION.

fruitless, *adj.* unavailing, unprofitable, vain; barren. See USELESSNESS.

frustrate, *v.t.* defeat, thwart, circumvent, cross, baffle, nullify. See HINDRANCE, DISAPPOINTMENT.

fry, *v.* sauté, panfry, deep-fry, frizzle, griddle, skillet-cook. *Slang,* get the [electric] chair. See HEAT, PUNISHMENT.

FUEL

Nouns—**1,** fuel, firing, combustible; inflammable, burnable; fossil fuel, peat, turf; ignite; bituminous, anthracite, glance, *or* cannel coal; coal dust, culm, coke, charcoal; OIL, kerosene, petroleum, gasoline, petrol; canned heat, paraffin; gas (see VAPOR); firewood, kindling, fagot, log; cinder, embers; atomic *or* nuclear fuel, plutonium, uranium. See HEAT, ENERGY, POWER.
2, tinder, punk, amadou, touchwood; brand, torch; fuse, detonator, cap; spill, wick, match, flint, lighter; candle.
Verbs—fuel, furnish with fuel; feed, fire, stoke.
Adjectives—combustible, inflammable, burnable; fiery.

Antonyms, see INCOMBUSTIBILITY.

fugitive, *adj.* runaway, fleeing; transient, ephemeral, evanescent, fleeting; transitory. —*n.* runaway, eloper, absconder; refugee, escapee. See AVOIDANCE, ESCAPE, TRANSIENTNESS.

fulfill, *v.t.* satisfy, realize, gratify; execute, discharge; effect, carry out. See COMPLETION.

full, *adj.* filled, sated, satiated, glutted, gorged; replete; whole, complete, entire; loose, baggy; sonorous; plump, rounded; brimming. See COMPLETION, SUFFICIENCY.

full-blooded, *adj.* thoroughbred, purebred, whole-blooded; virile. See PURITY, STRENGTH.

fulminate, *v.* boom, thunder, roar; detonate, explode; rail, berate, excoriate. See VIOLENCE, IMPRECATION, THREAT.

fulsome, *adj.* obnoxious, foul, noisome; unctuous, obsequious, fawning; cloying, excessive; tasteless, offensive. See SERVILITY, VULGARITY.

fumble, *v.* grope, paw; fluff, flub, muff, bungle. See UNSKILLFULNESS, TOUCH.

fume, *v.i.* chafe, fret, rage; smoke, reek. See EXCITABILITY, RESENTMENT, HEAT. —*v.i.* smoke (see ODOR); fret. See DISCONTENT.

fumigate, *v.t.* disinfect (see CLEANNESS).

fun, *n.* sport, diversion, AMUSEMENT. See WIT.

function, *n.* faculty, office, DUTY, rôle, province; observance. See AGENCY, BUSINESS, RITE. —*v.i.* operate, serve. See ACTION, USE.

functional, *adj.* useful, serviceable. See UTILITY.

functionary, *n.* official, administrator, bureaucrat. See DIRECTOR.

fund, *n.* resources, STORE, cache, reserve, accumulation; slush fund, kitty; (*pl.*) assets, MONEY, capital. —*v.t.* set aside, lay away, STORE; invest in, finance. See MEANS.

fundamental, *adj.* basic, essential, underlying, original, INTRINSIC, rudimentary.

funeral, *n.* obsequies; burial, INTERMENT, entombment.

funereal, *adj.* funebrial, mournful, sad, solemn, somber, lugubrious; black, dark. See DEJECTION, INTERMENT.

funnel, *n.* cone, bottleneck, channel, flue, chimney, shaft. See ROTUNDITY.

funny, *adj.* amusing, droll, comic; absurd, laughable, mirth-provoking, ludicrous; *colloq.,* strange, odd; (*pl.*) comics. See WIT, ABSURDITY.

fur, *n.* hide, pelt, coat, peltry, skin, pelage; hair, down. See COVERING, ROUGHNESS.

furies, *n.pl.* avengers, Erinyes, Eumenides, Dirae. See DEMON.

furious, *adj.* raging, violent, fierce, storming, turbulent, unrestrained; *colloq.,* mad, angry. See RESENTMENT, VIOLENCE.

furlough, *n.* leave [of ABSENCE], pass, shore leave, liberty. See PERMISSION.

furnace, *n.* See HEAT.

furnish, *v.t.* equip, outfit; provide, yield, supply. See PREPARATION, PROVISION.

furor, *n.* frenzy, commotion, disturbance, EXCITEMENT, hubbub, hullaballoo; craze, mania, fad. See FEELING, DESIRE.

FURROW

Nouns—furrow, groove, rut, scratch, stria, crack, score, incision, slit; chamfer, flute, fluting; channel, gutter, trench, ditch, moat, fosse, trough, kennel; ravine (see INTERVAL); seam, line. See FOLD.

Verbs—furrow, plow, plough; incise, score, cut, seam, channel; engrave (see ENGRAVING), etch, bite in; flute, chamfer; pucker, wrinkle, knit.

Adjectives—furrowed, ribbed, striated, fluted; corduroy.

Antonyms, see SMOOTHNESS.

---

further, *adj*. farther, more, additional. See ADDITION. —*v.t.* AID, advance, promote, expedite.

furthermore, *adv*. moreover, besides, in ADDITION.

furtive, *adj*. stealthy, sly, surreptitious, sneaking, skulking, covert. See CONCEALMENT.

fury, *n*. rage, frenzy; VIOLENCE, turbulence. See INSANITY, DEMON.

fuse, *v*. merge, unite, amalgamate, weld; melt, dissolve. See JUNCTION, COMBINATION, FUEL, UNITY.

fuss, *n*. ado, bustle, hubbub, confusion, AGITATION; fret, fidget. See ACTIVITY.

futile, *adj*. ineffectual, vain, idle, useless. See USELESSNESS, HOPELESSNESS.

FUTURITY

Nouns—futurity, future, hereafter, time to come; approaching *or* coming years *or* ages; millennium, doomsday, Day of Judgment, crack of doom; remote future; approach of time, advent, time drawing on, womb of time; DESTINY, POSTERITY, eventuality; prospect (see EXPECTATION); foresight. See PREDICTION, THREAT, SEQUENCE.

Verbs—approach, await; look forward, anticipate, expect (see EXPECTATION); foresee; come on, draw on; draw near; threaten, impend (see DESTINY).

Adjectives—future, to come, coming, impending (see DESTINY); next, near; near at hand, close at hand; eventual, ulterior, in prospect (see EXPECTATION).

Adverbs—in [the] future, prospectively, hereafter, tomorrow, the day after tomorrow; in course of time, in process of time, in the fullness of time; eventually, ultimately, sooner or later, in the long run; one of these days; after a while, after a time; from this time, henceforth, thence; thenceforth, whereupon, upon which; soon, on the eve of, on *or* at the point of, on the brink of; about to, close upon, around the corner, in the wind.

Antonyms, see PAST.

G

gabble, *v*. cackle; chatter, prattle, blab; gibber. *Colloq.,* gab. *Slang,* chin, jaw. See LOQUACITY.

gadget, *n*. contrivance, device, doohickey; invention, machine. *Colloq.,* thingamajig, whatchumacallit, contraption, doodad. See PLAN, INSTRUMENTALITY.

gaff, *n*. spear, hook. See ARMS.

gag, *v*. muffle, SILENCE; choke, strangle, retch. See EJECTION. —*n. colloq.,* joke. See WIT.

gaiety, *n*. merriment, frivolity, merrymaking, CHEERFULNESS.

gain, *n*. INCREASE, profit; amplification. —*v.i.* benefit; progress; put on weight. —*v.t.* earn, win; reach, attain; persuade. See ACQUISITION.

gainful, *adj*. profitable, lucrative. See UTILITY.

gainsay, *v.t.* contradict (see NEGATION).

gait, *n*. step, pace, stride; trot, gallop, walk, dogtrot; shuffle, saunter. See MOTION, METHOD.

gaiter, *n*. legging, spat[s]. See CLOTHING.

gala, *n*. festival. —*adj*. festive. See CELEBRATION.

galaxy, *n*. ASSEMBLAGE, MULTITUDE; Milky Way.

gale, *n*. WIND, storm, tempest. See REJOICING.

gall, *n*. bitterness, bile, rancor; *slang,* impudence, INSOLENCE. —*v*. irritate, chafe; annoy, exasperate; vex. See PAIN, RESENTMENT.

gallant, *n*. gigolo; squire, cavalier. See ACCOMPANIMENT. —*adj*. chivalrous, polite; brave, courageous; courteous, courtly. See ENDEARMENT.

gallery, *n.* balcony, corridor; veranda, loft; salon. See DRAMA, PAINTING, STORE.

gallop, *n. & v.* run, canter. See TRAVEL.

gallows, *n.* gibbet, scaffold, crosstree, hanging tree, yardarm. See PUNISHMENT.

galore, *adv.* in abundance. See SUFFICIENCY.

gambit, *n.* attack; stratagem, ruse, artifice, ploy. See CUNNING, GIVING.

gamble, *n.* CHANCE, wager, risk. —*v.* speculate, risk, bet.

gambler, *n.* speculator, gamester, tinhorn. *Slang,* piker. See CHANCE.

gambol, *v. & n.* LEAP, cavort, frolic, romp, play. See AMUSEMENT.

game, *n.* AMUSEMENT, diversion, sport, play; contest, match; plan, purpose; prey (see PURSUIT). See CONTENTION, CHANCE, ANIMAL. —*adj., slang,* sporty, gritty, plucky. See COURAGE, RESOLUTION.

gamin, *n.* urchin, street Arab. See YOUTH.

gamut, *n.* scale; scope, extent, compass. See SPACE, MUSIC.

gang, *n.* group, band; set, clique; mob, horde. See ASSEMBLAGE, PARTY.

gangling, *adj.* gangly, lanky, gawky, spindly; ungainly, awkward. See NARROWNESS, UNSKILLFULNESS.

gangrenous, *adj.* mortified, necrose. See DISEASE.

gangster, *n.* hoodlum, hooligan, thug, racketeer, tough; syndicate man. *Slang,* mobster, goon, hood. See EVILDOER.

gap, *n.* INTERVAL, vacancy, break, lacuna, hiatus. See NARROWNESS, DISCONTINUANCE.

gape, *v.* open, spread, yawn; stare, gaze. See OPENING, WONDER.

garage, *n.* carport; service station. See STORE, RESTORATION.

garb, *n.* See CLOTHING.

garbage, *n.* waste, refuse, trash, rubbish, junk, scraps; nonsense. See USELESSNESS, UNMEANINGNESS, UNCLEANNESS, FALSENESS.

garble, *v.* distort, misreport. See FALSENESS, DISTORTION.

garden, *n.* herbary, nursery, pleasance; flowerbeds. See AGRICULTURE.

garish, *adj.* showy, gaudy. See OSTENTATION.

garland, *n.* festoon, wreath, lei. See ORNAMENT, CIRCULARITY.

garment, *n.* CLOTHING, robe, dress, vestment, habiliment.

garner, *v.* harvest, collect, STORE.

garnish, *v.* ORNAMENT, trim, decorate, embellish; season, flavor (see TASTE).

garret, *n.* crawl space, loft, attic. See RECEPTACLE.

garrison, *n.* fort[ress], outpost, stronghold; camp, bivouac; billet, barracks, soldiery. —*v.* occupy, encamp, billet; defend, secure, protect, fortify. See DEFENSE, COMBATANT.

garrulity, *n.* LOQUACITY, wordiness, prolixity, verbosity.

gas, *n.* aeriform *or* elastic fluid; VAPOR, fume, reek; AIR, ether; FUEL, gasoline, petrol; bombast; gas attack. *Slang,* hot air.

gash, *n. & v.* slash, gouge, slit; cut; scratch, score. See DISJUNCTION, INTERVAL.

gasoline, *n.* petrol; leaded *or* no-lead gasoline. See FUEL, OIL.

gasp, *v.* pant, labor, choke; puff; exclaim. See WEARINESS.

gate, *n.* gateway, OPENING, portal; sluice, floodgate; *slang,* admission. See RECEIVING, EJECTION, PASSAGE.

gather, *v.* infer, conclude; congregate, group, amass; collect, harvest, cull, pick, glean; cluster, huddle, herd; pleat; fester, suppurate. See ASSEMBLAGE, SUPPOSITION, ACQUISITION.

gauche, *adj.* awkward, clumsy; uncultured. See UNSKILLFULNESS.

gaudy, *adj.* garish, showy, cheap, blatant, tawdry; gay, bright, flashy. See COLOR, OSTENTATION, VULGARITY.

gauge, *n.* measure, templet, template; caliber, SIZE. —*v.* measure, estimate, judge, evaluate. See MEASUREMENT, JUDGMENT.

gaunt, *adj.* haggard, bony, lean, emaciated. See NARROWNESS.

gauze, *n.* net, tulle, malines, scrim, marquisette, gossamer, cheesecloth, bandage. See TRANSPARENCY.

gay, *adj.* lively, vivacious, blithe; homosexual; convivial, festive; bright, colorful. See CHEERFULNESS, COLOR UNCONFORMITY.

gaze, *v.* stare, ogle, pore. See VISION.

gazebo, *n.* pavilion, summerhouse. See ABODE.

gazette, *n.* newspaper, tabloid, bulletin. See PUBLICATION.

gear, *n.* CLOTHING, dress; cogwheel; equipment, tools, apparatus; harness, *etc.* See INSTRUMENTALITY, PROVISION.

gelatin, *n.* gel, jelly, aspic, gelée; gluten, pectin, agar-agar. See COHERENCE.

gelid, *adj.* frozen, COLD; icy, frosty, ice-cold.

gem, *n.* jewel, stone; prize; work of art. See ORNAMENT, GOODNESS.

genealogy, *n.* pedigree, descent, ANCESTRY, lineage, stock, POSTERITY.

GENERALITY

Nouns—**1,** generality, generalization; universality, currency, broadness, collectivity; average; catholicity, catholicism; miscellany, miscellaneousness; prevalence; DISPERSION. *Colloq.,* dime a dozen.

2, everyone, everybody [and his *or* her brother *or* sister], every last man *or* woman, every man jack; all hands, all the world and his wife [*or* brother, *etc.*]; anybody; world community. *Colloq.,* whole kit and caboodle. *Slang,* the works.

Verbs—be general, prevail, be going about; generalize.

Adjectives—general, generic, collective, current; broad, comprehensive, extensive, sweeping; encyclopedic, widespread, dispersed; universal, catholic, common, all-inclusive, worldwide, global; ecumenical; transcendental; prevalent, prevailing, rife, epidemic, besetting; all over, covered with; every, each and every, every single *or* last, all; unspecified, impersonal; indiscriminate; customary (see HABIT).

Adverbs—generally, in general, generally speaking, on an average; always, for better or worse; for the most part, by and large, on the whole, in the main; in the long run; whatever, whatsoever; everywhere, wherever; to a man, one and all, all told. *Colloq.,* across the board.

Antonyms, see SPECIALITY.

---

generate, *v.* make, produce; proliferate, procreate, breed, impregnate; engender. See POWER, PRODUCTION, CAUSE.

generation, *n.* age, descent, lifetime; procreating, breeding, begetting. See PRODUCTION.

generosity, *n.* BENEVOLENCE, philanthropy, LIBERALITY, munificence, prodigality; altruism, magnanimity. See GIVING, UNSELFISHNESS.

genesis, *n.* creation, origin, formation, BEGINNING, birth. See PRODUCTION.

genetic, *adj.* genic, inherited, hereditary, innate. See PRODUCTION.

genial, *adj.* affable, cordial, jovial, friendly, hearty, pleasant. See CHEERFULNESS.

genie, *n.* imp, gnome; jinni. See DEMON, MYTHICAL DEITIES.

genius, *n.* spirit, pixy; brilliance, INTELLIGENCE; talent, bent, gift, ability. See SKILL, INTELLECT, MYTHICAL DEITIES.

genre, *n.* kind, category, species, type, CLASS.

genteel, *adj.* polite, elegant. See COURTESY, ELEGANCE.

gentile, *adj.* heathen, pagan; Christian; non-Jewish. See HETERODOXY.

gentility, *n.* refinement, ELEGANCE; COURTESY; NOBILITY. See FASHION.

gentle, *adj.* mild, calm; soothing, kindly, tolerant; considerate, courteous, well-bred, high-born; tame, docile. See COURTESY, MODERATION, NOBILITY, DOMESTICATION.

gentleman, *n.* aristocrat, cavalier, esquire. See MALE, PROBITY, NOBILITY.

gentleness, *n.* MODERATION, mildness; kindness, amenity, LENIENCY. See COURTESY.

gentry, *n.* See NOBILITY.

genuine, *adj.* true, right, real, authentic; sincere, real, unaffected; honest, valid. See GOODNESS, PURITY, TRUTH.

geometrical, *adj.* geometric, planimetric; patterned, designed, symmetric; formal, stylized. See ORDER, NUMERATION.

germ, *n.* microorganism; seed, embryo; microbe, bacterium; BEGINNING, rudiment; source, origin, CAUSE. See LITTLENESS.

germane, *adj.* relevant, pertinent, apropos, to the point. See RELATION.

germicide, *n.* germ-killer; bactericide, insecticide, antiseptic. See REMEDY.

germinate, *v.* impregnate; sprout, begin. See PRODUCTION.

gesticulate, *v.* gesture, motion, wave, pantomime, mime. See INDICATION.

gesture, *n.* motion, signal, gesticulation. —*v.i.* wave, signal, nod, beckon. See INDICATION.

get, *v.* secure, obtain, procure, acquire; win, earn, attain; understand, comprehend; produce, beget. See ACQUISITION, PRODUCTION, REPRODUCTION.

getaway, *n., slang,* ESCAPE, breakout, flight; head start.

getup, *n., colloq.,* rig, outfit, garb; costume. See CLOTHING.

gewgaw, *n.* trinket, knickknack, bauble. See ORNAMENT.

geyser, *n.* hot spring, spout, gusher; Old Faithful. See WATER.

ghastly, *adj.* pale, haggard, deathly, ashen, livid; horrible, terrible, fearsome, hideous. See UGLINESS, COLORLESSNESS, FEAR.

ghetto, *n.* quarter, slum. See ABODE.

ghost, *n.* apparition, phantom, spirit, shade, specter. See DEMON, INTELLECT.

ghostly, *adj.* ghostlike, spectral, phantasmal. See DEMON.

ghoul, *n.* grave robber, body snatcher; DEMON, vampire; blackmailer. See EVILDOER.

giant, *n.* jumbo, monster, titan, colossus. See SIZE.

gibberish, *n.* jargon, doubletalk. See ABSURDITY, UNMEANINGNESS.

gibe, *n.* sneer, taunt, jeer, RIDICULE. See DISRESPECT.

giddy, *adj.* frivolous, irresponsible; dizzy, flighty, capricious. See INSANITY, FOLLY.

gift, *n.* present, donation, favor, bounty; contribution, gratuity, tip, largess; talent, aptitude, ability. See GIVING, POWER, SKILL, LIBERALITY.

gifted, *adj.* talented (see SKILL).

gigantic, *adj.* titanic, huge, enormous, colossal, immense. See SIZE.

giggle, *v.* chuckle, titter. See REJOICING.

gigolo, *n.* fancy man. See IMPURITY.

gimmick, *n.* artifice, trick, angle. See PLAN.

gingerly, *adv.* carefully, prudently, timidly, charily, hesitantly. See CAUTION.

gird, *v.* bind, strap, secure; encircle, surround; equip, support, fortify. See CIRCUMSCRIPTION, PREPARATION, STRENGTH.

girdle, *n.* band, belt, girth; corset, cummerbund. See CLOTHING, CIRCUMSCRIPTION.

girl, *n.* lass, maid, damsel; SERVANT, clerk. See FEMALE, YOUTH.

girlfriend, *n.* sweetheart, girl, LOVE, date. *Colloq.,* steady. *Slang,* flame, moll.

girth, *n.* outline; circumference, belt, girdle, band. See CIRCUMSCRIPTION.

gist, *n.* MEANING, essence, significance, point. See INTRINSIC.

giveaway, *n.* disclosure, revelation, dead giveaway; premium, bonus, door prize, handout, come-on, something for nothing; loss leader. See GIVING.

GIVING

Nouns—**1,** giving, bestowal, donation; presentation, presentment; accordance; cession, concession; delivery, giveaway; consignment; dispensation; communication; endowment; investment, investiture; award; almsgiving, charity, LIBERALITY; generosity, philanthropy (see BENEVOLENCE).

2, gift, donation, present, *cadeau,* boon, favor; benefaction, grant; offering, oblation, sacrifice, immolation; gambit; bonus, bonanza.

3, allowance, contribution, subscription, subsidy, tribute; alimony, pension; fee, recompense (see PAYMENT); consideration; bribe, bait; peace offering.

4, bequest, legacy, devise, will; dot, appanage; voluntary settlement *or* conveyance, TRANSFER; amortization.

5, alms, charity, largess, bounty, dole; oblation, offertory; honorarium, gratuity, Christmas box, Easter offering, breadline; food stamps; tip, drink money, *pourboire,* lagniappe, premium. *Slang,* handout.

6, giver, grantor; contributor, donor, testator, testatrix; feoffer, settlor.

7, godsend, manna, windfall, blessing; pennies from heaven.

Verbs—**1,** give, donate, bestow, impart, confer, grant, accord, render, award, assign; present, give away, dispense, dispose of, deal, mete, *or* dole out (see APPORTIONMENT); pay *or* squeeze out; come across; make a present, chip in, contribute, subscribe; endow, settle upon, bequeath, will, leave, hand down, devise; hand *or* turn in; deliver, hand, pass, make, *or* turn over; entrust; consign, vest in; concede, cede, yield, part with, spend; pay (see PAYMENT).

2, furnish, supply, make available, help; administer *or* minister to; afford, spare; accommodate *or* favor with; shower down upon, lavish, pour, *or* thrust upon; cross, tickle, *or* grease the palm, bribe; tip; OFFER, sacrifice, immolate. *Colloq.,* fork over. *Slang,* kick in; cough up.

Adjectives—giving, given; allowed, allowable; donative, concessional; communicable; charitable, eleemosynary; liberal.

Antonyms, see RECEIVING, ACQUISITION.

---

glacial, *adj.* icy (see COLD).

glad, *adj.* happy, content, cheerful, joyful; blithe, beatific; pleased; blissful. See PLEASURE, REJOICING, CHEERFULNESS.

glade, *n.* clearing, glen, cañada. See MOISTURE.

glamour, *n.* charm, romance, enchantment, allure; sex appeal. See ATTRACTION.

glance, *n.* glimpse, *coup d'oeil;* ray, beam, look; ricochet, skim, stroke. —*v.i.* peek, glimpse, look; graze, brush, strike; gleam, flash. See VISION, LIGHT.

glare, *n.* scowl, frown, glower; stare. —*v.i.* flare, shine, glitter; blinding light. See LIGHT, VISION.

glaring, *adj.* fierce; bright, dazzling, showy; conspicuous, flagrant, obvious, notorious. See COLOR, VISIBILITY.

glass, *n.* crystal; mirror, lens, slide; beaker, tumbler, goblet, snifter; pane; stained glass, bottle glass, peloton, *etc.;* telescope, spyglass; (*pl.*) spectacles, eyeglasses. See OPTICAL INSTRUMENTS, RECEPTACLE, BRITTLENESS, TRANSPARENCY.

glassy, *adj.* glazed, vitreous, crystalline; mirrory, smooth, polished; clear, bright, transparent; fragile, brittle. See TRANSPARENCY, SMOOTHNESS, BRITTLENESS, UNMEANINGNESS.

glaze, *n.* luster, shine; coating; ice; glass, glassiness. See SMOOTHNESS, COVERING.

gleam, *n.* light, beam, flash, glimmer,

ray. —*v.i.* shine, glow, glitter, glimmer. See LIGHT.

glean, *v.* gather [in], harvest; deduce; cull, winnow. See AGRICULTURE, CHOICE, JUDGMENT.

glee, *n.* CHEERFULNESS, delight, joy, merriment, gaiety, mirth.

glen, *n.* valley, dale. See CONCAVITY.

glib, *adj.* facile, fluent, voluble, insincere. See LOQUACITY, FACILITY, AFFECTATION.

glide, *v.i.* float, flow, skim; slip, slide, coast; skate, swim, ski. See MOTION, AVIATION.

glimmer, *n.* glance, appearance, view, flash, sight. See VISION. —*v.i.* shine. See LIGHT, DIMNESS.

glimpse, *v.* & *n.* glance (see VISION).

glint, *n.* luster, brightness, gleam. —*v.i.* flash, gleam, glisten, scintillate. See LIGHT.

glisten, *v.i.* glister, gleam, glint, glitter, coruscate. See LIGHT.

glitter, *v.i.* & *n.* flash, gleam, twinkle, glisten, glint, sparkle. See LIGHT, OSTENTATION.

gloat, *v.i.* boast, exult, rejoice; stare, gape; revel, glory, delight. See PLEASURE, BOASTING.

global, *adj.* spherical; worldwide. See GENERALITY, ROTUNDITY.

globe, *n.* ball, sphere; earth; orb. See ROTUNDITY.

globule, *n.* glob, drop[let], bead, blob; spherule. See ROTUNDITY.

gloom, *n.* DEJECTION, sadness, dolefulness, melancholy; shadow, shade, dimness, DARKNESS, OBSCURITY; pessimism.

glorify, *v.* exalt, magnify, revere; exaggerate; praise, honor; transform; flatter. See REPUTE, EXAGGERATION, APPROBATION.

glory, *n.* aureole, halo, nimbus; radiance, brilliance; fame, dignity; effulgence; honor, kudos, renown. See BEAUTY, LIGHT, REPUTE.

gloss, *n.* luster, sheen, shine, finish, polish; glaze, veneer; DECEPTION, speciousness. See LIGHT, SMOOTHNESS, SHALLOWNESS.

glossary, *n.* [word]list, lexicon, vocabulary. See LIST.

glove, *n.* mitten, gauntlet. See CLOTHING.

glow, *n.* flush, sheen, LIGHT, radiance, warmth. —*v.* shine, gleam, flush, burn, blaze, flame. See HEAT, FEELING, COLOR, VIGOR.

glower, *n.* scowl, frown, glare. See RESENTMENT.

glue, *n.* mucilage, paste, cement, adhesive. —*v.* stick, attach, cement; adhere. See CONNECTION, COHERENCE.

glum, *adj.* morose, sullen, moody, gloomy, low, unhappy. See DEJECTION.

glut, *v.* stuff, cram, choke, pack, jam. —*n.* surplus, surfeit, plethora, saturation, satiety, redundance. See SUFFICIENCY.

GLUTTONY

Nouns—**1,** gluttony, gluttonousness, hunger, hoggishness; greed, greediness; voracity, rapacity, edacity, crapulence; epicurism; good *or* high living; guzzling; good cheer, blow out; feast; gastronomy. See DESIRE, PLEASURE.
2, epicure, bon vivant, gourmand, gourmandizer, gourmet; glutton, pig, cormorant; gastronome. *Colloq.,* hog.

Verbs—be gluttonous, gormandize, gorge; overgorge, overeat; engorge, eat one's fill, indulge one's appetite; cram, stuff; bolt, raven, wolf, devour, gobble up; eat out of house and home; have a tapeworm inside. *Colloq.,* eat like a horse. See FOOD.

Adjectives—gluttonous, greedy, hungry, voracious, ravenous, rapacious, edacious, omnivorous, crapulent, swinish, cormorant; gorged, overfed; insatiable.

Antonyms, see ASCETICISM, MODERATION.

---

gnarled, *adj.* knotty, burred, cross-grained; misshapen, deformed; rough, wiry, rugged. See DISTORTION, ROUGHNESS.

gnash, *v.t.* grind, champ, crunch, gnaw, bite. See RESENTMENT, LAMENTATION.

gnaw, *v.* chew, masticate, crunch; rankle, irritate, distress. See FOOD, PAIN.

gnome, *n.* dwarf, goblin, elf, kobold, gremlin; aphorism. See DEMON, MYTHICAL DEITIES, MAXIM.

go, *v.i.* leave, depart, withdraw, retire, exit; vanish, disappear, evaporate, evanesce; operate, work, run, function, succeed; proceed, pass; wend, stir; extend, reach; elapse, pass; wither, fade, die; burst, explode. See DEPARTURE, PASSAGE, DEATH, SUCCESS, MOTION, ENERGY.

goad, *v.* prick, stab, prod, poke, spur; urge, egg [on], incite, impel, drive. *Colloq.*, needle. See CAUSE.

go-ahead, *n.* approval, PERMISSION.

goal, *n.* object, end, aim, ambition; (*in games*:) finish line, home, cage, goalposts, end zone, basket; field goal, foul. See INTENTION, ARRIVAL.

gob, *n.* lump, dab, dollop (see DENSITY); (*pl.*) piles, lots, heaps, oodles. See MULTITUDE.

gobble, *v.* eat, devour, bolt, wolf, gulp; *slang,* engulf, swallow up, consume, exhaust, take over. See GLUTTONY, FOOD.

go-between, *n.* AGENT, intermediary, broker, middleman, dealer; pander. See BUSINESS.

goblet, *n.* cup, chalice. See RECEPTACLE.

goblin, *n.* gnome, gremlin. See MYTHICAL DEITIES.

goddess, *n.* DEITY, idol, divinity; Olympian. See MYTHICAL DEITIES.

godless, *adj.* unbelieving, faithless; atheistic, agnostic, skeptic[al]; heathen[ish], pagan, infidel; impious, irreligious. See IRRELIGION.

godly, *adj.* divine; pious, reverent, religious, devout. See PIETY.

godsend, *n.* miracle, blessing, manna [from heaven], windfall, boon, [lucky] break. See PROSPERITY.

go-getter, *n., slang,* doer, entrepreneur, drum-beater, hustler, operator; zealot, enthusiast. *Slang,* wheeler-dealer.

goings-on, *n., colloq.,* behavior, CONDUCT.

gold, *n.* MONEY, wealth; bullion, *aurum*; gilding, gilt, goldplate. See COLOR.

golden, *adj.* gilded, aureate, yellow; gold; precious, priceless; unequaled. See COLOR, DEARNESS.

gong, *n.* cymbal, tocsin, tam-tam. See MUSIC.

good-for-nothing, *n.* knave, rogue, ne'er-do-well, do-nothing; lazybones, loafer, sloth, wastrel, fainéant. *Slang,* bum. See INACTIVITY. —*adj.* no-account, useless, worthless, futile. See USELESSNESS.

good-looking, *adj.* handsome, pretty, comely. See BEAUTY.

goodly, *adj.* considerable, sizable; excellent, splendid. See SIZE, GOODNESS, BEAUTY.

good-natured, *adj.* easygoing, even-tempered, pleasant, agreeable, amiable, sociable. See CHEERFULNESS, BENEVOLENCE.

GOODNESS

Nouns—**1,** good, goodness; excellence, merit; value, worth, price; welfare, benefit, blessing. See VIRTUE, BENEVOLENCE, PROBITY, UTILITY.

2, masterpiece, *chef d'oeuvre,* prime, flower, cream, pride, elite, pick, classic, flower of the flock, salt of the earth, all wool and a yard wide; prime, heyday, zenith. See SUPERIORITY, PERFECTION.

3, gem [of the first water]; bijou, precious stone, jewel, diamond [in the rough], ruby, brilliant, treasure; good thing; *rara avis,* one in a million. *Slang,* something else, cat's meow *or* pajamas, living end.

4, good man, model, paragon, prince, angel.

Verbs—**1,** produce *or* do good, be beneficial, profit (see UTILITY); serve, help, avail, [confer a] benefit; be the making of, do a world of good, make a man *or* woman of; produce a good effect; do a good turn, improve (see IMPROVEMENT).

2, be good, stand the test; pass muster; challenge comparison, vie, emulate, rival.

Adjectives—**1,** good, beneficial, valuable, of value, excellent, divine, heavenly, goodly; serviceable, useful; advantageous, profitable, edifying, salutary, healthful (see HEALTH); genuine (see TRUTH); moderately good, tolerable (see MEDIOCRITY); elite, prime, tiptop, great, top-drawer, dandy; up to snuff, par, *or* the mark; above par. *Colloq.,* grand, topnotch, A-1, jim-dandy, out of this world, not half bad. *Slang,* bang-up, swell, all right, cool, copacetic.

2, harmless, unobnoxious, innocuous, innocent, inoffensive.

3, virtuous, moral, creditable, laudable, exemplary (see VIRTUE).

Adverbs—to the good, well and good, for the best, beneficially, in one's favor *or* interest[s].

Antonyms, see BADNESS, EVILDOER.

---

goods, *n.pl.* wares, merchandise, stock, effects, commodities; belongings, possessions. See POSSESSION.

goof, *n.* & *v.* See ERROR, FOLLY.

gore, *n.* blood (see FLUIDITY).

gorge, *n.* gully, ravine, canyon, pass; feast. See INTERVAL. —*v.* overeat, gormandize, stuff, bolt, gulp. See GLUTTONY.

gorgeous, *adj.* beautiful, superb, magnificent. See BEAUTY.

gory, *adj.* bloody; bloodthirsty, sanguinary. See KILLING.

gospel, *n.* good news, glad tidings; dogma, TRUTH. See SACRED WRITINGS, NEWS, RULE.

gossip, *n.* busybody, talebearer, chatterer; reports, rumors. —*v.i.* talk, report, tattle, whisper. See CURIOSITY, INFORMATION, SPEECH, NEWS.

gouge, *v.* scoop, channel, dig, groove, rout out; *colloq.,* defraud, cheat (see DECEPTION, STEALING). See CONCAVITY, FURROW.

goulash, *n.* stew; jumble, hash. See MIXTURE, FOOD.

gourmet, *n.* epicure, *bon vivant;* gastronome, gastrophile. See TASTE, GLUTTONY.

govern, *v.* RULE, reign, administrate, preside; hold power, sway, *or* the reins; guide, control; restrain, moderate, temper, curb, bridle, check. See RESTRAINT, AUTHORITY.

governess, *n.* nurse, nanny; preceptress, gouvernante. See TEACHING.

government, *n.* regime, administration; control, rule, regulation; state, economy; kingship, regency, *etc.* See AUTHORITY.

gown, *n.* peignoir, negligee, nightgown; dress, evening gown, robe; vestment, cassock, frock, smock, slip. See CLOTHING.

grab, *v.* take, snatch, seize, capture; clutch; annex. See ACQUISITION.

grace, *n.* delicacy, tact, culture; graciousness, COURTESY; attractiveness, charm; compassion, mercy, clemency; saintliness, PIETY. See PERMISSION, GRATITUDE, FORGIVENESS, ELEGANCE, PITY. —*v.* adorn, honor, decorate; improve. See BEAUTY, TASTE, ORNAMENT, ELEGANCE.

graceful, *adj.* lithesome, lissome, svelte, sylphlike, gainly; easy, fluent; willowy, pleasing, elegant, attractive. See BEAUTY, ELEGANCE.

graceless, *adj.* ungracious, tactless; inept, awkward, clumsy, ungainly; inelegant; sinful, corrupt. See UGLINESS, IRRELIGION, IMPENITENCE, INELEGANCE.

gracious, *adj.* gentle, courteous, tactful; kind, thoughtful, benign; affable, obliging; generous; charming, attractive. See BENEVOLENCE, COURTESY.

gradation, *n.* stage, DEGREE.

grade, *n.* level, quality, class; rank, standing; gradation, slope, tilt, slant. See OBLIQUITY, DEGREE.

gradual, *adj.* slow, progressive, moderate, leisurely. See DEGREE, SLOWNESS.

graduate, *n.* measure, beaker. *Slang*, grad. See DEGREE. —*v.* measure, classify, grade; calibrate; pass, commence. See ARRANGEMENT, MEASUREMENT, SCHOOL.

graffiti, *n.pl.* See WRITING.

graft, *v.* inoculate, bud, transplant, implant, join, crossbreed. See MIXTURE, INSERTION. —*n.* corruption, porkbarrel politics. See STEALING, IMPROBITY.

grain, *n.* fruit, cereal, seed, grist, kernel; TEXTURE, temper, TENDENCY; mite, speck, bit (see LITTLENESS).

GRAMMAR

Nouns—**1,** grammar; accidence, syntax, analysis, synopsis, praxis, punctuation, syllabi[fi]cation; parts of speech; participle; article, noun, substantive, pronoun, verb, adjective, adverb, preposition, postposition, interjection, conjunction; particle; prefix, suffix, combining form, element; inflection, inflexion, case, declension, conjugation.

2, tense: present, past, preterit, future; imperfect, perfect, past perfect, pluperfect; progressive, *etc*.

3, mood, mode: infinitive, indicative, subjunctive, imperative.

4, sentence, paragraph, clause, phrase.

5, style; philology, language; phraseology, wording, rhetoric, diction. See SPEECH; WRITING.

Verbs—parse, analyze, diagram; punctuate; conjugate, decline, inflect.

Antonyms, see ERROR.

grand, *adj.* large, impressive, magnificent, stately, majestic; pretentious, ostentatious; elegant, lofty. See GREATNESS, OSTENTATION, REPUTE.

grandeur, *n.* GREATNESS, magnificence; show, ostentation; splendor, majesty; eminence, stateliness, loftiness. See IMPORTANCE.

grandfather, *n.* grandpa, grandsire; gaffer, old man. See ANCESTRY, AGE.

grandiose, *adj.* grand; stately, pompous, bombastic. See BOASTING, OSTENTATION.

grandmother, *n.* granny, grandma, nana, nanny; old woman. See ANCESTRY, AGE.

grandstand, *n.* bleachers. See VISION.

grant, *n.* gift, allotment, contribution. —*v.* bestow, give, yield; concede; permit; contribute. See GIVING, PERMISSION, CONSENT, RIGHTNESS, TRANSFER.

granular, *adj.* granulated, grainy, mealy, gritty, sandy. See POWDERINESS.

grapevine, *n., colloq.,* rumor; rumor mill, pipeline, a little bird. See INFORMATION.

graph, *n.* diagram, chart, plot, PLAN; bar, circle, *etc*. graph.

graphic, *adj.* pictorial, descriptive; vivid, diagrammatic; delineative; picturesque. See REPRESENTATION, DESCRIPTION.

grapple, *v.* seize, grasp, clutch, struggle, contend. See OPPOSITION, CONTENTION.

grasp, *v.* hold, clasp, seize; comprehend, understand. See ACQUISITION, INTELLIGENCE, AUTHORITY, RETENTION.

grass, *n.* lawn, greenery, turf, sod, verdure. See VEGETABLE.

grassland, *n.* pasture, prairie, meadowland, plain. See LAND.

grate, *v.* scrape, grind, rasp, abrade, scratch, rasp. See FRICTION. —*n.* grating (see CROSSING).

grateful, *adj.* appreciative, thankful; welcome, agreeable, refreshing, soothing. See GRATITUDE, PLEASURE.

gratification, *n.* satisfaction, fulfillment; entertainment, diversion, feast; ease, comfort; indulgence, consummation. See PLEASURE, CONTENT.

grating, *n.* lattice, openwork, grillwork, grid. See CROSSING.

GRATITUDE

Nouns—gratitude, gratefulness, thankfulness; indebtedness; acknowledgment, recognition, thanksgiving; thanks, praise; paean, *Te Deum*, WORSHIP, grace; thank-offering; requital.

Verbs—be grateful, thank; give, render, return, offer, *or* tender thanks; acknowledge, requite; thank *or* bless one's [lucky] stars.

Adjectives—grateful, thankful, appreciative, obliged, beholden, indebted to, under obligation.

Interjections—thanks! much obliged! thank you! thank Heaven! Heaven be praised! thanks a million! *gracias! merci!*

Antonyms, see INGRATITUDE.

---

gratuitous, *adj.* baseless, uncalled for, unwarranted; free, gratis. See NONPAYMENT, SUPPOSITION.

gratuity, *n.* tip, largess; present, gift; fee. See LIBERALITY, GIVING, CHEAPNESS.

grave, *n.* sepulcher, tomb, mausoleum; DEATH. See INTERMENT. —*adj.* important, weighty, serious; sedate, dignified; momentous, solemn; dull, somber. See DEJECTION, IMPORTANCE, INEXCITABILITY.

gravel, *n.* stones, pebbles, calculi; rubble, scree; alluvium, detritus, attritus, ballast, shingle, beach. See LAND.

graveyard, *n.* cemetery, burial ground *or* mound. See INTERMENT.

GRAVITY

Nouns—**1,** gravity, gravitation; weight, weighing; heft, heaviness; ponderosity, pressure, burden; ballast, counterpoise; load, lading, freight; lead, millstone. See SIZE, ATTRACTION.

2, avoirdupois, troy, *or* apothecaries' weight; grain, scruple, dram, ounce, pound, load, stone, hundredweight, ton, carat, pennyweight.

3, balance, scales, steelyard, beam, weighbridge, weigh station, spring balance.

Verbs—be heavy; gravitate, weigh, press, cumber, load; weigh in at, tip the scales at; weight, weigh down; outweigh, overbalance; gain *or* put on weight.

Adjectives—**1,** gravitational.

2, weighty, weighted; weighing; heavy, ponderous, ponderable; loaded, sagging; lumpish, lumpy; cumbersome, burdensome; cumbrous, unwieldy, massive, hefty.

Antonyms, see LEVITY.

---

gravy, *n.* sauce, dressing; *slang,* profit, graft. See FOOD, INCREASE.

gray, *adj.* dun, mousy, slaty, *etc.;* clouded, overcast, drab, dingy, dull, depressing, bleak; aged, old, venerable. See COLOR, CLOUDINESS, DEJECTION, AGE.

graze, *v.* TOUCH, brush; scratch, abrade, rub; pasture, browse, feed, crop. See FOOD, FRICTION.

grease, *n.* OIL, fat; graphite; suet, lard, tallow. —*v.* lubricate; anoint; *slang,* FLATTERY, bribe. See SMOOTHNESS, PAYMENT.

GREATNESS

Nouns—**1,** greatness, magnitude; dimensions, number; immensity, enormity; might, STRENGTH; intensity, fullness. See SIZE, MULTITUDE, POWER, QUANTITY.
2, eminence, prominence, grandeur, distinction, IMPORTANCE; fame, REPUTE, notability.

Verbs—run high, soar, tower, transcend; rise to a great height; know no bounds; enlarge, INCREASE; expand.

Adjectives—**1,** great, grand, large, epic, considerable, fair, above par; ample, abundant; full, intense, strong; passing (*archaic*), heavy, plenary, deep, high, *etc.;* signal, at its height, in the zenith; marvelous (see WONDER).
2, goodly, noble, mighty, arch; profound, intense, consummate, utter; extraordinary, remarkable, noteworthy, spanking.
3, vast, immense, enormous, measureless, extreme. *Colloq.,* whopping, terrific.

Adverbs—greatly, much, in a great measure, to the *n*th degree, richly, to a large *or* great extent, on a large scale; mightily, powerfully, intensely; remarkably, notably, exceptionally, marvelously. *Colloq.,* terribly, awfully; no end, plenty, mighty, as you please; by far, far and away, by a long shot.

Antonyms, see LITTLENESS, UNIMPORTANCE.

---

greed, *n.* greediness, DESIRE, cupidity, avidity, avarice. See GLUTTONY, PARSIMONY.

green, *adj.* immature; inexperienced; new, recent; pale, wan. See COLOR, NEWNESS, YOUTH, CREDULITY.

greenhouse, *n.* hothouse, solarium, herbarium, conservatory, nursery. See AGRICULTURE.

greet, *v.* address, hail, salute; welcome, receive, entertain, admit. See COURTESY.

gregarious, *adj.* sociable (see SOCIALITY).

gremlin, *n.* goblin, gnome. See MYTHICAL DEITIES, DEMON.

grenade, *n.* bomb. *Slang,* pineapple, egg. See ARMS.

grid, *n.* gridiron, grate, network. See CROSSING.

grief, *n.* distress, bereavement, sorrow, dolor; affliction, disaster, trouble, tribulation. See PAIN, DEJECTION, FAILURE.

grievance, *n.* complaint, annoyance; injustice, WRONG; tribulation, injury. *Colloq.,* gripe. See EVIL.

grieve, *v.* distress, PAIN, hurt, sadden, injure; mourn, sorrow, deplore. See LAMENTATION.

grievous, *adj.* intense, sad; severe, flagrant, appalling, atrocious. See PAIN, BADNESS.

grill, *n.* gridiron, CROSSING; bar, tavern. —*v.* broil, roast, toast, sear, panfry, barbecue; question, rake over the coals. See INQUIRY, FOOD, HEAT.

grim, *adj.* fearful, stern, fierce, forbidding; inflexible; ruthless; grisly, horrible. See RESOLUTION, UGLINESS.

grimace, *n.* face, scowl, leer, expression, *moue.* See DISTORTION, DEJECTION.

grimy, *adj.* soiled, dirty, foul, filthy. See UNCLEANNESS.

grin, *n.* smile, smirk. —*v.* bare the teeth; smile; smirk; grin from ear to ear. See REJOICING.

grind, *v.* pulverize, crush; sharpen, whet, file, polish; masticate, chew, crunch; rasp, grate; oppress, harass. See FRICTION, POWDERINESS.

grip, *n.* handle; handclasp; hold, control; *colloq.,* suitcase, bag, satchel. —*v.* seize, grasp, clutch, hold. See ACQUISITION, RECEPTACLE, RETENTION.

gripe, *v., colloq.,* complain, grumble, mutter. See DISCONTENT.

grisly, *adj.* gruesome, frightful, grim. See UGLINESS.

grit, *n.* sand, roughage, gravel; COURAGE, pluck, stamina, endurance. See RESOLUTION, POWDERINESS.

groan, *n.* LAMENTATION, moan. —*v.i.* grumble, lament, moan.

grocery, *n.* grocery store, greengrocer[y], purveyor's; [super]market; (*pl.*) provisions, victuals, FOOD, supplies. See STORE, PROVISION.

grog, *n.* [hot] buttered rum; hot toddy; potion. See DRINKING.

groggy, *adj.* dizzy, stupefied, sleepy, half-asleep. *Colloq.,* punchy, out of it. See INATTENTION.

groom, *n.* bridegroom, benedict. See MARRIAGE, SERVANT. —*v.* dress, tend, polish, curry; coach, train. See DOMESTICATION, CLEANNESS.

groove, *n.* HABIT, routine, rut; FURROW; trench, channel, indentation.

grope, *v.i.* feel, essay, fumble; attempt; hunt, search. See FEELING, TOUCH.

gross, *adj.* bulky, large, fat, obese; coarse, crass; brutish, callous, unrefined, insensitive; vulgar, crude, obscene; total, whole; flagrant. See VULGARITY, SIZE, IMPURITY, INELEGANCE.

grotesque, *adj.* strange, unnatural, abnormal; bizarre, fantastic, odd; misshapen, distorted. See UNCONFORMITY, DISTORTION, INELEGANCE, UGLINESS.

grotto, *n.* cave, cavern; bower; crypt, vault; spelunk. See CONCAVITY, RECEPTACLE.

grouchy, *adj., colloq.,* cross, sharp, sulky, testy, grumpy, gruff, sullen, ill-tempered, sour, out of sorts. See IRASCIBILITY, DISCONTENT.

ground, *n.* earth, terra firma, soil; foundation, basis; CAUSE, reason; viewpoint. See COVERING. —*v.* base, establish; settle, fix; instruct. —*adj.* pulverized, grated; whittled, sharpened, abraded. See LAND, SUPPORT, POWDERINESS, REGION.

groundless, *adj.* unsubstantiated, baseless, unfounded. See INSUBSTANTIALITY.

grounds, *n.pl.* dregs, lees; property, land, estate, yard; motive, reason, CAUSE. See UNCLEANNESS, REMAINDER, EVIDENCE, POSSESSION.

groundwork, *n.* foundation, framework; inception, beginning; basis. See SUPPORT, CAUSE, PREPARATION.

group, *n.* ASSEMBLAGE, company, association; clique, set; collection, cluster, company. —*v.* collect, gather, classify, sort, combine, cluster. See ARRANGEMENT.

grove, *n.* thicket, coppice, copse. See VEGETABLE.

grovel, *v.* fawn, creep, cringe; wallow, humble (oneself). See SERVILITY, LOWNESS.

grow, *v.* mature, become, develop; increase, extend, expand, enlarge; nurture, raise, cultivate; germinate, breed, sprout; flourish, thrive. See AGRICULTURE, INCREASE, PROSPERITY, CHANGE.

growl, *v.* mutter, grumble, snarl; complain, howl. See LAMENTATION, THREAT.

growth, *n.* development, evolution, INCREASE; adulthood, maturity; harvest, crop, produce, yield; flora, VEGETABLE; tumor, cancer, node, polyp, mole, tubercule, cyst, excrescence, swelling, protuberance, wen. See DISEASE, CONVEXITY, EXPANSION.

grubby, *adj., colloq.,* dingy, dirty, shabby, scurvy; ignoble, base, mean. See UNCLEANNESS.

grudge, *v.* stint, dole; begrudge, withhold. See PARSIMONY, UNWILLINGNESS.

gruel, *n.* porridge, oatmeal, cereal, grout. See FOOD.

grueling, *adj.* arduous, exhausting, strenuous. See EXERTION, SEVERITY.

gruesome, *adj.* ghastly, fearful, grisly, hideous. See UGLINESS.

gruff, *adj.* bluff, surly, rough, harsh, coarse. See DISCOURTESY.

grumble, *v.* rumble, growl, complain, mutter. See DISCONTENT.

grumpy, *adj.* surly, glum. See IRASCIBILITY.

grunt, *v.* snort, rasp, oink; complain, lament. See LAMENTATION, CRY.

guarantee, *v.* vouch, undertake, warrant; pledge; PROMISE, insure, secure. See SECURITY, CERTAINTY.

guard, *n.* safeguard, shield, baffle; cover, protection; pad, hood; catch; protector, sentinel, watchman, sentry; escort, patrol, convoy; warder, warden; night watchman, keeper, guardian. —*v.t.* protect, defend, shield, watch, patrol. See DEFENSE, SAFETY, COMBATANT.

guardian, *n.* trustee, caretaker, warden. See SAFETY.

guerrilla, *n.* irregular, partisan, rebel; *franc-tireur,* sniper, terrorist, bush fighter. See WARFARE, COMBATANT.

guess, *n.* surmise, SUPPOSITION, assumption, conjecture, theory. —*v.* suppose, divine, predict, surmise, conjecture. See INTUITION.

guest, *n.* visitor, company, caller. See SOCIALITY.

guidance, *n.* direction, management. See TEACHING, ADVICE.

guide, *n.* tracker, leader, instructor, pilot; map, instructions; guidebook, chart, manual; cicerone, dragoman, escort. —*v.* lead, direct, regulate; train. See DIRECTION, INFORMATION, TEACHING, ADVICE, RULE.

guidebook, *n.* guide, manual; Baedeker, Michelin, atlas, *vade mecum*; gazetteer, directory; instructions, operating manual. See INFORMATION, DIRECTION.

guild, *n.* union, association, club, society. See PARTY.

guile, *n.* DECEPTION, deceitfulness; trickery, CUNNING, craftiness.

guileless, *adj.* artless, innocent, naïve, unsuspecting, ingenuous, honest. See INNOCENCE.

GUILT

Nouns—**1,** guilt, guiltiness, culpability, chargeability, criminality, IMPROBITY, sinfulness (see BADNESS). See ACCUSATION.

2, misconduct, misbehavior, misdoing, malpractice, transgression, dereliction, delinquency; misfeasance, misprision; malefaction, malfeasance.

3, fault, misdeed, sin, ERROR, lapse, flaw, blot, omission; failing; offense, trespass; misdemeanor, crime, felony; enormity, atrocity, outrage; deadly *or* mortal sin. See ILLEGALITY.

4, see EVILDOER.

Verbs—be guilty, have on one's head; plead guilty. *Slang,* cop a plea.

Adjectives—guilty, to blame, culpable, sinful, criminal; red-handed, derelict, at fault, censurable, reprehensible, blameworthy, exceptionable (see DISAPPROBATION).

Adverbs—guiltily; *in flagrante delicto*; in the act.

Antonyms, see INNOCENCE.

---

guiltless, *adj.* inculpable, innocent, blameless, faultless. See INNOCENCE.

guise, *n.* APPEARANCE, aspect, pretense, semblance; costume, mien; cloak, cover. See METHOD.

gulch, *n.* gully, ravine, canyon, arroyo, gorge; riverbed. See INTERVAL.

gulf, *n.* arm (of the sea), bay; chasm, abyss; rift, gap, separation, void, crevasse, pit, deep. See INTERVAL, WATER.

gullible, *adj.* See CREDULITY.

gully, *n.* arroyo, gulch, trench, ditch, wadi, gorge, ravine. See INTERVAL, CONCAVITY.

gulp, *v.* swallow; gulp, choke. See FOOD, CREDULITY, WIND.

gumption, *n., colloq.,* initiative, self-reliance; common sense. See CUNNING, RESOLUTION.

gun, *n.* firearm (see ARMS).

gunfire, *n.* gunplay, shooting, burst, volley, salvo. See ATTACK.

gunman, *n.* Slang, trigger man, torpedo. See EVILDOER.

gunner, *n.* carabineer, cannoneer, artilleryman; hunter; marksman. See COMBATANT.

gush, *v.* pour, flow, jet, spurt; effuse, issue, emit, spout. See EGRESS, WATER.

gust, *n.* puff, burst, flurry, blow, breeze, blast. See WIND.

gusto, *n.* PLEASURE, enthusiasm, enjoyment, relish, zest, delight. See FEELING.

gut, *v.* eviscerate, disembowel; burn out, lay waste, demolish. See DESTRUCTION.

guts, *n.pl.* bowels, entrails, innards, viscera; substance, gist, essence; *slang,* determination, endurance, intestinal fortitude, COURAGE. See INTERIOR.

gutter, *n.* curb, ditch, spillway, trough. See FURROW.

guttural, *adj.* throaty, rasping, husky, hoarse. See ROUGHNESS.

guzzle, *n.* swig (see DRINKING).

gymnasium, *n.* gym, gameroom; ARENA.

gymnastics, *n.pl.* athletics, acrobatics, exercises, calisthenics. See CONTENTION, EXERTION.

gyp, *n., slang,* cheat, swindle. See DECEPTION, STEALING.

gypsy, *n.* nomad, vagrant, idler; flirt, coquette. See TRAVEL.

gyrate, *v.* turn, whirl, twirl, spin, revolve, rotate. See ROTATION.

H

HABIT

Nouns—**1,** habit, habitude, wont, way; prescription, custom, USE, usage; practice; matter of course, prevalence, observance; conventionalism, conventionality; mode, vogue (see FASHION); CONFORMITY; RULE, standing order, precedent, routine; rut, groove, beaten path; banality, familiarity; bad habit, addiction; quirk, trick (see UNCONFORMITY); seasoning, hardening, inurement; second nature, acclimatization. See REGULARITY, GENERALITY, FREQUENCY, ORDER, PRECEDENCE.

2, habitué, addict, user, slave (to), frequenter, drunkard (see DRINKING). *Colloq.,* dope fiend. *Slang,* [hop]head, junkie, freak, mainliner, acidhead.

Verbs—**1,** be wont, fall into a custom, conform to (see CONFORMITY); follow the beaten path; get used to, make a practice *or* habit of, get the feel of, take to, get the knack of, learn.

2, be habitual, prevail; come into use, take root; become second nature.

3, habituate, inure, harden, season, caseharden; accustom, familiarize; naturalize, acclimatize; keep one's hand in; train, educate, domesticate; grow on, cling to, adhere to; repeat (see REPETITION); enslave. *Slang,* hook.

Adjectives—**1,** habitual, customary; accustomed; of everyday occurrence; wonted, usual, general, ordinary, common, frequent, everyday; well-trodden, well-known; familiar, hackneyed, trite, commonplace, conventional, regular, set, stock, established, routine, stereotyped; prevailing, prevalent; current; fashionable (see FASHION); deep-rooted, inveterate, chronic, besetting; ingrained.

2, wont; used to, given to, addicted to, habituated to; in the habit of; seasoned, imbued with; devoted to, wedded to.

Adverbs—habitually; always (see CONFORMITY); as usual, as is one's wont, as a rule, for the most part; all in a day's work; generally, of course, most often, frequently.

Antonyms, see DISUSE, IRREGULARITY.

---

habitat, *n.* habitation; ENVIRONMENT, native heath; quarters. See ABODE.

hack, *v.* chop, hew, slash, cut. —*n.* cough, stutter; hackney, cab. See DISJUNCTION, VEHICLE.

hackneyed, *adj.* trite, stale, used, banal, commonplace. See HABIT.

haft, *n.* handle. See SUPPORT.

hag, *n.* harridan, termagant, shrew, witch, crone. See EVILDOER.

haggard, *adj.* drawn, gaunt; cadaverous, skeletal. See UGLINESS.

haggle, *v.i.* cavil; bargain, chaffer, dicker. See BARTER.

hail, *n.* greeting, welcome; hailstones. See COLD. —*v.* salute, greet, call, summon; accost, address. See COURTESY, INDICATION.

hair, *n.* FILAMENT; hirsuteness; thatch; crowning glory, tresses; beard, whisker[s]; mop, locks, bristles; pile, nap. See ROUGHNESS, NARROWNESS.

haircut, *n.* barbering, trim, hairdo; crew cut, butch, flattop, fuzz-cut, razor cut. See BEAUTY.

hairdo, *n.* coiffure, hair style; set, cut, shape; permanent [wave]; bob, pigtail, ponytail, bangs, braids, ringlets; pageboy, chignon, gamin cut, *etc.* See BEAUTY.

hairdresser, *n.* coiffeur, coiffeuse, hair stylist; barber, tonsor; wigmaker, *perrugvier, perruqurère.* See BEAUTY.

hairless, *adj.* beardless; bald, bare; clean-shaven, smooth-faced. See DIVESTMENT.

hair-raising, *adj.* frightening, terrifying. See FEAR.

hairy, *adj.* hirsute; furry; *slang,* dangerous. See ROUGHNESS, DANGER.

halcyon, *adj.* calm, tranquil, peaceful, quiet, pleasant. See PLEASURE.

hale, *adj.* healthy, robust, hearty, vigorous, sound. See HEALTH. —*v.t.* haul, pull. See TRACTION.

half, *n.* hemisphere; bisection; moiety. See NUMERATION.

half-baked, *adj.* incomplete; immature. See INCOMPLETENESS, EARLINESS.

half-breed, *n.* mestizo, *métis[se],* mulatto; half-blood, half-caste; mule; hybrid, mongrel. See MIXTURE.

half-hearted, *adj.* indifferent, apathetic, listless, unenthusiastic; insincere; timid. See INDIFFERENCE.

halfway, *adj.* midway, equidistant, MIDDLE. —*adv.* half, part[ly], BETWEEN, en route; so-so. *Colloq.,* more or less. See INCOMPLETENESS.

half-witted, *adj.* unintelligent, foolish, feeble-minded, moronic; mentally retarded. See IGNORANCE.

hall, *n.* PASSAGE, corridor; auditorium, building; college; dormitory; edifice. See ABODE.

hallelujah! *interj.* praise the Lord! alleluia! hosanna! See RELIGION, REJOICING.

hallmark, *n.* imprint, badge, mark, cachet, stamp; guarantee, authority; characteristic, feature, attribute, trait, SPECIALITY. See INDICATION.

hallow, *v.* bless, sanctify, consecrate, enshrine. See PIETY, CELEBRATION.

hallucination, *n.* phantasm, phantom, mirage; fancy, delusion, chimera, illusion; deception. See ERROR, IMAGINATION.

hallway, *n.* vestibule, lobby, foyer, gallery; PASSAGE, corridor.

halo, *n.* corona, aura, nimbus, glory, aureole. See LIGHT, CIRCULARITY.

halt, *v.* stop, check, arrest, pause, cease. —*n.* stop, interruption, immobility. See END. —*adj., archaic,* crippled, disabled. See IMPOTENCE, DISEASE, STAMMERING.

halter, *n.* harness, bridle, tether,

hackamore; noose; shoulder strap, waist, brassiere. See CLOTHING, RESTRAINT.

ham, *n., slang,* hambone, ham actor, show-off, grandstand player. —*v., slang,* ham it up, overact, emote, chew the scenery, pull out all the stops. See DRAMA.

hamburger, *n.* chopped *or* ground meat, forcemeat, meatball, meat patty; meat loaf, Salisbury steak, steak tartar; beef- *or* cheeseburger. See FOOD.

hamlet, *n.* village, town. See ABODE.

hammer, *v.* strike, beat, drum, pound, ram. —*n.* mallet, gavel, sledge. See IMPULSE, REPETITION, INSTRUMENTALITY.

hamper, *v.* encumber, hinder, impede, trammel, obstruct, fetter, restrict. See HINDRANCE.

hand, *n.* fist, extremity; helper, workman, employee, laborer; handwriting; *colloq.,* applause, greeting. See WRITING, APPROBATION. —*v.* pass, deliver, convey, give, transmit. See GIVING, SIDE, AGENCY, TOUCH.

handbag, *n.* pocketbook, purse; valise, grip. See RECEPTACLE.

handbill, *n.* notice, announcement, flyer. See PUBLICATION.

handbook, *n.* guide[book], instructions, manual. See INFORMATION, PUBLICATION.

handcuff, *n.* manacle[s], bracelet[s]. —*v.* shackle, manacle, fetter. See RESTRAINT.

handful, *n.* fistful, grip; QUANTITY, few, some; *colloq.,* trouble, problem, nuisance, DIFFICULTY. *Slang,* pain in the neck.

handicap, *v.* penalize, encumber, inconvenience, burden, hamper. See HINDRANCE, EQUALITY.

handicraft, *n.* craftwork, handiwork; woodcraft, stonecraft, *etc.;* SKILL, workmanship, dexterity, artisanship, artistry, craftsmanship. See BUSINESS.

handily, *adv.* skillfully, neatly, easily, with dispatch. See FACILITY, SKILL.

handkerchief, *n.* nose cloth, sudarium; neckerchief; bandanna, foulard; scarf, headcloth, headkerchief. See CLOTHING.

handle, *n.* shaft, hilt, grip, knob; *slang,* name (see NOMENCLATURE). —*v.* manipulate, USE, wield; direct, control, manage; feel, paw, TOUCH; operate, direct, CONDUCT; deal in, trade. See DIRECTION, SALE, CONDUCT.

handler, *n.* trainer, coach; masseur; dealer, jobber, agent. See DOMESTICATION, AGENT.

handmade, *adj.* handcrafted, -wrought, -carved, *etc.;* individualized; crude, makeshift. See PRODUCTION.

hand-me-down, *adj.* secondhand, castoff, discarded. See OLDNESS.

handout, *n., slang,* alms, offering, charity; handbill. See GIVING, PUBLICATION.

handsome, *adj.* attractive, comely, good-looking, personable; fine; generous, ample; striking. See BEAUTY, LIBERALITY.

handwriting, *n.* calligraphy, penmanship. See WRITING.

handy, *adj.* convenient, near, available, ready; adept, dexterous, apt; competent, capable, expert. See SKILL, UTILITY.

handyman, *n.* jack-of-all-trades, odd-job man, factotum, janitor. See SKILL.

hanger-on, *n.* dependent, parasite. See SERVILITY, FLATTERY.

hangman, *n.* executioner. See PUNISHMENT.

hangout, *n.* resort, haunt, rendezvous, stamping ground, clubhouse; *slang,* saloon, dive, den. See ABODE.

hangover, *n., colloq.,* crapulence, nausea, katzenjammer, *gueule de bois;* holdover, atavism, survival, vestige, relic, remnant. See DRINKING, REMAINDER.

hang-up, *n., slang,* thing, obsession, preoccupation; phobia. See FEAR.

hanker, *v.* DESIRE, covet, crave, long for, yearn for.

haphazard, *adj.* CHANCE, casual, aimless, random; hit-or-miss.

hapless, *adj.* unlucky, unfortunate. See ADVERSITY.

happen, *v.* befall, eventuate, occur. See CHANCE, OCCURRENCE.

happy, *adj.* fortunate, lucky; gay, contented, joyous, ecstatic; felicitous, apt; glad. See AGREEMENT, CHEERFULNESS, PLEASURE, OCCASION.

happy-go-lucky, *adj.* unworried, irresponsible. See INDIFFERENCE.

harangue, *n.* SPEECH; tirade, scolding, diatribe; address, declamation.

harass, *v.* distress, badger, trouble, vex, plague, torment, irritate, heckle, beset; worry, afflict, depress, sadden. *Colloq.,* needle. See DISCONTENT, MALEVOLENCE.

harbinger, *n.* omen, sign, forerunner, precursor. See PREDICTION.

harbor, *n.* refuge; port, retreat; haven, shelter; mole. —*v.* protect, shield, shelter; cherish, keep. See SAFETY, ARRIVAL.

hard, *adj.* firm, rigid (see HARDNESS); unsympathetic, unloving, unfriendly, callous; strenuous, difficult, puzzling; severe, serious, short, intensive. See INSENSIBILITY.

hardboiled, *adj., colloq.,* disillusioned, sophisticated. See SKILL.

hard-core, *adj.* dedicated, faithful; severe, intense. See SENSIBILITY.

harden, *v.* anneal, fire; steel; congeal, thicken (see HARDNESS); accustom, inure, blunt. See HABIT, INSENSIBILITY.

hard-hearted, *adj.* cruel, pitiless, ruthless, merciless, uncompassionate, callous, unsympathetic, tough. *Colloq.,* hard as nails. See INSENSIBILITY.

hardly, *adv.* scarcely, barely; improbably; rarely. See RARITY, DIFFICULTY.

HARDNESS

Nouns—**1,** hardness, rigidity, inflexibility, temper, callosity; toughness; pertrifacation, lapidification, lapidescence; vitrification, ossification; crystallization. See DENSITY, STRENGTH.

2, Mohs scale: talc, gypsum, calcite, fluorite, apatite, feldspar, quartz, topaz, sapphire, diamond; horn, callus, flint, marble, rock, crag (see LAND), crystal, granite, adamant, iron, steel; brick; concrete.

Verbs—harden, stiffen, petrify, temper, ossify, vitrify; callous; set, congeal; bake.

Adjectives—hard, rigid, stubborn, stiff, firm; starch[ed]; stark, unbending, unlimber, unyielding; inflexible, tense; proof; diamondlike, diamantine, adamant[ine]; concrete, stony, marble, granitic, vitreous; horny, callous[ed], corneous; bony, osseous.

Antonyms, see SOFTNESS, ELASTICITY.

hardship, *n.* ADVERSITY, difficulties; calamity, affliction.

hard up, *adj., colloq.,* poor, needy (see POVERTY); frustrated, at one's wit's end; hungry, sex-starved, horny (see DESIRE). *Slang,* up against it.

hardware, *n.* housewares, tools, utensils; ironmongery, plumbing supplies, *etc.; slang,* guns, weaponry, ARMS. See INSTRUMENTALITY.

hardy, *adj.* sturdy, tough, vigorous; resolute, daring; durable. See COURAGE, DURABILITY, STRENGTH.

harem, *n.* seraglio; bridal suite. *Slang,* love nest. See ABODE.

hark, *v.* harken; hear, listen. See HEARING, ATTENTION.

harlot, *n.* strumpet, cocotte, prostitute; paramour, courtesan. See IMPURITY.

harm, *n.* DETERIORATION, EVIL, dishonor, mischief, injury. —*v.* damage, injure; desecrate, abuse, break. See MALEVOLENCE, WRONG.

harmful, *adj.* injurious, hurtful. See DISEASE, BADNESS.

harmless, *adj.* innocent, innocuous,

inoffensive. See INNOCENCE, SAFETY, GOODNESS.

harmony, *n.* AGREEMENT, concurrence, concord; accompaniment; ORDER, SYMMETRY; tunefulness, euphony; congruity; proportion; unison; peace, amity, friendship. See MUSIC, UNITY, FRIEND.

harness, *n.* bridle, traces, hackamore; gear. —*v.* control, utilize; curb, yoke. See DOMESTICATION, RESTRAINT, USE.

harp, *n.* lyre, psaltery. See MUSIC. —*v.* dwell on, repeat, din, iterate, nag, pester. See REPETITION.

harrowing, *adj.* distressing, wrenching, tragic, nerve-racking. See PAIN.

harry, *v.* plunder, pillage, ATTACK; distress, plague, harass, hound. See MALEVOLENCE.

harsh, *adj.* acrimonious, ungenial, severe, rough, ungracious; sharp, sour; discordant, hoarse, grating; brutal, heartless, cruel; austere, stern; rigorous, hard. See DISCOURTESY, DISCORD, SEVERITY, INELEGANCE.

harvest, *n.* crop, yield, product, issue, outcome. See EFFECT, STORE, AGRICULTURE.

hash, *n.* MIXTURE, medley, mix, jumble, mishmash, confusion; botch; rehash, review; *slang,* hashish, marijuana. See FOOD. —*v.t.* mince, chop, dice; botch, bungle; hash over, discuss. See INQUIRY, UNSKILLFULNESS.

hassle, *n., slang,* quarrel, squabble. See DISCORD.

HASTE

Nouns—haste, urgency; dispatch; acceleration, spurt, forced march, rush, dash; VELOCITY; precipitancy, precipitation, precipitousness; impatience, impetuosity; expedition, EARLINESS; hurry, drive, scramble, bustle.

Verbs—**1,** haste, hasten; make haste, hurry [up], rush, dart, dash, whip on, push on, press; sentry, scuttle along, step lively, dash off, bustle, hustle, scramble, plunge, bestir oneself (see ACTIVITY); lose no time, make short work of; work against time. *Colloq.,* make tracks, make good time, step on it. *Slang,* shake a leg, get cracking, make it snappy, get a move on.

2, speed [up], expedite; precipitate; quicken, accelerate. *Slang,* step on the gas, give 'er the gun, burn rubber; give the bum's rush.

Adjectives—hasty, hurried, cursory, precipitate, headlong, impulsive, impetuous, eager, impatient, hotheaded; pressed for time, hard-pressed, urgent.

Adverbs—hastily, precipitately, helter-skelter, slapdash, full-tilt, headlong, on the run; against time *or* the clock; apace, amain; all at once (see INSTANTANEITY); at short notice, immediately (see EARLINESS); express, posthaste; on the double. *Colloq.,* in a jiff[y].

Antonyms, see SLOWNESS.

---

hat, *n.* cap, headgear, bonnet; headdress; derby, bowler; turban, cloche. See CLOTHING.

hatch, *v.* invent, contrive, originate; incubate; concoct, devise. See FALSEHOOD, IMAGINATION, PLAN.

HATE

Nouns—**1,** hate, hatred, abhorrence, loathing; disaffection, disfavor; alienation, estrangement, coolness; enmity, hostility, animosity, RESENTMENT; spite, despite, bad blood; malice (see MALEVOLENCE); implacability (see RETALIATION); repugnance, DISLIKE, odium, unpopularity; detestation, antipathy, revulsion. See FEELING, PREPARATION.

2, abomination, aversion, *bête noire*; enemy (see OPPOSITION).

Verbs—**1,** hate, detest, despise, abominate, abhor, loathe; shrink from, view with horror, hold in abomination, revolt against, execrate; DISLIKE. *Colloq.*, have it in for, not be able to stand. *Slang,* hate one's guts.

2, excite *or* provoke hatred, be hateful; repel, envenom, incense, irritate, rile; horrify.

3, be unfriendly, on bad terms, estranged, *etc.*

Adjectives—**1,** averse, set against, hostile; bitter, acrimonious (see DISCOURTESY); implacable, revengeful; on the outs; invidious, spiteful, malicious (see MALEVOLENCE).

2, hated, despised, unloved, unbeloved, unlamented, unmourned, disliked; forsaken, rejected, lovelorn, jilted.

3, hateful, obnoxious, abhorrent, despicable, heinous, odious, abominable, repulsive, loathsome, offensive, disgusting, disagreeable; unfriendly.

Antonyms, see LOVE.

---

haughty, *adj.* overbearing, arrogant, supercilious, proud, lordly, superior. See CONTEMPT, INSOLENCE.

haul, *v.* drag, pull, draw; transport, deliver; lug; haul up, arraign. See TRANSPORTATION, TRACTION, LAWSUIT.

haunt, *n.* shade, ghost, spirit, spook; resort, rendezvous, retreat, den. *Slang,* hangout. —*v.* frequent, attend; obsess; visit. See FEAR, ABODE.

have, *v.* own, hold, retain, possess, keep, maintain. See POSSESSION.

haven, *n.* refuge, sanctuary, asylum, shelter; harbor, port, snuggery; protection. See SAFETY.

havoc, *n.* devastation, DESTRUCTION, wreckage; DISORDER, chaos, confusion; ravagement, vandalism; disaster, catastrophe.

hawk, *n.* falcon, buzzard, kite, harrier, *etc.;* [hard *or* racking] cough; *colloq.,* hard-liner, warmonger. See WARFARE, DISEASE. —*v.* peddle. See SALE.

hawker, *n.* street salesman, vivandière, street crier (see SALE).

haywire, *adj., slang,* confused, mixed-up, berserk, screwy; out of control, out of commission; balled *or* bollixed up. *Slang*, snafu. See DISORDER, INSANITY.

hazard, *n.* DANGER, CHANCE, risk, peril, gamble; accident, adventure, contingency. —*v.* risk, venture, gamble. See RASHNESS.

haze, *n.* film, opacity, mist, fog; dimness. OBSCURITY. See CLOUDINESS.

head, *n.* pate, poll; chief, DIRECTOR, manager, leader; title, heading, caption; talent, ability, JUDGMENT; CLASS, category, type, grouping; *slang,* user, addict (see HABIT). *Slang,* noggin, bean. See BEGINNING, INTELLECT, HEIGHT. —*v.* lead, direct, precede; guide, rule, control, manage. See DIRECTION, PRIORITY, AUTHORITY.

headache, *n.* migraine, megrim, splitting headache; hangover; problem, burden, difficulty, nuisance. *Colloq.*, the misery. See PAIN.

headdress, *n.* headgear, millinery; coiffure; plumage, warbonnet. See CLOTHING.

headland, *n.* promontory, spit, cape, spur. See CONVEXITY, HEIGHT.

headlong, *adj.* hasty, hurried; rash, precipitate; heedless, reckless. See RASHNESS, HASTE.

headmaster, headmistress, *n.* principal. See SCHOOL.

headquarters, *n.pl.* main office, base of operations, H.Q.; government, general staff, chief. See AUTHORITY, ABODE.

headstone, *n.* gravestone; foundation stone, cornerstone; cairn, dolmen, cromlech. See INTERMENT.

headstrong, *adj.* obstinate, willful, stubborn. See OBSTINACY, VIOLENCE.

headway, *n.* PROGRESSION, advance; gain, accomplishment, achievement; clearance. See SPACE.

heady, *adj.* exhilarating, intoxicating. See DRINKING, EXCITEMENT.

heal, *v.* mend, cure; repair, restore; ease. See RESTORATION.

HEALTH

Nouns—**1,** health, healthiness; mental health, SANITY; soundness; vim, vigor, and vitality; STRENGTH, robustness; bloom, prime; *mens sana in corpore sano;* hygeia; clean bill of health; convalescence, recovery, cure (see RESTORATION).
2, salubrity, healthfulness; hygiene, sanitation. See CLEANNESS.
3, health spa; sanitarium (see REMEDY). *Slang,* fat farm.

Verbs—**1,** be healthy; bloom, flourish; look oneself; be in *or* enjoy good health; convalesce, recuperate, recover (see RESTORATION); get better, improve (see IMPROVEMENT); take a new lease on life; cure, restore. *Colloq.,* feel like a million [dollars].
2, be salubrious, be healthful, agree with, be good for.

Adjectives—**1,** healthy, well, sound, hearty, sanguine, hale [and hearty], fresh, green, whole; florid, flush, hardy, stanch, brave, robust, vigorous; unscathed, uninjured, untainted; in shape *or* condition, in the pink [of condition]; sound as a bell, fit [as a fiddle]; fresh as a daisy *or* a rose, in fine feather *or* fettle, in one's prime. *Colloq.,* chipper. *Slang,* peppy.
2, salubrious, salutary, healthful, wholesome, prophylactic, benign, bracing, tonic, invigorating; good for; hygienic; innocuous, innocent, harmless, uninjurious, uninfectious, sanitary. See GOODNESS.

Antonyms, see DISEASE.

heap, *n.* pile, load, stack, mound, ASSEMBLAGE; *colloq.,* great deal. *Colloq.* heaps, oodles, piles. *Slang,* scads. See MULTITUDE.

HEARING

Nouns—**1,** hearing, sense of hearing; audition, auscultation; eavesdropping, audibility; acute ear, *etc.;* ear for music; otology; acoustics (see SOUND).
2, ear, auricle, acoustic organ, auditory apparatus, eardrum, tympanum; hearing aid, ear trumpet, speaking trumpet; amplifier, amplification, bone conduction.
3, hearer, auditor, listener, eavesdropper; audience.
4, hearing, interview, audition, audience; trial (see INQUIRY).

Verbs—**1,** hear, overhear, take in; eavesdrop; sit in on, audit; hark[en], listen, give *or* lend an ear, bend an ear, heed, attend, prick up one's ears. *Slang,* get a load of.
2, become audible, fall upon the ear, listen in, catch *or* reach the ear, be heard; ring, resound. *Colloq.,* be all ears, drink in.

Adjectives—audible, articulate, clear.

Antonyms, see DEAFNESS.

hearsay, *n.* NEWS, gossip, rumor, talk, report. See INFORMATION.

hearse, *n.* funeral wagon. See INTERMENT.

heart, *n.* center, substance; kernel, pith, gist, core; breast; spirit, COURAGE; sympathy, affection, understanding; nature, soul. See IMPORTANCE, MIDDLE, FEELING, INTERIOR.

heartache, *n.* sorrow, anguish. See DEJECTION.

heartbroken, *adj*. miserable, wretched, forlorn, disconsolate, anguished. See PAIN, DEJECTION.

heartburn, *n*. cardialgia, pyrosis, PAIN; rue, remorse, RESENTMENT. See JEALOUSY.

hearten, *v*. cheer, encourage, brighten, reassure, comfort, rally. See COURAGE, CHEERFULNESS.

heartfelt, *adj*. sincere, earnest; profound; meaningful, cordial; enthusiastic. See FEELING.

hearth, *n*. fireside, fireplace; ingle[nook]; family [circle]. See HEAT, ABODE.

heartless, *adj*. cruel, cold, unfeeling, uncaring, unsympathetic, callous; unkind, inconsiderate, insensitive. See INSENSIBILITY.

heart-rending, *adj*. harrowing; heartbreaking. See DEJECTION.

heart-to-heart, *adj*. intimate, confidential, private, off the record, *entre nous;* frank, candid. See SECRET, PROBITY.

hearty, *n*. comrade; sailor, tar. See FRIEND, NAVIGATION. —*adj*. sturdy, robust, strong, well, vigorous, healthy; friendly, cordial; substantial. See FEELING, HEALTH.

HEAT

Nouns—**1,** heat, caloric; warmth, ardor, fervor, fervency; incalescence, incandescence; flush, glow; temperature, fever; white heat, blood *or* body heat, fever heat.

2, fire, spark, scintillation, flash, combustion, flame, blaze; bonfire, campfire, smudge, forest fire, brand, wildfire, sheet of fire, lambent flame; devouring element; sun; fireworks, pyrotechnics; ashes, cinders.

3, torridity, hot weather, [mid]summer, dogdays; heat wave, hot spell, sirocco, simoom.

4, thermology, thermotics, thermodynamics, thermometer, thermostat, calorimeter. *Colloq*., mercury, glass. See MEASUREMENT.

5, heating, calefaction; heater, stove, range, cooktop, [convection *or* microwave] oven; [forced] hot air, steam heat, hot water, radiator, register; blast furnace, electric furnace; kiln; crematorium; forge, crucible, alembic; Bunsen burner; [acetylene *or* butane] torch, electric welder; crematory, pyre; incinerator; fireplace, hearth, grate, fender, fire screen; brazier; bed warmer, electric blanket, heating pad; chafing dish; heat pump; heliostat.

6, see FUEL.

Verbs—**1,** heat, warm [up], reheat; be hot, glow, flush, sweat, swelter, bask, smoke, reek, stew, simmer, seethe, boil, broil; go up in smoke; smolder; parch, fume, pant; thaw; cook (see FOOD).

2, ignite, set on fire, enkindle; burn, blaze, flame, char, burn to a crisp; cremate.

Adjectives—**1,** hot, warm; mild, genial; tepid, lukewarm, unfrozen; thermal, thermic, calorific; fervent, fervid, feverish; ardent, aglow; red-hot, white-hot, piping-hot; like a furnace *or* oven; hot as fire, like the fires of Hell.

2, sunny, torrid, tropical, estival, canicular; close, sultry, stifling, stuffy, sweltering, suffocating, oppressive; reeking; baking.

3, fiery, incandescent, incalescent; candent, glowing, smoking; on fire; blazing, in flames, alight, afire, ablaze; smoldering, in a glow, feverish, in a sweat; blood-hot, warm as toast; volcanic, plutonic, igneous; isothermal, isothermic.

Antonyms, see COLD.

---

heathen, *n.* pagan, infidel, unbeliever. —*adj.* irreligious, idolatrous, pagan, unconverted; atheistic. See IRRELIGION, IDOLATRY.

heave, *v.* lift, hoist, raise; throw, pitch, toss; swell, expand; undulate; vomit. See ELEVATION, PROPULSION.

HEAVEN

Nouns—**1,** heaven, kingdom of heaven *or* God; future state, eternal blessedness, eternity; Paradise, Eden, abode *or* isle of the blessed; celestial bliss, glory; hereafter, afterlife; Golden Age, Utopia, never-never land, millennium, land of Canaan, promised land. *Slang,* kingdom come. See PLEASURE.
2, Olympus; Elysium, Elysian fields, garden of the Hesperides, Valhalla, Nirvana, the happy hunting grounds, seventh heaven.
3, sky, firmament, welkin, blue empyrean, the ether, heavens. See UNIVERSE.
4, resurrection, translation, apotheosis, ascension, assumption.
5, see ANGEL, DEITY.

Adjectives—heavenly, celestial, supernal, unearthly, from on high, paradisiac[al], paradisaic[al], beatific, elysian, ethereal, Olympian.

Antonyms, see HELL.

heavenly, *adj.* celestial (see HEAVEN); blessed, angelic, saintly, holy; *colloq.*, delectable, delightful, wonderful, marvelous. See GOODNESS.

heavy, *adj.* weighty (see GRAVITY); oppressive, tedious, tiresome; dull, gloomy, overcast; strong, pressing, large; somber, dismal, dejected, sad, melancholy; slow, inert, sluggish; grievous, serious. See DEJECTION, IMPORTANCE.

heavy-duty, *adj.* durable, sturdy; tough, rugged. See DURABILITY.

heckle, *v.t.* plague, taunt, harass; challenge, interrupt. See DISCONTENT.

hectic, *adj.* feverish, febrile; excited, agitated, frenetic, wild, turbulent. See EXCITEMENT.

hector, *v.* bully, torment, plague, domineer, bluster. See INSOLENCE, THREAT.

hedge, *n.* shrubbery, hedgerow. See VEGETABLE, ENCLOSURE. —*v.* evade; protect, shelter; hem in, obstruct; temporize. See COMPENSATION.

heed, *n.* ATTENTION, notice, regard, consideration, CARE. —*v.* observe, CARE, notice, attend, regard; consider. See CAUTION.

heedless, *adj.* disregardful, remiss, careless, negligent, thoughtless; unobservant, unnoticing, undiscerning; reckless. See INATTENTION, RASHNESS.

heel, *n.* rear; tilt, cant; *slang,* cad, scoundrel. *Colloq,* bounder. *Slang,* rat, louse, s.o.b. See OBLIQUITY, EVILDOER. —*v.i.* turn around, pivot, swivel. —*v.t.* follow, pursue, go after; *slang,* shadow, tail; supply, furnish, outfit, PROVISION. See PURSUIT, DEVIATION, DISCOURTESY.

hefty, *adj.* weighty; bulky, burly, brawny; beefy, corpulent. See SIZE, GRAVITY.

HEIGHT

Nouns—**1,** height, altitude, ELEVATION; eminence, pitch; loftiness, tallness, stature, prominence (see CONVEXITY).
2, mount[ain]; headland, foreland; promontory, ridge, hogback; dune; vantage ground; down; moor[land]; Alp; uplands, highlands; watershed; heights; knoll, hummock, hill[ock], barrow, mound, mole, butte; steeps, bluff, cliff, frag, tor, pike, escarpment, edge, ledge, brae.

3, summit, top, vertex, apex, zenith, pinnacle, acme, peak, culmination; meridian; utmost height; capital; crown, point, crest, cap; mountain top; housetop, rooftop; head.

4, tower, pillar, column, obelisk, monument, steeple, spire, minaret, campanile, turret, dome, cupola, pole, pikestaff, maypole, flagstaff; aerial, mast; topmast, topgallantmast, moonraker; skyscraper, highrise; ceiling (see COVERING); derrick; attic, garret.

5, colossus, giant (see SIZE); mountain climber, mountaineer.

Verbs—be high, tower, soar, command; hover, cap, culminate; mount, perch, surmount; cover, crown; overtop, top off (see SUPERIORITY); stand on tiptoe; grow, upgrow, rise (see ASCENT); heighten, elevate (see ELEVATION).

Adjectives—high, elevated, eminent, exalted, lofty; tall; gigantic, towering, soaring, elevated, upper; highest, top[most], uppermost; capital, paramount; upland, hilly, mountainous, alpine, aerial; sky-high, tall as a steeple. *Colloq.,* high as a kite.

Adverbs—on high, high up, aloft, up, above, aloof, overhead; in the clouds; on tiptoe, on stilts.

Antonyms, see LOWNESS.

---

heinous, *adj.* dreadful, abominable; atrocious, hateful, monstrous. See BADNESS, HATE.

heir, heiress, *n.* legatee, inheritor, beneficiary. See POSSESSION, ACQUISITION.

heirloom, *n.* POSSESSION, keepsake, memento, souvenir.

heist, *n., slang,* burglary (see STEALING).

helicopter, *n.* autogiro, whirlibird. See AVIATION.

HELL

Nouns—**1,** hell, Hades, place of torment; Pandemonium, Tophet; hellfire, everlasting fire, fire and brimstone; underworld; purgatory, limbo, gehenna, abyss, bottomless pit; hell on earth.

2, Tartarus, Hades, Avernus, Styx, Stygian creek, pit of Acheron, Cocytus; infernal regions, inferno, realms of Pluto; Pluto, Rhadamanthus, Erebus; Charon; Satan (see DEMON).

Adjectives—hellish, infernal, Stygian, Plutonian.

Antonyms, see HEAVEN.

---

hello, *n.* greeting, salutation, welcome; reception. —*interj.* good day! good morning! good afternoon! good evening!; how are you? how do you do? *bonjour! buon giorno! guten Tag! aloha! Colloq.,* hi! hi there! howdy! how's tricks? ahoy! *ciao!* See COURTESY.

helm, *n.* tiller, wheel; authority, command, scepter. See DIRECTION.

helmet, *n.* headgear, skullcap, casque, headpiece; crest, morion. See CLOTHING, DEFENSE.

help, *n.* SERVANT[s], staff, employees; AID, assistance, succor; relief, REMEDY. —*v.* assist, serve, befriend; relieve, ameliorate, better. See AID, AUXILIARY.

helpful, *adj.* beneficial, contributory, favorable; useful, worthwhile, furthering, improving; serviceable, salutary; remedial. See IMPROVEMENT.

helpless, *adj.* impotent, powerless; defenseless, vulnerable, resourceless; prostrate, crippled; dependent. See IMPOTENCE.

helter-skelter, *adj.* confused, disorderly. See DISORDER.

hen, *n.* fowl, chicken, bird, pullet. See ANIMAL.

hence, *adv.* herefrom, away; henceforth, henceforward; so, therefore. See REASONING, DEPARTURE, ATTRIBUTION, EFFECT.

henchman, *n.* hireling, underling; flunky, lackey; tool, puppet; accomplice. *Slang,* stooge, yesman, ward heeler, errand boy. See SERVANT, AGENT.

henpecked, *adj.* hag-ridden; browbeaten, nagged, hounded; led by the nose, jumping through hoops. See OBEDIENCE, SUBJECTION.

hep, *adj., slang,* well-informed. *Slang,* hip, in the know, wise (to), up on, cool. See KNOWLEDGE.

herald, *n.* forerunner, precursor, announcer, messenger, harbinger. —*v.* proclaim, announce, declare; introduce; precede, warn. See PREDICTION, COMMUNICATION, PRECEDENCE.

heraldry, *n.* blazonry, emblazonment. See INDICATION.

herb, *n.* potherb, condiment. See VEGETABLE, REMEDY.

herd, *n.* group, flock, drove; gathering; troop, pack, crowd. See MULTITUDE. —*v.* drive, tend, collect; gather, assemble; corral, group. See ASSEMBLAGE.

herder, *n.* shepherd, shepherdess, cowherd, pasturer, herdboy, cowboy. See DOMESTICATION.

here, *adv.* hereabouts, hither, hitherward. See LOCATION.

hereafter, *adv.* subsequently, henceforth, henceforward, eventually, ultimately. See FUTURITY.

hereditary, *adj.* inheritable, transmissible, heritable, ancestral, patrimonial. See INTRINSIC, POSTERITY, TRANSFER.

heresy, *n.* dissent, HETERODOXY. See DOUBT, ERROR.

heritage, *n.* bequest, inheritance, legacy, hereditament, patrimony. See POSSESSION.

hermetic, *adj.* mystic, magic, alchemic; airtight, vacuum-packed. See CLOSURE.

hermit, *n.* anchorite, recluse, eremite, ascetic, solitary. See ASCETICISM, SECLUSION.

hero, heroine, *n.* victor, defender, champion, redeemer; inspiration, ideal, model, paragon; knight in [shining] armor; main character, protagonist, lead; darling, favorite, idol; submarine [sandwich], hoagie, grinder. *Slang,* big *or* hot shot. See COURAGE, DRAMA, FOOD.

heroic, *adj.* courageous, intrepid, valiant, brave, mighty, fearless, gallant. See COURAGE, BOASTING, UNSELFISHNESS.

heroin, *n.* diamorphine. *Slang,* [big] H, horse, snow, scag. See HABIT.

hesitate, *v.i.* falter, waiver, shrink, demur; pause. See DOUBT, STAMMERING, UNWILLINGNESS.

HETERODOXY

Nouns—**1,** heterodoxy, syncretism; sectarianism, nonconformity, UNCONFORMITY, secularism, denominationalism, cultism; heresy, schism, ERROR, false doctrine; schismaticism, recusancy; backsliding, apostasy, atheism, IRRELIGION.

2, bigotry (see OBSTINACY); fanaticism, zealotry, iconoclasm; hyperorthodoxy, precisianism, bibliolatry, sabbatarianism, puritanism, IDOLATRY; DISSENT, superstition.

3, sectarian, heretic, seceder, separatist, recusant, dissenter, dissident, nonconformist, nonjuror; gentile; zealot, fanatic.

4, sect, denomination, faction, division, schism, organization, group, school, church, following, fellowship, ism, faith.

Verbs—deviate, stray, err, fall into ERROR.

Adjectives—heterodox, sectarian, heretical, denominational, nonconformist, unorthodox, unscriptural, uncanonical, apocryphal; schismatic, recusant, iconoclastic, dissenting, dissident, secular; pantheistic, polytheistic; bigoted, prejudiced, exclusive, narrow, intolerant, fanatical, dogmatical; superstitious, ideological, visionary; idolatrous.

Antonyms, see RELIGION.

---

heterogeneous, *adj.* diverse, mixed, conglomerate; unlike, dissimilar. See DIFFERENCE, VARIEGATION.

hew, *v.t.* fell; chop, cut, hack; chip. See DISJUNCTION, FORM.

hex, *n.* spell (see SPELL).

heyday, *n.* prime, height, peak, zenith; glory, full bloom, top of one's form; halcyon, golden, *or* palmy days; golden age, YOUTH. See GOODNESS.

hiatus, *n.* INTERVAL, gap, interruption, lacuna, void.

hibernate, *v.i.* winter; become dormant. *Colloq.,* hole up. See INACTIVITY.

hick, *n., slang,* rustic, rube. See POPULACE.

hidden, *adj.* See CONCEALMENT.

hide, *n.* skin, pelt, coat; leather. See COVERING. —*v.* cover, secrete, cloak, veil; dissemble, falsify; hole up; disguise, camouflage. See CONCEALMENT, SECRET.

hideaway, *n.* hide-out, retreat, hiding [place]. See CONCEALMENT, SECLUSION, ABODE.

hidebound, *adj.* bigoted, prejudiced, narrow; illiberal; unyielding. See NARROWNESS.

hideous, *adj.* frightful, dreadful, horrible, repulsive, unsightly, revolting. See UGLINESS.

hierarchy, *n.* rank, officialdom; order, ranking, succession. See AUTHORITY.

high, *adj.* elevated, lofty, tall; towering, eminent; acute, sharp, shrill; prominent, important, directorial; costly, dear, expensive; overripe, gamy; *colloq.,* elated; *slang,* drunk. See HEIGHT, DRINKING.

highborn, *adj.* patrician, noble, royal, aristocratic. See NOBILITY.

highbrow, *n.* intellectual. *Slang,* egghead, longhair, brain. —*adj.* intellectual, intelligent, brainy, cultured. See KNOWLEDGE.

highest, *adj.* ultimate, supreme (see SUPERIORITY).

high-handed, *adj.* arrogant, authoritarian. *Colloq.,* pushy. See INSOLENCE.

high-strung, *n.* taut, tense, edgy, jumpy, temperamental, excitable; volatile. See EXCITABILITY.

highway, *n.* road, turnpike, highroad, thoroughfare. See PASSAGE.

highwayman, *n.* thief, robber, footpad, thug, bandit. See STEALING.

hijack, *v.t., slang,* highjack, steal. See STEALING.

hike, *n.* walk, tramp, jaunt, march; *colloq.,* raise, INCREASE. —*v.* walk, march; hitchhike, thumb a ride; raise, inflate, boost, hitch up, adjust higher. See ELEVATION, TRAVEL.

hilarity, *n.* CHEERFULNESS, mirth, amusement, enjoyment, gaiety, laughter, glee.

hill, *n.* grade, slope; rise, ASCENT; elevation, mound. See HEIGHT, CONVEXITY.

HINDRANCE

Nouns—**1,** hindrance, obstruction, stoppage; interruption, interception, impedition; retardment, retardation; embarrassment, coarctation, stricture, restriction, RESTRAINT, embargo; deterrent, inhibition, PROHIBITION; blockade, CLOSURE; DIFFICULTY. *Colloq.,* fly in the ointment.

2, interference, interposition (see BETWEEN), obtrusion; disadvantage; discouragement, DISSUASION.

3, impediment, let, obstacle, obstruction, knot, check, hitch, snag, contretemps; drawback, objection; stumbling block, blind alley, ill wind; head wind,

OPPOSITION; trammel, hobble, tether; counterpoise; bar, stile, turnstile, barrier; barrage; buffer; gate, portcullis; barricade (see DEFENSE); [brick *or* stone] wall, breakwater; bulkhead, block, hurdle, buffer, stopper, boom, dam, floodgate, weir; embolism.

4, encumbrance; clog, drag, stay, stop, detent, catch; preventive, prophylactic; load, burden, onus, handicap, millstone, *impedimenta;* dead weight; lumber, pack; incubus, old man of the sea; remora; red herring, false trail.

5, contraception, birth control, planned parenthood; rhythm method, prophylactic, sheath, condom, pessary, diaphragm, coil, loop, I.U.D., oral contraceptive, jelly, suppository. *Slang,* rubber, safe.

6, damper, wet blanket, hinderer, marplot, killjoy, interloper; opponent (see OPPOSITION).

Verbs—**1,** hinder, impede, delay, detain; embarrass, interpose, interfere, meddle; keep, fend, stave, *or* ward off; obviate; avert, turn aside, draw off, nip in the bud; forestall, retard, slacken, check, let; counteract, countercheck; debar, foreclose, deter, estop, inhibit (see PROHIBITION); shackle, restrain (see RESTRAINT); restrict. *Colloq.,* drag one's feet. *Slang,* stonewall.

2, obstruct, stop, stay, bar, block [up]; barricade; bar the door, dam up, close (see CLOSURE); put on the brake, put a spoke in the wheel; put a stop to (see END); interrupt, intercept; oppose (see OPPOSITION); fence, hem, *or* hedge in, cut off; cramp, hamper; clog, [en]cumber; choke; saddle *or* load with, overload, trammel, tie one's hands; inconvenience, incommode, baffle, faze, discommode. *Slang,* gum up, throw a monkey wrench in the works. *Colloq.,* cross up.

3, handicap; thwart, foil, frustrate, disconcert, balk, baffle; spoil, mar, clip the wings of, cripple (see DETERIORATION); dishearten, dissuade, deter, discourage; discountenance, throw cold water *or* a wet blanket on; cut the ground from under one, nip in the bud, take the wind out of one's sails, hang up, undermine; be *or* stand in the way of; act as a drag, be a millstone around one's neck. *Colloq.,* cook one's goose, spike one's guns. *Slang,* cramp one's style, louse up.

Adjectives—hindering, preventive, forbidding, deterrent; obstructive, impeditive, interceptive; in the way of, unfavorable; onerous, burdensome, cumbersome, cumbrous; binding, blocking, obtrusive; hindered, waterlogged, heavy-laden; hard-pressed; in one's hair, inhibitory, preclusive; prophylactic.

Antonyms, see AID.

---

hinge, *n.* joint, pivot, center, axis; crisis. See CAUSE, JUNCTION.

hint, *n.* intimation, suggestion, allusion, reference, implication; tip, trace, reminder, insinuation. —*v.i.* suggest, allude, imply, intimate. See INFORMATION, MEMORY, DISCLOSURE.

hinterland, *n.* country; inland, backwoods. *Colloq.,* the sticks. See REGION.

hip, *adj., slang,* wise, in, on to; swinging, jazzy; bohemian. *Slang,* cool, gone, beat; with it, making the scene. See KNOWLEDGE.

hippie, *n., slang,* hipster, beat[nik], yippie; bohemian, nonconformist. *Slang,* [cool] cat, swinger; hepcat; hip chick. See UNCONFORMITY.

hire, *n.* rental, employment; fee, remuneration. —*v.* rent, lease; employ, engage. See COMMISSION, PRICE.

hireling, *n.* mercenary, henchman, minion, SERVANT.

hiss, *n.* sibilation, fizz, sizzle; spit. —*v.* sibilate, fizz, sizzle; condemn. See DISAPPROBATION, DISRESPECT.

history, *n.* RECORD, chronicle, annals, biography; story, narrative, memoirs, autobiography. See DESCRIPTION.

histrionic, *adj.* theatrical; affected, exaggerated, dramatic. See DRAMA, AFFECTATION.

hit, *n., colloq.,* SUCCESS, smash; favorite; popularity. —*v.* strike, club, batter; touch, contact, reach, find; knock, smite; *slang,* bump off. See ARRIVAL, IMPULSE, KILLING.

hitch, *n.* HINDRANCE, knot, obstruction, obstacle, inconvenience, impediment; interruption, pause, stop; tug, jerk, pull; limp, hobble; accident, mischance. See DIFFICULTY. —*v.* hobble, shuffle, limp; tie, knot, fasten, yoke; attach. See JUNCTION.

hitchhike, *v.i., colloq.,* hitch, thumb [a ride], bum a ride. See TRAVEL.

hither, *adv.* here, nearer. See DIRECTION.

hoard, *n.* collection, STORE, reserve, stock, supply, savings. —*v.* save, preserve, retain, STORE, amass; treasure; hide; accumulate, collect.

hoarse, *adj.* throaty, raucous, husky, thick, croaking. See ROUGHNESS.

hoary, *adj.* old, aged, venerable, ancient; frosty, white; gray[ed]. See AGE.

hoax, *n.* DECEPTION, trick; deceit, fraud, fakery, humbug, canard. —*v.t.* dupe, deceive, trick, fool, swindle. *Slang,* sell.

hobble, *n.* shackle, bond, binding. —*v.* limp, stagger; halt, bind, shackle, handicap, limit. See RESTRAINT, SLOWNESS, FAILURE.

hobby, *n.* avocation, AMUSEMENT, fad, whim.

hobnob, *v.i.* consort, associate, socialize, mix. *Colloq.,* pal around, chum, hang out with. See SOCIALITY.

hobo, *n.* tramp, drifter, vagabond, vagrant; beggar, freight-hopper, rodrider; knight of the road, rolling stone. *Slang,* bum[mer], deadbeat, bo[e], vag. See POPULACE, TRAVEL.

hocus-pocus, *n.* magic, sleight-of-hand, SORCERY; trickery, deceit, DECEPTION.

hodgepodge, *n.* MIXTURE, medley, conglomeration; stew, hash, jumble.

hog, *n.* pig, swine, boar, sow; beast; *colloq.,* glutton (see GLUTTONY). See ANIMAL.

hogwash, *n., colloq.,* trash, nonsense. See UNMEANINGNESS.

hoist, *n.* elevator, lift, derrick, crane. —*v.t.* lift, raise, jack, rear. See ELEVATION.

hold, *n.* grasp, clutch, grip; tenure, POSSESSION; control, INFLUENCE, domination; ownership, keeping; anchor, rein. —*v.* have, occupy, retain, own, possess; restrain, repress, control, pinion, curb; check, stop, interrupt, pause; clutch, grasp, grip, seize; pin, clip, fasten; believe, declare, opine, state, think; insist, persist; last, endure, continue; cling, cleave, stick, adhere; keep, defend, protect, guard. See BELIEF, COHERENCE, DEFENSE, DURABILITY, RESTRAINT, RETENTION, STORE, SUPPORT, COMPOSITION, AUTHORITY.

holding, *n.* property, POSSESSION, tenure; claim, interest.

holdup, *n., colloq.,* theft, [armed] robbery. *Slang,* stickup, hijack[ing], heist. See STEALING.

hole, *n.* OPENING, aperture, gap, cavity; excavation, hollow; slot, puncture; dungeon; cave; space. See CONCAVITY, ABODE, INTERVAL.

holiday, *n.* vacation, festival, CELEBRATION, recreation. See AMUSEMENT, REPOSE.

hollow, *n.* CONCAVITY, depression, dent, cavity, hole; valley, gully, basin; channel, groove, furrow. —*adj.* thin, unresonant; sepulchral, deep, empty, void, unfilled, vacant; unsound, weak, uncertain, unconvincing; specious, false, unsubstantiated, inadequate. See ABSENCE.

holocaust, *n.* immolation, burnt offering; massacre, pogrom. See DESTRUCTION, KILLING.

holy, *adj.* consecrated, saintly; blessed, sacred, godly. See PIETY, DEITY.

homage, *n.* RESPECT, tribute, honor; deference, allegiance, devotion, veneration; SUBMISSION, reverence. See OBEDIENCE, WORSHIP.

home, *n.* domicile, residence, ABODE, dwelling; shelter, refuge, asylum, sanctuary; habitat, habitation, environment; homeland, native land, fatherland, country, homeland. *Colloq.,* stateside. See OBEDIENCE.

homecoming, *n.* return, ARRIVAL, journey's end.

homeless, *adj.* unhoused; nomadic; outcast, desolate. See DISPLACEMENT.

homely, *adj.* plain; simple, homespun, rustic, unpretentious, down-to-earth. See SIMPLENESS, UGLINESS.

homesick, *adj.* nostalgic, pining [for home], melancholy. See REGRET.

homicide, *n.* KILLING, murder, manslaughter, assassination.

homogeneity, *n.* uniformity, similarity, likeness. See SIMPLENESS, CONFORMITY, UNITY.

homosexual, *n.* gay, lesbian.—*adj.* gay, lesbian, homophile, homoerotic. See UNCONFORMITY.

honesty, *n.* candor, frankness; sincerity; trustworthiness, uprightness; truthfulness, veracity, PROBITY.

honor, *n.* PROBITY, integrity; REPUTE, glory, title, distinction, award; worship, RESPECT, deference. —*v.t.* revere, reward; elevate; recognize; RESPECT; accept (as payable).

honorarium, *n.* fee; gratuity, tip; reward. See GIVING, PAYMENT.

honorary, *adj.* nominal, in name only, titular, gratuitous, emeritus. See CHEAPNESS, REPUTE.

hood, *n.* COVERING; cape, cowl, coif; *slang,* hoodlum, gangster. See CLOTHING, EVILDOER. —*v.t.* shield, cover, protect; camouflage; blindfold.

hoodoo, *n.* Jonah, bad luck, jinx; witchcraft, voodoo, obeah; SORCERY.

hoodwink, *v.t.* delude, deceive, fool, hoax; blind. See DECEPTION, BLINDNESS, CONCEALMENT.

hoof, *n.* foot, ungula, dewclaw. See SUPPORT. —*v.* See TRAVEL.

hook, *n.* CURVATURE, crook, bend; gaff. —*v.t.* catch, fasten; curve, bend; link, join. See CONNECTION, PENDENCY.

hookup, *n., colloq.,* connection, JUNCTION; circuit, rigging; tie-up, union, alliance, merger, cooperation, partnership. See COMMUNICATION.

hooligan, *n., slang,* loafer; thug, strong-arm man, tough, ruffian. See EVILDOER.

hoop, *n.* ring, band. See CIRCULARITY.

hooray, *interj.* See REJOICING.

hop, *n.,* LEAP, spring; *colloq.,* dance. —*v.i.* jump, LEAP, bounce, spring, bound, dance. See AMUSEMENT.

HOPE

Nouns—**1,** hope, hopes, DESIRE; trust, confidence, optimism, reliance, faith, BELIEF; assurance, secureness, security; reassurance. See SAFETY.

2, good omen *or* auspices, promise; good, fair, *or* bright prospect; clear sky; ray of hope, cheer; silver lining; Pandora's box, balm in Gilead. *Slang,* pie in the sky.

3, assumption, presumption; anticipation, EXPECTATION; hopefulness, buoyancy, optimism, enthusiasm, aspiration.

4, castles in the air *or* in Spain, pot of gold at the end of the rainbow; Utopia, millennium, hope of Heaven; daydream, airy hopes, fool's paradise; mirage, chimera. See IMAGINATION.

5, optimist, Pollyanna; aspirant.

Verbs—**1,** hope, trust, confide, rely on, lean upon; pin one's hopes upon (see BELIEF); feel *or* rest assured, feel confident.

2, DESIRE, wish, anticipate; look on the bright side of, see the sunny side, make the best of it, hope for the best; put a good face upon; keep one's spirits up; take heart, be of good cheer; flatter oneself.

3, hope against hope, cross one's fingers, clutch *or* grasp at straws, count one's chickens before they are hatched, knock on wood; make a virtue of necessity.

4, give hope, encourage, cheer, [re]assure, buoy up, embolden; be hopeful, see daylight; promise, bid fair, augur well, look up.

Adjectives—**1,** hoping, in hopes, hopeful, confident; secure, certain (see BELIEF); starry-eyed; sanguine, in good heart, buoyed up, buoyant, elated, flushed, exultant, enthusiastic; fearless, undespairing, self-reliant.

2, within sight of; promising, propitious; of good omen; auspicious, encouraging, cheering, bright, rosy, roseate, rose-colored.

Adverbs—at [the] best, at worst.

Antonyms, see HOPELESSNESS.

HOPELESSNESS

Nouns—**1,** hopelessness, futility, IMPOSSIBILITY; despair, desperation; despondency, DEJECTION; pessimism; hope deferred, dashed hopes; vain expectation, DISAPPOINTMENT. *Slang,* fat chance. See USELESSNESS.

2, forlorn hope, ghost of a chance; bad job; slough of despond, cave of despair. *Slang,* dead duck.

3, pessimist, Job's comforter, bird of ill omen; cynic, killjoy.

Verbs—lose hope, lose heart, despair, give up *or* over; falter; despond, throw up one's hands, give way. *Colloq.,* throw in the towel *or* sponge.

Adjectives—**1,** hopeless, desperate, despairing, despondent, in despair, forlorn, inconsolable, dejected, brokenhearted.

2, out of the question, not to be thought of, futile, impracticable, impossible (see IMPOSSIBILITY); beyond hope, past mending, past recall; at the end of one's rope *or* tether, at one's wits' end; given up, incurable, beyond remedy, irreparable, irremediable; ruined, undone. *Colloq.,* all up.

Antonyms, see HOPE.

---

horde, *n.* mass, group, throng, mob, gang, crowd, pack. See MULTITUDE, ASSEMBLAGE, POPULACE.

horizon, *n.* skyline, sea line, azimuth, edge of the world; limit, circumscription, scope, range, sphere; reach; prospect, outlook. See EXPECTATION, DISTANCE.

HORIZONTAL

Nouns—**1,** horizontality, horizontalness, flatness; level, plane; stratum (see LAYER); horizon, azimuth; recumbency, lying down, reclination, proneness, supination, prostration; SMOOTHNESS.

2, plane surface; floor, platform, [billiard] table; terrace, esplanade, parterre, tableland, plain, plateau, prairie, ledge; plate, platter; tablet, slab; sea level.

Verbs—**1,** be horizontal, lie, recline, couch; lie down *or* flat; sprawl, loll.

2, lay [down *or* out]; level, flatten, smooth, even, equalize, align; steamroll[er], iron, press; prostrate, knock down, floor, fell, bowl over.

Adjectives—horizontal, level, even, plane, flush; flat [as a pancake *or* flounder], on an even keel; alluvial; calm; smooth as glass; recumbent, lying, prone, supine, couchant, prostrate.

Adverbs—horizontally, on a level, on one's back; on all fours.

Antonyms, see VERTICAL.

---

horn, *n.* antler, cornu, callus, nail; saddle horn, pummel, pommel; blower, tooter, tin horn, ram's horn, shofar, French horn, trumpet, *etc.* (see MUSIC); horn of plenty, cornucopia; powder horn. See HARDNESS, SHARPNESS, RECEPTACLE.

horny, *adj.* tough, callous[ed], sclerotic; *slang,* oversexed, lecherous, lascivious. *Slang,* hard up. See HARDNESS, DESIRE.

horrible, *adj.* alarming, dreadful, horrifying, appalling, frightful, horrendous, hideous, abominable, deplorable, revolting, execrable, dire. See FEAR.

horrid, *adj.* horrible, foul, shocking; troublesome, vexatious; nasty, bratty; unpleasant, disagreeable. See UGLINESS, BADNESS.

horror, *n.* terror; loathing, disgust, revulsion; detestation, abhorrence; dread, aversion. See HATE, FEAR.

hors d'oeuvres, *n.pl.* appetizers, canapés, antipasto, smorgasbord. See FOOD.

horse, *n.* equine; stallion, mare, colt, filly, foal, gelding; steed, mount; trotter, pacer, hackney; nag, hack, pony, charger, courser; dobbin, jennet; cavalry; sawhorse; bronco, mustang, cayuse; Arab. See ANIMAL, TRANSPORTATION, COMBATANT.

horseman, *n.* equestrian, rider; cavalryman, chevalier, jockey. See TRAVEL, COMBATANT.

hose, *n.* hosing, tubing; stockings, socks; tights, leotard. See CLOTHING, PASSAGE. —*v.t.* spray, sprinkle, WATER; extinguish, put out. See CLEANNESS.

hospice, *n.* shelter, retreat, rest house. See ABODE, SAFETY.

hospitable, *adj.* neighborly; receptive. See FRIEND, SOCIALITY.

hospital, *n.* sanitarium, sanatorium; clinic, pesthouse, infirmary. See REMEDY.

hospitality, *n.* SOCIALITY, cordiality, welcome, entertainment. See LIBERALITY.

host, *n.* MULTITUDE, throng, mass, horde, army, legion, array; element; innkeeper, boniface, hostess. See COMBATANT, RITE, SOCIALITY.

hostage, *n.* SECURITY, pledge, guarantee, bond.

hostel, *n.* shelter, lodgings; hotel, hostelry; hospice. See ABODE.

hostile, *adj.* antagonistic, opposed, warlike, unfriendly, belligerent. See OPPOSITION, HATE.

hot, *adj.* heated (see HEAT); peppery, biting. See TASTE, EXCITABILITY, PUNGENCY.

hotbed, *n.* source, CAUSE, generator, inciter; trouble spot, powderkeg.

hotel, *n.* inn, hostelry. See ABODE.

hotheaded, *adj.* hot, hotblooded, passionate; quick-tempered, peppery, irascible; willful, headstrong, rash, impetuous. See RASHNESS, IRASCIBILITY, EXCITABILITY.

hound, *n.* dog, beagle, basset, bloodhound, dachshund, greyhound, foxhound, *etc.; slang,* cur, wretch. See ANIMAL. —*v.t.* plague, worry, pursue, harass, bait, persecute; hunt; drive, incite. See MALEVOLENCE, PURSUIT.

hourly, *adj.* frequent, continual. See FREQUENCY.

house, *n.* ABODE, residence; chamber, legislature; firm, organization, company; family, ANCESTRY, lineage. See BUSINESS. —*v.t.* shelter, protect; cover, contain, harbor. See PARTY, COVERING.

housebroken, *adj.* tamed, domesticated, trained, disciplined. See DOMESTICATION.

household, *n.* establishment; domicile, family. See ABODE.

housekeeping, *n.* housewifery, ménage, ECONOMY.

housing, *n.* shelter, lodging; frame, COVERING. See ABODE, SUPPORT.

hovel, *n.* shanty, hut, cabin, shack,

den, shed. See ABODE.

hover, *v.i.* fly; poise, hang, linger; waver, vacillate. See DOUBT, NEARNESS.

how, *adv.* whereby, wherewith, why, however. See MEANS, COMPENSATION.

howl, *n.* bellow, shriek, yowl, bay, keen. —*v.i.* wail, complain, ululate, bawl, yowl. See CRY, LAMENTATION, WIND.

hub, *n.* center, midpoint, axis, focus, MIDDLE; nave.

hubbub, *n.* tumult, uproar, racket, disturbance, din. See LOUDNESS.

huddle, *v.i.* crowd, group, gather, bunch, collect. See ASSEMBLAGE, CONVERSATION, DISORDER.

hue, *n.* COLOR, tint, shade; tone, complexion, tinge.

huff, *n.* pique, nettle, tiff; offense, umbrage, petulance, tantrum, the sulks. See IRASCIBILITY, RESENTMENT.

hug, *v.* caress, embrace, enfold, clasp; cherish; press, fit. See LOVE, NEARNESS, ENDEARMENT.

huge, *adj.* gargantuan, enormous, gigantic, immense. See SIZE.

hull, *n.* husk, shell, calyx, COVERING. *v.t.* shuck (see DIVESTMENT).

hullabaloo, *n.* uproar, EXCITEMENT; publicity, ballyhoo, CRY.

hum, *n.* buzz, murmur, drone, bumble. —*v.i.* thrum, drone, buzz, murmur, croon, burr; sing. See REPETITION.

human, *adj.* mortal; earthly; humane, civilized. —*n.* man, woman, child, girl, boy; earthling. See HUMANITY.

humane, *adj.* kind, merciful, tender, sympathetic; civilized. See BENEVOLENCE, PITY.

HUMANITY

Nouns—**1,** humanity, human race, human species, *homo sapiens,* humankind; mankind, man, womankind; human nature, mortality, flesh [and blood], feet of clay; generation.

2, anthropology, anthropography, ethnography, ethnology, sociology.

3, human [being]; person, individual, creature, fellow creature; mortal; somebody, one; [living] soul; earthling; party; MALE, man; FEMALE, woman.

4, people; persons, folk; [African, Caucasian, Mongolian, *or* Australasian] race, nation; public, society, world, [world] community, general public, nationality, state, realm, commonweal[th], republic, body politic, population, POPULACE. See INHABITANT.

Adjectives—human; android, anthropoid; ethnic, racial; mortal, personal, individual; national, civil, communal, public, social; cosmopolitan, universal.

Antonyms, see ANIMAL.

---

humble, *adj.* lowly, unassuming, modest (see HUMILITY); poor, obscure, paltry, mean. —*v.t.* abase, shame, humiliate. See MODESTY, OBSCURITY, PIETY.

humbug, *n.* deceiver, imposter, pretender; DECEPTION, hoax, fraud; charlatanry. See FALSEHOOD.

humdrum, *adj.* dull, routine, monotonous, prosaic, tiresome; ordinary, unremarkable. See WEARINESS.

humid, *adj.* moist, damp, wet, dank. See MOISTURE.

humiliate, *v.t.* shame, degrade, debase, demean; humble (see HUMILITY). See DISREPUTE.

HUMILITY

Nouns—**1,** humility, humbleness; meekness, lowliness, lowness; [self-]abasement; SUBMISSION, resignation; MODESTY, blush, suffusion, confusion.

2, humiliation, degradation, mortification; letdown, comedown, setdown;

condescension, affability (see COURTESY). *Slang,* comeuppance. See SERVILITY.

Verbs—**1,** be humble, deign, vouchsafe, condescend; humble *or* demean oneself, stoop, submit; yield the palm; lower one's tone, sober down; not have a word to say for oneself; lose face, feel shame, eat dirt, crow, *or* humble pie; blush, redden, change color; swallow one's pride, hang one's head, come down off one's high horse, look foolish, feel small. *Colloq.,* sing small, draw in one's horns.

2, humble, humiliate, abase; let, set, *or* take down; bring to one's knees, cut down to size, put in one's place, put into the shade (see DISREPUTE); discountenance, stare out of countenance; confuse, mortify, deflate, disgrace, crush; take down a peg *or* notch.

Adjectives—humble, lowly, meek; modest, soberminded; unoffended; submissive, servile (see SERVILITY); humbled, downcast, bowed down, resigned, abashed, ashamed, dashed; out of countenance; down in the mouth; on one's knees, browbeaten; democratic, affable.

Adverbs—humbly, meekly, with one's tail between one's legs, with downcast eyes, on bended knee; on all fours.

Antonyms, see PRIDE.

---

humor, *n.* disposition, mood, temper; caprice, drollery, WIT; fun; jest; choler, melancholy, depression, anger; facetiousness. See FEELING. —*v.t.* indulge, favor, oblige, gratify. See PERMISSION, TENDENCY, FLATTERY.

humorist, *n.* comedian (see WIT).

hump, *n.* hunch, lump, bulge, knob, excrescence; humpback; pile, heap; ridge, hill. See CONVEXITY.

hunch, *n., colloq.,* intimation, sense, feeling; inkling, notion, SUPPOSITION, hint, intuition, guess.

hunger, *n.* DESIRE, craving; famine, hungriness, emptiness; appetite, voracity, greed. —*v.i.* DESIRE, crave, yearn; famish, starve. See GLUTTONY.

hunk, *n., colloq.,* piece, PART, chunk, clab, lump, mass. *Colloq.,* chaw.

hunt, *n.* chase, drag; PURSUIT, search. —*v.t.* chase, stalk, follow, trace, pursue, run, trail, hound. —*v.i.* shoot, poach, trap, snare, hawk, ferret. See INQUIRY.

hurdle, *n.* DIFFICULTY, HINDRANCE, snag, impediment; problem, obstacle, challenge.

hurl, *v.t.* throw, project, pitch, toss, fling, cast, dart. See PROPULSION.

hurricane, *n.* tempest, cyclone, typhoon, whirlwind; VIOLENCE, furor. See WIND.

hurry, *v.* press, rush, drive, force; hasten, speed, accelerate, quicken, facilitate, scurry. See HASTE, EXPEDITION.

hurt, *n.* damage, PAIN, ache, injury, wound, bruise, offense; loss, harm; distress, grief. —*v.* ache, PAIN, throb; injure, wound; damage, harm; offend, distress, grieve, bruise. See MALEVOLENCE, DETERIORATION, EVIL.

hurtful, *adj.* injurious, harmful. See BADNESS.

hurtle, *v.i.* rush, strike. See IMPULSE.

husband, *n.* mate, spouse; benedict, bridegroom; man. See MARRIAGE. —*v.* economize (see ECONOMY, RETENTION).

husbandry, *n.* frugality, ECONOMY; farming, AGRICULTURE. See CONDUCT.

hush, *n.* SILENCE, quiet, stillness, calm. —*v.t.* calm, stifle, muffle; soothe, allay, still; hide, suppress. See CONCEALMENT, MODERATION.

husk, *n.* shell, integument, rind, skin. See COVERING.

husky, *adj.* strong, sturdy, powerful, robust, healthy; harsh, throaty, hoarse. See STRENGTH, DRYNESS.

hussy, *n.* wanton, trollop, wench, tramp, slut, baggage. See IMPURITY.

hustle, *v.* jostle, jolt, poke, prod; rush, bustle, hasten; *slang,* push, promote, advertise; *slang,* con, swindle, fleece, deceive, inveigle, lead on, take, sucker, sell a bill of goods; *slang,* solicit, walk the streets. See DECEPTION, HASTE.

hustler, *n., colloq.,* go-getter, live wire, dynamo; *slang,* gambler, swindler, sharp[er]; *slang,* prostitute. See ACTIVITY, STEALING, IMPURITY.

hut, *n.* shack, shanty, hogan, hovel, shelter, cabin. See ABODE.

hybrid, *n.* MIXTURE, crossbreed, cross, mongrel; mestizo, mulatto, quadroon, octoroon, half-caste, half-breed, Creole. *—adj.* mixed, crossbred; mongrel; half-blooded. See UNCONFORMITY.

hygienic, *adj.* cleanly, sanitary, uncontaminated; wholesome, salutary; clean. See HEALTH, CLEANNESS.

hymn, *n.* song of praise *or* devotion; hallelujah, hosanna; canticle, sacred song, spiritual; psalm, paean; psalmody; chant, plainsong; anthem; response; evensong, vespers, matins; noël, nowell, Christmas carol. See RELIGION, MUSIC.

hypnotic, *adj.* mesmeric, fascinating, magnetic; soporific, narcotic, quieting, lethargic; irresistible. See SORCERY.

hypocrisy, *n.* deceit, dissembling, pretense, falsity, insincerity; sanctimony, cant, Phariseeism. See FALSEHOOD, IMPIETY.

hypothesis, *n.* condition, SUPPOSITION, theory, postulate, assumption.

hysterical, *adj.* uncontrolled, wild, emotional; convulsive; frenzied, frenetic. See EXCITABILITY.

I

ice, *n.* frost, rime; glacier; sherbet; icicle; *slang,* diamonds. *—v.* freeze, chill. See COLD.

iceberg, *n.* berg, floe, ice pack *or* sheet, glacier. See COLD.

icebox, *n.* refrigerator, Frigidaire. See COLD.

icy, *adj.* frosty, COLD.

idea, *n.* THOUGHT, concept, notion; opinion, conceit, BELIEF, impression; principle; invention, imagination.

ideal, *n.* model, paragon; idol, hero; perfect example. *—adj.* visionary; unattainable, Platonic, abstract, Utopian, perfect; impracticable. See IMAGINATION, NONEXISTENCE, PERFECTION.

idealist, *n.* visionary, dreamer; perfectionist, Utopian. See IMAGINATION, PERFECTION.

identify, *v.t.* recognize, distinguish, put one's finger on; associate; name. See MEMORY, IDENTITY, NOMENCLATURE.

IDENTITY

Nouns—**1,** identity, identicalness, oneness, sameness; coincidence, coalescence; convertibility; EQUALITY; identification; monotony, synonymity; tautology (see REPETITION); synonym, facsimile (see COPY); *alter ego* (see SIMILARITY); very *or* actual thing, no other, as much. See UNITY, INTRINSIC.

2, selfness, self, individuality, SPECIALITY; very thing; no other; personality; oneself, I, ego, myself, himself, *etc.*

Verbs—be identical, coincide, coalesce; treat as *or* render the same *or* identical; diagnose, identify; recognize the identity of.

Adjectives—identical; the same, selfsame, very same, one and the same; coincident, coalescent, coalescing; indistinguishable; one; synonymous, analogous, equivalent (see EQUALITY); much the same, much of a muchness; unaltered; tantamount.

Adverbs—each, apiece, one by one, in detail; identically, to scale.

Antonyms, see DIFFERENCE.

idiocy, *n.* imbecility, vacuity, cretinism, feeblemindedness; foolishness, vapidity, senselessness. See INSANITY, FOLLY.

idiom, *n.* dialect; language; idiotism, phrase. See SPEECH.

idle, *adj.* vain, useless, futile, fruitless, pointless, aimless; out of work, unemployed, inactive, at rest; vacant, empty. See INACTIVITY, USELESSNESS, UNIMPORTANCE.

IDOLATRY

Nouns—**1,** idolatry, idolism; demonism, demonolatry; idol, demon, devil, fire, *or* sun worship; zoölatry, fetishism; bibliolatry; deification, apotheosis, canonization; hero worship; animism. See HETERODOXY.

2, sacrifice, hecatomb, holocaust; human sacrifice, immolation, infanticide, self-immolation, suttee.

3, idolater, idol worshiper, devil worshiper, *etc.*

4, idol, golden calf, sacred cow, graven image, fetish, avatar, *lares et penates,* household gods.

Verbs—idolatrize, idolize, WORSHIP (idols, pictures, relics); deify; canonize, make sacrifice.

Adjectives—idolatrous, pagan, heathen; hero-worshiping.

Antonyms, see RELIGION, PIETY.

if, *conj.* supposing, in case that, provided; whether. See SUPPOSITION, QUALIFICATION.

ignition, *n.* firing, kindling; combustion. See HEAT.

ignoble, *adj.* vile, base; knavish; detestable, low, common. See VULGARITY, POPULACE, DISREPUTE.

ignominious, *adj.* shameful, disgraceful; degrading, humiliating. See DISREPUTE.

ignoramus, *n.* See IGNORANCE.

IGNORANCE

Nouns—**1,** ignorance, nescience; illiteracy; darkness, blindness; incomprehension, inexperience, simplicity, simpleness, INNOCENCE; stupidity; unawareness. See FOLLY, INSANITY, SHALLOWNESS.

2, unknown quantity, sealed book, *terra incognita,* virgin soil, unexplored ground; dark ages.

3, smattering, glimmering; dilettantism, superficiality; bewilderment (see DOUBT); incapacity; blind spot. See UNSKILLFULNESS.

4, innocent, ignoramus, dunce, dolt, know-nothing, dullard, moron; simpleton, oaf, lout, clod, bonehead, blockhead, halfwit, dimwit, idiot; greenhorn, novice (see BEGINNING). *Colloq.,* dummy. *Slang,* lowbrow, nitwit, dumbbell, dope, stupe.

Verbs—**1,** be ignorant, not know, have no idea, conception, *or* notion, not have the remotest idea; not know from Adam; ignore, be blind to; see through a glass darkly; not know what to make of. *Colloq.,* fly blind.

2, keep in the dark *or* in ignorance (see CONCEALMENT).

Adjectives—**1,** ignorant; unknowing, unaware, incognizant, unacquainted; unapprised, unwitting, witless; a stranger to; unconversant; uninformed, uncultivated, unversed, uninstructed, unlettered, none the wiser, uneducated, untaught, uninitiated, untutored, unschooled, unguided, unenlightened, crass; behind the times; in the dark, benighted; hoodwinked, misinformed; at sea (see DOUBT). *Colloq.,* out of it.

2, shallow, superficial, green, rude, empty, half-learned, illiterate; stupid, half-witted.

Adverbs—ignorantly, unaware[s], for anything one knows; not that one knows.

Antonyms, see KNOWLEDGE, INTELLIGENCE.

---

ignore, *v.t.* overlook, pass by, disregard; slight, omit, NEGLECT; snub.

ilk, *n.* kind, family, CLASS.

ill, *adj.* unwell, sick, indisposed; nauseous. See DISEASE. *—adv.* poorly, badly; wrongly, improperly; clumsily. See UNSKILLFULNESS, BADNESS. *—n.* See EVIL.

ill-advised, *adj.* unwise, imprudent. See FOLLY.

ill-bred, *adj.* unmannerly, impolite; boorish, rude, coarse, uncouth; ignoble, base. See DISCOURTESY, POPULACE.

ILLEGALITY

Nouns—**1,** illegality, lawlessness, unlawfulness, unconstitutionality; illegitimacy, bar sinister, bastardy; criminality; outlawry; extralegality; criminology. See DISOBEDIENCE, UNCONFORMITY, PROHIBITION, IMPROBITY, WRONG.

2, VIOLENCE, brute force; tyranny, despotism; mob, lynch, martial, *or* drumhead law, law of the streets, kangaroo court; anarchy, nihilism, law unto itself; rebellion, *coup d'état, Putsch,* REVOLUTION.

3, offense, crime, transgression, infringement, felony, misdemeanor, violation, breach, contravention, delinquency.

4, racketeering, confidence *or* bunco game, swindling, *etc.;* underworld. See DECEPTION.

5, undueness, invalidity, impropriety, absence of right, usurpation, encroachment.

6, criminal, outlaw, scofflaw (see EVILDOER); bastard, natural child.

Verbs—offend against, break, flout, contravene, *or* violate the law; take the law into one's own hands; smuggle, run, poach, encroach, usurp (see STEALING).

Adjectives—illegal, prohibited, unsanctioned, not allowed, *verboten, interdit,* unlawful, outlaw[ed], illegitimate, illicit, contraband, actionable, criminal, unchartered, unlicensed, unconstitutional; undue, unwarranted, unwarrantable; unauthorized, invalid; crooked, dishonest (see IMPROBITY); informal, unofficial, injudicial, extrajudicial; lawless, arbitrary, licentious; despotic, summary, irresponsible; unanswerable, unaccountable; null and void; bastard, born out of wedlock. *Slang,* hot.

Adverbs—illegally; with a high hand; in violation; outside *or* beyond the law.

Antonyms, see LEGALITY.

---

illegible, *adj.* unreadable, ill-written, scrawled; jumbled, pied. See UNINTELLIGIBILITY.

illegitimate, *adj.* See ILLEGALITY.

ill-fated, *adj.* ill-starred, doomed; unlucky. See ADVERSITY.

ill-gotten, *adj.* See IMPROBITY.

illicit, *adj.* illegal (see ILLEGALITY); clandestine, SECRET.

illiterate, *adj.* unlettered, unlearned. See IGNORANCE.

ill-mannered, *adj.* ill-bred, rude, coarse, boorish. See DISCOURTESY.

illness, *n.* sickness, DISEASE.

illogical, *adj.* unreasoned, fallacious, specious, implausible, absurd. See ERROR, ABSURDITY.

ill-treatment, *n.* abuse, cruelty, mistreatment, maltreatment; manhandling; carelessness. See MALEVOLENCE, SEVERITY, WRONG.

illuminate, *v.t.* LIGHT, illumine; clarify, elucidate, explain; decorate, ORNAMENT. See INTERPRETATION, COLOR.

illusion, *n.* delusion, hallucination, VISION, apparition; chimera, mirage, bubble, figment [of the mind *or* IMAGINATION]; dream, fool's paradise; misconception, self-delusion, ERROR; legerdemain. See DECEPTION.

illustrate, *v.t.* decorate; give as an example, exemplify; explain, clarify. See ORNAMENT, INTERPRETATION, PAINTING, REPRESENTATION.

illustrious, *adj.* renowned, eminent, distinguished, famous, celebrated. See REPUTE.

image, *n.* picture, reflection, double, counterpart, likeness; portrait, statue, figure; idea, concept. See SIMILARITY, APPEARANCE, REPRESENTATION, FIGURATIVE.

imagery, *n.* invention, fancy; tropes, metaphors, similes, analogies. See REPRESENTATION, FIGURATIVE.

IMAGINATION

Nouns—**1,** imagination, imaginativeness, originality, invention, fancy, creativeness, inspiration; mind's eye; verve, improvisation.

2, ideality, idealism; romanticism, utopianism, castle-building; dreaming; reverie, trance, somnambulism. See NONEXISTENCE, INSUBSTANTIALITY.

3, conception, concept, excogitation (see THOUGHT); cloudland, wonderland, dreamland, fairyland; flight of fancy, pipedream; brainstorm, brainchild; imagery; conceit, figment [of the imagination]; myth, dream, vision, shadow, chimera; phantasm, unreality, illusion, hallucination, mirage, fantasy; whim, whimsy; vagary, rhapsody, romance, extravaganza; bugbear, nightmare; castles in the air *or* Spain; Utopia, Atlantis, happy valley, millennium; fabrication, creation, coinage; fiction, stretch of the imagination (see EXAGGERATION).

4, imaginer, idealist, romanticist, visionary; romancer, dreamer; enthusiast; rainbow-chaser; tilter at windmills.

Verbs—imagine, fancy, conceive, visualize; idealize, realize; drum, make, *or* think up, dream (up), pull out of a hat; daydream; create, originate, cook up, devise, hatch, formulate, invent, coin, fabricate; improvise; set one's wits to work, strain one's imagination; rack, ransack, *or* cudgel one's brains; excogitate, work up, think out; give play to the imagination, indulge in reverie; conjure up a vision; suggest itself (see THOUGHT). *Colloq.,* see stars, see things.

Adjectives—imagined, made-up, imaginary; starry-eyed; imagining, imaginative; original, inventive, creative, fertile, fecund; fictitious; fabulous, legendary, mythical, mythological; chimerical, visionary; notional; fancy, fanciful, fantastic[al]; whimsical; fairy, fairylike; romantic, high-flown, flighty, extravagant, out of this world, enthusiastic, Utopian, quixotic; ideal, unreal, in the clouds; unsubstantial, out of thin air (see INSUBSTANTIALITY); illusory (see ERROR).

Antonyms, see TRUTH, WEARINESS.

imbalance, *n.* INEQUALITY, asymmetry, instability; difference, disparity.

imbecility, *n.* idiocy. See INSANITY.

imbue, *v.t.* saturate; tinge, COLOR, suffuse; instill, inspire. See TEACHING, MIXTURE.

IMITATION

Nouns—**1,** imitation; quotation, paraphrase, parody, travesty, burlesque; COPY, forgery (see FALSEHOOD); mockery, mimicry; simulation, pretense, sham, impersonation, imposture; REPRESENTATION; semblance; assimilation. *Colloq.*, take-off, Simon says, follow the leader.

2, model, prototype, pattern, mock-up; exemplar, paragon, original; type, standard. See CONFORMITY.

3, imitator, mimic, cuckoo, parrot, ape, monkey, mockingbird; counterfeiter, forger. *Colloq.*, copycat.

Verbs—imitate, COPY, catch; match, parallel; mock, take off, mimic, parrot, ape, simulate, [im]personate; act (see DRAMA); represent (see REPRESENTATION); counterfeit, parody, travesty, caricature, burlesque; feign, dissemble (see FALSEHOOD); follow, pattern after; follow suit; take after, model after; emulate, follow in one's footsteps *or* tracks.

Adjectives—imitated, imitating; mock; mimic; modeled after, molded on; quasi, pseudo; paraphrastic; literal; imitative; secondhand; imitable, unoriginal.

Adverbs—imitatively; literally, to the letter, *verbatim, literatim; sic;* word for word.

Antonyms, see UNCONFORMITY, IDENTITY.

---

immaculate, *adj.* clean, spotless, unsullied; chaste, pure, virgin, untouched. See CLEANNESS, PURITY, INNOCENCE, PERFECTION.

immanent, *adj.* INTRINSIC, innate, inherent; universal (as God).

immaterial, *adj.* unsubstantial, incorporeal, disembodied; impalpable, intangible; irrelevant, impertinent; trivial, unimportant, inconsequential. See INSUBSTANTIALITY, UNIMPORTANCE.

immature, *adj.* half-grown; unripe, green; undeveloped; raw, callow, young, hebetic; unready. See UNPREPAREDNESS, YOUTH, IMPERFECTION, NEWNESS.

immeasurable, *adj.* limitless (see INFINITY).

immediate, *adj.* prompt, instant, PRESENT; next, first. See EARLINESS, INSTANTANEITY.

immemorial, *adj.* prehistoric, beyond recollection. See OLDNESS.

immense, *adj.* vast, great, huge, infinite. See SIZE, INFINITY.

immerse, *v.* bathe, dip, baptize, duck, plunge, submerge. See WATER, INSERTION.

immigrant, *n.* newcomer, settler, colonist. See INGRESS.

imminent, *adj.* impending, close at hand, about to occur; near, threatening. See EARLINESS, APPROACH, EXPECTATION, THREAT.

immobile, *adj.* immovable; motionless. See STABILITY, REPOSE.

immoderate, *adj.* intemperate, excessive, extreme, extravagant. See INTEMPERANCE.

immodest, *adj.* forward, bold, vain (see VANITY); suggestive, risqué, revealing, low-cut; unseemly, indecorous, indecent. *Slang,* sexy. See IMPURITY.

immoral, *adj.* WRONG, EVIL; corrupt, lewd, bawdy; dissolute, licentious, loose, indecent, adulterous. See IMPURITY.

immortal, *adj.* everlasting; divine, godlike; deathless, imperishable. See DURABILITY, PERPETUITY.—*n.* [demi]god, great man. See REPUTE.

immovable, *adj.* fixed, unbudging; firm, steadfast, rocklike; stubborn, obdurate. See STABILITY.

immunity, *n.* EXEMPTION, FREEDOM (from); privilege.

imp, *n.* devil, DEMON; brat, YOUTH.

impact, *n.* brunt, shock, percussion, collision; contact, TOUCH, bump, slam. See IMPULSE.

impair, *v.t.* damage, weaken, wear [out], spoil, mar; vitiate. See DETERIORATION, WEAKNESS.

impale, *v.t.* transfix, pierce. See OPENING.

impart, *v.t.* share, lend; tell, disclose, divulge, reveal, communicate. See GIVING, INFORMATION.

impartial, *adj.* nonpartisan; unprejudiced, unbiased, fair; dispassionate, disinterested. See PROBITY, JUSTICE, LIBERALITY.

impasse, *n.* deadlock; blind alley, stone wall, dead end; standstill. See DIFFICULTY.

impassioned, *adj.* ardent, fervent, heated, passionate, frenzied, excited. See EXCITEMENT.

impassive, *adj.* stolid, phlegmatic, stoical, calm, undemonstrative. See INSENSIBILITY.

impatient, *adj.* eager, hurried, restive, restless; anxious, uneasy, intolerant. See EXCITABILITY, HASTE, DESIRE.

impeach, *v.t.* accuse, charge, indict, arraign; censure, cite, impute; try, court-martial. See ACCUSATION, LAWSUIT.

impeccable, *adj.* faultless, irreproachable (see PERFECTION).

impediment, *n.* HINDRANCE, obstacle.

impel, *v.t.* drive, push, urge; force, constrain; incite, compel, induce. See IMPULSE, MOTION.

impend, *v.i.* threaten, hang over. See APPROACH, THREAT, DESTINY.

impenetrable, *adj.* solid, dense; impermeable, impassable; proof; abstruse, mysterious, esoteric; incomprehensible, unfathomable. See DENSITY, UNINTELLIGIBILITY.

IMPENITENCE

Nouns—impenitence, irrepentance, recusance, remorselessness, gracelessness, incorrigibility; hardness of heart, induration, obduracy.

Verbs—harden the heart, steel oneself.

Adjectives—impenitent, uncontrite, obdurate; hard[ened]; seared, recusant; unrepentant; relentless, remorseless, graceless, shriftless; lost, incorrigible, irreclaimable; unreclaimed, unreformed; unrepented, unatoned.

Adverbs—impenitently; without regret, remorse, *or* qualms.

Antonyms, see PENITENCE.

---

imperative, *adj.* peremptory; obligatory, essential, necessary, compulsory; unavoidable. *—n.* command; imperative mood (see GRAMMAR). *Colloq.,* a must. See NECESSITY, DUTY.

imperceptible, *adj.* unnoticeable, indistinguishable; slight, minute, indiscerncernible. See INVISIBILITY, LITTLENESS.

IMPERFECTION

Nouns—**1,** imperfection, imperfectness, incompleteness, faultiness; deficiency; inadequacy, INSUFFICIENCY, peccancy (see BADNESS); immaturity; MEDIOCRITY, shortcoming, INFERIORITY; UGLINESS.

2, fault, defect, weak point; mar, blemish; flaw, snag, taint, stigma, attainder; bar sinister; WEAKNESS; half-blood; failing, foible, feet of clay; drawback, catch. *Colloq.,* no great shakes; fly in the ointment. *Slang,* bug.

3, deformity, disfigurement (see DISTORTION).

Verbs—**1,** not measure up, not pass muster, fall *or* come short, miss the mark, not come up to par.

2, impair, damage, mar (see DETERIORATION).

Adjectives—**1,** imperfect, deficient, defective; faulty, unsound, tainted; crude, jerry-built; out of order, out of tune; cracked, leaky; sprung; warped (see DISTORTION); lame, injured (see DETERIORATION); peccant, bad (see BADNESS); frail, weak, infirm; below par. *Colloq.,* not up to scratch, not much to boast of. *Slang,* on the blink; fouled (up), snafu.

2, blemished, pitted, discolored, impaired, marred, deformed.

Adverbs—imperfectly, almost, to a limited extent, rather (see LITTLENESS); pretty, only; considering, all things considered (see NEARNESS).

Antonyms, see PERFECTION.

---

imperialism, *n.* colonialism, expansionism; exploitation, "the White man's burden"; communism, capitalism. See AUTHORITY.

imperil, *v.t.* endanger, jeopardize, risk. See DANGER.

imperishable, *adj.* everlasting, indestructible, permanent, undying, immortal. See PERPETUITY.

impersonal, *adj.* removed, distant; impartial, fair, businesslike; general, abstract, unemotional. See GENERALITY, INSENSIBILITY, EXTRINSIC, JUSTICE.

impersonate, *v.t.* pose (as), imitate, take off, mimic; personify, play the impostor. See REPRESENTATION, DRAMA, IMITATION.

impertinent, *adj.* insolent, saucy, fresh, cheeky, impudent; irrelevant, inapt, inapposite. See INSOLENCE, DISAGREEMENT.

imperturbable, *adj.* See INEXCITABILITY.

impervious, *adj.* impenetrable, impermeable; safe, proof; invulnerable, immune; oblivious, indifferent, unaware. See DEFENSE, INSENSIBILITY, INDIFFERENCE.

impetuous, *adj.* impulsive, rash, headlong; rushing, unrestrainable. See EXCITABILITY, RASHNESS, VIOLENCE, FEELING, HASTE.

impetus, *n.* IMPULSE, force; stimulus, CAUSE, motive, incentive.

IMPIETY

Nouns—**1,** impiety, impiousness; sin; irreverence; profaneness, profanity, profanation; blasphemy, desecration, sacrilege; apostasy, iconoclasm; scoffing; hardening, fall from grace; backsliding, declension, perversion, reprobation, IRRELIGION.

2, assumed piety, hypocrisy (see FALSEHOOD); pietism, cant; pious fraud; lip service; misdevotion, formalism; sanctimony, sanctimoniousness; pharisaism; sabbatism, sabbatarianism; sacerdotalism.

3, sinner, EVILDOER; scoffer, blasphemer, profaner, sacrilegist; worldling; backslider, hypocrite, apostate; Pharisee, ranter, fanatic; sons of Belial, children of darkness.

Verbs—profane, desecrate, blaspheme, revile, scoff; swear (see IMPRECATION); commit sacrilege; fall from grace, backslide.

Adjectives—impious; irreligious; desecrating, profane, irreverent, sacrilegious, blasphemous; unhallowed, unsanctified, unregenerate; hardened, perverted, reprobate; hypocritical, canting, sanctimonious, unctuous, pharisaical, overrighteous.

Adverbs—impiously; under the mask, cloak, pretence, form, *or* guise of religion.

Antonyms, see PIETY.

---

implant, *v.t.* plant, embed, fix, set in; inculcate, instill; graft, engraft. See INSERTION.

implement, *n.* tool, utensil, instrument. —*v.* equip; affect, fulfill; enact, execute. See COMPLETION, INSTRUMENTALITY.

implicate, *v.t.* involve, entangle, embroil; incriminate; connect, associate. See ACCUSATION, INCLUSION, DIFFICULTY.

implication, *n.* involvement, allusion, inference; innuendo, suggestion. See MEANING, ACCUSATION, INFORMATION.

implicit, *adj.* unspoken, tacit, understood, implied, inferred. See MEANING, LATENCY.

implore, *v.t.* beg, beseech, entreat, plead. See REQUEST.

imply, *v.t.* hint, suggest, infer, intimate; involve, entail. See EVIDENCE, INFORMATION, LATENCY.

impolite, *adj.* rude, uncivil, ill-mannered. See DISCOURTESY.

import, *n.* MEANING, significance, IMPORTANCE; trend, drift, purport; importation, introduction. See INGRESS. —*v.* bring in, introduce; imply, indicate.

IMPORTANCE

Nouns—**1,** importance, import, consequence, moment, prominence, consideration, mark, materialness, primacy; significance, concern; emphasis, interest; distinction, prestige, grandeur, majesty, INFLUENCE, GREATNESS, SUPERIORITY, notability, REPUTE; weight, value, GOODNESS; usefulness (see UTILITY). See MEANING, PRECEDENCE.

2, gravity, seriousness, solemnity; no joke, no laughing matter; pressure, urgency, stress; matter of life and death; exigency.

3, memorabilia, notabilia, great doings; red-letter day, milestone, turning point. *Colloq.,* the big time.

4, essence, substance, gist; main chance, be all and end all, cardinal point; sum and substance, *sine qua non;* breath of life; cream, salt, core, kernel, heart, nucleus; key, keynote, keystone, cornerstone; trump [card]; salient points; essentials, fundamentals. *Colloq.,* where it's at, name of the game, the long and the short of it. See INTRINSIC.

5, personage, dignitary, figure, prima donna, chief, mogul, magnate, somebody. *Colloq.,* big fish in a small pond. *Slang,* big gun, shot, cheese, wheel, *or* daddy, V.I.P., bigwig.

Verbs—**1,** import, signify, matter, boot, be somebody, carry weight; cut a figure (see REPUTE); overshadow (see SUPERIORITY); count for something.

2, attach importance to, value, care for; set store by; mark (see INDICATION); underline; put in italics *or* capitals, capitalize, italicize; accentuate, emphasize, feature, point up, stress, lay stress on; get *or* come to the point, get down to brass tacks *or* to cases; make a fuss *or* stir about, make much *or* something of, play up; hit the high spots; hit the bull's-eye.

Adjectives—**1,** important; of importance, momentous, material, of consequence, consequential, crucial; not to be overlooked, not to be despised, not to be sneezed at; egregious; weighty, influential, big-time; of note (see REPUTE); prominent, salient, signal; memorable, remarkable; worthy of remark *or* notice; never to be forgotten; eventful, significant, telling, trenchant, emphatic, pregnant. *Colloq.,* earthshaking.

2, grave, serious, heavy; urgent, pressing, critical, instant, solemn, fateful, fatal. *Colloq.,* not to be sneezed at.

3, essential, vital, all-absorbing; cardinal, chief, main, prime, primary, principal, capital, foremost, overriding; in the front rank, first-rate; superior (see SUPERIORITY); considerable (see GREATNESS); marked. See PRIORITY.

Adverbs—importantly, materially, in the main, mainly, first and last *or* foremost. *Colloq.,* joking aside.

Antonyms, see UNIMPORTANCE.

impose, *v.t.* burden (with), inflict; force (upon); levy, tax; delude, take advantage (of), palm off, foist; obtrude. See DECEPTION, COMPULSION.

imposing, *adj.* dignified, awe-inspiring; impressive; grand, stately, commanding. See REPUTE.

imposition, *n.* nuisance, bother, inconvenience, intrusion, infringement, invasion of privacy. See DECEPTION, COMMAND, WRONG.

IMPOSSIBILITY

Nouns—impossibility, what can never be; HOPELESSNESS; impracticability, infeasibility, insuperability. *Colloq.*, no go. *Slang*, fat chance.

Verbs—have no chance; square the circle, skin a flint, make a silk purse out of a sow's ear, make bricks without straw, build castles in the air; bite off more than one can chew; be in two places at once; ask *or* cry for the moon, promise *or* give the moon.

Adjectives—impossible; absurd, contrary to reason (see ABSURDITY); unreasonable, incredible (see DOUBT); visionary, inconceivable (see IMPROBABILITY); unimaginable, unthinkable, impracticable, impractical, unachievable, unfeasible, unworkable, insuperable, insurmountable; unattainable, unobtainable, out of reach; out of the question; desperate, hopeless; out of print; inaccessible, impassable, impervious, unnavigable, inextricable, ineluctable, *etc.*

Adverbs—impossibly, *etc.;* when hell freezes over.

Antonyms, see POSSIBILITY.

impostor, *n.* fake[r]; masquerader, pretender, fraud. See DECEPTION.

imposture, *n.* masquerade, pretense; fraud, DECEPTION; impersonation.

IMPOTENCE

Nouns—**1,** impotence, inability, disability; disablement, impuissance, incapacity, incapability; inaptness, ineptitude, inefficiency, incompetence; disqualification. See WEAKNESS, UNSKILLFULNESS, INSUFFICIENCY.

2, inefficacy (see USELESSNESS); paralysis; helplessness, prostration, exhaustion, enervation.

3, emasculation, castration.

4, eunuch, *castrato;* cripple; blank cartridge, basket case, flash in the pan, dummy, dud, wimp.

Verbs—**1,** collapse, faint, swoon, drop. See DETERIORATION.

2, unman, unnerve, enervate; emasculate, castrate, geld; disable, disarm, incapacitate, disqualify, unfit, invalidate; deaden, cramp, exhaust, weaken, debilitate; demoralize, take the wind out of one's sails; muzzle, cripple, maim, lame, hamstring, hogtie, paralyze, pull *or* draw the teeth of; break the back of; unhinge, unfit. *Slang,* fix. See HINDRANCE.

Adjectives—**1,** impotent, powerless, unable, incapable, incompetent; inefficient, ineffective, ineffectual; inept, unfit[ted]; unqualified, disqualified, unendowed; crippled, halt, disabled, paralytic, paralyzed; emasculate[d], sexless, unsexed, fixed; on one's back; done up, dead beat, exhausted, shattered, demoralized; without a leg to stand on, *hors de combat,* out of commission.

2, harmless, helpless, unarmed; defenseless, unfortified; vincible, pregnable; null and void, nugatory, inoperative, good-for-nothing.

Antonyms, see POWER.

impound, *v.t.* jail, restrain; confine, corral, encage; seize, take, confiscate, expropriate, appropriate. See ENCLOSURE, RESTRAINT, ACQUISITION.

impoverish, *v.t.* pauperize; exhaust, drain; reduce, deplete, rob; weaken. See POVERTY, INSUFFICIENCY, WASTE.

impracticable, *adj.* unworkable, inexpedient, not feasible; idealistic, visionary; unrealistic. See DIFFICULTY, IMPOSSIBILITY, INEXPEDIENCE.

impractical, *adj.* impracticable; unwise, imprudent, unrealistic; unsound, illogical; harebrained. See IMAGINATION, IMPOSSIBILITY.

IMPRECATION

Nouns—imprecation, malediction, malison (*archaic*), curse, denunciation, execration; anathema, ban, fulmination; calumny, calumniation, contumely, invective, diatribe, jeremiad, tirade, vituperation, disparagement, obloquy; abuse, billingsgate, sauce; cursing, profanity, swearing, oath, expletive; THREAT. See DETRACTION, CONDEMNATION, DISAPPROBATION.

Verbs—imprecate, curse, damn, swear (at); execrate, beshrew, scold; anathematize; vilify, denounce; fulminate, thunder against; threaten; defame.

Adjectives—imprecatory, denunciatory, abusive, cursing, cursed, accursed.

Interjections—woe to! woe betide! damn! confound! blast! curse! devil take! hang! out with! a plague *or* pox upon! out upon!

Antonyms, see APPROBATION, WORSHIP.

impregnable, *adj.* invincible. See STRENGTH.

impregnate, *v.t.* fertilize, fecundate, pollinate, inseminate; infuse, soak, permeate, saturate. *Colloq.,* get in trouble, get in a family way. *Slang,* knock up. See REPRODUCTION, INSERTION, MIXTURE.

impresario, *n.* promoter, entrepreneur. See UNDERTAKING, DRAMA.

impress, *v.t.* stamp, mark, print, imprint; dint, dent; inspire, overawe; interest; strike; draft, compel (service), shanghai. See COMPULSION, PRINTING.

impression, *n.* PRINTING, ENGRAVING, mark, stamp; dent; opinion, FEELING; inkling, suspicion. See BELIEF, SENSIBILITY.

impressive, *adj.* imposing, awesome, majestic, stately, moving, stirring, weighty, large. See FEELING, OSTENTATION.

imprint, *n.* impress, stamp, impression; cachet, seal, symbol, device; result, effect. —*v.t.* impress, stamp, fix; inscribe, seal; make one's mark on. See INDICATION, PRINTING.

imprison, *v.t.* lock up, confine, detain; hold, jail, incarcerate. See CIRCUMSCRIPTION, RESTRAINT.

IMPROBABILITY

Nouns—improbability, unlikelihood, unlikeliness; small *or* long chance, Chinaman's chance, ghost of a chance; long odds, long shot; incredibility (see DOUBT). See HOPELESSNESS, IMPOSSIBILITY.

Verbs—be improbable *or* unlikely, be a strain on the imagination.

Adjectives—improbable, unlikely, contrary to all reasonable expectation, doubtful, farfetched; rare, infrequent (see RARITY); unheard-of, implausible, questionable, fishy. *Slang,* in a pig's eye.

Antonyms, see CHANCE, PROBABILITY.

IMPROBITY

Nouns—**1,** improbity; dishonesty, dishonor; disgrace, DISREPUTE; fraud, DECEPTION; lying, FALSEHOOD; bad faith, infidelity, inconstancy, faithlessness, Judas kiss, betrayal; breach of promise, trust, *or* faith; renegation, renegadism, disloyalty, [high] treason; apostasy (see CHANGEABLENESS). See GUILT, ILLEGALITY, WRONG.

2, villainy, baseness, abjection, debasement, [moral] turpitude, laxity; perfidy, perfidiousness, treachery, duplicity, double-dealing; knavery, roguery, rascality, foul play; trickery, venality; collaboration; nepotism, corruption, simony, barratry, graft, jobbery, malfeasance. *Slang,* dirty pool.

3, vice, depravity, looseness, profligacy. See IMPURITY.

4, knave (see EVILDOER); double-crosser, betrayer, informer; collaborator, Quisling. *Colloq.,* two-timer. *Slang,* rat, [rat]fink. See INFORMATION.

Verbs—**1,** play false; forswear, break one's word, faith, *or* promise, go back on one's word; betray, double-cross, stab in the back, sell out; jilt, cheat on, carry on; lie (see FALSEHOOD); live by one's wits; misrepresent; hit below the belt. *Colloq.,* two-time. *Slang,* rat (on), fink (on), blow the whistle (on).

2, sin (see BADNESS).

Adjectives—**1,** dishonest, dishonorable, unscrupulous, fly-by-night; fraudulent (see DECEPTION); knavish, disgraceful, unconscionable; disreputable (see DISREPUTE); wicked, sinful, vicious, criminal.

2, false-hearted, two-faced; crooked, insidious, Machiavellian, dark, slippery; perfidious, treacherous, underhand[ed], perjured; infamous, arrant, foul, base, abject, vile, ignominious, blackguard; corrupt, venal; recreant, inglorious, discreditable, improper; faithless, false, unfaithful, disloyal; treacherous, renegade; untrustworthy, unreliable, undependable, trustless; lost to shame, dead to honor.

Adverbs—dishonestly, like a thief in the night, underhandedly, by fair means or foul, by hook or crook.

Antonyms, see PROBITY.

---

impromptu, *adj.* extemporaneous. See UNPREPAREDNESS.

improper, *adj.* indecent, bawdy, lewd, risqué; WRONG, inapt, unsuitable, unfitting, incorrect, out of place, misplaced. See INEXPEDIENCE, DISAGREEMENT.

impropriety, *n.* misbehavior, VULGARITY, immodesty; bad manners, indecorum; unfitness, unsuitability. See INEXPEDIENCE, DISAGREEMENT, DISCOURTESY.

IMPROVEMENT

Nouns—**1,** improvement, uplift; melioration, amelioration, betterment; mend, amendment, emendation; advancement, advance, development, progress, PROGRESSION, ascent; promotion, preferment; elevation, INCREASE; evolution; cultivation, civilization, culture; crusade, crusading.

2, reform, reformation, revision; correction, refinement, enhancement; PERFECTION, purification (see CLEANNESS); repair, RESTORATION; recovery. See RELIEF.

3, reformer, radical, progressive, crusader; new man. *Colloq.,* do-gooder.

Verbs—**1,** improve; better, mend, amend; turn to good account, profit by, reap the benefit of; make good use of, make capital of; evolve, develop, advance, ascend, INCREASE; fructify, ripen, mature; come along, gain ground, pick up, come about, rally, take a turn for the better; turn over a new leaf, turn the corner; come a long way, recover. *Colloq.*, look up, snap out of it.

2, meliorate, ameliorate; palliate, mitigate; turn the tide; correct, rectify; enrich, mellow, fatten; promote, prefer; cultivate, advance, forward, enhance, refine (upon); update; bring forward, bring on; foster (see AID); invigorate, strengthen.

3, touch up, brush up, refurbish, renovate, polish, make the most of, set off to advantage; prune; repair, restore (see RESTORATION); put in order.

4, revise, edit, correct; debug; straighten out; doctor, purify; relieve, refresh, infuse new blood *or* life into; reform, remodel, retrofit, reorganize.

Adjectives—improving, on the mend; improved; progressive; better [off], better for; reformatory, emendatory; reparatory, restorative, remedial; corrigible, improvable.

Adverbs—for the better. *Colloq.*, over the hump, out of the woods.

Antonyms, see DETERIORATION.

---

improvise, *v.* invent, extemporize. See IMAGINATION, UNPREPAREDNESS.

imprudent, *adj.* careless, incautious, rash; unwise, injudicious, ill-advised; foolish. See RASHNESS, FOLLY, UNPREPAREDNESS.

impudence, *n.* INSOLENCE, gall, cheek, effrontery; boldness, DISCOURTESY.

IMPULSE

Nouns—**1,** impulse, impulsion, impetus, momentum; push, thrust, shove, jog, nudge, prod, jolt, brunt, throw; explosion (see VIOLENCE); PROPULSION; percussion, concussion, collision, pile-up, clash, encounter, shock, crash, bump; coup; impact; charge, ATTACK; beating, PUNISHMENT.

2, blow, dint, stroke, clap, knock, tap, rap, slap, smack, pat, wallop, dab; fillip; slam, bang; hit, whack, clout, cuff, clip, punch, bump, thump, pelt, kick; cut, thrust, lunge. *Colloq.*, bat, swat, lick. *Slang,* sock, the old one-two.

3, hammer, sledgehammer, maul, mallet, flail; ram, battering ram, pile driver, punch, bat; cudgel, weapon; ax.

4, impromptu, improvisation (see UNPREPAREDNESS).

Verbs—**1,** give impetus; impel, push; start, set going; drive, urge; thrust, prod; elbow, shoulder, jostle, hustle, hurtle, shove, jar, jolt; bump, run, *or* plow into; impinge; flounce.

2, strike, knock, hit, pelt, jab, clip, lambaste, wallop, tap, rap, slap, swipe, pat, thump, stub, beat, bang, slam, dash; sock, punch, whack; hit *or* strike hard; batter; pelt, buffet, bruise, belabor, rough up; fetch one a blow, throw a punch; poke at, lunge; kick, butt; make a pass at, take a punch, poke, *or* sock at, strike at, ATTACK; whip (see PUNISHMENT). *Colloq.*, swat, larrup, beat the [living] daylights out of. *Slang,* knock galley-west, knock off one's block, clobber, hang one on, waste, deck, paste.

3, collide; fall *or* run foul of; throw (see PROPULSION).

4, improvise (see UNPREPAREDNESS).

Adjectives—**1,** impelling, impellent; dynamic, impelled.

2, impulsive, impromptu, offhand, natural, unguarded; spontaneous, voluntary. See WILL, UNPREPAREDNESS.

Adverbs—impulsively, explosively, *etc.*

Antonyms, see THOUGHT, RECOIL.

---

impunity, *n.* EXEMPTION, immunity.

IMPURITY

Nouns—**1,** impurity, UNCLEANNESS; immodesty, grossness, indelicacy, indecency; pornography, obscenity, ribaldry, smut, bawdy, filth, *double entendre*.
2, laxity, looseness of morals, turpitude, depravity, pollution, profligacy, shame, vice. See BADNESS.
3, concupiscence, lust, carnality, flesh, salacity; pruriency, lechery, lasciviousness, lewdness, lubricity; incontinence, unchastity; debauchery, license, immorality, libertinism, fornication, liaison; wenching, venery, dissipation; incest; perversion; sodomy, pederasty; sadism, masochism; seduction, defloration, defilement, abuse, violation, rape, [criminal] assault; harlotry, whoredom, concubinage; cuckoldry, adultery, infidelity; blue *or* dirty movie.
4, brothel, bagnio, bawdyhouse, whorehouse, house of ill fame *or* pleasure, bordello; red-light district, combat zone.
5, a. libertine, voluptuary, rake, roué, playboy, debauchee, profligate; gigolo; lecher, satyr; pederast, dirty old man; pimp, pander, Don Juan, Casanova. *Colloq.,* rip. **b.** courtesan, call girl, doxy, prostitute, strumpet, harlot, bawd, procuress, whore, wanton, *fille de joie, putain,* streetwalker, lady of the evening, daughter of joy, fallen woman, concubine, demimondaine, camp follower; tart, chippy, wench, trollop, trull, doxy, jade, light o' love; nymphomaniac. *Slang,* chippy, floozy, hustler, pro, pickup, hooker, B-girl, V-girl.
6, adulteration (see DETERIORATION).

Verbs—debauch, defile, deflower, rape, ravish, ruin, seduce; prostitute, pander, cater, sell oneself, walk the streets; abuse, violate; adulterate (see DETERIORATION); commit adultery. *Slang,* sleep around, carry on, womanize.

Adjectives—**1,** impure, immoral, amoral; unclean; immodest, shameless; indecorous, indelicate, indecent; loose, coarse, gross, broad, earthy; smutty, foul, ribald, obscene, bawdy, erotic, pornographic, risqué, nasty, blue; concupiscent, prurient, lustful; lewd, lascivious, lecherous, libidinous, ruttish, salacious; unfaithful, adulterous; incestuous; unchaste, incontinent; light, wanton, licentious, rakish, debauched, dissipated, dissolute, fast; promiscuous, loose, meretricious, of easy virtue, on the streets; gay. *Colloq.,* off-color. *Slang,* sexy, sultry, raunchy.
2, vicious, immoral, dissolute, profligate, sinful, iniquitous.

Antonyms, see PURITY.

impute, *v.t.* ascribe, attribute. See ACCUSATION, ATTRIBUTION, DISREPUTE.

inability, *n.* IMPOTENCE, incapacity, powerlessness; UNSKILLFULNESS, incompetence, inefficiency.

inaccessible, *adj.* unapproachable, incommunicado; sheltered, guarded; restricted, taboo, sacrosanct; aloof, cold, cool, distant, withdrawn. See DISTANCE, PROHIBITION, SECLUSION.

inaccurate, *adj.* erroneous, fallacious, incorrect, WRONG; mistaken; inexact, unprecise; misleading. See ERROR.

INACTIVITY

Nouns—**1,** inactivity; inaction; inertness; lull, cessation (see REPOSE); idleness, sloth, laziness, indolence, vegetation; unemployment, dilatoriness, dawdling; malingering; passiveness, passivity, dormancy; stagnation; procrastination; time on one's hands; *laissez faire,* noninterference; *dolce far niente,* lotusland. See INSENSIBILITY, INDIFFERENCE, AVOIDANCE.

2, dullness, languor; sluggishness, SLOWNESS, delay (see LATENESS); torpor, torpidity, torpescence.

3, idler, drone, do-little; dummy, silent partner; fifth wheel; lounger, loafer; lubber, slowpoke (see SLOWNESS); opium eater, lotus eater; slug, laggard, sluggard, ne'er-do-well, do-nothing, fainéant; clock watcher, good-for-nothing. *Slang,* bum.

4, halt, pause, standstill, full stop; stalemate, impasse, block, check, checkmate; red light.

Verbs—**1,** let the grass grow under one's feet; take one's time, dawdle, lag, hang back, slouch, loll, lounge, loaf, laze, loiter, hang around; sleep at one's post *or* at the switch, flag, languish. *Slang,* hang out.

2, vegetate, lie fallow; waste, consume, kill, *or* lose time; twiddle one's thumbs; not lift a finger *or* hand; idle, trifle, fritter, *or* fool away the time, sit by, sit back, sit on one's hands, not move a muscle, lie down on the job; mark time, piddle, potter, putter, dabble, fiddle-faddle, dally, shilly-shally, dilly-dally; ride at anchor, rest on one's oars, rest on one's laurels; hang fire, postpone. *Colloq.,* cool one's heels. *Slang,* goof off.

Adjectives—**1,** inactive; motionless, quiescent, stationary; unoccupied, out of circulation, idle, off-duty, at leisure, on the bench, unemployed; indolent, shiftless, lazy, slothful, idle, remiss, slack, torpid, sluggish, languid, supine, heavy, dull, leaden, lumpish; inert, inanimate; listless; dilatory, laggard; lagging, slow; rusty, flagging, lackadaisical, pottering, irresolute.

2, torpid, lethargic, heavy, napping; tranquilizing, soporific, hypnotic; balmy, dreamy; sedative. *Slang,* dopey; out of this world.

Antonyms, see ACTIVITY, ACTION.

---

inadequate, *adj.* scant, wanting, short, below par; incomplete, partial, deficient, lacking. See INSUFFICIENCY.

inadvertent, *adj.* unintentional, adventitious, accidental, CHANCE; heedless, careless, regardless, thoughtless. See INATTENTION.

inadvisable, *adj.* inexpedient, not recommended; impracticable; ill-advised, unwise, imprudent, risky. See INEXPEDIENCE.

inane, *adj.* pointless, senseless, silly; empty, vacuous; idiotic. See UNMEANINGNESS, FOLLY.

inanimate, *adj.* inorganic; lifeless, insentient, unconscious, dead; listless, inactive, inert, supine, dormant, comatose. See DEATH, INACTIVITY.

inappropriate, *adj.* unbecoming, unsuitable, WRONG, improper; inapt, unfitting, inadvisable. See DISAGREEMENT.

inarticulate, *adj.* voiceless, speechless, mute, stammering; unexpressed, unspoken, indistinct; unjointed. See SILENCE, DISJUNCTION, STAMMERING, UNINTELLIGIBILITY.

INATTENTION

Nouns—inattention, inattentiveness; abstraction, absence of mind, preoccupation, distraction; reverie, woolgathering, daydreaming, brown study, detachment; inconsiderateness, oversight; inadvertence, inadvertency; nonobservance, disregard; thoughtlessness, heedlessness (see NEGLECT); insouciance,

INDIFFERENCE; RASHNESS. *Slang,* nobody home. See UNPREPAREDNESS, DISRESPECT, CONTEMPT, FOLLY.

Verbs—**1,** pay no attention, disregard, overlook; pass by, NEGLECT; ignore, think little of, wink at; close *or* shut one's eyes to; disdain, dismiss from one's thoughts *or* mind, reckon without; think no more of; set *or* put aside; turn a deaf ear *or* blind eye to, turn one's back upon, shrug off *or* away, laugh off; set aside; take no notice of. *Dial.,* pay no mind.

2, abstract oneself, dream, daydream, woolgather; play possum; moon.

3, escape notice *or* attention; go in one ear and out the other; fall on deaf ears.

4, divert, distract, turn one's head; disconcert, discompose; confuse, perplex, bewilder, fluster, muddle, dazzle; put off. *Colloq.,* fuddle, rattle, faze. *Slang,* ball up.

Adjectives—**1,** inattentive; unobservant, unmindful, unheeding, undiscerning; inadvertent, regardless, listless, indifferent; blind, deaf; cursory, percursory; inconsiderate, offhand, thoughtless; heedless, careless.

2, absent[-minded], abstracted, flighty, detached, distraught, distrait; lost in thought; rapt, in the clouds, in a fog; bemused, punch-drunk, slap-happy; preoccupied; engrossed; off [one's] guard; napping, dreamy, woolgathering, sleeping, asleep, groggy, dead to the world. *Colloq.,* asleep at the switch, out to lunch.

Antonyms, see ATTENTION, THOUGHT.

---

inaudible, *adj.* unhearable; faint, muffled. See SILENCE.

inaugurate, *v.t.* install, induct, invest; start, launch, initiate, institute, open. See BEGINNING.

inauspicious, *adj.* unpropitious, ill-omened, unfavorable, unlucky. See BADNESS.

inborn, *adj.* native, innate, inherent. See INTRINSIC.

incalculable, *adj.* inestimable, immeasurable; vast. See INFINITY.

incapable, *adj.* powerless, unable, incompetent; unqualified, unfitted, untrained. See IMPOTENCE.

incapacity, *n.* disability, IMPOTENCE, incompetence; inability, lack, deficiency. See IGNORANCE.

incarcerate, *v.t.* imprison (see RESTRAINT).

incarnate, *v.t.* shape, form, embody; animate, quicken. See SUBSTANCE.

incendiary, *n.* pyromaniac, firebug; arsonist. See DESTRUCTION.

incense, *v.t.* inflame, heat; infuriate, anger, ire; perfume, scent, thurify. See RESENTMENT. —*n.* perfume, fragrance, scent, ODOR, bouquet; frankincense, musk, myrrh, sandalwood. See FLATTERY, RITE.

incentive, *n.* stimulus, goad, spur; motive, CAUSE; provocation.

inception, *n.* start, BEGINNING.

incessant, *adj.* endless, continual, unceasing; uninterrupted. See FREQUENCY, CONTINUITY, REPETITION.

inch, *v.* creep, crawl; EDGE, worm. See SLOWNESS.

incident, *n.* occasion; event, episode, happening. See OCCURRENCE. —*adj.* dependent, pertaining; likely. See QUALIFICATION.

incidental, *adj.* secondary, minor, subordinate; casual, CHANCE; current. See CIRCUMSTANCE.

incinerate, *v.t.* burn, cremate. See HEAT, INTERMENT.

incipient, *adj.* See BEGINNING.

incision, *n.* cut, gash, notch. See FURROW, INTERVAL.

incite, *v.t.* stir, urge, impel; actuate, provoke, instigate; encourage, stimulate; spur, goad. *Colloq.,* fan the flames. See CAUSE, EXCITEMENT.

inclination, *n.* propensity, leaning, bent, predisposition; fondness, liking; predilection; slope, slant, ramp. See TENDENCY, WILL, OBLIQUITY.

incline, *v.* slant, slope, tilt; pitch, lurch; tend, influence, bias. See TENDENCY. *—n.* OBLIQUITY, grade; gradient, slant, bias, slope (see *v.*); ramp, ASCENT, upgrade; downgrade, DESCENT.

INCLUSION

Nouns—inclusion, admission, acceptance; comprehension, incorporation, subsumption; COMPOSITION, contents. See PART, GENERALITY.

Verbs—include, comprise, comprehend, embody, contain, admit, embrace, take in, receive, take up, subsume; inclose, circumscribe (see CIRCUMSCRIPTION); compose, incorporate, encompass; reckon *or* number among; cut *or* count in, implicate; refer to, place under, take into account *or* consideration; pertain *or* relate to.

Adjectives—included, including, inclusive; subsumptive; compendious, comprehensive, encyclopedic, omnibus; of the same class.

Adverbs—inclusively, comprehensively, *etc.*

Antonyms, see EXCLUSION.

incognito, *adj.* See CONCEALMENT.

incognizant, *adj.* unaware (of). See IGNORANCE.

incoherence, *n.* UNINTELLIGIBILITY, irrationality, inconsistency; incongruity; maundering, raving; immiscibility; looseness, FREEDOM. See DISJUNCTION.

INCOMBUSTIBILITY

Nouns—**1,** incombustibility, uninflammability.

2, [fire] extinguisher, fire engine, [automatic] sprinkler; carbon tetrachloride, foam, [wet] blanket; fireproofing, asbestos; fire wall *or* curtain.

3, fire fighter, fireman; fire *or* bucket brigade.

Verbs—fireproof, flameproof; extinguish, snuff, put *or* stamp out, quench, douse, smother, damp; burn *or* go out, die.

Adjectives—incombustible, non[in]flammable, flameproof, fireproof, unburnable; fire-resistant; quenched, [snuffed] out.

Antonyms, see FUEL.

income, *n.* revenue; dividends, interest; receipt[s], emoluments, fees, earnings; profit. See RECEIVING.

incomparable, *adj.* peerless, matchless, nonpareil, inimitable. See SUPERIORITY.

incompatible, *adj.* inharmonious, inconsistent, antipathetic, incongruous, uncongenial; clashing, discordant, disagreeing. See DISAGREEMENT.

incompetence, *n.* inability, inefficiency; IMPOTENCE; unfitness, incapability, incapacity, UNSKILLFULNESS.

INCOMPLETENESS

Nouns—**1,** noncompletion, nonfulfillment, nonperformance, nonexecution.

2, incompleteness, short measure, half measures, INSUFFICIENCY, deficiency, IMPERFECTION, inadequacy, DISCONTINUANCE; immaturity (see UNPREPAREDNESS). See PART.

3, deficit, want, lack, defalcation, omission, caret; INTERVAL, break, gap, missing link; loose end.

Verbs—**1,** be incomplete; fall short, lack, want; need (see INSUFFICIENCY).
2, leave unfinished, leave undone, let alone, let slide, let slip; lose sight of, hang fire, do things by halves, lie down on the job.

Adjectives—**1,** incomplete, uncompleted, unfinished, left undone, half-baked; imperfect, defective, deficient, partial, wanting, failing; in default, in arrears, short (of); hollow, meager, skimpy, poor, lame, half-and-half, perfunctory, sketchy, crude; mutilated, garbled, mangled, docked, lopped, truncated, catalectic.
2, unaccomplished, unperformed, unexecuted; in progress, going on, in hand, proceeding, under way, under construction.

Adverbs—incompletely; by halves, partly, partially; on paper, on the drawing board, in the blueprint *or* planning stage.

Antonyms, see COMPLETION.

---

incomprehensible, *adj.* unintelligible; unfathomable, abstruse, inscrutable. See UNINTELLIGIBILITY.

inconceivable, *adj.* unimaginable, unthinkable, incredible. See IMPOSSIBILITY, UNINTELLIGIBILITY.

incongruity, *n.* disharmony; inconsistency, incompatibility, absurdity. See DIFFERENCE, DISAGREEMENT.

inconsequential, *adj.* inconsequent, irrelevant; trivial. See UNIMPORTANCE, DISAGREEMENT.

inconsiderate, *adj.* careless, heedless, thoughtless; tactless, neglectful. See NEGLECT.

inconsistency, *n.* CHANGEABLENESS, fickleness; incompatibility; contrariness, contradiction.

inconspicuous, *adj.* unnoticeable, unobtrusive. See INVISIBILITY.

inconstant, *adj.* unstable, irregular; fickle, changeable, faithless. See CHANGEABLENESS.

inconvenient, *adj.* awkward, embarrassing, troublesome; inopportune, untimely. See INEXPEDIENCE, DIFFICULTY.

incorporate, *v.* embody; federate, merge, consolidate; unite, blend, join. See JUNCTION, INCLUSION, COMBINATION, SUBSTANCE.

incorrect, *adj.* WRONG, erroneous, fallacious; mistaken, false, untrue, inaccurate. See ERROR.

incorrigible, *adj.* irreclaimable, beyond redemption; intractable, hopelessly delinquent. See OBSTINACY, HOPELESSNESS.

INCREASE

Nouns—**1,** increase, augmentation, enlargement, extension; dilation, EXPANSION; advance, appreciation; gain, profit, increment, accretion; accession, ADDITION; development, growth; aggrandizement, aggravation; intensification, magnification, multiplication; rise, ascent; exacerbation; spread, DISPERSION; flood tide. *Slang,* gravy. See IMPROVEMENT.
2, booster; gains, profits.

Verbs—**1,** increase, augment, add to, enlarge, extend; supplement, eke out; dilate, sprout, expand, swell, burgeon, bud, puff up; grow, wax, get ahead, gain strength; fatten; advance; develop, grow, run up, shoot up; rise, ascend; amplify, build up, raise, step *or* jack up, punch up, hike. *Colloq.,* soup up.
2, aggrandize, exalt; deepen, heighten, strengthen, intensify, enhance, magnify, redouble; parlay; let out; accrue; aggravate, exasperate, exacerbate; add fuel to the flames, spread, disperse; appreciate, inflate, mushroom, escalate, go up. *Colloq.,* snowball.

Adjectives—increased, increasing, multiplying, enlarged, on the increase, undiminished; additional, extra, added (see ADDITION); swollen, turgid, tumid, bloated, distended; larger, bigger.

Adverbs—increasingly, *etc.;* even, all the; *crescendo.*

Antonyms, see DECREASE.

---

incredible, *n.* unbelievable, inconceivable; absurd, preposterous. See DOUBT, WONDER.

INCREDULITY

Nouns—**1,** incredulity, incredulousness, skepticism; want of faith (see IRRELIGION); DOUBT, distrust, suspicion, suspiciousness, scrupulosity, unbelief, disbelief; sophistication, ungullibility. See SURPRISE.

2, unbeliever, disbeliever, skeptic; infidel, heretic.

Verbs—distrust, DOUBT, disbelieve, refuse to believe, reject (see REJECTION); ignore, dispute, question. *Colloq.,* not swallow.

Adjectives—incredulous, skeptical; sophisticated, ungullible; unbelieving, unconvinced; doubtful, dubious, distrustful, questioning, quizzical, disputing; hesitant, uncertain, suspicious, scrupulous, apprehensive, wary, chary, qualmish; faithless, heretical. *Slang,* leery, not born yesterday.

Antonyms, see CREDULITY.

---

increment, *n.* growth, INCREASE.

incriminate, *v.t.* blame, indict, inculpate; impeach, put under suspicion; implicate, entangle. *Slang,* put the finger on, frame, pin the rap on. See ACCUSATION.

inculpate, *v.t.* accuse, incriminate. See ACCUSATION.

incur, *v.t.* acquire, bring about. See LIABILITY.

incurable, *adj.* hopeless, doomed; irremediable; unhealable. See DISEASE, HOPELESSNESS.

incursion, *n.* encroachment, inroad, invasion; ATTACK, foray, raid. See INGRESS.

indebted, *adj.* obligated, beholden. See DEBT, GRATITUDE.

indecent, *adj.* immoral, obscene, improper; salacious, lewd, lascivious, bawdy; immodest. See IMPURITY.

indecision, *n.* irresolution, hesitation, uncertainty, vacillation, shilly-shally. See DOUBT.

indecorous, *adj.* unseemly. See DISCOURTESY.

indeed, *adv.* in fact, truly. See EXISTENCE.

indefinite, *adj.* unclear, undefined, blurred; vague, uncertain, unspecified; indeterminate; equivocal. See OBSCURITY, DOUBT.

indemnity, *n.* protection, SECURITY; COMPENSATION, EXEMPTION.

indent, *v.t.* impress, hollow, dent, dint, notch; knock in, set in, incise, cut; pit, dimple. See CONCAVITY.

independence, *n.* FREEDOM, liberty; self-reliance; self-government, autonomy; self-sufficiency.

independent, *adj.* absolute, free, self-governing, self-reliant; unconnected, separate (from), exclusive (of); well off, comfortable, well-to-do. —*n.* nonpartisan; free lance, lone wolf. See FREEDOM.

indestructible, *adj.* unbreakable, invulnerable. See PERMANENCE.

index, *n.* measure, scale, table, LIST; pointer, INDICATION. —*v.t.* tabulate, categorize, post; catalogue, register, order; point out. See ARRANGEMENT.

INDICATION

Nouns—**1,** indication; symbolism, symbolization; denotation, connotation, signification; specification, designation; sign, symbol; index, indicator; dial; point[er], marker; exponent, note, token, symptom; manifestation, expression; type, figure, emblem, cipher, device; trademark; REPRESENTATION; epigraph, motto; lineament, feature, trait, characteristic, syndrome, earmark, peculiarity, property (see SPECIALITY); footprint, fingerprint; diagnosis (see IDENTITY). See EVIDENCE, RECORD.

2, gesture, gesticulation; pantomime; wink, glance, leer; nod, shrug, beck, touch, nudge; dactylology, sign language; cue, implication, suggestion, hint (see INFORMATION), clue, key; scent, track, spoor, hide or hair.

3, signal, rocket, blue light, watchfire, watchtower; telegraph, semaphore, flagstaff; cresset, fiery cross; calumet, white flag.

4, mark, line, stroke, dash, score, stripe, scratch, tick, dot, point, notch, nick; asterisk, star, dagger, obelisk, punctuation; period, comma, colon, semicolon, interrogation point, question mark, exclamation point, quotation marks, dash; parentheses, braces, [square] brackets; red letter, italics, sublineation, underlining, underscoring; accent, diacritical mark, acute, grave, circumflex, macron, dieresis, tilde, cedilla; degree.

5, identification, badge, caste mark; criterion; countercheck, countermark, countersign, counterfoil; tab, tally, label, ticket, coupon, billet, letter, counter, card, bill; button; stamp; imprint, colophon; trademark, service mark, brand, hallmark; signature, autograph; credentials; attestation; cipher; seal, signet; superscription, endorsement; title, heading, docket, caption; shibboleth, watchword, catchword, byword, password; open sesame; cachet; insignia, ensign; regalia; banner, flag, colors, streamer, standard, eagle, oriflamme, tricolor, Stars and Stripes; pennon, pennant, jack, ancient, (obsolete), gonfalon, union jack; bunting; heraldry; crest; [coat of] arms, armorial bearings, hatchment, scutcheon, escutcheon; shield, supporters.

6, beacon, cairn, road sign, post, staff, flagstaff, hand, pointer, vane, cock, weathervane, guidepost, signpost; landmark, lighthouse; polestar, lodestar; blaze; address, direction, name; plaque, sign[board], milestone; traffic signal *or* light, stoplight.

7, call, bugle, trumpet, bell, siren, alarum, cry; curfew.

Verbs—**1,** indicate, denote, betoken, imply, argue, testify (see EVIDENCE); connote, designate, specify, point out, manifest, reveal, disclose, exhibit; represent, stand for; typify, symbolize.

2, signal; warn, wigwag, semaphore, flag; beck[on], hail; nod; wink, glance, leer, nudge, shrug, gesticulate, gesture.

3, wave; unfurl, hoist *or* hang out a banner; wave the hand; give a cue, show one's colors; give *or* sound an alarm; sound the tocsin, beat the drum; raise a [hue and] cry.

4, note, mark, stamp, earmark; tab, label, ticket, docket; dot, spot, score, dash, trace, chalk; print.

Adjectives—indicating, indicative, indicatory; denotative; connotative; diacritical, representative, representational, significant, suggestive; typical, symbolic, symptomatic, characteristic, demonstrative, diagnostic, exponential, emblematic.

Adverbs—indicatively; in token of; symbolically.

Antonyms, see CONCEALMENT.

indict, *v.i.* accuse, charge, bring accusation against, bring *or* profer charges; impeach, arraign. See ACCUSATION, LAWSUIT.

INDIFFERENCE

Nouns—**1,** indifference, neutrality; coldness, frigidity (see INSENSIBILITY); unconcern, insouciance, nonchalance; INATTENTION, lack of interest, anorexia, apathy; supineness; disdain (see CONTEMPT); carelessness, NEGLECT.
2, sameness, equivalence, EQUALITY; MEDIOCRITY.

Verbs—be indifferent *or* neutral, be all the same *or* all one; take no interest in, have no desire, taste, *or* relish for, not care for, care nothing for *or* about, not give *or* care a hang, a rap, *or* a damn; not bat an eye[lash], not care a straw (see UNIMPORTANCE); not mind; set at naught, make light of; spurn, disdain (see CONTEMPT).

Adjectives—**1,** indifferent, neutral, cold, frigid, lukewarm; impervious; cool [as a cucumber]; on the fence, neither fish nor fowl, middle-of-the-road; unambitious, complacent; unconcerned, insouciant, dispassionate, easygoing, devil-may-care, happy-go-lucky, careless, listless, lackadaisical; half-hearted; unambitious, unaspiring, undesirous, unsolicitous, unattracted; all one (to).
2, unattractive, unalluring, undesired, undesirable, uncared for, unwished, unvalued; insipid; vain.

Adverbs—indifferently; for the devil of it, for aught one cares.

Interjections—never mind! who cares! what's the difference!

Antonyms, see DESIRE, CURIOSITY, TASTE.

indigenous, *adj.* native; innate, inborn; inherent, natural (to). See INTRINSIC, INHABITANT.

indigestion, *n.* dyspepsia, gastritis, heartburn, stomach-ache, sour stomach, acidosis, flatulence, colic. See DISEASE.

indignation, *n.* RESENTMENT, ire, wrath; displeasure, vexation.

indignity, *n.* slight, humiliation. See DISRESPECT.

indirect, *adj.* oblique; roundabout, circuitous; underhand, crooked, furtive; hinted, implied, inferential. See CIRCUITY, DEVIATION, OBLIQUITY.

indiscretion, *n.* carelessness, recklessness; blunder, *faux pas,* lapse, slip. See RASHNESS, WRONG.

indiscriminate, *adj.* random, heterogeneous, CHANCE; uncritical, injudicious. See MIXTURE, DISORDER, GENERALITY.

indispensable, *adj.* vital, needful, necessary; essential, required. See NECESSITY.

indisposed, *adj.* ill; unwilling. See DISEASE, DISSUASION.

indistinct, *adj.* inaudible; imperceptible, unclear, foggy, blurry, shadowy; vague, obscure, dim; faint. See DIMNESS, INVISIBILITY.

individual, *adj.* particular, single, peculiar, special; specific; personal, proper. —*n.* person; personality, entity; somebody, anybody. See SPECIALITY.

individuality, *n.* UNCONFORMITY, uniqueness; personality; peculiarity, originality; character. See SPECIALITY, IDENTITY, UNITY.

indivisible, *adj.* one; inseparable, indissoluble. See UNITY, WHOLE.

indoctrinate, *v.t.* inculcate; brainwash. See TEACHING, BELIEF.

indolence, *n.* sloth, idleness, laziness, sluggishness; INACTIVITY.

indomitable, *adj.* invincible, unconquerable. See STRENGTH.

indorse, *v.t.* See ENDORSE.

induce, *v.t.* CAUSE, bring about, incite; infer; urge, persuade, impel, influence; effect.

induction, *n.* inauguration, installation; inference, REASONING, conclusion; generalization. See COMMISSION.

indulge, *v.t.* pamper, spoil, favor, humor; gratify; take PLEASURE (in); revel. See INTEMPERANCE, PERMISSION, LENIENCY.

industrious, *adj.* active, busy, hardworking; diligent, assiduous, sedulous. See ACTIVITY.

industry, *n.* labor, work; occupation, trade, BUSINESS, ACTIVITY; diligence.

inebriate, *v.t.* intoxicate (see DRINKING).

ineffective, *adj.* useless, vain, unavailing; impotent, worthless; weak, inefficient. See USELESSNESS, FAILURE, IMPOTENCE.

ineffectual, *adj.* futile, unproductive, barren, ineffective. See USELESSNESS, FAILURE.

INELASTICITY

Nouns—inelasticity; flabbiness, limpness, flaccidity, laxity, SOFTNESS; inductibility, inflexibility, stiffness, HARDNESS; inextensibility.

Verbs—stiffen, rigidify, tense.

Adjectives—inelastic, unstretchable, inextensible; flabby, flaccid, limp, lax, soft; inductile, inflexible, irresilient, rigid, unyielding, unpliant.

Antonyms, see ELASTICITY.

INELEGANCE

Nouns—inelegance, gracelessness, harshness, tastelessness, VULGARITY; stiffness; barbarism; solecism; mannerism, artificiality (see AFFECTATION). See UNSKILLFULNESS.

Adjectives—inelegant, graceless, ungraceful; dowdy; harsh, abrupt; dry, stiff, cramped, formal, forced, labored; artificial, mannered, ponderous; turgid, affected, euphuistic; awkward, inept, clumsy (see UNSKILLFULNESS); slouching, ungainly, gawky, lumpish, lumbering, hulking, unwieldy; barbarous, barbaric, uncouth, vulgar, gross; grotesque, ludicrous; rugged, rough, gross, rude, crude, halting.

Antonyms, see ELEGANCE.

---

ineligible, *adj.* unqualified, disqualified, inadmissible; unfit, WRONG. See INEXPEDIENCE.

inept, *adj.* incompetent, unskilled, clumsy, all thumbs. See UNSKILLFULNESS, FOLLY, INELEGANCE.

INEQUALITY

Nouns—inequality, disparity, imparity, odds, DIFFERENCE; unevenness; imbalance, partiality; shortcoming; makeweight; SUPERIORITY; INFERIORITY. See INJUSTICE.

Verbs—be unequal, countervail; tip the scale; kick the beam; topple (over); overmatch; not come up to; trim, trim ship.

Adjectives—unequal, uneven, disparate, partial; off balance, unbalanced, overbalanced; topheavy, lopsided; unequaled, matchless, peerless, unique, inimitable.

Antonyms, see EQUALITY.

---

inertia, *n.* stillness; laziness, lethargy; passivity. See INACTIVITY, REPOSE.

inestimable, *adj.* priceless, invaluable, beyond price *or* value, too precious for words. See DEARNESS, USE.

inevitable, *adj.* inescapable, unavoidable. See CERTAINTY, DESTINY.

inexact, *adj.* unprecise, incorrect, wrong, erroneous; vague, loose, undefined, indefinite, unspecified. See ERROR, OBSCURITY.

INEXCITABILITY

Nouns—**1,** inexcitability, imperturbability; even temper, equanimity, equilibrium, tranquillity, dispassion; tolerance, patience; hebetude, hebetation; INSENSIBILITY. See SUBMISSION, MODERATION, RESTRAINT.

2, coolness, calmness, composure, placidity, indisturbance, imperturbation, aplomb, sangfroid, serenity; quiet, quietude; peace of mind.

3, staidness, gravity, sobriety, Quakerism; fortitude, stoicism; self-possession, self-control, self-command, self-restraint; presence of mind.

Verbs—**1,** not get excited, be composed, *laissez faire,* take things as they come; take it easy, live and let live; take in good part.

2, acquiesce, submit, yield (see SUBMISSION); resign *or* reconcile oneself to; brook, swallow, pocket, stomach; make light of, make the best of, make a virtue of necessity; put a good face on, keep one's countenance. *Slang,* keep one's cool.

3, compose, appease, moderate; repress, restrain; master one's feelings, keep one's head, keep one's wits about one; bite one's lips *or* tongue, count to ten; get it all together, calm *or* cool down. *Colloq.,* simmer down. *Slang,* hold one's horses, keep one's shirt on.

Adjectives—**1,** inexcitable, unexcitable; imperturbable; unsusceptible, insensible; dispassionate, coldblooded, enduring, stoical, Platonic, philosophical, staid, sober-minded; nonchalant, coolheaded, demure, sedate.

2, easygoing, peaceful, placid, calm; quiet, tranquil, serene; cool [as a cucumber], undemonstrative, temperate; composed, collected.

3, patient [as Job]; submissive; tame; content, resigned, chastened, subdued, lamblike; gentle [as a lamb]; mild [as milk]; armed with patience, long-suffering.

Adverbs—inexcitably, *etc.;* in cold blood.

Antonyms, see EXCITABILITY, EXCITEMENT.

inexcusable, *adj.* unpardonable, unforgivable, unjustifiable. See INJUSTICE.

inexhaustible, *adj.* limitless, endless, unfailing. See SUFFICIENCY, INFINITY.

INEXPEDIENCE

Nouns—inexpedience, inexpediency; undesirableness, undesirability; discommodity, impropriety, ineligibility, inaptitude; unfitness (see DISAGREEMENT); inconvenience; disadvantage, untimeliness.

Verbs—come amiss; embarrass, hinder (see HINDRANCE); inconvenience, put upon *or* out.

Adjectives—inexpedient, undesirable; inadvisable, unappropriate; improper, objectionable; deleterious; unapt, inconvenient, embarrassing, disadvantageous, unfit, ineligible; incommodious, discommodious, ill-contrived *or* -occasioned, inopportune, untimely, unseasonable; out of place, unseemly; ill-advised, injudicious; clumsy, awkward.

Antonyms, see EXPEDIENCE.

inexpensive, *adj.* See CHEAPNESS.

inexperienced, *adj.* green, raw, untrained, fresh; naïve. See UNSKILLFULNESS, YOUTH.

inexpressible, *adj.* unutterable, ineffable, beyond words, indescribably. See UNMEANINGNESS, WONDER, PIETY.

infallible, *adj.* reliable, dependable, trustworthy, right; unfailing, unerring, unerrable, certain. See CERTAINTY.

infamous, *adj.* shameful, abominable, disgraceful, unspeakable, contemptible; heinous, atrocious, base, discreditable. See IMPROBITY, DISREPUTE.

infancy, *n.* babyhood, childhood; BEGINNING, cradle, genesis. See YOUTH, IGNORANCE.

infant, *n.* baby (see YOUTH).

infantry, *n.* soldiery, troops, foot soldiers. See COMBATANT.

infatuation, *n.* enamorment, fascination (by); passion, folly, gullibility, dotingness. See LOVE.

infection, *n.* epidemic, contagion, plague, contamination; illness; taint, toxicity, gangrene, poisoning. See DISEASE, TRANSFER.

infectious, *adj.* contagious (see TRANSFER).

infer, *v.t.* gather, reason, deduce, conclude, opine; presume; construe. See REASONING.

INFERIORITY

Nouns—**1,** inferiority, minority, subordinacy; inadequacy, deficiency (see INSUFFICIENCY); minimum; smallness; IMPERFECTION; poorness, meanness; subservience. See INEQUALITY, MEDIOCRITY, LITTLENESS.

2, inferior, subordinate, junior, underling; second best, runner-up, also-ran; second fiddle. *Slang,* second-stringer, long shot.

Verbs—not pass [muster], not measure up to; play second fiddle; scrape the bottom of the barrel. *Colloq.,* take a back seat, get the short end of the stick.

Adjectives—inferior, smaller; minor, junior, less[er], deficient, minus, lower, subordinate, secondary; second-rate, second-class, imperfect; short, inadequate, out of depth; subaltern; abysmal; weighed in the balance and found wanting, below par; not fit to hold a candle to.

Adverbs—below; behind, beneath; below par; short of, in the hole; at the bottom of the scale; at a low ebb. *Colloq.,* not up to snuff.

Antonyms, see SUPERIORITY.

---

infernal, *adj.* hellish, Plutonian, Stygian; fiendish, diabolical, demoniac[al]; *colloq.,* annoying, troublesome. See DEMON, HELL.

infest, *v.t.* overrun, invade, pervade; molest, torment. See PRESENCE, DISEASE.

infidelity, *n.* betrayal, treachery; faithlessness, fickleness; adultery; skepticism, unbelief. See IMPROBITY, IRRELIGION.

infiltrate, *v.* penetrate, pervade, permeate; enter, worm in, mix with, assimilate into. See INGRESS, MIXTURE, PASSAGE.

infinitesimal, *adj.* tiny, minute (see LITTLENESS).

INFINITY

Nouns—infinity, infinitude, infiniteness; immensity, limitlessness, inexhaustibility, immeasurability, incalculability, illimitability, interminability; eternity, PERPETUITY; endlessness. See SPACE, UNIVERSE.

Verbs—be infinite, boundless, *etc.;* go on *or* endure forever; immortalize; have no bounds, limit, *or* end.

Adjectives—infinite, immense; numberless, countless, sumless, measureless; innumerable, immeasurable, incalculable, illimitable, interminable, endless, unfathomable, bottomless, inexhaustible; indefinite; without number, limit, end, *or* measure, beyond measure; incomprehensible; limitless, boundless; untold, unnumbered, unmeasured, unbounded; perpetual, eternal.

Adverbs—infinitely, *etc.; ad infinitum;* perpetually.

Antonyms, see LIMIT.

---

infirmary, *n.* clinic (see REMEDY).

infirmity, *n.* fault; feebleness, WEAKNESS; illness, DISEASE.

inflame, *v.* anger, excite, arouse; incite, animate, kindle; heat, blaze up; aggravate, provoke, irritate; redden, flush. See VIOLENCE, EXCITEMENT.

inflammable, *adj.* burnable, combustible. See FUEL.

inflate, *v.* puff *or* blow up, aerate; expand, dilate, swell, distend; exaggerate. See WIND, INCREASE, EXPANSION, EXAGGERATION.

inflect, *v.* bend, turn, curve; modulate, vary; conjugate, decline. See CURVATURE, CHANGE, GRAMMAR.

inflexible, *adj.* unbending, rigid, unyielding; firm, steadfast, stubborn; grim, stern. See HARDNESS, RESOLUTION, INELASTICITY.

inflict, *v.t.* burden *or* trouble with; impose, put upon; do (to); give. See PUNISHMENT, COMPULSION.

infliction, *n.* scourge, affliction; ADVERSITY; curse, disgrace; imposition; administering (to). See COMPULSION.

INFLUENCE

Nouns—**1,** influence, IMPORTANCE, weight, pressure, preponderance; predominance, predominancy (see SUPERIORITY); POWER, sway; ascendancy; hegemony, reign, control, AUTHORITY; bias, protection, patronage, auspices (see AID); purchase, support; play, leverage. *Colloq.,* clout. *Slang,* pull, drag. See CAUSE.

2, patron, friend at court, power behind the throne.

Verbs—**1,** have influence, be influential; carry weight, weigh, tell; have a hold upon, sway, bias, pull the strings, militate; bear *or* work upon; swing one's weight; gain headway, have, get, *or* gain the upper hand. *Colloq.,* have the inside track, have it all over. *Slang,* have an in.

2, affect, impact *or* play on, make an impression on; prejudice; bribe (see PAYMENT); bring into line, lead by the nose, have a way with; move, budge, prompt, persuade, motivate, lean on; prevail upon, outweigh, overweigh; override, overbear. *Slang,* have in one's pocket; cut ice.

Adjectives—influential, important (see IMPORTANCE); weighty; prevailing upon.

Adverbs—influentially, with telling effect.

Antonyms, see UNIMPORTANCE.

---

influx, *n.* inflow, INGRESS, infiltration; inroad, invasion, ARRIVAL; immigration.

informal, *adj.* casual, free, easy, unofficial; unconventional, unceremonious. See UNCONFORMITY, ILLEGALITY.

INFORMATION

Nouns—**1,** information, enlightenment, acquaintance, KNOWLEDGE; data; publicity (see PUBLICATION); COMMUNICATION, intimation; notice, notification;

word, ADVICE, annunciation; announcement; representation, presentment; case, estimate, specification, report, monition; release, communiqué, dispatch; tidings, bulletin, NEWS, intelligence, dope; returns, RECORD; account, DESCRIPTION; statement, AFFIRMATION. *Colloq.*, inside story, a thing or two, two cents. *Slang*, info, lowdown, scuttlebutt.

2, mention, acquainting; instruction, TEACHING; outpouring; intercommunication, communicativeness; hint, suggestion, innuendo, implication, allusion, inkling, whisper, passing word; word, bug, *or* flea in the ear; subaudition, cue, byplay; gesture (see INDICATION); gentle *or* broad hint; whisper campaign; word to the wise; insinuation; subliminal suggestion. *Slang*, hot tip.

3, informer, informant, authority, teller, spokesperson, intelligencer, publisher, broadcaster, newscaster, commentator, reporter, mouthpiece; informer, talebearer, scandalmonger, tattletale, tout, eavesdropper; detective, spy (see INQUIRY); crier, herald; newsmonger; messenger (see AGENT); *amicus curiae;* pilot, guide. *Colloq.*, squealer, tipster. *Slang*, snitcher, stool pigeon, nark, rat, fink.

4, guidebook, handbook; manual; map, PLAN, chart, gazetteer; itinerary (see TRAVEL). See DIRECTION.

5, rumor, gossip, hearsay; scandal, tidbit, canard; item, topic, talk of the town, common currency, byword, household word. *Colloq.*, earful.

Verbs—**1,** inform, tell, acquaint, impart, convey, make acquainted with, apprize, advise, enlighten, awaken; give a piece of one's mind, tell one plainly, speak volumes, open up; let fall, mention, express, intimate, represent, communicate, make known; publish (see PUBLICATION); notify, signify, specify, disclose (see DISCLOSURE); undeceive, correct, disabuse, open the eyes of; let one know; give one to understand; give notice; point out; instruct, teach; direct the ATTENTION to. *Colloq.*, fill one in on, put wise, cue *or* clue in.

2, announce, annunciate, report; bring, send, leave, *or* give word; retail, render, *or* give an account (see DESCRIPTION); state, affirm (see AFFIRMATION).

3, hint, give an inkling of, imply, insinuate, intimate, get *or* drive at; allude to, suggest, prompt, give the cue, breathe; get to; tattle, spill, whisper; have something on, get the goods on; inform on, betray, turn state's evidence. *Colloq.*, tip off; put a flea *or* bug in one's ear; tell on, let in on, spill the beans, let the cat out of the bag. *Slang*, rat, double-cross, squeal, fink; sell down the river, turn in, finger.

4, be informed, know (see KNOWLEDGE); learn, receive news, get wind *or* scent of; gather (from); awaken to, open one's eyes to; become alive *or* awake to; hear, overhear, find out, understand; come to one's ears, come to one's knowledge, reach one's ears. *Colloq.*, catch on. *Slang*, get wise to, wise up.

Adjectives—informative, informational, reported, published; expressive, explicit, open, clear, plainspoken; declaratory, expository; communicative, communicatory; informed, knowledgeable.

Antonyms, see CONCEALMENT.

---

infrequent, *adj.* rare, few; uncommon, unusual; scarce, odd. See RARITY.

infringement, *n.* trespass, encroachment; infraction, breach; plagiarism, violation. See ILLEGALITY, DISOBEDIENCE.

infuriate, *v.t.* enrage, anger, madden, incense; incite, provoke, nettle, peeve, rankle. *Colloq.*, rile, make one's blood boil. See RESENTMENT.

infuse, *v.t.* steep, soak; introduce, implant, instill; tinge, imbue; pour into, mix in. See MIXTURE, INSERTION.

ingenious, *adj.* clever, inventive. See IMAGINATION, SKILL.

ingenuity, *n.* SKILL; cleverness; inventiveness; originality.

ingenuous, *adj.* artless, naïve, simple; candid, frank, open; trusting, unsuspecting. See SIMPLENESS.

ingratiating, *adj.* charming, winsome, winning, captivating; attractive, pleasing. See COURTESY.

INGRATITUDE

Nouns—**1,** ingratitude, ungratefulness, unthankfulness.

2, ingrate, wretch, a serpent in one's bosom.

Verbs—look a gift horse in the mouth; bite the hand that feeds one.

Adjectives—ungrateful, unappreciative, unmindful, unthankful; thankless, ingrate; forgotten, unacknowledged, unthanked, unrequited, unrewarded; ill-requited.

Antonyms, see GRATITUDE.

ingredient, *n.* component, PART, element, constituent. See COMPOSITION.

INGRESS

Nouns—**1,** ingress; entrance, entry, entrée, introgression; influx; intrusion, inroad, incursion, invasion, irruption; penetration, interpenetration; import, infiltration; access, admission, admittance, reception; insinuation (see BETWEEN); INSERTION. See APPROACH.

2, port of entry; antechamber (see RECEPTACLE); inlet; way in; mouth, door, OPENING, path, way; conduit, channel, PASSAGE; immigration.

3, incomer, immigrant, colonist, alien; entrant; newcomer; fifth column.

Verbs—enter, step in[side]; go, come, pour, flow, creep, slip, pop, break, *or* burst in; gain entrée; set foot on; burst *or* break in upon; invade, intrude; insinuate itself *or* oneself; penetrate, interpenetrate; infiltrate; find one's way into, wriggle into, worm oneself into; trespass; give entrance to, receive, insert; bore from within. *Colloq.,* breeze in. *Slang,* crash [the gate].

Adjectives—ingressive; incoming, ingoing, inward; entrant.

Antonyms, see EGRESS.

INHABITANT

Nouns—**1,** inhabitant, habitant; resident, [in]dweller, roomer, occupier, occupant; householder, boarder, renter, lodger, tenant; inmate; incumbent, sojourner, *locum tenens,* settler, colonist, squatter, nester; backwoodsman, islander; mountaineer; denizen, citizen, burgher, burgess, townsman; villager, cottager; compatriot, fellow citizen. *Colloq.,* city slicker; sooner; hayseed. *Slang,* hick, rube. See LOCATION, ABODE.

2, native, indigene, aborigine; newcomer.

3, population, POPULACE, public, people (see HUMANITY); colony, settlement; household; garrison, crew.

Verbs—inhabit, be present (see PRESENCE); dwell, reside, sojourn, occupy, lodge; be *or* hail from; settle (see ABODE); squat; colonize, billet.

Adjectives—indigenous; native, natal; aboriginal, primitive; domestic, domiciled, naturalized, vernacular, domesticated; domiciliary.

inhale, *v.* breathe (in). See WIND.

inherent, *adj.* native, innate; INTRINSIC, essential.

inherit, *v.t.* succeed (to); get, acquire, receive; possess. See ACQUISITION.

inhibit, *v.* circumscribe, restrain; hamper, check, cramp; repress, suppress; forbid, prohibit. See RESTRAINT, PROHIBITION.

inhuman, *adj.* cruel, barbarous, bestial, brutal, savage; supernatural. See MALEVOLENCE.

iniquity, *n.* vice, immorality; sin, wickedness, transgression, crime, wrongdoing; injustice. See EVIL, WRONG, IMPROBITY, ILLEGALITY.

initial, *adj.* first, BEGINNING, introductory, primary.—*n.* letter, monogram.

initiate, *v.t.* admit, introduce, take in; start, commence, inaugurate, institute. See BEGINNING.

inject, *v.t.* insert, introduce; wedge *or* force in; inoculate; intersperse, interject. See INSERTION.

injudicious, *adj.* unwise, imprudent. See FOLLY.

injunction, *n.* COMMAND, order, admonition, direction; requirement; PROHIBITION.

injure, *v.t.* wound, hurt; damage, abuse, deface, mar, impair; WRONG, disgrace, dishonor, insult, mistreat, maltreat. See DETERIORATION, EVIL, MALEVOLENCE.

INJUSTICE

Nouns—injustice, unjustness, unfairness; bias, warp, twist, partiality, prejudice, inequity, inequitableness; bigotry, pedantry; unsportsmanlike conduct; disservice, injury, WRONG; favoritism, nepotism, partisanship; sexism, machismo; unjustifiability, *etc.* See IMPROBITY, ILLEGALITY, MISJUDGMENT.

Verbs—be unjust, unfair, *or* inequitable, do injustice to, favor, play favorites, show partiality, bias, warp, twist, prejudice; hit below the belt. *Slang,* give a raw deal.

Adjectives—unjust, unfair, unsporting, partial, prejudiced, jaundiced, shortsighted, bigoted, inequitable, partisan, nepotistic, biased, onesided; undue, unjustifiable, inexcusable, unpardonable, unforgivable, indefensible.

Antonyms, see JUSTICE.

---

inkling, *n.* clue, suggestion, hint, whisper; surmise. See INFORMATION, SUPPOSITION.

inlet, *n.* creek, cove; entrance, INGRESS; channel. See OPENING.

inmate, *n.* prisoner, détenu; tenant, occupant. See INHABITANT, PRISON.

inn, *n.* hotel, hostelry; tavern, bar and grill. See ABODE, DRINKING.

innate, *adj.* natural, inborn; inherent; congenital. See INTRINSIC, INTUITION.

inner, *adj.* inward, internal, INTERIOR, inside; private, concealed.

innkeeper, *n.* host, hostess; taverner, tavernkeeper; landlord; hotelier, boniface. See PROVISION.

INNOCENCE

Nouns—**1,** innocence, guiltlessness, blamelessness, incorruption, impeccability, clean bill of health, clean hands, clean slate; PURITY, VIRTUE, virginity, chastity; artlessness, naïveté, candor, SIMPLENESS; immaculacy, CLEANNESS. See PROBITY.

2, innocent, child, lamb, dove, saint, newborn babe; virgin, maid; babe in the woods.

Verbs—be innocent, have a clear conscience; exonerate, acquit, (see ACQUITTAL); exculpate (see VINDICATION); whitewash; keep one's nose clean.

Adjectives—innocent, not guilty, unguilty, guiltless, faultless, sinless, stainless, bloodless, spotless, *sans peur et sans reproche,* clean, immaculate, unspotted, unblemished, unerring; unsullied, undefiled (see PROBITY); unravished, virginal, pure, white as snow, virtuous; Arcadian, artless, guileless, naïve, simple, unsophisticated; inculpable, unculpable, unblamed, unblamable, blameless, above suspicion; irreproachable, irreprovable, irreprehensible; unexceptionable, unobjectionable, unimpeachable; harmless, inoffensive, innocuous; dovelike, lamblike; innocent as a lamb, saint, child, babe unborn, *etc.;* more sinned against than sinning, unreproved, unimpeached. *Colloq.,* in the clear.

Adverbs—innocently, *etc.;* with clean hands; with a clear conscience.

Antonyms, see GUILT.

---

innocuous, *adj.* harmless, mild, inoffensive. See HEALTH, INNOCENCE, GOOD.

innovation, *n.* CHANGE, NEWNESS, novelty; variation; departure.

innuendo, *n.* implication, intimation, allusion. See INFORMATION.

innumerable, *adj.* countless, uncountable; numberless. See INFINITY.

inoculate, *v.t.* vaccinate, variolate, immunize, infect. See INSERTION.

inoffensive, *adj.* innocuous, harmless; unaggressive; blameless. See INNOCENCE.

inopportune, *adj.* unseasonable, untimely, ill-timed; inconvenient, awkward. See INEXPEDIENCE.

INORGANIC MATTER

Nouns—**1,** inorganic matter, mineral, mineral world *or* kingdom, unorganized, inanimate, *or* lifeless matter, inorganization; lithification, petrification; petrifaction; brute matter; stone, metal, chemicals (see MATERIALS).

2, mineralogy, geology, geognosy, geoscopy, metallurgy, lithology, petrology; inorganic chemistry.

Verbs—mineralize, petrify, lithify; turn to dust.

Adjectives—inorganic, mineral, unorganized, inanimate, lifeless, azoic, inert, insentient, insensible, insensate, unfeeling.

Antonyms, see ORGANIC MATTER.

---

input, *n.* INFORMATION, knowledge; contribution. *Colloq.,* two cents.

inquietude, *n.* uneasiness, FEAR; restlessness, AGITATION.

INQUIRY

Nouns—**1,** inquiry, enquiry; question, REQUEST; search, research, quest, PURSUIT; examination, test, intelligence test; review, scrutiny, investigation, inspection, probe; trial, hearing; inquest, inquisition; exploration, ventilation; sifting, calculation, analysis, dissection; resolution; induction; Baconian method; autopsy, *post mortem;* strict, close, searching, *or* exhaustive inquiry; narrow *or* strict search; study, consideration. *Colloq.,* exam. See CURIOSITY, THOUGHT, LEARNING.

2, questioning, interrogation, grilling, third degree, interrogatory; interpellation; challenge, examination, cross-examination, catechism; questionnaire; feeler, Socratic method, leading question; discussion (see REASONING); reconnoitering, reconnaissance; prying, espionage.

3, question, query, problem, topic, talking point, proposition, *desideratum,* point to be solved, subject *or* field of inquiry, subject of controversy; point *or* matter in dispute; moot point; [question at] issue; bone of contention (see DISCORD); fair *or* open question; enigma (see SECRET); knotty point (see DIFFICULTY).

4, inquirer, investigator, inquisitor, inspector, querist, examiner, prober, cross-examiner; spy; detective, operative, private eye, house detective; catechist; analyst; busybody (see CURIOSITY). *Colloq.,* op. *Slang,* shamus.

Verbs—**1,** inquire, seek, search; look for, look about for, look out for; scan, reconnoiter, explore, sound, rummage, ransack, pry, peer, look round; cast about *or* around, scrounge around; scavenge; look *or* go through *or* over; spy; peer *or* pry into every hole and corner; trace; ferret out, unearth, leave no stone unturned; smell, sniff, feel, sound, seek, *or* search out, run down, hunt up, nose *or* poke about *or* around, seek a clue, hunt, track, trail, hound; follow the trail *or* scent; pick one's way; pursue (see PURSUIT); thresh *or* smoke out; fish, feel, *or* grope for.

2, investigate, check [up] on; follow up; look up, look at *or* into; preexamine; discuss, comb, canvass, agitate; browse; examine, study, consider, calculate; delve into, prove, sound, fathom; scrutinize, analyze, anatomize, dissect, sift, winnow; audit, review, take stock of; take into consideration (see THOUGHT); take counsel (see ADVICE). *Colloq.,* kick around, hash over.

3, ask, question, demand; ventilate; grapple with *or* go into a question; interrogate, catechize, quiz, grill, pump, cross-question, cross-examine, give the third degree; pick the brains of; frisk; feel out.

Adjectives—inquiring, inquisitive, curious; catechetical, inquisitorial, analytic; in search *or* quest of; on the lookout for, interrogative; in question *or* dispute, in issue, under discussion, investigation, *or* consideration; *sub judice,* moot, proposed; doubtful (see DOUBT).

Adverbs—what? why? wherefore? whence? whither? where? how goes it? how is it? what is the reason? what's the matter? what's in the wind? what on earth? when? who? how come? what's up? what's new?

Antonyms, see ANSWER.

---

inquisition, *n.* examination, questioning; tribunal; cross-examination; probe, investigation, INQUIRY. See SEVERITY.

inquisitive, *adj.* questioning; curious, prying, meddlesome, busybodyish. See CURIOSITY.

inroad, *n.* raid, encroachment. See ATTACK.

INSANITY

Nouns—**1,** insanity, lunacy, derangement, craziness, feeblemindedness; psychosis, psychopathy, schizophrenia, split personality, paranoia, *dementia praecox,* neurosis; madness, mental illness, abnormality, aberration; dementia, frenzy, raving, delirium, hallucination; lycanthropy; rabies, hydrophobia; disordered reason *or* intellect; diseased, unsound, *or* abnormal mind; idiocy, imbecility; anility, senility, dotage (see AGE). See UNCONFORMITY, FOLLY.

2, vertigo, dizziness, swimming; sunstroke, moon-madness; [nervous] breakdown, collapse.

3, mania; monomania, megalomania, nymphomania, bibliomania, pyromania, logomania, theomania, kleptomania, dipsomania, Anglomania; delirium tremens; hypochondriasis, melancholia, hysteria (see DEJECTION); obsession, fixation; shell shock; phobia (see FEAR). *Slang,* hangup.

4, madman, madwoman, maniac, bedlamite, lunatic; demoniac, dipsomaniac, megalomaniac; neurotic, psychotic, psychopath, schizophrenic, catatonic, paranoiac; idiot, imbecile, cretin, moron, lunatic. *Colloq.,* couch case. *Slang,* nut, crank, loon[y], bat, bug, screwball, oddball, case, crackpot.

5, insane asylum, sanitarium, sanatorium, mental hospital *or* institution, bedlam, madhouse, booby hatch; straight jacket, padded cell. *Slang,* nuthouse, bughouse, loony bin.

6, psychiatrist, alienist (see INTELLECT).

Verbs—**1,** be insane, be out of one's mind; lose one's senses *or* reason; lose one's faculties *or* wits; go mad, run mad *or* amuck, rave, rant, dote, ramble, wander; drivel; take leave of one's senses, go into a tailspin *or* nosedive, break *or* crack up, go to pieces; lose one's head. *Colloq.,* come apart at the seams. *Slang,* have a screw loose, have bats in the belfry, not have all one's marbles *or* buttons; go off one's nut *or* rocker, see things, flip [one's lid], flip *or* freak out.

2, drive mad *or* crazy, craze, distract, shatter, unhinge, madden, dement, addle the wits of, derange; infatuate, obsess, turn the brain, turn one's head, go to one's head.

3, commit, put away, institutionalize, lock up (see RESTRAINT); certify.

Adjectives—**1,** insane, mad, lunatic; crazy, crazed, *non compos mentis,* unhinged, unbalanced, disturbed; paranoid, manic, psychopathic, psychotic, psychoneurotic, manic-depressive; not right, touched; bereft of reason; unhinged, unsettled in one's mind; insensate, reasonless, beside oneself, demented, daft; frenzied, frenetic; possessed [of a devil]; far gone, maddened, moonstruck; scatterbrained, crackbrained, off one's head; maniacal; delirious, irrational, lightheaded, incoherent, rambling, doting, wandering; amuck, frantic, raving, stark mad, staring mad. *Slang,* crazy as a bedbug, loco, psycho, nutty [as a fruitcake], screwy, wacky, bananas, off the wall, off one's trolley *or* rocker, freaky, bonkers; tetched, pixilated, bughouse; mental (*Brit.*).

2, rabid, giddy, dizzy, cuckoo, daft, vertiginous, wild, slap-happy; mazed, flighty; distracted, distraught; mad as a hatter *or* March hare; of unsound mind; touched [in one's head], not in one's right mind; in a fog *or* haze; out of one's mind, head, senses, *or* wits; on the ragged edge. *Colloq.,* daffy. *Slang,* off one's nut, haywire, barmy, balmy.

3, fanatical, obsessed, infatuated; odd, eccentric (see UNCONFORMITY); hipped; hypochondriac; idiot, imbecile, silly.

4, monomaniacal, kleptomaniacal, *etc.* (see *Nouns, 3*).

Adverbs—insanely; like one possessed; maniacally, *etc.*

Antonyms, see SANITY.

---

insatiable, *adj.* greedy, voracious; insatiate, unappeasable, quenchless, unquenchable. See DESIRE, GLUTTONY.

inscribe, *v.t.* write; mark, engrave; enter, enroll, LIST. See WRITING, ENGRAVING.

inscrutable, *adj.* unfathomable (see UNINTELLIGIBILITY).

insect, *n.* bug; fly, moth, beetle, ant, *etc.* See ANIMAL.

insecurity, *n.* DANGER, uncertainty, risk, hazard, jeopardy.

INSENSIBILITY

Nouns—**1,** insensibility, insensibleness; impassibility, impassibleness, impassivity;

inappetency, apathy, phlegm, dullness, hebetude, supineness, lukewarmness. See OBLIVION.

2, coldness, cold fit, cold blood, cold heart; frigidity, *sangfroid;* stoicism; imperturbability, INEXCITABILITY; nonchalance, unconcern, dry eyes; insouciance, INDIFFERENCE; RASHNESS, callousness; heart of stone, marble, deadness; thickness of skin. See INACTIVITY.

3, coma, trance, sleep, suspended animation. See REPOSE.

4, numbness; unfeeling, anesthesia, analgesia, narcosis; acupuncture, acupressure; painkiller, novocaine, xylocaine, *etc.;* stupor, stupefaction, paralysis, palsy.

5, anesthetic, ether, chloroform, nitrous oxide, opium; refrigeration, cryotherapy.

Verbs—**1,** black *or* pass out, draw a blank; have a rhinocerous hide; show insensibility, not mind *or* care, not be affected by; have no desire for, not care a straw (see INDIFFERENCE); disregard (see NEGLECT); set at naught; turn a deaf ear to.

2, desensitize, blunt, obtund, [be]numb, paralyze, drug, chloroform, deaden, hebetate, stun, stupefy, daze, knock out; inure, harden [the heart]; steel, caseharden, sear.

Adjectives—**1,** insensible, senseless, unconscious; insensitive; impassive, impassible; dispassionate; blind, deaf, *or* dead to; unsusceptible, insusceptible; unimpressionable, passionless, spiritless, heartless, soulless, hardhearted; unfeeling, indifferent, lukewarm, careless, regardless; inattentive, neglectful.

2, callous, thickskinned, pachydermatous, impervious; hard, hardened, inured, casehardened; steeled against; proof against; imperturbable, inexcitable, unfelt; unconcerned, nonchalant, insouciant, *sans souci.*

3, unambitious; unaffected, unruffled, unimpressed, uninspired, unexcited, unmoved, unstirred, untouched, unshocked, unstruck; unblushing, shameless; unanimated, vegetative; apathetic, phlegmatic; dull, frigid; cold, coldblooded, coldhearted; cold as marble *or* charity; flat, obtuse, inert, supine, languid, half-hearted; numb[ed]; comatose; anesthetic, stupefied, chloroformed; dead to the world, dead[ened]; narcotic. *Colloq.,* out like a light, out cold.

Adverbs—insensibly, *etc.;* in cold blood; with dry eyes.

Antonyms, see SENSIBILITY.

INSERTION

Nouns—**1,** insertion, introduction, interpolation; injection, inoculation; implantation; ADDITION; INTERMENT; penetration. See BETWEEN.

2, insert, inset, inlay; entering wedge (see INGRESS); adjunct; parenthesis.

Verbs—insert, interpolate, inset, inlay; put, press, pack, *or* stuff in; inject, inoculate; introduce, insinuate, impregnate, implant, graft, bud; intervene (see BETWEEN); infuse, instill; add; bury, inter; immerse, submerge; pierce (see OPENING).

Adjectives—interpolative, parenthetical, *etc.*

Antonyms, see EXTRACTION.

---

insidious, *adj.* deceitful; treacherous. See DECEPTION, IMPROBITY.

insight, *n.* discernment, perceptiveness, perception; INTUITION; penetration, understanding. See KNOWLEDGE.

insignia, *n.pl.* badges [of office], emblems. See INDICATION.

insignificant, *adj.* meaningless; unimportant, inconsequential, trivial, small, worthless. See CHEAPNESS, UNIMPORTANCE.

insincere, *adj.* false, deceptive; hypocritical, two-faced; half-hearted, untrue, affected. See AFFECTATION, FALSEHOOD.

insinuate, *v.t.* hint, suggest, intimate; ingratiate (oneself), curry favor; insert, instill. See INFORMATION, INSERTION, BETWEEN.

INSIPIDITY

Nouns—insipidity, vapidity; tastelessness, weakness; dullness, MEDIOCRITY, INDIFFERENCE.

Adjectives—**1,** insipid, tasteless, flavorless, savorless, unseasoned, zestless; weak, stale, flat, mild, bland; milk-and-water, watery.

2, uninteresting, unentertaining, prosaic, prosy, jejune, tame, dull, dry; vapid, flat, banal; mawkish, wishy-washy; spiritless, lacklustrous, pointless, lifeless, amort, dead.

Antonyms, see TASTE, PUNGENCY.

---

insist, *v.i.* state, maintain, hold to; persist, urge, press; demand. See AFFIRMATION, COMPULSION, OBSTINACY.

insnare, *v.t.* See ENSNARE.

INSOLENCE

Nouns—**1,** insolence, arrogance; hauteur, haughtiness, airs; overbearance; presumption, assertiveness, bravado, pomposity, snobbery; DEFIANCE.

2, impertinence; sauciness, flippancy, petulance, bluster; familiarity; cheek, swagger[ing], bounce; impudence, assurance, audacity; hardihood, front, face, shamelessness, effrontery, PRIDE, VANITY. *Colloq.,* brass, sauce. *Slang,* gall, nerve, sass, crust, lip. See DISCOURTESY.

3, smart aleck. *Colloq.,* smart *or* wise guy. *Slang,* smarty pants, weisenheimer, minx, cool hand.

Verbs—**1,** bluster, vapor, swagger, swell, give oneself airs, snap one's fingers; swear (see AFFIRMATION); roister; arrogate; assume, presume; make bold, make free; take a liberty, patronize. *Slang,* have a nerve.

2, outface, outlook, outstare, outbrazen, outbrave; stare out of countenance; brazen out; lay down the law; talk *or* act big; talk back, get on a high horse; toss the head, carry with a high hand; overreach. See THREAT.

Adjectives—**1,** insolent, haughty, arrogant, imperious, high-handed, high and mighty, stuck-up, cocky, uppity; contumelious, supercilious, snobbish, overbearing, overweening, lordly, assertive, bold, high-flown; nervy. *Slang,* high-hat, fresh.

2, flippant, pert, cavalier, saucy, sassy, forward, impertinent, malapert; precocious, assuming, would-be, bumptious; bluff; brazen, shameless, aweless, unblushing, unabashed; boldfaced, barefaced, brazen-faced; familiar, impudent, audacious, presumptuous, free and easy; roistering, blustering, hectoring, swaggering, vaporing. *Colloq.,* flip.

Adverbs—insolently, *etc.;* with a high hand; where angels fear to tread.

Antonyms, see SERVILITY.

---

insolvency, *n.* FAILURE, bankruptcy; lack of funds. See DEBT.

insomnia, *n.* sleeplessness; wakefulness. See ACTIVITY.

inspect, *v.t.* examine, scrutinize; check (up); oversee; investigate, look into. See ATTENTION, VISION.

inspiration, *n.* breathing, inhalation; happy thought, brainstorm, brainwave. See CAUSE, FEELING, PIETY, IMAGINATION.

inspire, *v.* breathe (in); stimulate, animate, [en]liven; spur, give an incentive. See CAUSE, WIND.

instability, *n.* CHANGEABLENESS, unsteadiness, inconstancy.

install, *v.t.* put in, set up; induct, seat, inaugurate, invest. See LOCATION, CELEBRATION, BEGINNING.

installment, *n.* down payment, time payment, layaway plan; episode, PART; installation, setting up, putting in. See COMMISSION.

instance, *n.* case, example, illustration, demonstration. See CONFORMITY.

instant, *adj.* sudden, immediate, direct, instantaneous. See INSTANTANEITY. —*n.* second, moment; minute; twinkling, jiffy. See NECESSITY, PRESENT.

INSTANTANEITY

Nouns—**1,** instantaneity, instantaneousness, immediacy, precipitancy (see RASHNESS); suddenness, abruptness; moment, minute, second, instant, split second, nanosecond; twinkling, trice, flash, breath, crack, burst, flash of lightning, less than no time; jack-rabbit start. See TIME, EARLINESS, TRANSIENTNESS. **2,** very minute, very time, very hour; PRESENT time, right, true, exact, *or* correct time. *Colloq.,* jiffy. *Slang,* half a shake, sec. See CHRONOMETRY.

Verbs—think on one's feet; stop in one's tracks, stop on a dime.

Adjectives—instantaneous, momentary, sudden, instant, abrupt; extemporaneous; precipitate, immediate, hasty (see HASTE); quick as thought *or* lightning.

Adverbs—instantaneously, instantly, immediately, [right] now, right off, right away, then and there, here and now; in less than no time; presto, *subito,* instanter, suddenly, at a stroke, word, *or* blow, at the drop of a hat; in a moment, in the twinkling of an eye, in a flash, at one jump, in the same breath, [all] at once; plump, slap; at one fell swoop; at the same instant; straight off, directly, immediately, cold turkey, *ex tempore,* on the spot, on the spur of the moment; just then; slapdash. *Colloq.,* in a jiffy, like a shot, yesterday, in nothing flat, in two shakes, before one can say Jack Robinson. *Slang,* like a bat out of hell.

Antonyms, see LATENESS, PERPETUITY.

---

instead, *adv.* in place *or* lieu (of). See SUBSTITUTION.

instigate, *v.t.* incite, provoke; initiate, stimulate, urge, promote. See CAUSE.

instill, *v.t.* inculcate, implant, impart; pour in, mix in, infuse. See MIXTURE, TEACHING, INSERTION.

instinct, *n.* knack, aptitude; impulse, prompting, discernment; INTUITION. See INTRINSIC.

institute, *v.t.* found, inaugurate; organize, start, begin, commence; originate, organize. See BEGINNING. —*n.* institution; SCHOOL, college; foundation; society; museum; hospital, *etc.* See PARTY.

instruction, *n.* TEACHING, tutelage, education; training, coaching; COMMAND, order, direction, directive; ADVICE. See INFORMATION.

instrument, *n.* implement (see INSTRUMENTALITY); flute, oboe, *etc.* (see MUSIC); document, deed, paper, RECORD, charter; MEANS, AGENCY.

INSTRUMENTALITY

Nouns—**1,** instrumentality; instrument, AID; subservience, subserviency; vehicle, hand, expedient (see PLAN); MEANS, AGENCY.

2, stepping-stone; [master *or* skeleton] key, latchkey, passkey; open sesame; passport, *passe-partout,* safeconduct, pass, *etc.*

3, hardware, equipment; gadget, contraption; automaton, robot; instrument, tool, device, implement, appliance, apparatus, contrivance, machine; hammer, chisel, plane, saw, screw, nail, screwdriver, knife, rasp, file; lever, crowbar, pry, prize, jimmy, jack; motor, engine, treadle, pedal; gear, paraphernalia, machinery; pulley, block and tackle, crane, derrick; belt, conveyor belt; wheels, gears, cam, clockwork, cog, flywheel; can opener, scissors, shears, lawnmower, *etc.*

Verbs—be instrumental, subserve.

Adjectives—instrumental; useful (see UTILITY); ministerial, subservient.

Adverbs—instrumentality; through, by, per; whereby, thereby, hereby; by the agency of.

Antonyms, see USELESSNESS.

---

insubordinate, *adj.* disobedient, intractable; mutinous, insurgent; stubborn, obstinate. *Colloq.,* too big for one's britches. See DISOBEDIENCE, DEFIANCE.

INSUBSTANTIALITY

Nouns—**1,** insubstantiality; nothingness, nihility; nothing, naught, nil, nullity, zero, cipher, no one, nobody; never a one; no such thing, none in the world; nothing whatever, nothing at all, nothing on earth; not a particle (see LITTLENESS); all talk, moonshine, stuff and nonsense; shadow; phantom; dream (see IMAGINATION); *ignis fatuus;* [thin] air; bubble; mockery; hollowness, blank, void (see ABSENCE); inanity, fool's paradise. See NONEXISTENCE, UNIMPORTANCE.

2, immateriality, immaterialness, intangibility; incorporeality, disembodiment; spirit, soul, ego; spiritualism, spirituality.

Verbs—immaterialize, dematerialize; disembody, spiritualize (see DISAPPEARANCE).

Adjectives—insubstantial, unsubstantial; bodiless, incorporeal, spiritual, immaterial, intangible, unearthly; psychical, supernatural; visionary, imaginary (see IMAGINATION); dreamy; shadowy, ethereal, aerial, airy, spectral; weightless; vacant, vacuous, empty (see ABSENCE), blank, hollow; nominal, null; inane.

Antonyms, see SUBSTANCE.

---

insufferable, *adj.* unendurable, unbearable, insupportable, intolerable, past bearing *or* enduring, more than flesh and blood can bear; agonizing, excruciating. See PAIN.

INSUFFICIENCY

Nouns—**1,** insufficiency; inadequacy, inadequateness; incompetence, IMPOTENCE; deficiency, INCOMPLETENESS, IMPERFECTION, shortcoming, emptiness, poorness, depletion, vacancy, flaccidity; ebb tide; low water; bankruptcy, insolvency (see DEBT, NONPAYMENT).

2, paucity; stint; scantiness, smallness, none to spare; bare necessities, scarcity, dearth; want, need, deprivation, lack, POVERTY; inanition, starvation, famine, drought; dole, pittance; short allowance *or* rations, half-rations.

Verbs—**1,** not suffice, fall short of (see FAILURE); run dry, run *or* give out, run short; want, lack, need, require; be caught short, be in want, live from hand to mouth; miss by a mile.

2, exhaust, deplete, drain of resources; impoverish (see WASTE); stint, begrudge (see PARSIMONY); cut back, retrench; bleed white.

Adjectives—**1,** insufficient, inadequate; too little, not enough; unequal to; incompetent, impotent; weighed in the balance and found wanting; perfunctory (see NEGLECT); deficient, wanting, lacking, imperfect; ill-furnished, -provided, *or* -stored; badly off.

2, slack, at a low ebb; empty, vacant, bare; out of stock; short (of), out of, destitute (of), devoid (of), denuded (of); dry, drained; in short supply, not to be had for love or money, not to be had at any price; empty-handed; short-handed.

3, meager, poor, thin, sparing, spare, skimpy, stinted; starved, half-starved, famine-stricken, famished; jejune; scant, small, scarce; scurvy, stingy; at the end of one's tether; without resources (see MEANS); in want, poor (see POVERTY); in DEBT. *Slang,* shy of, fresh out of.

Adverbs—insufficiently, *etc.;* in default, for want of; failing.

Antonyms, see SUFFICIENCY.

---

insular, *adj.* isolated; islanded, insulated; aloof; narrow[minded], limited, illiberal; isolationist. See NARROWNESS.

insulate, *v.t.* cover, protect, shield; set apart, isolate, detach. See EXCLUSION, COVERING.

insult, *v.t.* slap, abuse, affront, offend. See DISCOURTESY. —*n.* outrage; slap, affront. See DISRESPECT.

insuperable, *adj.* insurmountable. See IMPOSSIBILITY.

insurance, *n.* guarantee, warranty, coverage, protection; insurance policy; assurance, SECURITY.

insurgent, *adj.* rebellious, insubordinate, mutinous, in revolt, uprising. —*n.* rebel, insubordinate, mutineer, revolutionary, insurrectionist. See REVOLUTION, DISOBEDIENCE.

insurmountable, *adj.* insuperable. See IMPOSSIBILITY.

insurrection, *n.* uprising, riot, eruption; mutiny, REVOLUTION, insurgence. See OPPOSITION, DISOBEDIENCE.

intact, *adj.* whole, unimpaired, uninjured; untouched. See PERFECTION, PRESERVATION.

intake, *n.* consumption, ingestion, assimilation; receipts. See RECEIVING.

intangible, *adj.* immaterial, vague, impalpable; unspecific; abstract. See INSUBSTANTIALITY.

integrate, *v.t.* unite, fuse; synthesize, blend; complete. See UNITY.

integrity, *n.* honor, honesty, PROBITY, uprightness; wholeness, completeness, oneness. See WHOLE.

INTELLECT

Nouns—**1,** intellect, intellectuality, mentality, brain[s], mind, understanding, reason (see REASONING), rationality; faculties, senses, consciousness, observation (see ATTENTION); perception, apperception, INTELLIGENCE; INTUITION, association of ideas; conception, JUDGMENT, wits, mental capacity, genius; logic, THOUGHT, meditation.

2, soul, spirit, psyche, ghost, inner man, heart, breast, bosom; seat of thought, brain; subconscious, id; head, cerebrum, cranium; gray matter. *Slang,* upper story, noodle.

3, psychology, psychopathology, psychotherapy, psychiatry, psychoanalysis, psychometry; ideology; philosophy; phrenology, craniology, cranioscopy; ideality, idealism; transcendentalism, spiritualism, immateriality.

4, psychologist, psychopathologist, alienist, psychiatrist, psychometrist, psychotherapist, psychoanalyst, analyst. *Slang,* head shrinker, shrink, head doctor.

Verbs—intellectualize (see THOUGHT); note, notice, mark; take notice, take cognizance; be aware *or* conscious; realize; appreciate; ruminate; fancy, imagine (see IMAGINATION).

Adjectives—intellectual, mental, rational, subjective, metaphysical, spiritual, ghostly; psychical, psychological; cerebral; percipient, aware, conscious; subconscious; immaterial; logical, reasoning, reasonable; thoughtful, thinking, meditative, contemplative.

Antonyms, see INSANITY.

INTELLIGENCE

Nouns—intelligence, capacity, comprehension, apprehension, understanding; parts, sagacity, [mother] wit, *esprit;* intelligence quotient, I.Q., acuteness, shrewdness, CUNNING; acumen, subtlety, penetration; perspicuity, perspicacity, percipience; discernment, good JUDGMENT; levelheadedness, discrimination; refinement (see TASTE); KNOWLEDGE; head, brains, mind, INTELLECT; eagle eye; genius, inspiration, soul; talent, aptitude (see SKILL). *Colloq.,* horse sense.

Verbs—be intelligent, have all one's wits about one; understand, grasp, comprehend, figure *or* make out; come to terms *or* grips with; take a hint; see through, take in, see at a glance, see with half an eye; dawn on one; penetrate; discern (see VISION). *Colloq.,* sink *or* soak in; catch *or* latch on (to).

Adjectives—intelligent, quick, keen, brainy, acute, alive, awake, bright, brilliant, sagacious, sharp; nimble- *or* quick-witted; wide awake; CUNNING, canny, arch, shrewd, astute; clear-headed *or* -eyed; far-sighted; discerning, perspicacious, penetrating, subtle, perceptive, piercing, sharp [as a tack]; alive to, aware of (see KNOWLEDGE); clever (see SKILL). *Colloq.,* not so dumb. *Slang,* not born yesterday.

Antonyms, see IGNORANCE.

---

intelligible, *adj.* clear, explicit; articulate, comprehensible; lucid, perspicuous; legible, precise; obvious. See MEANING.

INTEMPERANCE

Nouns—**1,** intemperance, indulgence, overindulgence, high living, self-indulgence; voluptuousness; epicurism, epicureanism, sybaritism (see GLUTTONY); drunkenness, DRINKING; prodigality (see WASTE); dissipation, licentiousness, debauchery; crapulence, incontinence; excess, too much; sensuality, animalism, carnality; PLEASURE, luxury, luxuriousness; lap of pleasure *or* luxury.

2, revel[s], revelry; debauch, carousal, jollification, drinking bout, wassail, saturnalia, orgy.

3, drunkard, addict, voluptuary, sybarite, glutton, rake, roué, gourmand, sensualist, *etc.*

Verbs—indulge, overindulge, exceed; live well *or* high, live on the fat of the land; wallow, plunge into dissipation; revel, rake, live hard, cut loose, run riot, sow one's wild oats; slake one's appetite *or* thirst; swill; pamper; burn the candle at both ends.

Adjectives—intemperate, inabstinent; sensual, self-indulgent; voluptuous, luxurious, licentious, wild, dissolute, dissipated, rakish, fast, debauched; brutish; crapulous, crapulent, swinish, piggish; epicurean, sybaritical; bred in the lap of luxury; indulged, pampered, full-fed, prodigal. *Slang,* off the wagon.

Antonyms, see MODERATION.

---

intend, *v.* See INTENTION.

intense, *adj.* violent, sharp, strong; passionate, ardent, vivid; deep, dark; poignant, keen, acute; extreme. See FEELING.

intensify, *v.* deepen, strengthen, heighten, sharpen; concentrate; aggravate (see INCREASE). See STRENGTH.

intensity, *n.* depth; feeling; power, force, strength, VIGOR; darkness, brilliance; extremity. See DEGREE, ENERGY, VIOLENCE.

intent, *n.* See INTENTION. *—adj.* earnest, sincere; absorbed, engrossed; bent (on). See ATTENTION, RESOLUTION.

INTENTION

Nouns—**1,** intention, intent, intentionality; purpose; project, PLAN, UNDERTAKING; predetermination; design, ambition; contemplation, mind, animus, view, purview, proposal; lookout; decision, determination, resolve, RESOLUTION; set *or* settled purpose, wish, DESIRE, motive. See WILL, MEANING.

2, final cause, *raison d'être,* end in itself; object, aim, end; drift, tenor, TENDENCY; goal, target, prey, quarry, game; destination, mark. See PURSUIT.

Verbs—intend, purpose, design, mean; have to; propose to oneself, harbor a design; have in view *or* mind; have an eye to; labor for; be after, aspire after, endeavor; aim *or* drive at; take aim, set before oneself; study to; hitch one's wagon to a star; take upon oneself, undertake, take into one's head; meditate, contemplate; think, dream, *or* talk of; premeditate; compass, calculate; plan *or* figure on, destine, propose, predetermine; project, PLAN, have a mind to (see WILLINGNESS); DESIRE, pursue.

Adjectives—intended, intentional, advised, studied, express, determinate, prepense, bound for; intending, minded; bent upon, earnest, resolute; at stake; on the fire, in view, in prospect.

Adverbs—intentionally, *etc.;* advisedly, wittingly, knowingly, designedly, purposely, on purpose, by design, studiously, pointedly; with intent; deliberately, with premeditation; with one's eyes open, in cold blood; to all intents and purposes; with a view *or* eye to; by way of, so as to, in order to *or* that, to the end that, with the intent that; for the purpose of, with the view of, in contemplation of, on account of; in pursuance of, pursuant to.

Antonyms, see CHANCE.

---

inter, *v.t.* bury, entomb, inearth. See INTERMENT.

intercede, *v.i.* mediate, arbitrate; intervene, interpose. See COMPROMISE.

intercept, *v.t.* stop, interrupt, check, hinder; catch, nab, seize; cut off. See HINDRANCE.

INTERCHANGE

Nouns—interchange, exchange, interchangeableness, interchangeability;

permutation, intermutation; reciprocation, reciprocity, transportation, shuffling, give and take; alternation; hocus-pocus; BARTER; a Roland for an Oliver, tit for tat, an eye for an eye, RETALIATION; crossfire, battledore and shuttlecock; *quid pro quo,* musical chairs; fungible. See TRANSFER, SUBSTITUTION.

Verbs—interchange, exchange, counterchange, transpose, bandy, shuffle, change hands, change partners, take turns, switch, swap, permute, reciprocate, commute; cash in; give *or* put and take, pay back, requite, return the compliment, put the shoe on the other foot, give a dose *or* taste of one's own medicine; retaliate (see RETALIATION). *Colloq.,* flip-flop.

Adjectives—interchanged, interchanging, interchangeable, fungible, reciprocal, mutual, communicative, intercurrent.

Adverbs—in exchange, *vice versa,* backward[s] and forward[s], by turns, turn and turn about; in exchange for, against, in consideration of; from hand to hand; in kind, in turn; each other, one another.

Antonyms, see IDENTITY.

---

intercourse, *n.* COMMUNICATION, CONVERSATION, converse, communion; coitus, [sexual] congress; SOCIALITY; fellowship, association; commerce, dealings, trade, BUSINESS.

interest, *v.* concern; touch, affect; fascinate, engross, intrigue; hold [the attention], engage, absorb. See EXCITEMENT. —*n.* concern; welfare, benefit; payment, sum, advantage, profit; PART, share, holding; claim, title. See DEBT, IMPORTANCE, POSSESSION.

interfere, *v.i.* butt in, meddle, interpose; hinder, hamper; clash, obstruct, collide, oppose. See HINDRANCE, BETWEEN.

interference, *n.* HINDRANCE; opposition, conflict; static, jamming.

interim, *n.* meantime (see BETWEEN).

INTERIOR

Nouns—interior, interiority; intrinsicality (see INTRINSIC); inside[s], subsoil, substratum; contents (see COMPOSITION), substance, bowels, belly, intestines, guts, chitterlings; womb; lap; [innermost] recesses; cave (see CONCAVITY).

Verbs—be inside *or* within; place *or* keep within; enclose, circumscribe (see CIRCUMSCRIPTION); intern; imbed, insert (see INSERTION); imprison (see RESTRAINT).

Adjectives—interior, internal; inner, inside, inward, inmost, innermost; deep-seated; intestinal; inland; subcutaneous; interstitial (see BETWEEN); inwrought; enclosed; intramural; domestic, indoor, vernacular; endemic.

Adverbs—internally, inwardly, inward[s], inly; herein, therein, wherein; indoors, within doors; at home, in the bosom of one's family.

Prepositions—in, inside, within.

Antonyms, see EXTERIOR.

---

interloper, *n.* intruder, trespasser; meddler, interferer, intermeddler. See BETWEEN.

interlude, *n.* intermission, intermezzo, entr'acte; pause, interval, episode, gap, space. See TIME, DRAMA.

intermediary, *n.* go-between, mediator; arbiter, arbitrator, umpire, referee; middleman. See BETWEEN.

intermediate, *adj.* BETWEEN; MIDDLE, intervening; halfway. See MEAN.

INTERMENT

Nouns—**1,** interment, burial, sepulture, inhumation.

2, obsequies, funeral [rites], last rites, extreme unction; wake; pyre, funeral pile, cremation, immolation; [death] knell, passing bell, tolling; dirge (see LAMENTATION); dead march, muffled drum; elegy, panegyric, funeral oration; epitaph; obituary, death notice; autopsy. *Colloq.,* obit.

3, grave clothes, shroud, winding sheet, cerement; coffin, casket, shell, sarcophagus, urn, pall, bier, hearse, catafalque, cinerary urn. *Slang,* dead *or* meat wagon.

4, grave, pit, sepulcher, tomb, vault, crypt, catacomb, mausoleum, golgotha, house of death, narrow house; cemetery, necropolis; burial place *or* ground; graveyard, churchyard; God's acre; cromlech, barrow, cairn; bonehouse, charnel house, morgue, mortuary; cinerarium, monument, marker, cenotaph, shrine; stele, gravestone, headstone, slab, tombstone; memorial, pyramid. *Slang,* boneyard, Boot Hill.

5, undertaker, embalmer, mortician; pallbearer, mourner; sexton; gravedigger.

Verbs—inter, bury; lay in the grave, consign to the grave *or* tomb, lay to rest; entomb, inhume; lay out; lie in state; perform a funeral; cremate, immolate; embalm, mummify. *Slang,* push up daisies.

Adjectives—funereal, funebrial; mortuary, sepulchral, cinerary; elegiac; necroscopic.

Adverbs—in memoriam; post-obit, *post-mortem;* beneath the sod.

Interjections—rest in peace! *requiescat in pace,* R.I.P.

Antonyms, see DISCLOSURE.

---

interminable, *adj.* endless (see CONTINUITY).

intermission, *n.* pause, interval, break; entr'acte. See DRAMA, DISCONTINUANCE.

intermittent, *adj.* fitful, off-and-on, recurrent; periodic, discontinuous, interrupted, broken; flickering. See IRREGULARITY, DISCONTINUANCE.

intern, *v.t.* detain, hold; shut up *or* in, confine. —*n.* interne, internee; prisoner; student *or* resident doctor. See RESTRAINT, REMEDY.

internal, *adj.* inner, enclosed, inside, INTERIOR; innate, inherent; domestic, inland. See INTRINSIC.

international, *adj.* worldwide, global, universal. See HUMANITY.

interpose, *v.* step in *or* BETWEEN; interfere, meddle; mediate, arbitrate; intervene, interrupt. See HINDRANCE, DISCONTINUANCE.

INTERPRETATION

Nouns—**1,** interpretation, definition; explanation, explication; solution, ANSWER; *rationale,* concept; strict interpretation; DEMONSTRATION; MEANING; acception, acceptation, acceptance; light, reading, lection, construction, version; semantics. See TEACHING.

2, translation, rendering, rendition, paraphrase, construct; literal *or* free translation; secret, clue; dissertation; ATTRIBUTION. *Colloq.,* trot, bicycle. *Slang,* pony.

3, exegesis; expounding, exposition; comment, commentary; inference, deduction (see REASONING); illustration, exemplification; glossary, annotation, scholium, note, elucidation; symptomatology; reading of signs, semeiology; diagnosis, prognosis; metoposcopy; paleography, philology; equivalent, synonym; polyglot.

4, decipherment, decodement; cryptography, cryptanalysis; key, solution, ANSWER, light.

5, lecture, sermon, tract; discussion, disquisition; treatise, discourse, exposition, study; critique, criticism; essay, theme, thesis.

6, interpreter, explainer, translator; expositor, exponent, expounder; demonstrator, definer, simplifier, popularizer; oracle, teacher; commentator, annotator, scholiast; constructionist; diagnostician; decoder, cryptographer, cryptanalyst.

Verbs—interpret, explain, define, construe, translate, render; do into, turn into; paraphrase, restate; read; spell *or* make out; decipher, unravel, disentangle; illuminate, clarify, find the key of, make sense of, make head or tail of, enucleate, resolve, solve, get at, clear up, get to the bottom of; read between the lines; account for; find *or* tell the cause of; throw *or* shed light on; clear up, elucidate; illustrate, exemplify; unfold, expound, comment upon, annotate, gloss; key; popularize; understand by, put a construction on, be given to understand; put *or* get across, get over, get through to. *Colloq.*, psych out.

Adjectives—interpretive, interpretative; definitive; inferential, deductive, explanatory, expository; explicative, explicatory, exegetical, illustrative; polyglot; literal; paraphrastic, metaphrastic; cosignificative, synonymous, equivalent.

Adverbs—interpretively, interpretatively, in explanation; that is to say, *id est, videlicet,* to wit, namely, in short, in other words; literally, strictly speaking, in plain words *or* English; more simply.

Antonyms, see UNMEANINGNESS, DISTORTION.

---

interrogation, *n.* INQUIRY, inquisition, questioning; probe, investigation, [cross]examination.

interrupt, *v.* stop, check; suspend, cut short, hinder, obstruct; butt in, interpose, break in. See HINDRANCE, DISCONTINUANCE.

intersect, *v.i.* cut, bisect; interrupt; meet, cross. See CROSSING.

intersperse, *v.* scatter (see BETWEEN, DISPERSION).

INTERVAL

Nouns—interval, interspace; separation, DISJUNCTION; break, fracture, gap; hole, OPENING; chasm, hiatus, caesura; interruption, interregnum; interstice, lacuna, cleft, mesh, crevice, chink, cranny, crack, chap, slit, fissure, scissure, rift, flaw, breach, rent, gash, cut, incision, leak; haha, gorge, defile, ravine, coulee, canyon, crevasse, abyss, abysm; gulf; inlet, firth, frith, strait, gulch, gully; pass, FURROW; parenthesis (see BETWEEN); void (see ABSENCE). See DEPTH, INCOMPLETENESS, DISCONTINUANCE.

Verbs—set at intervals, separate, space, gape, open.

Adjectives—with an interval, far between; spaced.

Adverbs—at intervals, discontinuously.

Antonyms, see CONTACT, COMPLETION, CONTINUITY.

---

intertwine, *v.* See CROSSING.

intervene, *v.i.* interfere, interrupt, interpose; come between; mediate, arbitrate; intercede; occur, happen, take place. See BETWEEN, DISCONTINUANCE.

interview, *v.t.* converse with, question. —*n.* questioning, CONVERSATION, consultation, meeting. See INQUIRY.

intimate, *adj.* close, friendly, familiar; private, personal. See NEARNESS. —*v.t.* hint, suggest, imply; announce, impart. See INFORMATION, DISCLOSURE. —*n.* FRIEND, crony, boon *or* bosom companion.

intimidate, *v.t.* subdue, cow, bully,

scare, frighten, overawe. See FEAR, THREAT.

intolerable, *adj.* beyond endurance, unbearable, insupportable, insufferable. See PAIN.

intolerance, *n.* bigotry, bias, prejudice; dogmatism, narrowness. See JEALOUSY, EXCITABILITY.

intoxicate, *v.* inebriate, [be]fuddle; exalt, elate, overjoy; poison. See DRINKING, EXCITEMENT.

intractable, *adj.* unmanageable, ungovernable; obstinate, perverse; refractory, rebellious. See OBSTINACY.

intrepid, *adj.* fearless, undaunted (see COURAGE).

intricate, *adj.* complicated, complex; involved, devious, cunning. See DISORDER, CONVOLUTION.

intrigue, *n.* plot, conspiracy, skullduggery; spying, espionage, scheming; love affair, amour. See LOVE. —*v.* fascinate, interest; plot, PLAN, scheme; spy. See ATTENTION.

INTRINSIC

Nouns—**1,** intrinsicality, inbeing, inherence, inhesion; subjectiveness; ego; essence, essentialness, essentiality, essential part, quintessence, incarnation; quiddity, gist, pith, core; marrow, sap, lifeblood, backbone, heart, soul; important part (see IMPORTANCE); principle. See PART.

2, nature, constitution, character, quality, property, crasis, diathesis; ring [of truth, *etc*.]. See IDENTITY.

3, habit, temper, temperament; spirit, humor, grain; moods, features, aspects; peculiarities (see SPECIALITY); idiosyncrasy; idiocrasy (see TENDENCY); diagnostics; endowment, capacity; capability (see POWER).

Verbs—inhere, be *or* run in the blood, be born to.

Adjectives—intrinsic[al]; subjective; fundamental, normal; implanted, inherent, essential, elementary, basic, natural; innate, inborn, inbred, ingrained, inwrought; radical; incarnate; thoroughbred, hereditary, inherited, immanent; congenital, connate, running in the blood; ingenerate, indigenous; in the grain, bred in the bone, instinctive; inward, internal, INTERIOR; to the manner born; virtual; characteristic; invariable, incurable, ineradicable, fixed, *etc*.

Adverbs—intrinsically, at bottom, in the main, in effect, practically, virtually, substantially, fairly.

Antonyms, see EXTRINSIC.

introduce, *v.t.* usher, bring in; present, acquaint (with); insert, interpolate; initiate, institute. See BEGINNING, PRECEDENCE, BETWEEN, INSERTION.

introduction, *n.* preface, forward, prelude; presentation, [new] acquaintanceship; INSERTION. See COURTESY, PRECEDENCE, DRAMA.

intrude, *v.i.* interlope, intervene, interfere; butt in, trespass, encroach; overstep, obtrude. See BETWEEN, INGRESS.

intrust, *v.t.* See ENTRUST.

INTUITION

Nouns—intuition, intuitiveness, insight, perceptivity, instinct; apprehension, presentiment (see EXPECTATION); rule of thumb; clairvoyance, sixth sense, extrasensory perception, E.S.P., second sight. See INTELLECT, KNOWLEDGE, PREDICTION.

Verbs—sense, feel; guess, hazard a guess, talk at random, play [it] by ear;

intuit. *Colloq.*, not have a leg to stand on; feel it in one's bones. *Slang,* fly by the seat of one's pants.

Adjectives—intuitive, instinctive, impulsive, automatic; perceptive; independent of reason, natural, innate, gratuitous, hazarded; unconnected. *Colloq.*, gut.

Adverbs—intuitively, instinctively, by intuition; illogically; without rhyme or reason.

Antonyms, see REASONING.

---

inundate, *v.t.* flood, deluge. See WATER, SUFFICIENCY.

inure, *v.t.* toughen, accustom, familiarize, harden, habituate. See HABIT, STRENGTHEN.

invade, *v.t.* enter, encroach, violate, penetrate, trespass; ATTACK, assail, harry. See INGRESS.

invalid, *adj.* void, null, worthless, useless, valueless, unusable. See NULLIFICATION.

invalid, *n.* sufferer, patient, case, shut-in; cripple. —*adj.* sickly, ill, unhealthy, unwell, weak. See DISEASE.

invalidate, *v.t.* nullify, cancel, annul, void. See NULLIFICATION.

invaluable, *adj.* inestimable, priceless. See DEARNESS, UTILITY.

invariable, *adj.* unvarying, constant, steady; fixed, uniform; monotonous; permanent. See PERMANENCE, STABILITY, REGULARITY.

invasion, *n.* encroachment, infringement, violation; invasion of privacy; ATTACK. See WARFARE, INGRESS, BETWEEN.

inveigle, *v.i.* lure, attract, ensnare, cajole, persuade, allure, entice. See DECEPTION.

invent, *v.t.* devise, conceive, contrive, originate; imagine, fabricate, improvise; create, spin, forge, design; feign. See IMAGINATION, FALSEHOOD.

inventory, *n.* tally, count; accounting, LIST; stock, goods, merchandise. See STORE.

INVERSION

Nouns—**1,** inversion, eversion, retroversion, introversion; contrariety, contrariness (see OPPOSITION); reversal; turn of the tide; overturn; somersault, somerset; revulsion; turnabout, about-face, *volte-face*. See CHANGE, INTERCHANGE.
2, transposition, metastasis, anastrophe; tmesis, parenthesis; metathesis; palindrome; pronation and supination.

Verbs—turn, go, *or* wheel around *or* about, cut *or* double back; backfire; turn *or* topple over; capsize; invert, retrovert, introvert, reverse, evert; overturn, upset, turn topsy-turvy; transpose, put the cart before the horse; turn the tables, turn turtle, keel over.

Adjectives—inverted, wrong side out; inside out, upside down; bottom upwards, bottoms up; on one's head, topsy-turvy; inverse; reverse, opposite; in reverse; top-heavy.

Adverbs—inversely, counter, heels over head, head over heels, end for end, *vice versa*.

Antonyms, see DIRECTION.

---

invest, *v.* endue, endow, clothe, array; surround, hem in, besiege, beleaguer; install, induct; dress, adorn; confer; spend. See CLOTHING, POWER, COMMISSION, ATTACK, PURCHASE.

investigate, *v.t.* inquire, examine, question; search, probe. See INQUIRY.

invigorate, *v.t.* strengthen, liven, refresh, enliven, restore, energize, animate. See POWER, STRENGTH, REFRESHMENT.

invincible, *adj.* unconquerable, indefatigable, unyielding, indomitable. See STRENGTH, POWER.

INVISIBILITY

Nouns—invisibility; nonappearance, imperceptibility, indistinctness; mystery, delitescence (see CONCEALMENT). See LATENCY, TRANSPARENCY.

Verbs—lurk, escape notice, blush unseen; conceal, veil, put out of sight; not see, lose sight of; dematerialize.

Adjectives—invisible, imperceptible, undiscernible, unapparent, nonapparent; out of sight, not in sight; behind the scenes *or* curtain; inconspicuous; unseen, covert, latent; eclipsed, under an eclipse; dim, faint (see DIMNESS); indistinct, indistinguishable; shadowy, indefinite, unseen; ill-defined *or* -marked; blurred, out of focus, misty (see OBSCURITY); clouded (see CLOUDINESS), veiled.

Antonyms, see VISIBILITY.

invite, *v.t.* summon, ask; tempt, attract, lure; solicit; bid; challenge; court. See REQUEST, OFFER.

invoice, *n.* LIST, bill, summation. See ACCOUNTING.

invoke, *v.t.* beseech, plead, beg; call, summon; utilize; wish, conjure; attest. See REQUEST, USE.

involuntary, *adj.* spontaneous, instinctive, automatic, reflex. See NECESSITY, UNWILLINGNESS.

involve, *v.t.* imply, entail, include; complicate, entangle, inculpate, implicate, incriminate, commit; mean. See COMPOSITION, DIFFICULTY, RELATION, DISORDER, ATTENTION, MEANING, ACCUSATION.

invulnerable, *adj.* impregnable, invincible; unassailable, impenetrable; immune, proof; perfect, flawless, unimpeachable. See DEFENSE, SAFETY, STRENGTH.

inward, *adj.* inside, private; in, interior, incoming; mental, spiritual, hidden. See INTERIOR.

iota, *n.* bit, jot, particle, tittle, mite. See LITTLENESS.

IRASCIBILITY

Nouns—**1,** irascibility, temper; crossness; petulance, irritability, pugnacity, contentiousness, EXCITABILITY; bad, hot, fiery, *or* quick temper, hot blood; ill humor, surliness, sullenness, churlishness, DISCOURTESY. *Colloq.,* crankiness; boiling point. See MALEVOLENCE, SENSIBILITY, DEJECTION.

2, fury, huff, miff, anger, RESENTMENT.

3, hothead, blusterer; shrew, vixen, virago, termagant, scold, Xanthippe; spitfire. *Colloq.,* fire-eater, crank, grouch, crosspatch. *Slang,* ugly customer, sourpuss, sorehead.

Verbs—have a temper, have a devil in one; flare *or* fire up, be angry (see RESENTMENT); sulk, mope, fret, frown, glower; get up on the wrong side of the bed. *Colloq.,* be *or* get sore.

Adjectives—irascible, bad-, quick-, *or* ill-tempered, hotheaded, irritable, crabbed; excitable; thin-skinned, edgy, sensitive; hasty, overhasty, quick, warm, hot, testy, touchy, huffy; pettish, petulant; waspish, snappish, cranky, disgruntled, out of sorts, cross, grumpy, peppery, fiery, passionate, choleric, shrewish; querulous, captious, moody, moodish; quarrelsome, contentious, disputatious; pugnacious, feisty, bellicose; cantankerous, churlish, discourteous (see

DISCOURTESY); fractious, peevish; in a bad temper; angry (see RESENTMENT). *Colloq.*, grouchy, ugly, sore, cross as two sticks, cross as a bear.
Adverbs—irascibly, irritably, *etc.;* against the grain.

Antonyms, see COURTESY, CHEERFULNESS.

---

irate, *adj.* See RESENTMENT.
iridescent, *adj.* opalescent, prismatic; colorful, glowing. See COLOR, VARIEGATION.
irk, *v.t.* annoy (see DISCONTENT).
irksome, *adj.* troublesome, irritating, tiresome, tedious, wearisome. See DIFFICULTY, DISCONTENT.
iron, *n.* flatiron, mangle. —*v.t.* press, mangle. See SMOOTHNESS.
irony, *n.* RIDICULE, satire, sarcasm. See FIGURATIVE.
irrational, *adj.* unreasonable, insensible; brainless, brutish, reasonless, absurd. See FOLLY.

IRREGULARITY

Nouns—irregularity, variability, DEVIATION, caprice, uncertainty; tardiness, unpunctuality (see LATENESS); intermittence, fitfulness, inconstancy. See CHANGEABLENESS, UNCONFORMITY, DISCONTINUANCE, ROUGHNESS, DISORDER.
Verbs—fluctuate, intermit, come and go; flare up.
Adjectives—irregular, uncertain, unpunctual, capricious, inconstant, desultory, fitful, intermittent, flickering; sporadic, erratic, eccentric, spasmodic, checkered, variable, unstable, changeable, unpredictable, undependable.
Adverbs—irregularly, by fits and starts, off and on, out of turn, from time to time.

Antonyms, see REGULARITY.

---

irrelevant, *adj.* inappropriate, unfitting, unrelated, inconsistent, inapplicable. See DISAGREEMENT.

IRRELIGION

Nouns—**1,** irreligion, irreligiousness, ungodliness, godlessness, IMPIETY; IDOLATRY; HETERODOXY.
2, skepticism (see DOUBT); unbelief, disbelief; lack *or* want of faith; agnosticism, atheism; materialism, positivism; nihilism, infidelity, freethinking, rationalism, heathenism, paganism; antichristianity.
3, atheist, skeptic, doubting Thomas; apostate, renegade; unbeliever, infidel; heathen, pagan, alien, gentile; freethinker, rationalist, materialist, positivist; nihilist; agnostic; heretic.
Verbs—disbelieve, lack faith; DOUBT, question; scoff; curse God [and die].
Adjectives—irreligious, undevout; godless, godforsaken, graceless, ungodly, unholy, unsanctified, unrighteous, unhallowed; atheistic, agnostic; skeptical, freethinking; unbelieving, unconverted; doubting, faithless; unchristian, non-Christian, antichristian; gentile; heathen, pagan; materialistic, worldly, mundane, earthly, earthbound, carnal; secular.

Antonyms, see RELIGION, PIETY.

---

irreparable, *adj.* irremediable, hopeless. See HOPELESSNESS.
irresistible, *adj.* overpowering, overwhelming, stunning, puissant. See POWER, NECESSITY.
irresolute, *adj.* infirm of purpose, of

two minds, half-hearted; dubious, undecided, unresolved, undetermined; hesitating, on the fence; at a loss; vacillating, unsteady, changeable, fickle, capricious, volatile; weak, timid, cowardly. See DOUBT, FEAR, CHANGEABLENESS.

irresponsible, *adj.* negligent, remiss; reckless, unburdened. See CHANGEABLENESS, IMPROBITY, NEGLECT.

irreverent, *adj.* See DISRESPECT.

irrevocable, *adj.* irreversible, past recall, done, absolute. See NECESSITY.

irrigate, *v.t.* WATER, moisten, flood, flush. See CLEANNESS.

irritable, *adj.* fretful, petulant, peevish, touchy, sensitive. See IRASCIBILITY.

irritate, *v.t.* annoy, provoke, vex, bother, trouble; irk, exasperate, chafe, nettle, ruffle. See EXCITEMENT, VIOLENCE, RESENTMENT.

island, *n.* isle, ait; cay, key; atoll, [coral] reef, ledge. See LAND.

isolate, *v.t.* segregate; insulate, separate, quarantine. See DISJUNCTION, EXCLUSION.

issue, *n.* product, offspring, progeny (see POSTERITY); discharge; outcome, result; question, dispute (see INQUIRY). —*v.* leave, depart, debouch, emerge; circulate, despatch, send, publish; emit, discharge, exude, eliminate; spout, spurt; flow, spring. See DEPARTURE, EFFECT, EGRESS, MONEY, PUBLICATION.

itch, *n.* itching, tickling, prickly sensation; mange, manginess; *cacoëthes, cacoëthes scribendi* (writer's itch); the itch, scabies, psora; itchiness; burning, tingling; DESIRE, craving, hankering. —*v.i.* tingle, prickle, burn; crave, long for, yearn, hanker. See SENSIBILITY.

item, *n.* piece, detail, particular; entry, article; term, paragraph, PART. See INFORMATION, UNITY.

itinerant, *adj.* wandering, nomadic, wayfaring, peripatetic, traveling. See TRAVEL.

itinerary, *n.* journey, route, circuit, course; guidebook. See TRAVEL, DIRECTION.

J

jab, *n. & v.* punch, blow; prod, poke. See IMPULSE.

jabber, *n.* gibberish, babble, blather, nonsense, jabberwocky; prattle, talk, gossip, chatter. —*v.i.* talk, rattle on, prattle, chatter, gibber, gabble. See UNMEANINGNESS.

jack, *n.* man, fellow; knave, bower; lever; sailor, hand; jack-of-all-trades; ass, mule, donkey, rabbit; *slang,* money; *slang,* applejack. See ANIMAL, ELEVATION, MALE.

jackal, *n.* wild dog, henchman, hireling. *Slang,* dog robber. See ANIMAL, SERVANT.

jacket, *n.* coat, sack *or* suit coat, dinner *or* smoking jacket, tuxedo, sport coat; jerkin; windbreaker, pea jacket *or* coat; peel, rind, skin. See CLOTHING, COVERING.

jackknife, *n.* pocket knife, penknife, switchblade. *Slang,* shiv. See SHARPNESS.

jackpot, *n.* [grand] prize, bonanza. See APPROBATION.

jaded, *adj.* weary, surfeited, blasé, dulled. See WEARINESS.

jagged, *adj.* sharp, rough, snaggy, notched, pointed, zigzag. See ROUGHNESS.

jail, *n.* See PRISON.

jam, *n.* crowd, press, crush; blockage, impasse; jelly, preserve; *slang,* predicament. See FOOD, DIFFICULTY. —*v.* crowd, press, crush; wedge, shove, push, cram; block. See HINDRANCE, IMPULSE.

jamboree, *n.* carousal, celebration. See AMUSEMENT.

jangle, *n.* DISCORD, clangor; ringing, jingle; bickering, dispute. —*v.* clash, clang, rattle, ring, jingle; upset. See DISCONTENT.

janitor, *n.* caretaker, superintendent, custodian; concierge. See CLEANNESS, SAFETY.

jar, *n.* clash, conflict, DISCORD; vessel, Mason jar, jug, cruse. —*v.* shock, jolt; jounce, shake, rattle; clash. See DISAGREEMENT, IMPULSE, RECEPTACLE.

jargon, *n.* lingo, shoptalk, patois, cant, argot; doubletalk; gibberish. *Slang,* jive. See CONCEALMENT, UNMEANINGNESS.

jaundice, *n.* jaundiced eye, JEALOUSY; bitterness, rancor, hate; prejudice, bias, bigotry, narrowness. *—v.t.* predispose, prejudice, bias, color, distort. See RESENTMENT.

jaunt, *n.* excursion, ride, escapade, lark, stroll. See TRAVEL.

jaunty, *adj.* stylish, sprightly, smart, dapper; gay, breezy, brisk, debonair; jolly, ebullient, vivacious, cavalier. *Colloq.,* sporty; cocky. See FASHION, CHEERFULNESS, OSTENTATION.

jaw, *n.* mandible, jawbone. *—v.i.* chatter, talk, jabber. See LOQUACITY.

jazz, *n.* ragtime, blues, hot jazz, *le jazz hot,* Dixieland, swing, bop, bebop; cool, progressive, West Coast, *or* modern jazz; *slang,* nonsense, foolishness. See MUSIC, UNMEANINGNESS.

JEALOUSY

Nouns—jealousy, envy, covetousness, cupidity, DESIRE, heartburn, jaundice, jaundiced eye; green- *or* yellow-eyed monster; distrust, mistrust, umbrage, spite, RESENTMENT; suspicion, DOUBT; anxiety (see CARE).

Verbs—**1,** envy, turn green, covet; distrust, resent; suspect, DOUBT.
2, fill with envy, put one's nose out of joint.

Adjectives—jealous, jaundiced, green [with envy], covetous, envious; distrustful, resentful; doubtful, suspicious; anxious, concerned; apprehensive, watchful; intolerant, zealous, umbrageous.

Antonyms, see BELIEF.

---

jeer, *v.* sneer, scoff, taunt, gibe, mock; RIDICULE, make fun of, belittle. *—n.* taunt, gibe, mockery; hoot, catcall, hissing. See CONTEMPT, DISRESPECT.

jelly, *n.* gelatin, aspic; jam, preserve; mush. See FOOD.

jeopardy, *n.* DANGER, risk, peril, hazard, THREAT.

jerk, *v.* twist, tweak, pull, snap; start, twitch, jitter, jump. *—n.* start, jump, twitch; spasm; pull, snap; *slang,* nitwit, fool, nobody. See EXCITABILITY, TRACTION, FOLLY.

jest, *n.* joke, jape; WIT, humor, clowning; practical joke; jocularity, pun, gag, wisecrack, witticism, *bon mot;* sport, fun; make-believe, fooling. *—v.i.* fool, joke; crack wise, gag; play the fool.

jester, *n.* WIT, joker, gagman, comedian; fool, clown, buffoon.

jet, *v.* stream, spurt, gush, shoot, spout, pour, rush, squirt. *—n.* stream, fountain; outgush, spurt; jet plane (see AVIATION). See WATER. *—adj.* black, pitch[y], ebon[y]. See COLOR.

jewel, *n.* stone, gem; diamond, ruby, sapphire, *etc.* See ORNAMENT, GOOD.

jewelry, *n.* gems, beads, trinkets, stones; bracelets, bangles, necklaces, *etc.* See ORNAMENT.

jiggle, *v.* fidget, twitch. See AGITATION.

jilt, *v.t.* reject *or* cast off (a lover); leave in the lurch. See DISAPPOINTMENT.

jingle, *n.* clink, tinkle, ring; jangle. See SOUND, POETRY.

jingo, *n.* See CHAUVINIST.

jinx, *n., colloq.,* curse, evil eye, bad luck, plague. *Slang,* [double] whammy. *—v.* curse, hex, bewitch, bedevil. See SORCERY.

jitter, *v.i.* twitch, fidget, jerk, jump, vibrate. *—n.* vibration; (*pl.*) heebie-jeebies, shakes, nervousness. See EXCITABILITY.

job, *n.* work, occupation, calling; piece of work, stint; position, situation, duty. See BUSINESS, ACTION.

jockey, *v.* maneuver; cheat, trick. See CUNNING, DECEPTION. —*n.* rider, racer (see VELOCITY).

jocularity, *n.* humor; mirth, laughter; jesting, joshing, kidding; WIT.

jog, *v.* jiggle, push, shake, jostle; trot, amble. See IMPULSE, TRAVEL.

join, *v.* unite (see JUNCTION); federate, associate, affiliate; become a member; marry. See CONTACT, UNITY.

joint, *n.* connection, link, juncture; articulation; *slang,* dive, den, haunt, hangout. See JUNCTION, ABODE. —*adj.* combined, shared, common [to both parties]. See PARTY.

joke, *n.* jest, gag, wisecrack, witticism, *bon mot;* fooling, kidding, joshing. —*v.i.* josh, jest, gag. See WIT.

jolly, *adj.* joyous, frolicsome, mirthful; buoyant, elated. See CHEERFULNESS.

jolt, *v.* shake [up], shock, stun; lurch, pitch; bump, collide, crash. *Slang,* give a kick in the pants. See IMPULSE, SURPRISE.

jostle, *v.t.* push, bump; elbow, shoulder; collide with. See IMPULSE.

journal, *n.* diary, daybook, RECORD, log; newspaper, magazine, periodical. See PUBLICATION, CHRONOMETRY, ACCOUNTING, DESCRIPTION.

journalist, *n.* newsman, newspaperman, reporter; writer, editor, copyreader. See RECORD, NEWS.

journey *n.* trip, tour; voyage, cruise, crossing; expedition; tramp, hike; pilgrimage, hadj; caravan; trek. —*v.* TRAVEL; voyage, sail, cross; tour, roam, range, venture, explore; ride, drive, motor. See MOTION.

jovial, *adj.* genial, cordial; gay, merry; jolly, convivial. See CHEERFULNESS.

joy, *n.* REJOICING; PLEASURE, happiness, delight, mirth, gaiety; *joie de vivre. Colloq.,* fun.

jubilant, *adj.* joyful; triumphant, exultant; elated, REJOICING, in high spirits. See CHEERFULNESS.

jubilee, *n.* CELEBRATION; anniversary; REJOICING.

judge, *n.* & *v.* See LAWSUIT, JUDGMENT.

JUDGMENT

Nouns—**1,** judgment, adjudication, arbitration; result, conclusion, upshot; deduction, inference, corollary (see REASONING); decision, determination, finding, opinion, ruling, verdict, settlement, award, decree, sentence; CONDEMNATION, doom, day of judgment, Judgment Day; *res judicata.*

2, judge; jurist, tribunal, court, *etc.* (see LAWSUIT); judgment seat.

3, estimation, valuation, assessment, appraisal, appreciation, consideration, judication; opinion, notion, THOUGHT, viewpoint, BELIEF; estimate, commentary, critique; diagnosis (see IDENTITY); CHOICE, vote; discernment, discretion, TASTE; INTELLIGENCE, INTELLECT, reason, sagacity; sense.

4, arbiter, umpire, referee; judicator; master, moderator, mediator, conciliator; censor, critic, commentator, connoisseur, authority, expert.

Verbs—**1,** judge, conclude; come to, arrive at, *or* draw a conclusion, find; make up one's mind; ascertain, determine, deduce; settle, give an opinion; decide, try, *or* hear a case *or* cause; pronounce, rule, pass judgment, sentence, condemn, doom (see CONDEMNATION); adjudge, adjudicate, arbitrate, sit in judgment; bring in a verdict; confirm, decree, award; pass under review; editorialize.

2, estimate, appraise, value, assess; deem, gauge; review, consider, believe; form an opinion about, take the measure of, jump to a conclusion, put two and two together; comment, criticize, examine, inquire. *Colloq.,* size up.

Adjectives—**1,** judicial, judiciary, forensic, legal; determinate, conclusive; censorious, condemnatory; tribunal.

2, discerning, discriminating, sensible, astute, judicious, circumspect; intelligent, rational, reasonable, sagacious, wise.

Adverbs—therefore, wherefore, this being so *or* the case; all things considered, in light *or* view of, all things being equal, on the whole; in one's opinion.

Antonyms, see ERROR, MISJUDGMENT.

---

judicious, *adj.* prudent, sound. See JUDGMENT.

jug, *n.* bottle, urn, pitcher, flagon, tankard. See RECEPTACLE.

juggle, *v.* manipulate; conjure; trick, cheat. See DECEPTION.

juicy, *adj.* moist, sappy, succulent; rich, tasty, tempting. See FLUIDITY.

jumble, *n.* mixup, confusion, DISORDER; pi. —*v.* mix up, disarrange, muddle, mess.

jumbo, *adj.* huge (see SIZE).

jump, *n. & v.* hop, LEAP, bound, spring, vault; start, twitch, jerk. See EXCITABILITY.

jumpy, *adj.* nervous, jittery. See EXCITABILITY.

JUNCTION

Nouns—**1,** junction, CONNECTION, conjunction, COHERENCE; joining, joinder, union, annex, annexation, attachment; ligation, accouplement, inosculation, anastomosis; MARRIAGE, knot, wedlock; hookup, network, communication, concatenation; fusion, blend, merger. See CROSSING, UNITY.

2, joint, joining, juncture, pivot, hinge, articulation, seam, suture, stitch; coupler, coupling; chain, link; miter, mortise, tenon, dovetail; interface.

3, see COMBINATION, MIXTURE.

Verbs—join, unite, knot, knit, conjoin, connect, hitch, affiliate, associate, couple; put, piece, *or* hold together; roll into one, combine, compound, incorporate; skewer; inosculate, anastomose; copulate. See CONNECTION.

Adjectives—**1,** joined, joint; conjoint, conjunct, conjunctive, corporate, compact, hand in hand; close-knit, conjugate.

2, segmented, jointed, articulate.

3, blent, blended, wedded, married, merged, fused. See MIXTURE.

Adverbs—jointly, in conjunction with, fast, firmly, intimately.

Antonyms, see DISJUNCTION.

---

juncture, *n.* joint, point, connection; contingency, emergency. See JUNCTION, CIRCUMSTANCE, OCCASION.

jungle, *n.* wilderness, bush. See VEGETABLE, DIFFICULTY, ABODE.

junior, *n. & adj.* younger, lesser, subordinate. See INFERIORITY.

junk, *n.* rubbish, waste, refuse, trash, discard, castoffs; scrap, salvage, wreck, wreckage; stuff, miscellany, claptrap. See SHIP, USELESSNESS. —*v.t.* scrap, wreck, tear down, dismember; salvage; discard, cast off, jettison. See DISUSE.

junket, *n.* picnic, excursion. See FOOD, TRAVEL.

junta, *n.* meeting, COUNCIL.

junto, *n.* cabal (see PARTY).

jurisdiction, *n.* judicature; administration; province, dominion, control; magistracy, AUTHORITY; municipality, corporation, bailiwick. See LEGALITY.

jurist, *n.* judge; legal expert. See LAWSUIT, LEGALITY.

jury, *n.* trial, grand, *or* petit jury; panel; board of judges. See LAWSUIT.

just, *adj.* fair, RIGHT; impartial,

nonpartisan; lawful, legal, legitimate; exact, accurate, precise. See PROBITY. —*adv*. precisely, exactly; almost, nearly, within an ace of. See JUSTICE.

JUSTICE

Nouns—**1,** justice, justness, fairness, fair treatment, impartiality, equity, equitableness; poetic justice, rough justice, deserts; nemesis (see PUNISHMENT); scales of justice; fair play, fair trial, trial by jury; affirmative action. *Colloq.,* square deal, straight shooting, fair *or* square shake. See LAWSUIT, LEGALITY, PROBITY.

2, due, dueness, rightfulness, RIGHTNESS, VINDICATION.

Verbs—**1,** do justice to, be fair, treat fairly, deal fairly with, be impartial, see justice done, play fair, give the devil his due. *Colloq.,* give a square deal, play the game, give a sporting chance.

2, be just, right, *or* due; have right, title, *or* claim to; be entitled to; have a claim upon, belong to, deserve, earn, merit, be worthy of. *Colloq.,* rate, have it coming.

3, demand, claim, call upon for, reclaim, exact, insist on, take one's stand, make a point of, require, lay claim to.

Adjectives—**1,** just, fair, impartial, equal, fair and square, dispassionate, disinterested, unbiased, even-handed.

2, having a right to, entitled to, deserving, meriting, worthy of; deserved, merited.

Adverbs—justly, rightfully, duly, by right, by divine right, fairly, in justice, as is just *or* fitting. *Colloq.,* on the level, aboveboard, on the square.

Antonyms, see INJUSTICE.

---

justify, *v*. exonerate, excuse, warrant, vindicate, acquit, absolve; prove right, free from blame. See VINDICATION.

jut, *v.i.* protrude, project, beetle, stand out, overhang. See CONVEXITY.

juvenile, *n*. youngster, minor, adolescent. —*adj*. puerile, young, undeveloped, immature; childish. See YOUTH.

juxtapose, *n*. See NEARNESS.

K

kaleidoscopic, *adj*. variegated, varying; colorful. See COLOR, CHANGEABLENESS.

kaput, *adj., colloq.,* ruined, done for, destroyed. See FAILURE, DESTRUCTION.

keel, *v*. turn (over), keel over, fall down, drop like a log. See OBLIQUITY, INVERSION. —*n*. bar *or* false keel; centerboard. See SHIP.

keen, *adj*. piercing, stinging, nippy; sharp, edged, cutting, razorlike; eager, enthusiastic, ardent; acute, clever, shrewd, quick. See DESIRE, SHARPNESS, FEELING, INTELLIGENCE, COLD.

keep, *v*. retain, hold, have, possess; receive, preserve; celebrate (holidays), maintain; sustain, continue; hold back, save, cling to, detain. See POSSESSION, PRESERVATION. —*n*. subsistence, maintenance; donjon, dungeon; PRISON, prison tower, cell, jail. See DEFENSE, FOOD.

keeper, *n*. custodian; jailer, warden, watchman, watchdog; gamekeeper, ranger; doorman, tiler; curator; protector, guardian; observer (of rites), celebrator, preserver; supporter, maintainer. See SAFETY, PRISON, DEFENSE.

keepsake, *n*. memento, souvenir, reminder, token. See MEMORY.

keg, *n*. barrel, cask. See RECEPTACLE.

ken, *n*. KNOWLEDGE, scope.

kennel, *n.* doghouse, stall; hovel, hut, hutch. See ABODE.

kernel, *n.* nub, gist, core, pitch, point, center, essence; grain, nut, seed, nucleus. See MEANING, IMPORTANCE, MIDDLE.

kettle, *n.* pot, caldron, boiler; teakettle. See RECEPTACLE.

key, *n.* answer, solution, code book, decipherment; pitch, tonality, register; cay. See SOUND, OPENING, INTERPRETATION, MUSIC, CAUSE, COLOR, INSTRUMENTALITY.

kibitz, *v.i.* advise, comment; butt in, interfere, meddle. See ADVICE, BETWEEN.

kick, *v.* punt; spurn; stamp; *slang,* complain, gripe, bellyache, grumble. —*n.* RECOIL; thrill, excitement, fun; *slang,* complaint, grievance, gripe. See IMPULSE, OPPOSITION.

kickback, *n., colloq.,* backfire; refund, discount, rebate; rakeoff; cut, commission; bribe, payoff, payola. See PAYMENT.

kid, *n.* kidling; kidskin; *colloq.,* child, YOUTH. —*v., slang,* tease, make fun of; deceive, fool. See DECEPTION.

kidnap, *v.* carry off, abduct. See STEALING.

KILLING

Nouns—**1,** killing, homicide, manslaughter, murder, assassination; bloodshed, bloodletting, slaughter, carnage, butchery, decimation, annihilation, genocide, pogrom, massacre, war, WARFARE; biocide; mercy killing, euthanasia. See DEATH.

2, death blow, finishing stroke, *coup de grâce,* quietus; gassing, electrocution, defenestration; execution; martyrdom; poisoning, suffocation, strangulation, garrote, hanging, decapitation, guillotine, violent death; traffic death, fatal accident, casualty, fatality. See PUNISHMENT.

3, butcher, slayer, murderer, Cain, assassin, cutthroat, garrotter, bravo, thug; executioner, hangman, headsman, firing squad; regicide, matricide, parricide, fratricide, infanticide; suicide, suttee, hara-kiri, immolation; germicide, insecticide. *Slang,* hatchet *or* finger man, necktie party.

4, hunting, coursing, shooting; sportsman, huntsman (see PURSUIT); slaughterhouse, shambles, abattoir; charnel house.

Verbs—**1,** kill, put to death, slay, shed blood; murder, assassinate, butcher, slaughter, immolate, massacre, annihilate; do away with, put an end to, put away; carry off, lay low; run over; pick off; dispatch, do for, put out of the way; sign one's death warrant. *Slang,* liquidate, bump off, brain, take for a ride, knock off, wipe out, zap, do in, rub out.

2, execute; strangle, garrote, hang, lynch, throttle, choke, stifle, poison, gas, electrocute, suffocate, smother, asphyxiate, drown, behead; put to the sword, stone, deal a death blow, wade knee-deep in blood; blow out one's brains, commit suicide, take one's own life; snuff out. *Slang,* string up.

Adjectives—**1,** killing, murderous, sanguinary, bloodstained, bloodthirsty, homicidal, redhanded; bloody, ensanguined, gory.

2, mortal, fatal, lethal, deadly, internecine, suicidal, biocidal.

Antonyms, see LIFE, REPRODUCTION.

---

kin, *n.* kin[s]folk, kinsman, kinswoman; blood relative *or* relation, family, clan; siblings, cousins. *Colloq.,* folks. See ANCESTRY, POSTERITY.

kind, *n.* sort, species, CLASS, type, ilk, breed, character, nature. —*adj.* kindly; gentle, tender, sympathetic, mild, friendly, obliging, benign, solicitous, lenient; helpful. See

BENEVOLENCE, LENIENCY.

kindergarten, *n.* nursery school, playschool. See SCHOOL.

kindle, *v.* ignite, start, fire, set ablaze; stir, excite, rouse, provoke. See EXCITEMENT, CAUSE.

kindling, *n.* tinder, FUEL, firewood, combustibles.

kindred, *n.* consanguinity; relatives, kinfolk[s], kinsmen; clan, tribe; brothers, sisters, cousins, parents, *etc.;* kindred spirits, congenial people. *—adj.* related, akin, allied; congenial. See RELATION, BENEVOLENCE.

king, *n.* ruler, monarch, emperor, sovereign; royalty. See AUTHORITY.

kingdom, *n.* domain, empire, realm. See REGION, AUTHORITY.

kingly, *adj.* royal, majestic, regal, imperial; noble, magnificent. See AUTHORITY.

kinsman, *n.* relative, blood relation; clansman. See ANCESTRY.

kiss, *n.* smack, osculation, caress, merest TOUCH. See ENDEARMENT. *—v.* caress, osculate; brush [lightly], TOUCH, graze.

kit, *n.* pack, sack, bag, knapsack; Dop kit; collection, gear, outfit, supplies; do-it-yourself kit. See RECEPTACLE.

kitchen, *n.* scullery, galley, cookhouse, kitchenette. See RECEPTACLE.

knack, *n.* adeptness, ability, aptitude, talent; dexterity, handiness, trick, SKILL.

knapsack, *n.* haversack, pack; mochila, rucksack, kit [bag], bag, case. *Slang,* poke, turkey, bindle. See RECEPTACLE.

knave, *n.* rogue, rascal, villain, scamp, scapegrace, blackguard, reprobate, miscreant; jack, bower; churl, menial, servant. See EVILDOER, CUNNING.

knead, *v.t.* press, squeeze, massage, manipulate, work. See MIXTURE, FORM, FRICTION.

kneel, *v.i.* bend (to pray), genuflect. See DEPRESSION.

knickknack, *n.* bric-a-brac, trifle, trinket, gewgaw. See ORNAMENT, UNIMPORTANCE.

knife, *n.* blade, edge, point, steel; carving knife; snickersnee, dagger, poniard, dirk, bodkin, stiletto; scalpel, lancet. *Slang,* shiv, toothpick. See ARMS, SHARPNESS. *—v.t.* stab, cut, slice, slash; wound; *colloq.,* knife in the back, betray. See IMPROBITY.

knight, *n.* knight-errant; cavalier, chevalier; paladin, champion, Galahad; Templar; noble. See DEFENSE, NOBILITY.

knit, *v.* weave, interlace; draw together, contract, FURROW, wrinkle. See JUNCTION.

knob, *n.* knot, lump, node, protuberance, boss; handle; hill. See CONVEXITY.

knock, *v.* pound, strike, hit, rap, tap; tamp; bump, collide; *colloq.,* belittle, depreciate. *—n.* stroke, bump; rap[ping]; *colloq.,* slur, aspersion. See IMPULSE, DISAPPROBATION.

knoll, *n.* hill, hillock, rise, mound, hummock. See HEIGHT.

knot, *n.* snarl, tangle; puzzle, problem; cluster, group; lump, node. *—v.* tangle, snarl; tie, bind, fasten. See DIFFICULTY, CROSSING, DENSITY, CONNECTION, ASSEMBLAGE.

know-how, *n.,* *colloq.,* expertise, SKILL. *Slang,* savvy.

KNOWLEDGE

Nouns—**1,** knowledge, cognizance, cognition, acquaintance, ken, privity, familiarity, comprehension, apprehension, recognition, appreciation; INTUITION, conscience, consciousness, awareness, perception, precognition; light, enlightenment; facts of life; glimpse, insight, inkling, glimmer, suspicion, impression.

2, science, philosophy, theory, doctrine, epistemology; encyclopedia; erudition,

LEARNING, lore, scholarship, reading, letters, literature, book learning, INFORMATION, store of knowledge, education, culture; attainments, accomplishments, proficiency, SKILL, wisdom, omniscience. *Colloq.*, know-how.

3, sage, wise man, luminary, magus, savant, philosopher, Nestor, Solon, pundit; highbrow; graduate, academician, academist; master, doctor; fellow, don; mathematician, scientist, *littérateur,* intellectual, intelligentsia; learned *or* literary man; man of learning, letters, *or* education; bookworm, scholar (see LEARNING). *Colloq.,* wise guy.

Verbs—**1,** know, ken, wot (*archaic*), be aware of; ween, trow; possess; apprehend, conceive, comprehend, realize, understand, appreciate, fathom, make out; recognize, discern, perceive, see, experience; feel *or* know in one's bones. See INTELLIGENCE.

2, know full well; have in one's head, have at one's fingertips, know by heart, be master of, know what's what, know one's way around, have been around, have one's eyes open. *Slang,* know the score, know one's stuff.

3, see one's way, discover, learn, study, ascertain.

Adjectives—**1,** knowing, cognitive, conscious, cognizant, aware, perceptive.

2, aware of, cognizant of, conscious of, apprised of, told, acquainted with, privy to, no stranger to, up to, alive to; proficient in, versed in, at home with; conversant *or* familiar with; not born yesterday, nobody's fool; sophisticated, cosmopolitan. *Slang,* hip, hep, wise, wised up, with it, in the know.

3, erudite, scholarly, instructed, learned, lettered, literary, educated, well-informed, well-read, well-grounded, well-educated, enlightened, shrewd; bookish, scholastic, solid, profound, accomplished, omniscient; sage, wise, intellectual; emeritus.

4, known, ascertained, well-known, recognized, proverbial, familiar, hackneyed, trite, commonplace.

5, knowable, cognizable, ascertainable, perceptible, discernible, comprehensible.

Antonyms, see IGNORANCE, FOLLY.

L

label, *n.* tag, tab, mark, sticker; slip, ticket; price tag; epithet, title; record, INDICATION. *Colloq.,* handle. —*v.t.* identify, tag, name; distinguish, describe. See NOMENCLATURE.

labor, *n.* work, toil, effort; travail, task; proletariat. See EXERTION, POPULACE.

laboratory, *n.* workplace; research center, lab. See BUSINESS.

laborious, *adj.* hard, arduous, tiresome, irksome; diligent, assiduous. See EXERTION.

labyrinth, *n.* maze, tangle, meander; complexity, intricacy. See DISORDER, CONVOLUTION, SECRET.

lace, *n.* cord, lacing; braid; openwork, network. See ORNAMENT. —*v.t.* weave, twine; interlace; bind, tie; flavor, mix, spike; *colloq.,* whip, lash. See MIXTURE, CROSSING, PUNISHMENT.

lacerate, *v.t.* tear, mangle; harrow, distress. See PAIN.

lack, *n.* want, deficiency, shortage, need. —*v.t.* need, require. See INSUFFICIENCY, POVERTY.

lackey, *n.* footman, SERVANT.

lackluster, *adj.* dull. See DIMNESS.

laconic, *adj.* concise, pithy. See SHORTNESS, DIFFUSENESS.

lad, *n.* boy, YOUTH, stripling.

ladle, *n.* spoon, dipper; metal pot. See RECEPTACLE.

lady, *n.* gentlewoman, madam, dowager; noblewoman. See NOBILITY, FEMALE.

ladylike, *adj.* womanly, feminine; genteel, well-bred. See FEMALE.

lag, *v.i.* linger, drag, fall behind, hang back. See SLOWNESS.

lagoon, *n.* laguna; pool, pond, cove; estuary, sound. See WATER.

lair, *n.* den, covert, burrow, cave. See ABODE.

LAITY

Nouns—**1,** laity, laic; flock, fold, congregation; assembly; churchgoers; parishioners; parish, brethren, people. See RELIGION.

2, lay person, layman, laywoman, lay brother *or* sister, catechumen.

Verbs—laicize, secularize, democratize, popularize.

Adjectives—lay, laic[al], nonclerical, nonreligious; secular, civil, temporal, profane, congregational, popular; nonprofessional, nonexpert, unprofessional.

Antonyms, see CLERGY.

---

lake, *n.* loch, lough; pond, pool, tarn, lakelet, mere. See WATER.

lame, *adj.* crippled, halt; weak, ineffectual. See DISEASE, FAILURE, WEAKNESS.

LAMENTATION

Nouns—**1,** lamentation, lament, wail, complaint, plaint, murmur, mutter, grumble, groan, growl, moan, whine, whimper, sob, sigh, cry, outcry, scream, howl. *Slang,* gripe, beef, bellyaching. See DEJECTION.

2, tears, weeping, lachrymation, languishment; condolence (see PITY).

3, mourning weeds, crepe, sackcloth and ashes; knell, dirge, coronach, keen, requiem, elegy, monody, threnody, jeremiad.

4, lamenter, mourner, grumbler, Niobe, Jeremiah, Rachel.

Verbs—**1,** lament, mourn, deplore, grieve, weep over, bewail; regret (see PENITENCE); condole with, commiserate; fret, wear mourning, wear sackcloth and ashes.

2, sigh, heave a sigh; wail, bawl, cry, weep, sob, greet (*archaic*), blubber, snivel, whimper, pule, shed tears; burst into tears, cry one's eyes out; scream, mew, growl, groan, grunt, moan, roar, bellow; frown, scowl, make a wry face, gnash one's teeth, wring one's hands, tear one's hair, beat one's breast.

3, complain, murmur, mutter, whine, grumble, clamor, make a fuss about. *Slang,* gripe, bellyache. See DISCONTENT.

Adjectives—lamenting, in mourning, in sackcloth and ashes, sorrowful, sorrowing, unhappy, mournful, tearful, lachrymose, plaintive, querulous, in tears, with tears in one's eyes; elegiac[al].

Interjections—alas! alack! O dear! too bad! sorry! woe is me! alas the day! alackaday! waly waly! what a pity! *O tempora, O mores!*

Antonyms, see CELEBRATION, REJOICING.

---

lamina, *n.* LAYER, stratum, sheet, plate, scale.

laminate, *v.t.* stratify, plate, veneer, overlay. See LAYER.

lamp, *n.* LIGHT, lantern, floor *or* table lamp; [light] bulb; headlamp.

lampoon, *n.* satire, spoof (see DETRACTION).

lance, *n.* dart, spear, pike, javelin, shaft. See ARMS. —*v.* spear; pierce, prick, puncture; hurl, throw, fling, propel, send flying. See OPENING, PROPULSION.

LAND

Nouns—**1,** land, earth, ground, dry land, *terra firma*.
2, continent, mainland, peninsula, delta; neck of land, isthmus, island; oasis, desert; lowland, highland; promontory; pasture, grassland; real estate, property, acres.
3, coast, shore, seashore, lakeshore, strand, beach, bank, lea, seaside, seacoast, rock-bound coast, alluvium. See EDGE.
4, soil, glebe, clay, loam, marl, mold, topsoil, sod, subsoil, clod; rock, crag, boulder, stone, shale, chalk, gravel, dust, sand.
5, geography, geology, geophysics, mineralogy; geographer, geologist, *etc.*
6, landlubber, landsman.
Verbs—land, light, alight, ground; disembark, come *or* go ashore. See ARRIVAL.
Adjectives—earthly, terrestrial; continental, midland, littoral, riparian, alluvial, landed, territorial; earthy.
Adverbs—ashore, on shore, land, *etc.;* aground, on solid ground.
Interjections—land ahoy!

Antonyms, see WATER, AIR.

---

landing, *n.* docking, alighting, landfall, disembarkation; wharf, dock, levee, pier; runway, airstrip; three-point landing. See ARRIVAL, SUPPORT.
landlord, landlady, *n.* proprietor, owner; host, innkeeper, boniface; landholder, landowner. See POSSESSION.
landlubber, *n.* landsman; raw seaman. See LAND, NAVIGATION.
landmark, *n.* milestone, marker, INDICATION; cairn, menhir, monolith; turning point, highlight.
landscape, *n.* countryside; vista, view; landscaping, park; cityscape. See APPEARANCE.
landslide, *n.* avalanche, landslip; sweep, runaway, no contest. *Colloq.,* walkover, shoo-in. See DESCENT, SUCCESS.
lane, *n.* path, byway, passageway; corridor, track. See PASSAGE.
language, *n.* See SPEECH.
languid, *adj.* weak, feeble, weary; listless, spiritless, apathetic. See INSENSIBILITY, WEARINESS.
languish, *v.i.* weaken, fail, fade, decline; pine, droop. See DISEASE, DEJECTION, WEAKNESS.
languor, *n.* WEARINESS, lassitude, listlessness; indolence, inertia. See INACTIVITY, SLOWNESS.
lank, *adj.* lanky; lean, spare, gaunt, bony. See NARROWNESS.
lantern, *n.* lamp, searchlight, torch, LIGHT; jack-o'-lantern.
lap, *v.* FOLD, wrap; lick; overlap; ripple. See SUPERIORITY, COVERING, DRINKING, TOUCH.
lapse, *n.* passage, interval; oversight, peccadillo, ERROR.—*v.i.* pass, glide away; deteriorate; err. See TIME, BADNESS, REVERSION, DESCENT, PAST.
larceny, *n.* theft, STEALING.
large, *adj.* big, huge, colossal, enormous, immense. See SIZE.
lariat, *n.* rope, lasso, line, riata. *Slang,* rawhide, cable, catgut. See FILAMENT.
lark, *n.* frolic, romp, gambol, caper, spree; prank, joke; caprice, whim, fancy, adventure, jaunt. See AMUSEMENT.
lascivious, *adj.* lustful, lewd, salacious, unchaste, wanton. See IMPURITY.
lash, *v.t.* beat, whip, flog, scourge; berate, rebuke, satirize. See PUNISHMENT, DISAPPROBATION.
lass, *n.* lassie; colleen, miss, maid, maiden. See FEMALE.

last, *v.i.* endure, persist, continue, abide. See TIME, DURABILITY. *—adj.* final, ultimate; latest. See END, NEWNESS, PAST.

latch, *n.* catch, latchet, hasp, clasp, lock; bolt, bar; coupling. See CLOSURE, CONNECTION.

late, *adj.* tardy (see LATENESS); new, recent; former, sometime; deceased. See NEWNESS, PAST, DEATH.

LATENCY

Nouns—latency, passivity, inertia, dormancy, abeyance; ambiguity, mystery, SECRET; INVISIBILITY, imperceptibility; CONCEALMENT; more than meets the eye *or* ear; POSSIBILITY.

Verbs—lurk, smolder, underlie; lie hidden; keep back, conceal, veil, hide; laugh up one's sleeve; still waters run deep.

Adjectives—latent, lurking, smoldering, delitescent; hidden, concealed; implied, unapparent, in the background, invisible, unseen; dark, unknown, unsuspected, undiscovered; unsaid, untold, unspoken, unsung, unwritten, unpublished, unexposed, undisclosed; undeveloped, potential; dormant, quiescent; suspended, in abeyance, inactive, inert; veiled, covert, obscure.

Adverbs—in secret, under cover, in the background, behind the scenes, behind one's back, between the lines, on the tip of one's tongue; in suspense.

Antonyms, see APPEARANCE, DISCLOSURE.

LATENESS

Nouns—**1,** lateness, tardiness, SLOWNESS, unpunctuality; delay, procrastination, deferring, deferment, postponement, adjournment, prorogation, retardation, respite; protraction, prolongation.
2, stop, stay, continuation, reprieve, moratorium; waiting list, rain check; afterthought; hang-up; lag (see SEQUENCE).
3, Johnny-come-lately, Sunday-morning quarterback.

Verbs—**1,** be late, tarry, wait, stay, bide, take time; dawdle, [dilly-]dally, linger, loiter, stick around, take one's time, drag one's feet *or* heels, gain time, bide one's time; hang fire, stand over, lie over; fall *or* get behind.
2, put off, defer, delay, lay over *or* aside, shelve, suspend, stave off, waive, retard, remand, postpone, put over, put on ice, adjourn, procrastinate, spin *or* draw out, prorogue, hold *or* keep back, tide over, temporize, play for time, get in under the wire, sleep on it; stand up, keep waiting, hold up.
3, lose an opportunity, be kept waiting, dance attendance; cool one's heels, [a]wait; miss *or* lose out, miss the boat *or* bus. *Slang,* sweat it out.

Adjectives—late, tardy, slow, behindhand, belated, backward, unpunctual, dilatory, delayed, delaying, procrastinating, in abeyance, on the shelf; untimely; eleventh-hour.

Adverbs—late, backward; late in the day, at the eleventh hour, at length, ultimately, finally, behind time, too late, after hours, *ex post facto;* in arrears (see DEBT); later on; slowly, leisurely, deliberately, at one's leisure; in the nick of time, about time; down to the wire; better late than never.

Interjections—too late! now or never!

Antonyms, see EARLINESS.

latent, *adj.* See LATENCY.

lateral, *adj.* sidelong. See SIDE.

latest, *adj.* last, freshest, newest; in fashion, *le dernier cri*. *Slang,* hot off the press, in. See NEWNESS.

lather, *n.* foam, froth, suds, spume,

bubbles; head; shaving cream; EXCITEMENT, AGITATION, frenzy, stew. *Slang,* tizzy.

latitude, *n.* range, extent, scope, FREEDOM, BREADTH, SPACE.

latter, *adj.* later, last mentioned. See PAST.

lattice, *n.* network (see CROSSING).

laud, *v.t.* praise, extol, eulogize. See APPROBATION.

laugh, *v.i.* guffaw, snicker, giggle, titter, chuckle. See REJOICING.

laughable, *adj.* ludicrous, amusing, comic, absurd; facetious, humorous. See ABSURDITY.

laughingstock, *n.* fool, target, butt, game, fair game, April fool; mockery, monkey, buffoon. *Slang,* fall guy. See RIDICULE.

laughter, *n.* laughing, guffaw, snicker, giggle, titter, chuckle. See REJOICING.

launch, *v.t.* float, start, get going; throw, cast, hurl. See BEGINNING, PROPULSION, ASTRONAUTICS.

launder, *v.t.* wash (see CLEANNESS).

lavatory, *n.* washroom; basin. See CLEANNESS.

lavish, *adj.* prodigal, profuse, bountiful, liberal. —*v.t.* give liberally; squander. See LIBERALITY.

law, *n.* statute, ordinance, regulation, mandate; RULE, MAXIM; precept, axiom, jurisprudence. See LEGALITY, PERMISSION.

law-abiding, *adj.* obedient, upright. See PROBITY.

lawbreaker, *n.* felon, miscreant, criminal, wrongdoer. See ILLEGALITY, EVILDOER.

lawful, *adj.* legal, legitimate; permissible; valid. See LEGALITY.

lawless, *adj.* disorderly, unruly, insubordinate, mutinous. See ILLEGALITY, DISOBEDIENCE.

lawn, *n.* green, greenyard, greensward. See AGRICULTURE.

LAWSUIT

Nouns—**1,** lawsuit, suit, action, cause, litigation, proceedings, dispute; hearing, trial; verdict, JUDGMENT, award; recovery, damages.

2, citation, arraignment, prosecution, impeachment; ACCUSATION, true bill, indictment; apprehension, arrest; commitment, committal; imprisonment; brief; writ, summons, subpoena, habeas corpus, pleadings, declaration, bill, claim, bill of right, affidavit, answer, replication, plea, demurrer, rejoinder, rebuttal, summation; appeal, motion, writ of error, case, decision, precedent, reports; plea bargaining. See RESTRAINT.

3, a. judge, justice, magistrate, surrogate, referee, chancellor; jurist, justice, [the] court; chancellor; judge of assize, recorder, justice of the peace, j.p., magistrate; his worship, his honor, his Lordship, Lord Chancellor, Chief Justice; archon, tribune, praetor; mufti, cadi, mullah; judge advocate. *Slang,* beak. **b.** coroner, sheriff, constable, bailiff, officer, policeman, gendarme. **c.** suitor, litigant, plaintiff, defendant, appellant, claimant. **d.** lawyer, legal adviser; district *or* prosecuting attorney, attorney general, prosecutor; advocate, barrister, solicitor, counsel, counselor[-at-law]; King's *or* Queen's counsel; attorney[-at-law]; bencher; bar; pleader; Portia; a Daniel come to judgment. *Colloq.,* D.A.; sea lawyer. *Slang,* mouthpiece, lip. **e.** jury, grand *or* petty jury; tribunal, court, forum, bench; circuit, juror, juryman, jury foreman. **f.** court, tribunal, judicatory; court of law, equity, chancery, *or* appeals, appellate court, Supreme Court; woolsack, drumhead; court-martial. *Slang,* kangaroo court. **g.** courtroom, chambers, dock jury-box, witness-box *or* -stand.

Verbs—sue, litigate; bring to trial, put on trial, accuse, hale to court; prefer a claim, file; serve, cite, apprehend, arraign, prosecute, bring an action against, indict, impeach, commit, arrest (see RESTRAINT), summon[s], call up, swear out a warrant, give in charge; empanel a jury, implead, join issue, try; set in judgment, plea-bargain; judge, adjudicate; rule, award, affirm, deny. *Slang,* cop a plea.

Adjectives—litigious, litigant, contentious; judicial, legal, appellate.

Adverbs—on trial, on the bench.

---

lawyer, *n.* See LAWSUIT.

lax, *adj.* loose, flaccid, limp, slack; remiss, careless, weak; relaxed, lawless, chaotic, disorderly; unbridled; anarchical, unauthorized. See LATENESS, SOFTNESS, NEGLECT, IMPURITY.

laxative, *n.* physic, cathartic, purgative, eliminant; enema, irrigation, cleansing. See REMEDY.

laxity, *n.* laxness, looseness, slackness, flaccidity, limpness; toleration, lenity, freedom, relaxation, remission, loosening, DISORDER, disorganization, chaos. See NEGLECT.

lay, *adj.* secular, noncleric, nonprofessional —*v.t.* put, place, deposit; allay, suppress; wager, bet; impose; impute, ascribe; present. See LOCATION, RELIEF, ATTRIBUTION, HORIZONTAL.

LAYER

Nouns—**1,** layer, stratum, couch, bed, zone, substratum, floor, stage, story, tier, slab, FOLD, flap, ply, veneer, lap, table, tablet, board, plank, platter, course. See HORIZONTAL.

2, plate, lamina, sheet, flake, foil, wafer, scale, coat, peel, membrane, film, leaf, slice, rasher, shaving, integument, seam, pane. See COVERING, PART.

3, stratification, shale, scaliness, squamosity, lamination.

Verbs—slice, shave, pare, peel; plate, coat, veneer, cover, laminate, stratify.

Adjectives—lamellar, lamellate, laminated, micaceous; schistose, scaly, squamous, filmy, membranous, flaky, scurfy, foliated, foliaceous, stratified, stratiform, tabular, discoid.

---

layman, laywoman, *n.* See LAITY.

lazy, *adj.* indolent, slothful; slow, sluggish. See INACTIVITY.

lead, *v.t.* conduct, direct; precede; open, start; bring; spend, pass. See AUTHORITY, DIRECTION, BEGINNING, PRECEDENCE.

leaden, *adj.* gray, somber; slow, heavy, gloomy, cheerless. See DIMNESS, INACTIVITY.

leader, *n.* guide, bellwether; DIRECTOR, conductor; head, commander, chief. See AUTHORITY, MUSIC, PRECEDENCE.

leadership, *n.* superintendence, chieftainship, stewardship, guidance. See AUTHORITY.

leaf, *n.* frond, blade; lamina, sheet, flake; sheet, page. See VEGETABLE, LAYER.

leafage, *n.* foliage, leaves, verdure. See VEGETABLE.

league, *n.* band, coalition, covenant, [con]federation, confederacy, junta, cabal. —*v.i.* confederate, unite, join. See PARTY.

leak, *v.i.* seep, ooze, escape. See EGRESS, DISCLOSURE, WASTE.

lean, *v.i.* slant, incline; depend, rely; tend. See SUPPORT, TENDENCY. —*adj.* spare, meager; lank, gaunt. See NARROWNESS.

LEAP

Nouns—**1,** leap, jump, hop, spring, bound, vault; bounce (see RECOIL).

2, dance, caper; curvet, prance, skip, gambol, frolic, romp, buck.

3, leaper, jumper, kangaroo, jerboa, chamois, goat, frog, grasshopper, flea, hoptoad; jumping bean, jumping jack, pogo stick; spring.

4, high jump, broad *or* long jump, pole vault; lover's leap; springboard; leap frog, hopscotch; hop, skip, and jump.

Verbs—leap, jump, hop, spring, bound, pounce, vault, cut capers, trip, skip, dance, prance, gambol, frolic, romp, cavort, caper, curvet, foot it, bob, bounce, flounce, frisk, start [up].

Adjectives—leaping, bounding, springy, saltatory, frisky, lively, bouncy, frolicsome, skittish.

Antonyms, see DESCENT.

LEARNING

Nouns—**1,** learning, assimilation, absorption; erudition, KNOWLEDGE; humanity, wisdom, breeding; study, education, schooling; reading, INQUIRY, contemplation; apprenticeship, pupilage, tutelage, novitiate, matriculation. *Colloq.*, school of hard knocks. See SCHOOL.

2, learner, beginner, novice, neophyte, adherent; student, scholar, pupil, schoolboy *or* -girl; apprentice, plebe, abecedarian; disciple, follower, apostle; self-taught man *or* woman.

3, scientist, savant, scholar, pedant, pedagogue; man of learning (see KNOWLEDGE); intelligentsia, literati, clerisy; bookworm, egghead. *Colloq.,* longhair.

Verbs—**1,** learn, acquire knowledge; master; learn by rote *or* heart, commit to MEMORY, memorize; acquaint oneself; sit at the feet of; learn by experience, learn the hard way (see DIFFICULTY); learn a lesson, run through; serve one's apprenticeship. *Colloq.,* learn the ropes; get the hang *or* knack of, catch on.

2, study, lucubrate, burn the midnight oil, keep one's nose in a book, cram. *Colloq.,* hit the books, crack a book, bone up. *Slang,* grind.

3, ascertain, hear (of), discover; come to one's knowledge.

Adjectives—learned, cultured, knowledgeable, erudite, literate; schooled, well-read, well-informed, wise; bookish; studious, scholastic, scholarly, academic, industrious; teachable, malleable.

Antonyms, see TEACHING.

---

lease, *n.* leasehold; contract. —*v.t.* rent, let, demise; hire. See COMMISSION.

leash, *n.* leader, thong; trio. See RESTRAINT, NUMERATION.

least, *adj.* smallest, minimum. See INFERIORITY, LITTLENESS.

leathery, *adj.* tough, tanned, coriaceous. See HARDNESS.

leave, *v.t.* abandon, surrender; quit, forsake; deliver; cease, desist, forego; bequeath; relinquish. See RELINQUISHMENT, GIVING. —*v.i.* go away, depart; omit, postpone. See DEPARTURE, NEGLECT. —*n.* PERMISSION; weekend, *etc.* pass.

leaven, *n.* yeast, ferment; CAUSE, generator. See LEVITY.

leave-taking, *n.* farewell, withdrawal, valediction; adieu, Godspeed. See DEPARTURE.

lecher, *n.* roué, rake, profligate, satyr. *Slang,* le[t]ch. See IMPURITY.

lecture, *v.t.* address, discourse, expound; reprove, rebuke, scold. See TEACHING, DISAPPROBATION, SPEECH.

ledge, *n.* shelf, rim, bench; berm, reef. See HEIGHT, HORIZONTAL.

leech, *n.* bloodsucker, parasite, bleeder; toady. See SERVILITY.

leer, *n.* smirk, wink, oblique look. —*v.* ogle, make eyes, grimace, look *or* eye askance. See VISION.

LEFT

Nouns—**1,** left, sinistrality, sinistration; left hand, left side, near side; port[side], larboard; verso. *Colloq.,* wrong side.
2, left wing, radical (see CHANGE); lefthander. *Slang,* lefty, southpaw, portsider.
Adjectives—left, sinister, sinistrous, left-hand[ed], awkward, near, port[side], larboard[ed]; counterclockwise.
Adverbs—port, left-handedly, leftward[s]. *Colloq.,* from left field (unexpectedly or unfairly).

Antonyms, see RIGHT.

leftover, *adj.* remaining, spare, surplus, extra, superfluous. —*n. (pl.)* REMAINDER, remains, leavings, scraps, odds and ends.

leg, *n.* limb, SUPPORT; course, tack, lap; side.

legacy, *n.* bequest (see GIVING).

LEGALITY

Nouns—**1,** legality, legitimacy, legitimateness, legalization, constitutionalism, constitutionality, lawfulness, legal process, due process of law.
2, legislation, legislature, law, code, codex, constitution, charter, enactment, statute, bill, canon, precept, ordinance, regulation; bylaw; decree, order; sanction, AUTHORITY.
3, jurisprudence, codification, equity; common, civil, statute, *or* constitutional law; ecclesiastical *or* divine law, law of Moses, unwritten law; military *or* maritime law; Uniform Code of Military Justice.
4, jurisdiction, administration, province, dominion, domain, bailiwick, magistracy, AUTHORITY, police power, eminent domain. See PERMISSION.
Verbs—**1,** legalize, legitim[at]ize, validate, authorize, sanction; enact, ordain, decree, order, pass a law, legislate; codify, formulate, regulate.
2, administer, govern, rule; preside, judge, arbitrate.
Adjectives—**1,** legal, legitimate, according to law, vested, constitutional, chartered, legalized, lawful, valid, permitted, statutory; official, *ex officio;* legislative. *Slang,* legit; kosher.
2, jurisdictional, judicatory, judiciary, judicial, juridical; judging, judicious; forensic.
Adverbs—legally, legitimately, by law, in the eye of the law. *Slang,* on the square, on the up and up, on the level.

Antonyms, see ILLEGALITY.

legate, *n.* AGENT. See COMMISSION.

legend, *n.* tradition, tale, saga; myth, edda; inscription, motto. See DESCRIPTION.

legendary, *adj.* fabled, storied; mythological, traditional, historical; unreal, illusory; famous, celebrated, of REPUTE. See IMAGINATION, DESCRIPTION.

leggings, *n. pl.* gaiters, spats, puttees, chaps. See CLOTHING.

legible, *adj.* readable, decipherable, clear, plain. See WRITING.

legion, *n.* horde, MULTITUDE; army, corps. See COMBATANT.

legislator, *n.* lawmaker, congressman, senator, parliamentarian. See COUNCIL.

legislature, *n.* congress, parliament. See COUNCIL.

legitimate, *adj.* lawful, legal; proper, valid; genuine, logical, justifiable. See LEGALITY, TRUTH.

leisure, *n.* spare time, idle hours, time on one's hands; holiday, vacation; SLOWNESS, deliberation; rest, ease, idleness, REPOSE. See TIME, OCCASION.

lemon, *n.* citron; *colloq.*, dud, FAILURE, bomb.

lend, *v.* advance, accommodate with, finance; loan; entrust; pawn; lend-lease; let, demise, lease, sublet. See DEBT, COMMISSION.

LENGTH

Nouns—**1,** length, lengthiness, longitude, span, extent, stretch, DISTANCE, dimension, footage, yardage, mileage. See MEASUREMENT, SPACE.

2, line, bar, stripe, string, row, streak; spoke, radius, diameter.

3, lengthening, prolongation, production, protraction, tension, extension, elongation.

4, line, nail, inch, hand, palm, foot, cubit, yard, ell, fathom, pole, rod, furlong, mile, league, chain; meter; centimeter, *etc.;* kilometer.

Verbs—**1,** stretch out, extend, sprawl, reach to, stretch to.

2, lengthen, extend, elongate, stretch, prolong, string out, produce, protract, let out, draw out, spin out.

3, enfilade, rake; look along; view in perspective.

Adjectives—**1,** long, lengthy, outstretched, lengthened, elongated, protracted, interminable, no end of, unshortened, over all.

2, linear, longitudinal, oblong, lineal.

Adverbs—lengthwise, at length, longitudinally, endwise, along, tandem, in a line, in perspective; from end to end, from stem to stern, from head to foot, from top to bottom, from head to toe; cap-a-pie; from dawn to dusk; fore and aft.

Antonyms, see SHORTNESS.

LENIENCY

Nouns—leniency, lenience, lenity, MODERATION, tolerance, toleration, mildness, gentleness, favor; indulgence, clemency, mercy, forbearance, quarter, patience; compassion, ruth, PITY. See LIBERALITY, RELIEF.

Verbs—tolerate, bear with, give quarter; spare, spare the rod [and spoil the child], PITY; indulge, put up with, bear with, baby, pamper, coddle, spoil. *Slang,* pull one's punches; let one down easy.

Adjectives—lenient, mild, gentle, soft, tolerant, indulgent; moderate, easygoing; clement, compassionate, forbearing, merciful.

Antonyms, see SEVERITY.

lens, *n.* refractor, eyeglass, magnifying glass, reading glass. See OPTICAL INSTRUMENTS.

less, *adj.* inferior, not so much, minor. —*adv.* under, short of. See INFERIORITY, DEDUCTION, ABSENCE.

lessen, *v.t.* reduce, diminish, mitigate, abate, shorten. See DECREASE, MODERATION.

lesson, *n.* instruction, task, exercise, example; admonition, reprimand. See TEACHING, WARNING.

lest, *conj.* for fear that. See LIABILITY.

let, *v.t.* allow, permit; propose, CAUSE; assign; lease, rent. See PERMISSION.

letdown, *n.* letup, abatement, fall; comedown, setback, drawback; DISAPPOINTMENT, disillusion; blow, anticlimax.

lethal, *adj.* deadly, fatal, mortal,

KILLING, toxic, poisonous; virulent, pernicious, noxious, hurtful, malignant, injurious.

lethargy, *n.* lassitude, sluggishness, indifference, apathy, stupor. See INACTIVITY, INSENSIBILITY, WEARINESS.

letter, *n.* character, symbol; cuneiform, hieroglyphic; capital, majuscule; small letter, minuscule; consonant, vowel, digraph, diphthong; missive, note. See WRITING, COMMUNICATION.

letup, *n.* lessening, slowup, slowdown, abatement, mitigation, alleviation; pause, lull, truce, cease-fire; interim, interlude, respite, relief; slack season, breathing spell. See MODERATION, REPOSE, DISCONTINUANCE, DECREASE.

level, *adj.* HORIZONTAL; flat; even; aligned; cool, well-balanced. —*v.t.* raze; flatten; equalize. See DESTRUCTION, SMOOTHNESS, EQUALITY.

lever, *n.* crowbar, pry, prize, jimmy; tool. See ELEVATION, INSTRUMENTALITY, INFLUENCE.

leverage, *n.* advantage; purchase, hold. See INFLUENCE.

LEVITY

Nouns—**1,** levity, lightness, buoyancy, imponderability, weightlessness, volatility, airiness, levitation; fermentation, effervescence, ebullience.

2, feather, fluff, down, thistledown, cobweb, gossamer, straw, cork, bubble, mote, dust, air, ether; lightweight, featherweight.

3, leaven, ferment, yeast, barm, baking soda *or* powder; zyme, enzyme, diastase, pepsin.

4, see CHEERFULNESS, UNIMPORTANCE.

Verbs—**1,** lighten, levitate, float, swim, rise, soar, hang, waft; uplift, upraise, buoy up, unburden.

2, leaven, raise, work, ferment; effervesce.

Adjectives—**1,** light, airy, feathery, fluffy, puffy, vapory, zephyry; subtle; weightless, ethereal, sublimated, volatile; buoyant, floating; portable; imponderable, imponderous.

2, foamy, yeasty, barmy, frothy; effervescent; fermentative, fermenting; zymotic, zymic, enzymic, diastatic, peptic.

Antonyms, see GRAVITY.

---

levy, *n.* assessment; tax; draft, conscription. See ASSEMBLAGE, PRICE.

lewd, *adj.* lascivious, obscene, salacious, indecent, unchaste. See IMPURITY.

lexicon, *n.* dictionary, vocabulary, wordbook. See PUBLICATION.

LIABILITY

Nouns—liability, liableness, responsibility, POSSIBILITY, probability, contingency, susceptibility; DUTY; liabilities, debts (see DEBT); drawback (see HINDRANCE). See TENDENCY.

Verbs—be liable, incur, lay oneself open to, risk, run the risk, stand a chance, lie under, expose oneself to, open a door to; be responsible for, answer for.

Adjectives—liable, subject, in danger, open to, exposed to, apt to, dependent on, responsible, answerable, accountable, incurring; contingent, incidental, possible, on *or* in the cards, at the mercy of.

Adverbs—responsibly, *etc.;* at the risk of. *Colloq.,* likely.

Conjunctions—lest, for fear that.

Antonyms, see EXEMPTION.

---

liaison, *n.* affair; CONNECTION. See LOVE.

liar, *n.* prevaricator, equivocator, falsifier, fibber, deceiver. See DECEPTION, FALSEHOOD.

libel, *n.* defamation, calumniation, aspersion. See DETRACTION.

LIBERALITY

Nouns—**1,** liberality, generosity, UNSELFISHNESS, munificence, largess, bounty; charity, hospitality, beneficence, philanthropy; prodigality; fullness, broadness, BREADTH.

2, tolerance, catholicity, bigness, broadmindedness, impartiality, lack of *or* freedom from bigotry, magnanimity. See JUSTICE.

3, gift, donation, present, gratuity, benefaction; giver, benefactor, philanthropist. *Colloq.,* big tipper. See GIVING, BENEVOLENCE.

Verbs—spend freely, shower down upon, open one's purse strings, spare no expense, give *carte blanche,* lavish; liberalize, broaden.

Adjectives—**1,** liberal, free, generous, handsome, charitable, beneficent, philanthropic; bounteous, bountiful, unsparing, ungrudging, unstinting, lavish, profuse; open- *or* free-handed, open- *or* large-hearted; hospitable, unselfish, princely, prodigal, munificent.

2, tolerant, catholic, progressive, broad- *or* large-minded, magnanimous, impartial, unbigoted, open-minded, receptive.

Adverbs—liberally, generously, *etc.;* with both hands.

Interjection—keep the change!

Antonyms, see ECONOMY, PARSIMONY, SELFISHNESS.

LIBERATION

Nouns—**1,** liberation, emancipation, enfranchisement, manumission, freeing; Emancipation Proclamation; ESCAPE, FREEDOM, liberty; deliverance, extrication, release, riddance; rescue, ransom; redemption, salvation, saving, absolution (see ACQUITTAL); discharge, dismissal, demobilization.

2, liberator, emancipator, freer, deliverer, rescuer; redeemer, savior.

Verbs—**1,** liberate, free [from bondage], set free, set at liberty, give one's freedom; disenthrall; emancipate, enfranchise, manumit; deliver, extricate, release, ransom, reclaim; snatch from the jaws of death; redeem, absolve, save; acquit. *Slang,* spring.

2, discharge, dismiss, disband, demobilize; parole; let go, turn, set, cut, *or* let loose, let out, let slip; turn *or* cast adrift; rid, shake off, be *or* get rid of; unfetter, untie, unleash, unloose[n], unlock, unbolt, unbar, uncork, unbind, unhand, unchain, unshackle; disengage, disentangle, disencumber; clear.

3, gain one's liberty, go [scot] free, get off *or* out, get clear *or* free of (see ESCAPE).

Adjectives—liberated, freed, saved, *etc.;* free, out of harness, unfettered, at liberty, off the hook, at large; out of bondage, on parole, free as a bird; liberative, liberatory.

Antonyms, see RESTRAINT.

libertine, *n.* See IMPURITY.

liberty, *n.* FREEDOM, independence, emancipation; right, license, privilege. See PERMISSION, EXEMPTION.

library, *n.* athenaeum, bookroom. See STORE.

libretto, *n.* script; scenario, book, dialogue, text, words; plot, story, synopsis, promptbook. See DRAMA, WRITING.

license, *n.* PERMISSION, authority; FREEDOM, licentiousness. See IMPURITY.

lick, *v.* lap (up), tongue; dart across (see TOUCH); *colloq.*, beat, thrash, flog; *colloq.*, overcome, defeat, rout. See IMPULSE, PUNISHMENT, SUCCESS. —*n.* lap, licking, sip, taste, sup; bit, jot, modicum; *slang*, try, essay, chance; *slang*, hot lick, blue note, vamp, improvisation, riff. See FOOD, TOUCH, MUSIC.

lid, *n.* top, cover, cap, crown, CLOSURE; censorship.

lie, *v.i.* prevaricate, falsify, deceive; recline, rest, be situated; extend. See FALSEHOOD, DECEPTION, LOCATION, HORIZONTAL.

lieutenant, *n.* deputy, assistant. See AGENT.

LIFE

Nouns—**1,** life, vitality, EXISTENCE, being, living, animation; vital force, flame, *or* spark; respiration, breath [of life], lifeblood, life force, vivification, revivification, resurgence. See REPRODUCTION, ORGANIC MATTER.

2, life sciences; physiology, biology, embryology, biochemistry, biophysics, *etc.*

3, the living, the quick (see HUMANITY).

Verbs—**1,** live, be alive, be, breathe, respire, subsist, exist, walk the earth.

2, see the light, be born, come into the world, draw breath, quicken, come to [life]. See RESTORATION.

3, give birth to, bring to life, put life into, [re]vitalize, revive, vivify, [re]animate, keep alive, keep body and soul together, keep the wolf from the door, support life.

Adjectives—**1,** living, alive, vital, existing, extant, in the flesh, in the land of the living, breathing, quick, animated, lively, alive and kicking.

2, life-giving, generative, fecund, seminal, germinal; vivifying, animative, invigorating, exhilarating.

Antonyms, see DEATH.

life-giving, *adj.* See LIFE.

lifeless, *adj.* inanimate, inert, sluggish, spiritless. See DEATH.

lifelike, *adj.* realistic, natural, accurate. See SIMILARITY.

life-preserver, *n.* lifesaver, life belt *or* jacket, Mae West, water wings, flotation device. See SAFETY.

lift, *v.t.* raise, elevate, exalt; uplift; *colloq.*, steal. See ELEVATION, STEALING.

ligature, *n.* bond, tie, slur, surgical thread. See CONNECTION.

light, *adj.* airy (see LEVITY); frivolous, jesting, jocular, lightsome; giddy, dizzy, flighty; wanton; nimble, agile; flippant, pert, insouciant; humorous; trivial. See CHEERFULNESS, UNIMPORTANCE, IMPURITY, CHANGEABLENESS.

LIGHT

Nouns—**1,** light, ray, beam, stream, gleam, streak, pencil; sunbeam, moonbeam, aurora, day, sunshine, light of day, sun, daylight, daybreak, noonday, sunlight; moonlight, starlight.

2, glow, glimmer[ing]; glitter, shimmer, flicker, glint; spark, scintilla, sparkle, scintillation, flash, blaze, coruscation, flame, fire, lightning bolt.

3, luster, sheen, gloss; tinsel, spangle; brightness, brilliancy, splendor, effulgence, dazzle, glare, resplendence, dazzlement, phosphorescence, incandescence, luminousness, luminosity, lucidity, radiation, irradiation, radiance, illumination, reflection, refraction.

4, photology, photometry, photics, optics, catoptrics, photography, heliography, radioscopy, holography.

5, luminary, illuminant; electric, fluorescent, neon, gas, *etc*. light; candlelight, lamplight, firelight; laser; candle, taper, lamp, torch, brand, flambeau, lantern, searchlight, flashlight; bulb, globe, mantle, jet; chandelier, candelabrum, sconce, candlestick; limelight, footlights, spotlight; rocket, flare, beacon; fireworks, pyrotechnics; halo, aureole, nimbus, gloriole, aura, glory. *Slang,* glim.

Verbs—**1,** shine, glow, glitter, spangle, glister, glisten, flicker, twinkle, gleam, flare, glare, beam, shimmer, glimmer, sparkle, scintillate, coruscate, flash, glint, blaze, be bright, reflect light, dazzle, radiate, shoot out beams; beat down.

2, lighten, enlighten; light [up], clear up, brighten, irradiate, shine, give *or* shed light, throw light upon, illume, illumine, illuminate; strike a light, kindle.

Adjectives—**1,** shining, alight, luminous, luminescent, lucid, lucent, luciferous, light, lightsome, bright, vivid, resplendent, lustrous, shiny, beamy, scintillant, radiant, lambent; glossy, sunny, cloudless, clear, unclouded; glinting, gleaming, beaming, effulgent, splendid, resplendent, glorious, blazing, brilliant, ablaze, meteoric, phosphorescent, glowing; lighted, lit, ablaze, on.

2, actinic, photographic, heliographic, optic, optical, holographic.

Antonyms, see DARKNESS.

---

lightness, *n.* LEVITY; gaiety, volatility; nimbleness, grace; paleness. See ACTIVITY, COLORLESSNESS.

lightning, *n.* thunderbolt, levin, firebolt, fulmination. See VELOCITY, LIGHT.

like, *adj.* similar, resembling, characteristic. See SIMILARITY. —*v.t.* enjoy, desire, fancy. See PLEASURE, LOVE, APPROBATION.

likely, *adj.* credible; suitable, promising. See LIABILITY, AGREEMENT, CHANCE, POSSIBILITY.

liken, *v.t.* compare. See RELATION.

likeness, *n.* portrait, effigy, counterpart; SIMILARITY; resemblance. See REPRESENTATION.

liking, *n.* fondness, inclination, preference. See DESIRE, LOVE.

limb, *n.* branch; arm, leg, member. See PART, INELASTICITY.

limber, *adj.* flexible, supple, pliable; lithe. See SOFTNESS.

limbo, *n.* land of the lost, no man's land, neither here nor there, nowhere, borderland, OBLIVION. See HELL.

limelight, *n.* spotlight, footlights; publicity, notoriety, fame. See PUBLICATION.

LIMIT

Nouns—limit, boundary, bounds, confines; curbstone, term, EDGE; compass; bourne, verge, pale; termination, terminus, END, terminal, extremity; stint; frontier, precinct, border, marches, boundary line, landmark, line of demarcation, point of no return, Rubicon, turning point; ceiling; deadline; Berlin wall, Iron *or* Bamboo Curtain. See RESTRAINT, CIRCUMSCRIPTION, QUALIFICATION.

Verbs—limit, restrict, bound, confine, define, circumscribe, restrain, qualify, draw the line.

Adjectives—definite, finite, determinate, terminal, frontier, limited, circumscribed, restricted, confined, earthbound.

Adverbs—thus far, so far and no further, just so far; to death; within bounds.

Antonyms, see FREEDOM, INFINITY.

---

limitless, *adj.* endless, inexhaustible, unbounded. See SUFFICIENCY, INFINITY.

limp, *adj.* limber, flaccid, flabby, soft. See SOFTNESS. —*v.t.* hobble, hitch; drag. See FAILURE.

line, *v.t.* interline, face; delineate. —*n.* mark; cord, string; crease, wrinkle; verse, note; route, system; vocation, calling; lineage; row, file. See INDICATION, FILAMENT, POETRY, BUSINESS, ANCESTRY, CONTINUITY, FURROW, LENGTH, NARROWNESS, STRAIGHTNESS.

lineage, *n.* ANCESTRY, family, pedigree, POSTERITY.

lineament, *n.* feature, characteristic, singularity. See APPEARANCE, FORM.

linear, *adj.* aligned, straight; lineal. See CONTINUITY.

lineup, *n.* program, calendar; batting order. See LIST, ARRANGEMENT.

linger, *v.i.* delay, dally, loiter, dawdle, poke; remain, persist. See LATENESS, DURABILITY, SLOWNESS.

lingerie, *n.* underthings, underwear. *Colloq.,* undies, unmentionables. See CLOTHING.

lingo, *n.* language, SPEECH, tongue; argot, cant, *etc.;* shop talk. *Slang,* jive.

linguist, *n.* polyglot, philologist, etymologist. See SPEECH.

lining, *n.* inner coating *or* COVERING, interlining; filling, stuffing; wainscot[ing]; gasket, washer; facing, sheathing, bushing; ceiling.

link, *n.* tie, bond; component, liaison. —*v.t.* join, unite, couple. See JUNCTION, RELATION, CONNECTION, PART.

lint, *n.* fluff, fuzz, threads; gauze, dressing. See COVERING, REMEDY.

lion, *n.* lioness, cat; hero, celebrity. See ANIMAL, REPUTE.

lip, *n.* EDGE, verge; labium, flange; *slang,* impertinence. See CONVEXITY, INSOLENCE.

LIQUEFACTION

Nouns—liquefaction, liquescence, liquidization, fluidization; melting, thaw; condensation, colliquation, dissolution, fusion; solution, infusion, lixivium, flux, decoction; solvent, menstrum, dissolvent, resolvent; liquefacient; liquefier. See FLUIDITY.

Verbs—liquefy, liquesce; run, melt, thaw, dissolve, resolve; deliquesce; liquidize, liquate, fluidize, condense; hold in solution, fuse, percolate, milk.

Adjectives—liquefied, fusil, condensed; melted, molten, thawed, *etc.;* in solution *or* suspension; liquefactive, liquescent, colliquative; liquifiable, soluble, dissoluble, dissolvable; solvent, melting.

Antonyms, see DENSITY, VAPOR.

---

liqueur, *n.* cordial, *digestif, pousse-café.* See FOOD, DRINKING.

liquid, *adj.* fluid, smooth, flowing. See FLUIDITY.

liquidate, *v.t.* pay, settle, wind up; *slang,* kill. See PAYMENT, KILLING.

liquor, *n.* liquid, fluid, broth, stock, juice, essence; spirits, *etc.* (see DRINKING). See FLUIDITY, FOOD.

lissome, *adj.* limber, lithe, agile. See SOFTNESS, ELASTICITY.

LIST

Nouns—**1,** list, catalog, beadroll, RECORD, register, cadastre, registry, directory;

tabulation, tally [sheet], file; tariff, schedule; docket, calendar; waiting list, honor roll, hit parade; lineup, roll, muster [roll]; enrollment, roster, slate, checklist; census, statistics, poll, ballot; bill [of lading], invoice, ledger, inventory; table, index; *catalogue raisonné;* glossary, vocabulary; wordbook, lexicon, dictionary, thesaurus; syllabus; portfolio, prospectus, canon, synopsis; Domesday Book, Blue Book, Social Register, Who's Who; Yellow, Blue, *or* White Pages; active, black, retired, sick, *etc*. list; registration, registry; matriculation. See CLASS.

2, registrar, cataloguer, indexer, tabulator; actuary, statistician; computer.

Verbs—**1,** list, catalog, RECORD, register, inventory; tally, file, tabulate; index, post, enter, set *or* jot down, inscribe; enroll, matriculate; itemize, schedule, chronicle; enumerate, rattle *or* reel off; blacklist.

2, list, incline, careen (see OBLIQUITY).

Adjectives—fair-trade, fixed, retail; inventorial.

---

listen, *v.i.* harken, attend; hear; grant; heed. See HEARING, ATTENTION.

listless, *adj.* indifferent, languid, spiritless, apathetic, lethargic. See INACTIVITY.

literal, *adj.* verbatim, word-for-word, exact, prosaic. See MEANING.

literary, *adj.* bookish, scholarly. *Slang,* long-haired. See KNOWLEDGE, WRITING.

literate, *adj.* lettered, educated. See LEARNING.

literature, *n.* books, belles-lettres, letters. See WRITING.

lithe, *adj.* lissome, supple, limber, flexible; spry, slender, willowy, sylphic, svelte. See SOFTNESS, ELASTICITY.

litigate, *v.* contest, dispute, sue, prosecute. See LAWSUIT.

litigious, *adj.* actionable; contentious, disputatious. See LAWSUIT.

litter, *n.* DISORDER, scraps; bedding; stretcher, palanquin; offspring, birth. See VEHICLE, USELESSNESS, POSTERITY.

LITTLENESS

Nouns—**1,** littleness, smallness, minuteness, diminutiveness; thinness, NARROWNESS; epitome, abstract, brief (see SHORTNESS); microcosm; rudiment, miniature; vanishing point. See INSUBSTANTIALITY, POWDERINESS, PART, INVISIBILITY.

2, animalcule, monad, mite, insect, fly, midge, gnat, shrimp, peewee, minnow, worm, maggot, entozoön, ameba, microbe, germ, bacterium, grub, tomtit, runt, mouse, small fry, mustard seed, peppercorn, pebble, grain of sand, molehill.

3, point; atom, molecule, ion, electron, neutron; fragment, particle, crumb, powder; pinpoint, dot, speck, mote, jot, iota; decimal, fraction; modicum, minimum; *minutiae;* trifle; *soupçon,* suspicion, shade, scintilla, smidgeon; grain, bit, fleck, scruple, granule, minim; sip, dab, drop[let], dash, driblet, sprinkling, tinge; bloom; scrap, tag, splinter, chip, sliver, morsel, crumb; bite, snick, snack; thimbleful; nutshell.

4, micrography, microscopy, micrology, microphotography; microscope, electron microscope, micrometer, vernier.

Verbs—belittle; dice; decrease, diminish, contract (see CONTRACTION).

Adjectives—**1,** little, small, minute, diminutive, microscopic, inconsiderable, exiguous, puny, wee, tiny; petty (see UNIMPORTANCE); petite, minikin, knee-high, miniature, pygmy, undersized, dapper, dwarf[ed], dwarfish, stunted, limited, cramped, Lilliputian; pocket[-size], portable, short; thin, weazened, scant, scrubby; granular, powdery, shrunken. *Colloq.*, pint-size. **2,** impalpable, imperceptible, invisible, infinitesimal, atomic, molecular.

Adverbs—little, slightly, in a small compass, on a shoestring, in a nutshell, on a small scale; partly, partially; some, rather, somewhat; scarcely, hardly, barely, less than; merely; at [the] least.

Antonyms, see SIZE, GREATNESS.

---

liturgy, *n.* ritual, RITE, ceremony, service, worship; prayer book.

live, *v.i.* exist, be alive; abide; subsist, survive. See LIFE, ABODE.

livelihood, *n.* living, living wage; MEANS, wherewithal, resources, support, [up]keep, subsistence, sustenance, daily bread, job. See BUSINESS.

liveliness, *n.* animation, vivacity, sprightliness. *Slang,* pep. See ACTIVITY, CHEERFULNESS, FEELING, VIGOR.

livid, *adj.* pallid, ashen. See COLORLESSNESS.

living, *adj.* [a]live, quick, existing. See LIFE. —*n.* See LIVELIHOOD.

lizard, *n.* lacerta, saurian; gecko, chameleon. See ANIMAL.

load, *n.* burden; cargo, lading, shipment; charge. See GRAVITY, TRANSPORTATION.

loafer, *n.* idler, lounger, vagrant. *Slang,* bum. See INACTIVITY.

loan, *n.* lending, borrowing; advance, credit; sinking fund; mortgage. *Slang,* touch. —*v., colloq.*, give *or* extend credit; underwrite, finance. See DEBT, MEANS.

loathe, *v.t.* detest, abhor, abominate. See HATE.

lobby, *n.* foyer, hall, vestibule; lobbyism; pressure group, bloc, party, lobbyists, advocates. See RECEPTACLE, INFLUENCE. —*v.* solicit, ask favors; promote, bring pressure [to bear]; plump for, root for, pull strings.

local, *adj.* restricted, narrow, provincial; native, endemic. See REGION.

locale, *n.* See LOCATION.

LOCATION

Nouns—**1,** location, localization, lodgment, stowage, collocation, packing, establishment, settlement, installation, fixation; placement, setting, insertion. **2,** place, situation, locality, locale, site, depot, position, post, stand, neighborhood, ENVIRONMENT, whereabouts, bearings, orientation; attitude, aspect, viewpoint, standpoint, spot; colony. See ABODE
3, colonization, domestication, habitation, naturalization.

Verbs—**1,** place, situate, locate, localize, make a place for, put, lay, set [down], posit, plunk down, slap down, seat, station, lodge, quarter, post, park, double-park, install, house, stow, establish, set up; fix, pin, root, graft, plant, lay down, deposit; cradle; moor, anchor, tether, picket; pack, tuck in; vest, replace, put back; billet on, quarter upon, saddle with, load, freight, put up.
2, inhabit, domesticate (see ABODE).

Adjectives—located, placed, situate[d], ensconced, embedded, rooted, domesticated, vested in.

Adverbs—here, there, here and there; hereabout[s], thereabout[s], whereabout[s]; in place.

Antonyms, see DISPLACEMENT.

---

lock, *v.t.* fasten, secure, make fast. See CLOSURE, JUNCTION.

locker, *n.* chest, cabinet, safe; lockbox, foot locker. See RECEPTACLE.

lodestone, *n.* loadstone; magnet, allurement. See ATTRACTION.

lodge, *v.i.* dwell, sojourn; settle; file. —*v.t.* shelter, harbor; deposit; file. —*n.* den; chapter, post. See ABODE, PARTY, LOCATION, STABILITY.

lodger, *n.* guest, roomer, boarder, transient; lessee, tenant. See INHABITANT.

lodging, *n.* accommodation. See ABODE.

loft, *n.* attic, garret; hayloft; studio. See ABODE, STORE.

lofty, *adj.* towering, high; haughty, patronizing; distinguished, noble; sublime; elevated; exalted. See HEIGHT, REPUTE.

log, *n.* timber, firewood; logbook, RECORD, diary, journal. See FUEL.

logical, *adj.* rational, reasonable, sane. See REASONING.

loincloth, *n.* breechclout, breechcloth. See CLOTHING.

loiter, *v.i.* linger, poke, dawdle, lag. See SLOWNESS.

loll, *v.i.* lounge, lie down, sprawl; idle. See INACTIVITY, HORIZONTAL.

lone, *adj.* solitary, lonely; single, unmarried. See SECLUSION, CELIBACY.

lonely, *adj.* lonesome, solitary, lone, desolate, alone. See SECLUSION.

long, *adj.* lengthy, elongated; tedious; extended, protracted. See LENGTH. —*adv.* in great degree, for a time. See DURABILITY.

longevity, *n.* See AGE, DURABILITY.

longing, *n.* yearning, craving, hankering, hunger. See DESIRE.

longshoreman, *n.* See STEVEDORE.

long shot, *n.* long odds, outside CHANCE, gamble. See IMPROBABILITY.

long-suffering, *adj.* forbearing, stoic, submissive, patient. See LIBERALITY, FORGIVENESS.

long-winded, *adj.* tedious. See DIFFUSENESS, WEARINESS.

look, *v.i.* behold; perceive, discern; inspect, scan; stare; seem, appear. —*n.* glance, view; APPEARANCE, aspect. See VISION, ATTENTION.

lookout, *n.* vigilance; observatory; watch, sentinel; prospect, vista; *colloq.*, concern. See VISION, WARNING, BUSINESS, CARE, EXPECTATION, DEFENSE.

loop, *n.* ring, circle, noose, eyelet, ambit. See CIRCULARITY.

loophole, *n.* peephole, OPENING; alternative, way out, escape hatch. See ESCAPE.

loose, *adj.* free, detached; flowing, unbound; vague, incoherent, diffuse; unrestrained, slack; dissipated, wanton, dissolute. See DISJUNCTION, IMPURITY. —*v.t.* free; unbind, undo; relax. See FREEDOM.

loot, *n.* booty, spoil, plunder. See ACQUISITION.

lop, *v.* chop, snip, clip, dock, nip, cut off. See SHORTNESS.

lopsided, *adj.* asymmetrical, askew, aslant; unbalanced, unequal; one-sided, off-center. *Slang,* cockeyed, gimpy. See INEQUALITY.

LOQUACITY

Nouns—**1,** loquacity, loquaciousness, talkativeness, volubility, garrulity, multiloquence, flow of words, gift of gab, eloquence, fluency. See SPEECH.
2, DIFFUSENESS, expatiation, dilation; REPETITION, prolixity.
3, jaw, gab[ble], jabber, chatter, prattle, patter, gossip, cackle, twaddle, blabber, blather, blarney, small talk. *Slang,* gas, hot air, yak[ety]-yak.
4, talker, chatterer, chatterbox, babbler, ranter, driveler, gossip, magpie, jay, parrot. *Slang,* windbag.

Verbs—run *or* go on, descant; protract, spin out, dwell on, harp on; talk glibly, patter, prate, palaver, chatter, prattle, blabber, drivel, jabber, jaw, babble, gabble, talk oneself hoarse; digress, perorate, maunder, ramble; gossip. *Slang,* shoot the breeze, shoot off one's mouth, run off at the mouth, gas.

Adjectives—loquacious, talkative, garrulous, voluble, fluent, gossipy; rambling; glib, effusive, gushy, eloquent, chattering, chatty, open-mouthed; long-winded, long-drawn-out, discursive; loudmouthed.
Adverbs—at length; *in extenso; ad nauseum.*

Antonyms, see TACITURNITY.

---

lordly, *adj.* noble, imposing; imperious, arrogant, insolent, dictatorial. See REPUTE, INSOLENCE, NOBILITY.

lore, *n.* erudition, scholarship, learning. See KNOWLEDGE.

LOSS

Nouns—loss; perdition; forfeiture, forfeit, lapse, detriment, privation, bereavement, deprivation, dispossession, riddance, WASTE, dissipation, expenditure, leakage; brain drain; DESTRUCTION. See NONEXISTENCE, DEJECTION.
Verbs—lose; incur *or* meet with a loss; miss, mislay, let slip, allow to slip through the fingers; forfeit, get rid of, WASTE, dissipate, squander; write *or* charge off. *Slang,* lose one's shirt.
Adjectives—**1,** losing, not having; shorn, deprived, rid *or* quit of, denuded, bereaved, bereft, minus, cut off, dispossessed, out of pocket.
2, lost, long-lost; dissipated, wasted, forfeited, missing, gone, irretrievable, destroyed, off one's hands.

Antonyms, see ACQUISITION.

---

lot, *n.* fate, DESTINY, fortune; batch, sum; parcel. See ASSEMBLAGE, CHANCE, QUANTITY.

lotion, *n.* wash, liniment; tonic, skin bracer. See REMEDY, OIL.

lottery, *n.* raffle, draw, lotto; allotment; fortune, CHANCE.

loud-mouthed, *adj.* See LOUDNESS.

LOUDNESS

Nouns—**1,** loudness, noisiness, vociference, sonorousness, vehemency, intensity, power; stridency, raucousness, cacophony. See ROTUNDITY.
2, resonance, reverberation, echo, ringing, tintinnabulation; roll, rumble, drumming, tattoo, rat-a-tat, rub-a-dub.
3, din, clamor, clang, clangor, fracas, bluster, rattle, clatter, noise, roar, uproar, racket, pandemonium, hubbub, shrillness, hullaballoo; charivari; trumpet blast, fanfare, ring, peal, toll, alarum, blast, boom, thunder, thunderclap; white noise; boiler factory; big mouth, loudmouth.
4, flashiness (see OSTENTATION, VULGARITY).
Verbs—peal, ring, swell, clang, boom, thunder, fulminate, roar, resound, pop, reverberate; shout, scream, CRY, vociferate, bellow, crack, crash, bang, blare, rend the air, detonate, fill the air, ring in the ear, pierce the ears, deafen, stun, make the rafters ring; drown out. *Colloq.,* raise the roof. *Slang,* belt out.
Adjectives—loud; sonorous, rotund; highsounding, big-sounding, deep, full, powerful, noisy, clangorous, thunderous, thundering, dinning, deafening, earsplitting, obstreperous, blatant, rackety, uproarious, boisterous, earth-shaking, shrill, clamorous, vociferous, stentorian, enough to wake the dead; loudmouthed, bigmouthed.
Adverbs—loudly, noisily, aloud, at the top of one's voice *or* lungs, lustily, to beat the band; in full cry.

Antonyms, see SOFTNESS.

---

lounge, *n.* sofa, settee, chaise longue, davenport, divan, daybed; lobby, bar. See SUPPORT, RECEPTACLE. —*v.* relax, REPOSE, loll, slouch, sprawl, make oneself comfortable. See INACTIVITY.

louse, *n.* vermin, bug, parasite; *slang,* lout, cad, rascal, bounder, dog, stinker, s.o.b., rat. See ANIMAL, EVILDOER.

lousy, *adj., slang,* see BADNESS.

lout, *n.* bumpkin, clod, oaf, boor. *Slang,* hick, rube. See POPULACE.

louver, *n.* turret, dome, cupola; air vent; shutter, blind, jalousie. See OPENING.

LOVE

Nouns—**1,** love, fondness, liking; inclination, DESIRE; regard, admiration, affection, tenderness, heart, attachment, yearning; gallantry; passion, flame, devotion, infatuation, adoration; spark, ardor; idolatry. See ENDEARMENT, FEELING, PLEASURE, MARRIAGE.

2, BENEVOLENCE, brotherly *or* sisterly love, mother *or* maternal love, father *or* paternal love, parental affection.

3, Cupid, Venus, Eros; true lover's knot, engagement ring, love token; love affair, amour, liaison, intrigue, romance, love story, plighted troth, courtship. *Colloq.,* calf *or* puppy love.

4, a. lover, suitor, follower, admirer, adorer, wooer, beau, honey, sweetheart, inamorato, swain, young man, boy friend, flame, love, truelove, fair-haired boy; Lothario, Romeo, Casanova, Don Juan, gallant, paramour, *amoroso;* fiancé. *Slang,* wolf, lover boy. **b.** inamorata, ladylove; idol, darling, duck, angel, goddess, true love, girl, sweetheart, beloved, girl *or* lady friend; betrothed, affianced, fiancée. *Colloq.,* steady, honeybunch, date, sweetie. **c.** favorite, apple of one's eye. **d.** lovers, lovebirds. **e.** lovers' lane, lover's leap.

Verbs—**1,** love, like, fancy, care for, favor, become enamored, fall *or* be in love with; go with, go together, keep company; revere, take to, make much of, hold dear, prize, hug, cling to, cherish, pet; adore, idolize, love to distraction, dote on, desire; throw oneself at, lose *or* give one's heart. *Colloq.,* go steady, pin. *Slang,* go for, fall for, take a shine to, shine up to, be sweet on, be nuts about, carry a torch for.

2, win, gain, *or* engage the love, affections, *or* heart, disarm; sweep off one's feet; keep company; take the fancy of; attract, endear, charm, fascinate, captivate, bewitch, seduce, enamor, enrapture, turn the head. *Colloq.,* throw oneself at the head of. See ATTRACTION.

Adjectives—**1,** loving, fond of; taken with, smitten, attached to, enamored, charmed, in love, lovesick, lovelorn; affectionate, tender, sweet on, amorous, amatory, amative, erotic, uxorious, ardent, passionate, romantic, rapturous, devoted. *Slang,* going steady, pinned; stuck on.

2, loved, beloved, well beloved, dearly beloved. See ENDEARMENT.

3, lovable, adorable, winsome. See BEAUTY, ATTRACTION.

Antonyms, see HATE, DISLIKE.

---

lovelorn, *adj.* lovesick; jilted. See LOVE, HATE.

lovely, *adj.* beautiful, delightful, comely, exquisite, captivating. See BEAUTY.

lover, *n.* suitor, wooer, sweetheart. *Colloq.,* beau. *Slang,* boyfriend. See LOVE.

lovesick, *adj.* languishing, lovelorn. See LOVE.

lowborn, *adj.* humble, plebeian, common. —*n., slang,* vulgarian, illiterate, idiot. See POPULACE.

lower, *v.i.* lour, glower, scowl; be imminent, impend, APPROACH. —*adj. & v.* See LOWNESS, DEJECTION.

lowland, *n.* bottom[land], marshland, downs; dale, dell. See LAND, LOWNESS.

lowly, *adj.* humble, meek. See HUMILITY, LOWNESS.

LOWNESS

Nouns—**1,** lowness, shortness, flatness, deepness, DEPTH; debasement, DEPRESSION, prostration. See INFERIORITY.

2, lowlands; basement, cellar, dungeon, ground floor, hold; low water; low tide, ebb tide, neap tide, bottom floor, bedrock; rock bottom.

3, [contr]alto, baritone, bass-baritone, bass; contrabass, tuba, *etc.* See SOUND, MUSIC.

Verbs—**1,** lie low, lie flat, underlie; crouch, slouch (see DEPRESSION); flatten, wallow, grovel, crawl. *Colloq.,* touch *or* hit bottom.

2, lower, depress, let *or* take down, debase, reduce, drop, sink; humble, humiliate. See HUMILITY, CONCAVITY.

Adjectives—low, neap, debased, nether, nethermost, sunken, fallen, flat, level with the ground, lying low, crouched, squat, prostrate, depressed, deep; bass, deep[-toned].

Adverbs—under, beneath, underneath, below, down, downward[s], at the foot of, underfoot, underground, downstairs, belowstairs, at a low ebb, lowly. See INFERIORITY.

Antonyms, see HEIGHT, ELEVATION.

low-priced, *adj.* See CHEAPNESS.

loyal, *adj.* faithful, true, devoted. See PROBITY, OBEDIENCE.

lubrication, *n.* greasing, oiling; oiliness; anointing, anointment, unction, unctuousness. See SMOOTHNESS, OIL.

lucid, *adj.* clear, limpid, transparent, understandable; sane, rational; shining. See TRANSPARENCY, SANITY.

luck, *n.* CHANCE, [good] fortune. See PROSPERITY, DESTINY.

lucky, *adj.* fortunate, opportune, auspicious; CHANCE, fortuitous. See OCCASION.

lucrative, *adj.* profitable, well-paying, gainful, moneymaking, productive. See ACQUISITION.

ludicrous, *adj.* ridiculous, absurd (see ABSURDITY).

lug, *v.* tote, transport, convey, carry; draw, drag. See TRACTION, TRANSPORTATION.

luggage, *n.* baggage, impedimenta, bag and baggage. See POSSESSION, TRANSPORTATION.

lukewarm, *adj.* tepid; moderate, temperate, insipid, so-so, neither here nor there, indifferent (see INDIFFERENCE). See HEAT.

lull, *n.* calm, intermission. See REPOSE.

lumber, *n.* wood, logs, timber; planks, boards, paneling, *etc.* See MATERIALS. —*v.* trudge, plod, hobble, bumble. See SLOWNESS.

luminary, *n.* heavenly body, sun, star, *etc.;* wise man, shining light; celebrity, notable. See UNIVERSE, KNOWLEDGE, REPUTE.

luminous, *adj.* luminary, lighted, glowing; incandescent, radiant, lit, alight, self-luminous; phosphorescent, luminescent; bright, resplendent; clear, lucid. See LIGHT, MEANING.

lump, *n.* protuberance, swelling, chunk, mass; consolidation, aggregation. See CONVEXITY, ASSEMBLAGE, DENSITY.

lunatic, *n.* madman, bedlamite, maniac, psychopath. See INSANITY.

lunch, *n.* luncheon, snack, collation, midday meal. *Colloq.*, spread, bite. See FOOD.

lung, *n.* lights, bellows. See WIND.

lunge, *v.i.* surge, thrust, jab; lurch, LEAP, plunge. —*n.* thrust, surge. See IMPULSE, ATTACK.

lurch, *v.i.* sway, pitch, stagger, stumble. See DESCENT.

lure, *v.t.* entice, decoy, tempt, coax. See ATTRACTION.

lurid, *adj.* pallid, ghastly; glaring, eerie; sinister, sensational. See DARKNESS, COLORLESSNESS.

lurk, *v.i.* skulk, slink, sneak, prowl. See CONCEALMENT, LATENCY.

luscious, *adj.* sweet, delicious, ambrosial. See SWEETNESS.

lush, *adj.* luscious, juicy, succulent; tender, ripe; luxurious. See SWEETNESS. —*n., slang,* drunkard, sot, barfly. See DRINKING.

lust, *n.* DESIRE, carnality, sex, sensuality, lasciviousness; satyriasis, nymphomania; voracity, avarice, greed, drive, itch. *Slang,* the hots, yen. —*v.i.* covet, crave, hunger, DESIRE, yearn, *etc.* See IMPURITY.

luster, *n.* gloss, sheen, brightness, splendor; radiance, brilliance, fame. See REPUTE, LIGHT.

lusty, *adj.* robust, vigorous, hearty, sturdy. See SIZE.

luxuriant, *adj.* lush, abundant, profuse; florid, fertile, rich. See SUFFICIENCY.

luxurious, *adj.* sumptuous, elegant; voluptuous, self-indulgent. See PLEASURE.

luxury, *n.* self-indulgence, prodigality; dainty; elegance, sumptuousness, extravagance. See PLEASURE, INTEMPERANCE.

lynching, *n.* hanging, murder; tar and feathering; mob rule. *Slang,* necktie party; kangaroo court. See PUNISHMENT, KILLING.

lyric, *n.* poem, song. See POETRY. —*adj.* melodic. See MUSIC.

M

macabre, *adj.* ghastly, grisly; eerie, weird; morbid, hideous, grotesque, gruesome. See DEATH.

machinate, *v.i.* plot, PLAN. See CUNNING.

machine, *n.* apparatus, contrivance, mechanism, device; motor, engine; airplane, car, bicycle, robot; organization, cabal; machinery. See VEHICLE, INSTRUMENTALITY, PARTY.

machismo, *n.* virility (see MALE).

mad, *adj.* crazy, insane; rabid; frantic, foolish, turbulent; *colloq.*, angry. See INSANITY, RESENTMENT.

madcap, *adj.* wild, flighty. See EXCITABILITY.

madden, *v.t.* infuriate, enrage, incense, craze; drive mad, derange; make one's blood boil. See RESENTMENT.

made-up, *adj.* fabricated, imagined, fanciful, make-believe, fictitious, made of whole cloth. See IMAGINATION, FALSEHOOD.

madhouse, *n.* asylum. See INSANITY.

madman, madwoman, *n.* See INSANITY.

magazine, *n.* storehouse, arsenal, reservoir; periodical, weekly, glossy. See STORE, PUBLICATION.

magic, *n.* SORCERY; witchery, glamour, spell; legerdemain. —*adj.* magic[al], mystic[al], occult; enchanting. See DECEPTION.

magician, *n.* witch, wizard, sorcerer; prestidigitator, conjurer. See SORCERY.

magisterial, *adj.* arbitrary, dictatorial; arrogant, pompous; authoritarian, imperious. See PRIDE, CERTAINTY.

magistrate, *n.* judge (see LAWSUIT).

magnanimous, *adj.* generous, high-minded, great-souled. See LIBERALITY, BENEVOLENCE.

magnate, *n.* mogul (see IMPORTANCE).

magnet, *n.* lodestone. See ATTRACTION, POWER.

magnetism, *n.* ATTRACTION, magnetic force; charm, animal magnetism. See POWER.

magnificent, *adj.* grand, splendid; awe-inspiring; noble, superb. See BEAUTY, OSTENTATION.

magnify, *v.t.* enlarge, augment; laud, glorify. See INCREASE, APPROBATION, EXAGGERATION.

magnitude, *n.* SIZE, bulk; extent; immensity. See GREATNESS.

maid, *n.* girl, lass, maiden, miss; virgin, spinster; SERVANT, domestic. See YOUTH, CELIBACY.

maidenly, *adj.* modest; gentle; girlish. See YOUTH, VIRTUE.

mail, *n.* post, letters, correspondence. —*v.t.* post, send, forward. See COMMUNICATION.

maim, *v.t.* cripple, disfigure, mutilate, lame, impair. See DETERIORATION.

main, *n.* conduit, pipe; strength, POWER; sea, ocean. —*adj.* chief, principal; sheer. See IMPORTANCE.

mainly, *adv.* principally, primarily; mostly, largely, on the whole; above all, more than anything. See IMPORTANCE.

mainstay, *n.* SUPPORT, supporter.

maintain, *v.t.* SUPPORT, carry; preserve, keep; possess, have; uphold, allege, affirm. See PRESERVATION, AGENCY, RETENTION, AFFIRMATION.

majestic, *adj.* noble, august, stately, imposing, grand. See OSTENTATION, PRIDE.

majesty, *n.* stateliness, grandeur; sovereignty. See GREATNESS, AUTHORITY, OSTENTATION.

major, *adj.* principal, chief; greater, senior. See SUPERIORITY.

majority, *n.* adulthood; preponderance, excess, SUPERIORITY.

make, *v.t.* create, produce; prepare; obtain, cause, compel; amount to. See PRODUCTION, COMPULSION, FORM.

make-believe, *n.* fantasy, unreality, fiction, imagination; pretense, feigning, imitation, fakery, DECEPTION. —*adj.* made-up; feigned, sham, whimsical, imitation. *Colloq.*, fake, phony. See FALSEHOOD.

makeshift, *n.* expedient, substitute, stopgap. See SUBSTITUTION.

make-up, *n.* COMPOSITION; personality; placement; cosmetics, beautification. See BEAUTY.

maladroit, *adj.* clumsy, inexpert, awkward, inept. See UNSKILLFULNESS.

malady, *n.* DISEASE, sickness, illness, infirmity.

malcontent, *n.* grumbler, faultfinder; insurgent, rebel. *Slang*, griper. See DISCONTENT.

MALE

Nouns—**1,** male, man, he, *homo,* gentleman, sir, master, yeoman, wight, swain, blade, chap, gaffer, husband, bachelor, Mr., mister, boy, stripling, YOUTH, lad; *homme; hombre;* macho; lady's man, ladykiller. *Colloq.*, fellow. *Slang,* guy, bloke (*Brit.*), bimbo, bozo, geezer, *etc.* See POPULACE, HUMANITY, MARRIAGE.

2, cock, drake, gander, dog, boar, stag, hart, buck, horse, stallion, tomcat, ram, billygoat, bull, rooster, cob, capon, ox, gelding, steer.

3, manhood, manliness, maleness, masculinity, virility, machismo.

Adjectives—male, masculine, manly, boyish, manlike, mannish; macho.

Antonyms, see FEMALE.

---

malediction, *n.* IMPRECATION, curse, anathema, execration.

malefactor, *n.* EVILDOER, wrongdoer, criminal, felon.

MALEVOLENCE

Nouns—**1,** malevolence; evil *or* bad intent; misanthropy, ill-nature; enmity, HATE; malignity, malice, malice aforethought, maliciousness, spite, RESENTMENT, venom, rancor, bitterness; virulence, spleen, mordacity, acerbity, churlishness, hardness of heart, obduracy; ill-treatment; cruelty, cruelness, brutality, savagery, ferocity, barbarity, barbarism, inhumanity; sadism, torture; truculence, ruffianism; heart of stone, evil eye, cloven foot *or* hoof, poison pen. See EVIL.

2, ill *or* bad turn; affront (see DISRESPECT).

3, misanthrope, misanthropist, man-hater, misogynist, woman-hater, cynic; sadist.

Verbs—**1,** bear *or* harbor a grudge, bear malice.

2, hurt, injure, harm, WRONG, do harm; malign, molest (see DISCONTENT); wreak havoc, do mischief, hunt down, hound, persecute, oppress, grind, maltreat, mistreat, bedevil, ill-treat, abuse, misuse, ill-use, do one's worst, show *or* have no mercy. *Colloq.,* have it in for. *Slang,* do one dirt, rub it in.

Adjectives—**1,** malevolent, ill-disposed, ill-intentioned, evilminded, misanthropic, malicious, malign, malignant, rancorous, spiteful, caustic, bitter, mordant, acrimonious, virulent, malefic, maleficent, venomous, invidious.

2, unkind, unfriendly, antisocial; coldblooded, coldhearted, hardhearted, stony-hearted, selfish, unnatural, ruthless, relentless. See DISCOURTESY, SELFISHNESS.

3, cruel, brutal, savage, ferocious, inhuman, sadistic, barbarous, fell, truculent, bloodthirsty, murderous, atrocious, fiendish, heinous, unrelenting, demoniacal, diabolic[al], devilish, infernal, hellish, Satanic.

Antonyms, see BENEVOLENCE.

---

malformation, *n.* DISTORTION, deformity.

malfunction, *v.i.* go amiss *or* wrong, fail. *Slang,* go haywire. —*n.* FAILURE, defect, misfire, miscarriage.

malice, *n.* MALEVOLENCE, spite, ill will, animosity.

malign, *v.t.* libel, slander, defame; calumniate, asperse, traduce, besmirch; backbite. See DETRACTION, MALEVOLENCE.

malignant, *adj.* malign, vicious, criminal; harmful, virulent, pernicious; fatal, incurable. See BADNESS.

malinger, *v.i.* feign, shirk, slack. *Colloq.,* goldbrick, soldier. See AVOIDANCE, DISEASE, FALSEHOOD.

mall, *n.* promenade, allée, avenue, parkway; shopping center. See PASSAGE, SALE.

malleable, *adj.* adaptable; tractable. See SOFTNESS, LEARNING.

mallet, *n.* hammer, club, maul. See SCULPTURE, INSTRUMENTALITY.

malnutrition, *n.* deficiency; emaciation, anemia, marasmus; cachexia, gout, scurvy, pellagra, hookworm; obesity. See DISEASE.

MALODOROUSNESS

Nouns—**1,** malodorousness, malodor, fetor, fetidness, bad smell, smelliness, bad ODOR, stench, stink, foul odor, rankness, goatishness, goatiness, mephitis, mustiness, rancidness, rancidity, foulness; opprobrium (see DISREPUTE); bad breath, halitosis. See UNCLEANNESS.

2, polecat, skunk, stoat, rotten egg, asafoetida, skunk cabbage, stinkpot, stinker, stink bomb; stinkweed.

Verbs—smell bad, reek, stink [in the nostrils], stink like a polecat, smell offensively. *Colloq.,* smell to high Heaven, smell up.

Adjectives—malodorous, fetid, smelling, stinking, stinky, smelly, high, bad, foul, strong, offensive, noisome, gassy, rank, rancid, gamy, tainted, fusty, musty, moldy, stuffy, putrid, suffocating, mephitic, goaty, goatish.

Antonyms, see ODOR.

malpractice, *n.* wrongdoing, misdemeanor, malfeasance, misconduct. See GUILT, ILLEGALITY.

maltreat, *v.t.* abuse, ill-treat, misuse. See MALEVOLENCE, WRONG.

mammoth, *adj.* huge, giant, gigantic, tremendous, prodigious, colossal, enormous. —*n.* elephant, behemoth. See SIZE.

man, *n.* See MALE, HUMANITY. —*v.* run, operate; staff. See DEFENSE.

manacle, *n.* shackle, handcuff. See RESTRAINT.

manage, *v.t.* administer, conduct; control; afford; contrive, bring about, manipulate. See AUTHORITY, SUFFICIENCY. —*v.i.* See PROVISION.

manageable, *adj.* tractable, docile, obedient; wieldy, governable. See FACILITY.

management, *n.* DIRECTION, control, administration; directorate, administrative body. See ORDER.

manager, *n.* See DIRECTOR.

mandate, *n.* COMMAND, edict, statute, ordinance; COMMISSION.

mandatory, *adj.* required, compulsory, binding, obligatory. See COMPULSION, NECESSITY.

maneuver, *n.* artifice, stratagem, tactic. See CUNNING, PLAN.

manger, *n.* trough, bin, crib, feed box. See RECEPTACLE.

mangle, *v.t.* break, crush, mutilate; disfigure, mar; press, iron. See DETERIORATION. —*n.* iron, press. See SMOOTHNESS.

mangy, *adj.* itchy, scurvy, scaly, scrofulous; shabby, seedy, shoddy, ragged; sordid, squalid, wretched. See DISREPUTE, TOUCH.

manhandle, *v.t.* maul, batter, paw, maltreat, push around. See MALEVOLENCE, WRONG.

manhood, *n.* adulthood, maturity; virility, manliness. See AGE, MALE.

manhunt, *n.* See PURSUIT.

mania, *n.* madness, frenzy, lunacy; INSANITY; obsession, craze. See DESIRE, EXCITABILITY.

maniac, *n.* madman (see INSANITY).

manic, *adj.* maniacal, insane, frenzied. See INSANITY.

manicure, *v.t.* trim, clip, cut, pare, file; polish, buff, lacquer. See BEAUTY.

manifest, *v.t.* bring forward, show, display, evidence, trot out, bring to light; demonstrate; proclaim, publish, disclose. —*adj.* apparent, obvious, evident; salient, striking, prominent; flagrant; pronounced; definite, distinct; conspicuous, unmistakable, plain, clear; open, overt; patent. See INDICATION, APPEARANCE.

manifestation, *n.* plainness, VISIBILITY; demonstration; exhibition; display, show[ing], showing off; indication, publicity, DISCLOSURE, revelation, openness, prominence, conspicuousness. See INDICATION.

manifesto, *n.* proclamation, statement, pronouncement; credo, theory, BELIEF.

manifold, *adj.* multiple, diverse, multiform; copied, repeated. See MULTITUDE.

manipulate, *v.t.* operate, control, manage; influence; juggle, falsify. See USE, CONDUCT, TOUCH.

manly, *adj.* masculine (see MALE).

mannequin, *n.* dummy, doll; [fashion] model. *Colloq.,* cover girl. See BEAUTY.

manner, *n.* kind, sort; habit; CLASS; style, mode; CONDUCT, behavior; way. METHOD.

mannerism, *n.* eccentricity, peculiarity, idiosyncrasy; AFFECTATION.

manners, *n. pl.* conduct, behavior, deportment; COURTESY, politeness. See FASHION.

manor, *n.* mansion, hall, hacienda; estate, territory, demesne. See ABODE.

manpower, *n.* working force, staff; strength, capacity, potential; warpower, army, fighting force; womanpower. See SERVANT, COMBATANT.

mansion, *n.* house, manor, hall, villa. See ABODE.

manslaughter, *n.* homicide, murder.

See KILLING.

mantle, *n.* COVERING; cloak, cape, robe. See CLOTHING.

manual, *adj.* nonautomatic, hand. —*n.* guide, handbook, text[book]; keyboard, control, dial; system, exercise, regimen. See INFORMATION, DIRECTION.

manufacture, *v.t.* make, produce, fabricate, invent. See PRODUCTION.

manure, *n.* fertilizer, compost, dung. See UNCLEANNESS.

manuscript, *n.* script, handwriting, [author's] original. See WRITING.

many, *adj.* numerous, multitudinous, manifold. See MULTITUDE.

many-sided, *adj.* versatile; multilateral, polyhedral. See SIDE.

map, *n.* PLAN, chart, projection; diagram; *slang,* FACE.

mar, *v.t.* disfigure, deface, blemish, scratch, impair. See DETERIORATION, IMPERFECTION.

marathon, *adj.* nonstop, continuous, arduous; long, endless. See VELOCITY, CONTENTION, DURABILITY.

maraud, *v.* raid, plunder, freeboot, pillage. See STEALING.

marble, *adj.* hard, vitreous, unyielding; lifeless, insensible, cold; white, pale, colorless; variegated, particolored, pied, striated, mottled. See COLOR, HARDNESS, INSENSIBILITY.

march, *v.i.* tramp, pace, parade, file, advance. See TRAVEL.

margin, *n.* EDGE, border, rim, brink, verge, limit; leeway. See SPACE, FREEDOM.

marijuana, *n.* marihuana; hemp, cannabis, hashish, bhang, ganja[h]. *Slang,* tea, pot, hay, grass, smoke, reefer, Mary Jane, Acapulco gold. See HABIT.

marina, *n.* boat basin, dock[age]. See SAFETY, NAVIGATION.

marine, *adj.* nautical, naval; pelagic, maritime. See NAVIGATION.

mariner, *n.* sailor, seaman. *Colloq.,* tar, salt. See NAVIGATION.

marionette, *n.* puppet; manikin. See REPRESENTATION.

marital, *adj.* hymeneal, spousal. See MARRIAGE.

maritime, *adj.* pelagic, oceanic; coastal, littoral, seaside; seafaring, nautical. See WATER, NAVIGATION.

mark, *n.* goal; imprint, stain; label, badge; token, symptom; symbol; standard, demarcation. See INDICATION. —*v.t.* inscribe, stain; note; check, indicate; delimit. See ATTENTION, SPECIALITY.

marked, *adj.* noticeable, conspicuous; watched, followed. See SPECIALITY, INDICATION, VISIBILITY.

marker, *n.* indicator, INDICATION, sign; counter, chip; *slang,* I.O.U., chit.

market, *n.* marketplace, mart (see BUSINESS); demand. See SALE.

marksman, *n.* sharpshooter, dead shot, crackshot. See PROPULSION.

maroon, *v.t.* abandon, isolate. See RELINQUISHMENT.

MARRIAGE

Nouns—**1,** marriage, matrimony, wedlock, union; intermarriage, nuptial tie, married state, bed and board, cohabitation, wedded bliss; mixed marriage; engagement. *Slang,* ball and chain, light housekeeping. See JUNCTION, UNITY, COMBINATION.

2, engagement, betrothal, understanding, proposal; wedding, nuptials, Hymen, espousal; leading to the altar; epithalamium; temple of Hymen; honeymoon; sea of matrimony.

3, fiancé[e], betrothed; bride, [bride]groom; bridesmaid, maid *or* matron of honor, best man, usher; spouse, mate, partner, helpmate, helpmeet; married man, Benedict, husband, man, good provider, consort, squaw-man; married woman, bride, wife, concubine, frau, goodwife, rib, better half, squaw, lady, matron; [married] couple, pair, husband and wife, bride and groom, newlyweds; Darby and Joan, Mr. and Mrs., lovebirds, loving couple; matchmaker, marriage broker. *Colloq.* old man *or* woman, little woman.

4, monogamy, bigamy, polygamy, polygyny, polyandry, Mormonism; morganatic marriage, common-law marriage, concubinage.

Verbs—**1,** marry, wive, take a wife; be married, be spliced; wed, espouse; rob the cradle; give away, give in marriage. *Slang,* get hitched, walk down the aisle, tie the knot.

2, marry, join, couple, unite, make one, tie the nuptial knot; join *or* unite in marriage; elope; live together. *Slang,* shack up with.

3, propose; betroth, affiance, plight troth; bespeak; pin; match; publish banns.

Adjectives—matrimonial, marital, conjugal, connubial; wedded, nuptial, hymeneal, spousal, bridal; engaged, betrothed, affianced; marriageable, nubile, available, eligible. See AGE.

Antonyms, see CELIBACY, DIVORCE.

---

marsh, *n.* swamp (see WATER).

marshal, *v.t.* array, dispose, order, arrange; mobilize, activate, assemble, collect, utilize. See ARRANGEMENT. —*n.* officer, AUTHORITY, sheriff.

mart, *n.* See BUSINESS.

martial, *adj.* military, warlike, soldierly. See WARFARE.

martyr, *n.* victim, sacrifice, scapegoat; symbol, example; sufferer; saint. See PUNISHMENT.

martyrdom, *n.* martyrship; sacrifice, suffering, PAIN, torture, agony; heroism, asceticism; saintliness, long-suffering. See KILLING, PUNISHMENT.

marvel, *n.* See WONDER.

marvelous, *adj.* wonderful, prodigious, surprising, extraordinary. See WONDER.

mascot, *n.* pet, talisman. See SORCERY.

masculine, *adj.* manly, virile. See MALE.

mash, *v.t.* crush, smash, squeeze, compress, bruise, batter. See POWDERINESS, SOFTNESS.

mask, *n.* false face, disguise, CONCEALMENT; effigy; shield; masquerade, pretense. —*v.t.* screen, conceal, hide. See DECEPTION.

masquerader, *n.* masker, domino, mummer; impostor. See DECEPTION, AMUSEMENT.

Mass, *n.* Divine Service, Eucharist, Communion. See RITE.

mass, *n.* bulk, SIZE; lump, wad, accumulation. See DENSITY, POPULACE.

massacre, *n.* KILLING, slaughter, butchery, carnage.

massage, *v.t.* rub [down]; knead, stroke; manipulate. See FRICTION, TOUCH.

massive, *adj.* bulky, ponderous, solid, imposing. See SIZE.

mast, *n.* pole, timber, upright, column, spar. See SHIP.

master, *n.* superior, DIRECTOR; crowned head, emperor (see AUTHORITY); expert, ARTIST, adept. See RULE, SKILL, MALE, POSSESSION.

masterful, *adj.* masterly, skillful; authoritative. See SKILL, AUTHORITY.

mastermind, *v.t.* PLAN, devise.

masterpiece, *n.* masterwork, *chef d'oeuvre*. See SKILL, GOOD, PERFECTION.

mastery, *n.* rule, victory; ascendency, supremacy; SKILL. See AUTHORITY.

mat, *n.* pad, rug, runner, doormat, doily. —*v.* tangle, snarl; plait, braid, weave, entwine. See CROSSING, TEXTURE.

match, *n.* lucifer, vesta; linstock, fuse; complement, equal, peer; contest, bout; union, matrimony. See EQUALITY, CONTENTION, MARRIAGE, SYNCHRONISM, IMITATION.

matchless, *adj.* unequaled, peerless, unrivaled. See SUPERIORITY, INEQUALITY.

matchmaker, *n.* marriage broker, go-between. See MARRIAGE.

mate, *n.* companion, chum, comrade; counterpart; consort, spouse; husband, wife. See FRIEND, MARRIAGE, AUXILIARY.

material, *adj.* bodily, corporeal (see SUBSTANCE). —*n.* cloth, fabric; matter, SUBSTANCE; written matter. See MATERIALS.

materialistic, *adj.* material, worldly; pleasure-seeking, hedonistic, sybaritic, epicurean; greedy, avaricious, mercenary. See IRRELIGION, PLEASURE, GLUTTONY.

materialize, *v.t.* produce, create, realize, give SUBSTANCE; conjure, call, *or* whip up, summon, produce [out of thin air]. —*v.i.* appear, enter, show. See APPEARANCE.

MATERIALS

Nouns—**1,** materials, raw materials, substances, stuff; stock, staples; FUEL; grist; stores, goods, provisions (see STORE); MEANS; baggage, personal property.

2, metal, stone, clay, brick, bricks and mortar, plaster, tile, shingle, siding, crockery, ceramics, composition; putty; concrete, cement (see COHERENCE); wood, lumber, timber; ore, iron, copper, *etc.* (see INORGANIC MATTER); steel; paper, pasteboard; artificial turf.

3, plastic[s]; synthetic resin; Celluloid, cellophane, vinyl, Vinylite, [poly]styrene, Bakelite; hard rubber, Neolite, Velon, nylon, Orlon, Dacron; synthetic rubber, butyl, butadiene; goods, fabric, cloth, material, plush, textiles (see TEXTURE); rayon, fiber, viscose, Celanese; urea, casein, lignite, lignin, wood flour; Teflon.

4, resin, rosin, gum, lac; bitumen, pitch, tar, asphalt, gilsonite.

Adjectives—plastic, synthetic; cloth, textile, wooden, woody, paper[y]; steel, *etc.*

maternal, *adj.* motherly, motherlike. See ANCESTRY, FEMALE.

mathematics, *n.* computation, calculation, reckoning, arithmetic. See NUMERATION.

matriarch, *n.* materfamilias, matron, dowager. *Colloq.,* queen bee. See FEMALE, AUTHORITY.

matrimony, *n.* MARRIAGE, espousal; nuptials. See RITE, MIXTURE.

matron, *n.* married woman, wife; widow. See FEMALE, MARRIAGE.

matter, *n.* SUBSTANCE, material; subject, topic, BUSINESS; affair; cause, ground; predicament, difficulty. —*v.i.* signify, import; count. See IMPORTANCE, THOUGHT.

matter-of-fact, *adj.* prosaic, unimaginative, formal. See SIMPLENESS, WEARINESS.

mattress, *n.* bedding; tick, bolster, pallet; futon; featherbed. See SUPPORT.

mature, *adj.* ripe, developed, full-grown, adult. —*v.i.* ripen, develop, grow up. See AGE, COMPLETION, CHANGE, PREPARATION, OLDNESS.

maudlin, *adj.* weepy, teary, sobby; sentimental; drunk. See FEELING.

maul, *v.t.* manhandle, pummel, batter, beat up. See PUNISHMENT.

maunder, *v.i.* digress, wander. See DIFFUSENESS.

mausoleum, *n.* vault, sepulcher; pyramid, mastaba. See INTERMENT, FEELING.

maverick, *n.* loner, lone wolf, nonconformist, dissenter. See UNCONFORMITY.

mawkish, *adj.* nauseous, offensive; effusive, maudlin. See REPULSION, FEELING.

MAXIM

Nouns—**1,** maxim, aphorism, gnome, apothegm, dictum, saying, adage, saw, proverb; sentence, *mot,* motto, word, moral, byword, household word; axiom, theorum, scholium, truism, TRUTH, formula, principle, law, conclusion, reflection, proposition, protasis; precept, RULE, golden rule; well-turned phrase; epigram, slogan, device; epitaph. See WIT.

2, commonplace, bromide, cliché; platitude, twice-told tale, text; wise, trite, *or* hackneyed saying. *Colloq.,* old song *or* story. *Slang,* chestnut.

Verbs—aphorize, epigrammatize.

Adjectives—aphoristic, proverbial, axiomatic, epigrammatic; sententious, bromidic, platitudinous, commonplace; terse, succinct.

Adverbs—aphoristically, proverbially, as the saying goes, as they say, to coin a phrase.

Antonyms, see ABSURDITY.

---

maximum, *adj.* supreme, utmost; greatest, highest. —*n.* most, utmost. See SUPERIORITY.

may, *v.* can; might; be allowed, permitted, *etc.* See PERMISSION.

maybe, *adv.* perhaps, mayhap, perchance; possibly, conceivably, feasibly. See DOUBT, POSSIBILITY.

mayhem, *n.* injury, mutilation, damage, harm, DESTRUCTION, violence.

mayor, *n.* administrator, president; burgomaster, magistrate, *major domo;* city manager. See AUTHORITY.

maze, *n.* labyrinth, network; bewilderment, perplexity. See DISORDER, CONVOLUTION, DIFFICULTY.

meadow, *n.* mead, lea, pasture, mowing. See LAND.

meager, *adj.* spare, scanty, sparse, poor; lean, gaunt. See INSUFFICIENCY, NARROWNESS.

meal, *n.* repast, refection; breakfast, dinner, lunch, *etc.;* powder, grits. *Slang,* feed, eats. See FOOD, POWDERINESS.

mealy, *adj.* powdery (see POWDERINESS).

mealymouthed, *adj.* evasive, insincere. See FALSEHOOD, COURTESY.

mean, *adj.* humble; ignoble; insignificant; stingy, miserly; sordid, niggardly. See PARSIMONY, SERVILITY, BADNESS.

MEAN

Nouns—mean, medium; average, normal, RULE, balance; MEDIOCRITY, generality; golden mean, middle course, middle compromise, neutrality, MODERATION, middle of the road. *Colloq.,* fence-sitting. See MIDDLE.

Verbs—split the difference, reduce to a mean, strike a balance, pair off; average, divide; take a middle course.

Adjectives—mean, intermediate, MIDDLE, medial, medium, average, mediocre, middle-class, commonplace, normal; median.

Adverbs—on the average, in the long run, taking all things together, in round numbers.

Antonyms, see INFERIORITY, SUPERIORITY, BEGINNING, END.

---

meander, *v.i.* wind, drift, twist, turn; go with the wind, the tide, *or* the current; float *or* move aimlessly; wander, roam, ramble. See DEVIATION, CONVOLUTION.

MEANING

Nouns—**1,** meaning, significance, signification, force; sense, expression; import, purport, implication, drift, tenor, spirit, bearing; scope, purpose, aim, intent, INTENTION, object; allusion, suggestion, synonym; INTERPRETATION, connotation. See IMPORTANCE.

2, matter, subject [matter], argument, text, sum and substance, gist, pith, kernel, meat.

Verbs—**1,** mean, signify, stand for, denote, express, import, purpose, convey, imply, connote, infer, indicate, tell *or* speak of; touch on; point *or* allude to, drive at, have in mind, put across, intend, aim at, declare; understand by, interpret (see INTERPRETATION).

2, have meaning, make sense, hang together. *Colloq.,* add up.

Adjectives—meaning, meaningful, expressive, suggestive, articulate, allusive, significant, eloquent, pithy, full of *or* pregnant with meaning; declaratory, intelligible, literal; synonymous, tantamount, equivalent; explicit, express, implied, implicit.

Adverbs—meaningly, significantly, *etc.;* to that effect, that is to say, to all intents and purposes; word-for-word.

Antonyms, see UNMEANINGNESS.

---

meaningless, *adj.* insignificant, without rhyme or reason; senseless, aimless; nonsensical. See UNMEANINGNESS, ABSURDITY.

MEANS

Nouns—means, resources, wherewithal, MONEY, wealth, capital, backing; MATERIALS, ways and means, stock in trade, PROVISION, STORE, appliances, conveniences; expedients, measures, two strings to one's bow, cards to play; aid, medium, instrument, INSTRUMENTALITY. *Colloq.,* ace in the hole; enough rope.

Verbs—have means, have the power; enable, empower; back, finance, underwrite, capitalize, fund.

Adverbs—by dint *or* means of, by virtue of, through the medium of, with, per, by all means; wherewith, herewith, therewith, wherewithal, how, in what manner, through, by the instrumentality of, with the aid of, by the agency of, with the help of; by fair means or foul; somehow or other, anyhow, somehow; by hook or crook.

Antonyms, see IMPOTENCE, POVERTY.

---

mean-spirited, *adj.* abject, groveling; contemptible, petty. See NARROWNESS.

meantime, *n.* meanwhile, interim. See BETWEEN.

measure, *n.* QUANTITY, extent; gauge; standard; amount, allotment; [legislative] bill; step, course. See MEASUREMENT, APPORTIONMENT, DEGREE, RULE.

measureless, *adj.* without measure, immeasurable, immensurable; infinite, endless, fathomless; vast, astronomical. See GREATNESS, INFINITY.

MEASUREMENT

Nouns—**1,** measurement, measure, admeasurement, mensuration, survey, valuation, appraisement, appraisal, metage, assessment, determination, assize, estimate, estimation; dead reckoning, reckoning, gauging. See SIZE, LENGTH, DISTANCE, QUANTITY, BREADTH, NUMERATION.

2, criterion, standard, benchmark; measure, standard, rule[r], foot-rule, yardstick, balance, sextant, quadrant, compass, calipers, gauge, meter, line, rod, check; level, plumb line, lead, log, tape, [T] square, index, scale; Beaufort scale (see WIND); engineer's, Gunter's, *or* surveyor's chain; graduated scale, vernier, anemometer, dynamometer, thermometer, barometer, bathometer, galvanometer, goniometer, speedometer, micrometer, hydrometer, tachometer, altimeter, hygrometer, ammeter, voltameter, voltmeter; pedometer; radiometer, potentiometer, sphygmomanometer, *etc.*

3, coordinates, ordinate and abscissa, polar coordinates, latitude and longitude, declination and right ascension, altitude and azimuth.

4, geometry, stereometry, chronometry, barometry, thermometry, hypometry; surveying, geodesy, geodetics, orthometry, topography, micrometry, altimetry, anthropometry, electrometry, craniometry.

5, measurer, surveyor, geometer, geodetist, topographer.

Verbs—measure, meter, value, assess, evaluate, rate, appraise, estimate, set a value on, appreciate, size up, span, pace, step; gauge, plumb, weigh, probe, sound, fathom; heave the lead; survey, graduate, calibrate.

Adjectives—measuring, metric[al], measurable; geodetic[al]; barometric[al]; latitudinal, longitudinal, *etc.*

---

meat, *n.* pith, essence, SUBSTANCE, core. See FOOD, MEANING.

mechanic, *n.* mechanician, repairman, serviceman. See AGENCY.

mechanical, *adj.* machinelike, automatic, power-driven, powered; involuntary, unreasoning. See POWER, NECESSITY.

mechanism, *n.* apparatus, contraption (see INSTRUMENTALITY).

medal, *n.* medallion, medalet; badge, decoration, order, prize, award, ribbon. See APPROBATION.

medallion, *n.* medal, plaque, relief, coin. See SCULPTURE, REPUTE.

meddle, *v.i.* tamper; interfere, intrude. See BETWEEN.

meddlesome, *adj.* officious, obtrusive, interfering. See BETWEEN, CURIOSITY.

media, *n.pl.* mediums; magazines, newspapers, journals, house organs; radio, television; billboards, posters, *etc.* See COMMUNICATION.

mediation, *n.* intermediation, intercession, intervention; interference; parley, negotiation, arbitration; COMPROMISE. See PACIFICATION, AGENCY.

medic, *n.* doctor, paramedic. *Colloq.*, medico. See REMEDY.

medicine, *n.* medicament, medication, REMEDY; therapy, physic; medical profession.

medieval, *adj.* feudal, knightly, courtly; antiquated, old-fashioned, outdated, quaint. See OLDNESS.

MEDIOCRITY

Nouns—mediocrity, middle course, moderate degree, medial standard, moderate *or* average circumstances; normality, average, golden MEAN; MODERATION, temperance, respectability; middle classes, bourgeoisie. See INFERIORITY, INSIPIDITY.

Verbs—jog on, go *or* get on tolerably, fairly, *or* quietly; get along, get by, pass [in the dark], muddle through.

Adjectives—mediocre, ordinary, commonplace, everyday; moderate, middling, normal, average, MEAN, medium, medial; indifferent, passable, tolerable, *comme ci comme ça*, presentable, bearable, better than nothing; second- *or* third-class; respectable, not bad, fair, so-so, second-rate, run of the mill *or* mine, of poor quality; pretty well *or* good; good *or* well enough; middle-class, bourgeois. *Colloq.*, no great shakes, fair to middling, nothing to write home about, namby-pamby, of sorts. *Slang,* no ball of fire.

Antonyms, see PERFECTION, SUPERIORITY.

---

meditate, *v.* muse, ponder, cogitate; PLAN, intend, contemplate, purpose. See THOUGHT.

medium, *n.* MEAN; surrounding; go-between, agent; agency, instrumentality, MEANS; spiritualist, clairvoyant. See BETWEEN, ENVIRONMENT, MEDIOCRITY.

medley, *n.* jumble, miscellany, variety, MIXTURE. See DISORDER.

meek, *adj.* subdued, humble, patient, submissive. See HUMILITY.

meet, *v.* encounter, intersect; oppose; greet, welcome; satisfy; refute; assemble, gather; contend. See AGREEMENT, ASSEMBLAGE, CONTACT. —*adj.* fitting See EXPEDIENCE.

meeting, *n.* encounter, assembly, JUNCTION; duel; tangency. See CONTACT, CONVERGENCE.

melancholy, *adj.* dejected, dispirited, sad, depressed. *Colloq.,* blue. See DEJECTION.

mélange, *n.* medley, MIXTURE.

melee, *n.* CONTENTION, combat, brawl, ruckus; DISORDER, turmoil.

mellow, *adj.* soft, rich, ripe; mellifluous; subdued, delicate. See SOFTNESS, AGE, DRINKING. —*v.* ripen, soften. See CHANGE.

melodious, *adj.* melodic, melic, melopoeic; tuneful, lilting, lyric[al], singable, cantabile; *bel canto.* See MUSIC.

melodrama, *n.* tragicomedy, seriocomedy; penny-dreadful, thriller, shocker; sentimentality, bathos; bravado, derring-do; *slang,* tear-jerker. See DRAMA.

melody, *n.* tune, theme, song, aria, air. See MUSIC.

melon, *n.* fruit, cantaloupe, honeydew, casaba, Persian melon, watermelon, *etc.; slang,* graft. See MONEY, FOOD.

melt, *v.* disappear, vanish; fuse, thaw, dissolve, soften; dwindle; blend. See PITY, DISAPPEARANCE, LIQUEFACTION.

member, *n.* unit, constituent, element, PART; fellow, adherent, partner, *etc.*

membership, *n.* members, body, whole, entirety; affiliation, participation, inclusion, admission. See PARTY.

membrane, *n.* film, lamina, sheet, sheath, LAYER.

memento, *n.* keepsake, souvenir, reminder, relic, token, memorial. See RECORD, MEMORY.

memoir, *n.* RECORD; reminiscence, autobiography. See DESCRIPTION, MEMORY.

memorable, *adj.* noteworthy, signal, outstanding; unforgettable. See IMPORTANCE, MEMORY.

memorandum, *n.* RECORD, note, reminder, memo.

memorial, *adj.* commemorative.—*n.* monument, shrine, tablet; anniversary; petition. See MEMORY, RECORD.

MEMORY

Nouns—**1,** memory, remembrance, RETENTION, retentiveness, reminiscence, recognition, recurrence, recollection, retrospect, retrospection, afterthought. See THOUGHT, PAST.

2, reminder, suggestion, prompting, hint, cue; token, memento, souvenir, keepsake, relic, memorandum, memo, memoir; memorial, commemoration, anniversary, Memorial, Veterans', Decoration Day, *etc.*; monument; memorabilia; flashback. See RECORD, CELEBRATION.

3, art of memory; artificial memory, mnemonics, mnemotechnics; Mnemosyne; retentive *or* photographic memory, total recall; rote, repetition;

flash *or* cue card, nudge; prompter. *Colloq.*, a string around a finger.

Verbs—**1,** remember, retain the memory of; keep in view, bear in mind, hold in memory, remain in one's memory, mind, *or* head; recur to the mind, flash across the memory; haunt, run in the head.

2, recognize, recollect, bethink oneself, recall, call up, identify, retrace, look *or* hark back, think back upon, review, call to mind, carry one's thoughts back, reminisce; rack one's brain.

3, suggest, prompt, put *or* keep in mind, remind, call *or* summon up; renew; tax, jog, refresh, *or* awaken the memory, ring a bell; dig up, exhume. *Slang,* rub it in (see REPETITION).

4, memorize; have, learn, know, *or* say by heart *or* rote; repeat, have at *or* on the tip of one's tongue; commit to memory; con, fix, make a note of. See LEARNING.

5, keep the memory alive, keep in memory, commemorate, memorialize, honor the memory of, enshrine.

Adjectives—remembering, remembered, mindful, reminiscent, retentive, retained in the memory, fresh, alive, green, unforgotten, within one's memory, indelible; uppermost in one's thoughts; memorable, memorial, commemorative.

Adverbs—by heart *or* rote, without prompting, word for word; in memory of, in memoriam.

Antonyms, see OBLIVION.

---

menace, *n.* THREAT, danger, hazard, peril. —*v.t.* threaten, intimidate, bully; impend, loom. See WARNING.

ménage, *n.* household; housekeeping, husbandry. See ABODE, ECONOMY.

menagerie, *n. Tiergarten,* zoo. See ANIMAL, DOMESTICATION.

mend, *v.* repair, restore, correct, improve. See IMPROVEMENT, RESTORATION.

mendacity, *n.* untruthfulness, untruth, FALSEHOOD, duplicity.

mendicant, *n.* beggar, pauper. See POVERTY.

menial, *n.* SERVANT, slave, flunky. —*adj.* humble, servile; degrading, mean. See SERVILITY.

menopause, *n.* change of life, climacteric; middle age. See CHANGE, AGE.

mental, *adj.* intellectual, cognitive, rational, psychological. See INTELLECT.

mentality, *n.* INTELLECT, intelligence, mind, understanding.

mention, *v.t.* communicate, designate, let fall; cite, speak of. See INFORMATION, SPEECH.

mentor, *n.* teacher (see TEACHING).

menu, *n.* bill of fare, fare, diet, list, carte. See FOOD.

mercantile, *adj.* commercial (see BARTER).

mercenary, *adj.* calculating, selfish, sordid, venal, grasping, avaricious. See PARSIMONY.

merchandise, *n.* wares, commodities. —*v.t.* buy, sell. See SALE.

merchant, *n.* trader, dealer. See SALE, PROVISION.

merciful, *adj.* compassionate; lenient. See LENIENCY, PITY.

merciless, *adj.* cruel, pitiless, relentless. See SEVERITY.

mercy, *n.* PITY, LENIENCY, forbearance, compassion.

mere, *adj.* nothing but, plain, bare, simple. See SIMPLENESS.

merely, *adv.* barely, simply, only, purely. See LITTLENESS.

merge, *v.* unite, blend, coalesce, absorb. See MIXTURE, JUNCTION, COMBINATION.

meridian, *n.* longitude; height, culmination, zenith, apex, apogee, summit; midday. See CIRCULARITY, CHRONOMETRY.

merit, *n.* desert[s], reward, due;

worth, excellence; VIRTUE. See GOODNESS.

merry, *adj.* jovial, mirthful, gay, vivacious. See CHEERFULNESS.

merry-go-round, *n.* carrousel, whirligig. See AMUSEMENT, ROTATION.

mesh, *n.* meshwork; network, web, net; lacework; tangle, snarl; lattice, trellis, grille, grate, gridiron, sieve. See CROSSING, INTERVAL.

mesmerize, *v.t.* hypnotize; fascinate, captivate. See SORCERY.

mess, *n.* DIFFICULTY, predicament; DISORDER, litter, jumble; botch. See FAILURE, FOOD.

message, *n.* COMMUNICATION, dispatch, note. See NEWS.

messenger, *n.* emissary, envoy, apostle, missionary; courier, carrier, bearer, errand boy, runner. *Slang,* gofer. See AGENT, COMMISSION.

messy, *adj.* untidy, sloppy. See DISORDER, UNCLEANNESS.

metal, *n.* mineral, element, alloy, ore. See INORGANIC MATTER.

metaphorical, *adj.* allegorical, FIGURATIVE.

metaphysical, *adj.* abstruse, speculative, esoteric, transcendental. See THOUGHT.

meteor, *n.* meteoroid, meteorite, shooting star. See UNIVERSE.

meteoric, *adj.* sudden, rapid, fast, shooting. See LIGHT, VELOCITY.

meter, *n.* rhythm, cadence, lilt; gauge. See POETRY, MEASUREMENT.

METHOD

Nouns—method, way, manner, wise; gait, form, mode, MEANS, style, FASHION, design, tone, behavior, guise; *modus operandi, modus vivendi,* procedure, process, practice, regimen, system, technique, methodology, strategy, tactics, routine, line of CONDUCT, life-style; system, PLAN, scheme, formula, RULE. See AGENCY, ORDER, USE.

Verbs—methodize, systematize, arrange, regularize, organize, formulate.

Adjectives—methodical, systematic, schematic, stylistic, modal, procedural, planned, arranged, orderly, routine.

Adverbs—how; in what way, manner, *or* mode; so, thus, in this way, after this fashion; one way or another, anyhow, by any means, somehow or other, however; by way of, via, on the high road to.

Antonyms, see DISORDER.

---

métier, *n.* profession, vocation; SPECIALITY. See BUSINESS.

metropolitan, *adj.* civil, urban, oppidan, city-wide, cosmopolitan, urbane, sophisticated, worldly. See ABODE.

mettle, *n.* spirit, temperament, COURAGE, disposition, VIGOR.

mettlesome, *adj.* high-strung, courageous, plucky. See COURAGE, EXCITABILITY.

microbe, *n.* bacterium, germ. See LITTLENESS.

microphone, *n.* pickup, lavaliere. *Colloq.,* mike. See COMMUNICATION.

microscopic, *adj.* minute, tiny, infinitesimal. See LITTLENESS.

midday, *n.* noon (see CHRONOMETRY).

MIDDLE

Nouns—**1,** middle, midst, MEAN, medium, middle term; center, core, hub, kernel; umbilicus; halfway house; nave, navel, nucleus; heart, axis, bull's-eye; marrow, pith; equidistance, bisection, half distance, equator, dead center; center, inner, *or* core city; midriff; interjacence (see BETWEEN).

2, centrality, centralness, focalization; concentration, focus (see CONVER-

GENCE); cynosure; magnetism; center of attraction; COMBINATION, merging.
Verbs—center (on), focus, concentrate; meet, unite, converge.
Adjectives—middle, medial, median, mean, mid; midmost, intermediate, equidistant, central, focal, axial, equatorial, concentric, convergent.
Adverbs—in the middle, midway, halfway, midships; *in medias res,* in the thick of it, smack dab in the middle.

Antonyms, see EXTERIOR, END.

---

middle-aged, *adj.* mature, in [one's] prime, *d'un certain âge*. See AGE.

middle-class, *adj.* common, ordinary; bourgeois, conservative, conventional. See MEDIOCRITY, PERMANENCE.

middleman, *n.* go-between, intermediary, AGENT. See COMPROMISE.

middling, *adj.* medium (see MEDIOCRITY).

midget, *n.* dwarf, pygmy, homunculus. *Slang,* shrimp. See LITTLENESS, SHORTNESS.

midmost, *adj.* central, MIDDLE, mean.

midnight, *n.* witching hour. See CHRONOMETRY, DARKNESS.

midst, *n.* center, MIDDLE.

midway, *adj.* halfway, MIDDLE. —*n.* carnival, side show. See AMUSEMENT.

mien, *n.* APPEARANCE, air, demeanor, bearing. See CONDUCT.

might, *n.* POWER, force, STRENGTH, VIGOR.

migrate, *v.i.* journey, TRAVEL; emigrate, immigrate.

mild, *adj.* gentle, easy, bland, soft, harmless; lenient, tolerant, merciful, humane, generous, forbearing; weak, neutral; placid, tranquil, temperate, moderate; comfortable, clement; meek, submissive, conciliatory. See MODERATION, INSIPIDITY, LENIENCY.

mildew, *n.* mold, decay, rot, must. See DETERIORATION.

milestone, *n.* landmark, milepost; giant step, progress, advance. See OCCURRENCE, INDICATION, IMPORTANCE.

milieu, *n.* ENVIRONMENT.

militant, *adj.* aggressive, warlike, pugnacious, bellicose. See WARFARE.

military, *adj.* martial, soldierly. See WARFARE.

militate, *v.i.* operate (for *or* against). See ACTION, INFLUENCE.

militia, *n.* standing army, reserves, minutemen, soldiery. See COMBATANT.

milk, *v.* extract; extort, bleed; get the most out of, exploit; interrogate, question. *Colloq.,* play for all it's worth. See EXTRACTION, STEALING, LIQUEFACTION.

milky, *n.* lacteal; white, pale, chalky; spiritless, timorous. See COLOR, FEAR.

mill, *n.* grinder, millstone, millrace; factory, plant, works, shop; (*pl.*) industry. See BUSINESS, CONTENTION. —*v.i.* stir, wander. See CIRCULARITY. —*v.t.* grind, pulverize. See POWDERINESS.

mimic, *v.t.* mime, imitate, impersonate; ape, COPY; mock. See IMITATION, DRAMA.

mince, *v.t.* chop, dice; moderate. See DISJUNCTION, MODERATION. —*v.i.* flounce. *Colloq.,* sashay. See AFFECTATION.

mind, *n.* consciousness, understanding; INTELLECT; purpose, intention, opinion. See WILL, DESIRE. —*v.t.* heed, obey; notice, tend; object to. See ATTENTION, CARE, BELIEF, DISLIKE.

mindful, *adj.* aware, heedful, cautious, careful; watchful, alert. See CAUTION, MEMORY, ATTENTION.

mindless, *adj.* thoughtless, heedless, careless, negligent, absent[-minded]; senseless, insane. *Colloq.,* blind, deaf, dumb. See INATTENTION.

mine, *n.* lode, vein, deposit; open pit, burrow, excavation; explosive, bomb; source, treasure trove. See

CONCAVITY, STORE.

mingle, *v.* blend, mix, merge, intermingle, conjoin; associate. See MIXTURE, SOCIALITY.

miniature, *adj.* diminutive, minuscule, minute, petite, minikin; dwarf, pygmy, Lilliputian. —*n.* scale model, reduction. See LITTLENESS.

minimize, *v.* reduce, lessen; belittle, gloss over, run down, deprecate, detract from. See DETRACTION, UNIMPORTANCE.

minimum, *n.* modicum; least amount *or* quantity. See LITTLENESS.

minion, *n.* subordinate; henchman. See SERVANT, SERVILITY, AGENT.

minister, *n.* legate, envoy, ambassador; cabinet officer, clergyman, pastor, *etc.* See CLERGY, AGENT. —*v.* attend, CARE for.

ministry, *n.* state officers; diplomatic service; priesthood, CLERGY.

minor, *adj.* lesser, inferior, secondary. See INFERIORITY, YOUTH.

minority, *n.* few, handful; smaller group; nonage, childhood. See YOUTH, INFERIORITY, RARITY.

minstrel, *n.* poet, troubadour, jongleur, bard. See POETRY, MUSIC.

mint, *v.t.* coin (see MONEY).

minus, *adj.* less, lacking; negative. See LOSS, ABSENCE, DEDUCTION.

minute, *adj.* minuscule, tiny; meticulous, precise, exact. See LITTLENESS, CARE. —*n.* moment; summary, draft; (*pl.*) RECORD, log. See TIME.

minutiae, *n.pl.* details, trivia. See UNIMPORTANCE.

miracle, *n.* WONDER, marvel, prodigy; impossibility, fluke, phenomenon; divine intervention, *deus ex machina*. See IMAGINATION.

miraculous, *adj.* preternatural, supernatural, prodigious, wondrous. See WONDER.

mirage, *n.* optical illusion, fata morgana. See DECEPTION, DISAPPOINTMENT, IMAGINATION.

mire, *n.* mud, muck, dirt; quagmire, marsh. See UNCLEANNESS, COHERENCE.

mirror, *n.* looking glass, glass, reflector; cheval *or* pier glass, *etc.* See OPTICAL INSTRUMENTS.

mirth, *n.* hilarity, jollity, merriment, glee. See CHEERFULNESS.

misanthrope, *n.* misanthropist, man-hater, cynic, egotist; woman-hater, misogynist. See MALEVOLENCE.

misapprehend, *v.t.* misunderstand, mistake, misinterpret. See ERROR.

misbegotten, *adj.* illegitimate, bastard; illicit, illegal. See DISCOURTESY, GUILT.

misbehavior, *n.* misconduct, mischief, disobedience, BADNESS, WRONG.

miscalculate, *v.t.* misjudge, err, misreckon. See MISJUDGMENT, DISAPPOINTMENT, SURPRISE.

miscarry, *v.i.* fail, go wrong, fall through; abort. See FAILURE.

miscellaneous, *adj.* heterogeneous, indiscriminate, mixed, many-sided; diversified, varied. See MIXTURE, GENERALITY.

miscellany, *n.* anthology, analecta; medley, MIXTURE.

mischief, *n.* harm, injury; trouble; prank. See EVIL.

misconception, *n.* delusion, mistake, misunderstanding. See ERROR, MISJUDGMENT.

misconduct, *n.* impropriety, misdemeanor, misbehavior, mismanagement. *Colloq.*, monkey business. See GUILT, WRONG.

miscreant, *n.* See EVILDOER.

misdeed, *n.* offense, WRONG, malefaction. See GUILT.

misdemeanor, *n.* crime, infraction, malfeasance. See ILLEGALITY.

miser, *n.* hoarder, niggard, money-grubber, skinflint. *Slang,* penny pincher, tightwad. See PARSIMONY.

miserable, *adj.* wretched, forlorn, doleful; mean, contemptible, paltry. See UNIMPORTANCE.

misery, *n.* wretchedness, POVERTY; distress, anguish. See PAIN.

misfire, *v.* fail, abort; fizzle, sputter; backfire. See FAILURE.

misfit, *n.* mismatch, poor fit; neurotic; rejectee, odd man [out]. *Slang,* schlemiel, oddball, schnook, jerk, queer. See UNCONFORMITY.

misfortune, *n.* mishap, disaster, calamity, catastrophe; bad luck; ADVERSITY. See EVIL.

misgiving, *n.* DOUBT, apprehension, premonition; qualm. See FEAR.

mishap, *n.* accident, mischance, misfortune. See ADVERSITY, EVIL.

mishmash, *n.* jumble, mess, farrago. See DISORDER.

misinformation, *n.* misintelligence; misteaching, misguidance, misdirection; misinstruction, misleading, perversion; sophistry. See DECEPTION.

misinterpretation, *n.* misunderstanding (see MISJUDGMENT); misrepresentation, perversion, exaggeration, false construction, falsification. See DISTORTION, ERROR.

MISJUDGMENT

Nouns—**1,** misjudgment, miscalculation, misconception, miscomputation, ERROR, hasty *or* snap conclusion, misinterpretation, misapprehension, misunderstanding, misconstruction, misapplication, mistake; overestimation, underestimation. See DISAPPOINTMENT.

2, prejudgment, prejudication, foregone conclusion, preconception, predilection, presumption, presentiment, preconceived idea, *idée fixe*.

3, partisanship, clannishness, provincialism; hobby, fad, quirk, crotchet; partiality, infatuation, blind side *or* spot, mote in the eye.

Verbs—**1,** misjudge, misestimate, misconceive, misreckon, miscompute, miscalculate, jump *or* rush to conclusions; overestimate, underestimate. *Colloq.*, bet on the wrong horse.

2, forejudge, prejudge, presuppose, prejudicate, dogmatize.

Adjectives—misjudging, wrongheaded, besotted, infatuated, fanatical, dogmatic, [self-]opinionated, crotchety, impractical, unreasoning.

Antonyms, see JUDGMENT.

mislay, *v.t.* misplace, lose. See LOSS.

mislead, *v.t.* deceive, delude, lead astray. See ERROR, DECEPTION.

mismanage, *v.t.* botch, mishandle; misconduct, maladminister. See UNSKILLFULNESS.

misnomer, *n.* misnaming (see NOMENCLATURE).

misplace, *v.t.* derange; mislocate, displace, mislay. See LOSS, DISPLACEMENT.

misprint, *n.* typographical ERROR. *Colloq.*, typo.

mispronounce, *v.t.* misspeak, missay; garble. See STAMMERING.

misquote, *v.t.* miscite, misrepresent; twist, garble, distort. See DISTORTION, FALSEHOOD.

misrepresentation, *n.* misstatement, DISTORTION, exaggeration, perversion, falsification; caricature, burlesque, travesty; mimicry, mockery, parody, takeoff, imitation. See FALSEHOOD.

misrule, *n.* mismanagement, misgovernment; confusion, tumult, DISORDER. See UNSKILLFULNESS.

miss, *v.* fail; omit, skip, overlook; avoid; escape; lose. See FAILURE, NEGLECT, DESIRE, LOSS.

misshapen, *adj.* deformed, malformed, distorted, grotesque. See DISTORTION, FORMLESSNESS, UGLINESS.

missile, *n.* projectile, trajectile; guided missile. See ARMS.

missing, *adj.* omitted; gone, absent; lacking. See ABSENCE, LOSS.

mission, *n.* errand, task, assignment; calling; deputation. See BUSINESS, COMMISSION.

missionary, *n.* evangelist, proselytizer, emissary. See CLERGY, COMMISSION.

misstatement, *n.* ERROR, mistake; misrepresentation, perversion, FALSEHOOD.

mist, *n.* fog, haze, vapor, drizzle. See CLOUDINESS, MOISTURE.

mistake, *v.t.* misunderstand, err, misidentify. —*n.* ERROR, blunder, misunderstanding, slip.

mistreat, *v.t.* maltreat; mishandle, abuse, neglect; treat shabbily, oppress, victimize, overburden. See SEVERITY, MALEVOLENCE, WRONG.

mistress, *n.* possessor, employer; matron, head, teacher; paramour, sweetheart. See TEACHING, EVILDOER, FEMALE.

mistrust, *n. & v.* See DISTRUST.

misunderstanding, *n.* misapprehension; quarrel, disagreement, falling out. See CONTENTION, ERROR, DISCORD, MISJUDGMENT.

misuse, *n.* misusage, misemployment, misapplication, misappropriation; abuse, profanation, perversion, prostitution, ill-use, ill-usage; desecration; WASTE. —*v.t.* misemploy, misapply, misappropriate; ill-use.

mite, *n.* louse, insect, chigoe, chigger, *etc.;* coin, penny, sou. See LITTLENESS.

mitigate, *v.t.* lessen, moderate, ameliorate, palliate, allay, relieve. See RELIEF, MODERATION, VINDICATION.

MIXTURE

Nouns—**1,** mixture, admixture, commixture, intermixture, alloyage; matrimony, JUNCTION, COMBINATION, union, amalgamation; permeation, imbuement, impregnation, infusion, suffusion, transfusion, infiltration; seasoning, sprinkling; adulteration; assortment, variety; miscegenation, interbreeding, intermarriage, mixed marriage; hybridization, crossing, crossbreeding. See BETWEEN, INSERTION.

2, tinge, tincture, sprinkling, spice, seasoning, infusion, *soupçon.* See LITTLENESS.

3, alloy, amalgam, compound, blend, mélange, miscellany, melting pot, medley, olio, mess, hodgepodge, brew, patchwork, odds and ends, jumble; salad, sauce; hash, mash; gallimaufry, salmagundy, potpourri, goulash, mosaic; crazy quilt, mishmash; pi; mixed blessing.

4, half-breed, half-caste, half-blood, mulatto; quadroon, octoroon; cross, hybrid, mongrel; ladino, mestizo; Eurasian; mustee, *métis, métisse.*

5, mixer, blender, food processor, eggbeater; social, John Paul Jones.

Verbs—mix, join, combine, commix, intermix, merge, mix up with, mingle, commingle, intermingle, stir up, knead, brew, impregnate with, intertwine, graft, interweave, associate with; instill, imbue, transfuse, infuse, suffuse, infiltrate, tinge, lace, tincture, season, sprinkle, blend, cross, allow, amalgamate, throw together with, compound, adulterate, contaminate, infect; run into.

Adjectives—mixed, composite, half-and-half; hybrid, mongrel; combined, united; amalgamated, alloyed; impregnated (with), ingrained; heterogeneous, motley, variegated, miscellaneous, promiscuous, indiscriminate, miscible.

Prepositions—among[st], amid[st], with, in the midst of.

Antonyms, see DISJUNCTION.

---

mixup, *n.* confusion, imbroglio, muddle, contretemps; mixture, hodgepodge; disagreement, CONTENTION, quarrel, brawl. *Slang,* hassle, rhubarb.

moan, *v.* wail, sigh, groan, bewail, lament. See LAMENTATION.

moat, *n.* trench. See FURROW, DEFENSE.

mob, *n.* rabble, riffraff; *hoi polloi;* common herd, *canaille;* crowd,

POPULACE. See ASSEMBLAGE.

mobile, *adj*. movable, loose, free, animate. See MOTION.

mobilize, *v*. motorize, activate, set in action; summon, muster, rally; arm, equip. See MOTION, WARFARE.

mobster, *n., slang,* gangster, racketeer. See EVILDOER.

mock, *v.t.* RIDICULE, mimic, tantalize, jeer at; disappoint. See DISRESPECT. —*adj*. false, IMITATION, sham, pseudo. See DECEPTION, SIMILARITY.

mod, *adj., colloq.,* modern, up-to-date. See NEWNESS.

mode, *n*. state, manner, METHOD, custom; FASHION, style.

model, *n*. prototype, pattern, mock-up; COPY, miniature, replica; style, type; mannequin, lay figure; exemplar, paragon. See REPRESENTATION, GOODNESS, FORM, PERFECTION, IMITATION, SCULPTURE.

MODERATION

Nouns—**1,** moderation, moderateness, temperance, continence, temperateness, gentleness; self-restraint, self-control, ASCETICISM, abstinence; teetotalism, soberness, sobriety; quiet, tranquility, INEXCITABILITY; relaxation, abatement, remission, mitigation, tranquilization, assuagement, PACIFICATION; letup, alleviation; *juste milieu,* golden MEAN. See RELIEF, DECREASE.

2, sedative, palliative, lenitive, balm, opiate, anodyne; lullaby; moderator, temperer.

3, LENIENCY, lenity, tolerance, toleration, clemency, PITY.

4, abstainer, nondrinker, teetotaler, dry, prohibitionist; W.C.T.U. (Women's Christian Temperance Union), Anti-Saloon League, Alcoholics Anonymous.

Verbs—**1,** keep within bounds, sober up, settle down, keep the peace, relent; abstain, be temperate, take the pledge, swear off; hold one's temper, take it easy, go easy. *Colloq.,* count to ten.

2, moderate, soften, mitigate, temper, mollify, dull, blunt, subdue, chasten, tone down, lessen, check, palliate; tranquillize, assuage, appease, lull, soothe, still, calm, cool, quiet, hush, quell, sober, pacify, tame, allay, slacken, smooth, alleviate, deaden, smother; pour oil on troubled waters; cool off, tone down, taper off, ease off *or* up, let up.

3, tolerate, bear with; indulge, spare the rod; spare; give quarter; PITY. *Slang,* pull one's punches; let one down easy.

Adjectives—moderate, lenient, gentle, easy, mild, soft, tolerant, easygoing, forbearing; sober, temperate, dry; tranquil, reasonable, tempered; tame, lulling, hypnotic, sedative, palliative. *Colloq.,* on the [water] wagon.

Adverbs—moderately, gingerly, within bounds *or* reason.

Antonyms, see VIOLENCE, INTEMPERANCE, DRINKING.

modern, *n*. contemporary; late, recent; up-to-date. See NEWNESS, PRESENT.

modernism, *n*. modernity, height of fashion; surrealism, dada, *etc.;* liberalism. See NEWNESS, PAINTING.

MODESTY

Nouns—modesty; HUMILITY; diffidence, timidity, bashfulness; shyness, unobtrusiveness; shame; reserve, constraint; demureness.

Verbs—**1,** be modest, retire, give way to, retire into one's shell, keep in the background, keep one's distance, hide one's light under a bushel; not dare to show one's face.

2, hide one's face, hang one's head, eat humble pie; blush, redden, change color; feel small. *Colloq.*, eat crow, draw in one's horns.

Adjectives—modest, diffident, humble, timid, timorous, bashful, shy, nervous; coy; sheepish, shamefaced, blushing; overmodest, unpretentious, unobtrusive, unassuming, unaspiring, reserved, demure, self-effacing, decent; common as an old shoe.

Adverbs—modestly, humbly, meekly; quietly, privately; without ceremony; with downcast eyes, on bended knee.

Antonyms, see VANITY.

---

modicum, *n.* little, pittance, bit. See LITTLENESS, APPORTIONMENT.

modification, *n.* CHANGE, alteration, mutation; limitation, QUALIFICATION, modulation.

modify, *v.t.* CHANGE, vary, alter; limit, reduce; temper, soften.

modish, *adj.* chic, stylish, fashionable, à la mode, smart. See FASHION.

modulation, *n.* regulation, abatement, inflection, modification. See CHANGE, SOUND.

module, *n.* unit, component, PART.

mogul, *n.* autocrat, ruler; capitalist, entrepreneur, financier, tycoon. *Slang,* bigwig, bigshot. See IMPORTANCE.

Mohammedan, *n.* Mussulman, Moslem, Islamite. —*adj.* Moslem, Islamic. See RELIGION.

MOISTURE

Nouns—**1,** moisture, moistness, humidity, dampness, wet[ness], dankness, clamminess; hygrometry. See WATER.

2, dew, fog, mist; marsh[land], swamp[land], glade; morass, moss, fen, [peat] bog; mire, quagmire, quicksand; slough; sump; wash, bottoms, mud, slush.

Verbs—moisten, wet, sponge, sprinkle, damp[en], bedew, saturate, soak, drench, water; soak [up].

Adjectives—moist, damp, watery, humid, wet, dank, clammy, muggy, dewy, juicy, wringing wet, wet through, wet to the skin, saturated; soggy, reeking, dripping, soaking, soft, sodden, sloppy, muddy, swampy, marshy.

Antonyms, see DRYNESS.

---

mold, *n.* matrix, die; FORM, shape, figure; stamp, cast; fungus, growth. —*v.t.* frame, shape, model, cast; knead, work. See SCULPTURE.

molding, *n.* necking, surbase, baseboard, platband; cornice, fillet, tringle, chaplet, *etc.;* edging, border, ornamentation. See ORNAMENT.

moldy, *adj.* musty, mildewed, fusty; stale, antiquated. See UNCLEANNESS, DETERIORATION, OLDNESS.

molecule, *n.* particle, atom, mite, micron. See LITTLENESS.

molest, *v.t.* disturb, annoy, vex, pester, harass. See PAIN, MALEVOLENCE.

mollify, *v.t.* placate, pacify, soothe, appease, calm; soften. See RELIEF, SOFTNESS.

mollycoddle, *n.* milksop, sissy. *Slang,* pantywaist. See COWARDICE. —*v.t.* pamper, coddle, spoil. See LENIENCY.

molt, *v.t.* shed; cast *or* slough off. See DIVESTMENT.

molten, *adj.* melted, fused, liquefied. See LIQUEFACTION, HEAT.

moment, *n.* IMPORTANCE, consequence, significance; instant, trice, flash; the PRESENT. See INSTANTANEITY.

momentous, *adj.* important, consequential, great, notable, signal; serious, solemn, memorable; influential. See IMPORTANCE.

momentum, *n.* impetus, moment. See IMPULSE.

monarch, *n.* sovereign, ruler, potentate, king. See AUTHORITY.

monastery, *n.* cloister, lamasery, abbey, convent, priory. See TEMPLE.

monasticism, *n.* monkhood, monachism, friarhood. See CLERGY.

MONEY

Nouns—**1,** money, finance, funds, treasure, capital, assets; ways and means, wherewithal, almighty dollar; money matters; resources, backing (see MEANS); purse strings. *Slang,* green power, fast *or* quick buck.

2, sum, amount; balance, balance sheet; proceeds, accounts, lump sum, round sum; principal, interest. See ACCOUNTING.

3, gold, silver, copper, nickel; bullion, ingot, nugget, gold brick; currency, circulating medium; coinage, specie, coin, cash, cold *or* hard cash; dollar, [pound] sterling, Mark, franc, yen, *etc.*; [legal] tender, money in hand, ready money; plastic money. *Colloq.,* folding money, boodle, [filthy] lucre, easy money, pelf, bundle. *Slang,* bread, dough, jack, brass, spondulix, gelt, lettuce, cabbage, kale, mazuma, filthy lucre, moolah, long green, shekels, simoleons, beans, chips, berries, bucks; the needful; pony, quid, bob, tenner, grand, century, sawbuck, two bits; bill, yard, G note, C note; red cent.

4, wealth, opulence, affluence, riches, fortune; competence, solvency; PROSPERITY; worth, substance; property; bonanza, mint, gold mine, Golconda, El Dorado, purse of Fortunatus. See POSSESSION.

5, petty cash; pocket, spending, mad, *or* pin money; change, small coin, stiver, mite, farthing, sou, penny, shilling, groat, guinea; wampum; paper money, money order, note, bank note, promissory note, I.O.U., bond, bill [of exchange]; draft, check, cheque, traveler's check; order, warrant, coupon, debenture, assignat, greenback. *Slang,* blue chips.

6, counterfeit, false, *or* bad money, stage money; base coin, flash note. *Colloq.,* slug. See DECEPTION.

7, DEARNESS, costliness.

8, rich man, capitalist, financier, millionaire, multimillionaire, billionaire; nabob, Croesus, Dives, Maecenas, Midas, Barmecide; plutocrat, tycoon, baron; carriage trade; heir[ess]. *Slang,* moneybags, zillionaire.

9, numismatics, science of coins, coin-collecting.

Verbs—**1,** monetize, issue, circulate; coin, mint; counterfeit, forge; amount to, come to, total.

2, have *or* roll in money, wallow in wealth, have a bundle, make a fortune, feather one's nest, strike it rich, burn a hole in one's pocket. *Colloq.,* have money to burn, hit the jackpot, make a killing. *Slang,* stink of money.

3, enrich, make rich, line one's pockets; cash a check.

Adjectives—**1,** monetary, pecuniary, fiscal, financial, numismatical.

2, wealthy, rich, affluent, opulent, well-to-do, well off, made of money, born with a silver spoon in one's mouth. *Colloq.,* flush. *Slang,* well-heeled, in the chips; filthy rich; loaded.

3, dear, expensive, costly; precious, extravagant, at a premium.

Antonyms, see POVERTY.

mongrel, *n.* crossbreed, hybrid, half-caste; cur, mutt, stray. *—adj.* crossed, mixed, hybrid; impure. See MIXTURE.

monitor, *n.* monitress; overseer, disciplinarian, censor; master, controller; watchdog, troubleshooter. *—v.* keep order, watch, oversee, supervise; check, regulate, sample; listen in (on). See CARE, COMMUNICATION, AUTHORITY, DIRECTOR.

monitory, *adj.* cautionary, WARNING.

monk, *n.* friar, brother, cleric; pilgrim, palmer, mendicant; ascetic, hermit, anchorite, cenobite, eremite, recluse, solitary; abbot, prior, father, abbé. See CLERGY, CELIBACY, ASCETICISM.

monkey, *n.* simian, primate, ape; imitator, mimic. See ANIMAL, IMITATION.

monocle, *n.* eyeglass, eyepiece, lens, lorgnon. See OPTICAL INSTRUMENTS.

monologue, *n.* recitation, monodrama; soliloquy, apostrophe; SPEECH; reverie, stream of consciousness. See DRAMA.

monopolize, *v.t.* engross, absorb, appropriate, corner. See ATTENTION.

monopoly, *n.* trust, cartel, syndicate, pool; corner. See RESTRAINT, POSSESSION.

monotonous, *adj.* wearisome, humdrum, tedious; unvaried, repetitious. REPETITION, WEARINESS.

monsoon, *n.* trade WIND; rainy season, rains. See WATER.

monster, *n.* monstrosity, freak; prodigy; giant; DEMON, brute. See UNCONFORMITY, SIZE, UGLINESS, EVILDOER.

monstrous, *adj.* huge, enormous; hideous, terrifying, revolting; fiendish, heinous; abnormal, freakish. See SIZE, UGLINESS, UNCONFORMITY, DISTORTION.

monument, *n.* memorial, cenotaph, tombstone. See INTERMENT, RECORD.

mooch, *v., slang,* cadge, borrow. *Colloq.,* sponge; lift. *Slang,* bum; snitch. See REQUEST.

mood, *n.* temper, humor, disposition, inclination. See TENDENCY, FEELING.

moody, *adj.* capricious, variable; gloomy, pensive, sad; peevish, testy; sullen, glum. See DEJECTION, IRASCIBILITY.

moon, *n.* satellite; month; lunation. See UNIVERSE.

moonshine, *n.* nonsense, idle talk; *colloq.,* home brew, bootleg. *Slang,* booze, hooch, white lightning, mountain dew. See DRINKING, DIMNESS.

moor, *n.* heath, moorland, down, brae. See HORIZONTAL, MOISTURE.

moot, *adj.* mooted, debatable, suspect. See DOUBT.

mop, *n.* floor mop, dry mop; brush, broom; tuft. —*v.t.* swab, wipe. See CLEANNESS.

mope, *v.i.* brood, fret, sulk, pout. See DEJECTION, IRASCIBILITY.

moral, *adj.* ethical; righteous, just, virtuous; logical, probable. See VIRTUE, DUTY.

morale, *n.* spirit, cheer, nerve, COURAGE, faith, hope; *esprit de corps;* gumption, RESOLUTION, determination.

morality, *n.* VIRTUE, righteousness, uprightness, rectitude, ethics, morals. See DUTY.

morass, *n.* marsh, bog. See MOISTURE.

moratorium, *n.* delay. See LATENESS.

morbid, *adj.* unhealthy, diseased; gloomy, unwholesome. See DISEASE.

mordant, *adj.* biting, sarcastic. See PUNGENCY, MALEVOLENCE.

more, *adj. & adv.* additional, in ADDITION, added, beside[s], to boot, over and above, further.

morgue, *n.* mortuary, death *or* charnel house, deadhouse; files, records, dead records file. See DEATH, RECORD.

moribund, *adj.* dying (see DEATH).

morning, *n.* morn, morningtide, forenoon, ante meridian, a.m., A.M., [crack of] dawn, daybreak, break of day; aurora; sunrise, sunup, cockcrow. See TIME, BEGINNING.

moron, *n.* simpleton, halfwit, imbecile. See IGNORANCE.

morose, *adj.* sulky, sullen, gloomy, crabbed, glum, dour. See DEJECTION, IRASCIBILITY.

morsel, *n.* mouthful, bite, crumb, scrap, bit. See LITTLENESS.

mortal, *adj.* human, ephemeral; fatal, deadly; dire; implacable. See HUMANITY, TRANSIENTNESS, KILLING.

mortar, *n.* cannon, howitzer; cement,

bond; vessel, cup; grinder, crucible. See ARMS, CONNECTION.

mortgage, *n.* pledge, SECURITY, encumbrance, loan, bond, debenture; PROMISE; hypothec. —*v.* borrow, pledge, hypothecate. See DEBT.

mortification, *n.* humiliation, vexation, embarrassment, chagrin. See ASCETICISM, HUMILITY.

mortify, *v.t.* humiliate, embarrass, chagrin; decay. See HUMILITY, DETERIORATION, ASCETICISM.

mortuary, *n.* morgue, funeral home. —*adj.* funerary, funereal. See INTERMENT.

mosaic, *n.* tilework, inlay, [in]tarsia; jigsaw puzzle; tesserae, tessellation; MIXTURE, montage, kaleidoscope. —*adj.* mosaical, motley; tessellated; pieced, joined. See ORNAMENT, VARIEGATION.

mosque, *n.* See TEMPLE.

moss, *n.* liverwort; club, peat, *etc.* moss. See VEGETABLE.

most, *adj.* greatest, most numerous; the majority of, nearly *or* almost all. See SUPERIORITY, MULTITUDE.

motel, *n.* motor court *or* hotel; stopover, inn; cabins. See ABODE.

motheaten, *adj.* worn, shabby, tattered, ragged. See DETERIORATION.

mother, *n.* parent, mamma; abbess, prioress; matron, matriarch. See ANCESTRY, CLERGY, FEMALE.

motif, *n.* [musical] theme; subject, topic, concept. See MUSIC, THOUGHT.

MOTION

Nouns—**1,** motion, movement, move, mobility, movableness; APPROACH; mobilization; restlessness, unrest; kinematics, kinetics.
2, progress, locomotion; journey, voyage, transit, TRAVEL; speed, VELOCITY, rate, clip. See PROGRESSION.
3, stream, flow, flux, run, course, flight, drift, DIRECTION. See FLUIDITY.
4, step, pace, tread, stride, gait, footfall, carriage.

Verbs—**1,** be in motion, move, go; hie; budge, stir; pass, flit, hover round; shift, slide, glide; roll on, flow, stream, run, drift, sweep along; wander, walk, get around; dodge; keep moving, pull up stakes.
2, put *or* set in motion, move, impel, propel, mobilize, motivate.
3, motion, signal, gesture, direct, guide (see INDICATION).

Adjectives—moving, in motion, astir, transitional, motory, motive, shifting, movable, mobile; mercurial, restless, changeable, nomadic, erratic; kinetic.

Adverbs—under way, on the move, on the wing, on the march.

Antonyms, see INACTIVITY, STABILITY.

---

motionless, *adj.* still, immobile, stationary, inert, fixed. See INACTIVITY.

motivate, *v.* induce, move; draw on, give an impulse to, inspire, prompt, stimulate, inspirit, [a]rouse, animate, incite, provoke, instigate, INFLUENCE, bias, sway; tempt, seduce; bribe, suborn; enforce, impel, propel, whip, lash, goad. See CAUSE.

motive, *n.* motivation, reason, ground, CAUSE; purpose, design; occasion; principle, mainspring, keystone; INTENTION, inducement, consideration, attraction; temptation, enticement; bewitchment, spell, fascination; influence, impulse, incitement, instigation; inspiration, encouragement; incentive, stimulus, spur, goad, bribe, bait; sop.

motley, *adj.* colorful, many-colored, variegated; assorted, jumbled, heterogeneous, diverse, kaleidoscopic, crazy-quilt, incongruous. See MIXTURE.

motor, *n.* engine (see POWER, INSTRUMENTALITY).

motorboat, *n.* speedboat, launch, cruiser; runabout, hydroplane. See SHIP.

motorcycle, *n.* motocycle, [motor]-scooter. *Slang,* motorbike, putt-putt. See VEHICLE.

motorist, *n.* automobilist; driver, chauffeur; speeder. *Colloq.,* Sunday driver, roadhog. See TRAVEL.

mottled, *adj.* spotted, blotched, dappled; motley. See COLOR.

motto, *n.* MAXIM, adage, precept, device.

mould, *n. & v.* See MOLD.

mound, *n.* heap, hillock, knoll, hill, tumulus. See HEIGHT.

mount, *v.t.* ascend, rise, soar, go up, climb; set, place. See ASCENT, HEIGHT.

mountain, *n.* hill, peak, elevation, alp, mount. See HEIGHT.

mountaineer, *n.* highlander, mountain climber. *Slang,* hillbilly. See ASCENT.

mountainous, *adj.* hilly, craggy, peaked; towering, sheer, lofty, precipitous; rugged, massive; Alpine, cordilleran. See HEIGHT.

mountebank, *n.* charlatan, quack. See DECEPTION.

mourn, *v.* lament, sorrow, grieve; bewail, bemoan, deplore. See LAMENTATION.

mourner, *n.* lamenter; mute, pallbearer. See INTERMENT, LAMENTATION.

mournful, *adj.* sorrowful; gloomy, dreary. See DEJECTION, LAMENTATION.

mousy, *adj.* drab, colorless; quiet. See COLOR, TACITURNITY.

mouth, *n.* oral cavity, lips; muzzle; entrance, exit, inlet, outlet. *Slang,* kisser, trap. See OPENING, EDGE, EGRESS, INGRESS.

mouthpiece, *n.* reed, embouchure, lip, bit, pipe stem, *etc.; slang,* spokesman, parrot, speaker, lawyer. See MUSIC, SPEECH, LAWSUIT.

movable, *adj.* portable, mobile; changeable. See CHANGEABLENESS, MOTION.

move, *v.* transport, impel, actuate, incite, arouse, INFLUENCE, propose; stir, act; remove. See CAUSE, EXCITEMENT, OFFER.

movement, *n.* MOTION, gesture; maneuver; progress; crusade, drive; works, workings. See ACTIVITY.

movie, *n.* motion picture (see DRAMA).

moving, *adj.* motile; stirring; touching, affecting; impressive, exciting. See MOTION, FEELING.

mow, *v.t.* cut, clip, reap, scythe. See AGRICULTURE, SHORTNESS.

much, *n.* abundance, ample, plenty, a lot, a great deal, a volume; wealth, sufficiency. —*adj.* many; abundant, ample, copious, plentiful, profuse. See GREATNESS.

muck, *n.* dirt, foulness, filth, slime, mud; pornography, smut, obscenity. See UNCLEANNESS.

muckraker, *n.* reformer, scandal- *or* gossipmonger. See DETRACTION.

mud, *n.* mire, muck, ooze, gumbo. See UNCLEANNESS, COHERENCE.

muddle, *n.* confusion, mess, DISORDER, befuddlement. See ABSURDITY.

mudslinger, *n.* slanderer, muckraker; character assassin. See DETRACTION.

muffin, *n.* bun, roll. See FOOD.

muffle, *v.t.* deaden, stifle, mute, dampen; wrap up, swathe, envelop. See SILENCE, CONCEALMENT.

muffler, *n.* scarf, comforter; silencer, deadener. See CLOTHING, SILENCE.

mug, *n.* cup, stein, tankard; *slang,* face, puss, kisser; *slang,* fool, dolt, clod; *slang,* gangster, mobster, thug. See RECEPTACLE, FRONT. —*v., slang,* pose, posture, make faces; assault, assail, attack, stick up, hold up. *Slang,* ham [it up]. See DRAMA, FEELING, STEALING.

muggy, *adj.* dank, oppressive, sultry, sticky. See MOISTURE.

mule, *n.* hinny, crossbreed; intransigent, pighead. See ANIMAL, OBSTINACY.

mull, *v.* think, reflect, consider, ruminate, ponder. See THOUGHT.

multiformity, *n.* variety, diversity; multifariousness, diversification. See DIFFERENCE.

multiple, *adj.* manifold, numerous. See MULTITUDE.

multiplication, *n.* procreation, REPRODUCTION; INCREASE, productiveness. See NUMERATION, MULTITUDE.

multiply, *v.* INCREASE, accrue; propagate proliferate; spread. See NUMERATION, REPRODUCTION.

MULTITUDE

Nouns—**1,** multitude, numerousness, multiplicity, profusion, plurality. See QUANTITY.

2, legion, host, horde, crowd, [great] numbers, quite a few, quite a number, good *or* great many, array, army, sea, galaxy, scores, peck, bushel, swarm, bevy, cloud, flock, herd, drove, flight, covey, hive, brood, litter, farrow. *Colloq.,* lots, gobs, stacks, heaps, scads, oodles, barrels, rafts, piles, millions, passel, any number. See POPULACE.

3, greater number, majority; INFINITY; multiplication. See INCREASE.

Verbs—be numerous, swarm, teem, crowd; outnumber, multiply, proliferate, swarm like locusts.

Adjectives—many, several, sundry, divers, various, not a few, many a; plural; ever so many, numerous, endless, countless, numberless, myriad, legion, profuse, manifold, multiplied, multitudinous, multiple, teeming, swarming, pullulating, populous, crowded, thick, studded; a world of, no end of, thick as fleas, infinite, untold. *Slang,* lousy with, alive with.

Adverbs—galore; in force, en masse; by the dozen, hundreds, *or* thousands; countlessly, numberlessly, infinitely, *etc. Colloq.,* hand over foot.

Antonyms, see RARITY, UNITY.

mumble, *v.t.* mutter, murmur, mouth. See STAMMERING.

munch, *v.* chew, masticate, crunch, nibble, eat. See FOOD.

mundane, *adj.* worldly, earthly; temporal, carnal. See IRRELIGION.

municipal, *adj.* civic, civil, city; local; governmental. See ABODE, AUTHORITY.

munificent, *adj.* generous, liberal, lavish, bounteous, bountiful, freehanded, openhanded; benevolent, philanthropic, charitable, altruistic; unsparing, princely, profuse. See LIBERALITY.

munitions, *n.pl.* See ARMS.

mural, *n.* wall painting, fresco; mosaic; shoji. See PAINTING.

murder, *n.* homicide, manslaughter. See KILLING.

murderer, *n.* assassin, manslayer, cutthroat; killer, butcher. See KILLING.

murderous, *adj.* bloodthirsty, sanguinary, deadly, brutal. See KILLING.

murk, *n.* gloom, haze, dusk, dark, blackness, obscurity. See CLOUDINESS, DARKNESS.

murmur, *v.i.* mumble, mutter, grumble; rustle, purl, ripple; whisper, breathe. See LAMENTATION.

muscle, *n.* thew, tendon, sinew; musculature, build, physique, huskiness, beef, weight, burliness; STRENGTH, brawn, power; armed might, arms, firepower.

muscular, *adj.* strong, brawny, sinewy, vigorous. See STRENGTH.

muse, *v.i.* ponder, meditate, dream, ruminate. See THOUGHT.

museum, *n.* gallery, repository, archives. See STORE.

mush, *n.* porridge, pottage, oatmeal, cereal; pap, sop; *colloq.,* sentimentality, emotionalism, romance. *Slang,* corn. See FEELING, SOFTNESS, FOOD.

mushroom, *v.i.* boom, INCREASE, expand, swell, puff up. *Colloq.,* snowball. See EXPANSION.

MUSIC

Nouns—**1,** music; classical *or* popular music; concert, light, *or* dinner music, *Tafelmusik* Muzak. *Colloq.*, longhair *or* pop music, canned music.
2, instrumental music; sonata, rondo, rondeau, pastorale, concerto, concert, musicale, overture, symphony; cadenza, cadence; fugue, toccata, round, canon; serenade, nocturne, prelude, adagio, minuet; lullaby; dirge, pibroch; march; composition, opus, arrangement, movement; full score, [musical] score; concert piece; acid, punk, hard metal, hard, *or* soft rock; soul [music], blues; swing, jive, boogie-woogie; progressive jazz, bop, bebop, third stream, stomp; hillbilly *or* country music, rockabilly; western music.
3, vocal music; [Gregorian *or* Anglican] chant, psalm, psalmody, plainsong, response; hymn, anthem; melody, strain, tune, air; song, canticle, lay, ballad, ditty, carol, pastoral, recitative, aria; sea chantey, work song, folk song, popular song, ballad, jingle; yodeling, crooning; part song, descant, glee, madrigal, catch, round, canon, chorus, antiphony; cantata, oratorio; [light *or* comic] opera, operetta, music[al] theater, musical comedy.
4, dance music, syncopation, ragtime, jazz; bolero, fandango, tango, mazurka, gavotte, minuet, polka, waltz, two-step, fox trot, reel, jig, hornpipe, conga, rumba, samba, cha-cha; rock [and roll].
5, a. musical instrument; band, orchestra. *Slang,* ax. **b.** strings, winds, drums, percussion, woodwinds, reeds, brass, horns. **c.** harp, lyre, lute, dulcimer, mandolin, guitar, gittern, cithern, cither, zither, theorbo, psaltery, ukulele, banjo; violin, fiddle, Cremona, Stradivarius, Amati, Guarnerius; [violon]cello, viol, viola, viola da braccio *or* da gamba, bass viol. **d.** piano[forte], grand, baby grand, spinet, upright [piano]; harpsichord, clavichord, virginal; fortepiano; celeste, keyboard glockenspiel. *Slang*, eighty-eights. **e.** [pipe *or* electronic] organ, harmonium, barrel organ; hurdy-gurdy, Aeolian harp, calliope; siren; pipe, pitchpipe, flute, fife, piccolo, flageolet, clarinet; oboe, hautboy, shawm, bassoon, bombarde; cornet, bugle, trumpet, [French] horn, serpent, saxhorn, trombone, sackbut, saxophone; accordion, concertina; bagpipes, whistle, ocarina; althorn, tuba; harmonica, Melodica; mouth organ, kazoo. *Slang,* squawk box; squeeze box; sax[e]; licorice stick; *etc*. **f.** cymbal, bell, gong, tambour, tambourine, snare *or* trap drum, bass drum, bongo, tomtom; kettledrum, tympanum; timbal, timbrel; steel drums; castanets; musical glasses, sounding board, rattle, bones; triangle; Jew's harp; xylophone, marimba, vibraphone *or* -harp; glockenspiel. **g.** baton, wand, stick; drumsticks; music stand, podium; metronome; tuning bar, box, fork, *or* hammer.
6, staff, key, bar, space, clef, signature, note, tone, rest, slur, pitch; barline; scale, gamut; tempo, rhythm; harmony, counterpoint; theme; chord; solo, duet, duo, trio, quartet, quintet; accompaniment, second. *Slang,* lick.
7, performance, execution; touch, expression, solmization, fingering; concert *or* recital hall; opera house.
8, a. musician, artist[e], performer, player. **b.** instrumentalist; organist, pianist; flutist, flautist, fifer, oboist, clarinetist, bassoonist, saxophonist; violinist, fiddler, violist, cellist, bassist; harper, harpist; bugler, trumpeter, horn player, trombonist; percussionist, tympanist, drummer; accordionist. **c.** vocalist, melodist, singer, warbler, minnesinger, troubadour, minstrel, bard, chanter, cantor, chantress, songstress, caroler, chorister; crooner, blues singer, folk singer, yodeler, calypso singer, scat singer, patter singer; soprano, mezzo[-soprano], [contr]alto, countertenor, tenor, baritone, bass-

baritone, bass, buffo, falsettist, castrato; songbird, nightingale, philomel, thrush, mockingbird; Orpheus, Apollo, the Muses, Euterpe, Terpsichore; siren, Lorelei. *Slang,* chorine. **d.** dancer, coryphée, ballet dancer, ballerina. See AMUSEMENT. **e.** conductor, bandmaster, choirmaster; leader, concertmaster, first violin; composer, arranger.

Verbs—compose, arrange, adapt, set to music, transpose, melodize, harmonize, orchestrate, score; accompany; execute, perform, play, sing, pipe, fiddle, beat the drum, blow *or* sound the horn, twang, plunk, pluck, pick, thrum, strum; strike up, tune up; keep time; sing, chant, hum, warble, carol, chirp, chirrup, trill, twitter, whistle, intone, lilt.

Adjectives—**1,** musical, instrumental, vocal, choral, singing, lyric, operatic; harmonious, melodious, tuneful, melodic, symphonic, orchestral; classical, popular. *Colloq.,* longhair, pop.

2, in tune, on pitch.

---

musket, *n.* firearm; flintlock, blunderbuss; brown Bess. See ARMS.

muss, *n.* DISORDER, tangle, confusion, mix-up, mess, muddle.

must, *v.* ought, should, had better, have [got] to, need, needs must, have no choice [but to]; be required, obliged, bound, compelled, doomed, destined, *etc.* See NECESSITY.

mustache, *n.* hairline, toothbrush, Charlie Chaplin, Hitler, Kaiser Wilhelm, waxed, handlebar, *or* walrus mustache. *Slang,* soup strainer, tickler, cookie duster. See ROUGHNESS.

muster, *v.t.* assemble, collect, gather, mobilize; poll. See ASSEMBLAGE.

mutation, *n.* CHANGE, variation, deviation; mutant, freak, aberrancy, monster.

mute, *v.* See SILENCE.

mutilate, *v.t.* maim, destroy, cripple; disfigure, deface, mar. See DISTORTION, DETERIORATION, FORMLESSNESS.

mutiny, *n.* rebellion, revolt, uprising, insurrection, insurgence. See DISOBEDIENCE.

mutter, *v.* murmur, grumble, mumble, growl. See LAMENTATION, STAMMERING.

mutual, *adj.* reciprocal, common, joint, correlative. See INTERCHANGE, PARTY.

muzzle, *v.i.* restrain, bridle, gag, SILENCE, throttle.

myriad, *adj.* innumerable, multitudinous, teeming. See MULTITUDE.

mystery, *n.* SECRET, enigma, puzzle, cabala; rite, sacrament. See CONCEALMENT, LATENCY, OBSCURITY, UNINTELLIGIBILITY.

mystic, *adj.* hidden, SECRET; mysterious; esoteric, occult. See CONCEALMENT.

mystify, *v.t.* puzzle, perplex, bewilder, obscure, confound, baffle. See CONCEALMENT, DECEPTION.

mystique, *n.* aura, mystery, charisma. See SPECIALITY.

myth, *n.* legend, tradition; phantasy, fiction. See IMAGINATION.

mythical, *adj.* unreal; fabulous, fictitious, mythological. See IMAGINATION, MYTHICAL DEITIES.

MYTHICAL DEITIES

Nouns—**1,** mythical deities, heathen gods and goddesses; god[dess], DEITY, divinity, demigod; pantheon, mythology, folklore.

2, *Greek:* Zeus, Apollo, Ares, Hephaestus, Hermes, Poseidon, Hades, Eros, Dionysus; Hera, Athena, Artemis, Aphrodite; Titans: Uranus, Gaea, Cronos, Oceanus, Coeus, Crius, Hyperion, Rhea, Mnemosyne, Themis, Phoebe, Dione, Cyclops, Helios.

3, *Roman:* Jupiter, Jove, Apollo, Mars, Vulcan, Mercury, Neptune, Pluto, Saturn, Cupid, Bacchus; Juno, Minerva, Diana, Venus.
4, *Norse:* Woden, Odin, Thor, Balder, Loki, Bragi; Freya; Sigurd, Brynhild, Gudrun, Fafnir, the Valkyries.
5, *Hindu:* Vishnu, Siva, Shiva, Brahma, Indra, Buddha.
6, *Egyptian:* Ra, Osiris, Horus, Set, Anubis, Thoth; Isis.
7, *Babylonian & Semitic:* Baal, Bel, Astarte, Ashtoreth, Ishtar, Ashur.
8, nymph, dryad, hamadryad, naiad, nereid, oread; sylph; salamander, undine; Pan, faun, satyr; mermaid, merman.
9, fairy, fay, sprite, elf, brownie, pixie, pixy, Puck, Robin Goodfellow, dwarf, gnome, troll, kobold, peri, hobgoblin, leprechaun; wee folk, little people; manitou; fairy godmother *or* -father.
10, familiar spirit, familiar, genius, genie, jinni; chimera; DEMON, incubus, succubus, vampire, harpy, werewolf; ogre, ogress.
Adjectives—mythical, mythological, legendary; fairylike, nymphlike, elfin, fey.

N

nab, *v.t., colloq.,* grab, catch, seize; latch on to; corner, tree, ensnare; take prisoner. *Slang,* collar; pinch. See RESTRAINT.

nag, *n., colloq.,* pony; jade, hack. *Slang,* plug. See ANIMAL.—*v.* pester, badger, scold; fret, complain; irritate, annoy, plague. See DISCONTENT, EVILDOER.

nail, *n.* fingernail, toenail, ungula; talon, claw; tack, brad, spoke; hobnail, clout; pin, peg. —*v.t.* pin, fix; *colloq.,* capture, catch. See JUNCTION, RESTRAINT.

naïve, *adj.* ingenuous, unsophisticated, unworldly, artless. See SIMPLENESS, CREDULITY.

naked, *adj.* uncovered, stripped, bare; nude, unclothed, unclad, unappareled; plain, undisguised. See DIVESTMENT, SIMPLENESS.

name, *n.* nomen (see NOMENCLATURE); reputation, fame, REPUTE. —*v.t.* [en]title, call, designate, christen; appoint, nominate; style; mention, specify. See COMMISSION.

nameless, *adj.* anonymous, unnamed; obscure, unknown, unchristened, illegitimate; untitled, inglorious, unnamable, abominable, indescribable. See NOMENCLATURE, DISREPUTE.

namely, *conj. & adv.* to wit, as follows, specifically, *viz., videlicet,* that is [to say], *i.e.* See SPECIALITY, INTERPRETATION.

nap, *n.* doze, sleep; pile, surface, TEXTURE. See REPOSE.

nape, *n.* scruff, scuff, nuque, scrag. See CONNECTION.

napkin, *n.* linen, serviette; towel, diaper, handkerchief; sanitary napkin, maxi- *or* minipad, tampon. *Slang,* wipe. See CLEANNESS.

narcotic, *n.* soporific, anesthetic; opiate, anodyne; dope, drug; sedative, tranquilizer. —*adj.* stupefying, narcotizing, tranquilizing. See INSENSIBILITY, REMEDY, HABIT.

narrate, *v.* describe, tell, relate; recount, recite; inform, rehearse; record, state, report, retail. See DESCRIPTION.

narrow-minded, *adj.* bigoted; intolerant. See NARROWNESS, MISJUDGMENT.

NARROWNESS

Nouns—**1,** narrowness, closeness, exiguity, LITTLENESS; thinness, tenuity, emaciation; narrowing; tapering, CONTRACTION; finger's- *or* hair's-breadth, line; strip, streak, vein.

2, shaving, chip; FILAMENT, thread, hair; skeleton, shadow, spindleshanks, lantern jaws, skin and bone; sylph; neck, waist, isthmus, hourglass; pass; ravine, narrows, gap; film, membrane (see LAYER).

3, narrow-mindedness, smallness, meanness (see INJUSTICE, MISJUDGMENT, SELFISHNESS).

Verbs—narrow, taper [off]; slice, shave, pare, trim, thin [down *or* out], slim, reduce, attenuate; waste away.

Adjectives—**1,** narrow, close; slender, thin, fine; threadlike, finespun, slim; wasp-waisted; scant[y]; tenuous, spare, delicate; contracted.

2, emaciated, lean, meager, gaunt, rawboned, lank[y], gangling, gangly, bony, weedy, skinny, thin as a rail; svelte; starved, attenuated, shriveled, worn to a shadow; slender-waisted, waspish.

3, confined, limited; cramped, pinched, close, tight, constricted; narrow-minded, prejudiced, illiberal, hidebound, insular, parochial, provincial; circumscribed, small. See INJUSTICE, MISJUDGMENT, SELFISHNESS.

Adverbs—barely, only, just.

Antonyms, see BREADTH, LIBERALITY.

---

nasty, *adj.* foul, filthy; distasteful, disgusting, horrid; dirty; nauseating, loathsome; indecent, obscene; ill-tempered, disagreeable, dangerous. See UNCLEANNESS, IMPURITY, DISCOURTESY.

nation, *n.* country, state, realm; republic, kingdom, empire; sovereignty, AUTHORITY, polity, body politic; commonwealth, community; tribe, people. See HUMANITY.

national, *adj.* federal, countrywide, nationwide; governmental, public; nationalistic, patriotic. See AUTHORITY. —*n.* citizen, subject. See INHABITANT, SUBJECTION.

nationalism, *n.* patriotism, civism, paternalism; chauvinism; socialism, totalitarianism. *Colloq.,* spread-eagleism. See PRIDE, AUTHORITY.

nationality, *n.* citizenship; nation. See HUMANITY, REGION.

native, *n.* INHABITANT, aborigine, countryman. —*adj.* indigenous; innate, inherent; aboriginal; endemic, natal, natural. See INTRINSIC.

nativity, *n.* birth. See REPRODUCTION, BEGINNING.

natty, *adj., colloq.,* smart, chic, stylish, modish, dapper. *Colloq.,* snappy. See FASHION.

natural, *adj.* unaffected, spontaneous, artless, unstudied; unsophisticated, naïve, ingenuous; normal, ordinary, regular; unadorned, unadulterated; inherent, innate, inborn. See SIMPLENESS, INTRINSIC, CONFORMITY, INTUITION, UNPREPAREDNESS.

naturalist, *n.* zoologist, herpetologist, botanist, horticulturalist, ichthyologist, geologist, arborist, arboriculturist, *etc.* See ANIMAL, VEGETABLE.

nature, *n.* character, type, sort, kind; essence, basis, essential; constitution, quality; disposition, structure; temperament, bent, CLASS, form; heart; creation, universe. See FEELING, INTRINSIC, TENDENCY.

naughty, *adj.* disobedient, wayward, mischievous, troublesome, perverse; improper. See DISOBEDIENCE, IMPURITY.

nausea, *n.* qualm, seasickness, queasiness; disgust, aversion, loathing. See DISEASE, DISLIKE.

nauseate, *v.t.* sicken, disgust, revolt. See PAIN, DISEASE.

nautical, *adj.* marine, maritime; oceangoing. See NAVIGATION.

NAVIGATION

Nouns—**1,** navigation; celestial navigation, dead reckoning; circumnavigation; pilotage, steerage; seamanship; navigability.

2, boating, yachting, yacht-racing, sailing, cruising, voyaging, seafaring; oarsmanship, rowing, sculling, crew, canoeing, paddling, kayaking. See SHIP, TRAVEL.

3, voyage, sail, cruise; leg; crossing; boat *or* yacht race, regatta (see CONTENTION); maneuvers.

4, progress, way; headway, sternway, leeway; sideslip; seaway, [inland *or* coastal] waterway, sea lane (see PASSAGE); buoy (see INDICATION).

5, navigator, sailor, mariner, seaman, seafarer, tar, jack, old salt, able seaman, A.B.; bluejacket, marine, naval cadet, midshipman, middy; captain, skipper, mate; ferryman, bargeman, bargee; longshoreman, stevedore; gondolier, rower, sculler, canoeist, paddler, oarsman; boatswain, coxswain, bosun, steersman, leadsman, helmsman, pilot (see DIRECTION); crew, watch, all hands. *Slang*, sea dog, barnacle.

6, anchorage, dock[age], [boat] basin, wharf, quay, port, harbor; marina.

Verbs—**1,** navigate, sail, steam, cruise; take bearings, pilot, steer, helm (see DIRECTION); cast off, set sail, put to sea, take ship, weigh anchor, get under way, spread sail, have sail (see DEPARTURE); make [head]way, plow the deep, buffet the waves, ride the storm, hug the shore; sail against *or* into the wind, warp, luff, scud, float, coast; hold a course; drift, yaw; careen, list (see OBLIQUITY); tack, jibe, come about; back water; heave into sight, heave to; nose in, bring to; lie *or* lay to; circumnavigate; put in, cast anchor, moor, dock (see ARRIVAL); shipwreck, beach, go aground; scuttle; capsize, founder, sink.

2, row, oar, paddle, feather, pull, scull, punt, raft, float.

Adjectives—sailing, seafaring, nautical, maritime, marine, naval, afloat; seagoing, ocean-going; adrift, afloat, aweigh; navigable.

Adverbs—under way, sail, canvas, *or* steam; before *or* against the wind; at anchor; aft, abaft, astern; aground; overboard; on board [ship], on deck, topside; aloft.

Interjections—ahoy! ship ahoy! avast! belay! steady as you go!

---

navy, *n.* fleet; ships, warships. See COMBATANT, WARFARE.

Nazi, *n. & adj.* fascist, Hitlerite, racist; National Socialist, N.S.D.A.P.; reactionary, economic royalist; brownshirt, blackshirt; authoritarian, totalitarian. See AUTHORITY.

NEARNESS

Nouns—**1,** nearness, closeness, proximity, propinquity, apposition, approximation, vicinity, neighborhood, adjacency; APPROACH, CONVERGENCE; likeness, SIMILARITY. See FUTURITY.

2, short distance, step, *or* way; shortcut; earshot; close-up, close quarters, close range, stone's throw, hair's-breadth; span.

3, purlieus, neighborhood, vicinage, environs, suburbs, outskirts, confines, borderland. See ENVIRONMENT.

4, bystander, neighbor; abutter, tangent (see CONTACT).

Verbs—**1,** adjoin, hang about, touch *or* border on, verge upon; stand by, approximate, tread on the heels of, cling to, clasp, hug; hover over.

2, near, draw *or* come near, APPROACH; converge, crowd, press.

Adjectives—near, nigh, close *or* near at hand; close, neighboring; adjacent, adjoining, proximate; impending, imminent, oncoming, at [close] hand, handy; near the mark; intimate, close to home.

Adverbs—**1,** near, nigh; hard, close, *or* fast by; close to, at the point of; within reach, call, *or* earshot, next door to, within an ace *or* inch of, on hand, at one's door[step], at one's elbow, but a step, not far from, at no great distance; on the verge *or* brink of; on the outskirts, in the neighborhood of, in the offing, around the corner, at one's fingertips, on the tip of one's tongue, under one's nose, on one's heels; within a stone's throw, in sight of, at close quarters; cheek by jowl; beside, alongside, side-by-side, tête-à-tête; in juxtaposition, at the threshold, bordering upon, in the way.

2, nearly, almost, about, thereabouts, *circa,* or so; roughly, in round numbers; approximately, more or less, as good as, well nigh; all but.

Antonyms, see DISTANCE.

---

nearsighted, *adj.* shortsighted, myopic. See VISION.

neat, *adj.* tidy, orderly; compact, trim, shapely; pure, unmixed; deft, skillful, adroit; pat, felicitous. See CLEANNESS, SIMPLENESS, ORDER.

nebulous, *adj.* nebular; cloudy, hazy; amorphous, indistinct, unclear, confused, vague, turbid. See DIMNESS, FORMLESSNESS.

NECESSITY

Nouns—**1,** necessity, necessitation, obligation, COMPULSION, subjection; needfulness, essentiality, indispensability; dire necessity, inexorable fate; what must be.

2, requirement, need, want, requisite, demand; urgency, exigency; bread and butter; *sine qua non,* matter of life and death; stress, pinch. See CERTAINTY, POVERTY, DESIRE.

3, DESTINY, fatality, foredoom, foreordination.

4, Fates, Parcae, three Sisters, book of fate; God's will, will of heaven, will of Allah; wheel of fortune; Hobson's choice; last shift *or* resort.

Verbs—**1,** lie under a necessity; be doomed *or* destined, be in for, be under the necessity of, have no choice *or* alternative, cannot [help] but, have one's back to the wall, be driven into a corner; burn one's bridges *or* boats. *Colloq.,* take it or leave it.

2, necessitate, demand, require, call for, entail; must; destine, doom, foredoom, predestine, preordain; compel, force, oblige, constrain.

Adjectives—**1,** necessary, needful, required, requisite, essential, imperative, indispensable, in demand; compulsory, obligatory, uncontrollable, inevitable, unavoidable, irresistible, irrevocable, inexorable, ineluctable; urgent, exigent, pressing, crying; instant.

2, fated, destined, preordained, fateful, doomed.

3, involuntary, instinctive, automatic, blind, mechanical, unconscious, unwitting, unthinking, impulsive.

Adverbs—necessarily, of necessity, of course, needs must, perforce, willing or unwilling, willy-nilly, compulsorily; like it or not.

Antonyms, see WILL, CHOICE.

---

neck, *n.* channel, isthmus, strait, pass; cervix; constriction, narrowing; scruff, nape. See NARROWNESS, CONVEXITY, CONNECTION. —*v.i., slang,* make love, pet. *Colloq.,* make out. *Slang,* smooch. See ENDEARMENT.

necklace, *n.* beads, chain, string, pearls; pendant, lavaliere; collar, choker. See PENDENCY, ORNAMENT, CIRCULARITY.

necktie, *n.* tie, cravat, scarf; string, bow, four-in-hand, Ascot, Windsor, half-Windsor, black, white, *etc.* tie; neckwear. See CLOTHING.

necrology, *n.* obituary. See DEATH.

necromancy, *n.* SORCERY, enchantment, magic.

nectar, *n.* honey[dew]. See SWEETNESS.

need, *n.* NECESSITY, requirement; DESIRE, want, privation, lack, POVERTY; USE. —*v.t.* require, crave, claim, demand, yearn; lack, want.

needle, *n.* obelisk, Cleopatra's needle; thorn, prickle; stylus; syringe. See SHARPNESS. —*v.t., colloq.,* rib, josh, tease, RIDICULE, heckle, prick, goad; *colloq.,* harass, torment, ride. See DISCONTENT.

needless, *adj.* unnecessary, pointless, purposeless, superfluous. See USELESSNESS.

needlework, *n.* darning, stitching, sewing, embroidery, lace[work], needlepoint, tatting, appliqué; sampler, brocade. See ORNAMENT.

needy, *adj.* in want, destitute, indigent, moneyless, impecunious, penniless, poverty-stricken; poor as a churchmouse. See POVERTY.

ne'er-do-well, *n.* wastrel, loafer, idler, do-nothing, fainéant, good-for-nothing. *Slang,* bum, deadbeat, no-good. See INACTIVITY.

nefarious, *adj.* evil, detestable, base, wicked. See BADNESS.

NEGATION

Nouns—negation, negativeness, abnegation, denial, disavowal, disclaimer, abjuration, contradiction, contravention, repudiation, retraction, refutation, rebuttal, disproof, CONFUTATION, REFUSAL, PROHIBITION. See NULLIFICATION, UNWILLINGNESS.

Verbs—negate, deny, contradict, contravene, controvert, gainsay, forswear, disown, disaffirm, disclaim, disavow, recant, revoke, abrogate, veto; dispute, impugn, traverse, call in question, doubt, give the lie to, disprove, explode, belie; repudiate, set aside, ignore, confute, rebut, refute, qualify, refuse.

Adjectives—negative, denying, denied, contradictory, contrary, recusant, dissenting.

Adverbs—no, nay, not, nowise, not a bit, not at all, not in the least, no such thing, nothing of the kind, quite the contrary, far from it, on no consideration, on no account, in no respect, by no means, for the life of me; let alone, less than; negatively, never, not ever; perish the thought, not for the world, anything but. *Dial.,* nohow. *Colloq.,* not on your life; nary a. *Slang,* like fun, fat chance, not by a long shot, nothing doing; in a pig's eye.

Antonyms, see AFFIRMATION.

NEGLECT

Nouns—**1,** neglect, negligence, carelessness, heedlessness, thoughtlessness, dereliction, delinquency; omission, oversight, laches, default; RASHNESS; procrastination. See INDIFFERENCE, INSUFFICIENCY.

2, laxity, laxness, slackness, looseness, slovenliness; UNPREPAREDNESS, improvidence, unreadiness; disregard, nonobservance, evasion (see AVOIDANCE); nonperformance, FAILURE. *Colloq.,* a lick and a promise. See RELINQUISHMENT.

3, INATTENTION, absence of mind, preoccupation, woolgathering.

4, neglector, trifler, procrastinator, waster, wastrel, drifter, slacker; Micawber.

Verbs—**1,** neglect, let slip, let go, lay aside, lose sight of, overlook, disregard, ignore, leave out of account; pass over, up, *or* by, elide; sit out; let pass, wink at, connive at, gloss over, blink at, eliminate, leave out in the cold; leave in the lurch.

2, be lax, loose, remiss, slack, *etc.;* relax; let be, ignore. *laisser faire;* hold a loose rein, give enough *or* too much rope.

3, scamp, do by halves, cut, slight, skimp, trifle with, slur, slur *or* skip over, skim the surface; miss, skip, omit; postpone, procrastinate (see LATENESS); close *or* shut one's eyes to, turn a deaf ear to, forget, be caught napping, let the grass grow under one's feet.

Adjectives—**1,** neglectful, negligent, lax, slack, heedless, half-baked, careless, forgetful, perfunctory, remiss, inconsiderate; unprepared, unready, off one's guard, unwary, unguarded, unwatchful, delinquent; casual, offhand, cursory; supine, asleep, indolent, inattentive, unobservant, unmindful, unheeding, thoughtless, inadvertent; indifferent, imprudent, slovenly, inexact, inaccurate, improvident, asleep at the switch.

2, neglected, unheeded, uncared for, unnoticed, unattended to, unmissed, shunted, shelved, unused, abandoned, unweighed, unexplored, hid under a bushel, unsung, out in the cold; fallow, untilled, uncultivated.

Adverbs—neglectfully, negligently, anyhow, in an unguarded moment.

Interjections—never mind! let it be!

Antonyms, see CARE, DUTY, SEVERITY.

---

negligee, *n.* deshabille, morning dress, peignoir, kimono, *robe de chambre,* nightgown. See CLOTHING.

negligent, *adj.* See NEGLECT.

negligible, *adj.* slight, insignificant. See LITTLENESS, UNIMPORTANCE.

negotiable, *adj.* conveyable, assignable, transferable; spendable. See TRANSFER, POSSIBILITY.

negotiate, *v.* accomplish, arrange; bargain, dicker, contract, overcome, achieve, effect; *colloq.,* handle. See BARTER, COMPROMISE.

Negro, *n.* African, Ethiopian, Sudanese, *etc.;* black, Afro-American. See HUMANITY.

neighbor, *n.* See FRIEND.

neighborhood, *n.* community, vicinity, district, REGION, environs, presence, venue. See NEARNESS, ENVIRONMENT, LOCATION.

neighborly, *adj.* hospitable; friendly. See FRIEND, SOCIALITY.

neither, *adj.* See NEGATION.

neology, *n.* neologism. See SPEECH.

neophyte, *n.* beginner, tyro, novice; initiate, debutant. *Colloq.,* greenhorn, greeny. *Slang,* rookie. See LEARNING, BEGINNING.

nepotism, *n.* favoritism, patronage; partiality, favor. See INJUSTICE.

nerve, *n.* COURAGE, STRENGTH, vigor, vitality; grit, determination, resolution. —*v.t.* embolden, steel, strengthen, invigorate.

nerveless, *adj.* listless; cowardly. See COWARDICE, WEAKNESS.

nervous, *adj.* jumpy, jittery, fidgety, uneasy; tense, fearful; sensitive, neurotic; high-strung; timid. See EXCITEMENT, AGITATION, FEAR.

nervy, *adj.* bold, brash. See COURAGE, INSOLENCE.

nest, *n.* aerie, hammock, lair, den; hotbed, coterie; nursery, cradle; resort, haunt, retreat. See CAUSE, ABODE.

nest egg, *n.* reserve [fund], savings; rainy-day fund, hope chest. See STORE, MONEY.

nestle, *v.i.* lodge, snuggle, lie, cuddle. See ENDEARMENT, ABODE.

net, *n.* seine, web, snare, mesh; trap, catch. See DECEPTION, CROSSING. —*n.* See REMAINDER.

nettle, *v.* trouble, irritate; prickle; ruffle, annoy, provoke; vex, offend. See DISCONTENT.

network, *n.* reticulation; net[ting], mesh, interlacing, openwork; hookup, web, interconnection. See CROSSING.

neurosis, *n.* nervous *or* mental disorder, illness, sickness, *or* disease; psychoneurosis, melancholia, nervous breakdown; phobia, mania, obsession, compulsion, hypochondria; psychosis, INSANITY. See FEAR.

neutral, *adj.* nonpartisan; indifferent, disinterested, unconcerned; undecided, irresolute, indeterminate; inert, inactive; impartial; neuter, asexual, sexless; barren, unfruitful, sterile. See INDIFFERENCE, LIBERALITY, MEDIOCRITY.

neutralize, *v.t.* nullify, cancel; offset, negate, counterbalance; destroy, defeat, overpower. See COMPENSATION, NULLIFICATION.

never, *adv.* ne'er, nevermore, not ever. See NEGATION, REFUSAL.

nevertheless, *adv.* nonetheless, anyway, still, yet, just the same, for all that, notwithstanding; in any event, however that may be, regardless. See COMPENSATION.

newcomer, *n.* immigrant, alien, foreigner; initiate. *Colloq.,* Johnny-come-lately. See ARRIVAL.

newfangled, *adj.* novel. See NEWNESS, FASHION.

NEWNESS

Nouns—**1,** newness, recentness, currency, freshness, greenness, novelty, immaturity, YOUTH; innovation, renovation; update; new blood; invention. See PRESENT, RESTORATION.

2, modernism, modernity; latest fashion, latest thing, last word; mushroom, *nouveau riche,* upstart, parvenu.

Verbs—renew, restore, modernize, renovate, remodel.

Adjectives—**1,** new, novel, recent, fresh, green, young, evergreen, raw, crisp, immature, virgin, untried, not dry behind the ears; untrodden, unbeaten.

2, late, modern, current, neoteric, new-fashioned, newfangled, just out, up to the minute, brand-new, vernal, renovated, fresh as a daisy, up to date, state of the art, abreast of the times; jet- *or* space-age; hot off the press, first run; a-go-go.

Adverbs—newly, freshly, afresh, anew, lately, just now, only yesterday, latterly, of late, not long ago, a short time ago.

Antonyms, see OLDNESS.

NEWS

Nouns—**1,** news, INFORMATION, intelligence, tidings, word, ADVICE; KNOWLEDGE, revelation; message, COMMUNICATION, account, dispatch, bulletin, communiqué; newscast; article, column; news flash, exposé; news channel; report, rumor, hearsay, buzz, bruit, fame, talk, gossip, table talk, town talk, scandal, tittle-tattle, canard, whisper; good news, glad tidings, gospel, evangel; story, copy, spot, piece; pipeline, earful, hot line. *Colloq.,* grapevine, scoop. *Slang,* beat. See PUBLICATION, WRITING, RECORD.

2, newsman, narrator, announcer, reporter, broadcaster, newscaster, anchor, commentator, news analyst; newsmonger, scandalmonger, informer, talebearer, telltale, tattletale; gossip, tattler, blabber, chatterer.

Verbs—report, disseminate, publish, notify, broadcast, televise; rumor, gossip, chatter, tattle, prate; make news, make the headlines. *Colloq.,* scoop.

Adjectives—reported, rumored, circulated, in circulation; rife, current, floating, going around, all over [the] town, the talk of the town, in every mouth, at second hand; newsworthy, fit to print, newsy.

Adverbs—as the story goes *or* runs, as they say, it is said.

---

newspaper, *n.* paper; daily, journal, weekly, gazette, sheet, tabloid. See PUBLICATION, RECORD, COMMUNICATION, NEWS.

New Testament, *n.* See SACRED WRITINGS.

next, *adv.* beside, nearest; after, later. —*adj.* adjacent, adjoining, bordering, contiguous; following, ensuing, succeeding, successive. See SEQUENCE, FUTURITY.

nib, *n.* point, END; beak, bill.

nibble, *v.* browse, gnaw, graze; nip, peck, pick at; snack, *nosh.* —*n.* nip, chew, bite, morsel, bit, snack. See FOOD.

nice, *adj.* pleasing, agreeable, attractive, enjoyable; tasteful, proper, genteel; precise, accurate, exact, meticulous; delicate, fine, sensitive, appealing; overrefined, critical, squeamish. See PLEASURE, TASTE.

niche, *n.* hollow, recess; corner, nook. See ANGULARITY.

nick, *n.* notch, chip, gouge, jag, indentation. —*v.t.* cut, chip, dent, jag, gouge. See FURROW.

nickname, *n.* pet name, diminutive, sobriquet; appellation. See NOMENCLATURE.

nifty, *adj., slang,* smart, stylish. See FASHION, GOODNESS.

niggardly, *adj.* cheap, stingy, miserly, close, parsimonious, ungenerous; grudging; tight; mean. See PARSIMONY, UNIMPORTANCE.

night, *n.* DARKNESS, evening, nightfall, midnight, nighttime, eventide.

nightclothes, *n.pl.* nightgown *or* -shirt, pajamas, *robe de nuit. Colloq.,* nightie, P.J.'s. See CLOTHING.

nightclub, *n.* cabaret, café, supper club; discotheque. *Colloq.,* nightspot. *Slang,* speakeasy, joint, nightery. See ABODE, DRINKING, AMUSEMENT.

nightmare, *n.* bad dream, hallucination; *cauchemar;* incubus, succubus, demon, night hag; terror, fright, daymare. See FEAR, IMAGINATION.

nimble, *adj.* spry, active, sprightly, supple, agile, lively, brisk, alert, acute, quick. See VELOCITY, SKILL, CUNNING.

nip, *v.t.* nibble, bite; cut, snip, pinch, chip, shorten; sip. —*n.* pinch, bite; sip; chill. See DEDUCTION, DISJUNCTION, CONTRACTION, COLD, STEALING.

nipple, *n.* dug, mammilla, pap[illa], teat; tit. See CONVEXITY.

nirvana, *n.* bliss, ecstasy, HEAVEN, paradise; nibbana.

nitwit, *n., slang,* bonehead, jughead, fool. *Slang,* dimwit. See FOLLY.

no, *adv.* none, not. See NEGATION.

NOBILITY

Nouns—**1,** nobility, aristocracy, quality, gentility, rank, condition, title, distinction, [blue] blood, [high] birth, high degree; pedigree, lineage. See POSTERITY, ANCESTRY, SUPERIORITY, PRIDE, FASHION.

2, the nobility, aristocracy, peerage, upper classes, *haut monde,* elite, *noblesse,* gentry, fashionable world, *beau monde,* high society.

3, noble[man], lord, peer, grandee, magnifico, hidalgo, don, aristocrat, gentleman, patrician. *Slang,* swell, nob, toff.

4, king, emperor, prince, crown prince, duke, marquis, marquess, earl, viscount, baron[et], knight, chevalier, squire, count, laird, thane, seignior, esquire, kaiser, czar, margrave; emir, sheik, rajah, maharajah, sultan. See AUTHORITY.

5, queen, empress, princess, begum, rani, ranee, maharani, sultana, czarina; duchess, marchioness, countess; lady, dame.

6, personage, *crème de la crème,* notable, celebrity, socialite; First Families. *Slang,* upper crust, four hundred. See IMPORTANCE, REPUTE.

Verbs—ennable, confer a title (on), knight, dub, esquire.

Adjectives—noble, exalted, princely, royal, lordly, titled, patrician, aristocratic, wellborn, highborn, of gentle blood, of family, genteel, blue-blooded.

Antonyms, see POPULACE.

---

nobody, *n.* nonentity, cipher, upstart, jackanapes. *Slang*, jerk, twirp. See UNIMPORTANCE.

nocturnal, *adj.* nightlike, nightly; nighttime; noctivagant, noctambulant; dark, black as night. See DARKNESS.

nocturne, *n.* night piece *or* music, evensong, *Nachtmusik;* serenade. See MUSIC.

nod, *n.* salute, greeting, recognition; sign, signal; permission, agreement. —*v.t.* dip, incline, bob. —*v.i.* greet, signal, sign; sleep, nap, doze, drowse. See COMMAND, INACTIVITY, INDICATION, ASSENT.

node, *n.* DIFFICULTY, nodus, Gordian knot; protuberance, CONVEXITY, lump, bump, knurl, gnarl; nodosity, nodule, tumescence. See DISEASE.

noise, *n.* uproar, hubbub, din, racket, clamor, pandemonium; crash, rattle, clatter. See LOUDNESS, SOUND.

noiseless, *adj.* soundless, quiet, silent, hushed. See SILENCE.

noisome, *adj.* destructive, harmful, baneful, EVIL; fetid, malodorous, rank, foul[-smelling]; disgusting, loathsome. See BADNESS, MALODOROUSNESS.

nomad, *n.* wanderer, gypsy, rover. See TRAVEL.

NOMENCLATURE

Nouns—**1,** nomenclature; naming, nomination, terminology, glossology, baptism, christening; nomenclator. See INDICATION.

2, name, appellation, appellative, designation, title, head[ing], denomination, byname, epithet; label; proper *or* Christian name, first name, cognomen, patronymic, nomen, praenomen, surname, nickname, maiden *or* birth name; synonym, antonym; honorific, title; signature; anonymity; alias, pseudonym, incognito, pen name, *nom de guerre, nom de plume;* misnomer, misnaming, malapropism. *Colloq.*, such-and-such, so-and-so. *Slang*, moniker, handle.

3, term, expression, noun, word, byword, technical term, cant.

Verbs—**1,** name, call, term, denominate, designate, identify, style, entitle, label, dub, christen, baptize, characterize, specify, label; misname, nickname.

2, be called, go by, answer to the name of.

Adjectives—named, [so-]called, hight, yclept; known as, alias, A.K.A., cognominal, titular, nominal; pseudonymous, *soi-disant,* self-styled; nameless, anonymous.

---

nominal, *adj.* titular, [so-]called, known as; in name only, token; slight, little; moderate, reasonable. See NOMENCLATURE.

nominate, *v.t.* propose, name; suggest; appoint. See COMMISSION.

nominee, *n.* appointee, designee, candidate, aspirant; grantee. See COMMISSION.

nonalcoholic, *adj.* abstemious, teetotal; nonintoxicating; unfermented. See MODERATION.

nonbeliever, *n.* See UNBELIEVER.

nonchalance, *n.* INDIFFERENCE, insouciance, unconcern; casualness, carelessness. See INATTENTION.

non-Christian, *adj.* pagan, heretic, heathen, infidel; Antichrist. See IRRELIGION.

noncommittal, *adj.* neutral, nonpartisan; ambiguous, vague; careful, cautious, circumspect, closemouthed, politic. See CAUTION.

nonconformity, *n.* See UNCONFORMITY.

nondescript, *adj.* indefinable, unclassifiable, indescribable, random; odd; casual, undistinguished. See UNCONFORMITY.

none, *pron.* no one, nothing. See NEGATION, NONEXISTENCE.

nonentity, *n.* nothing, negation; nobody; nullity. See NONEXISTENCE, UNIMPORTANCE.

nonessential, *adj.* unimportant, irrelevant, unnecessary, incidental. See UNIMPORTANCE.

nonesuch, *n.* rarity, unicum, paragon, exemplar; nonpareil, one in a thousand *or* million. See PERFECTION, UNCONFORMITY.

nonetheless, *adv.* however, nevertheless. See QUALIFICATION.

NONEXISTENCE

Nouns—**1,** nonexistence, inexistence, nonentity, nonsubsistence, negativeness, nullity, nihility, blank, nothingness, ABSENCE, no such thing, void, vacuum, OBLIVION. See DISAPPEARANCE, INSUBSTANTIALITY.

2, annihilation, extinction, obliteration, NULLIFICATION, DESTRUCTION.

3, nonperson, unperson.

Verbs—**1,** not exist, be null and void, cease to exist, pass away, perish, become extinct, die out; disappear, fade (see DISAPPEARANCE); go, be no more, die (see DEATH).

2, annihilate, render null [and void], nullify, abrogate, destroy, obliterate, extinguish, remove. See DESTRUCTION, KILLING.

Adjectives—**1,** nonexistent, inexistent, null [and void], negative, blank, missing, omitted, absent.

2, unreal, baseless, unsubstantial, imaginary, visionary, ideal, fabulous, legendary, chimerical, supposititious, vain. See IMAGINATION.

3, unborn, uncreated, unbegotten, unconceived, unproduced, unmade.

4, annihilated, extinct, exhausted, perished, gone, lost, departed, defunct.

Antonyms, see EXISTENCE.

nonfiction, *n.* reality; history, [auto]-biography, article, dissertation; journalism, exposé. See WRITING, PUBLICATION.

nonpareil, *adj.* unequaled, matchless, incomparable, in a class by itself. See PERFECTION, SUPERIORITY. —*n.* See NONESUCH.

nonpartisan, *adj.* neutral, uncommitted, disinterested; impartial, unbiased, broad-minded. —*n.* independent, neutral, freethinker, sideliner; judge, arbiter, umpire. See INDIFFERENCE.

NONPAYMENT

Nouns—**1,** nonpayment, default; protest, repudiation, evasion, reneging; unprofitableness; bad debt; cancellation, write-off, moratorium; insolvency, bankruptcy, INSUFFICIENCY, a run on the bank. See DEBT, POVERTY, ECONOMY.

2, free admission, free *or* complimentary seats, [free] pass, Annie Oakley; labor of love. *Slang,* comp, freebie. See CHEAPNESS.

3, bankrupt, insolvent, debtor; absconder, welsher, defaulter, lame duck, *etc.;* tax dodger. *Colloq.,* deadhead. *Slang,* deadbeat.

Verbs—**1,** not pay, stop payment; run up bills, go into debt *or* the red; go bankrupt, fail, crash, go under, fold [up]; protest, dishonor, repudiate, nullify; default; write off, wipe the slate clear, declare a moratorium, cancel; welsh. *Slang,* go broke, skip out, shoot the moon, fly kites.

2, give way, pass out [tickets, *etc.*]. *Colloq.,* paper the house.

Adjectives—**1,** defaulting, in default; insolvent, bankrupt; in DEBT, in arrears; unpaid, unrequited, unrewarded.

2, gratuitous, gratis, free, for nothing; without charge, untaxed; scot-free; free of cost, complimentary; honorary. *Colloq.*, on the house, dime a dozen; five-and-ten.

Antonyms, see PAYMENT, PRICE.

---

nonplus, *v.t.* perplex, confound, baffle; bring up short *or* to a standstill, stop dead [in one's tracks]. *Colloq.*, squelch, throw [for a loop]. See HINDRANCE, OBSCURITY, DIFFICULTY.

nonsense, *n.* ABSURDITY, senselessness, silliness, trash, foolishness. See UNMEANINGNESS.

nook, *n.* retreat, corner, cover, niche, recess. See ANGULARITY.

noon, *n.* noontime, midday, noonday, lunchtime. See CHRONOMETRY.

noose, *n.* hitch, catch; loop, halter, ring, lariat, lasso. See CIRCULARITY.

norm, *n.* normalcy; norma, model, standard, par, criterion, yardstick, rule of thumb; precept, canon, fashion. See CONFORMITY, MEASUREMENT.

normal, *adj.* ordinary, regular, average, usual, typical. See CONFORMITY, SANITY, INTRINSIC, MEAN, REGULARITY.

north, *adj.* northerly, northern, northward; arctic, polar. See DIRECTION.

nose, *n.* proboscis, snout, muzzle, beak; nasal *or* olfactory organ; nostrils. *Slang*, schnozzle. See CONVEXITY.

nosedive, *n.* plunge, DESCENT, fall; crash. See AVIATION.

nosegay, *n.* posy, bouquet, corsage. See ODOR.

nostalgia, *n.* homesickness; pathos, REGRET, wistfulness; nostomania.

nosy, *adj.* inquisitive, meddlesome, prying, snoopy. See CURIOSITY.

notable, *adj.* celebrated, noted, noteworthy, distinguished, renowned, famous, remarkable. See REPUTE, NOBILITY.

notarize, *v.t.* certify, attest, witness, stamp, validate. See RECORD.

notation, *n.* note; comment, annotation; entry. See WRITING, INDICATION, INTERPRETATION.

notch, *n.* nick, gut, gash, score; groove, rut, pit, pock; cleft, dent, dint, indentation; dimple; defile, pass, gap, opening, hole; serrature, tooth; crenel, scallop; embrasure, battlement, machicolation, castellation; tally, mark, DEGREE, calibration, step, peg. —*v.t.* nick, cut, gash, score, dent, indent, jag; scarify; crimp, scallop; crenelate; tally, calibrate, mark (in degrees), peg. See ANGULARITY, INDICATION, INTERVAL, FURROW.

note, *n.* letter, missive; acknowledgment, comment, reminder; observation, memo[randum], notation; explanation, remark, annotation; distinction, fame; tone, sound, pitch. See COMMUNICATION, ATTENTION, INDICATION, RECORD, REPUTE, MUSIC. —*v.t.* observe, notice, remark, attend, need, jot. See INTELLECT, MEMORY.

noted, *adj.* See NOTABLE.

noteworthy, *adj.* extraordinary, notable, remarkable, considerable, exceptional. See UNCONFORMITY, IMPORTANCE.

nothing, *n.* zero, cipher, nought, blank; nothingness; nonentity, bagatelle, trifle. *Slang*, zilch. See UNIMPORTANCE, INSUBSTANTIALITY, NONEXISTENCE.

notice, *n.* ATTENTION, observation, recognition, perception; circular, poster, bulletin; placard, announcement; WARNING, sign; consideration; review. See PUBLICATION, INFORMATION. —*v.t.* see, observe, perceive, regard, heed, detect, recognize, note. See VISION.

noticeable, *adj.* striking, conspicuous, perceptible, prominent, observable.

See VISIBILITY.

notify, *v.* inform, warn, apprise, advise, tell, acquaint. See INFORMATION, PUBLICATION.

notion, *n.* idea, THOUGHT, opinion; fancy, caprice, inclination; BELIEF, conception. See SUPPOSITION, CHANGEABLENESS.

notoriety, *n.* flagrancy, blatancy, notoriousness, DISREPUTE. See PUBLICATION.

notwithstanding, *adv.* nevertheless, although, however, yet. *—prep.* despite, even. See COMPENSATION.

nourish, *v.t.* nurture, sustain, feed, foster, support, maintain. See AID, FOOD, PROVISION.

novel, *n.* story, book, romance, epic. See DESCRIPTION, WRITING. *—adj.* new, unusual, different, remarkable, unique. See NEWNESS.

novelist, *n.* romancer, fictionist. See WRITING.

novelty, *n.* NEWNESS, originality, singularity, innovation, new departure, change, revolution; fad, fashion, *le dernier cri,* craze; marvel, freak, curiosity, neology, neoterism.

novice, *n.* beginner, student, amateur, probationer, neophyte, apprentice; tyro, greenhorn. See BEGINNING, LEARNING, PREPARATION.

now, *adv.* immediately, here, presently, today, yet. See PRESENT.

nowhere, *adv.* [in] no place, neither here nor there, absent. See ABSENCE.

noxious, *adj.* noisome, harmful, poisonous, injurious, deleterious, pernicious. See BADNESS.

nozzle, *n.* spout, outlet, vent, valve, faucet, nose, OPENING.

nuance, *n.* variation, modulation, shade, subtlety, nicety, fine point, distinction; suggestion, innuendo, hint. See DIFFERENCE.

nubile, *adj.* marriageable; pubescent, ripe, developed. See MARRIAGE.

nuclear, *adj.* atomic, thermonuclear. See POWER, MIDDLE.

nucleus, *n.* center, heart, core, kernel; basis, foundation. See MIDDLE, IMPORTANCE.

nude, *adj.* naked, stripped, bare, unclad, unclothed, exposed. *Colloq.*, raw. See DIVESTMENT.

nudge, *n.* push, poke, prod. *—v.t.* poke, prod, push, jog. See INDICATION, IMPULSE, MEMORY.

nugatory, *adj.* useless, ineffectual, worthless, futile; helpless. See USELESSNESS, IMPOTENCE.

nugget, *n.* lump, hunk; slug. See SIZE, MONEY.

nuisance, *n.* pest, annoyance, irritation, bore, bother. See EVIL.

NULLIFICATION

Nouns—nullification, abrogation, annulment, cancellation, revocation, repeal, rescission, defeasance, renege; dismissal, deposal, deposition, dethronement, establishment, disendowment, deconsecration; abolition, abolishment, dissolution; destruction; counterorder, countermand; *nolle prosequi;* thumbs down, veto. See NEGATION.

Verbs—**1,** nullify, abrogate, abjure, annul, cancel, destroy, abolish, revoke, repeal, reverse, retract, rescind, recall, overrule, override, set aside, dissolve, quash, invalidate, nol-pros, void, declare null and void, veto, disestablish, disendow, deconsecrate; delete, erase, cross [out], bleep *or* blip out; swallow *or* eat one's words, take back.

2, countermand, counterorder, set aside, do away with, throw overboard, throw to the dogs, scatter to the winds.

3, cast off, out, aside, away, *or* adrift, dismiss, discharge, discard; get rid of. *Colloq.*, fire. *Slang,* sack, bounce; send packing; give the gate *or* the boot *or* one's walking papers; give the pink slip.

4, depose, divest of office, throw down; cashier, displace, break, oust,

unseat, unsaddle, dethrone, unfrock, ungown, disbar, disbench; disinherit, disown, cut off.
Adjectives—[null and] void, invalid.

Antonyms, see AFFIRMATION, CELEBRATION.

---

nullity, *n.* nothingness, NONEXISTENCE.
numb, *adj.* unfeeling, deadened, frozen, benumbed; dazed, shocked; anesthetized, narcotized, drugged, paralyzed; dull, torpid, insensitive; desensitized; lifeless. —*v.t.* deaden, benumb, freeze; narcotize, drug, desensitize; stupefy, paralyze. See INSENSIBILITY, COLD.

NUMERATION

Nouns—**1,** numeration, numbering, counting, tally, enumeration, pagination, summation, reckoning, computation, calculation, cybernetics, MEASUREMENT; statistics, poll, census, roll call, recapitulation; recount.

2, mathematics; arithmetic, algebra, trigonometry, [differential *or* integral] calculus; addition, subtraction, multiplication, division; equation; [square, cube, *etc.*] root, power; exponent, index, prime; reduction, approximation, differentiation, integration; formula, function, series.

3, abacus, logometer, slide rule, table, Napier's rods, logarithm, log, antilogarithm; calculator, calculating machine, adder, adding machine, cash register; computer, electronic computer *or* brain, mainframe [computer], mini-, micro-, *or* personal computer, [micro]processor, punch-card *or* -tape reader. *Slang,* magic brain.

4, total, amount, QUANTITY; sum, difference, product, multiplier, multiplicand, coefficient, dividend, divisor, factor, quotient, subtrahend, fraction, mixed number, numerator, denominator, decimal, reciprocal; Arabic *or* Roman numbers *or* numerals; surd, imaginary number.

5, ratio, proportion, progression; arithmetic[al] *or* geometric[al] progression; percentage. See DEGREE.

6, a. UNITY; duality, dualism, biformity; triality, trinity; quaternity. **b.** duplication, duplicate; triplication, triplicate; trebleness, trine; quadruplication, quadruplicate, *etc.* **c.** bisection, bipartition, halving; trisection, tripartition; quadrisection, quadripartition, quartering, quarter; quinquesection; decimation.

7, a. number, symbol, numeral, figure, cipher, digit, integer, counter, round number; folio. **b.** one, single, unity, ace; two, deuce, couple, brace, pair, binomial, square; three, trey, triad, triplet, trio, leash, trinomial, third power, cube; four, tetrad, quartet, quaternion; five, quintet; six, sextet, half-a-dozen; seven, septet; eight, octet; nine, ennead; ten, decad[e], tithe; twelve, dozen; thirteen, baker's dozen; twenty, score; hundred, century, centenary; thousand, million, billion, trillion; zero (see INSUBSTANTIALITY).

8, mathematician, arithmetician, calculator, abacist, algebraist, statistician.

Verbs—**1,** number, count [off], tell [off], tally, enumerate, poll, count heads *or* noses, recapitulate; paginate, foliate; score, cipher, compute, calculate, figure, sum up, ring up, cast up, total, add, subtract, multiply, divide; round off.

2, check, prove, demonstrate, balance, audit, take stock (see ACCOUNTING); recount.

3, double, couple, pair [off *or* up], yoke, square; triple, treble, triplicate, cube; quadruplicate, *etc.*

4, bisect, halve, trisect, quarter, decimate.

Adjectives—**1,** numeral, numerical, arithmetic[al], geometric[al], analytic, algebraic, statistical, numerable, computable, divisible, reciprocal, whole, prime, fractional, decimal, proportional; Arabic, Roman; exponential, logarithmic, differential, integral, positive, negative; rational, irrational; radical, real, imaginary, impossible; approximate, round; exact; perfect.
2, one, first, annual, single, unique; two, second, double, duplicate, twain, dual, biannual, biennial, binary, binomial, twin, duplex; three, third, triple, treble, triform, trinary, trinal, trinomial, tertiary, trine, triplicate, threefold; four, fourth, quadruple, quadruplicate, quarter, quaternary, quaternal, quadratic; five, fifth, quintuple, quinary; sixth, sextuple; seventh, septuple. eight, octuple; tenth, decimal, tenfold; twelfth, dozenth, duodenary; hundredth, centennial, centenary, centuplicate; thousandth, millennial.
3, bisected, bipartite, bifid; trisected, tripartite, trifid; quartered, quadripartite; quinquepartite, quinquefid; octifid; tenth, decimal; twelfth, duodecimal; sixtieth, sexagesimal, sexagenary; hundredth, centesimal; thousandth, millesimal.
Adverbs—twice, double; thrice, trebly, triply, thirdly; fourthly; for one thing.
Prepositions—plus, minus, times.

Antonyms, see UNITY.

---

numerous, *adj.* many, myriad, multitudinous, plentiful, numberless, various, thick. See MULTITUDE.
numskull, *n.* numbskull, dolt, *Dummkopf. Slang,* meathead, bonehead. See IGNORANCE.
nun, *n.* sister, ecclesiastic, *religieuse.* See CLERGY.
nunnery, *n.* convent, cloister, cenacle, sisterhood, order. See TEMPLE.
nuptial, *adj.* connubial, bridal. —*n. (pl.)* MARRIAGE, wedding.
nurse, *n.* attendant, nursemaid. *Colloq.,* nanny. —*v.i.* foster, tend, serve, cherish; suckle, give suck; entertain, manage. See REMEDY.
nursery, *n.* nursery school, *crèche* (see SCHOOL); the cradle, infancy, babyhood; conservatory, green- *or* hothouse; hatchery, incubator; spawning ground. See AGRICULTURE.
nurture, *v.t.* sustain, support, feed, nourish; foster, cherish; educate, train, rear. See AID, PREPARATION, FOOD.
nut, *n.* kernel, stone, nutmeat; seed, core; *slang,* eccentric, crank. *Slang,* crackpot, kook. See FOOD, INSANITY.
nutritious, *adj.* nutritive, wholesome, digestible, nourishing. See FOOD, HEALTH.
nutshell, *n.* husk, hull, COVERING; synopsis, digest, minimum. See SHORTNESS.
nutty, *adj.* nutlike, meaty, rich, tasty; *slang,* crazy, insane. *Colloq.,* cracked. *Slang,* kooky, off one's nut, nuts. See INSANITY.
nuzzle, *v.* nose, muzzle; burrow, snuff, root, pry; suckle; cuddle, nestle, press, snuggle. See ENDEARMENT.
nymph, *n.* dryad, naiad, houri, undine. See MYTHICAL DEITIES.

O

oaf, *n.* lout, simpleton, dullard, dunce, blockhead, idiot. *Slang,* dope, jerk. See IGNORANCE.
oar, *n.* paddle, blade, sweep, scull, pole. See SHIP. —*v.* row, paddle, propel, stroke; scull. See NAVIGATION.
oarsman, *n.* rower, paddler, *etc.;* crewman, bowman, helmsman; gondolier; thalamite, zygite, thranite. See NAVIGATION.
oasis, *n.* waterhole, wallow; refuge, shelter. See SAFETY, RELIEF.
oath, *n.* curse, epithet, expletive, IMPRECATION, profanity; pledge, bond. See AFFIRMATION.
obdurate, *adj.* flinty, adamant, unyielding, inflexible; stubborn, adamantine, hardened, unshakable, unfeeling, hardhearted; firm. See IMPENITENCE, OBSTINACY.

OBEDIENCE

Nouns—**1,** obedience, compliance; SUBMISSION, nonresistance; malleability, tractability, ductility; acquiescence, observance; obsequiousness, SERVILITY. See SUBJECTION.

2, allegiance, loyalty, fealty, homage, deference, obeisance, devotion. See RESPECT.

Verbs—obey, comply, submit; observe, respect, abide by, meet, fulfill, carry out, make good; perform, satisfy, discharge (see COMPLETION); kneel *or* bow to, kowtow, salaam, make an obeisance; be at the beck and call of, do one's bidding, do what one is told, heel, walk the chalk [line], toe the line *or* mark; jump through a hoop; serve (see SERVANT).

Adjectives—obedient, observant, acquiescent, dutiful, complying, compliant, loyal, faithful, devoted; at one's command, at one's orders, at one's [beck and] call; tame[d], under control, in line; restrainable; resigned, passive; tractable, docile, submissive; henpecked; pliable, pliant, unresisting, ductile.

Adverbs—obediently, *etc.;* in compliance with, in obedience to; as you please, if you please; to heel.

Antonyms, see DISOBEDIENCE.

---

obeisance, *n.* homage, deference, OBEDIENCE; bow, salaam, kowtow, curtsy, genuflection; prostration. See COURTESY, SUBMISSION.

obelisk, *n.* monolith, needle, shaft; dagger, obelus. See HEIGHT, RECORD, INDICATION.

obese, *n.* fat, overweight, stout, plump, fleshy, bulky; corpulent, ponderous; adipose. See EXPANSION, ROTUNDITY.

obey, *v.* See OBEDIENCE.

obituary, *n.* obit, necrology; obsequies, exequy; eulogy. See DEATH.

object, *n.* thing, item; goal, aim, purpose, objective. See SUBSTANCE, INTENTION. —*v.i.* disapprove, demur, challenge, protest, resist, kick. See DISAPPROBATION, DISSENT, UNITY.

objection, *n.* remonstrance, protest; drawback, criticism; barrier, obstacle; exception, protestation. See DISAPPROBATION, HINDRANCE, DISSENT.

objectionable, *adj.* censurable, culpable; unpleasant, undesirable, obnoxious, offensive, harmful. See DISAPPROBATION.

objective, *adj.* unemotional, unprejudiced, unbiased, impersonal. See EXTRINSIC. —*n.* object, goal, aim, ambition. See INTENTION.

oblation, *n.* offering, sacrifice, corban; WORSHIP; expiation.

obligation, *n.* DUTY, PROMISE; DEBT; agreement, bond, incumbency, responsibility, liability, indebtedness; contract, mortgage. See COMPULSION; NECESSITY.

oblige, *v.* compel, force, constrain, bind, impel; accommodate, favor, assist, gratify, please. See AID, COMPULSION.

obliging, *adj.* accommodating, helpful, considerate. See COURTESY.

OBLIQUITY

Nouns—**1,** obliquity, obliqueness, DEVIATION, divergence; inclination, slope, slant; crookedness; leaning; bevel, tilt; bias, list, swag, cant, twist, DISTORTION; bend (see CURVATURE); ANGULARITY; tower of Pisa; indirectness (see CIRCUITY).

2, acclivity, rise, ASCENT, gradient, upgrade, rising ground, hill, bank;

ramp, incline, grade; steepness, diagonality; cliff, precipice (see VERTICAL); escarpment, scarp; declivity, downgrade, downhill, dip, fall, DESCENT.

3, clinometer; [co]sine, [co]tangent; angle, hypotenuse; diagonal; zigzag; talus.

Verbs—diverge, deviate; slope, slant, lean, incline, shelve, stoop; rise, ascend; decline, descend; bend, heel, careen, sag, cant, sidle; sway, bias; crook; tilt; distort.

Adjectives—**1,** oblique, inclined; sloping, tilted, recumbent, clinal, askew, aslant, indirect, wry, awry, crooked; knockkneed, distorted (see DISTORTION); beveled, out of the perpendicular; diagonal; transverse, CROSSING; curved (see CURVATURE).

2, uphill, rising, ascending, acclivitous; downhill, falling, descending; declining, anticlinal; steep, sheer, abrupt, precipitous, breakneck; not straight, not true.

Adverbs—obliquely, diagonally; on one side; askew, askant, askance, edgewise; out of plumb; at an angle; sidelong, sideways; slopewise, slantwise; by a side wind; out of kilter.

Antonyms, see DIRECTION, STRAIGHTNESS.

---

obliterate, *v.t.* efface, erase, expunge, cancel; rub, sponge, *or* scratch out, blot out, take out; dele, delete, strike out, wipe out, wash out; wipe away; deface, leave no trace. See DESTRUCTION, OBLIVION, NONEXISTENCE.

OBLIVION

Nouns—oblivion, obliviousness, forgetfulness, obliteration (of the past); INSENSIBILITY; failure, loss, *or* lapse of memory, amnesia; waters of Lethe *or* oblivion, nepenthe; limbo. See INATTENTION, NONEXISTENCE.

Verbs—**1,** forget, be forgetful, have on the tip of one's tongue; come in at one ear and go out the other; misremember; forget oneself; unlearn, efface, obliterate; think no more of; drown one's sorrows *or* troubles; get over, put behind one. *Colloq.,* file and forget, kiss *or* laugh off; draw a blank; blow *or* fluff one's lines.

2, fall, sink, *or* fade into oblivion; let the dead bury the dead; let bygones be bygones (see FORGIVENESS); slip *or* escape the memory; fade; lose, lose sight of.

Adjectives—oblivious, forgetful, mindless, nepenthean, Lethean; forgotten, unremembered, past recollection, bygone, buried *or* sunk in oblivion; clean forgotten; gone out of one's head.

Adverbs—in limbo; out of sight, out of mind.

Antonyms, see MEMORY.

---

oblong, *adj.* elongate, rectangular; elliptical, oval. See LENGTH.

obloquy, *n.* traduction, slander, calumny, denunciation, DETRACTION; odium, shame, disgrace, opprobrium, humiliation. DISREPUTE, ignominy.

obnoxious, *adj.* repulsive, loathsome, hateful, offensive, odious. See HATE, BADNESS, VULGARITY.

oboe, *n.* hautboy; English horn, shawm, schalmei, musette, oboe d'amore, heckelphone. See MUSIC.

obscene, *adj.* foul, lewd, dirty, indecent, coarse, smutty. See IMPURITY, UNCLEANNESS, VULGARITY.

OBSCURITY

Nouns—**1,** obscurity, DIMNESS, DARKNESS, obscuration, obfuscation, opacity; shade, cloud, gloom, duskiness, *etc.* See CONCEALMENT, INVISIBILITY, CLOUDINESS.

2, unclearness, indefiniteness, vagueness; UNINTELLIGIBILITY; ambiguity; intricacy, involution, CONVOLUTION; abstruseness, mystery.

3, lowliness, inconspicuousness; SECLUSION, privacy.

Verbs—obscure, shade, cloud, darken, conceal, hide; dim, bedim, becloud, befog, confuse, bewilder, baffle, befuddle, fluster, mystify, perplex, obfuscate. *Slang*, befuzz.

Adjectives—**1,** obscure, dim, unlighted, unilluminated, rayless, dusky, dark, darksome, muddy, muzzy; shadowy, murky, hazy, misty, seen through a mist, foggy, smoky, shaded, clouded, nebulous; gloomy, somber, opaque, indistinct, undiscernible, bleary; invisible.

2, unclear, indefinite, vague, undecided; unintelligible, ambiguous, enigmatical, equivocal, indefinable, doubtful, difficult; involved, confused, complex, intricate, abstruse, transcendental, indeterminate, inexact, inaccurate; mystic[al], mysterious, cabalistic, cryptic, recondite, hidden, concealed, blind.

3, nameless, unknown, unnoticed, unnoted, inconspicuous; undistinguished, uncelebrated, unhonored, renownless, inglorious; secluded, retired, remote, private.

Antonyms, see LIGHT, CERTAINTY, TRANSPARENCY.

---

obsequies, *n.pl.* funeral, burial. See INTERMENT.

obsequious, *adj.* abject, fawning, sycophantic, cringing, servile, truckling, compliant. See SERVILITY, RESPECT.

observance, *n.* performance, compliance, adhesion, OBEDIENCE; fulfillment, satisfaction, discharge; acquittance, acquittal; acknowledgment; fidelity; orthodoxy, ceremony, RITE, punctilio, protocol. See ATTENTION, VISION, HABIT.

observant, *adj.* attentive, mindful; vigilant. See ATTENTION, CARE.

observation, *n.* notice, perception, regard; comment, consideration, remark. See AFFIRMATION, ATTENTION, VISION.

observe, *v.* see (see VISION); comply with, respect, acknowledge, abide by; obey, cling to, adhere to, be faithful to, meet, fulfill; carry out, carry into execution, execute, perform, keep, satisfy, discharge, do one's duty; perform, fulfill, *or* discharge an obligation; acquit oneself; perform an office; keep one's word *or* promise; keep faith with; officiate. See CARE, ATTENTION.

obsess, *v.t.* haunt, beset, besiege. See INSANITY, SORCERY.

obsession, *n.* preoccupation, fixation, mania, phobia, compulsion, *idée fixe*. *Colloq.*, bee in one's bonnet. *Slang,* hang up. See INSANITY, SORCERY.

obsolescence, *n.* DISUSE, disappearance; antiquity. See OLDNESS.

obsolete, *adj.* past, extinct, outworn, disused, discarded, antiquated, dead, out of date. See OLDNESS, DISUSE.

obstacle, *n.* HINDRANCE, difficulty, barrier, obstruction, snag, impediment, barrage, baffle.

OBSTINACY

Nouns—**1,** obstinacy, stubbornness, TENACITY, doggedness; obduracy, obduration, insistence, RESOLUTION; intransigency, immovability, inflexibility, hardness, willpower; self-will, will of iron, will *or* mind of one's own; contumacy, pigheadedness, perversity, contrariness, recalcitrance, indocility. *Colloq.*, cussedness. See CERTAINTY, UNWILLINGNESS, RESISTANCE, DISOBEDIENCE, HETERODOXY.

2, pighead, stickler, mule, diehard, intransigent, holdout. *Colloq.*, bitter-ender, stand-patter, hard nut to crack, tough customer.

Verbs—be obstinate, stickle, insist, persist, persevere; fly in the face of facts, be wedded to an opinion, hug a belief; have one's own way *or* will; have the last word, die hard, fight to the last ditch, not yield an inch, stand firm. *Colloq.*, stand pat, fight city hall.

Adjectives—**1,** obstinate, stubborn, tenacious, persevering, pertinacious, persistent, dogged; obdurate, indurate, insistent, resolute, firm, sturdy, immovable, inflexible, unmoving, unyielding, unbending, not to be moved; rigid, set, settled, fixed, hard; unchangeable, intransigent, inexorable, determined; bullheaded, pigheaded, headstrong, *entêté,* mulish, stubborn as a mule, tough. *Colloq.*, bitter-end, diehard.

2, self-willed, willful, perverse, heady, headstrong, refractory, unruly, intractable, incorrigible, contumacious, difficult, balky, contrary, froward, cantankerous, recalcitrant; stiff-necked *or* -backed, hidebound; deaf to advice, impervious to reason; out of hand. *Colloq.*, cussed.

Antonyms, see UNCERTAINTY, CHANGEABLENESS.

---

obstreperous, *adj.* noisy, clamorous, vociferous; recalcitrant, unruly, riotous. See VIOLENCE, DISOBEDIENCE.

obstruct, *v.t.* block, stop, impede, choke, retard, clog; occlude, shut; dam, foul; barricade, blockade; delay; check, hedge, overgrow; encumber. See HINDRANCE, CLOSURE.

obtain, *v.t.* acquire, set; prevail. See EXISTENCE, ACQUISITION.

obtrude, *v.* intrude, thrust, interfere. See BETWEEN.

obtuse, *adj.* stupid, dull; blunt. See IGNORANCE, INSENSIBILITY, BLUNTNESS.

obviate, *v.t.* preclude, debar. See HINDRANCE.

obvious, *adj.* manifest, patent, clear, evident, plain; undisguised, unconcealed. See VISIBILITY, SHALLOWNESS.

OCCASION

Nouns—occasion, opportunity, opening, room; CIRCUMSTANCE, event, opportuneness; crisis, turn, juncture, psychological moment, conjuncture; turning point; given time; nick of time; chance of a lifetime, golden opportunity; clear field; spare time, leisure. *Colloq.*, new deal. See CAUSE.

Verbs—seize *or* take advantage of an opportunity; suit the occasion; strike while the iron is hot, make hay while the sun shines, take time by the forelock; take the bull by the horns. *Colloq.*, cash in on. *Slang,* get the jump on, jump the gun.

Adjectives—opportune, seasonable; providential, lucky, fortunate, happy, favorable, propitious, auspicious, critical; timely, well-timed; apropos, suitable (see AGREEMENT).

Adverbs—opportunely, *etc.;* in due time, course, *or* season, in proper time; for the nonce; in the nick of time, in the fullness of time; just in time, at the eleventh hour; now or never; by the way, by the by; *en passant, à propos;*

parenthetically, while on the subject; *ex tempore;* on the spur of the moment; on the spot (see EARLINESS); when the coast is clear.

Antonyms, see INEXPEDIENCE.

---

occasional, *adj.* incidental, irregular, casual. See RARITY, EXPEDIENCE, CIRCUMSTANCE.

occult, *adj.* mystic, mysterious, supernatural, SECRET, hidden. See SORCERY.

occupant, *n.* tenant, lodger, transient, occupier, INHABITANT, roomer. See POSSESSION.

occupation, *n.* tenure, occupancy, holding, tenancy, POSSESSION, habitation; work, trade, BUSINESS, employment, calling, profession, pursuit.

occupy, *v.t.* hold, inhabit, keep, fill, tenant, have; take, beset, garrison; interest, engage, engross, busy, employ. See ABODE, ATTENTION, BUSINESS, PRESENCE.

OCCURRENCE

Nouns—**1,** occurrence, eventuality, event, incident, affair, episode, milestone, transaction, proceeding, business, concern, CIRCUMSTANCE, particular; fact, matter of fact, phenomenon; happenstance, goings-on; adventure, happening; accident (see CHANCE), casualty.

2, the world, life, things, doings, affairs; things in general, affairs in general, the times, state of affairs, order of the day; course, tide, stream, current, run *or* march of events; ups and downs of life.

Verbs—**1,** occur, happen, take place, be; concur, accompany, coincide (see SYNCHRONISM); come, become of, come off, come true, come about, come into EXISTENCE, come into view, come to mind, come forth, come to pass, come on, pass; appear (see APPEARANCE), offer *or* present itself, be met with, be found, come one's way, meet the eye; fall, fall *or* turn out; run, be afoot; fall in, befall, betide, bechance; prove, supervene, eventuate, transpire, hap; draw on, turn up, crop up, spring up; issue, ensue, result (see EFFECT); arrive, arise, rise, start, hold, take its course. *Colloq.*, come off, go [off].

2, meet with, experience; fall to the lot of; be one's chance, fortune, *or* lot; find, encounter, undergo; pass *or* go through.

Adjectives—occurring, happening, going on, under way, current, prevailing; in the wind, afloat, on foot, at issue, in question; incidental, eventful, episodic, stirring, bustling, full of incident.

Adverbs—eventually, in the event of, in case; in the [natural] course of things; as things go, as times go, as the world goes, as the tail wags; as the tree falls, as the cat jumps; as it may turn out, as it may happen.

Antonyms, see INACTIVITY.

---

ocean, *n.* sea (see WATER).

ocular, *adj.* optic, visual; retinal, conjunctival; perceptible, visible. See VISION.

odd, *adj.* strange, unusual, unnatural; curious, quaint, queer, bizarre, droll; singular, single; casual, occasional; unmatched, unpaired, lone; extra, left. See REMAINDER, UNCONFORMITY.

oddity, *n.* curiosity, freak; singularity, strangeness, peculiarity; quaintness, eccentricity, oddness; crank, eccentric. See INSANITY, UNCONFORMITY.

odds, *n.* DIFFERENCE, probability,

advantage; disparity. See CHANCE, INEQUALITY.

ode, *n.* poem, lyric; psalm, canticle, hymn; monody. See POETRY.

odious, *adj.* disgusting, repugnant, detestable, offensive, loathsome, hateful. See HATE.

ODOR

Nouns—**1,** odor, odorousness, smell, scent, effluvium; emanation, exhalation; fume, essence, trail, redolence; PUNGENCY; fragrance, aroma, perfume, bouquet; sense of smell, olfaction. See MALODOROUSNESS.

2, incense; frankincense, myrrh; pastille; perfumes of Arabia; attar; bergamot, balm, civet, musk, potpourri; nosegay; scent, scentbag; sachet, smelling salts, vinaigrette; [eau de] Cologne.

Verbs—**1,** be fragrant, have an odor *or* perfume, smell sweet; smell of, exhale; give out a smell; scent, perfume, embalm.

2, smell, scent; snuff [up]; sniff; nose, inhale; get wind of.

Adjectives—odorous, odoriferous; [strong-]smelling; strong-scented; redolent, aromatic, fragrant, pungent, spicy, balmy, sweet-smelling *or* -scented, perfumed, fragrant as a rose; muscadine, ambrosial; reeking (see MALODOROUSNESS); olfactory.

Antonyms, see ODORLESSNESS, MALODOROUSNESS.

ODORLESSNESS

Nouns—**1,** odorlessness, inodorousness, scentlessness; deodorization, disinfection, purification, fumigation.

2, deodorizer, [stick, roll-on, *or* spray] deodorant, disinfectant; antiperspirant; fumigant; chlorophyll; mouth freshener, mouthwash.

Verbs—deodorize, fumigate, air, ventilate.

Adjectives—odorless, inodorous, scentless, unscented; deodorized.

Antonyms, see ODOR, MALODOROUSNESS.

odyssey, *n.* wandering, TRAVEL, journey; quest, pilgrimage.

offal, *n.* garbage, rubbish, refuse, waste; ordure, filth, excrement. See EXCRETION, UNCLEANNESS.

offbeat, *adj.* unfamiliar, unconventional, unorthodox, weird, queer. *Slang,* wacky, kooky. See UNCONFORMITY.

off-color, *adj., colloq.,* improper, indelicate; risqué, racy, dirty. See IMPURITY.

offend, *v.* break the law, err, WRONG, sin, trespass; give offense, displease, upset, vex, provoke, hurt; disgust; affront, spite, insult, hurt one's feelings. *Colloq.,* aggravate, rub the wrong way. See ILLEGALITY, PAIN, RESENTMENT, IMPROBITY.

offender, *n.* lawbreaker, culprit. See GUILT, ILLEGALITY.

offense, *n.* insult, affront, DISCOURTESY; aggression, ATTACK; transgression, fault, crime, sin, WRONG. See GUILT, ILLEGALITY.

OFFER

Nouns—**1,** offer, proffer, presentation, tender, bid, overture, advance; ultimatum, last word, final offer; proposal, proposition, motion, invitation; asking price; candidature, candidacy; offering (see GIVING). *Slang,* come-on. See WILL, PURCHASE, REQUEST.

2, bidder; by-bidder, Peter Funk. *Slang,* come-on man, capper.

Verbs—**1,** offer, proffer, present, tender, extend, hold forth, bid, make an offer; suggest, propose, prefer, move, make a motion; advance, make advances; serve up; invite, hold out, submit, exhibit, put forward, put up; place in one's way *or* at one's disposal, lay at one's feet; offer for SALE, hawk about; press, urge upon; furnish, propound, show, give.

2, offer *or* present oneself, volunteer, come forward, be a candidate, throw one's hat in the ring; stand for, seek; be at one's service; bribe (see PAYMENT).

Adjectives—offering, offered; on the market, for sale, to let, for hire.

Antonyms, see REQUEST.

---

offhand, *adv.* casually, impromptu, extemporaneously; abruptly, carelessly. *—adj.* casual, abrupt, extemporaneous, careless; unpremeditated, unplanned, impromptu. See UNPREPAREDNESS.

office, *n.* headquarters, department, bureau, room, branch; position, status, rank, function; post, job, duty, service. See AGENCY, BUSINESS, RITE.

officer, *n.* policeman; functionary, official, bureaucrat; president, vice-president, secretary, treasurer; registrar; mayor, governor. See DIRECTOR, AUTHORITY.

official, *n.* officer, functionary, dignitary. *—adj.* authoritative, functional, authentic, authorized; formal. See LEGALITY, AUTHORITY.

officiate, *v.* preside, serve, supervise, direct, function. See BUSINESS, RITE.

officious, *adj.* interfering, meddlesome, obtrusive, pushy, presumptuous; bossy. See BETWEEN, AUTHORITY, SEVERITY.

offset, *v.t.* neutralize, balance, counteract, cancel [out], counterbalance, counterpoise. See COMPENSATION.

offshoot, *n.* ramification, incidental, result; branch, shoot, sprout; scion. See EFFECT.

offspring, *n.* children (see POSTERITY); EFFECT.

off-the-record, *adj.* unofficial, informal. See UNCONFORMITY.

often, *adv.* ofttime[s], oftentime[s], frequently, repeatedly, recurrently, oft. See FREQUENCY.

ogre, *n.* giant[ess], maneater, cannibal; monster, beast, DEMON, fiend; cyclops; ogress, orgillon; bogy, bugbear, golliwog. See EVILDOER, FEAR.

OIL

Nouns—**1,** oil, fat, lipid, grease, wax; mineral, animal, *or* vegetable oil, ethereal, volatile, *or* essential oil; lubricant, lubricator; ointment, demulcent, liniment, lotion, embrocation, vaseline (*T.N.*), glycerine, pomade, brilliantine, unguent, emollient; suntan *or* tanning lotion *or* oil, face *or* cold cream, *etc.;* lard, tallow, beeswax, lanolin, spermaceti, paraffin; black gold, petroleum, gasoline, gas-oil, diesel oil, naphtha, benzine, kerosene (see FUEL); benzene, toluene. *Colloq.,* gas.

2, lubrication, oiling, oiliness; unction, unctuosity, lubricity; lubritorium, grease rack *or* pit. *Slang,* grease *or* lube job.

3, see FLATTERY, SMOOTHNESS, SERVILITY.

Verbs—oil, lubricant, grease; anoint; lather, soap, wax, slick [up], smear, smooth, butter, lard, make slippery.

Adjectives—oily, greasy, slippery, lubricous, slick, smooth, lubricant, emollient; fat[ty], adipose, gummy, mucous, slimy, soapy, oleose, sebaceous, oleaginous.

Antonyms, see DRYNESS.

ointment, *n.* unguent, balm, pomade, salve, cream. See REMEDY, OIL.

old-fashioned, *adj.* out-of-date, dated, out of style. See OLDNESS.

OLDNESS

Nouns—**1,** oldness, AGE, antiquity; maturity; decline, decay.
2, archaism, obsolescence; relic [of the past], missing link; antiquities, fossils; antiquarianism; antiquary (see PAST). *Colloq.*, backnumber, has-been.
3, tradition, prescription, custom, immemorial usage, common law (see HABIT, RULE).

Verbs—be old, have had *or* seen its day, have seen better days; become old, AGE, fade, obsolesce, whiten, turn gray *or* white; date.

Adjectives—**1,** old, older, oldest, eldest, ancient, antique; of long standing, time-honored, venerable.
2, prime; primitive, primeval, primordial, primordinate; medieval, olden, of old; aboriginal (see BEGINNING); diluvian, antediluvian; prehistoric, patriarchal, preadamite; fossil, paleozoic, preglacial, antemundane.
3, archaic, classic, medieval, pre-Raphaelite; immemorial, traditional, prescriptive, customary; inveterate, rooted; antiquated, obsolete, of other times, of the old school, out-of-date, out of fashion *or* style; stale, outmoded, old-fashioned, old-style, dated, superannuated, behind the times; exploded; gone out *or* by; passé, run out; timeworn; crumbling (see DETERIORATION); extinct; hand-me-down, secondhand, discarded, castoff; old as the hills, Methuselah, *or* history. *Colloq.*, old-fangled, rinky-dink, old hat.

Antonyms, see NEWNESS.

Old Testament, *n.* See SACRED WRITINGS.

old-timer, *n., colloq.,* veteran, old hand *or* soldier, war horse, oldster. See AGE.

oligarchy, *n.* clique, junta; aristocracy, autocracy. See AUTHORITY.

omen, *n.* WARNING, foreboding; portent, PREDICTION; presage, THREAT.

ominous, *adj.* inauspicious, bodeful, fateful. See WARNING, PREDICTION, THREAT.

omission, *n.* EXCLUSION, exception, elimination, cut; failure, NEGLECT, dereliction; apostrophe, ellipsis; deficit, shortage; evasion. See GUILT.

omit, *v.t.* NEGLECT, skip, spare, overlook; delete, remove, reject; evade, except, exclude, miss, drop; pass, forget.

omnibus, *n.* bus; collection, compilation; reader, portable. See VEHICLE, PUBLICATION. —*adj.* inclusive, catchall, comprehensive, all-embracing, extensive. See INCLUSION.

omnipotent, *adj.* all-powerful, almighty. See DEITY, POWER.

omniscient, *adj.* all-seeing, all-knowing. See DEITY, KNOWLEDGE.

omnivorous, *adj.* devouring, all-consuming, gluttonous. See FOOD, GLUTTONY, DESIRE.

on, *adv.* forward, onward, ahead. See PROGRESSION. —*prep.* upon, at; near; *colloq.,* at one's expense. See RELATION, LOCATION, CONTACT, HEIGHT, COVERING.

once, *adv.* formerly, previously, latterly. See TIME, PAST. —*conj.* as soon as, whenever. See TIME.

once-over, *n., slang,* glance, look, scrutiny, survey; run-through; the eye, sizing-up. *Slang,* double-O. See VISION, INQUIRY.

oncoming, *adj.* impending, menacing. See APPROACH, NEARNESS.

one, *adj.* individual, sole, only, solitary, single. See NUMERATION.

onerous, *adj.* difficult, troublesome, burdensome, wearing, oppressive. See DIFFICULTY.

onesided, *adj.* unfair, biased, partial,

prejudiced; unbalanced, lopsided, asymmetric, awry; unilateral. See DISTORTION, MISJUDGMENT, SIDE.

onlooker, *n*. spectator, observer, watcher, viewer, witness, bystander; nonparticipant. See PRESENCE, VISION.

only, *adv*. solely, singly, exclusively, merely, but. *—adj*. sole, solitary, apart, alone, unique. See UNITY, SIMPLENESS, LITTLENESS.

onset, *n*. ATTACK, onslaught; opening, BEGINNING, outbreak.

onslaught, *n*. onset, ATTACK, charge, assault, offensive, thrust, drive; blame, censure, accusation, DETRACTION.

onus, *n*. burden, charge. See DUTY, COMPULSION, HINDRANCE.

onward, *adv*. forward, ahead. See PROGRESSION.

ooze, *v*. seep, leak, filter; drip, percolate. See EGRESS.

opacity, *n*. opaqueness, nontransparency, DIMNESS, filminess, CLOUDINESS; UNINTELLIGIBILITY, obtuseness, OBSCURITY.

OPENING

Nouns—**1,** opening, hole, foramen; aperture, yawning, oscitancy, dehiscence; chasm (see INTERVAL); breach.

2, puncture, perforation, scuttle; pinhole, keyhole, loophole, porthole, peephole, pigeonhole; eye, eyelet, slot, oriel; porousness, porosity.

3, outlet, EGRESS; inlet, INGRESS; port; vent, vomitory; embouchure; crater, orifice, mouth, sucker, muzzle, throat, gullet; estuary; pore; nozzle, tap, spigot; bore, caliber.

4, door, doorway, entrance, entry, portal, porch, gate, astiary, postern, wicket, trapdoor, hatch; arcade; gateway, hatchway, gangway; embrasure, window, casement, light; dormer; lantern; skylight, fanlight; lattice, louver.

5, sieve, screen, filter, colander; honeycomb; notch, cleft, embrasure.

6, opener, key, skeleton key, passkey, master key; passe-partout; latch; passport, password, pass (see INDICATION); can opener; punch, gouge; piercer, borer, augur, gimlet, stylet, drill, awl, bradawl; corkscrew; dibble; trocar, trepan, probe; bodkin, needle, stiletto; reamer; warder; lancet; spear.

7, see LIABILITY.

Verbs—**1,** open, gape, gap, yawn, bilge; fly *or* hand open; ope (*poet.*); unfurl, unroll; dehisce.

2, perforate, pierce, run through, tap, bore, drill; mine; tunnel; transfix; enfilade, impale, spike, spear, gore, spit, stab, pink, puncture, lance, stick, prick, riddle, punch; stave in; cut a passage through, make way *or* room for, open up *or* out; cut, expose, lay *or* break open, breach, broach.

Adjectives—open, perforate[d], wide open, ajar, agape; unclosed, unstopped; ope (*poet.*), oscitant, gaping, yawning, cavernous; patent; tubular, cannular, fistulous; pervious, permeable; foraminous; vesticular, vascular, porous, follicular, honeycombed; notched, nicked, crenate; infundibular, riddled; tubulous, tubulated; opening; aperient.

Antonyms, see CLOSURE.

---

open-minded, *adj*. broad-minded, impartial, unbiased; candid, receptive, tolerant, understanding, worldly. See LIBERALITY.

opera, *n*. grand opera (see MUSIC); libretto. See DRAMA.

operate, *v*. conduct, manage, direct, go, run, work, function, act. See ACTION, AGENCY.

operative, *adj*. effective, operating, acting, working, functioning, effectual. See AGENCY. *—n*. workman; detective, spy. See INQUIRY, CONCEALMENT.

operator, *n.* worker, handler; speculator. See COMMUNICATION, AGENCY, EXERTION.

operetta, *n.* musical comedy (see MUSIC).

opiate, *n.* narcotic, palliative, drug, sedative, tranquilizer, analgesic. See INSENSIBILITY, REMEDY, HABIT.

opinion, *n.* idea, thought, BELIEF, conviction; theory, view, JUDGMENT; notion, mind, tenet, dogma; verdict; speculation; public opinion, poll, survey.

opinionated, *adj.* convinced; unconvincible, bigoted, dogmatic, prejudiced, hidebound, positive. See MISJUDGMENT.

opium, *n.* papavarine. *Colloq.*, poppy, hops, mud, the pipe. See REMEDY, HABIT.

opponent, *n.* See OPPOSITION.

opportune, *adj.* fortuitous, timely, seasonable, felicitous, suitable, apt, apropos. See OCCASION, EXPEDIENCE.

opportunism, *n.* See EXPEDIENCE.

opportunity, *n.* opening; chance, OCCASION; space, scope, place; leisure. See EXPEDIENCE.

oppose, *v.t.* contrast, confront; combat, counter, resist, hinder; contradict, refute, cross; repel, withstand; obstruct; contravene. See OPPOSITION, CONFUTATION, NEGATION, RESISTANCE.

OPPOSITION

Nouns—**1,** opposition, antagonism, antipathy; enmity, HATE; repugnance, oppugnancy, oppugnation, impugnation; contravention, contradiction; counteraction; counterplot; confrontation, showdown, face-off; crossfire, undercurrent, riptide, undertow, headwind; race; RESISTANCE; HINDRANCE; contrariness, DEFIANCE. See DISSENT.

2, opposition, contraposition, polarity; INVERSION; opposite side, reverse, inverse, converse; counterpart; antipodes, opposite poles, north and south, east and west, heads or tails, anode and cathode, feast or famine.

3, insurrection, rebellion, riot, REVOLUTION; strike, lockout, walkout; boycott.

4, enemy, foe, rival, opponent, adversary, antagonist, foeman; assailant; archenemy, nemesis; foil; disputant, competitor. See CONTENTION.

Verbs—**1,** oppose, counteract, run counter to, withstand, resist, counter, restrain, hinder (see HINDRANCE); antagonize, oppugn, fly in the face *or* teeth of, kick against, fall foul of; set *or* pit against; defy, face, confront, cope with; make a stand [against]; protest against, vote against, raise one's voice against; disfavor, turn one's back upon; set at naught, slap in the face, slam the door in one's face; freeze out; be *or* play at cross purposes; thwart, foil; play off.

2, stem, breast, encounter; stem *or* breast the tide, current, *or* flood, swim against the current *or* stream; beat up against; grapple with, contend (see CONTENTION); do battle (see WARFARE); contradict, contravene; belie; run *or* beat against; militate against; come in conflict with; emulate, compete, rival, vie with; side against.

3, be opposite, oppose, juxtapose, contrapose; subtend.

Adjectives—**1,** opposing, opposed; adverse, antagonistic; contrary; at variance (see DISAGREEMENT); at issue, at war with; unfavorable, unfriendly; hostile, averse, inimical, cross, unpropitious; up in arms; resistant; competitive, emulous.

2, opposite, reverse, inverse; head-on; antipodal; fronting, facing, diametrically opposite.

Adverbs—contrarily, conversely; to *or* on the contrary, then again; vice versa; at cross purposes; against the grain, stream, wind, tide, *or* current; with a head wind, in spite of, in despite of, in defiance of; in the way, teeth, *or* face of; across; athwart.

Prepositions—over, against; over *or* up against; face to face, *vis-à-vis;* counter to, in conflict with; *versus, contra.*

Antonyms, see COOPERATION, SIDE, FRIEND.

---

oppress, *v.t.* persecute, burden, crush, afflict, grieve, load, depress; overbear, compress, overtax, overburden; tyrannize. See MALEVOLENCE, BADNESS, SEVERITY, SUBJECTION, WRONG.

oppressive, *adj.* tyrannical, cruel, burdensome, onerous, grievous. See SEVERITY, BADNESS.

oppressor, *n.* persecutor, bully, boss, slave driver, Simon Legree, master; tyrant, martinet, dictator. See SEVERITY.

opprobrious, *adj.* abusive, insulting, offensive, slanderous, derogatory, contemptuous, malicious. See DISREPUTE, DETRACTION.

opt, *v.i.* decide; approve (of), vote for, elect, choose, select, pick, favor. See CHOICE.

OPTICAL INSTRUMENTS

Nouns—**1,** optical instruments, lens; spectacles, glasses, bifocals, *pince-nez,* eyeglass, monocle, lorgnette, goggles; Polaroid lenses, [hard *or* soft] contact lenses; sunglasses; spyglass, magnifying glass; opera glass, fieldglass, binoculars; glass eye; telescope, periscope, spectroscope, microscope; optics, optometry. *Slang,* specs, cheaters.

2, mirror, looking glass, pier glass, cheval glass; reflection.

3, camera, camera lucida, camera obscura; motion-picture camera; kinescope, television camera; stereoscope, stereopticon, viewer, magic lantern, kaleidoscope; projector.

4, optometrist; lens grinder; oculist, optician; microscopist, spectroscopist.

5, electric eye, photoelectric cell.

Adjectives—optic[al], optometrical; microscopic, telescopic, stereoscopic, three-dimensional, 3-D; [be]spectacled, monocled.

---

optimal, *adj.* optimum, prime, best. See GOODNESS.

optimism, *n.* hopefulness, HOPE, cheerfulness, enthusiasm; confidence, assurance.

option, *n.* CHOICE, preference, discretion, alternative; privilege, right; first call, choice, *or* say; put, call. See RIGHTNESS.

optional, *adj.* discretionary, voluntary, elective, nonobligatory. See CHOICE.

opulent, *adj.* wealthy; abundant. See MONEY, SUFFICIENCY.

oracle, *n.* prophet, seer (see PREDICTION).

oral, *adj.* verbal, vocal, spoken, unwritten. See SPEECH.

orange, *n.* tangerine, tangelo; sweet, blood, mandarin, navel, *etc.* orange. See VEGETABLE, COLOR.

oration, *n.* SPEECH, declamation, discourse, address.

oratory, *n.* SPEECH, elocution, declamation, eloquence, expression.

orbit, *n.* path, track, CIRCUIT, revolution, course; region, range, sphere, realm, scope; province, sphere of INFLUENCE. See ASTRONAUTICS, BUSINESS.

orchard, *n.* fruit garden, grove, vineyard, plantation. See AGRICULTURE.

orchestra, *n.* symphony, sinfonia; band; parterre, ground floor. See MUSIC, DRAMA.

ordain, *v.* install, appoint, invest, frock; decree, [pre]destine. See CLERGY, COMMISSION.

ordeal, *n.* trial, strain, cross, tribulation, test. See ADVERSITY, EXPERIMENT.

ORDER

Nouns—**1,** order, orderliness, REGULARITY, uniformity, SYMMETRY, harmony, precision; METHOD, system, disposition, ARRANGEMENT; composition; coordination, subordination; management, regimentation, discipline, ECONOMY; PLAN, FORM, array; course, routine, even tenor, HABIT. See CONFORMITY.
2, gradation, graduation, progression, series, sequence, classification, ordering; rank, place, step, DEGREE; CLASS, kind, sort, set; category, division. See CONTINUITY.
3, see COMMAND, REQUEST, PARTY.

Verbs—**1,** be in order; form, fall in, draw up; arrange, range, *or* place itself; fall into place *or* rank, take one's place, rally round.
2, [put in] order, make *or* restore order; organize, regulate, regularize; classify, alphabetize; arrange, range, array, align, trim, dispose, place; LIST, file [away], put away.

Adjectives—orderly, regular; in order, in good form, in trim, in place, in its proper place, fixed; neat, tidy, trim, spruce; methodical, classified, symmetrical, shipshape; cosmic; uniform, geometric[al]; businesslike, systematic, schematic. *Colloq.*, in apple-pie order.

Adverbs—orderly, in order; methodically, in [its] turn, step by step, by regular steps, stages, intervals, *or* gradations; *seriatim,* systematically, by *or* like clockwork.

Antonyms, see DISORDER.

---

ordinance, *n.* law, regulation, order, decree; appointment, destiny; RULE, enactment. See COMMAND.

ordinary, *adj.* usual, medium, average, unremarkable, commonplace, regular, common; inferior, low; middling, second-rate; mediocre, undistinguished. See CONFORMITY, HABIT, SIMPLENESS, MEDIOCRITY.

ordnance, *n.* guns, cannon, artillery. See ARMS.

organ, *n.* hand organ, hurdygurdy, barrel organ, organette, regal, organophone, harmonium, calliope; pipe *or* electronic organ; melodeon; PUBLICATION, journal; component, PART, member; gland, heart, *etc.* See MUSIC.

ORGANIC MATTER

Nouns—**1,** organic matter, organization, organized nature *or* world, animated *or* living nature, living beings; flora, fauna, biota; organic remains, fossils, petrified organisms. See ANIMAL, HUMANITY, VEGETABLE, LIFE.
2, organism, plankton; cell, plasma, protoplasm, cytoplasm, ectoplasm, *etc;* D.N.A., R.N.A., *etc.;* ovum, egg *or* sperm cell, spermatozoon, gamete, semen, seed; spore; nucleus; [X, Y, *or* Z] chromosome; cell division, mitosis. See REPRODUCTION.
3, biology, natural history; organic chemistry, anatomy, zoology, botany, *etc.;* cytology, chromosomology, genetics; biologist, zoologist, *etc.*

Adjectives—organic, vital, biotic, biological; protoplasmic, plasmic, plasmatic, cellular, nuclear; embryonic, germinal; structural, anatomic[al].

Antonyms, see INORGANIC MATTER.

---

organization, *n.* ARRANGEMENT, classification, CLASS; association, society, club, establishment, enterprise; organism. See PARTY, ORGA-

NIC MATTER, FORM.

orgasm, *n*. paroxysm, spasm; climax. See VIOLENCE.

orgy, *n*. debauch, carouse, dissipation; rite; revelry, carousal. See INTEMPERANCE.

orient, *v.t.* orientate; find one's bearings, locate; acquaint, familiarize, adapt, adjust; indoctrinate, educate, train. See DIRECTION.

orifice, *n*. See OPENING.

origin, *n*. BEGINNING, CAUSE, commencement; descent, source, fountainhead, derivation, rise, ANCESTRY.

original, *adj*. novel, unique; primary, initial; earliest, primal, aboriginal; creative, inventive. See BEGINNING, IMAGINATION, UNCONFORMITY, SPECIALITY.

originate, *v*. start, invent, begin, inaugurate, initiate, CAUSE; proceed, spring. See BEGINNING, IMAGINATION.

ORNAMENT

Nouns—**1,** ornament, ornamentation, ornateness; adornment, decoration, embellishment, dressing, décor.

2, garnish, polish, varnish, gilding, lacquer, enamel; cosmetics (see BEAUTY); ormolu.

3, pattern, diaper, powdering, paneling, lining, graining; detail, TEXTURE, richness; mosaic; tracery, filigree, molding, filet, flourish, fleur-de-lis, arabesque, fret, astragal, zigzag, acanthus, pilaster.

4, pargeting, embroidery, needlework; brocade, brocatel, lace, fringe, trapping, border, guilloche, edging, trimming, frill; hanging, tapestry, arras.

5, wreath, festoon, garland, chaplet, flower, nosegay, bouquet, posy, lei; crepe paper; tassel, shoulderknot, epaulet, braid, aiguillette, frog; star, rosette, bow; feather, plume, plumage, panache, aigrette, fine feathers.

6, jewelry, bijoutry; bijou, trinket, locket, diadem, necklace, bracelet, anklet, earring, carcanet, chain, chatelaine, brooch, pin, torque; slave bracelet, costume jewelry; jewel, gem, precious stone; diamond, brilliant, beryl, emerald, chalcedony, agate, heliotrope; girasol; onyx, sardonyx; garnet, lapis lazuli, opal, peridot, chrysolite, sapphire, ruby; spinel, topaz; turquoise; zircon, jacinth, hyacinth, carbuncle, rhinestone, amethyst; pearl, coral; sequin.

7, finery, frippery, gewgaw, gimcrack, tinsel, spangle, clinquant, brummagem, pinchbeck, paste, glass; knickknack, bric-a-brac, curio; gaudiness (see VULGARITY).

8, illustration, illumination, vignette; headpiece, tailpiece, scroll, flowers, rhetoric, work of art.

Verbs—**1,** ornament, embellish, decorate, adorn, grace, beautify, smarten; furbish, polish; blazon, beset; gild, varnish, whitewash, enamel, japan, lacquer, paint, grain, enrich, silver, chrome.

2, garnish, trim, [be]dizen, prink, primp, prank; trip out; [be]deck, [be]dight, array; dress up, [be]spangle, powder, embroider, work; chase, emboss, fret; stud; make up; emblazon, illuminate; illustrate. *Colloq.*, spruce up. *Slang*, doll up.

Adjectives—**1,** ornamented, beautified; ornate, rich, gilt, gilded; tasselated, festooned, ornamental, decorative, becoming, smart, gay, flowery, glittering; spangled. See BEAUTY.

2, pranked out, bedight, well-groomed, fresh as a daisy; in full dress *or* fashion, *en grande toilette;* in best bib and tucker, in Sunday best, showy, flashy, sporty, fancy; gaudy, garish (see OSTENTATION); gorgeous. *Slang*, sharp, snazzy, Sunday-go-to-meeting; in glad rags; dressed to kill, all dressed up like a Christmas tree.

Antonyms, see SIMPLENESS.

---

ornate, *adj.* See ORNAMENT.

orphan, *n.* waif, stray, gamin[e], urchin; foundling. See RELINQUISHMENT.

orphanage, *n.* home, foundlings' home, shelter, refuge. See ABODE.

orthodox, *adj.* approved, conventional; sound, strict, faithful; Christian; evangelical, scriptural, textual, literal, canonical. See RELIGION, BELIEF, CONFORMITY.

OSCILLATION

Nouns—**1,** oscillation; vibration, libration, nutation, undulation; pulsation, pulse; fluctuation, vacillation, wavering; wave, swing, beat, shake, wag, seesaw, dance; alternation, reciprocation; coming and going; ebb and flow, flux and reflux, ups and downs; trill, tremolo. See REGULARITY.

2, irresolution, indecision (see DOUBT, CHANGEABLENESS).

Verbs—**1,** oscillate; vibrate, librate, reciprocate, alternate, undulate, wave; rock, swing; flutter, pulsate, beat; wag; tick; play; fluctuate, dance, curvet, reel [to and fro], quake; quiver, quaver; shake, flicker; wriggle; roll, toss, pitch; flounder, stagger, totter; move *or* bob up and down; pass and repass, ebb and flow, come and go; waver, teeter, seesaw, vacillate; take turns, change off.

2, hesitate, shilly-shally, hem and haw, blow hot and cold.

Adjectives—oscillating, oscillatory, undulatory, pulsatory, libratory; vibratory, pendulous; wavering, fluctuating; every other; irresolute.

Adverbs—to and fro, up and down, back and forth, backward and forward, seesaw, zigzag, in and out, from side to side, from pillar to post.

Antonyms, see STABILITY.

---

ossify, *v.* harden, callous, horrify. See HARDNESS.

ostensible, *adj.* apparent, outward; professed, pretended. See APPEARANCE.

OSTENTATION

Nouns—**1,** ostentation, ostentatiousness, display, show, flourish, parade; pomp, array, state, solemnity; dash, splash, glitter, strut; bombast, pomposity (see BOASTING); tinsel, tawdriness; pretense, pretension, pretentiousness, flatulence; airs, showing off; showmanship; veneer, AFFECTATION; magnificence, splendor. *Colloq.,* front, dog. *Slang,* swank, side, ritz[iness], razzle-dazzle. See VANITY, PRIDE, ORNAMENT, VULGARITY.

2, pageant[ry], demonstration, panoply, exhibition, flying colors, tomfoolery; flourish *or* fanfare [of trumpets]; color guard; spectacle, procession; fete (see CELEBRATION).

3, dress; court dress, full dress, black tie, white tie [and tails], evening dress *or* gown, ball dress, fancy dress; full regalia, tailoring; millinery, frippery; foppery, equipage. *Slang,* glad rags, Sunday best. See CLOTHING, FASHION.

4, ceremony, ceremonial; ritual; form, formality; etiquette; punctilio, punctiliousness; stateliness, RITE; protocol.

5, exhibitionist, show-off; showman. *Slang,* grandstander. See AFFECTATION.

Verbs—put oneself forward, court attention, splurge; star, figure; make a show *or* display; glitter; show off, parade; display, exhibit, put forward; sport, brandish, blazon forth; dangle, flaunt, emblazon, prink, primp; set off, mount, have framed; put a good face upon. *Colloq.*, cut a figure, cut a dash, cut a wide swath, make a splash, play to the gallery, trot out, put on the dog, show off; wear one's heart on one's sleeve. *Slang,* grandstand, put on a front, strut one's stuff, doll up.

Adjectives—ostentatious, showy, dashing, pretentious, impressive; jaunty; grand, pompous, palatial; high-sounding, turgid, garish, gaudy [as a peacock]; conspicuous, flaunting, flashing, flamboyant, flaming, glittering, florid, flowery; gay, splendid, magnificent, sumptuous, grandiose, de luxe; theatrical, dramatic, spectacular; ceremonial, ritual; dressy, fancy; solemn, stately, majestic, formal, stiff, ceremonious, punctilious, starched; in best bib and tucker, in Sunday best, on parade; blatant. *Slang,* ritzy, artsy.

Adverbs—ostentatiously, pompously, *etc.;* with a flourish of trumpets, with flying colors; in a big way.

Antonyms, see SIMPLENESS, MODESTY.

---

ostracize, *v.t.* exclude, banish, bar, blackball; outcast. See EXCLUSION.

other, *adj.* different, separate, distinct; former; another, additional. See DIFFERENCE.

otherwise, *adv.* else, if not, besides; contrarily, contrariwise; conversely, vice versa; quite the contrary; alias. See DIFFERENCE.

otherworldly, *adj.* unworldly, religious, spiritual, supernatural, extramundane, unearthly; idealistic, unreal. *Slang,* out of this world. See UNCONFORMITY, UNIVERSE, HEAVEN.

oust, *v.t.* depose, evict, remove, dismiss, dislodge. See EJECTION.

out, *adv.* without, outside; outdoors; démodé. See EXTERIOR, DISUSE.

outbreak, *n.* outburst, eruption; rebellion, uprising, revolt, insurrection; disturbance. See DISOBEDIENCE, VIOLENCE, BEGINNING, ATTACK.

outburst, *n.* eruption, explosion, blowup; outpouring, flood, breakthrough; paroxysm, spasm, upheaval; uproar. See VIOLENCE.

outcast, *n.* pariah, derelict, exile; castaway, outsider, outlaw; leper. See UNCONFORMITY, DISPLACEMENT.

outclass, *v.t.* outdo, outrival. See SUPERIORITY.

outcome, *n.* issue, termination, end, result, consequence, outgrowth, upshot. See EFFECT.

outcry, *n.* clamor, tumult, exclamation, shout, uproar. See CRY, DISAPPROBATION.

outdistance, *v.t.* See OVERRUNNING.

outdo, *v.t.* excel, exceed, surpass, outstrip, beat. See SUPERIORITY.

outdoor, *adj.* open-air, out-of-door[s], alfresco; drive-in. See EXTERIOR.

outer, *adj.* outside, outward, external, EXTERIOR.

outfit, *n.* ensemble, garments, suit; group, unit; equipment, gear. See CLOTHING, PROVISION.

outflow, *n.* effluence, efflux, outpouring, issue, effusion, escape. See EGRESS.

outgoing, *adj.* extrovert; retiring. See COMMUNICATION, DEPARTURE.

outgrowth, *n.* development, result, outcome, offshoot; excrescence. See EFFECT, CONVEXITY.

outhouse, *n.* outbuilding; privy. See ABODE, UNCLEANNESS.

outing, *n.* excursion, junket, field day, picnic. See TRAVEL.

outlandish, *adj.* bizarre, *outré,* eccentric, foreign, grotesque, queer. See UNCONFORMITY.

outlast, *v.* outlive, survive, outwear. See DURABILITY.

outlaw, *n.* criminal, bandit, fugitive, outcast; desperado. See EVILDOER, ILLEGALITY.

outlet, *n.* loophole, port; sluice,

floodgate; faucet, tap, spout, conduit; exit, vent, OPENING. See EGRESS, ESCAPE.

outline, *n.* profile, tracing, tracery; bounds, boundary; EDGE, circumference, perimeter; [rough] sketch, PLAN, blueprint, schematic, scheme, drawing, draft; synopsis, summary, résumé; diagram, chart, map. —*v.t.* sketch; diagram; model, block in, PLAN; boil down, summarize, trace, draw, depict, delimit, design, picture, demonstrate. See APPEARANCE, DESCRIPTION, SHORTNESS, FORM.

outlive, *v.t.* survive, outlast. See DURABILITY.

outlook, *n.* APPEARANCE, prospect, probabilities, forecast; scene, view, vista. See EXPECTATION.

outlying, *adj.* distant, suburban, remote; frontier. See DISTANCE.

outmoded, *adj.* outdated, out-of-date; timeworn, stale; superseded. *Slang,* square. See OLDNESS, DISUSE.

out-of-date, *adj.* See OLDNESS.

out-of-the-way, *adj.* off the beaten track, secluded, isolated; bizarre, out of the ordinary, outlandish. See DISTANCE, UNCONFORMITY.

outpost, *n.* sentry, scout, picket, vanguard; border, march, frontier; outstation, fort. See DISTANCE, ENVIRONMENT, DEFENSE.

output, *n.* produce, yield, harvest, product. See PRODUCTION, EFFECT.

outrage, *n.* VIOLENCE, WRONG, affront, harm, damage, injury, abuse; transgression, infraction, violation. See EVIL, BADNESS, DISRESPECT.

outrageous, *adj.* offensive, shocking. See DISREPUTE.

outright, *adj.* complete, unqualified, unmitigated, consummate, out-and-out. See COMPLETION.

outrun, *v.t.* overtake, outdistance, outstrip. See SUPERIORITY.

outset, *n.* BEGINNING, start, commencement; DEPARTURE.

outshine, *v.t.* outdo, eclipse, excel, overshadow. See REPUTE.

outside, *adj.* EXTERIOR, outer, external, outward.

outsider, *n.* alien, stranger, foreigner; layman; onlooker, passerby, intruder, pariah, rebel, *etc.* See EXTRINSIC, LAITY.

outskirts, *n.pl.* suburbs, environs, surroundings; border, edge; purlieus. See NEARNESS, DISTANCE, ENVIRONMENT.

outsmart, *v.t.* See CUNNING.

outspoken, *adj.* frank, bluff, unreserved, blunt, loud, plainspoken. See SIMPLENESS, SPEECH.

outstanding, *adj.* prominent, exceptional, conspicuous, remarkable, noticeable, eminent; unpaid, uncollected, owing, due, unsettled. See DEBT, REMAINDER, CONVEXITY, IMPORTANCE, SUPERIORITY.

outstretched, *adj.* extended, proffered, offered; expanded, outspread. See BREADTH, OFFER.

outstrip, *v.t.* outspace, outrun, excel, exceed, outdo, outdistance; eclipse, surpass. See SUPERIORITY, OVERRUNNING.

outward, *adj.* EXTERIOR, outer, outside, out; visible (see VISIBILITY).

outweigh, *v.t.* overweigh, outbalance, overbalance, exceed. See SUPERIORITY.

outwit, *v.t.* frustrate, circumvent, outsmart. See DECEPTION.

oval, *adj.* elliptical, ovoid, ovate. See CIRCULARITY.

ovation, *n.* applause, kudos, tribute; acclamation, cheers, APPROBATION.

oven, *n.* stove, range, roaster, broiler; hearth; furnace, kiln; rotisserie, rotary oven, Dutch oven, hibachi; convection *or* microwave oven. See HEAT.

over, *adv.* past, across, by; again; beyond; extra, above, more, remaining, left. —*prep.* on, above. See END, OPPOSITION, REPETITION, SUPERIORITY.

overall, *adj.* blanket, all-inclusive. See INCLUSION.

overawe, *v.t.* intimidate, daunt, abash, cow; impress. See FEAR.

overbalance, *v.t.* surpass, unbalance,

overweigh. See SUPERIORITY.

overbearing, *adj.* domineering, bullying, lordly, arrogant, dictatorial; overwhelming. See INSOLENCE.

overcast, *adj.* cloudy, murky, shadowy, gloomy, dark, leaden. See CLOUDINESS.

overcautious, *adj.* overcareful, timorous, fearful, unenterprising. See CAUTION.

overcharge, *v.* rook, fleece, cheat, extort. *Colloq.*, scalp, gyp, do. See DEARNESS.

overcoat, *n.* greatcoat, duster, topcoat, ulster, raglan, petersham. See CLOTHING.

overcome, *v.* conquer, subdue, defeat, overthrow, surmount. See SUCCESS. —*adj.* subdued, conquered, defeated, broken, crushed, downcast. See FAILURE.

overconfident, *adj.* reckless, cocksure, cocky, complacent, brash, incautious. *Colloq.*, cheeky, nervy. See RASHNESS.

overestimation, *n.* See EXAGGERATION.

overflow, *v.* inundate, flood; brim *or* well over, boil over, run over. —*n.* inundation, flooding, deluge, alluvion; spate, profusion, excess. See SUFFICIENCY, WATER, OVERRUNNING.

overgrown, *adj.* overrun, weedy; swollen, bloated, oversize, outsize. See SIZE, EXPANSION, OVERRUNNING.

overhaul, *v.t.* examine, check, inspect; repair, renovate. See RESTORATION.

overhead, *n.* costs, expenditure, outlay, capital, investment. See PRICE. —*adv.* above (see HEIGHT).

overhear, *v.t.* catch; eavesdrop. See HEARING, CURIOSITY.

overjoyed, *adj.* delighted, enraptured. See PLEASURE.

overlap, *v.* imbricate, shingle; overhang, overlie; superimpose. See COVERING.

overlook, *v.t.* look out on, command [a view of]; oversee, manage, direct, supervise; pass over *or* by, ignore, omit, disregard, skip; forgive, indulge, excuse, condone, wink at. See DIRECTION, NEGLECT, FORGIVENESS.

overlord, *n.* master, liege [lord] (see AUTHORITY).

overpass, *n.* bridge, walkway. See PASSAGE.

overpower, *v.t.* overwhelm, subdue. See SUCCESS.

override, *v.t.* annul (see OVERRULE); prevail. See SUPERIORITY.

overrule, *v.t.* override, reverse, set aside, contravene, rescind, veto, cancel, countermand. See NULLIFICATION, REJECTION.

OVERRUNNING

Nouns—overrunning, overflowing, overspreading; overstepping, transgression, encroachment, incursion, intrusion, infringement, extravagation, transcendence; infestation; invasion. See EXAGGERATION.

Verbs—**1,** overrun, run *or* spread over, overspread, overgrow, infest, grow over, run riot; run down, run [roughshod] over, trample on; overswarm, overflow, overwhelm, deluge, inundate.

2, outrun, outstrip, outpace, outstride, outdistance, outrace, pass, go beyond, go by, shoot ahead of, override, outride; outrival, outdo, beat (see SUPERIORITY); overshoot [the mark].

3, overstep, transgress, trespass, encroach, infringe, intrude, invade.

Adjectives—overrun, infested, plagued; overspread, overgrown.

Adverbs—ahead, in advance, beyond the mark, beyond the pale.

Antonyms, see INSUFFICIENCY, FAILURE.

---

overseas, *adj*. transoceanic, ultramarine, foreign, colonial. *—adv*. beyond the sea, abroad, away. *Colloq*., over there. See DISTANCE.

oversee, *v.t.* manage, superintend, direct, supervise, command; overlook. See AUTHORITY.

overshoe, *n*. boot, arctic, galosh, rubber. See CLOTHING.

oversight, *n*. omission, ERROR, blunder, slip; management, directorship, supervision. See AUTHORITY, NEGLECT.

overstate, *v.t.* exaggerate, overclaim, overdo, overdraw, overembellish. See EXAGGERATION.

overstep, *v.i.* transgress, trespass, cross, encroach, exceed; intrude, infringe. See OVERRUNNING.

overtake, *v.t.* catch [up with], pass, reach, overhaul. See ARRIVAL.

overthrow, *v.t.* overcome, defeat, upset, abolish, confute; overturn, demolish, ruin. See DEPRESSION, SUCCESS, CONFUTATION, REVOLUTION.

overtone, *n*. suggestion, connotation, hint, implication, intimation, innuendo, insinuation, inference. See INFORMATION.

overture, *n*. advance, approach, proposal, bid; prelude, preliminary, introduction. See OFFER, PRECEDENCE.

overturn, *v.t.* invert, upset, reverse; overthrow, destroy. See CHANGE, CONFUTATION, DESTRUCTION, INVERSION.

overwhelm, *v.t.* overpower, crush, submerge, overcome. See DESTRUCTION, CONFUTATION, WATER.

overwork, *v*. overdo, tire, weary, exhaust, overtax, overburden, overtask. See EXERTION.

overwrought, *adj*. elaborate, pretentious, ornate; overworked, tired; distraught, hysterical, nervous, frenetic, high-strung. See ORNAMENT, EXCITEMENT.

ovum, *n*. cell, egg, seed. See ORGANIC MATTER, REPRODUCTION.

owe, *v.i.* be indebted, be in DEBT. See ATTRIBUTION.

own, *v*. admit, confess, concede, acknowledge; possess, have, hold. See DISCLOSURE, POSSESSION, SPECIALITY.

P

pace, *n*. rate, speed, VELOCITY; step, measuring step; stride; gait, amble, rack, single-foot. *—v*. walk, step, stride; walk to and fro; measure; lead, set the pace. See MOTION, PRECEDENCE, TRAVEL.

pachyderm, *n*. elephant, rhinoceros, hippopotamus. See ANIMAL.

PACIFICATION

Nouns—**1,** pacification, conciliation; reconciliation, reconcilement; propitiation, appeasement, mollification, mediation; shaking of hands, accommodation, arrangement, adjustment, COMPROMISE; shuttle diplomacy; deed of release.

2, peace offering; peace treaty; peace, truce, armistice, cease-fire; suspension of hostilities; breathing spell, détente; flag of truce, white flag, olive branch; peace pipe, calumet. *Slang,* flower power.

3, pacifier, peacemaker, conciliator. *Slang,* flower child.

Verbs—**1,** pacify, tranquilize, compose; allay (see MODERATION); reconcile, [re]unite, propitiate, placate, conciliate, meet halfway, hold out the olive branch, accommodate, heal the breach, make peace, restore harmony, bring to terms, pour oil on troubled waters, handle with kid gloves.

2, settle differences, arrange matters; set straight; make up (a quarrel), come to an understanding, come to terms; bridge over, hush up; make it up, make matters up; mend one's fences; patch up; shake hands. *Colloq.,* bury the hatchet, smoke the peace pipe.

3, disarm, demilitarize, sheathe the sword, denuclearize; raise a siege; lay down one's arms, beat swords into plowshares; come around.

Adjectives—pacific, peaceful, calm; peaceable, unwarlike, peace-loving, peace-making; pacifying, soothing, mollifying; appeasing; pacificatory, propitiatory, conciliatory; pacified, CONTENT.

Antonyms, see CONTENTION, WARFARE, RESENTMENT.

---

pack, *n.* stow, bale, package, packet; load, burden, bundle; knapsack; crowd, mob, multitude; herd, flock, bevy, covey. See ASSEMBLAGE. —*v.* stow, bale, package; cram, tamp; cake, solidify; add to; stuff; load, burden. See ARRANGEMENT.

package, *n.* parcel, pack[et], carton. See ASSEMBLAGE, ENCLOSURE.

packet, *n.* package; packet boat, *paquebot;* mail boat, steamer, coaster. See SHIP.

packing, *n.* contents, filler, stuffing, wadding; closure, stopper, bung, plug; pad, cushioning, buffer; lute, seal, gasket. See ENCLOSURE, COMPOSITION.

pact, *n.* compact, covenant, treaty; bargain, AGREEMENT.

pad, *n.* cushion, mat, buffer; [writing] tablet; *slang,* flat, room[s] (see ABODE). —*v.* cushion, stuff, wad; enlarge, overstate, inflate. See SOFTNESS, SUPPORT, WRITING.

padding, *n.* pads, cushion, wadding; fill-ins, additions; excess, extras, surplus; REPETITION, tautology; featherbedding. See COMPOSITION, COVERING.

paddle, *n.* oar, scull, sweep, flipper, pole.—*v.* canoe, row, ply the oar; backwater, feather, steer; beat, thrash, spank, drub; toddle, pad, waddle. See NAVIGATION, PUNISHMENT, TRAVEL.

pagan, *adj.* heathen, ungodly; idolatrous. —*n.* heathen, idolater. See IRRELIGION, IDOLATRY.

page, *n.* SERVANT, attendant, call boy, page boy, bellboy; folio, leaf. —*v.* summon, call; number pages, foliate, paginate. See NUMERATION, COMMAND.

pageant, *n.* exhibition, show, parade, display, spectacle. See OSTENTATION, CELEBRATION.

pail, *n.* bucket, can, canister, pot, pan, kettle. See RECEPTACLE.

PAIN

Noun—**1,** pain, suffering, sufferance; hurt, cut; discomfort, painfulness; discomfort, malaise; nightmare; anguish, agony, excruciation, torment, torture, rack; distress, affliction (see ADVERSITY). See DEJECTION, HELL, DISEASE, LAMENTATION.

2, aches and pains; ache, aching, sore[ness]; smart, sting, burn[ing], tingle; acute, sharp, piercing, throbbing, shooting, gnawing, *or* burning pain; twinge, pang, stab, pinch; cramp, paroxysm, spasm (see AGITATION, VIOLENCE); gripe, stomach-ache, heartburn, colic; headache, migraine; backache, earache, toothache, *etc. Colloq.,* tummy-ache.

3, shock, blow; distress, affliction, woe, bitterness; lovesickness; heartache; misery, tribulation, wretchedness, desolation; despair; extremity, prostration, depth of misery; hell on earth. See ADVERSITY.

Verb—**1,** feel, experience, suffer, endure, *or* undergo pain; suffer, ache, smart; sting, tingle, shoot; twinge, twitch, writhe, wince; make a wry face, cry out.

2, give, cause, *or* inflict pain; pain, hurt, wound, chafe, sting, bite, gnaw, gripe; pinch, tweak, grate, gall, fret, prick, pierce, wring, convulse; harrow, torment, torture, rack, agonize, crucify, excruciate; break on the wheel, put on the rack; spank, beat, thrash, flog (see PUNISHMENT).

3, sicken, disgust, revolt, nauseate, disenchant; repel, offend, shock, stink in the nostrils; turn the stomach; make one sick, set the teeth on edge; rankle, gnaw, corrode. See DISCONTENT.

Adjectives—**1,** in pain, suffering, pained, harrowed, afflicted, aching, griped, sore, raw; on the rack; agonized, tortured, crucified, racked, broken on the wheel.

2, painful, hurting, hurtful; dolorous; cutting, consuming, racking, excruciating, searching, grinding, grating, agonizing.

3, intolerable, insufferable, insupportable, unbearable, unendurable; more than flesh and blood can bear; enough to drive one mad.

4, distressing, afflicting, afflictive; grievous; woeful, rueful, mournful, deplorable, lamentable; affecting, touching. See ADVERSITY.

Antonyms, see PLEASURE.

---

painkiller, *n.* alleviative, lenitive, anodyne, paregoric, analgesic, [local *or* general] anesthetic, narcotic, morphine, Novocaine, codeine, sleeping pills. See RELIEF, INSENSIBILITY.

painless, *adj.* causing no pain; easy [to take]. See INSENSIBILITY, FACILITY.

pains, *n.pl.* EXERTION, labor, effort; attention, seriousness.

painstaking, *adj.* careful, particular, meticulous, scrupulous; diligent. See EXERTION, CARE.

PAINTING

Nouns—**1,** painting, depicting; drawing; drafting; design; chiaroscuro; composition, treatment, perspective, balance, technique; impasto; REPRESENTATION. See SCULPTURE, ENGRAVING.

2, school, style; the grand style, fine *or* high art, commercial art, genre, portraiture; classicism, romanticism, impressionism, postimpressionism, expressionism, realism, pointillism, Dada[ism], modernism, surrealism, cubism, minimalism, pop *or* op art.

3, palette, pallet; easel; [paint]brush, air brush, spray gun; palette knife, spatula; pencil, charcoal, crayons, chalk, pastel; paint, water color, oils, oil paint; varnish, gouache, tempera, distemper, [true *or* dry] fresco, enamel, encaustic painting; canvas, plaster, gesso; sketchbook.

4, painting, picture, piece, tableau, canvas; oil painting; fresco, cartoon; [pencil *or* watercolor] drawing; sketch, outline; study, scene, view; illustration; portrait, miniature, landscape, seascape, mural, still life, nude, study, scene; prospect; panorama; diorama; batik; finger painting.

5, picture *or* art gallery, museum; studio, atelier; exhibition, show[ing], retrospective.

6, painter, ARTIST, portrait *or* landscape painter, *etc.;* realist, surrealist, impressionist, cubist, pointillist, postimpressionist, *etc.*

7, house painting; latex, acrylic, *or* oil paint; flat, semi-gloss, *or* high-gloss paint, exterior *or* interior paint, enamel; varnish, lacquer, stain, polyurethane; brush, roller; drop cloth; house painter.

Verbs—paint, design, limn, draw, sketch, pencil, scratch, shade, stipple, hatch, crosshatch, hachure, dash off, block out, chalk out, square up; color, tint, dead-color; wash, varnish; illustrate; illuminate (see ORNAMENT); paint in oils; stencil; depict, represent; trace, copy. *Slang,* doodle.

Adjectives—pictorial, graphic, picturesque; painted; classic, romantic, realistic, impressionistic, *etc.;* pencil, oil, pastel, tempera, watercolor, *etc.;* freehand.

pair, *n.* couple, duo, brace; mates; two of a kind. —*v.* match, mate, couple, suit, unite. See NUMERATION, SIMILARITY.

pajamas, *n.* pyjamas. *Slang,* P.J.'s. See CLOTHING.

pal, *n., slang,* [bosom *or* boon] companion, crony, comrade, mate; sidekick, buddy, chum. See FRIEND.

palace, *n.* alcazar, chateau, mansion, great house, *palazzo, palais;* arena, pleasure dome, Crystal Palace. See ABODE.

palatable, *adj.* tasty, savory, toothsome, appetizing; pleasant, agreeable, easy to take. See TASTE, PLEASURE.

palaver, *n.* colloquy, conference, parley, CONVERSATION; babble, chatter; FLATTERY, nonsense, absurdity. *Colloq.,* soft soap. —*v.i.* converse, confer; dicker, BARGAIN; gossip, drivel, babble, chatter. See SPEECH, UNMEANINGNESS.

pale, *adj.* wan, waxen, ashy, ashen, colorless, bloodless; light, blond; faint, dim, vague; sickly. See COLORLESSNESS, DIMNESS. —*v.i.* whiten, blanch, blench; fade, dim. —*n.* stake, picket; border, boundary, LIMIT.

pall, *v.* jade, weary; cloy, sicken, satiate. See WEARINESS, SUFFICIENCY. —*n.* murk, smoke, smog, coffin. See COVERING, INTERMENT.

pallet, *n.* palette; mattress, bed; platform. See PAINTING, SUPPORT.

palliate, *v.t.* extenuate, excuse; mitigate, soften; relieve, ameliorate. See VINDICATION, MODERATION, RELIEF.

pallid, *n.* pale, bloodless, wan, sallow, white. See COLORLESSNESS.

palm, *n.* palmetto, palmyra; honor, prize, reward, trophy, guerdon, laurel[s]. See APPROBATION. —*v.* handle, TOUCH; conceal, hide, cover; steal, pilfer; palm off, impose *or* foist on, get rid of, deceive. See STEALING, DECEPTION.

palpable, *adj.* evident, plain, clear, manifest, obvious, apparent, unmistakable, definite, unquestionable, distinct. See FEELING, DISCLOSURE.

palpitate, *v.i.* beat, pulse, throb; vibrate; quake, shake. See AGITATION, FEAR.

palsy, *n.* paralysis. See DISEASE.

palter, *v.i.* equivocate; haggle; trifle. See BARTER, FALSEHOOD, UNIMPORTANCE.

paltry, *adj.* trifling, trivial, inconsequential, insignificant; mean, petty, worthless; contemptible, sorry, pitiable. See UNIMPORTANCE, BADNESS, CHEAPNESS.

pamper, *v.t.* humor, indulge, spoil, pet, coddle, gratify, overindulge. See LENIENCY.

pamphlet, *n.* booklet, folder, brochure, leaflet; monograph, manual. See PUBLICATION.

pamphleteer, *n.* essayist, propagandist. See WRITING.

pan, *n.* pot, kettle, saucepan; skillet, spider, grill; dishpan; utensil, vessel. See RECEPTACLE.

panacea, *n.* universal REMEDY, cure-all.

pancake, *n.* hotcake, flapjack, battercake, buckwheat cake, flannel cake, silver dollar, griddlecake; *crêpe* [*suzette, etc.*]; fritter. See FOOD.

pandemic, *adj.* universal, epidemic. See GENERALITY, DISEASE.

pandemonium, *n.* HELL, inferno; noise, racket, din; EXCITEMENT, DISORDER, convulsion, frenzy, bedlam, Babel, DISCORD. *Colloq.,* all hell breaking loose. See LOUDNESS.

pander, *v.* cater to; encourage (in bad habits); pimp. —*n.* pimp, go-between. See IMPURITY, SERVILITY.

pane, *n.* window[pane], light, skylight; sheet glass, plate glass; side, face, section, surface. See TRANSPARENCY.

panegyric, *n.* praise; encomium, eulogy; APPROBATION, laudation.

panel, *n.* jury, board of judges; board, table. See ASSEMBLAGE, LAYER.

pang, *n.* PAIN, twinge, shoot, throe, ache.

panhandle, *v., slang,* beg, solicit.

Slang, bum, [make a] touch. See REQUEST.

panic, *n.* terror, fright, FEAR, consternation; stampede. —*v.* alarm, frighten; stampede. See EXCITABILITY, FAILURE.

panoply, *n.* full armor, regalia, ARMS, arsenal, protection, shield; pageantry, pomp, OSTENTATION; array, spread, assemblage.

panorama, *n.* vista, view, scene, perspective; representation, cyclorama, diorama. See PAINTING, INCLUSION.

panpipe, *n.* syrinx, Pan's pipes. See MUSIC.

pant, *v.i.* gasp, puff, blow; yearn *or* long for. See DESIRE, WIND.

pantomime, *n.* mime, mimicry, chironomy; dumbshow, tableau, charades, silent film; gestures, gesticulation, hand talk; puppet show. See DRAMA, INDICATION.

pantry, *n.* STORE, cupboard, larder, kitchen, scullery; galley, cuddy; buttery, butlery; ewery, china closet. See RECEPTACLE.

pants, *n.pl.* trousers, breeches; slacks, flannels, jeans, Levis, dungarees; pantaloons, knickerbockers, knickers, plus-fours; shorts, pedalpushers, chinos, jodhpurs; bloomers, briefs, panties. See CLOTHING.

pap, *n.* spoon food, paste; teat, nipple; *slang*, patronage, plum, pork. See SOFTNESS, CONVEXITY, INFLUENCE.

papacy, *n.* the Vatican, Holy See. See CLERGY.

paper, *n.* writing paper, wallpaper, newsprint, rag paper, pulp paper, foolscap, *etc.;* paper money, bill, banknote; certificate, deed, document; newspaper, journal; monograph, article, composition. *Colloq.*, folding money. See COVERING, MONEY, PUBLICATION, RECORD, NEWS.

paperback, *n.* pocket book; penny dreadful, dime novel. —*adj.* softcover. See PUBLICATION.

par, *n.* EQUALITY, equal footing; par *or* face value; level.

parable, *n.* allegory, analogy; fable, moral tale; comparison, similitude. See FIGURATIVE, DESCRIPTION.

parachute, *n.* chute, drogue; parafoil; paraglider; airdrop, free fall. *Colloq.*, the silk. —*v.i.* bail out, drop, jump, leap. *Colloq.*, hit the silk. See AVIATION.

parade, *n.* show, display, pageant[ry]; march, procession; OSTENTATION, pretension. —*v.* show, display; march; air, vent; flaunt, show off.

paradise, *n.* Eden, HEAVEN, Promised Land, Canaan, land of milk and honey; Utopia, Arcadia; never-never land; bliss, happiness; Elysian fields, Elysium; Shangri-La.

paradox, *n.* inconsistency; ABSURDITY. See DIFFICULTY, UNINTELLIGIBILITY.

paragon, *n.* ideal, model, perfect example, pattern; nonesuch, nonpareil. See PERFECTION, GOODNESS.

paragraph, *n.* note, item; section, passage. See PART, GRAMMAR.

parallel, *n.* parallelism; coextension; analogy, comparison. —*adj.* coextensive, side by side; analogous, similar. See SIMILARITY, EQUALITY, SYMMETRY.

paralysis, *n.* stroke, disablement, paraplegia, hemiplegia, malfunction. See DISEASE, IMPOTENCE.

paralyze, *v.* cripple; demoralize; disable; deaden; bring to a stop. See IMPOTENCE, INSENSIBILITY.

paramount, *adj.* chief, first, supreme, all-important. See SUPERIORITY.

paramour, *n.* mistress, ladylove; lover. See LOVE, EVILDOER.

paranoid, *adj.* paranoiac; fearful, suspicious, distrustful. —*adj.* paranoiac; alarmist, pessimist. See INSANITY, FEAR.

parapet, *n.* wall, rampart, breastwork, embankment, DEFENSE; railing. See HINDRANCE.

paraphernalia, *n.pl.* apparatus, trappings, gear, equipment; belongings. See POSSESSION.

paraphrase, *n.* rendering, restatement. *Colloq.*, switch. —*v.* restate, alter, reword. See INTERPRETATION, IMITATION.

parasite, *n.* sycophant, fawner, hanger-on; leech, bloodsucker; inquiline, commensal; symbiont, symbiotic. *Colloq.,* free-loader. See SERVILITY, FLATTERY.

parasol, *n.* sunshade, umbrella. See COVERING.

paratrooper, *n.* paramarine, paramedic. *Colloq.,* chutist. See COMBATANT.

parboil, *v.t.* brew, simmer, seethe, coddle, HEAT. See FOOD.

parcel, *n.* package, bundle, pack[et]; PART, portion, piece; land, lot, division, section. See ENCLOSURE.

parch, *v.* dry [up], shrivel; roast, scorch. See DRYNESS.

parchment, *n.* vellum, sheepskin; pell, scroll; document, diploma; bond paper, rag paper. See WRITING, MATERIALS.

pardon, *v.t.* forgive, excuse; release; overlook, tolerate. —*n.* excuse, release, FORGIVENESS; indulgence; remission; toleration.

pare, *v.t.* peel, trim, cut, shave, slice; reduce, shorten. See LAYER, CONTRACTION, DIVESTMENT, DEDUCTION, NARROWNESS.

parent, *n.* begetter, procreator, progenitor; forebear, ancestor, father, mother; foster parent; fount, source. See ANCESTRY.

parenthetical, *adj.* in parentheses; inserted, interpolated, incidental; disconnected, irrelevant. See BETWEEN, INSERTION.

pariah, *n.* outcast; untouchable, outcaste. See POPULACE, EXCLUSION.

parish, *n.* fold, church, LAITY, congregation, flock; parsonage, vicarage, manse; territory, REGION, area. See ABODE.

parity, *n.* EQUALITY, equal basis; similarity, equivalence; par.

park, *v.* leave, deposit, place. See LOCATION. —*n.* parkway; playground; public, botanical, *or* zoological gardens, zoo; woodland, pleasance; grove; picnic grounds; village *or* bowling green, common; parking lot *or* space, parkade; amusement park, fair grounds, fun fair, theme park. See AMUSEMENT.

parkway, *n.* boulevard, roadway. See PASSAGE.

parlay, *v.* [re]bet (see CHANCE, INCREASE).

parley, *n.* conference, talk, discussion, CONVERSATION, council; palaver. —*v.* talk, confer, palaver, converse.

parliament, *n.* assembly, COUNCIL, convocation; assemblage, house.

parlor, *n.* living, front, *or* drawing room. See RECEPTACLE.

parochial, *adj.* provincial, local; narrow, illiberal; church-controlled, separate (*Canadian*). See REGION, RELIGION, NARROWNESS.

parody, *n.* take-off, IMITATION, travesty, burlesque. See COPY, RIDICULE.

parole, *n.* pledge, PROMISE; custody, release, FREEDOM, probation. —*v.t.* free, liberate, let go, release, put on probation. See LIBERATION.

paroxysm, *n.* fit, seizure, spasm; convulsion, attack; outburst, frenzy. See AGITATION, VIOLENCE, PAIN.

parrot, *n.* polly, parakeet; prater, chatterbox; imitator, mimic. —*v.t.* imitate, echo, mime, repeat, say by rote, prate. See IMITATION, LOQUACITY.

parry, *v.* fend *or* ward off, avert, turn aside, deflect; evade; fence. See DEFENSE.

PARSIMONY

Nouns—**1,** parsimony, parsimoniousness, stinginess, miserliness; illiberality, avarice, greed (see DESIRE). See SELFISHNESS, ECONOMY.

2, miser, niggard, churl, skinflint, scrimp, lickpenny, curmudgeon, harpy; extortioner, usurer; scrooge. *Slang,* tightwad, cheapskate, penny-pincher, piker.

Verbs—stint, [be]grudge, pinch, gripe, dole out, hold back, withhold, starve, live on nothing, pinch pennies, scrimp; drive a hard bargain; cheapen, beat down; have an itching palm, grasp, grab (see DESIRE).

Adjectives—parsimonious, penurious, stingy, miserly, mean, shabby, piddling, scrubby, pennywise, near, niggardly, close; close-, hard-, *or* tight-fisted, grasping; tight, sparing; chary; grudging, griping; illiberal, ungenerous; avaricious, greedy. *Colloq.*, skimping.

Antonyms, see GIVING, LIBERALITY

---

parson, *n.* clergyman; pastor, minister, preacher. See CLERGY.

parsonage, *n.* manse, rectory. See TEMPLE.

PART

Nouns—**1,** part, portion, sector, segment, fragment, fraction, item, particular, dose; aught, any; division, subdivision, section, ward, parcel, compartment, department, detachment, CLASS; county, REGION; partition, installment, interest, share (see APPORTIONMENT); chapter, verse, article, clause, paragraph; passage, excerpt, episode. See INCOMPLETENESS.

2, component *or* integral part, part and parcel; crux, kernel (see IMPORTANCE); element, factor, module, constituent, detail, ingredient, complement, material, specification, leaven; feature, principle, radicle. See COMPOSITION.

3, piece, lump, bit, chip, slab, chunk, dollop, slice, cut[ting]; shard, cob, crumb, flake, tatter; scale, lamina, LAYER; morsel, soupçon (see LITTLENESS); shred, snip, paring, shaving, scrap, remnant, sliver, splinter. *Colloq.*, hunk, smithereen.

4, member, limb, organ, lobe, lobule, arm, wing, fin, flipper; joint, link, offshoot, ramification, appurtenance; scion, branch, bough, twig, bush, spray, leaf[let], stump.

5, debris, odds and ends, oddments, flinders, detritus, matchwood. See REMAINDER.

6, rôle (see DRAMA); voice, instrument (see MUSIC); concern, interest, PARTICIPATION, business, work.

Verbs—part, divide, subdivide, break, disjoin (see DISJUNCTION); partition, share, parcel (see APPORTIONMENT); break up, disrupt, dismember, disconnect, disassociate, detach, terminate; chip, splinter, snip, snap, shred, tatter, flake; part company, separate.

Adjectives—**1,** part, partial, fractional, fragmentary, sectional, aliquot, incomplete; divided, cleft, multifid, separated, individual, in compartments; bipartite, tripartite, *etc.*, multipartite; broken, splintered, severed, disrupt[ed], scrappy; departmental; branch[y], branching, subsidiary.

2, component, constituent, INTRINSIC, integral; essential, inherent, innate; inclusive, comprehensive (see INCLUSION).

Adverbs—partly, in part, partially, piecemeal, part by part; by installments, by snatches, by inches, by driblets; in detail; bit by bit, inch by inch, foot by foot, drop by drop; in detail, in lots; somewhat.

Antonyms, see WHOLE.

---

partake, *v.* share [in] (see PARTICIPATE); take (food or drink); receive (part of). See COOPERATION.

partial, *adj.* incomplete, fractional, unfinished, PART; biased, partisan, onesided, prejudiced; favoring. See INCOMPLETENESS, INEQUALITY, INJUSTICE.

participate, *v.i.* partake; share [in], come in for a share; prorate; go shares *or* halves; share and share alike; have *or* own in common, possess *or* use jointly; join in; go in with, have a hand in; cooperate. *Colloq.*, go Dutch. *Slang,* kick in, feed the kitty. See COOPERATION.

particle, *n.* speck, iota, jot, whit, bit; atom, molecule; suffix, prefix, conjunction, preposition, interjection. See LITTLENESS, GRAMMAR.

particular, *adj.* demanding, painstaking, meticulous; definite, specific; fussy, finicky, per[s]nickety, overnice; special, outstanding; personal; precise, exact. See TASTE, IMPORTANCE. —*n.* fact, specification, datum, detail. See DESCRIPTION, CARE.

particularize, *v.* specify, itemize, mention particularly, detail. See DESCRIPTION.

parting, *n.* leavetaking, DEPARTURE; farewell, severance, separation; partition, division. See DISJUNCTION.

partisan, *adj.* partial, onesided, pro, favoring, interested. —*n.* supporter, ally, follower, adherent; aide; champion; guerrilla, underground fighter. See AUXILIARY, FRIEND, COMBATANT.

partisanship, *n.* party spirit, loyalty; unfairness, bias, prejudice; clannishness, closeness; provincialism. See INJUSTICE.

partition, *n.* wall, screen, diaphragm, barrier; separation, severance, cutting-off; section, portion, division. See PART, APPORTIONMENT, BETWEEN.

partly, *adj.* in part, not wholly; incompletely, partially, in a way, not quite. See PART.

partner, *n.* sharer, associate, co-owner, copartner, silent partner; spouse, mate. *Colloq.*, sidekick, pal, pardner. *Slang,* pard. See ACCOMPANIMENT, MARRIAGE, AUXILIARY, FRIEND.

partnership, *n.* co-ownership, [BUSINESS] association; COOPERATION, alliance. See ACCOMPANIMENT.

part-time, *adj.* spare-time, after-hours, temporary, occasional, odd. See RARITY.

PARTY

Nouns—**1,** party, faction, side; denomination, communion; community, body, fellowship, fraternity; confraternity; brotherhood, sisterhood; sodality; family, clan (see ANCESTRY).

2, gang, crew, band, clique, ring, set, camp, circle, coterie, club. See ASSEMBLAGE.

3, guild; syndicate, cartel, trust; joint account. See BUSINESS.

4, society, association; institute, institution, foundation; union, trade union; league, alliance, *Verein, Bund, Zollverein;* lodge, den, chapter, post; COMBINATION, coalition, federation; confederation, confederacy; junta, cabal, bloc, machine; freemasonry. See COOPERATION.

5, member, fellow, associate, cardholder, clubman *or* -woman, brother, sister, socius. *Colloq.*, joiner.

6, see SOCIALITY.

Verbs—become a member, join, go *or* come out for, sign up, enroll, affiliate with; be a member, belong; form a party, associate, league together.

Adjectives—in league, in partnership, in alliance; partisan, denominational; bonded, linked, *or* banded together; confederated, federative; joint, mutual; cliquish, clannish; factional, sectional.

Antonyms, see SECLUSION.

---

parvenu, *n.* pretender, newcomer, upstart, social climber, snob; *nouveau riche*. *Colloq.*, Johnny-come-lately, pusher. See NEWNESS, POPULACE.

pass, *n.* gap, gorge; way, opening, notch, defile, passage; free ticket; crisis, predicament, condition, CIRCUMSTANCE; leave [of absence]; *slang,* advance. See LOVE. —*v.* go through *or* by, bypass; get a passing mark, make the grade; do, pass muster; cross; hand over; admit, allow, tolerate; while away *or* spend; authorize, O.K., sanction, permit (see PERMISSION). See PASSAGE, MOTION, PAST.

passable, *adj.* navigable, traversable; allowable, acceptable, tolerable; passing fair, good enough. See IMPERFECTION, MEDIOCRITY.

PASSAGE

Nouns—**1,** passage, transmission; permeation; penetration; interpenetration; transudation, infiltration; osmosis, endosmosis, exosmosis; intercurrence; access, INGRESS, EGRESS.

2, road, highway, thoroughfare, boulevard, avenue, street; byway, lane, pike, alley, trail; high road, the King's highway; roadway; turnpike, thruway, expressway, interstate [highway], freeway, parkway, super-highway, dual *or* divided highway, limited-access highway; cross, through, one-way, *or* stop street; back *or* side street. *Colloq.,* main drag. See TRANSPORTATION.

3, esplanade, arcade, corridor, concourse, hall[way], way, aisle.

4, channel, gate, OPENING; way, path, footpath, thoroughfare; tube, pipe; vessel, tubule, canal, gutter, fistula; chimney, flue, tap, funnel, gully, tunnel, main; chute, artery; mine, pit, adit, shaft; gallery, alley, aisle.

5, see PROGRESSION, TRAVEL, NAVIGATION.

Verbs—pass [through]; perforate, penetrate, permeate, tread, enfilade; go through *or* across; go over, pass by, bypass, pass over; cut across; ford, cross; work *or* make one's way through; thread *or* worm one's way through; force one's way; find a way; transmit, make way; clear the course *or* track; traverse, go over ground.

Adjectives—passing, elapsing, progressive; intercurrent; transient, portable, assignable, movable.

Adverbs—in passing, *en passant,* in transit, under way.

Antonyms, see INACTIVITY, CLOSURE.

passé, *adj.* outmoded (see OLDNESS).

passenger, *n.* rider, commuter, fare; hitchhiker, pickup, stowaway. See TRAVEL.

passerby, *n.* man in the street, pedestrian, bystander. *Slang,* sidewalk superintendent. See PRESENCE, EVIDENCE.

passing, *adj.* cursory; fleeting. See TRANSIENTNESS, DISAPPEARANCE.

passion, *n.* LOVE; fervor, ardor, intensity, fever; infatuation, DESIRE; emotion, rage, anger, fury; EXCITEMENT; *colloq.,* predilection, preference. See FEELING, VIOLENCE.

passionate, *adj.* impassioned, vehement; irascible. See FEELING, EXCITABILITY, IRASCIBILITY.

passive, *adj.* nonresistant; inactive, inert, quiet; unemotional, untouched, unstirred, indifferent. See LATENCY.

passivity, *n.* passiveness, inaction, INACTIVITY, inertness; nonresistance, quiescence; indifference; neutrality, sluggishness, SUBMISSION. See RESIGNATION.

passkey, *n.* master *or* skeleton key. See OPENING.

passport, *n.* pass; safe-conduct. See PERMISSION, INSTRUMENTALITY.

password, *n.* countersign, shibboleth, watchword. See INDICATION.

PAST

Nouns—**1,** past, past tense, preterition; the past, yesterday; days of yore *or* of old; times past *or* gone by; bygone days; olden times, the good old days, yesteryear; auld lang syne, eld; water over the dam *or* under the bridge. See PRIORITY, OLDNESS.

2, antiquity, antiqueness; time immemorial; remote past; archaism, antiquarianism, medievalism, pre-Raphaelitism; retrospection; looking back; MEMORY; ANCESTRY. *Colloq.*, ancient history.

3, paleontology, paleography, paleology, archaeology.

4. antiquary, antiquarian; paleologist, archaeologist, medievalist.

5, ex. *Colloq.*, has-been.

Verbs—be past, have expired, have run its course, have had its day; pass; pass *or* go by, go *or* pass away, pass off; lapse; blow over; look back, trace back; turn *or* put back the clock; exhume, dig up.

Adjectives—past, gone, bygone, foregone; elapsed; lapsed, expired, no more, run out, blown over, that has been, extinct, never to return, exploded, forgotten, irrecoverable; obsolete (see OLDNESS); once, former, pristine, quondam, *ci-devant,* late; ancestral; foregoing; last, latter; recent, overgoing; perfect, preterite (see GRAMMAR); looking back; retrospective, retroactive; archaeological, *etc. Colloq.*, ex-.

Adverbs—formerly; of old, of yore; erst, erstwhile, whilom, erewhile, time was, ago; over; in the olden time; anciently, long ago, long since; a long time ago; yesterday; a while back; last year, season, *or* month; *ultimo;* lately, retrospectively; before now; hitherto, heretofore; no longer; at one time, once [upon a time]; from time immemorial, in the memory of man; time out of mind; already, yet, up to this time; *ex post facto*.

Antonyms, see FUTURITY, PRESENT.

---

paste, *n.* cement, bond, binder, glue, adhesive, mucilage; rhinestones, glass; gaudery, trinkery, frippery. See COHERENCE, CONNECTION, ORNAMENT. —*v.t.* paste up, cement, stick, glue; *slang,* lambaste, clout, wallop, punch, slug. *Slang,* sock. See COHERENCE, IMPULSE.

pasteboard, *n.* card-, paper-, pulp-, *or* chipboard, Bristol board. See MATERIALS. —*adj.* fake, phony, stagy, theatrical, simulated, lifeless; flimsy, unsubstantial. See FALSENESS, INSUBSTANTIALITY.

pastel, *adj.* pale, light, soft, delicate; tinted, hued, shaded. See COLOR, PAINTING.

pasteurize, *v.t.* sterilize, disinfect. See CLEANNESS.

pastime, *n.* AMUSEMENT, recreation, entertainment, play, diversion.

pastor, *n.* clergyman, minister, *etc.* (see CLERGY).

pastry, *n.* cake, crust, shell; pie, tart, strudel. See FOOD.

pasture, *n.* field, meadow, grassland; paddock, pasturage, range. See LAND, FOOD, VEGETABLE.

pasty, *adj.* doughy, soft; pallid, pale; gluey; viscid, glutinous. See COLORLESSNESS, SOFTNESS.

pat, *n.* caress, stroke; rap, tap; strike, beat, smack; patty. See ENDEARMENT, IMPULSE, DENSITY. —*adj.* apt, suitable, ready, appropriate, fitting; timely, fortuitous. See AGREEMENT.

patch, *n.* piece, segment, spot; repair, mend; field, lot. —*v.t.* repair, reconstruct, rebuild, revamp, adjust. See COMPROMISE, RESTORATION.

patent, *adj.* obvious, plain, clear, evident, apparent; noticeable; open. See VISIBILITY, DISCLOSURE. —*n.* & *v.* See PERMISSION.

paternal, *adj.* fatherly, patriarchal; ancestral, parental; indulgent, benign, benevolent; paternalistic, protective, autocratic; socialistic. See ANCESTRY.

paternity, *n.* fatherhood, fathership, parentage. See ANCESTRY.

path, *n.* trail, lane, road, footpath, route, way, course; lead, example. See DIRECTION, PASSAGE.

pathetic, *adj.* piteous, pitiable, saddening, touching; distressing, heartrending, sad; pitiful. See PAIN, BADNESS, PITY.

pathfinder, *n.* trail blazer, explorer, pioneer, frontiersman, scout, forerunner. See PREPARATION.

pathos, *n.* passion, warmth; sentiment, FEELING.

patience, *adj.* LENIENCY, tolerance; perseverance, persistence; forbearance, long-suffering, SUBMISSION, endurance; solitaire. See INEXCITABILITY, RESIGNATION.

patient, *n.* invalid, case, victim; out- *or* inpatient. See DISEASE.

patio, *n.* courtyard, enclosure, court, atrium; yard; terrace, piazza, veranda.

patriarch, *n.* forefather, forebear, elder, graybeard; leader, headman, chief, master; priest, primate, ecclesiarch, hierarch. See ANCESTRY, CLERGY, AUTHORITY.

patrician, *adj.* noble, well-born, aristocratic. See NOBILITY.

patrimony, *n.* heritage, estate. See POSSESSION.

patriot, *n.* chauvinist, flag-waver. See PRIDE.

patriotism, *n.* civic *or* national pride; loyalty, allegiance; love of country, civism, nationalism; chauvinism, jingoism, fascism; isolationism, provincialism, xenophobia. See PRIDE.

patrol, *n.* patrolman, guard, warden, ranger; lookout, sentinel, sentry; guardsman, picket; watch[man]; coast guard; vigilante, policeman *or* -woman. —*v.* guard, stand watch *or* guard, watch over, keep watch and ward; scout; walk the beat. See DEFENSE, SAFETY.

patrolman, *n.* policeman, night watchman (see SAFETY).

patron, patroness, *n.* customer; benefactor, supporter; saint, defender, backer, angel. See PURCHASE, FRIEND.

patronage, *n.* condescension, favor; custom, interest, support, assistance; auspices. See AID, AUTHORITY, INFLUENCE, PURCHASE.

patronize, *v.t.* support, endorse, AID; deal *or* do business with; buy from, frequent, go to, shop at; look down upon, show contempt *or* condescension, condescend toward. See HUMILITY, AID, BARTER.

patsy, *n., slang,* dupe, gull. See CREDULITY.

patter, *v.i.* chatter, mumble, ramble, babble, jabber, mutter; tap, pitter-patter. —*n.* dialect, cant, chatter, babble. See LOQUACITY, SOUND.

pattern, *n.* form, original; mold, example; design, PLAN, last; model, ideal. See PERFECTION, CONFORMITY, ORNAMENT.

paucity, *n.* scantiness, fewness (see INSUFFICIENCY).

paunch, *n.* stomach, abdomen, belly; fat. See CONVEXITY.

pauper, *n.* beggar, bankrupt, mendicant. See POVERTY.

pause, *n.* cessation, rest, hesitation, INACTIVITY; lull, stop, DISCONTINUANCE, suspension. —*v.i.* desist, halt, stop, cease, break. See DOUBT, REPOSE.

pave, *v.t.* coat, cover, floor, cobble, surface, tar, macadamize, concrete, asphalt; prepare. See COVERING, SMOOTHNESS, PREPARATION.

pavement, *n.* paving; road, street, sidewalk; macadam, asphalt, cement, tar, concrete, tile, bricks, stone, flagging, cobbles, pavestone, paving blocks, flagstone. See COVERING.

pavilion, *n.* tent, canopy, canvas;

kiosk; summerhouse. See COVERING, ABODE.

paw, *n.* forepaw; pad, mitt. —*v.* handle, TOUCH, finger; mishandle, rough up, maul; stamp, kick; feel, caress, stroke.

pawn, *v.t.* pledge. *Slang,* hock. See DEBT, SECURITY.

pawnshop, *n.* pawnbrokery, *mont-de-piété. Slang,* hockshop, spout, my uncle's. See DEBT.

PAYMENT

Nouns—**1,** payment, defrayment; discharge, remission; acquittance, quittance; settlement, clearance, liquidation, satisfaction, reckoning, arrangement, restitution, repayment, reimbursement; down payment, part payment, deposit; retribution; refund. *Colloq.,* a pound of flesh, an arm and a leg. See PURCHASE.

2, COMPENSATION, recompense, remuneration, bounty, reward, indemnity; expenditure, outlay; dividend; scholarship, fellowship, bursary; alimony, [child] support; welfare. *Slang,* palimony.

3, salary, stipend, wages, pay, paycheck, remuneration, emolument, allowance; bonus, premium, fee, retainer, honorarium, tip, scot, corkage, tribute, hire; bribe, blackmail, hush money. *Slang,* kickback, rake-off.

4, check, blank check, counter check, [bank] draft, money order; cash (see MONEY).

5, see PRICE.

Verbs—**1,** pay, defray, make payment; pay down, pay in advance; redeem; pay in kind; discharge, settle, quit, acquit oneself of; account, reckon, settle, be even *or* quits with; strike a balance; settle *or* square accounts with; wipe off old scores; satisfy; pay off, get even, pay in full; clear, liquidate; pay *or* put up.

2, pay one's way, pay the piper, pay the costs, pick up the check, do the needful; finance, set up; pay as one goes; ante up; expend; lay down; bribe (see PURCHASE). *Colloq.,* foot the bill, chip in, lay out, plunk down, lay *or* put on the line; go Dutch. *Slang,* kick *or* fork over, out, *or* up, tickle *or* grease the palm, dig down, cough up, kick in, shell out.

3, disgorge, make repayment, remit; expend, disburse; repay, refund, reimburse, retribute; reward, make compensation; spend money like water. *Slang,* pay through the nose, pay cash on the barrel-head *or* on the line; shoot one's wad; pay cold cash.

Adjectives—paying; paid, owing nothing, out of debt, quits, square.

Adverbs—to the tune of; on the nail; money down; in return.

Antonyms, see NONPAYMENT, RECEIVING.

peace, *n.* peacetime; amity, friendship, harmony, concord; tranquility, REPOSE, quiescence; truce; neutrality. See PACIFICATION, SILENCE, CONTENT, UNITY.

peaceful, *adj.* peaceable; quiet, tranquil; amicable. See REPOSE, PACIFICATION, FRIEND.

peak, *n.* summit, top, apex, pinnacle; point, crag; crest, HEIGHT; climax. See SHARPNESS.

peaked, *adj.* wan, worn, pale, haggard, tired, weary, fatigued; ailing, unwell, unhealthy, ill, poorly, sickly; thin, gaunt, frail. See WEARINESS, DISEASE.

peal, *n.* reverberation, ring, outburst. —*v.i.* ring, toll, reverberate, sound.

See LOUDNESS.

pearl, *n.* margarite, nacre, mother-of-pearl; artificial *or* cultured pearl; gem, treasure, jewel; pearl beyond price. See ORNAMENT, GOODNESS.

pearly, *adj.* nacreous, silvery, grayish, whitish; lustrous. See COLOR.

peasant, *n.* countryman; peon, *paisano, paisana,* coolie, boor, muzhik, fellah; farmer, laborer, worker; rustic. See POPULACE, AGRICULTURE.

pebble, *n.* pebblestone, nugget, stone. See LAND, HARDNESS.

peck, *v.i.* nip, bite, pick, snip; tap, rap. See IMPULSE, FOOD.

peculiar, *adj.* individual, indigenous, idiosyncratic; idiomatic; strange, odd, unusual, queer; particular, especial. See UNCONFORMITY, SPECIALITY.

pedagogical, *adj.* academic, educational, teacherly, professional, scholastic. See TEACHING.

pedal, *n.* treadle, lever. See INSTRUMENTALITY.

pedant, *n.* scholar, theorist, academician, doctrinaire; prig, bluestocking. See AFFECTATION.

pedantic, *adj.* precise, formal, narrow; bookish, stilted; affected, sophomoric. See AFFECTATION.

peddle, *v.* sell; canvass, hawk, retail. See SALE.

peddler, pedlar, *n.* hawker, huckster, colporteur, sutler, vendor, trader, dealer. See SALE.

pedestrian, *n.* walker, ambler, stroller, peregrinator, hiker. See TRAVEL. —*adj.* prosaic, dull. See WEARINESS.

pedigree, *n.* genealogy, lineage, ANCESTRY, descent, family; background. See NOBILITY.

peek, *v.i.* peep, glance, look, watch; pry. See VISION, CURIOSITY.

peel, *v.t.* strip, divest, bare, uncover, skin, pare. See DIVESTMENT, LAYER. —*n.* See COVERING.

peep, *n.* chirp, cheep, chirrup; glimpse. —*v.i.* peer, peek, look; spy, pry. See VISION, CURIOSITY.

peer, peeress, *n.* equal; nobleman, noblewoman; lord, lady; match. See EQUALITY, NOBILITY. —*v.i.* squint, stare, peep, pry; gaze, scrutinize. See VISION.

peerage, *n.* aristocracy, NOBILITY, the upper class[es].

peerless, *adj.* unequaled, matchless, unbeatable, supreme, unrivaled; indomitable. See SUPERIORITY.

peevish, *adj.* irascible, fretful, cranky, cross, irritable, touchy. See IRASCIBILITY.

peg, *n.* pin; DEGREE. See SUPPORT.

pellet, *n.* pill, tablet, capsule; missile, pebble, hailstone, bullet. See ARMS, ROTUNDITY.

pellmell, *adv.* madly, frantically; helter-skelter, hurry-scurry, breakneck, headlong. *Colloq.,* every which way. *Slang,* lickety-split. See DISORDER.

pelt, *n.* fur, hide, skin, peltry. See COVERING. —*v.* bombard, pepper, stone, strike; drive, beat; hurl, throw, pitch, fling. See IMPULSE, PROPULSION.

pen, *n.* stockade, ENCLOSURE, fold, stall, coop, cage, pound, corral, paddock; stylus, quill. See ABODE. —*v.t.* confine, jail, impound, enclose, restrain, cage, coop; write, indite, inscribe. See RESTRAINT, WRITING.

penalize, *v.t.* punish; fine, imprison, chastise, handicap, *etc.* See PUNISHMENT.

penalty, *n.* retribution, PUNISHMENT; pain, penance, atonement; the devil to pay; penalization; handicap, fine, amercement; forfeit[ure], damages, confiscation. *Slang,* rap.

penance, *n.* ATONEMENT, discipline, punishment; flagellation, fasting; price, suffering, repayment. See PENITENCE.

penchant, *n.* aptitude, leaning, inclination, flair, TENDENCY; predisposition, propensity, TASTE; DESIRE, longing, yearning. *Slang,* yen.

pencil, *n.* crayon, stylus, pastel, chalk. See WRITING, PAINTING.

pend, *v.i.* hang; depend, hang in the balance. See DOUBT, PENDENCY.

PENDENCY

Nouns—**1,** pendency, dependency, dependence, pendulousness, pendulosity, pensility; droop[ing], sag[ging], suspension, hanging, overhang.
2, pendant, drop, earring, eardrop, lavaliere, necklace; pedicel, pedicle, peduncle; hanging, lobe, wattle, tail, train, flag, tag, bob, skirt, tassel, swag; pigtail, queue; bell rope; pendulum, chandelier; appendage, appendix, ADDITION; suspender, belt, garter, fastening, button; peg, knob, hook, hanger, nail, stud, ring, staple, pothook, tenterhook, spar; clothesline, clothespin; gallows.

Verbs—**1,** be pendant, hang, drape, depend, swing, dangle, droop, sag, draggle; bag; flap, trail, flow, overhang, project, jut.
2, suspend, pend, hang [up], sling, hook up, hitch, fasten to, append.

Adjectives—pendent, pendulous, pensile; hanging, pending, drooping, cernuous, flowing, loose; suspended, dependent; overhanging, projecting, jutting; pedunculate, tailed, caudate.

Antonyms, see SUPPORT.

---

pendulum, *n.* oscillator, swing, bob, pendant. See PENDENCY, OSCILLATION.

penetrate, *v.t.* bore, burrow, pierce, enter; cut, perforate; permeate, invade; discern, perceive, understand, uncover. See INGRESS, INTELLIGENCE, PASSAGE, INSERTION.

penetrating, *adj.* astute, discerning, piercing; sharp, subtle, acute, penetrative. See FEELING, INTELLIGENCE.

peninsula, *n.* projection, chersonese, neck, tongue of land. See LAND, CONVEXITY.

PENITENCE

Nouns—**1,** penitence, contrition, compunction, repentance, remorse, regret.
2, self-reproach, self-reproof, self-accusation, self-condemnation, self-humiliation; pangs, qualms, prickings, twinge, *or* voice of conscience; awakened conscience.
3, acknowledgment, confession (see DISCLOSURE); apology, penance, ATONEMENT; recantation.
4, penitent, Magdalene, prodigal son, a sadder and a wiser man.

Verbs—repent, be penitent, be sorry for; rue; regret, think better of; recant; plead guilty; sing *miserere,* sing *de profundis;* confess oneself in the wrong; acknowledge, confess (see DISCLOSURE); humble oneself; beg pardon, apologize, do penance (see ATONEMENT).

Adjectives—penitent, regretful, regretting, sorry, contrite; regrettable, lamentable.

Antonyms, see IMPENITENCE.

---

penitentiary, *n.* PRISON, reformatory.

penmanship, *n.* chirography, handwriting. See WRITING.

pennant, *n.* banner, flag, streamer, pennon. See INDICATION.

penniless, *adj.* indigent, needy, bankrupt, impecunious, poor. *Slang,* broke. See POVERTY.

pension, *n.* allowance, annuity, allotment, settlement; boarding house. See GIVING, ABODE.

pensive, *adj.* thoughtful, reflective, meditative, musing; melancholy, sad, dejected. See THOUGHT, DEJECTION.

pent up, *adj.* held in, suppressed, repressed. See RESTRAINT.

penurious, *adj.* stingy, mean, miserly. See PARSIMONY.

penury, *n.* POVERTY, lack, indigence, destitution, pauperism.

people, *n.* See HUMANITY, POPULACE.

pep, *n., slang,* peppiness; ENERGY, vitality, VIGOR, vim, dash, zest; liveliness, pungency, sharpness, gusto. *Colloq.,* go, zing. *Slang,* pepper.

pepper, *n.* cayenne, black *or* white pepper; bell, hot, *or* sweet pepper. Slang, vim, VIGOR. See FOOD, PUNGENCY. —*v.t.* dot, stud; pelt; season. See DISPERSION, TASTE, ATTACK.

per, *prep.* by, as, by means *or* way of, through, via. See MEANS. —*adv., slang,* apiece, each, a head, per unit. See APPORTIONMENT.

perceive, *v.t.* apprehend, discern; observe, notice, see; comprehend, know. See KNOWLEDGE.

percentage, *n.* compensation, commission, discount; fee; allowance. See PAYMENT.

perceptible, *adj.* appreciable, discernible, visible; tangible, observable, sensible; cognizable. See KNOWLEDGE.

perceptive, *adj.* knowledgeable, observant, understanding; aware, sympathetic; knowing, cognitive. See KNOWLEDGE, INTELLIGENCE, INTUITION, SENSIBILITY.

perch, *n.* rest, roost, nest, seat. —*v.i.* poise, place, roost, settle, alight, sit. See LOCATION, ABODE.

percolate, *v.i.* drip, trickle, permeate; ooze, filter. See EGRESS, WATER.

percussion, *n.* impact, IMPULSE; drums, cymbals, *etc.* (see MUSIC).

perdition, *n.* DESTRUCTION, downfall, ruin, LOSS, fall. See FAILURE.

peremptory, *adj.* commanding, arbitrary, tyrannical, dogmatic; compulsory, binding; absolute, decisive, conclusive. See AUTHORITY, COMPULSION, SEVERITY.

perennial, *adj.* enduring, lasting, endless, persistent; successive, consecutive. See CONTINUITY, DURABILITY.

PERFECTION

Nouns—**1,** perfection, perfectness, indefectibility; impeccancy, impeccability, faultlessness, excellence. See GOODNESS.

2, paragon; ideal, paradigm; nonpareil; pink *or* acme of perfection; *ne plus ultra;* summit, model, standard, pattern, mirror; masterpiece; transcendence, transcendency, SUPERIORITY; quintessence.

3, perfectionist, idealist.

4, see COMPLETION, IMPROVEMENT.

Verbs—be perfect, transcend; bring to perfection, perfect, ripen, mature, consummate, complete, culminate.

Adjectives—perfect, faultless; indefective, indeficient, indefectible; immaculate, spotless, impeccable; unblemished, sound, scatheless, unscathed, intact; right as rain; consummate, finished, best, model, standard, state of the art; inimitable, unparalleled, nonpareil; superhuman, divine; *sans peur et sans reproche*.

Adverbs—to perfection, to a fare-thee-well; perfectly, *etc.;* to a T, to a turn, to the letter.

Antonyms, see IMPERFECTION.

---

perfidious, *adj.* treacherous, crooked, shifty, double-dealing; perjurious, lying, truthless; deceitful, insidious, snakelike. *Colloq.,* two-timing, double-crossing, like a snake in the grass. See IMPROBITY, FALSEHOOD.

perforate, *v.t.* bore, drill, pierce, puncture, penetrate, prick; punch, riddle; tunnel. See OPENING, PASSAGE.

perforce, *adv.* compulsorily, by *or* of NECESSITY; against one's will, in spite of oneself. See COMPULSION.

perform, *v.* enact, play, execute; fulfill, achieve, discharge; act, render, do; operate, work, conduct. See ACTION, AGENCY, COMPLETION, DRAMA, MUSIC.

performance, *n.* ACTION, representation, achievement; rendition, execution, touch; efficiency. See EFFECT, DRAMA.

perfume, *n.* fragrance, aroma; cologne, scent; sachet, attar, perfumery. See ODOR.

perfunctory, *adj.* formal, indifferent, careless; mechanical, crude; casual, superficial. See NEGLECT, INDIFFERENCE.

perhaps, *adv.* maybe, possibly, perchance, mayhap, conceivably. See CHANCE, POSSIBILITY, SUPPOSITION.

peril, *n.* DANGER, hazard, risk, chance, exposure. See THREAT.

perimeter, *n.* periphery, circumference, outline, contour; outside, border, boundary, limit; EDGE, rim, hem, margin, fringe. See CIRCUIT.

period, *n.* second, minute, hour; day, week, month; quarter, year, decade; lifetime, generation, TIME; century, age, milennium, era, epoch; [full] stop *or* pause, sentence; menstruation, monthlies. *Slang,* friend[s], the curse. See END, REGULARITY.

periodic, *adj.* recurrent, cyclic, intermittent, epochal; periodical, seasonal. See DISCONTINUANCE.

periodical, *n.* magazine, journal, quarterly, weekly, monthly. See PUBLICATION.

periodicity, *n.* REGULARITY, reoccurrence, cycle.

peripheral, *adj.* outer, EXTERIOR, neighboring; subsidiary, auxiliary, secondary, lesser; marginal. See LIMIT.

perish, *v.i.* expire, die, crumble. See DEATH, DESTRUCTION, NONEXISTENCE.

perishable, *adj.* impermanent, destructible; temporal, mortal; unenduring. See TRANSIENTNESS.

perjury, *n.* false swearing, FALSEHOOD, perversion, forswearing, fraud.

perk, *v.* perk up, cheer [up], brighten, animate, liven, show signs of life; *colloq.,* bubble, percolate. See CHEERFULNESS, REFRESHMENT.

PERMANENCE

Nouns—**1,** permanence, STABILITY, immutability, fixity; persistence, DURABILITY, duration; constancy, PERPETUITY, *status quo.*

2, PRESERVATION; conservatism, establishment; law of the Medes and the Persians; conservative, reactionary, stick-in-the-mud, diehard, fogy, right-winger, nonprogressive, Tory, Hunker, fixture. *Colloq.,* holdout, standpatter. *Slang,* mossback, fuddy-duddy.

Verbs—persist, remain, stay; hold [out], hold on; last, endure, [a]bide, maintain, keep; stand [fast]; subsist, survive; hold one's ground, hold good, stand pat.

Adjectives—permanent, stable, fixed, standing, immovable, immutable, established, settled, steadfast; constant, eternal, lifelong, lasting, durable, persistent, unending, perpetual, monotonous; unfading, unfailing, *etc.;* invariable, indelible, indestructible, inextinguishable, intact, inviolate; conservative, reactionary, right-wing; stationary; rootbound.

Adverbs—*in statu quo,* as usual; at a standstill, permanently, finally, for good, forever. *Slang,* until Hell freezes over.

Antonyms, see CHANGE.

---

permeate, *v.t.* pervade, saturate, overspread, infiltrate, penetrate. See PASSAGE, PRESENCE, MIXTURE.

PERMISSION

Nouns—**1,** permission, leave; allowance, sufferance; tolerance, toleration; FREEDOM, liberty, law, license, concession, grace; indulgence, lenity, LENIENCY; favor, ASSENT, dispensation, EXEMPTION, release; connivance; open door.
2, authorization, warranty, accordance, admission, permit, warrant, brevet, precept, fiat, imprimatur, sanction, AUTHORITY, firman, go-ahead; free hand, pass, passport; furlough, license, *carte blanche,* ticket of leave; grant, charter, patent. *Colloq.,* green light, signal, okay, O.K., blank check.

Verbs—**1,** permit; give permission, give power, entitle; let, allow, admit; suffer, bear with, tolerate, recognize; accord, vouchsafe, favor, humor, indulge, stretch a point; wink at, connive at, [let] pass; shut one's eyes to; give *carte blanche;* leave alone, leave to one's own devices, leave the door open; allow for, open the door to, open the floodgates, let loose; give the reins *or* free rein to. *Colloq.,* stand for.
2, grant, empower, character, enfranchise, confer a privilege, license, authorize, warrant; sanction; entrust, COMMISSION; sanctify, ordain, prescribe. *Colloq.,* okay, O.K., write one's own ticket.

Adjectives—permitting, permissive, indulgent; permitted, permissible, allowable, lawful (see LEGALITY); unconditional.

Adverbs—permissibly, by leave, with leave, on leave; under favor of; *ad libitum,* freely; with no holds barred.

Antonyms, see PROHIBITION.

permutation, *n.* See INTERCHANGE, CHANGE.

pernicious, *adj.* malign, ruinous, poisonous, detrimental, injurious, harmful; wicked. See BADNESS.

peroration, *n.* epilogue, conclusion; harangue. See DIFFUSENESS, END, SPEECH.

perpendicular, *adj.* erect, upright; sheer, precipitous; VERTICAL, plumb.

perpetrate, *v.t.* commit, inflict; perform, do, practice. See ACTION.

PERPETUITY

Nouns—perpetuity; everlastingness, unceasingness, *etc.;* eternity, INFINITY, aye, TIME without end, sempiternity; deathlessness, immortality, athanasia; incessance, CONTINUITY, DURABILITY, perpetuation, PRESERVATION. See STABILITY.

Verbs—last *or* endure forever, have no end, never end *or* die; perpetuate, eternalize, eternize, immortalize, continue, preserve.

Adjectives—perpetual, everlasting, unceasing, endless, ageless, unending, having no end; [co-]eternal, everliving, everflowing, sempiternal, continual, ceaseless, incessant, uninterrupted, interminable, infinite, neverending; unfailing, evergreen, amaranthine; deathless, immortal, undying, imperishable, perdurable; permanent, lasting, enduring; perennial, long-lived, dateless, illimitable, continued, constant.

Adverbs—perpetually, in perpetuity, always, ever[more], aye; forever, for evermore, for aye, for ever and a day, for ever and ever; in all ages, from age to age, without end, world without end, time without end; to the end of time, to the crack of doom; till death [do us part], till doomsday; constantly. *Colloq.*, for keeps, for good [and all], till Hell freezes over, till the cows come home.

Antonyms, see TRANSIENTNESS, TIME.

---

perplex, *v.* puzzle, bewilder, confuse, mystify, confound, nonplus; distract, disconcert. See DIFFICULTY, UNINTELLIGIBILITY, DOUBT.

perquisite, *n.* reward, bonus, gratuity, tip; bribe; due. *Slang,* perk. See ACQUISITION, GIVING, STEALING.

per se, *adv.* by itself, intrinsically, essentially; virtually, in the main; by nature, as a thing apart. See INTRINSIC, UNITY.

persecute, *v.t.* molest, oppress, maltreat, pursue, beset; abuse, injure; hound, annoy, trouble. See MALEVOLENCE, PAIN, BADNESS, WRONG.

perseverance, *n.* continuance, PERMANENCE; firmness, STABILITY; constancy, steadiness; TENACITY *or* singleness of purpose; persistence, plodding, patience; industry; pertinacity; gameness, pluck, stamina, backbone; indefatigability; bulldog COURAGE, sand, grit; determination. *Colloq.*, stick-to-itiveness. See RESOLUTION, FREQUENCY.

persist, *v.i.* persevere, continue, remain, endure, stand, abide, plod. See PERMANENCE, FREQUENCY, CONTINUITY.

person, *n.* individual, body, somebody, anybody; man, woman, child; human. See HUMANITY.

personable, *adj.* presentable; charming, [con]genial. See BEAUTY.

personage, *n.* dignitary, official, celebrity, notable, figure, somebody, bigwig. *Colloq.*, V.I.P., big wheel. See IMPORTANCE, NOBILITY.

personal, *adj.* private, individual, intimate, own, special, particular; invidious (of a remark). See SPECIALITY.

personality, *n.* character, individuality, self, ego; *colloq.*, celebrity, notable. See REPUTE, SPECIALITY, IDENTITY.

personify, *v.t.* embody, typify, symbolize, exemplify; represent, personate. See REPRESENTATION.

personnel, *n.* employees, workers, help; faculty, hands, squad, crew, gang, staff, team, rank and file; staffers. *Slang,* stable. See SERVANT.

perspective, *n.* view, angle, aspect, position; field of view *or* vision, vista, prospect, scene, vantage [point]; outlook, viewpoint, scope, grasp, appreciation, comprehension, point of view, judgment; remove, DISTANCE; context, orientation, insight. *Colloq.*, slant. See EXPECTATION, COLOR, APPEARANCE.

perspicacity, *n.* discernment, discrimination, acuteness, keenness; shrewdness; penetration, insight, acumen. See INTELLIGENCE.

perspicuity, *n.* intelligibility; manifestation; definiteness, definition; exactness. See INTELLIGENCE.

perspire, *v.* exude, sweat, exhale, excrete, swelter. See EXCRETION.

persuade, *v.t.* induce, prevail upon, win [over]; convince, satisfy, assure. See BELIEF, CAUSE, INFLUENCE.

persuasible, *adj.* docile, tractable, convincible; amenable, unresistant; persuadable. See INFLUENCE.

persuasion, *n.* argument, plea, exhortation; conviction; INFLUENCE, insistence. See BELIEF, CAUSE.

persuasive, *adj.* inducive; cogent, convincing, logical; winning. See BELIEF, CAUSE.

pert, *adj.* impudent, saucy, flippant; forward, bold, perky. *Slang,* fresh, flip, sassy. See DISCOURTESY, INSOLENCE.

pertain, *v.i.* apply, refer, bear upon; belong, relate; appertain, concern; affect. See RELATION.

pertinacious, *adj.* persevering, persistent; obstinate, unyielding, constant, resolute, firm. See RESOLUTION.

pertinent, *adj.* relevant, apposite,

applicable, apt. See RELATION.

perturbation, *n.* disturbance; disquiet, uneasiness, discomposure, apprehension, worry; trepidation, restlessness. See AGITATION, EXCITEMENT, FEAR.

peruse, *v.t.* read, con, study; examine. See INQUIRY, LEARNING.

pervade, *v.t.* fill, permeate, penetrate, imbue, overspread, impregnate, saturate; infiltrate. See PRESENCE, MIXTURE.

perverse, *adj.* contrary, stubborn, obstinate, self-willed; ungovernable, wayward; cross, petulant. See OBSTINACY, WRONG.

perversion, *n.* DISTORTION, misuse, misrepresentation, misconstruction; corruption, debasement. See DETERIORATION, IMPIETY, IMPURITY.

perversity, *n.* OBSTINACY, obduracy, perverseness; waywardness, unconformity; contumacy, wickedness. *Slang,* mulishness, cussedness. See IRASCIBILITY.

pervert, *v.t.* apostasize, distort, twist, garble, debase, misrepresent, corrupt, mislead, misinterpret, misstate; equivocate. See DISTORTION, FALSEHOOD.

pesky, *adj., colloq.,* troublesome, annoying. See DISCONTENT.

pessimism, *n.* DEJECTION; cynicism, morbidity. See HOPELESSNESS.

pest, *n.* plague, pestilence, epidemic; parasite, infestation; nuisance, trouble; bane, scourge, curse. See BADNESS, DISEASE.

pester, *v.t.* plague, annoy, trouble, vex, irritate, displease. See DISCONTENT.

pestilence, *n.* DISEASE, plague, epidemic.

pet, *n.* favorite, beloved, love, dearest, darling. —*v.t.* cherish, fondle, caress, embrace, stroke, cuddle. See ENDEARMENT, LOVE, FLATTERY.

petal, *n.* perianth; corolla, calyx, corona. See VEGETABLE.

peter out, *v.i.* diminish, DECREASE.

petite, *adj.* small, mignon, diminutive, trim, tiny. See LITTLENESS.

petition, *n.* plea, REQUEST, entreaty, supplication, prayer; asking, address. —*v.t.* ask, beg, entreat, REQUEST, plead, appeal, implore.

petrify, *v.t.* calcify, turn to stone, lapidify, fossilize; stun, astonish; stupefy, shock; stiffen, harden, paralyze. See DENSITY, HARDNESS, FEAR, INORGANIC MATTER.

petroleum, *n.* OIL. See FUEL.

petticoat, *n.* slip, chemise, underskirt, crinoline, camisole, balmoral, half-slip. See CLOTHING.

petty, *adj.* trivial, unimportant, small, mean, trifling; contemptible, spiteful. See UNIMPORTANCE.

petulant, *adj.* fretful, irritable, complaining, peevish. See IRASCIBILITY.

phantasm, *n.* apparition, specter; illusion. See IMAGINATION, DEMON.

phantom, *n.* specter, illusion, apparition, ghost, spirit, shade, shadow. See DEMON.

pharmacist, *n.* chemist, apothecary, druggist. See REMEDY.

phase, *n.* APPEARANCE, state, condition, situation, aspect; shape, FORM, angle. See CIRCUMSTANCE.

phenomenon, *n.* prodigy; marvel, WONDER; happening, OCCURRENCE.

philanderer, *n.* dallier, trifler, lecher, Romeo, Casanova, lover, rake, roué, libertine. *Colloq.,* playboy. *Slang,* sugar daddy; wolf. See ENDEARMENT, IMPURITY.

philanthropy, *n.* altruism, humanity, humanitarianism; BENEVOLENCE; generosity, LIBERALITY. See UNSELFISHNESS.

Philistine, *n.* vandal; bigot, yahoo, barbarian. See MEDIOCRITY, MISJUDGMENT.

philosophical, *adj.* contemplative, deliberative, thoughtful, speculative; imperturbable, calm; wise, rational; stoical, Platonic, Socratic, Aristotelian. See THOUGHT.

phlegmatic, *adj.* stolid, dull, apathetic; calm, imperturbable, languid, unemotional, inert, cold. See INSENSIBILITY.

phobia, *n.* FEAR, dread, aversion,

revulsion, repulsion, DISLIKE, antipathy; acrophobia, claustrophobia, *etc*. See INSANITY.

phonetic, *adj*. phonetical, phonic, phonal, sonant; vocal, voiced, lingual, tonic, oral, spoken. See SOUND, SPEECH.

phonograph, *n*. Gramophone, Graphophone, Panatrope, Victrola, record player; pickup, playback, turntable; dictating machine. See RECORD.

phony, *adj., colloq.*, spurious, fraudulent, sham, mock, trumped-up, forged; gimcrack, pasteboard; deceitful, false-hearted, lying; glib, canting, superficial. *Colloq.*, fake. *Slang*, put-on. —*n., colloq.*, counterfeit, fraud; charlatan, quack, impostor, mountebank. *Colloq.*, fake; faker. See DECEPTION.

photograph, *n*. picture; photo, film, snapshot, reproduction; portrait. See REPRESENTATION.

phrase, *n*. expression; sentence, paragraph, clause; figure of speech, euphemism; idiom; locution; motto, maxim. —*v.t.* express, word, term, couch; voice. See FIGURATIVE, WRITING, GRAMMAR.

physic, *n*. laxative, cathartic, purgative; drug, medicine; pill, dose. —*v.t.* purge, drench; treat, doctor. See REMEDY.

physical, *adj*. bodily, anatomical; material, substantial. See SUBSTANCE.

physician, *n*. doctor, medic, medico, surgeon, specialist; [general] practitioner, G.P.; consultant, adviser, healer. See REMEDY.

physique, *n*. frame, body, FORM; appearance, size; build, musculature. See SUBSTANCE.

piano, *n*. pianoforte, fortepiano, spinet, pianette, upright; clavier, [clavi]cembalo. *Slang*, eighty-eight. See MUSIC.

piazza, *n*. square, place, street; porch, veranda, portico. See ABODE, RECEPTACLE.

picaresque, *adj*. roguish, swaggering, adventurous; episodic. See DESCRIPTION.

picayune, *adj*. trifling (see UNIMPORTANCE).

pick, *n*. best, cream, flower, elite, CHOICE; selection; pick-ax. See SHARPNESS. —*v.t.* select, choose; pluck, garner, gather; cull. See GOODNESS, APPROBATION.

picket, *n*. post, pale, fence; sentry, guard, sentinel, patrol; striker, protester, goon. See WARNING, RESTRAINT, DISOBEDIENCE. —*v.* enclose, bar, fence; tether, restrain. See CIRCUMSCRIPTION.

pickle, *v.t.* preserve, salt, corn, brine, marinate. See PRESERVATION, SOURNESS.

pickpocket, *n*. thief, robber, cutpurse. *Slang*, dip. See STEALING.

picnic, *n*. excursion, junket, outing, festivity; cookout, barbecue, fishfry, *etc*. See AMUSEMENT, FOOD.

pictorial, *adj*. delineatory, graphic, depicting; illustrated. See PAINTING, REPRESENTATION.

picture, *n*. image, likeness, counterpart; portrayal, REPRESENTATION, view, scene, tableau, setting; drawing, PAINTING, photograph, sketch, etching, canvas. See APPEARANCE.

picturesque, *adj*. artistic, graphic, attractive; vivid; quaint. See BEAUTY, VIGOR.

pie, *n*. pastry, pasty, patisserie, tart; mud pie. See SWEETNESS, FOOD.

piece, *n*. scrap, morsel, bit; section, fragment, PART. —*v.t.* unite, combine, patch, repair. See JUNCTION, DRAMA.

piecemeal, *adv*. one at a time, one by one; gradually, little by little, bit by bit, step by step, in drops; by stages *or* degrees, by dribs and drabs. See PART, DEGREE, SLOWNESS.

pied, *adj*. mottled, brindled, piebald, dappled. See VARIEGATION.

pier, *n*. wharf, quay, mole, dock, breakwater; pillar, shaft, SUPPORT.

pierce, *v.t.* puncture, penetrate, perforate, bore, drill; stab, wound; affect; nip, chill. See OPENING.

piercing, *adj.* sharp, penetrating, keen, acute; discerning; cutting, biting; painful, affecting, chilling; high, shrill. See COLD, FEELING.

PIETY

Nouns—**1,** piety, piousness, devoutness; RELIGION, theism, faith, BELIEF; religiousness, holiness, saintliness; reverence, WORSHIP, veneration, devotion; grace, unction, edification; sanctity, sanctitude; consecration; theopathy. See VIRTUE.

2, beatification, canonization; sanctification; adoption, regeneration, palingenesis, conversion, justification, salvation, redemption; inspiration; pilgrimage (see TRAVEL); bread of life; body and blood of Christ.

3, believer, convert, theist, Christian, devotee, pietist, pilgrim; revivalist, evangelist; the good, the righteous, the just, the believing, the elect; saint, Madonna; the children of God, the Kingdom of light; born-again Christian. *Slang,* Jesus freak.

Verbs—**1,** be pious, have faith, believe, venerate, revere; be converted.

2, sanctify, beatify, canonize, inspire, hallow, bless, consecrate, enshrine, keep holy; convert, edify, redeem, save, regenerate.

Adjectives—pious, religious, devout, devoted, reverent, godly, humble, pure, holy, spiritual, pietistic; saintly, saintlike; seraphic, sacred, solemn; believing, faithful, Christian, Catholic; holier-than-thou; elected, adopted, justified, sanctified, beatified, canonized, regenerate[d], inspired, consecrated, converted, unearthly, inexpressible.

Antonyms, see IMPIETY.

pig, *n.* hog, sow, boar, swine; piglet; glutton; sloven, slob. See ANIMAL, GLUTTONY, UNCLEANNESS.

pigeon, *n.* dove, homer, squab, pouter, turbit, tumbler, roler, fantail, nun; *slang,* dupe, easy mark, sitting duck, gull. *Colloq.,* sucker, chump. *Slang,* pushover; clay pigeon. See CREDULITY, ANIMAL.

pigeonhole, *n.* cubbyhole, niche, compartment. See RECEPTACLE. —*v.t.* file away, file and forget; postpone, put off, delay; classify. See LATENESS CLASS.

piggyback, *adv.* pickaback. See SUPPORT.

pigheaded, *adj.* stubborn, tenacious, obstinate, *entêté*. See OBSTINACY.

pigment, *n.* COLOR, stain, dye, tint, paint, shade.

pigmy, *n.* See PYGMY.

pike, *n.* tip, point, spike; pikestaff, spear, lance, halberd, javelin. See ARMS, SHARPNESS.

piker, *n., slang,* pennypincher, tightwad, cheapskate, miser. See PARSIMONY.

pile, *n.* structure, building, edifice; nap; heap, mass, pyre; quantity. See ASSEMBLAGE. —*v.t.* accumulate, load, amass, furnish. See GREATNESS, COVERING, TEXTURE.

pilfer, *v.* filch, rob, steal, plunder, thieve; shoplift. See STEALING.

pilgrim, *n.* wayfarer, traveler, migrant; settler, pioneer, newcomer; hadji, palmer, devotee. See TRAVEL, PIETY.

pilgrimage, *n.* journey, crusade, mission, quest, hadj, expedition; life, lifetime. See TRAVEL, UNDERTAKING.

pill, *n.* bolus, tablet, capsule. *Slang,* goofball. See REMEDY.

pillage, *n.* spoliation, plunder, vandalism, theft, depredation. —*v.t.* plunder, rape, sack, thieve. See STEALING.

pillar, *n.* column, pedestal, SUPPORT, post, obelisk; mainstay. See STABILITY.

pillow, *n.* cushion, bolster, headrest, pad. See SUPPORT.

pilot, *n.* helmsman, steersman, guide; counselor; aviator, airman. See AVIATION, DIRECTION, INFORMATION, NAVIGATION.

pimp, *n.* procurer, solicitor, panderer, tout; white slaver; whoremonger; *maquereau*. *Colloq.*, hustler. *Slang*, cadet, fancy man. See EVILDOER.

pimple, *n.* pustule, boil, gathering, papule, pock, blackhead; blemish. See DISEASE, CONVEXITY.

pin, *n.* peg, spoke, dowel; fastener, bolt, toggle; needle, bodkin, skewer, style; brooch, scarf pin, fraternity pin, tie pin; badge. See ORNAMENT, SHARPNESS, MARRIAGE.—*v.t.* fasten, hold, bind, rivet, attach, secure; *colloq.*, engage. See JUNCTION, LOCATION.

pinch, *n.* stress, strain, pressure, emergency, DIFFICULTY, plight, predicament; pinching, nip; *slang*, arrest. See CIRCUMSTANCE, RESTRAINT. —*v.* nip, compress, tighten, squeeze; chill, bite, hurt. See CONTRACTION, PAIN.

pine, *v.i.* languish, long, crave; wither, droop. See DEJECTION, DISEASE, DESIRE.

pinnacle, *n.* summit, peak, spire, acme, crown. See HEIGHT.

pinpoint, *v.* locate, localize, place. *Colloq.*, pin down, nail. See LOCATION.

pinto, *adj.* mottled (see VARIEGATION).

pioneer, *n.* forerunner, settler; originator. See PRECEDENCE.

pious, *adj.* devout (see PIETY).

pipe, *n.* PASSAGE, tube, main; briar, corncob, meerschaum; flute, fife, bagpipe, flageolet. See MUSIC, OPENING, CRY.

piquant, *adj.* pungent, flavorful, strong, sharp; tart; keen, stimulating. See FEELING, EXCITEMENT, PUNGENCY.

pique, *v.t.* sting, cut, nettle, irritate, vex, offend; prick, jab; intrigue, stimulate, arouse interest. See EXCITEMENT.

pirate, *n.* buccaneer, marauder, corsair, freebooter, sea robber, privateer; plagiarist. —*v.t.* plunder, picaroon, appropriate; plagiarize, steal. See STEALING.

pistol, *n.* automatic, firearm, gun, derringer, revolver. *Colloq.*, shooting iron. *Slang*, gat, heater. See ARMS.

pit, *n.* hole, hollow, indentation, crater, excavation; abyss, HELL, Hades; mine, chasm; trap, snare. See CONCAVITY.

pitch, *n.* note, modulation, tone; roll, plunge, toss, dip, reel, lurch; slant, slope, drop; ascent, rise, grade, HEIGHT, range; resin, tar. —*v.t.* throw, toss; build, erect, set, establish; cast, heave. —*v.i.* roll, reel, plunge, toss; slope. See PROPULSION, SOUND, DEGREE.

pitcher, *n.* carafe, jug, jar, bottle, vessel, ewer, cruet, decanter; hurler, tosser, chucker, left- *or* righthander, spitballer, relief *or* starting pitcher. *Colloq.*, righty, lefty, portsider. *Slang*, arm; southpaw. See RECEPTACLE, PROPULSION.

piteous, *adj.* grievous, sorrowful; pitiable, pathetic; wretched, miserable. See PAIN, PITY.

pitfall, *n.* trap, snare, gin, pit; rocks, [coral] reefs, snags; [quick] sands, slippery ground; breakers, shoals, shallows; precipice. See DANGER.

pith, *n.* pulp, core, heart; essence, kernel, substance, gist. See MEANING, INTRINSIC, MIDDLE.

pithy, *adj.* concise; vigorous, forceful, powerful; meaningful; terse, brief, laconic. See MEANING.

pitiable, *adj.* miserable, paltry, wretched, deplorable; insignificant, woeful, pathetic. See BADNESS, PAIN, PITY, CONTEMPT.

pitiful, *adj.* compassionate (see PITY); deplorable, disreputable, pitiable, wretched; lamentable, piteous, paltry. See BADNESS, CONTEMPT, DISREPUTE.

pitiless, *n.* inclement, malevolent;

merciless, cruel, unfeeling, ruthless. See SEVERITY.

pittance, *n.* bit, mite, driblet; dole; pension, alms, allowance. See INSUFFICIENCY.

pitted, *adj.* blemished, variolate; honeycombed, favose, pocked, dented; cratered. See CONCAVITY.

PITY

Nouns—pity, compassion, commiseration, sympathy; LAMENTATION, condolence; empathy, fellow-feeling, tenderness, humanity, mercy, clemency; LENIENCY, charity, ruth, quarter, grace. See FEELING.

Verbs—**1,** pity; have, give, show, *or* take pity; commiserate, condole, sympathize, empathize; feel for, be sorry for; weep, melt, thaw, forbear, relax, relent, give quarter; give the *coup de grâce,* put out of one's misery; have mercy, have a heart, have one's heart go out to; be charitable; be lenient.
2, excite pity, touch, affect, soften; melt [the heart]; disarm; throw oneself at the feet of.

Adjectives—pitying, piteous, pitiful, pitiable; compassionate, sympathetic, affected, touched; merciful, clement, ruthful; humane; humanitarian, philanthropic, tenderhearted, softhearted, lenient; melting, weak.

Antonyms, see SEVERITY.

---

pivot, *n.* axis, turning point; gudgeon; joint, axle, hinge; focus; jewel. See CAUSE, JUNCTION. —*v.i.* swivel, turn, whirl; roll; hinge. See ROTATION.

pixilated, *adj.* eccentric, possessed. See INSANITY.

pixy, *n.* elf, sprite. See MYTHICAL DEITIES, DEMON.

placard, *n.* notice, poster, billboard, advertisement, bill. See PUBLICATION.

placate, *v.* soothe, quiet; pacify, conciliate; satisfy, give satisfaction, make it up. *Colloq.,* butter up, rub the right way. See PACIFICATION.

place, *n.* lieu, spot, point; niche, nook, hole; premises, precinct, station; locality; somewhere, someplace, anyplace; situation. —*v.t.* locate, identify; arrange; put, repose; employ, engage. See ABODE, LOCATION, BUSINESS, CIRCUMSTANCE, ARRANGEMENT.

placid, *adj.* serene, unruffled; calm, cool, collected; gentle, peaceful, quiet, undisturbed. See INEXCITABILITY.

plagiarize, *v.t.* pirate, infringe on, COPY, transcribe; imitate, simulate, ape; forge, counterfeit. *Colloq.,* crib, lift, sneak; pick one's brains. *Slang,* swipe, snitch, pinch. See STEALING.

plague, *n.* affliction, woe, visitation; nuisance, pest; bane, scourge, curse; pestilence, DISEASE, epidemic; bubonic plague, white *or* black death; cholera, tuberculosis, smallpox, typhoid, [Asian, *etc.*] flu. —*v.t.* annoy, tease, pester, molest, bother. *Colloq.,* be on one's back, get on one's nerves. See DISCONTENT.

plaid, *n.* plaidie, tartan, check; kilt, shawl. See VARIEGATION.

plain, *adj.* simple, unornamented (see SIMPLENESS); homely (see UGLINESS). —*n.* prairie, tableland, steppe, savanna, tundra, heath, pampas, mesa, llana; meadow, pasture, field. See LAND, HORIZONTAL.

plaintiff, *n.* litigant. See LAWSUIT, ACCUSATION.

plaintive, *adj.* mournful, wistful, sad, melancholy, sorrowful. See LAMENTATION.

PLAN

Nouns—**1,** plan, scheme, design, project, UNDERTAKING; aim, INTENTION;

proposal, proposition, suggestion; resolution, resolve, motion; precaution, provision, PREPARATION, calculation, meditation; operation, METHOD, way, setup, custom, *modus operandi*. See ORDER.

2, sketch, skeleton, outline, draft, diagram, blueprint, layout, schematic; architecture; delineation, pattern, format, representation, specifications, tabulation; chart, map, graph, atlas.

3, program, prospectus, syllabus, forecast, card, bill; protocol, order of the day, agenda; procedure, course, plank, platform; strategy, regime, line of CONDUCT, game plan, campaign; budget.

4, contrivance, invention, idea, conception, expedient, recipe, formula, nostrum; artifice, device, stratagem, ploy; trick (see CUNNING); alternative, loophole, makeshift; last resort; ace in the hole, card up one's sleeve. *Colloq.*, dodge. *Slang*, gadget, gimmick. See INSTRUMENTALITY, IMAGINATION.

5, plot, intrigue, cabal, counterplot, countermine, conspiracy, machination, collusion. *Slang*, racket.

6, schemer, strategist, machinator, tactician; planner, architect, promoter, organizer, designer; conspirator, plotter, conniver, dreamer, Machiavelli; junto, cabal (see PARTY).

Verbs—**1,** plan, scheme; design, frame, diagram, sketch, map, lay off, delineate, figure, represent.

2, contrive, project, schedule, forecast, aim, propose, suggest, premeditate, spring a project; devise, invent, concoct; chalk, cut, lay, block *or* map out, blueprint, lay down a plan; shape, mark, *or* set a course; [pre]concert, pre-establish, prepare; study, calculate, formulate, work out, envision, contemplate, cogitate, digest, mature, resolve, intend, destine, provide, take steps *or* measures; [re]cast, systematize, organize, arrange; hatch [a plot], plot, brew, counterplot, intrigue; machinate, incubate, rig, conspire. *Colloq.*, cook up, have something on. *Slang*, wheel and deal.

Adjectives—**1,** planned, arranged, *etc.;* on the table, on the agenda, laid out, under consideration; premeditated, deliberate, purposed, meant, intended, intentional; **2,** planning, strategic[al], systematic, schematic; conspiratorial, scheming, designing (see CUNNING); slated for. *Colloq.*, in the works, put-up.

Antonyms, see CHANCE.

---

plane, *n.* level, stratum, grade, surface; jointer, block, *or* jack plane. —*adj.* level, flat. —*v.t.* smooth, mill, even, traverse, shave, level. —*v.i.* glide. See AVIATION, HORIZONTAL, SMOOTHNESS.

planet, *n.* planetoid, asteroid. See UNIVERSE.

plank, *n.* board, timber; flooring, deck; gangplank *or* -board; platform, policy, PLAN, promise. See LAYER, MATERIALS.

plant, *n.* VEGETABLE, herb, organism, flower, seedling, shrub, sprout, shoot; machinery, factory, equipment. *Slang*, hoax, trick, frameup. See DECEPTION. —*v.* implant, deposit, settle; colonize; sow, seed, engender. See AGRICULTURE, LOCATION.

plantation, *n.* outpost, colony, settlement; farm[stead], ranch, spread; nursery, orchard, grove, vineyard, stand. See AGRICULTURE, ABODE.

plaque, *n.* tablet, sign, nameplate. *Colloq.*, shingle. See INDICATION.

plaster, *n.* plaster of Paris, mortar, parget, stucco, gesso; paste, lime; clay, adobe, mud; poultice, dressing, bandage. See MATERIALS, CONNECTION, REMEDY. —*v.t.* coat, cover, conceal, smear; caulk, repair, mend; stick up, paste. See COVERING.

plastered, *adj.*, *slang*, drunk. *Slang*,

tight, soused. See DRINKING.

plastic, *adj.* moldable, malleable, ductile, formable, pliant, impressionable, formative. See FORM, SOFTNESS.

plate, *n.* platter, dish, utensil, tray; slab, sheet, planch; coating, veneer, coat; denture. See RECEPTACLE, LAYER. —*v.t.* overlay, laminate; gild, silver, platinize; veneer; electroplate. See COVERING, LAYER.

plateau, *n.* plain, mesa; platform; highland, tableland. See HORIZONTAL.

platform, *n.* stand, dais, rostrum, pulpit, stage; foundation, base, basis; policy, PLAN. See SUPPORT, HORIZONTAL.

platitude, *n.* commonplace, cliché, truism, banality, MAXIM. See UNMEANINGNESS.

platonic, *adj.* idealistic, abstract, spiritual, intellectual; unsexual, uncarnal, chaste; pure, perfect. See THOUGHT, PURITY.

platter, *n.* trencher, tray, waiter, dish, plate. See RECEPTACLE, HORIZONTAL.

plaudit, *n.* acclaim, applause, encomium. See APPROBATION.

plausible, *adj.* credible, reasonable, believable; specious, colored; justifiable, defensible. See POSSIBILITY.

play, *n.* sport, frolic, fun, AMUSEMENT, game, recreation; DRAMA, comedy, tragedy; scope, FREEDOM, latitude, sweep, range. —*v.* operate, wield, ply; act, perform; compete; pluck, bow, strike, beat; move, caper, gambol, dally, idle, disport. See INFLUENCE, EXERTION, SPACE, MUSIC.

playboy, *n., slang,* idler, do-nothing, loafer; voluptuary, sensualist, pleasure seeker, sybarite, epicurean, hedonist. See PLEASURE.

player, *n.* performer, actor, musician, instrumentalist; participant, competitor. See DRAMA, MUSIC, ARTIST.

playful, *adj.* frolicsome, mischievous, sportive, frisky; roguish, prankish; jolly, rollicking. See AMUSEMENT, CHEERFULNESS.

playground, *n.* playing *or* athletic field. See AMUSEMENT, ARENA.

plaything, *n.* toy, doll, bauble; puzzle, kite, ball, top, *etc.;* bagatelle, trifle, trinket. See AMUSEMENT, UNIMPORTANCE.

playwright, *n.* playwriter, dramaturgist, dramatist, scenarist, librettist; farceur. See DRAMA.

plaza, *n.* piazza, forum, marketplace. See RECEPTACLE.

plea, *n.* REQUEST, petition; assertion, allegation, advocation, advocacy; pretext, pretense, subterfuge, feint, blind; excuse, VINDICATION. See LAWSUIT.

plead, *v.* allege, assert, state; take one's stand upon; beg, petition, urge, REQUEST. See VINDICATION, LAWSUIT.

pleasant, *adj.* agreeable (see PLEASURE).

pleasantry, *n.* WIT, jest, banter, chaff, chitchat, persiflage.

please, *adv.* if you please, pray, *s'il vous plaît, bitte, por favor, etc.;* kindly, do. See REQUEST. —*v.* gratify, satisfy, delight. See PLEASURE.

PLEASURE

Nouns—**1,** pleasure, enjoyment, gratification; voluptuousness, sensuality; luxuriousness; GLUTTONY; titillation, gusto; creature comforts, comfort, ease, [lap of] luxury; purple and fine linen; bed of down *or* roses, life of Riley; velvet, clover; treat; REFRESHMENT, feast; AMUSEMENT; fleshpots, epicureanism, sybaritism, hedonism. See CONTENT, FEELING.

2, delectation; relish, zest; satisfaction, contentment, complacency; well-being; good, snugness, comfort, cushion, *sans souci,* peace of mind.

3, joy, gladness, delight, euphoria; CHEERFULNESS; happiness, felicity, bliss; beatitude, beatification; enchantment, transport, rapture, ravishment, ecstasy;

summum bonum; HEAVEN; unalloyed happiness. *Colloq.*, one's cup of tea. *Slang*, bang, thrills, kicks, charge.

4, honeymoon, palmy *or* halcyon days; golden age *or* time; Arcadia, Eden, Utopia, happy valley, time of one's life; prime, heyday.

5, pleasurableness, pleasantness, agreeableness, delectability; sunny *or* bright side.

6, playboy, playgirl, voluptuary, sensualist, pleasure seeker, sybarite, epicure[an], hedonist. *Slang*, good-time Charlie *or* girl, sport, cutup.

Verbs—**1,** feel pleasure, be pleased, take pleasure in; revel, rejoice, *or* delight in, like, LOVE; enjoy oneself, give oneself up to; take to, take a fancy to; enjoy, relish, luxuriate in, riot in, bask in, swim in, wallow in; thrive *or* feast on; light up; gloat over, smack one's lips; be in clover, live on the fat of the land, walk on air, live in comfort, bask in the sunshine. *Colloq.*, live high off the hog; take the gravy train. *Slang*, have a ball, go into orbit; dig, get off (on), get a kick (from), lick one's chops.

2, cause, give, *or* afford pleasure; please, charm, delight, beguile, enchant, entrance, enrapture, enthrall, transport, bewitch; [en]ravish; bless, beatify; satisfy, gratify; slake, satiate, quench; indulge, humor, flatter, tickle [the palate], regale, refresh; enliven; treat; amuse; strike *or* tickle one's fancy; warm the cockles of the heart; do one's heart good, do one good; attract, allure, stimulate, interest; thrill. *Colloq.*, hit the spot, tickle pink. *Slang*, send; give a kick, bang, *or* charge.

Adjectives—**1,** pleased, glad[some]; pleased as Punch; happy as a king, as a lark, *or* as the day is long; thrice blest; in clover, in paradise, in raptures, on top of the world; overjoyed, entranced, *etc.*; ecstatic, beatific; unalloyed, cloudless. *Slang*, on cloud nine.

2, pleasing, pleasant, pleasurable; agreeable; grateful, gratifying, welcome [as the flowers in May]; to one's taste *or* liking, after one's own heart; sweet, delectable, nice, dainty; palatable; cozy, snug; sumptuous, sensuous, luxurious, voluptuous; empyrean, elysian, heavenly; palmy, halcyon. *Colloq.*, up *or* down one's alley. *Slang*, scrumptious, hunky-dory.

Adverbs—with pleasure; happily, delightedly, *etc.*

Antonyms, see PAIN, ASCETICISM.

---

pleat, *n.* plait, corrugation, wrinkle; FOLD, plicature, ply; doubling. —*v.t.* crease, gather, flounce, ruffle; FOLD over, play, pucker; corrugate.

plebeian, *adj.* unrefined, ill-bred, common, vulgar; lowborn, obscure, proletarian. See POPULACE.

plebiscite, *n.* referendum (see CHOICE).

pledge, *n.* PROMISE, SECURITY, gage, pawn, collateral, hostage, deposit; word, troth, vow, guarantee; bond, oath. See AFFIRMATION. —*v.t.* deposit, wage, pawn, hypothecate, mortgage; vow, PROMISE, undertake, engage, honor; toast. *Slang*, hock. See DEBT.

plenty, *n.* SUFFICIENCY, abundance, profusion, amplitude, copiousness; wealth, luxury.

pleonasm, *n.* redundance, verbosity, DIFFUSENESS, tautology, superfluity, circumlocution, wordiness.

plethora, *n.* superabundance (see SUFFICIENCY).

pliable, *adj.* plastic, ductile, malleable; flexible, supple, limber, yielding; docile, tractable, obedient, compliant. See SOFTNESS, OBEDIENCE.

pliant, *adj.* pliable, supple, flexible, malleable, compliant, yielding. See SOFTNESS, OBEDIENCE.

pliers, *n.pl.* pincers, pinchers; grippers, nippers, tongs, grip, clamp, forceps; wire cutter, tooth extractor. See RETENTION, EXTRACTION.

plight, *n.* quandary, predicament,

dilemma; trouble, DIFFICULTY, scrape, crisis; situation, condition; betrothal, PROMISE, engagement.

plod, *v.i.* persevere, persist; trudge, walk; labor, drudge, toil. See RESOLUTION, SLOWNESS, EXERTION.

plot, *n.* diagram, PLAN, outline; field, enclosure, paddock, lot; scheme, conspiracy, intrigue, collusion. See REGION. —*v.* conspire, machinate, scheme, intrigue; chart, PLAN, lay out. See CUNNING.

plow, plough, *v.* cultivate, dig, till, turn, break, FURROW. See AGRICULTURE.

ploy, *n.* maneuver, stratagem. See PLAN, CUNNING.

pluck, *n.* COURAGE, bravery, valor, stamina, endurance, grip, determination, WILL; twitch, tug, twang. See RESOLUTION. —*v.t.* pull, jerk; pick, twang; gather, garner; *slang,* rob, fleece. See TRACTION, STEALING, ACQUISITION.

plug, *n.* stopper, cork, dowel, plunger, tampon; quid, wad; wadding, padding, stopple, spigot. See CLOSURE.

plum, *n.* prune, sloe, damson; prize, haul, windfall, trophy; reward, patronage. See VEGETABLE, PAYMENT.

plumage, *n.* feathers, down, feathering. See COVERING, ORNAMENT.

plumb, *adj.* perpendicular, VERTICAL, erect; straight, true. —*adv., colloq.,* downright, utterly. See COMPLETION. —*v.t.* sound, fathom. See DEPTH.

plume, *n.* quill, feather, egret, panache, plumage. See COVERING, ORNAMENT.

plummet, *n.* weight, plumb, bob, lead. See VERTICAL. —*v.i.* fall, droop, plunge. See DESCENT.

plump, *adj.* corpulent, fat, chubby, stout, fleshy, buxom, pudgy, rotund; blunt, direct, unqualified. See SIZE. —*adv.* suddenly, directly. —*v.* fatten, fill, distend; blurt; fall; support, root (for); *colloq.,* plop [down]. See DESCENT, ROTUNDITY.

plunder, *n.* pillage, loot, sack, spoil, booty; advantage, gain; spoliation, rapine. —*v.* devastate, harry, despoil, strip, rifle, loot, forage, pillage, ransack, maraud, rob, depredate. See STEALING, ACQUISITION.

plunge, *v.* dip, submerge; dive; sink, fall, drop; douse, go *or* put under water; gamble, bet heavily; fling, jump. *Colloq.,* go off the deep end. —*n.* dive, swim, dip; submersion; *colloq.,* venture. See WATER, HASTE.

plural, *adj.* See MULTITUDE.

plus, *adj., adv., & prep.* and; additional, extra, added (to). See ADDITION.

plush, *n.* pile, nap, hair; plushette; velvet, fluff. See MATERIALS. —*adj., colloq.,* plushy, nappy, velvety, piled, woolly; rich, luxurious, posh, swank[y], elegant, high-toned. See SOFTNESS, OSTENTATION.

plutocrat, *n.* man of means, [multi]-millionaire, billionaire. See MONEY.

ply, *v.t.* exert, urge, attack, apply; play, work; USE, exercise, manipulate, wield. See EXERTION. —*n.* See LAYER.

poach, *v.* steal, thieve, filch, pilfer; encroach, infringe, trespass; boil, parboil, coddle. See STEALING, HEAT.

pocket, *n.* pouch, bin, purse; hollow, placket. See CONCAVITY, RECEPTACLE. —*v.t.* appropriate, take, steal. See STEALING.

pocketbook, *n.* purse, wallet; [hand]-bag; pouch, sporran. *Slang,* leather, kick. See RECEPTACLE.

pod, *n.* hull, husk, jacket, skin, shuck, shell, peapod; pouch; cabin. See COVERING.

podium, *n.* stand, dais, rostrum, platform. See SUPPORT.

POETRY

Nouns—**1,** poetry, *ars poetica,* poesy, balladry; Muse, Calliope, Erato; versification, rhyming, prosody, orthometry; poem, ode, epode, idyl, lyric, blank verse, free verse, *vers libre;* eclogue, pastoral, bucolic, dithyramb, anacreontic; sonnet, ode, roundelay, rondeau, rondo, roundel, ballade, villanelle, triolet, pantun, madrigal, canzonet, monody, elegy, haiku; epic, dramatic poetry, lyric poetry; opera, libretto; light verse, comic verse, *vers de société*. See WRITING.

2, song, ballad, lay; lullaby (see MUSIC); nursery rhymes; popular song.

3, doggerel, jingle, limerick, purple patches, macaronics.

4, canto, stanza, stich, verse, line; couplet, heroic couplets, triplet, quatrain; strophe, antistrophe.

5, rhyme, rime, assonance; meter, measure, foot, numbers, strain, rhythm; accentuation, stress, ictus; iamb[ic], dactyl, spondee, trochee, anapest; hexameter, pentameter, *etc.*

6, poet, poet laureate; bard, lyrist, skald, troubadour, trouvere, minstrel, minnesinger, meistersinger; versifier, poetaster. See MUSIC.

Verbs—poetize, sing, versify, make verses; rhyme; scan.

Adjectives—poetic[al], lyric; epic, heroic, bucolic, *etc.;* lofty, sublime, eloquent.

Antonymns, see WRITING, DESCRIPTION.

---

pogrom, *n.* KILLING, massacre, carnage, butchery, slaughter, genocide, hecatomb, mass murder; persecution.

poignant, *adj.* painful, pungent, intense, piercing, sharp, keen, biting. See FEELING, PUNGENCY.

point, *n.* object, meaning, significance, intent, aim; speck, dot, spot; place, location; pin, needle, prick, spike, prong, tip, END; limit; goal, site. See IMPORTANCE, SHARPNESS, LITTLENESS. —*v.* aim; face, tend, lead, indicate. See STRAIGHTNESS, DIRECTION, INDICATION.

point-blank, *adj.* close, straight, direct, undeviating; blunt, frank, candid, open. See STRAIGHTNESS.

pointed, *adj.* direct, concise, terse, pithy, brief; sharp, barbed, spiked. See SHARPNESS.

pointless, *adj.* meaningless, purposeless. See UNMEANINGNESS.

poise, *n.* equilibrium, balance, steadiness; bearing, self-possession, dignity, composure, imperturbability, coolness, nonchalance. See INEXCITABILITY.

poison, *n.* venom, toxicity, virus, bane. —*v.t.* corrupt, defile; intoxicate, drug, envenom; kill, murder. See DETERIORATION, KILLING.

poisonous, *adj.* venomous, toxic, deadly, virulent, noxious. See BADNESS.

poke, *v.* prod, nudge, stick, push; search, pry; dawdle; jab, punch. See IMPULSE, SLOWNESS, INQUIRY.

poker, *n.* fire iron, rod, branding iron, ramrod, salamander. See HEAT.

poker-faced, *adj., colloq.,* deadpan, frozen-faced, wooden, unrevealing, unreadable, secretive. See CONCEALMENT.

polar, *adj.* extreme, ultimate, furthest, outermost; magnetic, attracting; polarized; COLD, frigid, icy, frozen. See OPPOSITION.

polarize, *v.* orient, align, concentrate, gather; split, separate, dichotomize, oppose. See OPPOSITION.

pole, *v.* push, jab, prod, thrust, punch, nudge. See IMPULSE. —*n.* shaft, staff, post, stick, beam, mast; terminal, axis, hub, pivot; extremity, North *or* South Pole. See OPPOSITION.

polemic, *adj.* polemical, controversial, disputatious, eristic[al], dialectical; quarrelsome, contentious. —*n.* polemics, debate, discussion, contention, dialectics. See DISCORD.

polestar, *n.* lodestar, Polaris; guide; magnet, cynosure. See ATTRACTION, DIRECTION.

police, *n.* police force, constabulary; vigilantes, posse; F.B.I., Royal Canadian Mounted Police, military police, M.P., *sûreté*, Scotland Yard, *etc.* See SAFETY.

policeman, policewoman, *n*. patrolman *or* -woman, officer (see SAFETY).

policy, *n*. CONDUCT, administration, management; tactics, strategy; art, wisdom; platform, PLAN.

polish, *n*. sheen, luster, shine, glaze, gloss; refinement, culture; COURTESY tact, suavity, diplomacy; discernment, discrimination. —*v.t.* shine, buff, burnish; scrub, scour, brighten; refine, perfect. See SMOOTHNESS, ELEGANCE, ORNAMENT, FRICTION.

polite, *adj*. mannerly, civil, courteous, gracious; gallant, courtly, polished, well-bred, refined. See COURTESY, FASHION.

politic, *adj*. discreet, expedient, artful, strategic; prudent, wise, judicious; wary, calculating, shrewd, crafty. See CAUTION, INTELLIGENCE, TASTE, CUNNING.

politician, *n*. office-holder *or* -seeker; legislator, senator, *etc.;* diplomat, machinator, Machiavellian, strategist, wirepuller. See CUNNING.

poll, *n*. election, ballot; register; pate, head, skull. See CHOICE. —*v.t.* cut, crop, top; survey, canvass, tabulate. See NUMERATION.

pollute, *v.t* contaminate, foul, desecrate, taint, soil, defile, corrupt; demoralize. See IMPURITY, DETERIORATION, UNCLEANNESS.

poltroon, *n*. cad; dastard, craven, coward. See COWARDICE.

polygamy, *n*. bigamy, trigamy; Mormonism; polyandry, polygyny. See MARRIAGE.

pommel, *v.t.* See PUMMEL. —*n.* [saddle] horn. See SUPPORT.

pomp, *n*. grandeur, show, OSTENTATION, magnificence, display, splendor.

pompous, *adj*. self-important, ostentatious; high-flown, bombastic, stilted; haughty, vain, grandiose, puffed-up, arrogant. *Colloq.*, stuffy, snooty, stuffed-shirt. See BOASTING.

pond, *n*. lake, pool, fishpond, millpond, tarn. See WATER.

ponder, *v*. think, muse, cogitate; reflect, meditate, weigh, deliberate, consider. See THOUGHT.

ponderous, *adj*. heavy, weighty, bulky, massive; tedious. See GRAVITY, INELEGANCE.

pontiff, *n*. bishop, high priest; the Pope. See CLERGY.

pontificate, *v.i.* declaim, state; preach, orate, lecture. See LOQUACITY, OSTENTATION.

pontoon, *n*. float, raft; boat, bladder, floater, buoy. See SHIP.

pony, *n*. scrub horse; cob, cow pony, cayuse; glass, half-jigger, dram; *slang,* translation. *Colloq.*, crib, trot, horse. See RECEPTACLE, INTERPRETATION.

pool, *n*. association, amalgation, fund; pond, puddle; reservoir, lake; swimming pool, natatorium. —*v.t.* combine, cooperate, share, contribute. See WATER, PARTY, CHANCE.

poor, *adj*. indigent (see POVERTY); inferior, faulty, unsatisfactory, imperfect, defective; humble; weak, flimsy. See INSUFFICIENCY, IMPERFECTION, DISEASE.

pop, *n*. bang, shot, burst, explosion; soda [pop]. See LOUDNESS, DRINKING. —*v*. burst; explode.

POPULACE

Nouns—**1,** populace; the people, MULTITUDE, crowd, masses; bourgeoisie; commonalty; democracy; common people, lower classes, hoi polloi, rank and file, the ruck, folk, proletariat, *plebs,* great unwashed, silent majority; the common touch. See HUMANITY, VULGARITY, SERVANT.

2, mob, rabble, rout; horde, canaille; dregs; scum of society *or* the earth; riffraff, ragtag and bobtail; small fry.

3, commoner, man in the street, the average man, the little man, one of the people, democrat, plebeian, proletarian, republican, bourgeois; Mrs. Grundy,

Philistine, Babbitt; Joe Blow, Joe Doakes, John *or* Jane Doe, John *or* Jane Q. Public.

4, peasant, countryman, boor, churl, lout, villein, curmudgeon; serf; dockwalloper, longshoreman, navvy; swain, clown, clod, clodhopper; hobnail, yokel, bumpkin; plowman, rustic, tiller of the soil; white-collar man, woman, *or* worker; hewers of wood and drawers of water. *Colloq.*, hayseed. *Slang,* hick, jay, rube.

5, beggar, mudlark, *sans culotte,* raff, tatterdemalion, hobbledehoy, caitiff, ragamuffin, pariah; guttersnipe, urchin, street urchin *or* arab; tramp, hobo, knight of the road, vagabond, vagrant, bum, weary Willie. *Slang,* bindle stiff.

Adjectives—popular; plebeian, proletarian, common, democratic; homely, homespun; vulgar, lowborn, ignoble, illbred, baseborn, earthy; unknown to fame, obscure, untitled; rustic, countrified, provincial; loutish, boorish, clownish, churlish; barbarous, barbarian, barbaric.

Antonyms, see NOBILITY.

---

popular, *adj.* common, public, plebeian; acceptable, cheap; approved, liked, praised; elect, chosen; desirable; admired, famous. See APPROBATION, REPUTE, POPULACE.

population, *n.* people, residents; nation. See INHABITANT.

populous, *adj.* well-populated, thickly settled; teeming. See MULTITUDE, ASSEMBLAGE.

porcelain, *n.* china, ceramic. See MATERIALS.

porch, *n.* veranda, portico, piazza; entrance, portal; stoa. See OPENING, RECEPTACLE.

pore, *n.* breathing hole, skin hole, orifice; stoma, ostiole, porus; OPENING. —*v.i.* read, peruse, scan, scrutinize, examine closely; mull over, consider. See THOUGHT, INQUIRY, VISION.

pornography, *n.* erotica; prurience, sexuality; impudicity, obscenity, indecency, IMPURITY; VULGARITY, dirt, smut, filth. *Slang,* porn.

porous, *adj.* open; absorbent; perforated, honeycombed; sandy; permeable, loose, pervious. See OPENING.

porridge, *n.* pottage, stew, soup; gruel, mush, cereal, samp, pap, burgoo; stirabout, hasty pudding, pease porridge. See FOOD.

port, *n.* refuge, harbor, shelter, haven; OPENING, embrasure, porthole; APPEARANCE, bearing, deportment, demeanor; LEFT, larboard (*naut.*). See ARRIVAL.

portable, *adj.* portative, transportable, movable, carriable. See TRANSPORTATION.

portal, *n.* entrance, door, entry, doorway, portcullis. See OPENING.

portend, *v.t.* signify, presage, augur, forebode, foreshadow, omen, foretoken, mean. See PREDICTION, THREAT.

portent, *n.* wonder, marvel, phenomenon; sign, foreshadowing, foreboding, omen, token; importance, meaning. See PREDICTION, WARNING.

porter, portress, *n.* guard, gatekeeper, *concierge,* doorman, sentinel, warder; bearer. *Colloq.*, redcap. See TRANSPORTATION, SAFETY.

portfolio, *n.* briefcase, bag, portmanteau, attaché case; LIST, catalog. See RECEPTACLE.

portico, *n.* colonnade, stoa, veranda, porch. See RECEPTACLE.

portion, *n.* share, allotment, due, ration; PART, serving, morsel, fragment; fate, lot, destiny; dividend; section. —*v.t.* dower, apportion, divide, endow. See APPORTIONMENT, QUANTITY.

portly, *adj.* dignified, imposing, stately; fat, fleshy, stout, corpulent; bulky. See SIZE.

portmanteau, *n.* trunk, suitcase, valise; portfolio. See RECEPTACLE.

portrait, *n.* picture, likeness; depiction, DESCRIPTION; photograph, sketch. See PAINTING.

portray, *v.t.* picture, describe; enact, act out. See REPRESENTATION, DRAMA, DESCRIPTION.

pose, *n.* attitude, AFFECTATION; position, posture; aspect, figure. See FORM. —*v.* sit; attitudinize, affect; propound; question, puzzle, quiz, inquire, nonplus. See DIFFICULTY.

poser, *n.* puzzle[r], enigma; poseur, posturer. See UNINTELLIGIBILITY, AFFECTATION.

posit, *v.t.* place, dispose; stipulate. See SUPPOSITION, LOCATION.

position, *n.* situation, placement, point, spot, place, LOCATION, site; billet, berth, post, station, office, rank, status; caste; incumbency; dignity, honor. See BUSINESS, CIRCUMSTANCE, REPUTE.

positive, *adj.* certain, decided, emphatic, unqualified, absolute; inescapable, peremptory, firm. See AFFIRMATION, CERTAINTY.

posse, *n.* deputation, deputies, vigilantes; riot squad. See ASSEMBLAGE.

POSSESSION

Nouns—**1,** possession, ownership; proprietorship, lordship, fee, seigniorage, seigniory; empire, dominion (see AUTHORITY); interest, stake, estate, right, title, claim, demand, holding; tenure; vested, contingent, beneficial, *or* equitable interest; USE, trust, benefit; fee simple *or* tail; occupancy, occupation; hold[ing]; tenure, tenancy, feudality, dependency; monopoly, corner, RETENTION; heritage, inheritance, heirship, reversion; bird in hand; nine points of the law.

2, dower, dowry, dot; jointure, appanage; inheritance, heritage; patrimony; alimony; legacy (see GIVING).

3, assets, belongings, MEANS, resources, circumstances; wealth, MONEY; credit; patent, copyright; landed property, real property, real estate, realty, land[s], grounds; tenements; hereditaments; territory, state, kingdom, principality, realm, empire; dependence; protectorate, sphere of influence; manor, domain, demesne; farm, plantation, hacienda; freehold, leasehold; fixtures, plant; easement. See ABODE.

4, personal property *or* effects; personalty, chattels, goods, effects, movables; stock in trade; things, traps, gear, paraphernalia; equipage; parcels, appurtenances; impedimenta; luggage, dunnage, baggage; bag and baggage; pelf; cargo, lading, freight; heirloom; endowment.

5, possessor, holder; occupant, occupier; tenant; renter, lodger, lessee; owner; proprietor, proprietress; trustee; master, mistress, lord; landholder, landowner, landlord, landlady, yeoman; lord of the manor, laird; legatee, devisee; heir[ess], inheritress, inheritrix. See INHABITANT.

Verbs—**1,** possess, have, hold, occupy, enjoy; be possessed of, have on one's hands, own, command; inherit, come to, come in for; stake a claim; acquire (see ACQUISITION); retain. *Slang,* have dibs on.

2, belong to, appertain to, pertain to; be in one's possession; vest in.

Adjectives—**1,** possessing, having; worth; possessed of, seized of, master of, in possession of; in fee simple; outright; endowed with, blessed with, fraught with; possessed; on hand, by one; in hand, in store, in stock; in one's hands, at one's command, to one's name, at one's disposal; one's own.

2, retentive, retaining, tenacious; reserved, entailed.

3, landed, manorial, allodial; freehold, leasehold; feudal.

Antonyms, see POVERTY, DEBT, ACQUISITION.

POSSIBILITY

Nouns—possibility, potentiality, likelihood, LIABILITY; what may be, what is possible; compatibility (see AGREEMENT); reasonability; reasonableness (see REASONING); practicability, EXPEDIENCE, feasibility, potency, workability, workableness, accessibility, attainability; contingency, LATENCY, probability, CHANCE, hazard, outlook. *Colloq.*, toss-up, show, outside chance.

Verbs—be possible, stand a chance *or* show; admit of, bear; put in the way of; open up.

Adjectives—possible, potential, in *or* on the cards *or* dice, within the bounds of possibility, *in posse;* conceivable, imaginable, credible, thinkable, reasonable, plausible, presumable; compatible (see AGREEMENT); practicable, feasible, negotiable, workable, performable, achievable, accessible, superable, surmountable, attainable, obtainable, expedient, within reach; contingent, probably, likely; in the running; latent. *Colloq.*, liable, earthly.

Adverbs—possibly, by possibility; perhaps, perchance, peradventure; it may be, maybe, haply, mayhap; if [humanly] possible, [wind and] weather permitting, everything being equal, as luck may have it, God willing, *Deo volente,* D.V. *Colloq.*, on the off-chance, could be.

Antonyms, see IMPOSSIBILITY.

---

post, *n.* station, assignment, position; incumbency, place, office, mail; stake, picket, newel, pillar, pier. See BUSINESS, SUPPORT, COMMUNICATION, ACCOUNTING. —*v.* mail; inform, publish, RECORD, enter, transfer; speed, hurry. See LOCATION, VELOCITY, LIST.

postage, *n.* stamp, postmark, imprint. See COMMUNICATION.

poster, *n.* advertisement, placard, bill. See PUBLICATION.

posterior, *adj.* subsequent, later, succeeding, ensuing; postern, REAR, hindmost. See SEQUENCE. —*n.* buttocks, REAR.

POSTERITY

Nouns—**1,** posterity, progeny, issue, fruit, seed, offspring, young, flesh and blood; brood, litter, farrow, spawn, spat, clutch, seed, product; family, children, grandchildren, heirs; younger, rising, *or* succeeding generation. See FUTURITY.

2, child, son, daughter, grandchild, grandson, granddaughter, bantling, bairn, baby, infant; bastard, illegitimate *or* natural child; scion, shoot, sprout, sprit, [olive] branch, offshoot, offset, ramification; descendant, heir[ess]; heir apparent *or* presumptive; chip off the old block; foster child; stepchild, stepson, stepdaughter.

3, straight descent, sonship, line, lineage, succession, filiation, primogeniture, heredity; origin, extraction; tribe, clan, sept, nationality; genealogy; generation gap. See ANCESTRY, HUMANITY.

Verbs—run in the family, come down; pass on.

Adjectives—filial, sonly, daughterly, family; lineal, hereditary; tribal, national.

Antonyms, see ANCESTRY.

---

posthaste, *adv.* speedily, hastily, at top speed, apace, expeditiously, swiftly. See RASHNESS, VELOCITY, HASTE.

posthumous, *adj.* post-obit, postmortem; late; postponed, delayed. See DEATH, SEQUENCE.

postman, *n.* mail carrier, mailman, courier, mail clerk. See COMMUNICATION.

post-mortem, *adj.* See POSTHUMOUS. —*n.* autopsy, pathology, necropsy, necrotomy; *slang,* investigation, examination, INQUIRY, study, recapitulation.

postpone, *v.t.* procrastinate, delay, defer; shelve, adjourn, table. See LATENESS, NEGLECT.

postscript, *n.* ADDITION, appendix, afterthought; P.S., P.P.S.

postulate, *n.* proposition, axiom, SUPPOSITION; hypothesis, premise; fact, datum. —*v.* suppose, surmise, theorize, hypothesize.

posture, *n.* pose, attitude; bearing, position, carriage; mood, condition. See FORM, CIRCUMSTANCE.

pot, *n.* crock, jug, tankard; kettle, pan, vessel; mug; prize, pool. See WRITING.

potboiler, *n.* trash, dime novel. See WRITING, PUBLICATION.

potent, *adj.* powerful, strong, mighty; intense, influential; effectual, effective, forceful; capable, able. See POWER, VIGOR.

potentate, *n.* king, sovereign, ruler, monarch. See AUTHORITY.

potential, *adj.* dynamic, magnetic, charged; dormant, latent; unfulfilled, promising. See POWER, LATENCY, POSSIBILITY.

potion, *n.* potation; philter, elixir, brew, libation. See REMEDY, DRINKING.

potpourri, *n.* blend, medley, hodgepodge, miscellany, mélange; salmagundi, gallimaufry, pastiche. See MIXTURE, ODOR.

pottery, *n.* earthenware, china, porcelain, ceramics, ironstone; dishes, utensils. See MATERIALS.

pouch, *n.* bag, sack; purse, reticule, wallet; pocket, sac; marsupium. See RECEPTACLE.

poultry, *n.* chickens, ducks, geese, turkeys; fowl[s], hens, broilers, fryers, roosters; pigeons, squab. See ANIMAL.

pounce, *v.i.* spring, LEAP, jump; snatch, grasp, seize; ambush. See DESCENT.

pound, *v.* beat, thump, drum, bruise, tenderize; crush, pulverize. See POWDERINESS.

pour, *v.* flow, emerge; decant, fill; issue; rain, flood, shower. See EGRESS, WATER, SUFFICIENCY.

pout, *v.i.* sulk, grimace, moue. See DEJECTION, CONVEXITY.

POVERTY

Nouns—**1,** poverty, impecuniousness, indigence, penury, pauperism, destitution, want; need, neediness; lack, NECESSITY, privation, distress, difficulties; bad, poor, *or* needy circumstances; reduced *or* straitened circumstances, extremity; slender means, straits, bottom dollar; hand-to-mouth existence; beggary; mendicancy, loss of fortune, bankruptcy, insolvency (see DEBT). See ADVERSITY, INSUFFICIENCY, NONPAYMENT.

2, poor man, pauper, mendicant, beggar, starveling.

Verbs—**1,** want, lack, starve, live from hand to mouth, have seen better days, go down in the world, go to the dogs, go to wreck and ruin; not have a penny to one's name, be up against it; beg [one's bread]; tighten one's belt. *Slang,* go broke, lose one's shirt.

2, impoverish, reduce to poverty; pauperize, fleece, ruin, strip.

Adjectives—poor, indigent; poverty-stricken; poor as a church mouse; poor as Job's turkey; penniless, impecunious; hard up; out at elbows *or* heels; seedy, shabby; beggarly, beggared, down and out; destitute, bereft, in want, needy, necessitous, distressed, pinched, straitened; unable to keep the wolf from the door, unable to make both ends meet; embarrassed, involved;

insolvent, bankrupt, on one's uppers, on the rocks, on the beach. *Colloq.*, in the hole. *Slang*, broke, stony, stone-broke, flat [broke], down to the wire, looking for a handout.

Antonyms, see MONEY, PROSPERITY.

POWDERINESS

Nouns—**1,** powderiness; grittiness, sandiness; efflorescence; friability. See VAPOR.
2, powder, dust, sand, sawdust; grit; meal, bran, flour, farina; crumb, seed, grain; particle (see LITTLENESS); filings, debris, detritus, floc.
3, pulverization, grinding, comminution, attenuation, granulation, disintegration, trituration, levigation, abrasion, detrition, crystallization, limation; filing; erosion, corrosion (see DETERIORATION).
4, mill, grater, rasp, file, mortar and pestle, teeth, grinder, grindstone, quern. See FRICTION.
Verbs—pulverize, comminute, atomize, crystallize, granulate, triturate, levigate; scrape, file, abrade, rub down, grind, grate, rasp, pound, contuse, beat, crush, crunch, crumble; rust, shatter, disintegrate.
Adjectives—powdery, pulverulent, granular, ground, mealy, floury, farinaceous, branny, furfuraceous, flocculent, dusty, sandy; arenose, arenaceous; gritty; efflorescent; friable, crumbly, shivery; attrite; in pieces, shards, flinders, *etc.*

Antonyms, see COHERENCE, SIZE.

POWER

Nouns—**1,** power, potence, potency, potentiality; puissance, might, force, ENERGY, VIGOR; dint; right hand *or* arm; ascendancy, sway, control; prepotency; almightiness, omnipotence, AUTHORITY, STRENGTH; irresistibility, invincibility, *etc. Colloq.*, steam. See INTRINSIC.
2, ability, ableness; efficiency, efficacy; validity, cogency; enablement; vantage ground; INFLUENCE; capability, MEANS, capacity; faculty, endowment, virtue, gift, property, qualification, susceptibility. *Slang*, the stuff, something on the ball, what it takes. See AGENCY.
3, pressure, gravity, electricity, magnetism, electromagnetism; ATTRACTION; force of inertia, dead force, living force; energy, hydroelectric power, waterpower; atomic power, horsepower; friction, suction; torque, thrust.
4, powerhouse; engine, motor, dynamo, generator; battery; reactor; pump, mill, windmill; power plant; Diesel, gas, gasoline, internal combustion, *or* steam engine; reciprocating, rotary, Wankel, jet, *or* rocket engine; turbine.
Verbs—**1,** be powerful; be able; generate. *Slang.*, pack a wallop *or* punch. See STRENGTH, ENERGY, VIGOR.
2, see INFLUENCE.
Adjectives—**1,** powerful, puissant; potent, potential; capable, able; equal to, up to; cogent, valid; effective, effectual; efficient, efficacious, adequate; strong, omnipotent, all-powerful, almighty; electric, magnetic, dynamic; attractive; mechanical; energetic, forcible, forceful, incisive, trenchant, electrifying; influential.
2, resistless, irresistible; invincible, indomitable, invulnerable, impregnable, unconquerable; overpowering, overwhelming.
Adverbs—powerfully, strongly, irresistibly, *etc.*

Antonyms, see IMPOTENCE.

---

powerhouse, *n.* power plant, generating station; *colloq.,* tower of strength, muscle man. See POWER, STRENGTH.

powerless, *n.* impotent; paralyzed, incapable, weak, disabled. See IMPOTENCE.

powwow, *n.* conjurer, medicine man; *colloq.,* CONVERSATION, discussion. See SORCERY.

pox, *n.* smallpox, chicken pox, cow pox, variola, varicella, vaccinia; papules, maculas, vesicles, pustules; acne, eruption, breaking out; pocks, pockmarks; curse (see IMPRECATION). See DISEASE.

practicable, *adj.* possible, feasible; useful, practical; usable, workable, achievable. See POSSIBILITY, UTILITY, FACILITY.

practically, *adv.* actually, virtually; nearly, almost. See NEARNESS, INTRINSIC.

practice, *n.* training, drill, exercise; custom, HABIT; manner, METHOD, procedure. —*v.* exercise, apply; perform, act, do; drill, rehearse. See ACTION, TEACHING, USE, CONDUCT.

pragmatic, *adj.* practical, empirical; active, businesslike; materialistic, prosaic, pedantic, dogmatic, pedestrian. See UTILITY.

prairie, *n.* plain, grassland, mesa, steppe, llano, savanna. See HORIZONTAL, LAND.

praise, *n.* commendation, acclaim, approval, applause; eulogy; homage; benediction, thanksgiving, grace. —*v.t.* acclaim, approve, commend, extol, eulogize, applaud; glorify, laud. See APPROBATION, GRATITUDE.

praiseworthy, *adj.* commendable, laudable, meritorious, admirable. See APPROBATION.

prance, *v.i.* caper, cavort, spring, dance, slip; strut. See LEAP.

prank, *n.* caprice, frolic, caper, trick, jest, escapade. See AMUSEMENT.

prankster, *n.* trickster, joker, jokester, practical joker. See WIT.

prate, *v.i.* chatter, babble. See LOQUACITY.

prattle, *n.* chitchat, babbling, chatter. —*v.i.* murmur, chatter, babble, jabber. See LOQUACITY, SPEECH.

pray, *v.i.* implore, ask, beg, REQUEST, solicit, petition, entreat; WORSHIP.

preach, *v.* exhort, evangelize, lecture, sermonize, moralize. See RITE, TEACHING.

preacher, *n.* pastor; sermonizer (see CLERGY).

preamble, *n.* prologue, introduction, preface, prelude. See PRECEDENCE.

precarious, *adj.* dangerous, risky; critical; doubtful, uncertain, unsafe, insecure, unstable. See TRANSIENTNESS, DANGER.

precaution, *n.* CARE, CAUTION, warning; safeguard, PROVISION, protection; anticipation, forethought, foresight. See PREPARATION.

PRECEDENCE

Nouns—**1,** precedence, coming before; SUPERIORITY, IMPORTANCE, preference; PRIORITY, preexistence; antecedence, precedency, antecedency, anteposition, anteriority.

2, precession, leading, heading, forerunning, going before; going *or* being first; the lead, the van (see FRONT).

3, foreword, prelude, preamble, preface, prologue, prolusion, proem, prolepsis, prefix, introduction, heading, frontispiece, groundwork, PREPARATION; overture, voluntary, symphony.

Verbs—**1,** precede; come before, come first, antecede; introduce, usher in; set the fashion; take *or* have precedence; [out]rank; place before, prefix, premise, prelude, preface.

2, forerun; go before, go ahead, go in the van, go in advance; pioneer, herald, head, take the lead; lead [the way], get *or* have the start; steal a march; get before, get ahead, get in front of, outstrip. *Colloq.*, get in on the ground floor.

Adjectives—preceding, precedent, antecedent; anterior; prior, before; *avant-garde;* former, foregoing; above- *or* aforementioned, aforesaid, said; precursory, percursive, preliminary, prefatory, introductory; prelusive, prelusory, preludious, proemial, preparatory, forerunning.

Adverbs—in advance, before, ahead.

Antonyms, see SEQUENCE.

---

precept, *n.* instruction, charge; prescript, prescription; recipe, receipt; golden rule; MAXIM, RULE, canon, law, code, act, statute, rubric, regulation; form, formula, formulary, order, COMMAND.

precinct, *n.* neighborhood, district, area; enclosure, boundary, LIMIT, environs. See REGION, ENVIRONMENT.

precious, *adj.* priceless, costly; precise, overrefined, overnice; beloved, dear. See DEARNESS, AFFECTATION.

precipice, *n.* cliff, drop, bluff, declivity. See VERTICAL, OBLIQUITY.

precipitate, *adj.* rash, hasty, hurried, headlong, impetuous. See RASHNESS. —*v.* CAUSE, foment; hasten, speed, expedite; separate (as a chemical solution); fall (as rain, snow, *etc.*). See HASTE, EARLINESS, DESCENT, DENSITY.

precipitous, *adj.* steep, abrupt, cliff-like, sheer. See OBLIQUITY.

précis, *n.* summary, abstract. See SHORTNESS.

precise, *adj.* exact, accurate, definite, punctilious; fastidious; unbending, rigid; prim, precious. See RIGHTNESS, TRUTH.

preclude, *v.t.* prevent, stop, prohibit, obviate, check; forestall. See EXCLUSION, PROHIBITION.

precocious, *adj.* advanced, overforward, premature. See EARLINESS.

preconception, *n.* anticipation, prejudgment; prejudice. See MISJUDGMENT.

precursor, *n.* forerunner (see PRIORITY).

predacious, predatory, *adj.* robbing, ravening, plundering. See STEALING.

predecessor, *n.* forerunner (see PRIORITY); ancestor, antecedent, progenitor. See ANCESTRY.

predestine, *v.t.* foredoom, predestinate, preordain, foreordain. See DESTINY, NECESSITY.

predetermine, *v.t.* premeditate, preresolve, preconcert, prearrange; foreordain, predestine, doom; plan. *Colloq.*, stack the cards. See DESTINY, INTENTION.

predicament, *n.* condition, quandary, fix, corner, dilemma, mess, scrape, crisis, emergency. *Colloq.*, spot. See CIRCUMSTANCE, DIFFICULTY.

predicate, *v.t.* assert, declare; base, found. See AFFIRMATION, SUPPOSITION.

PREDICTION

Nouns—**1,** prediction, announcement; premonition, WARNING; prophecy, prognosis, prognostication, premonstration; augury, auguration; foreboding, presentiment, premonition, presage; ominousness; auspices, forecast; omen, horoscope, soothsaying; fortune-telling, crystal-gazing, chiromancy, palmistry; divination, prophetic vision, auspice; necromancy (see SORCERY); spiritualism; clairvoyance (see INTUITION); astrology, horoscopy; prefiguration, prefigurement.

2, foresight, precognition, prescience, foreknowledge, anticipation, prevision, foretoken, forethought; providence, prudence, PREPARATION; clairvoyance, second sight; foreboding, premonition, presentiment; foretaste, preview; foreshadowing, foretelling, forecasting, prophecy, prophetic vision. See CAUTION, FUTURITY.

3, prophet, seer, augur, oracle, fortune-teller, soothsayer, crystal-gazer; weatherman *or* -woman; herald; Cassandra, sibyl, Delphic oracle, Sphinx; sorcerer, interpreter.

4, crystal ball, tea leaves, divining rod, *etc.;* Ouija board.

Verbs—**1,** predict, prognosticate, prophesy, forecast, divine, foretell, soothsay, augur, tell fortunes; cast a horoscope; presage, [fore]bode, foretoken, portend, foreshadow; herald, announce; call the turn *or* shot.

2, bid fair; promise; lead one to expect; be the precursor *or* forerunner.

3, foresee, anticipate, foreknow, presurmise, expect. See EXPECTATION.

Adjectives—predicting, predictive, prophetic, oracular, sibylline; ominous, portentous; auspicious; prescient, farsighted; minatory, monitory, premonitory.

Antonyms, see CHANCE, SURPRISE.

---

predilection, *n.* partiality, preference, prejudice, bias. See TENDENCY, DESIRE.

predisposed, *adj.* inclined, prone, partial; prepared, ready, willing. See INFLUENCE, TENDENCY.

predominant, *adj.* prevalent, controlling, ascendant, ruling, supreme. See INFLUENCE, SUPERIORITY.

preeminent, *adj.* outstanding, notable, distinguished, renowned; foremost, paramount, superior, supreme. See REPUTE, SUPERIORITY.

preempt, *v.t.* commandeer, usurp, occupy, arrogate. See EARLINESS.

preen, *v.t.* groom, primp, prettify; strut. *Slang,* doll up. See VANITY.

prefabricated, *adj.* ready-built *or* -made. *Colloq.,* prefab. See PRODUCTION.

preface, *n.* foreword, prologue, preamble, introduction, prelude, preliminary. —*v.t.* introduce, open, premise, precede. See PRECEDENCE, BEGINNING.

prefect, *n.* magistrate; monitor, dean. See AUTHORITY, DIRECTOR.

prefer, *v.t.* select, fancy, choose, adopt; OFFER, promote, advance. See CHOICE, IMPROVEMENT.

preference, *n.* CHOICE, pick, desire, taste, liking. *Colloq.,* druthers. See PRECEDENCE.

preferment, *n.* promotion, advancement. See IMPROVEMENT.

pregnable, *adj.* vulnerable, assailable. See DANGER.

pregnant, *adj.* significant, weighty, potential; fertile, inventive; gravid, parturient; impregnated, big [with child], *enceinte. Colloq.,* in a family way. See IMPORTANCE, PRODUCTION.

prehistoric, *adj.* pristine, original; primeval, primal, primitive; archaic, lost to history, from before time; unrecorded, unwritten. See OLDNESS.

prejudge, *v.t.* presuppose, assume, presume. See MISJUDGMENT.

prejudice, *n.* partiality, bias, opinion; predilection, prepossession; detriment, injury; intolerance. —*v.t.* bias, INFLUENCE, color, jaundice. See MISJUDGMENT, INJUSTICE.

prelate, *n.* primate, bishop, cardinal. See CLERGY.

preliminary, *adj.* introductory, preparatory, prefatory. See PREPARATION, PRECEDENCE.

prelude, *n.* preface, foreword, prologue, introduction, precursor, overture. See MUSIC, PRECEDENCE.

premature, *adj.* untimely, underripe, immature, overhasty, precocious, unprepared, incomplete; forward. See EARLINESS.

premeditate, *v.t.* calculate, PLAN, predesign, resolve, prearrange. See INTENTION.

premier, *adj.* chief, foremost; earliest. See PRIORITY, SUPERIORITY. —*n.* prime *or* first minister. See AUTHORITY.

premiere, *n.* opening, debut, first night, inauguration, bow. See BEGINNING.

premises, *n.pl.* building, land, house, apartment, office, *etc.;* bases, data, testimony, facts. See EVIDENCE, REASONING, REGION, LOCATION.

premium, *n.* reward, prize, PAYMENT, recompense, gift, bounty, fee, bonus. See COMPENSATION.

premonition, *n.* foreboding, presentiment. See WARNING, PREDICTION.

preoccupied, *adj.* inattentive, prepossessed, distracted; absorbed, engrossed. *Colloq.,* in a brown study. See INATTENTION.

PREPARATION

Nouns—**1,** preparation, preparing; providing; PROVISION, providence, prearrangement, anticipation, foresight, forethought; precaution, predisposition; PLAN; rehearsal; training, education (see TEACHING); inurement, HABIT; novitiate (see LEARNING). See SAFETY, PRECEDENCE, EARLINESS.

2, ARRANGEMENT; tuning, adjustment (see AGREEMENT); equipment, outfit.

3, groundwork, keystone, cradle, steppingstone; foundation.

4, cuisine, cooking, cookery, culinary art (see FOOD); tilling, plowing, sowing, semination, cultivation; manufacture, PRODUCTION.

5, preparedness, readiness, ripeness, mellowness; maturity, EARLINESS.

6, prototype, original; model, pattern; precedent; standard, type; archetype; module, exemplary, example, paradigm; test, copy, design.

7, preparer, trainer, teacher; pioneer, pathfinder, trailblazer; forerunner, advanceman.

Verbs—**1,** prepare; get *or* make ready; make preparations, settle preliminaries, get up, predispose; set *or* put in order (see ARRANGEMENT); forecast, concoct, PLAN; lay the foundations, basis, *or* groundwork, pave the way; roughhew; nurture (see AID). *Colloq.,* dust off. *Slang,* prep.

2, equip, ready, set, prime, attune; adjust, put in working order, put in tune; pack; prepare for, train, teach, rehearse; make provision for; take steps, measures, *or* precautions; provide, provide against, set one's house in order; clear the decks for action, pave the way for.

3, prepare oneself, get set, line up; serve an apprenticeship; get into harness, gird up one's loins, hold on to one's hat, buckle on one's armor; wind up, shoulder arms, get up steam, draw *or* take a long breath; save for a rainy day; keep one's powder dry. *Colloq.,* get one's ducks in a row.

Adjectives—**1,** preparing, in preparation, in embryo, in hand; brewing, hatching, brooding; in store for, in reserve; precautionary, provident; preparative, preparatory; provisional; under revision; preliminary (see PRECEDENCE).

2, prepared, in readiness, at call, ready, handy, forthcoming; planned, strategic, schematic; in working order; of age, ripe; in practice; practiced, skilled; in battle array, in war paint; armed to the teeth, sword in hand; booted and spurred, rough and ready; on alert, vigilant, *semper paratus. Colloq.,* on the mark, all set, on tap, ready to roll, all systems go. *Slang,* loaded for bear.

Adverbs—in preparation, in anticipation of; against, for; under construction, afoot, afloat, under consideration, in the works, on foot. *Colloq.,* on the fire.

Antonyms, see NEGLECT, UNPREPAREDNESS.

---

preponderance, *n.* prevalence, predominance, supremacy, ascendancy. See INFLUENCE, SUPERIORITY.

prepossessing, *adj.* appealing, attractive; charming, winning, winsome, engaging. See BEAUTY.

preposterous, *adj.* ridiculous, absurd, nonsensical, idiotic; foolish, extravagant; improper, unsuitable. See ABSURDITY.

prerequisite, *n.* requirement, essential, necessity, proviso; stipulation, QUALIFICATION. *Colloq.,* must.

prerogative, *n.* franchise, right, privilege; birthright; liberty, advantage. See AUTHORITY.

presage, *n.* portent, prophecy, augury, forecast, omen; PREDICTION, precursor, harbinger, forerunner; inkling, promise.

prescribe, *v.* urge, suggest, advise; order, advocate, decree; appoint, institute; ordain. See ADVICE, COMMAND.

prescription, *n.* medicine; formula, recipe; mandate, decree, edict. See REMEDY, COMMAND, HABIT.

PRESENCE

Nouns—**1,** presence, attendance; ASSEMBLAGE; occupancy, occupation, habitation, inhabitancy, residence; permeation, pervasion; diffusion, dissemination; ubiety, ubiquity, omnipresence, EXISTENCE.

2, spectator, beholder, observer, looker-on, onlooker, watcher, viewer, [eye]witness, bystander, passerby; sightseer, rubberneck, sidewalk superintendent; inspector; attender, patron; house, audience; the gallery, grandstand, *or* bleachers; Johnny-on-the-spot; kibitzer. See VISION.

3, see INHABITANT, APPEARANCE.

Verbs—**1,** be present, assist at; exist; look on, witness, watch; kibitz; attend, remain; find *or* present oneself, turn out; show one's face; lie, stand. *Colloq.,* show up. *Slang,* make the scene.

2, frequent, haunt; dwell, reside, stay; tenant. *Slang,* hang out. See ABODE, INHABITANT.

3, fill, pervade, permeate; infest; be diffused, be disseminated; overspread, overrun; run across.

Adjectives—present; occupying, inhabiting; moored; resident[ial]; domiciled, domiciliary; ubiquitous, omnipresent; peopled, populated, inhabited.

Adverbs—here, there, where, everywhere, aboard, on board, at home, afield; on the spot, at the kill, on hand, on deck; face-to-face; here, there, and everywhere (see SPACE); in the presence of, before, in person, to one's face; under the eyes of, under the nose of; in the face of. *Colloq.,* in the flesh; live (*radio & T.V.*).

Antonyms, see ABSENCE.

PRESENT

Nouns—present time, day, moment, juncture, *or* occasion; the present, the times, the time being, the nonce; this day and age, existing times; nowadays; epoch, day, hour, age, TIME of life; now, the here and now, twentieth century; present tense, the historic[al] present (see GRAMMAR). See NEWNESS, CHRONOLOGY.

Adjectives—present, actual, instant, current, existing, living, immediate; up-to-date, latter-day, present-day, modern, contemporary, topical.

Adverbs—**1,** at this time, at this moment, immediately (see INSTANTANEITY); at the present time, at present, now; at this time of day, today, nowadays;

already, even now, but now, just now, as of now; on the present occasion; for the time being, for the nonce; on the spot; on the spur of the moment *or* occasion; until now, to this day, to the present day; in this day and age, in our time; forthwith, presently, soon, shortly, eventually (see FUTURITY).

2, to date, up to now, as yet, thus far, so far, hereunto.

Antonyms, see PRIORITY, SEQUENCE, FUTURITY, PAST.

---

present, *n.* gift, favor, gratuity, offering, bonus, donation. —*v.t.* award, endow, give, assign, deliver, proffer, tender, pass, bestow; introduce. See GIVING, OFFER.

presentable, *adj.* attractive, personable, engaging; decent; passable, tolerable, up to snuff *or* par. See BEAUTY, GOODNESS, MEDIOCRITY.

presentiment, *n.* PREDICTION, foreboding, anticipation, premonition, apprehension; foretaste, prescience, omen.

presently, *adv.* soon, shortly, immediately, eventually. See EARLINESS.

PRESERVATION

Nouns—**1,** preservation, conservation, safekeeping (see SAFETY); maintenance, support; ECONOMY. See RETENTION.

2, embalming; curing, pickling, salting, smoking, canning; dehydration; tanning; refrigeration, freezing, quick-freezing, freeze-drying.

3, preserver, conserver, preservative; brine, salt, formaldehyde, embalming fluid; lifesaver; reserve, reservation, park, preserve, sanctuary.

4, conserve, preserve, jelly, jam, marmalade. See FOOD.

Verbs—**1,** preserve, maintain, retain, keep, sustain, support; keep up, keep alive; bank up, nurse; save, rescue; make safe, take care of; guard, defend (see DEFENSE).

2, conserve; dry, cure, salt, pickle, corn, smoke; dehydrate, quick-freeze, freeze-dry; bottle, pot, tin, put up, can; tan; husband; embalm, mummify; immortalize.

Adjectives—preserving, put up; preservative; hygienic; preserved, unimpaired, unsinged, unmarred, unspoiled, safe and sound; intact, unscathed, with a whole skin.

Antonyms, see WASTE, DETERIORATION.

---

preside, *v.i.* supervise, superintend, control, rule, direct, manage; chair, head. See AUTHORITY.

president, *n.* head, chairperson, dean, principal, chief, ruler. *Slang,* prexy. See AUTHORITY.

press, *n.* crush, throng, crowd; pressure, urgency; closet, wardrobe, repository; ASSEMBLAGE; newspapers, news media, fifth estate. See PRINTING, PUBLICATION, COMMUNICATION, RECEPTACLE. —*v.* crush, push, iron, smooth; compel, force, urge, beg, persuade; conscript, draft; hug, embrace; squeeze, wring; solicit, entreat, importune. See COMPULSION, GRAVITY, SMOOTHNESS, HASTE.

pressing, *adj.* critical, important, urgent; exacting, demanding; persistent. See IMPORTANCE.

pressure, *n.* strain, COMPULSION, stress; persuasion, coercion, persuasiveness; affliction, trouble; distress; heaviness, compression. See ADVERSITY, GRAVITY, IMPORTANCE, INFLUENCE, POWER.

prestige, *n.* REPUTE, reputation, dignity, fame, note, importance.

presto, *adv.* quickly, rapidly; immediately. See INSTANTANEITY, MUSIC.

presume, *v.* impose, venture; deduce,

assume, infer, presuppose; infringe, take liberties. See SUPPOSITION, VANITY.

presumption, *n.* audacity, assurance, arrogance, haughtiness; impetuosity; deduction, conclusion, inference, guess, hypothesis. See INSOLENCE, BELIEF.

presuppose, *v.t.* assume, presume, imply. See SUPPOSITION.

pretend, *v.* sham, feign, dissemble, simulate; counterfeit, lie, fake; claim, aver. See FALSEHOOD.

pretender, *n.* claimant; impostor, fraud, humbug, hypocrite, deceiver. See DECEPTION.

pretense, *n.* show, pretension, AFFECTATION, sham, IMITATION, OSTENTATION; makeshift, simulation, excuse, pretext, evasion. See FALSEHOOD, VANITY.

pretext, *n.* subterfuge, pretense, excuse, justification, VINDICATION; cover, cloak, blind, sham, evasion. See FALSEHOOD.

pretty, *adj.* attractive, comely, good-looking; delicate, precise. See BEAUTY. —*adv., colloq.,* rather; moderately. See DEGREE.

prevail, *v.i.* preponderate, predominate, rule, obtain; exist, be; overcome; succeed, induce, persuade. See EXISTENCE, HABIT, SUCCESS.

prevalent, *adj.* customary, current; predominant, prominent, prevailing, preponderant; general, rife, current. See HABIT, FREQUENCY, GENERALITY.

prevaricate, *v.i.* lie, quibble, cavil, equivocate, palter. See FALSEHOOD.

prevent, *v.t.* preclude, hinder, stop, check, impede, forestall, avert, restrain, prohibit. See PROHIBITION, HINDRANCE.

preview, *n.* sneak preview, advance screening; trailer. See EARLINESS, DRAMA.

previous, *adj.* antecedent, anterior; preceding, foregoing, former, prior. See PRIORITY.

prey, *n.* victim, quarry, game, kill; loot, prize, spoil. —*v.i.* plunder, pillage, ravage; haunt, wear. See PURSUIT.

PRICE

Nouns—**1,** price, amount, cost, expense, prime cost, charge, figure, demand; fare, hire, bill, tab, rental; overhead, carrying charge *or* cost; rent charge, rackrent, quitrent; expenditure, outlay (see PAYMENT). *Slang,* damage[s], score, bad news, nick, ante, setback, shakedown, tune.

2, dues, duty, toll, [income, sales, excise, *or* value added] tax, cess, levy, impost; poll *or* head tax; custom, excise, assessment, tithe, tenths, exaction, ransom, salvage, tariff; brokerage, wharfage, freightage, carriage.

3, worth, rate, [face *or* book] value, valuation, appraisement, appraisal, estimate, evaluation, costliness; money's worth, pennyworth; current *or* market price, quotation, going rate, what it will fetch; pegged *or* fixed price, *prix fixe,* flat rate, package price. See DEARNESS, CHEAPNESS.

4, recompense, pay (see PAYMENT).

5, price index, [price] ceiling *or* floor, floor *or* ceiling price; price controls, guidelines, *or* supports; price fixing; escalator clause; inflation index.

Verbs—**1,** price; set, quote, fix, *or* peg a price; value, appraise, assess, estimate, rate, evaluate; charge, demand, ask, require, exact tax, levy, impose, apportion; have one's price.

2, amount to, come to, mount up to, fetch, sell for cost, bring in, yield, afford. *Colloq.,* stand one, stick for, set one back.

Adjectives—priced, appraised; taxable, dutiable; mercenary, venal.

Adverbs—to the tune of, at a price, for a consideration.

Antonyms, see CHEAPNESS.

priceless, *adj.* invaluable, precious; expensive, costly. See DEARNESS.

prick, *v.t.* puncture, pierce, stick; sting, wound; prod, urge, incite, goad, spur. See PAIN, SENSIBILITY, IMPULSE.

prickly, *adj.* thorny, barbed, bristly, spiny, thistly, burry; stinging, tingling, smarting. See ROUGHNESS, SHARPNESS, PAIN.

PRIDE

Nouns—**1,** pride, hauteur; dignity, self-respect, self-esteem, self-sufficiency, reserve.

2, arrogance, INSOLENCE; OSTENTATION; VANITY, vainglory, crest, airs, high notions; condescension; purse-pride; BOASTING, conceit, self-complacency, self-exaltation, self-glorification, self-satisfaction, self-importance, self-admiration, self-love, *amour-propre*. *Slang,* swelled head.

3, patriotism, nationalism, civic *or* national pride; loyalty, allegiance; love of country, civism; chauvinism, jingoism, fascism; flag-waving.

4, proud man, high flier, peacock; fine gentleman *or* lady; boast, pride and joy; patriot, chauvinist, jingo[ist], fascist. *Slang,* swellhead.

Verbs—**1,** be proud, look one in the face, lift *or* hold up one's head, hold one's head high, perk oneself up; pride oneself on, glory in, take pride in, stand upon, be proud of.

2, be conceited; plume, preen, *or* hug oneself; put a good face on, carry with a high hand; boast, swagger, strut, presume, look big; set one's back up, bridle, toss one's head, give oneself airs; condescend, talk down to, patronize, stoop, lower oneself. *Colloq.,* get on one's high horse. *Slang,* put on side *or* airs, put on the dog, put on the ritz.

3, fill with pride, puff up, swell, inflate, turn one's head. *Colloq.,* give a big head.

Adjectives—**1,** proud, exalted, lordly, noble (see NOBILITY); mettlesome, [high-]spirited; imposing, magnificent, splendid, majestic, grand.

2, arrogant (see INSOLENCE); vain, conceited (see VANITY); haughty, magisterial, puffed up, swollen, flushed, blown, vainglorious; supercilious, disdainful, contemptuous, presumptuous, condescending, cavalier; boastful, overweening, high and mighty; purse-proud; self-satisfied, self-confident, *etc.;* ego[t]istical; proud as a peacock *or* as Lucifer, bloated with pride, puffed up. *Colloq.,* uppish, uppity. *Slang,* high-hat.

3, stiff, formal, stiff-necked, starchy, prim, straitlaced; aristocratic (see NOBILITY); affected. *Colloq.,* stuck up.

4, patriotic, nationalistic, chauvinist[ic], jingo[ist], fascist.

Adverbs—proudly, haughtily; with dignity, with head erect, with nose in the air; in one's glory. *Colloq.,* on one's high horse.

Antonyms, see HUMILITY, MODESTY.

priest, priestess, *n.* father, clergyman, *etc.* See CLERGY.

priggish, *adj.* pedantic, affected; fastidious, prim, precious; conceited, egotistical. See AFFECTATION, VANITY.

prim, *adj.* precise, demure, formal, priggish; fussy, prudish. See AFFECTATION.

primary, *adj.* chief, original, initial, first, elementary; immediate; primitive, prime, principal. See BEGINNING, CAUSE, IMPORTANCE.

primate, *n.* chief, leader, head, master; bishop, archbishop, metropolitan, diocesan, suffragan, patriarch; man, ape, monkey, lemur, *etc.* See CLERGY, ANIMAL.

prime, *adj.* original, first, initial; primitive, primeval; chief, leading, main; choice, finest. See IMPORTANCE, OLDNESS, PREPARATION.

primitive, *adj.* primeval, aboriginal, crude, unpolished, unrefined; basic, primal, primary; prime; old, antiquated. See OLDNESS, INTRINSIC, VULGARITY.

primness, *n.* prudery, prudishness, priggishness; formality; preciousness, stiffness. See AFFECTATION.

primp, *v.* prink, preen, groom, bedizen, prettify, freshen up. *Colloq.,* deck out, put one's face on. *Slang,* doll up. See ORNAMENT.

prince, *n.* monarch, ruler, sovereign; noble[man]; chief; *slang,* swell guy. See AUTHORITY, GOODNESS.

princely, *adj.* regal, royal, titled, noble; magnanimous, generous, munificent. See NOBILITY.

princess, *n.* crown princess, queen. See AUTHORITY.

principal, *n.* chief, leader, head; constituent, client; buyer, seller; capital, *corpus.* See MONEY. *—adj.* foremost, chief, prime, greatest, main, leading. See IMPORTANCE.

principality, *n.* principate, dominion, domain, sovereignty, rule; princedom, satrapy, country, province, REGION; duchy, palatinate, margraviate; sheikdom, imamate, emirate, caliphate, sultanate.

principle, *n.* tenet, code, doctrine, conviction; theory, premise; postulate; rule, law, precept; equity, integrity, probity, nature, origin, source, CAUSE. See BELIEF, PART, SUBSTANCE, INTRINSIC.

prink, *v.* dress up, adorn, deck out. See ORNAMENT, CLOTHING.

PRINTING

Nouns—**1,** printing; typography, stereotype, electrotype; block printing; lithography, planography, collotype; offset, letterpress, gravure, rotogravure; instant printing, Xerox; photoprinting, photoengraving, Itek; intaglio; ENGRAVING; PUBLICATION; composition, typesetting, phototypesetting; Linotype, Monotype, Intertype, cold *or* hot type, computer typesetting; imposition; mat, matrix; reproduction; graphic arts. See COPY.

2, type, case, lower *or* upper case, capital; font; typeface, roman, italic, lightface, boldface; stick, stone; shank, serif, body, shoulder, beard; point *or* set size; Gothic, oldstyle, modern, *etc.* type; print.

3, impression, proof, galley, galley proof, page proof, repro[duction] proof, revise, run, rerun; plate, replate, cliché.

4, printing press, press, proof press; job press, flatbed press, cylinder press, rotary press.

5, printer, compositor, typographer, pressman, makeup man, proofreader, copyreader, copyholder; stone hand; printer's devil, proof boy.

Verbs—print, imprint, impress, run off; Xerox, offset; compose, impose, set, make up; proofread, revise; make ready; go to press.

Adjectives—printed; in type, in print; typographical; graphic; in black and white.

Antonyms, see WRITING.

PRIORITY

Nouns—**1,** priority, antecedence, anteriority, primogeniture; preexistence; precession; precursor, forerunner; PAST; premises. See PRECEDENCE, ANCESTRY, BEGINNING.

2, antecedent; head start. *Colloq.,* scoop.

3, precursor, forerunner, antecedent, precedent, predecessor, forebears; bellwether, herald, harbinger, announcer; HABIT, standard, model; prototype; custom, practice, usage; prefigurement, PREDICTION.

Verbs—**1,** precede, antecede, come *or* go before; lead; preexist; dawn; presage (see PREDICTION). *Colloq.,* beat one to it. *Slang,* get the jump on, beat to the punch *or* draw.

2, be beforehand, be early (see EARLINESS); steal a march upon, anticipate, forestall; have *or* gain a start; steal one's thunder, scoop. *Slang,* beat out, jump the gun.

Adjectives—prior, previous; preceding, precedent; anterior, antecedent; forehanded; preexisting, preexistent; former, foregoing; afore-mentioned, above-mentioned; aforesaid; said; introductory, precursory; preliminary; preparatory.

Adverbs—before, prior to; earlier; first[ly], first and foremost, in the first place; ere, heretofore, erstwhile, already, yet, beforehand; in advance, ahead; in the van *or* forefront; in front, foremost; on the eve of; *ante bellum;* before Christ, B.C.; antediluvian, before the fact. *Colloq.,* first off.

Antonyms, see SEQUENCE.

---

prismatic, *adj.* prismal; sparkling, coruscant, colorful, chromatic; kaleidoscopic; spectral, rainbowlike. See VARIEGATION, COLOR.

PRISON

Nouns—**1,** prison, penitentiary; jail, lockup, gaol, cage, coop, den, cell; cell block; stronghold, fortress, keep, dungeon, Bastille, oubliette; Sing Sing, Dartmoor, Alcatraz, Bridewell, house of correction, debtors' prison, prison farm, workhouse; guardroom, guardhouse; alimony jail; brig, hold; roundhouse, station house, station, police station; house of correction, reformatory, reform school, protectory; house of detention; pen, fold, corral, pound; ENCLOSURE; penal colony *or* settlement; stocks, stone walls. *Colloq.,* lockup. *Slang,* jug, can, calaboose, calabozo, hoosegow, pen, big house, stir, clink, cooler, school, quad, pokey. See RESTRAINT, PUNISHMENT.

2, concentration *or* detention camp, compound, stalag; extermination center, death camp; Auschwitz, Bergen-Belsen, Buchenwald, Dachau, Treblinka.

3, prisoner, captive, felon; convict, inmate, détenu, jailbird; trusty, parolee; prisoner of war, P.O.W.; ticket-of-leave man. *Slang,* lag, con.

4, warden, keeper, jailer, gaoler, turnkey, guard, warder. *Slang,* screw, roach. See SAFETY.

Verbs—imprison, immure, incarcerate, confine, entomb, put in irons; arrest, detain, take into custody, capture, pick up, apprehend, take prisoner, run in, lead into captivity; send to prison, commit; give in custody, subjugate. *Colloq.,* nab; put away. *Slang,* collar, haul *or* pull in, haul up.

Adjectives—imprisoned, pent up, under lock and key, behind bars; in custody, laid by the heels, under arrest, in hand. *Colloq.,* in lockup, inside. *Slang,* in stir, in the can *etc.*

Antonyms, see LIBERATION, FREEDOM.

---

prissy, *adj., colloq.,* priggish, prim; sissified, effeminate. See FEMALE.

pristine, *adj.* prime, first, dawnlike, primordial; fresh, dewy, pure, virginal, unspoiled. See BEGINNING, OLDNESS.

private, *adj.* personal, secluded, intimate, sequestered; privy, confidential, unofficial; individual, special. See SECLUSION.

privation, *n.* want, LOSS, POVERTY, indigence; deprivation, bereavement, dispossession.

privilege, *n.* option, franchise; prerogative, right; favor, EXEMPTION, exception, immunity, liberty. See RIGHTNESS.

privy, *adj.* personal, SECRET; privy to, apprised of, informed of. *Colloq.*, posted on, in on, on to, wise to. See CONCEALMENT, SPECIALITY.

prize, *n.* trophy, medal, award, decoration, laurel; premium, bonus, reward; advantage, privilege; pick, elite. —*v.t.* cherish, treasure, esteem, value. See APPROBATION, LOVE.

probably, *adj.* likely, hopeful, to be expected, in the cards, in a fair way; plausible, ostensible, well-founded, reasonable, credible, believable, presumable, presumptive, apparent, *prima facie*. See CHANCE, BELIEF, POSSIBILITY, LIABILITY.

probe, *v.t.* prod, pierce, stab; sound, fathom; search, investigate, sift, explore; verify. See INQUIRY, MEASUREMENT.

PROBITY

Nouns—**1,** probity, integrity, rectitude; uprightness; honesty, faith; honor; good faith, *bona fides;* clean hands; dignity, respectability; right, JUSTICE. See REPUTE, INNOCENCE, VIRTUE, RIGHTNESS, GOODNESS.

2, constancy; faithfulness, fidelity, loyalty; incorruption, incorruptibility; allegiance, devotion; trustworthiness, sincerity, candor, veracity. See TRUTH.

3, punctilio, delicacy, nicety, conscientiousness; scrupulosity, scrupulousness, scruple, point of honor; punctuality, honor system.

4, UNSELFISHNESS, disinterestedness, sublimity, chivalry.

5, gentleman, man of honor, honest man, man of his word, *fidus Achates;* truepenny, straight arrow. *Colloq.*, square-shooter, brick. *Slang,* trump, regular fellow, good egg, right guy, ace [of spades].

Verbs—deal honorably, squarely, impartially, *or* fairly, play fair; speak *or* tell the truth, speak one's mind, call a spade a spade; do one's duty; keep one's promise *or* word; be as good as one's word; keep faith with; one's word is one's bond; carry the torch. *Colloq.*, be on the level; be on the up and up; level, shoot straight *or* square. *Slang,* tell it like it is; go straight.

Adjectives—**1,** upright; honest, veracious, truthful; virtuous, honorable, law-abiding; upstanding; fair, right, just, equitable, impartial, square; open and aboveboard; straightforward, frank, candid, forthright, openhearted, man-to-man, heart-to-heart, straight from the shoulder. *Slang,* on the level, on the up and up, straight, square-shooting, upfront, legit, kosher.

2, constant, faithful, loyal, staunch; true, true-blue, true to the core; trusty, trustworthy; as good as one's word, reliable, dependable, to be depended on, steadfast, incorruptible, above suspicion. *Colloq.*, on the up and up, fair and square.

3, conscientious; disinterested, right-minded; high-principled, high-minded; scrupulous, religious, strict; nice, punctilious, correct, punctual; respectable, reputable, gentlemanly.

Adverbs—honorably, *bona fide;* on one's honor, on the square, from the heart, in good faith, honor bright, with clean hands.

Antonyms, see IMPROBITY, AFFECTATION.

---

problem, *n.* question, proposition, exercise; poser, puzzle, enigma, riddle; issue; query. See INQUIRY, SECRET.

problematical, *adj.* questionable, unsettled, perplexing; uncertain, enigmatic. See DOUBT.

proboscis, *n.* trunk, snout, nose. See CONVEXITY.

procedure, *n.* process, METHOD, tactics, proceeding, way, course; practice, CONDUCT; policy, ACTION, form. See PLAN.

proceed, *v.i.* continue, progress, advance; move, arise; emanate, result, issue. See PROGRESSION, EFFECT.

proceeding, *n.* ACTION, progress, move, measure, step, procedure. See OCCURRENCE, LAWSUIT.

proceeds, *n.pl.* balance, profit, gain, yield, earnings, receipts, issue, outcome, results; income. See MONEY, RECEIVING, EFFECT.

process, *n.* CONDUCT, METHOD, procedure, practice; course; outgrowth, protuberance, appendage, projection. See ACTION.

procession, *n.* cavalcade, parade, train, column, file; progression, sequence, succession. See CONTINUITY, TRAVEL.

proclaim, *v.t.* announce, declare, broadcast, circulate, publish, herald. See PUBLICATION.

proclivity, *n.* inclination, TENDENCY, propensity, proneness, predisposition.

procrastination, *n.* postponement, delay, dilatoriness; negligence, omission. See LATENESS, NEGLECT.

procreate, *v.* breed, reproduce, generate, beget, give birth. See REPRODUCTION.

proctor, *n.* monitor, overseer, housemaster; AGENT, steward. See DIRECTOR.

procure, *v.t.* acquire, PURCHASE, get, obtain; buy, hire; effect. See CAUSE.

procurer, procuress, *n.* pander, bawd, pimp; obtainer. See EVILDOER, PURCHASE.

prod, *v.t.* shove, goad, prick, spur, poke, jab; motivate, impel, instigate, incite. See IMPULSE.

prodigality, *n.* profligacy, WASTE; profusion, profuseness; extravagance, squandering; excess, lavishness; LIBERALITY. See SUFFICIENCY.

prodigious, *adj.* immense, enormous, vast, gargantuan, huge; remarkable, wonderful; monstrous; astonishing. See WONDER.

prodigy, *n.* phenomenon; WONDER, marvel, miracle; monster; curiosity, sight, spectacle; precocious child, child prodigy. *Slang,* boy *or* girl wonder, wiz kid. See UNCONFORMITY, SKILL.

produce, *n.* goods, yield, harvest; fruit, vegetables; stock, commodity, product. See AGRICULTURE, SALE. —*v.* show, exhibit; create, originate, bear, breed, hatch; make, fashion, manufacture. See PRODUCTION, REPRODUCTION.

product, *n.* yield, output, produce; outcome, EFFECT, result. See PRODUCTION, AGRICULTURE.

PRODUCTION

Nouns—**1,** production, creation, construction, formation, fabrication, manufacture; building, erection, edification; coinage; organization; putting together, establishment; workmanship, performance, operation; achievement, COMPLETION, authorship, PUBLICATION, works. See ACTION, PREPARATION.

2, product, output; edifice, building, structure, fabric; invention, composition; WRITING, book, PAINTING, MUSIC; flower, fruit, work, handiwork; *chef d'oeuvre,* opus.

3, productiveness, fecundity, fertility, luxuriance; pregnancy, pullulation, fructification, multiplication; fertilization.

4, producer, creator, originator, inventor, author, founder, generator, mover, architect, maker; contractor; construction worker, road gang, carpenter, *etc.*

5, manufacture, manufacturing, fabrication; mass production, assembly line; automation, robotics.

6, factory, plant, mill, foundry, works. See BUSINESS.

Verbs—produce, perform, operate, do, make, FORM, construct, fabricate, frame, contrive; mass-produce, hammer out, manufacture, turn out; weave, forge, coin, carve, chisel; build, raise, rear, erect, put together; set up, run up, establish, constitute, compose, organize, institute; achieve, accomplish, complete, perfect. See UTILITY.

Adjectives—produced, producing, productive; formative; fabricated, manufactured, synthetic, artificial, man-made, handmade *or* -crafted, machine-made, hand-built.

Antonyms, see DESTRUCTION, USELESSNESS.

---

profane, *adj.* vulgar; sacrilegious, impious, unhallowed. —*v.t.* debase, desecrate, defile, pollute; abuse. See IMPIETY.

profess, *n.* pretend, feign; teach, instruct; affirm, declare, avow; own, admit. See AFFIRMATION, FALSEHOOD.

profession, *n.* vocation, calling, occupation; sham, evasion, pretense; affectation, pretension; relief; acknowledgment, declaration, avowal. See AFFIRMATION, BUSINESS.

professor, *n.* academician, teacher, instructor, scholar, don, master. *Slang,* prof, doc. See TEACHING.

proffer, *v.t.* tender, OFFER.

proficient, *adj.* expert, adept, dext[e]rous, adroit; well-versed, practiced; masterly, skillful. See SKILL.

profile, *n.* outline, SIDE, shape, contour; sketch. See APPEARANCE, FORM.

profit, *n.* advantage, benefit, interest; gain, earnings, return. See INCREASE. —*v.* benefit; improve; gain, line one's pockets. See MONEY, UTILITY.

profitable, *adj.* remunerative, lucrative, paying, gainful; advantageous, productive; serviceable, useful. See UTILITY.

profiteer, *n.* extortionist, leech. *Colloq.,* highway robber. —*v.i.* overcharge, fleece, extort. *Colloq.,* hold up, skin, bleed. *Slang,* stick, sting. See STEALING.

profligate, *adj.* wanton, reckless, wild, intemperate; extravagant, wasteful. —*n.* roué, rake, libertine, lecher, reprobate; wastrel, spendthrift, squanderer. *Slang,* playboy. See WASTE, IMPURITY, EVILDOER.

profound, *adj.* erudite, learned, abstruse; heavy, weighty, deep; heartfelt, intense; complete, thorough. See FEELING, GREATNESS, KNOWLEDGE, DEPTH.

profusion, *n.* abundance, multiplicity; excess, waste, superfluity, extravagance; plenty. See MULTITUDE, SUFFICIENCY, DIFFUSION, LIBERALITY.

progenitor, *n.* forefather, ancestor; CAUSE. See ANCESTRY.

progeny, *n.* children, offspring, descendants. See POSTERITY.

prognosticate, *v.t.* prophesy, foretell, augur, predict. See PREDICTION.

program, *n.* playbill, prospectus, syllabus; agenda; forecast, draft, outline. See PLAN, CONDUCT.

PROGRESSION

Nouns—progression, progress, progressiveness; MOTION; advance, advancing, advancement; ongoing, chain; floodtide, headway; march (see TRAVEL); rise; improvement. See CONTINUITY, TIME.

Verbs—progress, advance, proceed; get on, get along, get under way; gain ground; go with the stream, current, *or* tide; hold *or* keep one's course; push *or* press on, forward, *or* ahead, go, move, go along, pass on; make one's way, work one's way; make progress *or* headway; make rapid strides; gain leeway. *Slang*, go great guns, get rolling, get cracking.

Adjectives—advancing, progressing, progressive, advanced.

Adverbs—progressively; forward, onward, along; forth, on, ahead; under way; en route, on one's way, on the move, on the [high] road; in progress.

Antonyms, see REGRESSION.

---

progressive, *adj*. enterprising, advanced, moving; improving, advancing; successive, continuing, continuous. See CONTINUITY, IMPROVEMENT, PROGRESSION.

PROHIBITION

Nouns—prohibition, inhibition, forbiddance, disallowance, restriction (see RESTRAINT); veto, injunction, interdict[ion], proscription; preclusion, EXCLUSION; embargo, ban, taboo, no-no, forbidden fruit; prevention, stoppage, HINDRANCE; intemperance act, Volstead Act, Eighteenth Amendment, dry law. See ILLEGALITY, MODERATION.

Verbs—**1,** prohibit, inhibit, forbid, disallow; veto, kill, ban, interdict; put *or* place under an interdiction *or* ban; taboo, proscribe, enjoin, deny, [de]bar, forfend; preclude, prevent, hinder; set *or* put one's foot down, have none of.
2, exclude, shut out, padlock, keep out; draw the color line, discriminate; shut *or* bolt the door; warn off; forbid the banns; disbar, unfrock.
3, see LIMIT, CIRCUMSCRIPTION, HINDRANCE.

Adjectives—**1,** prohibitive, prohibitory, prohibiting, forbidding, *etc*.
2, prohibited, forbidden, *verboten*, not permitted; unauthorized, unlicensed, illegal; banned, contraband, taboo; out of bounds, off limits.

Adverbs—on no account (see NEGATION).

Interjections—Heaven forbid! hands off! keep off! keep out! hold! stop! avast! no thoroughfare! no trespassing!

Antonyms, see PERMISSION.

---

project, *n*. PLAN, purpose, enterprise; endeavor. —*v*. protrude, bulge, jut; throw, hurl, pitch; devise, plan, scheme, intend. See CONVEXITY, PROPULSION, UNDERTAKING.

projectile, *n*. ball, pellet, bullet, missile, shell. See ARMS.

projection, *n*. extension, shelf; protuberance, protrusion; prominence, spur, eminence; transference, visualization. See CONVEXITY, ANGULARITY, OPTICAL INSTRUMENTS.

projector, *n*. magic lantern, stereopticon; slide projector; cinematograph. See OPTICAL INSTRUMENTS.

proletariat, *n*. working class, laborers, wage earners, labor force, POPULACE.

proliferate, *v.i*. spread, multiply. See MULTITUDE, REPRODUCTION.

prolific, *adj*. fruitful, fecund, productive, fertile; lavish. See PRODUCTION, IMAGINATION.

prolix, *adj*. lengthy, wordy, long-winded, discursive, verbose, diffuse; tedious. See DIFFUSENESS.

prologue, *n*. preface, introduction, proem, preamble, prelude. See DRAMA, PRECEDENCE.

prolong, *v.t*. extend, protract, hold; sustain, perpetuate, continue; lengthen. See LENGTH, DURABILITY.

promenade, *n*. mall, alameda, boulevard, esplanade, boardwalk; promenade deck; stroll, outing, march; dance, ball. —*v*. walk, stroll, saunter. See TRAVEL, AMUSEMENT.

prominent, *adj*. notable, important, salient, memorable; convex, raised, protuberant, projecting, jutting; influential, distinguished, eminent;

conspicuous, noticeable. See CONVEXITY, IMPORTANCE, REPUTE, ELEVATION, VISIBILITY.

promiscuous, *adj.* indiscriminate, mixed, miscellaneous, confused. See MIXTURE, DISORDER, IMPURITY.

PROMISE

Nouns—**1,** promise, UNDERTAKING, word, troth, pledge, parole, word of honor, vow, avowal; oath (see AFFIRMATION); assurance, warranty, guarantee; insurance, obligation, mortgage; covenant, contract, compact, commitment; engagement, affiance (see MARRIAGE). See SECURITY, EVIDENCE, DUTY.

2, fiancé[e]; man of his word; promised land.

Verbs—**1,** promise; give *or* make a promise, undertake, engage; make *or* enter into an engagement; bind, pledge, *or* commit oneself; take upon oneself; vow; give, pledge, *or* plight one's word, swear; plight one's troth; betroth, plight faith, take an oath; assure, warrant, guarantee; covenant, attest (see EVIDENCE); contract an obligation; become bound to, become sponsor for; answer for, be answerable for; secure; give security; underwrite; promise the moon. *Colloq.*, cross one's heart, swear to God.

2, extract a promise, adjure, administer an oath, put to one's oath, swear a witness, swear in.

Adjectives—promising, promissory; votive; under hand and seal, upon *or* under oath; contractual; promised, affianced, pledged, bound; committed, compromised; in for it.

Interjections—so help me! cross my heart [and hope to die]!

Antonyms, see REFUSAL.

promontory, *n.* spit, headland, cape. See HEIGHT, CONVEXITY.

promote, *v.t.* advance, further, AID; improve, dignify, elevate, raise; back, support, encourage. See IMPROVEMENT.

promoter, *n.* founder, organizer, planner; backer, supporter, encourager. See PLAN.

prompt, *v.t.* incite, induce, motivate; actuate; remind, suggest, mention. See INFORMATION, MEMORY, CAUSE, INFLUENCE. *—adj.* immediate, ready, punctual, unretarded; alert, quick, active; instant, instantaneous; reasonable, early. See EARLINESS.

prompter, *n.* reminder; note, tickler, cue card, teleprompter; promptbook. See MEMORY.

promulgate, *v.t.* publish, disseminate, proclaim, sponsor, advocate. See PUBLICATION.

prone, *adj.* inclined, disposed, likely, predisposed; recumbent, flat, prostrate, HORIZONTAL.

prong, *n.* tine, point, pincer, spike, tooth, fang; extension. See SHARPNESS.

pronounce, *v.t.* speak, say, utter, enunciate, articulate; deliver, judge, conclude; affirm, assert. See AFFIRMATION, SPEECH.

pronto, *adv., colloq.,* at once, immediately. See INSTANTANEITY.

pronunciation, *n.* utterance, saying, voicing, articulation, enunciation, orthoëpy. See SPEECH.

proof, *n.* EVIDENCE, substantiation, verification, confirmation; conclusiveness; corroboration, ratification; trial, test; sample, impression. See DEMONSTRATION, EXPERIMENT. *—adj.* impenetrable, impervious; invulnerable. See STRENGTH.

prop, *n.* SUPPORT, brace, stay, pillar, underpin, shore, column, block, base; foundation; mainstay, assistant, helper, staff; fulcrum; truss; property. See DRAMA, PROPULSION. *—v.t.* SUPPORT, uphold, brace, encourage, back; truss; shore, underpin, underset.

propaganda, *n.* publicity; persuasion, proselytization, movement. See INFORMATION, TEACHING.

propagate, *v.* breed, generate, produce, disseminate; spread, broadcast, publish, increase; multiply. See PRODUCTION, PUBLICATION.

propel, *v.t.* push, force, impel, thrust, shove, drive. See PROPULSION, ROTATION.

propeller, *n.* propulsor, impeller; rotor, blade, airfoil, screw. *Colloq.,* prop. See PROPULSION, ROTATION.

propensity, *n.* TENDENCY, aptitude, inclination, talent, bent, proclivity, disposition.

proper, *adj.* correct, fastidious; suitable, becoming; decorous, demure, chaste, delicate; individual, special, limited, own, appropriate, pertinent, apropos, meet; seemly, befitting; equitable, fair, right, just. See RIGHTNESS, SPECIALITY, ELEGANCE, EXPEDIENCE, JUSTICE.

prophecy, *n.* PREDICTION, prognosis, forecast, augury, divination.

prophet, *n.* oracle, soothsayer, prognosticator, sibyl; predictor, seer, diviner. See PREDICTION.

prophylactic, *adj.* preventive, precautionary, preservative, protective. See HEALTH.

propinquity, *n.* NEARNESS; vicinity, proximity; adjacency; RELATION; juxtaposition.

propitiate, *v.t.* pacify, conciliate, reconcile; intercede, calm, mediate; atone. See ATONEMENT, PACIFICATION.

propitious, *adj.* encouraging, auspicious; gracious; fortunate, prosperous, favorable; timely, opportune; thriving. See HOPE, PROSPERITY, OCCASION.

proponent, *n.* advocate, supporter; defender, champion, backer. See FRIEND, VINDICATION.

proportion, *n.* dimension, ratio, extent; share, part, quota, distribution, allotment; adjustment, uniformity; magnitude. See APPORTIONMENT, SYMMETRY, RELATION, SIZE.

proportional, *adj.* proportionate, commensurable, measurable. See NUMBER, EQUALITY.

proportionate, *adj.* commensurate, proportionable, proportional, according. See AGREEMENT, RELATION.

proposal, *n.* OFFER, statement, recommendation, proposition, motion, suggestion; REQUEST, overture, advance, PLAN.

propose, *v.* propound, advance, present, state; recommend, suggest; court, woo; intend; proffer, nominate. See ENDEARMENT, SUPPOSITION, SUBMISSION.

proposition, *n.* OFFER, PLAN, project, proposal, undertaking; axiom, hypothesis, theorem, postulate, problem, thesis, predication. See REASONING.

propound, *v.t.* propose, state, suggest. See SUPPOSITION.

proprietor, proprietress, *n.* manager, owner; master, mistress, lord, lady. See POSSESSION.

propriety, *n.* decorum, conventionality, suitability; aptness, fitness; fastidiousness, becomingness, delicacy, decorum, seemliness; prudery. See AGREEMENT, EXPEDIENCE, FASHION.

PROPULSION

Nouns—**1,** propulsion, projection; push (see IMPULSE); ejaculation; EJECTION; throw, fling, toss, shot.

2, propeller, driver, turbine (see POWER); shooter, archer, bowman, rifleman, marksman, pitcher; good shot, crack shot, sharpshooter.

Verbs—propel, project, throw, fling, cast, pitch, chuck, toss, jerk, heave, shy, hurl; dart, lance, tilt; jet, squirt, spurt, ejaculate; fulminate, bolt, drive, sling, pitchfork; send; send, let, *or* fire off; discharge, shoot; launch, catapult, send forth; let fly; dash; put *or* set in motion; set going, start; give a start, give an impulse to; impel, expel, put to flight, send flying, put [a shot].

Adjectives—propelled, propelling, propulsive, projectile; self-propelled, automotive, automobile.

Antonyms, see TRACTION, REPULSION.

---

prosaic, *adj.* unimaginative, dull, uninteresting, commonplace, prosy, plain, sober; unromantic. See WEARINESS, INSIPIDITY.

proscribe, *v.t.* outlaw, forbid, interdict, prohibit, condemn; excommunicate, exile, curse. See PROHIBITION, CONDEMNATION.

prose, *n.* WRITING, style; fiction, nonfiction, prose poem; journalese, hack work. *Colloq.,* deathless prose.

prosecute, *v.* urge, pursue, follow, continue, press; arraign, sue, indict, charge. See LAWSUIT, PURSUIT, ACCUSATION.

proselyte, *n.* convert, follower, neophyte. See CHANGE, PIETY.

prosody, *n.* metrics, poetics, versecraft; rhyme, rhythm, meter. See POETRY.

prospect, *n.* view, outlook, scene, landscape, vista, sight; promise, probability, HOPE, EXPECTATION, foresight. See APPEARANCE, FUTURITY.

prospective, *adj.* probably, foreseen, expected; coming; imminent. See EXPECTATION.

prospector, *n.* miner, gold panner, placer miner. *Colloq.,* desert rat, sourdough, forty-niner. See INORGANIC MATTER.

prospectus, *n.* presentation, brochure, catalog; description, sketch; design, scheme. See LIST, PLAN.

PROSPERITY

Nouns—prosperity, welfare, well-being; affluence, wealth, SUCCESS; thrift; good fortune, blessings, luck; sunshine; fair weather, fair wind; fat years, palmy days, halcyon days; boom, heyday; golden time, golden age; bed of roses, charmed life; lucky star; cornucopia, horn of plenty; fat of the land, milk and honey, good times; godsend, windfall, winning streak, manna from heaven; affluent society. *Colloq.,* land-office business; lucky break, streak *or* run of luck, Lady Luck. *Slang,* fat city. See MONEY, CHANCE.

Verbs—**1,** prosper, grow, multiply, thrive, flourish; be prosperous; go well, smoothly, *or* swimmingly; flower, blow, burgeon, blossom, bloom, fructify, bear fruit, pay off; fatten, batten; live high off the hog. *Colloq.,* look like a million dollars. *Slang,* clean up.

2, rise [in the world], get on in the world; climb the ladder of success; make one's way *or* fortune; feather one's nest; bear a charmed life; bask in the sunshine; have a run of luck, come on; have good fortune, have one's ship come in; take a favorable turn; live on the fat of the land, live in clover; win out, make a strike, make a hit, strike it rich, coin *or* make money. *Slang,* make one's pile, luck out, have it made, hit the jackpot.

Adjectives—prosperous; thriving; fruitful; well-to-do, in the chips, rich, wealthy, affluent; fortunate, lucky, in luck, in clover, in the lap of luxury, on easy street, in the clear; auspicious, propitious, providential; in the black; palmy, halcyon. *Slang,* in the chips *or* money, sitting pretty.

Phrases—every dog has his day; sitting on top of the world, born with a silver spoon in one's mouth, be fruitful and multiply; have money to burn.

Antonyms, see ADVERSITY.

---

prostitute, *n.* whore, harlot, tart (see IMPURITY).

prostrate, *adj.* recumbent, prone, flat, supine; debased, abased, humbled; helpless, powerless, resigned. See HORIZONTAL. —*v.t.* debase, abase, flatten; bow, submit. See DEJECTION, LOWNESS, SERVILITY.

prosy, *adj.* See PROSAIC.

protagonist, *n.* lead, hero[ine], headliner. See DRAMA.

protect, *v.t.* defend, guard, shelter, shield, screen; preserve, save, champion, secure. See SAFETY.

protection, *n.* safeguard, DEFENSE, shelter, screen; championship, custody, care, guard; foil. See INFLUENCE, RESTRAINT, SAFETY.

protégé, protégée, *n.* ward, charge; pupil, trainee. See LEARNING, SUBJECTION.

protest, *n.* objection, complaint, remonstrance, contradiction, disapproval, expostulation, protestation. —*v.t.* object, remonstrate, complain, contradict, repudiate, default; declare (see AFFIRMATION). See DISSENT, DISAPPROBATION, NONPAYMENT, REFUSAL.

Protestant, *n.* non-Catholic, dissenter; Presbyterian, Baptist, Methodist, *etc.* See RELIGION, DISSENT.

protocol, *n.* draft, RECORD; customs, procedures. See CONFORMITY.

prototype, *n.* original; model, pattern; precedent; standard, type; archetype; module, exemplary, example, paradigm; test, copy design; keynote, die, mold; matrix, last. See CONFORMITY, PREPARATION.

protract, *v.t.* extend, lengthen; prolong, continue; postpone, defer, delay; chart. See LENGTH, DURABILITY.

protrude, *v.* jut, bulge, extend, project. See CONVEXITY.

protuberance, *n.* projection, bulge, jut, protuberancy, prominence, excrescence, lump, swelling. See CONVEXITY.

proud, *adj.* See PRIDE.

prove, *v.t.* confirm, verify, substantiate, show, demonstrate, document, check, try, test. See EVIDENCE, CERTAINTY, FEELING.

provender, *n.* fodder, feed; FOOD, provisions.

proverb, *n.* MAXIM, axiom, adage, precept, saying.

provide, *v.* See PROVISION.

provided, *adv.* if, supposing, though. See CIRCUMSTANCE.

providential, *adj.* fortunate, lucky, fortuitous, timely, opportune, reasonable, auspicious. See PROSPERITY, OCCASION.

province, *n.* function, sphere; field, department, division, bailiwick, district; control; domain, jurisdiction. See BUSINESS, REGION.

provincial, *adj.* intolerant, illiberal; insular, narrow; local, rural, countrified; rustic. See NARROWNESS, MISJUDGMENT, ABODE.

PROVISION

Nouns—**1,** provision, purveyance, replenishment, reinforcement; subsidy, grant; stock, STORE; MEANS; equipment, furnishings, accoutrements, appurtenances, outfit, apparatus, gear, trappings; rig, tackle; matériel (see ARMS); grist [to the mill], FOOD, feed, fare, victuals, eatables, viands, nourishment, nutrition, provender.

2, PREPARATION, planning, arrangement, precaution, provident care.

3, provider, caterer, purveyor, supplier, commissary, commissariat,

quartermaster, feeder, batman, victualer, grocer, merchant, steward, manciple, purser, innkeeper, restaurateur, sutler; breadwinner.
4, see QUALIFICATION.

Verbs—**1,** provide, furnish, afford, supply, equip, fit out *or* up, gear, accouter; serve; arm; provision, victual, provender, cater, purvey, forage, feed, recruit, find; stock, lay in, come up with; make good, replenish, fill (up).
2, make provision for, take measures for, prepare *or* plan for; STORE, have in store, have in reserve; keep [handy *or* at hand]; have to fall back on, save for a rainy day.
3, provide for, make *or* earn a living, support, board; make one's way, make ends meet; manage. *Slang,* heel.

Adjectives—provided, prepared; well-stocked, -equipped, *etc. Slang,* [well-] heeled.

Antonyms, see WASTE, REFUSAL.

---

provisional, *adj.* conditional; temporary. See BETWEEN, QUALIFICATION.

proviso, *n.* condition[s], stipulation, clause, agreement; QUALIFICATION, reservation, covenant.

provisory, *adj.* provisional, conditional, dependent, subject. See QUALIFICATION.

provocation, *n.* aggravation, irritation, vexation, annoyance, indignity, affront. See DEFIANCE, EXCITEMENT.

provocative, *adj.* tantalizing, titillating; racy, piquant. See TASTE, ATTENTION, EXCITEMENT, ATTRACTION.

provoke, *v.t.* annoy, irritate, exasperate, nettle; excite, arouse; anger, incite, evoke, elicit; goad, vex. See CAUSE, EXCITEMENT, RESENTMENT.

prow, *n.* bow, FRONT, beak, nose, stem.

prowess, *n.* COURAGE, bravery, heroism; SKILL, competence.

prowl, *v.i.* ramble, wander, roam; lurk, slink, sneak; rove. See CONCEALMENT.

proximity, *n.* NEARNESS, vicinity, propinquity, neighborhood.

proxy, *n.* substitute, AGENT, delegate, representative; agency; procurator. See COMMISSION, SUBSTITUTION.

prude, *n.* formalist, puritan, prig. See AFFECTATION.

prudence, *n.* discretion, carefulness, CAUTION, circumspection, tact; policy, foresight; CARE, thoughtfulness, judiciousness. See VIRTUE.

prudent, *adj.* discreet, wary, circumspect, prudential, careful, heedful, chary, cautious; wise, politic. See CARE, CAUTION.

prudery, *n.* propriety; prudishness, stiffness, coyness, primness, preciousness. See AFFECTATION.

prudish, *adj.* prim, demure, precious, affected, precise. See AFFECTATION.

prune, *v.t.* trim, abbreviate, thin, lop; remove. See DEDUCTION.

pry, *v.* examine, search, seek, peer, ransack, peek, reconnoiter; raise, force, prize, lever. See CURIOSITY, INQUIRY, VISION.

pseudo, *adj.* spurious, counterfeit, simulated, false, fake, mock. See IMITATION, SIMILARITY.

pseudonym, *n.* sobriquet, alias, *nom de guerre*; pen name, *nom de plume*; byname, nickname, epithet; disguise, incognito, John Doe, Richard Roe. See CONCEALMENT, NOMENCLATURE.

psyche, *n.* soul, pneuma, anima; self-personality, spirit, inner being, essence, essential nature, id, ego and superego; INTELLECT.

psychiatrist, *n.* mental *or* mind doctor, [psycho]analyst *or* -therapist, alienist, psychiater. *Slang,* crazy *or* bug doctor, headshrinker, shrink. See INTELLECT.

psychic, *adj.* clairvoyant, prophetic, extrasensory, parapsychological, spiritualist, telepathic. —*n.* teleporter, mind reader, fortuneteller, seer, spiritualist, mentalist, clairvoyant, medium. See INTELLECT.

psychopath, *n.* neurotic, psychotic, madman. *Slang,* psycho. See INSANITY.

psychosis, *n.* neuropsychosis, schizophrenia, dementia praecox, *etc.* See INSANITY.

psychotherapy, *n.* psychotherapeutics, psychiatry. See INTELLECT.

psychotic, *adj.* psychopathic, demented (see INSANITY).

pub, *n.* tavern, public house. See FOOD, DRINKING.

puberty, *n.* pubescence, adolescence, nubility, maturity. See YOUTH.

public, *adj.* popular, common, general; civic, political, national; notorious, known, published; communal, free. See PUBLICATION, POPULACE, HUMANITY.

PUBLICATION

Nouns—**1,** publication; announcement; NEWS, INFORMATION; promulgation, propagation, proclamation; circulation; bulletin, edition; hue and cry; banns; notification; divulgation, DISCLOSURE; publicity, notoriety, currency; *vox populi;* report; newscast, broadcast, telecast, simulcast, radio; spotlight, limelight, white glare of publicity; public relations; blurb, plug, puff, write-up. *Slang,* P.R. See WRITING, PRINTING, DISCLOSURE.

2, the press; newspaper, journal, gazette, paper, organ; scandal sheet, yellow sheet, tabloid; daily, weekly; magazine, review, periodical; serial; monthly, bimonthly, *etc.;* issue, number, album, portfolio; annual, journal.

3, book, volume, folio, tome, opus; novel; tract, brochure; libretto; handbook, codex, manual, textbook, pamphlet, broadside, booklet, circular; edition, pocket edition, production; encyclopedia; dictionary, lexicon, glossary, thesaurus; anthology; gazetteer, almanac, digest, compilation.

4, advertisement; press *or* publicity release; handout, placard, bill, broadside; poster; billboard, hoarding, sandwich board; flier, circular, brochure, circular letter, [bulk] mailing; manifesto; public notice, skywriting. *Colloq.,* ad, want ad, classified ad; commercial, informercial, spot announcement; hitchhiker, cowcatcher; personal [ad].

5, publisher, publicist, journalist, columnist, press agent; announcer, broadcaster, commentator, analyst; writer, author (see WRITING). *Slang,* flack, P.R. man *or* woman.

Verbs—**1,** publish; edit; put, get, *or* bring out; come out, appear, hit the stands. *Colloq.,* put to bed.

2, make public, make known, publicize, advertise, circularize; air; voice, broach, utter; circulate, promulgate, propagate; spread abroad; disseminate; issue; bandy about; bruit abroad; drag into the open; raise a hue and cry; spread the word *or* the Gospel; put on the wire; wash one's dirty linen in public; make a scene; wear one's heart on one's sleeve; get around *or* about, go the rounds.

3, report; proclaim, herald, blazon; trumpet forth; announce; beat the drum; shout from the housetops; advertise, post; rumor, gossip, chatter, tattle; hang out one's shingle.

Adjectives—published, public, current, newsy, new, in circulation, afloat; notorious; flagrant, arrant, open; encyclical, promulgatory; broadcast.

Adverbs—publicly; in print, in public; in the air; on the air.

Antonyms, see SILENCE, CONCEALMENT.

---

publicity, *n.* notoriety, limelight; utterance, outlet, vent. See PUBLICATION.

pucker, *n.* wrinkle, crease, crinkle, ruffle, shirring. —*v.* contract; corrugate, crinkle, wrinkle, shirr, ruffle. See FOLD.

pudding, *n.* dessert, custard, junket. See FOOD.

puddle, *n.* pool, pond; mud puddle. See WATER, COHERENCE.

pudgy, *adj.* thickset, stocky, squat; plump, chubby, roly-poly. See SIZE.

puerile, *adj.* trivial, foolish, trifling, weak, nonsensical; childish, immature, boyish, juvenile. See YOUTH, IGNORANCE.

puff, *n.* swelling; blow, breath, cloud, wind, breeze; *colloq.*, gesture, praise. —*v.* brag, boast, praise, commend; blow, pant, gasp; inflate. See APPROBATION, BOASTING, INCREASE, FLATTERY.

pugilism, *n.* boxing, fisticuffs. See CONTENTION.

pugnacious, *adj.* combative, quarrelsome, militant, belligerent, contentious, bellicose. See CONTENTION, IRASCIBILITY.

pull, *n.* power, sway; jerk, wrench, tug; magnetism, gravity, ATTRACTION; *slang,* INFLUENCE. —*v.* tug, wrench, haul, drag, draw; extract; row, paddle; tow. See EXTRACTION, EXERTION, TRACTION.

pulp, *n.* paste, dough; curd; pap; jam, pudding; poultice; mush. See SOFTNESS.

pulpit, *n.* platform, rostrum, desk; priesthood, ministry. See TEMPLE.

pulsate, *v.i.* beat, throb; drum, palpitate. See OSCILLATION.

pulse, *v.i.* throb, beat, quiver, palpitate; thump; shudder, tremble; pulsate, vibrate. See OSCILLATION, AGITATION, REGULARITY.

pulverize, *adj.* crush, powder, crumble. See POWDERINESS.

pummel, *v.t.* pommel, beat, belabor. See IMPULSE, PUNISHMENT.

pump, *v.t.* draw, suck[out]; interrogate, question, catechize; inflate, puff up. See INQUIRY, WIND, EXTRACTION.

pun, *n.* wordplay, paronomasia, pundigrion, *calembour,* equivoque; quip, joke, *double entendre;* paragram. See WIT, SIMILARITY.

punch, *v.t.* strike, hit, poke, beat, knock; puncture, perforate, pierce. See IMPULSE, OPENING.

punchy, *adj., colloq.,* dazed, confused; punch-drunk. See INSENSIBILITY.

punctilious, *adj.* conscientious, scrupulous; exact, precise; formal, ceremonious; severe, strict. See OSTENTATION.

punctual, *adj.* prompt, regular, precise, punctilious; periodical; early, timely. See EARLINESS, REGULARITY.

punctuate, *v.t.* point, interpoint, interpunctuate; accentuate; interrupt. See GRAMMAR, IMPORTANCE.

puncture, *n.* perforation, hole, pinprick, OPENING. —*v.t.* pierce, jab, perforate, prick.

pundit, *n.* wise man, sage, savant. *Slang,* know-it-all, wise guy. See KNOWLEDGE, TEACHING, CLERGY.

PUNGENCY

Nouns—**1,** pungency, piquancy, poignancy, tang, raciness, *haut goût,* strong TASTE; sharpness, keenness, acrimony, acritude, acridity, astringency, acerbity, SOURNESS, gaminess; tartness, spiciness, heat, acidity, causticity, bite, tang. *Colloq.,* zip, nip, punch, ginger. See ODOR, MALODOROUSNESS.

2, mustard, cayenne, pepper, salt, brine, mace, onion, garlic, pickle, ginger, caviar; seasoning, spice, relish, condiment, catsup, curry, vinegar, *sauce piquante;* ammonia, smelling salts, niter; nicotine, tobacco, snuff, quid; cigarette, smoke, regular, king-size, long[-size], plain, oval, cork tip, filter tip, 100; cigar, cheroot, stogie, panatela, perfecto, corona, belvedere;

cigarillo. *Slang,* coffin nail, cig, fag, butt, gasper, tube, weed, reefer.
Verbs—be pungent, bite the tongue, sting; season, [be]spice, salt, pepper, pickle, curry, brine, devil; smoke, puff, chain smoke; chew, take snuff.
Adjectives—pungent, piquant, poignant, tangy, racy; sharp, keen, acrid, acerb, acrimonious, astringent, bitter; sour (see SOURNESS); unsavory (see TASTE); gamy, high, strong, high- *or* full-flavored, high-tasted; biting, stinging, mordant, caustic, pyrotic, burning, acid; odiferous (see ODOR); piercing, pricking, penetrating, stimulating, appetizing; tart, spicy, spiced, seasoned, peppery, hot [as pepper]; salt[y], saline, brackish, briny; nutty, zesty. *Colloq.*, zippy, snappy.

Antonyms, see INSIPIDITY, ODORLESSNESS.

PUNISHMENT

Nouns—**1,** punishment; chastisement, chastening; correction, castigation; discipline, infliction, trial; judgment, penalty; retribution; thunderbolt, nemesis; requital, RETALIATION; penology. See PAIN.

2, capital punishment, execution, electrocution, hanging, gassing, firing squad, decapitation, crucifixion, lynching, stoning; imprisonment (see PRISON, RESTRAINT); torture, rack, thumbscrew, question; transportation, banishment, expulsion, exile, ostracism, Coventry (see EJECTION); stocks, pillory; penal servitude, hard labor, solitary confinement; galleys; beating, hiding, rawhiding, flagellation, the lash, gauntlet, whipping post; rap on the knuckles, spanking, thrashing, box on the ear; blow (see IMPULSE); walking the plank, keelhauling; picket[ing]; martyrdom, *auto-da-fé;* harakiri, tarring and feathering, riding on a rail; fine, forfeit. *Colloq.*, the chair. *Slang,* hot seat, rope necktie, necktie party, kangaroo court, Judge Lynch, Jack Ketch.

3, scourge, whip, lash, *etc.*, drop, gallows, gibbet, scaffold, rope, noose, halter; block, ax; stake, cross; guillotine, electric chair, gas chamber.

Verbs—**1,** punish, penalize, chastise, chasten; fine, dock; castigate, correct, inflict punishment; retaliate, administer correction, deal out justice; visit upon; pay; make short work of, give short shrift, give a lesson to, serve one right, let one have it, give it to, make an example of; thrash, flog, spank, cane, whale away, whip; beat *or* mess up. *Colloq.,* give one his comeuppance; paddle; lower the boom; tan one's hide, skin alive; settle one's hash, throw the book at. *Slang,* give what for, give hell, make it hot for, work over.

2, strike, hit, *etc.* (see IMPULSE).

3, execute, electrocute; behead, decapitate, guillotine; hang, gibbet, bowstring; shoot; decimate; burn at the stake; boil in oil; break on the wheel; crucify; tar and feather; impale, flay; lynch; torture, put on the rack, picket. *Colloq.*, string up. *Slang,* burn, fry. See KILLING.

4, banish, exile, transport, expel, ostracize; rusticate; drum out; dismiss, disbar, disbench; demote; strike off the roll, unfrock; post. See EJECTION.

5, suffer punishment; take one's medicine, face the music; pay the piper, the fiddler, *or* the price. *Slang,* take it, take the rap.

Adjectives—punishing, penal, punitory, punitive; castigatory; capital.

Antonyms, see COMPENSATION.

---

punk, *n., slang,* hood, mug; henchman; kid, delinquent, snotnose [kid]. See YOUTH, EVILDOER.

puny, *adj.* small, underdeveloped, undersized, tiny; stunted. See LITTLENESS.

pupil, *n*. student, schoolchild, schoolgirl, schoolboy; learner, tyro, scholar. See LEARNING, SCHOOL.

puppet, *n*. marionette; manikin, doll; figure, tool, cat's-paw, hireling, henchman, vassal. See REPRESENTATION, AMUSEMENT, SERVANT.

puppy, *n*. pup, whelp, cub, youngling; child, tad, *etc*. See YOUTH.

purblind, *adj*. obtuse, dull, stupid; mole-eyed. See VISION.

PURCHASE

Nouns—**1,** purchase, buying, emption; purchasing power; bargain (see CHEAPNESS); installment buying *or* plan, time purchase plan, buying on time, deferred payment, layaway plan, revolving charge plan, hire-purchase (*Brit*.); ACQUISITION, acquirement, procurement, expenditure, PAYMENT; bribery, bribe, dealing. *Colloq*., buy. See OFFER.

2, purchaser, buyer, *emptor,* vendee; shopper, marketer, patron, employer; client, customer, consumer; constituency; trafficker; clientry, clientele, patronage. See BUSINESS.

Verbs—purchase, buy, invest in, procure, acquire; shop, market, go shopping, bargain for; rent, hire (see BORROWING); repurchase, redeem; buy in; pay (for), spend; make *or* complete a purchase; buy over *or* under the counter; buy out; be in the market for; keep in one's pay, bribe, buy off, suborn.

Adjectives—purchased; purchasable, buyable, available, obtainable; bribable, venal, commercial.

Phrase—*caveat emptor*.

Antonyms, see SALE.

purgative, *n*. cathartic, emetic, laxative, physic, aperient. —*adj*. purifying, cleansing; abstergent, evacuant, cathartic, expulsive, emetic, aperient, physic, laxative; restorative. See CLEANNESS.

purgatory, *n*. limbo, netherworld, underworld; ATONEMENT. See HELL.

purge, *v.t*. cleanse, clarify; flush, wash, clear; atone; pardon, absolve, acquit; expiate; evacuate, remove; liquidate, kill. See ATONEMENT, CLEANNESS, PURITY, KILLING.

puritanical, *adj*. strict, prudish, prim, severe, rigid. See ASCETICISM.

PURITY

Nouns—**1,** purity, pureness, clearness, *etc*. (see *Adjectives*); refinement, purification, clarification, cleansing; defecation, depilation; filtering, filtration; sublimation, distillation; percolation, leaching, lixiviation; elutriation; strain, sieve.

2, refinery; cleanser, clarifier, defecator, *etc.;* filter, sieve, colander, strainer, screen.

3, see VIRTUE, INNOCENCE, CLEANNESS.

Verbs—purify, make pure, free from impurity, decrassify; clear, clarify, clean, wash, cleanse; rectify; refine, purge, defecate, depurate, expurgate, sublimate; distill; strain (see CLEANNESS).

Adjectives—pure, unadulterated, unalloyed, unmixed, unpolluted, undefiled, untainted, uncorrupted; refined; genuine, real, true, simple, perfect, clear; fine; full-blooded, thoroughbred; clean, unspoiled, unblemished, untarnished, unviolated, wholesome; sinless, unerring (see VIRTUE).

Antonyms, see IMPURITY.

purlieus, *n.pl.* neighborhood, environs, surroundings, outskirts, limits, bounds, confines. See NEARNESS.

purple, *adj. & n.* See COLOR.

purport, *n.* MEANING, significance, import, sense.

purpose, *n.* INTENTION, determination, resolution, resolve; END, aim, view.

purposeful, *adj.* determined, resolved; intentional. See RESOLUTION, INTENTION.

purse, *n.* handbag, reticule, pocketbook, wallet, moneybag; MONEY, exchequer, funds; prize.

pursuant, *adj.* following; according. See INTENTION.

PURSUIT

Nouns—**1,** pursuit; pursuing, prosecution; pursuance; enterprise (see UNDERTAKING, BUSINESS); adventure, quest, INQUIRY; hue and cry; game, hobby. *Slang,* head-hunting. See SEQUENCE.

2, chase, hunt, steeplechase, coursing; safari; venery; foxhunt.

3, pursuer, hunter, huntsman, sportsman, Nimrod; hound, bloodhound; fisher, angler, fisherman *or* -woman.

Verbs—**1,** pursue, prosecute, follow, go after, go for; run, take, make, *or* chase after; gun for; carry on, engage in, undertake, set about; endeavor, court, REQUEST; seek, aim at, fish for; press on;

2, chase, give chase, chase *or* run after, course, dog, hunt [down], hound; track down; tread *or* follow on the heels of; run down; trail, shadow, dog. *Colloq.,* breathe down one's neck. *Slang,* tail.

Adjectives—pursuing, in search *or* quest of, in pursuit, in full cry, in hot pursuit; on the trail, track, *or* scent.

Adverbs—in pursuance of; at one's heels; after. *Colloq.,* on the prowl.

Antonyms, see AVOIDANCE.

---

purvey, *v.t.* deliver, yield, hand, give; provide, furnish, cater, PROVISION.

pus, *n.* matter, suppuration, purulence. See UNCLEANNESS.

push, *n.* nudge, thrust, shove; pressure, exigency; crisis, pinch; *colloq.,* endeavor, effort, drive, determination, perseverance, persistence, aggressiveness. See CIRCUMSTANCE. —*v.t.* drive, urge, force; propel, advance, impel; shove, encourage, hearten; prosecute. See IMPULSE, PROPULSION.

pushover, *n., slang,* easy mark. *Colloq.,* cinch, sucker. *Slang,* duck soup, set up. See FACILITY.

pushy, *adj.* aggressive. See ATTACK.

pusillanimous, *adj.* cowardly, mean-spirited. See COWARDICE.

put, *v.t.* place, locate, set, deposit, plant, fix, lay; cast, throw; thrust; impose, rest, stick. See LOCATION, PROPULSION.

putative, *adj.* thought, alleged, considered, supposed, reputed, presumed. See SUPPOSITION.

putdown, *n., slang,* insult, slight, rejection. See DETRACTION.

putrefy, *v.i.* rot, decay, decompose. See UNCLEANNESS.

putrid, *adj.* decomposed, decayed, rank, foul, rotten, corrupt. See UNCLEANNESS, BADNESS.

putter, *v.i.* dabble, dawdle, idle, loaf, tinker. *Colloq.,* fiddle, monkey. See INACTIVITY, UNIMPORTANCE.

puzzle, *n.* riddle, conundrum, poser, enigma; mystification, perplexity, complication; dilemma, bewilderment, confusion. —*v.t.* confound, perplex, bewilder, confuse, mystify. See DIFFICULTY, UNINTELLIGIBILITY, SECRET.

pygmy, *n.* pigmy, dwarf, midget, atomy; Lilliputian. See LITTLENESS.

pyramid, *n.* pyramidion, polyhedron;

progression, pile, accumulation, snowball. See INTERMENT, ANGULARITY, SHARPNESS, INCREASE.

Q

quack, *n.* charlatan, quacksalver, mountebank. See DECEPTION, FALSEHOOD, UNSKILLFULNESS.

quadrangle, *n.* rectangle, square, quad, quadrilateral; yard, compound, court[yard], ENCLOSURE. See ANGULARITY, ABODE.

quaff, *v.t.* drink; swill, guzzle. See DRINKING.

quagmire, *n.* quag, quicksand, marsh[land], mire, fen, morass, bog, slough; dilemma, problem, DIFFICULTY. See MOISTURE.

quail, *v.i.* shrink, cower, RECOIL, flinch. See FEAR, COWARDICE.

quaint, *adj.* old-fashioned, picturesque. See UNCONFORMITY.

quake, *v.i.* tremble, quiver, shake, shudder. See AGITATION, FEAR, COLD.

QUALIFICATION

Nouns—**1,** qualification, limitation, modification, restriction, coloring, leavening; allowance, consideration, extenuating circumstances; condition, proviso, provision, exception (see EXEMPTION); prerequisite, stipulation, specification, saving clause. See SUPPOSITION.

2, see ABILITY, REPUTE, SKILL.

Verbs—qualify, LIMIT, modify, leaven, allow for, make allowance for, take into account *or* consideration, consider, discount; take with a grain of salt.

Adjectives—qualifying, conditional, provisional, provisory; qualified, restrictive, contingent.

Adverbs—conditionally, admitting, admittedly, provided, if, unless, but, yet; nevertheless; according as; supposing; with the understanding, even, although, though, for all that, after all, at all events; with a grain of salt; wind and weather permitting; if possible; subject to; with this proviso, on condition that.

Prepositions—except for, but for.

Antonyms, see CERTAINTY.

qualified, *adj.* competent, fit; limited, restricted. See QUALIFICATION, JUSTICE, PREPARATION.

quality, *n.* attribute, property; excellence; trait, characteristic; status, brand, grade; NOBILITY, gentility. See ATTRIBUTION, FEELING, INTRINSIC, SPECIALITY.

qualm, *n.* twinge, pang, throe; misgiving, compunction, uneasiness, remorse. See FEAR, PENITENCE.

quandary, *n.* dilemma, plight, perplexity, bewilderment. See DOUBT, DIFFICULTY.

QUANTITY

Nouns—**1,** quantity, magnitude, amplitude; numbers, amount; content, mass, bulk, weight; sum, aggregate; MEASUREMENT; number, quantifier; MULTITUDE. See ASSEMBLAGE.

2, portion (see APPORTIONMENT); quantum; handful, armful, pocketful, mouthful, spoonful, *etc.;* batch, lot, stock, supply, STORE; some[what], aught, any, so much, so many.

Verbs—quantify, measure (see MEASUREMENT); count (see NUMERATION).

Adjectives—quantitative, quantitive, numerical, metrical; counted, weighed, figured, calculated, estimated; measurable, weighable, estimable; in bulk, mass, *or* quantity; certain; some, any, more, less; more *or* better than, more or less. *Colloq.,* to the tune of.

Antonyms, see UNITY.

---

quantum, *n.* QUANTITY, amount; substance, mass; particle, photon, phonon, magneton, light quantum, ENERGY. See APPORTIONMENT.

quarantine, *n.* detention, detainment, RESTRAINT, confinement, SECLUSION, segregation, sequestration, isolation; *cordon sanitaire.* —*v.t.* detain, segregate, separate, isolate, sequester. See EXCLUSION.

quarrel, *n.* altercation, wrangle, squabble; dispute, controversy, feud. *Colloq.,* spat. —*v.i.* dispute, disagree, wrangle, squabble; find fault. See DISCORD, DISAPPROBATION.

quarrelsome, *adj.* contentious, disputatious, pugnacious, combative. See IRASCIBILITY, CONTENTION.

quarry, *n.* prey, game; catch, bag, take; target, pursuit; lode, bed, [stone]pit, mine; STORE, source.

quarter, *n.* one-fourth; trimester; district, REGION, DIRECTION; lodging, billet; mercy. *Colloq.,* two bits. See SIDE, PITY, LENIENCY, ABODE. —*v.t.* quadrisect; divide, cut up; billet, station. See LOCATION, NUMERATION.

quarters, *n.pl.* ABODE, lodgings, residence; billet, barracks.

quash, *v.t.* suppress, subdue, crush; set aside, annul, void. See NULLIFICATION, RESTRAINT.

quasi, *adj.* apparent, seeming, so-called, pseudo, IMITATION, near, approximate. —*adv.* almost, in a sense, nearly, not quite; as though, as if, as it were, so to speak, seemingly. See SIMILARITY, SUPPOSITION.

quaver, *v.i.* quiver, shake, tremble; tremolo, warble, trill. See OSCILLATION, AGITATION.

quay, *n.* wharf, dock, pier, mole, levee. See ABODE.

queasy, *adj.* nauseous; squeamish, uneasy; timid, fearful, apprehensive; finicky, skittish. *Slang,* jittery. See DISEASE, FEAR.

queen, *n.* ruler, mistress; belle. See AUTHORITY, BEAUTY.

queer, *adj.* odd, singular, strange; giddy, faint. *Colloq.,* deranged. *Slang,* shady, counterfeit. See UNCONFORMITY.

quell, *v.t.* subdue, suppress, crush; quiet, allay. See DESTRUCTION, MODERATION.

quench, *v.t.* put *or* snuff out; extinguish; still; damp, chill; slake, sate, satisfy. See INCOMBUSTIBILITY, DISSUASION, PLEASURE.

querulous, *adj.* whining, complaining, fretful, petulant, peevish. See LAMENTATION, DISCONTENT.

query, *n.* INQUIRY, question, DOUBT.

quest, *n.* search, PURSUIT; probe, investigation, INQUIRY; adventure, mission, expedition; aim, goal, objective, desire.

question, *n.* problem, subject; query, interrogation; DOUBT, dispute. See INQUIRY. —*v.t.* interrogate, examine, cross-examine, quiz; dispute, challenge, DOUBT.

questionable, *adj.* doubtful, uncertain, debatable. *Colloq.,* fishy. See DOUBT, IMPROBITY.

questionnaire, *n.* form, blank; examination, interrogation; INQUIRY, survey, canvass, poll.

queue, *n.* cue, pigtail; line[up], file, rank. —*v.i.* line *or* queue up, form a line, fall in, wait. See CONTINUITY, SEQUENCE.

quibble, *n.* evasion, equivocation, sophism, cavil. See AVOIDANCE, DISSENT, FALSEHOOD.

quick, *adj.* rapid, swift, brief; prompt, alert; ready, unhesitating; hasty, irascible; sensitive, keen; alive, living, sentient. See VELOCITY, ACTIVITY, FEELING, IRASCIBILITY, INTELLIGENCE.

quicken, *v.t.* revive, refresh, arouse, animate; hasten, speed, accelerate. See VELOCITY, AGENCY, HASTE.

quicksand, *n.* quagmire, mire, morass, bog, slough. See MOISTURE.

quick-tempered, *adj.* impetuous, hotheaded, irascible, hot, peppery. See IRASCIBILITY.

quiddity, *n.* essence, quintessence, substance, kernel, pith; equivocation, quibble, hairsplitting. See INTRINSIC, WIT.

quiescent, *adj.* still, motionless, moveless, fixed, stationary; stagnant, becalmed, quiet; tranquil, unmoved, undisturbed, unruffled; calm, restful; sleeping, silent. See INACTIVITY, REPOSE, LATENCY.

quiet, *adj.* peaceful, tranquil, serene; hushed, silent; modest, restrained, subdued; gentle, calm; unostentatious. See REPOSE. —*n.* quietude, peacefulness, calm; SILENCE, hush. See MODERATION, INEXCITABILITY.

quill, *n.* feather; plume; pen; spine, bristle, seta, barb, spike, needle; pick, plectrum. See ROUGHNESS, SHARPNESS.

quilt, *n.* coverlet, patchquilt, comforter, goosedown, quilting. See COVERING.

quip, *n.* joke, witticism, retort, repartee. *Slang,* [wise]crack. See WIT.

quirk, *n.* flourish; quip, taunt, jibe; quibble, deviation, evasion; peculiarity, trick, eccentricity. See WIT, INSANITY.

quit, *v.* satisfy, requite; resign, abandon, relinquish, leave; cease, stop, desist. See PAYMENT, RELINQUISHMENT, DISCONTINUANCE, ACQUITTAL, RESIGNATION.

quite, *adv.* entirely, utterly, wholly; really, actually. *Colloq.,* rather, somewhat, very. See COMPLETION.

quittance, *n.* ACQUITTAL, freedom; receipt, quitclaim, relinquishment; retaliation, vindication, ATONEMENT; PAYMENT, recompense.

quitter, *n., colloq.,* shirker, evader, avoider. *Slang,* slacker, welsher. See AVOIDANCE.

quiver, *v.i.* tremble, shudder, shiver, flutter, vibrate, shake, quaver. See AGITATION.

quixotic, *adj.* visionary, unrealistic, whimsical; foolish, crazy. See RASHNESS.

quiz, *v.t.* interrogate, question, examine; tease, banter. See INQUIRY.

quorum, *n.* plenum, SUFFICIENCY, majority.

quota, *n.* allotment, share, proportion, percentage. See APPORTIONMENT.

quotation, *n.* citation, excerpt, REPETITION; PRICE.

quote, *v.t.* repeat, cite, instance, refer to, abstract. See EVIDENCE, REPETITION, PRICE.

R

rabbi, *n.* master, teacher; rabbin, rabbinist. See CLERGY.

rabble, *n.* crowd, proletariat, POPULACE, common herd, *hoi polloi;* mob, *canaille,* riffraff, scum. See ASSEMBLAGE.

rabblerouser, *n.* demagogue, agitator, troublemaker. See CAUSE.

rabid, *adj.* mad, furious; fanatical, overzealous. See FEELING, EXCITEMENT, EXCITABILITY.

rabies, *n.* hydrophobia, *lyssa;* foaming at the mouth. See DISEASE, INSANITY.

race, *n.* onrush, advance; competition; sprint, dash; stream; channel, millrace, tide, river; career; family, clan, tribe; people, ethnic group. —*v.* rush, career; hasten; compete; speed. See VELOCITY, ANCESTRY, CONTENTION, HUMANITY, OPPOSITION.

raceway, *n.* [race]track, racecourse, oval, turf. See AMUSEMENT, ARENA.

racial, *adj.* tribal, family; hereditary, ancestral. See HUMANITY.

racism, *n.* prejudice, bigotry; segregation, color line, apartheid; white *or* black supremacy, black nationalism; genocide. *Colloq.,* Jim Crow. See INJUSTICE, MISJUDGMENT.

rack, *v.t.* strain, exert; torture, distress, torment, agonize. See THOUGHT, PAIN. —*n.* single-foot, pace; frame[work]; wheel, Iron Maiden; scud, broken clouds. See MOTION, CLOUDINESS, SUPPORT.

racket, *n.* uproar, din, clatter, hubbub; frolic, carouse, rumpus, hurly-burly; battledore. See AMUSEMENT, LOUDNESS.

racketeer, *n.* mobster, gangster, hoodlum. See EVILDOER.

racy, *adj.* spirited, lively; piquant; *colloq.,* risqué, suggestive. See VIGOR, PUNGENCY, FEELING.

radiant, *adj.* shining, sparkling, glowing; splendid, resplendent, glorious. See LIGHT, BEAUTY.

radiation, *n.* DISPERSION, diffusion, emission, emanation; radiance, illumination. See LIGHT.

radical, *adj.* fundamental, INTRINSIC; extreme, drastic, thorough; sweeping, revolutionary. See COMPLETION. —*n.* liberal, leftist, left-winger (see CHANGE); reformer, rebel, revolutionary; anarchist, nihilist, Communist, Bolshevik. *Colloq.,* red, pink, parlor pink, fellow-traveler. *Slang,* Commie, pinko. See REVOLUTION.

radio, *n.* wireless, radio telegraphy, radio telephony; radiogram. See COMMUNICATION.

radius, *n.* half-diameter; spoke; range, scope, sphere, LENGTH. See BREADTH.

raffish, *adj.* rowdy (see VULGARITY).

raffle, *n.* drawing, door prize, lottery, sweepstake[s]. See CHANCE.

raft, *n.* flatboat, barge; float, pontoon; *colloq.,* MULTITUDE. See SHIP.

rafter, *n.* beam, timber, crosspiece, joist. See SUPPORT.

rag, *n.* shred, tatter, scrap, remnant; ragtime; (*pl.*) castoffs, hand-me-downs. See CLOTHING, MUSIC. —*v., slang,* tease, rib, kid, RIDICULE.

ragamuffin, *n.* tatterdemalion (see DETERIORATION).

rage, *n.* fury, frenzy, wrath, VIOLENCE; FASHION, fad, craze. See DESIRE. —*v.i.* storm, rave, bluster. See EXCITEMENT, EXCITABILITY.

ragged, *adj.* tattered, frayed, shabby, seedy, worn; in shreds; in patches; patched, torn, rough; tatterdemalion, ragamuffin; dogeared. See DETERIORATION, DIVESTMENT.

raid, *n.* ATTACK, invasion, onset, incursion; foray. See STEALING. —*v.t.* ATTACK, invade; pounce upon.

rail, *v.* rant, scold, chide; inveigh, carry on, harangue. See DISAPPROBATION.

railing, *n.* fence, barrier, balustrade. See ENCLOSURE.

raillery, *n.* banter, badinage, persiflage, quizzing. *Slang,* kidding, ribbing. See RIDICULE.

railroad, *n.* railway; main *or* trunk line, spur; model railroad; tramline, tramway, trolley *or* streetcar line, street railway, subway. See TRANSPORTATION. —*v., colloq.,* rush *or* push through, expedite. *Slang,* frame, jail. See INJUSTICE.

raiment, *n.* CLOTHING, apparel, attire, vesture, garb.

rain, *n.* shower, precipitation, rainstorm, downpour. —*v.* shower, pour, drizzle; bestow, lavish, shower upon. See WATER.

rainbow, *n.* arc, *arc-en-ciel;* spectrum. See VARIEGATION, COLOR.

raincoat, *n.* slicker, oilskin, poncho, mackintosh, trenchcoat, rainproof, plastic raincoat. See CLOTHING.

raise, *v.t.* lift, elevate; [a]rouse, stir up, incite; muster, collect; resurrect; erect, build, exalt, honor; INCREASE; cultivate, breed. See ELEVATION, EXCITEMENT, CONVEXITY.

rake, *v.t.* gather, collect; comb, ransack, search, rummage; enfilade, spray with bullets; incline, slope. See ASSEMBLAGE. —*n.* libertine, roué, rakehell; slope, ramp. See CLEANNESS, OBLIQUITY, AGRICULTURE.

rake-off, *n., slang,* rebate, refund, PAYMENT, return, kickback, payoff; payola, share, cut, percentage; bribe; extortion.

rally, *v.* muster, marshal, call together; revive, restore, rouse, encourage; banter, chaff. See COURAGE, ASSEMBLAGE.

ram, *v.t.* butt, batter, bump; pound, drive, tamp; cram, stuff. See IMPULSE.

ramble, *v.i.* stroll, saunter, stray, rove, wander; digress, maunder. See TRAVEL, LOQUACITY, DEVIATION, DIFFUSENESS.

rambunctious, *adj.* boisterous, pugnacious, quarrelsome. See IRASCIBILITY.

ramification, *n.* divergence, division, branching; PART, offshoot, spur. See DEVIATION.

ramp, *n.* incline, slant, slope. See OBLIQUITY.

rampage, *v.i.* ramp, rage, go berserk, run amuck, go crazy. —*n.* tantrum, VIOLENCE, disturbance, frenzy, turmoil.

rampant, *adj.* rife, widespread, raging, epidemic; luxurious, lush; wild, unrestrained, unchecked; turbulent, tempestuous. See FREEDOM, VIOLENCE.

rampart, *n.* parapet, fortification, wall, bulwark, embankment. See DEFENSE.

ramrod, *n.* ram[mer], stick, rod, poker, iron. See HARDNESS, STRAIGHTNESS.

ramshackle, *adj.* dilapidated, tumbledown, rickety. See DETERIORATION.

ranch, *n.* range, farm, grange, spread. See ABODE, AGRICULTURE.

rancid, *adj.* rank, stale, putrid, malodorous. See MALODOROUSNESS, SOURNESS.

rancor, *n.* spite, malice, bitterness, vengefulness, vindictiveness, MALEVOLENCE, hatred.

random, *adj.* haphazard, casual, CHANCE, fortuitous, aimless.

randy, *adj.* vulgar, bawdy. See VULGARITY.

range, *n.* row, series, chain; scope, extent; habitat; limit, span, latitude; compass, register; DISTANCE; stove[top], cooktop. See CONTINUITY, SPACE, BUSINESS, FREEDOM, DIRECTION, DEGREE.

rank, *adj.* lush, luxuriant, vigorous; coarse; malodorous, fetid, rancid, offensive; arrant, extreme, gross. —*n.* row, line; position, caste, quality; status, grade, standing, footing. See REPUTE, BADNESS, CLASS, HORIZONTAL, CONTINUITY.

rankle, *v.i.* fester, irritate, gall, PAIN.

ransack, *v.t.* rummage, scour, search diligently; rifle, loot, pillage. See INQUIRY, STEALING.

ransom, *v.t.* redeem. —*n.* redemption, release, LIBERATION. See ATONEMENT, PAYMENT, PRICE.

rant, *v.i.* rage, rave, scold, nag; harangue. See EXCITABILITY, SPEECH.

rap, *v.* tap, knock, blow, cuff, box, clout; criticize; *colloq.*, converse. *Slang,* swat, sock. See IMPULSE, DISAPPROBATION, CONVERSATION.

rapacious, *n.* greedy, ravenous, voracious. See DESIRE, GLUTTONY.

rape, *v.t.* seize, plunder; seduce, debauch, ravish. See IMPURITY, STEALING.

rapid, *adj.* swift, speedy, fleet, prompt, quick. See VELOCITY. —*n.* (*pl*). white water, chute, shoot. See WATER.

rapier, *n.* sword (see ARMS).

rapine, *n.* plunder (see STEALING).

rapport, *n.* touch, sympathy, understanding, communication; affinity, empathy, compatibility. See RELATION, AGREEMENT.

rapt, *adj.* ecstatic, enraptured, transported; absorbed, engrossed. See ATTENTION, THOUGHT, FEELING.

rapture, *n.* ecstasy, transport, bliss, joy, delight. See PLEASURE.

rare, *adj.* scarce, sparse; unusual, choice, remarkable; tenuous (see RARITY); underdone, half-done, half-cooked, raw (see UNPREPAREDNESS).

RARITY

Nouns—**1,** rarity, tenuity, subtlety, thinness, lightness, compressibility; rarefaction, attenuation, dilatation, inflation. See VAPOR.

2, rareness, scarcity, uncommonness, infrequency, infrequence; collector's item. See UNCONFORMITY.

Verbs—rarefy, expand, dilate, attenuate, thin out.

Adjectives—**1,** rare, subtle, thin, fine, tenuous, compressible, slight, light, ethereal; rarefied, unsubstantial.

2, scarce, unusual, infrequent, uncommon, few [and far between], scant, sporadic, occasional; part-time; unprecedented, unheard-of; odd, curious, singular.

Adverbs—rarely, infrequently, *etc.;* seldom, scarcely *or* hardly ever; once in a [great] while, once in a blue moon; now and then *or* again, from time to time, at times; once and for all.

Antonyms, see DENSITY, FREQUENCY, MULTITUDE.

---

rascal, *n.* scoundrel, knave, rogue, reprobate, blackguard; imp, scamp. See EVILDOER.

rascality, *n.* knavery, villainy, roguery, blackguardism. See IMPROBITY.

RASHNESS

Nouns—**1,** rashness, temerity, incautiousness, imprudence, indiscretion, recklessness, FOLLY; overconfidence, audacity, COURAGE, sporting blood; precipitancy, precipitation, impetuosity, foolhardiness, heedlessness, thoughtlessness, NEGLECT; desperation, Quixoticism; DEFIANCE; gaming, gambling; blind bargain, leap in the dark, fool's paradise. See DANGER.

2, desperado, hotspur, madcap, daredevil, fire-eater, bully, bravo, scapegrace, Don Quixote, adventurer; gambler, gamester; stunter, stuntman; speeder. *Slang,* speed demon.

Verbs—be rash, stick at nothing, play a desperate game, play with fire, walk on thin ice, go out of one's depth, ride for a fall, take a leap in the dark, buy a pig in a poke, tempt Providence, clutch at straws, lean on a broken reed; run the gauntlet; dare, risk, hazard, gamble, throw caution *or* discretion to the winds; put all one's eggs in one basket. *Slang,* take a flyer, go for broke.

Adjectives—rash, daring, incautious, indiscreet, imprudent, improvident, temerarious, heedless, careless, reckless, giddy, wild; madcap, desperate, devil-may-care, hotblooded, hotheaded, headlong, headstrong, breakneck; foolhardy, harebrained, precipitate, overconfident, adventurous, venturesome, quixotic, free-and-easy; risky, hazardous. *Colloq.,* quick on the trigger, trigger-happy.

Adverbs—rashly, recklessly, *etc.;* hotfoot, headlong, posthaste, head-over-heels, headforemost; at all costs, at all hazards.

Antonyms, see CARE, CAUTION, SAFETY.

---

rasp, *v.* scrape, file, grate; chafe, nag, worry, abrade. See FRICTION. —*n.* file, scraper, rasper, abrasive; hoarseness, huskiness. See ROUGHNESS.

rat, *n., slang,* sneak, polecat; traitor, turncoat, renegade; welsher, liar, informer. *Colloq.,* skunk. *Slang,* nark. See EVILDOER. —*v.i., slang,* betray, inform, spill the beans; desert, bolt, sell out. *Slang,* squeal. See INFORMATION, IMPROBITY.

rate, *n.* ratio, percent, DEGREE, proportion; rank, CLASS; PRICE, value; VELOCITY.

rather, *adv.* somewhat, passably, preferably, more correctly, sooner; considerably. See LITTLENESS, CHOICE, DEGREE, COMPENSATION.

ratify, *v.t.* approve, confirm, validate; endorse, verify. *Slang,* O.K. See EVIDENCE, ASSENT.

ratio, *n.* proportion, rate, percentage, value. See DEGREE, RELATION.

ration, *v.t.* apportion, allocate, allot, dole out; limit, restrict, withhold. See APPORTIONMENT, FOOD.

rational, *adj.* sound, sane, logical, sensible, reasonable. See REASONING, INTELLECT, SANITY.

rationale, *n.* theory, explanation, *raison d'être,* justification; METHOD, philosophy, principle.

rattle, *v.* clatter, chatter, clack; babble, prattle, gabble, jabber; fluster, befuddle, upset. See LOUDNESS, MUSIC, INATTENTION.

raucous, *adj.* harsh, grating, rasping, hoarse, strident. See LOUDNESS.

raunchy, *adj., slang,* obscene, indecent; lustful. See IMPURITY.

ravage, *v.t.* lay waste, pillage, plunder, sack, devastate. See DESTRUCTION.

rave, *v.i.* bluster, storm, rant, tear; ramble, wander. See EXCITEMENT, INSANITY, EXCITABILITY.

ravel, *v.* entangle, involve, unravel, fray, untangle, disentangle, separate. See DIFFICULTY, DISORDER.

ravenous, *adj.* rapacious, hungry, greedy, voracious, gluttonous. See DESIRE, GLUTTONY.

ravine, *n.* gorge, gulf, canyon, gully, coulee, gap, notch. See INTERVAL.

ravish, *v.t.* charm, captivate, enchant, enthrall; carry off, deflower, rape, violate. See PLEASURE, IMPURITY.

raw, *adj.* crude; unprepared, uncooked; undisciplined, unexperienced; skinned, scraped, abraded; bleak, piercing; harsh; naked; untrained; unpolished, boorish. See COLD, UNSKILLFULNESS, NEWNESS, UNPREPAREDNESS.

ray, *n.* skate; beam, gleam, radiation; stripe. See ANIMAL, LIGHT.

raze, *v.t.* demolish, level, tear down, obliterate. See DESTRUCTION.

razz, *v.* RIDICULE, heckle, scoff (at), jeer (at); *colloq.,* tease.

reach, *v.* touch, attain, gain, get to, arrive at, pass, influence; stretch, extend; strive; hand over, deliver. See DISTANCE, TRANSPORTATION. —*n.* stretch, span, range, expanse, DISTANCE, scope. See ARRIVAL.

reaction, *n.* response, revulsion, reflex, RECOIL. See COMPENSATION.

reactionary, *n.* conservative, recalcitrant, Tory, [John] Bircher, standpatter, diehard, fogy. See PERMANENCE.

reactor, *n.* nuclear reactor *or* pile, atom-smasher; breeder. See POWER.

read, *v.* peruse, con; interpret, decipher, predict; pronounce; study; teach, admonish. See INTERPRETATION.

reader, *n.* peruser; critic; elocutionist; proofreader; lecturer, prelector; textbook, anthology. See PRINTING, TEACHING.

readily, *adv.* willingly; easily, promptly. See WILL, FACILITY.

ready, *adj.* prepared, available, handy; prompt, quick; apt, ingenious; alert; ripe. See UTILITY, PREPARATION, SKILL, EARLINESS, EXPECTATION.

readymade, *adj.* ready-to-wear, prefabricated, ready-built, oven-ready, instant, precooked; unoriginal, cut and dried, derivative. See PREPARATION, PRODUCTION.

real, *adj.* actual, veritable, true, genuine; certain, sure, authentic. See EXISTENCE, TRUTH.

realism, *n.* actuality, naturalism, genre, verity. See PAINTING.

realistic, *adj.* lifelike, faithful, graphic. See SIMILARITY, CONFORMITY.

reality, *n.* TRUTH, actuality, verity, factuality, fact. See EXISTENCE, SUBSTANCE.

realize, *v.t.* comprehend, appreciate, understand; objectify, imagine; gain, net; produce, bring in; fulfill, attain, achieve. See KNOWLEDGE, COMPLETION, ACQUISITION, SALE, IMAGINATION.

really, *adv.* surely, indeed, truly, honestly, certainly, positively, absolutely; very, emphatically; genuinely, actually. See TRUTH.

realm, *n.* kingdom, empire, domain; sphere, bailiwick, province; land, REGION, AUTHORITY.

realty, *n.* real estate, property. See POSSESSION.

reap, *v.t.* mow, cut, gather, harvest; acquire. See AGRICULTURE, ACQUISITION, SHORTNESS.

reappearance, *n.* reincarnation, revival; rebirth, resurgence, return, comeback; rerun, reprint. See REGULARITY.

rear, *v.* erect, construct, establish; raise, elevate; foster, nurture, bring up; breed. See DOMESTICATION, TEACHING.

REAR

Nouns—**1,** rear, back, posteriority; rear guard; background, hinterland, back door; postern; rumble seat; reverse; END. See INVERSION, SEQUENCE.
2, nape, chine, heels, tail, tail *or* rear end, rump, croup, buttocks, posterior, backside; breech, loin, dorsal region, lumbar region, hindquarters; bottom, *derrière. Colloq.,* fanny, bottom.
3, stern, poop, afterpart, heelpiece, crupper, tail; wake, train; straggler.
Verbs—be behind, fall astern, bend backwards, straggle, bring up the rear, follow, heel; END, tail off; back [up], reverse.
Adjectives—back, rear, hind, hindmost, hindermost, postern, dorsal, after, caudal, lumbar, posterior, aftermost, aft.
Adverbs—behind, in the rear, in the background, behind one's back, back to back, backward, rearward, rearmost; after, aft, abaft, astern, aback.
Prepositions—[in] back of, behind.
Antonyms, see FRONT.

reason, *n.* SANITY, INTELLECT, common sense, JUDGMENT, explanation; ground, CAUSE.

reasonable, *adj.* sound, sensible; fair, moderate; rational, logical. See CHEAPNESS, MODERATION, SANITY.

REASONING

Nouns—**1,** reasoning, ratiocination, rationalism, deduction, dialectics, induction, generalization, logic, synthesis, analysis, rationalization. See INTELLECT, SANITY.
2, debate, polemics, discussion, INQUIRY; dissertation, exposition, explanation (see INTERPRETATION). See DISCORD.
3, argument, case, proposition, terms, premise, postulate, data, principle, inference, syllogism, hypothesis (see SUPPOSITION).
4, reasoner, logician, dialectician, disputant, controversialist, debater, polemicist, polemist, casuist, rationalist, rationalizer.
Verbs—reason, deduce, induce, infer, derive; argue, discuss, debate, philosophize, consider; stand to reason, make sense; talk over, work out.
Adjectives—**1,** reasoning, thinking, sapient; rationalistic; argumentative, controversial, dialectic, polemical, discursive; disputatious, forensic.
2, logical, relevant, rational; inductive, deductive, syllogistic; *a priori, a posteriori.*
Adverbs—for, because, hence, seeing that, since, so, inasmuch as, whereas, in consideration of; therefore, consequently, ergo, accordingly, *a fortiori;* Q.E.D., *quod erat demonstrandum; reductio ad absurdum;* in reason.
Antonyms, see INTUITION.

reassure, *v.* comfort, placate, set at rest, content; encourage. See COURAGE.

rebate, *n.* discount, refund, repayment, DEDUCTION.

rebel, *v.i.* revolt, resist, mutiny, rise

up. See DISOBEDIENCE.

rebellion, *n.* revolt, uprising, insurrection, insurgence, mutiny, sedition, REVOLUTION. See DISOBEDIENCE, DEFIANCE.

rebirth, *n.* resurrection, reincarnation, renascence, renaissance, revival; resurgence, upsurge; salvation, redemption; new life. See CHANGE, RESTORATION.

rebound, *v.i.* bounce, ricochet, react, bound back, RECOIL. See ELASTICITY.

rebuff, *n.* snub, slight, cut; repulse, rout, check. See FAILURE. —*v.t.* repel, repulse; snub, cut, slight. *Slang,* high-hat, cold-shoulder. See REJECTION, REPULSION.

rebuild, *v.t.* recreate, refashion, reform, restore. See RESTORATION.

rebuke, *n.* reproof, reprimand, admonition. —*v.t.* reprove, reprimand, chide, admonish, upbraid. See DISAPPROBATION.

rebus, *n.* picture puzzle, hieroglyphic, pictograph *or* -gram; charade. See SECRET.

rebut, *v.t.* ANSWER, contradict, oppose, refute. See NEGATION, CONFUTATION.

rebuttal, *n.* refutation, rejoinder, retort, ANSWER, defense; counterstatement, NEGATION, disclaimer. *Colloq.,* clincher, crusher, the perfect squelch.

recalcitrant, *adj.* refractory, stubborn, difficult, intractable; balky, mulish. *Colloq.,* cussed, cantankerous. See DISOBEDIENCE, OBSTINACY, RESISTANCE.

recall, *v.t.* recollect, remember; revoke, annul, withdraw; retract, countermand; revive, restore. See MEMORY, NULLIFICATION.

recant, *v.t.* withdraw, take back, renounce, retract, disavow, repudiate. See PENITENCE.

recapitulate, *v.t.* summarize, restate, review, rehearse. *Colloq.,* recap. See REPETITION, DESCRIPTION.

recast, *v.t.* recompose, reconstruct, refashion; remold; recompute. See REVOLUTION, CHANGE.

recede, *v.i.* retrograde, retrogress, retrocede; go, retire, withdraw; shrink, ebb, wane; move *or* drift away, move off, sheer off, fall back, depart, retreat, run away. See REGRESSION.

receipt, *n.* recipiency, reception, RECEIVING; recipe. See RULE.

RECEIVING

Nouns—**1,** receiving, reception, receipt, recipiency, ACQUISITION, acceptance, admission; absorbency, absorption.

2, receipts, share; income, revenue, intake, proceeds, return, net profits, yield, earnings, dividends; box office; salary, wages, remuneration (see PAYMENT); rent; pension; alimony, allowance; inheritance, legacy, bequest, patrimony, birthright, heritage. *Slang,* split, take, gate.

3, sales check *or* slip, stub, acknowledgment, voucher, quittance, discharge, release.

4, recipient, receiver, donee, grantee, lessee, beneficiary, assign[ee], devisee, pensioner, stipendiary; payee, endorsee; legatee, heir (see POSSESSION).

Verbs—**1,** receive, take, get, acquire, take in, catch, pocket, put into one's pocket, derive, come in for; throw open; come into one's own; accept, admit, take off one's hands, open doors to; absorb, inspire, suck in.

2, be received, come in, come to hand, go into one's pocket, fall to one's lot, accrue; yield, pay, return, bear.

Adjectives—receiving, recipient, receptive, pensionary; absorbent.

Antonyms, see GIVING, PAYMENT, EXCLUSION.

---

recent, *adj.* late, new, fresh, modern; newly come, just arrived *or* in; former, erstwhile, one-time. See NEWNESS, PAST.

RECEPTACLE

Nouns—**1,** receptacle, recipient, receiver; compartment, cell, follicle, hole, corner, niche, recess, nook, crypt, booth, stall, pigeonhole, cubbyhole, cove, bay, alcove.

2, capsule, vesicle, cyst, pod, calyx, utricle, arc; blister. See COVERING, TRANSPORTATION.

3, stomach, abdomen, paunch, ventricle, crop, craw, maw, gizzard, mouth, gullet, sac, bladder.

4, pocket, pouch, fob, sheath, scabbard, socket, folder, bag, sack, purse, wallet, portfolio, pocketbook, scrip, poke, knapsack, haversack, kit, briefcase, valise, suitcase, handbag, portmanteau, satchel, etui, reticule, quiver. *Colloq.,* grip. *Slang,* kick.

5, chest, box, carton, coffer, caddy, case, casket, caisson, bandbox, cage, manger, rack, snuffbox, vanity case.

6, vessel, bushel, barrel, canister, basket, pannier, hopper, creel, crate, cradle, bassinet, hamper, tray, hod, scuttle, utensil, carrier.

7, vat, caldron, tank, cistern, washstand, font; cask, puncheon, keg, tun, butt; firkin; carboy, amphora; bottle, jar, decanter, pitcher, ewer, cruse, vase, carafe, crock, flagon, magnum, demijohn, flask, stoup, jigger, noggin, pony; vial, phial, flacon, canteen; cruet; urn, tub, bucket, pail; pot, pan, tankard, jug, pitcher, mug; retort, alembic, test tube; tin, can, kettle, bowl, basin, punchbowl, cup, goblet, chalice, tumbler, glass; saucepan, skillet, tureen; vacuum bottle *or* jug.

8, plate, platter, dish, trencher, porringer, saucer, crucible.

9, shovel, trowel, spoon, spatula, ladle, dipper, scoop.

10, closet, commode, cupboard, cellaret, locker, chiffonier, bin, bunker, buffet, press, safe, showcase, whatnot, sideboard, desk, dresser, bureau, wardrobe, secretary, till, bookcase, cabinet, console.

11, chamber, apartment, room, cabin, office, court, hall; suite, flat, salon, parlor; dining, living, waiting, sitting, *or* drawing room; antechamber; stateroom; gallery, pew, box; boudoir, sanctum, bedroom, dormitory, refectory, playroom, nursery, schoolroom, library, study, studio; bathroom, lavatory, smoking room, den, lounge; rumpus room.

12, attic, loft, garret; cellar, basement, vault, hold; cockpit; kitchen, pantry, scullery; storeroom; dairy; laundry, bathroom, lavatory, outhouse; penthouse; lean-to, garage, hangar, shed, toolhouse, roundhouse.

13, portico, porch, veranda, lobby, court, hall, vestibule, foyer, corridor, PASSAGE.

14, conservatory, greenhouse, summerhouse, hothouse, alcove, grotto, arbor, bower; hermitage.

15, plaza, forum, piazza, place; market [place], agora; court[yard], square, quadrangle, *campo.*

---

reception, *n.* admission, admittance, entrée, entrance; importation; introduction, taking; party, affair. See RECEIVING, SOCIALITY.

receptionist, *n.* host[ess], greeter. See SOCIALITY.

receptive, *adj.* open-minded; impressionable. See LIBERALITY, TEACHING.

recess, *n.* alcove, niche, nook, bay; intermission, pause, interim, rest, break, breathing spell, coffee *or* lunch break. See RECEPTACLE, ANGULARITY, REPOSE.

RECESSION

Nouns—**1,** recession, receding, retirement, withdrawal, retrocession, DEPARTURE; retreat, flight (see ESCAPE); REGRESSION, regress, RECOIL.
2, depression, slowdown, temporary setback, hard times, decline, shakeout, bear market. *Colloq.,* slump. See DETERIORATION.

Verbs—**1,** recede, retrocede, regress, retire, withdraw; go [back]; move back, away, from, *or* off, sheer off; avoid; shrink, ebb, wane; drift *or* fade away, stand aside; fall back, RECOIL; retreat, run away, flee.
2, decline, slow down. *Colloq.,* slump.

Adjectives—recessive, receding, recedent; retiring, in retreat, retreating; ebbing, waning.

Antonyms, see APPROACH, PROGRESSION.

recherché, *adj.* uncommon, out of the ordinary, rare; esoteric, obscure; elegant, choice, refined. See FASHION.

recipe, *n.* receipt, formula, instructions, directions, method, prescription, ingredients. See MAXIM, RULE, REMEDY.

recipient, *n.* See RECEIVING.

reciprocal, *adj.* mutual, complementary, interchangeable, alternative, correlative. See RELATION, INTERCHANGE.

reciprocation, *n.* repayment, INTERCHANGE, exchange, reciprocity, alternation. See OSCILLATION, RETALIATION.

recital, *n.* telling, narration, rehearsal; account, recapitulation; concert, musicale. See MUSIC, DESCRIPTION.

recitation, *n.* declamation, elocution; recital, lesson. See SPEECH.

recite, *v.* rehearse, relate, repeat, declaim, detail, recapitulate. See SPEECH, DESCRIPTION.

reckless, *adj.* careless, foolhardy, incautious, heedless, rash, devil-may-care, daring. See RASHNESS.

reckon, *v.* calculate, count, compute, estimate; esteem, consider, believe; rely, depend; *colloq.,* think, suppose, guess. See PAYMENT, EXPECTATION, SUPPOSITION, NUMERATION.

reckoning, *n.* calculation, computation, count; accounting, settlement; bill, tally, score. See PAYMENT, NUMERATION, EXPECTATION.

reclaim, *v.t.* redeem, restore, reform, recover, retrieve; tame. See RESTORATION, ATONEMENT.

recline, *v.i.* lie, rest, couch, REPOSE, loll. See HORIZONTAL.

recluse, *n.* hermit, anchorite, ascetic, eremite. See SECLUSION, ASCETICISM.

recognize, *v.t.* acknowledge, concede, remember; perceive, realize, know, distinguish; salute, greet; commend, appreciate. See VISION, KNOWLEDGE, MEMORY, PERMISSION, GRATITUDE, ASSENT, COURTESY.

RECOIL

Nouns—recoil, reaction, retroaction, revulsion, rebound, ricochet, bounce, boomerang, kick, backlash, repercussion, reflex, return, repulse, REPULSION, reverberation, echo; reactionary, reactionist. See REVERSION, REGRESSION, LEAP.

Verbs—**1,** recoil, react, rebound, reverberate, echo, spring *or* fly back, kick, ricochet, reflect, boomerang, carom, bounce, shy; backfire.

2, cringe, cower, wince, flinch, quail, shrink; draw, fade, fall, *or* drop back, retreat (see RECESSION).

Adjectives—recoiling, refluent, repercussive, recalcitrant, reactionary; flinching, cowering, *etc.*

Antonyms, see IMPULSE.

---

recollection, *n.* remembrance, reminiscence, MEMORY, retrospection.

recommend, *v.t.* commend, advise, suggest; commit, entrust; urge, advocate. See ADVICE, APPROBATION.

recompense, *n.* reward, COMPENSATION, PAYMENT, requital. —*v.t.* requite, reward, repay, remunerate, indemnify, atone.

reconcile, *v.t.* conciliate, propitiate, placate, appease; harmonize, accord; settle. See PACIFICATION, AGREEMENT, COMPROMISE.

recondite, *adj.* mysterious, obscure, SECRET, abstruse, profound, esoteric, cryptic. See CONCEALMENT.

recondition, *v.t.* repair, renew, overhaul, renovate, restore, regenerate, rejuvenate. See RESTORATION.

reconnaissance, *n.* survey, surveillance, espionage, observation, inspection, INQUIRY; aerial reconnaissance. See VISION.

reconnoiter, *v.* investigate, survey, spy out, scout. *Slang,* case. See VISION.

reconsider, *v.* reexamine, review, think over *or* again, change one's mind, tergiversate. See THOUGHT, CHANGE.

reconstruct, *v.t.* rebuild; make over, redo, restore, renovate, recondition; overhaul; piece together, project. See REPRODUCTION, RESTORATION.

RECORD

Nouns—**1,** record, note, minute; register, poll, diptych, entry, memorandum, COPY, duplicate, docket; muniment, deed; document, chart, matter of record; testimony, deposition, affidavit, certificate; coupon, receipt (see RECEIVING); notebook, statistic; registry, registration, enrollment; tabulation, transcript, transcription, entry, booking, signature. See LIST, INDICATION, EVIDENCE, WRITING.

2, gazette, newspaper, magazine; almanac, calendar; diary, memoir, log, journal, daybook, album, ledger; yearbook, annual; archive, scroll, chronicle, annals; legend, history, biography. See PUBLICATION, NEWS.

3, monument, hatchment, slab, tablet, trophy, obelisk, pillar, column, monolith; memorial; memento, testimonial, medal; commemoration. See MEMORY.

4, trace, vestige, relic, remains, scar, footstep, footprint, track, mark, wake, trail, spoor, scent.

5, phonograph record, extended-play record, E.P., 45, long-playing record, L.P., 78; videodisc, Laserdisc, compact disc, digital *or* analog record[ing]; floppy disk, diskette, hard disk; wire *or* tape recording, transcription; disk, disc, waxing, platter; track, sector, field, record, groove.

6, recorder, registrar, register, notary, prothonotary, clerk, amanuensis, secretary, stenographer, scribe, bookkeeper; editor, author, journalist; annalist, historian, chronicler, biographer, antiquary, antiquarian, archivist; scorekeeper, scorer, timekeeper, timer.

7, recording instrument, recorder, ticker, ticker tape; tracer; timer, dater, stopwatch, speedometer (see MEASUREMENT, CHRONOMETRY); log, turnstile; seismograph; phonograph, record player, turntable; tape *or* wire recorder, dictating machine; adding machine, cash register (see NUMERATION); video [tape *or* cassette] recorder, V.T.R., V.C.R.

Verbs—record, put on record, chronicle, set down, hand down to posterity, commemorate, write, put in writing, take down; jot down, note, make a note; enter, book; post, make an entry of, enroll, register; check off, check in *or* out, sign in; notarize; make out; mark, sign, attest, file; wax, tape, transcribe; go down in history *or* records. *Colloq.*, chalk up.

Adjectives—recorded, recording; on record *or* file, on the books; documentary, in writing *or* print, in black and white.

Antonyms, see OBLIVION.

---

recount, *v.t* tell, recite, repeat, rehearse, relate, narrate, enumerate; recapitulate. See DESCRIPTION, NUMERATION.

recoup, *v.t.* regain, retrieve, indemnify, reimburse. See RESTORATION.

recourse, *n.* appeal, resort, resource, expedient; aid. See USE.

recover, *v.* regain, get back, redeem, retrieve, reclaim, salvage; get well, recuperate. See RESTORATION, IMPROVEMENT.

recreant, *adj.* cowardly, craven, dastardly, disloyal, false, treacherous; apostate, renegade. See COWARDICE, EVILDOER.

recreation, *n.* diversion, sport, pastime, REFRESHMENT. See AMUSEMENT.

recrimination, *n.* countercharge, RETALIATION, *tu quoque*, rejoinder, reply in kind; name calling, bickering. See ACCUSATION.

recruit, *v.t.* enlist, raise, furnish, supply, replenish; restore, renew. —*n.* conscript, draftee; newcomer, novice, tyro. *Slang,* rookie, boot. See COMBATANT, COMMISSION.

rectangular, *adj.* orthogonal, oblong, foursquare, square. See ANGULARITY.

rectify, *v.t.* correct, improve, repair, purify, redress, amend. See IMPROVEMENT, STRAIGHTNESS.

rectitude, *n.* uprightness, integrity, righteousness, goodness, VIRTUE, honesty. See PROBITY.

rector, rectress, *n.* pastor, parson; DIRECTOR, monitor, prefect. See CLERGY.

rectory, *n.* manse, parsonage, vicarage, parish house, deanery, presbytery; benefice. See ABODE, TEMPLE.

recumbent, *adj.* lying, reclining, leaning. See OBLIQUITY, HORIZONTAL.

recuperation, *n.* recovery, IMPROVEMENT, convalescence. See RESTORATION.

recur, *v.* return, come back, reoccur, repeat, intermit, revert. See REPETITION.

recusant, *n.* nonconformist, dissenter, schismatic, sectarian, Protestant; separatist, apostate. —*adj.* rebellious, dissenting, apostate, disobedient. See DISSENT, IMPENITENCE.

red, *n.* crimson, scarlet, *etc.;* radical, revolutionary. See COLOR, REVOLUTION, CHANGE.

redden, *v.* encrimson, incarmine; blush, flush, glow; bloody. See COLOR, MODESTY, RESENTMENT.

redecorate, *v.* renovate, refurbish, restore, remodel, do over. See RESTORATION.

redeem, *v.t.* ransom, recover, rescue, restore, liberate, deliver, convert, fulfill, perform. See RESTORATION, ATONEMENT, PIETY, PAYMENT.

redeemer, *n.* savio[u]r, Messiah, Christ, the Lord, *etc.;* emancipator. See LIBERATION.

redemption, *n.* salvation; deliverance; rescue; recovery. See RESTORATION, LIBERATION, ATONEMENT, PIETY.

redhanded, *adj.* in the act, *in flagrante delicto*. See GUILT.

red-hot, *adj.* intense; violent; fresh, new. See HEAT, NEWNESS.

redolent, *adj.* fragrant, odorous, aromatic, perfumed; heady, musky; reminiscent, remindful, having an aura (of). See ODOR.

redoubtable, *adj.* formidable. See FEAR.

redound, *v.* bounce back, rebound; do credit (to), accrue. See REPUTE, RECOIL, TENDENCY.

redress, *v.t.* right, correct, repair, reform, relieve, remedy. —*n.* amends, restitution, reparation, requital, COMPENSATION, relief. See RESTORATION, ATONEMENT.

red tape, *n.* bureaucracy, officialdom; paperwork; delay, HINDRANCE.

reduce, *v.* diminish, lessen, curtail, lower; allay, alleviate; set (a fracture); demote, abase, subjugate, subdue; diet, slenderize. See DECREASE, CONTRACTION, NARROWNESS.

redundance, *n.* redundancy; REPETITION, tautology; superabundance, superfluity, superfluence; profuseness, profusion, repletion, plethora; surfeit, surplus, surplusage; coals to Newcastle. See SUFFICIENCY.

reed, *n.* stem, stalk, straw, rush; pastoral pipe. See MUSIC.

reef, *n.* sandbar, shoal, bank, ledge. See CONVEXITY, SHALLOWNESS.

reek, *n.* vapor, fumes, ODOR; stench, stink, malodor, fetor, miasma. —*v.* stink, smell; give off, exude; sweat, perspire. See MALODOROUSNESS.

reel, *v.i.* sway, stagger, waver; spin, wheel. See AGITATION, ROTATION.

reestablish, *v.t.* restore, renew, revive, refound. See RESTORATION.

refashion, *v.t.* make over, remake, remodel, revolutionize. See REVOLUTION, CHANGE.

refer, *v.t.* submit, commit, send, direct, assign, ascribe, attribute. See EVIDENCE. —*v.i.* allude, advert, apply, concern, appeal. See RELATION, ATTRIBUTION.

referee, *n.* arbiter, arbitrator, umpire, mediator, moderator, judge. *Colloq.*, ref, ump. See JUDGMENT.

reference, *n.* citation, allusion; testimonial, credentials; consultation; bearing, concern, applicability; reference book, dictionary, encyclopedia, yearbook, atlas, almanac, catalog, concordance, thesaurus. See RELATION, EVIDENCE, PUBLICATION.

referendum, *n.* vote, plebiscite, initiative, *vox populi*. See CHOICE.

refill, *v.t.* See REPLENISH.

refine, *v.t.* purify, cleanse, educate, improve, polish, cultivate, elaborate. See PURITY, IMPROVEMENT.

refined, *adj.* well-bred, cultivated, polished; pure; subtle. See ELEGANCE, COURTESY, TASTE, PURITY.

reflect, *v.* throw back, cast back, mirror, imitate, reproduce, echo; meditate, ponder, muse, ruminate. See THOUGHT, LIGHT, DISAPPROBATION, COPY.

reflection, *n.* refraction, image, echo, duplication, counterpart, COPY; meditation, rumination, retrospection; comment; slur, insinuation, innuendo. See LIGHT, THOUGHT, DISAPPROBATION.

reflex, *n.* reaction, instinct, repercussion, RECOIL, rebound. —*adj.* reflective; involuntary, reactive, automatic, conditioned. See COPY, NECESSITY.

reflux, *n.* ebb, refluence, subsidence, backwater. See DECREASE, REGRESSION.

reform, *v.t.* better, reclaim, restore, improve, redeem, regenerate, convert. See CHANGE. —*n.* IMPROVEMENT, amendment, regeneration, reformation; crusade.

reformation, *n.* reform, IMPROVEMENT, betterment, correction; regeneration. See CHANGE, PIETY.

reformer, *n.* altruist, crusader, zealot, missionary. See IMPROVEMENT.

refraction, *n.* bending, deflection. See DEVIATION, VISION.

refractory, *adj.* unruly, unmanageable, obstinate, stubborn, intractable. See DISOBEDIENCE.

refrain, *v.t.* abstain, cease, desist, forbear. See AVOIDANCE. —*n.* chorus, burden, repetend. See REPETITION.

REFRESHMENT

Nouns—refreshment, invigoration, recuperation (see RESTORATION); ventilation; recreation, diversion, regalement, repast, FOOD, nourishment. *Colloq.*, pick-me-up, bracer. See RELIEF, PLEASURE.

Verbs—**1,** refresh, brace, strengthen, invigorate, stimulate; brisken, freshen (up), recruit, enliven; renew, revive, revivify, [re]animate; regale, cheer, cool, fan, ventilate, AIR, slake. *Colloq.*, give a new lease on life, buck up. **2,** breathe, respire, take a long breath; recuperate, revive, regain one's strength, come to oneself, perk (up).

Adjectives—refreshing, *etc.;* brisk, cool, restorative, recuperative, restful, pleasant, comfortable; refreshed, fresh, untired, unwearied.

Antonyms, see WEAKNESS, WEARINESS.

---

refrigerate, *v.* cool, ice, freeze, infrigidate; benumb, chill [to the marrow]; quickfreeze. See COLD.

refuge, *n.* asylum, sanctuary; hideout, hideaway; safe harbor; any port in a storm; last resort; support, seclusion; anchor[age]; home, hospital; retreat, den, lair. See SAFETY.

refugee, *n.* fugitive, misplaced person, evacuee, escapee, runaway. See ESCAPE, AVOIDANCE, DISPLACEMENT.

refund, *v.t.* return, give back, pay back, repay, reimburse. See PAYMENT, RESTORATION.

refurbish, *v.* redecorate, renovate (see RESTORATION).

REFUSAL

Nouns—refusal; nonacceptance, denial, declining, declination. See REJECTION, EXCLUSION, RESISTANCE, REPULSION, DISSENT, NEGATION, UNWILLINGNESS.

Verbs—refuse, reject, deny, decline; negate; [be]grudge, be deaf to; turn a deaf ear to, turn one's back on; discountenance, not hear of, turn [thumbs] down, vote down; wash one's hands of, stand aloof; pass up.

Adjectives—**1,** refusing, recusant; uncomplying, unaccommodating, unconsenting, deaf to; unwilling.

2, refused, rejected, ungranted, out of the question, not to be thought of, impossible.

Adverbs—no, on no account, never, by no [manner of] means.

Phrase—not for the world; no thank you. *Colloq.*, not a chance, not on your life, no way, nothing doing. *Slang,* no soap, no deal, no dice, no go, no sale.

Antonyms, see CONSENT.

---

refuse, *n.* trash, truck, rubbish, waste, leavings, garbage. See USELESSNESS.

refute, *v.t.* confute, controvert, disprove, deny, dispute. See NEGATION, CONFUTATION.

regain, *v.t.* recover, retrieve, get back [to]. See RESTORATION.

regal, *adj.* royal, splendid, stately, majestic; kingly, autocratic. See AUTHORITY.

regale, *v.t.* entertain, feast, wine and dine, treat; give PLEASURE. See FOOD.

regalia, *n.pl.* emblems, decorations, insignia; finery. See INDICATION.

regard, *v.t.* consider, deem, observe, mark, note; RESPECT, REPUTE, esteem; concern. —*n.* reference, concern, gaze, scrutiny, ATTENTION, deference, esteem. See RELATION, VISION.

regarding, *prep.* respecting, concerning. See RELATION.

regardless, *adj.* heedless, careless, indifferent, negligent. See INATTENTION, NEGLECT. —*adv.* notwithstanding, anyhow. See COMPENSATION.

regenerate, *adj.* reformed, reborn, converted. —*v.t.* make over, revivify; reform, convert. See RESTORATION, PIETY.

regent, *n.* viceroy, deputy, ruler, trustee. See AUTHORITY.

regime, *n.* rule, reign, sovereignty; rulers, incumbents; policy, program, PLAN, regimen. See AUTHORITY.

regimen, *n.* course, METHOD, prescription, program, procedure, schedule; drill, training; diet[etics]. See FOOD, REMEDY.

regiment, *n.* corps, troop[s], army, company; multitude, assemblage. See COMBATANT. —*v.t.* muster, enlist; organize, systematize, train, drill, discipline; harness, enslave. See RESTRAINT, ARRANGEMENT.

REGION

Nouns—**1,** region, sphere, ground, soil, area, hemisphere, latitude, meridian, zone, clime, climate; quarter, district, beat, orb, circuit, circle; vicinity, neighborhood, premises, precinct, pale, department, domain, bailiwick, dominion, section, tract, territory. See LOCATION, SPACE, ABODE, PART.

2, country, state, canton, county, shire, province, city, conurbation, arrondissement, parish, township, borough, hundred, riding, principality, duchy, realm, kingdom, empire.

3, arena, march; patch, plot, enclosure, enclave, field, court.

Adjectives—regional, sectional, territorial, local, parochial, vicinal, provincial, topographical.

---

register, *n.* RECORD, roll, LIST; registration, enrollment. —*v.t* enroll, LIST; mark, RECORD; express, indicate. See ARRANGEMENT.

REGRESSION

Nouns—**1,** regression, retrogression, retrogradation, retroaction, retreat, return, REVERSION; relapse, RECESSION, recess; recidivism, backsliding, fall, DETERIORATION. See FAILURE.

2, reflux, refluence, backwater, regurgitation, ebb; resilience, reflection, RECOIL.

Verbs—**1,** regress, retrogress, recede, return, revert, retreat, retrograde; [re]lapse; back down, off, *or* out, rebound; lose ground, fall astern, back water, put about, wheel, countermarch; turn, turn tail, about-face, turn around, turn one's back upon; retrace one's steps, beat a retreat, go home; backslide. *Slang,* pull in one's horns.

2, ebb, flow back, regurgitate.

Adjectives—**1,** regressive, retrograde; retrogressive, refluent, reflex, recidivous, crablike, reactionary, recessive, receding.

2, relapsing, backsliding, recrudescent; reversionary, atavistic.

Adverbs—back, backward[s], reflexively, in retreat, on the run, behind.

Antonyms, see PROGRESSION.

REGRET

Nouns—regret, remorse, qualms, compunction, contrition, attrition, repentance, PENITENCE; LAMENTATION, mourning; heartache, sorrow, grief, bitterness,

DISAPPOINTMENT, DISCONTENT; repining, homesickness, nostalgia, *mal du pays*.

Verbs—regret, deplore, feel sorry *or* contrite, think better of; sorrow, grieve, repent, repine, rue [the day]; weigh *or* prey on the mind, leave an aching void. *Colloq.*, kick oneself.

Adjectives—**1,** regretting, regretful, sorry, contrite, remorseful, rueful, mournful, penitent, ashamed; repining, homesick, nostalgic.

2, regretted, regrettable, deplorable, unfortunate, lamentable; culpable, blameworthy, opprobrious.

Interjections—what a pity! what a shame! too bad! *Slang,* tough luck.

Antonyms, see CONTENT, REJOICING.

REGULARITY

Nouns—**1,** regularity, periodicity; evenness, steadiness, constancy, consistency, invariability, punctuality; intermittence, alternation (see OSCILLATION); beat, pulse, pulsation, cadence, swing, rhythm. See REPETITION.

2, round, bout, turn, period, CIRCUIT, cycle, routine; period, menstruation; menses, catamenia.

3, ORDER, RULE, system, even tenor; SYMMETRY, uniformity, proportion. See HABIT.

4, anniversary, jubilee; diamond, golden, silver, wooden, paper, *etc.* anniversary; holiday, Christmas, Easter, Thanksgiving, New Year's Day, Independence Day, Memorial Day, Labor Day, Dominion Day, Bastille Day, Boxing Day, *etc.;* centennial, biennial, *etc.;* feast, festival, CELEBRATION, fast day, birthday, saint's day, holy day.

Verbs—recur, return, reappear, come again, come [a]round, come in its turn, revolve, circle; beat, pulsate, throb, alternate, intermit, oscillate; come and go. *Colloq.*, roll around.

Adjectives—regular, steady, constant, uniform, even, symmetrical, consistent, punctual, systematic, methodical, orderly, unvarying, congruous; periodic[al], serial, recurrent, cyclical, seasonal, rhythmic[al], intermittent, remittent, alternate, every other; fixed, established, settled, continued, permanent; normal, natural, customary, habitual, usual, conventional, ordinary, typical, correct; hourly, diurnal, daily, quotidian, tertian, weekly, biweekly, fortnightly, monthly, yearly; annual, biennial, triennial, centennial; secular, paschal, lenten; menstrual, catamenial.

Adverbs—regularly, normally, periodically, constantly, punctually; at regular intervals, like clockwork, at fixed periods, at stated times, from day to day, day by day; by turns, in turn, in rotation, alternately, every other day, off and on, round and round, year after year.

Antonyms, see IRREGULARITY.

---

regulate, *v.t.* ORDER, manage, legislate, rule, direct; adjust, rectify, fix, organize, systematize, tranquilize, moderate. See CONFORMITY, ARRANGEMENT, AGREEMENT, AUTHORITY.

regulation, *n.* adjustment (see REGULATE); law, RULE, order, ordinance. See LEGALITY.

regurgitate, *v.t.* vomit, disgorge; ebb. See EJECTION, REGRESSION.

rehabilitate, *v.t.* restore, reinstate, reestablish. See RESTORATION.

rehash, *v.t.* review, repeat, restate; summarize, recapitulate, sum up. *Colloq.*, chew one's cud; recap. See REPETITION.

rehearse, *v.t.* repeat, recite, enumerate; drill, practice, prepare. See REPETITION, PREPARATION, DESCRIPTION, DRAMA, MUSIC.

reign, *v.i.* rule, govern, command, hold sway.—*n.* rude, sway; currency, prevalence; INFLUENCE. See AUTHORITY, GENERALITY.

reimburse, *v.t.* repay, compensate, indemnify, restore, refund. See PAYMENT, RESTORATION.

rein, *n.* curb, check, control; (*pl.*) lines, RESTRAINT, guidance.

reincarnation, *n.* rebirth, resurrection. See RESTORATION.

reinforce, *v.t.* strengthen, support, buttress, replenish. See STRENGTH.

reinforcements, *n.pl.* replenishment, AID, recruits, auxiliaries. See PROVISION.

reinstate, *v.t.* restore, put back, reinstall, rehabilitate. See RESTORATION.

reiterate, *v.t.* repeat, iterate (see REPETITION).

REJECTION

Nouns—rejection, repudiation, EXCLUSION, REPULSION, rebuff; REFUSAL, declination; disallowance, disavowal; veto; disbelief (see DOUBT); ostracism (see EXCLUSION); relegation, dismissal, discard (see DISUSE). *Colloq.,* kick in the pants *or* teeth. *Slang,* brush-off, cold shoulder. See RELINQUISHMENT.

Verbs—**1,** reject, repudiate, abandon, renounce, exclude, except, repulse, repel, rebuff, scorn, spurn, slight; set *or* lay aside, pass over, give up, cast off, dump, discard, cast behind one, cast to the winds, set at naught, throw to the dogs, toss overboard, throw away, wash one's hands of, have done with; scrap, dismiss, cashier, deport, eject, relegate, resist; jilt. *Colloq.,* brush off; opt out.

2, refuse, disallow, disapprove, disclaim, overrule, abnegate, abjure; veto, be deaf to.

Adjectives—rejected, repudiated, refused, not chosen, not granted, out of the question, impossible; unaccepted, unloved, unwelcome, discarded, castaway, excluded, jilted; rejective, repudiative.

Antonyms, see APPROBATION, CHOICE.

REJOICING

Nouns—**1,** rejoicing, exultation, triumph, jubilation, joy, revelry, reveling, merrymaking, festivity, jubilee, CELEBRATION, paean, acclamation, thanksgiving, CONGRATULATION.

2, smile, simper, smirk, gloat, grin; laughter, giggle, titter, snigger, snicker, crow, chuckle, horse laugh; fit, shout, roar, gale, *or* peal of laughter; risibility; laugh track. *Colloq.,* canned laughter.

3, cheer, hurrah, hooray, shout, yell, hallelujah.

Verbs—**1,** rejoice, thank one's [lucky] stars, congratulate oneself, clap one's hands, fling up one's cap; dance, skip; sing, chirrup, hurrah; cry *or* leap for joy, leap with joy, exult, glory, triumph, celebrate; be tickled.

2, make merry, smile, simper, smirk, grin, laugh, giggle, titter, snigger, crow, snicker, chortle, chuckle, cackle; cheer; hurrah, yell, shout, roar, split one's sides. *Colloq.,* crack a smile.

3, enjoy, revel in, delight in, be glad.

Adjectives—rejoicing, jubilant, exultant, triumphant, flushed, glad, gladsome, elated, laughing, bursting *or* convulsed with laughter; risible, laughable. *Colloq.,* in stitches.

Interjections—hurrah! hooray! three cheers! hail! Heaven be praised! *Slang,* swell! great! oh, boy!

Antonyms, see LAMENTATION.

---

rejoin, *v.t.* reply, retort, respond; reunite, reassemble. See ANSWER, ASSEMBLAGE.

rejoinder, *n.* ANSWER, reply, retort, response.

rejuvenate, *v.* renew, refresh, reinvigorate. See YOUTH, RESTORATION.

relapse, *n.* recurrence (of illness or behavior); DETERIORATION, backsliding; REGRESSION. —*v.i.* lapse, fall back, backslide.

relate, *v.t.* tell, recount, report, narrate; connect, assoccate (see RELATION). See DESCRIPTION.

RELATION

Nouns—**1,** relation, relationship, bearing, reference, connection, concern, dependence, cognation; correlation, analogy, SIMILARITY, affinity, reference; kinship, consanguinity, blood [tie], brotherhood, sisterhood; parentage, paternity, maternity (see ANCESTRY); alliance, homogeneity, association, approximation, affiliation, interest, relevancy; propinquity; comparison, ratio, proportion, link, tie, bond of union. See INTERCHANGE, DEGREE.

2, kin, kinfolk, kinsman, kinswoman, relation[s]; family, ilk, breed; stock, strain; lineage, line; root, branch, tree; tribe, clan; generation; offspring, children, progeny (see POSTERITY); house[hold], kith and kin; cousins, *etc.*

Verbs—**1,** be related, relate to, refer to, bear upon, regard, concern, touch, affect, have to do with; pertain *or* belong to *or* with, interest; correspond.

2, relate, bring into relation with, bring to bear upon, connect, associate, ally, draw a parallel, link, compare; allude to, refer to, speak of, deal with; correlate, interrelate, TOUCH.

Adjectives—**1,** relative, correlative, cognate, relating, referable; belonging, appurtenant.

2, related, connected, implicated, associated, affiliated, allied to; akin, like, similar; relevant, pertinent, germane; reciprocal; mutual, common, correspondent, interchangeable, alternate.

3, approximating, proportionate, proportional, allusive, comparable.

Adverbs—relatively, pertinently, comparatively; *en rapport,* in touch with; for that matter.

Prepositions—as to, as for, as regards, regarding, about, concerning, anent, relating to, relative to, with relation to, touching, with reference to, with regard to, apropos of, on the score of; under the head of, in the matter of, in re, re; compared to, alongside.

Antonyms, see DISAGREEMENT, DIFFERENCE.

---

relative, *n.* RELATION, kinsman; comparative, dependent.

relax, *v.* rest, relent, slacken, loosen, unbend, abate, relieve, ease, mitigate. See SOFTNESS, PITY, REPOSE, MODERATION.

relaxation, *n.* ease, REPOSE, diversion, recreation; abatement, loosening. See AMUSEMENT, MODERATION.

relaxed, *adj.* loose, slack; not tense, at ease. See REPOSE.

relay, *n.* replacement, substitute, shift; intermediary, medium, go-between, agent, agency. —*v.* forward, advance, transmit. See SUBSTITUTION, TRANSPORTATION.

release, *v.t.* free, liberate, give out, relinquish. See LIBERATION, ACQUITTAL. —*n.* EXEMPTION; DEATH.

relegate, *v.t.* consign, commit, assign,

refer, banish. See EJECTION, EXCLUSION.

relent, *v.i.* soften, yield, submit. See SOFTNESS, PITY.

relentless, *adj.* pitiless, merciless, implacable, remorseless; inexorable, indefatigable. See RESOLUTION, RETALIATION, SEVERITY.

relevant, *adj.* pertinent, fitting, apposite, applicable, apropos, germane, appropriate. See RELATION.

reliable, *adj.* trustworthy, dependable, trusty, responsible. See CERTAINTY, PROBITY.

reliance, *n.* dependence, trust, confidence, faith, credence. See BELIEF.

relic, *n.* memento, souvenir, keepsake, token, antique, remains. See MEMORY, RECORD, REMAINDER, OLDNESS, RITE.

RELIEF

Nouns—**1,** relief, deliverance, easement, softening, alleviation, mitigation, MODERATION, palliation, soothing, assuagement, slaking. See REFRESHMENT, IMPROVEMENT, RESTORATION.

2, solace, consolation, comfort. See AID, CONTENT.

3, lenitive, restorative, palliative, alleviative, anodyne, tranquilizer, painkiller, analgesic; cushion, oasis. See LENIENCY, REMEDY.

Verbs—**1,** relieve, ease, alleviate, mitigate, palliate, soothe, salve, soften, mollify; poultice; spell (see SUBSTITUTION); assuage, allay, disburden, lighten; quench, slake.

2, cheer, comfort, solace; REMEDY, cure, refresh.

3, be relieved, breathe more freely, take comfort, breathe a sigh [of relief].

Adjectives—**1,** relieving, consolatory, comforting, soothing, assuaging, assuasive, balmy, lenitive, palliative, remedial, curative.

2, at [one's] ease, comfortable, CONTENT, contented; relaxed.

Antonyms, see INCREASE.

RELIGION

Nouns—**1,** religion, faith; theology, divinity, deism, theism, monotheism, polytheism; hagiology; BELIEF, truth, creed, doctrine, dogma; cult; canonicity; declaration, profession, *or* confession of faith; articles of faith; conformity, orthodoxy, strictness. See PIETY.

2, Christianity, Catholicism, Protestantism (Presbyterianism, Methodism, Lutheranism, Quakerism, Mormonism, Christian Science, *etc.*); Judaism; Mohammedanism, Moslemism, Islam; Buddhism, Shintoism, Confucianism, Hinduism, Brahmanism, Sikhism, Lamaism, *etc.*

3, the Church, Holy Church, Established Church; temple of the Holy Ghost, Universal Church, Apostolic Church, Roman Catholic Church, Greek Orthodox Church; Church of Christ, Scientist; Church of the New Jerusalem; Presbyterian, Methodist, Protestant Episcopal, *etc.* Church; Society of Friends; Church of Jesus Christ of Latter-Day Saints; Church of Christ.

4, true believer, Christendom, Christians; Islam; Jewry; Christian, Catholic, Protestant (Presbyterian, Christian Scientist, Swedenborgian, Moravian, *etc.*), Quaker, Friend, Mormon; Jew; Moslem; Buddhist; Brahman, Hindu, *etc.*

5, scriptures, canons, SACRED WRITINGS; catechism; Apostles' Creed, Nicene Creed, Athanasian Creed; Articles of Religion.

6, WORSHIP, prayer, hymn, hymnody, psalmody; sacrifice, oblation, incense, libation, offering, offertory; disciple, fasting, asceticism; RITE, divine service, office, duty, Mass, matins, evensong, vespers.

7, CLERGY, clergyman; theologian, theist, monotheist; churchwarden, altar boy, acolyte, chorister; congregation, flock, worshiper, communicant, celebrant; presbyter, elder, vestryman, usher.

Verbs—WORSHIP, pray, invoke, supplicate, say one's prayers, tell one's beads; return thanks, say grace; praise, glorify, magnify; bless, give benediction; attend services, attend Mass, go to church; communicate, take communion.

Adjectives—religious, Godfearing; reverential (see RESPECT); orthodox, sound, strict, canonical, authentic, faithful, catholic; theological; doctrinal, dogmatic, denominational, sectarian; Christian, Catholic, Protestant, Lutheran, Calvinistic, *etc.;* evangelical, scriptural; divine, true (see DEITY); Jewish, Judaic, Hebrew, Hindu, Mohammedan, *etc.*

Antonyms, see IRRELIGION, IDOLATRY, HETERODOXY, LAITY.

RELINQUISHMENT

Nouns—**1,** relinquishment, abandonment, expropriation, dereliction; cession, surrender, dispensation; RESIGNATION, abdication; abnegation, REJECTION; riddance.

2, desertion, defection, secession, withdrawal; DISCONTINUANCE, DISUSE.

3, derelict, foundling, outcast, castaway.

Verbs—**1,** relinquish, give up, surrender, release, yield, abnegate, cede, let go, spare, drop, resign, forgo, renounce, abandon, give away, dispose of, part with, lay aside, lay on the shelf, lay down, throw up *or* over, discard, cast off, dismiss, get rid of, eject, divest oneself of, wash one's hands of, throw overboard, throw to the winds; sweep away, jettison, maroon; defect.

2, desert, forsake, leave in the lurch, depart from, secede from, renege, withdraw from, back out of, turn one's back on, walk out on, take leave of, walk out on, leave holding the bag, leave, quit, vacate. *Colloq.,* leave flat. *Slang,* ditch, give the gate, rat out on.

Adjectives—**1,** relinquished, abandoned, cast off, high and dry, out in the cold; derelict, forlorn, unowned, unappropriated, left; dropped.

2, renunciatory, abjuratory, abdicant; relinquishing, *etc.*

Antonyms, see POSSESSION, ACQUISITION.

---

relish, *n.* zest, gusto; flavor, TASTE; spice, condiment, appetizer; liking, fondness. See PLEASURE, DESIRE, PUNGENCY.

reluctance, *n.* UNWILLINGNESS, hesitation, aversion, disinclination, DISLIKE.

rely, *v.i.* trust, depend (on), count (on). See BELIEF.

remain, *v.i.* stay; endure, last; continue. See REMAINDER, DURABILITY, CONTINUITY, ABODE.

REMAINDER

Nouns—**1,** remainder, residue, hangover, result; remains, remnant, vestige, rest, relic, leavings, crumbs, heeltap, odds and ends, leftovers, debris, cheese parings, orts, residuum, dregs, lees, grounds, silt, sediment, slag, refuse, chaff, stubble, fag end, ruins, wreck, butt, rump, carcass, skeleton, stump, alluvium, deposit; precipitate; dross, cinder, ash, clinker. *Colloq.,* shank. See UNCLEANNESS.

2, surplus, surplusage, overplus, excess, balance, superfluity, survival. *Colloq.*, money to burn.

Verbs—remain, be left, be left over, exceed, survive.

Adjectives—remaining, left; left over, left behind, residual, residuary, over, odd, unconsumed, sedimentary, surviving; net, exceeding, over and above; superfluous.

Antonyms, see COMPLETION, END, DECREASE.

---

remand, *v.* send *or* order back, recommit, recall, return to custody. See COMMAND.

remark, *v.t.* note, observe; comment on, mention. See ATTENTION. —*n.* observation, statement, comment. See SPEECH.

remarkable, *adj.* noteworthy, notable, extraordinary, striking, unusual, singular, uncommon. See UNCONFORMITY, WONDER.

REMEDY

Nouns—**1,** remedy, help, redress, RESTORATION; antidote, counterpoison, counterirritant, counteragent, antitoxin, antibody, prophylactic, antiseptic, corrective, restorative, sedative, palliative, febrifuge; germicide, specific, emetic, cathartic, carminative; narcotic, sedation (see INSENSIBILITY). See RELIEF.

2, antibiosis; antibiotic, wonder drug, miracle drug; toxin, antitoxin, penicillin, gramicidin; bacitracin, Chloromycetin, dihydrostreptomycin, erythromycin, gumagillin, magnamycin, neomycin, polymycin, streptomycin, terramycin; sulfa, sulfonamide, sulfadiazine, sulfanilamide, sulfapyridine, sulfathiazole.

3, physic, medicine, simples, drug, potion, draught, draft, dose, pill, bolus, tincture, medicament.

4, nostrum, receipt, recipe, prescription; panacea, sovereign remedy, cure-[-all], elixir, *elixir vitae,* philosopher's stone, balm, balsam, cordial, ptisan, tisane, patent medicine, herb.

5, salve, ointment, OIL, lenitive, lotion, cosmetic, emollient, embrocation, liniment, depilatory; compress, bandage, poultice, plaster, dressing.

6, treatment, therapy, regimen; diet; appliance; dietetics; bloodletting, bleeding, venesection, phlebotomy, cupping, leeches; surgery, operation, section; plastic surgery; acupuncture, acupressure.

7, pharmacy, pharmacology, pharmaceutics; chemotherapy; shock treatment, therapeutics, pathology, neurology, homeopathy, allopathy, hydrotherapy, surgery, orthopedics, osteopathy, chiropractic, dentistry, midwifery, obstetrics, psychiatry.

8, hospital, infirmary, pesthouse, lazaretto, dispensary, clinic, sanitarium, sanatorium, spa, halfway house; Red Cross.

9, doctor, physician; dentist; surgeon, general practitioner, neurologist, pathologist, psychiatrist, oculist, *etc.;* resident, interne; anesthetist; attendant; apothecary, pharmacist, druggist; leech, *accoucheur, accoucheuse,* midwife, oculist, dentist, aurist, nurse, sister, visiting nurse; paramedic. *Slang*, sawbones, bone crusher, pill pusher, quack.

Verbs—remedy, doctor, dose, physic, nurse, operate, minister to, treat, attend; dress the wounds, plaster; prevent, relieve, cure, heal, clear up, palliate, restore (see RESTORATION); bleed; respond to treatment.

Adjectives—remedial, restorative, corrective, curative, palliative, healing, sanatory, sanative; cathartic; antitoxic, antiseptic, prophylactic, medical, medicinal, surgical, therapeutic, tonic, analeptic, balsamic, anodyne, hypnotic, neurotic, narcotic, sedative, lenitive, demulcent, emollient, detergent; antibiotic, bactericidal, bacteriostatic; disinfectant, febrifugal, laxative, dietetic, alimentary, nutritious, nutritive, peptic; curable, remediable.

Antonyms, see DISEASE.

---

remember, *v.t.* recollect (see MEMORY); observe, acknowledge.

remind, *v.t.* prompt (see MEMORY).

reminiscent, *adj.* retrospective, suggestive. See MEMORY.

remiss, *adj.* lax, slack, neglectful, dilatory. See NEGLECT.

remission, *n.* annulment, cancellation; pardon, FORGIVENESS; suspension, respite, abatement. See PAYMENT.

remit, *v.t.* forgive, pardon, excuse, exempt, relax, slacken; restore, replace; discharge, pay, send. See FORGIVENESS, RESTORATION, PAYMENT.

remnant, *n.* REMAINDER, residue, fragment, scrap, vestige.

remodel, *v.t.* rearrange, rebuild, modernize; renovate, rehabilitate, refurbish, make over, recondition. See NEWNESS, RESTORATION, CHANGE.

remonstrance, *n.* protest, objection; reproof, expostulation. See DISSUASION, DISAPPROBATION.

remorse, *n.* self-reproach, REGRET, compunction, contrition, PENITENCE.

remorseless, *adj.* impenitent, hardened, callous, obdurate; hard, cold, ruthless. See IMPENITENCE.

remote, *adj.* distant, secluded, alien; slight, inconsiderable. See DISTANCE, SECLUSION.

remove, *v.* depart, go away, move; displace, excise, shift, eliminate, take off, discharge, evict. See EJECTION, DEPARTURE, DEDUCTION, EXTRACTION, TRANSFER, TRANSPORTATION, DISPLACEMENT.

remunerate, *v.t.* pay, reimburse, recompense, requite, reward. See PAYMENT.

remunerative, *adj.* profitable, paying, rewarding, compensatory, gainful, lucrative; worthwhile. See UTILITY.

renaissance, *n.* renascence, rebirth, revival. See RESTORATION.

rend, *v.t.* tear, shred, rip, rive, split; harrow, cut, cleave. See DISJUNCTION.

render, *v.t.* give, pay, deliver, furnish, supply, yield, produce, perform; express, translate, interpret; reduce, melt; return, present. See GIVING, INTERPRETATION.

rendezvous, *n.* tryst, appointment, date, meeting, assignation. See SOCIALITY, ASSEMBLAGE.

rendition, *n.* rendering; execution, performance, REPRESENTATION; view, version, INTERPRETATION, reading, paraphrase.

renegade, *n.* traitor, turncoat, apostate, defector; mutineer. See EVILDOER. —*adj.* treacherous, disloyal; rebellious, mutinous. See IMPROBITY.

renege, *v., colloq.,* break one's word *or* promise, disavow, disclaim, take back, go back (on), cancel, back out. See NULLIFICATION, NEGATION, NONPAYMENT.

renew, *v.t.* revive, restore; resume, continue; replace, renovate, replenish. See RESTORATION, NEWNESS.

renounce, *v.t.* abjure, disclaim, disown, repudiate, reject, give up, abandon, surrender. See REJECTION.

renovate, *v.t.* renew, restore, repair, freshen, purify. See RESTORATION.

renown, *n.* REPUTE, fame, reputation, glory, distinction, kudos.

rent, *n.* tear, slit, fissure; split, division, rupture, schism; payment, return, rental. *Colloq.,* tenement. See INTERVAL.

reorganize, *v.t.* resystematize, remodel, reform, rehabilitate, reestablish. See CHANGE, RESTORATION.

repair, *v.* betake oneself, go; mend, renovate, restore; amend, remedy. See TRAVEL. —*n.* RESTORATION, renovation, mending, redress. See ATONEMENT.

reparation, *n.* amends, redress, restitution, indemnity. See ATONEMENT.

reparative, *adj.* mending, restorative, remedial, corrective, compensatory. See COMPENSATION, RESTORATION, RETALIATION.

repartee, *n.* [witty] retort, [clever] rejoinder, sally, persiflage, banter. *Slang*, [snappy] comeback. See ANSWER, WIT.

repast, *n.* meal, collation, snack; feast, banquet, spread. See FOOD.

repay, *v.t.* reimburse, indemnify, refund; recompense, requite. See PAYMENT, RETALIATION.

repeal, *v.t.* revoke, recall, annul, nullify, vacate, abrogate. See NULLIFICATION.

repeat, *v.t.* iterate, quote, recite; redo, duplicate. See REPETITION.

repel, *v.t.* repulse, resist, reject, scatter, drive apart; disgust, revolt. See PAIN, DISLIKE.

repellent, *adj.* repulsive, resistant, forbidding, distasteful. See RESISTANCE, UGLINESS.

repent, *v.* rue, REGRET. See PENITENCE.

repercussion, *n.* rebound, RECOIL, impact, reverberation, kick; result, EFFECT.

repertory, *n.* repertoire; LIST, catalogue, collection, store, stock; acts, routines. *Colloq.,* bag of tricks, one's paces. See DRAMA.

REPETITION

Nouns—**1,** repetition, reiteration, harping; recurrence, reappearance; résumé, recapitulation, run; tautology, monotony, rhythm, periodicity, redundance, alliteration; DIFFUSENESS. See REGULARITY, FREQUENCY, IDENTITY, HABIT.

2, echo, burden of a song, refrain, repetend, encore, rehearsal; drone, monotone; reverberation, reverb, drumming, chimes; twice-told tale, old story, second edition; double duty; old wine in new bottles. *Slang,* chestnut. See MEMORY.

3, reproduction, duplication, reduplication; retake; COPY; SIMILARITY.

Verbs—**1,** repeat, [re]iterate, reproduce, duplicate, retake, refilm, retape, renew, echo, reecho, drum, pulsate, harp upon, keep after, dwell (upon), drill, hammer, redouble. *Colloq.,* beat into one's head. *Slang,* rub it in, ding.

2, recur, revert, return, reappear, redound, resume, rehearse, retell, go over the same ground, rehash, return to, [re]capitulate, reword; chew one's cabbage twice, repeat oneself, ring the changes. *Colloq.,* double in brass.

Adjectives—repeated, repetitive, repetitious, recurrent, recurring, frequent, incessant; monotonous, harping, iterative, chiming, retold, aforesaid, abovementioned, habitual.

Adverbs—repeatedly, often, again, anew, over again, afresh, once more, ditto, encore, over [and over], time after time, time and [time] again, frequently; *da capo.*

Interjections—come again? bis!

Antonyms, see END.

---

repine, *v.i.* fret, complain, mope, grieve, despond. See DISCONTENT, DEJECTION.

replace, *v.t.* put back; supplant, succeed, supersede; substitute; restore, return; move. See SUBSTITUTION.

replenish, *v.t.* refill, restock, renew; stock up. See PROVISION, SUFFICIENCY.

repletion, *n.* surfeit, satiety, overfullness, glut, engorgement. See SUFFICIENCY.

replica, *n.* image, double, twin, likeness; facsimile, COPY, reproduction, imitation, duplicate, model;

photostat, print, transfer, impression.

reply, *n.* ANSWER, response, retort, rejoinder; countermove.

report, *v.t.* state, review; rehearse, give tidings, announce, give notice of, proclaim. See INFORMATION, PUBLICATION. —*n.* record, account, statement; news; rumor; hearsay; fame, repute; bang, blast, detonation. See INFORMATION, NEWS.

reporter, *n.* news gatherer, journalist, newspaperman. *Slang,* leg man, newshound, newshawk. See NEWS, COMMUNICATION.

REPOSE

Nouns—**1,** repose, rest, INACTIVITY, relaxation, breathing time *or* spell, letup, halt, pause, respite, breather.

2, sleep, slumber, somnolence, sound *or* heavy sleep; Morpheus; coma, swoon, trance; catalepsy; dream; hibernation, estivation; nap, catnap, doze, siesta; land of nod; beauty sleep. *Colloq.,* forty winks, snooze, shut-eye.

3, leisure, spare time, idleness, ease; coffee break; time out, shore leave.

4, quiescence, quiet, stillness, tranquillity, calm, peace, composure; stagnation, stagnancy, immobility.

5, day of rest, Sabbath, Sunday, Lord's day, holiday, vacation, recess; pause, lull.

6, sedative, tranquillizer, sleeping draft *or* pill, soporific, opiate (see REMEDY). *Slang,* knockout drops.

7, slumberer, sleepyhead, dormouse.

Verbs—**1,** repose, rest, take one's ease, recline, lie down, go to bed, turn in, go to sleep, sleep, slumber, sleep a wink; snore; put to bed; hibernate; oversleep; sleep like a top *or* log; doze, drowse, snooze, nap; dream; snore; nod, yawn. *Colloq.,* drop off. *Slang,* saw wood, conk out, flop, sack out *or* in, hit the hay *or* sack, pound the ear.

2, relax, unbend, slacken, take breath, rest upon one's oars, pause; loaf, idle, while away the time, take a holiday, shut up shop. *Colloq.,* take it easy, let down, let go, take a breather, take time out, kill time; let one's hair down, catch one's breath.

Adjectives—**1,** reposing, reposed, reposeful, calm, quiet, restful, relaxed, unstrained, tranquil; quiescent, dormant; quiet; leisurely, slow, unhurried, calm.

2, asleep, sleeping, comatose; in the arms of Morpheus; sleepy, drowsy, somnolent; napping, dozing; laid-back. *Colloq.,* out like a light, dead to the world.

Adverbs—at rest, at ease, calmly, peacefully; at a standstill; at [one's] leisure, unhurriedly.

Antonyms, see EXERTION, MOTION, ACTIVITY.

---

repose, *v.* lay, place, entrust, deposit, put. See SUPPORT.

repository, *n.* vault, warehouse, museum. See STORE.

reprehensible, *adj.* blameworthy, censurable. See DISAPPROBATION.

REPRESENTATION

Nouns—**1,** representation, IMITATION, illustration, delineation, depiction, depictment, imagery, portraiture, design, designing, art, fine arts, PAINTING, drawing, SCULPTURE, ENGRAVING, photography, holography; collage, montage; expression. See DESCRIPTION.

2, personation, personification, impersonation; rendition; motion picture, movie, *etc*. See DRAMA.

3, picture, drawing, sketch, draft, tracing, COPY, photograph, daguerreotype; hologram; image, likeness, icon, portrait, effigy, facsimile; enlargement, blowup.

4, figure, puppet, marionette, doll, figurine, manikin, model, dummy, waxwork, bust, statue, statuette, figurehead, effigy.

5, map, plan, chart, graph, ground plan, blueprint, projection, elevation; diagram, cartography, atlas, outline, view.

6, ARTIST, designer, sculptor, draftsman, delineator.

Verbs—**1,** represent, delineate, depict, portray; photograph, figure, picture, describe, draw, sketch, trace, graph, COPY, mold, illustrate, symbolize, paint, carve, engrave, *etc*.

2, personate, personify, impersonate, embody, pose as, act [out], play, mimic, imitate.

Adjectives—representative, representing, depictive, illustrative, imitative, figurative, like, graphic, descriptive.

Antonyms, see DISTORTION.

---

representative, *adj*. typical, characteristic, illustrative, descriptive, exemplary; democratic, legislative, popular, republican. —*n*. delegate, nominee, agent, deputy; Congressman, Assemblyman, legislator, Member of Congress *or* Parliament, M.P. See AGENT, SUBSTITUTION, AUTHORITY.

repress, *v.t.* suppress, restrain, curb, control, quell, stifle, smother, crush. See RESTRAINT.

reprieve, *n*. delay, stay, respite, suspension; pardon. See LATENESS, FORGIVENESS, ACQUITTAL.

reprimand, *n*. reproof, rebuke, censure, admonition, reprehension. See DISAPPROBATION.

reprint, *n*. reissue, new edition, revision; COPY, replica. See PUBLICATION.

reprisal, *n*. RETALIATION, revenge, requital, indemnity.

reproach, *v.t.* blame, rebuke, upbraid, censure; stigmatize. —*n*. reproof, blame, disgrace, discredit, dishonor. See DISAPPROBATION, DISREPUTE, ACCUSATION.

reprobate, *n*. sinner, scoundrel; rogue, blackguard. See IMPIETY.

REPRODUCTION

Nouns—**1,** reproduction; [re]generation, propagation, multiplication, reenactment, REPETITION, procreation, fructification, breeding, begetting. See RESTORATION.

2, bringing forth, parturition, birth, childbirth, delivery, confinement, travail, labor, midwifery, obstetrics; gestation, evolution, development, growth; genesis, generation, procreation, progeneration, propagation; fecundation, impregnation; parthenogenesis, spontaneous generation; biogenesis, abiogenesis.

3, fecundity, fertility, pregnancy, multiplication; fertilization.

4, reconstruction, REPRESENTATION, IMITATION, offprint, illustration.

Verbs—**1,** reproduce, reconstruct; multiply, propagate, procreate, revivify, breed, populate, crop up; produce, flower, bear fruit, fructify; teem, ean, yean, farrow, drop, whelp, pup, kitten; bear, lay, bring forth, give birth to, lie in, be delivered of; evolve, pullulate, usher into the world.

2, create; mother, father, beget, get, generate, fecundate, impregnate; proliferate, progenerate, fertilize, spermatize, conceive; bud, bloom, blossom, burgeon; engender.

3, COPY, portray, duplicate, repeat, reprint, transcribe.

Adjectives—**1,** reproductive, reproduced, recreative, procreative, generative.

2, fertile, fecund, creative; genetic, genital; pregnant; *enceinte,* big with; teeming, parturient, puerperal. *Colloq.,* expectant, in the family way.

Antonyms, see IMPOTENCE, CELIBACY, HINDRANCE.

---

reprove, *v.t.* admonish, censure, rebuke, chide, criticize. See DISAPPROBATION.

reptile, *n.* saurian, crocodilian, serpent, lizard, *etc.;* toady, bootlicker. See ANIMAL, SERVILITY.

republic, *n.* democracy, free state, commonwealth, *res publica;* self-government, *vox populi;* people's republic, soviet; country. See HUMANITY, AUTHORITY.

repudiate, *v.t.* renounce, disavow, disclaim, disown, divorce, deny. See DISSENT, NEGATION, NONPAYMENT, REJECTION.

repugnance, *n.* DISLIKE, aversion, antipathy, disgust; inconsistency, contradictoriness; OPPOSITION. See HATE.

repugnant, *adj.* distasteful, repulsive; incompatible, contrary, antagonistic. See DISAGREEMENT, DISLIKE.

REPULSION

Nouns—**1,** repulsion, repulse, repellency; REJECTION, rebuff, spurning; diamagnetism; RESISTANCE.

2, abhorrence, revulsion, aversion (see DISLIKE).

Verbs—**1,** repulse, repel, drive from, beat back; push *or* send away; send, ward, beat, fend, fight, *or* drive off; fling *or* throw back; chase, dispel, scatter, rout, disperse.

2, rebuff, reject, refuse, discard, snub, spurn, kick aside; keep at arm's length, turn one's back upon, give the cold shoulder to. *Colloq.,* cold-shoulder. *Slang,* freeze.

Adjectives—repulsive, repelling, repellent, abhorrent, repugnant, loathsome, odious, offensive, mawkish, nauseating, revolting; diamagnetic. See UGLINESS.

Antonyms, see ATTRACTION.

REPUTE

Nouns—**1,** repute, reputation, distinction, mark, name, figure; note, notability, celebrity, fame, famousness, renown, popularity, credit, prestige, glory, honor; luster, illustriousness, account, regard, face, reputableness, respectability, good *or* fair name. See PROBITY.

2, dignity, GREATNESS, IMPORTANCE, eminence, preeminence.

3, rank, standing, station (see CLASS).

4, elevation, ascent, exaltation, dignification, aggrandizement; dedication, consecration, enthronement, canonization, celebration, enshrinement, glorification.

5, hero, man of mark, celebrity; lion, luminary, notability, somebody, pillar of the church *or* the community; chief, first fiddle, flower, pink, pearl, paragon, star. *Colloq.,* personality. *Slang,* V.I.P., big wheel.

6, ornament, honor, feather in one's cap, halo, aureole, nimbus, blaze of glory, laurels.

7, memory, posthumous *or* lasting fame, immortality, immortal name.

Verbs—**1,** shine [forth], figure, cut a figure, [make a] splash, live, flourish, glitter, gain honor, play first fiddle, take precedence, win laurels, win [one's] spurs, leave one's mark, star, come into vogue, look to one's laurels.

2, rival, surpass, outshine, outrival, outvie, emulate, eclipse, cast into the shade, overshadow.

3, enthrone, immortalize, deify, exalt; consecrate, dedicate, enshrine, lionize, crown with laurel; honor, confer honor, do honor *or* credit to, accredit, dignify, glorify, look up to, aggrandize, elevate. *Colloq.,* do proud, put on the map. *Slang,* build up.

Adjectives—**1,** reputable, creditable, honorable, respectable, decent, in good order, in high favor.

2, distinguished, *distingué,* noted, of note, honored, popular; fashionable; remarkable, notable, celebrated, renowned, talked of, famous, famed, legendary, conspicuous, foremost, in the ascendant; illustrious, glorious, splendid, brilliant, radiant, bright.

3, eminent, prominent, lofty; peerless, superior, preeminent; great, dignified.

4, imperishable, deathless, immortal, neverfading, time-honored, sacrosanct.

Antonyms, see DISREPUTE.

REQUEST

Nouns—**1,** request, requisition, petition, plea, suit, prayer; motion, overture, application, proposition, proposal, OFFER, canvass, address, appeal, apostrophe, orison, incantation. *Slang,* touch, shakedown, bite. See PURSUIT, INQUIRY.

2, mendicancy; asking, begging, postulation, solicitation, invitation, entreaty, importunity, beseechment, supplication, imploration, obtestation, invocation, interpellation; fund raising, telethon, radiothon; charity case.

3, requester, petitioner, cadger, beggar, solicitor, canvasser, door-to-door salesman; applicant, supplicant, suitor, demander, importuner; bidder, asker. *Colloq.,* sponger. *Slang,* moocher, free-loader, panhandler.

Verbs—**1,** request, ask, beg, crave; sue, pray, petition, solicit; invite, beg, beg leave, crave *or* ask a boon; speak for, apply to, call upon, call for, commandeer, enlist, requisition, ask a favor; coax (see FLATTERY).

2, entreat, beseech, plead, conjure, supplicate, implore, adjure, cry to, kneel to, appeal to; invoke, ply, press, urge, beset, importune, dun, cry for help; raise money; hound; whistle for. *Colloq.,* buttonhole. *Slang,* put the bite, sting, *or* touch on; fly a kite.

3, beg from door to door, go a-begging, cadge, pass the hat. *Colloq.,* sponge. *Slang,* mooch, panhandle, free-load.

Adjectives—**1,** requesting, precatory, suppliant, supplicant, supplicatory.

2, importunate, clamorous, urgent, cap in hand, on bended knee, on one's knees.

Adverbs—prithee, do, please, pray, be so good as, be good enough, if you please, for the asking.

Antonyms, see OFFER.

---

requirement, *n.* want, NECESSITY; the necessary *or* requisite; requisition, demand; needfulness, essentiality, indispensability; urgency, exigency, *sine qua non,* matter of life and death. See COMPULSION, COMMAND.

requisite, *adj.* necessary, required; imperative, essential, indispensable, urgent, pressing. See NECESSITY.

requisition, *n.* demand, order, claim, exaction, REQUEST. See COMMAND.

requite, *v.t.* retaliate, avenge; repay, indemnify, make amends, reward. See RETALIATION, GRATITUDE.

rescind, *v.t.* revoke, repeal, recall, abrogate, annul. See NULLIFICATION.

rescue, *v.t.* liberate, set free, deliver, save; recover, reclaim. See LIBERATION.

research, *n.* INQUIRY, investigation, study, exploration.

resemblance, *n.* SIMILARITY, likeness, similitude.

RESENTMENT

Nouns—**1,** resentment, displeasure, animosity, anger, wrath, indignation, exasperation; pique, umbrage, huff, miff, soreness, dudgeon, acerbity, virulence, bitterness, acrimony, asperity, spleen, gall, rankling; ill humor, temper (see IRASCIBILITY); HATE, irritation, bile, choler, ire, fume, dander, ferment, ebullition, pet, tiff, slow burn, passion, fit, tantrum. See MALEVOLENCE, JEALOUSY, DISCONTENT.

2, sullenness, moroseness, sulks, black looks, scowl, chip on one's shoulder, hard feelings.

Verbs—**1,** resent, take amiss, take to heart, take offense, take in bad part, fly into a rage, bridle, bristle, flare up; sulk, pout, frown, scowl, simmer, lower, glower, snarl, growl, gnarl, gnash, snap, look daggers, grind one's teeth; chafe, fume, kindle, seethe, boil [with indignation], get one's back up, rage, storm, have a fit, foam [at the mouth], vent one's spleen, take it out on, lose one's temper, quiver with rage; burst with anger. *Colloq.*, blow one's top, a fuse, a gasket, *or* one's stack, take hard, fly off the handle, see red, burn up. *Slang,* flip one's lid *or* wig, hit the ceiling *or* roof, go into orbit.

2, anger, affront, offend, displease, give umbrage, hurt the feelings, tread *or* step on one's toes, insult, fret, ruffle, frazzle, nettle, chafe, wound, incense, inflame, enrage, aggravate, envenom, embitter, exasperate, get one's goat, infuriate, rankle, put out of humor, put one's nose out of joint, raise one's dander, make one's blood boil, drive one mad. *Slang,* get a rise out of.

Adjectives—**1,** resentful, offended, sullen; wrought up, worked up, indignant, hurt. *Colloq.,* sore.

2, angry, irate; wrathful, wroth, cross, sulky, bitter, virulent; acrimonious, warm, burning; boiling, fuming, raging; foaming at the mouth; convulsed with rage; in a stew, fierce, wild, rageful, furious, mad with rage, fiery, rabid, savage; flushed with anger, in a huff, in a passion, up in arms, in high dudgeon. *Colloq.,* hot under the collar, steamed up, blue in the face, fit to be tied, mad as a hornet *or* wet hen, on the warpath, teed off.

Adverbs—resentfully, angrily, *etc.;* in the heat of passion, in the heat of the moment.

Antonyms, see GRATITUDE.

---

reservation, *n.* exception, QUALIFICATION, misgiving; booking, engagement. See COMMISSION.

reserve, *n.* restriction, qualification; restraint, caution, reticence, dignity; STORE, stock. See SILENCE, MODESTY, ECONOMY, TACITURNITY.

reserved, *adj.* undemonstrative, diffident, distant, reticent; set aside. See MODESTY, SILENCE, STORE.

reservoir, *n.* cistern, reserve, source, supply. See STORE.

reside, *v.i.* live, dwell, abide, sojourn, lodge. See ABODE, INHABITANT.

residual, *adj.* left over, extra, surplus; future, continuing. See REMAINDER.

residue, *n.* REMAINDER, rest, remnant, leavings.

RESIGNATION

Nouns—**1,** resignation, demission, retirement, abdication, withdrawal, surrender, quitting; RELINQUISHMENT. See SUBMISSION.

2, resignedness, patience, forbearance, long-suffering, sufferance, acquiescence; passiveness, meekness, stoicism. See INEXCITABILITY.

Verbs—**1,** resign, withdraw, demit, yield, surrender, resign oneself, grin and bear it, submit, desert, retire, tender one's resignation, lie down, give up, throw in the towel *or* sponge, quit, take it on the chin; make a virtue of necessity.

2, abrogate, abdicate, vacate, step down; walk the plank.

Adjectives—**1,** resigning, renunciatory, abjuratory, abdicant; retired, in retirement. *Colloq.,* out to pasture.

2, resigned, submissive, patient, long-suffering, acquiescent, unresisting, complying, yielding, uncomplaining, reconciled, philosophical, stoical.

Antonyms, see OBSTINACY.

---

resilient, *adj.* elastic, pliable, rubbery, tensile, ductile, malleable; recuperative, tough, rugged; irrepressible, indestructible; resistant, renitent; buoyant, youthful. See ELASTICITY.

resin, *n.* rosin, gum, lac, sealing wax, amber; bitumen, pitch, tar, asphalt, asphaltum; varnish, copal, mastic, lacquer, japan. See COHERENCE.

RESISTANCE

Nouns—**1,** resistance, OPPOSITION, oppugnance, renitence, stand, front; recalcitrance, OBSTINACY; impeding, kicking, parrying, imperviousness, endurance, fastness, immunity, immovability; REPULSION, REFUSAL; impedance; FRICTION. See UNWILLINGNESS, DURABILITY.

2, strike, turnout, lockout, walkout, tieup, slowdown, boycott; sit-down strike, passive resistance, [civil] DISOBEDIENCE. See REVOLUTION.

Verbs—**1,** resist, withstand, stand [firm], stand one's ground, hold one's own, stick to one's own guns, hold out, make a stand, take one's stand, show a bold front. *Colloq.,* stick it out.

2, oppose, defy, face, confront, stand up against, strive against, bear up against; balk, kick (against), grapple with, keep at bay; obstruct, impede (see HINDRANCE).

3, fight, struggle, put up a fight, attack, defend, persevere, die hard, sell one's life dearly, fight to the last ditch. See TENACITY.

4, strike, walk out, turn out, boycott, picket, remonstrate, disobey, sabotage; riot, rebel, revolt.

Adjectives—resisting, resistant, renitent, resistive, refractory, recalcitrant, disobedient; repellent, repulsive, proof against, up in arms; unconquerable, irresistible, resistless, indomitable, unyielding, invincible; stubborn, obstinate, obdurate, dogged, firm, uncompromising.

Antonyms, see OBEDIENCE, SUBMISSION.

RESOLUTION

Nouns—**1,** resolution, resoluteness, determination, WILL, decision, strength of mind, resolve, firmness, steadfastness, ENERGY, pluck, grit, backbone, morale, gumption, COURAGE, devotion, devotedness.

2, mastery over self, self-control, self-command, self-possession, self-reliance, moral courage, perseverance, TENACITY, OBSTINACY, doggedness. See INTENTION, STRENGTH.

Verbs—**1,** resolve, determine, have determination, be resolved, make up one's mind, WILL, decide, form a resolve; conclude; devote oneself to, set one's teeth, put one's foot down, take one's stand; stand firm, steel oneself, stand no nonsense; put one's heart into, take the bull by the horns, go in for, insist upon, make a point of, set one's heart upon; stick at nothing, go the limit. *Colloq.,* go all out, go the whole hog, stick to one's guns, make no bones about.

2, persevere, persist; apply oneself; stick with, stick it out, see it through, see out, bear up, hold out, hang on, die hard, fight, insist, never say die. *Colloq.,* mean business, hang in [there].

Adjectives—resolute, resolved, determined, strong-willed, grim, self-possessed, decided, decisive, definitive, pertinacious, peremptory, unhesitating, unflinching, firm, indomitable, game, inexorable, do-or-die; tireless, untiring, indefatigable, unwearied; relentless, unshakable, inflexible, obstinate, steady, persevering, steadfast. *Colloq.,* together.

Adverbs—resolutely, in earnest, seriously, earnestly, heart and soul, at any risk, at any price, cost what it may, all or nothing, rain or shine, sink or swim, come hell or high water, through thick and thin.

Antonyms, see DOUBT.

---

resolve, *n.* determination, RESOLUTION. —*v.* determine, decide; separate, solve. See INQUIRY, CHANGE, JUDGMENT.

resonance, *n.* vibration; reverberation, resounding, rebound; reflection, echo; ringing, tintinnabulation; ring, boom, rumble. See LOUDNESS, SOUND.

resort, *v.i.* gather, flock, frequent; turn to; have recourse to. —*n.* haunt, meeting place; refuge, resource. See USE, ABODE, AMUSEMENT.

resound, *v.i.* echo, reecho, ring, reverberate, peal. See LOUDNESS, SOUND.

resourceful, *adj.* ingenious, inventive, imaginative, versatile, skillful; adaptable, resilient, prepared; devious, CUNNING. See SKILL.

resources, *n.pl.* assets, wealth, PROSPERITY; ingenuity, expedients. See MONEY, MEANS.

RESPECT

Nouns—**1,** respect, regards, consideration, COURTESY, ATTENTION, deference, reverence, honor, esteem, estimation, veneration, admiration; APPROBATION, devotion, homage. See WORSHIP, OBEDIENCE.

2, homage, fealty, obeisance, genuflection, genuflexion, kneeling, prostration, obsequiousness, salaam, kowtow, bow, salute. See RELIGION.

3, respects, regards, duty, devoirs; feather in one's cap.

Verbs—**1,** respect, regard, admire, consider; think a great deal, a lot, *or* much of, revere, reverence, hold in reverence, honor, venerate, esteem, think much of, look up to, defer to, pay attention to, do honor, hail, salute, pay tribute to, take one's hat off to; kneel to, bow to, bend the knee to, prostrate oneself, WORSHIP.

2, command *or* inspire respect; awe, overawe; dazzle; impress.

Adjectives—**1,** respectful, deferential, decorous; reverent, reverential, worshipful, obsequious, ceremonious.

2, respected, respectable, worthy, estimable, in high esteem, on a pedestal, time-honored, venerable, emeritus; creditable.

Adverbs—deferentially, *etc.;* with due respect, in honor (of), in homage (to).

Antonyms, see DISRESPECT.

---

respectable, *adj.* worthy, reputable, estimable; moderate, fairly good, decent. See REPUTE.

respective, *adj.* particular, individual, several. See SPECIALITY, APPORTIONMENT.

respectively, *adv.* severally, one by one, each to each; in order. See APPORTIONMENT.

respire, *v.i.* breathe (see WIND).

respite, *n.* postponement, pause, reprieve, cessation, intermission. See LATENESS, REPOSE.

resplendent, *adj.* shining, lustrous, radiant, splendid, gleaming. See LIGHT, BEAUTY.

response, *n.* ANSWER, reply, rejoinder; reaction; responsory. See MUSIC, FEELING.

responsible, *adj.* trustworthy, dependable; answerable, accountable, liable, chargeable; solvent. See DUTY, LIABILITY.

responsive, *adj.* sympathetic, sensitive, receptive, adaptable; antiphonal. See SOFTNESS, ANSWER.

rest, *n.* REMAINDER, remains, balance, residuum; REPOSE; DEATH.

restaurant, *n.* café, eating house, coffee house, roadhouse, cafeteria, diner, automat, canteen, grill. See FOOD.

restful, *adj.* soothing, quiet, reposeful, tranquil. See REPOSE.

restitution, *n.* RESTORATION, reparation, amends, *amende honorable;* atonement, redemption; remuneration; recovery, repossession; return, compensation; making good; rehabilitation; indemnification; retrieval; repair. See PAYMENT.

restive, *adj.* nervous, skittish, balky; refractory, disobedient, unruly; uneasy, impatient; restless. See AGITATION, DISOBEDIENCE.

restless, *adj.* nervous, restive, impatient; fidgety, skittish, jumpy, unquiet, disturbed. See AGITATION, CHANGEABLENESS, FEAR.

RESTORATION

Nouns—**1,** restoration, reinstatement, replacement, rehabilitation, reestablishment, reconstruction, renovation, renewal, revival, REFRESHMENT, resuscitation, reanimation, revivification, second wind *or* breath; reorganization. See IMPROVEMENT, NEWNESS.

2, renaissance, renascence, second youth, rejuvenescence, resurrection, resurgence, rebirth, recrudescence, new birth; regeneration, regeneracy, reconversion; comeback; reincarnation.

3, recovery, convalescence, recuperation, cure, repair, reparation, reclamation, retrieval, RELIEF, healing, rectification, cicatrization. See REMEDY.

4, restitution, return, rendition, redemption, reinvestment, ATONEMENT; redress, replevin, REVERSION; *status quo ante*.

5, restorer, refinisher; repairer, repairman *or* -woman, mechanic; adjuster; service station; halfway house, convalescent home.

Verbs—**1,** restore, put back, reinstate, rehabilitate, reestablish, reinstall, reconstruct, rebuild, reorganize, reconstitute, reconvert; renew, renovate, regenerate; redecorate, remodel; make *or* do over.

2, recover, rally, convalesce, revive, come to, come around, pull through, be oneself again, come to one's senses, get well, rise from the grave, survive, live again, get over. *Colloq.*, snap out of it.

3, redeem, reclaim, recover, retrieve, rescue, salvage.

4, redress, cure, heal, REMEDY, doctor, physic, medicate; bring [a]round, set on one's legs; resuscitate, bring to, reanimate, revivify, resurrect, reinvigorate, refresh, freshen, strengthen, pick up; make whole, recoup, make good, make all square, rectify, put to rights, clear up, set straight, correct, put in order, put one's house in order; refit, recruit, reinforce.

5, repair, mend, fix, retouch, touch up, recondition, overhaul, [re]vamp, tinker, patch [up], darn, stop a gap, staunch, caulk, splice, bind up wounds.

6, return, give back, bring back, render up, give up, let go, disgorge, reimburse, refund, remit; get back, revert. *Slang,* cough up, kick back. See RELINQUISHMENT.

Adjectives—**1,** restored, renewed, convalescent, on the mend, none the worse, on one's feet, all better; refreshed.

2, restoring, restorative, recuperative, sanative, curative, remedial, sanatory, salubrious (see HEALTH); refreshing, bracing.

3, restorable, recoverable, retrievable, curable.

Antonyms, see DESTRUCTION, ACQUISITION.

RESTRAINT

Nouns—**1,** restraint, inhibition, repression, discipline, control, check, curb, rein; limitation, restriction; PROHIBITION; monopoly. See CIRCUMSCRIPTION, LIMIT, SUBJECTION, RETENTION, PUNISHMENT, DISSUASION.

2, HINDRANCE, confinement, durance, duress; imprisonment, incarceration, solitary confinement; isolation ward, quarantine; entombment; limbo; captivity; embargo, blockade, siege, besiegement, beleaguerment.

3, arrest, custody, keep, CARE, charge, ward, protection.

4, bond[s], irons, chains, pinions, gyves, fetters, shackles, manacles, handcuffs, bracelets; straitjacket; seat *or* lap belt, car seat, air bag, passive restraint; muzzle, gag, yoke, collar, halter, harness, reins; bit, brake, curb, snaffle, bridle, seine; martingale, lead; tether, hobble, picket, band, leash; bolt, bar, lock, latch; bars, PRISON. See CLOSURE.

5, detainee; prisoner (see PRISON).

Verbs—**1,** restrain, check, put under restraint, enthrall, enslave, restrict, contain, debar, hinder, clip one's wings; curb, control, govern, hold back, hold in, put down, hold in check *or* leash, harness; withhold, keep under, keep *or* clamp down, repress, suppress, smother, pull *or* rein in; prohibit, inhibit, dissuade. *Colloq.,* hold one's horses, cramp one's style.

2, enchain, fasten, fetter, shackle, trammel; tie one's hands; bridle, gag, pinion, manacle, handcuff, hobble, bind, pin down, tether, picket, tie up *or* down, secure; moor, anchor, belay. *Colloq.,* hogtie.

3, confine; shut up, lock up, box, bottle up, cork up, seal up, hem in, bolt in, wall in, rail in; trap, bring to bay, corner; impound, pen, coop, enclose, cage; snow in. See ENCLOSURE.

Adjectives—**1,** restrained, in check, constrained, pent up, jammed in, wedged in; bound; muscle-bound; icebound, snowbound.

2, stiff, restringent, straitlaced, hidebound, reserved.

Antonyms, see FREEDOM.

---

restrict, *v.t.* check, LIMIT, confine, restrain, circumscribe, hinder, impede. See CIRCUMSCRIPTION, HINDRANCE, RESTRAINT.

result, *n.* consequence, conclusion, outcome, upshot, fruit, EFFECT, product. See JUDGMENT.

resume, *v.t.* recommence, reoccupy, retake, reassume; continue. See REPETITION, CONTINUITY.

résumé, *n.* abstract, summary, compendium, condensation, digest, brief, précis, outline, review, synopsis; job summary, *[curriculum] vitae*. See REPETITION, SHORTNESS.

resurgence, *n.* reappearance, renewal, revival; recovery, refreshment, RESTORATION; improvement, growth, increase, rise, surge.

resurrect, *v.t.* restore, revive, rebuild, reestablish, renew, rehabilitate; reanimate; disinter. See RESTORATION.

resuscitate, *v.t.* revive, restore, reanimate; refresh, revivify. See RESTORATION.

retail, *v.t.* sell, dispense, vend, peddle, spread (gossip). See SALE, INFORMATION.

retain, *v.t.* See RETENTION.

retainer, *n.* emolument, remuneration, PAYMENT; adherent, SERVANT; hireling, henchman; guardian, bodyguard; (*pl.*) household, retinue. See ACCOMPANIMENT.

retake, *v.t.* resume; recover, recapture, retrieve; refilm. See REPETITION.

RETALIATION

Nouns—**1,** retaliation, reprisal, requital, counterstroke, retribution, COMPENSATION, reciprocation, reciprocity, retort, counterattack, recrimination, tit for tat, give and take, blow for blow, *quid pro quo,* measure for measure, the biter bit, comeuppance, just deserts. *Slang,* the hair of the dog [that bit one]. See PUNISHMENT.

2, revenge, vengeance, avengement; vendetta, feud, grudge fight; an eye for an eye.

3, vengefulness, vindictiveness, implacability; spite, rancor (see RESENTMENT).

4, avenger, vindicator, Nemesis, Eumenides, Furies, Erinyes.

Verbs—**1,** retaliate, strike back, retort, requite, repay, turn upon, pay back, return in kind, pay in the same coin, cap, reciprocate, turn the tables upon, return the compliment, give as good as one gets, give and take, scratch one's back, be quits, be even with, pay off old scores; call *or* make it quits. *Colloq.,* give one a dose of his own medicine.

2, revenge, avenge, take one's revenge, get even, get back at, settle the score, square *or* settle accounts, wreak vengeance; feud with.

3, have a bone to pick, harbor a grudge, bear malice, rankle in the breast. *Colloq.,* have it in for.

4, get what's coming to one, have it coming.

Adjectives—**1,** retaliative, retaliatory, recriminatory, retributive.

2, revengeful, vengeful, vindictive, rancorous, ruthless, unforgiving, implacable, relentless.

Antonyms, see FORGIVENESS.

---

retard, *v.t.* delay, slow down, check, hinder, impede, postpone, hold up. See SLOWNESS, HINDRANCE.

retarded, *adj.* delayed; mentally deficient *or* handicapped, brain-damaged, moronic; backward, slow. See SLOWNESS, INSANITY.

retch, *v.i.* vomit (see EJECTION).

RETENTION

Nouns—**1,** retention, retaining, holding, keeping, custody, maintenance, PRESERVATION; hold, grasp, gripe, grip, clutch[es]; snare, trap. See POSSESSION, RESTRAINT, TENACITY.

2, retentiveness, retentivity, MEMORY.

3, fangs, teeth, claws, talons, nails, hooks, tentacles, nipper, pincer, tusk; paw, hand, finger, digit, fist, jaws; tongs, forceps, tweezers, pincers, nippers, pliers, clasp, dog, wrench, cramp, clamp, chuck, vise, Visegrip; grapnel, grappling iron *or* hook.

Verbs—**1,** retain, hold, keep, maintain, restrain, hold fast *or* tight, hold one's own; clinch, clench, grasp, grip, gripe, hug, hand *or* hold on to; save, preserve, secure, husband, reserve, STORE, withhold, hold *or* keep back, keep close, have a firm hold on, have in stock; keep on; entail, tie up, settle.

2, remember, recall, recollect, bear in mind (see MEMORY).

Adjectives—retentive, retaining, keeping, holding, prehensile; unforfeited, undeprived, undisposed, incommunicable, uncommunicated, inalienable; unforgetting, dependable, tenacious, of good memory.

Antonyms, see RELINQUISHMENT, LOSS.

---

reticence, *n.* reserve, TACITURNITY, muteness. See CONCEALMENT.

retinue, *n.* train, following, suite, cortege, attendants, retainers. See ACCOMPANIMENT, CONTINUITY, SERVANT.

retire, *v.* withdraw, retreat, leave, resign, rusticate, lie low, keep aloof; put out [to pasture]; go to bed. See SECLUSION, DEPARTURE, RECESSION, RESIGNATION, REPOSE.

retiring, *adj.* modest, unassuming, self-effacing, bashful, withdrawn, shy, diffident. See MODESTY, HUMILITY.

retort, *n.* reply, rejoinder, witticism, sally; alembic. *Slang,* comeback. See ANSWER, WIT, RETALIATION.

retract, *v.t.* withdraw, recall, take back, recant, disavow, repudiate, revoke. See NULLIFICATION, NEGATION.

retreat, *n.* withdrawal, retirement; seclusion; shelter, asylum; refuge, resort. See ABODE. —*v.i.* withdraw, retire, fall back. See REGRESSION, DEPARTURE, ESCAPE.

retrench, *v.* cut [down], reduce, decrease, curtail; economize; cut back. See ECONOMY, DEDUCTION.

retribution, *n.* compensation, redress, reparation, reprisal, reciprocation; nemesis; amends. See RETALIATION, PAYMENT.

retrieve, *v.t.* recover, regain, reclaim, repair, restore, make amends, fetch. See RESTORATION, LIBERATION, TRANSPORTATION.

retroactive, *adj.* retrospective, regressive, *ex post facto*. See PAST.

retrograde, *adj.* retreating, retrogressive, reversed, deteriorating, degenerate, decadent. See REGRESSION.

retrogress, *v.i.* revert, decline. See REVERSION, REGRESSION, DETERIORATION.

retrospect, *n.* reminiscence, remembrance, retrospection, review. See MEMORY.

retrospective, *adj.* looking backward, reminiscent; retroactive. See PAST. —*n.* exhibition, showing. See PAINTING.

return, *v.* restore, put back, bring back, echo, yield, render, reply, ANSWER, reciprocate; nominate, elect; come back, recur, reappear, revert. See RESTORATION. —*n.* ARRIVAL, homecoming, REVERSION, recurrence, reappearance, rebound, ANSWER, reply, recovery, RETALI-

ATION, restitution, compensation; profit, yield. See REPETITION, RECOIL, REGULARITY.

reunion, *n.* gathering, assembling, convention; reconciliation. See SOCIALITY, RESTORATION.

revamp, *v.t* do *or* make over; recast, rework, rewrite; rehash, remodel, redesign, modernize, improve. See CHANGE, RESTORATION.

reveal, *v.t.* disclose, show, divulge, announce, display, exhibit, expose, bare. See DISCLOSURE, VISIBILITY.

revel, *v.i.* disport, gambol, romp, carouse; delight in, enjoy. See PLEASURE. —*n.* lark, spree, carouse. See AMUSEMENT, REJOICING.

revelation, *n.* DISCLOSURE, manifestation, exposition, revealment; Bible. See SACRED WRITINGS.

revelry, *n.* merrymaking, festivity, conviviality, jollification. See AMUSEMENT, REJOICING.

revenge, *n.* & *v.* See RETALIATION.

revenue, *n.* income, receipts; earnings, profits, net, yield, dividends; taxes, tariff, customs, duties. See RECEIVING.

reverberate, *v.i.* reecho, respond, be reflected. See SOUND, LOUDNESS, RECOIL.

revere, *v.t.* venerate, honor, RESPECT, esteem, admire; WORSHIP. See LOVE, PIETY.

reverend, *adj.* venerable, worshipful. See RESPECT, CLERGY.

reverent, *adj.* respectful; devout. See RESPECT, PIETY.

reverie, *n.* daydream, musing, fancy, brown study, wool-gathering. See IMAGINATION, INATTENTION.

reversal, *n.* setback; turnabout, tit-for-tat; INVERSION; repeal; upset; abrogation. See CHANGE, REVERSION.

reverse, *n.* antithesis, converse, opposite; misfortune, setback, comedown, defeat; tail, back (of coin), about-face, rightabout. See OPPOSITION. —*v.t.* transpose, invert, evert, turn around; back; revoke, annul, set aside. See NULLIFICATION.

REVERSION

Nouns—**1,** reversion, reverse, reversal, return[ing], reconversion; atavism, reversion to type; turning point, turn of the tide; REGRESSION, relapse, recurrence; RESTORATION; INVERSION; RECOIL, reaction, backlash. See TRANSFER. **2,** throwback, revenant, atavist; repeater, recidivist, backslider; escheat, lapse, succession; reversionist.

Verbs—revert, return, reverse; turn, hark, *or* go back; recur, recidivate, recrudesce, relapse; restore; retreat, RECOIL; turn the tide *or* scale[s]; regress, retrogress, backslide, escheat, lapse.

Adjectives—reversionary, reversive, reversional, regressive, retrogressive, recidivist; reactionary; atavistic; reversionable.

Antonyms, see CHANGE.

---

review, *v.t.* reexamine, reconsider, revise, recall, rehearse, criticize, inspect. See INQUIRY, MEMORY, ATTENTION. —*n.* retrospection, recollection; critique, criticism; inspection, parade; résumé, recapitulation, summary. See DRAMA, REPETITION, THOUGHT, JUDGMENT.

revile, *v.t.* abuse, vilify, malign, asperse, calumniate, deride. See CONTEMPT, DETRACTION.

revise, *v.t.* alter, correct, reconsider, edit, amend, rewrite. See IMPROVEMENT.

revision, *n.* redaction; emendation, IMPROVEMENT; new version, remake, rewrite, new edition; old wine in new bottles; innovation, enlargement.

revival, *n.* resuscitation, revivification, reanimation; WORSHIP, camp meeting; reestablishment, reintroduction.

See RESTORATION.

revivalist, *n.* evangelist, gospel shouter, jubilee singer. See PIETY.

revive, *v.* reanimate, revivify; refresh; bring back, reestablish; rally, perk up. See RESTORATION.

revoke, *v.t.* recall, repeal, annul, rescind, withdraw, abrogate; recant, repudiate, disavow. See NULLIFICATION.

revolt, *n.* uprising, rebellion, insurgence, insurrection, mutiny, sedition; demonstration. See DISOBEDIENCE, REVOLUTION.

revolting, *adj.* disgusting, repellent, loathsome, repulsive. See UNCLEANNESS.

REVOLUTION

Nouns—**1,** revolution, radical *or* sweeping CHANGE, clean sweep; coup, *coup d'état,* uprising, counterrevolution, shakeup, breakup, upset, overthrow, reversal, debacle, cataclysm, upheaval, convulsion, revulsion. See DESTRUCTION.

2, insurrection, rebellion, revolt, insurgence, mutiny; RETALIATION; riot, uprising, DISORDER, sabotage. See RESISTANCE, WARFARE.

3, revolutionary, rabblerouser, rebel; anarchist; red, Bolshevik, Jacobin, Fenian, *etc.*

4, see ROTATION.

Verbs—**1,** revolutionize, change radically, remodel, recast, refashion, reform, change the face of, break with the past.

2, rebel, revolt. *Slang,* kick over the traces.

Adjectives—revolutionary, anarchic, rebellious, insurgent, radical, revulsionary, cataclysmic; Bolshevist, Fenian.

Antonyms, see INACTIVITY, PERMANENCE.

revolve, *v.* rotate, roll, circle, spin, recur. See ROTATION.

revolver, *n.* handgun, pistol, repeater. *Colloq.,* six-shooter, sixgun. See ARMS.

revue, *n.* review, vaudeville; Follies, New Faces, *etc.* See DRAMA.

revulsion, *n.* DISLIKE, distaste, aversion, repugnance, disgust, repulsion.

reward, *n.* recompense, remuneration, meed, prize, guerdon; indemnity, indemnification; quittance; compensation, reparation, redress (see RESTORATION); perquisite; spoils; salary, pay, PAYMENT; tribute, bonus, tip, premium, fee, honorarium. *Slang,* jackpot, payoff. —*v.* recompense, repay, requite, remunerate, compensate; enrich, indemnify, satisfy; pay off.

rhapsody, *n.* ecstasy, exaltation, transport, rapture; effusion, tribute, eulogy, panegyric, lyricism. See PLEASURE, POETRY.

rhetoric, *n.* oratory, eloquence, elocution, declamation, floridity. See SPEECH.

rheumatism, *n.* inflammation, ache; rheumatoid arthritis, sciatica, gout, bursitis, lumbago, backache; neuritis, rheumatic fever. *Colloq.,* rheumatics, the rheumatiz, the misery. See DISEASE.

rhyme, *n.* alliteration, assonance; verse, poesy, doggerel; agreement, harmony, concord, SIMILARITY. See POETRY.

rhythmic, *adj.* metrical, pulsating, periodic, recurrent. See REGULARITY.

rib, *v.t., colloq.,* tease, kid. *Colloq.,* razz. *Slang,* roast. See WIT.

ribald, *adj.* coarse, low, broad, vulgar; profane, blasphemous. See IMPURITY, VULGARITY.

ribbon, *n.* riband, strip; badge; (*pl.*) shreds, tatters. See FILAMENT, REPUTE, DISJUNCTION.

rich, *adj.* wealthy, affluent, opulent; fruitful, fertile, luxuriant; vivid;

fattening; abundant, bountiful; sumptuous; gorgeous; sonorous, mellow. See MONEY, ORNAMENT.

riches, *n.pl.* wealth, possession, fortune, affluence, opulence. See MONEY.

rich man, *n.* Croesus, Midas, Dives, [multi]millionaire, capitalist, moneybags. See MONEY.

rickety, *adj.* shaky, infirm, weak, ramshackle; rachitic. See WEAKNESS, DISEASE.

ricochet, *n.* bounce, rebound, carom, RECOIL. —*v.i.* bounce off, carom, cannon (*Brit.*), glance off, deflect, reflect, skip, skim, RECOIL.

rid, *v.t.* free, disburden, disencumber. See EJECTION, LIBERATION, LOSS.

riddle, *n.* conundrum, enigma, puzzle; problem, poser. See SECRET, DIFFICULTY, UNINTELLIGIBILITY.

ride, *v.i.* drive, tour, journey, travel; jog, gallop, trot, *etc.;* cycle, pedal. —*v.t.* be borne; sit (a horse); mount, straddle; tease, harass. See SUPPORT, TRAVEL, RIDICULE.

rider, *n.* postscript, codicil, ADDITION; horseman, cyclist, passenger, *etc.* See TRAVEL.

ridge, *n.* fold, welt, wrinkle, flange; arete, spine, esker. See HEIGHT.

RIDICULE

Nouns—**1,** ridicule, derision, scoffing, mockery, quiz, banter, irony, persiflage, raillery, chaff, badinage; sarcasm; squib, lampoon, satire, skit, quip, grin, leer. See CONTEMPT.

2, parody, burlesque, travesty, farce, caricature; buffoonery, practical joke. See WIT.

3, ridiculousness, *etc.*, ABSURDITY; laughingstock, fool, object of ridicule, fair game, April fool, jest, joke, queer *or* odd fish, mockery, monkey, buffoon. *Slang*, goat, gag. See FOLLY.

Verbs—**1,** ridicule, deride, jeer; laugh, grin, *or* smile at; snigger, snicker, scoff, banter, rally, chaff, joke, twit, gibe, rag, mock, tease, poke fun at, play tricks on, fool, show up; satirize, parody, caricature, lampoon, burlesque, travesty, make fun of, make game of, make a fool of. *Colloq.*, give a bad time. *Slang,* roast.

2, be ridiculous, play the fool, make a fool of oneself, commit an absurdity, raise a laugh.

Adjectives—derisive, derisory, mock; sarcastic, cutting, facetious; ironical, quizzical, burlesque, satirical, scurrilous.

Antonyms, see RESPECT.

---

ridiculous, *adj.* laughable, absurd, preposterous. See ABSURDITY.

riding, *n.* horsemanship, motoring; district, bailiwick (both *Brit.*). See TRAVEL, REGION.

rife, *adj.* prevalent, current, widespread, epidemic; abundant, plentiful, profuse, teeming. See NEWS, GENERALITY.

riffraff, *n.* rabble, *canaille,* dregs of society. See POPULACE.

rifle, *n.* gun, firearm; piece, carbine, automatic rifle; [sub]machine gun; *chassepot,* culverine, needle gun; flintlock, wheel lock, matchlock. See ARMS.

rift, *n.* crack, cleft, crevice, fissure; schism, breach. See INTERVAL.

rig, *v.* equip, furnish, fit out; improvise, jury-rig; appoint; scheme, manipulate, maneuver. *Colloq.,* fix; clothe, outfit. *Slang,* frame. —*n.* rigging, ropes, ropework, cordage, ratlines, shrouds, stays, wires; equipment, outfit, fittings, furnishings; VEHICLE; apparatus, machinery, pump, derrick, well. See PLAN, PROVISION.

RIGHT

Nouns—**1,** right; rightness, dextrality; right hand *or* side, dexter, starboard (*naut.*), recto, decanal side, off side. See SIDE.

2, conservativism, reactionarism, Toryism, *etc.* (see PERMANENCE).

3, conservative, reactionary, Tory; right-hander.

Adjectives—right, dextral, dexter, off [side], starboard, recto; rightist, conservative, Tory, antileftist, reactionary; right-handed; clockwise.

Adverbs—rightward[s], right-handedly, starboard.

Antonyms, see LEFT.

RIGHTNESS

Nouns—**1,** rightness, right, what ought to be, what should be, fitness, propriety; due[ness], rightfulness; morality, PROBITY, honor, VIRTUE, lawfulness. See AGREEMENT.

2, right, privilege, prerogative, title, claim, grant; franchise, license; human *or* civil rights, bill of rights; suffrage, woman's rights, feminism; affirmative action. See PERMISSION, POSSESSION, FREEDOM.

3, [civil, woman's, *etc.* rights] activist; suffragist, feminist, suffragette (*archaic*).

4, correctness, accuracy, precision; exactness, TRUTH.

Verbs—**1,** be right *or* just, stand to reason.

2, right, make right, correct, remedy, see justice done, play fair, do justice to, recompense, hold the scales even, give every one his due.

Adjectives—**1,** right, upright, good; rightful, just, equitable, due, square, fit[ting], meet, seemly, reasonable, suitable, becoming; decorous, creditable; allowable, lawful, legal, legitimate, licit, in the right.

2, right, correct, proper, precise, exact, accurate, true. *Slang,* right on.

Adverbs—rightly, justly, fairly, correctly; in justice, in equity, in reason, without distinction of persons, on even terms; just so.

Antonyms, see WRONG, INJUSTICE.

righteous, *adj.* godly, upright, just, moral, good; puritanical; devout, virtuous. See VIRTUE.

rightful, *adj.* See RIGHTNESS.

rigid, *adj.* stiff, inflexible, unyielding; set, firm, obdurate, strict; rigorous, cleancut. See HARDNESS, SEVERITY, OBSTINACY.

rigor, *n.* harshness, hardness, austerity, SEVERITY, stringency, rigorousness, strictness, rigidity, inflexibility, sternness.

rile, *v.t., colloq.,* annoy, vex. See DISCONTENT.

rill, *n.* brook, stream. See WATER.

rim, *n.* EDGE, border, margin, curb, brink.

rime, *n.* ice, [hoar]frost. See COLD.

rind, *n.* skin, peel, epicarp, integument. See COVERING.

ring, *v.* encircle, girdle, environ, encompass, hem in; toll, chime, clang, peal, tinkle; resound, reverberate, re-echo. See SOUND. —*n.* circlet, circle, annulet, hoop, signet, girdle; machine, gang, clique; ARENA; ringing, peal, chime. See PARTY, CIRCULARITY.

ringer, *n., slang,* dead ringer, double, look-alike; substitute; pretender, fraud, poseur. See SIMILARITY, DECEPTION, SUBSTITUTION.

ringleader, *n.* rabblerouser, demagogue. See CAUSE.

rink, *n.* course, drome, skating palace; icedrome, rollerdrome.

See ARENA, AMUSEMENT.

rinse, *v.* rewash, dip, splash; tint, color, touch up. See CLEANNESS. —*n.* conditioner, hairdressing, hair rinse.

riot, *n.* brawl, uprising; DISORDER, row, fracas, uproar, tumult. See DISOBEDIENCE, VIOLENCE.

rip, *v.t.* tear, split, rend, slit, sever, part. See DISJUNCTION.

ripe, *adj.* mature[d], perfect[ed], complete, mellow, consummate, ready. See PREPARATION, AGE, COMPLETION.

ripen, *v.t.* mature, prepare, perfect, mellow, season, temper. See CHANGE, COMPLETION.

ripoff, *n., slang,* DECEPTION, swindle.

riposte, *n.* thrust, counterthrust *or* -stroke, parry, stroke; repartee, witticism, mot. *Slang,* [wise]crack. See WIT, ANSWER.

ripple, *v.i.* gurgle, babble, purl. —*n.* riffle, wavelet. See AGITATION, WATER.

rise, *v.i.* arise, ascend, soar; slope upward; loom, appear; INCREASE, augment; originate, spring from; get up; prosper; revolt, rebel. —*n.* ASCENT; acclivity, slope; origin, source; appreciation, INCREASE; promotion, advancement; revolt; *slang,* reaction. See OBLIQUITY, BEGINNING, CAUSE, PROGRESSION, DISOBEDIENCE.

risible, *adj.* laughable; jovial, merry. See CHEERFULNESS, ABSURDITY.

risk, *v.t.* CHANCE, venture, hazard, gamble, jeopardize; invest. See DANGER, RASHNESS.

risqué, *adj.* suggestive, indelicate, off-color, racy, spicy, sexy, daring. See IMPURITY.

RITE

Nouns—**1,** rite, ceremony, ceremonial, ordinance, observance, CELEBRATION, duty, form, function, office, solemnity, sacrament; service. See RELIGION, WORSHIP, OSTENTATION.

2, ministration, preaching, sermon, homily, preachment. See TEACHING.

3, seven sacraments: baptism, christening, immersion; confirmation, laying on of hands; Eucharist, Lord's supper, communion, consecration, transubstantiation, consubstantiation, Mass; penance, ATONEMENT, repentance, confession; extreme unction, last rites; holy orders, ordination; matrimony, MARRIAGE.

4, canonization, transfiguration, telling of beads, processional, purification, incense, holy water, aspersion, offertory, burial, excommunication.

5, relics, rosary, beads, reliquary, host, cross, crucifix, pax, pyx, *agnus Dei,* censer, rood, chrys[o]m.

6, ritual, rubric, canon, ordinal, liturgy, prayer book, Book of Common Prayer, litany, lectionary, missal, breviary, Mass book; psalter, hymn book, hymnal, psalmody, chant.

7, ritualism, ceremonialism, Sabbatarianism; ritualist, Sabbatarian.

8, holy day, feast, fast, Sabbath, Passover, Pentecost, Advent, Christmas, Epiphany, Lent, Holy Week, Easter, Whitsuntide, Michaelmas.

Verbs—perform service, celebrate [the mass], minister, officiate, baptize, christen, confirm, lay hands on, administer *or* receive the sacrament; administer *or* receive extreme unction, anoint, anele; preach, sermonize, lecture, deliver a sermon, homily, *etc.*

Adjectives—ritual, ritualistic, ceremonial, liturgical, baptismal, eucharistical, sacramental.

---

ritzy, *adj., slang,* classy, swell, swank[y], plush, posh. See OSTENTATION.

rival, *n.* competitor, contender, antagonist, emulator. —*v.t.* vie *or* cope with; emulate; exceed, excel. See OPPOSITION, CONTENTION, REPUTE.

river, *n.* waterway (see WATER).

rivet, *n.* pin, bolt. —*v.t.* fasten, bolt, pin; arrest *or* engage the ATTENTION. See CONNECTION.

road, *n.* way, path, track, PASSAGE, highway, roadway, thoroughfare, trail; anchorage. See ABODE.

roam, *v.i.* wander, range, ramble, rove, stray, stroll. See DEVIATION, TRAVEL.

roar, *v.i.* shout, bellow, howl, bawl; resound, roll, rumble, thunder; guffaw. —*n.* uproar, vociferation; roll, rumble, boom, rote; guffaw. See LOUDNESS, CRY, LAMENTATION, REJOICING.

roast, *v.t.* grill, barbecue, broil, bake, toast, parch; *slang,* tease, RIDICULE. See HEAT, FOOD.

rob, *v.t.* plunder, rifle, pillage, steal, purloin, burglarize; defraud. See STEALING.

robe, *n.* cloak, mantle, gown, vestment, robe of state; purple. See CLOTHING.

robot, *n.* automaton, golem, mechanical man, cybernaut; slave, drudge, worker; pawn, cat's-paw, puppet, dummy. See SERVANT, INSTRUMENTALITY, NECESSITY.

robust, *adj.* vigorous, healthy, lusty, strong, sturdy, stalwart; rude, boisterous, rough. See HEALTH, STRENGTH.

rock, *v.i.* swing, sway, oscillate, teeter. See OSCILLATION. —*n.* crag, boulder, cliff, stone; refuge, haven, support, defense; *slang,* diamond, jewel, gem. See LAND, STABILITY.

rock-bottom, *adj.* basic, fundamental. See LOWNESS, SUPPORT.

rocket, *n.* projectile, missile; propulsor; rocket *or* space ship; skyrocket, firework. See ASTRONAUTICS, ARMS, VELOCITY.

rocky, *adj.* rugged, stony, hard; unfeeling; dizzy, shaky. See ROUGHNESS.

rod, *n.* wand, pole, staff, switch, scepter, caduceus; *slang,* pistol (see ARMS). *Slang,* gat. See SUPPORT.

rogue, *n.* vagabond, scoundrel, cheat, scamp; imp. See EVILDOER.

roguery, *n.* knavishness, rascality, mischief. See IMPROBITY, BADNESS.

roguish, *adj.* dishonest; mischievous, prankish, waggish. See AMUSEMENT, IMPROBITY.

roil, *v.t.* disturb, vex, annoy. See DISCONTENT.

roister, *v.i.* bluster, swagger, bully; rollick, frolic, make merry, riot; rejoice, celebrate. *Colloq.,* paint the town [red], carry on, raise hell. See BOASTING, AMUSEMENT.

rôle, *n.* PART, character, career, function, business. See CONDUCT, DRAMA.

roll, *n.* drumming, rumble, rattle, clatter, patter, toll; trill, chime, beat; reverberation, echoing, thunder; tattoo, rat-a-tat, rub-a-dub, pitter-patter, dingdong, ticktock, charivari, quaver, peal of bells; biscuit, bun, muffin, gem, popover, scone (see FOOD). —*v.* drum, rumble (see *n.*); reverberate, re-echo, resound; whirl, twirl. See SOUND, LOUDNESS, ROTATION, CONVOLUTION, ROTUNDITY.

rollback, *n.* reduction, retrenchment. See DECREASE, REGRESSION.

roller, *n.* cylinder, wheel, roll, rouleau, platen, mill; breaker. See ROTATION, ROTUNDITY, WATER.

romance, *n.* novel, love story; exaggeration, fiction, tall story; love affair, gest, fantasy. See DESCRIPTION, IMAGINATION, FALSEHOOD.

romantic, *adj.* sentimental, heroic, picturesque, idealistic; dreamy, poetic, fantastic, visionary, quixotic, fanciful. See IMAGINATION, SENSIBILITY.

romp, *v.i.* frolic, caper, cavort, gambol, frisk. See AMUSEMENT.

roof, *n.* COVERING, housetop, rooftop,

shelter, ceiling; home, rooftree; top, summit. See ABODE, HEIGHT.

rookie, *n., slang,* beginner, novice, greenhorn, tenderfoot. See BEGINNING.

room, *n.* chamber, hall, apartment; SPACE, capacity, elbow-room; lodging. RECEPTACLE, ABODE. —*v.* lodge, put up (see ABODE).

roomer, *n.* tenant, lodger, occupant, boarder, INHABITANT.

roommate, *n.* berth *or* bunk mate. *Colloq.,* bunkie. *Slang,* roomie. See FRIEND.

roomy, *adj.* spacious, commodious, capacious, ample. See SPACE.

roost, *n.* perch, foothold, limb, branch; nest, rookery; *colloq.,* ABODE, residence, refuge, place, berth, bunk, niche. —*v.i.* alight, land, perch on; stay, remain, settle, nestle, bed down; *colloq.,* lodge, inhabit. See LOCATION.

root, *n.* rootlet, radicle, radicel, taproot; radical; base, origin, essence, source; etymon. See NUMERATION, CAUSE. —*v.* plant, implant, fix; eradicate, extirpate; take root; *colloq.,* acclaim, cheer. See LOCATION, ABODE, APPROBATION.

rope, *n.* cord, line; hawser, painter, lanyard; lasso, riata; hangman's noose, execution; string, twist. See FILAMENT.

rosary, *n.* beads, beadroll; garland, bed of roses. See RITE.

roseate, *adj.* rosy, blooming; optimistic, promising, propitious. See COLOR, HOPE.

roster, *n.* LIST, register, roll call, muster; membership; schedule, program; census, count, tally, record, catalog, slate. See PLAN, PREPARATION.

rostrum, *n.* platform, dais, podium, stand, floor, pulpit, lectern. See SUPPORT.

rosy, *adj.* blushing, blooming, bright, promising, hopeful. See COLOR, HOPE.

rot, *v.i.* decay, decompose, putrefy; degenerate, waste. See DETERIORATION. —*n.* decay, decomposition, putrefaction; *slang,* nonsense, twaddle (see UNMEANINGNESS). *Slang,* piffle, baloney.

ROTATION

Nouns—**1,** rotation, revolution, gyration, turning, circulation, roll; circumrotation, circumvolution, circumgyration, turbination, CONVOLUTION.

2, whir, whirl, turn, wheel, pirouette, eddy, vortex, whirlpool, cyclone, tornado; vertigo; maelstrom.

3, wheel, screw, whirligig, windmill, propeller, top, roller, flywheel; caster; axis, axle, spindle, pivot, pin, hinge, pole, swivel, bobbin, mandrel, reel; turbine; carrousel, merry-go-round; rotor, arbor; crank; capstan.

Verbs—rotate, roll, revolve, spin, turn, turn around, swivel, circulate, gyrate, wheel, whirl, twirl, eddy, trundle, bowl, roll up, furl, spin like a top; whirl like a dervish; pivot; crank; turn on one's heel, turn on a dime.

Adjectives—rotary, rotating, rotatory, rotational, rotative, whirling, circumrotatory, trochilic, dizzying, vertiginous, gyratory, vortical; centrifugal, centripetal.

Antonyms, see DIRECTION, STRAIGHTNESS.

---

rotten, *adj.* decomposed, putrefied, putrid; unsound, treacherous; corrupt, dishonest; offensive, disgusting. See UNCLEANNESS, DETERIORATION, BADNESS.

ROTUNDITY

Nouns—**1,** rotundity, roundness, cylindricity, sphericity, spheroidicity, orbicularity, globosity, globularity. See CIRCULARITY, CURVATURE.
2, cylinder, cylindroid, barrel, drum, roll, rouleau, roller, column, rundle; sphere, globe, ball, spheroid, ellipsoid, drop, spherule, globule, blob, bubble, vesicle, bulb, bullet, pellet, bead, pill, B.B. shot, marble, pea, knob, pommel; cone, conoid, funnel, cornet; pear-, egg-, *or* bell-shape.
3, corpulence, obesity, *embonpoint,* stoutness, plumpness. See CONVEXITY, SIZE.
4, resonance, sonority, grandiloquence, magniloquence (see LOUDNESS).

Verbs—round [out], fill out, sphere, form into a sphere, ball, roll into a ball; snowball, bead; round off.

Adjectives—**1,** rotund[ate], round, circular; cylindric[al], columnar; conic[al], funnel-shaped, infundibular; spherical, orbicular, globular, global, globous, gibbous; beadlike, moniliform; pear-shaped, pyriform; egg-shaped, oval, ovoid, oviform, elliptical; bulbous, fungilliform; bell-shaped, campanulate, campaniform; eccentric.
2, corpulent, obese, fat, stout, plump, chubby, pudgy, buxom, full, full-fleshed, well-padded, roly-poly.
3, resonant, sonorous, rounded, grandiloquent, magniloquent (see LOUDNESS).

Antonyms, see ANGULARITY, LAYER.

---

roué, *n.* rake, libertine. See IMPURITY.

roughage, *n.* fodder, bulk (see FOOD).

roughneck, *n.* boor, rowdy. See VULGARITY, EVILDOER.

ROUGHNESS

Nouns—**1,** roughness, unevenness, ruggedness, asperity, rugosity, corrugation, nodosity, nodulation, hairiness, arborescence, tooth, grain, TEXTURE, ripple.
2, brush, hair, beard, shag, mane, whiskers, mustache, imperial, toupée, goatee, tress, lock, curl, ringlet, bangs, bun; plumage, plumosity, bristle, plume, crest, feather, tuft, fringe.
3, plush, corduroy, nap, pile, floss, fur, down, moss, bur. See SOFTNESS.
4, raspiness, harshness, *etc.* (see *Adjectives*); rasp.

Verbs—rough[en], ruffle, crisp, crumple, corrugate, make one's hackles stand up; rub the wrong way; rumple; go against the grain; grate, rasp, grate [on the ears]; scrabble. See FRICTION.

Adjectives—**1,** rough, uneven, scabrous, knotted, rugged, angular, irregular, crisp, gnarled, unpolished, unsmooth, roughhewn, craggy, cragged, scraggy; prickly, bristling, sharp; lumpy, bumpy, knobbed, ribbed, corduroy.
2, feathery, plumose, tufted, hairy, ciliated, filamentous, hirsute; bushy, leafy, whiskery, bearded, pilous, pilose, filar, shaggy, shagged, fringed, setaceous, bristly.
3, raspy, harsh, coarse, hoarse, husky, throaty, guttural, raucous, croaking.

Antonyms, see SMOOTHNESS.

---

round, *adj.* circular, annular, spherical, globular, cylindrical; approximate. See CIRCULARITY, ROTUNDITY, NUMERATION. —*n.* revolution, cycle; CIRCUIT, ambit, course, itinerary, beat; series, catch, rondeau; routine, rut. See CONTINUITY, ROTATION, BUSINESS.

roundabout, *adj.* circuitous, indirect. See CIRCUITY, DEVIATION, DIFFUSENESS.

roundly, *adv.* vigorously, earnestly. See COMPLETION.

roundup, *n.* gathering; summation. See ASSEMBLAGE.

rouse, *v.* waken, arouse, animate, stir, stimulate, excite, incite, inflame. See CAUSE.

roustabout, *n.* longshoreman (see STEVEDORE); circus hand, ranch hand, odd-job man. See EXERTION.

rout, *v.t.* stampede, panic; discomfit, defeat, repulse. See SUCCESS, FAILURE, POPULACE.

route, *n.* path, road, way, course, passage, track, itinerary. See CIRCUIT, TRAVEL.

routine, *n.* practice, procedure, system, HABIT, round, rut. See BUSINESS, METHOD.

rove, *v.i.* wander, ramble, meander. See DEVIATION, TRAVEL.

roving, *adj.* vagrant, restless, vacillating. See CHANGEABLENESS, TRAVEL.

row, *v.* paddle, scull, oar. See NAVIGATION. —*n.* rank, file, tier, range; quarrel, brawl, rumpus, melée. See CONTINUITY, LENGTH, DISORDER, CONTENTION.

rowboat, *n.* skiff, dinghy, dory, longboat, whaleboat, shell, punt, gig. See SHIP.

rowdy, *n.* ruffian, tough, hoodlum, bully, thug. See EVILDOER, VULGARITY.

rower, *n.* oarsman, oar, sculler, galley slave, waterman, gondolier. See NAVIGATION.

royal, *adj.* regal, imperial, princely, magnificent. See AUTHORITY, NOBILITY.

rub, *v.t.* buff, abrade, scour, polish; chafe, massage, stroke, graze; annoy, disturb. See FRICTION, SMOOTHNESS, DISCONTENT.

rubber, *n.* eraser, eradicator; latex, Lastex, gum arabic, buna, neoprene, caoutchouc, foam rubber; vulcanite; overshoe, galosh, arctic boot, wader, hipboot; rubber band; session, game, series. See MATERIALS, CLOTHING, ELASTICITY.

rubberneck, *n., slang,* sightseer, busybody. See CURIOSITY, VISION.

rubbish, *n.* trash, waste, debris, litter, junk. See USELESSNESS.

rubble, *n.* rubbish, litter, trash, refuse, waste; ruins, debris, remains, detritus, wreckage, shards, pieces. See HARDNESS, USELESSNESS, REMAINDER.

rubdown, *n.* massage (see FRICTION).

rube, *n., slang,* countryman, rustic, hick. See POPULACE.

rude, *adj.* barbarous, crude, primitive, rough, rustic; harsh, rugged; coarse, uncouth; discourteous, uncivil, insolent. See VULGARITY, COURTESY, INELEGANCE, FORMLESSNESS.

rudiment, *n.* element, germ, embryo, root. See CAUSE, BEGINNING.

rudimentary, *adj.* elementary, abecedarian; embryonic, undeveloped, imperfect, vestigial. See BEGINNING, UNPREPAREDNESS.

rueful, *adj.* sorrowful, regretful, doleful; pitiable, deplorable, pathetic. See DEJECTION, PAIN, REGRET.

ruffian, *n.* rowdy, bully, tough, thug. See EVILDOER.

ruffle, *v.t.* gather, shirr, crinkle, corrugate, plait; agitate, ripple, tousle, rumple, disarrange; vex, irritate. See AGITATION, EXCITEMENT, DISORDER, ROUGHNESS, FOLD.

rug, *n.* mat, drugget, shag [rug], throw [rug]; carpet[ing]; lap robe. See COVERING.

rugged, *adj.* craggy; shaggy, rough, unkempt; harsh, stern, austere; hilly, uneven; unpolished, uncultivated; fierce, tempestuous; *colloq.,* robust, hale. See ROUGHNESS, FORMLESSNESS, VIOLENCE, SEVERITY.

ruin, *n.* DESTRUCTION, downfall, perdition; wreck, remains, relic. See FAILURE, REMAINDER. —*v.t.* wreck, raze, demolish; impoverish, seduce, *etc.* See IMPURITY, POVERTY.

ruinous, *adj.* dilapidated, rundown; disastrous, calamitous, desolating, tragic. See DETERIORATION, PAIN, ADVERSITY.

RULE

Nouns—**1,** rule, law, ordinance, regulation, canon, code, act, measure, statute; decision, ruling (see JUDGMENT); commandment, COMMAND; guide, gospel, formula, form, standard, model, precept, convention; MAXIM, aphorism, axiom; natural *or* normal state, normality, average (see MEAN); order of things; standing order, parliamentary law, Procrustean law, law of the Medes and the Persians, hard and fast rule.

2, REGULARITY, uniformity, constancy, consistency, CONFORMITY; punctuality, exactness; routine, custom, HABIT, system, METHOD.

3, see AUTHORITY, MEASUREMENT.

Verbs—settle, fix, establish, determine, decide, adjudicate, judge (see JUDGMENT).

Adjectives—**1,** regular, uniform, symmetrical, constant, steady, systematic, methodical, according to rule; customary, conformable, natural, habitual, normal.

2, conventional, formalistic, rigid, legalistic, ceremonious. See CONFORMITY.

Adverbs—by the rule; as a rule; normally, usually.

Antonyms, see DISOBEDIENCE.

---

ruler, *n.* sovereign (see AUTHORITY); rule, straightedge, folding rule, slide rule. See MEASUREMENT.

rumble, *n.* roll, hollow roar, reverberation. See LOUDNESS.

ruminate, *v.i.* meditate, ponder; chew, chew the cud. See FOOD, THOUGHT.

rummage, *v.* hunt, ransack; junk, odds and ends. See INQUIRY, USELESSNESS.

rumor, *n.* report, hearsay, gossip, common talk. See INFORMATION, NEWS.

rump, *n.* croup, buttocks; REMAINDER, fag, end; steak. See REAR, FOOD.

rumple, *v.t.* muss, dishevel, tousle, wrinkle, crumple. See ROUGHNESS, DISORDER.

run, *v.* scurry, hasten, travel, abscond; ply, flow; liquefy; act, function, extend, complete, pass into, continue, elapse; operate, work; ravel; thrust, compete; smuggle. *Colloq.,* streak. See MOTION, VELOCITY, ILLEGALITY. —*n.* swift pace, race; trip, current, flow; TENDENCY; sequence, course, progress; demand; yard; brook, rill. See PROGRESSION, WATER.

runaway, *n.* fugitive, escapee, truant, renegade; refugee, turntail, fly-by-night, hit and run; landslide, no contest. *Colloq.,* walkover, whitewash. *Slang,* lam[mi]ster. See COWARDICE, ESCAPE, SUCCESS. —*adj.* fugitive; uncontrollable, wild, speeding. See AVOIDANCE, VELOCITY, FREEDOM.

run-down, *adj.* dilapidated, broken-down, tumbledown; weakened, weary, debilitated. *Colloq.,* done up, used up, in a bad way. See DETERIORATION. —*n., colloq.,* narrative, DESCRIPTION.

rung, *n.* rundle, round, spoke; step, degree. See SUPPORT.

runner, *n.* race horse, racer, sprinter; messenger, courier, solicitor; blade, skid; rotor; rug, mat, scarf; operator; sarmentum; tackle. See CONTENTION, COMMUNICATION, SMOOTHNESS, COVERING.

runt, *n.* dwarf, pigmy. —*adj.* stunted, underdeveloped, tiny, wee. See LITTLENESS.

rupture, *n.* DISCORD, schism, split, falling-out; break, rift, breach; hernia. See DISJUNCTION, DISEASE.

rural, *adj.* rustic, provincial, countrified, bucolic, pastoral, arcadian, agrarian. See AGRICULTURE, POPULACE.

ruse, *n.* trick, stratagem, artifice, wile, subterfuge. See CUNNING.

rush, *v.* hurry, scurry, dash, speed, gush, surge; hasten, expedite, precipitate, urge, drive; assault, attack; advance; *colloq.*, court, woo (see LOVE); *colloq.*, pledge, recruit. —*n.* HASTE, run, dash, precipitation; surge, gush, onrush; stampede. See VELOCITY.

rust, *v.* corrode, oxidize; deteriorate. See DETERIORATION, COLOR.

rustic, *adj.* rural, countrified, bucolic; artless, unsophisticated; unpolished, rude, backwoods. See UNSKILLFULNESS. —*n.* peasant, farmer, bumpkin, boor. See POPULACE, AGRICULTURE.

rustle, *v.i.* crackle, swish, whisk, whisper. *Colloq.*, steal (cattle). See SOFTNESS, STEALING.

rusty, *adj.* reddish-brown; timeworn, frowsy, antiquated; out of practice. See INACTIVITY, DETERIORATION, UNSKILLFULNESS.

rut, *n.* groove, beaten path, track, FURROW; HABIT, routine; heat (see FEMALE).

ruthless, *adj.* relentless, merciless, inexorable, cruel. See SEVERITY.

S

Sabbath, *n.* day of rest, Lord's Day; Sunday, Saturday; First Day. See RITE.

sabbatical, *n.* sabbatical year *or* leave, vacation. See REPOSE.

saber, *n.* sabre; sword, scimitar, broadsword, cutlass. See ARMS.

sabotage, *n.* DESTRUCTION, vandalism; subversion. —*v.t.* destroy, cripple, disable, undermine, scuttle. *Colloq.*, throw a monkey wrench in the works. See HINDRANCE.

sac, *n.* pouch, pocket, cyst; vesicle; sound, bladder. See RECEPTACLE.

saccharine, *adj.* sweet, sickening, cloying, sugary, fulsome. See SWEETNESS.

sack, *n.* bag; destruction, pillage; wine. —*v.t.* ravage, plunder, pillage, despoil. See STEALING, RECEPTACLE.

sacrament, *n.* RITE, ceremony; host, consecrated bread *or* wine.

sacred, *adj.* hallowed, sanctified, sacrosanct, holy; consecrated, dedicated, inviolable. See DEITY, PIETY.

sacred cow, *n.* idol, god; tradition; taboo, superstition. See IDOLATRY.

SACRED WRITINGS

Nouns—**1,** scripture, the Scriptures, the Bible, the Book, the Good Book, Holy Writ, Holy Scriptures; Gospel; revelation, inspiration; text; King James Bible, Douay Bible, Vulgate; Talmud, Masorah, Torah; Haggadah, Halakah; exegesis (see INTERPRETATION).

2, Old Testament, Septuagint, Pentateuch; Octateuch; the Law, Jewish Law, the Prophets; major *or* minor Prophets; Hagiographa, Hagiology; Hierographa, Apocrypha.

3, New Testament; Gospels, Evangelists, Acts, Epistles, Apocalypse, Revelation.

4, Koran, Alcoran; the Eddas; Zend-Avesta; Veda, Upanishad, Bhagavad-Gita; Book of Mormon.

5, prophet (see PREDICTION); evangelist, apostle, disciple, saint; the Apostolic Fathers; Holy Man; Gautama Buddha, Zoroaster, Lao-tse, Mohammed, Confucius, Joseph Smith.

Adjectives—scriptural, biblical, sacred, prophetic; evangelical, evangelistic, apostolic, inspired, apocalyptic, ecclesiastical, canonical, textuary; exegetic, Masoretic, Talmudic; apocryphal.

Antonyms, see IMPIETY.

sacrifice, *n.* oblation, offering, hecatomb, holocaust; immolation, self-denial. —*v.t.* renounce, give up; immolate. See GIVING, IDOLATRY, ATONEMENT, DESTRUCTION.

sacrilege, *n.* desecration, profanation,

blasphemy, IMPIETY, irreverence, disrespect; defilement; sin, trespass, transgression; vandalism.

sacrosanct, *adj.* hallowed (see SACRED); saintly, snow-white; sanctimonious. *Slang*, lily-white. See DEITY.

sad, *adj.* sorrowful, downcast, dejected, unhappy, woeful, woebegone, depressed, disconsolate; melancholy, gloomy, cheerless, somber, dismal; heavy[-hearted]; regrettable, shameful. *Colloq.*, blue, down; weepy. See DEJECTION, PAIN, BADNESS.

saddle, *n.* seat, pad; packsaddle, panel, pillion; back, joint, ridge, hump, crest. *Slang*, rig, hull. See SUPPORT. —*v.t.* harness; load, encumber, embarrass; blame, accuse. See DUTY.

sadistic, *adj.* cruel, brutal, fiendish; malicious, pernicious. See MALEVOLENCE.

safari, *n.* journey, expedition, trek; caravan. See TRAVEL, PURSUIT.

safeguard, *n.* DEFENSE, protection, shield, egis; passport, safe-conduct, convoy. See SAFETY.

safekeeping, *n.* care, custody, guardianship, protection. See SAFETY.

SAFETY

Nouns—**1,** safety, safeness, SECURITY, surety, assurance; impregnability, invulnerability, invulnerableness; ESCAPE, safety valve; safeguard, passport, safe conduct; confidence (see HOPE).

2, guardianship, wardship, wardenship; tutelage, custody, safekeeping; PRESERVATION, protection, auspices, egis.

3, protector, guardian; keeper, warden, warder; preserver, custodian; duenna, chaperon; escort, convoy; guard, shield (see DEFENSE); guardian angel, tutelary saint; watchman; mother, father; janitor, sentinel, sentry, ranger, scout (see WARNING); garrison, watchdog; Cerberus, doorman, doorkeeper.

4, policeman *or* -woman, patrolman *or* -woman, officer; peace officer, traffic *or* motorcycle officer; constable, sheriff, deputy, state trooper; detective, plainclothesman; mountie, gendarme, bobby; police *or* riot squad, SWAT [team]; shore patrol. *Slang*, cop, copper, flatfoot, bull, flic, Smokey [the bear], fuzz, pig, the Man, nark, Fed.

5, life preserver, lifeline; fender, bumper, buffer; safety zone, island, *etc.* *Colloq.*, security blanket.

6, refuge, asylum, sanctuary; hideout, hideaway; haven, hospice, shelter, safe harbor; any port in a storm; last resort; anchor[age]; home, hospital; retreat, den, lair; precaution (see PREPARATION); quarantine, *cordon sanitaire*.

Verbs—**1,** be safe; ride out *or* weather the storm; land upon one's feet; bear *or* live a charmed life; fall back on; ESCAPE. *Colloq.*, be over the hump. *Slang*, save one's bacon.

2, safeguard, protect; take care *or* charge of (see CARE); preserve, cover, screen, shelter, shroud, flank, ward; ensure; guard (see DEFENSE); escort, convoy, ride herd on; garrison; stand over, watch, mount guard, patrol; take precautions (see PREPARATION); take shelter *or* refuge. *Slang*, hole up.

Adjectives—**1,** safe, secure; in safety *or* security; on the safe side; under the shield *or* egis of; under the wing of; under cover, under lock and key; out of danger, out of harm's way; on sure ground, at anchor, high and dry, above water; unthreatened, unmolested; protected; safe and sound; scatheless, unscathed; out of danger, in the clear.

2, snug, seaworthy; weatherproof, waterproof, fireproof, bulletproof, bombproof; defensible, tenable, proof (against), invulnerable; unassailable, unattackable, impregnable, inexpugnable.

3, harmless (see GOOD); not dangerous; protecting, guardian, tutelary, custodial; preservative; trustworthy.

Adverbs—safely, with safety, with impunity, without risk.

Antonyms, see DANGER.

---

sag, *v.* droop, buckle, warp, curve; slouch, slump; weaken, wilt; decline, languish; lapse, fall off. See OBLIQUITY, PENDENCY, CURVATURE.

saga, *n.* epic, prose narrative. See DESCRIPTION.

sagacious, *adj.* penetrating, shrewd, astute. See INTELLIGENCE.

sage, *n. & adj.* See KNOWLEDGE.

sail, *v.* cruise, voyage; navigate, traverse. See NAVIGATION. —*n.* canvas; moonsail, moonraker; jib, foresail, lateen, lug, mainsail, mizzen, spanker, topsail. See SHIP.

sailboat, *n.* See SHIP.

sailor, *n.* seaman, mariner (see NAVIGATION).

saint, *n.* hallow, pietist, apostle; votary; saintess, patroness; martyr; pir; saintling, saint-errant. *Colloq.,* angel, paragon. See PIETY, INNOCENCE, VIRTUE.

sainted, *adj.* saintly; hallowed, sacred. See PIETY, VIRTUE.

sake, *n.* purpose, motive, reason; behalf, regard, good. See INTENTION.

salad, *n.* greens, herb, lettuce; tossed salad, cole slaw, aspic. See FOOD.

salary, *n.* stipend, pay, remuneration, wage[s], hire, compensation, PAYMENT. See RECEIVING.

SALE

Nouns—**1,** sale, selling, disposal; auction, vendue, market, custom, BARTER; BUSINESS; salesmanship; vendibility, vendibleness, salability; sales talk.

2, clearance sale, liquidation, white sale, end-of-month sale; bargain basement *or* counter; closeout, fire sale; black market, gray market; garage, yard, *or* tag sale, flea market; close-out sale, going-out-of-business sale; land-office business. See CHEAPNESS.

3, consumer goods *or* items, merchandise, wares, commodities; effects; goods, articles; stock [in trade]; supplies, stores, cargo; produce, *etc.*

4, seller, vendor, vender; merchant, trader, dealer, tradesman, merchandiser; shopkeeper, storekeeper; businessman *or* -woman; retailer, wholesaler, middleman, jobber; salesperson, -woman, -girl, -lady, *or* -man, [sales] clerk, monger, solicitor, huckster, hawker, peddler, pedlar; sutler, costermonger, fishmonger; canvasser, agent, door-to-door salesman; traveling salesman, roadman, sales agent; cashier; auctioneer. See AGENT.

5, purveyor, supplier, caterer, commissary, sutler; grocer, druggist, soda jerk, *etc.;* quartermaster; batman, steward, purser, supercargo (see PROVISION).

6, shopping center, mall; store, department store, shop, five-and-dime, mart, market, emporium, commissary, bazaar, fair.

Verbs—sell, vend, dispose of, effect a sale; trade, merchandise, market, OFFER, BARTER, distribute, dispense, wholesale, retail; deal in, handle; traffic (in); liquidate, turn into money, realize, auction (off); bring under the hammer; put up [at auction *or* for sale]; hawk, peddle, bring to market; undersell; sell out; make *or* drive a bargain. See SUCCESS.

Adjectives—salable, marketable, vendible; unsalable, unpurchased, unbought; commercial; cut-rate, bargain-counter.

Adverbs—for sale, on sale, on the market, over *or* under the counter;

marked up *or* down, under the hammer, on the [auction] block; in *or* on the market.

Antonyms, see PURCHASE.

---

salient, *adj.* outstanding, prominent, striking, conspicuous; notable, momentous, signal. See IMPORTANCE, ANGULARITY, CONVEXITY.

saliva, *n.* spit, spittle, sputum. See EXCRETION.

salivate, *v.i.* drool, slaver. See EXCRETION.

sallow, *adj.* yellow, muddy; sickly, pallid, wan, jaundiced. See COLOR, COLORLESSNESS.

sally, *n.* sortie, raid, foray, ATTACK; excursion, expedition, trip; outburst, outbreak; banter, riposte, repartee. See WIT, DEPARTURE.

salmon, *n.* kipper, lox; alevin, parr, smolt, samlet, *etc.* See FOOD, ANIMAL.

salon, *n.* drawing room, parlor, ballroom; gathering, reception, exhibition; gallery, studio, atelier, workshop, showroom; beauty parlor. See SOCIALITY, RECEPTACLE, BEAUTY.

saloon, *n.* bar, tavern, taproom, bistro; hall, dining room, main cabin; sedan, four-door. *Slang,* oasis. See DRINKING, FOOD, VEHICLE.

salt, *v.t.* salinize; season; pickle, brine, drysalt, preserve, souse; *colloq.,* salt away, invest, bank, save. See PRESERVATION, STORE.

salty, *adj.* briny, brackish, saline; corned, salted; racy, pungent. See TASTE, PUNGENCY.

salubrity, *n.* healthfulness, wholesomeness. See HEALTH.

salutary, *adj.* healthful, salubrious, wholesome; healing, medicinal, sanatory; tonic; beneficial, good. See HEALTH, GOODNESS.

salutation, *n.* salute, address, greeting, welcome; reception, respects, salvo; salaam, bow, curtsy. See COURTESY.

salute, *v.* welcome, greet, hail; uncover, bow, curtsy, present arms, dip colors. See COURTESY, CONGRATULATION, RESPECT.

salvage, *n.* salvation, rescue, retrieval, recovery, reclamation; flotsam, jetsam. —*v.t.* rescue, save, recover, retrieve, redeem, reclaim, rehabilitate; snatch from the jaws of death. See RESTORATION, LIBERATION.

salvation, *n.* redemption, deliverance, reclamation, salvage. See PIETY, RESTORATION.

salve, *n.* ointment, balm, unguent; REMEDY, lenitive, emollient.

salvo, *n.* volley, gunfire, burst; discharge, broadside, fusillade, rafale; strafing, shellfire; peppering, riddling; fanfare, salute; proviso, QUALIFICATION. See ATTACK, CELEBRATION.

same, *adj.* identical, selfsame, interchangeable, alike, equivalent; monotonous. See IDENTITY.

sample, *n.* specimen, example, exemplar, pattern; prototype, archetype; trial, portion, TASTE, teaser. See CONFORMITY.

sanatorium, *n.* sanitarium, health resort, retreat, hospital, rest home. See REMEDY, INSANITY, ABODE.

sanctify, *v.t.* consecrate, bless, hallow, purify, beatify; sanction, authorize. See DEITY, PIETY, PERMISSION.

sanctimonious, *adj.* pietistic, sacrosanct; self-righteous, holier-than-thou; hypocritical. *Colloq.,* goody-goody. See IMPIETY.

sanction, *n.* PERMISSION, confirmation, ratification, approval, APPROBATION; interdiction, penalty, punishment. See LEGALITY.

sanctuary, *n.* chancel; refuge, asylum, immunity. See TEMPLE, ABODE.

sand, *n.* grit, granules; particle, grain, speck; beach, strand, desert, dune; abrasive; silica, otolith; COURAGE, pluck, spunk. See LAND, POWDERINESS. —*v.* sprinkle, dust, powder; smooth, polish, abrade, sandpaper. See SMOOTHNESS, FRICTION.

sandal, *n.* slipper; thong, flip-flop; loafer. See CLOTHING.

sandwich, *n.* combination, club, deli, hero, *etc.* sandwich; lamination. —*v.t.* insert; laminate. See FOOD, BETWEEN.

sane, *adj.* rational (see SANITY).

sanguinary, *adj.* sanguineous, gory, bloody; bloodthirsty, murderous, savage, cruel. See KILLING.

sanguine, *adj.* cheerful, confident, hopeful; ruddy. See HOPE, CHEERFULNESS, HEALTH.

sanitarium, *n.* See SANATORIUM.

sanitary, *adj.* hygienic, clean, sterilized, germfree, safe, aseptic, antiseptic. See CLEANNESS, HEALTH.

SANITY

Nouns—sanity, saneness, soundness, reason; rationality, normality, sobriety; lucidity; senses, sound mind, *mens sana [in corpore sano]*. See INTELLECT.

Verbs—be sane, keep one's senses *or* reason, have it all together; come to one's senses, sober up; bring to one's senses. *Slang,* have all one's marbles *or* buttons.

Adjectives—sane, rational, reasonable, *compos mentis*, of sound mind; self-possessed; sober, in one's right mind; in possession of one's faculties. *Colloq.*, all there *or* here, hitting on all cylinders.

Adverbs—sanely, reasonably, *etc.;* in reason, within reason.

Antonyms, see INSANITY.

---

sap, *n.* plant juice, lifeblood; vigor, vitality; trench, furrow; *slang,* fool (see IGNORANCE). See FLUIDITY, INTRINSIC. —*v.t.* undermine; tunnel; enfeeble, debilitate, devitalize. See CONCAVITY, DETERIORATION, WEAKNESS.

sapid, *adj.* savory (see TASTE).

sapling, *n.* seedling, treelet, treeling; stripling, youngster. See YOUTH.

sarcastic, *adj.* scornful, contemptuous, withering, cynical, satiric, ironical, sardonic. See RIDICULE, DISRESPECT.

sardonic, *adj.* scornful, derisive; caustic, malicious, twisted. See DISAPPROBATION.

sash, *n.* casement, casing; waistband, cummerbund, scarf; obi, baldric. See CLOTHING, SUPPORT, CIRCUMSCRIPTION.

Satan, *n.*, **satanic,** *adj.* See DEMON.

satchel, *n.* bag, carpetbag, schoolbag. See RECEPTACLE.

satellite, *n.* hireling, dummy, puppet; moon; artificial satellite, space station; slave state. See ASTRONAUTICS, UNIVERSE, ACCOMPANIMENT, AUXILIARY.

satiate, *v.* sate, satisfy; cloy, jade, make blasé; quench, slake, pall; glut, gorge, surfeit, bore; spoil. See SUFFICIENCY.

satire, *n.* RIDICULE, sarcasm, irony, mockery, travesty, burlesque.

satirical, *adj.* cutting, bitter, sarcastic, wry, ironic, sardonic, lampooning, cynical. See DISAPPROBATION.

satisfaction, *n.* COMPENSATION, gratification, enjoyment, CONTENT, contentment; ATONEMENT, reparation, redress, amends; fulfillment. See PLEASURE, PAYMENT, SUFFICIENCY.

satisfy, *v.t.* CONTENT, set at ease; gratify, sate, appease; convince, assure; pay, liquidate, discharge; fulfill, meet; suffice, do, ANSWER. See PLEASURE, BELIEF, PAYMENT, SUFFICIENCY.

saturate, *v.t.* soak, fill, drench, impregnate, imbue. See COMPLETION, MOISTURE, SUFFICIENCY.

saturnalia, *n.* festival, carnival; revel[ry], rejoicing, celebration. See AMUSEMENT.

saturnine, *adj.* morose, phlegmatic. See DEJECTION.

satyr, *n.* faun, goat-man, panisc, demigod, godling; sensualist, lecher, rake, roué, wanton. See MYTHICAL

DEITIES, IMPURITY, DEMON.

sauce, *n.* dressing, dip, gravy; compote; fillip, flavor, zest, TASTE; *slang,* liquor; *colloq.,* INSOLENCE. See FOOD, DRINKING.

saucy, *adj.* pert, impertinent, impudent, bold; smart, chic, piquant. See INSOLENCE.

saunter, *v.i.* stroll, loiter, amble, meander, ramble. See TRAVEL, SLOWNESS.

sausage, *n.* frankfurter, *Wurst,* kielbasa, salami, pepperoni; liverwurst, bratwurst, *etc. Colloq.,* hot dog, wienie. *Slang,* frank. See FOOD.

savage, *adj.* wild, untamed, uncivilized, uncultivated; barbarous, ferocious, fierce, feral, cruel, rude; angry, enraged. See VIOLENCE, MALEVOLENCE, EVILDOER.

save, *v.t.* rescue, deliver, preserve, salvage, safeguard; STORE, lay up, keep, hoard; redeem, convert; spare, avoid; economize, conserve. See PRESERVATION, PIETY. —*prep.* saving, except[ing], barring, but, excluding. See EXCLUSION, LIBERATION.

savings, *n.pl.* backlog, reserves, nest egg, bank account. See STORE, ECONOMY.

savior, *n.* rescuer, liberator; *cap.,* Saviour, Christ, Jesus [of Nazareth], Messiah, the [Lord's] Anointed, Redeemer, Son of God, [our] Lord. See LIBERATION, DEITY.

savory, *adj.* tasty (see TASTE).

saw, *n.* proverb, MAXIM; blade, handsaw, hacksaw, ripsaw, *etc.;* serration. See SHARPNESS. —*v.t.* cut, kerf; scratch, scrape, rasp, grate. See DISJUNCTION, FRICTION.

say, *v.t.* speak, tell, declare, state, aver, affirm, mention, allege, recite; decide. See SPEECH, AFFIRMATION.

saying, *n.* saw, MAXIM, proverb, adage, epigram, dictum, *ipse dixit.* See AFFIRMATION.

scab, *n.* crust, cicatrice, eschar, incrustation; strikebreaker. *Slang,* fink. See COVERING.

scabbard, *n.* sheath, case. See COVERING.

scaffold, *n.* framework, scaffolding, platform; gallows, gibbet. See SUPPORT.

scald, *v.* [par]boil, steam, broil, stew, cook; burn, scorch, scathe, sear, seethe, simmer. See HEAT.

scale, *n.* balance, steelyard; lamina, flake, scab, incrustation, horny plate, squama, lamella, eschar; degree, graduation, table, ratio, proportion; gamut. See MEASUREMENT, LAYER, COVERING, MUSIC, CONTINUITY, GRAVITY. —*v.* weigh; peel, husk, exfoliate, flake; climb, surmount. See DIVESTMENT, ASCENT.

scalp, *n.* hair, epicranium. See COVERING. —*v.t.* strip, flay; fleece, gouge, overcharge. See DIVESTMENT.

scamp, *n.* good-for-nothing, rogue, rascal, scalawag. See EVILDOER. —*v.t.* skimp, scrimp; slight, botch, work carelessly. See NEGLECT.

scamper, *v.i.* run, scurry, scuttle, skitter, scoot, flit, dash, dart. *Colloq.,* skip, hotfoot. *Slang,* skiddoo. See VELOCITY.

scan, *v.t.* examine, study, scrutinize; look over, peruse, survey; contemplate. *Slang,* take a gander at, give the once-over. See VISION, INQUIRY, POETRY.

scandal, *n.* disgrace, infamy, shame, humiliation, stigma; defamation, slander, backbiting, calumny; gossip. See DISREPUTE, DETRACTION, INFORMATION, NEWS.

scandalize, *v.* insult, defame, calumniate, stigmatize; horrify, shock, appall, outrage. See DISAPPROBATION, WRONG.

scant, *adj.* scanty, limited, meager, inadequate, sparse. See INSUFFICIENCY.

scapegoat, *n.* goat, whipping boy; butt, tool, victim, dupe. See SUBSTITUTION.

scar, *n.* blemish, flaw, cicatrix, pock; scab, crust; precipice, rock, crag, cliff. See RECORD. —*v.* cicatrize, mark, pit, scarify, blemish, disfigure, deface, mutilate; mar, damage, dent, scratch. See INTERVAL,

INDICATION, DETERIORATION.

scarce, *adj.* rare, uncommon, deficient, scanty, few. See INSUFFICIENCY, RARITY.

scarcely, *adv.* hardly, barely. See RARITY, LITTLENESS.

scarf, *n.* muffler, neckerchief, shawl; boa; sash, cornet, fichu, choker, veil, stole; cravat; snood, wimple, babushka; prayer shawl, talith. See CLOTHING.

scathe, *v.t.* injure, harm, hurt, scorch; castigate, denounce. *Colloq.,* tear apart, lash into. *Slang,* lambaste. See DETERIORATION.

scatter, *v.t.* strew, disperse, disseminate, dispel, dissipate. See DISPERSION.

scatterbrained, *adj.* absent-minded, flighty, harebrained, daft. *Colloq.,* dizzy, daffy. *Slang,* barmy (*Brit.*). See FOLLY.

scavenge, *v.* look (for), comb, pick, sift, hunt, cull, ransack, glean; dig, grub, root, scratch. *Slang,* scrounge. See INQUIRY.

scenario, *n.* plot, script, text, book, libretto; summary, skeleton, screenplay, photoplay; typescript. See DRAMA, WRITING.

scene, *n.* view, vista, landscape, panorama; site, location, setting; episode, event; outburst, tantrum; picture, tableau, pageant. See APPEARANCE, DRAMA.

scenery, *n.* prospect, landscape, view, scene; *mise en scène,* setting, backdrop, wings, borders, *etc.* See APPEARANCE, DRAMA.

scenic, *adj.* picturesque, theatrical, dramatic, stagy. See DRAMA, APPEARANCE.

scent, *v.t.* smell, detect; perfume. —*n.* ODOR, fragrance, aroma; sachet, perfume; track, trail, spoor.

scepter, *n.* staff, mace, rod, baton, wand; rod of empire; insignia of AUTHORITY.

schedule, *n.* LIST, catalogue, inventory, record, docket; agenda, outline, register; timetable, calendar, time sheet. —*v.t.* PLAN, order, program, slate, book, TIME, docket, designate, appoint.

scheme, *n.* PLAN, plot, project, design, intrigue; system, METHOD; CUNNING.

schism, *n.* DISJUNCTION, division, DISSENT, separation, split; HETERODOXY; factionalism, faction, sect, subdivision.

scholar, *n.* savant, sage (see KNOWLEDGE); bookworm; man of learning, letters, *or* education; pedant, pedagogue; student. See SCHOOL, LEARNING.

scholarship, *n.* learning, erudition, KNOWLEDGE; scholastic *or* financial AID, fellowship, bursary.

SCHOOL

Nouns—**1,** school, academy, university, alma mater, college, seminary, yeshiva, lyceum; institute, institution, institution of [higher] learning; gymnasium; class, semester.

2, day, boarding, primary, elementary, grammar, grade, secondary, junior high, high, summer, [college] preparatory, *or* graduate school; parochial, separate, denominational, public, *or* private school; kindergarten, nursery school; crèche; reformatory, reform school; law *or* medical school; teachers' college, dental college; normal school; correspondence *or* night school; extension school; vocational, technical, trade, business, secretarial, finishing, *or* music school, conservatory; art, dramatic, *or* dancing school; military school *or* academy. *Colloq.,* prep school.

3, campus, quadrangle, grounds.

4, matriculation, graduation, commencement; curriculum, course; tuition; catalog; class, form, grade, seminar; classroom, lecture room *or* hall, home room; desk, blackboard; textbook, schoolbook; slate, chalk, eraser; three R's, ABC's.

5, learner, student (see LEARNING); undergraduate, freshman, sophomore, junior, senior, plebe, yearling, collegian, upperclassman; graduate, alumnus, alumna; bachelor, doctor; faculty, professorship, chair, fellowship; master, proctor; teacher, instructor (see TEACHING); provost, dean, bursar.

6, see ASSEMBLAGE.

Verbs—go to school, attend; matriculate, enroll, register; graduate, be graduated; teach, learn.

Adjectives—scholastic, academic, collegiate; educational, curricular, extracurricular.

---

schooling, *n.* education, LEARNING.

science, *n.* KNOWLEDGE, SKILL, efficiency, technology.

scientific, *adj.* systematic, accurate, exact, sound. See KNOWLEDGE.

scintillate, *v.* glisten, twinkle, sparkle, glitter, coruscate, shine; be charming *or* witty, effervesce. *Slang,* turn on the charm. See LIGHT, INTELLIGENCE, WIT.

scion, *n.* sprout, shoot, twig, cutting, graft; heir, descendant. See POSTERITY.

scissors, *n.pl.* shears, trimmer, cutter, clipper, secateur. See SHARPNESS.

scoff, *v.t.* jeer, be contemptuous *or* derisive (of), flout, laugh (at). See CONTEMPT, DISRESPECT.

scold, *v.* reprove, rebuke, rate, chide, berate, tongue-lash. *Slang,* bawl out. See DISAPPROBATION.

scoop, *n.* scooper, ladle, dipper, spoon; *slang,* NEWS, story, beat, lead, exclusive. *Slang,* dope.—*v.* dig out, lade, hollow, rout, gouge, excavate; *slang,* beat out. See CONCAVITY.

scoot, *v.i., colloq.,* dash, run, dart, scurry, scamper; leave, depart, go, decamp, exit. *Slang,* beat it, scram, vamoose, get lost. See VELOCITY.

scope, *n.* extent, range, sweep, compass, SPACE, sphere, field. See BREADTH, DEGREE, FREEDOM.

scorch, *v.t.* char, singe, brown, blacken, toast, roast, parch, shrivel, wither; denounce, upbraid; *colloq.,* speed. *Colloq.,* burn up the road. See DRYNESS, HEAT.

score, *n.* account, reckoning, tally, record; reason; twenty; music, orchestration, arrangement; notch, scratch. *Slang,* chart. See DEBT, MUSIC, CREDIT, FURROW.

scorn, *n.* CONTEMPT, disdain, superciliousness; derision, ridicule. —*v.t.* despise, disdain, contemn, spurn, neglect. See REJECTION, DISRESPECT.

scoundrel, *n.* knave, villain, rascal, rogue, blackguard. See EVILDOER.

scour, *v.t.* scrub, abrade, polish, cleanse; search, range. See FRICTION, CLEANNESS, INQUIRY.

scourge, *n.* whip, strap, belt, lash, horsewhip; PUNISHMENT, curse, affliction, bane, nuisance, plague. —*v.t.* whip, lash, flay, beat; punish, afflict, plague. See EVIL, BADNESS.

scout, *n.* spy, observer, spotter, outrider, reconnoiterer, forerunner. See PRECEDENCE, INQUIRY.

scowl, *v.i.* frown; lower, glower. See DISAPPROBATION.

scraggly, *adj.* irregular, ragged. See ROUGHNESS.

scramble, *v.i.* clamber, swarm, struggle, scrabble, tussle, scuffle. See CONTENTION, DISORDER, HASTE.

scrap, *n.* bit, crumb, morsel; splinter, fragment, chip; whit, tittle, jot, speck; *slang,* fight, bout, tussle. See LITTLENESS, CONTENTION.

scrapbook, *n.* album, looseleaf. See RECORD.

scrape, *v.* graze, brush; scratch, rasp, abrade, grind; grate; curtsy, bow. See FRICTION. —*n.* abrasion, scratch; DIFFICULTY, plight, predicament.

scratch, *v.* score, gash, scrape, rasp, wound, lacerate, deface; erase, withdraw, reject; scribble, scrawl;

irritate; sputter. See FRICTION, WRITING, FURROW, SHALLOWNESS.

scrawl, *v.t.* scribble, scratch. See WRITING.

scrawny, *adj.* underweight, puny, rawboned, bony, meager, lean. See NARROWNESS.

scream, *v.i.* shriek, screech, shrill, yell, CRY. See LOUDNESS.

screen, *n.* partition, curtain, shield, mask, protection, shelter; netting, mesh; sieve, sifter, bolter; cinema, movies, silver screen. —*v.t.* shelter, shield, protect, hide, conceal, veil, shroud; sift, sort; film, exhibit. See DEFENSE, CONCEALMENT, CLASS, CLEANNESS, CHOICE, DRAMA.

screw, *n.* spiral, helix, volute; twist; propeller, prop, jack; pressure, coercion; extortionist, niggard, skinflint; *slang,* jailer, turnkey. See ROTATION, CONNECTION, PRISON.

scribble, *v.* scrawl, scratch. —*n.* scrawl, hen tracks. See WRITING.

scribe, *n.* scrivener, secretary, amanuensis, clerk, copyist; writer, author. See WRITING.

scrimmage, *n.* free-for-all, fracas, scuffle, tussle, brawl. See CONTENTION.

scrimp, *v.* curtail, limit, pinch, tighten, reduce; economize, skimp, stint, save, niggardize. See ECONOMY, PARSIMONY.

script, *n.* handwriting, penmanship, calligraphy, cursive, round hand; scenario, libretto, book, screenplay, dialogue. See WRITING, DRAMA.

scriptural, *adj.* biblical, sacred; prophetic, evangelical, evangelistic, apostolic, inspired, apocalyptic, ecclesiastical. See SACRED WRITINGS.

Scriptures, *n.pl.* See SACRED WRITINGS.

scroll, *n.* roll, list, memorial; volute, flourish. See ORNAMENT, WRITING.

scrounge, *v.* pilfer, sponge. See STEALING.

scrub, *v.t.* rub, scour, holystone, swab, mop. See FRICTION, CLEANNESS.

scrubby, *adj.* wretched, shabby; undersize, stunted. See SHORTNESS, UNIMPORTANCE.

scruffy, *adj.* unkempt, shabby. See UNCLEANNESS.

scruple, *n.* DOUBT, perplexity, misgiving, reluctance, UNWILLINGNESS, qualm, conscience. See PROBITY.

scrupulous, *adj.* exact, careful; fastidious, meticulous, punctilious; conscientious; upright, moral. See PROBITY.

scrutiny, *n.* examination, inspection, investigation, INQUIRY.

scuff, *v.t.* scratch, abrade, scrape; disfigure. See FRICTION.

scuffle, *n.* strife, tussle, struggle, contest, CONTENTION, fray, fracas, brawl; shuffle.

SCULPTURE

Nouns—**1,** sculpture, sculpting; plastic arts; carving; statuary, statue, statuette, bust, head (see REPRESENTATION); cast (see FORM); relief, relievo; high *or* low relief, bas relief; intaglio, cameo; anaglyph; medal, medallion.

2, marble, bronze, terra cotta, clay, alabaster; ceramics, ceramic ware, pottery, procelain, china, earthenware.

3, sculptor, sculptress, carver, chiseler, modeler. See ARTIST, ENGRAVING.

Verbs—sculpture, carve, grave, chase, cut, chisel, model, FORM, mould; cast.

Adjectives—sculptured; carven, graven; in relief; ceramic, marble, anaglyptic.

---

scum, *n.* froth, foam; slag, dross; mother (in fermentation); riff-raff. See UNCLEANNESS, POPULACE, LAYER.

scurfy, *adj.* flaky, scabby, squamous, flocculent, furfuraceous. See LAYER.

scurrilous, *adj.* abusive, foulmouthed, vituperative, insulting, offensive, coarse, vulgar, opprobrious. See DETRACTION, DISRESPECT.

scurry, *v.i.* hasten, dash, scuttle,

scoot. See HASTE.

scurvy, *n.* scorbutus, scurf, Werlhof's *or* Barlow's disease. —*adj.* scorbutic, scurfy; villainous, mean, low, nasty, vile. See DISEASE, IMPROBITY.

scuttle, *n.* hod, RECEPTACLE, pail, bucket; scoop, shovel; hatch[way], hole, OPENING. —*v.i.* flee, escape, run, scurry. —*v.t.* sink, scupper, swamp, destroy, sabotage; demolish, overthrow, suppress. See DESTRUCTION, VELOCITY, HASTE.

sea, *n.* ocean, main, lake; wave, billow, swell; profusion, MULTITUDE. See WATER.

seacoast, *n.* seashore, seaside, seaboard. See LAND.

seal, *n.* die, stamp, signet; embossment, wafer, stamp; guarantee, confirmation; safeguard, stopper. —*v.t.* stamp, ratify, confirm; fasten, secure, occlude; close, confine. See COMPLETION, CLOSURE.

seam, *n.* ridge, JUNCTION; scar, wrinkle, FURROW; stratum, bed, LAYER.

seaman, *n.* mariner, sailor, salt, tar, seadog, seafarer. *Slang,* gob. See NAVIGATION.

seamstress, *n.* sewer, stitcher; dressmaker, tailor[ess]. See CLOTHING.

seamy, *adj.* sordid, worst. See UNCLEANNESS.

séance, *n.* session, gathering, sitting, COUNCIL; spiritualism, spirit-rapping. See ASSEMBLAGE.

seaplane, *n.* flying boat; hydroplane, amphibian, water plane, aeroboat, supermarine. See AVIATION.

sear, *adj.* sere, dry, arid, desiccated, waterless, dry-as-dust; barren, sterile, effete; yellow, pale, colorless. See DRYNESS, USELESSNESS. —*v.* dry, dehydrate, dessicate; singe, burn, scorch; brand, cauterize; wither, blast; fade, yellow. See HEAT, DRYNESS.

search, *v.t.* hunt, seek, look for; explore, examine, penetrate; probe; test. —*n.* quest, pursuit; INQUIRY, examination, investigation, scrutiny, exploration.

searching, *adj.* penetrating, keen, sharp; rigorous, unsparing. See SEVERITY.

seashore, *n.* seaside, shore, strand, beach; [sea]coast, littoral, coastline, waterfront. See LAND.

seasickness, *n. mal de mer,* naupathia; nausea, queasiness, qualm. See DISEASE.

season, *n.* period, TIME, spell, interval. —*v.t.* harden, acclimate, habituate, inure, accustom; prepare, AGE, cure, ripen, dry out; imbue; spice, flavor. See HABIT, PUNGENCY, CHRONOMETRY.

seasonable, *adj.* suitable, opportune, timely. See EXPEDIENCE, AGREEMENT.

seat, *n.* chair, bench, howdah, *etc.* (see SUPPORT); site, location, ABODE; villa, estate; membership; *colloq.,* buttocks, rump (see REAR).

seaweed, *n.* algae, fucus, kelp, conferva, carrageen. See VEGETABLE.

secede, *v.i.* withdraw, separate, bolt. See RELINQUISHMENT.

SECLUSION

Nouns—**1,** seclusion, privacy; retirement; reclusion, recess; rustication, *rus in urbe;* solitude; solitariness, isolation; loneness, withdrawal, hermitism, ermitism, anchoritism, voluntary exile, aloofness; inhospitality, inhospitableness; unsociability; quarantine; domesticity. See OBSCURITY, CONCEALMENT, UNITY, ASCETICISM.

2, cell, hermitage; cloister, convent; holy of holies, Most Holy Place, *sanctum sanctorum;* depopulation, desertion, desolation; desert, wilderness; retreat, refuge (see SAFETY). See ABODE.

3, recluse, hermit, cenobite, eremite, anchoret, anchorite; St. Anthony; Simeon Stylites; Timon of Athens; solitaire, ruralist, cynic, Diogenes. *Colloq.,* lone wolf, loner. See ASCETICISM.

Verbs—be secluded, keep aloof, stand in the background; shut oneself up, creep into a corner, keep to oneself, keep one's own counsel, withdraw; rusticate; sequester, seclude, retire; take the veil, take orders.

Adjectives—secluded, sequestered, retired, private; conventual, cloistered, out of the world; remote, inaccessible, out of the way; snug, domestic, stay at home; unsociable, unsocial, antisocial; inhospitable, solitary; lone, lonely, lonesome; isolated, single; unfrequented, uninhabited, uninhabitable; tenantless; abandoned.

Adverbs—by oneself; in private, in one's shell, in a world of one's own.

Antonyms, see SOCIALITY.

---

second, *n.* moment, instant, trice, twinkling; backer, supporter, assistant. See INSTANTANEITY, AUXILIARY.

secondary, *adj.* subordinate, minor, inferior, second-rate; resultant, consequent. See INFERIORITY, EFFECT.

second-guess, *v.t.* anticipate, predict. See EXPECTATION.

secondhand, *adj.* used, hand-me-down; indirect, hearsay, unoriginal. See OLDNESS.

second-rate, *adj.* inferior, lesser, secondary, next best; mediocre, second-class. *Colloq.*, also-ran. See INFERIORITY, MEDIOCRITY.

SECRET

Nouns—secret; dead secret, profound secret; mystery; sealed *or* closed book; skeleton in the closet; confidence; problem, enigma, riddle, puzzle, crossword puzzle, [double] acrostic, jigsaw puzzle, nut to crack, conundrum, charade, rebus, logogriph, anagram (see DIFFICULTY); Sphinx, riddle of the Sphinx; labyrinth; UNINTELLIGIBILITY; *terra incognita; arcanum,* esotery, esotericism, occult, occultism. See CONCEALMENT, WONDER, SORCERY, LATENCY.

Verbs—secrete, hide, conceal, disguise; classify; keep to oneself, keep under one's hat, hush up. *Colloq.*, sit on.

Adjectives—**1,** secret, concealed, clandestine, underhand[ed], arcane, enigmatical, recondite, privy, mysterious, puzzling, labyrinthine, veiled, hidden, problematical, paradoxical, inscrutable, unintelligible; esoteric, occult, mystic. *Colloq.*, hush-hush, under the counter.

2, classified; restricted, confidential, secret, top secret, most secret, eyes only.

3, secretive, evasive; uncommunicative, poker-faced, reticent (see TACITURNITY).

Adverbs—secretly, on the sly, like a thief in the night; under one's breath; *sub rosa. Colloq.*, on the q.t. See CONCEALMENT.

Antonyms, see DISCLOSURE, INFORMATION.

---

secretary, *n.* amanuensis, clerk; minister, administrator; desk, escritoire. See WRITING, RECEPTACLE, AUXILIARY, SERVANT.

secrete, *v.t.* hide, conceal, mask; separate, prepare, excrete. See CONCEALMENT, EXCRETION.

sect, *n.* denomination, faction, following, school, fellowship. See CLASS, HETERODOXY.

sectarian, *adj.* denominational; nonconformist, unorthodox, heterodox, heretical; dissident, schismatic, recusant, iconoclastic. See DISSENT, HETERODOXY.

section, *n.* separation, DISJUNCTION, division; segment, PART, portion, cross-section; book, chapter; land, subdivision, sector, REGION; subdivision, subgenus, group, CLASS. —*v.t.* disjoin, divide, separate, bisect, slice, dismember, partition, distribute.

secular, *adj.* lay, temporal, profane, mundane, worldly, earthly. See IRRELIGION, LAITY.

SECURITY

Nouns—**1,** security, guaranty, guarantee; gage, warranty, bond, tie, pledge, plight, mortgage, debenture, hypothecation, bill of sale, lien, pawn; stake, deposit, earnest, collateral. See PROMISE.

2, promissory note; bill [of exchange]; I.O.U.; covenant, acceptance, endorsement, signature; execution, stamp, seal; sponsor, sponsorship; surety, bail; hostage; recognizance; indemnity; authentication, verification, warrant, certificate, voucher, RECORD; probate, attested copy; receipt, acquittance; discharge, release.

3, title deed, instrument; deed, deed poll; assurance, insurance, indenture; charter, compact; paper, parchment, settlement, will, testament, last will and testament; codicil.

4, see SAFETY, JUSTICE.

Verbs—secure; give security, give bail, go bail; put up, deposit, pawn, mortgage, hypothecate; guarantee, pledge, ensure, warrant, assure; accept, endorse, underwrite, insure; execute, stamp; sign, seal.

Antonyms, see DANGER.

sedan, *n.* VEHICLE, automobile, limousine, landau[let], closed *or* touring car; litter, palanquin, palkee. See SUPPORT.

sedate, *adj.* staid, calm, inexcitable, serious, dignified, serene, demure, decorous, composed. See INEXCITABILITY.

sedation, *n.* alleviation; narcosis, hypnosis; sedative. See REMEDY.

sedative, *n.* sedation; tranquilizer, bromide, calmant; sleeping pill; drug, narcotic, opiate, morphine; hypnotic; painkiller, barbiturate, analgesic; Demerol, Nembutal. *Slang,* goof ball. See REMEDY, INACTIVITY, MODERATION.

sedentary, *adj.* stationary, seated; inactive, sluggish, passive; nonmigratory, white-collar, desk, office. *Colloq.,* stay-at-home. See INACTIVITY.

sediment, *n.* alluvium, silt, settlings, precipitate, lees, dregs, heeltap. See REMAINDER, UNCLEANNESS.

sedition, *n.* incitement, insurgence, disloyalty. See DISOBEDIENCE.

seduce, *v.t.* lead astray, lure, entice, corrupt, inveigle; debauch, betray. See IMPURITY, ATTRACTION.

sedulous, *adj.* diligent, industrious, assiduous, persevering, persistent. See ACTIVITY, TENACITY.

see, *v.* view, descry, behold; discern, perceive, comprehend; observe, note; know, experience; ascertain, make sure; consider; meet; escort, attend. See VISION, KNOWLEDGE.

seed, *n.* germ, ovule, semen, milt; CAUSE, origin; offspring, children, descendants; grain, corn. See BEGINNING, ORGANIC MATTER, POSTERITY.

seedy, *adj.* gone to seed *or* to pot; shabby, rundown, shoddy; broken-down, ramshackle; poor, indigent. *Colloq.,* grubby, grimy. See DETERIORATION, POVERTY, DISEASE.

seek, *v.t.* search for, hunt, pursue; request, solicit; try, attempt, endeavor. See INQUIRY, PURSUIT.

seem, *v.i.* appear, look. See APPEARANCE.

seemly, *adj.* decorous, proper, becoming, decent, fitting. See EXPEDIENCE, BEAUTY.

seep, *v.* leak, ooze, drain, drip, exude; trickle. See EGRESS.

seer, seeress, *n.* prophet, crystal-gazer, clairvoyant; soothsayer, oracle. See PREDICTION.

seesaw, *v.i.* teeter[-totter]; waver, vacillate, dilly-dally; crossruff. See OSCILLATION.

seethe, *v.* boil, stew, simmer; steep, soak; fume, chafe. See HEAT, RESENTMENT, AGITATION, EXCITABILITY.

segment, *n.* slice, portion; component, member, branch, PART.

segregate, *v.t.* separate, set *or* keep apart, single out, discriminate; quarantine, isolate; exclude. See EXCLUSION, DISJUNCTION.

seize, *v.t.* grasp, clutch; capture, arrest, appropriate, confiscate; afflict; attach, distrain; comprehend, understand. See STEALING, INTELLIGENCE, ACQVISITION.

seizure, *n.* confiscation, appropriation, arrest, capture; attack, fit, spell, stroke. See ACQUISITION, DISEASE, RESTRAINT.

seldom, *adv.* rarely, not often, infrequently. See RARITY.

select, *v. t.* choose, pick, prefer, elect, opt, specify, designate. See CHOICE.

self, *n.* ego, I; being, essence; personality, IDENTITY, individuality, persona; mind, soul, spirit, self-esteem; inner self *or* being, inner man *or* woman.

self-centered, *adj.* egotistic; selfish. See SELFISHNESS, VANITY.

self-confident, *adj.* self-reliant *or* -assured, sure of oneself, poised, cocky, cocksure, smug. See CERTAINTY, INEXCITABILITY.

self-conscious, *adj.* self-aware, introspective; shy, embarrassed; unsure, hesitant; unnatural, stylized, theatrical. See AFFECTATION.

self-control, *n.* self-discipline, -possession, *or* -restraint; poise, composure; reserve. See RESOLUTION.

self-defense, *n.* self-preservation; martial arts, karate, judo, *etc.* See DEFENSE.

self-denial, *n.* self-sacrifice, abnegation, renunciation, asceticism. See UNSELFISHNESS.

self-effacing, *adj.* diffident, modest. See MODESTY.

self-esteem, *n.* PRIDE, self-respect; egotism, conceit, VANITY.

self-governing, *adj.* autonomous, independent, sovereign. See AUTHORITY.

self-indulgent, *adj.* unrestrained, selfish, sensual, voluptuous, unbridled, sybaritic. See SELFISHNESS.

SELFISHNESS

Nouns—**1,** selfishness, self-indulgence, self-interest; egotism, egoism; VANITY; nepotism; worldliness; egomania, megalomania; illiberality; meanness, PARSIMONY. See MALEVOLENCE.

2, self-seeker, fortune-hunter, worldling; egotist, egoist, monopolist, nepotist; dog in the manger; spoiled child *or* brat.

Verbs—be selfish; indulge oneself; look after one's own interests; feather one's nest; take care of number one; have an eye to the main chance; know on which side one's bread is buttered; give an inch and take an ell.

Adjectives—selfish, self-seeking, self-indulgent, self-interested, self-centered; egotistic, egotistical; mean, mercenary, venal; earthly, mundane; worldly, materialistic, worldly-wise.

Adverbs—selfishly, ungenerously.

Antonyms, see UNSELFISHNESS, LIBERALITY.

---

selfless, *adj.* See UNSELFISHNESS.

self-made, *adj.* autogenous, spontaneous; self-educated, self-taught, autodidactic; raised up by one's own bootstraps. See PRODUCTION, KNOWLEDGE.

self-righteous, *adj.* smug, priggish; supercilious; sacrosanct, sanctimonious; hypocritical, holier than thou. See IMPIETY.

sell, *v.* See SALE.

sellout, *n., colloq.,* deception, betrayal, treachery, double-dealing; depletion, exhaustion; clearance, liquidation, closeout, fire sale; SUCCESS, hit, smash, full house, standing room only, S.R.O. See SALE.

semblance, *n.* likeness, resemblance, aspect; counterfeit, COPY, IMITATION; APPEARANCE, seeming, similitude, show, pretext. See SIMILARITY.

semiliquidity, *n.* stickiness, viscidity, viscosity; glutinosity; adhesiveness; inspissation, incrassation; thickening, gelatinousness; muddiness, miriness, slushiness. See COHERENCE, SOFTNESS.

seminal, *adj.* germinal; rudimentary, fundamental; productive, creative, catalytic, far-reaching. See CAUSE, ORGANIC MATTER.

seminar, *n.* study group, tutorial. See SCHOOL.

seminary, *n.* SCHOOL, academy; theological school; seminar.

senator, *n.* legislator, congressman *or* -woman; solon, lawgiver, statesman. See COUNCIL.

send, *v.t.* dispatch, forward, transmit, broadcast; impel, drive; *slang,* excite, move (see EXCITEMENT). See TRANSFER, PROPULSION.

send-off, *n.* farewell, good-bye; outset, BEGINNING. See DEPARTURE.

senility, *n.* dotage, second childhood, superannuation, old age, degeneration, decrepitude. See AGE, INSANITY, WEAKNESS.

senior, *adj.* elder, older; superior, top-ranking. See AGE.

sensation, *n.* FEELING, perception, consciousness, impression; furor. See SENSIBILITY.

sensational, *adj.* melodramatic, thrilling, startling; lurid, yellow. See EXCITEMENT.

sense, *n.* MEANING, import; perception, feeling; judgment, appreciation; opinion, consensus. See INTELLECT, INTUITION.

senseless, *adj.* unconscious; foolish, stupid, dull; meaningless, unreasonable, absurd. See INSENSIBILITY, ABSURDITY.

SENSIBILITY

Nouns—**1,** sensibility, sensitivity, sensitiveness; FEELING, perceptivity, esthetics; sensation, impression; consciousness (see KNOWLEDGE); sensorium.

2, sensibleness, impressionableness, affectibility; susceptibleness, susceptibility, susceptivity; tenderness, softness; sentimentality, sentimentalism. *Slang,* mush, corn, schmaltz. See IRASCIBILITY, EXCITABILITY.

3, sensation, tickle, tickling, titillation, itch[iness], itching; formication; aura; tingling, prickling; pins and needles; sore spot *or* point; allergy.

Verbs—**1,** be sensible of; feel, perceive; sharpen, cultivate, tutor; impress. See TOUCH.

2, have a tender, warm, *or* sensitive heart, be sensitive; take to, treasure; shrink; touch to the quick, touch the heart.

3, itch, tingle, creep, thrill, sting; prick[le], formicate; tickle, titillate.

Adjectives—sensible, sensitive, sensuous; esthetic, perceptive, sentient; conscious; acute, sharp, keen, vivid, lively, impressive; impressionable; susceptive, susceptible; alive to; gushing; warmhearted, tenderhearted, softhearted; tender, soft, sentimental, romantic; enthusiastic, high-flying, spirited, mettlesome, vivacious, lively, expressive, mobile, excitable; oversensitive, thin-skinned; fastidious; alert, aware. *Slang,* corny, cornball, mushy, sappy.

Antonyms, see INSENSIBILITY.

---

sensitive, *adj.* perceptive, conscious, impressionable, tender, susceptible, sentient; alert, aware; sentimental. See SENSIBILITY.

sensual, *adj.* voluptuous, carnal; salacious, lewd; sybaritic, epicurean. See INTEMPERANCE, PLEASURE.

sensualist, *n.* voluptuary; epicure; libertine. See INTEMPERANCE, PLEASURE.

sensuous, *adj.* sensitive, esthetic, hedonistic; emotional, pleasurable. See SENSIBILITY, PLEASURE.

sentence, *n.* statement, expression; JUDGMENT, decision, penalty. See SPEECH, CONDEMNATION, WRITING.

sententious, *adj.* terse, laconic, pithy, succinct, curt; didactic. See MAXIM, TACITURNITY.

sentient, *adj.* perceptive, sensitive, feeling, responsive, alive. See SENSIBILITY, FEELING.

sentiment, *n.* opinion, FEELING; sensitivity, delicacy, sympathy; motto, toast. See BELIEF, SENSIBILITY.

sentimental, *adj.* emotional, romantic, simpering, maudlin, mawkish. See SENSIBILITY.

sentinel, *n.* sentry, watchman, guard, lookout, picket. See DEFENSE.

separate, *v.* divide, disunite, disconnect, part, detach, sever, keep apart, isolate, segregate, sift, screen; part company. —*adj.* disconnected, distinct, alone, isolate, unconnected, individual. See DISJUNCTION, DIVORCE, EXCLUSION, INTERVAL.

sepulcher, *n.* tomb, vault, crypt, mausoleum, sarcophagus. See INTERMENT.

sequel, *n.* upshot, outcome, continuation; consequence, appendix, postscript; epilogue, afterword. See SEQUENCE.

SEQUENCE

Nouns—**1,** sequence, coming after; going after, following, consecutiveness, succession, extension, continuation, order of succession, successiveness; CONTINUITY. See REAR, PURSUIT, ACCOMPANIMENT.

2, successor, sequel, continuance; FUTURITY, posteriority.

Verbs—**1,** succeed; come after, come on, come next; follow (up), ensue, step into the shoes of; alternate; place after, suffix, append (see ADDITION).

2, pursue, go after, fly after; attend, beset, dance attendance on, dog; hang on the skirts of; tread on the heels of; lag, get behind.

Adjectives—**1,** succeeding, successive; sequent, subsequent, consequent; ensuing, proximate, next; consecutive, alternate; latter, posterior; chronological (see CHRONOLOGY).

2, following, attendant, trailing, in line.

Adverbs—after, subsequently; behind, in the rear of, in the wake of; successively; sequentially, consequentially, consequently; after which, whereupon; as follows, next; as soon as.

Antonyms, see PRIORITY, PRECEDENCE.

---

sequester, *v.* seclude, isolate, separate; cloister, shut up *or* away, immure, confine; confiscate, commandeer, expropriate. See SECLUSION.

sequin, *n.* spangle (see ORNAMENT).

sere, *adj.* withered, dry. See DRYNESS.

serenade, *n.* serenata, cassation, nocturne, shivaree. See MUSIC. —*v.* sing to, entertain, perform for; court, woo. See ENDEARMENT.

serene, *adj.* calm, placid, tranquil, unperturbed; clear, unclouded. See

INEXCITABILITY, CONTENT.

serf, *n.* bondman, esne, villein, vassal; peasant. See SERVANT, POPULACE, SUBJECTION.

sergeant, *n.* noncommissioned officer, N.C.O.; staff sergeant, sergeant, major, *etc. Colloq.,* top sergeant, top. *Slang,* [top] kick, gunny. See COMBATANT.

serial, *adj.* seriatim; sequential, continuous, ordered, ranked, episodic; consecutive; to be continued. See CONTINUITY, PART, REGULARITY.

series, *n.* sequence, set, succession, chain, progression, cycle. See CONTINUITY.

serious, *adj.* grave, momentous, solemn; earnest, resolute; important, weighty; alarming, critical. See IMPORTANCE.

sermon, *n.* homily, lecture, discourse, dissertation, exhortation. See RITE, TEACHING, DISAPPROBATION, SPEECH.

serpentine, *adj.* snaky, reptilian, herpetic; sinuous, slithery; winding, tortuous, snaking; cunning, wily, venomous, cold-blooded. See CONVOLUTION.

serrate, *adj.* serrated, saw-edged *or* -toothed, dentate; jagged; crenulate, scalloped. See SHARPNESS.

serried, *adj.* crowded, packed, dense. See DENSITY.

serum, *n.* antitoxin, vaccine; antigen, agglutinin; plasma; whey, WATER. See FLUIDITY.

SERVANT

Nouns—**1,** servant, servitor, domestic, menial, help; retainer, follower, henchman, subject, liegeman; retinue, suite, cortege, staff, entourage, court; majordomo, chamberlain. See AUXILIARY, ACCOMPANIMENT.

2, employee, staff, personnel, manpower, workforce, human resources; secretary; clerk; subsidiary; AGENT.

3, attendant, servitor, squire, usher, page; waiter, butler, steward; livery servant, lackey, footman, flunky, factotum, bellboy, valet, *valet de chambre;* man; equerry, groom; jockey, hostler; orderly, messenger; [hired] hand. *Slang,* jack, slavey.

4, maid[servant], handmaid[en]; lady's maid, nurse, *bonne,* ayah, wet nurse, nursemaid, housemaid, parlor maid, waitingmaid, chambermaid, kitchen maid, scullery maid; *femme* or *fille de chambre,* abigail, girl; *chef de cuisine,* cook, scullion; maid of all work, hired hand, laundress, charwoman; [baby]sitter.

5, serf, vassal, slave, minion, bondsman *or* -woman; bondslave; villein; pensioner, dependent; hanger-on, satellite; parasite (see SERVILITY); protégé[e], ward; hireling, underling, mercenary, puppet, creature, henchman, cat's-paw, myrmidon, errand *or* office boy *or* girl; batman, dog robber.

Verbs—serve, work for, tend, minister to; wait at *or* on table, wait on, attend (upon), squire (see OBEDIENCE).

Adjectives—serving, ministering, tending; in the train of, in one's pay *or* employ, on the payroll; at one's call (see OBEDIENCE); in bondage.

Antonyms, see AUTHORITY, DIRECTOR.

---

serve, *v.* attend, wait on (see SERVANT); replace; AID; avail, be of use; supply; suffice. See UTILITY, PROVISION, SUFFICIENCY.

service, *n.* aid, help, duty; servitude, ministration, employment; worship, ritual, armed forces; wear, usefulness, USE; set, equipment; serving, helping. See BUSINESS, UTILITY, RITE.

SERVILITY

Nouns—**1,** servility, obsequiousness, subserviency; abasement (see HUMILITY); prostration, genuflection; fawning, ingratiation; tuft-hunting, time-serving, flunkyism; sycophancy, FLATTERY. *Slang,* apple-polishing.

2, sycophant, parasite; toady, freeloader, tuft-hunter; snob, flunky, slavey, lapdog; hanger-on, leech, sponger; clinging vine; time-server, fortune-hunter; flatterer, lick-spittle; henchman, hireling, tool, cat's-paw; courtier. *Slang,* yesman, handshaker, baby-kisser, back-slapper, apple-polisher. See SERVANT.

Verbs—**1,** cringe, bow, stoop, kneel, bend the knee; sneak, crawl, crouch, cower; truckle to, curry favor with; grovel, fawn, lick the feet of, kiss the hem of one's garment, throw oneself at the feet of; freeload.

2, pay court to, make up to; dance attendance on, wait on hand and foot, hang on the sleeve of, fetch and carry, do the dirty work of. *Colloq.,* sponge. *Slang,* polish the apple, play up to.

Adjectives—servile, obsequious, abject; soapy, oily, unctuous; flattering, adulatory, fulsome; pliant, cringing, subservient, fawning, slavish, groveling, sniveling, mealy-mouthed; beggarly, sycophantic, parasitical; base, mean, sneaking, skulking.

Adverbs—servilely, abjectly, *etc.;* with hat in hand; abased.

Antonyms, see INSOLENCE.

---

session, *n.* sitting, meeting; period, term, semester; conference, hearing, convocation. See ASSEMBLAGE, COUNCIL.

set, *v.* place, put, station; arrange, prepare; establish; mount; adjust, regulate; fix, assign, appoint; plant, set out; overthrow, unsettle; sink, go down; solidify, jell, harden; start out. See LOCATION, COMMAND, DESCENT, DENSITY. —*n.* clique, coterie, group; collection, series, outfit; TENDENCY, trend, drift; carriage, posture; agglutination, solidification; scenery. See COHERENCE, DIRECTION, PARTY, ASSEMBLAGE, CLASS, FORM, DRAMA.

setback, *n.* backslide; relapse, reverse, reversion, regression; defeat, LOSS, upset, check, discouragement.

settee, *n.* seat, settle, bench, form, sofa, lounge. See SUPPORT.

setting, *n.* background, backdrop; LOCATION, place[ment], site, locale, scene, ENVIRONMENT, milieu, region; mounting, base, frame, monture, collet, chape. See APPEARANCE.

settle, *v.* define, fix, confirm, appoint; agree upon; resolve, determine, decide, conclude; tranquilize, calm; reconcile, adjust, compose; discharge, square, pay, set at rest; place, establish; people, colonize, defeat, outwit; locate, settle down, take residence; sink, subside, sag, solidify; precipitate; alight; arrange, agree. See STABILITY, AGREEMENT, PAYMENT, ABODE, CERTAINTY, DESCENT.

settlement, *n.* arrangement; disposition, reconciliation, COMPROMISE, agreement, JUDGMENT; colony, base, outpost, LOCATION; bestowal, PAYMENT, discharge, award.

settler, *n.* colonist, pioneer, emigrant, homesteader. See INHABITANT.

set-to, *n., colloq.,* fight, brawl. See CONTENTION.

setup, *n.* arrangement, situation, facilities, plant, layout; makeup, PLAN, COMPOSITION, rig; *slang,* gull. *Slang,* frameup, fix; fall guy.

sever, *v.t.* cut off, cleave, separate, sunder, part; disjoin, dissolve. See DISJUNCTION.

several, *adj.* individual, distinct, separate, particular; different, various; few, sundry. See MULTITUDE, DISJUNCTION.

SEVERITY

Nouns—**1,** severity; strictness, harshness, rigor, stringency, austerity, straight face; ill-treatment; inclemency, pitilessness, arrogance. See INSOLENCE, VIOLENCE, AUTHORITY.

2, arbitrary power, absolutism, despotism; dictatorship, autocracy, tyranny, domineering, oppression; inquisition, reign of terror, martial law; iron heel *or* hand; brute force *or* strength; coercion, COMPULSION; strong hand.

3, tyrant, dictator, disciplinarian, martinet, stickler, despot, taskmaster, hard master, Draco, oppressor, inquisitor, extortioner, harpy, vulture, Simon Legree, slavedriver, drillmaster.

Verbs—be severe, give no quarter, domineer, bully, tyrannize; rack, put the screws on, be hard on, mistreat; come down on; ill-treat; rule with a rod of iron; oppress, override; trample [under foot], tread upon, crush under an iron heel, crack the whip, crack down, ride roughshod over; keep a tight rein; work in a sweatshop.

Adjectives—severe, strict, hard, harsh, astringent, tough, dour, rigid, stiff, stern, rigorous, uncompromising, unyielding, heavy-handed, exacting, exigent, inexorable, inflexible, obdurate, hardboiled, hard-as-nails, austere, relentless, merciless, pitiless, unforgiving, Draconian, Spartan, stringent, strait-laced, searching, unsparing, hard-fisted, ironhanded, peremptory, high-handed, absolute, positive, imperative; hard-and-fast, coercive, puritanical, dictatorial, tyrannical, extortionate, grinding, withering, oppressive, inquisitorial; inclement, ruthless, cruel, grueling; cut-throat; haughty, arrogant. *Slang,* hard-nosed.

Adverbs—severely, *etc.;* with a high *or* heavy hand; at sword's point.

Antonyms, see MODERATION, NEGLECT, PITY.

---

sew, *v.t.* stitch, mend, baste, seam. See JUNCTION.

sewage, *n.* refuse, garbage, rubbish, waste, offal; drainage. See UNCLEANNESS.

sewer, *n.* seamstress; drain, cloaca, culvert, conduit, PASSAGE, sluice. See CLEANNESS.

sex, *n.* gender; sexuality; MALE, FEMALE, masculine, feminine. See CLASS.

sexism, *n.* sexual discrimination; machismo. See INJUSTICE.

sexless, *adj.* neuter, asexual; gelded, castrated, emasculated, spayed, altered; impotent; cold, frigid, passionless. *Colloq.,* fixed. See IMPOTENCE.

sexton, *n.* sacristan, verger; vestryman, beadle. See CLERGY.

sexual, *adj.* carnal, sensual; erotic. See DESIRE, MALE, FEMALE, IMPURITY.

sexy, *adj., slang,* voluptuous, seductive, erotic; lewd, lascivious; wanton, sensational, bold; pornographic, X-rated. See IMPURITY.

shabby, *adj.* dilapidated, seedy, rundown, threadbare; mean, sorry, pitiful, contemptible. See DETERIORATION, UNIMPORTANCE.

shack, *n.* hut, shanty, shed, hovel. See ABODE.

shackle, *n.* fetter, hobble, manacle, gyve, handcuff, bond; check, curb. —*v.t.* bind, restrain; handcuff, manacle, chain. See RESTRAINT.

shade, *n.* shadiness, shadow, umbrage, gloom, gloaming, DIMNESS, DARKNESS; OBSCURITY; duskiness; shading, tone; curtain, veil, film, haziness, haze, misti[ness], CLOUDINESS; COLOR, hue, tint; nuance, DEGREE; blind, curtain, shutter, Venetian blind; spirit, ghost, phantom, specter, apparition, haunt (see DEMON). —*v.t.* hide, conceal; darken, shadow; cover, veil; COLOR, tinge, tint. See COVERING, CONCEALMENT.

shadow, *n.* umbra, silhouette, shade; spy, follower; reflection; shelter, protection; trace, suggestion; ghost. *Slang,* tail. See ACCOMPANIMENT, IMAGINATION. —*v.t.* overcast, darken, shade; foreshadow, adumbrate; trail, dog. *Slang,* tail. See PURSUIT, DARKNESS, CLOUDINESS, COPY, DIMNESS.

shady, *adj.* shadowy, indistinct; *colloq.,* uncertain, questionable, sinister. See CLOUDINESS, IMPROBITY.

shaft, *n.* arrow, spear; beam, ray; handle; bar, axle; thill; column, pillar; well, pit. See ARMS, DEPTH, SUPPORT.

shaggy, *adj.* nappy, fuzzy, wooly; unkempt, scragg[l]y, stubbly, bearded, hirsute; matted, tangled; rough[hewn], crude. See ROUGHNESS.

shake, *v.* vibrate, agitate, shiver, brandish, flourish, rock, sway, wave, rattle, jolt, worry, jar; unsettle, disillusion, impair, unnerve; tremble, quiver, quaver, quake, shudder, flutter, vibrate. See AGITATION, EXCITEMENT, FEAR, OSCILLATION, WEAKNESS.

shakedown, *n., slang,* extortion (see STEALING).

shakeup, *n.* agitation, disturbance; reorganization, overhaul, REVOLUTION, change, reformation, rearrangement, reconstruction.

SHALLOWNESS

Nouns—**1,** shallowness, shoalness, flatness; superficiality; inanity, FOLLY; banality, insipidity, dullness, vapidity; IGNORANCE; triviality, frivolity. See UNIMPORTANCE.

2, shallow, shoal, flat, shelf, sandbank, bar, [coral] reef, ford; façade, gloss, veneer, scratch, pinprick; surface *or* flesh wound; trivia.

Verbs—scratch the surface, skim over, touch upon.

Adjectives—shallow, shoal[y], depthless, flat; empty, superficial, cursory; skin-, angle-, *or* knee-deep; flighty, silly, slight, unintelligent, simple, foolish, ignorant; banal, fatuous, inane, insipid, puerile, jejune, vapid; trivial, frivolous, trifling, flimsy, obvious, dull.

Antonyms, see DEPTH, IMPORTANCE.

---

sham, *n.* counterfeit, IMITATION, fake; pretense, dissimulation; humbug; imposture. —*adj.* make-believe, spurious, bogus, fake. See DECEPTION, FALSEHOOD, AFFECTATION.

shambles, *n.pl.* slaughterhouse, abattoir (see KILLING); wreck, chaos, mess. See DISORDER.

shame, *n.* humiliation, mortification, abashment; ignominy, reproach, disgrace, dishonor. —*v.t.* humiliate, mortify, abash, disgrace. See DISREPUTE, IMPURITY, WRONG.

shameless, *adj.* brazen, barefaced, unblushing, graceless, wanton, immodest. See INSOLENCE, IMPURITY.

shanghai, *v.t.* abduct, kidnap, impress, commandeer. See COMPULSION.

shank, *n.* leg, shin; shaft, stem; handle; *colloq.,* END, REMAINDER. See SUPPORT.

shanty, *n.* shack, shed; hovel, tumbledown; hutch, bungalow. See ABODE.

shape, *n.* FORM, figure, contour; pattern, mold; state, condition.

shapeless, *adj.* amorphous, vague, ill-defined; disorganized; misshapen, distorted; unshapely, blobby. See FORMLESSNESS.

shapely, *adj.* well-built, -proportioned, *or* -developed; handsome, beautiful, gainly, svelte, lissome, lithe; buxom, voluptuous. *Colloq.,* curvaceous, chesty, busty. *Slang,* stacked. See BEAUTY, SYMMETRY.

shard, *n.* potsherd; fragment, piece, splinter. See PART.

share, *n.* portion, part, allotment, quota, dole. *Slang,* cut. —*v.* apportion, allot, assign, mete; partake, participate. See APPORTIONMENT.

shark, *n.* dogfish, hammerhead, *etc;* sharper, swindler; *slang,* expert. See ANIMAL, STEALING.

sharper, *n.* cardsharp, slicker, cheat[er], swindler. *Colloq.,* chiseler, crook. *Slang,* con man, gyp; shark, mechanic. See DECEPTION.

SHARPNESS

Nouns—**1,** sharpness, acuity, acumination; spinosity; PUNGENCY, acerbity.

2, point, spike, spine, spiculum; needle, pin; prick, prickle; spur, rowel; barb, barbwire; spit, cusp; horn, antler; snag, thorn, briar, bramble, thistle; bristle; tine, prong; nib, tooth, tusk, fang; spoke, cog, ratchet.

3, crag, crest, *arête,* cone, peak, sugarloaf, pike; spire, pyramid, steeple.

4, wedge; knife, blade, edge, point, steel, carving knife; snickersnee; dagger, poniard, dirk, bodkin, stiletto; jackknife; scalpel, lancet; cutting edge, blade, razor; probe; plowshare; hatchet, ax, pickax, mattock, pick, adz, bill; billhook, cleaver, slicer, cutter; scythe, sickle, scissors, shears; sword (see ARMS); perforator; saw. *Slang,* shiv, toothpick. See ARMS, ANGULARITY.

5, sharpener, hone, strop; grindstone, whetstone, steel; abrasive.

Verbs—be sharp, have a point; bristle with; sharpen, point, aculeate, whet, barb, spiculate, set, strop, grind; cut (see DISJUNCTION).

Adjectives—sharp, keen, cutting; acute, acicular, aciform; aculeate[d], acuminated; pointed; tapering; conical, pyramidal; spiked, spiky, ensiform, peaked, salient; cusped, cuspidate, cornute; prickly, spiny, spinous; thorny; bristling; studded; thistly, briary; craggy, rough, snaggy; digitated, two-edged, fusiform; dentiform; toothed, odontoid; starlike, stellate; arrow-headed; arrowy, barbed, spurred; cutting; sharp-edged, knife-edged; sharpened.

Antonyms, see BLUNTNESS.

sharpshooter, *n.* marksman *or* -woman, crack shot; sniper. See COMBATANT, ARMS.

shatter, *v.* splinter, shiver, smash, disintegrate; destroy; madden, craze; crash, shatter. See BRITTLENESS, DISJUNCTION, INSANITY, DESTRUCTION.

shave, *v.t.* pare, plane, crop; skim, graze; cheapen, mark down, trim. See DEDUCTION, LAYER, NARROWNESS, SHORTNESS.

shaving, *n.* slice, paring, scale, LAYER. See PART, FILAMENT.

shawl, *n.* scarf, stole, mantle, serape, mantilla, wrap; tallith. See CLOTHING.

sheaf, *n.* bundle, fagot; cluster, batch, bunch; quiver; fascicle, packet, bale. —*v.t.* sheave; bundle, tie, bind; gather. See ASSEMBLAGE.

shear, *v.* clip, scissor; cut, lop, snip, trim, prune; shave, mow, fleece; despoil, strip, denude, rob of. See DIVESTMENT, SHARPNESS, SHORTNESS.

shears, *n.pl.* scissors, clippers. See SHARPNESS.

sheath, *n.* scabbard, sheathing, case, envelope, casing; involucre, capsule, fascia, lorica. See COVERING, RECEPTACLE.

shed, *n.* shelter, lean-to; shack, shanty, hangar, train shed. See ABODE. —*v.t.* spill, pour out; drop, cast off; molt, slough off; spread, diffuse, scatter. See DIVESTMENT, EJECTION, DISPERSION.

sheen, *n.* LIGHT, gleam, luster, shine, glow, shimmer, splendor. See SMOOTHNESS.

sheep, *n.* ram, ewe, lamb; bighorn,

karakul; mutton; congregation, parish; follower. See ANIMAL, LAITY, MODESTY.

sheepish, *adj.* shamefaced, blushing, downcast, coy. See MODESTY.

sheer, *adj.* utter, absolute; mere, simple; thin, diaphanous; perpendicular, precipitous, VERTICAL, steep. See TRANSPARENCY, SIMPLENESS.

sheet, *n.* bedsheet; shroud, winding sheet, cerement; page, leaf, folio; plane, surface, plate, lamina, LAYER, membrane; rope, mainsheet. See COVERING, HORIZONTAL, INTERMENT, NAVIGATION.

shelf, *n.* ledge, mantel, mantelpiece; sandbank, reef. See SUPPORT.

shell, *v.t.* bomb, bombard, cannonade, strafe, pepper; shuck, strip, pod, hull. See ATTACK, DIVESTMENT. —*n.* case; carapace; husk, seashell; bomb, grenade, explosive, shrapnel, torpedo; boat, cockleshell, racing boat. See COVERING, DEFENSE.

shell shock, *n.* combat fatigue; psychosis, neurosis; amnesia. See INSANITY, FEAR.

shelter, *n.* refuge, retreat, sanctuary, asylum; cover, security, protection, SAFETY. See COVERING, DEFENSE.

shelve, *v.t.* put aside *or* off, postpone. See DISUSE, LATENESS.

shepherd, *n.* herder, sheepherder, herdsman; pastor, clergyman; Good Shepherd. See DOMESTICATION, CLERGY, DEITY.

sherbet, *n.* ice, sorbet, granita. See SWEETNESS.

sheriff, *n.* peace officer, marshal. See SAFETY.

shield, *n.* armor, safeguard, screen; protection, protector, egis; arms, escutcheon. See DEFENSE, COVERING, INDICATION.

shift, *v.* veer, vary, CHANGE; equivocate; contrive, get along; transfer; substitute. —*n.* CHANGE, SUBSTITUTION, dislocation; expedient, subterfuge, trick. See DEVIATION, CUNNING.

shiftless, *adj.* lazy, indolent, improvident, thriftless, negligent. See INACTIVITY, UNPREPAREDNESS.

shifty, *adj.* unreliable, tricky; CUNNING; evasive, slippery; alert, resourceful. See AVOIDANCE.

shimmer, *n.* flicker, glimmer, gleam, sheen, glint, twinkle. See LIGHT.

shin, *n.* shinbone, tibia, shank, leg. See PART. —*v.* climb, creep up, clamber, scale; kick. *Colloq.,* shinny. See ASCENT.

shindig, *n., slang,* party, gala, affair, celebration, spree. *Slang,* shindy. See SOCIABILITY, AMUSEMENT.

shine, *v.* glow, gleam, scintillate; excel; polish, wax, burnish. See LIGHT, REPUTE.

shingle, *n.* roof *or* wall slate; signboard; beach gravel; bob. See COVERING, MATERIALS.

SHIP

Nouns—**1,** ship, vessel, sail; craft, bottom; airship (see AVIATION).

2, navy, marine, fleet, flotilla; shipping, merchant marine; coast guard.

3, transport, tender, storeship; freighter, merchant ship, merchantman; packet; whaler, slaver, collier, coaster, lighter; fishing *or* pilot boat; dragger, trawler; hulk; yacht; liner; tanker, oiler.

4, bark, barque, brig, brigantine, barkantine; schooner; sloop, cutter, corvette, clipper, yawl, ketch, sharpie, smack, lugger; barge, scow; cat[boat], sailer, sailing vessel; steamer, steamboat, steamship; paddle steamer; tug, tugboat; hovercraft, hydrofoil, hydroplane.

5, boat, pinnacle, launch; rowboat, shallop; lifeboat, longboat, jollyboat, bumboat, flyboat, cockboat, canalboat, ferryboat; shallop, gig, skiff, dinghy, scow, cockleshell, wherry, punt, outrigger; float, raft, pontoon; fireboat, motorboat; cabin cruiser; houseboat; class boat.

6, catamaran, coracle, gondola, carvel, caravel; felucca, caique; dugout, canoe; kayak, faltboat; bireme, trireme; galley, hooker, argosy, carrack; galliass, galleon, galliot; junk, praam, proa, prahu, saic, sampan, xebec, dhow; dahabeah.

7, marine, navy, naval forces, fleet, flotilla, armada, squadron; man-of-war, ship of the line, ironclad, warship, frigate, gunboat, flagship, cruiser; privateer; troopship, transport, corvette, torpedo boat, submarine, battleship, scout, dreadnaught, aircraft carrier, flattop, destroyer.

8, oar, paddle, scull, screw, sail, gaff, canvas, fish's tail; paddle wheel, side, *or* stern wheel; rudder, leeboards, rigging, sail, sheet, line, rope, mainsheet; mast, boom, pole; beam; keep; deck, quarterdeck, forecastle, fo'c'sle; after, boat, flight, *etc.* deck; bow, stern.

Verbs—sail, cruise, steam, drift, navigate (see NAVIGATION).

Adverbs—afloat, aboard, on board, aboardship, on shipboard, amidship[s].

---

shipment, *n.* delivery, conveyance, carriage, truckage; load, cargo, freight, lading; order, consignment. See TRANSPORTATION.

shipshape, *adj.* trim, tidy, neat, orderly, spruce; prepared, set; methodical; taut, seaworthy; tiptop, in the pink, perfect. See ORDER.

shipwreck, *n.* derelict, castaway, wreckage, flotsam, hulk; ruin, bankruptcy, *etc.* —*v.* wreck, ruin, scuttle, sink, capsize, run ashore; ground; shatter, destroy, fail. See DESTRUCTION.

shirk, *v.* evade, shun, neglect; slack, soldier, malinger. *Slang,* goldbrick. See AVOIDANCE.

shirt, *n.* blouse, chamise[tte], camisole, shift, plastron. See CLOTHING.

shiver, *v.i.* tremble, shudder, quiver, shake; shatter, splinter, burst. See AGITATION, BRITTLENESS, COLD, DISJUNCTION, FEAR.

shoal, *n.* school, multitude, host, horde; shallow, sandbar. See ASSEMBLAGE, LOWNESS.

shock, *v.t.* shake, jar, jolt; startle, surprise, horrify, scandalize, disgust; paralyze, stun; galvanize, electrify. —*n.* concussion, jar, impact; brunt, onset, assault; earthquake, temblor; prostration, stroke, paralysis, shellshock, apoplexy; ordeal, calamity; stack, stook; crop, thatch, mop (of hair). See DISEASE, ASSEMBLAGE, PAIN, VIOLENCE, SURPRISE, DISAPPROBATION, IMPULSE.

shocking, *adj.* distressing, horrible, abominable, odious, opprobrious, ghastly, indecent, dire, frightful, fearful, appalling, horrendous. See FEAR, DISREPUTE, VULGARITY.

shoddy, *adj.* inferior, low-grade, shabby; tawdry, gimcrack; sham, vulgar, common; low, mean, ignoble. See VULGARITY.

shoe, *n.* footwear; footgear; sandal, espadrille, boot, loafer, casual, sneaker; runner, [tire] casing; [brake] lining. See CLOTHING.

shoemaker, *n.* cobbler, bootmaker. See PRODUCTION.

shoo, *v.t.* chase, disperse, scatter, dispel. —*interj.* scat! get away! get out! go away! *Slang,* scram! beat it! blow! See DEPARTURE.

shoot, *v.* rush, dart; sprout, burgeon, grow; fire, discharge; detonate, explode; kill, wound, hit; propel, drive, emit. See VELOCITY, PROPULSION.

shop, *n.* mart, market, store, bazaar, emporium; office, workshop, shoppe, works, factory, mill. See BUSINESS.

shopkeeper, *n.* tradesman, merchant, dealer, retailer. See SALE.

shoplifter, *n.* thief, kleptomaniac. See STEALING.

shore, *n.* coast, beach, coastline; bank, strand, shingle, seaside. See LAND.

shortage, *n.* deficiency, shortcoming. See INSUFFICIENCY.

short-change, *v.t., colloq.,* cheat, gyp. See DECEPTION.

shortcoming, *n.* failing, foible, weakness, fault; deficiency, defect, default; delinquency, failure, inadequacy, INSUFFICIENCY, shortage, lack. See IMPERFECTION.

shortening, *n.* fat, lard, butter, suet, [oleo]margarine, OIL.

shorthand, *n.* stenography, phonography, stenotypy, stenology; Pitman, Gregg, Speedwriting. See WRITING.

shorthanded, *adj.* understaffed, short. See INSUFFICIENCY.

short-lived, *adj.* transitory, impermanent, mortal, perishable, ephemeral, fugitive, evanescent; doomed. See TRANSIENTNESS.

shortly, *adv.* soon; briefly, concisely, curtly. See EARLINESS, SHORTNESS.

SHORTNESS

Nouns—**1,** shortness, brevity, briefness, conciseness; shortening, abbreviation, abridgement, retrenchment, curtailment; compression, condensation, CONTRACTION; reduction, epitome, digest, synopsis, compendium; butt, stub; short cut. *Colloq.,* short haul.

2, see LITTLENESS.

Verbs—be short, shorten, curtail, abridge, boil down, abstract, condense, digest, abbreviate, take in, reduce; compress, contract; epitomize; retrench, cut short, scrimp, cut, chop up, hack, hew; cut down; clip, dock, lop, prune, bob; take up; cut corners; shear, shave; mow, reap, crop; snub; truncate, stunt, nip in the bud, check the growth of; foreshorten; come to the point.

Adjectives—short, brief, curt, succinct, short and sweet, crisp, epitomized, compendious, compact, concise, summary, stubby, shorn, stubbed; stumpy, thickset, pug; squat, dumpy; dwarfed, dwarfish, little; oblate; sawed-off.

Adverbs—shortly, in short; for short, concisely, in brief, in fine, in a nutshell, in a word, in a few words; to come to the point, to make a long story short, to be brief; abruptly.

Antonyms, see LENGTH, LOQUACITY.

shortsighted, *adj.* myopic, nearsighted; improvident, unimaginative, lacking foresight. See VISION.

short-term, *adj.* brief, temporary. See TRANSIENTNESS.

short-winded, *adj.* dyspn[o]eic, broken-winded, asthmatic, wheezy. See WEARINESS.

shot, *adj.* propelled, struck (see PROPULSION); interspersed, interwoven. —*n.* bullet, ball, pellet; discharge, stroke, attempt; *slang,* injection, inoculation, hypodermic, hypo. See ARMS, REMEDY.

shoulder, *n.* scapula; projection, abutment. See ANGULARITY, CONVEXITY. —*v.* assume, bear, carry; sustain, maintain, SUPPORT; jostle, poke (see IMPULSE).

shout, *v. & n.* scream, call, bawl, bellow, yell; whoop, cheer, roar. See CRY, REJOICING, LOUDNESS.

shove, *v.* push, hustle; urge, thrust, force; crowd, cram, wedge; shoulder, jostle, jog, jar, elbow, nudge. See IMPULSE.

shovel, *n.* spade, digger; scoop[er], excavator, trowel, scuttle. —*v.* dig, excavate, unearth; ladle, dip. See CONCAVITY.

show, *v.* exhibit, display; explain, teach; demonstrate, prove, guide, escort; appear, stand out. See EVIDENCE, DISCLOSURE. —*n.* display, exhibition, play, entertainment, pageant, spectacle; pomp, OSTENTATION; semblance, APPEARANCE, pretext. See DRAMA, VISIBILITY, DEMONSTRATION.

showcase, *n.* display case *or* window;

vitrine, *étalage;* exhibition; repository, reliquary; étagère, whatnot, mantelpiece. See RECEPTACLE.

showdown, *n.* confrontation, face-off; climax, denouement; settling of accounts, putting one's cards on the table, show of hands. See OPPOSITION, DISCLOSURE.

shower, *n.* rain, sprinkle, drizzle; spate; volley; fall. See WATER, ASSEMBLAGE, CLEANNESS.

showing, *n.* performance; display, exhibition. See DISCLOSURE, OSTENTATION.

showman, *n.* exhibitor, impresario, producer. See DRAMA, OSTENTATION.

showmanship, *n.* skill, stagecraft; dramaturgy, histrionics; OSTENTATION, style, garishness, exhibitionism, fanfare, pageantry, display, theatricality. See DRAMA.

show-off, *n.* display, OSTENTATION; exhibitionist, peacock. *Slang,* hotshot, ham.

showy, *adj.* conspicuous, colorful; ornate, florid, flashy, gaudy, pretentious, ostentatious, imposing. See COLOR, VULGARITY, OSTENTATION.

shred, *n.* strip, tatter, remnant, snippet, scrap; modicum, bit, particle, speck; trace, vestiges. —*v.t.* grate; macerate, mangle, lacerate; tear, rip. See PART, FILAMENT, DISJUNCTION.

shrew, *n.* termagant, scold, virago, vixen, fishwife, henpecker, beldame. See EVILDOER, FEMALE.

shrewd, *adj.* clever, keen, farsighted, astute; CUNNING, wily, artful; sharp, acute, piercing. See SKILL.

shriek, *v.i.* scream, screech, shrill, squeal. See CRY.

shrill, *adj.* sharp, piercing, strident, high-pitched, piping, penetrating, poignant. See LOUDNESS, CRY.

shrine, *n.* altar, TEMPLE; RECEPTACLE (for sacred objects), reliquary; tomb.

shrink, *v.* contract, shrivel, diminish, wizen; flinch, draw back, RECOIL, wince, quail, cower; compress, reduce, DECREASE. See CONTRACTION, FEAR.

shrivel, *v.* shrink, wrinkle, wizen, pucker; wither, sear. See CONTRACTION, FOLD.

shroud, *n.* winding sheet, graveclothes; pall; screen, cloak, veil. See INTERMENT, CONCEALMENT.

shrub, *n.* shrubbery; scrub, bush, arbuscle, hedge, treelet. See VEGETABLE.

shrug, *v.* raise the shoulders. See INDICATION, DISAPPROBATION, DISLIKE.

shudder, *v.i.* tremble, quake, quiver, shiver, vibrate. See COLD, FEAR.

shuffle, *v.* rearrange, switch, shift, mix, intermingle, jumble; scuff, drag; fidget; scuffle, shamble, slouch; equivocate, quibble, evade. See INTERCHANGE, SLOWNESS, CHANGEABLENESS.

shun, *v.t.* avoid, elude, evade, eschew; cut, ignore; steer clear of. See AVOIDANCE.

shunt, *v.t.* turn aside, sidetrack, get rid of. See DEVIATION.

shut, *v.t.* close, fold; imprison, confine; silence; cease operations, terminate; bar, exclude, blockade. See CLOSURE.

shutdown, *n.* stoppage, cessation, end, termination, halt; layoff, sitdown strike, closing, foreclosure; lockout, walkout; CLOSURE. See DISCONTINUANCE.

shutter, *n.* blind[s], louver, persiennes; screen, grille. See CONCEALMENT.

shuttle, *n.* See OSCILLATION, TRANSPORTATION.

shy, *adj.* bashful, reserved, retiring, demure; cautious, suspicious, wary; timid, skittish, fearful; short, lacking. See MODESTY, FEAR, INCOMPLETENESS. —*v.* start, RECOIL. See DEVIATION, FEAR.

sibilant, *adj. & n.* hissing; whispering; whistling. See SOUND.

sick, *adj.* ill, ailing, diseased; nauseated; disgusted; bored. *Slang,* fed up. See DISEASE, DISLIKE.

sicken, *v.* ail; languish, droop, waste away; cloy, weary; make ill, afflict; nauseate, revolt. See DISEASE, PAIN, DISLIKE.

sickly, *adj.* invalid, ailing, unwell; debilitated, languid, peaked; wan, pale, washed out, faint; mawkish, nauseating. See DISEASE, WEAKNESS, COLORLESSNESS.

SIDE

Nouns—**1,** side, flank, quarter, lee, leeward, weather, windward; skirt, EDGE; hand; cheek, jowl; wing; profile; temple; loin, haunch, hip; laterality; gable[-end]; broadside; outside, inside (see EXTERIOR, INTERIOR); east, west (see DIRECTION); orientation, aspect.

2, see RIGHT, LEFT, PARTY.

Verbs—be on one side, flank, outflank; sidle; skirt, border.

Adjectives—**1,** side, lateral, sidelong; collateral; parietal, flanking, skirting; flanked; bordering; lee[ward], weather, windward; askance; shoulder-to-shoulder. See NEARNESS.

2, onesided, many-sided, multilateral; bilateral, trilateral, quadrilateral.

Adverbs—sideways, sidewise, sidelong; laterally; broadside on; on one side, abreast, abeam, alongside, beside, aside; by, by the side of; side by side; cheek by jowl; to windward, to leeward; right and left.

Antonyms, see MIDDLE.

---

sidestep, *v.* avoid, circumvent, evade; jockey, parry; equivocate. See AVOIDANCE.

sidetrack, *v.t.* divert, distract. See DEVIATION, INATTENTION.

sidewalk, *n.* walk, footwalk, crosswalk, pavement; footpath, footway, banquette; boardwalk, *trottoir,* promenade, mall. See PASSAGE.

siding, *n.* sidetrack, [track] spur; paneling, boarding. See COVERING, DEVIATION.

sidle, *v.* EDGE, crab; sidestep, skirt, flank; slither. See DEVIATION, OBLIQUITY, SIDE.

siege, *n.* investment, encirclement; besiegement, blockade, beleaguerment; period, long spell. See ATTACK, RESTRAINT.

siesta, *n.* nap, snooze, doze, rest. See REPOSE.

sieve, *n.* riddle, colander, sifter, screen, strainer, bolter. See OPENING.

sift, *v.t.* separate, bolt, screen, sort; examine, scrutinize, segregate, eliminate. See CHOICE, CLEANNESS, TASTE.

sigh, *v.i.* suspire, sough, moan; long, yearn, *or* grieve (for). See WIND, DESIRE, LAMENTATION.

sight, *n.* VISION, eyesight; view, vista, scene; APPEARANCE, aspect, look; spectacle, display; visibility; aim, observation; eyesore (see UGLINESS). *Colloq.,* lots, heap (see QUANTITY).

sightless, *adj.* blind, eyeless, unseeing; amaurotic; invisible, imperceptible. See BLINDNESS, INVISIBILITY.

sightseeing, *n.* tour[ing], tourism; excursion, expedition; globetrotting, vacationing. *Slang,* rubbernecking. See CURIOSITY, TRAVEL.

sign, *n.* omen, portent; INDICATION, symptom, token, mark; symbol, emblem; gesture, signal; trace, vestige; signboard, shingle; guidepost. See INDICATION, DIRECTION.

signal, *n.* sign, watchword, cue; alarm, WARNING, direction, order; traffic light, beacon, foghorn, wigwag; trace, vestige. See INDICATION. —*adj.* memorable, conspicuous, momentous. See IMPORTANCE. —*v.t.* signalize, speak, hail, call, beckon, gesticulate; semaphore, wigwag; radio, broadcast, beam. See INDICATION.

signalize, *v.* indicate, point out; celebrate. See INDICATION, CELEBRATION.

signatory, *n.* signer, signator; witness, testifier; subscriber, party, underwriter, endorser, co-signer, co-maker. See ASSENT.

signature, *n.* autograph, hand, sign manual; subscription; mark, endorsement; identifying theme, music, letters, *etc.;* identification; attestation. *Slang,* fist, John Hancock, John Henry. See INDICATION, NOMENCLATURE.

significant, *adj.* important, consequential; meaningful, expressive. See IMPORTANCE, MEANING.

signify, *v.t.* show; declare, portend; mean, denote, express, connote, indicate. See MEANING, IMPORTANCE.

SILENCE

Nouns—**1,** silence; stillness, quiet, peace, hush; inaudibility.

2, muteness, dumbness, aphony, voicelessness; TACITURNITY, reticence; deadness, dullness.

3, silencer, muffler, damper, mute; gag, muzzle.

4, mute, deafmute.

Verbs—**1,** silence, baffle, strike dumb, quiet, still, hush (up); stifle, muffle, stop, cut one short, cut off; drown (out); smother, muzzle, mute, gag, put to silence; dampen, deaden. *Colloq.,* shush, squelch. *Slang,* shut up, slap down, put the kibosh on, soft-pedal.

2, hold one's tongue, speak softly, whisper. *Colloq.,* save one's breath, keep one's mouth shut. *Slang,* button *or* zip one's lip, clam up.

Adjectives—**1,** silent; still, stilly; quiet, noiseless, soundless; hushed, soft, solemn, awful, tomblike, deathlike, silent as the tomb *or* grave; inaudible, faint; soundproof, muted, muffled, noiseproof.

2, mute, dumb, mum, tongue-tied, tongueless, voiceless, speechless; aphonic; tacit; unspoken; silent, gagged, muzzled; inarticulate; taciturn (see TACITURNITY).

Adverbs—silently, mutely, *etc.;* with bated breath, under one's breath, *sotto voce; tacet. Slang,* on the q.t.

Interjections—hush! silence! shut up! cat got your tongue? mum is the word! *Slang,* dry up! belay that! stow it!

Antonyms, see SOUND, LOUDNESS.

---

silhouette, *n.* shadow [figure], shadowgram, skiagraph *or* -gram; outline, profile, cutout, cameo. See FORM.

silky, *adj.* silken, sericeous; satiny, lustrous; flossy, sleek, smooth, luxurious; suave, mellifluous. See SMOOTHNESS, SOFTNESS.

sill, *n.* windowsill, ledge, shelf; threshold, base, SUPPORT; frame, beam.

silly, *adj.* witless, foolish, stupid, childish; fatuous, inane; senseless, absurd, ridiculous; stunned. See ABSURDITY, CREDULITY, FOLLY.

silo, *n.* grainery, granary, grain elevator; crib, bin; storehouse (see STORE).

silt, *n.* sediment, deposit, alluvium, loess, clay. See UNCLEANNESS, REMAINDER.

silver, *n.* argentum, sterling, silver plate; [small *or* loose] change, cash; pin *or* hard money; silverware. —*adj.* argent[al]; silvery, silver-gray; eloquent, silver-tongued, mellisonant. See MINERAL, COLOR.

SIMILARITY

Nouns—**1,** similarity, resemblance, likeness, similitude, semblance; affinity, approximation, parallelism; AGREEMENT; analogy; family likeness; alliteration, rhyme, pun. See IMITATION, NEARNESS, CONFORMITY.

2, REPETITION; sameness, IDENTITY; uniformity, EQUALITY; parallel; simile, image; counterpart; striking, speaking, *or* faithful likeness; double, twin, picture. *Colloq.*, chip off the old block. *Slang,* [dead] ringer, spit and image. See COPY.

Verbs—**1,** look like, look alike, resemble; bear resemblance; smack of; approximate, partake of; parallel, match; take after; imitate; assimilate.

2, compare, identify, parallel, relate. See RELATION.

Adjectives—similar; resembling, like, alike; twin, analogous, analogical; parallel, of a piece; so; much the same; near, close, something like; comparable; akin; mock, pseudo, simulating, representing; exact, lifelike, faithful; true to nature, true to life, the very image, the very picture of; like two peas in a pod, cast in the same mold, in the same boat.

Adverbs—similarly, as if, so to speak, as it were, quasi, just as, a la; such as.

Antonyms, see DIFFERENCE, DEVIATION.

---

simile, *n.* figure of speech, comparison. See FIGURATIVE.

simmer, *v.* boil, cook, bubble, parboil; effervesce, fizz; fume, chafe, brood, fret, ferment. See HEAT, RESENTMENT.

simper, *v.i.* smile, smirk; strut, prance. See AFFECTATION, REJOICING.

SIMPLENESS

Nouns—**1,** simpleness, classicism; PURITY, homogeneity; CLEANNESS.

2, simplicity, artlessness, INNOCENCE; plainness, homeliness; undress; chastity, SEVERITY; ELEGANCE. See CREDULITY.

Verbs—simplify; clear, purify, clean; disentangle (see DISJUNCTION); come down to earth; call a spade a spade, lay on the line.

Adjectives—**1,** simple, homogeneous, single, pure, clear, sheer, neat, mere; bare, austere; classic; unmixed, uncomplex; simplistic, oversimplified; elementary; unadulterated, unsophisticated, unalloyed; pure and simple; free from, exempt from; exclusive; no-frills, severe, chaste; naïve.

2, plain, homely, homespun; Anglo-Saxon; dry, unvaried, monotonous; earthy; down-to-earth; ordinary; bald, flat; dull, artless, ingenuous, unaffected, free from affectation *or* ornament; chaste, severe; unadorned, unornamented, ungarnished, unvarnished, unarranged, untrimmed.

3, outspoken, blunt, direct, forthright, straight from the shoulder, down to brass tacks; in plain words, in plain English.

Adverbs—simply, purely; solely, only; unadornedly, in the raw; in plain terms, words, English, *etc.*, in words of one syllable, in no uncertain terms; bluntly, point-blank, right out, straight. *Colloq.*, flat-out.

Antonyms, see ORNAMENT, DISORDER, AFFECTATION, LOQUACITY.

---

simpleton, *n.* dunce, blockhead, moron, ninny, nincompoop, innocent, fool. *Slang,* nitwit, dope, jerk. See FOLLY, IGNORANCE.

simplistic, *adj.* naïve; oversimplified. See SIMPLENESS, IGNORANCE.

simulate, *v.t.* imitate, resemble, mimic; feign, counterfeit, pretend. See FALSEHOOD, IMITATION.

simultaneous, *adj.* coincident, concurrent, contemporaneous, in concert, in unison, synchronous. See TIME, SYNCHRONISM.

sin, *n.* IMPIETY, sacrilege, transgression, wickedness, IMPURITY, iniquity, vice; offense, crime, fault, error, peccadillo. —*v.i.* transgress, err, offend. See GUILT, WRONG, BADNESS, EVIL.

since, *adv.* ago, later, subsequently,

afterwards. —*conj.* because, inasmuch as; after. See CAUSE, ATTRIBUTION, CIRCUMSTANCE, REASONING.

sincere, *adj.* honest, genuine; ingenuous, forthright, unreserved, candid; cordial, hearty, earnest. See TRUTH, FEELING, PROBITY.

sinecure, *n.* easy job. *Slang,* snap, cinch, gravy. See FACILITY.

sinewy, *adj.* fibrous, wiry, stringy; strong, well-knit. See STRENGTH.

sing, *v.* troll; chant, carol, intone, warble; laud, praise; vocalize; yodel; versify; hum, whistle. See MUSIC, POETRY, DISCLOSURE.

singe, *v.t.* scorch, sear. See HEAT.

singer, *n.* vocalist, songster (see MUSIC).

single, *adj.* one, separate, solitary, individual; unmarried; unique, sole; detached, alone; sincere, honest, unequivocal. See CELIBACY, UNITY, SECLUSION.

single-handed, *adj.* alone, solo; by oneself, independent, unassisted, one-man; with one hand tied behind one's back. See UNITY.

single-minded, *adj.* one-track, narrow[-minded]; resolute, stubborn, determined; obsessive, monomaniacal; undeviating. See RESOLUTION.

singular, *adj.* unique, individual; peculiar, unusual, odd, eccentric; exceptional, rare; extraordinary. See UNCONFORMITY, SPECIALITY.

sinister, *adj.* ominous, unlucky, portentous; LEFT; evil, bad; unpropitious, baleful, injurious; ill-starred; malicious, harmful, corrupt. See BADNESS.

sink, *v.* founder, drown, go down; ebb, wane, decline, lapse, settle, subside, precipitate; retrograde, go downhill; languish, droop, flag; despond; fail, deepen, dig, lower; debase, abase, bring low; suppress, overwhelm; submerge, immerse, bury; discourage, dampen; invest, risk, venture. See DEPTH, DESCENT, DETERIORATION, DEJECTION, FAILURE.

sinless, *adj.* impeccable, virtuous, innocent, immaculate; absolved, shriven, purified, forgiven; unfallen, prelapsarian. See PURITY, INNOCENCE.

sip, *v.* drink, imbibe, taste; siphon, suck. —*n.* taste, soupçon, sampling; drink, draft; modicum. See FOOD, DRINKING.

sire, *v.* beget, father. See ANCESTRY.

siren, *n.* water nymph, temptress, Circe, Lorelei, Delilah, Jezebel; alarm, warning, signal. *Slang,* vamp, vampire, gold digger. See DEMON, ATTRACTION, FEMALE.

sissy, *n., colloq.,* weakling, milksop, milquetoast, mama's boy, mollycoddle; effeminate, transvestite. *Slang,* chicken, scaredy-cat. See WEAKNESS, COWARDICE.

sister, *n.* kinswoman; nun, sister of mercy, *religieuse;* associate, *soror,* fellow; nurse; counterpart. See CLERGY, SIMILARITY, RELATION.

sit, *v.i.* sit down, perch; pose; hold session, convene; fit, suit; brood; be situated. See LOCATION.

site, *n.* position, LOCATION.

sitting, *n.* session; séance. See ASSEMBLAGE.

situate, *v.* place, locate; set, station, put; lie, be situated. See LOCATION.

situation, *n.* place, LOCATION; position, site; state, predicament, plight, case, CIRCUMSTANCE; job, office, post, station, employment. See BUSINESS.

SIZE

Nouns—**1,** size, magnitude, dimension, bulk, volume; largeness, GREATNESS; expanse, SPACE; extent, scope (see DEGREE); AMPLITUDE; mass, DENSITY; proportions, MEASUREMENT; capacity, tonnage, caliber; corpulence, obesity, plumpness, fatness, *embonpoint,* avoirdupois, girth, corporation; hugeness, enormousness, immensity, monstrosity. See EXPANSION, ROTUNDITY.

2, giant, titan, Brobdingnagian, Antaeus, Goliath, Anak, Gog and Magog,

Gargantua, Cyclops; monster, mammoth, whale, porpoise, behemoth, leviathan, elephant, hippopotamus; colossus. *Colloq.,* whopper, bumper.

Verbs—expand, enlarge; grade, assort, graduate (see DEGREE).

Adjectives—**1,** large, big, great; considerable, goodly, hefty, bulky, voluminous, ample, massive, mammoth, massy; capacious, comprehensive, vast; spacious, towering, magnificent; tremendous, huge, immense, enormous, mighty; monstrous, titanic, gigantic, elephantine, jumbo; giant, stupendous, colossal; Cyclopean, Brobdingnagian, Gargantuan; gross; life-size, big *or* large as life.

2, corpulent, stout, fat, plump, full, lusty, strapping, bouncing; portly, burly, well-fed, full-grown; stalwart, brawny, fleshy; goodly; lumbering, unwieldy; whopping, thumping, thundering, hulking; overgrown, bloated; big as a house.

Antonyms, see LITTLENESS.

---

sizzle, *v.* crepitate, fizz, crackle, sp[l]utter; scorch, broil, fry, sear; burn, swelter. See HEAT.

skein, *n.* coil; tangle, twist, snarl. See CONVOLUTION.

skeleton, *n.* frame[work]; outline, diagram; bones, bony structure. See SUPPORT, PLAN, REMAINDER.

skeptic, *n.* doubter, agnostic, freethinker, doubting Thomas, questioner; infidel; unbeliever. See IRRELIGION, DOUBT.

sketch, *v.t.* draw, outline, block out, rough in; state briefly; draft, chart, map. See REPRESENTATION, FORM, PAINTING, PLAN.

skew, *adj.* oblique, distorted. See OBLIQUITY.

skewer, *n.* spit, pin. See JUNCTION.

skid, *n.* sideslip; incline; runner, check, curb, brake; skidway, travois; (*pl.*) *slang,* skid row, downfall, bankruptcy. —*v.* slide, [side]slip, spin; swerve; grip, brake, lock. See DESCENT, SIDE, DEBT, POVERTY.

SKILL

Nouns—**1,** skill, skillfulness, address; dexterity, dexterousness; adroitness, expertise, proficiency, adequacy, competence, [handi]craft, finesse, *savoir-faire,* FACILITY, knack; mastery, mastership; professionalism; excellence, ambidexterity, versatility, virtuosity, prowess; artistry, wizardry.

2, accomplishment, acquirement, endowment, attainment (see SUCCESS); art, science, touch, flair; technicality, technology; KNOWLEDGE, experience; discretion, diplomacy; delicacy; craftiness, CUNNING; management. See LEARNING.

3, cleverness, talent, ability, ingenuity, capacity, parts, faculty, endowment, forte, turn, gift, genius; INTELLIGENCE, sharpness; aptness, aptitude; capability, qualification; trick of the trade. *Colloq.,* knowhow. *Slang,* the goods, what it takes.

4, masterpiece, master stroke, coup, *coup de maître, chef d'oeuvre, tour de force;* trump card.

5, expert, adept, connoisseur, virtuoso, master; man of arts; artisan; master hand, top sawyer (*Brit.*), prima donna, first fiddle, old hand; practiced eye, marksman, crack; conjuror; veteran, champion, ace; old stager *or* campaigner; handyman; genius, mastermind, tactician, strategist, diplomat. *Slang,* sharp, shark, wizard, whiz.

Verbs—be skillful, excel in, be master of; have a turn for, play one's cards well *or* right, hit the nail on the head; have all one's wits about one; have one's hand in; have a lot on the ball. *Slang,* know one's stuff; have been around.

Adjectives—**1,** skillful, dexterous; adroit, expert, apt, handy, quick, deft, ready, smart, proficient, good at, up to, at home in, master of, a good hand at; masterly, crack, accomplished, versed in, conversant (see KNOWLEDGE); versatile; sophisticated, experienced, practiced, skilled, [well] up in, dry behind the ears; in practice; competent, efficient, qualified, capable, fitted for, up to the mark, trained, initiated, prepared, primed, finished.

2, clever, able, ingenious, felicitous, gifted, talented, endowed; inventive, shrewd, sharp, intelligent; ambidextrous, sure-footed; artistic, workmanlike, businesslike, statesmanlike.

Adverbs—skillfully, handily, well, artistically; with skill.

Antonyms, see UNSKILLFULNESS.

---

skillet, *n.* frying pan, frypan, spider; saucepan, casserole. See RECEPTACLE.

skim, *v.* scum; strain, cream, separate; scan, thumb through; glide, skip, skid, graze, brush, TOUCH. See VELOCITY.

skimp, *v.* scrimp, stinge, stint; economize. See ECONOMY, NEGLECT.

skin, *v.t.* flay, peel, decorticate; *slang,* fleece, cheat. See DIVESTMENT, STEALING. —*n.* integument, cuticle, dermis, epidermis; pelt, hide; rind; veneer, plating, lamina; parchment. See COVERING.

skinflint, *n.* niggard, scrimp, hoarder, tightwad. See PARSIMONY.

skinny, *adj.* thin, lean, slim, slender. See NARROWNESS.

skip, *v.* caper, spring, LEAP, hop, trip, frisk, gambol, frolic; omit, pass over, stay away; ricochet. *Slang,* decamp, play truant. See NEGLECT, ABSENCE.

skipper, *n.* captain, master, pilot; commodore, commander. See NAVIGATION, AUTHORITY.

skirmish, *n.* clash, brush, tilt, encounter, engagement. See CONTENTION.

skirt, *n.* overskirt, kilt, petticoat, farthingale, coattail; purlieu, borderland, EDGE, margin, outskirts; *slang,* woman, girl. See CLOTHING, FEMALE.

skit, *n.* burlesque, satire, parody, lampoon, pasquinade; sketch, playlet, vignette, tableau. See RIDICULE, DRAMA.

skittish, *adj.* lively, frisky, spirited; excitable, restive, nervous; timorous, fearful; coy, bashful; capricious, fickle. *Slang,* jittery. See EXCITABILITY.

skulduggery, *n.* trickery, DECEPTION.

skulk, *v.i.* lurk, sneak, slink, malinger, steal, hide; cower. See CONCEALMENT, COWARDICE.

sky, *n.* firmament, heavens, HEAVEN, welkin. See AIR.

skyline, *n.* horizon (see HORIZONTAL).

skyscraper, *n.* high-rise, tower. See ABODE.

slab, *n.* slice, wedge, section, piece, cut; plate, board, plank, shingle; tablet, gravestone. *Colloq.,* hunk, chunk. See PART, INTERMENT, HORIZONTAL, LAYER.

slack, *adj.* careless, lax, negligent, remiss; loose, limp, flaccid, relaxed; sluggish, stagnant; dull, slow, not busy, light. See NEGLECT, INACTIVITY, SOFTNESS, INSUFFICIENCY.

slacken, *v.* retard, diminish, lessen; loosen, relax; abate; languish, decline; ease up, dwindle. See MODERATION, REPOSE, SLOWNESS, DECREASE.

slacker, *n.* shirker, quitter, evader. See AVOIDANCE.

slake, *v.t.* quench, satisfy, appease, allay, abate, sate. See PLEASURE, REFRESHMENT, RELIEF.

slam, *v.* shut, close; swat, pound, batter. *Colloq.,* bash, slug. —*n.* impact, closing, crash, clang; buffet. See IMPULSE.

slander, *n.* scandal, aspersion, defamation, calumny, disparagement. See DETRACTION.

slang, *n.* argot, jargon, cant, lingo, patois, vernacular; dialect; colloquialism, neologism, vulgarism. See SPEECH.

slant, *n.* OBLIQUITY, slope, inclination, declination, tilt, pitch; bias, leaning, TENDENCY.

slap, *v.t. & n.* hit, smack, swat, cuff; insult. See IMPULSE, RIDICULE, PUNISHMENT.

slapdash, *adj.* precipitate, hasty, careless, hit or miss; superficial, sketchy, rough, hack, sloppy. See HASTE.

slap-happy, *adj., slang,* dazed, groggy; silly, foolish. See INSANITY, INATTENTION.

slash, *v.* hack, cut, gash, cleave, sever, sunder, slice, carve; whip, scourge; mark down, reduce, lower. See DISJUNCTION, DECREASE.

slat, *n.* lath, strip. See NARROWNESS, FILAMENT, LAYER, MATERIALS.

slate, *n.* LIST, ballot, ticket; blackboard; slab, rock, roof. See MATERIALS.

slattern, *n.* sloven; slut, trollop. See UNCLEANNESS.

slaughter, *n.* butchering; butchery, massacre, carnage, murder. See KILLING.

slaughterhouse, *n.* abattoir, shambles, butchery. See KILLING.

slave, *n.* bondsman, bond servant, thrall, serf; drudge, peon, vassal, menial; addict, victim. See SERVANT. —*v.i.* toil, drudge; overwork. See EXERTION.

slaver, *v.i.* slobber, drivel; fawn. See EXCRETION, SERVILITY.

slavery, *n.* bondage; forced labor; servitude, chains, captivity; drudgery, toil; addiction, submission. See SUBJECTION.

slay, *v.t.* kill, slaughter, dispatch; murder, assassinate. See KILLING.

sleazy, *adj.* flimsy, gauzy; shabby; shoddy, cheap, unsubstantial. See WEAKNESS, INSUBSTANTIALITY.

sled, *n.* sledge, sleigh; bobsled; dogsled; skid, cutter, pung. See VEHICLE.

sleek, *adj.* slick, oily, smooth, glossy; well-groomed; chic, soigné, elegant, suave, urbane, skillful, adroit. See SMOOTHNESS.

sleep, *n.* slumber, somnolence, nap, doze, drowse, rest, REPOSE; coma; hypnosis. —*v.i.* slumber, repose, doze, nap; be dead *or* dormant.

sleeping pill, *n.* barbiturate, opiate; tranquillizer, sedative. *Slang,* goof ball.

sleepless, *adj.* wakeful, insomniac, restless; alert, vigilant. See CARE, ACTIVITY.

sleepwalker, *n.* somnambulist, noctambulist, nightwalker. See TRAVEL.

sleepy, *adj.* drowsy; languid; lethargic. See REPOSE, INACTIVITY.

sleeve, *n.* COVERING, envelope, pipe; mandrel, quill, bushing, coupling, union.

slender, *adj.* slim, thin, skinny, attenuated; tenuous, slight, meager; scanty, weak. See NARROWNESS.

sleuth, *n.* bloodhound; detective, hawkshaw, gumshoe; plainclothesman; shadow, operative, [private] investigator. *Slang,* dick, private eye, shamus, op. See CONCEALMENT.

slice, *v.t.* cut, slash, carve, shave, skive. See LAYER.

slick, *adj.* glossy, shiny, polished; oily, slippery, greasy; unctuous, obsequious; sophisticated, urbane; *colloq.,* crooked, cheap, glib; sly, ingenious, CUNNING, tricky. See SMOOTHNESS, OIL, KNOWLEDGE.

slicker, *n.* raincoat, waterproof, poncho, oilcoat, oilskin; *colloq.,* swindler. See CLOTHING.

slide, *v.i.* glide, slip, coast, skim; steal, pass. See MOTION, DESCENT.

slight, *adj.* slender, slim, frail, delicate; trivial; meager, scant. See UNIMPORTANCE. —*v.t.* ignore, cut, snub, rebuff; scamp, NEGLECT, disdain. —*n.* snub, rebuff, cut. See CONTEMPT.

slim, *adj.* slender, thin, slight; frail, weak, meager. See NARROWNESS.

slime, *n.* ooze, mire, sludge, mud, muck; primordial slime; filth. See UNCLEANNESS.

sling, *v.t.* propel, fling, catapult; shoot, pitch; hang, fasten up, suspend. *Colloq.,* chuck, peg. See PROPULSION, PENDENCY. —*n.* slingshot, catapult, perrier, ballista; bandage, strap, suspensory, SUPPORT. See ARMS.

slink, *v.i.* sneak, steal, skulk, slither; creep, snoop. See CONCEALMENT, COWARDICE.

slip, *v.* glide, slide; misstep; steal; ESCAPE, elapse; blunder, err; don. —*n.* misstep, slide; blunder, ERROR; scion, graft; *faux pas,* indiscretion; undergarment; pillowcase; dock; strip, sheet; chit, girl; ceramic, cement. See DESCENT, CLOTHING, TRAVEL.

slippery, *adj.* slimy, greasy, slick, glassy, shifty, elusive, unreliable; sly, insecure. See SMOOTHNESS, DANGER.

slipshod, *adj.* negligent, slovenly, careless. See NEGLECT, DISORDER.

slit, *v. & n.* cut, gash, slash, slice. See INTERVAL, FURROW.

slither, *v.* slink, sinuate, worm; crawl, creep; slide, slip. See SMOOTHNESS, DESCENT.

sliver, *n.* splinter, shive; slice, chip, shaving; shard, fragment. See PART, FILAMENT.

slob, *n., slang,* sloven, slattern; pig, slovenly Peter. See UNCLEANNESS.

slobber, *v.i.* slaver, drivel, dribble, drool. See EXCRETION, MOISTURE.

slogan, *n.* watchword, shibboleth, password, byword, motto, MAXIM.

slop, *n.* spillage, muck, slush, slime; spillings, refuse, garbage, swill, waste, sewage; puddle; *slang,* chow, FOOD; *slang,* gush, sloppiness, schmaltz. —*v.* spill, overflow, splash. See UNCLEANNESS, MOISTURE.

slope, *n.* slant, tilt, pitch, inclination; incline, grade, gradient, ramp, ascent, rise. See OBLIQUITY.

sloppy, *adj.* untidy, messy; maudlin; slovenly. See DISORDER, NEGLECT, FEELING.

slosh, *v.* splash, slop, spill. See WATER, MOISTURE.

slot, *n.* aperture, slit, OPENING; groove, notch, nick, channel, PASSAGE.

sloth, *n.* laziness, idleness, INACTIVITY, inertia; slowness, sluggishness, indolence.

slouch, *v.* droop, flag, slump, sag, bend; shamble, shuffle, lounge, loll. See SLOWNESS, INACTION, DEPRESSION.

slovenly, *adj.* slatternly, sluttish; untidy, unkempt, disorderly; slipshod, lax. *Colloq.,* sloppy, tacky. See DISORDER, UNCLEANNESS, NEGLECT.

SLOWNESS

Nouns—**1,** slowness, languor, INACTIVITY; leisureliness; retardation; slackening; delay, LATENESS; walk, stroll, saunter, snail's pace, jog-trot, dog-trot; slow motion, slowdown. *Colloq.,* slowup.

2, dullness, flatness, monotony, boredom. See WEARINESS.

3, laggard, lingerer, loiterer, sluggard, tortoise, plodder; snail; dawdler. *Slang,* slowpoke. See IGNORANCE.

Verbs—**1,** move slowly, creep, crawl, lag, linger, loiter, straggle, stroll, saunter, walk, plod, trudge, inch, stump along, lumber; trail, drag; dawdle, worm one's way, steal along; toddle, waddle, slouch, shuffle, halt, hobble, limp, shamble; flag, falter, totter, stagger; take one's time; hang fire (see LATENESS). *Colloq.,* take one's own sweet time, laze along. *Slang,* get no place fast, mosey along, hold one's horses.

2, slow, retard, relax; slacken, check, moderate, rein in, fall behind, slow down, curb; reef; strike, shorten, *or* take in sail; set back; put on the drag, brake, apply the brake; clip the wings; reduce the speed; slacken speed *or* one's pace; lose ground; slack off *or* down; step down.

Adjectives—slow, slack; tardy; dilatory, inactive, gentle, easy, leisurely; deliberate, gradual; dull, uninteresting; languid, sluggish, snail- *or* slow-paced, snaillike, creeping. *Colloq.*, slow as molasses.

Adverbs—slowly, leisurely; at half speed, under easy sail; at a snail's pace; in slow time; in slow motion; gradually, by degrees *or* inches, step by step, drop by drop, inch by inch, bit by bit, little by little.

Antonyms, see VELOCITY, HASTE.

---

sludge, *n.* mud, mire, filth; ooze, slime, slush; slag; sewage. See UNCLEANNESS.

slug, *v.* hit, swat, belt; bash, smash, whale. See IMPULSE.

sluggish, *adj.* inactive, stagnant, torpid, slow; lazy, slothful, dull, indolent; languid, apathetic, lethargic. See INACTIVITY, SLOWNESS.

sluice, *n.* channel (see EGRESS).

slum, *n.* tenements, skid row, wrong side of the tracks; ghetto. See ABODE, POVERTY, UNCLEANNESS.

slumber, *n.* sleep, nap, doze, quiescence. See REPOSE.

slump, *v.i.* fall, settle, sink, drop; slouch, lounge, sprawl; sag, droop; decline, diminish, wane, languish; fail, collapse. —*n.* decline; setback, depression, RECESSION, regression, reversion, comedown, collapse, failure; *colloq.*, slowdown, slack season.

slur, *v.t.* slight, disparage, calumniate, traduce, asperse; skim, skip, gloss over; ignore; elide. See DISREPUTE, NEGLECT.

slush, *n.* slosh, sludge, slop; gush, effusiveness, drivel; bribery. See COHERENCE, SENSIBILITY.

slut, *n.* sloven, slattern, slob; prostitute. *Slang,* doxy, chippy. See IMPURITY.

sly, *adj.* CUNNING, furtive, wily; crafty, deceitful, stealthy, underhand; roguish, mischievous. See CONCEALMENT.

smack, *n.* clap, whack, slap; kiss, buss; savor, tastiness, flavor, gusto, relish, TASTE. See IMPULSE, ENDEARMENT. —*v.* slap, strike, smite, whack; TASTE, savor; smack of, recall, call to mind. See SIMILARITY, MEMORY.

small, *adj.* little, tiny, short, wee; dwarfish, undersized, stunted; lowercase; humble; minute, infinitesimal; dainty, petite; trivial, unimportant, petty; puny, slight, weak; mean, paltry, unworthy; pygmy, Lilliputian, minikin. See LITTLENESS, HUMILITY, UNIMPORTANCE.

small-time, *adj., slang,* minor, unimportant, trivial, petty; one-horse, jerkwater, tinhorn, minor-league. See UNIMPORTANCE.

smart, *adj.* chic, stylish, jaunty, dapper; severe, sharp, keen; witty, pert, sparkling; brisk, energetic, fresh; shrewd, clever. See SKILL, FEELING, WIT. —*v.i.* sting, PAIN, rankle.

smash, *v.t.* shatter, crush; hit, strike; ruin, destroy, disintegrate. See DESTRUCTION, SUCCESS.

smash-up, *n.* crash, collision, wreck, crackup, pileup; accident; calamity, catastrophe, disaster. See IMPULSE.

smattering, *n.* superficiality, sciolism. See IGNORANCE.

smear, *v.t.* [be]daub, besmirch, smudge; grease, anoint, defame; slander; soil, sully. See COVERING.

smell, *v.* scent; stink; sniff, snuff, inhale; detect, nose out. See ODOR, MALODOROUSNESS.

smile, *v.i.* grin, simper, smirk; beam, look with favor; sneer, RIDICULE. See REJOICING.

smirk, *n.* simper, grin, leer; smug look, grimace. See REJOICING, RIDICULE.

smite, *v.t.* strike, hit, cuff, pummel; affect, captivate, enamor, entrance; afflict. See IMPULSE, FEELING.

smith, *n.* blacksmith, tinsmith, tinker. See EXERTION.

smock, *n.* blouse, housecoat, house dress; coverall, apron. See CLOTHING.

smog, *n., colloq.,* [weather] inversion. See CLOUDINESS.

smoke, *v.* reek, fume, smolder; steam; puff, inhale, chain-smoke; smoke-dry, cure; fumigate; begrime, pollute. See DRYNESS, UNCLEANNESS, PUNGENCY, PRESERVATION.

smoky, *adj.* hazy, cloudy. See OBSCURITY.

smolder, *v.i.* reek, fume, smoke; hang fire, be latent, lurk. See HEAT, LATENCY.

SMOOTHNESS

Nouns—**1,** smoothness, polish, gloss, glaze, sheen; slickness, slipperiness; blandness; evenness. See TEXTURE, FRICTION.

2, level, velvet, silk, satin; glass, ice; flatness. See HORIZONTAL.

3, plane, roller, steamroller; sandpaper, abrasive; buffer, burnisher, polisher; wax, varnish; iron, mangle; Teflon, graphite; OIL.

Verbs—**1,** smooth, plane; file; mow, shave; level, roll; unroll, unfurl; pave; polish, rub, shine, buff, burnish, calender, glaze; varnish, wax; iron, press; lubricate; sand.

2, slip, slide, glide (see TRAVEL, DESCENT).

Adjectives—**1,** smooth; polished, even; level; plane, flat, HORIZONTAL; sleek, glossy; silken, silky; downy, velvet[y]; slippery, glassy; greasy, oily; soft, unwrinkled; smooth as glass, silk, ice, *or* velvet; slippery as an eel; bald [as an egg *or* billiard ball].

2, slippery, greasy, oily, slick, unctuous, lubricating.

Antonyms, see ROUGHNESS.

smother, *v.t.* suffocate, stifle; suppress, repress; extinguish, deaden. See KILLING, RESTRAINT, DEATH.

smudge, *n.* soot, grime, dirt, blotch, smear, blot, smutch; smolder. —*v.* soil, smear, mark, daub, dirty; stain, blacken. See HEAT, UNCLEANNESS.

smug, *adj.* sleek, trim, neat; self-satisfied, complacent; priggish, conceited. See AFFECTATION, VANITY.

smuggler, *n.* contrabandist, bootlegger, runner. See ILLEGALITY.

smut, *n.* soot, smudge, spot, blemish; dirt, filth, pornography; fungus, rot, mildew. See IMPURITY. —*v.* blacken, sully, smudge. See UNCLEANNESS.

snack, *n.* repast, collation, refreshment, coffee break. See FOOD.

snag, *n.* catch, detent, snaggle-tooth; HINDRANCE, difficulty. —*v.* catch, fix, entangle; snarl, impede, hamper, hinder. See IMPERFECTION.

snake, *n.* serpent, reptile, ophidian; snake in the grass, deceiver, double dealer. See ANIMAL, DECEPTION.

snap, *n.* crackle, rapping, pop, crack, report, clap, smack; vigor, pep, verve, dash, élan; smartness, spruceness, crispness; spell (of weather); *colloq.,* sinecure, cinch, soft job. —*v.* break, crack, crackle; knock, rap, tap; snarl, bark, scold; bite, nip. See DISJUNCTION, DISCOURTESY, SOUND, BRITTLENESS.

snappy, *adj.* brisk, COLD; *colloq.,* smart, quick, crisp. See FASHION.

snare, *n.* trap, springe, gin; artifice, pitfall, ambush. See DECEPTION, RETENTION.

snarl, *v.i.* growl, gnarl, grumble; entangle. See DISCOURTESY, THREAT.

snatch, *v.t.* grab, seize, grasp, clutch, jerk, twitch, pluck, wrench; steal; *slang,* kidnap. See STEALING.

sneak, *v.i.* slink, skulk, crawl, steal. —*n.* skulker, sneak thief; coward. See COWARDICE.

sneer, *v.* smile, jeer, taunt, scoff; flout, deride. See CONTEMPT.

sneeze, *n.* sternutation. See WIND.

snicker, *v.i.* snigger, titter, laugh, giggle, chuckle; RIDICULE.

snide, *adj.* spiteful, malicious, sarcastic, cynical, derogatory; mean, invidious. See DISREPUTE, BADNESS.

sniff, *v.* sniffle; smell, scent; breathe, inhale, detect. See ODOR, WIND.

snip, *v.* cut, slice, shear, scissor; prune, trim, lop. See DISJUNCTION.

sniper, *n.* marksman, sharpshooter; critic. See COMBATANT, DISAPPROBATION.

snitch, *v., slang,* swipe, filch; inform. See STEALING, INFORMATION.

snivel, *v.i.* snuffle, sniff, blubber; whimper, cry, weep; cower, grovel, crawl, cringe. See LAMENTATION.

snob, *n.* sycophant, toady, fawner, bounder, upstart; parvenu, social climber. See SERVILITY, VULGARITY.

snoop, *v.i., colloq.,* pry; investigate, probe; meddle; play detective. —*n.* snooper, pry; meddler, busybody. See CURIOSITY.

snooze, *n.* nap, doze, sleep, forty winks. See INACTIVITY.

snore, *n.* stertor, wheeze, rhoncus, rale, zzz. See SOUND, LOUDNESS.

snort, *v.* grunt, snortle, guffaw. See CRY. —*n.* grunt, laugh; drink, draft, dram, jigger. *Colloq.,* shot. See DRINKING.

snout, *n.* nose, nostrils, muzzle, beak, bill, trunk. See CONVEXITY.

snow, *n.* snowfall, snowflake, flurry; snowstorm, blizzard; snowslide, drift, avalanche; hail, sleet. —*v.* snow in *or* under; swamp, flood, inundate; *slang,* impress, flatter. *Slang,* do a snow job on. See COLD, FLATTERY.

snowball, *v.i., colloq.,* accelerate, gain momentum, pick up speed. See INCREASE.

snub, *v.t.* cut, ignore, slight, rebuff, cold-shoulder; check, curb, halt. —*n.* rebuff, slight, cut. —*adj.* turned-up, blunt, retroussé. See CONTEMPT, REPULSION.

snuff, *v.t.* extinguish, put out; sniff, inhale; smell, scent; snuffle, sniffle. See WIND, ODOR, INCOMBUSTIBILITY.

snug, *adj.* cozy, comfortable; sheltered; trim, compact, neat. See PLEASURE, CLOSURE, CONTENT, SAFETY.

snuggle, *v.i.* nestle, cuddle, lie snug. See ENDEARMENT.

soak, *v.t.* wet, drench, saturate, steep; absorb; permeate; drink, tipple; *slang,* overcharge, bleed. See WATER, MOISTURE, DRYNESS, DRINKING, DEARNESS.

soap, *n.* cleanser, cleansing agent; lather; detergent; shampoo; *slang,* softsoap, corniness, sentimentality. See CLEANNESS, SENSIBILITY.

soar, *v.i.* fly, fly high; tower; glide. See AVIATION, HEIGHT, ASCENT.

sob, *v.i.* weep, cry, sigh; moan. See LAMENTATION.

sober, *adj.* grave, quiet, sedate, staid, serious; abstemious; drab, plain, severe, unadorned; calm, moderate; thoughtful; subdued; inconspicuous; demure; earnest; solemn, somber. See MODERATION, INEXCITABILITY, DEJECTION, SANITY.

sobriquet, *n.* nickname. See NOMENCLATURE.

sob story, *n., slang,* tearjerker, melodrama, human interest; tale of woe, hard-luck story. *Slang,* mush, schmaltz. See FEELING.

social, *adj.* gregarious, friendly; fashionable; communal, public. See SOCIALITY, PARTY, HUMANITY.

socialism, *n.* public ownership, communism, collectivism; communalism. See AUTHORITY, LEFT.

socialite, *n.* See FASHION.

SOCIALITY

Nouns—**1,** sociality, sociability, sociableness, friendship; social intercourse, community; fellowship, fraternity, companionship, camaraderie; familiarity, intimacy; association, brotherhood; communion; gregariousness. See CONVERSATION, AMUSEMENT.

2, conviviality, good fellowship, joviality, jollity, *savoir vivre,* festive board.

3, hospitality, cheer; welcome, greeting; hearty *or* warm welcome *or* reception; urbanity (see COURTESY).

4, social circle, sewing circle, family circle; coterie, society; club; social [gathering], assembly (see ASSEMBLAGE); party, entertainment, reception, salon, levee, at home, *conversazione, soirée;* garden party; house-warming; reunion; coffee *or* happy hour; debut, visit[ing]; call; affair; appointment, tryst, date. *Colloq.,* get-together, hen party, stag party, coming-out party, mixer, be-in.

5, social person, good company, companion, crony, *bon vivant. Colloq.,* joiner; good mixer, back-slapper, hand-shaker, hail-fellow-well-met. *Slang,* good egg *or* scout.

Verbs—**1,** be sociable, know; be acquainted, associate with, keep company with, club together, consort, bear one company, join; make acquaintance with; make advances, fraternize, socialize, tie up with, take up with, rub shoulders *or* elbows, hobnob, mix with, mingle with; embrace; be, feel, *or* make oneself at home with; date, double-date; make free with; be hospitable; roll out the red carpet. *Colloq.,* throw a party; fix someone up with.

2, visit, pay a visit; call [up]on, drop in, look in on; look one up; entertain, give a party, hold court, be at home, keep open house, do the honors, receive with open arms, welcome, bid one welcome, give a warm reception to; kill the fatted calf; see one's friends, drop by *or* around, stop by.

Adjectives—sociable, companionable, friendly; conversable, cozy, chatty, conversational; social, neighborly, gregarious, affable; convivial, festive, festal; jovial, jolly, hospitable; welcome; free and easy. *Colloq.,* clubby, chummy.

Adverbs—socially, companionably, intimately, *etc.*

Antonyms, see SECLUSION.

---

society, *n.* HUMANITY, mankind, folk; culture, civilization, group; community; companionship, fellowship; *bon ton,* elite, aristocracy; sodality, solidarity, association, league, union, alliance; parish, congregation. See SOCIALITY, PARTY, FASHION.

sock, *n.* [half] hose, anklet, stocking; *slang,* slug, punch, clout, wallop, jab. —*v.t., slang,* strike, slug, *etc.* See CLOTHING, IMPULSE.

socket, *n.* holder, cup, RECEPTACLE, CONCAVITY, hole, pit.

sod, *n.* turf, sward, glebe; clod, divot. See VEGETABLE, LAND.

soda, *n.* carbonated water, [soda] pop, seltzer, fizz, mineral water. See DRINKING.

sodden, *adj.* soaked, saturated, soggy, doughy, dull; drunken, befuddled, bloated. See MOISTURE, DRINKING.

sofa, *n.* couch, seat, lounge, divan, settee, love seat. See SUPPORT.

SOFTNESS

Nouns—**1,** softness, pliableness, pliancy, pliability, flexibility; malleability; ductility, tractility; extendability, extensibility; plasticity; flaccidity, flabbiness, laxity; sensitivity, responsiveness, susceptibility (see SENSIBILITY).

2, clay, wax, butter, dough, pudding; cushion, pillow, featherbed, down, padding, wadding; foam rubber.

3, softening, modification; mellowness, relaxation (see MODERATION).

4, faintness, lowness; murmur, whisper; hum, buzz; rustle. See SOUND.

Verbs—**1,** soften, mollify, mellow, relax, temper; mash, knead, squash; melt, liquefy; bend, yield, relent, give.
2, whisper, murmur, rustle, mutter, hum, buzz.

Adjectives—**1,** soft, tender, supple, pliant, pliable; flexible, flexile; sensitive, responsive, susceptible; lithe[some], lissom, limber, plastic; ductile; tractile, tractable; malleable, extensile; yielding, flabby, limp, flimsy; flaccid, flocculent, downy, feathery, fleecy, spongy, doughy; mellow, velvet[y], silky, satiny.
2, faint, low, dim, feeble, indistinct; muffled, muted (see SILENCE); whispering, murmuring, *etc.*

Adverbs—**1,** soft as butter, soft as down, soft as silk; yielding as wax.
2, softly, faintly, *etc.;* piano, pianissimo; *sotto voce,* under one's breath, in a whisper; muted, *à la sourdine.*

Antonyms, see HARDNESS, INELASTICITY.

---

soft-soap, *v.t., colloq.,* flatter, feed a line to. *Slang,* snow. See FLATTERY.

soft-spoken, *adj.* unassertive, quiet, gentle, kindly. See COURTESY.

soggy, *adj.* saturated, soaked, soppy; sodden, doughy. See MOISTURE.

soil, *n.* loam, earth, sod, topsoil, dirt, mold, ground; stain, blotch, smudge, smear, filth. —*v.t.* besmear, dirty, daub, stain; defile, sully. See LAND, REGION, UNCLEANNESS.

sojourn, *v.i.* tarry, abide, stay, lodge, stop over, visit. See ABODE.

solace, *n.* comfort, consolation, RELIEF. —*v.t.* soothe, calm, comfort; cheer, console; assuage, mitigate.

solder, *v.* spelter, fuse, braze, weld; bond, cement, mend. See JUNCTION, COHERENCE, CONNECTION.

soldier, *n.* warrior, fighting man. See COMBATANT.

soldierly, *adj.* military, martial; brave, courageous; gallant, snappy, spruce; erect. See WARFARE.

sole, *adj.* only, one, single, unique, exclusive, individual. See UNITY, EXCLUSION.

solecism, *n.* ERROR, lapse, slip, blunder; grammatical error; barbarism, *faux pas,* social error, impropriety; incongruity, mistake. See INELEGANCE.

solemn, *adj.* awesome, impressive; grave, serious, dignified; sober; formal, ceremonious; reverent, ritualistic. See IMPORTANCE, DEJECTION, PIETY, OSTENTATION.

solemnize, *v.t.* celebrate, perform, observe. See CELEBRATION, RITE.

solicit, *v.t.* REQUEST, invite, ask, entreat, importune, beg, canvass, petition.

solicitous, *adj.* considerate; anxious, concerned; eager, careful. See CARE.

solicitude, *n.* CARE, concern, anxiety; consideration; uneasiness. See DESIRE, FEAR.

solid, *adj.* dense, compact, hard, firm, rigid; substantial; united, unanimous, reliable; unbroken, undivided, whole, intact; sound, valid; stable, solvent; genuine, real. See DENSITY, SUBSTANCE, CERTAINTY, TRUTH.

solidarity, *n.* union, fellowship. See UNITY.

soliloquy, *n.* monologue; apostrophe. *Colloq.,* aside. See SPEECH.

solitary, *adj.* alone, lonesome; sole, single, individual, lone; deserted, remote, unfrequented; unsocial, retiring. See SECLUSION.

solitude, *n.* SECLUSION, privacy, isolation; remoteness; loneliness; wilderness.

solo, *n.* single; aria, arietta; recital, solo flight. —*adj.* lone, single, singlehanded; one-man; unaided. See UNITY.

soluble, *adj.* dissolvable (see LIQUEFACTION).

solution, *n.* ANSWER, explanation,

INTERPRETATION, key, clue; disintegration, dissolution; lixivium, decoction; LIQUEFACTION.

solve, *v.t.* explain, interpret; ANSWER; resolve, clear up; decipher, decode. See DISCLOSURE.

solvent, *adj.* financially sound, moneyed; responsible, reliable; soluble, separative, dissolvent, diluent. —*n.* dissolvent, dissolver, liquefier. See LIQUEFACTION, MONEY.

somber, *adj.* gloomy, dark, overcast, dull; sad, dismal, leaden, depressing, funereal. See DARKNESS, DEJECTION.

some, *adj.* several, [a] few, a number of; one, any; certain, divers, various, sundry. *Colloq.,* what a, quite a. —*pron.* any, a few, one or more, someone, somebody. —*adv.* about, around, approximately, nearly, almost, in a way; to a degree. See QUANTITY.

somebody, *n.* one, someone; person, individual; bigwig, personage. See IMPORTANCE.

somehow, *adv.* some way, by some means. See METHOD.

somersault, *n.* See INVERSION.

something, *n.* thing, object, anything; matter, part; affair, event. See SUBSTANCE.

sometimes, *adv.* occasionally, now and then. See OCCASION, FREQUENCY.

somewhere, *adv.* someplace; anywhere, somewhere about; approximately. See LOCATION.

somnolent, *adj.* sleepy, drowsy, slumb[e]rous; dozing; lethargic. See INACTIVITY.

son, *n.* male child, boy, offspring; descendant, inheritor. See POSTERITY.

song, *n.* lyric, ballad, popular song; aria, chanson, cavatina; carol, lilt, madrigal, glee, ditty; minstrelsy, poem, chanty, lay, birdsong, folksong, spiritual, *etc.* See MUSIC, POETRY.

sonorous, *adj.* resonant, deep-toned, rich, majestic; grandiloquent, high-flown. See LOUDNESS, SOUND.

soon, *adv.* anon, presently; promptly, quickly; readily, willingly. See EARLINESS.

soot, *n.* smoke, carbon dust, smut, grit, coal dust; lampblack; smog, smaze. See UNCLEANNESS.

soothe, *v.t.* calm, quiet, tranquilize; relieve, assuage, mitigate, allay, console, comfort. See MODERATION, RELIEF, CONTENT, FLATTERY.

sop, *n.* morsel, pacifier; bribe, inducement, compensation, propitiation, token; milksop. See PAYMENT, MODERATION. —*v.* steep, dunk, dip, soak; wet, moisten. See MOISTURE.

sophisticate, *n.* worldling; cosmopolitan, man-about-town, man of the world. See SKILL, KNOWLEDGE.

sophistication, *n.* affectation; worldliness, veneer. See AFFECTATION, SKILL, KNOWLEDGE.

sophistry, *n.* sophism; false *or* specious reasoning; casuistry; fallaciousness, paralogism; shift, subterfuge, equivocation; absurdity, inconsistency; hair-splitting. See FALSEHOOD.

sophomoric, *adj.* immature, callow; inane, foolish. See FOLLY.

soporific, *adj.* sedative, narcose, soothing; lethargic, torpid, dull, slow, sluggish; tedious, wearisome. See REPOSE, WEARINESS.

SORCERY

Nouns—**1,** sorcery; the occult; magic, the black art, necromancy, theurgy, thaumaturgy; demonology, diablerie, bedevilment; voodoo, obeah, hoodoo, witchcraft, witchery; alchemy; white *or* black magic; black Mass; fetishism, vampirism; conjuration; bewitchery, enchantment, mysticism, second sight, mesmerism, animal magnetism; od *or* odylic force; clairvoyance (see INTUITION); spiritualism, spirit-rapping, table-turning; divination (see PREDICTION); sortilege, hocus-pocus (see DECEPTION). See SECRET.

2, spell, charms, hex, incantation, cabala, runes, abracadabra, open sesame, mumbo-jumbo, evil eye. *Colloq.*, jinx, Indian sign.

3, exorcism; countercharm; bell, book, and candle; talisman, amulet, periapt, phylactery, philter; fetish, *agnus Dei*.

4, wand, caduceus, rod, divining rod, magic lamp *or* ring, wishing cap, Fortunatus' cap, magic carpet; philosophers' stone.

5, sorcerer, magician; thaumaturgist, theurgist; conjuror, voodooist, necromancer, seer, wizard, witch; lamia, hag, warlock, charmer; medicine man; alchemist; shaman, medium, clairvoyant, mesmerist; *deus ex machina;* soothsayer, oracle; Cagliostro, Mesmer; Circe, siren, weird sisters. See DEMON.

Verbs—practice sorcery, conjure, charm, enchant; bewitch, bedevil; entrance, mesmerize, magnetize; exorcise; fascinate; taboo; wave a wand; rub the ring *or* lamp; cast a spell; hold a seance, call up spirits, raise spirits from the dead. *Colloq.*, jinx. *Slang*, hoodoo.

Adjectives—magic, magical; occult; SECRET, mystic, weird, cabalistic, talismanic, phylacteric, incantatory; charmed, bewitched; spellbound, haunted.

Antonyms, see RELIGION.

---

sordid, *adj.* mean, base, ignoble; covetous, niggardly; mercenary, self-seeking; squalid, dirty, foul. See PARSIMONY, UNCLEANNESS.

sore, *adj.* painful, tender, sensitive; grieved, distressed; harsh, severe, intense, dire; *slang*, aggrieved, resentful, disgruntled. See PAIN, DISCONTENT, RESENTMENT. —*n.* wound, abrasion, ulcer, chancroid, sore spot. See DISEASE.

sorrow, *n.* grief, sadness, dolor, distress; contrition, remorse, penitence; affliction, woe. See DEJECTION.

sorry, *adj.* rueful, regretful, penitent; sympathetic, sorrowful; pitiful, deplorable; shabby, paltry, wretched, mean. See PENITENCE.

sort, *n.* CLASS, kind, variety, group, category, description. —*v.t.* segregate, separate, isolate; size, grade, group, match; assort, arrange, classify; sift, screen. See ARRANGEMENT.

sortie, *n.* sally, mission, ATTACK.

so-so, *adj.* passable, fair; *comme ci, comme ça*. See MEDIOCRITY.

sot, *n.* drunkard (see DRINKING).

soubrette, *n.* actress, ingenue, comedienne; coquette, flirt. See DRAMA.

soul, *n.* psyche, spirit, mind; vital principle; essence; person, mortal, individual; ego; nobility, courage, heart, fire, élan; genius. See HUMANITY, INTELLECT.

soulful, *adj.* emotional, affective. See FEELING.

sound, *adj.* whole, undamaged; healthy, robust; logical, true, valid, reliable, honorable, trustworthy; solvent; strong, firm; thorough; unbroken. See PERFECTION, HEALTH, STABILITY. —*n.* inlet, channel, bay, gulf. —*v.* fathom, plumb, measure; probe; investigate, examine; utter; investigate. See DEPTH, INQUIRY.

SOUND

Nouns—**1,** sound, noise, strain; accent, twang, intonation, tone; cadence; sonorousness, resonance, audibility (see HEARING); resonance, voice; sound effects; sine, square, *etc.* wave, sound wave, white noise; decibel, phon. See SPEECH.

2, tone, tonality, intonation, inflection, modulation; pitch, key, timbre, tone color; monotone; overtone, fundamental; homophony, polyphony.

3, acoustics, phonics, phonetics, phonology, phonography; diacoustics, diaphonics, telephonics, radiophony; acoustician, acoustical engineer.

4, vociferation, roar, CRY, utterance, voice; snap, crash, bang, boom, roll, clatter, detonation, explosion; sonic boom. See LOUDNESS.

Verbs—**1,** sound, ring, resound; make a noise; give out *or* emit sound.

2, speak (see SPEECH); snap, roll, reverberate, detonate, *etc.;* buzz. See LOUDNESS.

Adjectives—sounding; soniferous, sonorous, resonant; audible, distinct; sonant, stertorous; sonic, sub- *or* supersonic; phonetic; acoustic, phonic; sibilant.

Antonyms, see SILENCE.

---

soundless, *adj.* silent (see SILENCE).

soundly, *adv.* completely, thoroughly. See COMPLETION.

soundproof, *adj.* insulated, sound-absorbing; muted, muffled, noise-proof; noiseless, quiet, silent. See SILENCE.

soup, *n.* stock, broth, bouillon, consommé; potage, purée, bisque, chowder. See FOOD.

source, *n.* CAUSE, origin, fountainhead, fount, derivation. See BEGINNING.

SOURNESS

Nouns—**1,** sourness, acid[ity], acerbity, acridity, astringency, tartness, rancidness, UNSAVORINESS. See TASTE, PUNGENCY, DISCORD.

2, vinegar, acetum, verjuice, acetic acid, alum; lemon, lime, crab, pickle, sauerkraut; sour milk *or* cream, buttermilk, *crème fraiche,* yogurt; sour grapes.

3, moroseness, sullenness, *etc.* (see DISCONTENT); IRASCIBILITY, ill-humor.

Verbs—**1,** sour, turn sour, ferment, set the teeth on edge; acidify, acidulate, curdle, clabber, turn.

2, exasperate, exacerbate, irritate (see RESENTMENT).

Adjectives—**1,** sour, acid, subacid, acidulous; acetic, acerbic, astringent, acrid, acetous, acetose; tart, crabbed, vinegary; sourish, sour as vinegar, sour as a pickle *or* lemon; green, unripe; styptic, hard, rough, caustic, bitter; distasteful; soured, rancid, curdled, coagulated, turned, spoiled, musty, bad.

2, morose, sullen, surly, churlish, currish, crusty, crabbed, peevish, pettish, cross; acrimonious, ill-humored, -natured, *or* -tempered, fretful, petulant, testy, snarling, irascible; glum, gloomy, dismal, sad, austere.

Antonyms, see SWEETNESS.

---

southern, *adj.* southerly, austral. See DIRECTION.

souvenir, *n.* memento, keepsake, relic. See MEMORY.

sovereign, *n.* monarch, ruler; potentate; king, queen, emperor, empress. See AUTHORITY, SUPERIORITY.

sow, *v.t.* strew, scatter, disseminate, broadcast; plant, seed. See AGRICULTURE, DISPERSION.

spa, *n.* mineral spring, watering place, thermal spring, mudbaths, balneum, hydro, *Bad,* waters; health club; resort. See REMEDY.

SPACE

Nouns—**1,** space, extension, extent, superficial extent, area, expanse; sphere, range, latitude, field, way, EXPANSION, compass, gamut, sweep, play, swing, spread, capacity, stretch; open *or* free space; void, emptiness; waste, wild, wilderness, wide open spaces; moor, prairie, campagna, champaign;

abyss, unlimited space, INFINITY, UNIVERSE, creation; heavens, sky; interplanetary space; length and breadth of the land. See ASTRONAUTICS.

2, room, scope, spare room, elbow room; margin; leeway, headway. *Slang*, room to swing a cat.

3, proportions, dimensions, acreage, acres, BREADTH, width; square inches, feet, yards, *etc*. See LENGTH, MEASUREMENT, SIZE, TIME.

Verbs—extend, reach, stretch, cover, spread, sweep, range; give *or* make room *or* way, open up [on].

Adjectives—spatial; spacious, roomy, commodious, extensive, expansive, capacious, ample; widespread, vast, worldwide, uncircumscribed; unlimited, endless; infinite, universal; boundless, unbounded, shoreless, trackless, pathless, bottomless.

Adverbs—extensively, wherever; everywhere; far and near, far and wide, right and left, all over, all the world over; throughout the world; under the sun, in every quarter, in all quarters, in all lands; here, there, and everywhere; from pole to pole, from end to end; on the face of the earth, in the wide world, from all points of the compass, to the four winds, to the uttermost parts of the earth; infinitely, *ad infinitum*.

Antonyms, see CIRCUMSCRIPTION, RESTRAINT.

---

space-age, *adj.* twentieth-century, modern, contemporary. See NEWNESS.

spacecraft, *n.* spaceship, rocket, transport (see ASTRONAUTICS).

spade, *n.* shovel, spud. —*v.* dig, delve, shovel, excavate. See CONCAVITY.

span, *v.t.* measure; encircle; stretch over, bridge. —*n.* bridge; extent; period; lifetime; nine-inch spread; team, yoke. See MEASUREMENT, SPACE, JUNCTION, DISTANCE, LENGTH, TIME.

spangle, *n.* sequin, paillette, ORNAMENT, bead, gem, stud, bauble, trinket, sparkler. —*v.t.* bespangle, jewel, stud, ORNAMENT, decorate. —*v.i.* sparkle, glitter, glisten, scintillate, coruscate. See LIGHT.

spank, *v.t.* slap, paddle, wallop; punish, chastise. See PUNISHMENT.

spanking, *adj.* brisk, lively, fresh; exceptional. See ACTIVITY, GREATNESS. —*n.* PUNISHMENT, hiding, thrashing.

spar, *v.i.* box; stall, play for time; bandy words, argue, bicker, wrangle, dispute. See CONTENTION. —*n.* mast, pole, gaff, boom, sprit, yard, bowsprit; varnish. See SHIP.

spare, *v.t.* be lenient; save; refrain, abstain, forbear, withhold; exempt; give up, surrender, forego, relinquish. See RELINQUISHMENT. —*adj.* lean, gaunt, bony; meager; extra, reserve; frugal. See NARROWNESS, STORE, LENIENCY, DISUSE, ECONOMY, EXEMPTION.

spark, *n.* flash; inspiration; iota, jot; *colloq.*, beau, swain, gallant. See HEAT, LOVE.

sparkle, *v.i.* glisten, spark, twinkle, flash, glitter, scintillate; effervesce, bubble. See LIGHT, CHEERFULNESS.

sparse, *adj.* scattered, sporadic; thin, few, meager, scanty. See RARITY.

spasm, *n.* throe, paroxysm, convulsion, seizure; fit, furor. See AGITATION, IRREGULARITY, PAIN, VIOLENCE, DISCONTINUANCE.

spat, *n.* quarrel, dispute; slap, smack; gaiter. See DISCORD, IMPULSE, CLOTHING.

spate, *n.* freshet, storm. See WATER.

spatial, *adj.* dimensional. See SPACE.

spatter, *v.t.* splash, sprinkle; besprinkle, bedraggle, bespatter; sully, soil. See UNCLEANNESS.

spawn, *v.* deposit, lay; propagate, breed, beget; produce, bring forth, give birth to, engender. —*n.* eggs, roe, ova; products, handiwork; offspring, scions, progeny, brood.

See POSTERITY, REPRODUCTION.

speak, *v.* talk, converse; lecture, discourse, orate; say, utter, pronounce; express, communicate. See SPEECH.

speaker, *n.* presiding officer, chairperson, orator, spokesman; loudspeaker. See SPEECH, AUTHORITY.

spear, *n.* lance, pike, javelin, blade; shoot. See ARMS, VEGETABLE.

SPECIALITY

Nouns—**1,** speciality, individuality, originality, particularity, peculiarity, distinction; state, trait, feature, mark, stamp, property, attribute (see ATTRIBUTION); IDENTITY, character (see INTRINSIC); personality, characteristic, hallmark, TENDENCY, mannerism, trick, idiosyncrasy, the nature of the beast, *je ne sais quoi*; fingerprint, voice print; aroma, mystique, aura, charisma; technicality, singularity (see UNCONFORMITY). See DIFFERENCE, UNITY.

2, specialty, specialization; hobby, métier; specialist. *Colloq.*, keynote, bit.

3, particulars, details, items, counts, circumstances, ins and outs.

4, I, self, I myself, me, ego, psyche. *Colloq.*, number one. See IDENTITY.

Verbs—specialize, specify, be specific, particularize, individualize, individuate, realize; pick out, designate, lay *or* put one's finger on, name, detail, earmark, show clearly, clarify; give particulars, go into detail, come to the point. *Colloq.*, get down to cases *or* brass tacks.

Adjectives—special, particular, individual, specific, singular, exceptional, extraordinary, original, unique, uncommon, unlike, picked, marked, distinct, distinctive, *sui generis;* proper, own, personal, private, privy, partial, party; respective, certain, definite, express, determinate, detailed, diagnostic; especial, esoteric, endemic, idiomatic, idiosyncratic, characteristic; in character, true to form, appropriate, typical, exclusive, several; tailor-made, made to measure *or* order. See EXCLUSION.

Adverbs—specially, in particular, on *or* for my part, personally, *ad hominem;* each, apiece, one by one, severally, individually, respectively, each to each; seriatim, in detail, bit by bit; namely, that is to say, *videlicet, viz.*, to wit.

Antonyms, see GENERALITY.

species, *n.* variety, sort, CLASS, category.

specific, *adj.* special, distinct (see SPECIALITY); limited, exact, precise, absolute, unequivocal, right; explicit, definite. —*n.* REMEDY, medicine, medicament, cure, treatment. See CIRCUMSTANCE.

specify, *v.* name, mention, identify, enumerate, indicate, stipulate, define, state, itemize, detail; order, request. See SPECIALITY, INDICATION, DESCRIPTION, QUALIFICATION.

specimen, *n.* sample, example, representative, instance, pattern, taster. See CONFORMITY.

specious, *adj.* plausible, ostensible, apparent, casuistic, insincere; deceptive. See FALSEHOOD, IMAGINATION.

speck, *n.* blemish, speckle, spot, macula; particle, iota, mite, mote, dot. See LITTLENESS.

spectacle, *n.* sight, phenomenon, pageant, parade, show; exhibition, scene, display. See APPEARANCE, OSTENTATION, DRAMA.

spectacles, *n.pl.* [eye]glasses, goggles; lorgnette. *Slang,* specs, cheaters. See OPTICAL INSTRUMENTS.

spectator, *n.* observer, onlooker (see PRESENCE).

specter, *n.* ghost, spirit, apparition, vision, shadow, shade; wraith, phantom, phantasm, haunt, spook; aura, emanation, materialization, reincarnation, illusion, delusion, hallucination. See DEMON, IMAGINATION.

spectrum, *n.* rainbow; color gamut. See COLOR, VARIEGATION.

speculate, *v.i.* ponder, contemplate, meditate, theorize, conjecture, surmise; gamble, play the market. See THOUGHT, CHANCE, BARTER.

SPEECH

Nouns—**1,** speech, talk, faculty of speech; locution, parlance, expression, vernacular, oral COMMUNICATION, word of mouth, parole, palaver, prattle; effusion, discourse; soliloquy; interlocution, CONVERSATION; LOQUACITY. *Colloq.*, gab, confab, powwow, corroboree. See SOUND.

2, formal speech, speechifying, oration, recitation, delivery, peroration, valedictory, monologue, sales talk; oratory, elocution, eloquence; rhetoric, declamation; bombast, grandiloquence; burst of eloquence; fecundity; flow *or* command of language; power of speech, gift of gab, blarney. *Slang*, spiel, line, earful, pep talk.

3, allocution, exhortation, appeal, harangue, lecture, sermon, tirade, diatribe, invocation.

4, language, tongue, lingo, vernacular, mother tongue; idiom, parlance, phraseology; wording; dialect, patois, cant, jargon, slang, argot; pig *or* dog Latin, pidgin English, *bêche-de-mer;* Esperanto, Ito, Basic English, lingua franca; academese, journalese. *Slang,* jive, gobbledygook. See MEANING, COMMUNICATION.

5, linguistics, GRAMMAR, lexicography, etymology; semantics, general semantics, MEANING, denotation, connotation; WRITING, literature, philology, classics, letters, *belles lettres,* humanities, Muses.

6, word, phone, phoneme, syllable, stem, root; phrase, sentence; syntax, idiom; utterance, remark, statement, pronouncement, observation, comment, *obiter dictum*; question, INQUIRY; ANSWER, reply; aside, apostrophe, rhetorical question.

7, vocalization, enunciation, articulation, delivery; expression, utterance; vociferation, exclamation, ejaculation; clearness, distinctness; whisper, stage whisper; ventriloquism, ventriloquy. See CRY.

8, [public] speaker, spokesman; prolocutor, interlocutor; mouthpiece, orator; Demosthenes, Cicero; rhetorician; stump *or* platform orator; speechmaker, patterer, improvisator, monologist; gossip; singer (see MUSIC).

9, linguist, philologist, grammarian; semanticist, etymologist, lexicographer.

10, accent, accentuation; inflection, intonation; tone of voice; emphasis, stress; brogue, burr; pronunciation, euphony.

11, voice, vocality; speaking *or* singing voice; larynx, voice box, glottis, vocal cords; voice print (see SPECIALITY); lung power.

Verbs—**1,** speak, talk, speak of; say, utter, pronounce, deliver, comment, remark, recite, voice, give utterance to, vocalize; breathe, let fall, come out with; rap out, blurt out; chatter, open one's mouth; lift *or* raise one's voice; speak one's mind; state, assert, declare. *Colloq.*, gab, shoot one's mouth off, shoot the breeze, talk a blue streak.

2, hold forth; make *or* deliver a speech, speechify, orate, declaim, stump, flourish, spout, rant, recite, discourse, have *or* say one's say, say *or* speak one's piece; expatiate, be eloquent, have the gift of gab.

3, soliloquize, apostrophize, talk to oneself; tell, impart, inform (see INFORMATION); converse, speak to, talk together; communicate; divulge (see DISCLOSURE); express, phrase, put into words; translate, interpret.

4, allocute, exhort, appeal, harangue, lecture, preach, invoke, sermonize.

5, enunciate, pronounce, articulate, verbalize, emit, give voice, let out, mention, bring up, expound, spell [out]; accentuate, aspirate; express oneself, think out loud *or* aloud, exclaim, ejaculate, CRY; shout, yell, mouth. *Colloq.*, pipe up.

Adjectives—**1,** speaking, spoken; vocal, oral, lingual, phonetic, outspoken; eloquent, elocutionary; oratorical, rhetorical, flamboyant; declamatory, bombastic, grandiloquent; talkative (see LOQUACITY).

2, lingual, linguistic; verbal, idiomatic, colloquial, dialectic, vernacular, provincial; polyglot; literary.

Adverbs—orally; vocally; by word of mouth, *viva voce,* from the lips of; loudly, out loud, aloud; softly, *sotto voce*.

Antonyms, see SILENCE, WRITING.

---

speechless, *adj.* aphonic, mute, dumb. See SILENCE, TACITURNITY.

speed, *v.i.* HASTE, hasten, hurry, accelerate. —*n.* VELOCITY, dispatch, expedition, swiftness.

speedway, *n.* expressway, superhighway; racecourse, track, dragstrip. See PASSAGE, CONTENTION.

spell, *n.* charm, trance; talisman; incantation, SORCERY, magic; witchery, allure, glamour; enchantment; spellbinding; term, period, interval; TIME; turn, stretch; breathing spell, respite. See SUBSTITUTION, REPOSE.

spend, *v.t.* disburse, pay out, expend; consume, exhaust; pass, employ. See EJECTION, WASTE.

spendthrift, *n.* wastrel, prodigal, profligate, squanderer. See WASTE.

spent, *adj.* used up, exhausted, fatigued, dead-tired, fagged; effete, worn-out, impotent. See WEARINESS.

sperm, *n.* semen, seed, germ. See REPRODUCTION.

spew, *v.* vomit, regurgitate, retch, throw up; gush, shoot, spout, eject, emit, expel; spit; discharge. See EJECTION.

sphere, *n.* orb, globe, ball; environment, province, status, field, range. See BUSINESS, REGION, ROTUNDITY, SPACE.

sphinx, *n.* prophetess; enigma, riddle. See PREDICTION, SECRET.

spice, *v.t.* season, flavor; make piquant. See EXCITEMENT, TASTE, ODOR, PUNGENCY.

spigot, *n.* faucet. See PASSAGE.

spike, *n.* cleat, skewer, spindle; projection; goad, prod. See SHARPNESS. —*v.* pierce, gore; nail, rivet, impale, transpierce; *slang,* lace (with); needle. See CONNECTION, OPENING, DRINKING.

spill, *v.* overturn, upset; splash; brim over, slop, pour out; *slang,* tell, let slip. See EJECTION, DISCLOSURE, DESCENT, WATER.

spin, *v.* twirl, whirl, rotate; protract, draw out; gyrate, swirl, reel, eddy; fabricate. See ROTATION, LOQUACITY, IMAGINATION.

spindle, *n.* axis, axle, shaft; stick, spike, mandrel, arbor; stalk, stem. See ROTATION.

spine, *n.* backbone; ridge, *arête;* thorn, prickle, spike, spiculum, quill, barb. See SHARPNESS.

spineless, *adj.* invertebrate, boneless; pliant, limp, flabby; irresolute, cowardly, craven. *Slang,* gutless, yellow. See COWARDICE.

spinster, *n.* maid[en], old maid; spinner. See CELIBACY.

spiral, *adj.* coiled, winding, helical, turbinate, cochlear. See CONVOLUTION.

spire, *n.* steeple, minaret; flèche; point, pinnacle, peak; pyramid, obelisk; epi, finial, aiguille. See HEIGHT, SHARPNESS.

spirit, *n.* vitalness, essence; soul; ghost, fairy, ANGEL, DEMON; disposition, temper, mood, humor; energy, vivacity, élan, verve, intrepidity, enthusiasm, dash, gallantry, intent; (*pl.*) liquor. See MEANING, ACTIVITY, VIGOR, FEELING,

CHEERFULNESS, DRINKING, INTELLECT.

spirited, *adj.* animated, lively, mettlesome, bold, ardent; blithe, debonair, jaunty; sparkling, racy. See ACTIVITY, CHEERFULNESS.

spiritual, *adj.* immaterial, incorporeal, insubstantial, fleshless; divine, exalted, celestial, holy, sacred; religious; inspired, supernatural, virtuous, platonic; occult. See INSUBSTANTIALITY, PIETY, VIRTUE.

spit, *v.* impale, transfix, pierce, stab; sprinkle, drizzle, discharge (bullets); sputter, expectorate, hiss. See OPENING, EXCRETION.

spite, *n.* malice, ill-will, grudge, malignity, MALEVOLENCE.

spitfire, *n.* firebrand, hothead, tigress, hellcat. See IRASCIBILITY.

splash, *v.* splatter, [be]spatter; dash, plop, spill; slop, splash, dabble, paddle. See WATER, UNCLEANNESS, OSTENTATION.

spleen, *n.* RESENTMENT, wrath, choler; anger, malice, spite, MALEVOLENCE.

splendid, *adj.* gorgeous, magnificent; heroic, glorious; resplendent; admirable, grand, excellent. See BEAUTY, REPUTE.

splice, *v.t.* join, unite, interweave; *slang,* marry. See JUNCTION, MARRIAGE.

splint, *n.* splinter; slat, strip; support, cast, brace, bracket. See REMEDY.

splinter, *n.* splint; shard, sliver, shaving, shive; fragment, particle, toothpick, matchwood. See PART, LITTLENESS. —*v.* sliver, rend, smash, fragmentize, fracture. See DISJUNCTION, BRITTLENESS, FILAMENT.

split, *v.t.* rive, rend, cleave, splinter; divide, separate, disunite, divorce; apportion; *slang,* leave, depart. See DISJUNCTION, BRITTLENESS, DEPARTURE.

splurge, *n., colloq.,* extravagance, waste, expense. —*v., colloq.,* indulge (oneself), extravagate, lavish. *Slang,* shoot the works, go [the] whole hog. See OSTENTATION.

spoil, *v.* damage, ruin, impair; overindulge, humor; despoil, plunder, sack, pillage, rob; decay, putrefy, rot, mold, ferment. See DETERIORATION. —*n.* plunder, loot, booty, spoliation. See ACQUISITION.

spoke, *n.* ray; rung, rundel, stave. See SUPPORT.

spoken, *adj.* oral, vocal; verbal. See SPEECH.

spokesperson, spokesman, spokeswoman, *n.* voice, mouthpiece; front, figurehead; representative, go-between, proxy, AGENT, delegate, advocate. See SPEECH.

sponge, *n.* swab, blotter, dryer; *colloq.,* hanger-on, parasite, leech, dependent. *Slang,* moocher, scrounge, freeloader. See CLEANNESS, SERVILITY, DRINKING. —*v.* sop, soak up, mop, swab, blot, absorb, dry, suck in, drink up. *Colloq.,* touch, live off. *Slang,* scrounge, mooch, freeload. See DRYNESS, MOISTURE.

sponsor, *n.* patron, backer; surety, guarantor; godparent; advertiser. See SECURITY.

spontaneous, *adj.* instinctive, automatic, involuntary; extemporaneous, uninhibited, unforced, natural. See IMPULSE, WILL, FREEDOM.

spoof, *n., slang,* jest, joke, banter, hoax; satire, burlesque, parody, take-off, caricature, lampoon. —*v., slang,* deceive, hoodwink, fool; needle, josh, kid; lampoon, parody, satirize. See DECEPTION, COPY.

spook, *v.* frighten. —*n., colloq.,* ghost, specter. See DEMON, FEAR.

spool, *n.* spindle, bobbin, reel. See CIRCULARITY.

spoon, *v.* ladle, dip; *colloq.,* pet, make love. See TRANSFER, ENDEARMENT.

sporadic, *adj.* occasional; irregular. See RARITY, IRREGULARITY.

sport, *n.* recreation, athletics, pastime, angling, hunting, chase; jesting, merriment, fun, diversion; mockery, ridicule; freak, mutant; gamester, gambler. *Slang,* spender. See AMUSEMENT, EXERTION.

sportsman, *n.* sportswoman, Nimrod, hunter, angler; athlete, ballplayer, golfer, *etc*. See PURSUIT.

spot, *n*. place, locality, site; blotch, dapple, speckle, macula; smear, spatter, daub, blot; blemish, flaw, stain, stigma. See LOCATION, DISREPUTE.

spotless, *adj*. clean, unsullied, immaculate; pure, unblemished, impeccable. See PERFECTION, CLEANNESS, INNOCENCE.

spotlight, *n*. limelight, spot[lamp], searchlight, beacon, headlamp; notoriety, attention. —*v.t.* feature, star, play up. See PUBLICATION, DRAMA, LIGHT.

spouse, *n*. mate, husband, wife, consort. See MARRIAGE, ACCOMPANIMENT.

spout, *n*. tube, pipe, trough, nozzle, rainspout, gargoyle; jet, spurt, geyser, waterspout. See EGRESS, WATER.

sprain, *v.t.* wrench, strain, twist. See EXERTION.

sprawl, *v*. spread, extend, slump, slouch, lounge, loll. See LENGTH, HORIZONTAL.

spray, *n*. spindrift, spume, scud; fusillade, barrage; sprinkler, atomizer; sprig. —*v.t.* sprinkle, atomize; pepper, riddle (with bullets). See VAPOR, VEGETABLE, DISPERSION.

spread, *v*. scatter, strew; disseminate, diffuse, circulate; cover; unfold, stretch; part, separate; show, display; expand, disperse, deploy. —*n*. diffusion, EXPANSION; extent, expanse; bedspread, coverlet; meal, banquet, collation; layout; ranch. See COVERING, FOOD, INCREASE, PUBLICATION.

spree, *n*. frolic, lark, escapade, fling, revel; carousal, saturnalia. *Slang*, souse, jag, toot, binge, bat, bust. See AMUSEMENT, DRINKING.

sprig, *n*. branch, shoot, spray. See VEGETABLE, PART.

sprightly, *adj*. gay, brisk, vivacious, animated; scintillating, smart. See CHEERFULNESS, WIT.

spring, *v*. LEAP, bound, dart, start; bounce, RECOIL, rebound; arise, rise; result *or* derive from; release; detonate; reveal, disclose; bend, twist; *slang*, release, bail. See LIBERATION. —*n*. LEAP, bound; ELASTICITY, RECOIL; well, fount, origin, source; coil. See CAUSE.

sprinkle, *v*. scatter, spread, sow; spray, wet; speckle, mottle, powder; drizzle, shower. See WATER, DISPERSION, MOISTURE.

sprint, *n*. run, dash; speed, rush; bolt, dart, tear. *Colloq*., hotfoot. See VELOCITY, CONTENTION.

sprite, *n*. elf, fairy. See DEMON, MYTHICAL DEITIES.

sprout, *v.i*. germinate, shoot, bud, burgeon. See INCREASE, EXPANSION.

spruce, *adj*. trim, neat, tidy, shipshape; smart, dapper, chic. See CLEANNESS.

spry, *adj*. lively, alert, athletic, nimble, agile. See ACTIVITY.

spunky, *adj*., *colloq*., plucky, mettlesome, brave, intrepid. See COURAGE, RESOLUTION.

spur, *n*. spine; rowel; incentive, goad, stimulus; projection, headland, siding. See SHARPNESS, CAUSE.

spurious, *adj*. false, counterfeit, sham, specious; bastard, illegitimate. See DECEPTION, ERROR, FALSEHOOD.

spurn, *v.t.* flout, scout, reject, repudiate, repel, contemn, scorn, disdain; kick. See CONTEMPT, DISRESPECT.

spurt, *v.i*. gush, squirt, spray; burst. See WATER, HASTE, REPULSION, EJECTION, TRANSIENTNESS.

sputter, *v*. spit, spew, splutter, spatter, eject, splash; blurt, babble, jabber, stammer; misfire, fizzle. See STAMMERING, ACTIVITY, AGITATION.

spy, *n*. secret agent, scout, undercover man, informer, stool pigeon. *Slang*, mole. See INFORMATION, CONCEALMENT.

spyglass, *n*. telescope. See OPTICAL INSTRUMENTS.

squabble, *v.i*. quarrel, bicker, altercate, fall out. —*n*. falling out, quarrel, dispute, wrangle, spat, argument. See CONTENTION, DISCORD.

squad, *n.* band, patrol; squadron, wing, unit; crew, team. See ASSEMBLAGE, COMBATANT.

squalid, *adj.* filthy, dirty, foul, sordid, repulsive, wretched, degraded. See UNCLEANNESS, UGLINESS.

squall, *n.* gust, blow, blast; turmoil; scream, CRY. —*v.i.* blow, bluster; scream, bawl, wail. See WIND, VIOLENCE.

squalor, *n.* dirt, filth, decay, UNCLEANNESS, misery, poverty. See DISORDER.

squander, *v.t.* WASTE, lavish, dissipate.

square, *n.* tetragon, quadrilateral, equilateral rectangle; block; quadrangle; plaza, court; T square; *slang,* misfit, fogy. See NUMERATION, MEASUREMENT, ANGULARITY, PERMANENCE. —*v.t.* quadrate; balance, settle, reconcile; set, adjust. See AGREEMENT, VERTICAL.

squash, *v.t.* crush, mash, squeeze, flatten; squelch; *colloq.,* suppress, SILENCE. See DESTRUCTION.

squat, *adj.* dumpy, stocky, pudgy. See SHORTNESS, LOWNESS.

squawk, *v.* CRY, call, scream, screech; *colloq.,* complain. *Slang,* kick, gripe, grouse. —*n.* outcry, squeak, croak, caw, screech. See DISCONTENT.

squeak, *v.* creak, CRY; *colloq.,* squeak by, just make it, pull through. See ESCAPE.

squeal, *v.* yell, CRY, yelp, shriek, screech; *slang,* confess, inform, blab, tattle, tell (on), spill [the beans]. *Slang,* stool, sing. See DISCLOSURE.

squeamish, *adj.* queasy, qualmish, nauseous; fearful, skittish, nervous; fastidious, picky; hypercritical. See UNWILLINGNESS, TASTE.

squeeze, *v.t.* press, compress; express, extract; stuff, cram; exact, extort, blackmail. See EXTRACTION, CONTRACTION.

squelch, *v.t.* disconcert, discomfit, rout, crush; silence, stifle, muffle. See DESTRUCTION.

squint, *n.* cross-eye, strabismus; peek, peering, glance. See VISION.

squire, *n.* landed gentleman; esquire; attendant, escort. —*v.t.* attend, escort. See ACCOMPANIMENT, NOBILITY.

squirm, *v.i.* twist, turn, thrash (about); wriggle, writhe. See AGITATION, EXCITEMENT.

squirt, *v.* spray, jet, douche, hose, spatter. See EJECTION. —*n.* spurt, jet, stream[let]; syringe, spray[er], atomizer; *colloq.,* upstart, runt, shrimp, imp. *Slang,* half pint, snotnose. See UNIMPORTANCE.

stab, *v.t.* pierce, puncture, perforate, stick, prick, pink; distress, hurt. See OPENING, PAIN, ATTACK.

STABILITY

Nouns—**1,** stability; immutability, unchangeableness, constancy, firmness, equilibrium, immobility, soundness, vitality, stiffness, solidity, aplomb; establishment, fixture; PERMANENCE; obstinacy, RESOLUTION. See DURABILITY.
2, rock, pillar, tower, foundation, leopard's spots; rock of Gibraltar.

Verbs—**1,** be *or* stand firm; stick fast; weather the storm, hold up; settle down, take root; entrench oneself, hold the line, stand pat, stay put; hold *or* stand one's ground, hold one's own. *Colloq.,* hold the fort.
2, establish, settle, fix, set, retain, keep *or* take hold, pin down; make good *or* sure; perpetuate (see PERPETUITY); mark time.

Adjectives—**1,** stable, fixed, steadfast, firm, fast, steady, balanced; confirmed, valid, immovable, irremovable, riveted, rooted; settled, established, vested; incontrovertible; tethered, anchored, moored; firm as a rock; firmly seated *or* established; deep-rooted, ineradicable; inveterate; stuck fast, aground, high and dry, stranded. See OBSTINACY.

2, unchangeable, immutable; unaltered, unalterable; changeless, constant, permanent; invariable, undeviating; durable, perennial.
3, conservative, Tory, reactionary, diehard (see PERMANENCE).

Adverbs—in statu quo; at a standstill; as is.

Antonyms, see CHANGEABLENESS, MOTION.

---

stable, *n.* barn, stall, mews. See ABODE.

stack, *n.* pile, heap, mound; rick, sheaf, faggot; chimney, flue. *Colloq.,* piles, heaps, lots. See ASSEMBLAGE, MULTITUDE. —*v.* pile, heap, bundle; doctor, rig, prearrange; fix, load. See DECEPTION.

stadium, *n.* See ARENA.

staff, *n.* walking stick, cane, cudgel; scepter, wand, baton, truncheon, crosier; flagpole; assistants, crew, aides, associates, personnel, force. See SUPPORT, SERVANT, ARMS.

stage, *n.* platform, rostrum, scaffold; DRAMA, theater; ARENA, field, scene; degree, step, phase; period, stretch, interval, span; stagecoach, diligence, omnibus. See SUPPORT, VEHICLE, LAYER.

stagger, *v.* reel, sway, falter, totter, lurch; waver, hesitate; surprise, stun, jar, shock, startle, take aback; alternate. See AGITATION, OSCILLATION.

staging, *n.* direction, *mise en scène,* production; scaffolding. See DRAMA, SUPPORT.

stagnant, *adj.* static, inert; foul; sluggish, dull, torpid. See INACTIVITY, REPOSE.

staid, *adj.* demure, serious, sedate, settled, inexcitable, sober. See INEXCITABILITY, MODERATION.

stain, *n.* COLOR, dye, dyestuff; discoloration; blotch, blot, smear, smudge; blemish, tarnish; stigma, taint, brand. See UNCLEANNESS, DISREPUTE.

stairway, *n.* stairs, steps, staircase, Escalator; companionway, ladder. See ASCENT.

stake, *n.* post, peg, pile; palisade; burning, execution; wager, bet, ante, pot; SECURITY, earnest, deposit; interest, claim, holding; prize, reward. See CHANCE, PROPERTY.

stale, *adj.* passé; rancid, dried up, tasteless, insipid, flat, vapid; trite, dull, banal. *Colloq.,* old hat. *Slang,* corny. See INSIPIDITY, WEARINESS.

stalemate, *n.* draw, deadlock, standoff, tie; stall; RESISTANCE, opposition; impasse, standstill; check, hindrance, bottleneck, jam. See DIFFICULTY.

stalk, *n.* stem, pedicle, petiole. See SUPPORT.

stall, *n.* stable, manger; ENCLOSURE, chamber; booth, concession, kiosk; alcove, niche; *colloq.,* pretext, evasion. See RECEPTACLE, AVOIDANCE. —*v.* stick, stand still, bog down; fail, go dead; *colloq.,* delay, dodge, play for time, put *or* hold off, stave off.

stallion, *n.* stud[horse], entire [horse]. See ANIMAL.

stalwart, *adj.* strong, brawny, husky; dauntless, steadfast. See STRENGTH, SIZE.

stamina, *n.* staying power, hardiness, force, VIGOR; vitality, STRENGTH; grit, pluck, backbone; endurance, durability, resilience.

STAMMERING

Nouns—stammering, stuttering, *etc.;* hesitancy, broken voice; speech impediment; lisp, drawl; mispronunciation, slip of the tongue, *lapsus linguae.*

Verbs—stammer, stutter, falter, sputter, splutter, stumble, halt, hesitate, pause, balbutiate, hem and haw, trip over one's tongue, be unable to put two words together; mumble, mutter, dither; lisp, speak thickly, swallow one's words, mispronounce, missay. *Colloq.,* mushmouth.

Adjectives—inarticulate, indistinct, hesitant, halting; guttural, nasal, husky, throaty, tremulous, tongue-tied.

Antonyms, see SPEECH.

---

stamp, *n.* impression, symbol, device, seal, trademark, brand; authorization, certification, approval, assent; postage; die, rubber stamp; certificate, wafer, label; kind, sort, quality. See INDICATION, FORM, CLASS, SPECIALITY.

stampede, *n.* flight, charge, rampage, onrush. —*v.* panic, rout, scare, alarm, incite, inflame. See FEAR.

stance, *n.* foothold, placement, post, station; posture, carriage, bearing; pose, form, appearance; standpoint, view[point]. *Colloq.,* slant. See SUPPORT, LOCATION, VISION.

stanch, *adj.* loyal, reliable, faithful, constant, steadfast; seaworthy, strong. See PROBITY.

stand, *v.* abide, tolerate, endure, SUPPORT; last, persist; remain upright; pause, halt, stop; be, remain; stagnate; be valid; put, place; bear, undergo; stand for, represent, mean. See DURABILITY, INDICATION, EXISTENCE, PERFECTION, RESISTANCE.

standard, *n.* emblem, ensign; criterion, measure, grade, exemplar, norm, canon, prototype, ethics. —*adj.* regulation, normal, conventional. See CONFORMITY, RULE, MEASUREMENT, DEGREE.

stand-by, *n.* mainstay, ally, supporter; staple; alternate, replacement, substitute. See AUXILIARY.

stand-in, *n.* substitute (see SUBSTITUTION).

standing, *n.* station, rank, REPUTE; duration, continuance; status, rating. See DURABILITY, CIRCUMSTANCE. —*adj.* continuing, permanent. See PERMANENCE.

stand-off, *n.* tie, draw. See EQUALITY.

standpoint, *n.* vantage [point]; viewpoint, point of view. See LOCATION, VISION.

standstill, *n.* full *or* dead stop, halt, suspension, impasse. See DISCONTINUANCE, REPOSE.

stanza, *n.* verse, stave, strophe. See POETRY.

staple, *adj.* chief, principal; stable, established, regular; marketable, popular. See CONNECTION. —*n.* commodity, raw material (see MATERIALS).

star, *n.* sun, celestial body; pentagram, asterisk; prima donna, *primo uomo,* leading man *or* lady, chief performer; DESTINY; planet. See INDICATION, DRAMA, REPUTE.

stare, *v.i.* gaze, gape, gawk; stand out. See VISION, CURIOSITY.

stark, *adj.* sheer, downright; rigid; desolate, naked. See COMPLETION, HARDNESS, DIVESTMENT.

starry, *adj.* spangled, stellar, stellate, star-studded; starlit; shiny, glittering. See UNIVERSE.

start, *v.* begin, commence, set out; jerk, jump, shy; loosen, crack; originate; get going; startle, rouse. See BEGINNING, PROPULSION, IMPULSE, DEPARTURE, FEAR.

startle, *v.t.* start, alarm, frighten, shock, surprise, amaze. See SURPRISE, DOUBT, FEAR.

starve, *v.* hunger, famish, fast; pine; pinch, scrimp, deny. See PARSIMONY, POVERTY.

stash, *v.t., slang,* put away, hide. See CONCEALMENT.

state, *n.* condition, category, estate, lot; case, mood, disposition, temper; pickle, contretemps, quandary, dilemma, plight; aspect, appearance; constitution, habitude, frame; pomp, dignity, formality, CIRCUMSTANCE; mode, modality; form, tone, tenor, turn; fashion, style, character, rank, situation, position, status; nation, country, government; commonwealth. *Colloq.,* make-up; kilter; shape. —*v.* allege, say, assert, declare, avow, aver, express, make a statement. See AFFIRMATION, OSTENTATION.

stately, *adj*. impressive, imposing, grand; dignified, noble, lofty. See OSTENTATION, PRIDE, NOBILITY.

statement, *n*. assertion, declaration, AFFIRMATION; report; bill, account. See ACCOUNTING, SPEECH.

statesman, *n*. legislator, diplomat, solon, Draco; politician. See DIRECTOR.

static, *adj*. immobile, motionless, inert, passive, inactive; unchanging, the same, conservative; fixed, stationary, stagnant. See REPOSE. —*n*. interference, noise; crackling, snow, ghosts, jamming. See COMMUNICATION.

station, *n*. place, position; office, situation, rank, standing; depot, terminal; headquarters, stopping place, post. See LOCATION, REPUTE, BUSINESS, CLASS. —*v.t.* set, place, assign, post. See LOCATION.

stationary, *adj*. fixed, rooted, planted, immovable; constant, unchanging, static. See PERMANENCE, INACTIVITY.

statistics, *n*. data, charts, computations, graphs. See NUMERATION.

statue, *n*. SCULPTURE, effigy, image, statuette. See APPROBATION.

statuesque, *adj*. monumental, marmoreal; dignified, majestic, tall, well-proportioned. See BEAUTY, SCULPTURE.

stature, *n*. size, HEIGHT, form; standing, rank, status, importance, repute.

status, *n*. position, rank, standing; state, condition. See CIRCUMSTANCE, CLASS.

statute, *n*. law, ordinance, enactment; RULE. See LEGALITY.

staunch, *adj*. See STANCH.

stave, *n*. slat, strip. See MATERIALS, SUPPORT, MUSIC. —*v.t.* break (up), penetrate, puncture, pierce; stave *or* fend off, hold off *or* back, avert. See OPENING, DEFENSE, CONTENTION.

stay, *v*. check, halt, stop; restrain, detain, delay; suspend, defer; support, brace; appease; outlast; linger, tarry, remain; endure, last; dwell, sojourn; stick, stay put; continue. See HINDRANCE, PRESENCE, ABODE, PERMANENCE, RESTRAINT.

steadfast, *adj*. firm, unswerving, constant, stanch, resolute, industrious. See RESOLUTION, PERMANENCE, PROBITY, STABILITY.

steady, *adj*. firm, secure, stable; constant, unvarying, uniform; regular, habitual; trustworthy. See STABILITY, REGULARITY.

steak, *n*. beefsteak; club, flank, tenderloin, Swiss, New York, porterhouse, *etc*. steak, filet mignon. See FOOD.

STEALING

Nouns—**1,** stealing, theft, thievery, robbery; abduction, kidnaping; abstraction, appropriation; plagiarism; rape, depredation, poaching, raid; spoliation, plunder, pillage, sack, rapine, brigandage, foray; extortion, blackmail; graft; piracy, privateering, buccaneering; burglary; housebreaking; peculation, pilfering, embezzlement; fraud, swindle (see DECEPTION); kleptomania; grand *or* petty larceny; pickpocketing, shoplifting, highway robbery; holdup, stick-up, mugging; hijacking. *Colloq.,* haul. *Slang,* make, heist, snatch, snitch, touch, inside job, score, rip-off.

2, thief, robber, crook, sneak thief, pickpocket, cracksman, pilferer; swindler, confidence man; shoplifter, housebreaker, kleptomaniac; stealer, pirate, purloiner, filcher; highwayman, brigand; burglar, second-story man, *etc*. *Slang*, apache, cat bandit, dip, stick-up artist, yegg.

Verbs—**1,** steal, thieve; rob, purloin, pilfer, filch, cop, crib, palm; scrounge, sponge; abstract, appropriate, plagiarize; abduct, kidnap; make, walk, *or* run off *or* away with; seize, take; spirit away; plunder, pillage, rifle, sack, loot, ransack; mug; prey on; spoil, spoliate, despoil, strip, sweep, gut, forage; blackmail, pirate, maraud, poach, smuggle, run; hold up, stick up, hijack, skyjack. *Colloq.*, swipe, do out of, rob the till, have one's hand in the till. *Slang*, heist, rip off, knock off, snitch, take to the cleaners, roll, dip. **2,** swindle, peculate, embezzle, extort; sponge, mulct, rook, bilk, milk, pluck, fleece, defraud; obtain under false pretenses; live by one's wits; rob Peter to pay Paul; set a thief to catch a thief. *Colloq.*, rook, gouge, shake down. *Slang*, wrangle, hustle.

Adjectives—stealing, thieving, thievish, sticky- *or* light-fingered, furtive; piratical, predaceous, predacious, predatory; stolen. *Slang*, hot.

Interjections—Slang, reach for the sky! stick 'em up!

Antonyms, see PROBITY, RESTORATION.

---

stealth, *n.* furtiveness, secrecy, skulking, stalking. See CONCEALMENT.

steam, *n.* VAPOR, water vapor, mist, fog, gas, evaporation. —*v.* cook, boil, simmer; soften, moisten; clean, renovate; progress, speed. See HEAT.

steamer, *n.* river boat, steamboat, steamship, launch, liner, packet boat, side wheeler, stern-wheeler, paddle-wheeler. See SHIP.

steed, *n.* horse, mount, charger. See TRANSPORTATION.

steel, *v.t.* plate, armor, coat; temper, anneal, caseharden; harden, inure, strengthen, toughen; brace, gird, fortify. See HARDNESS, STRENGTH.

steep, *v.t.* soak, saturate, macerate. See WATER. —*adj.* precipitous, abrupt, sheer, declivitous; VERTICAL; *colloq.*, expensive (see DEARNESS).

steeple, *n.* spire, finial, flèche, belfry, campanile. See HEIGHT, TEMPLE, SHARPNESS.

steer, *v.t.* guide, pilot, control; manage, direct; follow (a course). See DIRECTION.

stellar, *adj.* starry, astral, celestial; radiant, glorious; feature[d], top, star[ring]. See UNIVERSE.

stem, *n.* tree trunk, stalk, petiole, pedicle; tube, shaft; cutwater, prow; lineage, extraction, derivation. See ANCESTRY, FRONT.

stench, *n.* fetor, stink, mephitis, fetidness, malodor, (strong) smell. See MALODOROUSNESS.

stenography, *n.* See SHORTHAND.

step, *n.* pace, stride, football; footprint; gait, tread; stair, rung; interval, gradation; (*pl.*) measures, action. See DEGREE, AGENCY, NEARNESS, TRAVEL.

stereotype, *n.* plate, mold (see PRINTING); pattern, type; cliché, convention; preconception. —*v.t.* reproduce, print, copy; stylize, type, conventionalize, conform. See CONFORMITY.

sterile, *adj.* barren, unproductive, unfruitful, unfertile; aseptic, germfree. See USELESSNESS, CLEANNESS.

sterling, *adj.* genuine, unalloyed, pure; noble, excellent, exemplary; silver. See TRUTH, VIRTUE.

stern, *adj.* rigorous, austere; forbidding, grim; strict, harsh, uncompromising. See SEVERITY. —*n.* poop, counter, REAR.

stevedore, *n.* longshoreman, roustabout; lader, stower, docker, navvy, loader, lader, dockman, dockwalloper. See EXERTION.

stew, *v.* simmer, seethe, [pressure-] cook, steam; *colloq.*, worry, fret, fume, stew in one's own juice. —*n.* pepperpot, ragout, goulash, fricassee, bouillabaisse; *colloq.*, agitation, dither, sweat, tizzy. See FOOD, DIFFICULTY, EXCITEMENT.

steward, *n.* agent, manager, trustee; provider, caterer; SERVANT, waiter. See STORE, DIFFICULTY.

stick, *v.t.* stab, puncture, prick; put, place, thrust; glue; transfix, impale; *colloq.*, puzzle, stump. See OPENING, COHERENCE, DIFFICULTY. —*v.i.* adhere, cling; stay, remain, tarry; stall, freeze, be immobile. See COHERENCE, STABILITY. —*n.* piece, branch; cane, staff, cudgel, rod, baton. See SUPPORT.

stickler, *n.* purist, pedant, quibbler; puritan, prig; perfectionist; poser, puzzle, enigma, baffler. See OBSTINACY, SEVERITY, DIFFICULTY.

sticky, *adj.* adhesive, mucilaginous, glutinous, viscous, tenacious; humid, muggy; sweaty; tacky. See COHERENCE.

stiff, *adj.* rigid, inflexible, firm, nonfluid; strong, brisk; difficult, hard; severe, excessive; formal, unreserved; awkward, stilted. See HARDNESS, SEVERITY, AFFECTATION, INELEGANCE, RESTRAINT, PRIDE.

stifle, *v.t.* smother, suffocate; extinguish, put down, suppress; repress, check. See KILLING, CONCEALMENT, SILENCE.

stigma, *n.* blemish, birthmark; brand, blot, stain, reproach. See DISREPUTE, IMPERFECTION.

stigmatize, *v.t.* denounce, reproach, brand, vilify. See DISREPUTE.

stiletto, *n.* dagger, dirk. See ARMS.

still, *adj.* silent, quiet, hushed; calm, peaceful, tranquil; motionless, at rest, stationary. See SILENCE. —*adv.* yet, nevertheless. See COMPENSATION.

stilted, *adj.* formal, stiff; unnatural, affected, mannered, prim; inflated, florid, flowery, pedantic. *Colloq.*, stuffy. See AFFECTATION, INELEGANCE.

stimulant, *n.* excitant, stimulus, bracer, tonic, spur; liquor. See ENERGY.

stimulate, *v.t.* excite, rouse, animate, stir, spur, invigorate, exhilarate. See EXCITEMENT, CAUSE, REFRESHMENT, STRENGTH.

sting, *v.* smart, tingle; irritate, trouble, PAIN; bite, wound; nettle, gall, goad. See RESENTMENT. —*n.* wound, prickle, smart, irritation; stimulus, goad; stinger, prickle, nettle. See PAIN, PUNGENCY, SENSIBILITY.

stingy, *adj.* penurious, miserly, niggardly; scanty, meager. *Colloq.*, near, tight, close. See PARSIMONY.

stink, *n. & v.* See MALODOROUSNESS.

stint, *v.* restrain, restrict, LIMIT; scrimp, skimp, economize. —*n.* RESTRAINT, LIMIT; turn, shift, bout; task, chore, job. See PARSIMONY.

stipend, *n.* compensation, wage, pay, salary. See PAYMENT.

stipple, *v.* mottle, speckle, pepper; splatter, dapple. See VARIEGATION.

stipulate, *v.t.* specify, demand, insist upon, require, negotiate. See QUALIFICATION.

stir, *v.t.* move, budge, circulate; agitate, incite, arouse; animate, stimulate, provoke. See AGITATION, MOTION, EXCITEMENT.

stitch, *n.* seam, suture. —*v.t.* sew, knit, crotchet, tack, smock, overcast; staple; darn, mend. See JUNCTION.

stock, *n.* stem, bole, trunk; race, family; livestock, cattle; [gun] butt; capital; broth; merchandise, goods; raw MATERIALS; repertory; *colloq.*, BELIEF. See ANCESTRY, STORE, DRAMA, PROVISION, QUANTITY.

stockade, *n.* palisade, palings, ENCLOSURE; wall, barrier, barricade, fort, fortification; pen, compound, PRISON.

stockpile, *n.* reserve, STORE; hoard, cache; materials, surplus.

stocky, *adj.* thickset, sturdy, chunky, squat. See SHORTNESS.

stodgy, *adj.* short, thickset, stocky; sluggish, slow, obstinate, stolid; tedious, dull, unimaginative; backward, old-fashioned. See PERMANENCE, WEARINESS.

stoic, *adj.* stoical; self-controlled, impassive, unfeeling; long-suffering, ascetic. See INEXCITABILITY, RESIGNATION.

stoke, *v.* tend, poke, prod, stir; FUEL, fire, feed. See HEAT.

stole, *n.* scarf, cape, mantle, fur piece; surplice. See CLOTHING.

stolid, *adj.* inexcitable, impassive, dull, lethargic, sluggish. See IGNORANCE, INEXCITABILITY.

stomach, *n.* appetite, hunger; DESIRE, craving, inclination; maw, craw.

Colloq., belly, paunch, corporation. See RECEPTACLE.

stomach-ache, *n.* colic, gastralgia, gripe. See PAIN.

stone, *n.* coblestone, pebble; mineral; gem, jewel; gravestone, tombstone, millstone, whetstone, hearthstone, flagstone, *etc.;* pit, endocarp, pyrene; concretion, calculus. See DENSITY, ORNAMENT.

stoned, *adj., slang,* intoxicated. *Colloq.,* high, out of it. See DRINKING.

stooge, *n., colloq.,* dupe, butt, tool; straight man, yes man; SERVANT, henchman, lackey. *Colloq.,* sucker; sidekick. *Slang,* fall guy, patsy. See SERVILITY, MEANS, AGENT.

stool, *n.* cricket, hassock; seat; footrest, footstool; prie-dieu, kneeling stool; piano stool, milking stool, ducking stool. See SUPPORT.

stool pigeon, *n., slang,* decoy, informer, betrayer. See INFORMATION.

stoop, *v.i.* bend, bow, crouch; condescend, deign; submit. See SERVILITY, HUMILITY, SUBMISSION.

stop, *v.* close; obstruct; stanch; arrest, halt, impede; inhibit; delay, hold up, detain; discontinue, suspend; END, terminate, conclude; cease, desist. —*n.* halt, standstill, pause; DISCONTINUANCE, stoppage; stay, sojourn; stopping place, station; period, punctuation mark; brake, catch, skid, detent, curb. —*interj.* halt! belay! avast! stay! cease! See END, CLOSURE, LATENESS.

stopgap, *n.* expedient, makeshift; substitute. See SUBSTITUTION.

stopper, *n.* plug, cork (see CLOSURE).

stopple, *n.* stopper, plug, cork. See CLOSURE.

stopwatch, *n.* timer, chronograph. See CHRONOMETRY.

STORE

Nouns—**1,** store, accumulation, hoard; mine, vein, lode, quarry; spring, wellspring; treasure, reserve, savings, nest egg; fund, savings bond, stamp, account, *etc.;* stock [in trade], merchandise; supply, heap (see ASSEMBLAGE); crop, harvest, vintage; supplies, provisions. See PROPERTY, PROVISION, MEANS, ACQUISITION, QUANTITY.

2, storage, conservation; storehouse, storeroom, depository; depot, warehouse, cache, repository, magazine, arsenal, armory; buttery, larder, pantry, closet; garage; stockpile; bank, vault, safe-deposit box, treasury, piggy bank; museum, gallery, conservatory; silo, grain elevator, granary; menagerie; zoo; reservoir, tank, cistern, pond, millpond. See RETENTION.

3, store, storekeeper (see SALE).

Verbs—store; put, set, *or* lay by, lay *or* stow away, set *or* lay aside; store, lay, heap, put, *or* save up, accumulate, amass, hoard, garner, save; reserve, keep *or* hold back; save, bank, deposit; husband [one's resources] (see ECONOMY); stow, stack, load; harvest; heap, collect, stockpile, stock up, lay in store, keep, file; lay in, provide; preserve. *Colloq.,* salt away. *Slang,* stash.

Adjectives—stored, in store, in reserve; on hand, in stock (see PRESENCE); spare, supernumerary; extra.

Antonyms, see WASTE, POVERTY.

---

storehouse, *n.* See STORE.

storm, *n.* hurricane, tempest, tornado; spate, flood; cloudburst, blizzard; outburst, commotion; assault, onslaught, ATTACK. —*v.* assault, assail, ATTACK; rage, rant; bluster; blow violently, pour, rain, snow. See RESENTMENT, WIND, VIOLENCE.

story, *n.* tale, narrative, yarn; report, account, news article; plot; storey, floor, stage, level. See DESCRIPTION, NEWS, LAYER.

stout, *adj.* stalwart, robust, brawny, firm; doughty, bold, dauntless, resolute; determined, stubborn; stocky, thickset, portly. See COURAGE, SIZE, ROTUNDITY, STRENGTH.

stove, *n.* oven, range[tte], cookstove, cooker; heater, furnace; kiln, etna, hot plate, rotisserie. See HEAT.

stow, *v.t.* put away, conceal, stash, STORE; fill, cram, park; chuck, can, junk. *Slang,* stop, leave off. See LOCATION, CONCEALMENT.

straddle, *v.t.* bestride, bestraddle; equivocate; be neutral, sit on the fence. See SUPPORT.

strafe, *v.* ATTACK, fusillade, pepper, riddle; castigate, assail, chasten, chastise. See DISAPPROBATION.

straggle, *v.* drag, dawdle, bring up the rear, trail, drag one's feet; disperse; meander, wander, rove, stray. See SLOWNESS, DEVIATION.

STRAIGHTNESS

Nouns—**1,** straightness, directness (see *Adjectives*); rectilinearity, alignment, truing; straight, direct, *or* right line, straight angle; beeline, short cut; inflexibility, stiffness (see INELASTICITY); verticality, perpendicularity (see VERTICAL).

2, straightedge, ruler; T-square, carpenter's square; straightaway.

3, honesty, fairness, reliability, dependability (see PROBITY).

Verbs—be straight, not turn, not bend, *etc.;* go straight, steer for, aim for, head for (see DIRECTION); sit up, straighten, rectify, set straight; line, align, true, level; unbend, uncurl, unravel, unfold, unwrap.

Adjectives—straight, rectilinear, rectilineal; direct, even, right, true, near, short; linear, in a line, straightaway, straightforward, straight as an arrow *or* a die, point-blank; unbent, invariable, inflexible, unbroken; VERTICAL, perpendicular.

Adverbs—straight[way], straightforward[s], in line, in a straight line, as the crow flies; continuously, through; correctly, rightly, bluntly, point-blank; upright.

Antonyms, see CURVATURE.

---

strain, *v.t.* stretch, make taut; strive, exert; sprain; overtax, overstretch; filter, percolate. See CLEANNESS, EGRESS, EXAGGERATION. —*n.* effort, EXERTION; pressure; line of descent, stock, ANCESTRY; streak, trace; sprain; section, passage (see MUSIC, POETRY).

strainer, *n.* sieve, sifter, colander, screen, filter, percolator; cheesecloth, tamis, riddle. See PURITY, CLEANNESS.

strait, *n.* straits, narrows; DIFFICULTY. See NARROWNESS.

strait-laced, *adj.* severe, stern, dour, stiff; proper, formal, self-righteous; prim, prudish, fastidious; strict, puritanical. *Colloq.,* bluenosed. See SEVERITY.

strand, *n.* thread, string, fiber, rope, FILAMENT. See LAND.

stranded, *adj.* aground, stuck, left high and dry, grounded; embarrassed, penniless. See STABILITY, DIFFICULTY.

strange, *adj.* unusual, odd, unfamiliar; queer, fantastic; alien, foreign, extraneous, outlandish, exotic; eccentric, mysterious. See UNCONFORMITY.

stranger, *n.* newcomer, foreigner, alien, outsider. See EXTRINSIC.

strangle, *v.t.* choke, garrotte, stifle, suffocate; suppress, repress; squeeze, constrict. See KILLING, CLOSURE.

strap, *n.* band, bond, strip, tape, tether; strop, thong, rope; rein; cinch, girdle. —*v.t.* secure, tether, fasten, tie, support, lash; thrash, flagellate; strop, hone. See FILAMENT, CONNECTION, PUNISHMENT.

stratagem, *n.* trick, subterfuge, artifice, ploy, ruse, guile, wile. See DECEPTION, CUNNING.

strategy, *n.* generalship, maneuvering, CONDUCT, warcraft, artifice. See WARFARE, METHOD, PLAN.

stratum, *n.* LAYER, bed; lamella.

stray, *v.i.* wander, straggle, roam, rove, ramble; digress; deviate, err. See DEVIATION, ERROR.

streak, *n.* band, stripe, smear; vein, layer; disposition; run; trait, idiosyncrasy. See NARROWNESS, INTRINSIC, VELOCITY, INDICATION, LENGTH.

stream, *n.* river, streamlet, rivulet, rill; gush; trickle; creek, brook, runnel, runlet; current, flow, flux, course, flood, tide, race; shower, outpouring, downpouring. —*v.i.* issue; pour out, forth, *or* down; flow, run, rush; shed; blow, extent, run across *or* along; drift, tend; jet, spurt, gush. See WATER, MOTION, WIND, LIGHT, COURSE.

streamer, *n.* pennant, banner, bunting; banner headline. See INDICATION.

streamlined, *adj.* efficient, simplified; smooth, fast, speedy; trim, tapering; up-to-date, modernized. See NEWNESS, SIMPLENESS.

street, *n.* thoroughfare, avenue, boulevard, alley; roadway. See PASSAGE.

streetcar, *n.* tram[car], tramway, trolley, street railway. See TRANSPORTATION, VEHICLE.

streetwalker, *n.* prostitute (see IMPURITY).

STRENGTH

Nouns—**1,** strength, POWER, ENERGY, VIGOR; might, main [force], physical *or* brute force, manpower, horsepower; spring, ELASTICITY, tone, tonicity, tension; stamina; brawn, muscle, muscularity, sinew, gristle, thews and sinews, pith[iness], physique; HEALTH, virility, vitality. *Slang,* beef, grit. See REFRESHMENT, RESTORATION.

2, strong man *or* woman, tower of strength, powerhouse; athlete, gymnast, acrobat, equilibrist; Atlas, Hercules, Antaeus, Samson, Cyclops, Goliath; amazon; horse, ox; oak, rock; iron, steel, nails; iron grip, grit, bone, horn; feats of strength, athletics, athleticism, gymnastics, calisthenics. *Colloq.,* he-man, muscleman.

3, see COURAGE, RESOLUTION, TENACITY, HARDNESS.

Verbs—strengthen, fortify, harden, caseharden, steel, toughen, indurate, roborate, brace, nerve, gird, train; set on one's legs, gird up one's loins; build (up), reinforce, restore, consolidate; confirm, corroborate (see DEMONSTRATION); invigorate, vitalize, stimulate, enliven, energize, animate, encourage, lift, reman; enhance, heighten, brighten, intensify; regain strength, rally, grow, wax (see INCREASE). *Colloq.,* beef up. *Slang,* give a shot in the arm, pep up.

Adjectives—**1,** strong, powerful; robust, stout, stalwart, strapping, hardy, burly, husky, leathery, brawny, thewy, sturdy, sinewy, virile, muscular, wiry, limber, hale, hearty, healthy, vibrant; hard as nails, hard-fisted; athletic, gymnastic, able-bodied, broad-shouldered, well-built, -knit, *or* -developed, strong as a lion, horse, *or* ox; titanic, gigantic, Herculean; mettlesome, in fine feather *or* fettle. *Slang,* beefy.

2, strengthening, refreshing, bracing, tonic, roborant.

3, irresistible, invincible, impregnable, unconquerable, indomitable, more than a match for, heavy-duty; proof; airtight, waterproof, *etc.;* foolproof, fail-safe.

4, strong-smelling, pungent, piquant, *etc.* (see ODOR).

5, intense, concentrated, brilliant, bright, vivid, dazzling, *etc.*

6, alcoholic, spirituous, hard, bodied, heady, proof (see DRINKING).
Adverbs—by [main] force, by main strength, with might and main.
Antonyms, see WEAKNESS.

---

strenuous, *adj.* vigorous, energetic, dynamic; arduous, exhausting, straining, laborious. See EXERTION.

stress, *n.* pressure, strain, compulsion; emphasis, urgency, IMPORTANCE; accent. See NECESSITY.

stretch, *v.* extend, lengthen, spread, expand, INCREASE; stretch out, sprawl; *colloq.,* exaggerate, strain, force. —*n.* EXPANSION, reach, range; LENGTH, field, expanse; ELASTICITY; long run, distance, home- *or* backstretch; overstatement, EXAGGERATION; *slang,* sentence, hitch. See EXERTION, PUNISHMENT.

stretcher, *n.* litter, carrier; frame, brace. See SUPPORT, TRANSPORTATION.

strew, *v.* scatter, disperse, disseminate; throw to the winds. See DISPERSION.

stricken, *adj.* hurt, ill, disabled; knocked out, afflicted, beset. See PAIN.

strict, *adj.* exact, precise; rigid; accurate, meticulous, scrupulous, punctilious, conscientious, nice; stringent, exacting; strait-laced, puritanical. See TRUTH, SEVERITY.

stricture, *n.* censure, criticism, blame, reprehension, restraint; compression, constriction, contraction. See DISAPPROBATION, DISTANCE, HINDRANCE.

stride, *n.* step, pace; (*pl.*) progress, improvement. —*v.* walk, march, step; straddle. See TRAVEL, MOTION.

stridency, *n.* stridulation; shrillness, harshness; DISCORD, dissonance, LOUDNESS, roughness, sharpness; noise, noisiness, raucousness, cacophony; clangor, clamor.

strife, *n.* CONTENTION, emulation, rivalry; altercation; dissension, discord, dispute, quarrel; war, warfare; struggle, conflict.

strike, *v.* hit, smite, beat, thump; give, deliver, deal; affect, TOUCH, impress, occur to; blast; lower, take down; collide, bump; conclude, agree upon; ATTACK; collide; walk out, quit, rebel, cancel; print. See IMPULSE, EXCITEMENT, AGENCY, DISOBEDIENCE, SUCCESS, NULLIFICATION.

striking, *adj.* impressive, remarkable; attractive; dramatic. See WONDER, EXCITEMENT.

string, *n.* twine, thread, cord; catgut; series, row, line, chain; set, stud of horse. See FILAMENT, CONTINUITY, MUSIC, LENGTH.

stringent, *adj.* severe, strict, stern. See COMPULSION, SEVERITY.

strip, *v.* divest, denude, decorticate, peel, pull off; dismantle; plunder, fleece; dispossess, deprive; disrobe, undress; cut in strips. *Slang,* skin. See STEALING, DIVESTMENT. —*n.* hue, stripe, bend, fillet, shred; lath, ribbon; *slang,* comic [strip]. See FILAMENT, NARROWNESS, WIT.

stripe, *n.* line, band, streak, belt; CLASS, ilk. *Slang,* hash mark. See LENGTH, VARIEGATION.

stripling, *n.* lad, boy, teenager, YOUTH. *Colloq.,* shaver, kid, nipper.

strive, *v.i.* endeavor, strain, ESSAY; struggle, contend; quarrel. See CONTENTION, EXERTION.

stroke, *n.* blow, impact, beat, throb, pulsation, bolt, blast, coup; seizure, apoplexy, shock; feat, exploit, coup; mark, flourish; caress. See DISEASE, TOUCH, ENDEARMENT.

stroll, *n.* ramble, saunter, promenade, walk. *Colloq.,* constitutional. See TRAVEL, SLOWNESS.

strong, *adj.* See STRENGTH.

stronghold, *n.* refuge; fort[ress], citadel; blockhouse; fastness, bulwark. See DEFENSE, PRISON.

structure, *n.* building, edifice, construction, fabrication; framework, makeup, arrangement, COMPOSITION, anatomy, constitution. See FORM.

struggle, *v.i.* strive, strain, endeavor, contend, labor; flounder, writhe, squirm; fight, battle. —*n.* endeavor, effort, CONTENTION, essay; fight, conflict, warfare. See EXERTION.

strut, *v.* swagger; stalk, peacock. See VANITY, OSTENTATION, TRAVEL.

stub, *n.* stump, end, stubble; receipt, record; butt. See SHORTNESS, RECEIVING, REMAINDER. —*v.t.* bump, hit, strike. See IMPULSE.

stubble, *n.* stumps, stalks, stubs, remnants; beard, bristles. See REMAINDER, ROUGHNESS.

stubborn, *adj.* perverse, obstinate; dogged, persistent; intractable, unyielding; tough. See OBSTINACY, HARDNESS.

stubby, *adj.* thickset; bristly. See SHORTNESS, ROUGHNESS.

stuck-up, *adj.* vain, conceited, aloof, snooty. See VANITY.

stud, *n.* boss, knob, projection, jewel; timber, SUPPORT; studhorse, breeder. —*v.t.* bestud, ORNAMENT, bejewel, spangle; dot, scatter. See DISPERSION, REPRODUCTION, CONVEXITY.

student, *n.* learner, pupil, apprentice, schoolboy *or* -girl; scholar, schoolman *or* -woman, pedant. See SCHOOL, LEARNING.

studied, *adj.* deliberate, careful. See CARE, INTENTION.

studio, *n.* atelier, salon, workshop; study; station. See BUSINESS.

studious, *adj.* scholarly, thoughtful, speculative, contemplative, bookish. See THOUGHT, LEARNING.

study, *n.* meditation, research, examination, investigation; library, atelier, den; PLAN; sketch, cartoon; étude. —*v.* investigate, weigh, consider, examine; scrutinize; con; memorize; ponder. *Colloq.,* grind. See THOUGHT, INQUIRY, ATTENTION, REPRESENTATION, LEARNING, PAINTING.

stuff, *v.* cram, pack, jam, fill; pad, wad; plug, block; gormandize, gorge, overeat. See GLUTTONY, EXPANSION. —*n.* fabric, cloth, material; nonsense; SUBSTANCE; rubbish. *Slang,* the goods, the ability.

stuffing, *n.* dressing, filling, forcemeat, farce; contents. See COMPOSITION.

stuffy, *adj.* ill-ventilated, close, stifling, airless; sultry, oppressive, musty; dull, stiff, stodgy. See DENSITY, HEAT, PERMANENCE.

stumble, *v.i.* trip, stub one's toe; hobble, stagger, lumber; blunder, flounder, stammer; err, slip, backslide. See DESCENT, AGITATION, ERROR, STAMMERING.

stumbling block, *n.* obstacle, HINDRANCE.

stump, *n.* stub, butt, snag, remnant, fag end; rostrum, pulpit; hobble, heavy tread; *colloq.,* electioneer. See REMAINDER, SHORTNESS. —*v.t.* confound, puzzle, nonplus. See DOUBT.

stun, *v.t.* benumb, deaden, daze, stupefy; dizzy; dumfound, astound, astonish, bewilder. See INSENSIBILITY, SURPRISE.

stunning, *adj., colloq.,* striking, lovely. See BEAUTY.

stunt, *v.* dwarf; cramp, retard, check; perform feats, do tricks, grandstand. See SHORTNESS, CONTRACTION. —*n.* trick, feat, daredevil[t]ry, *tour de force*. See ACTION.

stupefy, *v.t.* deaden, dull, numb, narcotize; stun, astound, daze, dumfound. See INSENSIBILITY, SURPRISE.

stupendous, *adj.* prodigious, enormous, astounding, amazing, wonderful, immense, vast, colossal, overwhelming. See WONDER.

stupid, *adj.* slow-witted, dull, obtuse; benumbed, bemused; absurd, inane; banal, tiresome, tedious, dull. See IGNORANCE, CREDULITY, FOLLY.

stupor, *n.* lethargy, torpor, apathy, coma, daze. See INSENSIBILITY, WONDER.

sturdy, *adj.* stalwart, hardy, husky, robust; durable, long-wearing; firm, stubborn, unyielding. See STRENGTH.

stutter, *v.i.* See STAMMERING.

sty, *n.* pigpen, pigsty; pen; hovel, shed; stable. See ENCLOSURE, UNCLEANNESS, ABODE.

style, *n.* form, manner, METHOD, way; FASHION; smartness, vogue, mode, chic; craze, fad, rage, last word;

practice, habit, [characteristic] behavior, air; diction, phraseology, wording, rhetoric; distinction, ELEGANCE. See GRAMMAR.

stymie, *v.* hinder, obstruct, impede; thwart, frustrate, puzzle, perplex, put at a loss, baffle. *Colloq.,* throw, floor. See HINDRANCE.

suave, *n.* urbane, bland, courteous, gracious; oily, smooth, ingratiating. See COURTESY, FASHION.

subconscious, *adj.* subliminal, nonconscious, unconscious, automatic. —*n.* subliminal self, id, unconscious. See INTELLECT.

subdue, *v.t.* tame, overcome, master; vanquish, conquer; repress, restrain; soften, tone down. See MODERATION.

subject, *n.* topic, theme; matter; liege, vassal, citizen. See SERVANT. —*v.t.* reduce, control, restrain, tame; treat, expose. See SUBJECTION, THOUGHT. —*adj.* liable, conditioned (upon). See LIABILITY.

SUBJECTION

Nouns—**1,** subjection; dependence, dependency; subordination; thrall, thraldom, enthralment, subjugation, oppression, bondage, serfdom; feudalism, vassalage, villeinage; slavery, enslavement, servitude; constraint, yoke, RESTRAINT; OBEDIENCE. See SUCCESS, SUBMISSION.

2, subject, citizen; serf, slave (see SERVANT).

Verbs—**1,** be subject, be at the mercy of; depend, lean, *or* hang upon; fall a prey to, fall under, not dare to call one's soul one's own; drag a chain; serve (see SERVANT); obey, comply, submit.

2, subject, subjugate, hold down, bring to terms, break in, tame; master; tread down, tread under foot; enthrall, enslave, take captive; take into custody; rule (see AUTHORITY); drive into a corner, hold at sword's point; keep under; hold in bondage; tie to one's apron strings.

Adjectives—subject, dependent, subordinate; feudal, feudatory, in harness; subjected, enslaved, constrained, downtrodden, under the lash, led by the nose; henpecked; the puppet *or* plaything of; under orders *or* command; under one's thumb; a slave to; in the toils; in the power, hands, *or* clutches of, at the mercy of; over a barrel; at the feet of; at one's beck and call (see OBEDIENCE).

Antonyms, see FREEDOM, LIBERATION.

subjective, *adj.* nonobjective; personal, individual, selfish; introspective, introverted. See INTRINSIC.

subjugate, *v.t.* conquer, vanquish, master, subdue; overthrow; enslave. See SUBJECTION.

sublime, *adj.* inspiring, impressive; noble, lofty, exalted, elevated; superb, magnificent, glorious. See BEAUTY, GREATNESS, PLEASURE.

submarine, *adj.* suboceanic, undersea *or* -water. —*n.* torpedo boat; U-boat, submersible. *Colloq.,* sub. *Slang,* pigboat. See DEPTH, SHIP.

submerge, *v.* drown, sink, plunge, dive, submerse, immerse, engulf, inundate; be overshadowed, subordinate to, play second fiddle to. See WATER, DEPTH, INFERIORITY.

SUBMISSION

Nouns—**1,** submission, submissiveness, OBEDIENCE, RESIGNATION, patience, HUMILITY, self-abasement, compliance, pliancy, docility, passivity, acquiescence, sufferance, conformity, SUBJECTION; capitulation, surrender, cession, yielding. See INEXCITABILITY, SERVILITY.

2, obeisance, homage, kneeling, curtsy, kowtow, salaam; white flag.

Verbs—**1,** submit, succumb, yield, comply, acquiesce, accede, resign, bend, stoop, obey, defer to, be subject, be submissive.

2, capitulate, surrender, cede, come to terms, retreat, lay down *or* deliver up one's arms, lower, haul down *or* strike one's flag *or* colors; show the white flag; give up *or* in, give up the ship, give way, give ground, cave in, bend before the storm; throw up one's hands; knuckle down *or* under. *Colloq.,* throw in the towel *or* sponge. *Slang,* say uncle.

3, be submissive, eat dirt, humble pie, *or* crow; bite *or* lick the dust; throw oneself at the feet of, be *or* fall at one's feet, swallow the pill, kiss the rod, turn the other cheek; crouch before, kneel to, bow to, pay homage to, cringe to; truckle to, bend the neck *or* knee; kneel, fall on one's knees, curtsy, kowtow, salaam, make an obeisance, bow submission, bow and scrape; lick one's boots. *Slang*, eat one's dust, take it [lying down].

4, endure, tolerate, put up with, bear with, be reconciled to, resign oneself, swallow the insult, pocket the affront, grin and bear it, submit with a good grace.

Adjectives—submissive, subdued, yielding, unresisting, tractable, compliant, dutiful, long-suffering, patient, passive, acquiescent, unassertive, manageable, governable, docile, agreeable; obsequious, slavish, servile, fawning, deferential, defeatist, self-abasing, lowly; prostrate, crouching, downtrodden, on bended knee, down on one's legs.

Antonyms, see DEFIANCE, RESISTANCE.

---

submit, *v.* yield (see SUBMISSION); propose, state; refer. See SUPPOSITION, OFFER.

subordinate, *adj.* lower, inferior, secondary; dependent, subservient. See INFERIORITY, UNIMPORTANCE, SUBJECTION.

subpoena, *n.* summons, writ, order, monition, citation. See COMMAND.

subscribe, *v.* sign, endorse, contribute; ASSENT, AID, abet, back, patronize; undertake, contract.

subsequent, *adj.* succeeding, following, sequent, later, ensuing, consequent. See SEQUENCE.

subservient, *adj.* servile, submissive, obsequious, cringing, abject; subordinate, contributory, instrumental, subsidiary. See SERVILITY, INSTRUMENTALITY.

subside, *v.i.* sink, fall, ebb, lower; abate, lessen; settle, precipitate. See DESCENT, DECREASE.

subsidiary, *adj.* branch, incidental; helpful; supplementary; secondary. See PART, AID, AUXILIARY.

subsidize, *v.t.* AID, support, promote; patronize, finance, underwrite, back, pay for, subscribe to; endow, invest in; encourage. See PROVISION.

subsist, *v.i.* exist, live, be, continue, survive, abide; eke out a living. See EXISTENCE, PERMANENCE, SUBSTANCE.

subsistence, *n.* EXISTENCE, being, continuance; maintenance, livelihood, sustenance. See FOOD.

SUBSTANCE

Nouns—**1,** substance, matter; *corpus,* frame, protoplasm, principle; person, thing, object, article; incarnation, embodiment, avatar; something, a being, an existence, entity; creature, body, stuff, clay. See HUMANITY, TEXTURE.

2, substantiality, materiality, materialness, essence, reality, corporeality; tangibility; flesh and blood.

3, physics, physical science; somatology, somatics; materialism; materialist, physicist.

Verbs—embody, incorporate, incarnate, actualize, materialize, subsist, be; substantiate.

Adjectives—substantive, substantial; concrete, sound, solid; personal; bodily, tangible, corporeal, real, material; appreciable.

Adverbs—substantially, bodily, essentially, *etc.;* on solid ground; in the flesh.

Antonyms, see INSUBSTANTIALITY.

---

substantiate, *v.t.* embody (see SUBSTANCE); evidence, CORROBORATE, verify, bear out, demonstrate, confirm, support. See DEMONSTRATION, TRUTH.

SUBSTITUTION

Nouns—**1,** substitution, commutation; supplanting, supersedure, supersession, replacement; metonymy (see FIGURATIVE); INTERCHANGE; TRANSFER.

2, makeshift, *pis aller,* stopgap, expedient, jury mast, *locum tenens;* palimpsest; *quid pro quo,* alternative; [make]shift, apology *or* excuse for.

3, substitute, understudy, replacement, delegate, deputy, AGENT; surrogate, alternate, representative; viceroy, viceregent, vicegerent; dummy, scapegoat, whipping boy; double; changeling; supplanter; alternate; backup, understudy, cover, stand-in, pinch-hitter, bench-warmer, ghost writer. *Colloq.,* sub. *Slang,* patsy, ringer, fall guy, goat.

Verbs—**1,** substitute, put in the place of, change for; deputize; make way for, give place *or* way to.

2, substitute *or* be deputy for; represent; stand for, appear *or* answer for; fill, step into, *or* stand in the shoes of, fill in for, do duty for; take the place of, supplant, supersede, replace, cut out; rob Peter to pay Paul. *Colloq.,* pinch-hit. *Slang,* cover up for; be the goat; ghost-write.

Adjectives—substitutive, substituted, vicarious, temporary, deputy, acting; vice, viceregal; jury (*Naut.*).

Adverbs—instead; in the place of, on behalf of, in lieu of, in the stead of, in one's shoes *or* boots, *in loco parentis*; *faute de mieux,* by proxy; for want of something better.

Antonyms, see IDENTITY.

---

subterfuge, *n.* ruse, shift, pretext, artifice, device, stratagem, CUNNING; evasion. See AVOIDANCE.

subterranean, *adj.* underground; infernal, Stygian, nether; hidden. See DEPTH.

subtle, *adj.* sly, artful, crafty, wily, CUNNING; discerning, acute, penetrating; elusive, unobvious, abstruse, delicate; dainty, fragile, rarefied, ethereal, unsubstantial. See INTELLIGENCE, RARITY.

subtract, *v.* deduct, take away; remove, detract. See DEDUCTION.

suburban, *adj.* out-of-town, rural, provincial. See ABODE, REGION.

suburbs, *n.* suburbia, outskirts, environs, purlieus. See NEARNESS, ABODE, ENVIRONMENT.

subversion, *n.* overthrow, defeat, disruption, disorder, mutiny, rebellion. See REVOLUTION.

subvert, *v.i.* overthrow, overturn, upset; ruin, fell, raze. See DESTRUCTION.

subway, *n.* underground, subrailway, *Métropolitain;* underpass. *Colloq.,* tube, *Métro.* See VEHICLE.

succeed, *v.* follow, come after; displace, supplant; thrive (see SUCCESS). See SEQUENCE.

SUCCESS

Nouns—**1,** success, successfulness; good fortune, luck, run of luck; PROSPERITY; accomplishment (see COMPLETION).

2, great success, land-office business; hit, stroke [of luck], breakthrough, windfall; [lucky] strike; master stroke; *coup de maître;* checkmate; half the battle, prize; trump card. *Colloq.,* smash [hit]; sleeper, dark horse; fast track.

3, victory, triumph, advantage; landslide, runaway, sweep; upper *or* whip hand; ascendance, ascendancy, SUPERIORITY; expugnation, conquest, subjugation, SUBJECTION.

4, winner, champion; conqueror, conquistador, victor; master of the situation, king of the mountain.

Verbs—**1,** succeed; be successful, gain one's end *or* ends, make the grade; crown with success; gain, carry, *or* win a point; manage to, contrive to; accomplish, effect (see COMPLETION); do *or* work wonders; score a success, make one's mark; deliver the goods. *Colloq.,* pan out, click, make a go of, pull off, come off, go over, make out. *Slang,* set the world on fire.

2, make progress, advance, get ahead, go places, go to town; win, make, *or* find one's way; prosper (see PROSPERITY); reap the fruits *or* benefit of; reap *or* gather the harvest; make one's fortune, turn to good account. *Colloq.,* hit one's stride, do a land-office business. *Slang,* sell like hotcakes; wow them, knock them dead.

3, win, prevail, triumph, be triumphant; gain *or* obtain a victory *or* advantage; master; get *or* have the best *or* better of; get *or* have the upper hand, ascendancy, *or* whip hand; distance, surpass (see SUPERIORITY); come off well, rise to the occasion, come off with flying colors; make short work of; take *or* carry by storm; win out; win one's spurs; win the battle; win *or* carry the day, win *or* gain the prize *or* palm; have the best of it, have it all one's own way, call the turn, set the pace, have the world at one's feet; carry all before one, remain in possession of the field; bear *or* carry off the palm. *Colloq.,* come through. *Slang,* win in a walk; romp home; score standing up, walk off with.

4, defeat, conquer, vanquish, discomfit; overcome, overthrow, overpower, overmaster, overmatch, overset, override, overreach; outwit, outdo, outflank, outmaneuver, outgeneral, outvote; take the wind out of one's sails; beat, rout, lick, drub, floor, best, worst, dispose of; put down, put to flight *or* rout, run into the ground, pin one's ears back; shout down; bring to terms (see SUBMISSION); edge out; snow under. *Colloq.,* nose out, polish off. *Slang,* whip, trash, beat all hollow, clobber, mop the floor with.

5, surmount *or* overcome a difficulty *or* obstacle; make headway against; stem the torrent, tide, *or* current; weather the storm; turn a corner, keep one's head above water, tide over.

6, answer [the purpose], avail, take effect, do, turn out well, work well, take, tell, bear fruit; hit the mark, hit the nail on the head; turn up trumps, make a hit; find one's account in. *Colloq.,* do *or* turn the trick, bring down the house. *Slang,* take the cake.

Adjectives—succeeding, successful, fortunate; prosperous (see PROSPERITY); triumphant; flushed *or* crowned with success; victorious; set up, in the ascendant; unbeaten; felicitous, effective.

Adverbs—successfully, with flying colors, in triumph, swimmingly.

Antonyms, see FAILURE.

---

succession, *n.* series; SEQUENCE, progression; heirship, inheritance, heritage, primogeniture, REVERSION; lineage, family. See POSTERITY.

successor, *n.* follower; heir[ess]; replacement. See SEQUENCE.

succinct, *adj.* terse, concise, brief, crisp, laconic, meaty, pithy, sententious. See SHORTNESS.

succor, *v.t.* help, AID, assist, serve, comfort.

succulent, *adj.* juicy, succulous, fleshy, tender; savory, tasty, toothsome; wet, watery, moist; interesting, spicy, piquant. See TASTE, FLUIDITY.

succumb, *v.* give in, yield, submit, surrender, assent; die, expire, give up the ghost. See WEAKNESS, SUBMISSION, FAILURE, DEATH.

such, *adj.* like, suchlike, similar, of the same kind; such and such, aforementioned; such a, some, one who. —*adv., colloq.,* so, thus, that; very; such as, like, resembling. See SIMILARITY.

suck, *v.* draw, extract, absorb, pull in, sponge up; pump; nurse, suckle; drain, leech, bleed, extort; suck in, seduce, lure; inhale. See EXTRACTION, RECEIVING.

sucker, *n., colloq.,* lollipop, all-day sucker, sourball; *slang,* dupe, gull, pushover, [easy] mark, soft touch. See CREDULITY, SWEETNESS.

suckle, *v.* give suck, nurse, nurture; wet-nurse, breast-feed. See FOOD.

suction, *n.* inhalation, EXTRACTION; absorption, siphonage, capillarity.

sudden, *adj.* abrupt, unexpected; hasty, quick, unpremeditated; instantaneous; precipitate; hot-tempered, rash. See SURPRISE, INSTANTANEITY.

suds, *n.* lather, foam, bubbles, froth, spume. See AGITATION.

sue, *v.* prosecute, bring suit, petition; beg, solicit, REQUEST; court, woo. See LAWSUIT, ENDEARMENT.

suffer, *v.t.* endure, encounter, undergo, experience, sustain; allow, permit, tolerate. See FEELING, PERMISSION. —*v.i.* endure pain, be troubled, ache; ail, be ill. See PAIN, DISEASE.

SUFFICIENCY

Nouns—**1,** sufficiency, adequacy, enough, satisfaction, competence; MEDIOCRITY; fill, fullness, completeness; plenitude, plenty; abundance, copiousness; amplitude, profusion, prodigality; full measure; luxuriance, affluence (see PROSPERITY); quorum; outpouring; flood. *Colloq.,* lots, oodles, rafts. *Slang,* scads, loads.

2, satiety, satiation, saturation, repletion, glut, excess, surfeit, superfluity (see REMAINDER); feast, deluge, overkill; too much of a good thing, a drug on the market.

Verbs—**1,** suffice, do, just do, satisfy, pass muster, make the grade; make ends meet, have enough to go around, make do, get by, manage, get along; eat, drink, *or* have one's fill, sate, be satiated, have enough; fill, charge, load, saturate, replenish, piece *or* eke out. *Colloq.,* gas up.

2, run over, burst at the seams; roll, wallow, *or* swim in; abound, exuberate, teem, flow, stream, rain, shower down; pour [in]; swarm, bristle with; cloy; run into the ground.

Adjectives—**1,** sufficient, enough, adequate, up to the mark, commensurate, competent, satisfactory, full, complete; ample, plenty, plentiful, plenteous; copious, abundant, abounding, replete, enough and to spare, flush; chock-full, well-stocked, well-provided; liberal; unstinted, unstinting; stintless;

without stint; all kinds of; unsparing, unmeasured, lavish, wholesale; rich; luxuriant; affluent, wealthy; big with, pregnant.

2, satiated, sated, gorged; blasé, jaded; sick (of), fed up; *de trop*.

Adverbs—sufficiently, amply, full, galore, in abundance, in full measure; to one's heart's content; *ad libitum,* without stint; enough is enough; to a fault.

Antonyms, see INSUFFICIENCY.

---

suffix, *n.* affix, addition, ending. See ADDITION, END.

suffocate, *n.* smother, stifle, asphyxiate; choke; extinguish; strangle. See KILLING, DEATH.

suffrage, *n.* franchise, right to vote; [the] vote, ballot. See CHOICE, RIGHTNESS.

suffuse, *v.* spread [out], overspread, pervade; permeate, imbue; wash, dye, tinge. See COLOR, MIXTURE.

sugar, *n.* sweetening, sucrose, lactose, glucose, dextrose, maltose, fructose, *etc.* See SWEETNESS.

suggest, *v.t.* intimate, hint, insinuate; propose, submit; imply, connote; recommend, advise, advocate. See INFORMATION, ADVICE, OFFER.

suggestive, *adj.* indicative, expressive; thought-provoking, stimulating; remindful, mnemonic; risqué, indecent. See MEANING, SUPPOSITION.

suicide, *n.* self-destruction, self-ruin; *felo-de-se,* harakiri. See KILLING.

suit, *n.* petition, appeal, prayer; courtship, wooing; suite, retinue, train; outfit, set, group, sequence; LAWSUIT, action, litigation. See REQUEST, ENDEARMENT, CLOTHING, CONTINUITY, CLASS. —*v.t.* satisfy, please; become, befit; fit, adapt. See AGREEMENT.

suitable, *adj.* fitting, appropriate, proper, convenient, apropos, becoming, fit[ted], compatible. See AGREEMENT, EXPEDIENCE.

suitcase, *n.* bag, valise, grip; (*pl.*) luggage, baggage. See RECEPTACLE.

suite, *n.* company, train, retinue, following, escort; set, series, group; apartment. See CONTINUITY, RECEPTACLE.

suitor, *n.* lover, wooer. *Colloq.,* beau, swain, admirer, boy friend. See LOVE.

sulk, *v.i.* be sullen, pout, mope; grumble, gripe, grouch. See IRASCIBILITY, REJECTION.

sullen, *adj.* sulky; ill-tempered, ill-humored; out of sorts, temper, *or* humor; crusty, crabbed; sour, surly, discourteous; moody; spleenish, splenetic; resentful; cross[-grained]; perverse, wayward, forward; dogged, stubborn; grumpy, glum, grim, morose; scowling, glowering, growling; peevish, irascible. See DISCOURTESY, RESENTMENT.

sully, *v.* soil, stain, tarnish, smear; defile, dishonor, blemish, stigmatize. See UNCLEANNESS, DISREPUTE.

sultan, *n.* caliph, imam, khan, emir. See AUTHORITY.

sultry, *adj.* hot, oppressive, sweltering, humid, muggy, stifling, close; voluptuous, sensual, sexy. See HEAT, IMPURITY.

sum, *n.* QUANTITY, amount; total, aggregate, sum total; substance, gist; problem; summary. See WHOLE, MONEY.

summary, *n.* compendium, abridgment, abstract, brief, epitome, résumé, digest. —*adj.* prompt, expeditious, speedy, fast, immediate; brief, concise, compact, condensed. See TRANSIENTNESS, SHORTNESS, DESCRIPTION, ILLEGALITY.

summer, *n.* summertime, summertide; high point, zenith, acme, *etc.* See CHRONOMETRY.

summit, *n.* top (see HEIGHT); maximum, climax; culminating, high, crowning, *or* turning point; tiptop; extremity. See PERFECTION, SUPERIORITY.

summon, *v.t.* call [for], send for; cite, arraign, subpoena; convoke;

rouse, invoke, evoke. See COMMAND, LAWSUIT, EXTRACTION.

sumptuous, *adj.* lavish, luxurious, splendid, imposing, grand; costly. See OSTENTATION.

sun, *n.* daystar, Sol; sunshine, sunlight; prosperity, happiness; star. See UNIVERSE.

Sunday, *n.* day of rest, Lord's Day, holy day, sabbath; day off, holiday. See REPOSE, RELIGION.

sunder, *v.t.* break, separate, sever, dissever, divide. See DISJUNCTION, PART.

sundial, *n.* sun-clock, solarium, dial; gnomon, style. See CHRONOMETRY.

sundown, *n.* dusk, nightfall, twilight. See CHRONOMETRY.

sundry, *adj.* various, divers; several, numerous; (*pl.*) notions, knickknacks, toiletries, cosmetics, *etc.* See MULTITUDE, SALE.

sunny, *adj.* warm, bright, sunshiny; cheerful, cheery, blithe; prosperous, palmy, halcyon. See HEAT, CHEERFULNESS.

sunrise, *n.* dawn, prime, daybreak, dayspring, aurora, cockcrow, sunup. See CHRONOMETRY.

sunset, *n.* twilight, sundown, dusk, nightfall, curfew, eventide. See CHRONOMETRY.

sunshade, *n.* parasol, umbrella; awning; sunscreen. See COVERING.

sunstroke, *n.* insolation, heatstroke, prostration; siriasis, heliosis. See DISEASE.

superb, *adj.* magnificent, impressive, stately; admirable, excellent; costly, rich, gorgeous, sumptuous. See BEAUTY, OSTENTATION.

supercilious, *adj.* disdainful, contemptuous, scornful; arrogant, cavalier. See INSOLENCE, CONTEMPT.

superficial, *adj.* shallow, cursory, dilettante, slight, slender, trivial, inane; surface, skin-deep. See EXTERIOR, SHALLOWNESS, IGNORANCE.

superfluous, *adj.* unnecessary, needless; excessive, overmuch. See REMAINDER.

superhighway, *n.* interstate [highway], *autoroute,* divided highway, turnpike. See PASSAGE.

superhuman, *adj.* sublime, divine; Olympian, Jovian; herculean, preterhuman, phenomenal, extraordinary. See UNCONFORMITY, SUPERIORITY.

superimpose, *v.* superpose, stratify, overlay, cover. See COVERING, ADDITION.

superintend, *v.t.* oversee, direct, control; boss, manage. See AUTHORITY.

SUPERIORITY

Nouns—**1,** superiority; excellence (see GOODNESS); majority, plurality; advantage; preponderance, preponderation; vantage point *or* ground, prevalence, partiality; lead, gain; NOBILITY. *Colloq.,* edge, inside track. See INEQUALITY, OVERRUNNING.

2, supremacy, primacy, preeminence, PRECEDENCE; whip *or* upper hand; victory, triumph (see SUCCESS); championship; maximum; climax; culmination, summit, transcendence, transcendency, prepotence, *ne plus ultra*; lion's share, excess, surplus; PERFECTION, sovereignty (see AUTHORITY).

3, cream of the crop, number one; ace; elite. *Colloq.,* first string.

Verbs—excel, exceed, transcend; outdo, better, outbalance, outweigh, outrival; pass, surpass, get ahead of; overtop, override, overpass, overbalance, overweigh, overmatch; top, cap, beat, cut out, steal a march on, upstage; beat hollow; outstrip, eclipse, throw into the shade, run circles around, put one's nose out of joint; have the upper hand, have the whip hand, have the advantage, hold all the trumps; have at one's feet (see SUBMISSION); turn the scale, play first fiddle (see IMPORTANCE); preponderate, predominate, prevail; precede, take precedence, come first; come to a head, culminate; beat all others, bear the palm, break the record. *Colloq.,* get the drop on, have it [all] over (someone), have an edge on, have the last laugh. *Slang,* pull rank; have something going for one.

Adjectives—**1,** superior, greater, major, higher, premier; exceeding; great, distinguished, ultra; vaulting; more than a match for; supreme, greatest, utmost, paramount, preeminent, foremost, crowning; first-rate, first-class, top-notch, important, excellent; increased, enlarged; one up. *Colloq.,* of the first water; ahead of the game. *Slang,* tops, top-drawer.

2, superlative, inimitable, incomparable, sovereign, without parallel, *ne plus ultra;* unrivaled, peerless, matchless; champion, second to none, nonpareil; unparalleled, unequaled, unapproached, unsurpassed; beyond compare *or* comparison; culminating, topmost; transcendent; superhuman.

Adverbs—beyond, more, over; over *or* above the mark; above par, at the top of the scale, on top, at its height; eminently, preeminently, surpassing, prominently, superlatively, supremely, above all, *par excellence, [summa] cum laude,* exceedingly, principally, especially, particularly, peculiarly, even, yea, still more.

Antonyms, see INFERIORITY.

---

superlative, *adj.* See SUPERIORITY.

supernatural, *adj.* miraculous, preternatural; abnormal, unearthly, superhuman, occult. See DEMON.

supernumerary, *n.* bit [player], subordinate, walk-on, stand-in, extra. *Colloq.,* super. See DRAMA, SUBSTITUTION.

supersede, *v.t.* replace, displace, supplant, succeed. See SUBSTITUTION, DISUSE.

superstition, *n.* irrationality, CREDULITY; fear, phobia; paganism, witchcraft, animism; old wives' tale, fairy tale, folklore. See HETERODOXY.

supervision, *n.* oversight, surveillance, superintendence. See AUTHORITY, DIRECTOR.

supine, *adj.* recumbent, reclining, prostrate; apathetic, sluggish, torpid; indifferent, passive. See INACTIVITY, INSENSIBILITY, HORIZONTAL.

supper, *n.* meal, repast, refection; banquet, feast, entertainment. See FOOD.

supplant, *v.* supersede, succeed, replace (see SUBSTITUTION).

supple, *adj.* limber, lithe, pliant, flexible; yielding, compliant, adaptable; fawning, servile. See SOFTNESS.

supplement, *n.* adjunct, ADDITION, addendum, appendix, complement, conclusion. See AUXILIARY.

supplicate, *v.t.* entreat, petition, pray, beg, beseech. See REQUEST, WORSHIP.

supply, *v.t.* provide, furnish, give, afford, present, contribute. See PROVISION, STORE, QUANTITY.

SUPPORT

Nouns—**1,** support, maintenance, upkeep, sustenance. See AID.

2, ground, foundation, groundwork, substratum, base, basis; *terra firma;* purchase, grip, footing, hold, foothold, toehold, handhold; landing, landing stage, landing place; stage, platform; block; rest, resting place, basement, supporter, prop, stand; anvil, bearing; fulcrum, rowlock, oarlock; stay, shore, skid, rib, lap; bar, rod, boom, sprit, outrigger. See STABILITY.

3, staff, stick, crutch, alpenstock, baton, walking stick; handle, heft.

4, post, pillar, shaft, column, pilaster, stud, sash, pier, atlas, atlantes (*pl.*), caryatid; pediment, pedicle, stalk; prop; pedestal; plinth, shank, leg,foot;

[flying] buttress, jamb, mullion, abutment; baluster, banister, stanchion; balustrade, railing; bracket.

5, frame, framework, gantry, trellis; scaffold[ing], skeleton, beam, rafter, girder, lintel, joist, travis, trave, cornerstone, summer, transom; spoke, rung, round, step, sill, tholepin.

6, backbone; keystone; axle[tree]; axis; arch, mainstay.

7, board, ledge, shelf, hob, bracket, trevet, trivet, arbor, rack; mantel, mantelpiece; mantelshelf; slab, console; counter, dresser; flange, corbel; table, trestle; shoulder; perch; stand, [saw]horse; easel, desk.

8, seat, throne, dais; divan; chair, bench, form, stool, sofa, sedan, lounge, settee, stall, armchair, easy chair, rocking chair, Morris chair; love seat, couch, *fauteuil,* ottoman, settle, bench; saddle; pillion; saddle; pommel.

9, bed, waterbed, berth, bunk, pallet, tester, crib, cot, hammock, shakedown, cradle, litter, stretcher, bedstead; bedding, mattress, futon, paillasse, box spring, spring, pillow, bolster; mat, rug, carpet, linoleum, cushion, four-poster, truckle bed, platform bed; chair bed, sofa bed, convertible.

10, footstool, hassock; tabouret; tripod; platform, stand, rostrum, dais, podium, pulpit, lectern.

11, Atlas, Persides, Hercules.

Verbs—**1,** lie, sit, recline, lean, loll, rest, stand, step, repose about, bear *or* be based on; have at one's back.

2, support, bear, carry, hold (up), sustain, shoulder; hold, back, bolster, shore up, buttress; uphold, prop; underpin; bandage, tape, brace.

3, give *or* support foundations; found, base, ground, imbed, embed.

4, maintain, keep on foot.

Adjectives—supporting, supported, braced, propped, bolstered; founded, based, basic, grounded, built on; fundamental, bottom, undermost; pickaback, piggyback.

Adverbs—astride, astraddle.

Antonyms, see PENDENCY.

SUPPOSITION

Nouns—supposition, assumption, postulation, condition (see QUALIFICATION); presupposition, hypothesis, postulate, theory, data; proposition, position; thesis, theorem; proposal; conceit; conjecture, cast; guess[work], rough guess, shot [in the dark]; surmise, suspicion, inkling, notion, suggestion, association of ideas; presumption (see BELIEF); divination, speculation. *Colloq.,* hunch. See REASONING.

Verbs—**1,** suppose, conjecture, gather, surmise, suspect, guess, divine; theorize; presume, presuppose; assume, beg the question, fancy, take it; give a guess, speculate, believe, dare say, take it into one's head, take for granted.

2, put forth, propound, propose; start, put *or* give a case, move, make a motion; hazard a suggestion *or* conjecture; put forward a suggestion; submit; allude to, suggest, hint, put it into one's head.

Adjectives—supposing, supposed, given, postulatory; assumed, suppositive, supposititious; speculative, conjectural, hypothetical, theoretical, supposable, presumptive, putative, academic, gratuitous; impractical; suggestive.

Adverbs—supposedly, theoretically, on paper, seemingly, if, if so be; on the supposition of, in case of, in the event of; quasi, as if, provided; perhaps; for all one knows; for the sake of argument.

Antonyms, see KNOWLEDGE, CERTAINTY.

suppress, *v.t.* put down, quell, subdue; repress, restrain; conceal; quash; withhold; abolish, ban; stanch, check. See RESTRAINT, CONCEALMENT.

suppurate, *v.i.* run, fester, putrefy, rankle; pustulate, ulcerate. See EXCRETION.

supremacy, *n.* mastery, SUPERIORITY, ascendancy, AUTHORITY.

supreme, *adj.* highest, utmost, paramount, prime, chief, dominant. See SUPERIORITY.

sure, *adj.* certain, positive; dependable, trustworthy; safe, secure; confident, convinced; unfailing, infallible. See CERTAINTY, SAFETY.

surf, *n.* sea, waves, breakers, rollers, whitecaps, white horses, billows, surge, spume, sea-foam, froth, spindrift, spray. See WATER, AGITATION.

surface, *n.* outside, EXTERIOR, superficies.

surfeit, *n.* excess, glut, superfluity, superabundance, plethora; satiety, repletion, engorgement. See SUFFICIENCY.

surge, *v.i.* rise, swell, billow, seethe, swirl; sweep, rush, stream, gush. See WATER, ASSEMBLAGE.

surgeon *n.* chirurgeon (*archaic*). *Slang,* sawbones, medic, knife man. See REMEDY.

surly, *adj.* sullen, morose, churlish, gruff, uncivil. See DISCOURTESY.

surmise, *v.t.* guess, conjecture, suppose, suspect, presume. See BELIEF, SUPPOSITION.

surmount, *v.t.* overtop, rise above; master, surpass, transcend; crown, cap, top; scale, climb over; overcome, conquer. See HEIGHT, ASCENT, SUCCESS.

surname, *n.* family name, cognomen, patronymic. See NOMENCLATURE.

surpass, *v.t.* exceed, excel, overtop, outshine, outdo, outclass, eclipse, outstrip. See SUPERIORITY, REPUTE.

surplus, *n.* surplusage; excess, oversupply, glut; REMAINDER, overage; profit, balance. See SUFFICIENCY.

SURPRISE

Nouns—surprise, nonexpectation, unexpectedness, the unforeseen, unforeseen contingency *or* circumstances, miscalculation, astonishment, WONDER, thunderclap, turn, blow, shock, bolt from the blue, eye opener. See INATTENTION. See FEAR, UNPREPAREDNESS.

Verbs—**1,** not expect, be taken by surprise, miscalculate, not bargain for. *Colloq.,* do a double take, sit up and take notice.

2, burst, steal, creep, *or* sneak up on one, be unexpected, come unawares, turn *or* pop up, drop from the clouds, take by surprise, take unawares, catch napping, catch with one's pants down, boggle the mind, beat all, beat the Dutch. *Slang,* come from left field.

3, surprise, astonish, amaze, astound; dumfound, startle, dazzle; strike with WONDER *or* awe; raise eyebrows, daze; stun, stagger, strike dumb, stupefy, flabbergast, turn the head, make one's heart skip a beat, hit between the eyes, knock off one's feet, make one's jaw drop, take away one's breath; make one's hair stand on end, make one's eyes pop, take by surprise, set one back on one's heels; ambush, waylay. *Colloq.,* bowl over, explode a bombshell. *Slang,* knock *or* throw for a loop, throw a curve.

Adjectives—**1,** surprised, nonexpectant, unsuspecting, unwarned, off one's guard, inattentive. See WONDER.

2, surprising, unexpected, unlooked for, unforeseen, unhoped for, beyond expectation, unheard of, startling, sudden, breathtaking.

Adverbs—surprisingly, unexpectedly, abruptly, plump, pop, unawares, without warning, out of a clear [blue] sky, out of nowhere, like a bolt from the blue, suddenly. *Colloq.*, smack.

Interjections—dear me! do tell! you don't say! for crying out loud!

Antonyms, see EXPECTATION.

---

surrender, *n.* capitulation, cession; RELINQUISHMENT, abandonment, SUBMISSION. —*v.* capitulate, yield, give up; cede, renounce, relinquish. See RESIGNATION.

surreptitious, *adj.* stealthy, clandestine. See CONCEALMENT.

surround, *v.t.* encompass, enclose, hem in, encircle; ring; circumscribe; environ; invest, besiege; embrace. See CIRCUMSCRIPTION, ENVIRONMENT.

surveillance, *n.* watch, observation, scrutiny, vigilance, CARE, attention; oversight, supervision, superintendence; lookout, patrol, guardianship; espionage, reconnaissance, watch and ward. *Colloq.,* keeping tabs on. *Slang,* stakeout. See VISION.

survey, *v.t.* view, examine, inspect, appraise; measure, lay out, plot. See VISION, MEASUREMENT.

survive, *v.* outlive, outlast; live; escape [with one's life]; continue, persist, remain, endure, abide, last. See DURABILITY, PERMANENCE.

susceptible, *n.* liable; allergic; vulnerable, impressionable, sensitive. See LIABILITY, SENSIBILITY, TENDENCY.

suspect, *v.t.* surmise, infer, conjecture, imagine, suppose, believe; mistrust, DOUBT. See SUPPOSITION.

suspend, *v.t.* hang, dangle; defer, postpone, stave off; adjourn, recess, intermit, prorogue, interrupt; debar, exclude. See LATENESS, DISCONTINUANCE, LATENCY, PENDENCY.

suspenders, *n.pl.* braces, garters, elastics. *Colloq.,* galluses. See PENDENCY.

suspense, *n.* anxiety, apprehension; uncertainty, indecision, hesitation; DISCONTINUANCE, interruption, pause; inaction, abeyance. See EXPECTATION, LATENCY.

suspicion, *n.* mistrust, distrust, apprehension; DOUBT, misgiving, JEALOUSY; SUPPOSITION, inkling, intimation, hint; trace, touch, shade, modicum. See LITTLENESS, FEAR, FEELING.

sustain, *v.t.* bear up, SUPPORT; endure; maintain, prolong, protract; nourish; corroborate, confirm, ratify, substantiate; assist. See AID, AGENCY.

sustenance, *n.* FOOD, nourishment; SUPPORT, maintenance, subsistence.

svelte, *adj.* slim, narrow-waisted; lithe. See NARROWNESS, BEAUTY.

swab, *n.* mop; swab stick, applicator, Q-tip; sponge. —*v.* mop, scrub, cleanse; wipe, dab, daub. See CLEANNESS.

swagger, *v.i.* strut, stalk, bluster, boast, bully. —*n.* arrogance, braggadocio, pomposity. *Colloq.,* swank, side. See VANITY, BOASTING.

swallow, *v.t.* ingest, gulp, devour, consume; absorb, engulf, assimilate, envelop; retract; bear, endure, submit to; believe, accept. See FOOD, CREDULITY, RECEIVING.

swamp, *n.* swampland, marsh, bog, wetland, moor, slough, fen, morass, quagmire. —*v.t.* submerge, sink, flood, inundate, immerse, drench, deluge; overwhelm, snow under. See MOISTURE, WATER.

swanky, *adj., slang,* showy, ostentatious, smart, elegant, fancy. *Colloq.* posh, plush. *Slang,* swell, ritzy, classy. See OSTENTATION.

swap, *n. & v.* exchange, BARTER. See INTERCHANGE.

swarm, *n.* group, crowd, MULTITUDE, horde, colony, hive. See ASSEMBLAGE, SUFFICIENCY.

swarthy, *adj.* dark, swart, dusky; dark-complexioned. See DARKNESS, COLOR.

swastika, *n.* fylfot, gammadion. See CROSSING.

swat, *v.t., colloq.,* slap, clip, slug. See IMPULSE.

swatch, *n.* sample (see CONFORMITY).

swath, *n.* strip, belt; window. See CONTINUITY, FILAMENT.

sway, *v.* swing, rock; INFLUENCE, direct, control, rule, bias, prejudice, warp; lurch, rock, roll, reel, dangle. See CAUSE, AGITATION.—*n.* domination, rule; INFLUENCE; OSCILATION. See AUTHORITY, POWER.

swear, *v.i.* affirm, depose, depone, vow; testify, witness; blaspheme, curse. See AFFIRMATION, IMPRECATION.

sweat, *v.* perspire; run, exude, secrete, ooze, drip; bead, dew, wet; *colloq.,* drudge, overwork; suffer, extract; force out; exploit. —*n.* perspiration, *sudor,* exudation; *colloq.,* EXERTION, toil, sweat of one's brow, AGITATION, stew, excitement. See EXCRETION.

sweater, *n.* knitwear, jersey, guernsey, pullover, cardigan. See CLOTHING.

sweep, *v.* brush, clean, vacuum; push, drive, blow, impel; trail; scan; strum; bend, curve; stream, glide, skim. See CLEANNESS, CURVATURE, MOTION, VELOCITY, SPACE.

sweeping, *adj.* comprehensive; extensive, wide-ranging. See INCLUSION, GENERALITY.

sweepstakes, *n.* lottery, draw, raffle, CHANCE; winner-take-all; contest.

sweetheart, *n.* lover, love, suitor, beloved, truelove, ladylove. *Colloq.,* beau, swain, boy friend, girl, best girl. *Slang,* gal, sweetie, flame, steady. See LOVE, ENDEARMENT.

SWEETNESS

Nouns—**1,** sweetness, sugariness, saccharinity; sweetening, sugar, molasses, honey, sirup, syrup; saccharin, aspartame, sugar substitute, artificial sweetener; nectar.

2, a. sweets, confection, confectionery, confectionary; fondant; conserve, preserve, confiture, marmalade, jam, julep; licorice, jujube; caramel, candy, candy bar; lollipop, lemon drops, jawbreaker; chewing gum, chicle; sugarplum, bonbon, comfit, sweetmeat; taffy, butterscotch; mint, spearmint, peppermint; chocolate, fudge, *etc. Colloq.,* sucker. **b.** nectar, mead, liqueur, cordial, sweet wine, punch, soda [water *or* pop], lemonade, carbonated drink (see DRINKING). **c.** dessert, pastry, pie, tart, cake, torte, cream puff, custard, pudding, *etc.;* ice cream, sherbet, frozen custard.

3, amiability, gentleness (see FRIEND, COURTESY).

Verbs—sweeten, sugar[-coat], candy, mull.

Adjectives—sweet, saccharine; dulcet, candied, honeyed; luscious, lush; sweetened; sweet as sugar, honey, *or* candy; sugar-coated, sirupy.

Antonyms, see SOURNESS.

swell, *v.i.* expand, dilate, bulge, protrude; billow; INCREASE, grow, surge. See WATER, FEELING, PRIDE. —*n.* swelling, INCREASE; billow, wave, groundswell, sea, roller; rise, slope, knoll. See CONVEXITY, EXPANSION, NOBILITY.

swelter, *v.i.* perspire, sweat. See HEAT, EXCRETION.

swerve, *v.i.* turn aside, deviate, shift, sheer, veer, yaw; dodge. See DEVIATION, CHANGE.

swift, *adj.* quick, rapid, fast, fleet, speedy; expeditious. See VELOCITY, HASTE.

swig, *v.t., colloq.,* guzzle, toss off *or* down. *Slang,* chug-a-lug. See DRINKING.

swill, *v.* flood, drench, swamp, soak, slosh; wash, rinse; guzzle, swizzle, swallow. *Colloq.,* swig. —*n.* garbage, refuse, waste, slop[s], mess, filth; eyewash, hogwash. See UNCLEANNESS, DRINKING.

swim, *v.* paddle, crawl, stroke, float, kick, tread water; feel dizzy, faint, swoon, reel, whirl; soak, be saturated, steep. See WATER.

swimmingly, *adv.* easily; prosperously. See FACILITY, SUCCESS.

swindle, *v.t.* defraud, hoax, cheat, fleece, victimize, trick. *Slang,* gyp. See STEALING, DECEPTION.

swine, *n.* pig, hog, porker, sow, boar; scoundrel, sloven, wretch. See ANIMAL, EVILDOER.

swing, *v.i.* oscillate, sway, wag; depend, dangle; pivot, turn; *colloq.,* be hanged; *slang,* [wife- *or* husband-]swap. See OSCILLATION, PUNISHMENT, IMPURITY. —*n.* sweep, sway, OSCILLATION; rhythm, lilt, scope, range, latitude, FREEDOM; REGULARITY, PENDENCY.

swipe, *v.* strike, hit, thwack; *colloq.,* steal, grap, snatch, pilfer, lift, filch, cop, borrow. *Slang,* snitch. See IMPULSE, STEALING.

swirl, *v.* whirl, eddy, twist. See ROTATION.

swish, *v.* whisk, flourish; rustle. See SOFTNESS, AGITATION.

switch, *n.* twig, sprig, spray; rod, cane, birch; shunt; paraphrase; CHANGE, new version. —*v.t.* cane, whip, lash; shunt, deflect, turn, shift; paraphrase, modify, CHANGE; transpose. See INTERCHANGE, VEGETABLE, PUNISHMENT.

swivel, *v.* turn, pivot, rotate, wheel, veer, swing. See ROTATION.

swoop, *v.* sweep up, catch up, clutch, carry off; pounce, hawk, souse, fly, fall on, descend, sweep down, dive. See DESCENT, ACQUISITION.

sword, *n.* blade, broadsword, falchion, glaive; rapier, foil, épée, saber, cutlass, *etc.;* war, vengeance, DESTRUCTION. See ARMS, WARFARE.

sybarite, *n.* sensualist, voluptuary, hedonist. See PLEASURE.

sycophant, *n.* parasite, toady, bootlicker, lickspittle, flatterer, fawner, truckler. See SERVILITY, FLATTERY.

syllable, *n.* sonant, phone; (*pl.*) tone, accent, inflection. See SPEECH.

syllabus, *n.* outline, schedule, PLAN, calendar; prospectus; abstract, compendium. See PUBLICATION.

sylvan, *adj.* forest, wooded, wood[s]y, arboreous; rural, bucolic. See VEGETATION.

symbol, *n.* token, emblem, mark, badge, device, character, letter. See INDICATION, FIGURATIVE, NUMERATION.

symbolize, *v.t.* represent, indicate, signify, typify, mean, betoken, express, imply. See INDICATION.

SYMMETRY

Nouns—symmetry, proportion, balance, parallelism; uniformity, correspondence, congruity, REGULARITY, regular ARRANGEMENT; ORDER, harmony, eurythmy; shapeliness, FORM, BEAUTY, eurythmics.

Verbs—symmetrize, make symmetrical, balance, proportion, regularize, harmonize, coordinate, equalize.

Adjectives—symmetric[al], proportional, balanced, bilateral, parallel, coextensive; corresponding, congruent, consistent, coordinate, equal (see EQUALITY); even, regular, uniform, orderly, harmonious, eurythmic; shapely, well-set, well-formed, finished, beautiful, classic.

Antonyms, see DISTORTION, IRREGULARITY.

sympathize, *v.i.* feel for, sorrow for; condole; understand; feel sorry for, commiserate. See PITY, BENEVOLENCE.

sympathizer, *n.* upholder, supporter, advocate, champion, well-wisher; commiserator, condoler, FRIEND. See PITY, AUXILIARY.

sympathy, *n.* agreement, understanding, accord; compassion, PITY, condolence, commiseration, fellow-feeling; empathy. See FEEL-

ING, BENEVOLENCE.

symphony, *n.* consonance, harmony, concert, concord; sinfonia, sinfonietta, symphony orchestra, philharmonic. See MUSIC.

symposium, *n.* banquet, collation, feast; panel [discussion], colloquium, colloquy, round table, forum; gathering, social. See ASSEMBLAGE, COUNCIL, CONVERSATION.

symptom, *n.* sign, INDICATION, token, mark. See WARNING.

synagogue, *n.* tabernacle, TEMPLE.

SYNCHRONISM

Nouns—synchronism, synchronization, coexistence, coincidence, concurrence; simultaneity, coinstantaneity, concomitance, unity of TIME, isochronism; simulcast.

Verbs—synchronize, agree in time, be simultaneous; coexist; coincide, agree, concur, match, correspond, harmonize, mesh, dovetail, work together, accompany, go hand in hand, keep pace with; cooperate, coordinate, intermesh, interlock, interact; syncromesh, synthesize, synthetize, syncretize, contemporize. *Colloq.*, gee, sync, jibe, fit to a T.

Adjectives—synchronous, synchronal, synchronical, synchronistical; simultaneous, coinstantaneous, coexistent, coexisting, coincident, concomitant, concurrent; coeval, contemporary, contemporaneous, coetaneous; coeternal; isochronous.

Adverbs—at the same time, at *or* in one fell swoop, at a time, at once, at one time, simultaneously, contemporaneously, during the same time, in concert, together, in the same breath; at the very moment.

Antonyms, see DISAGREEMENT.

---

syncopation, *n.* syncope; jazz, blues, ragtime. See MUSIC.

syndicate, *n.* cartel, combine, pool, monopoly, trust; directorate. See PARTY, COMBINATION, COUNCIL.

syndrome, *n.* characteristics (see INDICATION, SPECIALITY).

synod, *n.* council, convocation, congregation, conclave. See ASSEMBLAGE, CLERGY.

synonymous, *adj.* similar, equivalent, analogous. See IDENTITY, MEANING.

synopsis, *n.* condensation, abridgment, digest. See SHORTNESS.

synthesis, *n.* COMBINATION, composite, amalgamation, unity; construct, fabrication; blend, marriage; syncretism.

synthetic, *adj.* artificial, manmade, unnatural. See PRODUCTION.

syringe, *n.* sprinkler, atomizer, spray[er]; enema, clysma, clyster, douche; needle, hypodermic; syringium. See WATER, CLEANNESS.

syrup, *n.* concentrate, extract, elixir; glucose, sugar water; sorghum, molasses, treacle. See SWEETNESS, COHERENCE.

system, *n.* coordination, organization, routine, ARRANGEMENT, METHOD, scheme, plan; classification; complex. See ORDER, REGULARITY.

systematic, *adj.* methodic[al], orderly. See ORDER, REGULARITY.

T

---

tab, *n.* flap, tag, strip, lug, label; earmark, ticket; tabulation, bill, check, charge, reckoning. —*v.t., colloq.*, appoint, select, designate, nominate, choose, pick [out]. *Slang,* finger. See INDICATION, ADDITION.

tabernacle, *n.* synagogue, TEMPLE.

table, *n.* board, slab; desk, counter; FOOD, diet, fare, cuisine, menu; index, compendium, catalog, chart, tabulation, LIST, schedule; tableland, plateau, mesa. See HORIZONTAL.

tableau, *n.* group; picture, scene, backdrop, set, diorama; arrangement, array. See DRAMA, PAINTING, APPEARANCE.

tablet, *n.* slab, stone, memorial; slate, plaque, signboard; pad, booklet; pill, lozenge, pastille, wafer. See HORIZONTAL, RECORD.

tabloid, *n.* yellow journal, scandal sheet, tattler. *Slang,* rag, blat. See PUBLICATION.

taboo, *n.* tabu, PROHIBITION, interdiction, forbiddance. —*v.t.* forbid, prohibit, keep inviolate. —*adj.* forbidden; untouchable, unprofanable, inviolate.

tabulate, *v.t.* chart, graph; LIST, catalog; calculate, figure, enumerate, tally; enroll, RECORD. See ARRANGEMENT.

tacit, *adj.* unspoken, unexpressed; silent, mute; implied, understood. See SILENCE, TACITURNITY.

TACITURNITY

Nouns—**1,** taciturnity, uncommunicativeness, reticence, reserve, closeness, curtness; SILENCE, muteness, pauciloquy, laconicism; secrecy, CONCEALMENT. **2,** man of few words, mouse. *Slang*, oyster, clam.

Verbs—be taciturn *or* silent, keep SILENCE, not speak, say nothing; hold *or* put a bridle on one's tongue, hold one's peace, bottle up, seal the lips, close the mouth, keep one's tongue between one's teeth, lose one's tongue, lay a finger on the lips, not let a word escape one, make no sign, keep a secret, not have a word to say, cat's got one's tongue. *Slang,* pipe down, clam up.

Adjectives—taciturn, uncommunicative, reticent, reserved, close, close-mouthed *or* -tongued, tight-lipped, short-spoken, unconversable, unsociable, short, curt, laconic, sparing of words, mousy; silent, still, mute, speechless; pauciloquent, concise, terse, sententious; secretive.

Antonyms, see LOQUACITY.

tack, *n.* thumbtack, carpet tack, *etc.;* nail; change of course, yaw, veer; route, course, path; FOOD, fare. —*v.* change course *or* direction; yaw; zigzag; baste. See CONNECTION, DIRECTION, DEVIATION.

tackle, *n.* pulley; gear, equipment, apparatus, instruments; luggage. —*v.t.* grasp, grapple with; seize; address, attach; attempt, try, undertake. See UNDERTAKING, PROVISION.

tacky, *adj., colloq.,* shabby, shoddy, seedy, cheap, tawdry, sleazy, in poor taste; sticky, adhesive. *Slang,* cheesy. See COHERENCE, DETERIORATION.

tact, *n.* diplomacy, finesse, discretion, consideration. See TASTE, CONDUCT.

tactics, *n.pl.* strategy, generalship, CONDUCT; maneuvering; policy, diplomacy; mode, METHOD. See WARFARE.

tactile, *adj.* tangible; tactual. See TOUCH.

tactless, *adj.* thoughtless, insensitive, inconsiderate; callous, unfeeling, blunt, direct. See INDIFFERENCE.

tag, *n.* stub, tab, flap; tail, tassel, pendant; slogan, phrase, name, catchword; tatter, shred, rag. See ADDITION, END, INDICATION.

tail, *n.* appendage, END; cauda; tip, extremity; REAR, rudder, queue, pigtail, train. *Slang,* shadow. See PENDENCY, PURSUIT.

tailor, *n.* sartor, clothier, costumier, dressmaker, seamstress. —*v.* fit, design, make, cut, trim, alter; sew, stitch, style, fashion, shape, drape, hand-tailor, finish. See CLOTHING, FORM, AGREEMENT.

taint, *v.* corrupt, spoil, poison; tarnish, stain, sully; pollute, infect, contaminate. —*n.* corruption; spoilage; stigma, dishonor, defilement; fault, flaw, blemish; contamination. See DISEASE, DISREPUTE, IMPERFECTION, BADNESS, DETERIORATION.

take, *v.* catch, capture (see ACQUISITION); plagiarize, pirate (see STEAL-

ING); take by storm; snap *or* pick up; do; work, be effective; snap a picture. —*n.* taking; *colloq.*, receipts. *Colloq.*, haul. *Slang*, gate, swag. See RECEIVING.

take-off, *n.* lift-off; *colloq.*, IMITATION, parody, satire, burlesque, skit. See ASCENT.

taking, *n.* reception, RECEIVING; appropriation (see ACQUISITION); extortion, theft (see STEALING). —*adj.* fetching, winning, endearing. See PLEASURE, BEAUTY.

tale, *n.* story, account, recital; count[ing], tally; report; fable, yarn, legend; rumor. See DESCRIPTION, INFORMATION.

talent, *n.* gift, faculty, ability, power; turn, knack, aptitude; genius. See SKILL.

talisman, *n.* lucky piece; charm, amulet, fetish. See SORCERY.

talk, *n.* CONVERSATION; chatter, chat, gossip; SPEECH, lecture, discourse; rumor, hearsay. —*v.* say, speak, chat, converse, gossip. See NEWS, INFORMATION.

talkative, *adj.* talky, verbose (see LOQUACITY).

tall, *adj.* high, lofty, towering; long, long-limbed; *colloq.*, exaggerated. See HEIGHT, EXAGGERATION.

tally, *n.* count, tale, counting; score, check; tag, label; match[ing]; roll call. —*v.* count, tell; record, register, score; tag; suit, correspond, agree, harmonize; check. See LIST, NUMERATION, INDICATION, AGREEMENT, CREDIT.

tame, *adj,* tamed, domestic, domesticated; broken, subdued; meek, gentle; docile, tractable; dull, insipid; flat; spiritless, feeble. —*v.t.* subdue, cow, break; harness; domesticate. See DOMESTICATION, SUBJECTION, INSIPIDITY.

tamper, *v.i.* meddle, intermeddle, interfere; bribe, seduce, corrupt, taint; CHANGE, alter. *Colloq.*, doctor, monkey (with). See DETERIORATION.

tang, *n.* savor, flavor, TASTE, zest; sharpness, PUNGENCY, tanginess; bite, nip, twang, snappiness.

tangent, *n.* divergence, DEVIATION. —*adj.* touching (see CONTACT).

tangible, *adj.* material, real; touchable, palpable; concrete, perceptible. See FEELING, SUBSTANCE, TOUCH.

tangle, *n.* snarl, mixup, jumble, mattedness; complication, involvement. —*v.* mat, snarl; knot, mix inextricably; snare, trap, enmesh; catch, perplex; embroil, complicate. See DISORDER, DIFFICULTY.

tank, *n.* reservoir, cistern; boiler; panzer; pond, swimming pool; (*pl.*) armor. See STORE, ARMS.

tankard, *n.* cup, mug. See RECEPTACLE.

tantalize, *v.* tease, tempt, excite, provoke; balk. See DESIRE.

tantamount, *adj.* equivalent (see EQUALITY).

tantrum, *n.* fit, outburst; display (of ill temper); rage, frenzy, paroxysm. See RESENTMENT, VIOLENCE.

tap, *n.* spigot, faucet, valve; plug, bung, stopper; outlet; knock, rap; tapping, tap dance, soft shoe; taproom, bar, saloon. —*v.* knock, rap, pat, strike, TOUCH; tapdance; broach, draw off (liquor, *etc.*); wiretap; draw upon, nominate. See IMPULSE, OPENING, EGRESS, CHOICE.

tape, *n.* band, strip, ribbon; cellophane, Scotch, masking, electrical, *or* friction tape; tapeline. See MEASUREMENT. —*v.* bind, bandage, swaddle, mummify; *colloq.*, tape-record, copy. See FILAMENT.

taper, *v.* narrow; come to a point; lessen, slacken, slack off, diminish. —*n.* candle, LIGHT; pyramid, cone, spire, *etc.* See NARROWNESS.

tapestry, *n.* weaving, rug; mosaic, montage. See COVERING, REPRESENTATION.

tar, *n.* asphalt, pitch, resin, bitumen; goo, sludge. —*v.* besmirch, stain, blacken, defame; tar and feather. See NAVIGATION, COVERING, PUNISHMENT.

tardy, *adj.* overdue, late, behind-time; slow, slack, dilatory, sluggish. See LATENESS, LATENCY.

target, *n.* aim, mark; goal; bull's-eye; quarry, object; butt. See INTENTION.

tariff, *n.* duty, customs, impost; price list; PRICE, cost. See PAYMENT.

tarnish, *v.* smirch, taint; dishonor; stain, sully, besmirch; defame; dull, smudge, dim, spot, blemish; discolor. See DISREPUTE, UNCLEANNESS.

tarpaulin, *n.* tarp, canvas, oilcloth, tent; poncho, slicker. See COVERING.

tarry, *v.i.* linger, stay, wait; idle, dawdle; visit (with); bide a while, sojourn; delay, dally. See LATENESS, DURABILITY.

tart, *adj.* acid, sour; sarcastic, acerbic, snappy, sharp, astringent. —*n.* pie; *slang,* strumpet. See SOURNESS, DISCOURTESY, PUNGENCY, IMPURITY.

tartan, *n.* plaid, check; kilt, trews, filibeg. See VARIEGATION.

task, *n.* work, stint, job, labor; lesson, assignment, charge, DUTY, chore; drudgery, burden. —*v.t.* strain, tax, overburden, overwork; impose, assign, charge. See EXERTION, COMMISSION, COMMAND, BUSINESS.

taskmaster, *n.* overseer, martinet, slavedriver. See SEVERITY.

TASTE

Nouns—**1,** taste, tastefulness; good *or* cultivated taste; delicacy, refinement, tact, finesse, flair; nicety, discrimination; distinction, polish, ELEGANCE; virtu, connoisseurship, dilettantism; fine art; culture, cultivation, fastidiousness; esthetics. See FASHION, INTELLIGENCE, JUDGMENT.

2, sample; tinge, bit, trace, scrap, soupçon; tasting, gustation, degustation; palate, tongue, tooth, stomach. See PART, LITTLENESS.

3, flavor, gusto, savor, zest; sapor, sapidity, aftertaste, tang; savoriness, tastiness, palatability; unsavoriness, unpalatability, austerity, INSIPIDITY; SWEETNESS; SOURNESS, acidity, acerbity; PUNGENCY.

4, seasoning, condiment; spice, relish; tidbit, dainty, delicacy, morsel, appetizer, *hors d'oeuvres,* antipasto, delicatessen; sauce; ambrosia; nectar; rue, hemlock, myrrh, aloes, gall and wormwood. See FOOD.

5, man of taste, connoisseur; epicure, gourmet; judge, critic, virtuoso; amateur, dilettante.

Verbs—**1,** have good taste, appreciate, have an eye for; judge, criticize, discriminate, distinguish, particularize; single out, draw the line, sift, estimate, weigh, consider, diagnose; pick and choose, split hairs, know which is which.

2, savor, taste, sample; relish, like, enjoy, smack the lips; tickle the palate; turn the stomach, disgust; pall, stale, spoil; sour, curdle, ferment, turn.

3, season, spice, garnish.

Adjectives—**1,** in good taste; tasteful, unaffected, pure, chaste, classical, cultivated, refined; dainty, delicate, esthetic, artistic; meticulous, precise, exact, precious; elegant; euphemistic; choosy, fussy; astute, keen; fastidious, finicky, finical, crotchety, per[s]nickety, squeamish; [over]nice, particular, discriminating, discriminative, discerning, perceptive; to one's taste, after one's fancy; *comme il faut, de rigueur. Colloq.,* picky.

2, tasty, flavorful, toothsome, sapid, saporific; palatable, gustable, gustatory, tastable; pungent, strong; flavored, spicy, hot; sweet, sour, salt[y], bitter, nutty; savory, unsavory.

Adverbs—tastefully, elegantly; purely, esthetically, *etc.*

Antonyms, see VULGARITY, INSIPIDITY, NEGLECT, DISORDER.

---

tasteless, *adj.* insipid, flat; inelegant; inept, clumsy, vulgar, savorless, unappetizing. See INSIPIDITY, VULGARITY, INELEGANCE.

tatters, *n.pl.* rags, odds and ends, fragments. See PART.

tattle, *v.* prattle, prate; chat[ter]; jabber, talk, gossip; reveal (a secret), inform. *Colloq.,* peach, tell on, tell tales. *Slang,* blab; spill the beans. See ACCUSATION, DISCLOSURE.

taunt, *v.* RIDICULE, scoff, jeer, twit; provoke, mock, flout, deride. See ACCUSATION.

taut, *adj.* tight, stretched, tense, strained; keyed up, on edge; snug, tidy, shipshape, neat. See HARDNESS, ORDER.

tautology, *n.* REPETITION, reiteration, redundance, verbosity.

tavern, *n.* inn, hostel, restaurant, café; saloon, bar. See FOOD, DRINKING.

tawdry, *adj.* cheap, showy, flashy; loud, garish; tinsel, gimcrack. See VULGARITY, OSTENTATION.

tax, *n.* assessment, levy, duty, tariff, excise, toll, tithe; impost, custom; rate, income tax, internal revenue; *colloq.,* charge. See PAYMENT. —*v.* assess, rate, COMMAND; charge, accuse; take to task; strain, overwork, burden, fatigue. See ACCUSATION, COMPULSION, EXERTION.

taxi, *n.* taximeter cab, taxicab; hack[ney], jitney; taxiplane; fiacre, droshky, [jin]rickshaw, pedicab. See VEHICLE, TRANSPORTATION.

tea, *n.* pekoe, souchong, oolong, *etc.* tea; beef tea, broth, bouillon; collation, afternoon *or* five-o'clock tea, high tea, snack. See DRINKING.

TEACHING

Nouns—**1,** teaching, instruction, edification, education, tuition; tutorship, tutelage; DIRECTION, guidance; PREPARATION, training, upbringing, schooling; discipline; exercise, drill, practice; indoctrination, inculcation, inoculation; explanation, INTERPRETATION. See SCHOOL, LEARNING.

2, lesson, catechism; lecture, sermon; apologue, parable; discourse, prelection, preachment; exercise, task.

3, teacher, educator, trainer, instructor, master, tutor, director, coach, disciplinarian; professor, lecturer, reader, prelector, prolocutor; preacher, pastor (see CLERGY); schoolmaster, dominie, pedagogue, abecedarian; schoolmistress, governess; monitor; expositor, interpreter; preceptor, guide, mentor; adviser (see ADVICE); exponent; pioneer, apostle, missionary, propagandist. *Colloq.,* schoolmarm.

Verbs—**1,** teach [a lesson], instruct, edify, school, tutor; cram, prime, coach; enlighten, inform; inculcate, indoctrinate, inoculate, infuse, instill, infiltrate; imbue, impregnate, implant; graft, sow the seeds of, disseminate; give an idea of; put up to, set right, sharpen the wits, broaden one's horizon, open the eyes, bring forward, improve; direct, guide; direct attention to, impress upon the mind *or* memory; convince (see BELIEF). *Colloq.,* beat into [the head].

2, expound, set forth, develop; interpret, lecture, editorialize, hold forth, preach; sermonize, moralize.

3, train, discipline; bring up, educate, form, ground, prepare, qualify, drill, exercise, practice; nurture, breed, rear, take in hand; break [in]; tame; preinstruct; initiate, inure, habituate; brainwash (see DECEPTION). *Colloq.,* show the ropes.

Adjectives—teaching, taught, educational; scholastic, academic, doctrinal;

disciplinal, disciplinary; teachable, receptive; instructive, didactic, homiletic; professorial, pedagogical.

Antonyms, see LEARNING.

---

team, *n.* crew, side, aggregation; nine, five, eleven (baseball, basketball, and football teams); rig, span (of horses); combat team, group; brace, pair, foursome, *etc.* See COOPERATION, NUMERATION.

teamster, *n.* wagonmaster, muleteer; carter, drayman, wagoner; truck driver, truckman, trucker, vanman, carrier. See TRANSPORTATION.

teamwork, *n.* coordination, collaboration, COOPERATION.

tear, *v.* rip, rend, lacerate, tatter, shred; split, burst, break, part, separate, remove, raze, wrench; give; snatch, race; speed, dash, fly. —*n.* break, rent, split; wound; crack, fissure, gap; (*pl.*) teardrops, weeping, crying, LAMENTATION; *slang,* spree. *Slang,* binge, toot, bender, jag. See DISJUNCTION, PART, VELOCITY, INTEMPERANCE.

tearful, teary, *adj.* weeping, sorrowful. See DEJECTION, LAMENTATION.

tease, *v.* plague, annoy, vex, harass; taunt, mock; beg; tantalize; titillate, excite. See RIDICULE, MALEVOLENCE.

technical, *adj.* scientific, technological; professional, skilled. See KNOWLEDGE, BUSINESS, SKILL.

technicality, *n.* fine point, minutiae (*pl.*); nuance, detail, subtlety, formality; law, rule, rubric; loophole, letter of the law; procedure, problem. See SKILL.

technique, *n.* technic, execution, style, METHOD.

technology, *n.* technics; knowledge, information, craft, science, engineering, mechanics; SKILL, practice; automation, mechanization. *Colloq.,* know-how.

tedious, *adj.* wearisome, wearing, dry, dry-as-dust, boring, tiresome, irksome, dull, monotonous, prosy, uninteresting. See WEARINESS.

teem, *v.i.* swarm, abound; multiply, pullulate; rain heavily, pour; bear, generate, produce. See PRODUCTION, SUFFICIENCY.

teeming, *adj.* swarming, abounding, abundant, plentiful; crowded, chock-full, jam-packed; replete, fraught, full, pullulating; raining. See MULTITUDE.

teenager, *n.* YOUTH, adolescent. *Colloq.,* bobbysoxer, teen. *Slang,* teeny-bopper.

teepee, *n.* wigwam, hut, lodge. See ABODE.

teeter, *v.i.* seesaw, rock, sway, totter, tremble; hesitate, vacillate. See OSCILLATION, DOUBT.

teetotal, *adj.* absolute, entire; abstinent; dry, prohibitionist; *colloq.,* all, entire, whole. See WHOLE, MODERATION.

telegram, *n.* message, wire, cable. See COMMUNICATION.

telegraph, *n.* telegram; wireless, Morse, wire, cable, semaphore, heliograph, pantelograph, phototelegraph. —*v.t.* signal, wire, radio, cable; *colloq.,* betray, disclose, reveal. See COMMUNICATION, INDICATION.

telepathy, *n.* psychic COMMUNICATION, thought transference, extrasensory perception, ESP; psi.

telephone, *v.* call [up], phone, dial, get through to. See COMMUNICATION.

telescope, *n.* glass, fieldglass, spyglass. —*v.* collapse, fold; [fore]-shorten, condense, abridge. See OPTICAL INSTRUMENTS, DISTANCE.

television, *n.* video, TV; telefilm, kinescope; [video]tape; station, studio, channel, network, syndicate; closed-circuit, cable, *or* pay television; telecast; CATV. See COMMUNICATION.

tell, *v.* recount, relate, narrate; inform, apprise, acquaint; explain; weigh, matter, influence; reveal, disclose, own, confess, acknowledge; discern, distinguish, make out, see, recognize; count, number, reckon, rally; speak, state, declare. See INFORMATION, DESCRIPTION, DISCLOSURE, SPEECH, INFLUENCE.

teller, *n.* bank clerk, cashier. See STORE.

telling, *adj.* effective, striking. See EFFECT, POWER, IMPORTANCE.

telltale, *adj.* significant, revealing. —*n.* tattler, talebearer. See INFORMATION.

temerity, *n.* RASHNESS, boldness, audacity, recklessness, daring. *Slang,* nerve, gall, brass, cheek.

temper, *n.* temperament, nature, disposition; mood, humor, tone; tantrum, passion, rage; mettle, quality; calmness, composure, equanimity. See IRASCIBILITY, FEELING, INTRINSIC. —*v.t.* moderate, soften; harden, anneal, toughen. See HARDNESS, SOFTNESS, CHANGE.

temperament, *n.* constitution, disposition, nature, humor. See FEELING, SENSIBILITY.

temperamental, *adj.* irritable, sensitive; constitutional, innate. See IRASCIBILITY, INTRINSIC.

temperance, *n.* See MODERATION.

temperate, *adj.* moderate, ascetic, cautious, mild, sober, abstemious, abstinent, continent; Pythagorean; vegetarian. See MODERATION.

tempest, *n.* storm, gale, hurricane, squall, blizzard; excitement, tumult, disturbance; maelstrom. See WIND, VIOLENCE.

tempestuous, *adj.* stormy, raging, furious; gusty, blowy, squally; violent, tumultuous, turbulent. See WIND, VIOLENCE.

TEMPLE

Nouns—**1,** temple, place of worship; house of God, house of prayer; cathedral, minister, church, kirk, chapel, meetinghouse, tabernacle, basilica, holy place, chantry, oratory; synagogue; mosque; marabout; pantheon; pagoda. See ABODE.

2, altar, shrine, sanctuary, Holy of Holies, *sanctum sanctorum,* communion table; pyx; baptistery, font; sedilia; reredos; rood-loft, rood-screen; chancel, nave, aisle, transept, vestry, sacristy, crypt, cloisters, churchyard, golgotha, calvary; stall, pew; pulpit, ambo, lectern, reading-desk, confessional; apse, oriel, belfry, steeple.

3, parsonage, parish house, rectory, vicarage, manse, deanery, presbytery, Vatican, bishop's palace.

4, monastery, priory, abbey, friary, convent, nunnery, cloister; sanctuary.

Adjectives—churchly, claustral, cloistral, cloistered; monastic, conventual.

---

tempo, *n.* time, beat, rate, pace, rhythm. See MUSIC.

temporal, *adj.* worldly, mundane, secular; civil, political, profane, unsacred; temporary, ephemeral, impermanent. See TRANSIENTNESS.

temporary, *adj.* impermanent, irregular, seasonal, provisional, momentary, brief, fleeting, transitory; stopgap, makeshift, ersatz. See TRANSIENTNESS.

temporize, *v.i.* adapt oneself, maneuver; vacillate, procrastinate, stall, delay, hedge. *Colloq.,* blow hot and cold, play for time. See LATENESS, DURABILITY.

tempt, *v.t.* entice, cajole, fascinate, lure, decoy, seduce; provoke, defy, incite, appeal, attract. See DESIRE, ATTRACTION.

temptation, *n.* ATTRACTION, enticement, allurement; bait; siren song; provocativeness. See DESIRE.

TENACITY

Nouns—tenacity, cohesion, COHERENCE; holding, STRENGTH; viscidity, viscosity; pertinacity, perseverance, persistence, RESOLUTION, patience; OBSTINACY, RESISTANCE, constancy, RETENTION. *Colloq.*, stick-to-itiveness.

Verbs—adhere (to), stick (to), cling (to); persevere, persist, hold on *or* out, never say die, fight to the last ditch, be in at the death, stick to one's guns; keep on, hold one's course *or* ground, bear *or* keep up, continue, plod, follow through *or* up. *Colloq.*, stick it out, muddle through, see it through, hang on for dear life, keep a stiff upper lip, keep one's chin up.

Adjectives—tenacious, cohesive, adhesive, clinging, holding, fast, resisting, strong; sticky, gummy, tacky, waxy, glutinous, viscous, viscid; pertinacious, persistent, persevering, dogged, determined, unyielding, uncompromising, unwavering, unfaltering; obstinate, stubborn, intransigent, opinionated, positive, single-minded; steady, steadfast, firm, resolute, constant, purposeful, relentless; retentive. *Colloq.*, pigheaded, never-say-die.

Adverbs—tenaciously, *etc.*; through thick and thin, rain or shine.

Antonyms, see WEAKNESS, SUBMISSION.

---

tenant, *n.* occupant, occupier, resident, INHABITANT, renter; inmate. See POSSESSION, ABODE.

tend, *v.* mind, watch, care for, guard, keep; attend, serve, wait on, incline, bend, bear toward, lean, gravitate. See SERVANT, TENDENCY, UTILITY.

TENDENCY

Nouns—tendency; aptness, aptitude; proneness, proclivity, predilection, bent, turn, tone, tenor, bias, set, leaning, penchant, [pre]disposition, inclination, propensity, susceptibility; likelihood, LIABILITY; nature, temperament; idiosyncrasy; cast, vein, grain; humor, mood; trend, drift, the way the wind blows; conduciveness, conducement; applicability. See SPECIALITY, INTRINSIC, DIRECTION.

Verbs—tend, contribute, conduce, lead, dispose, incline, verge, lean, bend to, trend, affect, carry, redound to, bid fair to, gravitate toward; be liable.

Adjectives—tending, conducive, working toward, in a fair way to, calculated to; liable, prone; useful, subsidiary.

Antonyms, see OPPOSITION.

---

tender, *v.t.* present, OFFER, proffer, hold out; propose, suggest; volunteer. —*adj.* gentle, kind; sentimental; affectionate, tenderhearted, loving, amorous; immature; sympathetic, soft; humane, merciful; young; fragile, delicate; pathetic, touching; painful, sore. See BENEVOLENCE, LOVE, SOFTNESS, FEELING, PITY, YOUTH. —*n.* MONEY; supply ship; supply car, coal car. See SHIP, VEHICLE.

tenderfoot, *n.* newcomer, recruit, novice. *Colloq.*, greenhorn. See BEGINNING.

tenebrous, *adj.* dark, gloomy. See DARKNESS.

tenement, *n.* apartment house; flat, dwelling, ABODE; slum.

tenet, *n.* dogma, BELIEF, opinion, creed, doctrine.

tenor, *n.* drift, purport, TENDENCY, import, MEANING, significance; gist, sense; course, manner, nature, mood; DIRECTION. See MUSIC.

tense, *adj.* taut, rigid; intent; excited;

high-strung, nervous, strained. See HARDNESS. —*n.* time, verb form, inflection. See GRAMMAR.

tensile, *adj.* stretchable, ductile, flexile; resilient, pliable. See ELASTICITY.

tension, *n.* strain, pressure, tensity, tenseness; stretching; anxiety, nervousness. See LENGTH, TRACTION, HARDNESS, FEAR.

tent, *n.* canvas, wigwam, teepee, pavilion, shelter. See COVERING, ABODE.

tentacle, *n.* process, feeler, palp; (*pl.*) power, grasp. See RETENTION.

tentative, *adj.* experimental, provisional, conditional, temporary, makeshift. See EXPEDIENCE, EXPERIMENT.

tenuous, *adj.* unsubstantial, flimsy; thin, slender; rarefied. See NARROWNESS, RARITY.

tenure, *n.* holding, tenancy, occupancy, occupation, habitation, POSSESSION.

tepid, *adj.* lukewarm, mild; indifferent. See HEAT, INDIFFERENCE.

term, *n.* word, expression, locution; LIMIT, bound; period, TIME, tenure, duration; semester. See NOMENCLATURE.

terminal, *adj.* final; closing, concluding. See END. —*n.* station, terminus. See LOCATION, ARRIVAL.

termination, *n.* END, ending, conclusion; LIMIT, bound; result, outcome, consequence, completion; suffix.

terminology, *n.* See NOMENCLATURE.

terms, *n.* provisions, limitations, stipulations, conditions, agreement; relationship, footing. See COMMAND, QUALIFICATION.

terrace, *n.* level, plateau, plane; parterre, esplanade, promenade; porch, patio, balcony, embankment. See HORIZONTAL.

terrestrial, *adj.* earthly; worldly, mundane, secular, temporal. See LAND.

terrible, *adj.* terrifying, dreadful; awesome, appalling, frightful, horrible, shocking, fearful, alarming. *Colloq.*, excessive. See FEAR.

terrific, *adj.* terrible (see FEAR); *colloq.*, sensational, wonderful, fabulous, stupendous. *Slang,* out of this world. See GREATNESS.

terrify, *v.t.* terrorize, frighten, alarm; appall, dismay; cow, intimidate; panic, stampede. See FEAR.

territory, *n.* REGION, district; possession; kingdom, state, realm, province; jurisdiction; field, ground. See KNOWLEDGE..

terror, *n.* FEAR, dread; fright, alarm; dismay, horror; panic.

terrorism, *n.* oppression, tyranny, anarchy, revolution, bolshevism, nihilism; VIOLENCE, destruction, sabotage, intimidation, agitation. See FEAR, THREAT.

terse, *adj.* concise, brief, curt; pithy, laconic, succinct; short, compact. See MAXIM, SHORTNESS.

test, *n.* examination; trial, essay; criterion; EXPERIMENT.

testament, *n.* will, last will and testament, probate; covenant, AGREEMENT. See GIVING.

testify, *v.* affirm, declare, state, depose, swear, avow, witness. See EVIDENCE.

testimonial, *n.* recommendation, reference; certificate. See RECORD, APPROBATION, EVIDENCE.

testimony, *n.* declaration, affirmation, profession, attestation; witness, EVIDENCE; Scriptures.

testy, *adj.* irritable, irascible, petulant, cross. *Colloq.*, ornery. See IRASCIBILITY.

tether, *v.t.* picket, stake, tie, fasten. See RESTRAINT.

text, *n.* composition; matter; textbook; topic, subject, theme. See WRITING, PUBLICATION, TEACHING.

TEXTURE

Nouns—**1,** texture, quality, fabric, surface, fiber, nap, tooth, tissue, weave, warp and woof, weft, grain, fineness *or* coarseness of grain; SMOOTHNESS, ROUGHNESS. See ORNAMENT.

2, SUBSTANCE, stuff, staple (see MATERIALS); mat, web[bing], braid, plait, trellis, mesh, lattice[work], tissue. See CROSSING.

Verb—texture; braid, plait, *etc.*; coarsen, grain.

Adjectives—textured, textural, textile, woven; structural, anatomic[al], organic; coarse, grainy, coarse-grained, homespun; shaggy, nappy; fine, fine-grained; delicate, subtle, filmy, downy, gossamery, smooth.

Antonyms, see SMOOTHNESS.

---

thankful, *adj.* grateful, appreciative; much obliged. See GRATITUDE.

thankless, *adj.* ungrateful, unthankful, unappreciative, ingrate, ungracious; unrewarding, unpleasant. See INGRATITUDE, DISCONTENT.

thanks, *n.pl.* GRATITUDE; acknowledgment, appreciation; thank you; grace.

thanksgiving, *n.* grace, prayer, praise. See GRATITUDE.

thaw, *v.* melt, dissolve, liquefy; soften, unbend. See HEAT, LIQUEFACTION.

theater, *n.* stage, ARENA, field [of action]; DRAMA; playhouse, motion-picture house, studio. See AMUSEMENT.

theatrical, *adj.* dramatic, melodramatic; histrionic; scenic; showy, stagy, affected; vivid, moving. See AFFECTATION, DRAMA, OSTENTATION.

theft, *n.* larceny, STEALING.

theme, *n.* subject, topic, text; essay, thesis, treatise, dissertation; composition; melody, motif. See MUSIC, THOUGHT.

then, *adv.* soon, next, immediately; consequently, therefore, evidently, again; afterwards. See CIRCUMSTANCE, SEQUENCE.

theology, *n.* RELIGION; creed, BELIEF; doctrine, dogma.

theoretical, *adj.* speculative, hypothetical, conjectural; unapplied; pure, abstract. See SUPPOSITION.

theory, *n.* speculation, surmise, conjecture; contemplation; principle, philosophy, doctrine; hypothesis; guess, idea, plan. See SUPPOSITION.

therapy, *n.* therapeutics, REMEDY, healing, cure; rehabilitation, RESTORATION; physical therapy, psychotherapy, *etc.*

thereafter, *adv.* after[wards], after that; subsequently, [t]henceforth, from that moment; after which; later, in the future. See SEQUENCE.

therefore, *adv.* consequently, ergo, hence, wherefore, so, accordingly. See REASONING, ATTRIBUTION, CIRCUMSTANCE, EFFECT.

thermometer, *n.* thermostat, pyrometer, calorimeter; mercury, glass. See MEASUREMENT, HEAT.

thesaurus, *n.* treasury; repository, lexicon, dictionary. See PUBLICATION.

thesis, *n.* proposition, topic, argument; affirmation; postulate; statement; composition, treatise, dissertation. See THOUGHT.

thick, *adj.* broad, wide, massive, thickset, stout, fat; dense, solid; populous, crowded; heavy, viscous, creamy; foggy, smoky, hazy; hoarse, guttural, throaty; slow[-witted], witless. *Slang,* gooey. See BREADTH, DENSITY, MULTITUDE.

thicket, *n.* brush, underbrush; grove, coppice, covert. See VEGETABLE.

thick-skinned, *adj.* insensitive, callous[ed], hard. See INSENSIBILITY.

thief, *n.* robber (see STEAL).

thin, *adj.* slender, lean, narrow (see NARROWNESS); watery, weak, diluted; attenuated; faint, dim, threadlike; fine, delicate; poor, lame (as an excuse); flimsy, sheer, filmy. See RARITY, WEAKNESS, TRANSPARENCY, INSIPIDITY.

thing, *n.* affair, matter, circumstance; deed, act, occurrence; entity, person; possession, belonging, chattel; item, object, detail, article. See SUBSTANCE.

think, *v.* See THOUGHT.

thirst, *n.* DRYNESS; craving, DESIRE; dipsomania, thirstiness, parchedness.

thirsty, *adj.* dry, parched, unslaked, unquenched, arid; greedy, avid. See DRYNESS, DESIRE.

thorn, *n.* spine, prickle, briar, bramble; annoyance, irritation. See SHARPNESS, DISCONTENT.

thorough, *adj.* thoroughgoing, painstaking, exact, careful; complete, absolute, unqualified, arrant, out-and-out; exhaustive, deep, sweeping. See COMPLETION.

thoroughbred, *adj.* purebred, full-blooded, pedigreed; blueblooded, noble, aristocratic; to the manor born; well-bred *or* -mannered. See PURITY, FASHION, NOBILITY.

thoroughfare, *n.* avenue, highway, street; PASSAGE, way; thruway, stop street, boulevard, turnpike.

though, *conj.* although, even if, nevertheless, yet. See COMPENSATION.

THOUGHT

Nouns—**1,** thought, thoughtfulness; reflection, cogitation, consideration, meditation, study, lucubration, speculation, deliberation, pondering; headwork, brainwork; cerebration; deep reflection, rumination, close study, application, ATTENTION; abstract thought, abstraction; contemplation, musing, preoccupation, brown study, reverie, Platonism; self-counsel, self-communing, self-consultation; association, succession, *or* flow of ideas; train *or* current of thought. See JUDGMENT, INTELLECT, REASONING.

2, afterthought, mature thought, reconsideration, second thought; retrospection, hindsight; MEMORY; excogitation; examination (see INQUIRY); invention (see IMAGINATION).

3, idea, concept, notion; opinion, conceit, belief, impression; principle; topic, subject of thought, material *or* food for thought; subject [matter], matter, theme, thesis, text, business, affair, matter in hand, argument; motion, resolution; head, chapter; case, point; proposition, theorem (see SUPPOSITION); field of inquiry; moot point, problem.

Verbs—**1,** think, reflect, cogitate, cerebrate, excogitate, consider, think over, deliberate, lucubrate; rationalize, speculate, contemplate, meditate, ponder, muse, dream, ruminate; brood upon; animadvert, study; bend *or* apply the mind; digest, discuss, weigh; realize, appreciate; fancy; think on one's feet. *Slang,* beat one's brains (out), use one's head, bean, noodle, *or* noggin.

2, take into consideration; see about *or* to; take counsel, commune with oneself, bethink oneself; collect one's thoughts; revolve, turn over *or* run over in the mind; sleep on; rack one's brains; set one's wits to work; puzzle *or* pore over; take into one's head; bear in mind; reconsider, think better of; put on one's thinking cap. *Colloq.,* sweat over, chew the cud, mull over. *Slang,* kick around.

3, occur, present, *or* suggest itself; come into one's head; strike one, cross *or* pass through the mind, occupy the mind; have on one's mind; make an impression; sink in, penetrate the mind; engross the thoughts; come to think of it. *Colloq.,* take a notion.

Adjectives—thinking, thoughtful, pensive, meditative, reflective, musing, wistful, contemplative, speculative, deliberative, studious, sedate, introspective, platonic, philosophical, metaphysic[al]; rational; lost in thought, engrossed, absorbed, rapt, preoccupied; in the mind, under consideration; on one's chest. *Slang,* on the brain.

Adverbs—thoughtfully, reflectively; all things considered.

Antonyms, see RASHNESS, INATTENTION.

---

thoughtful, *adj.* considerate, kind, tactful; meditative. See THOUGHT, ATTENTION, CARE.

thoughtless, *adj.* rash, reckless, heedless; casual; inconsiderate, unthinking, mindless; unreasoning; careless, indifferent. See RASHNESS.

thousand, *n.* fifty score, M. *Slang,* thou, yard, grand, G. See NUMERATION.

thrash, *v.t.* beat, spank, whip, flog, strike; defeat, overcome, conquer; thresh. See SUCCESS, PUNISHMENT.

thread, *n.* FILAMENT, fiber, hair; string; yarn; linen, cotton, silk, lisle, nylon, *etc.*; course, drift, train (of thought). See CONTINUITY, NARROWNESS.

threadbare, *adj.* frayed, tattered, worn[-out]; jaded, weary; trite, hackneyed; scanty. See DETERIORATION, DIVESTMENT, WEARINESS.

THREAT

Nouns—**1,** threat, menace, intimidation, commination, minacity, TERRORISM; empty threat, fulmination, sword- *or* sabre-rattling; DEFIANCE; yellow menace *or* peril; blackmail, extortion. See FUTURITY, FEAR, WARNING.

2, thunder[bolt], gathering clouds, red sky in the morning; foreboding, imminence, omen, WARNING; notice; peril, jeopardy, DANGER.

Verbs—**1,** threaten, menace, intimidate, comminate, fulminate; terrorize, frighten, hector, cow, bully, browbeat; snarl, growl, mutter, bark, thunder, bluster, brandish; jeopardize, imperil, endanger; blackmail, extort; talk big, look daggers, shake the fist at; carry a big stick. *Slang,* shake down.

2, portend, presage, augur, omen, [fore]bode, foreshadow (see PREDICTION), impend, be imminent, overhang, lower, lour, loom, hang over one's head.

Adjectives—threatening, menacing, intimidative, denunciatory, fulminatory, bullying; WARNING, cautionary, dangerous, perilous, jeopardous; ominous, foreboding, lowering, looming, *etc.*; baleful, baneful, thundery, dire[ful], awful, sinister, dark, black.

Antonyms, see SAFETY.

---

threshold, *n.* sill, doorsill, entrance; outset, BEGINNING; limen, threshold of pain, *etc.* See EDGE.

thrift, *n.* thriftiness, ECONOMY, frugality, saving; providence, husbandry; vigor, growth, thriving.

thrifty, *adj.* frugal, saving; sparing; economical; foresighted; provident. See ECONOMY.

thrill, *n.* EXCITEMENT; tremor, vibration; sensation; tingle. *Slang,* kick, charge. —*v.* throb, tingle, shiver; stir, excite, move deeply; vibrate, tremble. See FEELING, SENSIBILITY.

thriller, *n.* chiller, shocker; pulp story, dime novel, cloak-and-dagger *or* spy story; swashbuckler. *Slang,* whodunit. See DESCRIPTION.

thrive, *v.i.* prosper, batten, succeed, grow, flourish, bloom, flower. See PROSPERITY.

throat, *n.* neck, gullet, gorge, maw; windpipe; throttle. See OPENING.

throb, *v.i.* beat, pulsate, vibrate, palpitate; quiver, shudder, tremble; ache, hurt. See AGITATION, FEELING.

throe, *n.* pang, spasm, paroxysm, PAIN, AGITATION.

throne, *n.* royal seat, chair; sovereignty, scepter. See AUTHORITY.

throng, *n.* multitude, crowd, mob, horde; army, host. See ASSEMBLAGE.

throttle, *v.* choke, strangle, suffocate; silence, stifle; close. See CLOSURE, KILLING.

through, *prep. & adv.* among, via,

by way of; during, throughout; by; with. See DIRECTION, MEANS.

throughway, *n.* thruway, turnpike, superhighway. See PASSAGE.

throw, *v.* pitch, toss, cast, fling, hurl, sling; propel, project, unhorse, unseat; *slang,* stop, disconcert, confound. See PROPULSION.

thrust, *v.* push, drive, shove, propel; lunge, plunge, ram; stab, pierce; compel, drive, force; interpose, interject. —*n.* blow, jab, poke; ATTACK, sortie; dig; repartee; POWER. See IMPULSE.

thug, *n.* cutthroat, assassin, killer; ruffian, hooligan, tough. *Colloq.,* hoodlum. *Slang,* mugger, hood, goon, yegg, torpedo, gorilla. See EVILDOER.

thunder, *v.* shout, bellow; resound, peal, boom, roar, roll, crash. See LOUDNESS.

thus, *adv.* so; consequently, hence. See CIRCUMSTANCE.

thwart, *v.t.* oppose, baffle, foil, frustrate, defeat, block, contravene. See HINDRANCE.

tiara, *n.* diadem, coronet. See ORNAMENT.

tick, *n.* click, beat; check, dot; mite; *colloq.,* score, account. See INDICATION, CREDIT, ANIMAL.

ticket, *n.* notice, memorandum, record; license; label, tag; list, slate, ballot; admission ticket. *Slang,* ducat. See INDICATION, CHOICE.

tickle, *v.t.* excite; gladden, delight, overjoy; please; titillate; amuse, gratify, divert. See PLEASURE.

ticklish, *adj.* tickly, excitable, sensitive; unstable, touchy; delicate, critical, risky, dangerous. See SENSIBILITY, DANGER.

tidbit, *n.* morsel, bite, snack; goody, treat, bonbon; gem, pearl, jewel; news, INFORMATION, juicy bit. See FOOD.

tide, *n.* flow, current, flood, riptide. See WATER.

tidings, *n.pl.* NEWS, message, intelligence, INFORMATION.

tidy, *adj.* neat, orderly, trim, prim; *colloq.,* sizable, considerable (see GREATNESS). —*v.* arrange, put in order, straighten. See CLEANNESS, ARRANGEMENT, ORDER.

tie, *n.* bond, obligation; shoelace; necktie, cravat, four-in-hand *or* bow tie; fastening, ligature; draw, tied score, dead heat; beam, post; sleeper. —*v.t.* fasten, attach, join; bind, restrict, constrain, confine; knot; equal. See CLOTHING, DUTY, JUNCTION, CONNECTION, EQUALITY.

tier, *n.* rank, row, level, LAYER; gallery, boxes, balcony.

tie-up, *n.* halt, stoppage, blockade, impediment, snarl, [traffic] jam, impasse; *colloq.,* association, connection, tie-in, liaison. See COOPERATION, HINDRANCE.

tiff, *n.* temper, fit, tantrum; squabble, spat. *Colloq.,* miff. See CONTENTION, DISCORD.

tight, *adj.* close, compact, hermetic, impervious; snug, close-fitting; hemmed-in; strict, stringent; scarce, in short supply; *colloq.,* stingy, parsimonious; *slang,* intoxicated, inebriated, loaded. See CLOSURE, CONTRACTION, NARROWNESS, PARSIMONY, DRINKING.

tight-fisted, *adj.* stingy, frugal, parsimonious, grudging, niggard[ly], miserly, moneygrubbing, avaricious. *Colloq.,* tight, cheap. See PARSIMONY.

till, *prep.* until, up to, down to. See TIME. —*v.* cultivate, plow, farm. See AGRICULTURE.

tilt, *v.* tip, slant, incline, slope; joust. —*n.* joust, tournament; altercation, dispute; speed; slant, slope; awning, canopy. See CONTENTION, OBLIQUITY, COVERING.

timber, *n.* wood, lumber, log, beam; forest, woodland, stand of timber, timberland. See MATERIALS.

timbre, *n.* resonance, tonal quality, SOUND, tone color, ring, clang.

TIME

Nouns—**1,** time, duration; period, term, stage, space, span, spell, season; fourth dimension; the whole time; era, epoch, age, eon; time of life; moment, instant, INSTANTANEITY, SYNCHRONISM; anachronism; course, progress, flow, march, stream, *or* lapse of time; slow *or* standard time; Time, Father Time, ravages of time.See PAST, FUTURITY.

2, intermediate time, while, interim, interval, pendency; intermission, intermittence, interregnum, interlude; leisure, spare time; respite. See DISCONTINUANCE, BETWEEN.

3, anniversary, jubilee, recurrence (see REGULARITY).

4, see CHRONOMETRY.

Verbs—continue, last, endure, go on, remain, persist; intervene, elapse, lapse, pass, flow, advance, roll on, go by, go on; flit, fly, slip, slide, *or* glide by; take [up] time, fill *or* occupy time; pass, spend, waste, while away, *or* consume time; live out; talk against time; tide over; seize an opportunity, take time by the forelock; make a day *or* night of it.

Adjectives—continuing; permanent, perpetual, eternal; regular, steady, periodic, intermittent; elapsing, passing, aoristic; timely, untimely, punctual, fast, slow, leisurely, unhurried, early, late. See EARLINESS, LATENESS, SLOWNESS, HASTE.

Adverbs—during, pending; in passing, during the time; during the time *or* interval; in the course of time; for the time being, day by day; in the time of, when; from time immemorial; meantime, meanwhile; in the meantime, in the interim, from day to day, from hour to hour; hourly, always; for a time *or* season; till, until, up to, yet, as yet; the whole time, all the time; all along; throughout, for good; hereupon, thereupon, whereupon; then; *anno Domini,* A.D., before Christ, B.C., once upon a time; in a time, in due time, in season, in the fullness of time, some fine day; out of season.

Antonyms, see PERPETUITY.

---

timeless, *adj.* endless, perpetual, everlasting, deathless, immortal; dateless, ageless, immemorial, prehistoric, legendary. See PERPETUITY.

timely, *adj.* well-timed, seasonable, opportune; auspicious, right. See TIME, EARLINESS, OCCASION, EXPEDIENCE.

timepiece, *n.* clock, watch, chronometer (see CHRONOMETRY).

timetable, *n.* schedule (see CHRONOMETRY).

timeworn, *adj.* out-of-date; worn, impaired. See OLDNESS, DETERIORATION.

timid, *adj.* fearful, cowardly, afraid, fainthearted, timorous; shrinking, bashful, shy, retiring, diffident; irresolute, hesitant; weak. See FEAR, MODESTY.

timorous, *adj.* timid, fearful. See FEAR, MODESTY.

tincture, *n.* trace, vestige, touch, dash; tinge, tint, shade; soupçon. See COLOR, MIXTURE.

tinder, *n.* touchwood, punk, amadou. See FUEL.

tine, *n.* prong, branch, point, tip; skewer, spike, bodkin, barb. See SHARPNESS.

tinge, *n.* tint, shade, COLOR, dye, stain; flavor, cast. See MIXTURE.

tingle, *v.i.* sting, prickle; thrill. See PAIN, FEELING.

tinhorn, *n.* gambler, piker. See CHANCE.

tinker, *n.* handyman, jack-of-all-trades; blunderer, bungler. *Colloq.,* Mr. Fixit. —*v.* mend, repair; botch; tamper, putter. *Colloq.,* doctor;

fiddle, fuss, play, *or* monkey with. See RESTORATION, UNSKILLFULNESS.

tinsel, *n.* tawdriness, gaudiness, frippery, show; baubles, gewgaws. See ORNAMENT, DECEPTION, OSTENTATION.

tint, *n.* COLOR, tinge, hue, dye, shade; tone, cast, nuance.

tiny, *adj.* minute, miniature, small, diminutive, wee; microscopic. *Slang,* halfpint. See LITTLENESS.

tip, *v.* overturn, capsize, upset; incline, slant, tilt, topple; reward. See PAYMENT. —*n.* point, END; apex, summit; clue, hint, warning, pointer; gratuity, gift, fee, perquisite, *pourboire.* See HEIGHT, GIVING, COVERING.

tipsy, *adj.* intoxicated. *Slang,* high, tight. See DRINKING.

tiptoe, *v.i.* steal, sneak, walk on tiptoes; creep, sidle. See CAUTION, TRAVEL.

tirade, *n.* harangue, screed, diatribe, jeremiad; SPEECH, sermon; outpouring, flood, spate. See DISAPPROBATION.

tire, *v.* weary, fatigue, bore, exhaust, jade, fag. See WEARINESS.

tireless, *adj.* untiring, indefatigable, unwearied. See RESOLUTION.

tiresome, *adj.* tedious, wearying, boring. See WEARINESS.

tissue, *n.* gauze, fabric, web, net, mesh; membrane, cartilage, muscle; tissue *or* crepe paper; structure. See CROSSING, TEXTURE.

titillate, *v.t.* tickle; excite. See TOUCH, DESIRE, EXCITEMENT.

title, *n.* name; form of address; subheading, subtitle; appellation, designation, caption; legend; epithet; honorific, peerage; status, degree; cognomen, surname. *Colloq.,* handle. —*v.* name, call. See NOMENCLATURE, NOBILITY, AUTHORITY, POSSESSION, RIGHTNESS.

toady, *n.* fawner, sycophant, truckler. *Colloq.,* bootlicker. See SERVILITY, FLATTERY.

toast, *v.t.* brown, heat, warm; drink to, pledge, honor. —*n.* toasted bread, zwieback, rusk; health, pledge. See HEAT, CELEBRATION.

tobacco, *n.* smoking; leaf, perique, Burley, latakia, Turkish, Havana, Virginia; cigar, cigarette, caporal; snuff, plug, chew. *Colloq.,* weed, Lady Nicotine. See PUNGENCY.

to-do, *n.* ado, turmoil, bother, bustle, commotion. See EXCITEMENT.

together, *adv.* mutually, reciprocally, unitedly; coincidentally, concurrently, simultaneously. See ACCOMPANIMENT, SYNCHRONISM.

toil, *n.* labor, drudgery; task, work; effort, exhaustion. —*v.* work, drudge, moil, labor; strive. See EXERTION.

toilet, *n.* toilette, prinking, makeup; powder room, washroom, bathroom, lavatory, restroom, comfort station, watercloset, W.C., cabinet; outhouse, latrine, privy; chamberpot, bidet, slop pail. *Slang,* john, head, can. See UNCLEANNESS.

toils, *n.pl.* snare, net, trap, mesh, web; grip, clutches. See DECEPTION.

token, *n.* sign, symbol, emblem; feature, trait; souvenir, memento, keepsake; badge, evidence; slug; earnest, INDICATION. See MEMORY.

tolerable, *adj.* endurable, bearable; passable, not bad. See CONTENT, GOODNESS.

tolerance, *n.* toleration, allowance; MODERATION, temperance, endurance, forbearance, sufferance, laxity; clemency, LENIENCY. See PERMISSION, FEELING, INEXCITABILITY, LIBERALITY.

toll, *n.* tax, import, charge, fee. See PAYMENT, PRICE.

tomb, *n.* grave, sepulcher, mausoleum, vault, catacombs. See INTERMENT.

tomboy, *n.* hoyden, romp. See FEMALE.

tomorrow, *adv.* on the morrow, the next day, henceforth, mañana. See FUTURITY.

tone, *n.* SOUND; quality; accent, pitch, inflection, modulation, intonation; strain, key, spirit; elasticity, resilience; tension, firmness, tonus; condition; frame of mind, mood; ELEGANCE, stylishness; tint, shade, hue. See COLOR, FEELING, METHOD.

tongs, *n.pl.* pincers, nippers, pliers, forceps. See RETENTION.

tongue, *n.* communication, SPEECH, language, dialect; pole; flap, projection. See SUPPORT, CONVEXITY.

tongue-lashing, *n.* scolding (see DISAPPROBATION).

tongue-tied, *adj.* silent, mute, inarticulate, STAMMERING; bashful, shy.

tonic, *adj.* invigorating, bracing, refreshing; voiced, sonant; stressed, accented. See HEALTH, REMEDY. —*n.* medicine, stimulant; quinine; key, keynote. See STRENGTH.

too, *adv.* also, likewise; over; additionally, excessively. See ADDITION.

tool, *n.* instrument, implement, utensil, device, machine; cat's-paw, dupe, henchman, intermediary. See INSTRUMENTALITY.

tooth, *n.* fang, tusk, canine, incisor, molar, cuspid, bicuspid, eyetooth; tine, cog; TASTE, relish; fondness. *Colloq.,* grinder, chopper. See SHARPNESS, CONVEXITY.

toothsome, *adj.* toothy, palatable, appetizing; delicious, luscious, dainty, delectable. See TASTE.

top, *n.* crown, head; acme, summit, pinnacle; pick, elite; lid, cover. —*v.* crown, cap; prune, excel, dominate. See SUPERIORITY, HEIGHT.

topcoat, *n.* overcoat, greatcoat. See CLOTHING.

topflight, *adj.* first-rate, superior. See SUPERIORITY.

topic, *n.* subject, theme, thesis, subject matter; item, question; business, point [of argument]; proposition, statement. See INQUIRY, INFORMATION, THOUGHT.

topping, *n.* sauce, coating; layer, COVERING. See FOOD.

topple, *v.i.* fall over *or* down, tumble, somersault, pitch, plunge; fail, collapse, go bankrupt. *Slang,* fold. —*v.t.* push, trip, knock over *or* down; overturn, upset; overthrow, subvert, defeat, smash. See DESCENT, DESTRUCTION, FAILURE.

torch, *n.* LIGHT, torchlight, brand; flambeau; flashlight; *slang,* firebug, arsonist. See HEAT, FUEL.

torment, *n.* languish, distress; torture, agony, PAIN —*v.t.* torture, distress, agonize, rack, afflict. See DISCONTENT, PUNISHMENT.

tornado, *n.* WIND, windstorm, twister, cyclone, typhoon. See VIOLENCE, ROTATION.

torpid, *adj.* dormant, sleepy; numb; inert, unmoving, still, stagnant; dull, stupid, apathetic, slothful, sluggish, lethargic; listless. See INACTIVITY.

torrent, *n.* cascade, deluge, downpour; current, rapids; outburst, outbreak, spurt, spate, surge, flood, Niagara. See VELOCITY, VIOLENCE, WATER.

torrid, *adj.* hot, burning, arid, parched, sizzling, scorching; equatorial, tropical; ardent, passionate. See HEAT, FEELING.

torso, *n.* trunk (see SUBSTANCE).

tortuous, *adj.* spiral, snaky, sinuous, serpentine; winding, crooked. See CONVOLUTION.

torture, *n.* PAIN, excruciation, agony, torment; martyrdom, crucifixion; anguish; cruelty. —*v.t.* punish; torment, rack, agonize, martyr; garble, distort, twist, misrepresent. See PUNISHMENT, BADNESS.

toss, *v.* fling, buffet, jerk; agitate, stir; throw, cast; tumble, sway; pitch, roll. See AGITATION, PROPULSION, EXCITABILITY.

total, *adj.* complete, entire, utter, absolute, WHOLE. —*n.* sum, amount, aggregate, quantity, WHOLE. —*v.t.* add, reckon, tot up; amount to; constitute; *slang,* wreck, destroy. See NUMERATION.

totter, *v.* shake, tremble, rock, reel, waver; falter, stumble, stagger. See OSCILLATION, WEAKNESS.

TOUCH

Nouns—**1,** touch, tact[us], CONTACT, impact, taction; tactility, palpability, tangibility, tangency; FEELING, sensation; manipulation, massage; stroke, tap, feel, brush, graze, glance, tickle, caress, kiss, osculation, lick, pat, rap, hit, handclasp. *Slang,* soft touch.

2, hand, finger, palm, paw, toe, tongue; feeler, antenna, flipper, vibrissa, palp[us], barbel.

3, see COMMUNICATION, CORRESPONDENCE, SKILL, SENSIBILITY.

Verbs—**1,** touch, feel, contact, handle, finger, thumb, palm, paw, toe; caress, kiss, lick, lap, pat, tap; fumble, grope; brush, graze, glance, skim; palpate, manipulate, wield, massage, rub, knead.

2, border on, be contiguous to, impinge, meet, reach, come to, abut, adjoin, neighbor, juxtapose. See NEARNESS, CONTACT.

3, touch upon (see RELATION).

4, touch up, delineate lightly, refine, improve, correct (see IMPROVEMENT).

5, move, stir, melt, soften, mollify, arouse PITY. See SENSIBILITY.

Adjectives—touching, FEELING, tactual, tactile; tangible, touchable, palpable; lambent, licking; adjacent, bordering, tangent, abutting, neighboring, contiguous; affecting, moving, melting, distressing, heartrending, pitiable, tender, pathetic, impressive.

---

touchy, *adj.* irritable; risky, delicate. See IRRITABILITY, SENSIBILITY, DANGER.

tough, *adj.* strong, firm; stiff, resilient; vigorous, robust, hardy; stubborn, intractable; violent, severe; unyielding, hardened, incorrigible; *colloq.,* vicious, rowdy, unruly, difficult, troublesome. See SEVERITY, STRENGTH, DIFFICULTY, EVILDOER.

toupee, *n.* hairpiece; wig. See ROUGHNESS.

tour, *n.* trip, journey, expedition, excursion, junket, jaunt; turn, shift, tour of duty. See TRAVEL, SUBSTITUTION.

tourist, *n.* traveler, voyager, sightseer; ugly American. See TRAVEL.

tournament, *n.* tourney, jousting, contest, match. See CONTENTION.

tousled, *adj.* disheveled, untidy, unkempt, rumpled, tangled, snarly. See DISORDER.

tow, *v.t.* draw, pull, drag, haul; take in tow. See TRACTION.

toward, *prep.* See DIRECTION.

towel, *n.* dishtowel, bath- *or* hand-towel, *etc.* See DRYNESS, CLEANNESS.

tower, *n.* fortress, castle; skyscraper; campanile, belfry, spire. —*v.i.* rise, soar; loom, transcend. See DEFENSE, ASCENT, HEIGHT, STABILITY.

town, *n.* hamlet, burg[h], village. See ABODE.

toxic, *adj.* poisonous, venomous, virulent, noxious. See DISEASE, BADNESS.

toy, *n.* plaything, trinket, trifle; doll, puppet. —*v.* trifle *or* play (with); fiddle, dally. See AMUSEMENT, UNIMPORTANCE, ENDEARMENT.

trace, *v.* draw, sketch, delineate, COPY; track, trail, follow, scent, detect; investigate; deduce. See INQUIRY, REPRESENTATION, INDICATION. —*n.* course, path; track, footprint, trail; hint, shade, vestige. See INDICATION, RECORD, COPY.

track, *v.t.* trail, follow, scent; explore; traverse. See PURSUIT. —*n.* trace, trail, wake; vestige; footprints, spoor, scent; path, course; succession; rails; race track, course, turf, cinders; footracing. See INDICATION, CONTENTION.

tract, *n.* expanse, area, REGION; composition, dissertation, treatise. See PUBLICATION.

tractable, *adj.* docile, well-behaved, manageable, adaptable, yielding, compliant; malleable, plastic. See FACILITY, SOFTNESS, OBEDIENCE.

TRACTION

Nouns—traction; drawing, dragging, *etc.* (see *Verbs*); draft, draw, drag, pull, haul, tow, tug, jerk, twitch; suction (see EXTRACTION); grip, FRICTION; tension, ATTRACTION; tractor, traction engine, Caterpillar [tractor].

Verbs—draw, drag, draggle, haul, pull, tow, trail, lug, tug, take in tow; jerk, twitch, heave, wrench, yank.

Adjectives—tractional, tractive; tractile; attractive; in tow.

Antonyms, see PROPULSION, REPULSION.

---

trade, *n.* BUSINESS, profession, occupation; livelihood; craft; merchandising; commerce, traffic, BARTER; clientele; purchase and sale, deal. —*v.t.* BARTER, buy and sell, bargain. See SALE.

trademark, *n.* brand [name], cachet; logo[type], colophon, label. See INDICATION.

tradesman, *n.* shopkeeper, merchant. See SALE.

tradition, *n.* belief, practice, usage, custom, culture, folklore. See OLDNESS.

traditional, *adj.* conventional, customary, formal. See CONFORMITY.

traduce, *v.* slander, calumniate, vilify, defame, asperse, malign, disparage. See DETRACTION.

traffic, *n.* trade, BARTER, commerce, business. TRANSPORTATION; dealings, familiarity, intercourse, fraternization. —*v.* trade, deal, have dealings. See SALE.

tragedy, *n.* DRAMA; disaster, calamity, catastrophe; crushing blow. See EVIL.

tragic, *adj.* dramatic, melodramatic; dire, disastrous. See DRAMA.

trail, *n.* track, spoor, footprints; tire, *etc.*, tracks; vestige, scent; path, wake; train. —*v.* track, scent; hang; lag, dawdle, crawl, straggle; drag, draw. See SLOWNESS, PURSUIT.

train, *n.* retinue, suite, entourage, procession, cortège; order, sequence, sequel, succession; railroad cars. See VEHICLE. —*v.t.* instruct, discipline, drill; educate. See TEACHING, DOMESTICATION, PENDENCY, CONTINUITY, PREPARATION.

trait, *n.* quality, characteristic, peculiarity, idiosyncrasy; custom; feature. See INDICATION, ATTRIBUTION, SPECIALITY.

traitor, *n.* betrayer, turncoat, renegade, deserter, conspirator; informer, Judas, fifth columnist, quisling. See EVILDOER.

trajectory, *n.* orbit, curve, arc, parabola; CIRCUIT, course.

trammel, *n.* net; tether, manacle, chain, fetter; impediment, shackle, HINDRANCE; confinement, RESTRAINT. —*v.t.* entangle, catch, trap; bind, hobble, tether, shackle, bridle, manacle, chain; restrain, imprison; impede, hinder.

tramp, *n.* traveler, vagabond, hobo, vagrant, bum, panhandler; jaunt, journey, hike, freighter; tread, walk, stroll; *slang,* prostitute. See POPULACE, IMPURITY. —*v.i.* walk, tread, step, plod, trudge, travel, hike; trample, stamp. See TRAVEL.

trample, *v.t.* crush, tread, grind, squash, stamp on. See OVERRUNNING.

trance, *n.* daze, stupor; abstraction, ecstasy; somnambulism, sleepwalking; coma, catalepsy; hypnosis. See INSENSIBILITY, IMAGINATION.

tranquil, *adj.* calm, quiet, undisturbed, composed, serene, placid, peaceful. See MODERATION, REPOSE, INEXCITABILITY.

tranquillize, *v.* pacify, soothe, appease; calm, still. See PACIFICATION, CONTENT.

transact, *v.* negotiate, deal; CONDUCT, bring about, do, perform, execute. See BUSINESS, ACTION.

transaction, *n.* deal, proceeding, ACTION, affair; CONDUCT, act, deed. See BARTER, OCCURRENCE.

transcend, *v.* exceed, overpass, surpass, excel, outstrip, outdo. See SUPERIORITY, OVERRUNNING.

transcribe, *v.* COPY, write, reproduce, engross; decode, decipher; transliterate, RECORD. See INTERPRETATION.

TRANSFER

Nouns—**1,** transfer, transference, transmission, transmittal, transmittance, consignment; transfusion, DISPLACEMENT, dislodgment; metastasis; shift, CHANGE, removing, removal, remotion, relegation, deportation, extradition; convection, conduction; contagion, infection. See TRANSPORTATION.

2, conveyance, assignment, assignation, alienation; enfeoffment, cession, grant, deed, quitclaim; conveyancing, bargain and sale, lease and release; exchange, INTERCHANGE, BARTER, SUBSTITUTION, delegation; succession, accession, REVERSION; demise, devise, bequest, legacy, gift.

Verbs—transfer, convey, assign, alienate; grant, cede, deed, confer (see GIVING), consign, enfeoff, sequester; sell, rent, let, lease, charter (see SALE); carry over; make *or* sign over, hand down, pass (on *or* down), transmit, negotiate, change hands; hand, turn, fork, *or* give over; demise, devise, bequeath, will, leave, give; devolve, succeed, come into possession, acquire (see ACQUISITION); rub off; substitute (see SUBSTITUTION). *Colloq.*, wish off on.

Adjectives—transferable, transmittable, assignable, conveyable; negotiable; contagious, catching, infectious, communicable; metathetic[al], metastatic.

Antonyms, see POSSESSION.

transfigure, *v.t.* transform, transmute; exalt. See CHANGE, ELEVATION.

transfix, *v.* pierce, fasten, impale. See OPENING, STABILITY.

transformation, *n.* CHANGE, alteration, transmutation; conversion, transfiguration; metamorphosis; wig, switch.

transfuse, *v.t.* set into, insert, infuse, instill; pour, inject. See MIXTURE, TRANSFER.

transgression, *n.* trespass, sin, violation, fault, offense, crime, misdeed, slip, misdemeanor; infraction, infringement. See ILLEGALITY, GUILT, WRONG.

TRANSIENTNESS

Nouns—transientness, transience, evanescence, impermanence, fugacity, mortality, span; nine days' wonder, bubble, ephemerality; short term; spurt; temporary arrangement, interregnum; brevity, SHORTNESS; suddenness (see INSTANTANEITY); CHANGEABLENESS. *Slang,* flash in the pan.

Verbs—be transient, flit, pass away, fly, gallop, vanish, evanesce, fade, evaporate; blow over; one's days are numbered.

Adjectives—transient, transitory, transitive; passing, evanescent, volatile, fleeting, elusive, elusory; flying; fugacious, fugitive; shifting, slippery; spasmodic; temporal, temporary; provisional, provisory; cursory, short-lived, meteoric, ephemeral, deciduous; perishable, mortal, precarious; impermanent; brief, quick, extemporaneous, summary; sudden, momentary, short and sweet.

Adverbs—temporarily, *pro tempore;* for the moment, for a time, for the nonce, for the time being; awhile, *en passant,* briefly.

Phrases—tempus fugit, time flies; here today, gone tomorrow.

Antonyms, see DURABILITY.

---

transit, *n.* passage, change, transition, conveyance, TRANSPORTATION, MOTION.

transition, *n.* passage, passing; CHANGE, development, flux, modulation; break, graduation, rise, fall; metastasis, metabasis.

transitory, *adj.* See TRANSIENTNESS.

translate, *n.* transfer; decipher, decode, render; construe, [re]interpret; transform, transmute, CHANGE.

translucent, *adj.* lucid, clear, diaphanous, hyalescent, semi-opaque, frosty. See TRANSPARENCY.

transmission, *n.* conveyance, transference, sending, communication, conductance; gearshift, gears, torque converter. See PASSAGE, INSTRUMENTALITY, TRANSFER.

transmit, *v.* send, TRANSFER, convey, forward, post, mail, wire, telegraph; impart, hand down; admit, conduct; emit, broadcast, communicate. See TRANSPORTATION.

TRANSPARENCY

Nouns—**1,** transparency, translucency, transpicuity, diaphaneity, lucidity, pellucidity, limpidity, clearness, sheerness, thinness. See INVISIBILITY.

2, glass, crystal, lucite, cellophane, [window]pane, prism, water, lymph, gauze, veil. *Colloq.,* goldfish bowl.

3, see COHERENCE, SIMPLENESS.

Verbs—show through; be transparent, diaphanous, *etc.*

Adjectives—transparent, translucent, transpicuous, diaphanous, lucid, pellucid, lucent, limpid; glassy, hyaline, hyaloid, vitreous, crystal[line], clear as crystal, crystal-clear; gauzy, flimsy, see-through, thin, sheer, gossamer; serene, unclouded.

Antonyms, see OBSCURITY

---

transpire, *n.* transude, exhale, pass through, ooze *or* leak out, sweat, perspire; come to light, issue, unfold, crop up; occur, happen, come to pass, take place. See DISCLOSURE, OCCURRENCE, EXCRETION.

transplant, *v.t.* replant, repot, graft; relocate, resettle; colonize. See TRANSFER, AGRICULTURE.

transport, *n.* transformation, conveyance, movement; emotion, ecstasy, rapture; troopship; airplane, carrier. —*v.* convey, carry, move, ship; transfer; delight, overjoy. See TRANSPORTATION, PLEASURE.

TRANSPORTATION

Nouns—**1,** transportation, transport, TRANSFER, transference, transmission, conveyance; movement, PASSAGE, transit, removal, delivery; carriage, portage, cartage, *etc.,* shipment, postage, express, messenger service; mass *or* public transportation. See TRAVEL, COMMUNICATION.

2, common carrier, mass transit, commuter transport; cart, wagon, stagecoach; [omni]bus, coach, jitney, charabanc; car pool; taxicab, taxi, cab, hack, gypsy cab; truck, van; railroad, railway, train; local, express, limited, freight [train]; streetcar, trolley [car], tram, subway, tube, el, elevated line, interurban, rapid transit; monorail; airline, air shuttle, airliner, transport, airplane (see AVIATION); sledge, cart, dray, truck, trailer, semitrailer; SHIP, ferry, troopship, transport. See VEHICLE.

3, carrier, porter, bearer; redcap, skycap; stevedore; conveyer, conductor, transporter; freighter, shipper; courier, messenger, runner; coolie; postman, mailman, letter carrier (see COMMUNICATION); helper, expressman.

4, a. driver, coachman, whip, charioteer, postillion, postboy; cabdriver; engineer; chauffeur. **b.** rider, fare; commuter; ridership.

5, beast of burden; horse, draft horse, packhorse, carthorse; ass, burro, jackass, hinny, jennet, donkey, mule; camel, dromedary, ox, llama, elephant; reindeer, dog, husky; carrier pigeon, passenger pigeon, homing pigeon.

6, shipment, traffic, freight, haul, cargo, lading, goods, baggage, luggage.

7, basket, box, carton, tray, *etc.* (see RECEPTACLE).

Verbs—transport, convey, transmit, TRANSFER, remove, move; carry, bear, cart, haul, truck, drive, ship, transship, ferry; fetch, call for, drop off; conduct, convoy, bring, take, pull, lug, pack, reach; run, smuggle (see ILLEGALITY); freight, express, railroad, forward, deliver, TRAVEL. See PASSAGE.

Antonyms, see STABILITY.

---

transpose, *v.* exchange, INTERCHANGE, reverse, rearrange, invert; substitute, transliterate; CHANGE. See INVERSION, MUSIC.

transverse, *adj.* crossing, cross, athwart, oblique. See OBLIQUITY.

trap, *n.* pitfall, snare, net, deadfall; ambush; carriage; trapdoor; (*pl.*) equipment, luggage. —*v.* catch, entrap, [en]snare, net, enmesh, fool, ambush. See DECEPTION, VEHICLE.

trappings, *n.pl.* caparison, regalia, habiliments, outfit, rigging, panoply, vestments, decorations; indications, earmarks. See CLOTHING, ORNAMENT.

trash, *n.* rubbish, garbage, refuse, offal, litter, debris; junk, scrap, waste. See USELESSNESS, POPULACE.

trauma, *n.* traumatism, injury; shock. See DETERIORATION, DISEASE.

travail, *n.* labor, work, drudgery, toil; agony, pain. See EXERTION.

TRAVEL

Nouns—**1,** travel; traveling, wayfaring, itinerancy, tourism; journey, voyage, excursion, expedition, safari, tour, trip, trek, crossing, cruise, grand tour, CIRCUIT; procession, caravan; odyssey; discursion; sightseeing; pilgrimage; ambulation; sleepwalking, somnambulism. *Colloq.,* globe-trotting. See NAVIGATION, PROGRESSION, AVIATION, MOTION, TRANSPORTATION.

2, walk, promenade, stroll, saunter, tramp, ramble, jog-trot, turn, perambulation, pedestrianism; driving, riding, posting, motoring, touring; outing, ride, drive, airing, jaunt; constitutional, hike, spin. See VEHICLE.

3, roving, vagrancy, nomadism; vagabondism; vagabondage; gadding; flitting; migration, emigration, immigration, intermigration.

4, itinerary, course, route, road, path; bypass, detour, loop; handbook, road map; Baedeker, Michelin, guidebook.

5, traveler, wayfarer, voyager, itinerant, passenger, rider, motorist, tourist, excursionist; explorer, adventurer, mountaineer; peregrinator, wanderer, rover, straggler, rambler; bird of passage; gadabout, vagrant, tramp, vagabond, hobo, nomad, Bohemian, gypsy, Arab, Wandering Jew, hadji, pilgrim, palmer; peripatetic; somnambulist; emigrant, fugitive, refugee; runner, courier; pedestrian, walker, cyclist, passenger; rider, horseman *or* -woman, equestrian, jockey. *Colloq.,* road hog.

Verbs—**1,** travel, journey, course; take a journey; voyage, cruise; take a walk, go for a walk, have a run; take the air; flit, take wing; migrate, emigrate, immigrate; rove, prowl, roam, range, knock about *or* around, kick around, go about, patrol, make rounds, pace up and down, traverse; perambulate, circumambulate; nomadize, wander, trek, ramble, stroll, saunter, go one's rounds, gad [about]; cover [the] ground. *Slang*, hit the road.

2, walk, march, step, tread, pace, plod, wend; promenade, trudge, tramp, hike; stalk, stride, strut, foot it, bowl along, toddle; paddle; tread a path; jog on, shuffle on; pace, walk the floor; bend one's steps; make, wend, pick, thread, plow *or* find one's way; slide, glide, skim, skate; march in procession; go to, repair to, hie oneself to, betake oneself to. *Colloq.*, hitchhike, thumb [a ride], hotfoot, stump, pound the pavement. *Slang*, stir one's stumps, hoof.

3, ride, take horse, drive, trot, amble, canter, prance, gallop; drive, fly; commute; go by car, train, rail, *or* air. *Colloq.*, joyride. *Slang*, burn up the road.

Adjectives—traveling, ambulatory, itinerant, peripatetic, roving, rambling, gadding, discursive, vagrant, migratory, nomadic; footloose; equestrian; on the wing, on the road, on the move; locomotive, automotive; wayfaring; travel-stained.

Adverbs—on foot, on horseback, on shanks' mare; abroad; en route.

Antonyms, see REPOSE.

---

traverse, *v.* cross, ford, range, patrol; contradict, obstruct. See TRAVEL, PASSAGE.

travesty, *n.* caricature, burlesque, farce, parody, lampoon; fiasco; ABSURDITY. *Colloq.*, takeoff. *Slang*, spoof. See RIDICULE, IMITATION.

trawl, *n.* net, dragnet, seine. —*v.* beam *or* otter trawl, fish, net, haul, drag, seine. See TRACTION, PURSUIT.

tray, *n.* platter, salver, server, trencher; galley. See TRANSPORTATION, RECEPTACLE.

treachery, *n.* treason, perfidy, faithlessness, disloyalty, infidelity, falsity, falseness. See IMPROBITY, DECEPTION.

tread, *v.* walk, step, pace; trample, crush; stamp, tramp; dance. See TRAVEL, MOTION.

treason, *n.* betrayal, disloyalty, faithlessness, sedition, treachery. See IMPROBITY.

treasure, *n.* hoard, STORE; wealth, riches. —*v.* value, prize, cherish, appreciate; remember. See MONEY, GOODNESS.

treasurer, *n.* bursar, purser; financier, banker, cashier, teller; receiver; steward, trustee; paymaster. See MONEY.

treasury, *n.* bank, exchequer; depository, vault, safe, safe-deposit box; till, strongbox, cash register; coffer, chest; purse, wallet, handbag, pocketbook. See STORE, MONEY.

treat, *v.* negotiate, bargain, deal, parley; entertain, pay for; deal with, discuss, teach; dose, attend, doctor. See REMEDY, PLEASURE, CONDUCT.

treatise, *n.* book, textbook; exposition, discussion, composition, commentary, tract, monograph, dissertation. See PUBLICATION.

treaty, *n.* compact, pact, covenant, concordat, entente, AGREEMENT.

tree, *n.* plant, sapling, scrub, shrub, bush; timber; whiffletree; stake; gibbet, gallows; family tree, pedigree, lineage. See VEGETABLE, ANCESTRY.

trek, *v.i.* walk, hike, TRAVEL, tramp, trudge. —*n.* journey, hike, migration, expedition.

trellis, *n.* lattice, grill[e]; network, screen, espalier, grid; arbor, bower, pergola, gazebo. See CROSSING, SUPPORT.

tremble, *v.* shake, shiver; vacillate; vibrate, totter, quake, quaver; shudder, pulsate. See FEAR, AGITATION, WEAKNESS.

tremendous, *adj.* stupendous, colossal, gigantic, huge; extraordinary. See SIZE.

tremolo, *n.* tremolando; trill, twitter, warble, crack. See OSCILLATION.

tremor, *n.* trembling, shivering, shaking, quivering, vibration. See FEAR, AGITATION.

tremulous, *adj.* trembling, unsteady; fearful, timid, irresolute. See AGITATION, FEAR.

trench, *n.* ditch, fosse, dugout; FURROW.

trenchant, *adj.* cutting, incisive, penetrating; thoroughgoing; clearcut, keen, sharp, biting, crisp; energetic. See POWER, FEELING.

trend, *n.* direction, course, TENDENCY, inclination, drift, tide.

trepidation, *n.* quaking, trembling; alarm, FEAR, AGITATION, perturbation, dread, dismay.

trespass, *v.i.* sin, offend, transgress; encroach, infringe, intrude, invade. See IMPROBITY, BADNESS.

tress, *n.* strand, curl, ringlet, lock; (*pl.*) locks, hair. See ROUGHNESS.

trial, *n.* test, EXPERIMENT, probation, hearing; hardship, ordeal; cross, tribulation, affliction; effort, attempt. See ADVERSITY, INQUIRY, LAWSUIT, PUNISHMENT.

triangle, *n.* trigon, delta, pyramid, triquetra; gore, gusset; triad, trio, threesome; the eternal triangle. See ANGULARITY, NUMERATION.

tribe, *n.* race, people, sect, group; clan, nation, society; lineage, family stock. See ASSEMBLAGE, ANCESTRY, CLASS.

tribulation, *n.* sorrow, woe; care, trouble, ordeal. See PAIN.

tribunal, *n.* court; board, forum; bench, judicatory; court of justice *or* law, court of arbitration, inquisition; seat of judgment *or* justice, bar [of justice]; drumhead, court-martial. *Slang,* kangaroo court. See JUDGMENT, COUNCIL.

tribune, *n.* dais, pulpit, rostrum; gallery. See SUPPORT.

tributary, *n.* stream, source, affluent; prayer of tribute. *—adj.* subject, subordinate; contributory. See WATER.

tribute, *n.* PAYMENT, tax, contribution; gift, offering, service; praise, encomium, compliment. See GIVING, APPROBATION.

trick, *n.* artifice, stratagem, craft; illusion; wile, ruse, subterfuge, fraud, imposture, DECEPTION; tour, shift, turn; trait, idiosyncrasy, peculiarity. See UNCONFORMITY.

trickle, *v.i.* drip, dribble, seep. See WATER, EGRESS.

tricky, *adj.* ticklish, intricate; deceitful, evasive, artful, shifty. See DECEPTION.

trifle, *n.* bagatelle, nothing, triviality; gewgaw, trinket, knickknack, gimcrack; particle, bit, morsel, trace. See LITTLENESS, UNIMPORTANCE. —*v.i.* toy, play, dally, fool. See NEGLECT.

trill, *n.* vibration, tremor, quaver, tremolo, vibrato. —*v.* sing; quaver; warble. See MUSIC, OSCILLATION.

trim, *adj.* neat, well-ordered, compact, tidy, spruce, smart. —*v.* ORDER, tidy, adjust, dress, arrange; decorate, ORNAMENT, adorn; defeat; cheat; balance, equalize; cut, lop, shear, prune, barber; *colloq.,* defeat. See CLEANNESS, DISAPPROBATION, EQUALITY, NARROWNESS.

trinket, *n.* toy, plaything, bauble, gewgaw. See ORNAMENT.

trip, *n.* journey, excursion, voyage; slip, ERROR; *slang,* hallucinations, *etc.* —*v.* skip; stumble; offend, err; obstruct, halt. See LEAP, IMAGINATION.

trite, *adj.* commonplace, ordinary; hackneyed, stale, old; boring, dull; banal. *Slang,* corny, Mickey Mouse. See HABIT, WEARINESS.

triumph, *n.* joy, exultation, celebration; success, victory, conquest; accomplishment. —*v.i.* win, conquer, succeed; celebrate, rejoice. See REJOICING, SUCCESS, CELEBRATION.

triumphant, *adj.* triumphal, victorious (see SUCCESS).

trivial, *adj.* insignificant, unimportant, trifling, picayune, paltry; mean, piddling, small, petty. See UNIMPORTANCE, CHEAPNESS.

trolley, *n.* pulley, truck; trolley car, streetcar. See CIRCULARITY, TRANSPORTATION.

trollop, *n.* harlot, whore; slut, hussy, baggage. See IMPURITY.

troop, *n.* group, number, party, company, crowd, ASSEMBLAGE. —*v.i.* march, tramp, go. See TRAVEL.

trooper, *n.* soldier; [mounted] policeman, state trooper. *Colloq.*, mountie. See COMBATANT, SECURITY.

trophy, *n.* medal, prize (see APPROBATION, RECORD).

tropical, *adj.* torrid, hot, fiery; equatorial. See HEAT.

trot, *v.i.* run, jog, lope; hasten. See TRAVEL, VELOCITY.

troubadour, *n.* trouvère, poet, bard, minstrel, jongleur, meistersinger, minnesinger, balladeer, streetsinger; laureate; serenader. See POETRY, MUSIC.

trouble, *n.* affliction, distress, misfortune, ADVERSITY, calamity; disorder, unrest; DIFFICULTY; pains, EXERTION, effort, anxiety, perturbation, sorrow, worry. —*v.* disturb, disquiet, perturb; annoy, molest, harass, agitate; worry, distress, grieve; afflict, ail, plague; inconvenience.

troublesome, *adj.* disturbing, annoying, distressing; vexatious, burdensome, grievous, worrisome; difficult. See DIFFICULTY.

trough, *n.* manger, hutch, bin; trench, ditch, FURROW. See RECEPTACLE.

trounce, *v.* thrash, beat, flog. See SUCCESS.

troupe, *n.* troop, band, group, party, company; *dramatis personae*. See DRAMA.

trousers, *n.pl.* breeches, pantaloons, pants; [blue]jeans, slacks, chinos, Levis. See CLOTHING.

truant, *n.* shirker, absentee, deserter. See ABSENCE, AVOIDANCE.

truce, *n.* armistice, peace, respite, delay; cessation, lull. See PACIFICATION.

truck, *n.* VEHICLE; lorry, van, pick-up, dump, panel, rack; six-, *etc.* wheeler, half-track; cart, wagon, dray; barrow, dolly; dealings, BARTER.

truculent, *adj.* fierce, savage, deadly, bestial; vitriolic, scathing, mean; overbearing, cruel. *Colloq.*, with a chip on one's shoulder. See MALEVOLENCE.

trudge, *v.* march, slog, tramp, walk, plod. See SLOWNESS, TRAVEL.

true, *adj.* faithful, loyal, constant, sincere; certain, correct, accurate; truthful; sure, reliable; actual, genuine; legitimate, rightful; real, straight, undeviating. See PROBITY, TRUTH, STRAIGHTNESS.

truelove, *n.* sweetheart, lover. See LOVE.

truism, *n.* platitude. See MAXIM, UNMEANINGNESS.

trumpet, *n.* cornet, bugle, horn; ear trumpet. See MUSIC. —*v.* bellow, roar; blow, toot, blare; proclaim. See PUBLICATION.

truncate, *v.* abridge, reduce, shorten, curtail. See SHORTNESS, DEDUCTION, FORMLESSNESS.

truncheon, *n.* baton, staff, club. See AUTHORITY.

trundle, *v.* roll, wheel, revolve, rotate. See ROTATION.

trunk, *n.* stem, bole; body, torso; proboscis, snout; chest, box; circuit; (*pl.*) breeches, shorts. See RECEPTACLE, ANCESTRY.

truss, *v.t.* gird[le], belt; tie, bind, *or* do up; lace, button, strap, buckle; skewer, sew, stitch; support, strengthen, bandage. —*n.* fasten, pack, bundle, bale; holder, fastening; supporter, belt. See JUNCTION, ASSEMBLAGE.

trustee, *n.* guardian, fiduciary, overseer, supervisor. See POSSESSION.

trustful, *adj.* confiding, trusting. See CREDULITY, BELIEF.

trustworthy, *adj.* reliable, dependable, faithful, trusty, responsible, credible, believable; constant, true, loyal. See PROBITY, BELIEF, CERTAINTY.

TRUTH

Nouns—**1,** truth, fact, reality; verity, gospel, authenticity; plain, unvarnished, sober, *or* naked truth, matter of fact; the Gospel truth; the truth, the whole truth and nothing but the truth. *Slang,* the [real] McCoy, the goods. See RIGHTNESS, MAXIM.

2, truthfulness, veracity; fidelity; accuracy, exactitude; exactness, preciseness, precision. See PROBITY, CERTAINTY.

Verbs—**1,** be true, be the case; stand the test; hold good *or* true, have the true ring; render *or* prove true, substantiate (see EVIDENCE); get at the truth. *Colloq.,* hold water, hit the nail on the head.

2, be truthful; speak *or* tell the truth; not lie; speak one's mind; make a clean breast (see DISCLOSURE); cross one's heart. *Slang,* say a mouthful.

Adjectives—**1,** true, factual, real, actual, existing; veritable, certain (see CERTAINTY); unimpeachable; unrefuted, unconfuted; genuine, authentic, legitimate; pure, sound, sterling, unadulterated, unvarnished, uncolored; well-grounded, well-founded; solid, substantial, tangible, valid; undistorted, undisguised, honest-to-goodness; unaffected, unexaggerated, unromantic, unflattering. *Colloq.,* all wool and a yard wide.

2, exact, accurate, definite, precise, well-defined, just, right, correct, strict; literal; undisguised; faithful, constant, unerring.

3, truthful, veracious; sincere, pure, guileless, bona fide, true blue. *Slang,* up front. See PROBITY.

Adverbs—**1,** truly, verily, indeed, really, in reality; with truth, certainly, actually, for real; exactly, verbatim, word for word, literally, *sic,* to the letter, chapter and verse, to an inch; to a nicety, to a hair, to a turn, to a T; neither more nor less, in so many words; in every respect, in all respects; at any rate, at all events; strictly speaking; *de facto. Colloq.,* on the nose, smack-dab. *Slang,* on the button.

2, truthfully, *etc.*; at heart, from the bottom of one's heart; honor bright.

Antonyms, see ERROR, FALSEHOOD.

---

try, *v.* essay, endeavor, attempt, undertake; test, examine, assay, EXPERIMENT; refine, purify, afflict, beset; strain, tax; judge, hear. See LAWSUIT, EXERTION, USE, UNDERTAKING.

trying, *adj.* dull, wearisome, boring; annoying, bothersome, galling, irritating. See WEARINESS.

tryout, *n.* trial; audition, hearing; test, dry run; EXPERIMENT. See HEARING.

tryst, *n.* assignation, meeting, appointment, rendezvous. See SOCIALITY.

tsar, *n.* See CZAR.

tub, *n.* pot, vat, cauldron; washtub, bathtub; *slang,* tramp, freighter (see SHIP). See RECEPTACLE.

tube, *n.* pipe, hose, conduit; tunnel, subway; *slang,* television. See PASSAGE.

tuck, *n.* FOLD, pleat, lap.

tuft, *n.* cluster, clump, wisp, bunch, brush; tussock; fetlock, topknot, crest. See ROUGHNESS.

tug, *v.* pull, strain, drag, haul, tow; toil, labor, strive, drudge. See EXERTION, TRACTION.

tuition, *n.* tutelage, training, coaching,

education; fees, cost, charge, bill. See TEACHING, PRICE.

tumble, *v.* fall, roll; leap, spring; throw, overturn, disarrange, dishevel, tousle; toss, pitch. See DESCENT, AGITATION.

tumbler, *n.* glass, vessel, goblet; acrobat, gymnast, juggler; lever, cog, *etc.* See RECEPTACLE, DRAMA, INSTRUMENTALITY.

tumid, *adj.* turgid, swollen, distended, enlarged; protuberant, bulging; bombastic, pompous, inflated; teeming, bursting. See CONVEXITY, EXPANSION.

tumor, *n.* tumefaction, swelling, wen, cyst, tubercle, growth; neoplasm, sarcoma, cancer, carcinoma. See EXPANSION, CONVEXITY, DISEASE.

tumult, *n.* commotion, AGITATION, turbulence, DISORDER. See VIOLENCE.

tune, *n.* melody, air; harmony, concord. See MUSIC. —*v.* modulate, adjust, attune; harmonize. See AGREEMENT.

tunic, *n.* blouse. See CLOTHING.

tunnel, *n.* passageway, burrow, crosscut, subway, tube. See OPENING, CONCAVITY, CONNECTION, CROSSING.

turbid, *adj.* roiled, muddy, cloudy, clouded, opaque; confused, muddled. See CLOUDINESS.

turbine, *n.* rotator, rotor, rotary wheel; propeller, turboprop *or* -jet. See PROPULSION, ROTATION, POWER.

turbulence, *n.* disorder, VIOLENCE, unrest, disturbance, EXCITEMENT, AGITATION.

turf, *n.* sod, sward; peat; racetrack. See ARENA, VEGETABLE.

turgid, *adj.* See TUMID.

turmoil, *n.* confusion, tumult, turbulence, disturbance, AGITATION, commotion; DISORDER.

turn, *n.* ROTATION, revolution; twirl, twist; deflection, diversion; coil, CONVULSION; CHANGE; crisis; aptitude, ability, SKILL; act, skit; spell, shift, tour, trick. —*v.* revolve, rotate, pivot; reel; rebel, retaliate; shape, round, finish; CHANGE, move; invert, reverse; upset, derange; deflect, divert, veer, shift; pervert, prejudice, repel; avert; curdle, ferment, sour. See INVERSION, FORM, CURVATURE, OCCASION, DEVIATION, SOURNESS, REGULARITY.

turnabout, *n.* reversal, return; reversion. See INVERSION.

turncoat, *n.* renegade, deserter, traitor; apostate, recreant. See EVILDOER.

turnpike, *n.* tollroad, pike, throughway, thruway, skyway. See PASSAGE.

turpitude, *n.* depravity, baseness, wickedness. See IMPURITY.

turret, *n.* tower, gazebo, belvedere, cupola. See HEIGHT.

tussle, *n.* scuffle, struggle. See CONTENTION.

tutor, *n.* teacher, instructor, coach; guardian. See TEACHING.

tuxedo, *n.* dinner jacket, dress suit, smoking jacket. *Colloq.*, black tie, tux. *Slang,* tuck, monkey suit, soup-and-fish. See CLOTHING.

twaddle, *n.* gabble, nonsense, fustian. See ABSURDITY.

twice, *adv.* doubly, twofold. See NUMERATION.

twig, *n.* shoot, branch, tendril, slip, scion. See PART.

twilight, *n.* dusk, gloaming, nightfall; shade, shadow. See TIME, DIMNESS.

twin, *adj.* double, twofold; fraternal, identical; like. See SIMILARITY, NUMERATION.

twine, *n.* cord, string, line. See FILAMENT, CONNECTION, CONVOLUTION, CROSSING.

twinge, *n.* pinch, throb; qualm, doubt. See AGITATION, PAIN.

twinkle, *v.* blink, wink; scintillate, sparkle, shine. See LIGHT.

twirl, *v.* twist, spin, rotate, turn, whirl; wind, coil. See CONVOLUTION, ROTATION.

twist, *v.* wind, wreathe, twine, interlace; coil; wrench, contort; wring, screw; pervert; misinterpret, misapply; distort, warp. See CONVOLUTION, DEVIATION, DISTORTION.

twister, *n.* tornado, cyclone. See VIOLENCE, ROTATION.

twit, *v.t.* taunt, reproach. See ACCUSATION, RIDICULE.

twitch, *v.* jerk, writhe, shake, pull; tug, vellicate; pinch, squeeze; twinge. See TRACTION, EXCITABILITY, PAIN.

two-faced, *adj.* hypocritical, deceitful, double-dealing; faithless, false. See FALSEHOOD, DECEPTION.

tycoon, *n.* shogun; *colloq.*, magnate, millionaire. See MONEY, AUTHORITY.

tympani, *n.pl.* kettledrums (see MUSIC).

type, *n.* sign, emblem; kind, CLASS, sort, nature; standard, model, example, ideal; group; letter, figure, character. See INDICATION, PRINTING, FORM. —*v.* type, CLASS; symbolize; typewrite, touchtype, hunt and peck. See WRITING.

typewriter, *n.* teletype[writer], stenotype. See WRITING.

typhoon, *n.* hurricane, tornado, cyclone. See WIND.

typical, *adj.* emblematic, symbolic; characteristic, representative, model, ideal, conforming. See CONFORMITY, INDICATION.

typify, *v.* symbolize, exemplify, embody, represent; prefigure. See INDICATION, CONFORMITY.

tyranny, *n.* despotism, autocracy, totalitarianism; SEVERITY, rigor, harshness, oppression. See AUTHORITY, ILLEGALITY.

tyrant, *n.* despot, autocrat, oppressor. See AUTHORITY, SEVERITY.

tyro, *n.* beginner, novice, amateur, learner. See LEARNING.

U

ubiquitous, *adj.* ubiquitary, omnipresent; inescapable. See PRESENCE, DEITY.

U-boat, *n.* submarine. See SHIP.

udder, *n.* mamma, bag. See CONVEXITY.

UGLINESS

Nouns—**1,** ugliness, deformity, disfigurement, blemish; INELEGANCE; want *or* lack of symmetry, DISTORTION; IMPRESSION; homeliness, plainness, unloveliness; grotesqueness; unsightliness, gruesomeness; loathsomeness, hideousness; sordidness, squalor (see UNCLEANNESS).

2, eyesore, sight, fright, specter, scarecrow, hag, harridan, satyr, witch, toad, baboon, monster; ugly duckling; Quasimodo, Caliban; gargoyle.

Verbs—be ugly, look unprepossessing; make faces; render ugly, uglify; deface; disfigure; distort, blemish.

Adjectives—**1,** ugly [as sin]; plain, homely, ordinary, unornamental, inartistic; squalid, unsightly, unseemly, uncomely, unshapely, unlovely; not fit to be seen; unbeautiful; beautiless; foul, dingy.

2, gruesome, misshapen, repulsive, hideous, loathsome, disgusting, nauseating, misproportioned, deformed, disfigured, monstrous; gaunt, thin; dumpy, ill-made, ill-shaped, ill-favored, ill-proportioned; crooked, distorted, hard-featured; unattractive, unbecoming, ill-looking, unprepossessing.

3, grisly, ghastly; ghostlike, deathlike; cadaverous, frightful, repellent, grotesque, horrid, horrible.

Antonyms, see BEAUTY.

ulcer, *n.* abscess, infection, sore, fistula. See DISEASE.

ulterior, *adj.* beyond, farther; further, remote; hidden, unavowed. See DISTANCE, FUTURITY.

ultimate, *adj.* farthest, most remote; extreme, last; maximum; terminal, final, conclusive; elemental; eventual. See END.

ultimatum, *n.* demand, requirement, exaction. See COMMAND, OFFER.

ultra, *adj.* radical, extreme; superlative, excessive. See SUPERIORITY.

ululate, *v.i.* howl, wail, CRY, hoot, bark, mewl, mew, meow, bellow, moo, roar, caterwaul.

umbrage, *n.* RESENTMENT, offense, dudgeon, pique, huff; foliage. See JEALOUSY.

umbrella, *n.* shade, screen; parasol, sunshade, bumbershoot; canopy, COVERING.

umpire, *n.* referee, arbiter, arbitrator; linesman. *Colloq.,* ump. See JUDGMENT.

unabashed, *adj.* shameless, brazen, unblushing, unashamed. See INSOLENCE.

unabated, *adj.* tireless, relentless, ceaseless, constant. See CONTINUITY.

unable, *adj.* incapable, unfit. See IMPOTENCE, UNSKILLFULNESS.

unacceptable, *adj.* unsatisfactory; objectionable. See DISAPPROBATION.

unaccompanied, *adj.* alone, unattended, solitary, lone. See UNITY.

unaccountable, *adj.* inexplicable, mysterious, strange; not responsible, unanswerable. See UNCONFORMITY, UNINTELLIGIBILITY.

unaccustomed, *adj.* unwonted, unused (to); a stranger (to); uncommon, unusual, rare, strange. See UNSKILLFULNESS, DISUSE.

unacquainted, *adj.* ignorant, unknowing, uninformed; never introduced, strange. See IGNORANCE.

unadorned, *adj.* bare, severe, austere, unornamented, plain, simple; naked, blank; terse, trenchant. See SIMPLENESS.

unadulterated, *adj.* clear, simple, pure, undiluted; genuine, true. See PURITY, TRUTH, SIMPLENESS.

unaffected, *adj.* natural, simple, plain; genuine, sincere; ingenuous, artless; untouched, uninfluenced, unmoved. See INSENSIBILITY, SIMPLENESS.

unafraid, *adj.* See FEARLESS.

unaided, *adj.* unsupported; single[-handed]. See UNITY.

un-American, *adj.* anti-American, subversive, fascist, unpatriotic. See ILLEGALITY.

unanimity, *n.* agreement, consent, accord. See COOPERATION, UNITY.

unanticipated, *adj.* unexpected, unforeseen; surprising, startling. See SURPRISE, INSTANTANEITY.

unappetizing, *adj.* unsavory, distasteful, repugnant; tasteless, insipid. See DISCOURTESY, UNSAVORINESS.

unapproachable, *adj.* inaccessible; cold, cool, forbidding, distant. See IMPOSSIBILITY, TACITURNITY, SECLUSION.

unarmed, *adj.* weaponless, unprepared, defenseless. See IMPOTENCE.

unasked, *adj.* voluntary, spontaneous; gratis, free; uninvited. See WILL, DISLIKE.

unassuming, *adj.* modest, retiring, reserved. See MODESTY.

unattached, *adj.* loose, independent, alone; unengaged, fancy-free. See DISJUNCTION, CELIBACY.

unattractive, *adj.* ugly, homely, plain, unsightly. See UGLINESS.

unauthorized, *adj.* unwarranted, unsanctioned; illegal; illegitimate, unconstitutional. See ILLEGALITY, PROHIBITION.

unavailable, *adj.* unattainable, not to be had for love or money. See IMPOSSIBILITY.

unavailing, *adj.* useless, vain, futile; ineffectual, bootless. See USELESSNESS.

unavoidable, *adj.* inevitable, certain, unpreventable, necessary. See CERTAINTY, NECESSITY.

unaware, *adj.* unwary, unwarned; oblivious, ignorant. See IGNORANCE.

unbalanced, *adj.* unpoised, lopsided, out of kilter; unhinged, deranged. *Slang,* off one's rocker. See INSANITY, INEQUALITY.

unbearable, *adj.* unendurable, intolerable, insufferable, odious. See PAIN.

unbeaten, *adj.* undefeated, unconquered. See SUCCESS.

unbecoming, *adj.* indecorous, unseemly, unfitting; ugly, unattractive, ill-suited, inharmonious. See UGLINESS, DISAGREEMENT.

unbelievable, *adj.* incredible; unthinkable, unimaginable, farfetched, implausible, impossible. See DOUBT.

unbeliever, *n.* skeptic, doubter, infidel, agnostic, heretic. See DOUBT, IRRELIGION.

unbiased, *adj.* impartial, unprejudiced, objective, dispassionate; fair, just, equitable. See JUSTICE.

unbounded, *adj.* boundless, limitless, unlimited, infinite. See SPACE, FREEDOM, INFINITY.

unbreakable, *adj.* indestructible; shatterproof, tough, durable. See HARDNESS.

unbridled, *adj.* unrestrained; violent, licentious; unruly, intractable. See FREEDOM, ILLEGALITY.

unbroken, *adj.* intact, WHOLE; continuous, constant, uninterrupted, even; untamed, unsubdued. See CONTINUITY, VIOLENCE.

unburden, *v.t.* unload; lighten, relieve; disclose, reveal. See EJECTION, LEVITY, DISCLOSURE.

uncalled-for, *adj.* undue, unnecessary, superfluous, gratuitous; ill-timed, untimely, inopportune. See USELESSNESS, INEXPEDIENCE.

uncanny, *adj.* mysterious, eery, ghostly, weird, unnatural. See DEMON, DEATH, FEAR.

unceasing, *adj.* continuous, uninterrupted; perpetual, eternal, endless. See CONTINUITY.

uncertainty, *n.* incertitude, DOUBT.

unchanged, *adj.* unaltered, *etc.* (see CHANGE); pristine, erstwhile, undiminished, good as new, the same, as of old; continuous, maintained. See PERMANENCE.

unchaste, *adj.* lewd, incontinent, wanton, lascivious, lecherous, dissolute, immoral; unfaithful, adulterous. See IMPURITY.

uncivil, *adj.* rude, impolite, unmannerly. See DISCOURTESY.

uncivilized, *adj.* primitive, simple; barbarous, savage, barbaric. See VIOLENCE.

UNCLEANNESS

Nouns—**1,** uncleanness, IMPURITY; filth, defilement, contamination, soilure; abomination; taint; MALODOROUSNESS; decay, putrescence, putrefaction; corruption, mold, must, mildew, dry rot; slovenliness, squalor, sordidness. See UGLINESS.

2, offal, garbage, carrion; EXCRETION; feces, excrement, ordure, dung; slough; pus, matter, gangrene, suppuration; sewage, sewerage; muck, guano, manure, compost. See DECOMPOSITION.

3, dross, scoria; ashes, cinders, clinkers, scum, froth; swill, hogwash; ditchwater, dishwater, bilgewater; rinsings, offscourings, sweepings; scurvy, scurviness, scurf[iness]; dandruff, tartar. See REMAINDER.

4, dirt, filth, soil, slop; dust, cobweb, smoke, soot, smudge, smut, grime; muck, mud, mire, quagmire, alluvium, silt, sludge, slime, slush.

5, drab, slut, slattern, sloven, slob, pig, riffraff; vermin, louse, flea, cockroach. *Slang,* litterbug.

6, dunghill, dungheap, midden, bog, sink, latrine, outhouse, head, privy, cesspool; sump, slough, dump, dumpheap, cloaca, scrapheap, junkyard, boneyard; drain, sewer; sty, pigsty, lair, den, Augean stables, sink of corruption; slum, rookery.

7, spot, taint, mark, stain, blot; smear, smudge.

8, foul-mindedness, obscenity, foulmouthedness; evil-mindedness, dirtiness; foul, evil, *or* dirty mind, filthiness; foul play. *Slang,* dirty fighting, dirty deal.

Verbs—**1,** rot, putrefy, fester, rankle, reek, stink (see MALODOROUSNESS); mold, go bad, spoil, become tainted.

2, dirty, soil, smoke, tarnish, spot, smear, daub, blot, blur, smudge, smirch; drabble, draggle; spatter, besmear, bemire, beslime, begrime, befoul; splash, stain, sully, pollute, defile, debase, contaminate, taint, corrupt (see DETERIORATION). *Colloq.*, foul.

Adjectives—**1,** unclean, dirty, filthy, grimy; soiled; dusty, smutty, sooty, smoky; thick, turbid, slimy; uncleanly, scruffy, slovenly, untidy, dingy, draggled, slatternly, sluttish, draggletailed; uncombed, unkempt, frowzy; unscoured, unswept, unwiped, unwashed, unpurified; squalid, rotten, seamy, nasty, coarse, foul, impure, offensive, abominable, nasty, piggish, beastly, reeky, sweaty, fetid, obscene; disgusting, nauseating, stomach-turning, revolting, sordid, corrupt. *Colloq.*, grubby. *Slang*, grungy.

2, moldy, musty, mildewed, rusty, motheaten, rancid, bad, gone bad, fusty; scabrous, scrofulous, leprous; rotten, corrupt, tainted; gamy, high, flyblown, verminous, maggoty; putrid, putrescent, putrefied; purulent, carious, infected, infested, peccant, fecal, scurfy, impetiginous; gory, bloody; rotting, crapulous.

Antonyms, see CLEANNESS.

---

unclouded, *adj.* unobscured, clear, LIGHT. See DISCLOSURE.

uncomfortable, *adj.* uneasy; cramped; disturbed, restless; embarrassing, difficult; unpleasant, distressing. See DISCONTENT.

uncommon, *adj.* unusual, rare, infrequent, sporadic; scarce; remarkable, extraordinary, strange; exceptional, original, unconventional. See RARITY, UNCONFORMITY.

uncommunicative, *adj.* taciturn, reticent; secretive. See TACITURNITY, SECRET.

uncompromising, *adj.* inflexible, unyielding; rigid, strict. See SEVERITY.

unconcerned, *adj.* indifferent, uninterested, disinterested, detached, aloof; unmoved, uncurious. See INSENSIBILITY, INDIFFERENCE.

unconditional, *adj.* absolute, unreserved, unqualified; full, plenary; free. See FREEDOM.

unconfined, *adj.* unrestrained, free, unhampered. See FREEDOM.

UNCONFORMITY

Nouns—**1,** unconformity, nonconformity, unconventionality, informality, abnormality; anomaly, anomalousness; exception, peculiarity, IRREGULARITY; infraction, breach, violation, *or* infringement of law, custom, *or* usage (see ILLEGALITY); eccentricity, oddity, twist, trick, quirk; conversation piece, something to write home about; DISAGREEMENT. *Colloq.*, one for the books. See DISSENT, HETERODOXY.

2, individuality, SPECIALITY, idiosyncrasy, originality, mannerism; unusualness, strangeness; aberration; variety, singularity; EXEMPTION; mannishness, eonism, homosexuality, bisexuality, Lesbianism. *Slang*, third sex.

3, nonconformist, nondescript, original; nonesuch, monster, prodigy, wonder, miracle, curiosity, *rara avis;* alien, foreigner (see EXTRINSIC); beatnik, hippie, yippie; mongrel, hybrid (see MIXTURE); hermaphrodite; transsexual; homosexual, Lesbian; transvestite; bisexual; invert, pervert; monstrosity, rarity, freak, crank; maverick, misfit, fish out of water; freak of nature; neither one thing nor another; neither fish, [flesh,] nor fowl; one in a million; outcast, pariah, outlaw. *Colloq.*, character, card. *Slang*, crackpot, screwball, oddball, flake, fluke, queer fish, wack, kook; homo, fairy, nance, pansy, fag[got], queer, ladylover, dike; flower child.

4, phoenix, chimera, hydra, sphinx, minotaur; griffin, centaur; hippogriff;

cockatrice, roc, dragon, sea-serpent; mermaid; unicorn; Cyclops, Medusa, Hydra. See MYTHICAL DEITIES.

Verbs—leave the beaten track *or* path, go one's [own] way; baffle *or* beggar description. *Slang,* beat the Dutch.

Adjectives—**1,** unconformable, exceptional, abnormal, anomalous, out of place *or* keeping; irregular, arbitrary; alien, foreign; lawless, aberrant, peculiar, unnatural, eccentric, uncommon, extraordinary, outside the pale. **2,** unusual, uncommon; rare, singular, unique, curious, odd, extraordinary, off the beaten track, out of the ordinary, strange, monstrous; wonderful, unaccountable; informal; unofficial; out of step, out of one's element; outré, out-of-the-way, remarkable, noteworthy; queer, quaint, *sui generis;* original, unconventional, unfashionable; unprecedented, unparalleled, unexampled, unheard of, nondescript; fantastic, grotesque, bizarre, kinky; pixilated; outlandish, exotic, offbeat, off-center, weird, out of this world; preternatural; superhuman, inhuman; unsymmetric. *Colloq.,* offtrail. *Slang,* far-out, wacky, flaky, kooky.

Adverbs—unconformably; except, unless, save, barring, beside, without, let alone; however, yet, but.

Antonyms, see CONFORMITY.

---

unconquerable, *adj.* indomitable, invincible, irresistible, impregnable. See POWER, STRENGTH.

unconscionable, *adj.* unscrupulous, wrong, unethical; extravagant, excessive; immoderate, inordinate, intolerable. See IMPROBITY.

unconscious, *adj.* unaware, insensible; stupefied, asleep, out; uninformed, ignorant; submerged, subconscious, suppressed, repressed. *Colloq.,* blotto. See INSENSIBILITY.

unconstitutional, *adj.* illegal, unfair, unjust, against one's rights; un-American. See ILLEGALITY.

unconventional, *adj.* uncommon, unusual. See UNCONFORMITY.

uncooperative, *adj.* reluctant, resistant, recalcitrant, obstinate, stubborn, difficult, contrary. See OBSTINACY.

uncouple, *v.t.* unyoke, disconnect. See DISJUNCTION.

uncouth, *adj.* boorish, rude, crude, common, vulgar, uncultivated; ill-mannered, clumsy; strange, unusual; awkward, gauche, ungraceful. See VULGARITY, INELEGANCE.

uncover, *v.t.* open, unclose, unseal; disclose, discover; reveal, lay bare, expose; undress, denude, bare. See DISCLOSURE, DIVESTMENT.

unction, *n.* anointing; unguent, ointment; unctuousness, gushing; fervor. See FEELING.

uncultivated, *adj.* uncultured, unrefined, uncouth, rough; illiterate; wild, untilled, primeval. See IGNORANCE, UNPREPAREDNESS.

undaunted, *adj.* courageous, undismayed; bold, intrepid, dauntless, cool, reckless. See COURAGE.

undeceive, *v.t.* disabuse, disillusion, correct. See INFORMATION.

undecided, *adj.* undetermined, unresolved, unsettled, uncertain, irresolute, doubtful, hesitant. See DOUBT, OBSCURITY.

undefeated, *adj.* See UNBEATEN.

undemonstrative, *adj.* restrained, reserved; impassive, inexpressive, stolid, apathetic, calm. See TACITURNITY.

undeniable, *adj.* indisputable, incontestable, unquestionable, incontrovertible, irrefutable. See CERTAINTY

under, *prep & adj.* below, beneath, underneath; subject to, controlled by; inferior, subordinate. See LOWNESS, SUBJECTION, INFERIORITY.

underage, *adj.* immature, premature; minor, in one's minority. See YOUTH.

underbrush, *n.* bush, thicket, brake, bracken, scrub, shrubbery, boscage; furze, gorse, heather. See VEGETABLE.

underclassman, *n.* freshman, sophomore; lowerclassman. *Colloq.*, plebe, frosh. See SCHOOL.

underclothes, *n.* See UNDERWEAR.

undercover, *adj.* masked, in disguise, incognito; [top-]secret, clandestine, *sub rosa*. See CONCEALMENT.

undercurrent, *n.* undertow; undertone, innuendo. See DANGER.

undercut, *v.t.* undersell. See SALE.

underdog, *n.* loser, victim. See FAILURE.

underestimate, *v.* underrate, undervalue, underreckon; depreciate, disparage, detract from; not do justice to; misprize, disprize; slight, neglect; slur over; make light of, play down, underplay, understate, take no account of; minimize, belittle. See DETRACTION, MISJUDGMENT, CONTEMPT.

undergo, *v.t.* suffer, experience, endure, sustain, bear, stand, withstand. See CIRCUMSTANCE, PAIN, OCCURRENCE.

undergraduate, *n.* freshman, sophomore, junior; lowerclassman. *Colloq.*, undergrad, plebe, frosh, soph. See SCHOOL.

underground, *n.* subway, tube, Métro; [the] resistance, partisans, guerrillas, Maquis. *—adj.* subterranean, buried, interred. See CONCEALMENT, DEPTH.

underhand, underhanded, *adj.* hidden, secret; deceitful, fraudulent, unfair, tricky; stealthy, sly, clandestine, furtive, devious. See SECRET, DECEPTION, IMPROBITY.

underline, *v.t.* underscore; accent, emphasize, urge. See INDICATION, IMPORTANCE.

underling, *n.* subordinate, assistant, inferior, deputy, apprentice; SERVANT, menial, flunky, retainer. See INFERIORITY.

undermine, *v.t.* excavate, mine, sap; honeycomb; subvert, weaken, demoralize, thwart, frustrate. See CONCAVITY, HINDRANCE, DETERIORATION, WEAKNESS.

underneath, *prep. & adv.* beneath, below, lower, under. See LOWNESS.

underpass, *n.* underwalk, tunnel, tube, viaduct. See CROSSING.

underprivileged, *adj.* impoverished, deprived, depressed, downtrodden, unfortunate; un[der]developed. See ADVERSITY.

underrate, *v.t.* undervalue (see UNDERESTIMATE); disparage, belittle. See DETRACTION.

underscore, *v.t.* See UNDERLINE.

underside, *n.* underneath, [under] belly, downside. See LOWNESS.

undersigned, *n.* signer, subscriber, endorser, petitioner. See ASSENT.

understand, *v.t.* know, comprehend, grasp, catch; perceive, discern, penetrate, apprehend; interpret, construe, fathom; gather, infer, assume; realize, believe; sympathize (with). See MEANING, INTELLIGENCE, SUPPOSITION.

understanding, *n.* discernment, comprehension, INTELLIGENCE, knowledge, insight, perception; sympathy; agreement. See INTELLECT.

understate, *v.* underestimate, undervalue, underrate; play *or* tone down, palliate, belittle, degrade, deprecate; whitewash. *Colloq.*, soft-pedal. *Slang,* pull one's punches. See DISTORTION, DETRACTION.

understudy, *n.* alternate, substitute, stand-by, stand-in, second, double. See DRAMA, SUBSTITUTION.

undertaker, *n.* funeral director, mortician; sexton; embalmer. See INTERMENT.

UNDERTAKING

Nouns—**1,** undertaking; compact, engagement, PROMISE; enterprise, emprise, project; endeavor, venture, pilgrimage, adventure; matter in hand, BUSINESS;

move, first move, beginning; caper. *Colloq.*, tall order. See EXPERIMENT, INTENTION.

2, entrepreneur, man *or* woman of action, founder, launcher; contractor; adventurer.

Verbs—undertake, tackle; engage in, embark on; launch *or* plunge into; volunteer; apprentice oneself to, devote oneself to, take up, take in hand; set *or* go about; set to, fall to, fall to work; try one's hand, take the plunge, launch forth; set up shop; put in hand, put in execution; set forward; put *or* turn one's hand to, throw oneself into; begin; broach, institute, originate; put one's hand to the plow, put one's shoulder to the wheel; have in hand, have many irons in the fire; move heaven and earth. *Colloq.*, bite off more than one can chew, go in for, go off the deep end, give it a whirl, take the bull by the horns.

Adjectives—venturesome, adventurous. *Slang,* on the make.

Adverbs—on *or* in the fire. *Colloq.*, in the works.

Antonyms, see REFUSAL.

---

undertow, *n.* riptide, undercurrent, backlash; eddy, vortex. See WATER, OPPOSITION.

underwear, *n.* underclothes, undergarments, underthings, lingerie, drawers, union suit, B.V.D.'s, briefs, panties, pantyhose; foundation [garment], girdle, pantygirdle, brassiere, bra, corset. *Colloq.*, unmentionables. See CLOTHING.

underworld, *n.* netherworld, infernal regions, HELL, Hades; world of crime, criminals, gangsters. *Colloq.*, gangland. See ILLEGALITY.

underwrite, *v.t.* insure, guarantee, warrant, indemnify; sanction, authorize; sponsor, finance, subscribe to, support, back; defray, pay (for). *Colloq.*, stake, grubstake. *Slang,* bankroll. See SECURITY, MEANS.

undesirable, *adj.* disagreeable, distasteful, objectionable, disliked; inadvisable, inexpedient. See INEXPEDIENCE, DISLIKE.

undignified, *adj.* discreditable, inelegant, ludicrous, awkward, *gauche;* mean, degrading; indecorous, ill-bred. See INELEGANCE, VULGARITY.

undisciplined, *adj.* wild, chaotic; lawless, licentious; primitive, savage; spontaneous, capricious, erratic. See CHANGEABLENESS, ILLEGALITY.

undisguised, *adj.* true, genuine; evident, obvious; candid, frank, open. See TRUTH.

undisputed, *adj.* unchallenged, indisputable, accepted, agreed. See BELIEF, CERTAINTY.

undivided, *adj.* concentrated, exclusive, WHOLE, intact, entire; single, united.

undo, *v.t.* loose, unlock, unfasten, untie, release; annul, reverse, cancel, neutralize; spoil, destroy, ruin. See DISJUNCTION, DESTRUCTION.

undoing, *n.* downfall, defeat, ruin, reversal. See FAILURE.

undoubted, *adj.* undisputed, *etc.* (see DOUBT); accepted, sure, assured, certain. See CERTAINTY.

undress, *v.* strip, disrobe, unclothe, dismantle, expose. *Slang,* peel. See DIVESTMENT.

undue, *adj.* unjust, inequitable; improper, inappropriate; extreme, excessive, immoderate, inordinate, exorbitant, unwarranted. See INJUSTICE.

undulate, *v.* surge, fluctuate, ripple, pulsate, wave. See OSCILLATION, CONVOLUTION.

undying, *adj.* deathless, immortal, unending. See PERPETUITY.

unearth, *v.t.* exhume, disinter; expose, disclose, discover, uncover; eradicate, uproot, dig up. See EXTRACTION, INTERMENT, DISCLOSURE.

unearthly, *adj.* supernatural, uncanny, ghostly, spectral, eerie, weird; appalling, hair-raising. *Colloq.*, exceptional, unusual. See DEMON.

uneasy, *adj.* restless, restive; disturbed, perturbed, disquieted, uncomfortable; anxious, apprehensive, fearful; constrained; fidgety, jittery, on edge, jumpy; uncertain, unstable, touch-and-go. See AGITATION, EXCITEMENT, EXCITABILITY, FEAR.

uneducated, *adj.* ignorant, untaught, untutored, illiterate. See IGNORANCE.

unemotional, *adj.* apathetic, calm, cool, impassive, unfeeling. See INSENSIBILITY, INDIFFERENCE.

unemployed, *adj.* idle, jobless, out of work; loafing, at leisure, at liberty, free, available; looking [around]. See INACTIVITY.

unequal, *adj.* disparate, disproportionate; inadequate; uneven, mismatched, one-sided; inequitable, unfair. See DIFFERENCE.

unequivocal, *adj.* unmistakable, unqualified; clear, definite, yes or no, black and white. See CERTAINTY.

uneven, *adj.* variable, odd, unequal, disparate; rough, lumpy, broken, rugged. See ROUGHNESS, INEQUALITY.

uneventful, *adj.* monotonous, humdrum, dull. See INACTIVITY.

unexpected, *adj.* unforeseen; sudden, SURPRISE, abrupt, accidental, coincidental, contingent, chance; from nowhere, out of the blue.

unfailing, *adj.* constant, steadfast, unfaltering, sure. See CERTAINTY, PERMANENCE.

unfair, *adj.* unjust, unreasonable, inequitable; unsporting; disingenuous; partial, biased, prejudiced, discriminatory. See WRONG, IMPROBITY, INJUSTICE.

unfaithful, *adj.* disloyal, faithless; adulterous, philandering, cheating, untrue, fickle; inaccurate, untrustworthy. See IMPROBITY, WRONG.

unfamiliar, *adj.* unknown, uncommon, strange, novel, new; unacquainted. See UNCONFORMITY, NEWNESS, IGNORANCE.

unfashionable, *adj.* dowdy, old-fashioned, out-of-date; passé, antiquated. *Slang,* corny, old hat, out. See UNCONFORMITY, OLDNESS.

unfasten, *v.t.* loose[n], disconnect, unbind, unfix, unpin; liberate. See DISJUNCTION.

unfathomable, *adj.* fathomless, bottomless, unplumbed, unsounded; unintelligible, inexplicable, incomprehensible. See DEPTH, INFINITY, UNINTELLIGIBILITY.

unfavorable, *adj.* adverse, disadvantageous, inauspicious, unpropitious, unlucky; unfriendly, antagonistic; negative, contrary; inclement; inopportune, untimely. See INEXPEDIENCE, PREDICTION, ADVERSITY, DISAPPROBATION.

unfeasible, *adj.* impracticable, impossible, unthinkable. See IMPOSSIBILITY.

unfeeling, *adj.* hard[-hearted], cold[-blooded], cruel; heartless, inhuman, callous, dispassionate; merciless, pitiless, unmerciful, relentless, adamant. See INSENSIBILITY, MALEVOLENCE.

unfettered, *adj.* unchained, unrestrained, at liberty. See FREEDOM.

unfinished, *adj.* crude, raw, sketchy, rough; incomplete; amateurish, inept; unpainted, *etc.* See UNPREPAREDNESS, INCOMPLETENESS, UNSKILLFULNESS.

unfit, *adj.* incapable, unqualified, *etc.;* incapacitated, unhealthy, in poor condition; unsuitable, inappropriate, *etc.* See UNSKILLFULNESS, DISAGREEMENT.

unfold, *v.* open, unroll, smooth out; disclose, expose, announce; develop, progress. See DISCLOSURE.

unforeseen, *adj.* unexpected, unanticipated, out of the blue; sudden. See SURPRISE.

unforgettable, *adj.* memorable, notable. See IMPORTANCE.

unforgivable, *adj.* inexcusable, unpardonable. See INJUSTICE.

unforgiving, *adj.* relentless, unrelenting, implacable, unappeasable, inexorable; merciless, pitiless; vengeful. See SEVERITY, RETALIATION.

unfortunate, *adj.* unlucky, hapless, ill-fated, ill-starred, star-crossed, luckless, unsuccessful, abortive, disastrous, ruinous. *Slang,* short *or* out of luck, S.O.L., behind the eight ball, jinxed, hexed. See ADVERSITY, INEXPEDIENCE.

unfounded, *adj.* baseless, vain, groundless, ungrounded. See FALSEHOOD.

unfriendly, *adj.* hostile, inimical, antagonistic; unfavorable. See MALEVOLENT, DISAPPROBATION.

unfrock, *v.t.* dismiss, discharge, oust, disgrace. See PUNISHMENT.

unfruitful, *adj.* barren, unproductive, infertile, sterile; fruitless. See USELESSNESS.

unfurl, *v.t.* unroll, open, spread out, fly, wave; display. See OPENING, SMOOTHNESS.

ungainly, *adj.* awkward, clumsy; gawky, ungraceful, lumbering; grotesque. See UGLINESS, UNSKILLFULNESS.

ungenerous, *adj.* illiberal; mean, harsh, exacting. See SELFISHNESS, MALEVOLENCE.

ungodly, *adj.* godless, pagan, freethinking; profane, unholy, impious; satanic, diabolic; *colloq.,* bad, outrageous. See IRRELIGION, BADNESS.

ungovernable, *adj.* unbridled, irrepressible, unruly, headstrong, uncontrollable, unmanageable, incorrigible; licentious. See DISOBEDIENCE, OBSTINACY.

ungrateful, *adj.* unthankful, ingrate, unappreciative, thankless, forgetful; unwanted, unpleasing, unwelcome. See INGRATITUDE, DISCONTENT.

unguarded, *adj.* inadvertent, thoughtless, incautious; with one's guard down; not guarded. See DANGER, INATTENTION.

unhand, *v.t.* let go, release. See RELINQUISHMENT.

unhappy, *adj.* unlucky, unfortunate; sad, sorrowful, wretched, miserable, dolorous, despondent, disconsolate, inconsolable, gloomy, joyless; inappropriate, dismal; calamitous, disastrous, catastrophic. See DEJECTION, ADVERSITY.

unhealthy, *adj.* sickly, infirm, ailing, invalid; delicate, frail; undesirable, inauspicious, ominous. See DISEASE.

unheard-of, *adj.* unprecedented, unexampled; unbelievable, inconceivable. See UNCONFORMITY, IMPOSSIBILITY.

unhinge, *v.t.* unsettle, derange, unbalance, craze. See INSANITY.

unholy, *adj.* unhallowed, unconsecrated, unsanctified; wicked, profane; ungodly, impious, irreligious; *colloq.,* frightful, extreme, unseemly. See IRRELIGION, BADNESS.

uniform, *adj.* homogeneous, homologous; of a piece, consistent; monotonous, even, invariable, changeless; stable. See SYMMETRY, ORDER, UNITY. —*n.* livery, outfit, caparison; regimentals, blues, whites, khaki, sailor suit, *etc.* See CLOTHING.

unify, *v.t.* consolidate, combine, amalgamate, join. See UNITY.

unimaginative, *adj.* uninventive, uncreative, uninspired; imitative, stereotyped, hack, pedestrian, prosaic. See WEARINESS, SIMPLENESS.

unimpeachable, *adj.* irreproachable, above reproach; innocent, faultless; reliable, authoritative. See INNOCENCE, CERTAINTY.

UNIMPORTANCE

Nouns—**1,** unimportance, insignificance, nothingness, immateriality, inconsequentiality, inconsequence; triviality, levity, frivolity, froth; paltriness, USELESSNESS; matter of indifference; no object. See FOLLY, MEDIOCRITY, SHALLOWNESS.

2, trivia, trifle, minutiae, [minor] details; drop in the ocean *or* bucket, pinprick, fleabite, molehill; nothing [worth speaking of], nothing particular, nothing to boast *or* speak of; bosh; small matter, no great matter, trifling matter; mere joke, mere nothing; hardly *or* scarcely anything; no great shakes; child's play; small beer *or* potatoes.

3, toy, plaything, gimcrack, gewgaw, bauble, trinket, bagatelle, kickshaw, knickknack, trifle; trumpery, trash, rubbish, stuff, frippery; chaff, froth, bubble, smoke, cobweb; weed, refuse, scrum; joke, jest, snap of the fingers; fudge, fiddlesticks; pack of nonsense, straw, pin, fig, button, feather, two cents, halfpenny, penny, [brass] farthing; peppercorn, jot, rap, pinch of snuff, old song. *Colloq.,* red cent, row of pins, hill of beans.

4, nobody, nonentity, nonperson, unperson, cipher, mediocrity, small fry, pipsqueak, nine days' wonder, flash in the pan, dummy, straw man; every Tom, Dick, and Harry. *Colloq.,* lightweight, no great shakes. *Slang,* squirt. See NONEXISTENCE.

Verbs—not matter, signify nothing, not matter a straw; trifle, palter, fiddle, mess around, idle; make light of; dispense with; underestimate, belittle, downplay, play down, think *or* make little of, minimize, set no store by, not care a straw about; catch at straws, overestimate, not see the wood for the trees. *Colloq.,* not give a damn, continental, rap, *or* hang.

Adjectives—**1,** of little, small, *or* no account *or* importance, unimportant; inconsequential, immaterial, unessential, nonessential; indifferent; subordinate, inferior, mediocre, average; small-time.

2, trifling, trivial, slight; puerile; airy, shallow; frivolous, petty, niggling, picayune, piddling; inane, ridiculous, ludicrous, farcical; finical, namby-pamby, wishy-washy, milk and water; inappreciable.

3, poor, paltry, pitiful; shabby, miserable, wretched, vile, scrubby, niggardly, scurvy, beggarly, worthless, cheap; not worth the pains, not worthwhile, not worth mentioning, not worth speaking of, not worth a thought, damn, *or* straw; beneath notice *or* consideration; futile, vain. *Slang,* measly, punk. See CHEAPNESS.

Adverbs—slightly, rather, somewhat, pretty well, tolerably.

Interjections—no matter! tut-tut! pshaw! pooh[-pooh]! bosh! humbug! fiddlesticks! fiddlededee! never mind! what of it! what's the odds! stuff and nonsense! *Colloq.,* skip it! *Slang,* nuts! baloney! bunk! big deal!

Antonyms, see IMPORTANCE.

---

uninhabited, *adj.* unpopulated, unpeopled, unsettled, vacant. See ABSENCE.

uninhibited, *adj.* unhampered, free [and easy], natural, spontaneous. See FREEDOM.

UNINTELLIGIBILITY

Nouns—**1,** unintelligibility, incoherence; OBSCURITY, ambiguity; uncertainty, intricacy, perplexity; confusion, DISORDER; mystification.

2, paradox, enigma, poser, mystery, riddle [of the Sphinx], [Chinese] puzzle (see SECRET); sealed book; cryptography, steganography, code; cacography (see WRITING); gibberish, jargon (see UNMEANINGNESS), Greek, Hebrew, Dutch, *etc.*

Verbs—**1,** pass comprehension; veil, obscure, obfuscate; confuse, perplex, mystify, speak in riddles.

2, not understand, lose [the clue], miss [the point]; not know what to make of, be able to make nothing of, give up; not be able to account for, not be able to make heads or tails of, be at sea; see through glass darkly, not understand one another, work at cross purposes.

Adjectives—**1,** unintelligible, unaccountable, incomprehensible, inapprehensible, unrecognizable, unfathomable, fathomless, undiscoverable, inexplicable, inscrutable, impenetrable, unsolvable, meaningless; incoherent, irrational; illegible, undecipherable, unexplained, as Greek to one; enigmatic[al], paradoxical, puzzling, baffling, intricate.

2, inconceivable, beyond comprehension, beyond one's depth, over one's head. *Colloq.,* clear as mud.

3, inarticulate, mumbled.

Phrases—I don't understand; it's Greek to me.

Antonyms, see MEANING.

---

unintentional, *adj.* accidental, involuntary, inadvertent, unpremeditated, spontaneous. See CHANCE.

uninteresting, *adj.* dull, dreary, tedious, humdrum. See WEARINESS.

union, *n.* UNITY, concord, uniting, joining, connection; COMBINATION, fusion, coalescence; marriage; [con]federation, association, alliance. See AGREEMENT, JUNCTION, MIXTURE, PARTY.

unique, *adj.* sole, single; singular, only, *sui generis;* unequaled, matchless, unparalleled, unprecedented, unusual, rare. See UNCONFORMITY, EXCLUSION, INEQUALITY, UNITY.

unison, *n.* harmony, concord, AGREEMENT, union, unanimity, UNITY.

UNITY

Nouns—**1,** unity, oneness, individuality; indivisibility, inseparability, homogeneity, integrality; solitude, isolation, SECLUSION; IDENTITY, sameness, uniformity, consistency, COHERENCE; unification, amalgamation, consolidation, integration, coalescence, fusion, JUNCTION.

2, harmony, concurrence, AGREEMENT, accordance, accord, concord, consonance, concert, peace; unison, union, unanimity, solidarity.

3, unit, one, ace, solo, monad, module, integer, integrant, figure, number; individual, person, entity, none else, no other; detail, particular; item, object, thing, article, WHOLE, ensemble.

Verbs—be one *or* alone, isolate, unite, unify, join, merge, mix, blend, fuse, weld, cement, consolidate, solidify; marry, wed; reconcile, harmonize, attune, fraternize.

Adjectives—**1,** one, single, sole, solo, solitary, monistic; individual, apart, alone, unaccompanied, unattended, unaided, unassisted; singular, odd, unique, azygous, unrepeated, first and last, three in one; isolated, insulated, insular; single-handed, singleminded.

2, inseparable, inseverable, indivisible, indissoluble, indiscerptible, irresolvable, integral, uniform, compact; unipartite, one-piece, unilateral, unilinear, unipolar, *etc.,* united, unified, joined, combined, connected, unseparated, undivided, homogeneous.

3, harmonious, concordant, unanimous. See AGREEMENT.

4, unifying, uniting, connective, conjunctive, combinative, coalescent.

Adverbs—singly, individually, independently, severally, separately; solely, simply, alone, by oneself, by the piece, each, apiece, by itself, only apart, *per se;* in the singular, in the abstract, one by one, one at a time, as an individual, as one man, in unison. *Colloq.,* high and dry.

Antonyms, see MULTITUDE.

---

universal, *adj.* comprehensive, catholic, ecumenical; popular, general; cosmic; global, world-wide. See GENERALITY, UNIVERSE, KNOWLEDGE, THOUGHT.

UNIVERSE

Nouns—**1,** universe, cosmos, celestial sphere, macrocosm; infinity, span, [all] creation, earth and heaven, [all the] world, ether; ecosphere. See SPACE.
2, HEAVEN, the heavens, sky, empyrean, firmament, vault *or* canopy of heaven, celestial spaces, outer space, ceiling.
3, heavenly bodies, luminaries, starry host; nebula, galaxy, Milky Way; constellation, zodiac (Aries, Aquarius, Cancer, Capricorn, Gemini, Leo, Libra, Pisces, Sagittarius, Scorpius, Taurus, Virgo); Great *or* Little Bear, Ursa Major *or* Minor, Big *or* Little Dipper; Andromeda, Auriga, Boötes, Canis Major *or* Minor, Cassiopeia, Centaurus, Cepheus, Cygnus, Draco, Hercules, Lyra, Orion, Perseus, Pleiades; star, Achenar, Arcturus, Aldebaran, Altair, Antares, Betelgeuse, Canopus, Capella, Centauri, Pollux, Procyon, Rigel, Sirius, Vega; falling *or* shooting star, nova, double star, cluster.
4, solar system, sun, orb; planet, Mercury, Venus, Earth, Mars, Jupiter, Saturn, Uranus, Neptune, Pluto; planetoid, asteroid, satellite, moon, Luna, man in the moon, new moon, half moon, crescent, first, *etc.*, quarter, comet, meteor[ite]; Earth, Terra, [terrestrial] globe, sphere, oblate, spheroid, world; cosmic rays, sunspots, aurora borealis *or* australis, northern *or* southern lights; artificial satellite, bird, space station.
5, astronomy, astrometry, astrophysics, astrochemistry, spectroscopy, cosmography, cosmogony, cosmology, geography, geodesy, geology, geognosy, geophysics; almagest, ephemeris, star atlas *or* map, nautical almanac; observatory, planetarium.
6, see GENERALITY.

Adjectives—**1,** universal, cosmic, empyrean, ethereal, celestial, heavenly; stellar, astral, sidereal, starry; solar, lunar, planetary, nebular; earthly, terrestrial, mundane.
2, astronomical, astrometrical, astrophysical, spectroscopic, *etc.*; geocentric, heliocentric, Copernican, Ptolemaic; 1st, 2nd, *etc.* magnitude.

Adverbs—under the sun.

---

university, *n.* college, SCHOOL, academy, seminary, institute, institution [of higher learning]; campus. *Colloq.*, U.

unjust, *adj.* unfair, inequitable, undue, biased. See WRONG.

unkempt, *adj.* uncombed, disordered, ill-kept; slovenly, untidy, bedraggled. See VULGARITY, DISORDER.

unkind, *adj.* pitiless, merciless, hardhearted, cruel, brutal, harsh, inhuman. See MALEVOLENCE.

unknown, *adj.* incognito, unrecognized, unperceived, unfamiliar. See OBSCURITY, LATENCY.

unlatch, *v.t.* open, unfasten. See OPENING.

unlawful, *adj.* See ILLEGALITY.

unleash, *v.t.* uncage, unshackle, [un]loose, release, set loose. See LIBERATION.

unless, *conj. & prep.* if [not], but, save, except[ing], other than, aside from, let alone, without, barring. See CIRCUMSTANCE, QUALIFICATION.

unlike, *adj.* dissimilar, diverse, different, disparate; distinct, separate. See DIFFERENCE.

unlikely, *adj.* improbable, doubtful, dubious; farfetched, inconceivable;

impracticable, implausible; unpromising, inauspicious. See IMPROBABILITY.

unlimited, *adj.* undefined, indefinite, boundless, limitless, uncounted, infinite, full, absolute, unconfined, unconstricted, unrestrained. See FREEDOM, INFINITY.

unload, *v.t.* empty, disgorge, discharge, offload, unpack. See EJECTION.

unlock, *v.t.* unfasten, unbolt, disengage, undo; open; release, uncover, solve (a mystery, *etc.*). See LIBERATION, ANSWER.

unlucky, *adj.* unfortunate, ill-starred, ill-omened, hopeless, disastrous; regrettable. See ADVERSITY, BADNESS.

unman, *v.t.* emasculate, devitalize, unnerve, enervate, weaken; effeminize. See IMPOTENCE, FEAR, DEJECTION.

unmanageable, *adj.* unruly, ungovernable, refractory. See OBSTINACY, DIFFICULTY.

unmanly, *adj.* cowardly; ignoble; effeminate. See COWARDICE, FEMALE.

unmannerly, *adj.* rude, uncivil, ill-mannered; caddish, discourteous. See DISCOURTESY.

unmarried, *adj.* bachelor, spinster, maiden, virgin; widowed, divorced; celibate, single, unwed. See CELIBACY.

unmask, *v.t.* disclose, lay bare, reveal. See DISCLOSURE.

UNMEANINGNESS

Nouns—**1,** unmeaningness, meaninglessness, senselessness, *etc.;* ABSURDITY, inanity; ambiguity (see UNINTELLIGIBILITY).

2, nonsense, verbiage, mere words, empty sound, dead letter; gibberish, jargon, academese, jabber, babble, drivel, palaver, double-talk, hocus-pocus, mumbo-jumbo, gobbledy-gook, Jabberwocky; balderdash, rigmarole, flummery, humbug, moonshine, fiddle-faddle, wish-wash, stuff [and nonsense]; fustian, rant, bombast, rodomontade; platitude, truism; scribble, scrabble, doodle. *Colloq.,* hogwash, poppycock, flapdoodle, buncombe. *Slang,* tommyrot, applesauce, baloney, hooey, blah, malarkey.

Verbs—mean nothing, not mean a thing; jabber, babble, twaddle (see *Nouns*); scrabble, scribble, scrawl, doodle; drivel, slaver, drool. *Slang,* bull, gas, talk through one's hat, run off at the mouth.

Adjectives—unmeaning, meaningless, senseless, reasonless, nonsensical, void of sense, without rhyme or reason; unintelligible, illegible, inexpressive, expressionless, vacant, blank, inane, vague, ambiguous; inexpressible, glassy, ineffable, undefinable, incommunicable. *Slang,* deadpan.

Antonyms, see MEANING.

unmentionable, *adj.* ineffable, unutterable, unspeakable, nameless, despicable. See DISREPUTE.

unmerciful, *adj.* merciless, pitiless, inhuman, cruel; unfeeling, relentless, unrelenting; stern, hard-hearted, cold-blooded, callous. See MALEVOLENCE, SEVERITY.

unmistakable, *adj.* obvious, evident, manifest, patent, clear, apparent, plain, open; downright, overt, certain. See CERTAINTY.

unmitigated, *adj.* unalleviated; downright, utter, sheer, out-and-out. See GREATNESS, COMPLETION.

unmoved, *adj.* unaffected, impassive, unsympathetic, *etc.;* unconvinced, firm, unwavering, unshaken, steadfast. See INSENSIBILITY.

unnatural, *adj.* artificial, factitious; affected, stagy, insincere; strange, abnormal, foreign; monstrous, freakish, misshapen; merciless, cold. See AFFECTATION, MALEVOLENCE, UNCONFORMITY.

unnecessary, *adj.* useless, needless,

inessential, superfluous, dispensable. See USELESSNESS.

unnerve, *v.t.* unhinge, disconcert, frighten. *Colloq.,* rattle. *Slang,* give the jitters. See FEAR, IMPOTENCE, EXCITABILITY.

unnumbered, *adj.* uncounted; countless, innumerable. See INFINITY.

unobtrusive, *adj.* unassertive, unpretentious, shy, modest, retiring, timid. See MODESTY.

unoccupied, *adj.* empty, vacant, tenantless; unemployed. See ABSENCE, INACTIVITY.

unofficial, *adj.* unauthorized, unauthoritative; tentative. *Slang,* off the cuff *or* record, not for publication. See ILLEGALITY, UNCERTAINTY.

unorthodox, *adj.* unconventional; heretical. See UNCONFORMITY, HETERODOXY.

unpack, *v.t.* unwrap, uncover, open; unload, put away. See EJECTION.

unpaid, *adj.* owing, due, unsatisfied; unsalaried, volunteer. See DEBT, NONPAYMENT.

unpalatable, *adj.* distasteful, unsavory, unappetizing; insipid; inedible, uneatable, tasteless. See UNSAVORINESS.

unparalleled, *adj.* unequaled, peerless, unmatched, inimitable. See SUPERIORITY.

unpardonable, *adj.* See UNFORGIVABLE.

unpleasant, *adj.* disagreeable, offensive, displeasing, unpleasing, bad, nasty, sickening; noisome; unattractive, unsatisfactory; surly, unfriendly. See DISCOURTESY, UNSAVORINESS.

unpopular, *adj.* disliked, unloved; distasteful; out of favor. See DISLIKE.

unprecedented, *adj.* new, novel, unheard-of, original. See UNCONFORMITY.

unprejudiced, *adj.* impartial, dispassionate, unbiased, uninfluenced. See LIBERALITY.

unpremeditated, *adj.* extempore, impromptu, extemporary, impulsive, spontaneous. See IMPULSE, UNPREPAREDNESS.

UNPREPAREDNESS

Nouns—**1,** unpreparedness, unreadiness, improvidence, imprudence; inadvertence (see INATTENTION); negligence; improvisation, unpremeditation (see IMPULSE); immaturity, prematurity. See EARLINESS, NEGLECT.

2, [state of] nature, absence of art; virgin soil, fallow ground, unweeded garden; raw material, diamond in the rough; rough copy; embryo, germ.

Verbs—lie fallow, live from hand to mouth, take no thought of tomorrow; extemporize, improvise; take aback (see SURPRISE). *Colloq.,* cook up, go off half-cocked.

Adjectives—**1,** unprepared, unready, untutored, undrilled, unexercised; untaught, uneducated, uncultured; unqualified, disqualified, unfit[ted], ill-fitted, unsuited, ineligible; unorganized, unarranged, unfurnished, unprovided, unequipped, untrimmed. *Colloq.,* flatfooted.

2, immature, unripe, raw, green; uncooked, unboiled, unconcocted, undigested, ill-digested, unmellowed, unseasoned, unleavened; crude, coarse, rough[cast], roughhewn, in the rough; unhewn, unformed, unfashioned, unwrought, unpolished.

3, rudimentary, rudimental, embryonic, *in ovo,* vestigial, inchoate, abortive, premature; undeveloped, unhatched, unfledged, unlicked, unnurtured; incomplete, imperfect.

4, fallow, unsown, untilled, uncultivated, unplowed, idle; in a state of nature, natural; undressed, in dishabille, *en déshabillé.*

5, shiftless, improvident, empty-handed; negligent, unguarded, thoughtless, caught napping.

6, unpremeditated, improvised, improvisatory, improviso, extemporaneous, extempore, extemporary, impromptu, offhand; unintentional; off the top of one's head. *Colloq.,* off the cuff.

Adverbs—unpreparedly, extemporaneously, extempore, impromptu, off-hand, without preparation, on the spur of the moment.

Antonyms, see PREPARATION, EXPECTATION.

---

unprincipled, *adj.* unscrupulous, thievish, rascally; lawless, perfidious, dishonest, fraudulent; wicked, evil. See IMPROBITY.

unproductive, *adj.* inoperative; barren, unfertile, unprolific; arid, dry, sterile, unfruitful; fruitless, bootless; fallow; impotent, issueless; unprofitable, useless; null and void, of no effect. See USELESSNESS, IMPOTENCE.

unprofitable, *adj.* profitless, unbeneficial, unproductive; useless, futile, bootless, fruitless; costly, expensive; unwise, inexpedient. See USELESSNESS.

unpromising, *adj.* discouraging, disappointing, hopeless. See PREDICTION.

unqualified, *adj.* unfit, unsuited, ineligible; straight, thoroughgoing; certain, out-and-out, outright, unconditional, consummate, complete. See CERTAINTY, UNSKILLFULNESS.

unquenchable, *adj.* quenchless, insatiate; thirsty, parched, arid. See DESIRE.

unquestionable, *adj.* indubitable, indisputable, certain, sure, undeniable, irrefutable, incontrovertible. See CERTAINTY.

unquiet, *adj.* disturbed, agitated; restless, unpeaceful. See AGITATION.

unravel, *v.t.* ravel, untwine, disentangle, untangle; develop, explain, unfold. See INTERPRETATION, DISCLOSURE, DISJUNCTION.

unread, *adj.* illiterate; unlearned, uneducated; unintellectual. See IGNORANCE.

unreal, *adj.* imaginary, illusionary, illusory, shadowy; imponderable, unsubstantial, fanciful, fictitious; ideal; *slang,* unbelievable. See IMAGINATION, NONEXISTENCE.

unreasonable, *adj.* irrational, illogical, absurd, senseless, preposterous, ridiculous; immoderate, excessive, extravagant, exorbitant; stubborn, obstinate. See FOLLY, IMAGINATION, CHANGEABLENESS, DEARNESS.

unrefined, *adj.* unpurified, crude, raw, natural, native; unfastidious, uncultivated, rude, coarse, inelegant, vulgar, common. See VULGARITY, INELEGANCE, IGNORANCE.

unrelenting, *adj.* relentless, inexorable, unyielding, rigorous, obdurate, remorseless, stern. See MALEVOLENCE, VULGARITY.

unreliable, *adj.* untrustworthy, irresponsible, unstable, treacherous, inconstant; unsure, uncertain, fallible. See IMPROBITY, CHANGEABLENESS, DOUBT.

unremitting, *adj.* unrelieved, unceasing, unending; endless, relentless, perpetual, continuous, chronic. See CONTINUITY.

unrequited, *adj.* unrewarded, unanswered; ignored, scorned. See INGRATITUDE, NONPAYMENT.

unreserved, *adj.* frank, outspoken; demonstrative, cordial; unrestricted, absolute. See COMPLETION, COMMUNICATION, PROBITY.

unresisting, *adj.* nonresistant, yielding, acquiescent, submissive, passive. See OBEDIENCE.

unrest, *n.* restlessness, disquiet, uneasiness; agitation, insurgence, rebellion. See CHANGEABLENESS, AGITATION.

unrestrained, *adj.* unbridled, unchecked, uncurbed, untrammeled, unbounded, free; inordinate, uninhibited, wanton, lax, loose, rampant. See FREEDOM.

unrestricted, *adj.* unlimited, unconfined, unqualified. See FREEDOM.

unrighteous, *adj.* wicked, ungodly; unjust. See EVIL, IRRELIGION.

unripe, *adj.* premature, immature; precocious, crude. See UNPREPAREDNESS.

unruffled, *adj.* serene, calm, placid, poised, undisturbed. See INEXCITABILITY, SMOOTHNESS, REPOSE.

unruly, *adj.* unmanageable, insubordinate, obstreperous, fractious, refractory, ungovernable, turbulent, boisterous, balky. See DISOBEDIENCE.

unsafe, *adj.* insecure, precarious, dangerous, risky, perilous; untrustworthy. See DANGER.

unsatisfactory, *adj.* inadequate; intolerable. See MEDIOCRITY, DISCONTENT.

UNSAVORINESS

Nouns—unsavoriness, tastelessness, INSIPIDITY; unpalatableness, distastefulness, roughness, acridity, acridness, acerbity, SOURNESS; gall and wormwood. See DISLIKE, DISCONTENT.

Verbs—be unsavory *or* unpalatable; sicken, repel, disgust, nauseate, pall, turn the stomach.

Adjectives—**1,** unsavory, insipid, tasteless; unpalatable, ill-flavored, distasteful, harsh, rough, bitter, acrid, acerb, acrimonious.

2, offensive, repulsive, repugnant, obnoxious, unpleasant, objectionable, disagreeable, uninviting, nasty, sickening, nauseous, loathsome, disgusting, vile, foul, revolting.

3, disreputable, unprepossessing (see DISREPUTE, UGLINESS).

Antonyms, see TASTE.

---

unscathed, *adj.* unharmed, uninjured. See PERFECTION.

unschooled, *adj.* uneducated, untaught. See IGNORANCE.

unscientific, *adj.* instinctive, intuitive, subjective; trial-and-error, untrue, unsound, unproved. See IMAGINATION, INTUITION.

unscramble, *adj.* untangle, disentangle, unmix; decode, decipher, disclose, solve. *Colloq.,* crack. *Slang,* dope out. See SIMPLENESS, ANSWER.

unscrupulous, *adj.* unprincipled, conscienceless, dishonest. See IMPROBITY.

unseasonable, *adj.* untimely, inopportune; inapt. See INEXPEDIENCE, DISAGREEMENT.

unseat, *v.t.* displace; depose. See DISPLACEMENT.

unseemly, *adj.* unbecoming, unsuitable, unfitting, improper, indecent, indecorous, tasteless. See UNCONFORMITY, VULGARITY.

unseen, *adj.* imperceptible, invisible. See INVISIBILITY.

UNSELFISHNESS

Nouns—unselfishness, generosity, disinterestedness, selflessness, devotion (to others); LIBERALITY, liberalism, magnanimity; BENEVOLENCE; high-mindedness, nobility; impartiality, fairness, lack of prejudice; loftiness of purpose, chivalry, heroism (see COURAGE); altruism, self-denial, -abnegation, *or* -sacrifice; Good Samaritanism, good works; self-immolation, martyrdom, suttee; labor of love. See GIVING.

Verbs—be disinterested *or* generous, make a sacrifice, put oneself in the place of others, do as one would be done by.

Adjectives—unselfish, disinterested, selfless, benevolent, altruistic; chivalrous, heroic; charitable, liberal, generous, magnanimous, large-hearted, high- *or* noble-minded; objective; self-denying, self-sacrificing. See BENEVOLENCE.

Antonyms, see SELFISHNESS.

---

unsettle, *v.t.* upset, disturb, disarrange, displace; unhinge, derange, unbalance. See DISORDER, SURPRISE.

unsettled, *adj.* outstanding, unpaid; disturbed, troubled; unfixed, indeterminate. See IRREGULARITY, CHANGEABLENESS, INSANITY, DOUBT, EXCITEMENT.

unsightly, *adj.* ugly, unattractive. See UGLINESS.

UNSKILLFULNESS

Nouns—**1,** unskillfulness, incompetence; inability, inexperience; quackery, maladroitness, ineptness, clumsiness, awkwardness, two left feet.

2, mismanagement, misconduct; maladministration; misrule, misgovernment, misapplication, misdirection, misfeasance.

3, bungling, FAILURE; too many cooks, blunder, mistake, ERROR; gaucherie, act of folly, botch[ery]; bad job. *Slang,* snafu.

4, blunderer, bumbler, botcher, butcher, bungler, fumbler, duffer, klutz; bull in a china shop; butterfingers; greenhorn, palooka; Mrs. Malaprop.

Verbs—**1,** blunder, bungle, boggle, fumble, botch, flounder, stumble, trip, hobble; tinker, make a mess *or* hash of, play havoc with; make a fool of oneself; play the fool; lose one's head. *Colloq.,* put one's foot in it; foul up. *Slang,* mess, ball, hash, *or* louse up, snafu.

2, err, make a mistake (see ERROR); mismanage, misconduct, misdirect, misapply; do things by halves; work at cross purposes; put the cart before the horse; not know what one is about; not know a hawk from a handsaw; kill the goose that lays the golden eggs; cut one's own throat, burn one's fingers; run one's head against a stone wall; fall into a trap, catch a Tartar, bring down the house about one's ears; too many irons in the fire.

Adjectives—**1,** unskillful, unskilled, inexpert, bungling, awkward, ungainly, clumsy, lubberly, gangling, gauche, maladroit; left-handed, heavy-handed, heavy-footed; inapt, unapt, inept; neglectful; all thumbs; stupid, incompetent; unqualified, ill-qualified; unfit; quackish; raw, green, inexperienced; amateur, jackleg; half-baked.

2, unaccustomed, rusty, out of practice, unused, untrained, uninitiated, unconversant, ignorant (see IGNORANCE); unadvised, ill-advised, misguided. *Colloq.,* wet behind the ears.

Antonyms, see SKILL.

---

unsociable, *adj.* reserved, aloof, distant, shy, solitary, retiring. See SECLUSION.

unsolicited, *adj.* unsought (for), undue, unlooked for; voluntary. See WILL.

unsophisticated, *adj.* ingenuous, innocent, simple, guileless, artless. See INNOCENCE, SIMPLENESS.

unsound, *adj.* unhealthy, diseased, sickly; deranged, unbalanced, unsettled; invalid, unreliable; untrue, incorrect, faulty, imperfect, illogical; decayed. See DISEASE, ERROR, IMPERFECTION.

unspeakable, *adj.* shocking, dreadful, horrible, execrable, unutterable, inexpressible, unimaginable. See WONDER, UNMEANINGNESS.

unspoiled, *adj.* perfect, intact, whole, wholesome; untouched, pristine; ingenuous. See PURITY.

unspoken, *adj*. tacit, implied; unsaid. See SILENCE, LATENCY.

unstable, *adj*. irregular, fluctuating, unsteady; inconstant, vacillating, fickle, changeable, variable. See CHANGEABLENESS.

unsteady, *adj*. fluctuating, waving, shifting, vacillating, irresolute, shaky, tottery, wobbly, infirm. See INEQUALITY, CHANGEABLENESS, AGITATION.

unstinting, *adj*. unsparing, generous, lavish; unbounded. See LIBERALITY.

unstrung, *adj*. unhinged, unnerved, distraught, agitated. *Slang*, jittery. See EXCITABILITY.

unsuccessful, *adj*. unprosperous, unfortunate, unavailing, unproductive. See FAILURE.

unsuitable, *adj*. unsuited, inappropriate, unfitting, unbecoming. See DISAGREEMENT.

unsullied, *adj*. immaculate, spotless, unspotted, pure, flawless, untarnished. See CLEANNESS, INNOCENCE, PURITY.

unsung, *adj*. neglected, slighted, ignored. See LATENCY, NEGLECT.

unsurpassed, *adj*. unexcelled, incomparable, nonpareil, nonesuch, preeminent, superlative. *Colloq*., tops. See SUPERIORITY.

unsuspecting, *adj*. trusting, trustful, unsuspicious, credulous, unquestioning, artless. See BELIEF, CREDULITY, INNOCENCE.

untangle, *v*. disentangle, [un]ravel, disengage; free, extricate; comb, tease, card, straighten [out]; clear up, interpret. See DISJUNCTION, ANSWER.

untaught, *adj*. illiterate, unlettered, uneducated. See IGNORANCE.

untenable, *adj*. indefensible, insupportable, inconsistent, illogical. See FALSEHOOD.

unthinkable, *adj*. inconceivable, unimaginable, impossible; repugnant, out of the question; beyond belief, unbelievable. See IMPOSSIBILITY.

untidy, *adj*. slovenly, careless, di- orderly; messy, littered; dow frumpy, slipshod; unkempt. See DISORDER, UNCLEANNESS.

untie, *v.t* loosen, free, unbind, unknot. See LIBERATION, DISJUNCTION.

until, *prep*. till, to, up to [the time of]. See TIME.

untimely, *adj*. inopportune, unseasonable; intrusive; inexpedient, early, late, anachronistic. See DISAGREEMENT, EARLINESS, LATENESS, INEXPEDIENCE.

untiring, *adj*. tireless, indefatigable, unwearied, unremitting, unrelaxing. See RESOLUTION.

untold, *adj*. unknown, unrevealed, undisclosed; countless, measureless, legion, innumerable. See CONCEALMENT, MULTITUDE, INFINITY.

untouchable, *adj*. inaccessible, out of reach; immune, exempt, sacrosanct, taboo. —*n*. pariah, outcast[e]. See PROHIBITION.

untoward, *adj*. inconvenient, perverse, troublesome; vexatious; ungraceful, awkward; unfavorable. See ADVERSITY, BADNESS.

untrained, *adj*. unbroken, untamed; raw, inexperienced, green. See UNSKILLFULNESS.

untrue, *adj*., **untruth,** *n*. See DECEPTION, FALSEHOOD.

unused, *adj*. See UNACCUSTOMED.

unusual, *adj*. uncommon, rare; out-of-the-way, curious, odd, queer, singular; abnormal, anomalous, exceptional, extraordinary; irregular, bizarre, peculiar; unwonted, unaccustomed. See UNCONFORMITY, RARITY, DISUSE. NSPEAKABLE.

unutterable, *adj*. S veal, uncover.

unveil, *v.t*. disclo

See DISCLOS unjustified, un-

unwarrante arrantable, unjust.

called-f , ILLEGALITY, DEAR-

See rash, unwise, indiscreet,

NE it, unguarded, injudicious.

u GLECT, RASHNESS.

, *adj*. ailing, sick, indisposed, invalid, diseased. See DISEASE.

unwieldy, *adj.* clumsy, awkward, cumbersome, ungainly, bulky, ponderous. *Colloq.*, hulking. See GRAVITY, SIZE.

UNWILLINGNESS

Nouns—unwillingness, indisposition, disinclination, aversion, DISLIKE; nolleity, nolition, renitence; reluctance; indocility, OBSTINACY, noncompliance, REFUSAL; scrupulousness, fastidiousness, delicacy; scruple, qualm, demur, shrinking; hesitancy, irresolution, indecision, UNCERTAINTY. See RESISTANCE, REFUSAL.

Verbs—be unwilling, grudge, DISLIKE, not have the stomach to; scruple, stickle, stick at, boggle at, shy at, demur, hesitate, hang back, hang fire, lag, RECOIL, shrink; avoid (see AVOIDANCE); oppose, refuse. *Slang*, duck.

Adjectives—unwilling, not in the mood *or* vein; loath, disinclined, indisposed, averse, renitent, reluctant, recalcitrant, balky, demurring, objecting, unconsenting, refusing, grudging, dragging, adverse, opposed, laggard, backward, remiss, slack, slow (to); scrupulous, squeamish, fastidious; involuntary, forced; repugnant.

Adverbs—unwillingly, grudgingly, with bad grace, with an ill will; against one's will, *à contre-coeur,* against one's wishes; against the grain, with a heavy heart; *nolens volens,* willy-nilly; in spite of oneself, *malgré soi;* perforce, under protest; no. See NEGATION.

Phrases—not for the world; *Colloq.*, not on your life.

Antonyms, see WILL, DESIRE.

---

unwind, *v.i.* relax, let down one's defenses, let one's hair down. See REPOSE, MODERATION.

unwise, *adj.* foolish, injudicious, imprudent, ill-advised; senseless, impolitic, indiscreet. See FOLLY.

unwitting, *adj.* unknowing, unaware, thoughtless, heedless; involuntary, inadvertent; blind, deaf. See IGNORANCE, NECESSITY.

unwonted, *adj.* unusual, uncustomary; unused, unaccustomed. See UNCONFORMITY, DISUSE.

unworkable, *adj.* inoperable, impractical; futile, no good. See IMPOSSIBILITY.

unworthy, *adj.* undeserving, worthless; un[illegible]; shameful; [illegible]ming, disgraceful, derogatory, [illegible]able, discreditable, [illegible]SREPUTE.

unyielding, *adj* [illegible]ing, rigid, inf[illegible]able, unbending, indomitable, ob[illegible] firm; grim, obstinate, relentle[illegible] stubborn, ing; pertinacious, [illegible]promising, table, perverse. See [illegible] intractable [illegible]STINACY, SEVERITY.

up, *adv.* upward[s], aloft, ASCENT, HEIGHT.

upbeat, *adj., colloq.,* lively, brisk. See ACTIVITY.

upbraid, *v.t.* reprove, chide, admonish, rebuke, reprimand, scold; accuse, charge, revile. See DISAPPROBATION.

upbringing, *n.* rearing, breeding, training, education. See TEACHING.

update, *v.t.* make current, modernize; revise, re-edit. See NEWNESS.

upgrade, *v.t.* improve, better; raise, increase; dignify. See IMPROVEMENT.

upheaval, *n.* cataclysm, debacle; agitation, unrest, REVOLUTION. See VIOLENCE, EXCITEMENT.

uphill, *adj.* ascending, rising; precipitous; laborious; difficult, strenuous. See EXERTION, OBLIQUITY.

uphold, *v.t.* maintain, sustain; champion; advocate, confirm; approve, encourage. See AID, SUPPORT, DEMONSTRATION.

upkeep, *n.* care, maintenance; sustenance; overhead, expenses; pension. See SUPPORT, PAYMENT.

uplift, *n.* ELEVATION; IMPROVEMENT, refinement, inspiration.

upon, *prep.* on, on top of, above; by, by the act of, through; touching, against; about, regarding, concerning. See CONTACT, COVERING, MEANS, RELATION.

upper, *adj.* higher, superior. See HEIGHT.

upper-class, *adj.* fashionable, elite; moneyed, propertied; exclusive. *Slang,* classy. See NOBILITY, MONEY.

upperclassman, *n.* junior, senior. See SCHOOL.

uppish, *adj.* insolent, haughty, uppity. See INSOLENCE.

upright, *adj.* VERTICAL, perpendicular, erect; honorable, conscientious, upstanding, honest, righteous. *Colloq.,* straight. See PROBITY, RIGHTNESS.

uprising, *n.* revolt, REVOLUTION, rebellion, insurrection, [civil] war, coup.

uproar, *n.* tumult, hubbub, discord, pandemonium, bedlam, ado, bustle, din, clamor. *Colloq.,* hullabaloo. See DISORDER, LOUDNESS.

uproot, *v.t.* extirpate, eradicate, root out, abolish, destroy. See EXTRACTION, DESTRUCTION.

upset, *v.t.* overthrow, overturn, capsize; disturb, bother, discompose, disconcert; spoil; perturb; disarrange, unbalance; demoralize. —*n.* reversal, overturn, disorder. See DESTRUCTION, INVERSION, CHANGE, REVOLUTION.

upshot, *n.* outcome, conclusion, result, EFFECT, meaning. See JUDGMENT.

upside-down, *adj.* reversed, inverted, head over heels, standing on one's head, bottom-side up; upended, capsized. See INVERSION, DISORDER.

upstage, *v.* show up, overshadow. *Slang,* one-up. See SUPERIORITY.

upstanding, *adj.* upright, honorable. See PROBITY.

upstart, *n.* parvenu. *Colloq.,* pusher. See NEWNESS.

upswing, *n.* IMPROVEMENT, upturn, uptrend, betterment, recovery. *Colloq.,* pickup. See ASCENT.

up-tight, *adj., slang,* tense, nervous. See EXCITABILITY.

up-to-date, *adj.* modern, new, fresh, current, timely; fashionable, modish, stylish; restored, renovated, revised, modernized. See NEWNESS, RESTORATION.

upward, *adv.* higher, aloft, upwards; more. See ASCENT, HEIGHT, INCREASE.

urban, *adj.* city, town, metropolitan, civil. See ABODE, REGION.

urbane, *adj.* suave, sophisticated, debonair; civil, polite, affable. See COURTESY.

urchin, *n.* hedgehog; child, imp, brat. See YOUTH, DEMON.

urge, *v.* solicit, plead, importune, advocate, exhort, incite, instigate; press, push. —*n.* IMPULSE, desire, ambition. See NECESSITY, REQUEST, CAUSE.

urgent, *adj.* important, imperative, exigent, necessary, critical; importunate, insistent, pressing. See IMPORTANCE, REQUEST, HASTE, NECESSITY.

urn, *n.* vase, ves... pot, amphora, ...ar; cinerary urn, jardiniere; sa... ...e RECEPTACLE, INTERMENT.

USE

Nouns—**1,** use, employ[ment]; exercise, ap...n, appliance; adhibition, avail; utilization, service, disposal; consumption; usufruct; recours...IT; usefulness (see UTILITY); wear; usage, function, practice, meth... exploitation, sexism. See POSSESSIO...

2, user, employer, applier, consu...r, purchaser, enjoyer.

Verbs—**1,** use, make use of, utiliz... employ, put to use; put in action, operation, *or* practice; set in ...to work; ply, work, wield, handle, maneuver, manipulate; play ...on; exert, exercise, practice, avail oneself of, make free with, seize on, make the most of, do with, profit by; resort to, look to, have recourse to, betake oneself to; take advantage of, exploit, trade on; try.

2, render useful, apply, turn to account, utilize; bring into play; press into service; bring to bear (upon), devote, dedicate, consecrate; apply, adhibit, dispose of; make a cat's-paw of; fall back upon, make shift with; make the most *or* best of.

3, use up, consume, absorb, dissipate (see WASTE); finish off, exhaust, drain; expend; tax, wear.

4, be used up *or* expended, run out.

Adjectives—in use, in effect; used; well-worn, well-trodden; functional, utilitarian, useful (see UTILITY).

Antonyms, see NEGLECT, WASTE, DISUSE.

USELESSNESS

Nouns—**1,** uselessness, inutility; inefficacy, futility; impracticableness, impracticality; inefficiency, IMPOTENCE; worthlessness, vanity, inanity, UNIMPORTANCE. See UNSKILLFULNESS, HOPELESSNESS.

2, unproductiveness, unprofitableness; infertility, infecundity, barrenness, aridity; labor lost, wild-goose chase.

3, WASTE; desert, Sahara, wilderness, wild, tundra, marsh; litter, rubbish, odds and ends, cast-offs; junk, dross, shoddy, rags, orts, trash, refuse, sweepings, scourings, rubble, debris; stubble, leavings; dregs; weeds, tares; white elephant; rubbish heap. See REMAINDER.

Verbs—**1,** be useless *or* unproductive; come to nothing; fall; seek *or* strive after impossibilities; roll the stone of Sisyphus; bay at the moon, preach to the winds; lock the barn door after the horse is stolen; cast pearls before swine; carry coals to Newcastle; cry over spilled milk; beat one's head against a wall. *Colloq.,* chase rainbows.

2, disable, hamper (see HINDRANCE); cripple, lame; spike guns, clip the wings; put out of gear; decommission, dismantle, disassemble, break up, tear down, raze, demolish, destroy; wear out; pull the fangs *or* teeth of, tie one's hands, put in a straitjacket.

Adjectives—**1,** useless, inutile, inefficacious, futile, unavailing, bootless; ineffectua[illegible] ineffective, effete; inoperative, unproductive, barren, infertile, sterile, fall[illegible]y; unprofitable, null and void; inadequate, insufficient; unskillful (see UNS[illegible]LFULNESS); superfluous, dispensable, disposable, throwaway; thrown awa[illegible]vasted; abortive.

2, worthless, [illegible]gatory, valueless, unsalable; not worth a straw; vain, empty, inane; [illegible]less, profitless, fruitless; unserviceable, unprofitable; ill-spent; obsole[illegible] [illegible]od for nothing, no-good; of no earthly use; not worth having, not worth [illegible]t, unnecessary, unneeded. *Slang,* not worth a tinker's damn.

Adverbs—uselessly, to [illegible] purpose, to no purpose, to little or no purpose; to no avail.

Anto[illegible] see UTILITY, PRODUCTION.

---

usher, *v.t.* escort, introd[illegible] nounce, induct. —*n.* d[illegible] escort, groomsman, vestrym[illegible] BEGINNER, RELIGION.

usual, *adj.* customary, accustomed, habitual, ordinary, wonted, normal, regular, everyday; traditional. See HABIT, CONFORMITY.

usurp, *v.t.* seize, expropriate, arrogate, appropriate; conquer, annex, snatch, grab. See ILLEGALITY, STEALING.

usury, *n.* overcharge, extortion. See DEARNESS, DEBT.

utensil, *n.* implement, instrument; vessel, container. See INSTRUMENTALITY, RECEPTACLE.

utilitarian, *adj.* See USE, UTILITY.

UTILITY

Nouns—utility; usefulness, efficacy, efficiency, adequacy; service, stead, avail, benefit; help, AID; convenience, availability; applicability, function, value; worth, GOODNESS; productiveness; utilization (see USE). See EXPEDIENCE.

Verbs—avail, serve; subserve; conduce, tend; answer *or* serve a purpose; bear fruit, produce (see PRODUCTION); profit, remunerate, benefit, do good; perform *or* discharge a function; do *or* render a service; bestead, stand one in good stead; be the making of; help, AID. *Colloq.*, come in handy.

Adjectives—useful, of use; serviceable, good for; instrumental, conducive, tending; convenient; subsidiary, helping, advantageous, beneficial, profitable, gainful, remunerative, worth one's salt; valuable, invaluable; prolific, productive; practical, practicable; at one's service; pragmatic, functional; adequate; efficient, efficacious; effective, effectual; expedient, applicable, available, ready, handy, at hand, tangible; commodious, adaptable.

Adverbs—usefully, efficiently, *etc.; pro bono publico*. *Colloq.*, on tap.

Antonyms, see USELESSNESS.

---

utmost, *adj.* most, greatest, farthest, furthest; last, final; total, unlimited, full, complete. See COMPLETION, SUPERIORITY.

Utopian, *adj.* ideal[istic], optimistic, visionary, romantic; rosy; perfect; unrealistic, unworldly; Quixotic, Arcadian. —*n.* utopianist; dreamer, idealist, optimist, visionary, romantic; Quixote. See IMAGINATION.

utter, *adj.* total, complete, entire; extreme, unusual; unqualified; stark, sheer, downright, absolute. See COMPLETION, GREATNESS, CERTAINTY. —*v.t.* speak, voice; pronounce, express, enunciate, deliver; issue, emit. See SPEECH, DISCLOSURE.

V

vacancy, *n.* emptiness, void, vacuum, space; inanity, stupidity, idleness. See ABSENCE.

vacant, *adj.* empty; open, free, untenanted, unoccupied, to let; blank, void, hollow; shallow, brainless, inane, idle, disengaged; stupid, vacuous. See ABSENCE, IGNORANCE, INATTENTION.

vacate, *v.* move out; leave, decamp; abandon, relinquish, surrender, quit; evacuate, leave empty; annul, cancel, invalidate, quash. See RELINQUISHMENT, DEPARTURE.

vacation, *n.* holiday, rest, time off, leave [of absence]; recess, respite; abandonment, DEPARTURE. See REPOSE.

vaccinate, *v.t.* jennerize, variolate; inoculate, inject; immunize; prick, scratch, scarify. *Colloq.*, give shots. See REMEDY.

vaccine, *n.* bacterin, serum, antitoxin, immunotoxin. See REMEDY.

vacillation, *n.* uncertainty; fluctuation; hesitation, faltering, shilly-shallying. See DOUBT, OSCILLATION, CHANGEABLENESS.

vacuum, *n.* void, vacancy, emptiness, nothingness; space. See ABSENCE, NONEXISTENCE.

vagabond, *n.* hobo, tramp, vagrant, wanderer, idler, beggar. *Colloq.*, bum, knight of the road. See TRAVEL, POPULACE.

vagary, *n.* fancy, notion, caprice, whim; quirk, foible. See CHANGE-

ABLENESS, IMAGINATION.

vagrant, *n.* tramp, hobo (see VAGABOND). —*adj.* wandering, aimless, wayward, roving; erratic, capricious. See TRAVEL, POPULACE.

vague, *adj.* unclear, blurred, blurry; amorphous, shapeless; undefined, uncertain, indistinct, inexact, indefinite, obscure. See FORMLESSNESS, OBSCURITY.

vain, *adj.* proud, conceited; futile, fruitless; trivial. See VANITY.

vainglorious, *adj.* vain, proud, boastful. See VANITY, BOASTING.

valediction, *n.* farewell speech, valedictory; farewell, good-bye, adieu. See DEPARTURE, SPEECH.

valet, *n.* SERVANT; manservant, gentleman's gentleman, attendant.

valiant, *adj.* valorous, brave, courageous, gallant; daring, intrepid, dauntless, lionhearted; noteworthy. See COURAGE.

valid, *adj.* sound, logical; legal, binding, well-grounded, just. See DEMONSTRATION, TRUTH, LEGALITY, POWER.

validate, *v.t.* confirm; legalize. See LEGALITY, EVIDENCE, ASSENT.

valise, *n.* traveling bag, satchel. See RECEPTACLE.

valley, *n.* vale, river land, dale, dell, glen, canyon, hollow. See CONCAVITY, LOWNESS.

valor, *n.* COURAGE, intrepidity, fearlessness; prowess, heroism, gallantry; daring, derring-do.

valuable, *adj.* precious, costly; worthy, meritorious, estimable; useful. See UTILITY.

value, *n.* usefulness, worth; PRICE, cost, rate, rating; estimation, valuation, merit; import; significance; shade, tone, emphasis. —*v.t.* esteem, prize, treasure, regard highly; appraise, evaluate, assess, rate. See IMPORTANCE, GOODNESS, MEASUREMENT, APPROBATION.

valueless, *adj.* worthless (see USELESSNESS).

valve, *n.* damper, cutoff, cock, butterfly, pallet, poppet; ventil, side valve; plug, piston, cusp. See CLOSURE.

vamp, *n., slang,* flirt, coquette. See ENDEARMENT.

vampire, *n.* bloodsucker, bat; ghoul; parasite; *slang,* siren, seducer, vamp, temptress. See EVILDOER, DEMON.

van, *n.* truck, lorry, moving van; forefront, vanguard, *avant garde;* FRONT, head. See VEHICLE.

vandalism, *n.* pillage, depredation, plundering; DESTRUCTION, mutilation, defacement; sabotage; desecration, profanation; barbarianism.

vane, *n.* girouette, anemometer; cone, sleeve, sock; arm, plate, fin, blade. See WIND, INDICATION.

vanguard, *n.* van; spearhead, front line, shock troops; Marines; *avant garde;* forerunner, leader; innovators, modernists. See PRECEDENCE, FRONT, NEWNESS.

vanish, *v.i.* disappear, fade out; dissolve; *slang,* decamp, vamoose. See DISAPPEARANCE, DEPARTURE.

VANITY

Nouns—**1,** vanity, conceit, conceitedness; immodesty, self-esteem, self-love, self-praise; complacency, smugness, *amour-propre;* ego trip. See BOASTING, SELFISHNESS.

2, [false] PRIDE, airs, pretensions; egotism, egoism; priggishness; coxcombery, vainglory, pretense, OSTENTATION; INSOLENCE.

3, egotist, egoist, prig, pretender, fop, coxcomb, know-it-all.

4, vainness, futility (see USELESSNESS).

Verbs—be vain, put oneself forward; fish for compliments; give oneself airs; boast; presume, swagger, strut; plume *or* preen oneself; turn one's head, go to one's head, have a big head, flatter oneself. *Colloq.,* get on one's high horse. *Slang,* put on side, the dog, *or* the ritz.

Adjectives—vain [as a peacock], conceited, immodest, overweening, pert, forward; haughty, puffed-up (see PRIDE); prideful, vainglorious, high-flown, ostentatious; self-satisfied, self-centered, full of oneself, smug, complacent, opinionated; imperious, arrogant, cocky, too big for one's britches, immodest, pretentious, priggish; egotistic; *soi-disant;* unabashed, unblushing. *Colloq.*, swell-headed, stuck-up.

Adverbs—vainly, priggishly, pridefully, proudly, haughtily, *etc.*

Antonyms, see MODESTY.

---

vanquish, *v.t.* conquer, subdue, subjugate, overcome; quell, silence; worst, rout; master. See SUCCESS.

vantage, *n.* advantage; rise, vantage ground *or* point. See SUPERIORITY, HEIGHT.

vapid, *adj.* flat, tasteless, insipid; tame, spiritless, lifeless, dull. See INSIPIDITY.

VAPOR

Nouns—**1,** vapor, vaporousness, vaporization, volatilization; gaseousness, gaseity; evaporation; distillation, aeration, sublimation, exhalation; fumigation, steaming; volatility. See INSUBSTANTIALITY, RARITY.

2, gas, elastic fluid; oxygen, ozone, hydrogen, nitrogen, argon, helium, fluorine, neon; natural gas, coal gas, illuminating gas; sewer gas, poison gas; damp, chokedamp; air, vapor, ether, steam, fume, reek, effluvium, miasma, flatus; flatulence; cloud (see CLOUDINESS). See FUEL.

3, vaporizer, atomizer, still, retort; spray, spray gun, airbrush, sprayer.

4, pneumatics, pneumostatics; aerostatics, aerodynamics.

Verbs—vaporize, volatize, distill, sublime; evaporate, exhale, transpire, fume, reek, steam, fumigate; give off; atomize, spray.

Adjectives—vaporous, volatile, volatilized, gaseous, gassy, reeking; aeriform, evaporable, vaporizable.

Antonyms, see DENSITY.

---

variable, *adj.* changeable, alterable; inconstant. See CHANGEABLENESS, IRREGULARITY.

variance, *n.* change, alteration; DIFFERENCE, DISAGREEMENT, DISCORD; jarring, dissension; variation, UNCONFORMITY.

variation, *n.* variance, alteration, CHANGE, modification; diversification; divergence, deviation, aberration; innovation. See DIFFERENCE.

VARIEGATION

Nouns—**1,** variegation, diversification, diversity, heterogeneity; spottiness, maculation, striation, streakiness, marbling, elaboration, discoloration; parti- *or* party-color, dichroism, dichromatism, polychrome; iridescence, iridization, opalescence, play of colors; counterchange. See COLOR.

2, stripes, bands, streaks, striae; vein, thread, line; check, plaid, tartan, motley, tricolor; marquetry, parquetry, mosaic, tessellation, tesserae; chessboard, checkerboard; confetti, patchwork, crazy quilt, harlequin, Joseph's coat [of many colors]; spectrum, rainbow, iris, tulip; peacock, chameleon, butterfly, zebra, leopard, piebald; tortoiseshell, mother-of-pearl, nacre, opal, marble, mackerel sky; kaleidoscope; color organ.

Verbs—variegate, vary, variate, varify, diversify; stripe, striate, streak, line, checker, counterchange; [be]spot, dot, mottle, dapple, brindle, pie, [be]speckle, freckle, [be]sprinkle, stipple, maculate, fleck, pepper, powder; inlay, tessellate, tattoo, damascene; vein, marble[ize], water; embroider, figure, braid, quilt, fret, lace, interlace.

Adjectives—variegated, varied, various, diverse, diversified; many-colored *or* -hued, multi- *or* varicolored, parti- *or* party-colored, divers-colored; bicolor, tricolor, versicolor, polychromatic, dichromatic, kaleidoscopic[al]; chameleonic; iridescent, opalescent, opaline, prismatic, rainbow-hued, rainbowlike, nacreous, nacre, pearly, chatoyant, cymophanous, tortoiseshell, shot; pied, paint, pinto, piebald; mottled, motley, harlequin, marbled, dappled, clouded, paned, pepper-and-salt, calico; spotted, spotty, dotted and speckled, freckled, studded, flecked, peppered, powdered, punctuated; striped, listed, streaked, streaky, banded, barred, cross-striped, grizzled; mosaic, tessellated, plaid, tartan, checkered, checked, embroidered, daedal; brindle[d], tabby; blotchy.

Antonyms, see UNIFORMITY, COLOR.

---

variety, *n.* variation, diversity, DIFFERENCE; assortment; kind, CLASS; brand; multifariousness; vaudeville. See MIXTURE, DRAMA.

various, *adj.* diversified, multiform, diverse; different; many, several, manifold, numerous, sundry; changeable, unfixed. See DIFFERENCE, MULTITUDE.

varnish, *n.* shellac, lac, lacquer; spar; gloss, mitigation, whitewash, excuse. —*v.t.* shellac, lacquer, *etc.;* palliate, gloze, gloss, excuse, whitewash; finish. See SMOOTHNESS, COVERING.

vary, *v.* CHANGE, alter; fluctuate; differ, disagree; diversify. See DIFFERENCE, DISCORD, DISAGREEMENT.

vase, *n.* urn, cup, chalice, jug, amphora, ampulla. See RECEPTACLE.

vassal, *n.* liege, liegeman; thrall, bondman, subject; [feudal] tenant, serf. See SERVANT.

vast, *adj.* huge, immense; infinite, boundless, immeasurable; tremendous, enormous. See SIZE, SPACE, BREADTH.

vat, *n.* vessel, cistern, tank, drum, caldron; tub, tun, puncheon, bac[k], barrel, cask, hogshead, keg, butt. See RECEPTACLE.

vaudeville, *n.* turns, acts, variety; burlesque, music hall. See DRAMA.

vault, *n.* arch, dome, cupola; bank vault, safe; tomb, sepulcher, catacomb; dungeon, cell, cellar; LEAP, jump, pole-vault. See INTERMENT, STORE. —*v.* arch; LEAP over, jump; pole-vault. See CONVEXITY, CURVATURE.

vaunt, *v.* boast, brag, vapor, talk big. See BOASTING.

veer, *v.i.* swerve, shift; deviate; jibe, come about, yaw. See CHANGE, DEVIATION.

VEGETABLE

Nouns—**1,** vegetable kingdom, vegetation, vegetable life; plants, flora, verdure; growth, biome.

2, vegetable, plant; tree, shrub, bush, hedge; vine, creeper; herb[age]; grass; annual, perennial, biennial, triennial.

3, timber, timberland, forest; wood[lands]; park, chase, greenwood, brake, grove, copse, coppice, thicket, spinney; underbrush, brushwood; tree, shade tree, *etc.*

4, brush, jungle, prairie; heather, heath; fern, bracken; furze, gorse, grass, sod, turf; pasture, pasturage; sedge, rush, weed; fungus, mushroom, toadstool; lichen, moss; growth.

5, foliage, foliation, branch, bough, ramage, leaf; flower, bloom, blossom, bine; pulse, legume, bean, root, bulb.

6, botany, vegetable physiology, phytology; horticulture; AGRICULTURE, agronomy; silviculture; botanist, plant physiologist, horticulturist, *etc.;* botanical gardens, herbarium, arboretum.

Adjectives—vegetable, vegetal, herbaceous, botanic; sylvan, arboreous, arborescent, dendritic, woody, grassy, verdant, verdurous; floral; mossy; lignous, ligneous, xyloid; wooden; woodsy, leguminous; endogenous, exogenous.

Antonyms, see ANIMAL, INORGANIC MATTER.

---

vegetarian, *n.* cerealist, herbivore, granivore, nutarian, lactovegetarian; phytophagan; food faddist. *Colloq.,* health nut. —*adj.* Lenten, meatless; herbivorous, vegetivorous, plantivorous; grain-eating, granivorous; uncarnivorous. See FOOD.

vegetate, *v.i.* stagnate, exist. See EXISTENCE, INACTIVITY.

vegetation, *n.* VEGETABLE life; flora, verdure, greenery.

vehemence, *n.* VIOLENCE, VIGOR, impetuosity, force; ardor, fervor, warmth, zeal. See EXERTION, FEELING.

VEHICLE

Nouns—**1,** vehicle, machine, conveyance, equipage, turnout, cart, rig, car, wagon. See PASSAGE, TRAVEL, TRANSPORTATION.

2, carriage, coach, chariot, chaise, phaeton, berlin, landau, barouche, victoria, hard-top, brougham, sulky; jalopy; two-wheeler, dogcart, trap, buggy. *Slang,* bucket of bolts.

3, stage[coach], diligence, mailcoach; hackney, hack; omnibus, bus, cab, taxi[cab], hansom; jinrickishaw. *Colloq.,* jitney, ricksha.

4, sled, sledge, pung, sleigh, bobsled, toboggan, travois, Alpine slide, luge.

5, handcart, pushcart, barrow, wheelbarrow, handbarrow; sedan chair; gocart, baby carriage, perambulator, stroller; wheelchair, litter, stretcher. *Colloq.,* pram.

6, cycle, bicycle, two-wheeler; tricycle, velocipede, three-wheeler; motorcycle, motor scooter, scooter; motor bicycle, moped. *Colloq.,* bike, trike, wheel, motorbike.

7, automobile, auto, car, motorcar; sedan, coupé, limousine, cabriolet, phaeton, convertible, roadster, touring car; stock car; trailer, caravan; racing car; patrol car, squad *or* police car, patrol wagon, Black Maria; ambulance, hearse; station wagon, beach wagon, suburban; dune buggy; Jeep; motor coach, charabanc; truck, panel truck, lorry, tractor, van, moving van, semitrailer; wrecker. *Colloq.,* paddy wagon. *Slang,* bus, flivver, [hot] rod; heap, jalopy; prowl car.

8, train, locomotive, passenger train, streamliner, turbo[liner], light rail vehicle, LRV; express, local, limited, freight train; subway [train], underground, tube, Métro; trolley, streetcar, cable car, interurban, tram, trackless trolley; freight car, boxcar, Pullman, sleeper, refrigerator car, tender, tank car, caboose; dining, smoking, lounge, *etc.* car, day coach. *Colloq.,* iron horse.

9, space vehicle (see ASTRONAUTICS).

10, driver, operator, busman, cabbie, carter, coachman; engineer; [bi]cyclist. See TRANSPORTATION, DIRECTION.
Verbs—start, turn over; drive (see DIRECTION).
Adjective—vehicular.

---

veil, *n.* net, mesh, curtain, screen, cloak, cover; film, haze, CLOUDINESS. —*v.t.* conceal, becloud, disguise, shield, cover, shroud. See CONCEALMENT, CLOTHING.

vein, *n.* blood vessel, rib (of a leaf); streak, stripe, marbling; [ore] deposit, lode, seam, ledge, leader; thread; bent, humor, disposition, temper. See FILAMENT, FEELING, NARROWNESS.

vellum, *n.* parchment, skin, sheepskin; papyrus; manuscript, document. See MATERIALS, WRITING.

VELOCITY

Nouns—**1,** velocity, speed, celerity, swiftness, rapidity, expedition (see HASTE); acceleration; hurry, spurt, rush, dash; smart, lively, swift, *or* spanking pace; flying, flight; gallop, canter, trot, run, scamper; race, horserace, steeplechase; sweepstakes, Derby; handicap; foot race, marathon, relay race. See HASTE, MOTION.

2, lightning, light, electricity, wind; cannonball, rocket, arrow, dart, quicksilver; whirlwind; telegraph, express train; torrent; hustler; eagle, antelope, courser, racehorse, gazelle, cheetah, greyhound, hare, deer, doe, jackrabbit, squirrel; jockey.

Verbs—**1,** speed, hasten, post, scuttle; scud, scour, scoot, scamper; run, fly, race, cut away, shoot, tear, whisk, sweep, whiz, skim, brush; bowl along; rush, dash, bolt; trot, gallop, bound, flit, spring, charge, dart; march in double time; ride hard, cover the ground. *Colloq.,* cut along, step along, step lively, zip, cut and run, make it snappy, cover ground, burn up the road, drive like Jehu. *Slang,* go all out, go hell-bent for election, go like a bat out of hell; watch one's dust *or* smoke; skedaddle; go hell-for-leather, burn up the road; hightail it, make tracks, lay rubber.

2, hurry, hasten (see HASTE); accelerate, quicken, step up; wing one's way; spur on; crowd on sail; gain ground; show a clean pair of heels; overtake, overhaul, outstrip. *Slang,* stir one's stumps, step on the gas, give her the gun, boot home.

Adjectives—fast, speedy, swift, rapid, quick, fleet; nimble, agile, expeditious, express; meteoric, breakneck, fast and furious; flying, galloping, light- *or* nimble-footed; winged, mercurial, electric, telegraphic; light of heel; swift as an arrow; quick as lightning *or* thought. *Colloq.,* flat-out.

Adverbs—swiftly, apace; at a great rate, at full speed, full tilt, posthaste; all sails crowding, heeling over, full steam ahead; trippingly; instantaneously; in seven league boots; with whip and spur; as fast as one's legs will carry one; at top speed; by leaps and bounds. *Colloq.,* on the double, at a fast clip, like mad, like sixty, like all possessed, like greased lightning, to beat the band, like a [blue] streak. *Slang,* P.D.Q., lickety-split, like a bat out of hell; jet-propelled.

Antonyms, see SLOWNESS.

---

velvet, *n.* silk, plush, velour, velure, velveteen; mossiness; SMOOTHNESS, SOFTNESS; *slang,* surplus, winnings, profit, graft. —*adj.* velvety, mossy;

smooth, soft, mild, soothing, bland; light, caressing.

venal, *adj.* money-loving, mercenary, sordid; corrupt, bribable, purchasable (of persons). See IMPROBITY.

vend, *v.* sell, purvey (see SALE); publish, issue.

vendetta, *n.* feud, grudge fight, vengeance. See CONTENTION, RETALIATION.

veneer, *n.* facing, overlay, coating, shell; superficial polish, façade. See LAYER, SHALLOWNESS, COVERING.

venerable, *adj.* aged, hoary; patriarchal; respected, revered. See AGE, OLDNESS.

veneration, *n.* esteem, RESPECT; admiration, WORSHIP; awe. See PIETY.

venereal, *adj.* sexual, genital, coital; syphilitic, luetic; gonorrheal, chancrous; aphrodisiac, cantharidian. See IMPURITY, PLEASURE.

vengeance, *n.* RETALIATION, revenge; vengefulness; reprisal, retribution; nemesis.

venial, *adj.* excusable, pardonable, slight, trivial. See VINDICATION.

venomous, *adj.* poisonous; envenomed, noxious, toxic, virulent, deadly; spiteful, malicious, malignant. See MALEVOLENCE, DISEASE, BADNESS.

vent, *v.t.* utter, express; let out, let off, emit, expel, discharge. *—n.* ventilator, OPENING, airhole, air pipe, outlet, funnel; emission; blowhole; utterance, expression. See EGRESS, DISCLOSURE, WIND.

ventilate, *v.t.* AIR; freshen; disclose, publish. See WIND, REFRESHMENT.

venture, *v.* dare, risk; speculate; undertake; presume, hazard, stake, take a chance. *—n.* enterprise, UNDERTAKING; adventure; speculation, hazard, risk. See CHANCE, COURAGE.

veracity, *n.* See TRUTH.

veranda, *n.* porch, gallery, piazza, portico. See RECEPTACLE.

verbal, *adj.* spoken, oral, unwritten; literal, verbatim, word-for-word. See SPEECH.

verbalize, *v.* express in words, phrase; expatiate. See SPEECH, FIGURATIVE, DIFFUSENESS.

verbatim, *adj.* word-for-word, literal, verbal, letter-perfect; unchanged, unedited. *—adv.* word for word, *sic, literatim.* See TRUTH.

verbose, *adj.* wordy, prolix, repetitive, talkative. See DIFFUSENESS.

verdant, *adj.* green, grassy; fresh, springlike; inexperienced, naïve, artless. See COLOR, VEGETABLE, UNSKILLFULNESS.

verdict, *n.* JUDGMENT, ruling, finding, decision, opinion, decree; determination, conclusion; award, sentence. See LAWSUIT.

verdure, *n.* grass, growth, greenness, greenery. See VEGETABLE.

verge, *n.* EDGE, brink, rim, marge, margin; point, eve; LIMIT. *—v.i.* be on the point (of); border, skirt, approach, touch; tend, incline. See TENDENCY, NEARNESS.

verify, *v.t.* corroborate, substantiate, confirm, prove, make certain, establish; identify. See EVIDENCE, DEMONSTRATION.

veritable, *adj.* real, genuine, authentic; proven, valid. See TRUTH.

vermin, *n.* pests, insects, rats, mice; scum, riffraff. See ANIMAL.

vernacular, *n.* tongue, dialect; argot, slang. See SPEECH.

versatile, *adj.* many-sided; adaptable; skilled. See SKILL, CHANGEABLENESS.

verse, *n.* versification; POETRY, prosody, poesy; line; stanza; meter, measure; poem, doggerel; passage. See PART.

versed, *adj.* skilled, skillful; knowledgeable; accomplished, trained, conversant. See SKILL, KNOWLEDGE.

version, *n.* rendition, account; translation. See INTERPRETATION.

vertex, *n.* top, apex, head, cap, crown, pinnacle; HEIGHT; acme, zenith.

VERTICAL

Nouns—**1,** vertical, perpendicular, upright; verticality, plumbness, aplomb, perpendicularity, orthogonality, ELEVATION, erection; right angle, normal, azimuth circle; square, plumb, plumbline, plummet. See STRAIGHTNESS, OBLIQUITY.

2, wall, precipice, cliff, steep, bluff, crag, escarpment, palisade.

Verbs—stand up, on end, erect, *or* upright, be vertical, draw up, get up, get to one's feet; erect, rear, raise; set, stick, cock, *or* raise up; upraise, upend, raise on its legs; true, plumb, square.

Adjectives—vertical, upright; erect, perpendicular, plumb, true, straight, bolt upright, up-and-down; sheer, steep; rampant, standing up; normal, rectangular, orthogonal, longitudinal.

Adverbs—vertically, uprightly, erectly, up, on end, right on end, *à plomb,* endways, endwise; on one's legs *or* feet; at right angles, square.

Antonyms, see HORIZONTAL.

vertigo, *n.* dizziness, giddiness, vertiginous. See INSANITY, ROTATION.

verve, *n.* gusto, vivacity, dash, fervor, elan, VIGOR. See FEELING.

very, *adv.* exceedingly, highly; emphatically, decidedly, notably; unusually, remarkably, uncommonly; extremely, surpassingly. See GREATNESS.

vessel, *n.* container; vase, urn, jug; boat, SHIP. See RECEPTACLE.

vest, *v.t.* furnish, endow, invest; clothe; give the power *or* right, enfranchise, authorize. See GIVING. —*n.* waistcoat; bodice; weskit. See CLOTHING, PROVISION.

vestibule, *n.* foyer, lobby, hall[way], reception hall; passage, entry[way]; anteroom *or* -chamber, alcove; narthex; porch, portico. See RECEPTACLE.

vestige, *n.* trace, REMAINDER, evidence, relic.

vestments, *n.pl.* canonicals (see CLOTHING).

vestry, *n.* vestiary, sacristy; chapel. See COUNCIL.

veteran, *n.* old man, elder, patriarch, graybeard; grandfather, grandmother; old campaigner, seasoned *or* old soldier, ex-soldier; octogenarian, nonagenarian, centenarian. *Colloq.,* oldster, old-timer, codger, gaffer. See COMBATANT, AGE.

veterinarian, *n.* veterinary, animal *or* horse doctor. *Colloq.,* vet. See DOMESTICATION.

veto, *n.* NULLIFICATION; no, *nyet;* pocket veto; disapproval, PROHIBITION. —*v.t.* turn thumbs down; forbid; disallow, prevent, disapprove, prohibit, negate; kill, quash. See REJECTION.

vex, *v.* tease, plague, harass, torment; roil, pique; fret, chafe, irritate, annoy, provoke, nettle. *Colloq.,* peeve, rile. See RESENTMENT, DISCONTENT.

via, *prep.* through, along, on, by way of, by means of, per. See DIRECTION.

viable, *adj.* fertile, capable; possible, potential; alive, living, vibrant; workable, practical. See LIFE, POSSIBILITY.

viaduct, *n.* trestle, bridge, span, arch. See CONNECTION.

vial, *n.* phial, flask, *flacon,* vessel, ampoule, test tube. See RECEPTACLE.

vibrant, *adj.* pulsing, athrob, seismic; resonant, sonorous; robust, healthy, dynamic, energetic, vital; vibratory. See VIGOR, OSCILLATION, AGITATION.

vibration, *n.* vibrating, shaking, shimmying; thrill, quiver, throb, pulsation; agitation, trembling; rattling. See OSCILLATION.

vicar, *n.* priest; deputy, AGENT. See

CLERGY, SUBSTITUTION.

vicarious, *adj.* substitutive; once removed, secondhand, indirect; proxy, deputy; imaginary, fictive, fictional. See SUBSTITUTION.

vice, *n.* viciousness, evildoing, wrongdoing, wickedness, iniquity, sin, sinfulness; crime, criminality; prostitution; defect, vice; immorality, IMPURITY, looseness of morals; demoralization, [moral] turpitude, depravity, degradation; weakness [of the flesh], fault, frailty, error; besetting sin; delinquency; sink of iniquity. See EVIL, BADNESS, IMPROBITY, WRONG.

vice versa, *adv.* oppositely, contrariwise, conversely, turnabout. See OPPOSITION.

vicinity, *n.* neighborhood, locality, vicinage; NEARNESS, proximity, environs, ENVIRONMENT.

vicious, *adj.* sinful, wicked, iniquitous, immoral, WRONG; criminal, disorderly; vile, felonious, nefarious, infamous, heinous; demoralized, corrupt, depraved, perverted; evil-minded, shameless; abandoned, debauched, degenerate, dissolute; reprobate, beyond redemption. See EVIL, IMPROBITY, IMPURITY.

vicissitude, *n.* CHANGE; change of fortunes; fluctuation.

victim, *n.* prey; sufferer, dupe, gull, cat's-paw; sacrifice, martyr. See CREDULITY, PURSUIT, RIDICULE.

victimize, *v.t.* cheat, dupe, swindle, hoax, fool, gull, deceive, hoodwink. *Colloq.*, sell, bamboozle. See DECEPTION.

victor, *n.* champion, winner; conqueror, vanquisher. See SUCCESS.

victory, *n.* conquest, triumph, SUCCESS; winning, mastery; the palm, laurel, wreath, award, trophy, prize, pennant.

victuals, *n.pl.* See FOOD.

vie, *v.i.* rival, emulate; contend, strive, compete. See CONTENTION.

view, *n.* sight; panorama, vista, prospect, scene; inspection, survey; purpose, aim; viewpoint, angle; opinion, BELIEF, notion; APPEARANCE, aspect. See VISIBILITY. —*v.t.* see; survey, scan; watch, witness; consider, regard, study. See VISION.

viewpoint, *n.* attitude, point of view, standpoint; outlook. See LOCATION, BELIEF, VISION.

vigil, *n.* watch, surveillance; wake; wakefulness. See CARE, ATTENTION, ACTIVITY.

vigilant, *adj.* alert, wary, watchful, wakeful, unsleeping; careful, cautious, circumspect; on the lookout, on the *qui vive*. See CARE.

vignette, *n.* decoration, ornament; picture, illustration, depiction, sketch, squib, piece, DESCRIPTION.

VIGOR

Nouns—**1,** vigor, force, might, vim, POWER, STRENGTH, ENERGY, potency, efficacy, ACTIVITY, vitality, virility; HEALTH, stamina; spirit, verve, warmth, exuberance, glow, sap, pith, bloom, tone, mettle, ELASTICITY. *Colloq.*, zip, get-up-and-go. *Slang,* pep, punch.

2, ardor, fire, enthusiasm, piquancy, pungency, intensity, trenchancy; vehemence, point, cogency.

Adjectives—**1,** vigorous, strong, mighty, powerful, potent, energetic, mettlesome, active, virile; healthy, hardy, hearty, hale, robust, SOUND, sturdy, stalwart, muscular, lusty, strenuous, well, buxom, brisk, alert, glowing, sparkling, in good health; thrifty, fresh, flourishing. *Slang,* peppy.

2, spirited, lively, racy, bold, nervous, trenchant, piquant, pungent, biting, slashing, sharp, severe; incisive, forcible, forceful, effective, cogent, pithy, pointed, full of point; picturesque, vivid, poetic. *Slang,* full of beans.

Adverbs—vigorously, powerfully, *etc.;* emphatically, in glowing terms.

Antonyms, see IMPOTENCE, WEARINESS.

---

vile, *adj*. base, debased, low, lowly, mean; repulsive, odious; foul, nasty; paltry; evil, villainous, corrupt, wicked, depraved. See BADNESS, DISREPUTE, UNIMPORTANCE.

vilify, *v.t.* vilipend, revile, calumniate, traduce, slander, libel, defame, decry, belittle, slur. See DETRACTION.

villa, *n*. mansion, chalet, chateau. See ABODE.

village, *n*. town, hamlet. See ABODE.

villain, *n*. blackguard, scoundrel; knave, rascal, rogue; badman; EVILDOER; *slang,* heavy, bad guy (see DRAMA).

villainy, *n*. roguery, rascality; criminality, depravity, wickedness, wrongdoing. See IMPROBITY.

vim, *n*. zest, ENERGY, VIGOR. *Colloq.,* pep, zip, ginger.

VINDICATION

Nouns—**1,** vindication, justification, warrant; exoneration, exculpation; acquittal; whitewashing; extenuation; palliation, softening, mitigation. See JUSTICE.
2, reply, defense, demurrer, exception; apology, plea, pleading; excuse, extenuating circumstances; allowance, argument. *Colloq.,* alibi.
3, vindicator, apologist, justifier, defender, defendant; proponent.

Verbs—**1,** vindicate, justify, warrant; exculpate, acquit (see ACQUITTAL); clear, set right, exonerate, whitewash; extenuate, palliate, excuse, soften; apologize, put a good face upon, smooth over, explain away; mince; gloss over, bolster up. *Colloq.,* give a clean bill of health.
2, defend; advocate; stand, stick, *or* speak up for; bear out, support; plead, say in defense; put in a good word for; talk up. *Slang,* go to bat for.
3, make allowance for, take the will for the deed, do justice to; give one his due, give the devil his due; make good; prove one's case.

Adjectives—vindicated, vindicating, vindicatory, vindicative; palliative; exculpatory; apologetic, vindicable; excusable, defensible, pardonable; venial, specious, plausible, justifiable.

Antonyms, see ACCUSATION, GUILT.

---

vindictive, *adj*. vengeful, spiteful, bitter; resentful; implacable, rancorous; bearing a grudge. See RETALIATION.

vine, *n*. climber, creeper, runner, twiner, tendril, vinelet; liana, bine, stem, shoot; grapevine, ivy, wisteria, *etc*. See VEGETABLE, AGRICULTURE.

vinegar, *n*. acetum, pickle; condiment, preservative. See SOURNESS.

vintage, *n*. crop, produce, harvest; viticulture, viniculture; [vintage] wine, *vin du pays;* time, age, style, period. See AGRICULTURE.

violate, *v*. break, breach; outrage, profane, desecrate; disrespect; transgress, infringe; usurp, encroach; rape, ravish. See ILLEGALITY, IMPURITY, BADNESS, DISOBEDIENCE, WRONG.

VIOLENCE

Nouns—**1,** violence, vehemence, intensity, impetuosity; boisterousness; turbulence, riot, row, rumpus, devil to pay, the fat in the fire; turmoil, DISORDER; AGITATION; storm, tempest, rough weather; squall, earthquake, upheaval, cataclysm, volcano, thunderstorm, cyclone, tornado, hurricane; maelstrom, whirlpool. See ILLEGALITY, EXCITABILITY, IMPULSE.

2, SEVERITY, ferocity, ferociousness, fierceness, rage, fury; fit, frenzy, paroxysm, orgasm; force, brute force; outrage, strain, shock, spasm, convulsion, throe; hysterics, tantrum, passion, EXCITEMENT.

3, outbreak, outburst; burst, discharge, volley, explosion, blast, detonation, backfire, rush, eruption, blowup; torrent; storm center.

4, explosive, cap, fuse, proximity fuse, detonator; powder, gunpowder, smokeless powder, guncotton; cordite, melinite, lyddite, dynamite, nitroglycerine, TNT (trinitrotoluene).

5, fury, fiend, dragon, demon, tiger; wild beast; fire-eater, hellion, hellcat, virago, termagant, beldame; madcap; rabble rouser, lynch mob, terrorist, agitator, *agent provocateur;* thug, tough, strongarm man, gunman.

Verbs—**1,** be violent, run high; ferment, effervesce; rampage; run wild, run riot; break the peace; run amuck, raise a riot; lash out, make the fur fly; bluster, rage, roar, riot, storm; seethe, boil [over]; fume, foam, come in like a lion, wreak, wreck, spread havoc, ride roughshod, out-Herod Herod; spread like wildfire. *Colloq.,* make *or* kick up a row, raise the devil, raise Cain, raise the roof; roughhouse; fly off the handle; blow one's top, let off steam.

2, break, fly, *or* burst out; explode, implode, go off, fly, detonate, thunder, blow up, flash, flare, burst; shock, strain.

3, stir up, excite, incite, urge, lash, stimulate; inflame, kindle, foment, fulminate, touch off, set off; convulse, infuriate, madden, lash into *or* goad to fury; fan the flames, add fuel to the flames.

Adjectives—**1,** violent, vehement; ungentle, boisterous, rough-and-tumble, wild, untamed; impetuous, frenetic, bestial, barbaric; rampant; dog-eat-dog.

2, turbulent; disorderly, blustering, raging, troublous, riotous, tumultuous, obstreperous, uproarious; extravagant, unmitigated; ravening, frenzied, desperate (see RASHNESS); infuriated, furious, outrageous, frantic, hysterical; fiery, flaming, scorching, [red-]hot; seething; savage, fierce, ferocious, barbarous; headstrong, ungovernable, uncontrollable; convulsive, explosive; volcanic; stormy.

Adverbs—violently, *etc.;* amain; by storm, by force, by main force; with might and main; tooth and nail; with a vengeance; headlong.

Antonyms, see MODERATION.

---

violin, *n.* fiddle; string; Amati, Stradivarius, Strad, Guarnerius; violinist; (*pl.*) string section. See MUSIC.

viper, *n.* adder, snake, serpent; traitor, turncoat, Judas [Iscariot], Iago, double dealer; viperess. *Slang,* rat. See ANIMAL, IMPROBITY.

virago, *n.* termagant, vixen, shrew, maenad, hellcat. See IRASCIBILITY.

virgin, *n.* maiden, celibate, vestal; spinster. —*adj.* chaste, untouched; maidenly, fresh, virginal, pure; new, uncut, unexplored, primeval. See CELIBACY, NEWNESS, PURITY.

virile, *adj.* manly, masculine, macho; vigorous, potent; fully-sexed. See STRENGTH, VIGOR.

virtual, *adj.* practical; implied, implicit; substantial; true, veritable; potential. See INTRINSIC.

VIRTUE

Nouns—virtue; virtuousness, GOODNESS; morality; moral rectitude; integrity, PROBITY; nobleness; prudence; morals, ethics, DUTY; cardinal virtues; merit, worth, excellence, credit; self-control; fortitude, self-denial; good deeds, good behavior; discharge, fulfillment, *or* performance of duty; INNOCENCE. See RIGHTNESS, GOODNESS, PIETY.

Verbs—practice, virtue; do, fulfill, perform, *or* discharge one's duty; redeem one's pledge; behave; command *or* master one's passions; keep on the straight and narrow path; set an example, be on one's good *or* best behavior.

Adjectives—virtuous, good, innocent; meritorious, deserving, worthy, correct; dutiful, duteous, moral, right, righteous, right-minded; well-intentioned, creditable, laudable, commendable, praiseworthy; above *or* beyond praise; excellent, admirable; sterling, pure, noble, exemplary, matchless, peerless; saintly, saintlike; heaven-born, angelic, seraphic.

Antonyms, see EVIL, IMPROBITY.

---

virtuosity, *n.* dilletantism, dabbling; SKILL, mastery, proficiency, technique, know-how, expertise; finesse, flair, dexterity. *Slang,* chops.

virtuoso, *n.* consummate ARTIST, artiste; connoisseur. See TASTE.

virulent, *adj.* poisonous, venomous; deadly; toxic, noxious; malignant, malevolent; caustic, acrimonious. See BADNESS, DISEASE, RESENTMENT.

vìrus, *n.* venom, poison, contagium, germ, microorganism. See DISEASE.

visa, *n.* endorsement, validation, stamp. See ASSENT.

visage, *n.* face, countenance, physiognomy; semblance, look, aspect, guise. *Slang,* puss, phiz, map. See APPEARANCE, FRONT.

vis-à-vis, *adv.* face-to-face, *tête-à-tête,* facing. —*prep.* opposite, contra, versus, against; contrasted to, as opposed to. See OPPOSITION.

viscous, *adj.* viscid; ropy, glutinous, slimy; mucid; sticky, mucilaginous; oleaginous, greasy. See COHERENCE.

vise, *n.* clamp, gripper, clinch. See RETENTION.

VISIBILITY

Nouns—visibility, perceptibility; conspicuity, precision; APPEARANCE, manifestation, exposure [to view]; ocular proof, evidence, *or* demonstration; field of view, range; high *or* low visibility, visibility zero; view, prospect, horizon. See VISION.

Verbs—**1,** appear, show, gleam, glimmer, glitter, glare, meet *or* catch the eye, materialize; present, show, manifest, produce, discover, reveal, expose, *or* betray itself; stand out *or* forth, peep *or* peer out, crop out; start, spring, show, turn, *or* crop up; float before the eyes, be conspicuous, be prominent, attract the attention, speak for itself. *Colloq.,* stand out like a sore thumb.

2, expose to view; bring out; show, display, reveal, expose, disclose (see DISCLOSURE).

Adjectives—visible, visual, perceptible, perceivable, noticeable, observable, discernible, external, outward, seeable, to be seen; in [full] view, in sight, in the open, exposed to view; distinct; apparent, manifest, evident, obvious, unhidden, unclouded, conspicuous, prominent, in the public eye, in view, glaring, staring, standing out; before one, before one's eyes, under one's nose. *Colloq.,* plain as the nose on one's face.

Adverbs—visibly, perceptibly, *etc.;* in sight of, before one's eyes, *à vue d'oeil,* as large as life.

Antonyms, see INVISIBILITY.

VISION

Nouns—**1,** vision, sight, optics, eyesight, seeing; view, look, espial, glance, ken; glimpse, glimmer, peep, *coup d'oeil;* focus; gaze, stare, leer; perception, contemplation; regard, survey; observance, observation, examination, half an eye, surveillance; inspection (see INQUIRY); reconnaissance, watch, espionage, autopsy; ocular inspection; sightseeing; perspicacity, discernment. *Slang,* look-see; once-over; eyeful.

2, 20-20 vision, *etc.;* farsightedness, eagle eye; nearsightedness, myopia; myosis, astigmatism, presbyopia; double vision, colorblindness, Daltonism, night *or* day blindness, nyctalopia, hemeralopia; strabismus, cross-eyes, cock-eyes; squint, cast, cataract, opthalamania; goggle-eyes, wall-eyes.

3, point of view, viewpoint; vantage point; stance; observatory; gazebo, loophole, crow's nest; belvedere, watchtower; peephole, lookout post; field of view; grandstand, bleachers; theater, amphitheater, arena, vista, horizon; VISIBILITY; prospect, perspective (see APPEARANCE); commanding view, bird's-eye view; periscope; spectator, viewer (see PRESENCE).

4, visual organ, organ of vision; eye; eyeball; naked eye; retina, pupil, iris, cornea, white, canthus. *Colloq.,* optics, orbs, peeper, peeled *or* weather eye.

5, refraction, distortion; illusion, optical illusion, mirage, phantasm, specter, apparition; reflection, mirror, image.

Verbs—**1,** see, behold, discern, perceive, have in sight, descry, sight, make out, spot, lay *or* set eyes on, catch sight of, pick out, discover, distinguish, recognize, spy, espy, get *or* catch a glimpse of; command a view of; watch, witness, look on; cast one's eyes on; see at a glance.

2, look, view, eye; lift up one's eyes, open one's eyes, look around, survey, scan, inspect, contemplate, take the measure of; run one's eye over, reconnoiter, glance around, direct one's eyes to, observe, peep, peer, pry, take a peep; stare [down]; strain one's eyes; fix *or* rivet eyes on, feast one's eyes on; gaze; pore over; leer, ogle, glare; goggle, stare, gape, gawk, gawp; cock one's eye. *Slang,* get a load of, give the once-over, size up.

3, dazzle, blind (see BLINDNESS); wink, blink, squint; screw up one's eyes; have a mote in the eye; see through a glass darkly.

Adjectives—visual, ocular, seeing; optic[al]; ophthalmic; shortsighted, blear; farsighted; clear-sighted; eagle-, hawk-, lynx-, Argus-, *or* keen-eyed; visible; misty, dim.

Adverbs—visibly; in sight of, with one's eyes open; at [first] sight, at a glance; out of the corner of one's eye; at first blush; *prima facie.*

Antonyms, see BLINDNESS.

---

visionary, *adj.* idealistic, unpractical, quixotic, Utopian; imaginary, delusory, chimerical. —*n.* dreamer, idealist, theorist, theorizer. See IMAGINATION, HETERODOXY, NONEXISTENCE.

visit, *n.* call; interview, appointment; stopover, sojourn. —*v.* call on, drop in; stop, stay, tarry; sojourn; afflict, assail. See ARRIVAL, SOCIALITY.

visitation, *n.* visit; calamity, misfortune; seizure, stroke, blow; disaster; bad luck, hardship. See ADVERSITY, DISEASE.

visor, *n.* beaver, vizard, mask, domino, [eye] shield, eyeshade, sunshade, peak, brim. See COVERING.

vista, *n.* view, prospect, scene; landscape; panorama. See APPEARANCE, VISION.

visualize, *v.t.* picture, envision; imagine, project. See IMAGINATION.

vital, *adj.* essential, indispensable, necessary; life-supporting; vivifying, invigorating; alive, live, vibrant, animate; fatal. See LIFE, ORGANIC MATTER, NECESSITY.

vitality, *n.* LIFE; VIGOR, energy, virility; viability. See STRENGTH.

vitiate, *v.t.* adulterate, weaken; impair, spoil; destroy, void, invalidate; corrupt, contaminate, pollute; deteriorate. See DETERIORATION.

vitreous, *adj.* glassy, crystalline, vitriform; brittle, hard; transparent, translucent. See TRANSPARENCY, BRITTLENESS.

vituperate, *v.t.* vilify, abuse, revile; reproach, inveigh (against), rebuke, scold, upbraid; objurgate, tongue-lash. See DETRACTION, DISAPPROBATION.

vivacious, *adj.* lively, animated, sprightly; gay, breezy, spirited; frolicsome, sportive, cheerful. See ACTIVITY, CHEERFULNESS.

vivid, *adj.* striking; telling; picturesque; animated, bright; lifelike, realistic; lively, vital; vibrant, glowing; fresh, intense, unfaded, brilliant. See COLOR, LIGHT, VIGOR.

vixen, *n.* harridan, shrew, witch, scold, virago, harpy. See FEMALE, EVILDOER.

vocabulary, *n.* words, glossary, wordlist; dictionary, lexicon; language. See SPEECH.

vocal, *adj.* articulate; spoken, [to be] sung; choral, lyric; verbal, oral. See SPEECH, MUSIC.

vocalist, *n.* singer; tenor, alto, *etc. Slang,* crooner, warbler, songstress, thrush, nightingale. See MUSIC.

vocation, *n.* profession; work, trade; calling, occupation. See BUSINESS.

vociferous, *adj.* loud, noisy, clamorous; blatant, obstreperous, loudmouthed. See LOUDNESS, CRY.

vogue, *n.* mode, style, FASHION; practice, custom, usage; favor, HABIT.

voice, *n.* vocality; speaking *or* singing voice; inflection, intonation; tone of voice; ventriloquism, ventriloquy; lung power; vocal cords, vocalization (see SPEECH); CRY, expression, utterance, vociferation, enunciation, articulation; accent[uation]; emphasis, stress; singer (see MUSIC); representation, vote, participation (see CHOICE). —*v.t.* speak, utter; give voice, utterance, *or* tongue to; shout, CRY, exclaim, ejaculate; express; vocalize, articulate, enunciate, pronounce, enounce, announce; accentuate; deliver, mouth. See PUBLICATION.

void, *adj.* empty, vacuous, blank; unoccupied, untenanted; devoid, lacking, unfilled; ineffectual; null, invalid; not binding; vain, unreal, unsubstantial. —*v.t.* vacate; abrogate, nullify, negate; evacuate, eject, cast off. See EJECTION. —*n.* emptiness, SPACE, nothingness; vacuum; abyss, chasm. See ABSENCE, NULLIFICATION, INSUBSTANTIALITY, NONEXISTENCE.

volatile, *adj.* gaseous, vaporizable; fickle, changeable, mercurial; unstable, transient; light, giddy; lively; capricious; buoyant, airy. See VAPOR, CHANGEABLENESS, TRANSIENTNESS.

volition, *n.* WILL, CHOICE, voluntariness; option, preference, willingness.

volley, *n.* broadside, salvo, fusillade, raking, round; burst. See ATTACK.

voluble, *adj.* talkative, verbose; fluent, glib. See LOQUACITY.

volume, *n.* book, tome; contents, capacity; bulk, mass, dimensions, SIZE, QUANTITY. See GREATNESS, PUBLICATION.

voluminous, *adj.* capacious, big, bulky, copious; prolix; ample. See SIZE.

voluntary, *adj.* free-will, volunteered, willing, spontaneous, willed, unasked; unforced; deliberate, intentional. See WILL, CHOICE.

volunteer, *n.* enlister; offerer. —*v.* enlist; OFFER, proffer; give, donate. See WILL, UNDERTAKING.

voluptuous, *adj.* sensual, carnal, fleshy, meretricious; epicurean, worldly. *Slang,* sexy. See PLEASURE, INTEMPERANCE.

vomit, *v.t.* throw up, disgorge; belch, spew, eject. See EJECTION.

voodoo, *n.* wanga, obeah, fetishism, witchcraft, black magic; witch doctor, shamanist, medicine man, sorcerer. See SORCERY.

voracious, *adj.* ravenous, omnivorous; rapacious; starving, famished, hungry; gluttonous, edacious. See GLUTTONY, DESIRE.

vortex, *n.* eddy, whirlpool; maelstrom; whirl; storm center. See ROTATION, WATER.

votary, *n.* votarist, devotee, disciple, follower, enthusiast, adherent, zealot. *Colloq.,* fan. —*adj.* votive, dedicated; consecrated; pledged; devoted. See DESIRE, AUXILIARY.

vote, *n.* poll, ballot; franchise, suffrage; CHOICE, voice, option, election; referendum, plebiscite. —*v.* cast a ballot; choose, select, elect, establish, enact, ratify, veto, nullify. See ASSENT.

vouch, *v.* guarantee, warrant; affirm, declare; answer for, attest; certify; support, back, bear witness. See AFFIRMATION, EVIDENCE, SECURITY.

voucher, *n.* receipt, stub; warrant, testimonium, EVIDENCE, record, support. See SECURITY.

vow, *v.* swear, take oath; vouch, affirm; pledge, PROMISE; dedicate, devote; take vows. —*n.* dedication, devotion; oath, swearing; pledge, PROMISE; consecration. See AFFIRMATION.

voyage, *n.* cruise, sea trip, crossing, sail, excursion. See TRAVEL, MOTION.

voyeur, *n.* Peeping Tom; lecher, pervert, psychopath. See CURIOSITY.

VULGARITY

Nouns—**1,** vulgarity, vulgarism; barbarism; offense, bad taste; INELEGANCE, indelicacy; gaucherie, ill-breeding, DISCOURTESY, incivility; coarseness, indecorum, boorishness; rowdyism, blackguardism; ribaldry, obscenity, pornography; risqué story, *double-entendre*.

2, gaudiness, tawdriness, finery, frippery, brummagem, tinsel, gewgaws, knickknacks (see OSTENTATION).

3, vulgarian, rough diamond; tomboy, hoyden, cub, unlicked cub; lout, churl, knave, clown, cad, roughneck, barbarian; snob, parvenu, frump, slattern, slut. *Colloq.,* bounder.

Verbs—offend, coarsen, vulgarize; misbehave, roughhouse. *Slang,* gross out.

Adjectives—**1,** vulgar, in bad taste, crass, crude; distasteful, fulsome, unrefined, coarse, indecorous, ribald, gross; unseemly, unpresentable; common, boisterous, loud, rough and ready; tasteless, obnoxious; backwoods.

2, uncourtly; uncivil, discourteous, ill-bred, bad-mannered, ill-mannered; ungentlemanly, unladylike, unfeminine; unkempt, uncombed, frowzy, unpolished, uncouth, rude, savage, blackguard, rowdy, barbarous, barbaric; low, vile, ignoble, monstrous, shocking; obscene. See POPULACE.

3, bizarre, outré, outlandish; affected, meretricious, ostentatious, extravagant; gaudy, tawdry, flashy, showy; cheap; shoddy; obtrusive.

Antonyms, see TASTE.

---

vulnerable, *adj.* open (to attack); weak, defenseless, assailable, susceptible. See DANGER, WEAKNESS.

vulpine, *adj.* foxlike; foxy, crafty, wily, CUNNING.

vulture, *n.* predator, scavenger; condor, buzzard, griffon; extortionist, bloodsucker, vampire, parasite, jackal, harpy. See EVILDOER, ANIMAL.

W

wacky, *adj., slang,* erratic, odd, demented. See INSANITY, UNCONFORMITY.

wad, *n.* lump, plug, stuffing, filling, batting, wadding; bankroll. See SIZE, MONEY.

waddle, *n.* toddle, shamble, lurch, waggle, sway, duck walk. See SLOWNESS.

wade, *v.* walk through, traverse, ford; wallow, slog, slosh; stand up to one's ankles (in); *colloq.,* wade into, attack, undertake. See WATER, UNDERTAKING.

wafer, *n.* biscuit, cracker, cookie; lozenge, tablet, troche. See FOOD, NARROWNESS, LAYER, RITE.

waft, *v.* float, buoy, convey, transport, carry; roll, wave. See WIND, TRANSPORTATION.

wag, *v.* wave, shake, sway, jerk, waggle, wigwag, nod. See OSCILLATION, AGITATION. —*n.* WIT, humorist; shake. See OSCILLATION.

wage, *v.t.* wager; conduct, make, carry on, engage in, undertake. See WARFARE, UNDERTAKING, CHANCE.

wager, *n. & v.* bet, stake, gamble, risk, hazard, gage. See CHANCE.

wages, *n.pl.* pay, PAYMENT, hire, compensation, remuneration; earnings, salary, income.

wagon, *n.* cart, dray, buckboard, wain; truck, lorry, car; van. See VEHICLE, TRANSPORTATION.

waif, *v.i.* stray, foundling; [street] Arab; homeless child; vagrant. See TRAVEL, RELINQUISHMENT.

wail, *v.i.* lament, CRY, moan, bewail; howl, ululate, caterwaul; complain. See LAMENTATION.

waist, *n.* girth, middle, midriff, loin, waistline; bodice, blouse, shirt, tunic. See CLOTHING.

wait, *v.* stay, linger, tarry, abide, remain, bide [one's time]; dally, procrastinate, delay; serve, attend; await, expect, look for. *Slang,* sit tight; cool one's heels; sweat it out. See EXPECTATION.

waiter, *n.* SERVANT, *garçon,* attendant, steward, servitor, waitress, carhop; tray, salver (see RECEPTACLE).

waive, *v.* relinquish, renounce, give up, forgo, disclaim, surrender (a right or claim); defer. See DISUSE, RELINQUISHMENT.

waiver, *n.* quitclaim (see RELINQUISHMENT).

wake, *n.* path, track, trail, swath; vigil, watch. See REAR, INTERMENT, PASSAGE. —*v.* [a]rouse, awak[en]; stir, excite, animate. See ACTIVITY, EXCITEMENT.

wakeful, *adj.* alert, watchful, on guard, on the *qui vive,* vigilant; restless, sleepless, insomniac. See CARE, ACTIVITY.

walk, *n.* ramble, stroll, promenade, wander, saunter, TRAVEL (on foot), march, parade, tramp, hike; path[way]; gait, carriage, tread, pace, step; calling, occupation; sphere, province, department, BUSINESS. *Colloq.,* constitutional. See MOTION, SLOWNESS, PASSAGE.

wall, *n.* side, partition, bulkhead, flange, splashboard; rampart, DEFENSE; barrier; fence; cliff, precipice; levee, dike, seawall; (*pl.*) PRISON. See ENCLOSURE, HINDRANCE, VERTICAL, CIRCUMSCRIPTION.

wallet, *n.* purse, pocketbook, billfold; bag, pouch, sack, moneybag; pack, knapsack. See RECEPTACLE.

wallop, *v.* thrash, beat, strike, punch, hit, clout. See IMPULSE.

wallow, *v.i.* tumble, grovel, roll, flounder, welter, toss; revel, delight in, luxuriate in. See LOWNESS, PLEASURE, INTEMPERANCE.

wan, *adj.* pale, pallid, waxen, waxy, ashen, ashy, bloodless. See COLORLESSNESS.

wand, *n.* rod, caduceus, mace, scepter; staff, stick, baton; divining rod, dowsing stick; withe. See SORCERY.

wander, *v.i.* rove, ramble, stroll, walk, range; digress, swerve, deviate, stray; rave, maunder, be delirious;

moon; straggle, forage. See TRAVEL, DEVIATION, INSANITY, MOTION.

wane, *v.i.* DECREASE, lessen, ebb, fade, diminish, peter out, dwindle; abate, subside; decline, sink, fail, slacken. —*n.* failure, ebb, decline, decay, DECREASE.

wangle, *v., colloq.,* wheedle, inveigle, coax; extort, wring, wrench; contrive, get by hook or crook. *Slang,* con, rustle up. See STEALING, ACQUISITION.

want, *n.* need; POVERTY, indigence; lack, dearth, deficiency, ABSENCE; shortage, inadequacy, scarcity; NECESSITY, requirement. —*v.* lack, need; be in need; require, DESIRE, wish, crave; fall short of, be deficient, miss, omit, neglect, fail. See INSUFFICIENCY.

wanting, *adj.* lacking, missing, absent. See ABSENCE.

wanton, *adj.* lewd, licentious, loose, dissolute, immoral; frolicsome, abandoned, capricious, willful; wild; heartless, malicious; heedless, reckless, wayward, perverse; luxuriant, rampant, exuberant. See IMPURITY. —*n.* libertine; flirt, baggage, hussy, trollop. See EVILDOER, FREEDOM.

war, *n. & v.* See WARFARE.

warble, *v.* trill, sing, quaver. See MUSIC.

ward, *v.t.* watch, guard, defend, protect; fend, parry, stave [off]. —*n.* watch, guard, DEFENSE, protector; CARE, charge, custody; protégé[e], dependent, minor; precinct, district; hospital room. See REPULSION, REGION, REMEDY, PRISON, SUBJECTION.

warden, *n.* keeper; game warden, church warden; custodian, curator; ranger; jailer, turnkey; superintendent. See SAFETY, AUTHORITY.

warder, *n.* keeper; gatekeeper; warden; guard; mace, staff. See SAFETY.

wardrobe, *n.* CLOTHING, outfit, togs, duds, apparel, attire, livery, uniforms, finery; clothes closet, cloakroom, vestry. See RECEPTACLE.

warehouse, *n.* STORE, depot, supply dump, storehouse.

wares, *n.pl.* merchandise, goods, commodities; products, stock in trade, provisions, kitchenware, tableware, *etc.* See SALE.

WARFARE

Nouns—**1,** warfare, state of war, fighting, hostilities; war, combat; ARMS, force of arms, the sword; appeal to arms; baptism of fire, ordeal of battle; war to the death, open war, internecine war, civil war; world *or* global war; war to end war; revolutionary war, REVOLUTION, religious war, crusade; underground warfare; guerrilla warfare; chemical, germ, *or* bacteriological warfare; trench warfare, war of position, war of attrition; aerial, naval, conventional, nuclear, *or* atomic warfare; Mars, Ares, Odin, Bellona; cold *or* hot war; nuclear deterrent, first-strike capability; balance of power, deterrence. See KILLING.

2, campaign[ing], crusade, expedition, invasion; investment; siege; battle, fighting (see CONTENTION); call to arms, mobilization; trumpet, clarion, bugle, pibroch; slogan; war cry, war whoop; rebel yell, battle cry; beat of drum; tom-tom; password, watchword; muster, rally; service, active service, action; inactive service. See ATTACK.

3, battlefield, battleground, field; theater, front; camp, encampment, bivouac, billet; flank, center, salient, line; beachhead, airhead. See ARENA.

4, art of war, tactics, strategy, generalship, soldiership; ballistics, ordinance, gunnery; chivalry; weapons (see ARMS); logistics.

5, warrior, soldier (see COMBATANT); camp follower.

6, warlikeness, belligerence, bellicosity, combativeness, contentiousness; militarism; chauvinism, jingoism (see PRIDE); warmonger.

Verbs—**1,** war, go to war; declare war, carry on *or* wage war, let slip the dogs of war; cry havoc; take the field, give *or* join battle; set *or* fall to, engage, measure swords with, cross swords; come to blows, come to close quarters; fight, combat; contend (see CONTENTION); battle with; fight it out, fight hand to hand; sell one's life dearly. *Colloq.*, flex one's muscles.

2, arm; raise troops, mobilize; enroll, enlist, sign up; draft, conscript, call to the colors, recruit; serve, be on active service; campaign; wield the sword, bear arms; live by the sword, die by the sword; take up arms; shoulder a musket, smell powder, be under fire; spill blood. *Colloq.*, join up. See COMPULSION.

Adjectives—**1,** warring, battling, contending, contentious; armed [to the teeth], sword in hand; in *or* under arms, up in arms; at war with; in battle array, in open arms, in the field; embattled, beleaguered, besieged.

2, warlike, belligerent, combative, bellicose, martial; military, militant; soldierlike, soldierly; chivalrous; strategic, tactical.

Adverbs—at war, in the thick of the fray, in the cannon's mouth; at swords' points; on the warpath.

Antonyms, see PACIFICATION.

---

warhorse, *n.* charger, courser, destrier (*archaic*); *colloq.*, veteran, vet, war dog, old-timer; *slang*, standby, old reliable. *Slang*, chestnut. See SKILL, COMBATANT.

warlock, *n.*, *archaic*, wizard, sorcerer, necromancer. See SORCERY.

warm, *adj.* hot, tepid, lukewarm; sunny, mild, summery; close, muggy; ardent, fervid, fervent, passionate; new, fresh; earnest, intimate; warmhearted, responsive, glowing, enthusiastic, hearty, affectionate, cordial; lively, excitable, feverish, hasty, quick; alive, living. See HEAT, FEELING, EXCITEMENT, BENEVOLENCE, FRIEND.

warmonger, *n.* [war] hawk, war dog; war lord, militarist, mercenary; drumbeater, flagwaver, saber-rattler, firebrand, instigator; jingo[ist], xenophobe, rabblerouser. See WARFARE, COMBATANT.

WARNING

Nouns—**1,** warning, forewarning, CAUTION, *caveat;* notice; premonition, foreboding, PREDICTION; lesson; admonition, monition; alarm; THREAT. See DISSUASION.

2, warning sign, handwriting on the wall; *mene, mene, tekel, upharsin;* red flag; tip-off; foghorn; monitor, warning voice, Cassandra, signs of the times, Mother Carey's chickens, stormy petrel, bird of ill omen; gathering clouds, clouds on the horizon; symptom; watchtower, beacon, lighthouse; a cloud no bigger than a man's hand; straw in the wind. See SAFETY, INDICATION.

3, sentinel, sentry, lookout; watch[man]; patrol, picket, scout, spy, advance guard, rear guard; watchdog, housedog; Cerberus.

Verbs—**1,** warn, caution; forewarn, prewarn; admonish, premonish, exhort; forebode; give notice *or* warning; menace; threaten, look black; put on one's guard; sound the alarm; cry wolf; ring the tocsin. *Colloq.*, tip off.

2, beware, take warning, take heed; keep watch; stop, look, and listen.

Adjectives—warning, premonitory, monitory, cautionary; admonitory, admonitive;

symptomatic; ominous, foreboding; warned, on one's guard, careful, cautious.
Interjections—beware! take care! look out! watch out! *cave canem! caveat emptor!*

Antonyms, see RASHNESS.

---

warp, *v.* twist, bend, serve, distort; bias, prejudice; pervert, deviate; incline. See DISTORTION. —*n.* bias; deflection, tendency; torsion, twist, malformation. See DEVIATION.

warrant, *n.* warranty, guaranty; pledge, SECURITY, surety; authority; summons, writ, permit, pass; sanction; justification. —*v.t.* guarantee, indemnify, vouch for, answer for, certify, secure; affirm; state, maintain; assure, support, sanction, authorize, justify. See PERMISSION, VINDICATION, AFFIRMATION, EVIDENCE.

warren, *n.* hutch, rabbitry; slum[s], tenement, shantytown. See ABODE.

warrior, *n.* See COMBATANT.

warship, *n.* See SHIP, ARMS.

wart, *n.* growth, blemish, excrescence, callous, protuberance. See CONVEXITY.

wary, *adj.* guarded, watchful, alert, cautious, suspicious, discreet, prudent, chary, scrupulous. See CARE, CAUTION.

wash, *v.* clean, cleanse, deterge, bathe, lave; wet, soak, rinse, drench; purify; irrigate, inundate, flood; scrub, swab, launder; paint, tint, COLOR; sweep; lap, lick; brim over, overflow. See CLEANNESS, PAINTING, WATER.

washout, *n., slang,* FAILURE.

washroom, *n.* lavatory, wash-up, bathroom, restroom. See CLEANNESS.

washstand, *n.* sink, washbowl, washbasin, lavabo, lavatory, commode, washpot, water butt. See CLEANNESS, RECEPTACLE.

waspish, *adj.* snappish, petulant, irascible; slender-waisted. See IRASCIBILITY, NARROWNESS.

WASTE

Nouns—**1,** waste, wastage; dissipation; DISPERSION; ebb; leakage, LOSS; wear and tear; extravagance, wastefulness, prodigality, conspicuous consumption; *jeunesse dorée;* misuse; wasting, DETERIORATION. See USE, INSUFFICIENCY, WEAKNESS.

2, waster, wastrel, spendthrift, spender, prodigal, squanderer, profligate. *Colloq.,* sport.

Verbs—**1,** waste, spend, misspend, expend, USE, MISUSE, use up, consume, swallow up, overtax, exhaust; impoverish; spill, drain, empty; disperse; cast, fool, throw, fling, *or* fritter away; burn the candle at both ends; go *or* run through, squander; waste powder and shot, labor in vain; pour water into a sieve; leak, run out; ebb, melt away, run dry, dry up; deteriorate; throw to the winds; cast pearls before swine; throw good money after bad. *Colloq.,* blow.

2, be wasted, give out; go to waste, go for nothing.

Adjectives—wasted, thrown away; wasteful, penny-wise and pound-foolish; prodigal, profligate, improvident, thriftless, unthrifty, extravagant, lavish, consumptive.

Phrase—easy come, easy go.

Antonyms, see STORE, PARSIMONY, ECONOMY.

---

wasteland, *n.* wilderness, desert, barren land. See USELESSNESS.

wastrel, *n.* spendthrift (see WASTE).

watch, *v.* look (at), scrutinize, examine; view, stare, ogle; regard, follow, survey; be alert, guard; chaperone, tend, babysit; oversee, superintend; wait, guard, patrol. —*n*. vigil, surveillance, sentry duty; guardianship, CARE; supervisor; guard, watchman, sentinel, lookout; timepiece, pocket watch, wristwatch. See SAFETY, VISION, CHRONOMETRY.

watchdog, *n*. bandog, bloodhound, mastiff; police dog; censor, monitor, policeman; guard[ian]. See DEFENSE, SAFETY.

watchful, *adj*. alert, vigilant, observant. See ATTENTION, CARE.

watchtower, *n*. beacon, lighthouse; lookout *or* observation post. See VISION, INDICATION.

watchword, *n*. countersign, shibboleth; password, catchword; slogan. See INDICATION.

WATER

Nouns—**1,** water, MOISTURE, wetness; drinking water, spring water, mineral water; sea *or* salt water, fresh water; serum, serosity; lymph; rheum; diluent; dilution, maceration, lotion; washing, immersion, infiltration, infusion, irrigation; douche, bath; baptism, rain, deluge, spate, flood, high water, flood tide. See FLUIDITY, CLEANNESS.

2, a. river, waterway, stream, tributary, branch, fork, creek, brook, watercourse, spring, fount, fountain, rill, rivulet, streamlet, runnel, tributary; channel (see PASSAGE); riverbed, wadi, arroyo; torrent, rapids, flood, freshet; current, tide, race. **b.** waterfall, falls, cascade, linn; cataract; jet, Niagara; rapids, white water, shoot, chute; fountain, geyser. **c.** gulf, bay, cove, harbor, arm (of the sea), fiord. **d.** ocean, sea, great sea, high seas; Atlantic, Pacific, Indian, Arctic *or* Antarctic ocean; *mare nostrum*, Mediterranean, Arabian, Caribbean, *etc*. sea; salt water, deep water, blue water; the [bounding] main, the [briny] deep; the Seven Seas, the frozen seas; the billow, wave, tide, *or* flood; the deep blue sea, wine-dark sea; Father Neptune, Poseidon; the watery waste; lake, lagoon, pond, pool, tarn, lakelet, mere; undertow. **e.** marsh, swamp (see MOISTURE). **f.** well, cistern, tank; reservoir, dam. See PASSAGE.

3, rain, rainfall, precipitation; cloudburst, downpour; thunderstorm; shower, drizzle; rainstorm, monsoon, rainy season; deluge, flood, inundation, spate, torrent, cataclysm.

4, wave, billow, surge, swell, ripple, rollers, surf, breakers, heavy sea; undercurrent, eddy, vortex, whirlpool, maelstrom; waterspout; jet, spurt, squirt, spout; splash, plash; rush, gush, sluice.

5, hydraulics, hydrodynamics, hydrology, hydrokinetics, hydrostatics, hydroponics.

Verbs—**1,** be watery; be awash *or* afloat; swim (in), brim.

2, water, wet; moisten; dilute; dip, immerse, submerge, plunge, souse, douse, dunk, duck, drown; go under; drench, soak, steep, macerate, pickle; wash, sprinkle, lave, bathe, splash; slop; irrigate, inundate, deluge; syringe, douche, inject, gargle.

3, flow, run; issue, gush, pour, spout, roll, stream; rain, drizzle; drop, drip, dribble, drain, trickle, percolate; bubble, gurgle, spurt, ooze; spill, overflow.

Adjectives—**1,** watery, liquid, aqueous, aquatic, lymphatic; balneal, diluent; brimming, drenching, diluted; weak; wet, moist, soppy, sopping, soaked, wet to the skin, waterlogged.

2, oceanic, marina, maritime, briny; tidal, fluent, flowing, streaming, meandering; riparian, alluvial; lacustrine; marshy, swampy, boggy, paludal, miry, sloppy; showery, asea, under water.

Antonyms, see LAND, AIR.

---

watercourse, *n.* river (see WATER).

waterfall, *n.* cascade, falls (see WATER).

waterproof, *adj.* water-repellent *or* -resistant, watertight; leakproof, impermeable; seaworthy, hermetic, sealed. See DRYNESS, SAFETY, CLOSURE.

watershed, *n.* runoff, catchment basin; basin, reservoir; crisis, crux, crossroad[s], milestone. See HEIGHT, IMPORTANCE.

watertight, *adj.* water-repellent, waterproof; airtight, safe, binding, legal, ironclad, unbreakable. See DRYNESS, CLOSURE.

waterway, *n.* channel (see WATER).

wave, *v.* wag, shake, sway, flutter, stream (in the wind); signal, motion, gesture, indication; roll, undulate; ripple, swell, billow, flood, surge; flaunt, flourish. —*n.* sea, tide, WATER, ripple, billow, *etc.*, wavelet, undulation; signal, gesture, flourish; CONVOLUTION, curl; marcel, permanent, finger wave. See OSCILLATION, FASHION.

waver, *v.i.* vacillate, fluctuate, hesitate; sway, tremble, totter; undulate; teeter. See DOUBT, OSCILLATION.

wax, *v.* cere, grease, coat, smooth, polish; grow, INCREASE, strengthen. See SMOOTHNESS. —*n.* tallow, paraffin, beeswax, cerumen, OIL.

way, *n.* PASSAGE, road, route, path, roadway, highway, channel, street, avenue; journey, progression, transit; trend, tendency; approach, access, gateway; METHOD, manner, mode, style, fashion; SPACE, interval, stretch, distance; usage, custom, HABIT, practice, wont; course, routine; PLAN; CONDUCT, form; behavior; scheme, device; knack; charm, winsomeness.

wayfarer, *n.* traveler, walker, hiker, rambler, wanderer, pilgrim, journeyer. See TRAVEL.

waylay, *v.t.* accost, buttonhole, detain; attack, SURPRISE. See HINDRANCE.

wayward, *adj.* perverse, willful, forward; delinquent; capricious, changeable, wanton; rebellious; irregular, accidental. See CHANGEABLENESS, DISOBEDIENCE.

weak-minded, *adj.* moronic, idiotic, imbecilic, feebleminded; brainless, foolish, witless, empty-headed, vacuous; vacillating, irresolute, fickle. See IGNORANCE, DOUBT.

WEAKNESS

Nouns—**1,** weakness, feebleness, debility, debilitation, infirmity, decrepitude, inanition; WEARINESS, enervation, IMPOTENCE; paleness, COLORLESSNESS; disability, attenuation, senility, superannuation, malnutrition, atony, asthenia, adynamia, cachexia, hyposthenia, anemia; invalidity, delicacy, frailty, foible, fragility, flaccidity, vapidity; invalidation, adulteration, dilution; vulnerability, perishability, accessibility; Achilles' heel. See DETERIORATION.
2, reed, thread, rope of sand, house of cards, house built on sand; child, baby, kitten, cat, chicken; water, milk and water, gruel.
3, weakling, softling, poor specimen, wimp; invalid, asthenic, hypochondriac; deficient, defective, dunce, imbecile, lackwit, wreck, runt; faintheart, jellyfish; weathercock. *Colloq.*, sissy, softy, betty, baby, crybaby, whiner; pantywaist, mollycoddle, milksop, namby-pamby, softhead, weak sister, nebbish. *Slang,* doormat, pushover, fancy pants.
4, see UNCERTAINTY, IMPERFECTION, BRITTLENESS, COWARDICE, DOUBT, CHANGEABLENESS.

Verbs—**1,** be weak, faint, drop, crumble, droop, sag, fade, fail, flag, pine, decline, languish, give way, give in; deteriorate, waste, falter, halt, limp; black out; soften, relent, relax, yield, submit, succumb; totter, tremble, dodder, potter, shake, have one foot in the grave. *Colloq.,* keel over, cave in.

2, weaken, enfeeble, debilitate, enervate, emasculate, devitalize, take the edge off, take the starch out of, wear down; deplete, WASTE; bate, soften up, slacken, blunt; disintensify; undermine, sap, impair, damage, cripple, lame, maim, disable, paralyze.

3, dilute, thin, cut, water [down], attenuate, adulterate, debase; reduce, depress, lower, lessen, impoverish, invalidate.

Adjectives—weak[ly], feeble, infirm, invalid, debile, senile, decrepit; sickly, poorly, unhealthy, unsound; weakened, enfeebled, *etc.;* strengthless, impotent, defenseless; anemic, asthenic, atonic, cachectic, hyposthenic, adynamic, bloodless, short-winded; out of shape; faltering, drooping, *etc.;* unsteady, shaken, palsied, laid low, weak as a child, baby, *or* kitten; flimsy, flabby, frail, fragile; effeminate; vulnerable, assailable, indefensible; unsupported, unaided, unassisted. *Colloq.,* doddering, namby-pamby, wish-washy; on one's last legs, on one's knees. *Slang,* woozy.

Antonyms, see STRENGTH, POWER, VIGOR, RESOLUTION.

---

wealth, *n.* riches, fortune, opulence, affluence; PROSPERITY; MEANS, resources, property, MONEY; plenty, plenitude, luxuriance, excess, plethora, sufficiency.

wealthy, *adj.* rich, affluent, opulent, moneyed; worth a fortune; well-to-do, well-off; rich as Croesus. *Colloq.,* made of money, rolling in money; flush, in funds. *Slang,* well-heeled, in the chips, in the money, loaded, filthy rich; rolling in dough; in the big time; rolling high. See MONEY, PROSPERITY.

wean, *v.* separate, withdraw, deprive; estrange, grow up; alienate. See DISUSE.

weapon, *n.* See ARMS.

wear, *v.* last, endure; USE, show, display; tire, fatigue, weary; bear, don, put on; carry, have on; waste, consume, spend; rub, chafe, fray, abrade; jibe, tack, veer, yaw. See WEARINESS, FRICTION. —*n.* CLOTHING, garb; USE, usage, hard usage; impairment, wear and tear. See DETERIORATION.

WEARINESS

Nouns—**1,** weariness, tiredness, exhaustion, lethargy, lassitude, fatigue; drowsiness, languor, languidness; WEAKNESS, faintness. See DEJECTION, INDIFFERENCE.

2, bore, proser, nuisance. *Colloq.,* wet blanket. *Slang,* drip, creep, pain in the neck, deadhead.

3, wearisomeness, tedium, tediousness, dull work, boredom, ennui, sameness, monotony, twice-told tale; heavy hours, time on one's hands.

Verbs—**1,** weary; wear, wear *or* tire out, tire, fatigue, jade; bore, weary, *or* tire to death; send *or* put to sleep; wear thin, frazzle, exhaust; run ragged, burn out; weigh down; harp on, dwell on. *Slang,* do in.

2, be weary of, never hear the last of; be tired of; gasp, pant; yawn. *Colloq.,* peter out. *Slang,* climb the wall, be fed to the gills *or* teeth, have had it, crump out.

3, bore [to tears]. *Slang,* bore stiff.

Adjectives—**1,** wearying, wearing, arduous, fatiguing, tiring; wearisome, tiresome, irksome; uninteresting, stupid, bald, devoid of interest, dry, monotonous, dull, drab, dreary, tedious, trying, humdrum, flat, wooden; prosy, soporific, somniferous.

2, weary, tired, spent, fatigued; toilworn, footsore; winded, out of breath; drowsy, played out, sleepy; uninterested, flagging; used up, worn out; dog-tired, ready to drop, more dead than alive, played out; exhausted, breathless, short-winded, dead tired, dead on one's feet; prostrate, on one's last legs, *hors de combat*. *Colloq.*, fed up, all in. *Slang*, done up, pooped [out], bushed, fagged, beat, tuckered out, zonked out.

3, bored, sick and tired, blasé, jaded.

Adverbs—wearily, boringly, tiresomely, *etc.; ad nauseam.*

Antonyms, see ENERGY, AMUSEMENT.

---

weasel, *n.* ermine, suck-egg; sneak, skulker, trickster, hedger. See ANIMAL, AVOIDANCE. —*v., colloq.,* equivocate, bandy words, hem and haw, hedge, renege. *Slang,* pussyfoot, welsh. See FALSEHOOD.

weather, *n.* clime, climate. See AIR.

weatherbeaten, *adj.* weathered, seasoned, inured, acclimatized, casehardened. See DETERIORATION.

weathercock, *n.* girouette, weathervane; opportunist. See CHANGEABLENESS.

weatherman, *n.* meteorologist, weather forecaster. See PREDICTION.

weave, *v.* interlace, intertwine, twine, entwine; loom, spin, fabricate; plait, pleat, pleach, braid, mat; contrive, construct. See CROSSING, PLAN.

web, *n.* cobweb, spiderweb; weaving, TEXTURE, mesh, net; network, hookup; trap, snare, scheme, plan; tissue, gossamer. See CROSSING.

wed, *v.* marry, espouse; couple, blend, join. See MARRIAGE, UNITY.

wedge, *n.* quoin, chock, sprag, block, shim. See ANGULARITY.

wee, *adj.* tiny, little, minute, small; infinitesimal, microscopic; diminutive, petite. *Colloq.,* teenyweeny. See LITTLENESS.

weed, *v.t.* root out, extirpate, clear (of weeds); cull; remove, eliminate. See CLEANNESS, EXCLUSION. —*n.* pest, nuisance; *colloq.,* tobacco, smoking. See VEGETABLE, AGRICULTURE, PUNGENCY.

weeds, *n.pl.* mourning, black, widow's weeds. See LAMENTATION.

week, *n.* seven-night (see TIME).

weep, *v.* shed tears, CRY, lament, wail, sob, blubber; mourn, grieve; rain, flow, drip. See LAMENTATION.

weigh, *v.* measure (weight); lift, heft; balance, scale, counterbalance; examine, ponder, consider, mull over, estimate; tell, count; weigh down, be heavy, drag, load, press; oppress, burden, depress; overbalance, bear down. See GRAVITY, MEASUREMENT, ELEVATION, INFLUENCE.

weight, *n.* heaviness; heft; overweight, avoirdupois, tonnage, poundage; GRAVITY; ballast; measurement; IMPORTANCE, INFLUENCE; significance; pressure, load, burden. See QUANTITY. —*v.* ballast, load, burden; favor; adjust, compensate. See COMPLETION.

weightless, *adj.* light, feathery; disembodied, immaterial, incorporeal, intangible; floating, drifting, lighter than air. See LEVITY, INSUBSTANTIALITY.

weighty, *adj.* ponderous, heavy; burdensome, onerous; influential. See GRAVITY, IMPORTANCE, INFLUENCE.

weird, *adj.* uncanny, eldritch, eerie; ghostly, spectral, unearthly; supernatural. *Colloq.,* spooky. See UNCONFORMITY, DEMON.

welcome, *n.* greeting, salutation, cordial reception. *Slang,* glad hand. —*v.t.* greet, salute; embrace, receive (gladly), hail. —*adj.* pleasing, agreeable, acceptable, wanted, gratifying. See COURTESY, SOCIALITY, PLEASURE.

weld, *v.t.* fuse, unite, join, fasten; blend. See JUNCTION, UNITY.

welfare, *n.* well-being; PROSPERITY, advancement, profit, sake, benefit; social work; happiness, success. See GOODNESS, PAYMENT.

well, *adj.* healthy, robust, strong, hale, hearty, in good health. —*adv.* rightly, properly; thoroughly, skillfully, accurately; amply, sufficiently, fully, adequately; favorably, worthily; very much; quite, considerable; easily, handily. See HEALTH, SUFFICIENCY, SKILL. —*n.* fount, font, wellspring, wellhead, reservoir, spring; source, origin; hole, pit, shaft. See WATER, CONCAVITY. —*v.i.* issue, gush, brim, flow, jet, rise. See EGRESS.

well-being, *n.* good, PROSPERITY; euphoria, good health, SANITY, robustness, CONTENT, PLEASURE, contentment.

wellbred, *adj.* well-behaved *or* -brought-up; noble, wellborn, gentle; courteous, polished, sauve, polite. See COURTESY, NOBILITY.

well-heeled, *n., slang,* see WEALTHY.

well-informed, *adj.* well-read, well-versed. See KNOWLEDGE.

well-known, *adj.* familiar, recognized, famous, renowned; notorious. See KNOWLEDGE.

well-meaning, *adj.* well-intentioned, with the best intentions, kind[ly], well-disposed, sympathetic. See BENEVOLENCE.

well-nigh, *adv.* very nearly, almost. See NEARNESS.

well-off, *adj.* prosperous, fortunate; wealthy. See PROSPERITY, MONEY.

well-read, *adj.* learned, erudite, scholarly, bookish, educated; well-informed. See LEARNING, KNOWLEDGE.

well-rounded, *adj.* complete, thorough. See COMPLETION.

wellspring, *n.* fountainhead, wellhead, *fons et origo,* source. See CAUSE.

well-to-do, *adj.* comfortable, well-off; prosperous, affluent, wealthy, rich. See MONEY.

welsh, *v.* welch; default on, fail, hedge, renege; leave high and dry, leave holding the bag. See NONPAYMENT.

welt, *n.* wale, weal; edging, rim; binding; cord, ridge, rib. See EDGE, CONVEXITY, DISEASE.

welter, *n.* confusion, turmoil; jumble, hodgepodge, mishmash; ruck, masses; ferment. —*v.i.* wallow. See DEPRESSION, ROTATION, AGITATION.

wench, *n.* girl, maiden, lass[ie], servant; maid; slut, slattern, tart, trollop, harlot. *Slang,* broad, piece. See IMPURITY, FEMALE.

werewolf, *n.* wolf-man, lycanthrope, *loup-garou;* changeling. See DEMON.

west, *n.* Occident; Europe; wild west. See DIRECTION.

wet, *adj.* damp, moist, dewy; clammy, dank, humid, dripping; rainy, showery, foggy, misty; soaked, drenched, saturated; watery, waterlogged. —*v.t.* soak, moisten, dampen, drench, saturate; immerse, dip, sprinkle; rain upon. —*n.* wetness, WATER; rain, fog, dew, mist; dampness, MOISTURE, clamminess, *etc.;* antiprohibition.

wet blanket, *n., slang,* spoilsport, killjoy; Cassandra, pessimist, alarmist; prophet of gloom *or* doom, crepehanger. *Slang,* party pooper. See DEJECTION, HINDRANCE, WEARINESS.

whale, *n.* cetacean; finback; blue, humpback, killer, sperm, sulphur-bottom, *or* right whale; orca, rorqual, narwhal, blackfish, dolphin, porpoise, grampus; Moby Dick. *Colloq.,* whopper. See SIZE, ANIMAL.

wharf, *n.* dock, pier, quay, landing; waterfront. See EDGE.

what, *pron.* that which; sort of, kind of; which; how; whatever, whatsoever, whichever. See GENERALITY.

whatnot, *n.* thing, something, what have you, whatever; cabinet, étagère, china closet. *Colloq.,* contraption, doodad. *Slang,* thingumabob, blankety-blank; doohickey, dingbat, gismo. See RECEPTACLE.

wheedle, *v.t.* coax, cajole, persuade; court, humor, flatter. See SERVILITY, FLATTERY.

wheel, *n.* disk, circle, roller; roulette *or* fortune's wheel; bike, bicycle; *slang,* V.I.P., big wheel, bigwig. See CIRCULARITY, VEHICLE, IMPORTANCE. —*v.* roll; trundle, cycle; rotate, revolve, spin, twirl; pivot, about-face, turn, gyrate, whirl, wind. See ROTATION, DEVIATION.

wheelbarrow, *n.* pushcart, barrow. See TRANSPORTATION.

wheeze, *v.* breathe hard, gasp, puff, choke. —*n.* old joke, gag, chestnut. See WIND, WIT.

when, *adv.* at what time?, at the same time; whereupon, just then, whenever. See TIME.

whence, *adv.* See ATTRIBUTION.

where, *adv.* in what place; whereabouts, whither; in what direction, from what source, place, *etc.* See LOCATION, INQUIRY.

whereabouts, *n.* locality, LOCATION.

whereas, *conj.* inasmuch as, since, while, as, in view of, forasmuch as, in consideration of, considering that, seeing that. See ATTRIBUTION, CAUSE.

whereupon, *adv.* whereat, after which. See SEQUENCE.

wherewithal, *n.* MEANS, resources; MONEY, funds, cash, capital, assets; power, ability, competence. *Colloq.,* the stuff, the goods, what it takes.

whet, *v.t.* sharpen, hone, whetstone, grind; excite, stimulate, provoke, stir up, kindle, quicken, inspire. See SHARPNESS, EXCITEMENT, DESIRE.

whether, *conj.* if, in case; if it is so; in either case. See QUALIFICATION.

whiff, *n.* puff, waft, blast; inhalation. See ODOR, WIND.

while, *conj.* during, as long as, whilst, whereas; although. —*v.* pass the time, kill time. See TIME.

whim, *n.* caprice, fancy, DESIRE, vagary; notion, quirk, crotchet, whimsy; freak; impulse. See WIT, IMAGINATION.

whimper, *v. & n.* cry, whine. See LAMENTATION.

whimsical, *adj.* curious, odd, peculiar, freakish; humorous, waggish, droll; crotchety, capricious, queer, quaint. See CHANGEABLENESS, WIT.

whine, *v.i.* CRY, whimper, complain, moan, snivel. *Slang,* gripe, bellyache. See LAMENTATION.

whip, *n.* lash, scourge; quick motion, snap. —*v.t.* lash, beat, flog; thrash; conquer, subdue; defeat. See SUCCESS.

whirl, *n.* spin[ning], gyration, turn; flutter, tizzy, confusion; pirouette. —*v.* spin, twirl, turn, rotate, revolve, gyre, gyrate; dance, pirouette. See ROTATION.

whirligig, *n.* merry-go-round, carrousel; rotor, roller, *etc.;* top. See ROTATION.

whirlpool, *n.* eddy, swirl; vortex, maelstrom. See WATER, ROTATION.

whirlwind, *n.* tornado, twister, cyclone, typhoon, hurricane, windstorm. See WIND. —*adj.* fast, speedy, headlong, breakneck, dizzying. See VELOCITY.

whisk, *n.* [egg]beater; whiskbroom. —*v.* whip, froth, beat; sweep; swish, whish; zip. See AGITATION, VELOCITY.

whiskers, *n.pl.* beard, hair, stubble; hirsuteness; mustache, sideburns, goatee, Vandyke, muttonchops, *etc.;* bristles; feelers, antennae. See ROUGHNESS.

whiskey, *n.* [hard] liquor, spirits; bourbon, rye, corn; firewater. *Colloq.,* booze, moonshine, bootleg. *Slang,* hooch, white mule, rotgut, redeye. See FOOD, DRINKING.

whisper, *n.* murmur, whispering, sigh, breath; hint, intimation, rumor, gossip, plot; aside, stage whisper. See INFORMATION, NEWS, SPEECH, SOFTNESS. —*v.* murmur, breathe, divulge, reveal, hint, intimate. See DISCLOSURE, CONCEALMENT.

whistle, *n. & v.* pipe, piping, flute.

See WIND, LOUDNESS, SOUND, MUSIC.

white, *adj.* snow-white (see COLOR, COLORLESSNESS); cleansed, purified; Caucasian, Caucasoid. See HUMANITY. —*n.* whiteness, purity; hoariness, grayness (of age); lime, paper, milk, ivory, snow, sheet, alabaster; albinoism, blondness, fairness; pallor, ashiness, waxiness, bloodlessness; bleach, etiolation; silveriness; glare, LIGHT, lightness; INNOCENCE, stainlessness.

white elephant, *n.* nuisance, embarrassment; dead weight, deadwood, drag, burden, impediment; plague, cross. *Slang,* lemon. See GIVING, USELESSNESS.

whitewash, *v.t.* calcimine, kalsomine; whiten; vindicate, exonerate; *colloq.,* shut out, blank. *Slang,* skunk. See COVERING, VINDICATION, FLATTERY.

whittle, *v.* shape, carve; pare, cut, slice, shave; deduct, curtail, dock, diminish; dwindle, eat away, erode. See DISJUNCTION.

who, *pron.* which one?; that. See INQUIRY.

WHOLE

Nouns—**1,** whole, totality, totalness, integrity; entirety, ensemble, collectiveness; UNITY, completeness, indivisibility, integration, embodiment; integer.

2, the whole, all, everything, total, aggregate, one and all, gross amount, sum, sum total, *tout ensemble,* length and breadth of, alpha and omega, be-all and end-all; bulk, mass, lump, tissue, staple, body, trunk, bole, hull, hulk, skeleton. *Colloq.,* ball game. *Slang,* whole kit and caboodle, whole show, whole shebang, whole shooting match; the works.

Verbs—form *or* constitute a whole; integrate, embody, amass; aggregate, assemble; amount to, come to, add up to.

Adjectives—**1,** whole, total, integral, entire, all, complete; one, individual; wholesale, sweeping.

2, unbroken, uncut, undivided, unsevered, unclipped, uncropped, unshorn; seamless; undiminished; undemolished, undissolved, undestroyed; indivisible, indissoluble, indissolvable.

Adverbs—wholly, altogether; totally, completely, entirely, all, all in all, wholesale, in a body, collectively, all put together; in the aggregate, in the mass, in the main, in the long run; *en masse,* on the whole, bodily, throughout, every inch, substantially, by and large.

Antonyms, see PART.

wholesale, *adj.* bulk, job-lot, jobbing; extensive, indiscriminate; at a discount, cheaper; mass, sweeping, general, widespread. See WHOLE, GENERALITY, BARTER.

wholesome, *adj.* healthy, beneficial. See HEALTH, PURITY.

whore, *n.* prostitute, harlot, bawd, strumpet, streetwalker, call girl, B-girl, daughter of joy. See EVILDOER, IMPURITY.

why, *adv.* wherefore? what for? for what cause? *Slang,* how come? See CAUSE, ATTRIBUTION.

wicked, *adj.* EVIL, bad; criminal, depraved, iniquitous; cruel, heartless, sinful, vicious, immoral; difficult, disagreeable; *colloq.,* mischievous. See WRONG.

wicker, *n.* twig, vimen, shoot, rod, osier, willow, withe, sallow; rattan, straw, buri, raffia; wickerware. See CROSSING.

wicket, *n.* gate, door; window; hoop, arch; turnstile. See OPENING.

wide, *adj.* spacious, widespreading, comprehensive; generous, ample, all-embracing; broad, large, roomy, extensive; vast, open; general. See BREADTH, EXPANSION.

widespread, *adj.* general, common, rife, universal, prevalent; ubiquitous; extensive, inclusive, all-embracing; global. See GENERALITY, DISPERSION, EXPANSION.

widow, *n.* survivor (of a husband), relict, dowager; divorcée, grass widow. See DIVORCE.

width, *n.* BREADTH, broadness; wideness, span, beam; extent, expanse.

wield, *v.t.* handle, manipulate, ply; brandish, flourish, wave, shake; employ, control, manage. See USE, OSCILLATION.

wife, *n.* married woman; mate, spouse, *Frau;* housewife, helpmeet, helpmate. *Slang,* the Mrs., madam, little woman, old lady, ball and chain, better half. See MARRIAGE.

wig, *n.* toupée, toupet; peruke, periwig, switch, transformation; fall; headdress. *Slang,* doily, divot, rug. See COVERING, ORNAMENT.

wiggle, *v.i.* squirm, shake, wriggle, wobble, wag, shimmy. See AGITATION.

wigwam, *n.* hut, lodge; teepee. See ABODE.

wild, *adj.* savage, untamed, uncivilized; feral, bloodthirsty, fierce; uncontrolled, amuck, frenzied; inaccurate, intemperate, unwise, foolish; eager, impetuous, stormy, violent, unrestrainable, desert, uninhibited; rank, thick, junglelike, luxuriant; untended, uncultivated; shy, skittish; daring, reckless, rash, breakneck; freak. See VIOLENCE, EXCITABILITY.

wildcat, *n.* lynx, puma, mountain lion, panther, ocelot. See ANIMAL. —*adj., colloq.,* risky, speculative, venturesome, shoestring; unauthorized, splinter, spontaneous. See DANGER, ILLEGALITY, RASHNESS.

wilderness, *n.* wasteland, waste[s], wilds, badlands; desert, sands, Sahara. See SPACE, USELESSNESS.

wild-goose chase, *n.* fool's errand, chasing rainbows; red herring, snipe hunt, chasing one's own tail, tilting at windmills. See USELESSNESS.

wile, *n.* stratagem, subterfuge, ploy; trick, dodge. See CUNNING.

WILL

Nouns—will, free will, volition, conation, velleity; FREEDOM, discretion; option, CHOICE; voluntariness, spontaneity, spontaneousness; pleasure, wish, mind; frame of mind, disposition, proclivity, inclination, willingness, readiness, willing mind *or* heart; INTENTION, predetermination; self-control, determination, RESOLUTION.

Verbs—will, see fit, think fit; determine, resolve, settle, choose, volunteer; have a will of one's own; have one's own way; exercise one's discretion; take responsibility; take upon oneself, find it in one's heart; do of one's own accord.

Adjectives—**1,** voluntary, volitional, willful, intentional; free, optional; discretionary; prepense; intended; arbitrary; autocratic; unbidden, unspontaneous; original (see CAUSE).

2, willing, minded, disposed, inclined, favorable; favorably inclined *or* disposed to; nothing loath; in the mood *or* humor; ready, forward, earnest, eager; bent upon, desirous, predisposed; voluntary, unasked, unforced.

Adverbs—voluntarily, at will, at pleasure; *ad libitum,* as one thinks proper, according to one's lights; with good grace; of one's own accord *or* free will; by choice, purposely, intentionally, deliberately.

Antonyms, see NECESSITY, UNWILLINGNESS.

---

willful, *adj.* self-willed, arbitrary; headstrong, wayward, obstinate, stubborn, unruly; intentional, deliberate, premeditated. See WILL.

willing, *adj.* minded, disposed (see WILL); bent upon, desirous, predisposed; docile, agreeable, easygoing, tractable, pliant; cordial, hearty; content, assenting, voluntary, gratuitous, spontaneous. See ASSENT.

willingness, *n.* voluntariness (see WILL); penchant, DESIRE; docility, pliability; good will; alacrity, eagerness; ASSENT, compliance, CONSENT; PLEASURE.

will-o'-the-wisp, *n.* ignis fatuus; illusion, chimera. See IMAGINATION, LIGHT.

willy-nilly, *adv.* will I, nill I; *nolens volens;* like it or not, whether or not; perforce, inescapably. See COMPULSION, NECESSITY.

wilt, *v.i.* droop, sag; weaken, languish, wither; collapse. See DETERIORATION.

wily, *adj.* designing, tricky, crafty, foxy; deceitful, crooked, Machiavellian; clever, subtle, CUNNING.

wimp, *n.* weakling (see WEAKNESS, IMPOTENCE).

win, *v.* beat, conquer, master; gain, obtain, get; achieve, accomplish, reach; persuade, sway, convince, influence; succeed, triumph, surpass. See ACQUISITION, SUCCESS, BELIEF.

wince, *v.i.* flinch, RECOIL; shy, quail, shrink. See FEAR, PAIN.

winch, *n.* See WINDLASS.

wind, *v.* twist, [en]twine; coil, curl, spiral; bandage, loop; enfold, infold; wreathe, roll; crank, reel; sinuate, meander, wander. See CONVULSION, DEVIATION, ROTATION.

WIND

Nouns—**1,** wind, windiness, draught, draft, flatus, afflatus, AIR; breath [of air]; puff, whiff, blow, drift; aura; stream, current, undercurrent; [in]sufflation, inflation; blowing, fanning, ventilation.

2, gust, blast, flurry, breeze, zephyr, squall, gale, half a gale, storm, tempest, hurricane, whirlwind, tornado, samiel, cyclone, twister, typhoon, simoom; harmattan, khamsin, chinook, monsoon, trade wind, sirocco, mistral, bise, tramontane, foehn, levanter; capful of wind; fresh *or* stiff breeze; blizzard; rough, foul, *or* dirty weather; dirty sky, mare's tail.

3, anemography, aerodynamics; wind gauge, anemometer, pneumatics; weathercock, [weather]vane; Beaufort scale, Fujita-Pearson scale.

4, breathing, respiration, sneezing, sternutation; hiccough, hiccup; catching of the breath.

5, Aeolus, Boreas, Eurus, Zephyr, Notus, cave of the winds.

6, airpump, lungs, bellows, blowpipe, fan, ventilator, vacuum cleaner, wind tunnel; air pipe (see PASSAGE); funnel; sailboat, windjammer (see SHIP).

Verbs—**1,** blow, waft; stream, issue; freshen, gather; storm; blow up, bluster; sigh, moan, scream, howl, whistle; breeze.

2, breathe, respire, inhale, exhale, puff, pant; whiffle, gasp, gulp, wheeze; snuff[le], sniff[le]; sneeze, cough; expire.

3, fan, ventilate; inflate; blow up, pump up.

Adjectives—windy, blowing, breezy, gusty, squally; stormy, tempestuous, blustering; boisterous; pulmonic, pulmonary, pneumatic.

Antonyms, see REPOSE.

---

windbag, *n., slang,* bag of wind; braggart, blusterer; gossip, chatterer. *Slang,* gasbag, gasser, big mouth, blabbermouth. See LOQUACITY, BOASTING.

windfall, *n.* bonus, prize, blessing, boon; treasure trove, find; pennies *or* manna [from heaven], godsend, discovery. See ACQUISITION.

windjammer, *n.* sailboat, sailing SHIP;

sailor (see NAVIGATION).

windlass, *n.* hoist, lifter; moulinet, reel, capstan, pinion, winch, crank. See ELEVATION.

window, *n.* casement, dormer, OPENING; pane; bay window, oriel; port[hole]; skylight; embrasure, loophole.

windpipe, *n.* airpipe, trachea; throat, throttle; weasand. See PASSAGE.

windup, *n., colloq.,* END, termination, conclusion, closure, settlement, climax, denouement, resolution, outcome, upshot; preliminaries, preparation. See COMPLETION.

wine, *n.* the grape; drink, liquor; DRINKING, intoxication; stimulant, alcohol; nectar.

wing, *n.* pinion, [feathered] limb, pennon, ala; arm, sail; flank; ell, annex, extension; airfoil; flight, flying. —*v.* fly; disable, wound. See ADDITION, AVIATION, COMBATANT, DRAMA, SIDE.

wink, *v.* blink, nictitate, nictate, squint, twinkle; overlook, ignore, condone. See VISION, FORGIVENESS, NEGLECT, INDICATION.

winning, *adj.* conquering, victorious, triumphant; winsome, captivating, charming, engaging, entrancing, prepossessing, comely, attractive; persuasive, convincing. See LOVE, SUCCESS, BEAUTY.

winnow, *v.t.* select, cull, sift, separate, glean, pick; ventilate, fan. See CHOICE, CLEANNESS.

winsome, *adj.* gay, merry, lively, sportive; charming, winning, captivating; lovable, adorable, pleasant, attractive. See LOVE, ENDEARMENT.

winter, *n.* wintertime, COLD; hibernation. See CHRONOMETRY.

wipe, *v.t.* clean, rub, brush, dust, mop; dry, towel. See CLEANNESS, DRYNESS.

wire, *n.* (metal) thread, FILAMENT; flex, cord, line; telephone, telegraph, cable; cablegram, telegram. See COMMUNICATION.

wireless, *n.* radio; radiogram, marconigram. See COMMUNICATION.

wiry, *adj.* filamentous, filar, threadlike; strong, muscular, sinewy; tough; flexible. See FILAMENT, STRENGTH.

wise, *adj.* sage, sagacious; learned, profound, deep; judicious, well-advised; *colloq.,* impudent, rude. See KNOWLEDGE, INSOLENCE. —*n.* manner, METHOD.

wisecrack, *n., slang,* crack, quip, witticism, comeback, answer. See WIT.

wish, *n.* DESIRE, WILL; pleasure; craving, yearning, want, hankering; INTENTION. —*v.* want, long for, dream of, hope for, ask [for], yearn, crave, hanker. See HOPE, DESIRE.

wishy-washy, *adj.* washed-out, anemic, colorless; weak-kneed *or* -willed, spineless, irresolute, feeble, vacillating. See INSIPIDITY, WEAKNESS.

wisp, *n.* bundle; tuft, lock. See ASSEMBLAGE.

wistful, *adj.* musing, pensive, thoughtful; desirous, wishful, hopeful; eager; craving, yearning. See DESIRE, FEELING, THOUGHT.

WIT

Nouns—**1,** wit, wittiness; Atticism; salt; sense of humor, funny bone, esprit, point, fancy, whim, humor, drollery, pleasantry; comedy; jocularity, jocosity, jocoseness; levity, facetiousness; waggery, waggishness; comicality. *Colloq.,* crazy bone.

2, farce, buffoonery, clowning, fooling, tomfoolery; harlequinade; broad farce, broad humor, slapstick; fun; smartness, banter, badinage, retort, repartee, riposte; RIDICULE; horseplay. *Slang,* monkey business.

3, witticism, jest, joke, conceit, quip, one-liner, quirk, quiddity, pleasantry; sally, wheeze; flash of wit, scintillation; *mot, bon mot,* smart saying, epigram; dry wit, cream of the jest. *Slang,* comeback, gag, [wise]crack, running gag.

4, wordplay, play on words, pun, punning, *double entendre,* equivocation; conundrum, riddle (see SECRET); trifling. *Slang,* chestnut.

5, wit, wag; joker, jester, buffoon; comedian, comic, humorist, punster; merry-andrew, fool; practical joker, funmaker. *Colloq.,* gagman. *Slang,* wisecracker.

Verbs—be witty, joke, jest; crack a joke; pun; make fun of, make sport of; retort; banter. *Colloq.,* kid. *Slang,* wisecrack, come back at.

Adjectives—witty, Attic, quick-witted, nimble-witted; smart, jocular, jocose, droll, funny, waggish, facetious, whimsical, humorous; playful, merry, pleasant, sprightly, sparkling, epigrammatic, pointed, comic.

Adverbs—jokingly, jestingly, *etc.;* in jest, in sport, in play; in fun; not seriously.

Antonyms, see WEARINESS.

---

witch, *n.* hag, beldam[e], crone; shrew, scold, dragon; sorceress, enchantress; charmer. See UGLINESS, BEAUTY, SORCERY, EVILDOER.

witch hunt, *n.* vigilantism, persecution, baiting; purge, investigation, inquisition, McCarthyism, redbaiting, superpatriotism. See WRONG, INQUIRY, INJUSTICE.

with, *prep.* by, by means of, through; accompanying, alongside, among[st], amid[st], beside, plus; upon, at, thereupon, *etc.* See ACCOMPANIMENT, MIXTURE.

withdraw, *v.* remove, separate, subduct; retire, retreat, disengage, draw off; abstract, subtract; recall, rescind, recant; resign, relinquish; abdicate, decamp, depart; shrink, recoil, drop out, back out. See DEPARTURE, RECESSION, SECLUSION, RELINQUISHMENT.

wither, *v.* waste, decline, droop, wilt, fade, decay; contract, shrivel, pine, decline, languish; blast, destroy, burn, scorch; cut, scathe. See DETERIORATION, DRYNESS.

withhold, *v.t.* keep back, restrain, detain; check, hold back; hinder; suppress, repress, reserve. See CONCEALMENT, RESTRAINT.

within, *adj. & prep.* outside, outdoor[s], indoor[s]; internal. See INTERIOR.

without, *adv. & prep.* outside, outdoor[s], outward, beyond; minus. See EXTERIOR, ABSENCE, CIRCUMSTANCE, DEDUCTION, EXEMPTION.

withstand, *v.t.* face, confront; fight off, oppose, defy. See OPPOSITION.

witless, *adj.* senseless, brainless; silly, foolish, pointless, idiotic, moronic, imbecilic; half-witted, dull, thick, stupid, scatterbrained, muddleheaded. *Slang,* dumb, dopy. See IGNORANCE.

witness, *n.* testimony, proof, EVIDENCE, corroboration; deponent, eyewitness; testifier, attestor; beholder, observer. —*v.t.* see, observe; attest, sign, subscribe to, bear witness to. See PRESENCE.

wizard, *n.* wonder-worker, conjuror; Merlin, magician, sorcerer; *colloq.,* master, expert. See SORCERY, SKILL.

wobble, *v.* roll, rock, stagger, reel, lurch, yaw, sway; teeter, totter, flounder; hesitate, waver, quaver. See OSCILLATION, AGITATION.

woe, *n.* trouble, tribulation; sorrow, grief; unhappiness, misery. See PAIN, DEJECTION.

wolf, *n.* canid, wolfkin, cub, whelp; hyena; werewolf, wolfman; *slang,* philanderer, rake, roué, womanchaser, ladykiller. See ANIMAL, LOVE. —*v.t.* raven, gulp, bolt, gobble. See FOOD.

woman, FEMALE, lady, gentlewoman; wife. See HUMANITY.

womanish, *adj.* effeminate, emasculated; unmanly; shrill, vixenish; soft, weak. See FEMALE.

WONDER

Nouns—wonder, wonderment, marvel, miracle, miraculousness, astonishment, amazement, bewilderment; amazedness, admiration, awe; stupor, stupefaction; fascination; sensation, phenomenon; SURPRISE. See UNINTELLIGIBILITY, SECRET.

Verbs—**1,** wonder, marvel, admire; be surprised, start; stare, open *or* rub one's eyes; gape, hold one's breath; look *or* stand aghast, stand in awe of; not believe one's eyes, ears, *or* senses.

2, be wonderful, beggar *or* baffle description; stagger belief.

3, SURPRISE, astonish, startle, shock, take aback, electrify, stun, stagger, bewilder.

Adjectives—**1,** wonderful, wondrous; miraculous; surprising, unexpected, unheard of; mysterious, indescribable, inexpressible, ineffable; unutterable, unspeakable; monstrous, prodigious, stupendous, marvelous; inconceivable, incredible; unimaginable, strange, uncommon, passing strange, striking, overwhelming. *Slang,* out of sight.

2, surprised, aghast, agog, breathless, agape; open-mouthed; awestruck, thunderstruck; round-, wide-, *or* large-eyed; spellbound; speechless, at a loss [for words]; lost in amazement, wonder, *or* astonishment; unable to believe one's senses. *Slang,* bug-eyed.

Adverbs—wonderfully, fearfully; for a wonder; strange to say, *mirabile dictu,* to one's great surprise; with wonder.

Interjections—lo! lo and behold! O! what! wonder of wonders! will wonders never cease! what will they think of next!

Antonyms, see EXPECTATION.

---

wonderful, *adj.* miraculous, marvelous, amazing, astounding. *Colloq.,* great, swell, dandy; colossal, terrific. See WONDER, GOODNESS.

wont, *n.* custom, use, HABIT, routine, practice, usage.

woo, *v.* court, make love to; seek, pursue, solicit; importune. See ENDEARMENT.

wood, *n.* forest, grove, timber, copse, coppice, thicket, spinny, bosque, *bois;* woods, woodland; board, plank, log, lumber. See MATERIALS.

woodcut, *n.* wood block, woodprint; xylograph, lignograph, pyrograph, wood ENGRAVING.

wooded, *adj.* sylvan, forested, timbered. See VEGETABLE.

wooden, *adj.* wood[y], ligneous, xyloid; oaken, mahogany, ash, pine, teak, walnut, *etc.;* frame, clapboard, shingle[d]; stiff, rigid, inflexible; expressionless, lifeless, unimaginative. See MATERIALS, UNMEANINGNESS, HARDNESS, WEARINESS.

woodsman, *n.* woodcutter, lumberman, lumberjack, logger, timberjack; conservationist, forester, ranger; frontiersman, backwoodsman. See AGRICULTURE.

woodwind, *n.* flute, clarinet, oboe, bassoon, saxophone. See MUSIC.

woodwork, *n.* molding, paneling, baseboard, didoes, frames, jambs, sashes; doors. See ORNAMENT.

woof, *n.* weft, filling; fabric, TEXTURE. See CROSSING.

wool, *n.* fleece; down, hair; worsted, yarn. —*adj.* woolen; knitted; woolly, hairy, fleecy, downy, fluffy, flocculent. See COVERING, SOFTNESS, MATERIALS.

word, *n.* expression, utterance; syllable, phone, ideophone, phoneme; stem, root, derivative, inflected form (see GRAMMAR); particle, article; prefix, suffix, combining form, element; compound, phrase (see

SPEECH); neologism, coinage, nonce word; barbarism, corruption (see ERROR); PROMISE; password, watchword (see INDICATION); NEWS, INFORMATION. See WRITING, NOMENCLATURE.

word game, *n.* acrostic, palindrome, anagram[s], crossword puzzle, ghosts, riddles, word square, double acrostic; spelling bee; rebus, charades; Scrabble, Jotto, Boggle, *etc.*; Guggenheim, categories, wordplay, *etc.* See AMUSEMENT.

wording, *n.* phrasing, expression, phraseology. See FIGURATIVE, SPEECH.

wordy, *adj.* verbose, talkative, loquacious, prolix, garrulous; rambling, circumlocutory, windy, longwinded. See DIFFUSENESS.

work, *n.* job, occupation, calling, trade, profession; task, stint, employment; drudgery, toil, moil, grind, routine; function; craftsmanship, workmanship; arts and crafts, craft, handicraft; opus, PRODUCTION, WRITING, book PUBLICATION; office; management; manufacture. See BUSINESS. —*v.* toil, moil, labor, plod, plug, drudge; run, act, operate, function; leaven, ferment, yeast; use, employ; succeed, perform, do; effect, exert, strain; embroider, embellish, decorate. *Colloq.*, use elbow grease. See ACTION, SUCCESS, EXERTION, AGENCY, EFFECT.

workable, *adj.* feasible, practicable; tractable. See POSSIBILITY, SOFTNESS.

workaday, *adj.* everyday, quotidian, common[place], matter-of-fact, homespun, humdrum; routine, orderly. See BUSINESS, EXERTION, SIMPLENESS.

worker, *n.* laborer, workman; artisan, craftsman; operator, doer, performer; journeyman, yeoman; Trojan; drudge; mechanic; toiler, moiler. See EXERTION.

workmanlike, *adj.* well-done, expert, professional. See SKILL.

workmanship, *n.* craftsmanship, handiwork, SKILL, technique, expertness, competence; performance, execution, construction; finish, polish, art. See PRODUCTION.

workout, *n.* trial, essay; practice, rehearsal, run-through. See EXERTION, EXPERIMENT.

works, *n.pl.* factory, plant, mill, workshop, shop; mechanism, machine; fort, rampart, breastworks, earthworks, barricade; *colloq.*, everything. See AGENCY, PUNISHMENT, COMPLETION.

workshop, *n.* workhouse, sweatshop; laboratory, factory, manufactory, mill, rolling mill, sawmill; works, steelworks, ironworks, foundry, furnace; mint; seminar, clinic; forge, loom; cabinet, atelier, studio, bureau, office, store, shop, plant. See BUSINESS.

world, *n.* creation, nature; earth, cosmos (see UNIVERSE).

worldly, *adj.* experienced, sophisticated; earthly, mundane; terrestrial; profane, secular, carnal; sordid, mercenary; proud, selfish, material, materialistic, unspiritual, irreligious. See SELFISHNESS, IRRELIGION.

worldwide, *adj.* universal, widespread; general, all-embracing, unlimited. See GENERALITY.

worm, *n.* earthworm, angleworm; maggot, larva, grub, caterpillar; insect; crawler, nightcrawler; flatworm, platyhelminth, tapeworm, cestode, nematode, roundworm, ascarid, pinworm, annelid; wretch; screw, spiral. See ANIMAL. —*v.* crawl; creep, belly; insinuate (oneself), bore; writhe, wriggle. See CONVOLUTION, INSERTION.

worn, *adj.* used, secondhand; frayed, shabby, threadbare; shopworn; weary. See DETERIORATION, WEARINESS.

worry, *n.* care, anxiety, mental anguish, uneasiness, FEAR, apprehension; concern, misgiving. —*v.* tease, plague, vex; disturb, fret, upset; torment, torture, trouble, bait, badger; maul, chew, mangle; get gray hairs. See MALEVOLENCE, DISCONTENT, CARE.

WORSHIP

Nouns—**1,** worship, adoration, devotion, homage, service; religious rites *or* observance; RESPECT, reverence, veneration; cult; deification, idolization. See IDOLATRY, GRATITUDE, RELIGION, RITE.

2, a. liturgy; prayer, orison, invocation, supplication, devotion[s], rogation, intercession, beseeching, entreaty, petition (see REQUEST); thanksgiving, grace; praise, laudation, exaltation, glorification, benediction; Magnificat, doxology, hosanna, hallelujah, alleluia, Te Deum, Trisagion; paean, psalm, psalmody, hymn, anthem, plainsong, chant (see MUSIC). **b.** (*Christian:*) collect, litany, miserere, Lord's prayer, paternoster, Ave Maria, Hail Mary, rosary, prayer wheel, missal. **c.** (*Jewish:*) Shoma, Kol Nidre, Kaddish. **d.** (*Moslem:*) Aliahu akbar, Fatihah, shahada, rak'ah. **e.** (*Hindu:*) Ram, Ram, Siva, Siva.

3, divine service, office, duty; Mass, Eucharist, Communion, Lord's Supper; morning prayer, matins, evening prayer, evensong, vespers, vigils, compline, prime [song], tierce, lauds, sext, nones; prayer meeting, revival. See RITE.

4, worshiper, adorer, venerator, reverer, glorifier; religionist, churchman, churchgoer, devout person, congregation; communicant, celebrant, votary, pietist; idolizer, devotee, deifier, deist; idolator, idolatress, fetishist, pagan. *Colloq.,* psalmsinger. See CLERGY, RELIGION, PIETY.

Verbs—**1,** worship, adore, reverence, revere, inspire, aspire, lift up one's heart; pay homage, humble oneself, kneel, genuflect, bend *or* bow one's knee, fall on one's knees, prostrate oneself, bow down and worship; be devout.

2, RESPECT, adulate, idolize, lionize; deify, enshrine, immortalize.

3, pray, invoke, supplicate; offer up prayers, tell one's beads; return *or* give thanks, say grace, bless; praise, laud, glorify, magnify, exalt, extol, sing praises; give benediction, lead the choir, intone; go to church, attend service, attend Mass, communicate.

Adjectives—worshipful, adoring, prayerful, devout, devotional, pious, reverent, religious, spiritually-minded, paying homage; pure, solemn, fervent, fervid, heartfelt; reverential, venerating, obeisant.

Interjections—hallelujah! alleluia! hosanna! praise the Lord! *Deo gratias!* glory be to God! pray God that! lift up your hearts! *sursum corda!*

Antonyms, see IRRELIGION, DISRESPECT, IMPRECATION.

---

worst, *v.t.* best, defeat, conquer. See SUCCESS.

worth, *n.* merit, value, PRICE, cost, estimation; worthiness, importance, VIRTUE, credit; character. See MONEY, UTILITY, GOODNESS.

worthless, *adj.* useless, no good, good-for-nothing; base, vile; valueless; poor, miserable; trashy; unserviceable; trifling; characterless. *Colloq.,* no-account. *Slang,* lousy. See USELESSNESS, CHEAPNESS, UNIMPORTANCE.

worthwhile, *adj.* beneficial, salubrious, good; gainful, profitable, lucrative; meritorious, worthy. See EXPEDIENCE, USE.

worthy, *adj.* deserving, meritorious; virtuous, good; estimable, honest, upright, reputable. See VIRTUE, SKILL, REPUTE.

would-be, *adj.* hopeful, aspiring;

pretended, so-called, self-styled, *soi-disant;* fraudulent. See PRIDE, NOMENCLATURE, DECEPTION.

wound, *n.* injury, hurt; painfulness. —*v.t.* injure, hurt, lame, cripple; PAIN; shoot, stab, cut, lacerate, tear, wing; insult, offend, gall, mortify. See DETERIORATION, RESENTMENT.

wraith, *n.* ghost, specter. See DEMON, IMAGINATION.

wrangle, *v.i.* quarrel, bicker, squabble, dispute, altercate, argue, brawl. See DISCORD, CONTENTION.

wrap, *n.* robe, shawl, serape, cloak, coat, cape, cover, wrapper, blanket. —*v.t.* swathe, swaddle, clothe, cover, envelop, enclose; hide, muffle, conceal; fold, lap, wind; pack[age]. See COVERING, ENVIRONMENT.

wrath, *n.* choler, anger, ire, indignation; vengeance; fury, rage. See RESENTMENT.

wreath, *n.* garland, lei, chaplet, festoon; laurel wreath, garland of bays; floral ring, decoration. See ORNAMENT, APPROBATION, CIRCULARITY.

wreck, *n.* DESTRUCTION, ruin, undoing; accident, collision, crack-up, smash-up, crash; shipwreck; derelict; ruined person, human wreckage; break-up; ruins, demolition, wreckage, junk. —*v.t.* smash, crash, crack up; ruin, tear down, demolish, raze, destroy; shipwreck, strand, cast away; shatter, blight, blast. *Slang,* bust up. See REMAINDER.

wrench, *v.t.* twist, wring; yank, pull; extort, wrest, snatch; sprain, strain, dislocate; distort. —*n.* monkey wrench, spanner; twist, yank, *etc.* See EXTRACTION, DISJUNCTION, RETENTION.

wrest, *v.t.* turn, pull, twist; tear away, snatch, grab. See DISTORTION, ACQUISITION, EXTRACTION.

wrestle, *v.* grapple, strive, struggle with, contend. See CONTENTION.

wretch, *n.* sufferer; beggar, outcast, pariah; knave, villain; rogue, rascal. See EVILDOER, DISCONTENT.

wretched, *adj.* beggarly, worthless, miserable; paltry, mean, pitiful; unhappy, unfortunate; woebegone, tormented, afflicted; shabby, disreputable, deplorable. See BADNESS, UNIMPORTANCE.

wriggle, *v.* wiggle, shake, squirm, writhe, shimmy. See AGITATION.

wring, *v.t.* wrench, twist; rack, PAIN; squeeze, compress; extort. See CONVOLUTION, EXTRACTION, ACQUISITION.

wrinkle, *n.* FURROW, crease, pucker, FOLD, corrugation, rumple; crinkle, crow's-foot; *colloq.,* angle, development, gimmick. —*v.t.* crease, rumple, FOLD.

writ, *n.* process, summons, warrant. See LAWSUIT.

writhe, *v.i.* wriggle, squirm, twist, contort. See DISTORTION, PAIN.

WRITING

Nouns—**1,** writing, chirography, calligraphy, pencraft, penmanship, hand, handwriting, uncial writing, cuneiform, rune, hieroglyph[ic], letter; alphabet; black and white; stroke of the pen, pen and ink; shorthand, stenography, typewriting; cryptography, code, steganography; pneumatography, spirit writing. See SPEECH, PUBLICATION, DESCRIPTION.

2, cacography, bad hand, illegible hand, scribble, scrawl; writer's cramp. *Slang,* hen tracks. See UNINTELLIGIBILITY.

3, word, syllable, phrase, sentence, paragraph; authorship, composition; prose, POETRY.

4, manuscript, codex, document, ms., mss., COPY, transcript, rescript, typescript, rough copy *or* draft; fair copy; autograph, monograph, holograph.

5, a. writing paper, parchment, manila [paper], newsprint, onionskin, rice paper, bond [paper]; papyrus; tablet. **b.** pencil, pen; fountain, ball[-point], felt-tip, laundry, *etc.* pen; manual, electric, *or* electronic typewriter, printer, dot-matrix *or* daisy-wheel printer, draft- *or* letter-quality printer.

6, writer, author[ess], litterateur, essayist, novelist, short-story writer, playwright, dramatist, poet; editor; lexicographer, annotator, commentator; journalist, newspaperman, critic, reviewer, correspondent; hack [writer], ghostwriter; librettist; screenwriter; scribe, amanuensis, scrivener, secretary, clerk, stenographer, stenotypist, penman, copyist, transcriber; typewriter, typist; calligrapher. *Colloq.*, free lance, inkslinger, penny-a-liner.

Verbs—write, pen, COPY, engross; write out, transcribe; scribble, scrawl, scratch; interline; write down, record, sign; compose, indite, draw up, dictate; inscribe, dash off, draft, formulate; take pen in hand; typewrite, type; write shorthand.

Adjectives—writing, written, holographic, manuscript; shorthand, stenographic; in writing, in black and white; uncial, runic, cuneiform, hieroglyphic, hieratic; handwritten, cursive, printed, lettered; legible; Spencerian, backhand.

Antonyms, see SPEECH, PRINTING.

WRONG

Nouns—**1,** wrong, wrongfulness, INJUSTICE, imposition, oppression, corruption, foul play; ILLEGALITY, miscarriage of justice. See ERROR.

2, wrongdoing, wickedness, sinfulness, BADNESS, EVIL, sin, vice, iniquity, immorality, GUILT, reprehensibility, miscreancy, IMPROBITY; blackguardism; transgression, felony, trespass, misdeed, misbehavior, misdoing, indiscretion, crime, violation, offense, misdemeanor, tort, injury, grievance, outrage, the matter, malefaction, shame, blame.

3, wrongdoer, transgressor (see EVILDOER).

Verbs—**1,** wrong, harm, injure, damage, maltreat, mistreat, ill-treat, abuse, hit below the belt, oppress, persecute, outrage, offend, dishonor, misserve, do wrong to, do injury to, do injustice to, get at, treat unjustly, sin against; scandalize.

2, do wrong, transgress, be unjust, be inequitable, show partiality.

Adjectives—**1,** wrong[ful], bad, EVIL, immoral, sinful, wicked, vicious, grievous, iniquitous, scandalous, reprehensible, blameworthy, guilty, criminal; harmful, deleterious, injurious, hurtful, detrimental, pernicious, perverse, perverted.

2, unjust, unfair (see INJUSTICE); unreasonable, unallowable, impermissible; unjustified, unlawful, illegal; illegitimate.

3, improper, inappropriate, inapposite, inapt, incongruous, unsuitable, unfit. See DISAGREEMENT.

4, inaccurate, incorrect (see ERROR).

Adverbs—wrong[ly], falsely, in the wrong; improperly, faultily, amiss, awry, bad; mistakenly, erroneously, inaccurately, incorrectly, in error.

Antonyms, see RIGHTNESS.

wrongheaded, *adj.* misguided, stubborn, obstinate. See OBSTINACY.

wry, *adj.* crooked, twisted; askew, awry; ironic, distorted, contorted; warped. See DISTORTION, OBLIQUITY.

X

xanthic, *adj.* yellow[ish]; fulvous, tawny. See COLOR.

xanthous, *adj.* blond[e], fair, light-skinned; fair-, yellow-, *or* golden-haired; yellowish; Mongolian. See COLOR.

x-ray, *n.* Roentgen ray; radiation; radiograph. See REMEDY.

xylograph, *n.* woodcut, wood engraving. See ENGRAVING.

xyloid, *adj.* wood[y], ligneous. See VEGETABLE.

xylophone, *n.* marimba, gamelan[g], vibraphone, vibraharp, glockenspiel, orchestra bells, sticcado-pastrole, gigelira, straw fiddle. See MUSIC.

Y

yacht, *n.* sailboat, pleasure boat; houseboat; sloop, yawl, ketch; cruiser. See SHIP.

yahoo, *n.* lout, knave. See VULGARITY.

yammer, *v., colloq.,* complain, wail, whine, whimper, pule; cry, howl; desire, crave, yearn; lament. *Slang,* gripe, grouse. See LAMENTATION.

yank, *n. & v.* pull, twist, jerk. See TRACTION.

yap, *v.i.* See YELP.

yard, *n.* ENCLOSURE, court[yard], patio.

yardstick, *n.* ruler; standard, criterion, rule, test, measure. See MEASUREMENT.

yarn, *n.* thread, worsted, spun wool; tale, fib, tall story. See FILAMENT, DESCRIPTION, EXAGGERATION.

yaw, *v.i.* drift, deviate; jibe, tack. See DEVIATION, NAVIGATION.

yawn, *v.i.* gape, open wide; split, part. See OPENING, WEARINESS.

yea, *adv.* yes; indeed, truly. See ASSENT.

year, *n.* twelvemonth; fiscal year, calendar year. See CHRONOMETRY.

yearbook, *n.* annual, annuary, calendar, almanac; journal, diary, RECORD.

yearling, *n.* teg; youngling, colt, filly, whelp, cub. See YOUTH, ANIMAL.

yearn, *v.i.* pine, long, hanker; grieve, mourn. See DESIRE, LAMENTATION.

yeast, *n.* leaven, ferment, barm; spume, froth, foam. See AGITATION.

yell, *v. & n.* shout, CRY, scream, shriek, bawl, call; yelp, bark; bellow, roar, hoot. *Colloq.,* squawk, holler.

yellow, *adj.* fair, blond[e], flaxen, light-haired (see COLOR); Mongolian, Mongoloid; jaundiced; jealous, envious; *colloq.,* cowardly, craven, fearful, lily- *or* white-livered, afraid, unmanly, pusillanimous; lurid, sensational, melodramatic, scandalmongering. See COWARDICE.

yelp, *n. & v.* bark, squawk, CRY, yap, yip.

yen, *n., colloq.,* DESIRE, craving, longing, hankering, yearning; taste, hunger, relish; passion; tendency, appetite.

yeoman, *n.* freeholder, commoner, farmer; guardsman, beefeater; attendant, retainer; petty officer. See POSSESSION, AGRICULTURE, MALE.

yes, *adv.* yea, aye; indeed, true, verily; agreed, surely, certainly, of course, that's right. See ASSENT, CONSENT.

yeshiva, *n.* Talmudic academy, rabbinical seminary; Hebrew SCHOOL.

yesterday, *n.* day before; the PAST.

yet, *conj.* nevertheless, notwithstanding, still, however. See COMPENSATION. —*adv.* still, besides, thus far, hitherto, till now, up to now *or* this time. See PRIORITY, PAST.

yield, *n.* crop, harvest, product. See AGRICULTURE. —*v.* surrender, cede, abandon, give up; give in, succumb; produce, bear, bring; furnish, supply, afford; soften, relax, give [way]; assent, comply, obey. See RELINQUISHMENT, CONSENT, RECEIVING, RESIGNATION, SUBMISSION.

yielding, *adj.* soft, pliant, tractable, docile; submissive, compliant, acquiescent; supple, plastic, flexible; productive, fertile. See SOFTNESS, FACILITY.

yodel, *v.i.* warble (see MUSIC).

yoke, *n.* union, bond, chain, link, tie; bondage, slavery, oppression, servitude, enslavement, thralldom, vassalage; couple, pair, team. See SUBJECTION. —*v.t.* couple, join, pair, wed; bind, tie, link; bracket, connect, associate. See JUNCTION.

yokel, *n.* rustic, peasant, countryman. *Colloq.,* hick, hayseed, rube; bumpkin; yahoo. See POPULACE.
yonder, *adj.* yon, that. *—adv.* in that place, thither, there, beyond; in the distance, afar, far away. See DISTANCE.
yore, *n.* antiquity, old times, olden days, time immemorial; yesterday; bygone[s], history, the PAST. *Colloq.,* good old days.
young, *adj.* youthful; puerile; ageless; green; foundling; adolescent, juvenile, teen-age; fresh, new; inexperienced, immature. See YOUTH. *—n.* offspring, children. See POSTERITY.

YOUTH

Nouns—**1,** youth, juvenility, juvenescence, immaturity, juniority; childhood, boyhood, maidenhood, girlhood, youthhood; minority, nonage, teen-age, teens, tender age, bloom; prime of life, flower of life; heyday of youth; school days; adolescence, puberty; growing pains; greenness, callowness; *jeunesse dorée*; inexperience, puerility. See NEWNESS, POSTERITY.
2, babyhood, infancy, cradle, nursery, apron strings.
3, infant, baby, babe, suckling, nursling; bairn, *enfant,* papoose; offspring, young; brat, tot, toddler. *Colloq.,* kid[dy], chick, *bambino;* big baby, thumbsucker, crybaby. *Slang,* mama's boy.
4, child, boy, girl, lad, maid, youth, hobbledehoy, stripling, teen-ager, adolescent; cherub, brat, imp, gamin, urchin; sapling; foster child, fosterling. *Colloq.,* kid; bobby soxer, juvenile. *Slang,* spring chicken.
5, See ANIMAL. Pup, whelp, kitten, cub, foal, colt, lamb.
Verbs—rejuvenate, make young; rob the cradle.
Adjectives—young, youthful, juvenile, tender, immature, green, callow, budding, sappy, unfledged, underage, teen-age, in one's teens; hebetic, adolescent, pubescent; immature; younger, junior; boyish, beardless; maidenly, girlish; infant, infantile, newborn, babyish, childish, puerile.
Antonyms, see AGE.

Z

zany, *n.* clown, madcap, buffoon, comic, fool, comedian, jester, merry-andrew, Punch, pickle-herring; nitwit, dunce. See FOLLY, WIT.
zeal, *n.* earnestness, devotion, dedication; passion; soul, spirit, ardor, fervor, verve, enthusiasm, eagerness, warmth, energy; zealotry, fanaticism. See ACTIVITY, FEELING.
zealot, *n.* fanatic; visionary, dreamer, enthusiast; bigot; devotee, partisan. *Colloq.,* addict, fan. See HETERODOXY, PIETY.
zenith, *n.* summit, top, acme, apex, pinnacle, apogee; climax, culmination; prime, heyday. See HEIGHT.
zephyr, *n.* breeze, breath, gentle wind, west wind. See WIND.
Zeppelin, *n.* dirigible [balloon], airship. See AVIATION.
zero, *n.* nothing; naught, nought; cipher, none; (*in games*) love, blank; nobody, not a soul. *Colloq.,* zip. *Slang,* goose-egg, zilch. See INSUBSTANTIALITY.
zest, *n.* relish, gusto, appetite, enthusiasm, enjoyment, thrill, titillation, exhilaration; tang, twang, PUNGENCY, piquance, savor, sauce, edge. *Colloq.,* kick, zip. See TASTE, PLEASURE, EXCITEMENT.
zigzag, *adj.* back-and-forth, tacking, serrated, jagged; crooked, tortuous. See DEVIATION, ANGULARITY.
zip, *n., colloq.,* zero; VIGOR, zest, ENERGY. *Colloq.,* ginger, whiz, ping, swish. *Slang,* pep. *—v.* flash; swish, whiz; close (a zipper). See VELOCITY.
zipper, *n.* slide fastener. See CONNECTION.

zither, *n.* zitter, cittern, cithara; koto. See MUSIC.

zodiac, *n.* constellations; horoscope, circle, circuit. See UNIVERSE.

zombie, *n.* walking dead, living ghost; automaton; monster. *Slang,* stooge; eccentric, oddball, nut, weirdo. See DEATH, DEMON.

zone, *n.* REGION, clime, climate; district, ward, area; belt, girdle, band, girth, cincture. See CIRCULARITY, LAYER.

zoo, *n.* zoological park *or* garden; menagerie; vivarium, vivary; aviary, birdhouse; serpentarium; bear pit; aquarium. See ANIMAL, DOMESTICATION.

FOREIGN WORDS AND PHRASES

Translated, with reference to the applicable English categories

ab initio, *Lat.*, from the beginning. See BEGINNING.
ad infinitum, *Lat.*, to infinity; without end. See INFINITY, PERPETUITY, SPACE.
ad libitum, *Lat.*, at [one's] pleasure. See WILL.
ad nauseam, *Lat.*, to the point of nausea; boringly. See WEARINESS.
ad valorem, *Lat.*, according to value. See RELATION, PRICE.
affaire d'amour, *Fr.*, love affair. See LOVE.
a fortiori, *Lat.*, all the more. See REASONING.
agent provocateur, *Fr.*, professional agitator. See REVOLUTION, VIOLENCE.
Agnus Dei, *Lat.*, Lamb of God. See DEITY.
al fresco, *Ital.*, in the open air; outdoors. See AIR.
alter ego, *Lat.*, another I; intimate friend. See FRIEND.
amicus curiae, *Lat.*, a friend of the court. See LAWSUIT.
amour-propre, *Fr.*, self-esteem. See VANITY, PRIDE.
ancien régime, *Fr.*, the old order. See OLDNESS.
ante bellum, *Lat.*, before the war. See PRIORITY.
a posteriori, *Lat.*, from effect to cause. See REASONING.
a priori, *Lat.*, from cause to effect. See REASONING.
arrière-pensée, *Fr.*, mental reservation; hidden motive. See CONCEALMENT.
au contraire, *Fr.*, on the contrary. See OPPOSITION.
au courant, *Fr.*, up-to-date; informed. See KNOWLEDGE.
au fait, *Fr.*, well-informed. See KNOWLEDGE.
au naturel, *Fr.*, nude. See DIVESTMENT.
ave atque vale, *Lat.*, hale and farewell. See DEPARTURE.
Ave Maria, *Lat.*, Hail Mary! See WORSHIP.
à votre santé, *Fr.*, to your health. See CONGRATULATION.

beau geste, *Fr.*, fine deed. See COURAGE, AFFECTATION.
beau monde, *Fr.*, fashionable society. See FASHION.
belles-lettres, *Fr.*, fine literature. See WRITING.
bête noire, *Fr.*, object of dislike or dread. See HATE.
billet-doux, *Fr.*, love letter. See COMMUNICATION, ENDEARMENT.
bon mot, *Fr.*, witty saying. See WIT.
bon ton, *Fr.*, good manners or breeding. See COURTESY, FASHION.
bon vivant, *Fr.*, epicure; good companion. See GLUTTONY, SOCIALITY.
bon voyage, *Fr.*, happy trip; farewell. See DEPARTURE.

cantus firmus, *Lat.*, fixed melody; chant or musical theme. See MUSIC.
carpe diem, *Lat.*, make use of the [present] day. See ACTIVITY.
carte blanche, *Fr.*, unlimited authority. See PERMISSION.
casus belli, *Lat.*, event provoking war. See CONTENTION.
caveat emptor, *Lat.*, let the buyer beware. See CAUTION.
cave canem, *Lat.*, beware the dog. See CAUTION.
chacun à son goût, *Fr.*, each to his own taste. See JUDGMENT.

chef d'oeuvre, *Fr.*, masterpiece. See SKILL, GOODNESS, PRODUCTION.
che sera sera, *Ital.*, what will be, will be. See CERTAINTY, NECESSITY.
comme ci, comme ça, *Fr.*, so-so. See MEDIOCRITY.
comme il faut, *Fr.*, as is required; as it should be. See TASTE, FASHION.
compos mentis, *Lat.*, sane. See SANITY.
corpus delicti, *Lat.*, the facts connected with a crime. See EVIDENCE.
coup de grâce, *Fr.*, merciful finishing blow. See KILLING, COMPLETION, PITY.
coup de maître, *Fr.*, master stroke. See SKILL, SUCCESS.
coup d'état, *Fr.*, political stroke. See REVOLUTION.
coup d'oeil, *Fr.*, glance. See VISION.
crème de la crème, *Fr.*, the cream of the cream; the very best. See SUPERIORITY.
cum laude, *Lat.*, with [the highest] praise. See APPROBATION, SUPERIORITY.

danse macabre, *Fr.*, dance of DEATH.
de facto, *Lat.*, in fact; actual; realistically. See EXISTENCE, TRUTH.
Dei gratia, *Lat.*, by the grace of God. See JUSTICE.
déjà vu, *Fr.*, already seen. See IMAGINATION, MEMORY.
de jure, *Lat.*, by right; lawfully. See LEGALITY.
de novo, *Lat.*, from the BEGINNING.
Deo gratias, *Lat.*, thank God. See GRATITUDE.
Deo volente, *Lat.*, God being willing. See CHANCE, POSSIBILITY.
de profundis, *Lat.*, out of the depths. See PENITENCE, WORSHIP.
de rigueur, *Fr.*, obligatory. See COMPULSION, FASHION, TASTE.
dernier cri, *Fr.*, the last word; modern. See NEWNESS, FASHION.
de trop, *Fr.*, too much. See SUFFICIENCY.
deus ex machina, *Lat.*, contrived or supernatural device. See PLAN, SORCERY.
Dies Irae, *Lat.*, day of wrath; JUDGMENT day.
dolce far niente, *Ital.*, sweet idleness. See INACTIVITY.
double-entendre, *Fr.*, double meaning. See VULGARITY, WIT.
dramatis personae, *Lat.*, the characters in a DRAMA.

en déshabillé, *Fr.*, not dressed for receiving company. See UNPREPAREDNESS.
en famille, *Fr.*, at home; informally. See UNCONFORMITY.
enfant terrible, *Fr.*, unruly child. See DISOBEDIENCE.
en masse, *Fr.*, all together; in a group. See ASSEMBLAGE, WHOLE.
en passant, *Fr.*, in passing; by the way. See OCCASION, TRANSIENTNESS.
en rapport, *Fr.*, in harmony. See AGREEMENT.
entre nous, *Fr.*, [just] between us. See DISCLOSURE, NEARNESS.
esprit de corps, *Fr.*, group spirit; morale. See COURAGE, CHEERFULNESS.
ex cathedra, *Lat.*, from the seat of AUTHORITY. See CERTAINTY.
exempli gratia, *Lat.*, for example; e.g. See CONFORMITY.
ex officio, *Lat.*, by right of office. See AUTHORITY, LEGALITY.
ex parte, *Lat.*, from one side only. See MISJUDGMENT, EVIDENCE.
ex post facto, *Lat.*, after the deed [is done]. See LATENESS.
ex tempore, *Lat.*, out of the time; offhand. See OCCASION.

fait accompli, *Fr.*, accomplished fact. See COMPLETION.
faux pas, *Fr.*, a false step; ERROR.
femme fatale, *Fr.*, dangerous woman; seductress. See ENDEARMENT, ATTRACTION.
festina lente, *Lat.*, make haste slowly. See CAUTION.
fidus Achates, *Lat.*, faithful Achates; a devoted FRIEND. See PROBITY.
fin de siècle, *Fr.*, end of the century; decadent. See DETERIORATION.

flagrante delicto, *Lat.*, during the commission of the crime. See GUILT, ACTION.

grand prix, *Fr.*, first prize. See APPROBATION, SUPERIORITY.

haute couture, *Fr.*, high FASHION.
haut monde, *Fr.*, upper classes; high society. See FASHION, NOBILITY.
hic jacet, *Lat.*, here lies. See INTERMENT.
hors de combat, *Fr.*, out of the fight; disabled. See IMPOTENCE, WEARINESS.

ibidem, *Lat.*, in the same place. See IDENTITY.
idée fixe, *Fr.*, fixed idea; obsession. See BELIEF, MISJUDGMENT.
ignis fatuus, *Lat.*, will-o'-the-wisp. See INSUBSTANTIALITY.
in absentia, *Lat.*, in or during [one's] ABSENCE.
in camera, *Lat.*, privately. See CONCEALMENT.
in esse, *Lat.*, in EXISTENCE.
in extremis, *Lat.*, at the very end; near DEATH.
infra dignitatem, *Lat.*, beneath one's dignity. See DISREPUTE.
in loco parentis, *Lat.*, in the place of a parent. See SUBSTITUTION.
in medias res, *Lat.*, in the MIDDLE of things.
in ovo, *Lat.*, in the egg. See UNPREPAREDNESS.
in posse, *Lat.*, in POSSIBILITY.
in re, *Lat.*, in the matter of; concerning. See RELATION.
in statu quo, *Lat.*, in the same condition. See STABILITY, PERMANENCE.
interdit, *Fr.*, forbidden. See ILLEGALITY.
inter nos, *Lat.*, [just] between us. See DISCLOSURE.
in toto, *Lat.*, in full; wholly. See COMPLETION.
ipse dixit, *Lat.*, he himself has said it. See AUTHORITY.
ipso facto, *Lat.*, [by virtue of] the same fact. See EXISTENCE.

je ne sais quoi, *Fr.*, I don't know what; an indefinable something. See SPECIALITY, INTRINSIC.
jeunesse dorée, *Fr.*, gilded youth. See WASTE, YOUTH.
joie de vivre, *Fr.*, joy of life; enthusiasm. See CHEERFULNESS.

laissez faire, *Fr.*, noninterference. See PERMISSION, FREEDOM, INACTIVITY, NEGLECT.
lapsus linguae, *Lat.*, slip of the tongue. See ERROR.
lettre de cachet, *Fr.*, sealed letter (ordering arrest). See RESTRAINT.
loco citato, *Lat.*, in the place cited; loc. cit. See LOCATION.
locum tenens, *Lat.*, substitute. See SUBSTITUTION, INHABITANT.

magnum opus, *Lat.*, masterpiece. See SKILL.
mal de mer, *Fr.*, seasickness. See DISEASE.
mal de siècle, *Fr.*, world-weariness. See DEJECTION.
mañana, *Span.*, tomorrow. See LATENESS.
mare nostrum, *Lat.*, our sea. See WATER.
mea culpa, *Lat.*, I am to blame. See GUILT.
mens sana in corpore sano, *Lat.*, a healthy mind in a healthy body. See HEALTH, SANITY.
mirabile dictu, *Lat.*, marvelous to relate. See WONDER.
mise en scène, *Fr.*, stage setting. See DRAMA, APPEARANCE.
modus operandi, *Lat.*, METHOD of working. See PLAN.
modus vivendi, *Lat.*, way of living or getting along. See METHOD.

ne plus ultra, *Lat.*, that which is peerless; the ultimate. See PERFECTION, DISTANCE.
n'est-ce pas?, *Fr.*, isn't it [true]? See INQUIRY.
nicht wahr?, *Ger.*, [is it] not true? See INQUIRY.
nil desperandum, *Lat.*, despairing

of nothing. See COURAGE.

noblesse oblige, *Fr.*, noble rank requires [honorable conduct]. See DUTY.

nolens volens, *Lat.*, willy-nilly. See NECESSITY, UNWILLINGNESS.

nom de guerre, *Fr.*, pseudonym. See NOMENCLATURE.

nom de plume, *Fr.*, pen name. See NOMENCLATURE.

non compos mentis, *Lat.*, not of sound mind. See INSANITY.

non sequitur, *Lat.*, it does not follow [logically]. See UNMEANINGNESS.

nota bene, *Lat.*, note well. See INDICATION.

nouveau riche, *Fr.*, [one who is] newly rich; snob. See VULGARITY.

obiter dictum, *Lat.*, passing remark; comment. See SPEECH.

on dit, *Fr.*, they say. See INFORMATION.

par excellence, *Fr.*, above all others. See SUPERIORITY.

particeps criminis, *Lat.*, accomplice. See AUXILIARY.

passim, *Lat.*, here and there. See DISPERSION.

pater noster, *Lat.*, our father (the Lord's prayer). See WORSHIP.

pax vobiscum, *Lat.*, peace be with you. See DEPARTURE.

peccavi, *Lat.*, I have sinned. See PENITENCE.

per annum, *Lat.*, by the year. See TIME.

per capita, *Lat.*, by the head; each. See APPORTIONMENT.

per diem, *Lat.*, by the day. See APPORTIONMENT, PAYMENT.

per se, *Lat.*, by itself. See INTRINSIC, UNITY.

persona grata, *Lat.*, acceptable person. See FRIEND.

persona non grata, *Lat.*, unacceptable person. See DISLIKE.

pièce de résistance, *Fr.*, the main dish, event, etc. See GOODNESS, FOOD.

pied-à-terre, *Fr.*, lodging. See ABODE.

pis aller, *Fr.*, last resort. See SUBSTITUTION.

prima facie, *Lat.*, at first sight. See EVIDENCE, VISION.

prix fixe, *Fr.*, [at a] fixed PRICE.

pro bono publico, *Lat.*, for the public good. See UTILITY.

pro forma, *Lat.*, as a matter of form. See CONFORMITY.

pro tempore, *Lat.*, for the time being. See TRANSIENTNESS.

quid pro quo, *Lat.*, something in return. See COMPENSATION, RETALIATION, SUBSTITUTION, INTERCHANGE.

quien sabe?, *Span.*, who knows? See DOUBT.

qui vive, *Fr.*, alertness. See CAUTION, EXCITEMENT.

quod erat demonstrandum, *Lat.*, which was to be proved. See DEMONSTRATION.

quod vide, *Lat.*, which see; q.v. See ATTRIBUTION.

raison d'être, *Fr.*, reason for being. See INTENTION.

rara avis, *Lat.*, rare bird; unusual thing. See UNCONFORMITY, GOODNESS.

reductio ad absurdum, *Lat.*, reduction to absurdity. See CONFUTATION, REASONING.

requiescat in pace, *Lat.*, may he rest in peace. See INTERMENT.

res gestae, *Lat.*, things done; exploits. See COMPLETION, PRODUCTION.

rigor mortis, *Lat.*, the stiffness of DEATH.

sanctum sanctorum, *Lat.*, Holy of Holies. See TEMPLE.

sang-froid, *Fr.*, cold blood; calmness; composure. See INEXCITABILITY, CAUTION.

sans souci, *Fr.*, without care. See CONTENT, INSENSIBILITY, PLEASURE.

sans peur et sans reproche, *Fr.*, fearless and irreproachable. See PERFECTION, INNOCENCE, PURITY.

sauve qui peut, *Fr.*, save [himself]

who can; a disorderly retreat. See ESCAPE.

savoir-faire, *Fr.*, knowledge of what to do; know-how. See KNOWLEDGE, SKILL.

semper fidelis, *Lat.*, ever faithful. See PROBITY.

semper paratus, *Lat.*, ever ready. See PREPARATION.

shalom aleichem, *Hebrew,* peace be with you. See DEPARTURE.

s'il vous plaît, *Fr.*, if you please. See REQUEST.

sine die, *Lat.*, without [setting] a day [to meet again]. See TIME, LATENESS.

sine qua non, *Lat.*, without which, nothing; something indispensable. See IMPORTANCE.

soi-disant, *Fr.*, self-styled. See BOASTING.

sotto voce, *Ital.*, under the breath. See SOFTNESS, CONCEALMENT, SILENCE.

status quo, *Lat.*, existing condition. See STABILITY, PERMANENCE.

status quo ante, *Lat.*, the way things were before. See RESTORATION.

sub judice, *Lat.*, before the court; under consideration. See LAWSUIT.

sub rosa, *Lat.*, secretly. See SECRET, CONCEALMENT.

sui generis, *Lat.*, of its own kind; unique. See UNCONFORMITY, SPECIALITY.

tableau vivant, *Fr.*, [posed] living tableau. See REPRESENTATION.

tempus fugit, *Lat.*, time flies. See TRANSIENTNESS.

terra firma, *Lat.*, solid ground; LAND, SUPPORT.

terra incognita, *Lat.*, unknown territory. See IGNORANCE, SECRET.

tête-à-tête, *Fr.*, private CONVERSATION.

tour de force, *Fr.*, feat of skill or strength. See SKILL, CUNNING.

tout à fait, *Fr.*, entirely. See COMPLETION.

tout de suite, *Fr.*, immediately. See INSTANTANEITY.

vade mecum, *Lat.*, go with me; summons. See LAWSUIT, INFORMATION.

vae victis, *Lat.*, woe to the vanquished. See RETALIATION.

verbum sapienti, *Lat.*, a word to the wise. See ADVICE.

verboten, *Ger.*, forbidden. See ILLEGALITY, PROHIBITION.

vis-à-vis, *Fr.*, face to face. See OPPOSITION.

viva voce, *Lat.*, aloud; orally. See SPEECH.

volte-face, *Fr.*, reversal. See INVERSION.

vox populi, *Lat.*, the voice of the people. See AGREEMENT, POPULACE, PUBLICATION.

wie geht's?, *Ger.*, how does it go?; how are you? See INQUIRY.